ONLY BOOK WITH **GRADED EXERCISES**

The Hand on Guide to

ANALYTICAL REASONING & LOGICAL REASONING

For CAT, MAT, CMAT, IIFT, BANK (PO/CLERK), SSC (CGL/CPO)
UPSC (CSAT) & Other State PCS Exams etc.

PEEYUSH BHARDWAJ

ARIHANT PUBLICATIONS (INDIA) LTD.

ARIHANT PUBLICATIONS (INDIA) LTD.

卐 Administrative & Production Offices

Corporate Office: 'Ramchhaya' 4577/15, Agarwal Road, Darya Ganj, New Delhi -110002
Tele: 011- 47630600, 43518550; Fax: 011- 23280316

Head Office: Kalindi, TP Nagar, Meerut (UP) - 250002
Tele: 0121-2401479, 2512970, 4004199; Fax: 0121-2401648

All disputes subject to Meerut (UP) jurisdiction only.

卐 Sales & Support Offices

Agra, Ahmedabad, Bengaluru, Bhubaneswar, Bareilly, Chennai, Delhi, Guwahati, Haldwani Hyderabad, Jaipur, Jalandhar, Jhansi, Kolkata, Kota, Lucknow, Meerut, Nagpur & Pune

卐 ISBN 978-93-5203-854-1

卐 Price : ₹ 310

PO No. : TXT-59-T063417-02-25

Typeset by Arihant DTP Unit at Meerut

PRINTED & BOUND BY
ARIHANT PUBLICATIONS (I) LTD. (PRESS UNIT)

For further information about the products from Arihant log on to **www.arihantbooks.com** or email to **info@arihantbooks.com**

PREFACE

Books play an important role in the preparation of any examination and one cannot prepare or score well without the help of books in any competitive exam. This book Analytical Reasoning and Logical Reasoning will help you score better in any competitive exam. As Reasoning basically tests one's thinking power and mind applicability skills. Books for Analytical Reasoning and Logical Reasoning can be the source to get the concepts related to various topics which will help in going through the examination.

Importance of reasoning is increasingly moving centre stage in today's competitive examinations. The questions that are asked in different examinations are not easy to solve and one cannot solve these problems without having a better practice, once you know the basic concept behind it, you can solve it in least time.

The Hand on Guide Analytical Reasoning & Logical Reasoning has been prepared after a comprehensive research on the teachers involve in Analytical and Logical Reasoning.

This book covered all the types of question patterns which are generally faced by the students in different competitive examinations. The value point incorporated in this book make it stand far apart from other books available in the market.

However, I have put my best efforts in preparing this book, but if any error or whatsoever has been skipped out, I will by heartly welcome your suggestions. Apart from all those, who helped in the compilation of this book a special note of thanks goes to Mr Amogh Goel, Miss Sapna and Mr Amit Jha without their support, the book could not have come to its shape.

Ravi Shankar and Ravindar Rawat have given their expertise in the layout of the book. The contribution of Mr Sachin Kumar and Ms Gaura Sharma for this book is also very special worthy of great applause.

Peeyush Bhardwaj

Features of this Book

- Each chapter begins with a brief introduction that will make the students understand different concepts clearly and completely.
- Clear indication of the Types of Questions along with proper guidelines to solve them. Each type has its specific and detailed solution.
- The Exercises of each chapter have been graded as per the type of questions and at the end, cumulative exercise has been given which is divided into two parts i.e. Base and Advance level.
- Base level and Advance level exercise covers all types of questions i.e. asked in previous years examinations.
- Questions of different competitive examinations like CAT, MAT, CMAT, XAT, IIFT, SNAP, MHT-CET, Bank (PO & Clerk) Railways, UPSC, SSC (CGL & CPO) etc, upto 2015 have been covered.

CONTENTS

Analytical Reasoning

Logical Reasoning

Understanding **Analytical Reasoning** & **Logical Reasoning**

An Introduction

In any general, competitive or entrance exam, the section **'Analytical and Logical Reasoning'** tests your **decision making** ability and **speed** using limited input and time. It measures a candidate's ability to analyse a given structure of arbitrary relationship and to deduce new information from that structure. It represents judgements made upon statements that are based on own content. No particular experience, beyond an understanding of the meanings of word used, is necessary for analytical reasoning.

The problem from this topic basically tests two attributes

1. You will be required to think logically, on the basis of a set of rules.

2. You will be asked to analyse the situations using your common sense.

The Logical Reasoning test items will be intended to measure your ability to understand, analyse and evaluate the arguments. Your strategy would consist in determining, what has been specifically stated and drawing inferences, on the basis of the facts stated.

First of all, determine the assumptions made by the author when jumping from evidence to conclusion.

On the other hand, Analytical Reasoning questions would be testing your ability to understand a given structure of arbitrary relationships among fictitious persons, places, things or events and deducing new information from the relationships given. Regular practice is required for tackling such questions. Don't make undue haste in tackling these questions.

Types of Problem

From this topic, usually, two types of problems are asked.

FIRST one in which problems are usually **all-or-nothing** type, in the sense that, if you crack the problem you will have answers to all the questions that follow and if you don't, you will not be able to answer even a single question. This is because, if the logic to the problem is apparent to you, the questions that follow are trivial. Hence, proper selection of problems to tackle is crucial.

The most important and first step to solve a reasoning problem is to write down all of the information given in a box, table or diagram e.g. if the problem involves seating arrangements at a round table, always draw the table first and then try various permutations and combinations of people seated around it. Once you have drawn the figure for the problem, you are free to think with an uncluttered mind

SECOND type of problems, questions are **not given in the form of a set *i.e.*, they are separate**. These are statement based questions and based on real life situations. To understand and to solve these type of questions, one should have the proper knowledge of definitions and terms used in logical reasoning.

As this section is clear to you, you will find that it is one of the high scoring sections. So, you can look to it for help in improving your overall score, if you had a good proportion of practice time to it. In such questions, the accuracy can be highest and time spent on solving them can be quite less, if one has done a heavy amount of practice.

HOW TO PREPARE

Analytical Reasoning & Logical Reasoning

Hence, we are going to tell you, how to tackle and crack this section in any exam and what points should be remembered for it. Usually the students make the strategy, plan their way of practice and then follow it. Even then they forget some points, which can be considered as their weak points. So, you are advised to follow some points.

Point 1 : Do the Perfect Practice

As in all other sections, the most important part of preparation is practice, you are advised to practice seriously and regularly. For it, you should take tests but remember, that taking untimed tests holds no value, that means taking test without looking at the watch will only hamper your preparation.

For practicing, start with topical tests in the initial stage of preparation. When you gain confidence in all it's areas, start taking full-length tests. Always analyse your performance after every test you took and use tests as a valuable feedback mechanism. If you feel that you require more work in one or more topics, keep going back and take 1-2 more specific tests at that topic.

An important thing you need to work on is the judicious selection of questions. Use practice sets for this purpose.

Point 2 : Don't Take Questions as Difficult

Most students perceived that this section is difficult but it is not so. Infact, they are very easy. Actually, the questions are framed in such a way that they seems difficult, but if you are able to understand it's language, it will be easy for you. *e.g.*, 'Rohan is the most intelligent person of the class' may be written as' No one in the class has as much intelligence as Rohan Here, both of the statements are same.

Point 3 : Real Life and Your Views

Analytical reasoning is the primary tool used in solving problems of every kind, which we face in real life situations. Mostly some situations from the real life experience would put forward and options would provided to check clarity of thought, decision making and problem solving abilities of the candidates. So, try to construct as much situational examples as possible from real life happenings. e.g., when you read a newspaper thoroughly, try to put yourself in same situations underlying the occured events. Also, construct some options yourself and try to find out that option that comes high unbiased and morals.

Before starting any **Logical Reasoning** problem, it is advised to keep some point in your mind. Normally, all the candidates know these points but sometimes, they don't use them or we can say that they don't know their importance. It's not enough to know the point only but to understand and use them is also necessary. These points are given below

1. Study the question carefully.
2. Don't assume any information that the question fails to give you.
3. Read all the response choices carefully before choosing one.
4. Pay special attention to words like all, some, none, unless, other than, only etc. These words play an important role in precisely specifying the facts to be used in LR.

Logical Reasoning skills find its importance in a variety of settings and have many applications. A correct approach and regular practice would make you gradually develop and deepen these skills. Each of us has these skills and we use them in all aspects of daily life without consciously being aware of it.

ANALYTICAL REASONING

1

Seating Arrangement

The process of making a group of people to sit as per a prefixed manner is called ***Seating Arrangement.***

These type of questions are the most common in various examinations like CAT, XAT, IIFT, FMS and Bank PO. These questions generally involve five to eight individuals arranged in a certain pattern. They may have to be arranged in a row or in a circle.

In some questions we will also deal with other arrangements like, square, pentagonal, hexagonal etc.

Sometimes these questions are made more difficult by allowing an individual to a particular position with some conditions.

General Guidelines to Solve 'Seating Arrangement' Questions

Guideline 1 First of all take a quick glance on the given information. After performing this step, you would get an idea of the situation of people or objects.

Guideline 2 Next, determine the usefullness of each information and classify them accordingly into 'definite information', 'comparative informaton' and 'negative information'.

Guideline 3 When the place of any person or object is definitely mentioned then we say that it is a **definite information.**

e.g. A is sitting on the right end of the bench.

These persons or objects are placed directly at the mentioned position.

Guideline 4 When the place of any person or object is not mentioned definitely but mentioned only in the comparison of another person or object, then we say that it is a **comparative information.**

e.g. A is sitting second to the right of E. This type of information can be helpful when we can get the definite information about E.

And the persons or objects are placed according to the person or object whose position is definite.

Guideline 5 A part of definite information may consist of **negative information**. A negative information does not tell us anything definitely but it gives an idea to eliminate a possibility.

e.g. C is not sitting on the immediate left of A.

According to this information, we find the remaining possible places where the person or object may be placed.

Case **Five friends A, B, C, D and E are sitting on a bench facing North.**

(i) C is sitting next to the right of D. (Comparative information)
(ii) D is sitting at extreme left position. (Definite information)
(iii) A is sitting to the left of B. (Comparative information)
(iv) B is not at the extreme right position. (Negative information)

Here, first of all we will consider the statement (ii)

D _ _ _ _

Now, from statement (i)

D C _ _ _

From statements (iii) and (iv)

D C A B _

Now, the remaining person, i.e. E will sit at remaining position.

D C A B E

Types of Questions Asked in Different Examinations

There are multiple types of questions which are asked from the chapter 'Seating Arrangement', so it is quite difficult to predict exact type of questions that are asked, but on the basis of **Observation, Analysis and Experience.** Here, we are giving different types of questions that are usually asked in the examination. Almost all the questions in this chapter can be categorised into these types. Also, this description of type will make your study easy and streamlined.

Type 1 Linear Arrangement

In this type of arrangement, we arrange people or objects in a line or row. The arrangement is done only on one 'axis' and hence, the position of people or objects assumes importance in terms of order like first position, second position... last position. In this type of arrangement, we take directions according to our left and right.

There are few words which must be paid adequate attention, i.e. 'between' means sandwiched, **'immediate left' is different from 'to the left'.**

To understand it, let us see some pictorial representation.

One Row Sequence

(A) When direction of face is not clear, then we take ourself as base and then the diagram will be as follows

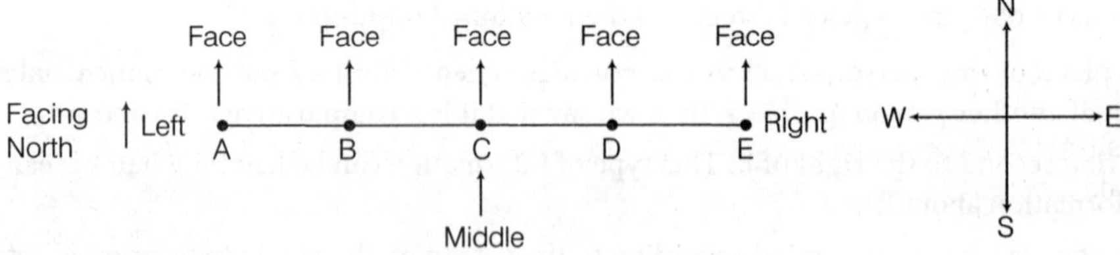

From the above diagram, it is clear that

(i) B, C, D, E are **right** of A but **only** B is to the **immediate right** of A.
(ii) D, C, B, A are **left** of E but **only** D is to the **immediate left** of E.
(iii) C, D, E are **right** of B but **only** C is to the **immediate right** of B.
(iv) C, B, A are **left** of D but **only** C is to the **immediate left** of D.
(v) D and E are **right** of C but **only** D is to the **immediate right** of C.
(vi) B and A are **left** of C but **only** B is to the **immediate left** of C.
(vii) A is the **immediate left** of B **while** E is to the **immediate right** of D.

The correct form is 'B is to the to immediate right of A'.

(B) When direction of face is towards you, then the diagram will be as follows

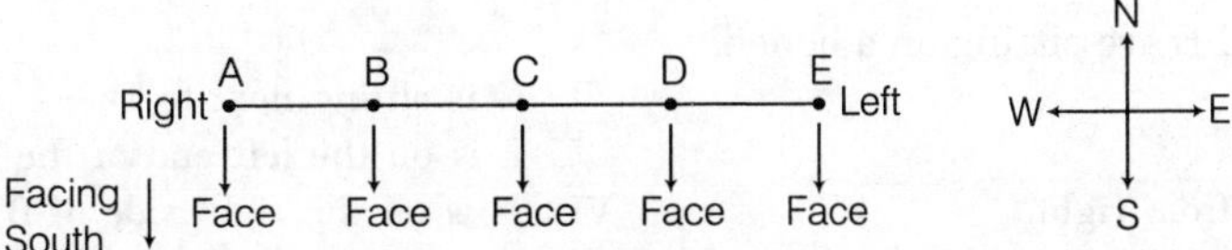

From the above diagram, it is clear that

(i) Left of A = B, C, D and E

(ii) Right of E = D, C, B and A

(iii) B is immediate left of A; C is immediate left of B; D is immediate left of C and E is immediate left of D.

(iv) D is immediate right of E; C is immediate right of D; B is immediate right of C; and A is immediate right of B.

Two Rows Sequence

Let us see 6 persons seating in two rows

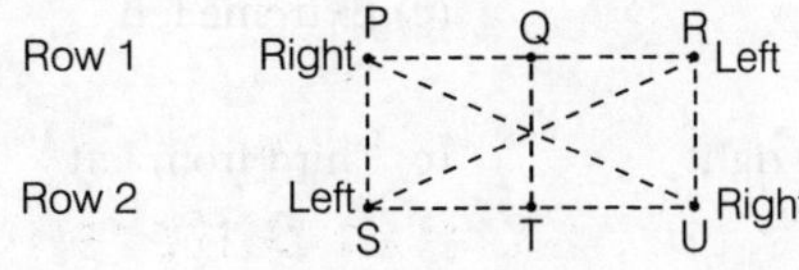

From the above diagram, it is clear that

(i) P is sitting opposite S.

(ii) Q is sitting opposite T.

(iii) R is sitting opposite U.

(iv) P and U are sitting at diagonally opposite positions.

(v) S and R are sitting at diagonally opposite positions.

Examples Based on Type 1

Ex **1.** A, B, C, D, E, F, G and H are sitting in a row facing North.

I. A is fourth to the right of E

II. H is fourth to the left of D

III. C and F, which are not at the ends, are neighbours of B and E respectively.

IV. H is next to the left of A and A is the neighbour of B,

Who are sitting at the extreme ends?

(a) E and D (b) F and B (c) B and D (d) None of these

Sol. (*a*) From information I, we get that there are three persons between A and E.

E __ __ __ A

In the information IV, it is given that H is next to the left of A and B is the neighbour of A. Using the information with (i), we get E ___ H A B

By the information II, E ___ H A B __ D

By the information III,

Left E F G H A B C D Right — Facing North

So, E and D are sitting at the extreme ends.

Ex **2.** Four children are sitting in a row. A is occupying the seat next to B but not next to C. If C is not sitting next to D, who is/are occupying seat/seats adjacent to D? **CSAT 2014**

(a) B (b) A (c) B and A (d) Impossible to tell

Sol. (*b*) The arrangement, as per the given information, is possible only if C is sitting next to B and D is sitting next to A.

∵ Two possible arrangements are D A B C or C B A D

Clearly, only A is sitting adjacent to D.

Ex **3.** Six persons M, N, O, P, Q and R are sitting in two rows with three persons in each row. Both the rows are in front of each other. Q is not at the end of any row. P is second to the left of R. O is the neighbour of Q and diagonally opposite to P. N is the neighbour of R. Who is in front of N?

(a) R (b) Q (c) P (d) M

Sol. (*b*) Arrangement according to the question is as follows

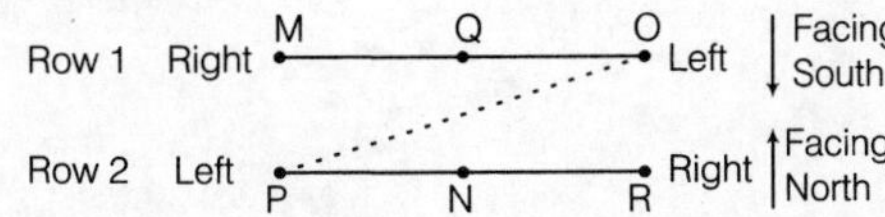

The dotted line in the above figure shows that P is diagonally opposite to O. Clearly, Q is sitting opposite to N.

Direction (Examples 4-7) *Read the following information carefully and then answer the questions given below it.*

Five friends A, B, C, D and E are sitting on a bench.

I. A is sitting next to B.
II. C is sitting next to D.
III. D is not sitting with E.
IV. E is on the left end of the bench.
V. C is on second position from right.
VI. A is on the right side of B and to the right side of E.
VII. A and C are sitting together.

Ex 4. At what position is A sitting?
(a) Between B and C (b) Between D and C (c) Between E and D (d) Between C and E

Ex 5. Who is sitting at the centre?
(a) A (b) B (c) C (d) D

Ex 6. What is the position of B?
(a) Second from right (b) Centre (c) Extreme left (d) Second from left

Ex 7. What is the position of D?
(a) Extreme left (b) Extreme right (c) Third from left (d) Second from left

SOLUTION (Examples 4-7) Arrangement according to the information is as follows

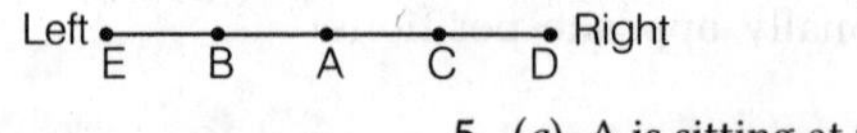

4. (*a*) A is sitting between B and C.
5. (*a*) A is sitting at the centre.
6. (*d*) B is sitting second from left.
7. (*b*) D is at the extreme right

Direction (Examples 8-11) *Study the following information carefully to answer the given questions.*

Twelve persons are sitting in two parallel rows containing six persons each, in such a way that there is an equal distance between adjacent persons. In row— 1, A, B, C, D, E and F are seated (but not necessarily in the same order) and all of them are facing South. In row— 2, P, Q, R, S, T and V are seated (but not necessarily in the same order) and all of them are facing North. Therefore, in the given seating arrangement each person seated in a row faces another person of the other row.

A sits third to the left of E. The person facing A sits second to the left of T. Two persons are sitting between T and P. C and D are immediate neighbours. C and D do not sit at any of the extreme ends of the line. Only one person sits between B and C. The person facing D is an immediate neighbour of Q. V is not an immediate neighbour of P. S does not face A.

Ex 8. Who amongst the following sits second to the right of the person who faces R?
(a) C (b) D (c) B (d) E
(e) Cannot be determined

Ex 9. Which of the following statements regarding B is true?
(a) B sits second to the left of C
(b) A sits to immediate left of B
(c) T faces B
(d) D is an immediate neighbour of B
(e) The person who faces B is an immediate neighbour of S

Ex 10. Who amongst the following faces P?
(a) A (b) D (c) C (d) E
(e) Cannot be determined

Ex 11. Four of the following five are alike in a certain way based on the given seating arrangement and thus form a group. Which is the one that does not belong to the group?
(a) F (b) Q (c) T (d) C
(e) E

SOLUTION (Examples 8-11) On the basis of given information, the sitting arrangement of twelve persons in two parallel rows is shown below

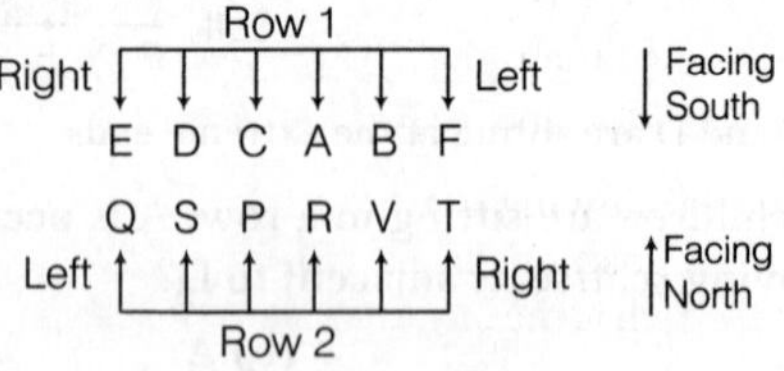

8. (*b*) A faces R. D sits second to the right of A.
9. (*a*) B sits second to the left of C. A sits to the immediate right of B.
V faces B.
A and F are immediate neighbours of B.
V faces B. R and T are immediate neighbours of V.
10. (*c*) C faces P.
11. (*d*) Except C, all others are seated at extreme ends of the lines.

Intro Exercise 1 (Based on Type 1)

1. There are five houses P, Q, R, S and T. P is right of Q and T is left of R and right of P. Q is right of S. Which house is in the middle? **IIFT 2013**

(a) P (b) Q (c) T (d) R

2. Six friends A, B, C, D, E and F are sitting in a row facing towards North, C is sitting between A and E, D is not at the end, B is sitting at immediate right of E, F is not at the right end, but D is sitting at 3rd left of E. Which of the following is sitting to the left of D? **SSC (CPO) 2013**

(a) A (b) F (c) E (d) C

3. Seven children A, B, C, D, E, F and G are standing in a row. G is to the right of D and to the left of B. A is on the right of C, A and D have one child between them. E and B have two children between them. D and F have also two children between them. Who is exactly in the middle? **UPPSC (Pre) 2013**

(a) A (b) C (c) D (d) G

Direction (Q. Nos. 4-8) *Study the following information to answer the given questions.* **IBPS (PO) 2011**

A, B, C, X, Y and Z are seated in a straight line facing North. C is third to the right of Z and B sits second to the right of C. X sits to the immediate right of A.

4. Which of the following represents the pair of persons sitting exactly in the middle of the line?

(a) XB (b) ZB
(c) BX (d) XC
(e) XY

5. What is X's position with respect to Z?

(a) Immediate right of Z
(b) Second to the left
(c) Third to the right
(d) Second to the right
(e) None of the above

6. Four of the following five are alike in a certain way based on their sitting positions in the above arrangement and so form a group. Which is the one that does not belong to the group?

(a) ZA (b) XC
(c) CY (d) YB
(e) XA

7. How many persons are seated between A and C?

(a) One (b) Two
(c) Three (d) Four
(e) None of these

8. If A : X and Z : A, then Y: ?

(a) Y (b) B
(c) A (d) X
(e) None of these

Direction (Q. Nos. 9-13) *Study the following information carefully and answer the given questions following it.*

I. Eleven students A, B, C, D, E, F, G, H, I, J and K are sitting in the first row of a class facing the teacher.
II. D, who is to the immediate left of F, is second to the right of C.
III. A is second to the right of E, who is at one of the ends.
IV. J is the immediate neighbour of A and B and third to the left of G.
V. H is to the immediate left of D and third to the right of I.

9. Who is sitting in the middle between E and H ?

(a) J (b) B (c) I (d) G
(e) None of these

10. Which of the following statements is not true in the context of the above seating arrangements?

(a) There are seven students sitting between K and D
(b) G is the immediate neighbour of I and C
(c) H is the immediate neigbour of D and F
(d) K is between E and A
(e) F is third to the right of C

11. To obtain the respective seats of all the persons which statement given above is not required?

(a) I (b) II (c) III (d) IV
(e) None of these

12. Besides E, who among the following is at the extreme end?

(a) K (b) F (c) B
(d) Cannont be determined (e) None of these

13. Which of the following groups is at the left of I?

(a) AJB (b) GCH (c) HDF (d) GCH
(e) None of these

Direction (Q. Nos. 14-16) *Read the following information carefully and answer the questions given below.*

I. There are five friends.
II. They are standing in a row facing South.
III. Jayesh is to the immediate right of Alok.
IV. Pramod is between Bhagat and Subodh.
V. Subodh is between Jayesh and Pramod.

14. Who is at the extreme left end?

(a) Alok (b) Bhagat
(c) Subodh (d) Data inadequate

15. Who is in the middle?

(a) Bhagat (b) Jayesh (c) Pramod (d) Subodh

16. To find answers of the above two questions, which of the given statements can be dispensed with?

(a) Only I (b) Only V (c) Only III (d) Only II

17. Six students are sitting in a row in an examination hall. K is sitting between V and R. V is sitting next to M. M is sitting next to B. B is sitting on the extreme left and Q is sitting next to R. Who are sitting adjacent to V? **FMS 2010**
(a) M and R (b) M and K
(c) K and R (d) M and Q

Direction (Q. Nos. 18-22) *Study the following information to answer the given questions.*

P, Q, R, S, T, V, X and Y are seated in a straight line facing North. P sits fourth to the left of V. V sits either sixth from the left end of the line or fourth from the right end of the line. S sits second to right of R. R is not an immediate neighbour of V. T and Q are immediate neighbours of each other but neither T nor Q sits at extreme ends of the line. Only one person sits between T and X. X does not sit at the extreme end of the line.

18. What is the position of Q with respect to P?
(a) Fifth to the right (b) Immediate neighbour
(c) Second to the right (d) Third to the left
(e) None of these

19. Which of the following represents persons seated at the two extreme ends of the line?
(a) P, V (b) Y, S (c) R, V (d) Y, P
(e) R, Y

20. How many persons are seated between R and T?
(a) One (b) Two (c) Three (d) Four
(e) None of these

21. If P is related to Q and S is related to T in a certain way, to which of the following would V be related to following the same pattern?
(a) Y (b) P (c) R (d) S
(e) X

22. Who amongst the following sits exactly in the middle of the persons who sit second from the left and the person who sits fifth from the right?
(a) V (b) Q (c) T (d) S
(e) P

Direction (Q. Nos. 23-25) *Read the following information carefully and answer the questions given below.*

Six girls A, B, K, D, E and P are standing in a row. B is between D and P. A does not stand next to either P or D. K does not stand next to D. E stands between A and K.

23. P stands between
(a) B and K (b) E and A (c) D and B (d) A and K
(e) Cannot be determined

24. Who occupy the extreme ends of the row?
(a) D and E (b) D and A (c) A and P (d) B and E
(e) None of these

25. K stands between
(a) P and B (b) P and D (c) P and E (d) E and A
(e) None of these

Direction (Q. Nos. 26-30) *Study the following information carefully to answer the given questions.*

Eight members P, Q, R, S, T, V, H and L are sitting in two rows with equal number of members in each row. Members of one row are facing North and those in the other row are facing South. Each member in one row is sitting exactly opposite to a member in the other row.

P sits in the row facing North, to the immediate right of H who is exactly opposite of R. L is to the immediate right of R and S is exactly opposite of T who is to the immediate right of P. V does not sit at any of the ends of any row.

26. Which of the following members sit at the ends of the same row?
(a) TH (b) SR (c) LQ (d) LT
(e) None of these

27. Who sits opposite of P?
(a) L (b) Q
(c) V (d) Cannot be determined
(e) None of these

28. Which of the following members sit exactly opposite to each other?
(a) VQ (b) LV (c) VH (d) RH
(e) None of these

29. Who is to the left of V?
(a) T (b) S (c) R (d) L
(e) None of these

30. Who sits to the right of Q?
(a) H (b) L (c) V (d) R
(e) None of these

Direction (Q. Nos. 31-35) *Study the following information to answer the given questions.* **PNB (PO) 2010**

Seven friends T, U, V, W, X, Y and Z are sitting in a straight line facing North. W sits fifth to the right of T. W does not sit at any of extreme ends. Two people sit between Z and X. Y sits third to the left of U. Y sits exactly in the middle. Z is not an immediate neighbour of Y.

31. What is Z's position with respect to W?
(a) Second to the left (b) Third to the right
(c) Fourth to the left (d) Third to the left
(e) Fourth to the right

32. Who is second to the right of T?
(a) Y (b) X
(c) U (d) V
(e) None of these

33. Four of the following five are alike in a certain way based on their sitting positions in the above line and so form a group. Which of the one that does not belong to the group?
(a) UW (b) XV
(c) ZT (d) YV
(e) WX

34. If all the seven friends are made to sit alphabetically from right to left, then positions of how many will remain unchanged?
(a) None (b) One (c) Two (d) Three
(e) Four

35. Who sit at the extreme ends of the line?
(a) XZ (b) VX (c) YZ (d) XT
(e) TU

Direction (Q. Nos. 36-40) *Study the following information carefully and answer the questions that follow.*

I. Seven members of a family J, K, L, M, N, O and P are to be seated in a row from left to right. (The one standing at the left end will be called the 1st; the one standing at the right end, the 7th.)
II. Their professions are lawyer, accountant, social worker, IAS, housewife, commissioner and student, though not necessarily in that order.
III. The third person is the housewife.
IV. M, who is not the commissioner, will stand after the person who immediately follows N.
V. J is the social worker.
VI. The lawyer stands sixth.
VII. The accountant stands to the immediate left of the commissioner.
VIII. P stands to the immediate right of O and to the immediate left of K.
IX. N, the student, stands fifth.

36. The person standing first from left is
(a) O (b) social worker
(c) P (d) commissioner
(e) L

37. The person standing to the immediate left of M is
(a) housewife (b) J
(c) lawyer (d) K
(e) commissioner

38. Which of the following correctly matches a person with his/her profession?
(a) O-IAS (b) K-housewife
(c) L-commissioner (d) P-lawyer
(e) M-accountant

39. Suppose, P has to go on account of an emergency and the family brings in the family servant Q, who stands to the immediate right of L. The sixth person from the left is now
(a) K (b) J
(c) N (d) Q
(e) M

40. If in addition to the changes described in Q. 39 the housewife and her husband, the IAS, agree to interchange places, which of the following will be true?
(a) M will stand after O but before J
(b) K wil be the only person to the right of L
(c) There will be an equal number of persons to the left and to the right of J
(d) There will be only one person to the right of N and to the left of K
(e) The first and last person will be the same as before

41. In a college party, 5 girls are sitting in a row. P is sitting to the left of M and to the right of O. R is sitting to the right of N but to the left of O. Who is sitting in the middle? **SSC (10+2) 2010**
(a) O (b) R (c) P (d) M

Direction (Q. Nos. 42-45) *Read the following information carefully and answer the questions given below.*

Six persons A, B, C, D, E and F are sitting in two rows, three in each.
I. E is not at the end of any row.
II. D is second to the left of F.
III. C the neighbour of E, is sitting diagonally opposite to D.
IV. B is the neighbour of F.

42. Which of the following are sitting diagonally opposite to each other?
(a) F and C (b) D and A (c) A and C (d) A and F
(e) A and B

43. Which of the following are in the same row?
(a) A and E (b) E and D (c) C and B (d) A and B
(e) C and E

44. Which of the following are in one of the two rows?
(a) FBC (b) CEB
(c) DBF (d) AEF
(e) ABF

45. After interchanging seat with E, who will be the neighbours of D in the new position?
(a) C and A (b) F and B
(c) Only B (d) Only A
(e) Only C

Direction (Q. Nos. 46-47) *Study the following information carefully and answer these questions.*

I. Six children B, D, C, M, J and K are split into two groups of three each and are made to stand in two rows in such a way that a child in one row is exactly facing a child in the other row.
II. M is not at the end of any row and is to the right of J, who is facing C. K is to the left of D, who is facing M.

46. Who is to the immediate left of B?
(a) M
(b) J
(c) D
(d) Data inadequate

47. Which of the following groups of children is in the same row?
(a) BDC
(b) BMD
(c) MJK
(d) None of the above

Type 2 Circular Arrangement

Arrangement Around a Closed Path

In this type of questions, we are given some clues regarding arrangement. We have to apply these clues on a closed path and using these information, we have to find the solutions of questions associated with them. In this type, the arrangement of the closed path could be of any shape i.e. square, rectangle, circular etc.

1. Circular Arrangement

In this arrangement, some persons are sitting around a circle and they are facing the centre or in the direction opposite to the centre.

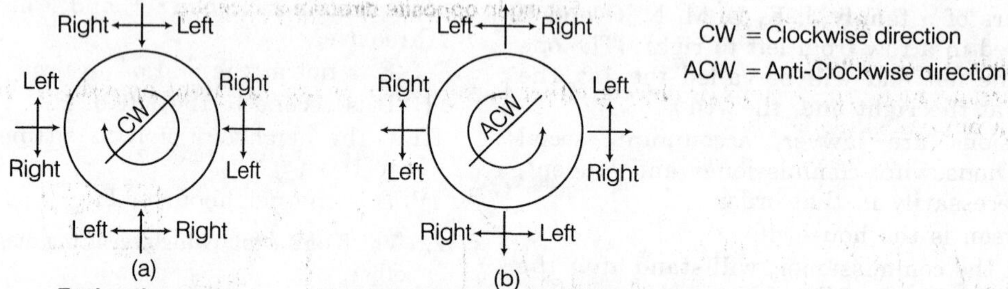

(a) Facing the centre (b) Facing in opposite directions to centre

The above presentation is for 4 persons lent for any number of persons, the direction is take in the same manner.

2. Square/Rectangular Arrangement

In this arrangement, some persons are sitting at the corners, middle and both around the square/rectangular table and they are facing the centre and facing in the direction opposite to the centre.

(i) Sitting at the corners

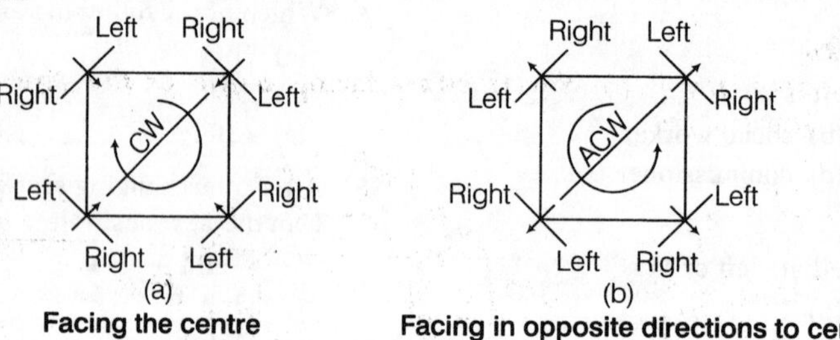

(a) Facing the centre (b) Facing in opposite directions to centre

(ii) Sitting at the middle

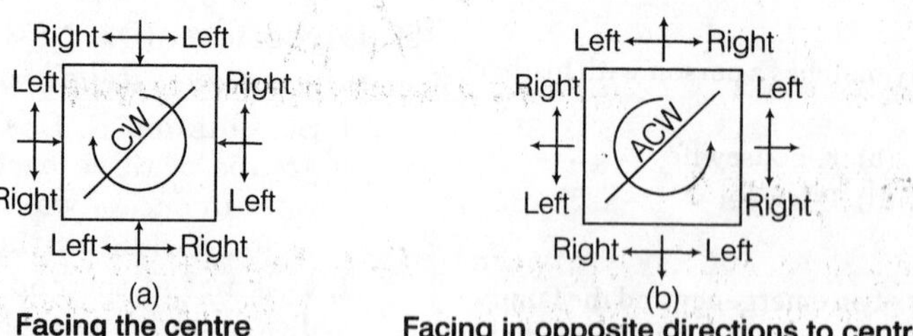

(a) Facing the centre (b) Facing in opposite directions to centre

(iii) Sitting at both sides

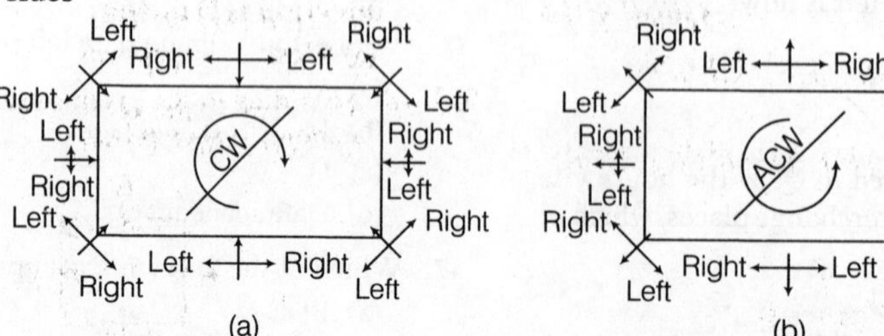

(a) Facing the centre (b) Facing in opposite directions to centre

Sometimes persons are sitting around square/rectangle table and facing the centre and in directions opposite to centre alternatively and may be depends on the information.

3. Pentagonal/Hexagonal/Octagonal Arrangement

(i) Pentagonal Arrangement

In this arrangement, five persons or objects, either facing centre or the direction opposite to the centre, are arranged around a pentagonal plane.

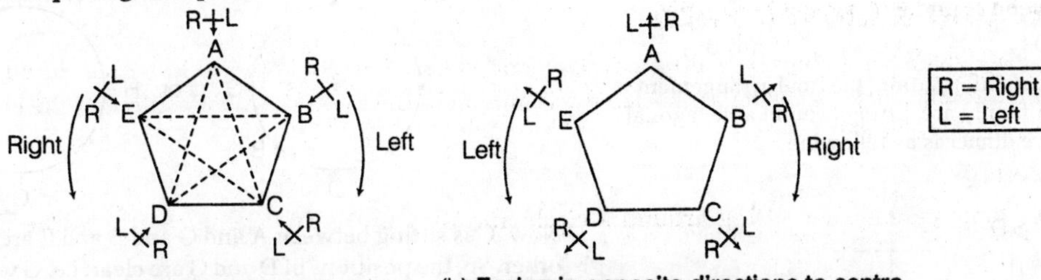

(a) Facing the centre (b) Facing in opposite directions to centre

(ii) Hexagonal Arrangement

In this arrangement, six persons or objects, either facing centre or the directions opposite to the centre, are arranged around a hexagonal plane.

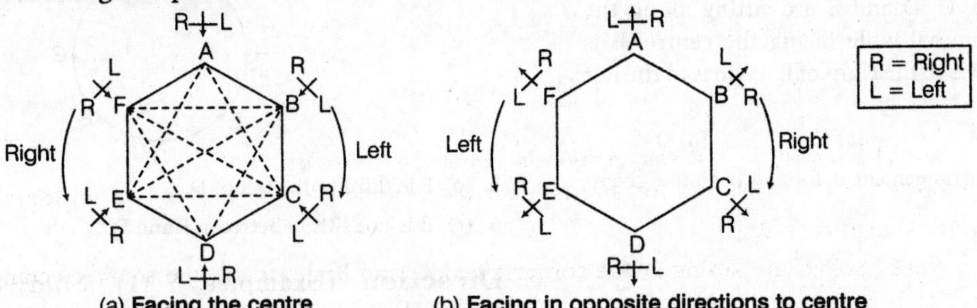

(a) Facing the centre (b) Facing in opposite directions to centre

(iii) Octagonal Arrangement

In this arrangement, eight persons or objects either facing centre or the directions opposite to the centre, are arranged around a octagonal plane.

R = Right
L = Left

(a) Facing the centre (b) Facing in opposite directions to centre

Examples Based on Type 1

***Ex* 1.** Five students are standing in a circle. Abhinav is between Alok and Ankur. Apurva is on the left of Abhishek. Alok is on the left of Apurva. Who is sitting next to Abhinav on his right? **CGPSC 2014**

(a) Apurva (b) Ankur (c) Abhishek (d) Alok
(e) None of these

Sol. (*d*) According to the question, seating arrangement of the students is as follows

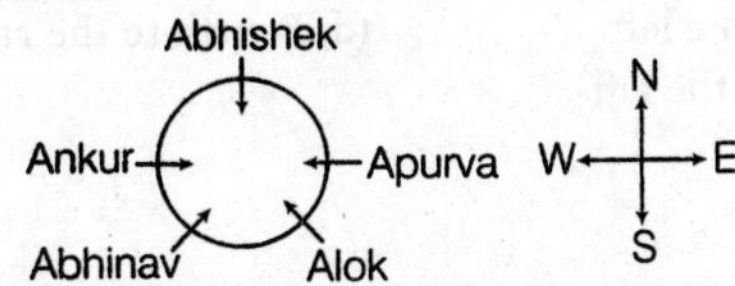

Hence, Alok is sitting next to Abhinav on his right.

***Ex* 2.** Four students A, B, C and D are playing carrom. In this game, A makes a pair with C and B makes a pair with D. D is to the right of C whose face is towards west. Which direction is D facing?

(a) West (b) East (c) South (d) North

Sol. (*c*) According to the given information, the arrangement of four students is shown below

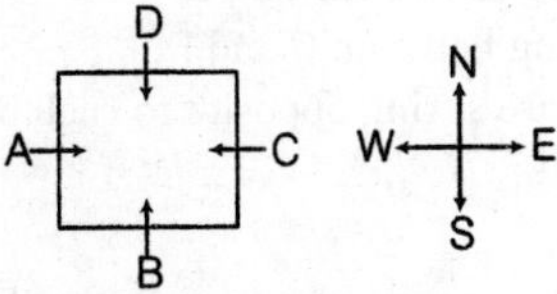

It is clearly shown that, the face of D is towards South.

Ex 3. There are six members in a family. They are A, B, C, D, E and F who are sitting around a hexagonal dinning table to have dinner. B is sitting between F and C, A is sitting between E and D and F is sitting to the left of D. Who is sitting between A and F?

(a) E (b) D (c) C (d) B

Sol. (*b*) According to the given information, the final arrangement of six members in a family are sitting around a hexagonal dinning table to have dinner is as following

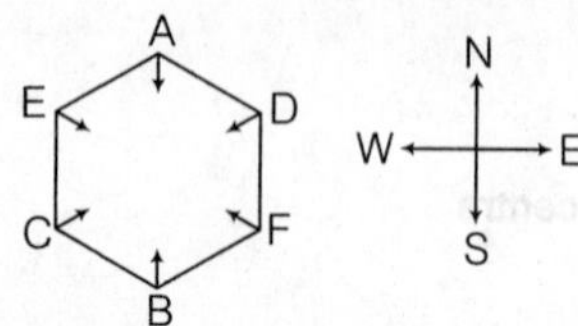

It is clearly shown that, D is sitting between A and F.

Ex 4. Five children A, B, C, D and E are sitting along the corners of a pentagonal table facing the centre. B is between E and C. D is to the right of E. Who is to the left of C?

(a) B (b) A (c) C (d) D

Sol. (*b*) Following seating arrangement is formed from the given information.

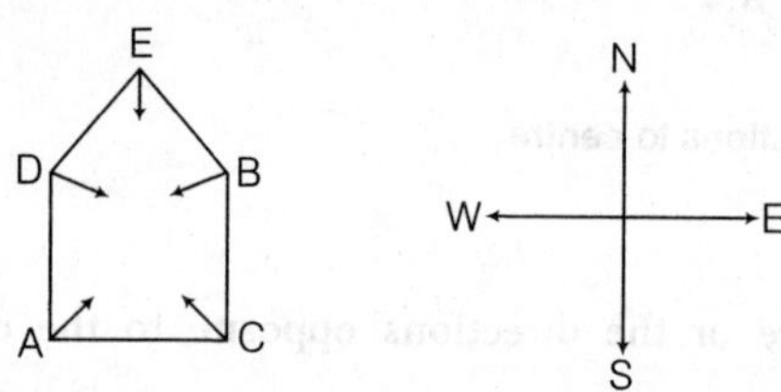

Clearly, A is to the left of C.

Direction (Examples 5-6) *Read the following information and answer the questions based on it.*

Eight friends A, B, C, D, E, F, G and H are sitting in a circle facing the centre. B is sitting between G and D. H is third to the left of B and second to the right of A. C is sitting between A and G and B and E are not sitting opposite to each other.

Ex 5. Who is third to the left of D?

(a) F
(b) E
(c) A
(d) Cannot be determined
(e) None of the above

Ex 6. Which of the following statements is not correct?

(a) D and A are sitting opposite to each other
(b) C is third to the right of D
(c) E is sitting between F and D
(d) A is sitting between C and F
(e) E and C are sitting opposite to each other

SOLUTION (Examples 5-6) First of all draw possible circular figures having eight persons. Now, B is sitting between G and D. H is third to the left of B and second to the right of A.

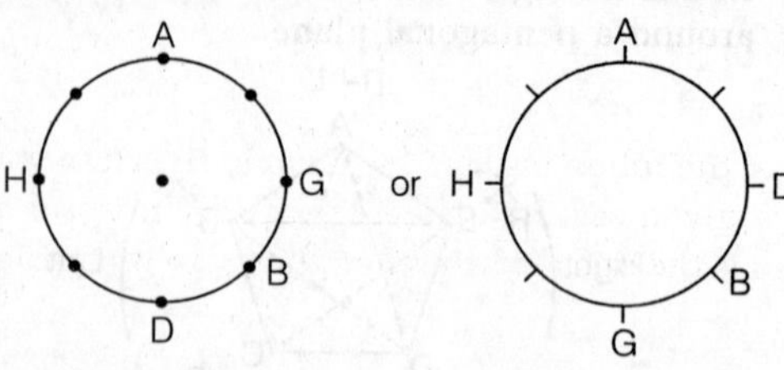

Now, C is sitting between A and G and B and E are not opposite to each other. So, the positions of D and G are clear, i.e. G will be to the right of B and D will be to the Left of B.

Now, the final arrangement will be as following

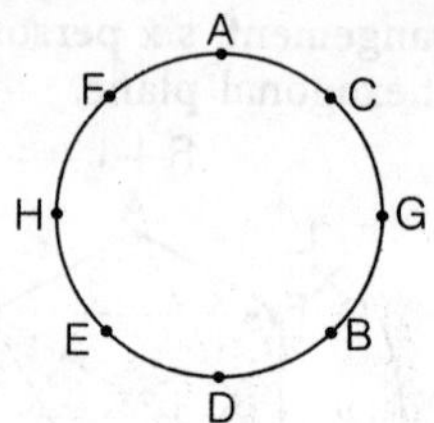

5. (*a*) F is third to the left of D.

6. (*c*) E is not sitting between F and D.

Direction (Examples 7-11) *Study the information carefully and answer the given questions.* **IBPS (Clerk) 2013**

S, T, U, V, W, X, Y and Z are sitting around a circle area, with equal distance amongst each other but not necessarily in the same order.

Only two people face the centre and the rest face outside (i.e. in a direction opposite to the centre).

Y sits second to left of W. S sits second to left of Y. Only one person sits between S and Z. T sits to immediate right of S. T is not an immediate neighbour of Y. V is not an immediate neighbour of Y.

Both the immediate neighbours of X face the centre.

Ex 7. Who is sitting to immediate right of Z?

(a) Y (b) V (c) T (d) X
(e) W

Ex 8. Which of the following is true regarding U as per the given seating arrangement?

(a) X sits second to left of U
(b) Only three people sit between U and Y
(c) Z is one of the immediate neighbours of U
(d) U faces the centre
(e) S sits to immediate left of U

Ex 9. What is T's position with respect to Y?

(a) Second to the right (b) Second to the left
(c) Fifth of the left (d) Fourth to the right
(e) Third to the left

Ex **10.** Which of the following groups represents the immediate neighbour of X?

(a) WY (b) VW
(c) TZ (d) VZ
(e) SU

Ex **11.** Four of the following five are alike in a certain way based on the given seating arrangement and so form a group. Which is the one that does not belong to that group?

(a) Z
(b) T
(c) Y
(d) V
(e) X

SOLUTION (Q. Nos. 7-11) From the given information, seating arrangement of all the persons is as follows

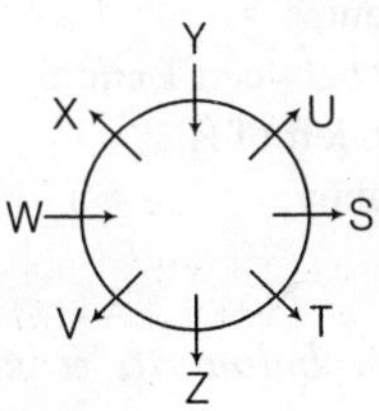

7. (*b*) V is immediate right of Z.
8. (*a*) X sits second to left of U.
9. (*e*) T is third to the left of Y.
10. (*a*) W and Y are the immediate neighbours of X.
11. (*c*) Except Y, all other are facing outside, while Y is facing inside.

Intro Exercise 2 (Based on Type 2)

Direction (Q. Nos. 1-5) *Study the following information carefully and answer the questions given below.* **IOB (PO) 2010**

A, B, C, D, E, F, G, H and J are sitting around a circle facing centre. C is third to the left of A. E is fourth to the right of A. D is fourth to the left of J, who is second to the left of J, who is second to the right of A. F is third to the right of B. G is not an immediate neighbour of A.

1. What is H's position with respect to E?

(a) Third to the left (b) Fourth to the left
(c) Fifth to the right (d) Fifth to the left
(e) Sixth to the left

2. Who is third to the right of G?

(a) B (b) D
(c) A (d) Data inadequate
(e) None of these

3. Who is fifth to the right of E?

(a) F (b) C
(c) H (d) A
(e) None of these

4. Who is second to the left of H?

(a) A
(b) F
(c) D
(d) Data inadequate
(e) None of these

5. Who is the immediate right of D?

(a) F
(b) C
(c) A
(d) Data inadequate
(e) None of the above

Direction (Q. Nos. 6-10) *Study the following information carefully and answer the given questions.* **IBPS (PO) 2011**

Eight friends P, Q, R, S, T, V, W and Y are sitting around a square table in such a way that four of them sit at four corners of the square while four sit in the middle of each of the four sides. The ones who sit at the four corners face the centre while those who sit in the middle of the sides face outside.

P who faces the centre sits third to the right of V. T, who faces the centre, is not an immediate neighbour of V. Only one person sits between V and W. S sits second of right of Q. Q faces the centre. R is not an immediate neighbour of P.

6. Who sits second to the left of Q?

(a) V (b) P (c) T (d) Y
(e) Cannot be determined

7. What is the position of T with respect of V?

(a) Fourth to the left (b) Second to the left
(c) Third to the left (d) Third to the right
(e) Second to the right

8. Four of the following five are alike in a certain way and so form a group. Which is the one that does not belong to that group?

(a) R (b) W
(c) V (d) S
(e) Y

9. Which of the following will come in place of the question mark based on the given seating arrangement?

WP TR QW RS ?

(a) YT (b) VY
(c) VQ (d) PY
(e) QV

10. Which of the following is true regarding R?
(a) R is an immediate neighbour of V
(b) R faces the centre
(c) R sits exactly between T and S
(d) Q sits third to left of R
(e) None of the above

Direction (Q. Nos. 11-15) *Read the information given below to answer the given questions.* **CLAT 2013**

A, B, C, D, E, F, G and H want to have a dinner on a round table and they have worked out the following seating arrangement.

I. A will sit beside C.
II. H will sit beside A.
III. C will sit beside E.
IV. F will sit beside H.
V. E will sit beside G.
VI. D will sit beside F.
VII. G will sit beside B.
VIII. B will sit beside D.

11. Which of the following is wrong?
(a) A will be to the immediate right of C
(b) D will be to the immediate left of B
(c) E will be to the immediate right of A
(d) F will be to the immediate left of D

12. Which of the following is correct?
(a) B will be to the immediate left of D
(b) H will be to the immediate right of A
(c) C will be to the immediate right of F
(d) B will be to the immediate left of H

13. A and F will become neighbours, if
(a) B agrees to change her seating position
(b) C agrees to change her seating position
(c) G agrees to change her seating position
(d) H agrees to change her seating position

14. During sitting
(a) A will be directly facing C
(b) B will be directly facing C
(c) A will be directly facing B
(d) B will be directly facing D

15. H will be sitting between
(a) C and B
(b) A and F
(c) D and G
(d) E and G

Direction (Q. Nos. 16-20) *Study the following information carefully and answer the given questions.* **RBI (PO) 2011**

A, B, C, D, E, F, G and H are sitting around a square table facing the centre in such a way that four of them sit at four corners of the square while four sit in the middle of each of the four sides.

I. A sits second to right of F. F sits in the middle of one of the sides of the table.
II. G who does not sit at any of the corners of the table sits second to the right of D.
III. Only two people sit between D and B (taken from one side).
IV. C is not an immediate neighbour of G.
V. H is sit second to left of B.
VI. E is not an immediate neighbour of G or F.

16. Who sits exactly between F and A?
(a) B (b) C (c) E (d) H
(e) None of these

17. How many persons sit between A and H when counted in anti-clockwise direction from A?
(a) None (b) One (c) Two (d) Three
(e) Four

18. Four of the following five are alike in a certain way based on their seating positions in the above arrangement and so form a group. Which is the one that does not belong to that group?
(a) D (c) F (c) A (d) E
(e) G

19. What is the position of F with respect to C?
(a) Third to the left (b) Immediate right
(c) Second to the left (d) Third to the right
(e) Immediate left

20. What will come in place of the question mark (?) based upon the given seating arrangement?

AE EH HF ?

(a) FE (b) HC (c) FD (d) DB
(e) FH

Direction (Q. Nos. 21-25) *Study the following information carefully and answer the questions given below.* **Corporation Bank (PO) 2010**

P, Q, R, S, T, V, W and Z are sitting around a circle facing the centre. T is second to the right of R who is third to the right of P. S is second to the left of P and fourth to the right of Q. Z is third to the right of V who is not an immediate neighbour of P.

21. In which of the following combinations is the first person seating between the second and the third persons?
(a) VTS (b) TZS (c) QRV (d) PWQ
(e) VRT

22. Who is second to the right of T?
(a) S (b) Z
(c) P (d) R
(e) None of these

23. What is P's position with respect to S?
(a) Fourth to the left (b) Fourth to the right
(c) Fifth to the left (d) Sixth to the left
(e) Third to the right

24. Who is the immediate left to Z?
(a) T (b) P
(c) S (d) V
(e) None of these

25. Who is second to the right of W?
(a) R (b) Q
(c) Z (d) S
(e) None of these

Direction (Q. Nos. 26-30) *Study the following information carefully and answer the questions given below.* **Allahabad Bank (PO) 2010**

Eight people-A, B, C, D, E, F, G and H are sitting around a circular table. A and B are facing towards the centre while other six people are facing opposite to the centre. A is sitting second to the right of H. B sits third to the left of A. D sits second to the right of G. G is immediate neighbour of neither B nor A. E and F are immediate nighbours and are facing outside.

26. What is the position of C with respect to D?
(a) Third to the right
(b) Third to the left
(c) Fourth to the left
(d) Fourth to the right
(e) Second to the left

27. Who is sitting to the immediate right of G?
(a) C (b) D
(c) F (d) H
(e) None of these

28. Which of the following pairs represents the people who are immediate neighbours of C?
(a) B and G (b) B and H
(c) G and H (d) D and G
(e) None of these

29. Who is sitting third to the left of G?
(a) A (b) D
(c) E (d) F
(e) Either E or F

30. How many people are there between B and D?
(a) Two
(b) Four
(c) Three
(d) One
(e) None

Direction (Q. Nos. 31-35) *Study the following information carefully and answer the questions given below.*

Eight persons A, B, C, D, E, F, G and H are sitting around a rectangular table in such a way that two persons sit on each of the four sides of the table facing the centre. Persons sitting to opposite sides are exactly opposite to each other. D faces North and sits exactly opposite to H . E is to the immediate left of H. A and G sit on the same side. G is exactly opposite to B who is to the immediate right of C. A is next to the left of D.

31. Who is sitting opposite to A?
(a) G (b) D
(c) E (d) A
(e) None of these

32. Who is next to E in clockwise direction?
(a) G (b) B
(c) F (d) A or F
(e) None of these

33. Which of the following pairs of persons has both the persons sitting on the same side with first person sitting to the right of second person?
(a) DF (b) CB
(c) FC (d) AG
(e) None of these

34. Who is sitting opposite to E?
(a) D (b) A
(c) F (d) A or D
(e) None of these

35. Which of the following statements is/are definitely true?
(a) A is facing North
(b) E is sitting opposite to F
(c) F is to the left of G
(d) C is to the left of A
(e) None of the above

Direction (Q. Nos. 36-40) *Study the following information to answer the given questions.*

I. Eight persons E, F, G, H, I,J, K and L are seated around a square table-two on each side.
II. There are three lady members and they are not seated next to each other.
III. J is between Land F.
IV. G is between I and F.
V. H, a lady member is second to the left of J.
VI. F, a male member is seated opposite to E, a lady member.
VII. There is a lady member between F and I.

36. Who among the following are the three lady members?
(a) E, H and J (b) E, G and J
(c) G, H and J (d) Cannot be determined
(e) None of these

37. Which of the following is true about J?
(a) J is a male member
(b) J is a female member
(c) Sex of J cannot be determined
(d) Position of J cannot be determined
(e) None of the above

38. Who among the following is seated between E and H?
(a) I (b) J
(c) F (d) Cannot be determined
(e) None of these

39. Who among the following is to the immediate left of F?
(a) G (b) J
(c) I (d) Cannot be determined
(e) None of these

40. How many persons are seated between K and F?
(a) One
(b) Two
(c) Three
(d) Cannot be determined
(e) None of the above

41. Five people A, B, C, D and E are seated about a round table. Every chair is spaced equidistant from adjacent chairs.
1. C is seated next to A. **UPSC CSAT 2014**
2. A is seated two seats from D.
3. B is not seated next to A.

Which of the following must be true?
I. D is seated next to B.
II. E is seated next to A.

Select the correct answer from the codes given below.
(a) Only I (b) Only II
(c) Both I and II (d) Neither I nor II

42. Some friends are sitting at an octagonal place. Each person is sitting at one corner facing the centre. Mahima is sitting slantly in front of Ram. Ram is to the right of Sushma. Ravi is sitting beside Sushma and in front of Giridhar. Giridhar is to the left of Chandra. Savitri is not to the right of Mahima but is in front of Shalini. Who is sitting to the right of Shalini?
SSC (CPO) 2010
(a) Ravi (b) Mahima
(c) Giridhar (d) Ram

Cumulative Exercise

Base Level

1. There are five different houses, A to E, in a row. A is to the right of B and E is to the left of C and right of A, B is to the right of D. Which of the houses is in the middle? **IB (ACIO) 2013**
(a) A (b) B
(c) C (d) D

2. Five friends P, Q, R, S and T are sitting in a row facing North. Here, S is between T and Q and Q is to the immediate left of R. P is to the immediate left to T. Who is in the middle? **SSC (FCI) 2012**
(a) S (b) T
(c) Q (d) R

3. Six children A, B, C, D, E and F are standing in a row. B is between F and D. E is between A and C. A does not stand next to either F or D. C does not stand next to D. F is between which of the following pairs of children? **SSC (FCI) 2012**
(a) B and E (b) B and C
(c) B and D (d) B and A

4. Five boys are standing in a row facing East. Pavan is to the left of Tavan, Vipin, Chavan. Tavan, Vipin and Chavan are to the left of Nakul. Chavan is between Tavan and Vipin. If Vipin is fourth from left, then how far is Tavan from the right? **CLAT 2014**
(a) First (b) Second
(c) Third (d) Fourth

5. Five children are sitting in a row. S is sitting next to P but not T. K is sitting next to R, who is sitting on the extreme left and T is not sitting next to K. Who is/are sitting adjacent to S? **NIFT (UG) 2014**
(a) K and P (b) R and P
(c) Only P (d) P and T

6. In a gathering seven members are sitting in a row. C is sitting left to B but on the right to D. A is sitting right to B. F is sitting right to E but left to D. H is sitting left to E. Find the person sitting in the middle. **SSC (10+2) 2013**
(a) C
(b) D
(c) E
(d) F

Direction (Q. Nos. 7-8) *Read the following information carefully and answer the questions that follow.* **SNAP 2014**

There are 3 females A, B and E and 4 males C, D, F and G standing in a straight line. No two females are together. B is to right of C, F and D are not together as A is placed between them. G is not near B or E but E and F are together. D is not to the right of B.

7. Who are in the extreme ends?
(a) G and B (b) C and F
(c) B and D (d) None of these

8. Who is exactly in the middle?
(a) A (b) F
(c) E (d) None of these

Direction (Q. Nos. 9-14) *Study the following information to answer the given questions.* **Bank of Maharashtra (PO) 2010**

A, B, C, D, E, F, G and H are sitting around a circular table facing the centre. No two males or two females are immediate neighbours of each other.

A is wife of H. A sits third to the left of E. F sits second to the right of D. D is not an immediate neighbour of A or E. H and C are immediate neighbours of each other. F is not an immediate neighbour of his wife B.

9. Which of the following is true about G?
(a) G is a male
(b) G sits exactly between F and H
(c) G sits third to the left of E
(d) G sits second to the right of B
(e) None of the above

10. Who sits third to the left of B?
(a) F (b) H (c) D (d) A
(e) None of these

11. How many persons sit between B and F when counted in anti-clockwise direction from B?
(a) One (b) Two (c) Three (d) Four
(e) More than four

12. Four of the following five are alike in a certain way and so form a group. Which is the one that does not belong to that group?
(a) H (b) F (c) E (d) G
(e) D

13. Which of the following groups consists of only female members of the group?
(a) A, B, H (b) G, F, C (c) C, H, G (d) D, H, C
(e) None of these

14. If all the persons are made to sit in alphabetical order in clockwise direction, starting from A, the position of how many (excluding A) will remain unchanged as compared to their original seating positions?
(a) None (b) One (c) Two (d) Three
(e) Four

Direction (Q. Nos. 15-16) *Study the information carefully to solve the questions given below.*

Six friends P, Q, R, S, T and U are sitting around the hexagonal table each at one corner and are facing the centre of the hexagonal. P is second to the left of U. Q is neighbour of R and S. T is second to the left of S.

15. Which one is sitting opposite to P?
(a) R (b) Q
(c) T (d) S

16. Who is the fourth person to the left of Q?
(a) P (b) U
(c) R (d) Data inadequate

17. Four boys and four girls are sitting around a square facing the centre. One person is sitting at each corner and at the mid-point of each side of the square. Madhu is sitting diagonally opposite to Usha who is to the right of Geeta. Ram who is to the left of Geeta is diagonally opposite to Gopi who is to the left of Bose. Position of Suma is not to the right of Madhu but in front of Prema. Who is sitting opposite to Bose?
(a) Geeta (b) Prema
(c) Getta (d) Madhu

Direction (Q. Nos. 18-20) *Read the following information carefully to answer the questions that follow.*

Six girls are sitting in a circle. Sonia is sitting opposite to Radhika. Poonam is sitting right of Radhika but left of Deepti. Monika is sitting left of Radhika. Kamini is sitting right of Sonia and left of Monika. Now, Deepti and Kamini, Monika and Radhika mutually exchange there position.

18. Who will be opposite to Sonia?
(a) Radhika (b) Monika
(c) Kamini (d) Sonia

19. Who will be sitting left of Kamini?
(a) Poonam (b) Deepti
(c) Radhika (d) Sonia

20. Who will be sitting left of Deepti?
(a) Sonia (b) Monika
(c) Radhika (d) Poonam

Direction (Q. Nos 21-22) *Read the following information carefully and answer the questions that follow.*

Eight friends A, B, C, D, E, F, G and H are sitting in a circle facing the centre. B is sitting between G and D. H is third to the left of B and second to the right of A. C is sitting between A and G and B and E are not sitting opposite to each other.

21. Who is third to the left of D?
(a) F (b) E
(c) A (d) Cannot be determined

22. Which of the following statements is not correct?
(a) D and A are sitting opposite to each other
(b) C is third to the right of D
(c) B is sitting between H and D
(d) A is sitting between C and F

Direction (Q. Nos. 23-27) *Study the following information carefully and answer the questions given below.* **IOB (PO) 2010**

P, Q, R, S, T, V, W, Y and Z are sitting around a circle facing the centre. V is second to the left of P who is third to the left of Y. S is fourth to the left of P. T is third to the right of Q who is the immediate right of V. W is fourth to the right of Z.

23. Who is third to the left of S?
(a) Y (b) W
(c) T (d) Data inadequate
(e) None of these

24. In which of the following pairs is the first person sitting to the immediate right of the second person?
(a) VQ (b) ZV
(c) SZ (d) RS
(e) YT

25. In which of the following combinations is the first person sitting between the second and the third person?
(a) RSZ (b) YTW
(c) WPQ (d) VZQ
(e) PQV

26. Who is third to the right of W?
(a) S (b) R
(c) V (d) Z
(e) Data inadequate

27. Who is second to the right of Z?
(a) Q
(b) P
(c) W
(d) Data inadequate
(e) None of the above

Direction (Q. Nos. 28-32) *Study the given information carefully and answer the questions that follow.*

I. A, B, C, D, E, F and G are sitting on a wall and all of them are facing East.
II. C is on the immediate right of D.
III. B is at an extreme end and has E as his neighbour.
IV. G is between E and F.
V. D is sitting third from the South end.

28. Who is sitting to the immediate right of E?
(a) A (b) C
(c) D (d) None of these

29. Which of the following pairs of people is sitting at the extreme ends?
(a) AB (b) AE (c) CB (d) FB

30. Name the person who should change places with C, so that he gets the third place from the North end.
(a) E (b) F (c) G (d) D

31. Immediately between which of the following pairs of people is D sitting?
(a) AC (b) AF (c) CE (d) CF

32. Which of the conditions I to V given above is not required to find out the place in which A is sitting?
(a) I (b) II
(c) III (d) All are required

Direction (Q. Nos. 33-37) *Read the following information to answer the given questions.*

I. A, B, C, D, E, F and G are sitting in a circle facing at the centre and playing cards.
II. E is neighbour of A and D.
III. G is not between F and C.
IV. F is to the immediate right of A.

33. Which of the following does not have the pair of persons sitting adjacent to each other?
(a) BA (b) CB (c) DE (d) GD
(e) None of these

34. Which of the following pairs has the second person sitting immediately to the right of the first?
(a) AB (b) CB (c) EA (d) DG
(e) None of these

35. What is the position of F?
(a) Third to the left of C
(b) Second to the right of C
(c) To the immediate left of A
(d) To the immediate right of B
(e) None of the above

36. Who are the neighbours of B?
(a) A and F (b) C and D
(c) F and C (d) Data inadequate
(e) None of these

37. Which of the following persons are sitting adjacent to each other from left to right in the order as shown?
(a) BGC (b) FBC
(c) CDG (d) EGD
(e) None of these

Direction (Q. Nos. 38-40) *Study the following information to answer the given questions.*
IBPS (PO) 2011

L, M, N, O, P, Q and R are sitting around a circle facing the centre. O is sitting between L and R. Q is second to the right of R and P is second to the right of Q. N is not an immediate neighbour of R.

38. Which of the following is not correct?
(a) R is second to the right of L
(b) M is second to the left of N
(c) L sits exactly between O and P
(d) P and N are immediate neighbours
(e) P sits to the opposite of N

39. How many persons are seated between L and Q if we count anti-clockwise from L to Q?
(a) One (b) Two (c) Three (d) Four
(e) More than four

40. Who is to the immediate left of P?
(a) L (b) N (c) M (d) O
(e) None of these

Direction (Q. Nos. 41-42) *Four of the following five are alike in a certain way based on their seating positions in the above arrangement and so form a group.* Which is the one that does not belong to the group?

41. (a) QPN (b) MNQ (c) LRO (d) RQM
(e) ROL

42. (a) LP (b) RM
(c) MQ (d) NP
(e) OR

Direction (Q. Nos. 43-47) *Study the following information carefully and answer the given questions.*
OBC (PO) 2010

Seven persons A, B, C, D, E, F and G are sitting in a straight line (not necessarily in the same order) facing North.

I. Only two persons sit between F and G and G sits second to the left of B.
II. D sits third to the left of C.
III. E sits exactly between G and B and B sits at the extreme right end of the row.

43. Who amongst the following sits at the extreme left of the line?
(a) F (b) D
(c) C (d) E
(e) G

44. Four of the following five are alike in a certain way based on their seating positions in the above arrangement and so form a group. Which is the one that does not belong to that group?
(a) AG (b) CE (c) DA (d) AF
(e) GB

45. How many persons sit between F and E?
(a) One (b) Two
(c) Three (d) Four
(e) Five

46. Who amongst the following sits exactly in the middle of the line?
(a) A (b) C
(c) E (d) G
(e) F

47. What is the position of E with respect to A?
(a) Third to the right (b) Second to the right
(c) Second to the left (d) Fourth to the right
(e) Immediate left

Direction (Q. Nos. 48-52) *Study the following information carefully and answer the questions given below.* **IBPS (Clerk) 2011**

P, T, V, R, M, D, K and W are sitting around a circular table facing the centre. V is second to the left of T. T is fourth to the right of M. D and P are not immediate neighbours of T. D is third to the right of P. W is not an immediate neighbour of P. P is to the immediate left of K.

48. Who is second to the left of K?
(a) P (b) R (c) M (d) W
(e) Data inadequate

49. Who is to the immediate left of V?
(a) D (b) M
(c) W (d) Data inadequate
(e) None of these

50. Who is the third to the right of V?
(a) T (b) K
(c) P (d) M
(e) None of these

51. What is R's position with respect to V?
(a) Third to the right
(b) Fifth to the right
(c) Third to the left
(d) Second to the left
(e) Fourth to the left

52. Four of the following five are alike in a certain way based on their positions in the above seating arrangement and so, form a group. Which of the following does not belong to that group?
(a) DW (b) TP
(c) VM (d) RD
(e) KR

Direction (Q. Nos. 53-57) *Study the following information carefully and answer the questions given below.* **IBPS (PO) 2011**

A, B, C, D, E, F, G and H are sitting around a circular table facing the centre not necessarily in the same order. F is fourth to the left of A and second to the right of C. B is second to the left of A and A is to the immediate right of G. E, who is not an immediate neighbour of B is fourth to the left of D.

53. Which of the following is correct?
(a) F is third to the left of B
(b) H is third to the left of D
(c) C is third to the left of B
(d) E is third to the left of F
(e) All of the above

54. What is H's position with respect to G?
(a) Fifth to the right (b) Third to the left
(c) Third to the right (d) Fifth to the left
(e) Fourth to the left

55. Who is second to the right of E?
(a) C (b) H (c) G (d) A
(e) Data inadequate

56. Who is to the immediate right of F?
(a) D (b) H (c) B (d) C
(e) None of these

57. Which of the following pairs represents the immediate neighbours of A?
(a) EB (b) GC (c) EG (d) ED
(e) None of these

Direction (Q. Nos. 58-62) *Read the following information and answer the questions based on it.* **MAT 2012**

Ten students A, B, C, D, E, F, G, H, I and J are sitting in a row facing West.

I. B and F are not sitting on either of the edges.
II. G is sitting to the left of D and H is sitting to the right of J.
III. There are four persons between E and A.
IV. I is to the North of B and F is to the South of D.
V. J is in between A and D and G is in between E and F.
VI. There are two persons between H and C.

58. Who is sitting at the seventh place counting from left?
(a) H (b) C
(c) J (d) Either H or C

59. Who among the following is definitely sitting at one of the ends?
(a) C (b) H
(c) E (d) Cannot be determined

60. Who are immediate neighbours of I?
(a) BC (b) BH
(c) AH (d) Cannot be determined

Advanced Level

Direction (Q. Nos. 1-6) *Study the following information to answer the given questions.*
PNB (PO) 2010

Nine friends L, M, N, O, P, Q, R, S and T are sitting around a circle facing the centre. T sits fifth to the right of R. N is not an immediate neighbour of either R or T. M sits between S and P. N sits fourth to left of the P. O sits second to the right of Q. S is not an immediate neighbour of T.

1. Who is second to the right of M?
(a) R (b) T
(c) L (d) Cannot be determined
(e) None of these

2. If all the nine friends are made to sit alphabetically in the clockwise direction starting from L, positions of how many will remain unchanged (excluding L)?
(a) None (b) One (c) Two (d) Three
(e) Four

3. Four of the following five are alike in a certain way based on their seating positions in the above arrangement and so form a group. Which is the one that does not belong to the group?
(a) LP (b) SP (c) TS (d) LN
(e) QO

4. Which of the following is O's position with respect to M in the anti-clockwise direction starting from M?
(a) Fourth to the left (b) Fifth to the right
(c) Third to the right (d) Fifth to the left
(e) None of these

5. If S : Q, then N : ?
(a) R (b) O (c) L (d) T
(e) None of these

6. Who is to the immediate left of T?
(a) O (b) Q
(c) L (d) Cannot be determined
(e) None of these

Direction (Q. Nos. 7-11) *Study the following information carefully and answer the given questions.*
NABARD (PO) 2009

Eight persons I, J, K, L, M, N, O and P are sitting around a circular table but not necessarily in the same order. Three of them are facing outward while five are facing towards the centre.

M is third to the right of K. N is sitting third to the left of M. Three persons are sitting between N and J. O is sitting third to the right of N, who is not facing the centre. L is sitting third to the right of I, who is not facing the centre.

7. Who sits between N and I?
(a) J (b) K
(c) M (d) O
(e) None of these

8. Who among the following is second to the right of J?
(a) L (b) K
(c) M (d) N
(e) None of these

9. Which of the following statements is/are true with respect to P?
(a) P is opposite of O
(b) P is fourth to the right of O
(c) P is fourth to the left of O
(d) All are true
(e) None of the above

10. Which of the following groups represents the group, of those facing away from the centre?
(a) IKN (b) KNL
(c) IJK (d) LMN
(e) None of these

11. What is the position of K with respect of P?
(a) K is third to the right of P
(b) K is second to the left of P
(c) K is third to the left of P
(e) K is in front of P
(e) None of the above

Direction (Q. Nos. 12-14) *Study the given information and answer the given questions.*

Six people– K,L,M,N,O and P live on six different floors of a building not necessarily in the same order. The lower most floor of the building is numbered 1, the one above is numbered 2 and so on till the top most floor numbered 6. L lives on an even numbered floor. L lives immediately below K's floor and immediately above M's floor. P lives immediately above N's floor. P lives on an even numbered floor. O does not live on floor number 4.

12. Four of the following five are alike in a certain way based on the given arrangement and hence form a group. Which of the following does not belong to that group?
(a) MN (b) OL (c) KM (d) LP
(e) PK

13. Who amongst the following live on floor number 2?
(a) K (b) P (c) L (d) M
(e) O

14. On which floor does N live?
(a) 4 (b) 3 (c) 5 (d) 1
(e) 2

77. What will come in place of the question mark according to the above seating arrangement?

OJKN?

(a) L (b) P (c) Q (d) O
(e) M

78. What is the position of L with respect to K in the above arrangement?
(a) Third to the left (b) Immediate left
(c) Fifth to the right (d) Immediate right
(e) Second to the left

79. Who sits second to the left of M?
(a) K (b) Q (c) J (d) O
(e) P

80. Who amongst the following sits exactly between N and J?
(a) M (b) P (c) Q (d) O
(e) Cannot be determined

Direction (Q. Nos. 81-85) *Study the given information carefully and answer the given questions.*

IBPS (Clerk) 2012

Eight people P, Q, R, S, T, U, V and W are sitting around a circular table facing the centre not necessarily in the same order. T is sitting third to the right of P. W is sitting second to the right of S. S is not an immediate neighbour of either P or T. U and Q are immediate neighbours of each other. Q is not an immediate neighbour of P. V is not an immediate neighbour of W.

81. What is R's position with respect to V?
(a) Second to the left (b) Second to the right
(c) Third to the right (d) Third to the left
(e) None of these

82. Four of the following five are alike in a certain way based on their seating position in the above arrangement and so form a group. Which one does not belong to the group?
(a) RQ (b) PV
(c) TP (d) US
(e) WT

83. Who is sitting second to the right of the one who is sitting to the immediate right of W?
(a) U (b) R
(c) V (d) P
(e) Q

84. How many people are sitting between U and W when counted from the left side of U?
(a) Three (b) None
(c) More than three (d) Two
(e) One

85. Who is sitting exactly between T and S?
(a) U (b) Q (c) W (d) V
(e) R

Direction (Q. Nos. 86-90) *Study the given information carefully and answer the given questions.*

IBPS (PO) 2012

Eight people A, B, C, D, E, F, G and H are sitting in a straight line facing North not necessarily in the same order. F is sitting fifth to the right of A. D is sitting fifth to the right of E. E is to the immediate right of A. H is third to the left of D. B is third to the right of G. G is an immediate neighbour of A.

86. What is E's position with respect to C?
(a) Second to the left (b) Third to the right
(c) Fourth to the right (d) Third to the left
(e) None of these

87. Who is sitting third to the right of the one who is sitting sixth from the right end of the above arrangement?
(a) D (b) C (c) E (d) H
(e) None of these

88. Who amongst the following are sitting at the extreme ends of the line?
(a) G and D (b) A and D
(c) G and F (d) E and D
(e) A and B

89. Four of the following five are alike in a certain way based on their seating positions in the above arrangement and so form a group. Which one does not belong to the group?
(a) HD (b) BE (c) EC (d) AH
(e) GB

90. If all eight persons are asked to sit in an alphabetical order from right to left, the positions of how many will remain unchanged as compared to their original seating position?
(a) Three (b) More than three
(c) One (d) Two
(e) None

Advanced Level

Directions (Q. Nos. 1-6) *Study the following information to answer the given questions.*

PNB (PO) 2010

Nine friends L, M, N, O, P, Q, R, S and T are sitting around a circle facing the centre. T sits fifth to the right of R. N is not an immediate neighbour of either R or T. M sits between S and P. N sits fourth to left of the P. O sits second to the right of Q. S is not an immediate neighbour of T.

1. Who is second to the right of M?
(a) R (b) T
(c) L (d) Cannot be determined
(e) None of these

2. If all the nine friends are made to sit alphabetically in the clockwise direction starting from L, positions of how many will remain unchanged (excluding L)?
(a) None (b) One (c) Two (d) Three
(e) Four

3. Four of the following five are alike in a certain way based on their seating positions in the above arrangement and so form a group. Which is the one that does not belong to the group?
(a) LP (b) SP (c) TS (d) LN
(e) QO

4. Which of the following is O's position with respect to M in the anti-clockwise direction starting from M?
(a) Fourth to the left (b) Fifth to the right
(c) Third to the right (d) Fifth to the left
(e) None of these

5. If S : Q, then N : ?
(a) R (b) O (c) L (d) T
(e) None of these

6. Who is to the immediate left of T?
(a) O (b) Q
(c) L (d) Cannot be determined
(e) None of these

Direction (Q. Nos. 7-11) *Study the following information carefully and answer the given questions.*

NABARD (PO) 2009

Eight persons I, J, K, L, M, N, O and P are sitting around a circular table but not necessarily in the same order. Three of them are facing outward while five are facing towards the centre.

M is third to the right of K. N is sitting third to the left of M. Three persons are sitting between N and J. O is sitting third to the right of N, who is not facing the centre. L is sitting third to the right of I, who is not facing the centre.

7. Who sits between N and I?
(a) J (b) K
(c) M (d) O
(e) None of these

8. Who among the following is second to the right of J?
(a) L (b) K
(c) M (d) N
(e) None of these

9. Which of the following statements is/are true with respect to P?
(a) P is opposite of O
(b) P is fourth to the right of O
(c) P is fourth to the left of O
(d) All are true
(e) None of the above

10. Which of the following groups represents the group, of those facing away from the centre?
(a) IKN (b) KNL
(c) IJK (d) LMN
(e) None of these

11. What is the position of K with respect of P?
(a) K is third to the right of P
(b) K is second to the left of P
(c) K is third to the left of P
(e) K is in front of P
(e) None of the above

Direction (Q. Nos. 12-14) *Study the given information and answer the given questions.*

Six people– K,L,M,N,O and P live on six different floors of a building not necessarily in the same order. The lower most floor of the building is numbered 1, the one above is numbered 2 and so on till the top most floor numbered 6. L lives on an even numbered floor. L lives immediately below K's floor and immediately above M's floor. P lives immediately above N's floor. P lives on an even numbered floor. O does not live on floor number 4.

12. Four of the following five are alike in a certain way based on the given arrangement and hence form a group. Which of the following does not belong to that group?
(a) MN (b) OL
(c) KM (d) LP
(e) PK

13. Who amongst the following live on floor number 2?
(a) K (b) P (c) L (d) M
(e) O

14. On which floor does N live?
(a) 4 (b) 3 (c) 5 (d) 1
(e) 2

Direction (Q. Nos. 15-19) *On the basis of the information provided below, answer these questions.*

Six people A, B, C, D, E and F are sitting on the ground in a hexagonal shape. All the sides of the hexagon so formed are of same length. A is not adjacent to B or C. D is not adjacent to C or E. B and C are adjacent F is in the middle of D and C.

15. Which of the following is not a correct neighbour pair?
(a) A and F (b) D and F (c) D and E (d) C and F

16. Who is at the same distance from D as E is from D?
(a) B (b) C (c) D (d) F

17. Which of the following is in the right sequence?
(a) A, F, B (b) F, A, E (c) B, C, F (d) D, A, B

18. If one neighbour of A is D, who is the other one?
(a) B (b) C (c) E (d) F

19. Who is placed opposite to E?
(a) B (b) C (c) D (d) F

Direction (Q. Nos. 20-23) *Answer the questions based on the following information.*

A leading socialite decides to organise a dinner and invited a few of her friends. Only the host and the hostess were sitting at the opposite ends of a rectangular table, with three persons along each side. The prerequisite for the seating arrangement was that each person must be seated such that atleast on one side it has a person of opposite sex. Maqbool is opposite of Shobha who is not the hostess. Ratan has woman on his right and is sitting opposite of a woman. Monisha is sitting to the hostess's right, next to Dhirubhai. One person is seated between Madhuri and Urmila, who is not the hostess. The men were Maqbool, Ratan, Dhirubhai and Jackie, while the women were Madhuri, Urmila, Shobha and Monisha.

20. The eighth person present, Jackie must be
I. the host.
II. seated to Shobha's right.
III. seated opposite of Urmila.
(a) Only I (b) Only III (c) I and II (d) II and III

21. Which of the following persons is definitely not seated next to a person of the same sex?
(a) Maqbool (b) Madhuri
(c) Jackie (d) Shobha

22. If Ratan would have exchanged seats with a person four places to his left, which of the following would have been true after the exchange?
I. No one was seated between two persons of the opposite sex (e.g. No man was seated between two women).
II. One side of the table consisted entirely of persons of the same sex.
III. Either the host or the hostess changed their seats.
(a) Only I (b) Only II
(c) I and II (d) II and III

23. If each person is placed directly opposite of her spouse, which of the following pairs must be married?
(a) Ratan and Monisha
(b) Madhuri and Dhirubhai
(c) Urmila and Jackie
(d) Ratan and Madhuri

Directions (Q. Nos. 24-28) *Study the following information to answer the given questions.*
MHT CET MBA 2011

Twelve cars *viz.* Mercedes, Swift, Santro, Accord, Innova, Polo, Punto, Figo, Civic, City, Ferrari and Landrover are parked in two parallel rows containing six cars each, in such a way that there is an equal distance between adjacent cars. The cars parked in row-1 are parked in such a manner that the driver seated in the cars would face the South. In row-2, cars are parked in such a manner that the drivers seated in these cars would face the North. Therefore, in the given parking arrangement each car parked in a row faces another car of the other row.

I. Mercedes being a big car must be parked at one of the extreme ends. Mercedes is parked second to the left of Santro. Santro faces Figo.
II. Punto and Innova are parked immediately next to each other. Neither is parked next to Figo or Santro.
III. Civic is parked in such a manner that its driver when seated in the parked car would face South. Civic is parked third to the left of Polo.
IV. City is parked in such a manner that it faces Ferrari. Ferrari is parked second to the left of Landrover. Landrover faces North and is not parked next to Figo.
V. Swift is parked third to the right of Ferrari and faces Innova.

Left and right parking directions are with reference to the driver as if the driver is seated in the car.

24. How many cars are parked between Santro and Civic?
(a) One (b) Two (c) Three (d) Four
(e) Both cars are parked in different rows

25. Polo is related to Ferrari in the same way as Innova is related to Accord. To which of the following is city related to, following the same pattern?
(a) Mercedes (b) Innova (c) Santro (d) Punto
(e) Landrover

26. Which of the following cars are parked at extreme ends of the rows?
(a) Landrover, Punto (b) Innova, Polo
(c) Polo, Accord (d) Landrover, Innova
(e) Ferrari, Swift

27. Which of the following cars faces Polo?
(a) Mercedes
(b) Civic
(c) Landrover
(d) Punto
(e) Accord

28. Which of the following is true regarding Figo?
(a) A driver seated in the parked Figo would face North
(b) Swift is parked second to the right of the car facing Figo
(c) Punto and Ferrari are parked immediately next to Figo
(d) Mercedes and Accord are parked at the extreme ends of the row in which Figo is parked
(e) None of the above

Direction (Q. Nos. 29-30) *Four of the following five are alike in a certain way based upon the given parking arrangement and so form a group.*

Which is the one that does not belong to that group?

29. (a) Ferrari (b) Civic
(c) Swift (d) Mercedes
(e) Landrover

30. (a) Polo-Figo (b) Accord-Landrover
(c) Figo-Innova (d) Mercedes-City
(e) Santro-Swift

Direction (Q. Nos. 31-34) *Refer to the data below and answer the questions that follow.*

A group of 7 people, Salman, Shahrukh, Aamir, Ranbir, Imran, Shahid and Akshay are to be arranged in a row of 7 chairs (not necessarily in the same order), such that 2 adjacent chairs are facing opposite directions but not facing each other.

Given below are some of the conditions to be followed for the seating arrangement.

I. Akshay sits in a chair whose direction is opposite to that of Imran.
II. None of Salman, Shahrukh or Aamir can sit adjacent to each other.
III. Ranbir and Shahid are best friends, so they always sit together.
IV. Imran has 4 people sitting to his right.
V. Aamir is sitting two positions to the right of Ranbir.

31. Which of the following can never occupy adjacent chairs?
(a) Akshya and Imran (b) Ranbir and Salman
(c) Shahrukh and Shahid (d) Aamir and Imran

32. If Ranbir is 3 places to the right of Imran, then who is 2 places to the left of Akshay?
(a) Salman
(b) Aamir
(c) Either Shahrukh or Salman
(d) Either Aamir or Shahrukh

33. If Akshay is 3 places to the left of Shahid, then who can occupy the corner positions (in any order)?
(a) Salman and Aamir (b) Shahrukh and Salman
(c) Shahrukh and Aamir (d) None of these

34. Whose position is always fixed?
(a) Imran (b) Akshay
(c) Shahid (d) None of these

Direction (Q. Nos. 35-36) *Read the following information carefully and mark the correct answer to the questions given below.*

Sampada Apartment is a housing society formed by a group of professors of a university. It has six flats on a floor in two rows facing North and south which are allotted to Prof Purohit, Prof Qureshi, Prof Usman, Prof Qureshi gets a North facing flat and it is not next to Prof Sawant's flat. Prof Sawant and Prof Usman get their flats which are diagonally opposite to each other. Prof Rathor gets a South facing flat which is next to Prof Usman's flat. Prof Tripathy's flat is North facing.

35. Which of the following professors get South facing flats?
(a) Prof Qureshi, Prof Tripathy and Prof Sawant
(b) Prof Usman, Prof Tripathy and Prof Purohit
(c) Prof Usman, Prof Rathor and Prof Purohit
(d) None of the above

36. If the flats of Prof Tripathy and Prof Purohit are interchanged, whose flat will be next to that of Prof. Usman?
(a) Prof Rathor (b) Prof Tripathy
(c) Prof Usman (c) None of these

Direction (Q. Nos. 37-44) *Study the following information carefully to answer the given questions.*
MHT CET MBA 2012

Eight people are sitting in two parallel rows containing four people each, in such a way that there is an equal distance between adjacent persons. In row 1 A, B, C and D are seated and all of them are facing South. In row 2 E, F, G and H are seated and all of them are facing North. Therefore, in the given sitting arrangement each member seated in a row faces another member of the other row. Each one of them also has a different profession, *viz.* Engineer, Doctor, Teacher, Pilot, Businessman, Banker, Lawyer and Builder but not necessarily in the same order.

B sits second to right of the Builder. G faces the immediate neighbour of the Builder. Only one person sits between G and the Pilot. Two people sit between H and the Lawyer. D faces the immediate neighbour of the Pilot. Only one person sits between the Teacher and C. Teacher does not sit at any of the extreme ends. Immediate neighbour of D faces the Doctor. E faces the Engineer. F is not the Banker.

37. Who amongst the following sit at extreme ends of the rows?
(a) B and the Pilot (b) C and the Builder
(c) The Builder and G (d) G and the Engineer
(e) A, G

38. Who amongst the following is the Banker?
(a) A (b) B (c) C (d) E
(e) G

39. Who is/are seated between the Lawyer and the Doctor?
(a) Pilot only
(b) G and the Businessman
(c) F, E
(d) Businessman and the Banker
(e) No one

40. Who amongst the following faces the Businessman?
(a) A (b) Doctor (c) F (d) Teacher
(e) Builder

41. Which of the following is true regarding G?
(a) D faces G
(b) The pilot is an immediate neighbour of G
(c) G faces the person who is second to left of the Banker
(d) G is the doctor
(e) G sits at one of the extreme ends of the line

42. F is related to Builder in the same way as H is related to Banker based on the given arrangement. To who amongst the following is G related to following the same pattern?
(a) Businessman (b) Teacher
(c) Lawyer (d) Engineer
(e) Pilot

Direction (Q. Nos. 43-44) *Four of the following five are alike in a certain way based on the given sitting arrangement and thus form a group. Which is the one that does not belong to that group?*

43. (a) B (b) Banker (c) Pilot (d) D
(e) Lawyer

44. (a) Lawyer (b) Banker
(c) Pilot (d) Businessman
(e) Doctor

Direction (Q. Nos. 45-48) *Answer the questions based on the following information.*

Mr Bankatlal acted as a judge for the beauty contest. There were four participants, *viz.* Ms Andhra Pradesh, Ms Uttar Pradesh, Ms West Bengal and Ms Maharashtra, Mrs Bankatlal, who was very anxious about the result asked him about it as soon as he was back home. Mr Bankatlal just told that the one who was wearing the yellow saree won the contest. When Mrs Bankatlal pressed for further details, he elaborated as follows

I. All of them were sitting in a row.
II. All of them wore sarees of different colours, viz. green, yellow, white, red.
III. There was only one runner-up and she was sitting beside Ms Maharashtra.
IV. The runner-up was wearing the green saree.
V. Ms West Bengal was not sitting at the ends and was not the runner-up.
VI. The winner and the runner-up are not sitting adjacent to each other.
VII. Ms Maharashtra was wearing white saree.
VIII. Ms Andhra Pradesh was not wearing the green saree.
IX. Participants wearing yellow saree and white saree were at the ends.

45. Who wore the red saree?
(a) Ms Andhra Pradesh
(b) Ms West Bengal
(c) Ms Uttar Pradesh
(d) Ms Maharashtra

46. Ms West Bengal was sitting adjacent to
(a) Ms Andhra Pradesh and Ms Maharashtra
(b) Ms Uttar Pradesh and Ms Maharashtra
(c) Ms Andhra Pradesh and Ms Uttar Pradesh
(d) Ms Uttar Pradesh only

47. Which saree was worn by Ms Andhra Pradesh?
(a) Yellow (b) Red (c) Green (d) White

48. Who was the runner-up?
(a) Ms Andhra Pradesh (b) Ms West Bengal
(c) Ms Uttar Pradesh (d) Ms Maharashtra

Directions (Q. Nos. 49-55) *Study the following information carefully and answer the given questions.*
OBC (PO) 2010

Eight friends, P, Q, R, S, T, V, W and Y are sitting around a square table in such a way that four of them sit at four corners of the square while four sit in the middle of each of the four sides. The ones who sit at the four corners face the centre while those who sit in the middle of the sides face out side.

S sits third to the right of P. P faces the centre. Y is not an immediate neighbour of P or S. T sits third to the right of R. R does not sit in the middle of any of the sides and also P is not an immediate neighbour of Y. Only one person sits between P and V. Q is not an immediate neighbour of V.

49. If all the persons are made to all in alphabetical order in clockwise direction, starting from P, the positions of how many (excluding P) will remain unchanged as compared to their original seating positions?
(a) None (b) One (c) Two (d) Three
(e) Four

50. Which of the following is true regarding Y?
(a) T is not an immediate neighbour of Y
(b) Y sits in the middle of one of the sides
(c) R sits second to left of Y
(d) P and V are immediate neighbours of Y
(e) None of the above is true

51. Who amongst the following sits fourth to the left of V?
(a) Y (b) R
(c) T (d) Q
(e) W

52. What is the position of Q with respect to R?
(a) Immediate left
(b) Second to the left
(c) Third to the left
(d) Third to the right
(e) Immediate right

53. Four of the following five are alike in a certain way and so form a group. Which is the one that does not belong to that group?
(a) T (b) W
(c) V (d) S
(e) Q

54. Who sits third to the right of W?
(a) R (b) S (c) Q (d) Y
(e) Cannot be determined

55. How many people sit between T and Q?
(a) None (b) One (c) Two (d) Three
(e) Four

Direction (Q. Nos. 56-60) Study the information carefully and answer the questions.
MHT CET MBA 2014

S, T, U, V, W, X, Y and Z are seating around a circle area, with equal distance amongst each other, but not necessarily int he same order.

Only two people face the centre and the rest face outside (i.e. in a direction opposite to the centre).

Y sits second to left of W. S sits second to left of Y. Only one person sits between S ad Z. T sits to immediate right of S. T is not an immediate neighbour of Y. V is not an immediate neighbour of Y.

Both the immediate neighbour of X face the centre.

56. Who is sitting to immediate right of Z?
(a) Y (b) V (c) T (d) X
(e) W

57. Which of the following is true regarding U as per the given seating arrangement?
(a) X sits second to left of U
(b) Only three people sit between U and Y
(c) Z is one of the immediate neighbours of U
(d) U faces the centre
(e) S sits to immediate left of U

58. What is T's position with respect of Y?
(a) Second to the right (b) Second to the left
(c) Fifth of the left (d) Fourth to the right
(e) Third to the left

59. Which of the following groups represents the immediate neighbours of X?
(a) WY (b) VX
(c) TZ (d) VZ
(e) SU

60. Four of the following five are alike in a certain way based on the given seating arrangement and so form a group. Which is the one that does not belong to that group?
(a) Z (b) T
(c) Y (d) V
(e) X

Answers with Explanations

Intro Exercise 1

1. (*a*) According to the question, the houses can be arranged as

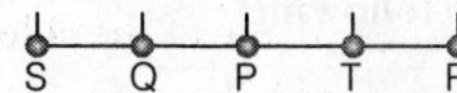

Clearly, the house P is in the middle of all the house.

2. (*b*) According to the question, arrangement of A, B, C, D, E and F is as follows

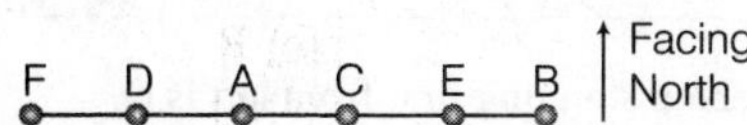

Clearly, F is sitting to the left of D.

3. (*c*) The sequence of children in the row is as follows

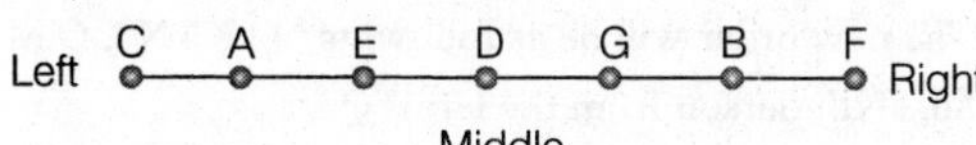

Clearly, D is exactly in the middle.

Solution (Q. Nos. 4-8) According to the given information, the final arrangement is as following

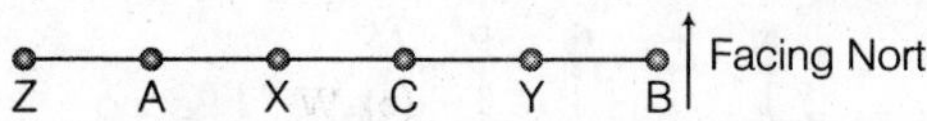

4. (*d*) X and C are sitting exactly middle of the line.

5. (*d*) X is second to the right of Z.

6. (*e*) XA does not belong to that group because in this pair, second person is sitting to the immediate left of first person, while in others second person is sitting to the immediate right of first person.

7. (*a*) Only X is sitting between A and C.

8. (*b*) In the given two pairs, second person is sitting to the immediate right first person. B is sitting immediate right of Y.

Solution (Q. Nos. 9-13)

From III, A is second to the right of E, who is at one of the ends. So, E is at the left end.

From IV, J is the immediate neighbour of A and B, it implies that J is sitting on the immediate right of A and B is sitting immediate right of J.

E _ AJB _ G ...(i)

From II and IV, we get the following arrangement

I _ CHDF ...(ii)

From the arrangements (i) and (ii), we can get the final arrangement

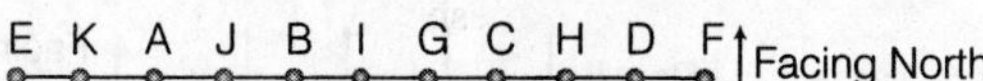

9. (*b*) There are seven persons which are sitting between E and H. B is in the midway of them.

10. (*c*) H is not the immediate neighbour of D and F.

11. (*e*) To get the final arrangement, we require all the statements.

12. (*b*) F is at the extreme end.

13. (*a*) A, J and B are at the left of I.

Solution (Q. Nos. 14-16) According to the given information, the final arrangement is as following

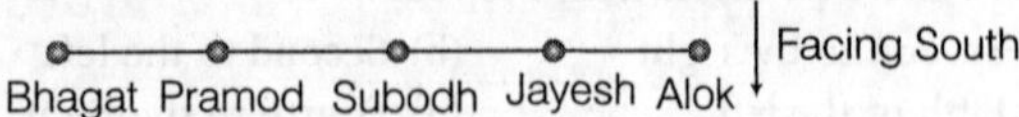

14. (*a*) Alok is at the extreme left end.

15. (*d*) Subodh is in the middle.

16. (*a*) Statement I is superfluous.

17. (*b*) According to the given information, the final arrangement is as following

So, M and K are sitting adjacent to V.

Solution (Q. Nos. 18-22) According to the given information, the final arrangement is as following

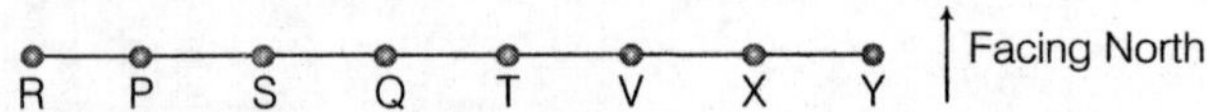

18. (*c*) Q is second to the right of P.

19. (*e*) R and Y are sitting on the extreme ends of line.

20. (*c*) Three persons P, S and Q are seated between R and T.

21. (*a*) In the given pairs, second person is seated second to the right of first person. So, V be related to Y as Y is sitting second to the right of V.

22. (*d*) Second from the left is P and fifth from the right is Q. S is sitting between P and Q.

Solution (Q. Nos. 23-25) From the given information, B is between D and P. So, DBP or PBD.

E stands between A and K. So, AEK or KEA.

A does not stand next to either P or D and K does not stand to next D. So, the final arrangement will be as following

23. (*a*) P stands between B and K.

24. (*b*) D and A occupy the extreme ends of the row.

25. (*c*) K stands between P and E.

Solution (Q. Nos. 26-30) According to given information, the final arrangement is as following

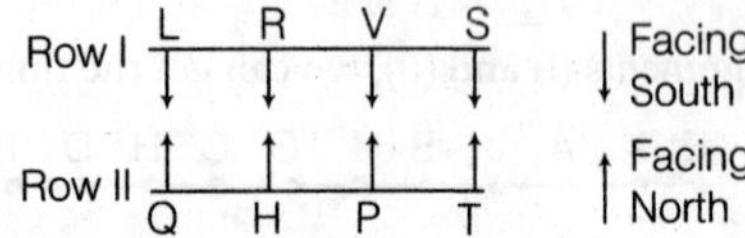

26. (*e*) LS and QT sit at the ends of same row.

27. (*c*) V sits opposite of P.

28. (*d*) R and H sit exactly opposite to each other.

29. (*b*) S is to the left of V.

30. (*a*) H sits to the right of Q.

Solution (Q. Nos. 31-35) According to given information, the final arrangement is as following

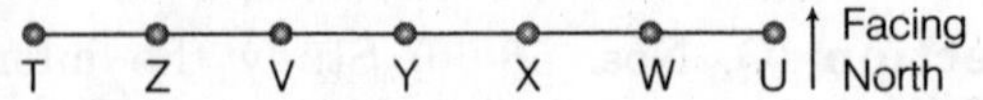

31. (*c*) Z is fourth to the left of W.

32. (*d*) V is second to the right of T.

33. (*b*) XV does not belong to the group because they are not immediate neighbours while other pairs are immediate neighbours.

34. (*a*) Actual position TZVYXWU

Alphabetical position ZYXWVUT

So, the position of none of the friends will remain unchanged.

35. (*e*) T and U sit at the extreme ends of line.

Solution (Q. Nos. 36-40) From statements III, VI and IX, we can get the following arrangement

Position	1	2	3	4	5	6	7
Name					N		
Profession			House wife		Student	Lawyer	

Now, from Statements IV and VII,

Position	1	2	3	4	5	6	7
Name					N		M
profession	Acc.	Comm.	House wife		Student	Lawyer	

J must be at position 4 and from statement VIII, O, P and K are together. So, they are at positions 1, 2 and 3. respectively. The final arrangement will be as following

Position	1	2	3	4	5	6	7
Name	O	P	K	J	N	L	M
Profession	Acc.	Comm.	House wife	Social worker	Student	Lawyer	IAS

36. (*a*) The person standing first from left is O.

37. (*c*) The person standing to the immediate left of M is the lawyer.

38. (*b*) K is the housewife.

39. (*d*) The new order will be as following OKJNLQM

So, sixth person from the left is Q.

40. (*a*) The new order will be as following OMJNLQK

So, M will stand after O but before J.

41. (*a*) According to the given information arrangement of 5 girls sitting in a row shown below

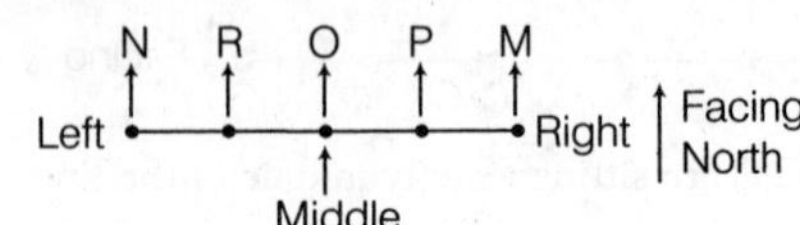

It is clearly shown that , O is sitting in the middle.

Solution (Q. No. 42-45) As per the given information, the seating arrangement of given person is as follows

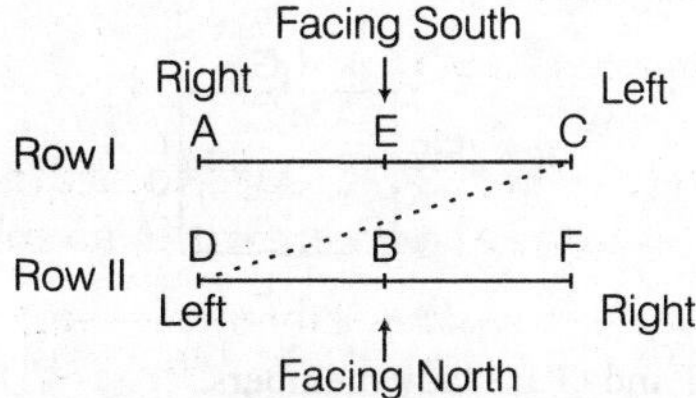

The dotted line in the above diagram shows that D is diagonally opposite to C.

42. (*d*) Clearly, A and F are sitting diagonally opposite to each other.

43. (*a*) Clearly, A and E are in the same row.

44. (*c*) Clearly, from amongst the given alternatives, D, B and F are sitting in one of the two rows.

45. (*a*) As neighbours of E are A and C. So, on interchanging the seat with E, new neighbours of D will be A and C.

Solution (Q. Nos. 46-47) As per the given information, standing arrangement of six children in two rows is as follows

Row I	B	M	J	Facing South
Row II	K	D	C	Facing North

46. (*a*) Clearly, M is to the immediate left of B.

47. (*d*) BMJ and KDC are two sets of children in the same row.

Intro Exercise 2

Solution (Q. Nos. 1-5) According to given information, the final arrangement is as following

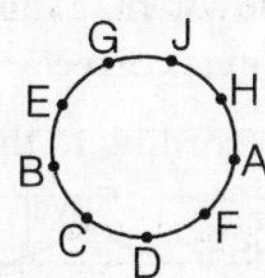

1. (*a*) H's position with respect to E is third to the left.

2. (*e*) C is third to the right of G.

3. (*d*) A is fifth to the right of E.

4. (*b*) F is second to the left of H.

5. (*a*) F is to the immediate right of D.

Solution (Q. Nos. 6-10) On the basis of given information, the seating arrangement is as following

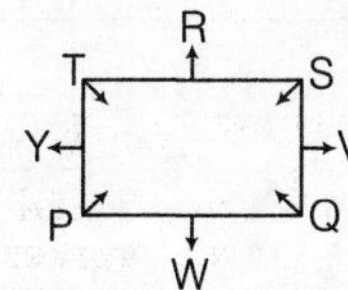

6. (*b*) Q faces center and P is second to the left of Q.

7. (*c*) T is third to the left of V.

8. (*d*) R, W, V and Y are sitting in the middle of the sides of the table. S is sitting at the corner.

9. (*a*) WP and TR represent neighbours. There are two persons between Q and W as well as R and S. Now, we have to choose such pair in which there would be three persons between the two.

10. (*e*) None of the statements is true.

Solution (Q. Nos. 11-15) Following seating arrangement is formed from the given information.

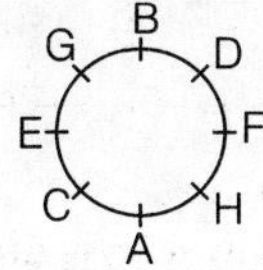

11. (*c*) Clearly, E is not to immediate right of A.

12. (*b*) Clearly, H will be to the immediate right of A.

13. (*d*) A and F will become neighbours, if H agrees to change her seating position.

14. (*c*) Clearly, A will be directly facing B.

15. (*b*) Clearly, H is sitting between A and F.

Solution (Q. Nos. 16-20) According to given information, the final arrangement is as following

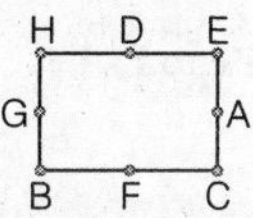

16. (*b*) C is between F and A.

17. (*c*) There are two persons E and D that are sitting between A and H, when counted in anti-clockwise direction from A.

18. (*d*) E does not belong to this group because E is sitting on a corner while all others are sitting in the middle of each side.

19. (*e*) F is to the immediate left of C.

20. (*c*) One more person sits in each successive pair of persons. Hence, three persons (C, A and E) are sitting between F and D.

Solution (Q. Nos. 21-25) According to given information, the final arrangement is as following

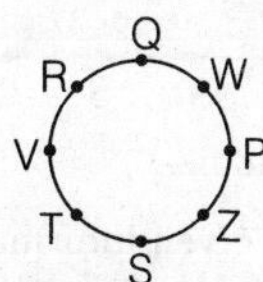

21. (*e*) V is sitting between R and T.

22. (*b*) Z is second to the right of T.

23. (*d*) P is sixth to the left of S.

24. (*c*) S is to the immediate left of Z.

25. (*a*) R is second to the right of W.

Solution (Q. Nos. 26-30) According to given information, the final arrangement is as following

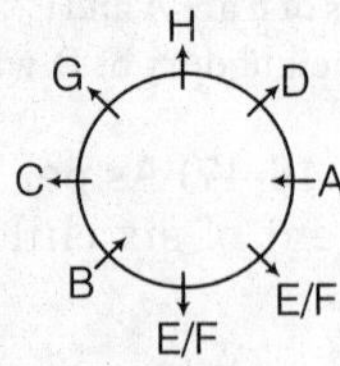

26. (*b*) C is third to the left of D.
27. (*d*) H is sitting to the immediate right of G.
28. (*a*) B and G are immediate neighbours of C.
29. (*e*) Either E or F is sitting third to the left of G.
30. (*c*) There are three people between B and D.

Solution (Q. Nos. 31-35) On the basis of given information the arrangement of 8 persons sitting around a rectangular table is shown below

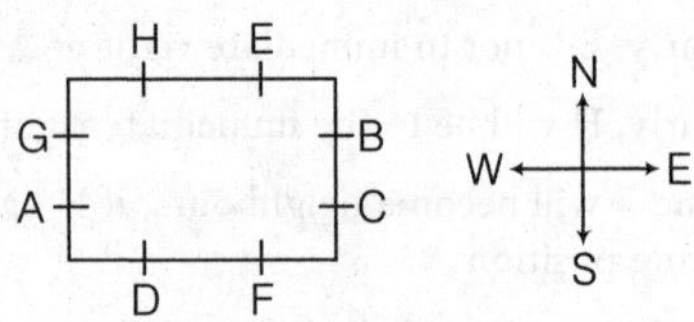

31. (*e*) C is sitting opposite to A.
32. (*b*) B is next to E in clockwise direction.
33. (*d*) A and G are sitting on the same side and A is to the right of G.
34. (*c*) F is sitting opposite to E.
35. (*b*) E is sitting opposite to F.

Solution (Q. Nos. 36-40) According to given information, the final arrangement is as following

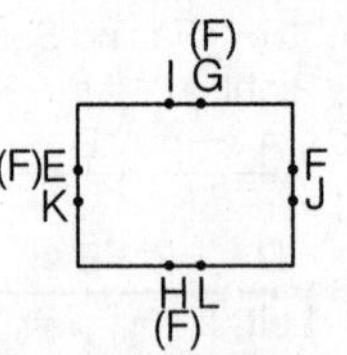

36. (*e*) E, H and G are lady members.
37. (*a*) J is a male member.
38. (*e*) K is sitting between E and H.
39. (*b*) J is to the immediate left of F.
40. (*c*) Three persons (H, L and J) are seated between K and F.
41. (*c*) On the basis of given information, the arrangement is shown below

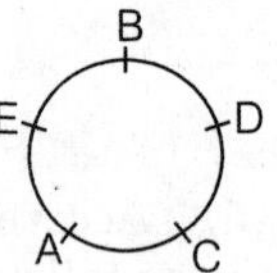

It is clearly shown that, both statements must be true. Hence, option (c) is correct.

42. (*a*) Arrangement according to the information is as follows

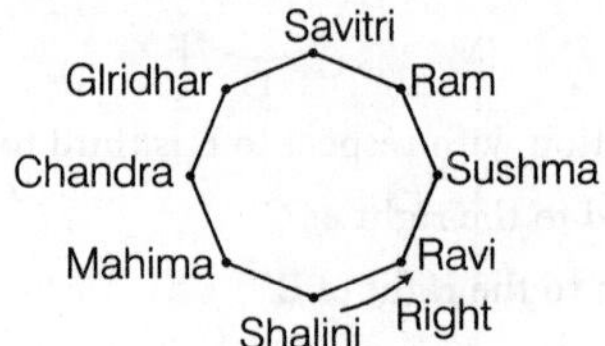

Clearly, Ravi is to the right of Shalini.

Cumulative Exercise

Base Level

1. (*a*) According to the given information, houses in the row are arranged as follows

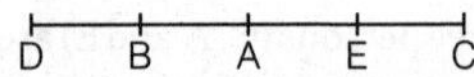

Clearly, the house in the middle is A.

2. (*a*) According to the question, seating arrangement of all the five friends is as follows

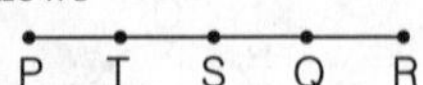

Hence, S is the middle.

3. (*b*) According to the given information, the arrangement in which children are standing in the row is as follows

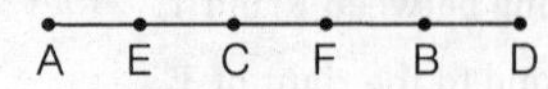

Clearly, F is standing between B and C.

4. (*d*) Five boys standing in a row are Pavan, Tavan, Vipin, Chavan and Nakul

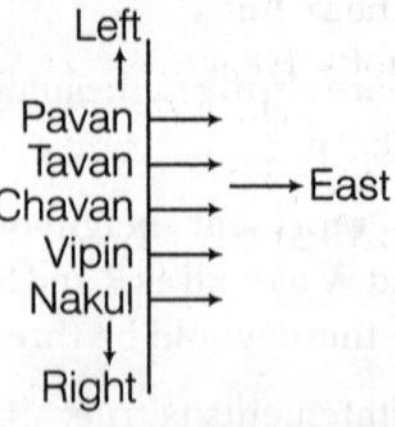

From the given information, the five boys are standing in the row as shown above. Clearly, Tavan is fourth from the right end.

5. (*a*) According to the question, if we arrange the children in a row, then we get

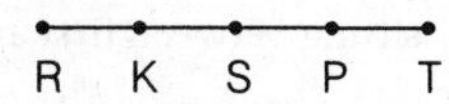

K and P are sitting adjacent to S.

Hence, P and T are sitting adjacent to S.

6. (*b*) According to the question,

Arranging the seven members in a row,

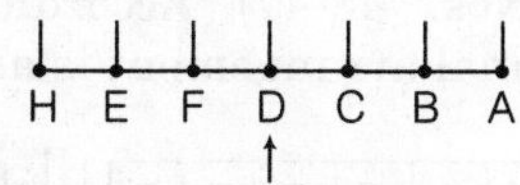

Hence, D is sitting in the middle.

Solution (Q. Nos. 7-8) Standing persons in a straight line is as follows

G D A F E C B ↑ Facing North

7. (*a*) G and B are in the extreme ends.
8. (*b*) F is exactly in the middle.

Solution (Q. Nos. 9-14) According to the given information, the final arrangement is a following

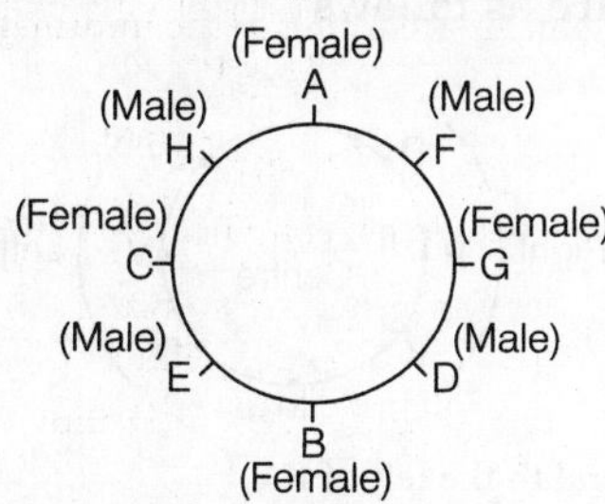

Here, A is wife of H. B is wife of F.

9. (*d*) G is a female who sits second to right of B.
10. (*b*) H sits third to the left of B.
11. (*b*) Two persons D and G sit between B and F when counted in anti-clockwise direction from B.
12. (*d*) G is a female while all others are males.
13. (*e*) Female members are A, G, B and C.
14. (*c*) H and D remain unchanged as compared to their original seating positions. Hence, option (c) is correct.

Solution (Q. Nos. 15-16) According to the given information, the final arrangement is as following

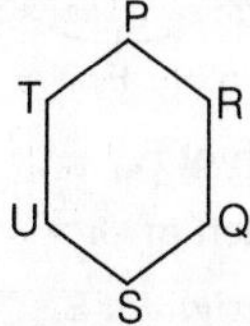

15. (*d*) S is sitting opposite to P.
16. (*a*) P is the fourth person to the left of Q.
17. (*a*) Arrangement according to the question is as follows

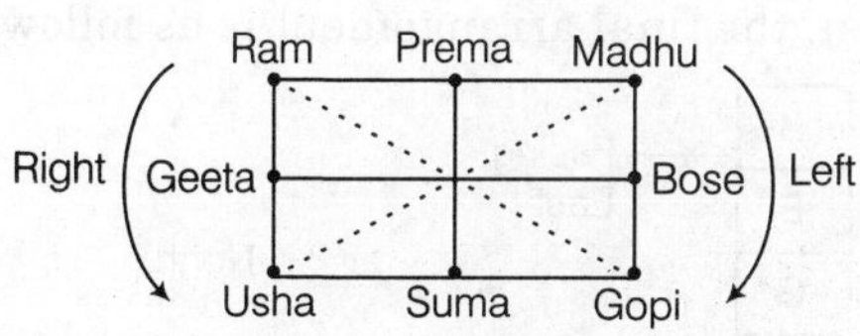

Clearly, Geeta is sitting opposite to Bose.

Solutions (Q. Nos. 18-20) Arrangement according to the question are as follows

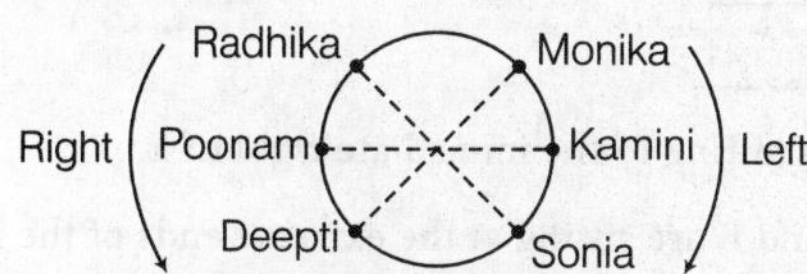

Original positions

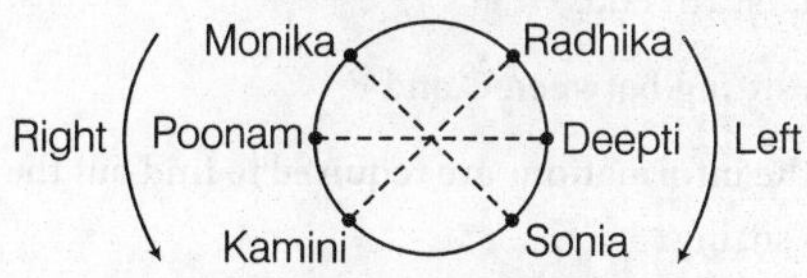

New arrangement

18. (*b*) Clearly, Monika will be opposite to Sonia.
19. (*a*) Clearly, Poonam will be sitting left of Kamini.
20. (*a*) Clearly, Sonia will be sitting left of Deepti.

Solution (Q. Nos. 21-22) On the basis of given information, the correct position of persons sitting around the circular table is as follows

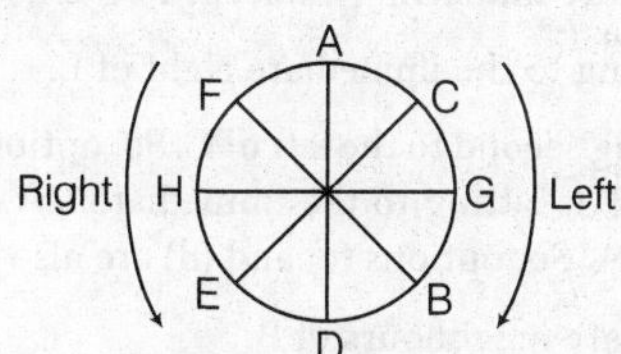

21. (*a*) Clearly, F is third to the left of D.
22. (*c*) E is sitting between H and D. Hence, statement (c) is not correct.

Solution (Q. Nos. 23-27) According to the given information, the final arrangement is as following

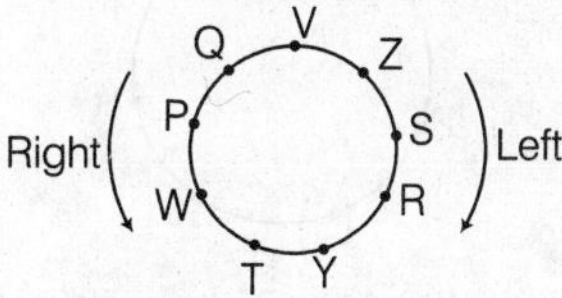

23. (*c*) T is third to the left of S.
24. (*e*) Y is sitting to the immediate right of T.
25. (*d*) V is sitting between Z and Q.
26. (*b*) R is third to the right of W.
27. (*a*) Q is second to the right of Z.

Solution (Q. Nos. 28-32) According to the given information, the final arrangement is as following

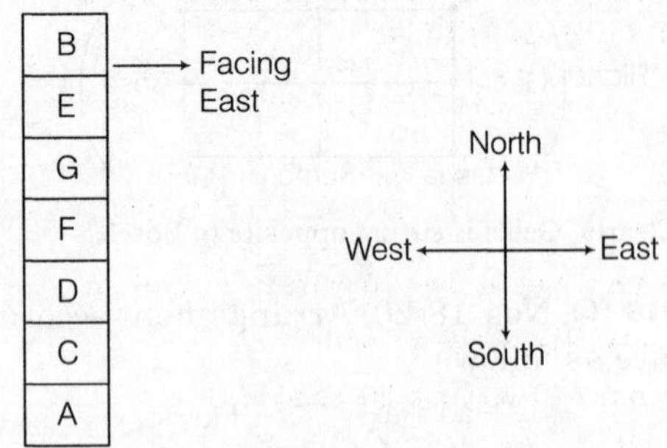

28. (*d*) G is sitting to the immediate right of E.

29. (*a*) A and B are sitting at the extreme ends of the row.

30. (*c*) C should interchange his position with G to get third place from North end.

31. (*d*) D is sitting between C and F.

32. (*d*) All the informations are required to find out the place in which A is sitting.

Solution (Q. Nos. 33-37) According to the given information, the final arrangement is as following

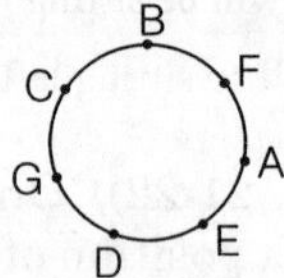

33. (*a*) B and A are not sitting adjacent to each other.

34. (*c*) A is sitting to the immediate right of E.

35. (*e*) F is sitting second to the left of C. So, options (a) and (b) are not correct. F is sitting to the immediate left of B and immediate right of A. So, options (c) and (d) are also not correct.

36. (*c*) C and F are neighbours of B.

37. (*b*) F, B and C are sitting adjacent to each other from left to right.

Solution (Q. Nos. 38-40) According to the given information, the final arrangement is as following

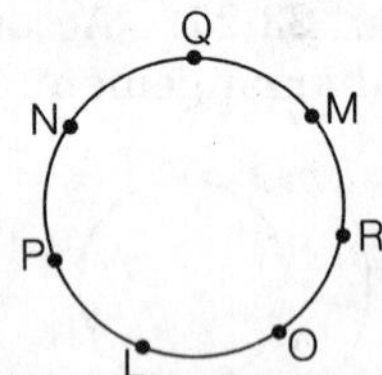

38. (*e*) P is not sitting opposite of N, he is sitting to the immediate right of N.

39. (*c*) Three persons O, R and M are seated between L and Q, if we count anticlockwise from L to Q.

40. (*b*) N is to the immediate left of P.

41. (*e*) ROL does not belong to this group because in this second person is sitting between first and third person while in others third person is sitting between first and second person.

42. (*a*) LP does not belong to this group because in this pair, second person is sitting to the immediate left of first person while in other pairs, second person is sitting to the immediate right of first person.

Solution (Q. Nos. 43-47) According to the given information, the final arrangement is as following

D	F	A	C	G	E	B

↑ Facing North

43. (*b*) D is sitting at the extreme left of the line.

44. (*d*) AF does not belong to this group because A and F are sitting adjacent to each other while in other pairs, one person is sitting between them i.e. they are not sitting adjacent to each other.

45. (*c*) Three persons A, C and G are sitting between F and E.

46. (*b*) C sits exactly in the middle of the line.

47. (*a*) E is third to the right of A.

Solution (Q. Nos. 48-52) Eight persons' seating arrangements are as follows

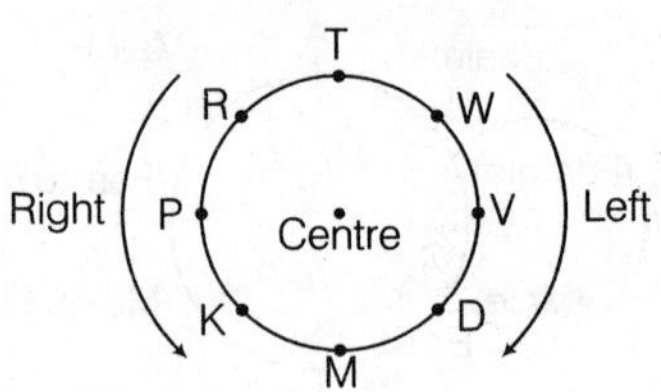

48. (*b*) R is second to the left of K.

49. (*a*) D is the immediate left of V.

50. (*e*) R is third to the right of V.

51. (*a*) Third to the right.

52. (*d*) R and D are opposite to each other.

Solution (Q. Nos. 53-57) According to the given information, the final arrangement is as following

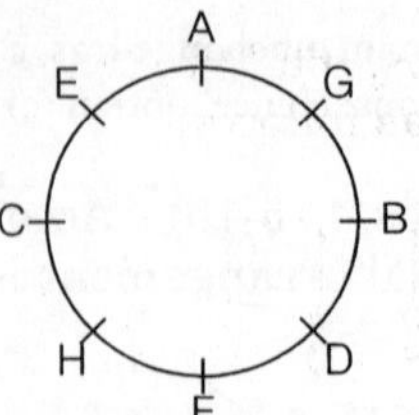

53. (*d*) E is third to the left of F.

54. (*e*) H is fourth to the left of G.

55. (*b*) H is second to the right of E.

56. (*a*) D is to the immediate right of F.

57. (*c*) E and G represent the immediate neighbours of A.

Solution (Q. Nos. 58-62) On the basis of the information given in the question, exact positions of C and H cannot be determined. However, they will sit either on first or fourth positions.

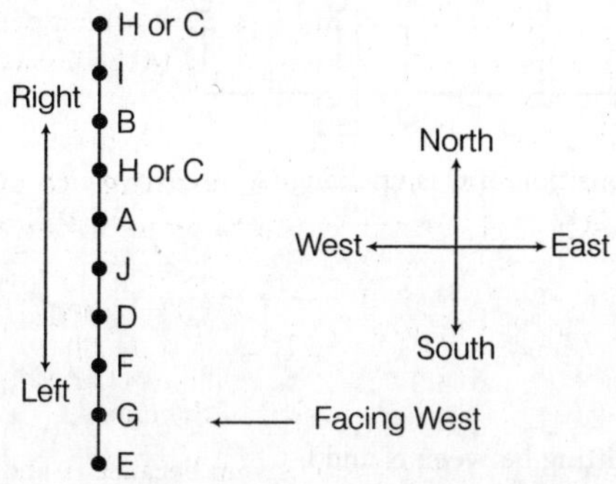

58. (*d*) Either H or C will occupy seventh position from the left.

59. (*c*) E is sitting at one of the ends.

60. (*d*) Cannot be determined because the position of H and C cannot be fixed.

61. (*a*) G is sitting to the second left of D.

62. (*c*) A will become the immediate neighbour of E.

63. (*c*) The following figures show the seating arrangements of six persons.

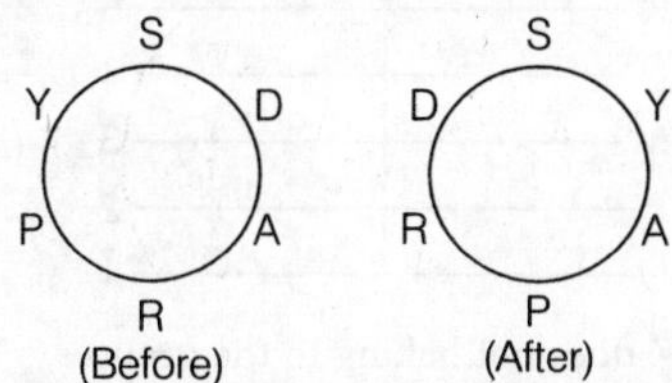

Hence, Suresh is sitting to the left of Dhiraj.

64. (*d*) "Facing you" means facing South directions according to the guidelines

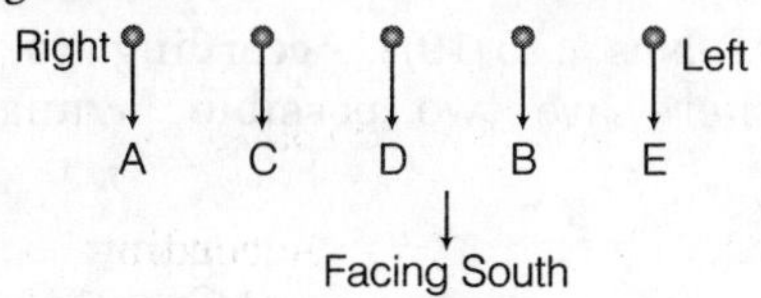

Hence, D is sitting at the centre.

Solution (Q. Nos. 65-70) Seven friends' seating arrangements are as follows

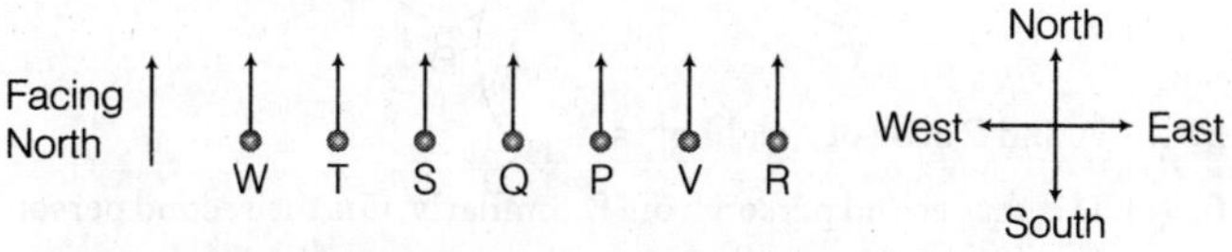

65. (*b*) WR are sitting at the extreme ends of the line

66. (*c*) P is sitting second to the right of S.

67. [illegible] S is exactly between T and Q.

68. (*c*) Q has as many people sitting to his right as to his left.

69. (*d*) QP (only QP is immediate neighbour).

70. (*c*) S is third to the right of V.

Solution (Q. Nos. 71-75) Eight persons' seating arrangements are as follows

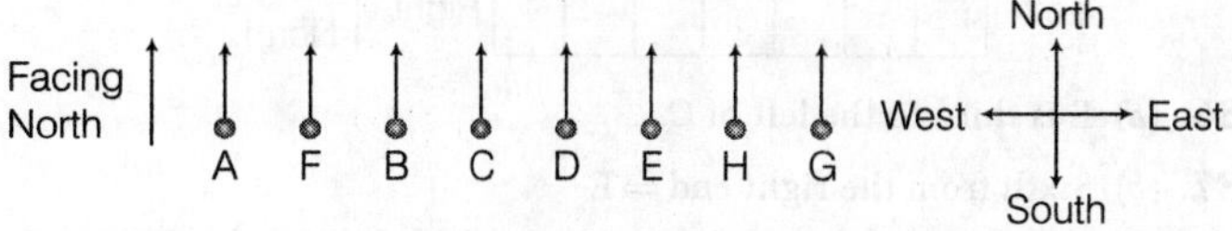

71. (*c*) A, G are sitting at the two extreme ends of line.

72. (*a*) H sits exactly between E and G.

73. (*d*) Only one person (G) to the right of H.

74. (*a*) Third to the left.

75. (*e*) Five persons are seated between A and H.

Solution (Q. Nos. 76-80) Eight persons' seating arrangements are as follows

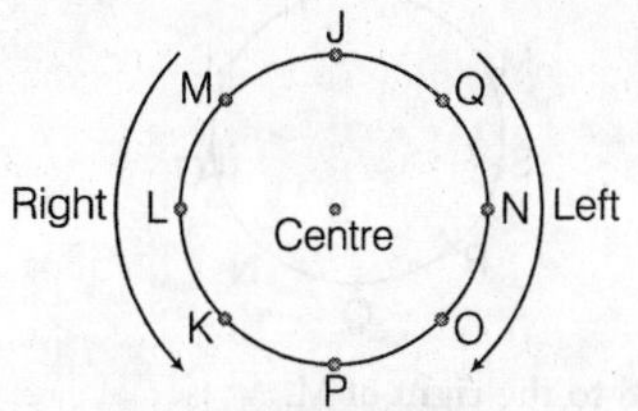

76. (*d*) N, P are immediate neighbour of O.

77. (*e*) The pattern is

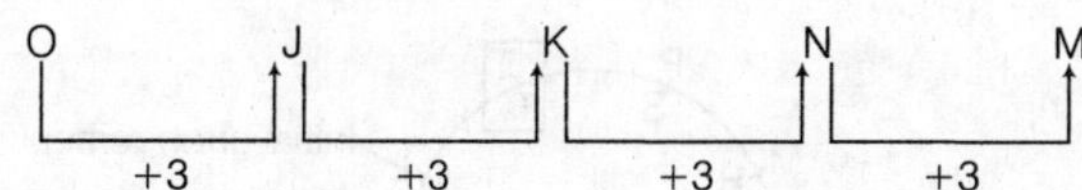

78. (*b*) Immediate left.

79. (*b*) Q sits second to left of M.

80. (*c*) Q exactly between N and J.

Solution (Q. Nos. 81-85) According to the given information, the final arrangement is as following

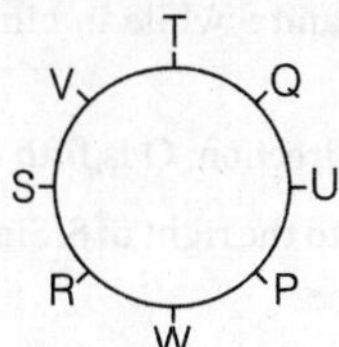

81. (*b*) R is second to the right of V.

82. (*c*) Except TP, in all other pairs one person is just opposite to the other person.

83. (*e*) P is sitting to the immediate right of W. Q is sitting second to the right of P.

84. (*e*) Only P is sitting between V and W, when counted from the left side of U.

85. (*d*) V is sitting exactly between T and S.

Solution (Q. Nos. 86-90) According to the given information, the final arrangement is a following

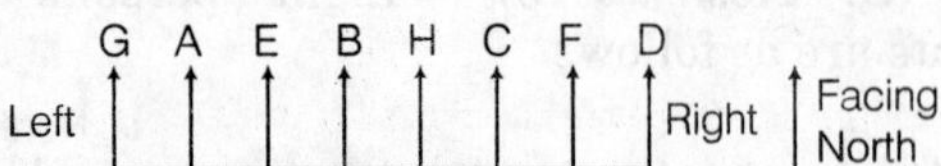

86. (*d*) E is third to the left of C.
87. (*b*) Sixth from the right end ⇒ E
    C is third to the right of E.
88. (*a*) G and D are sitting at the extreme ends of line.
89. (*b*) E is the immediate neighbour of B. In all other, the first person is third to the right of the second person.
90. (*c*)

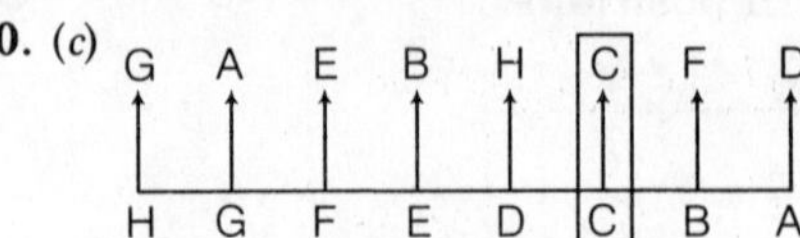

The position of C is unchanged.

Advanced Level

Solution (Q. Nos. 1-6) According to the given information, the final arrangement is as following

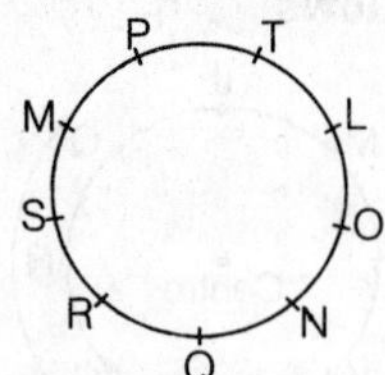

1. (*a*) R is second to the right of M.
2. (*c*) According to the question, the arrangement will be as following

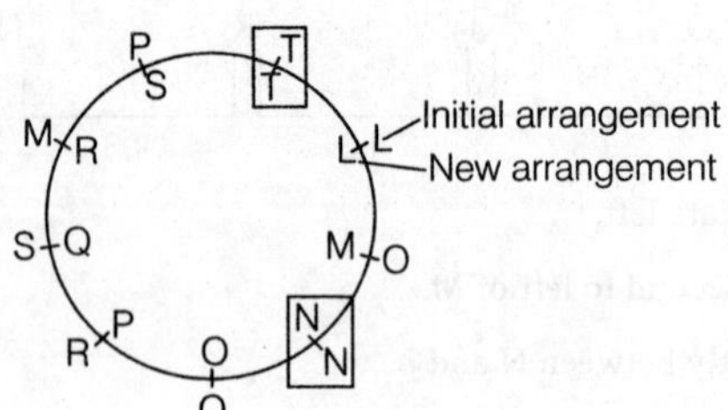

So, the position of N and T will not changed.

3. (*c*) TS does not belong to this group because two persons are sitting between T and S while in others, one person is sitting between them.
4. (*b*) In anti-clockwise direction, O is fifth to the right of M.
5. (*c*) Q is sitting second to the right of S. Similarly, L is sitting second to the right of N.
6. (*c*) L is the immediate left of T.

Solution (Q. Nos. 7-11) According to the given information the final arrangement of eight persons are sitting around a circular table is shown below

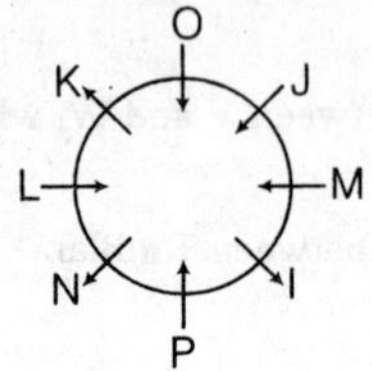

7. (*e*) P is sitting between N and I.
8. (*b*) K is sitting second to right of J.
9. (*d*) All statements are true with respect to P.
10. (*a*) I, K and N facing away from the centre.
11. (*c*) K is third to the left of P.

Solution (Q. Nos. 12-14) Arrangement according to the information is as follows

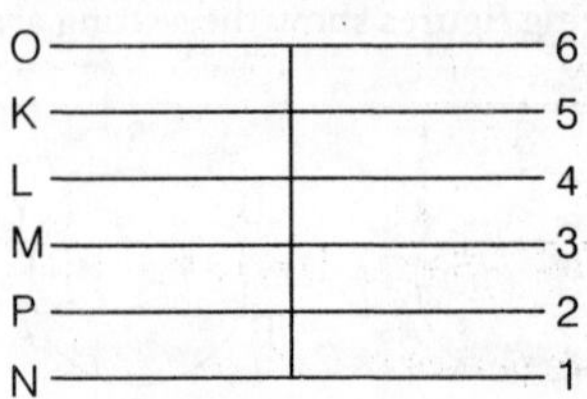

12. (*e*) Clearly, PK does not belong to the group.
13. (*b*) Clearly, P lives on floor number 2.
14. (*d*) Clearly, N lives on floor number 1.

Solution (Q. Nos. 15-19) According to the given information, there are two possible arrangements as shown below

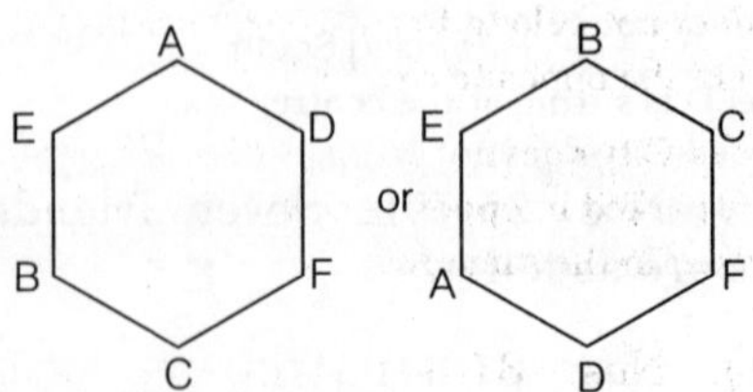

15. (*a*) A and F are not neighbours.
16. (*b*) D is the second person from E. Similarly, C is the second person from D.
17. (*c*) B,C and F are sitting in a sequence.
18. (*c*) The other neighbour of A is E.
19. (*d*) F is placed opposite to E.

Solution (Q. Nos. 20-23) It is clear that Shobha, Monisha and Urmila are not the hostess. So, Madhuri is the hostess. Now, the arrangement will be as following

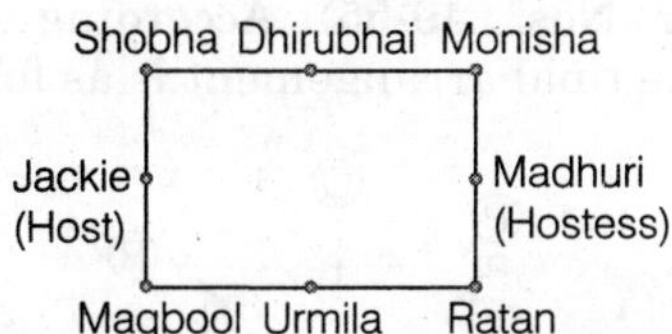

20. (*c*) Jackie must be the host and seated to Shobha's right. So, I and II are correct. Jackie is seated opposite to Madhuri. So, IV is not correct.

21. (*d*) Shobha is sitting between Dhirubai and Jackie. So, she is not sitting next to the person of the same sex.

22. (*a*) Four places to the left of Ratan is Shobha. If they interchanged their seats, then no one will be seated between two persons of the opposite sex.

23. (*a*) Ratan and Monisha are seated opposite to each other. So, they must be a married couple.

Solution (Q. Nos. 24-30) According to the given information, the final arrangement is as following

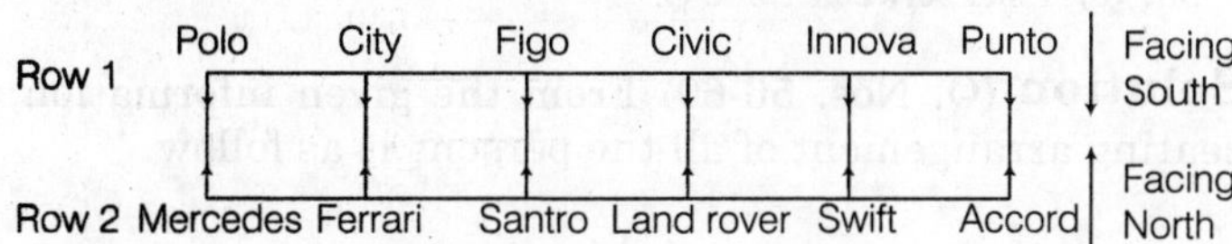

24. (*e*) Both cars are parked in different rows.

25. (*c*) Car parked opposite to Polo is Mercedes and Ferrari is to the immediate right of Mercedes. Similarly, Ferrari is parked opposite to city and Santro is to the immediate right of Ferrari.

26. (*c*) Polo and Accord are parked at the extreme ends of the rows.

27. (*a*) Mercedes faces Polo.

28. (*b*) Swift is parked second to the right of the car facing figure i.e. Santro.

29. (*b*) Civic does not belong to this group because all other cars are parked in the opposite row of Civic.

30. (*d*) Mercedes-City does not belong to this group because these two cars are parked in opposite rows while in all other pairs, cars are parked in the same row.

Solution (Q. Nos. 31-34) On the basis of given information, there can be many arrangements. Two of them are given below

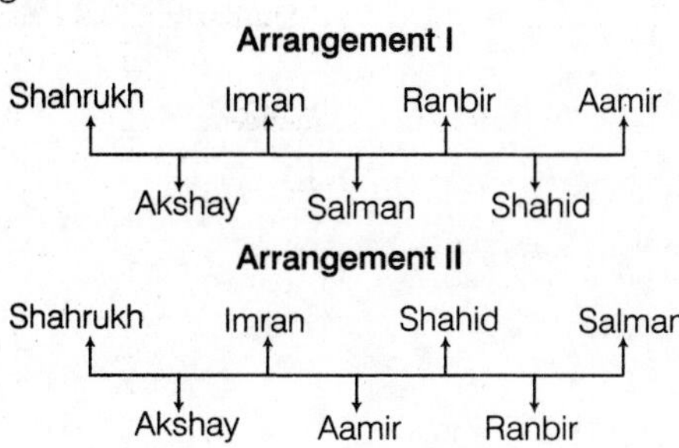

31. (*c*) From the all possible arrangements, we can find that Shahrukh and Shahid can never occupy adjacent chair as Shahid is always between Aamir and Ranbir.

32. (*b*) If Ranbir is 3 places to the right of Imran, then arrangement II will follow. Thus, Aamir will be 2 places to the left of Akshay.

33. (*b*) If Akshay is 3 places to the left of Shahid, Shahrukh and Salman can occupy the corner positions.

34. (*d*) None of the persons has fixed position. If you have confusion with the position of Imran, consider the following arrangement.

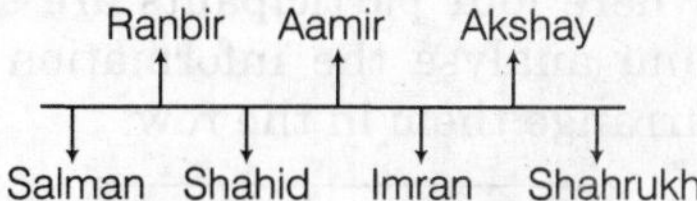

Solution (Q. Nos. 35-36) According to the given information, the arrangement of all the professors' flats is as follow

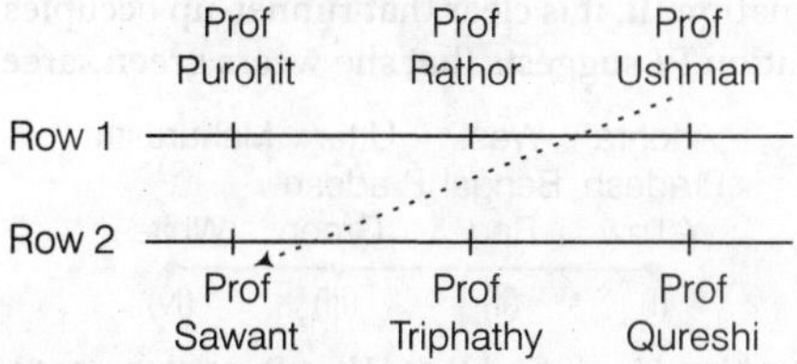

The dotted line shows that Prof Sawant is diagonally opposite to Prof Ushman.

35. (*c*) Prof Purohit, Prof Rathor and Prof Usman have South facing flats.

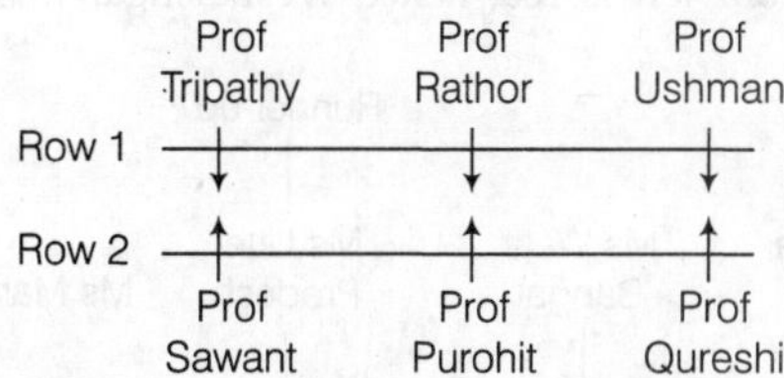

Prof Rathor flats is next to Prof Ushman.

36. (*a*) Interchanging the flats of Prof Tripathy Prof Purohit does not effect the neighbour of Prof Usman, i.e. Prof Rathor will remain in the flat next to that of Prof Usman.

Solution (Q. Nos. 37-44) According to the given information seating arrangement is given below

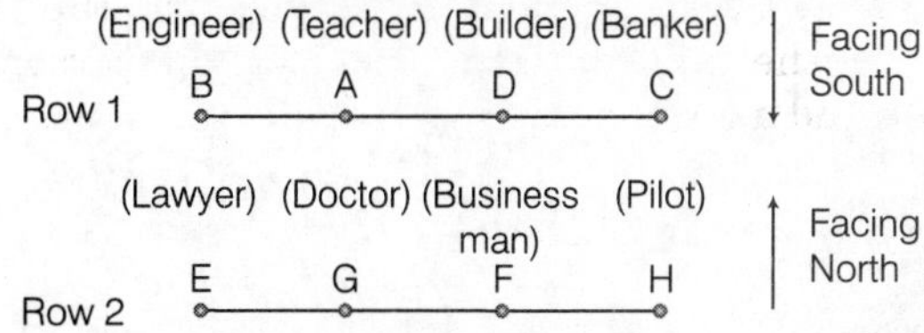

37. (*a*) From the given options, only B and the pilot (i.e. H) sit at the extreme ends of the row.

38. (*c*) C is the banker.

39. (*e*) The lawyer and the doctor are adjacent sitters. So, no one sit between them.

40. (*e*) D i.e. the builder faces the businessman.

41. (*d*) G is the doctor (from the arrangement).

42. (*b*) As F faces the builder and H faces the banker, similarly G faces the teacher.

43. (*d*) Except builder (d) all are at extreme ends.

44. (*b*) Except banker, all other are sitting in the same row.

Solution (Q. Nos. 45-48) Line given on the adjacent side represents the row, with four positions marked by (i), (ii), (iii), and (iv) where four participants are sitting. Let us now classify and analyse the information given in the question and arrange them in the row.

From information (i), it is clear that participants wearing yellow and white sarees occupy positions (i) and (iv), respectively. From information I it is clear that Maharastra wears white saree.

From information III, it is clear that runner-up occupies position (iii) and information IV suggests that she wears green saree.

Andhra Pradesh	West Bengal	Uttar Pradesh	Maharastra
Yellow	Red	Green	White
(i)	(ii)	(iii)	(iv)

From information V, we find that West Bengal cannot be at either (i) place as it is one of the ends or (iii) place as it is occupied by runner-up, hence the only place left is (ii).

From information (viii), Andhra Pradesh was not wearing green saree, hence she occupies position Ist and remaining position (iii) is occupied by Ms Uttar Pradesh.

The only colour left is red, hence West Bengal was wearing red colour saree.

Winner		Runner-up	
Ms Andhra Pradesh	Ms West Bangal	Ms Utter Pradesh	Ms Maharashtra
(i)	(ii)	(iii)	(iv)

45. (*b*) Ms West Bengal wore the red saree.

46. (*c*) Ms West Bengal was sitting adjacent to Ms Andhra Pradesh and Ms Uttar Pradesh.

47. (*a*) Ms Andhra Pradesh wore Yellow saree.

48. (*c*) Ms Uttar Pradesh was the runner-up.

Solution (Q. Nos. 49-55) According to the given information, the final arrangement is as following

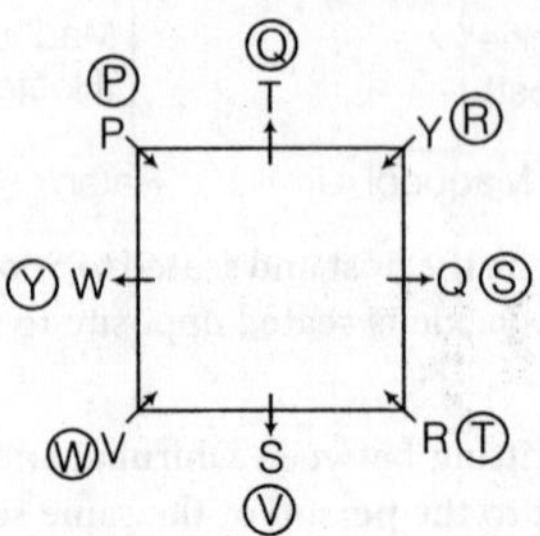

49. (*a*) None

50. (*c*) R sits second to the left of Y.

51. (*a*) Y sits fourth to the left of V.

52. (*e*) Q is to immediate right of R.

53. (*c*) Except V, all others are sitting in the middle of the sides.

54. (*d*) Y sits third to the right of W.

55. (*b*) Y sits between T and Q.

Solution (Q. Nos. 56-60) From the given information, seating arrangement of all the persons is as follow

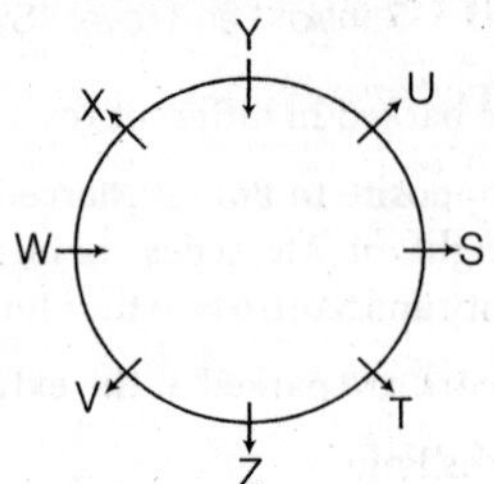

56. (*b*) V is sitting to the immediate right of Z.

57. (*a*) X sits second to the left of U.

58. (*e*) T is third to the left of Y.

59. (*a*) WY are immediate neighbours of X.

60. (*c*) Y faces centre while others are facing outside.

2

Complex Arrangement

This chapter is an extension of previous chapter 'Seating Arrangement'. Here, an object may contain two or more characteristics, so these questions are more complex than those of Seating Arrangement.

In this type of questions, a series of inter-linked information would be given and you would be expected to logically analyse the data in order to reach certain conclusions. So, you should make some diagrams or charts on the basis of the given information in the question which will help you to understand the situation. Hence, the key links or points can be highlighted to make it easier to solve the questions.

Types of Information

To understand the types of information. Let us see the following

(i) There are six cities L, M, N, O, P and Q.

(ii) L is not a hill station.

(iii) M and P are not historical places.

(iv) O is not a industrial city.

(v) L and O are not historical cities.

(vi) L and M are not alike.

Now, we can categorise all the above information as follows

(A) **Useful Secondary Information** The basic informations given in first one or few sentences. In the above information, (i) is the useful secondary information as it gives the general idea of the situation.

(B) **Actual Information** A part from useful secondary information(s), all other informations are actual information. In the above informations [(ii) to (vi)] are actual informations.

(C) **Negative Information** They are part of actual information in the form of negative sentences. In the above informations, all the actual informations [(ii) to (vi)] are negative sentences and hence, they are negative informations.

➘ Questions of 'Complex Arrangement' can be easily solved by making truth table/sitting or placing around linear or circular arrangements.

Types of Questions Asked in Different Examinations

There are multiple types of questions which are asked from the chapter 'Complex Arrangement', so it is quite difficult to predict exact type of questions that are asked but on the basis of **Observation, Analysis and Experience.** Here, we are giving different types of questions that are usually asked in the examination. Almost all the questions at this chapter can be categorised into these types. Also, this description of type will make your study easy and streamline.

Type 1 Problems of Categorisation

In this type of questions, you are supposed to analyse the given data and simply place different items in different categories according to the given information. These questions (are based on classification, seating/placing arrangement and basec on family etc.) can be easily and quickly solved by constructing a truth table or sitting/placing around linear or circular arrangements as per the given information.

Examples Based on Type 1

Direction (Examples 1-3) *Read the following information carefully to answer these questions.*

A, B, C, D, E, F and G are the names of two rivers, three canals and two valleys. B, G and D are not canals. E and F are not rivers. C is a canal but A is a valley. B, F and G are not valleys.

***Ex* 1.** Which are the two rivers?

(a) A and D (b) B and D
(c) B and G (d) A and G

***Ex* 2.** Which are the three canals?

(a) A, C and E (b) C, E and F
(c) A, C and F (d) E, F and G

***Ex* 3.** Which are the two valleys?

(a) A and D (b) D and E
(c) D and G (d) A and B

SOLUTION (Examples 1-3) According to the given information

I. B, G, D are not canals.
II. E, F are not rivers.
III. C is a canal.
IV. A is a valley
V. B, F, G are not valleys.

If B is neither a valley nor a canal, then it is a river.
If F is neither a river nor a valley, then it is a canal.
If G is neither canal nor a valley, then it is a river.

Canal	River	Valley
C	B	A
F	G	D
E		

1. (*c*) B and G are two rivers.
2. (*b*) C, E and F are three canals.
3. (*a*) A and D are two valleys.

Direction (Examples 4-6) *Examine carefully the following statements and answer the three items that follow.* **CSAT 2013**

Out of four friends A, B, C and D, A and B play football and cricket, B and C play cricket and hockey, A and D play basketball and football, C and D play hockey and basketball.

***Ex* 4.** Who does not play hockey?

(a) D (b) C
(c) B (d) A

***Ex* 5.** Who plays football, basketball and hockey?

(a) D
(b) C
(c) B
(d) A

***Ex* 6.** Which game do B, C and D play?

(a) Basketball
(b) Hockey
(c) Cricket
(d) Football

SOLUTION (Examples 4-6)

First of all construct a truth table and arrange the four friends according to the given information in the question.

From the information, we get the following arrangement.

Friends	Football	Cricket	Hockey	Basketball
A	✓	✓		✓
B	✓	✓	✓	
C		✓	✓	✓
D	✓		✓	✓

4. (*d*) 'A' does not play hockey.
5. (*a*) 'D' plays football, basketball and hockey.
6. (*b*) B, C and D play hockey.

Direction (Examples 7-11) *Study the following information and answer the given questions.*

IBPS (PO) 2013

J, P, Q, R, S, T, U and V are four married couples sitting in a circle facing the centre. The profession of the males within the group are lecturer, lawyer, doctor and scientist. Among the males, only R (the lawyer) and V (the scientist) are sitting together. Each man is seated besides his wife. U, the wife of the lecturer is seated second to the right of V. T is seated between U and V. P is the wife of the doctor. Q is not the doctor. S is a male.

Ex **7.** Which of the following is P's position with respect to S?
- (a) Second to the right
- (b) Second to the left
- (c) Immediate right
- (d) Immediate left
- (e) Third to the left

Ex **8.** Which of the following is J's position with respect to T?
- (a) Third to the left
- (b) Fourth to the right
- (c) Third to the right
- (d) Oppsite T
- (e) Second to the right

Ex **9.** Which of the following is not true regarding the couples?
- (a) P is the wife of S
- (b) T is the wife of Q
- (c) R is the husband of J
- (d) J and S are seated adjacent to each other
- (e) All are true

Ex **10.** The wives of which two husbands are immediate neighbours?
- (a) UT
- (b) SR
- (c) VQ
- (d) RV
- (e) None of the above

Ex **11.** Four of the following are alike in a certain way based on their seating position in the above arrangement and so form a group. Which is the one that does not belong to the group?
- (a) RSJ
- (b) TRV
- (c) UTV
- (d) SQP
- (e) UPQ

SOLUTION (Examples 7-11)

First of all draw a circular figure having eight persons i.e. (J, P, Q, R, S, T, U and V). Now, place then according to the given information with their profession and genders.

Here, on the basis of given information, the sitting arrangement can be drawn as shown below.

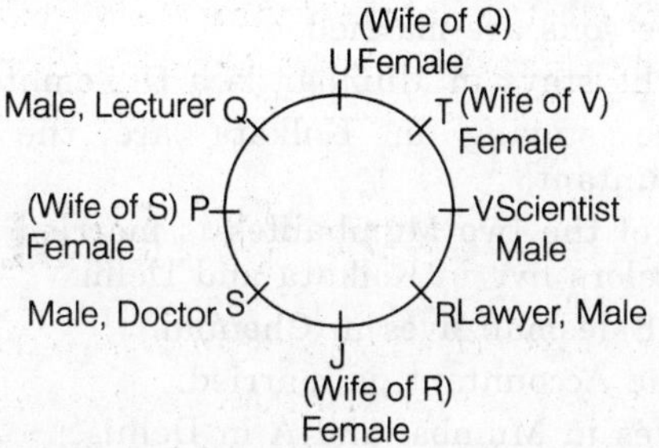

7. (*d*) P is to the immediate left of S.

8. (*a*) J is third to the left of T.

9. (*b*) T is the wife of Q.

10. (*c*) Wives of Q and V are immediate neighbours.

11. (*c*) Except in UTV, in all others the third person is sitting between the first and the second persons. In UTV, the second person is sitting between the first and the third persons.

Direction (Examples 12-14) *Read the following passage and answer the questions that follow.*

A, B, C, D and E are members of the same family. There are two father, two sons, two wives, three males and two females. The teacher was the wife of a lawyer who was the son of a doctor. E is not a male, neither also a wife of a professional. C is the youngest person in the family and D is the eldest. B is a male.

Ex **12.** How is D related to E?

(a) Husband (b) Son (c) Father (d) Wife

Ex **13.** Who are the females in the group?

(a) C and E (b) C and D (c) E and A (d) D and E

Ex **14.** Whose wife is the teacher?

(a) C (b) D (c) A (d) B

SOLUTION (Examples 12-14) According to the given information, the arrangement can be drawn is as following.

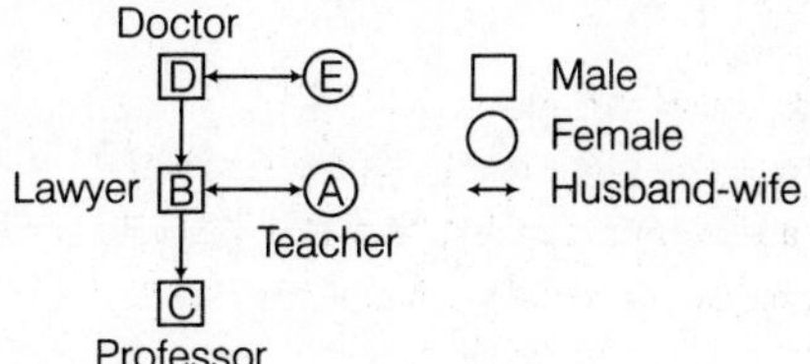

12. (*a*) D is husband of E.

13. (*c*) A and E are females.

14. (*d*) B's wife A is the teacher.

Direction (Examples 15-18) *Read the following information carefully and answer the questions given below it.*

I. A man has six sons A, B, C, D, E and F, who stay in four metros.
II. They are Cricketer, Salesman, Diplomat, Pilot, Accountant and Driver.
III. Three sons are married.
IV. D, who stays in Mumbai, is a Diplomat.
V. Those staying in Kolkata are the Pilot and the Accountant.
VI. One of the two Mumbaiites is married while two of the bachelors live in Kolkata and Delhi.
VII. The Salesman lives in Chennai.
VIII. E, the Accountant, is married.
IX. F lives in Mumbai and A in Delhi.
X. B is a Pilot and Pilots don't marry.

Ex **15.** Who among the following is a Salesman?
(a) C (b) D
(c) E (d) Cannot be determined
(e) None of these

Ex **16.** If the Cricketer is a bachelor, who is the driver?
(a) A (b) E
(c) F (d) Cannot be determined
(e) None of these

Ex **17.** Who among the following is definitely not married?
(a) D (b) E (c) B (d) C
(e) Cannot be determined

Ex **18.** Where does C live?
(a) Delhi (b) Mumbai
(c) Kolkata (d) Chennai
(e) Cannot be determined

SOLUTION (Examples 15-18) From I, IV, VII, IX and X, we get the following arrangement

Person	Profession	Marital status	City
A			Delhi
B	Pilot	Bachelor	
C			
D	Diplomat		Mumbai
E	Accountant	Married	
F			Mumbai

From (V) B and E live in Kolkata.

Now, only C is left, so he lives in Chennai and from (VII) he is a Salesman.

From (VI) A is Bachelor while among D and F, one is married while other is bachelor.

From (III) C is married.

Now, two professions (Cricketer and Driver) are remaining and they go to A and F. So, the final arrangement will be as following.

Person	Profession	Marital status	City
A	Cricketer/Driver	Bachelor	Delhi
B	Pilot	Bachelor	Kolkata
C	Salesman	Married	Chennai
D	Diplomat	M/B	Mumbai
E	Accountant	Married	Kolkata
F	Driver/Cricketer	B/M	Mumbai

15. (*a*) C is a Salesman.

16. (*d*) It is not known that who is a Cricketer or Driver. So, the answer cannot be determined.

17. (*c*) B is definitely not married.

18. (*d*) C lives in Chennai.

Intro Exercise 1 (Based on Type 1)

Direction (Q. Nos. 1-3) *Read the following information carefully and answer the questions given below.* **MAT 2013**

Rajneesh, Kavita, Suresh, Gambhir and Mahesh are friends and good players. Rajneesh and Kavita are good in hockey and volleyball. Suresh and Rajneesh are good in hockey and tennis. Gambhir and Kavita are good in cricket and volleyball. Suresh, Gambhir and Mahesh are good in football and tennis.

1. Who is good in hockey, volleyball and cricket?
(a) Rajneesh (b) Suresh (c) Kavita (d) Gambhir

2. Who is good in tennis, cricket, volleyball and football?
(a) Suresh (b) Kavita
(c) Rajneesh (d) Gambhir

3. Who is good in tennis, volleyball and hockey?
(a) Gambhir (b) Kavita
(c) Suresh (d) Rajneesh

Direction (Q. Nos. 4-8) *Study the following information carefully and answer the questions that follow.*

M, T, J, R, D, W and Q are seven friends travelling in three cars A, B and C with atleast two persons in each car. There are three females among them one in each car. T travels with only her best friend Q in car B. M travels in car A. D and W do not travel in car C. J is not a female and W is a female. **IBPS (Clerk) 2014**

4. J travels in which car?
(a) A (b) C
(c) A or C (d) Data inadequate
(e) None of these

5. In which car do three of them travel?
(a) C (b) B
(c) A (d) Data inadequate
(e) None of these

6. D travels in which car?
(a) B (b) A
(c) A or C (d) Data inadequate
(e) None of these

7. Which of the following groups represents the three females?
(a) WQR (b) DQR
(c) DTR (d) Data inadequate
(e) None of these

8. Which of the following combinations of car-person is not correct?
(a) A-M (b) B-Q
(c) C-R (d) A-D
(e) All are correct

Direction (Q. Nos. 9-13) *Read the information carefully and answer the questions.*

I. In a family of six persons, there are people from three generations. Each person has separate profession and also each one likes different colours. There are two couples in the family.
II. Charan is a CA and his wife neither is a doctor nor likes green colour.
III. Engineer likes red colour and his wife is a teacher.
IV. Vanita is mother-in-law of Namita and she likes orange colour.
V. Mohan is grandfather of Raman and Raman, who is a principal, likes black colour.
VI. Sarita is granddaughter of Vanita and she likes blue colour. Sarita's mother likes white colour.

9. Who is an Engineer?
(a) Sarita (b) Vanita (c) Namita (d) Mohan

10. What is the profession of Namita?
(a) Doctor (b) Engineer
(c) Teacher (d) Cannot be determined

11. Which of the following is the correct pair of two couples?
(a) Mohan—Vanita and Charan—Sarita
(b) Vanita—Mohan and Charan—Namita
(c) Charan—Namita and Raman—Sarita
(d) Cannot be determined

12. How many ladies are there in the family?
(a) Two (b) Three
(c) Four (d) None of these

13. Which colour is liked by CA?
(a) White (b) Blue
(c) Black (d) None of these

Direction (Q. Nos. 14-18) *Read the given information carefully to answer these questions.*

A Teacher's Training Institute has to conduct a refresher course for teachers of seven different subjects.

History, Geography, Political Science, Hindi, Sanskrit, Music and English from 12th December to 19th December.

I. The course should start with Geography.
II. 13th December being a Sunday, should be a holiday.
III. Music should be on the day previous to English.
IV. The course should end with History.
V. Political Science should be immediately after the holiday. Sanskrit follows Political Science.
VI. There should be a gap of one day between Sanskrit and English and between Music and Hindi.

14. Which subject is followed by Music?
(a) English (b) Geography
(c) Political Science (d) Sanskrit

15. How many days gap is there between Music and Political Science?
(a) One (b) Two (c) Three (d) Four

16. Which subject precedes History?
(a) Sanskrit (b) English
(c) Political Science (d) Hindi

17. Which subject will be on Tuesday?
(a) History (b) English
(c) Sanskrit (d) None of these

18. Which refresher course will start three days before English subject?
(a) Geography (b) History
(c) Political Science (d) Sanskrit

Direction (Q. Nos. 19-23) *Study the following information carefully and answer the questions given below.* **SBI (Clerk) 2015**

P, Q, R, S, T, V, W and Y are four married couples sitting in a circle facing the centre. The profession of the males with in the group are Engineer, Editor, Teacher and Columnist. Among the males, only S (the Editor) and Y (the Teacher) are sitting together. Each man is seated besides his wife. W, the wife of the Engineer is seated second to the right of Y. V is seated between W and Y. Q is the wife of the columnist. R is not the columnist. T is a male.

19. Which of the following is Q's position with respect to T?
(a) Second to the right (b) Second to the left
(c) Immediate right (d) Immediate left
(e) Third to the left

20. Which of the following is P's position with respect to V?
(a) Third to the left (b) Fourth to right
(c) Third to the right (d) Opposite to T
(e) Second to the right

21. Which of the following is not true regarding the couples?
(a) Q is the wife of T
(b) V is the wife of R
(c) S is the husband of P
(d) P and T are seated adjacent to each other
(e) All are true

22. The wives of which two husbands are immediate neighbours?
(a) W, V (b) T, S (c) Y, R (d) S, Y
(e) None of these

23. Four of the following are alike in a certain way based on their seating position in the above arrangement and so form a group. Which is the one that does not belong to the group?
(a) STP (b) VSY (c) WVY (d) TRQ
(e) WQR

Direction (Q. Nos. 24-27) *Study the following information carefully and answer the questions given below.* **IBPS (PO) 2014**

P, Q, R, S, T, V and W are seven students of a college. Each of them has a favourite subject from Physics, Chemistry, English, Biology, History, Geography and Philosophy not necessarily in the same order. Each of them also has a favourite sport from Football, Cricket, Hockey, Volleyball, Badminton, Table Tennis and Basketball not necessarily in the same order.

R likes Philosophy and his favourite sport is Hockey. The one who likes Football likes English. T's favourite sport is not Badminton or Table Tennis. V does not like either History or Biology. The one whose favourite sport is Basketball does not like Physics. W likes Chemistry and his favourite sport is Volleyball, S likes Geography. Q's favourite sport is Badminton. V does not like English and his favourite sport is not Basketball. P's favourite sport is Cricket. The one whose favourite sport is Badminton does not like Biology.

24. Who likes History?
(a) P (b) R (c) Q (d) V
(e) Data inadequate

25. Whose favourite sport is Basketball?
(a) S (b) W
(c) Q (d) Data inadequate
(e) None of these

26. Which subject does T like?
(a) Biology (b) Physics
(c) Chemistry (d) Data inadequate
(e) None of these

27. What is Q's favourite sport?
(a) Cricket (b) Table Tennis
(c) Football (d) Badminton
(e) None of these

Direction (Q. Nos. 28-32) *Study the following information and answer the questions that fallow.* **SBI (PO) 2010**

I. In a family of 6 persons, there are two couples.
II. The Lawyer is the head of the family and has only two sons-Mukesh and Rakesh-both Teachers.
III. Mrs Reena and her mother-in-law both are Lawyers.
IV. Mukesh's wife is a Doctor and they have a son, Ajay.

28. Which of the folowing is definitely a couple?
(a) Lawyer-Teacher (b) Doctor-Lawyer
(c) Teacher-Teacher (d) Cannot be determined
(e) None of these

29. What is the profession of Rakesh's wife?
(a) Teacher
(b) Doctor
(c) Lawyer
(d) Cannot be determined
(e) None of the above

30. How many male members are there in the family?
(a) Two (b) Three
(c) Four (d) Cannot be determined
(e) None of these

31. What is/was Ajay's Grandfather's occupation?
(a) Teacher (b) Lawyer
(c) Doctor (d) Cannot be determined
(e) None of these

32. What is the profession of Ajay?
(a) Teacher (b) Lawyer
(c) Doctor (d) Cannot be determined
(e) None of these

Direction (Q. Nos. 33-38) *Study the following information carefully and answer the questions that follow.* **SBI (PO) 2011**

Eight colleagues, A, B, C, D, E, F, G and H are sitting around a circular table facing the centre but not necessarily in the same order. Each one of them holds a different post viz. Manager, Company Secretary, Chairman, President, Vice-President, Group Leader, Financial Advisor and Managing Director.

A sits third to right of the Managing Director. Only two people sit between the Managing Director and H. Vice-president and the Company Secretary are immediate neighbours of each other. Neither A nor H is a Vice-president or a Company Secretary. Vice-president is not an immediate neighbour of the Managing Director. Manager sits second to left of E. E is not an immediate neighbour of H. The Manager is an immediate neighbour of both Group Leader and the Financial Advisor. Financial Advisor sits third to right of B. B is not the Vice-president. C sits to the immediate right of the Chairman. A is not the Chairman. F is not an immediate neighbour of A. G is not an immediate neighbour of the Manager.

33. Who amongst the following sits third to the left of E?
(a) The Manager (b) G
(c) A (d) The Financial Advisor
(e) B

34. Four of the following five are alike in a certain way based on the given arrangement and thus form a group. Which is the one that does not belong to that group?
(a) F–Chairman (b) G–President
(c) D–Manager (d) A–Financial Advisor
(e) B–Managing Director

35. Who amongst the following is the President of the Company?
(a) A (b) C (c) H (d) G
(e) D

36. Which of the following is true with respect to the given seating arrangement?
(a) The Group Leader of the Company is an immediate neighbour of the Vice-president
(b) G sits second to right of D
(c) The Group Leader and the Company Secretary are immediate neighbours of each other
(d) The Chairman of the Company sits to the immediate left of the Managing Director
(e) The Group Leader sits second to the left of D

37. Which of the following posts does B hold in the Company?
(a) Chairman (b) Manager
(c) Company Secretary (d) Vice-president
(e) Financial Advisor

38. Who amongst the following sit exactly between the Managing Director and H?
(a) H and the Chairman
(b) B and G
(c) The Chairman and C
(d) F and C
(e) E and the Group Leader

Direction (Q. Nos. 39-44) *Read the following information carefully and answer the questions that follow.*

Six persons A, B, C, D, E and F are expert in six different fields P, Q, R, S, T and U (not respectively), won different prizes-Kalinga Award, Gandhi Peace Prize, Vyas Samman, Kabir Samman, Iqbal Samman and Saraswati Samman though not respectively, for the year 2000.

C and F have not won Gandhi Peace and Iqbal Samman. The winner of Kabir Samman is expert in the field S but he is certainly not E and B. D and A have won Kalinga Award and Kabir Samman though not, respectively. The experts of the field Q and E have won Gandhi Peace Prize and Iqbal Samman though not, respectively. A is expert in field P and winner of Iqbal Samman is expert in the field T.

39. Who has won the Vyas Samman?
(a) B (b) C
(c) F (d) Either C or F
(e) None of these

40. The winner of the Saraswati Samman is an expert in the field
(a) R (b) U
(c) Either R or U (d) Data inadequate
(e) None of these

41. D has expertise in which of the following fields?
(a) S (b) Q
(c) T (d) Cannot be determined
(e) None of these

42. Who is the winner of Gandhi Peace Prize?
(a) A (b) B
(c) C (d) Cannot be determined
(e) None of these

43. The person, who is expert in the field P, has won
(a) Saraswati Samman (b) Kabir Samman
(c) Vyas Samman (d) Data inadequate
(e) None of the above

44. Which of the following combinations is definitely true?
(a) E-Q-Iqbal Samman
(b) A-P-Kalinga Award
(c) D-S-Kalinga Award
(d) E-T-Gandhi Peace Prize
(e) None of the above

Direction (Q. Nos. 45-47) *Read the following informations carefully and answer the questions that follow.*

Surinder, Prem, Wasim, Bishamber and Chauhan are five players of a college cricket team and their home towns are Sikandrabad, Panipat, Waranga, Banaras and Chennai (not in the order of their names). The five specialist slots of spinner, pace-bowler, wicket-keeper, batsman and captain are held by them (not in order of their names stated above). Their names, home towns and specialities donot start with the same letter. Neither Prem nor Wasim is the captain and they do not belong to either Sikandrabad or Banaras. Panipat is not Bishamber's home town. The player who hails from Banaras is a wicket-keeper. The captain's town is Panipat while the batsman does not hail from Warangal. Surinder is neither a wicket-keeper nor a batsman.

45. Who is the wicket-keeper?
(a) Wasim (b) Bishamber
(c) Chauhan (d) Surinder

46. The spinner's home town is
(a) Chennai (b) Banaras
(c) Warangal (d) Panipat

47. Who is the pace bowler?
(a) Prem (b) Bishamber
(c) Surinder (d) Chauhan

Direction (Q. Nos. 48-50) *Read the following information carefully and answer the questions that follow.* **FMS 2010**

In a business school, four students Dinakaran, Sumit, Tarun and Amul exhibit a very strange mix of hobbies and subject interests. One of them studies Commerce and plays Golf and Lawn Tennis. Dinakaran and Sumit study Psychology. Dinakaran plays Billiards. Both the Psychology students play Chess. Tarun is a student of Physics. The Physics student plays Chess and Badminton. All the friends play two games each and study one subject each. One of the students also does Weight Training.

48. Who does not play Chess?
(a) Dinakaran (b) Sumit
(c) Tarun (d) Amul

49. Who studies Psychology and plays Billiards?
(a) Dinakaran (b) Sumit
(c) Tarun (d) Amul

50. How many games are played and subjects studied by all the four students?
(a) 2, 1 (b) 3, 2
(c) 6, 3 (d) 5, 4

Direction (Q. Nos. 51-53) *Read the following information carefully and answer the questions that follow.* **FMS 2011**

P, Q, R, S, T and X are six persons who decided to start a partnership business in computer hardware. Q, R and T are ladies and the rest are men. P, Q, R and X are well versed in hardware but the others do not know much about hardware. Q, S and X know marketing but the others do not know anything about marketing.

51. The male partner who knows marketing but does not know computer hardware
(a) S (b) P
(c) X (d) Q

52. The female partner who is well versed in computer hardware but does not know marketing
(a) X (b) Q
(c) T (d) R

53. The female partner who neither knows hardware nor marketing
(a) R (b) Q (c) T (d) X

54. Five Friends A, B, C, D and E have different jobs. They work with either Bank or Cinema or Pharma or Sales or Jewellery. Pick the right job in which they are employed if B is neither concerned with Bank nor with Sales. E has nothing to do with Cinema or Jewellery. C is not in Bank or Cinema. D has nothing to do in Sales or Pharma. Cinema has not given a chance to B or D nor E is bank employee. C is not in Sales nor B is in Jewellery.

Which of the following is correct?
(a) A-Cinema, B-Sales, C-Jewellery, D-Pharma, E-Bank
(b) A-Cinema, B-Sales, C-Pharma, D-Bank, E-Jewellery
(c) A-Cinema, B-Sales, C-Jewellery, D-Bank, E-Pharma
(d) A-Cinema, B-Pharma, C-Jewellery, D-Bank, E-Sales

Type 2 Sequential Order of Things

In this type of questions, some points in jumbled form are given regarding the occurrence of certain events. You are required to analyse the given information and answer the questions accordingly.

Steps to Solve Sequential Order Questions

Step I Analyse the given situation.

Step II Frame the right sequence of different points.

Step III Check the sequence framed by you. It should be clear understable.

Step IV Now, answer the questions asked on the basis of given information.

Examples Based on Type 2

Direction (Examples 1-6) *Study the following informatin carefully and answer the questions that follow.* **SBI (PO) 2014**

An organisation decided to distribute seven types of laptops on week days starting from Monday to Sunday. The seven laptops to be distributed are of Sony, Acer, Asus, Lenovo, Dell, HP and HCL but non-necessarily in the same order. Dell laptops are to be given on Saturday. Lenovo laptops are given just after Asus laptops and Asus laptops are not given on Wednesday. HP laptops are given two days after the distribution of Asus laptop. Acer laptops are distributed just after Sony laptop. HCL laptops are distributed before Acer laptops. HP laptops are distributed after Dell laptops.

Ex 1. On which day of the week Lenovo laptops are distributed?
(a) Tuesday (b) Wednesday
(c) Friday (d) Sunday
(e) Monday

Ex 2. Which laptops are distributed just between the days when Lenovo and HP are distributed?
(a) Asus (b) Dell
(c) Sony (d) HCL
(e) None of these

Ex 3. Which laptops are distributed on Wednesday?
(a) Acer (b) Lenovo (c) HCL (d) HP
(e) Sony

Ex 4. On which day of the week Asus are distributed?
(a) Monday (b) Sunday
(c) Tuesday (d) Wednesday
(e) None of these

Ex 5. If HCL is related with Tuesday, Sony is related with Wednesday, similarly Lenovo is related with which day?
(a) Thursday (b) Friday
(c) Saturday (d) Sunday
(e) None of these

Ex 6. Which laptops are distributed in the middle of the week?
(a) Acer (b) Asus (c) Lenovo (d) HCL
(e) None of these

SOLUTION (Examples 1-6) As per the given information, arrangement of days and laptops is as follow.

Days	Laptops
Monday	HCL
Tuesday	Sony
Wednesday	Acer
Thursday	Asus
Friday	Lenovo
Saturday	Dell
Sunday	HP

1. (*c*) On Friday lenovo laptops are distributed.
2. (*b*) Dell laptops are distributed just between the lenovo and HP are distributed.
3. (*a*) Acer laptops are distributed on Wednesday.
4. (*e*) Asus are distributed on Thursday.
5. (*c*) Lenovo is related with Saturday.
6. (*b*) Asus laptops are distributed in the middle of the week.

Direction (Examples 7-9) *Read the following information carefully and answer the questions that follow.*

Five friends Satish, Rajesh, Rehman, Rakesh and Vineet each presents one paper to their class on Physics, Zoology, botany, English or Geology. One day a week, Monday through Friday.

I. Vineet does not present English and does not given his presentation on Tuesday.
II. Rajesh makes the Geology presentation and does not do it on Monday or Friday.
III. The Physics presentation is made on Thursday.
IV. Rehman makes his presentation, which is not on English, on Wednesday.
V. The Botany presentation is on Friday and not by Rakesh.
VI. Satish makes his presentation on Monday.

Ex 7. What day is the English presentation made?
(a) Friday (b) Monday
(c) Tuesday (d) Wednesday

Ex 8. What presentation does Vineet do?
(a) English (b) Geology
(c) Physics (d) Botany

Ex 9. What day does Rakesh make his presentation on?
(a) Monday (b) Tuesday
(c) Wednesday (d) Thursday

SOLUTION (Examples 7-9) Following table can be drawn from the given information

Names	Papers					Days				
	Physics	Zoology	Botany	English	Geology	Monday	Tuesday	Wednesday	Thursday	Friday
Satish	✗	✗	✗	✓	✗	✓	✗	✗	✗	✗
Rajesh	✗	✗	✗	✗	✓	✗	✓	✗	✗	✗
Rehman	✗	✓	✗	✗	✗	✗	✗	✓	✗	✗
Rakesh	✓	✗	✗	✗	✗	✗	✗	✗	✓	✗
Vineet	✗	✗	✓	✗	✗	✗	✗	✗	✗	✓

7. (*b*) English presentation made on Monday.
8. (*d*) Botany
9. (*d*) Rakesh make his presentation on Thursday.

Direction (Examples 10-13) *Study the following information and answer the questions given below.*

Bihar Kshetriya (GBO) 2012

Six play K, L, M, N, O and P are to be staged. Each play is to be staged in a different month starting from March to August of the same year.

Play K will be staged in a month that has only thirty days. Two plays will be staged between play L and play K. Three plays will be staged between play P and play O. The month in which play P will be staged does not have thirty one days. Play N will not be staged immediately before or immediately after play P.

Ex 10. Which play will be staged in April?
(a) Play K
(b) Play L
(c) Play O
(d) Play P
(e) None of the above

Ex 11. Three of the following four are alike in a certain way based on the given information and hence form a group. Which of the following does not belong to that group?
(a) Play N (b) Play P
(c) Play L (d) Play O
(e) None of these

Ex 12. Play M will be staged in which of the following months?
(a) August
(b) April
(c) June
(d) May
(e) None of the above

Ex 13. How many play will be staged before play N?
(a) One
(b) Three
(c) Four
(d) Two
(e) None of the above

SOLUTION (Examples 10-13) Following table can be drawn from the given information

March 31 days	April 30 days	May 31 days	June 30 days	July 31 days	August 31 days
L	P	M	K	N	O

10. (*d*) Play P will be staged in April.
11. (*b*) Except play P, all others will be staged in month having 31 days.
12. (*d*) Play M will be staged in May.
13. (*c*) Four play L, P, M and K will be staged before play N.

Intro Exercise 2 (Based on Type 2)

Direction (Q. Nos. 1-5) *Examine the information given in the following paragraph and answer the items that follow.*

Guest lectures on five subjects *viz.* Economics, History, Statistics, English and Mathematics have to be arranged in a week from Monday to Friday. Only one lecture can be arranged on each day. Economics cannot be scheduled on Tuesday. Guest faculty for History is available only on Tuesday. Mathematics lecture has to be scheduled immediately after the day of Economics lecture. English lecture has to be scheduled immediately before the day of Economics lecture.

1. Which lecture is scheduled on Monday?
   (a) History (b) Economics
   (c) Mathematics (d) Statistics

2. Which lecture is scheduled between Statistics and English?
   (a) Economics (b) History
   (c) Mathematics (d) No lecture

3. Which lecture is the last one in the week?
   (a) History (b) English
   (c) Mathematics (d) Economics

4. Which lecture is scheduled on Wednesday?
   (a) Statistics (b) Economics
   (c) English (d) History

5. Which lecture is scheduled before the Mathematics lecture?
   (a) Economics (b) History
   (c) Statistics (d) English

Direction (Q. Nos. 6-11) *Read the following information carefully and answer the questions that follow.* **FMS 2011**

In a Public Sector Undertaking Township, there are five Executives– Ambrish, Amit, Rohit, Manu and Tarun. Two of them play Cricket while the other three play different games *viz.* Football, Tennis and Chess. One Cricket player and a Chess player stay in the 3rd flat, whereas the other three different flats. i.e. 2nd, 4th and 5th.

Two of these five players are mechanical engineers while the other three are quality inspector, design engineer and power engineer, respectively. The Chess player is oldest in age while one of the Cricket players, who plays at the national level, is the youngest in age. The age of the other Cricket player, who plays at the regional level lies between the Football player and the Chess player. Manu is a regional level player and stays in the 3rd flat while Tarun is a quality inspector and stays in the 5th flat. The Football player is a design engineer and stays in the 2nd flat. Amit is a power engineer and plays Chess while Ambrish is the mechanical engineer and plays Cricket at the national level.

6. Who stays in the 4th flat?
   (a) Ambrish (b) Amit (c) Rohit (d) Manu

7. What does Tarun play?
   (a) Chess (b) Football (c) Cricket (d) Tennis

8. Who plays Football?
   (a) Ambrish (b) Amit (c) Rohit (d) Manu

9. Agewise who among the following lies between Manu and Tarun?
   (a) Quality inspector (b) Mechanical engineer
   (c) Power engineer (d) Design engineer

10. Who stay in the same flat?
    (a) Ambrish and Amit (b) Manu and Tarun
    (c) Amit and Manu (d) Rohit and Tarun

11. The Chess player is a
    (a) Power engineer (b) Mechanical engineer
    (c) Design engineer (d) Quality inspector

Direction (Q. Nos. 12-17) *Study the following information and answer the given questions.* **IBPS (PO) 2011**

Six lectures are scheduled in a week starting from Monday and ending on Sunday of the same week. Computer Science is not on Tuesday or Saturday. Psychology is immediately after Organisational Behaviour. Statistics is not on Friday and there is one day gap between Statistics and Research Methods. One day prior to the schedule of Economics there is no lecture. (as that day is the 'off' day and Monday is not the off day.)

12. Which of the following is the last lecture scheduled?
    (a) Statistics (b) Research Methods
    (c) Psychology (d) Cannot be determined
    (e) None of these

13. If Wednesday is the 'off' day, then the code would be 2-4, if Thursday was the 'off' day, then the code would be 3-3. Taking into acccount the 'off' day which of following code is correct?
    (a) 2-4 (b) 3-3
    (c) 4-2 (d) Cannot be determined
    (e) None of these

14. Which lecture is scheduled on Friday?
    (a) Economics (b) Psychology
    (c) Computer Science (d) Cannot be determined
    (e) None of these

15. How many lectures were scheduled between Economics and Psychology?
    (a) One (b) Two
    (c) Three (d) Cannot be determined
    (e) None of these

16. Which day is Computer Science scheduled?
(a) Monday (b) Wednesday
(c) Thursday (d) Cannot be determined
(e) None of these

17. Which day is the 'off' day?
(a) Tuesday (b) Wednesday
(c) Friday (d) Cannot be determined
(e) None of these

Direction (Q. Nos. 18-22) *Study the following information and answer the questions that follow.*

CBI (PO) 2010

I. Six plays are to be organised from Monday to Sunday– One play each day with one day when there is no play. 'No play' day is not Monday or Sunday.
II. The plays are held in sets of 3 plays each in such a way that 3 plays are held without any break i.e. 3 plays are held in such a way, that there is no 'No play' day between them but immediately before this set or immediately after this set it is 'No play' day.
III. Play Z is held on 26th and play X was held on 31st of the same month.
IV. Play B was not held immediately after play A (but was held after A, not necessarily immediately) and play M was held immediately before Q.
V. All the six plays were held in the same month.

18. Which play was organised on Monday?
(a) Z (b) M
(c) Q (d) Cannot be determined
(e) None of these

19. Which day was play Z organised?
(a) Tuesday (b) Monday
(c) Wednesday (d) Cannot be determined
(e) None of these

20. Which date was a 'No play' day?
(a) 26th (b) 28th
(c) 29th (d) Cannot be determined
(e) None of these

21. Which of the following is true?
(a) Play B is held immediately before play M
(b) Play Z is held after play B
(c) There was a gap after 2 plays and then 4 plays were organised
(d) First play was organised on the 25th
(e) Play B was held on Friday

22. Which day was play Q organised?
(a) Friday (b) Wednesday
(c) Saturday (d) Cannot be determined
(e) None of these

Direction (Q. Nos. 23-27) *Read the following information and answer the questions that follow.*

Davis Cup is held every year to decide top tennis playing country. Six countries namely Russia, Sweden, Holland, America, France and Spain won the cup held at six different cities *viz*, Dallas Barcelona, Athens, Florence, Madrid and Stockholm between 2005 and 2010, not necessarily in the same order. It is known that.

I. Country won at Florence in a year, which is a multiple of two but not of five.
II. America and France won in two consecutive years but not in 2006.
III. Country at Florence won in the year 2008.
IV. Russia won at Stockholm in the year 2007 and Sweden won at Athens.
V. Sweden, Russia and France won in an odd numbered year.
VI. Spain won in a year, which is a multiple of five.
VII. The game at Dallas was held before it was held at Madrid.

23. In which of the following cities the game was not held in two consecutive years?
(a) Florence, Barcelona
(b) Athens, Dallas
(c) Florence, Madrid
(d) Florence, Stockholm

24. Which of the following combination of city-country-year is correct?
(a) Florence-Holland-2008
(b) Barcelona-France-2009
(c) Dallas-Spain-2005
(d) None of the above

25. Which country won the cup just the year before Russia had won?
(a) Sweden
(b) Holland
(c) France
(d) Cannot be determined

26. Which of the following pairs of countries won in two consecutive years?
(a) Sweden and Holland
(b) Sweden and Spain
(c) Russia and Spain
(d) None of the above

27. Which of the following are the respective cities in which America and France won?
(a) Madrid and Dallas
(b) Florence and Barcelona
(c) Florence and Dallas
(d) None of the above

Direction (Q. Nos. 28-32) *Read the following passage and answer the questions based on this.* **CGPSC 2014**

Four families decided to go for picnic to Banarsi Bagh and agreed to meet at a place called Narhi before moving for the picnic. One family has no kid, while others have atleast one kid each.

Amongst each family with kids atleast one kid goes to picnic. The following is the information about the families

I. The family with two kids came just before the family with no kid.

II. D who does not have any kid reached just before C's family.

III. P and his wife reached last with their only kid.

IV. Q is not B's husband.

V. Q and S are fathers.

VI. C's and A's daughters go to same school.

VII. B came before D and not A when she reached the fixed place.

VIII. R stays farthest from the place and he is a good singer.

IX. S explained that his son could not come because of exams.

28. Who amongst the females arrived third?

(a) A (b) C
(c) B (d) D
(e) None of these

29. Which is the correct pair of husband and wife?

(a) S and D (b) P and C
(c) Q and C (d) S and A
(e) None of these

30. Whose daughters go to the same school?

(a) Q and R
(b) P and R
(c) P and Q
(d) Q and S
(e) None of the above

31. Whose family has definitely more than one kid?

(a) R
(b) S
(c) Q
(d) P
(e) None of the above

32. Among the males who arrived second?

(a) P
(b) Q
(c) R
(d) S
(e) None of the above

Direction (Q. Nos. 33-35) *Study the information carefully and to answer the questions that follow.* **MAT 2011**

Five persons, Amrinder, Bishamber, Chidambaram, Digamber and Inder of a family eat grapes, apples, cherries, mangoes and pineapples not in the order as mentioned, after lunch, from Tuesday to Saturday. No member eats any fruit on Sunday and Monday. Each member eats only one fruit on one day and does not repeat it during the same week. No two members can eat the same fruit on the same day.

I. Inder does not eat cherries or grapes on Wednesday.

II. Amrinder eats cherries on Tuesday.

III. Digamber eats apples on Tuesday.

IV. Inder does not take pineapples on Tuesday but takes apples on Thursday.

V. Bishamber eats pineapples on Friday.

VI. Chidambaram eats grapes on Saturday, cherries on Wednesday and mangoes on Thursday.

VII. Digamber eats pineapples on Wednesday.

33. Which fruit does 'Inder' eat on Wednesday?

(a) Apples
(b) Pineapples
(c) Grapes
(d) Mangoes

34. Who eats 'mangoes' on 'Tuesday'?

(a) Bishamber
(b) Amrinder
(c) Inder
(d) None of the above

35. Which fruit can Chidambaram take on Tuesday?

(a) Apples
(b) Cherries
(c) Grapes
(d) Pineapples

Cumulative Exercise

Base Level

Direction (Q. Nos. 1-3) *Read the passage given below and answer the questions that follow.*

A, B, C, D, E, F are members of a family. They are engineer, stenographer, doctor, draughtsman, lawyer and judge (not in order). A, the engineer is married to the lady stenographer. The judge is married to the lawyer. F, the draughtsman is the son of B and brother of E. C, the lawyer is the daughter-in-law of D. E is the unmarried doctor. D is the grandmother of F. There are two married couples in the family.

1. What is the profession of B?
   (a) Judge (b) Lawyer
   (c) Draughtsman (d) Cannot be determined

2. Which of the following is/are a couple/ couples?
   (a) Only AD (b) Only BC
   (c) AD and BC (d) AC and BD

3. What is the profession of D?
   (a) Judge (b) Stenographer
   (c) Doctor (d) Cannot be determined

Direction (Q. Nos. 4-6) *Read the following information carefully and answer the questions that follow.*

Six members of a family G, H, I, J, K and L are an Accountant, clerk, Lawyer, Jeweller, Doctor and Engineer but not in the same order. Doctor is the grandfather of L who is an accountant. Clerk J is married to G. I, who is a jeweller, is married to the lawyer. H is the mother of L and K. There are two married couples in the family.

4. What is the profession of K?
   (a) Doctor (b) Clerk
   (c) Engineer (d) Accountant

5. How many male members are there in the family?
   (a) Two (b) Three
   (c) Four (d) Cannot be determined

6. How is G related to L?
   (a) Wife
   (b) Father
   (c) Grandmother
   (d) Grandfather

Direction (Q. Nos. 7-9) *Study the information below to answer the questions.* **MAT 2011**

L, M, N, O and P are five important cities of our country out of which, three are industrial cities, two are port cities, one is a hill station and three cities have a university each. Every hill cities has a university but has no port. 'O' is not a port city. No port city has a university. 'M' is a port city. Two industrial cities have universities and 'N' and 'O' are not industrial cities. The industrial cities with universities donot have ports. None of the industrial cities is a hill station 'O' is a hill station and 'P' has a university.

7. Which city has industries as well as a port but does not have a university?
   (a) L and O (b) O and M (c) M (d) N

8. Which city has neither industries nor a university nor a hill station?
   (a) M (b) N (c) L (d) P

9. Which two cities have ports?
   (a) L and M (b) M and N (c) L and O (d) N and P

Direction (Q. Nos. 10-14) *Study the following information carefully and answer the questions that follow.* **NIACL 2014**

P, Q, R, S, T and M are six students of a school, one each studies in class I-VI. Each of them has a favourite colour from Red, Black, Yellow, Pink, Blue and Green not necessarily in the same order.

Q likes Black and does not study in class IV or V. The one who studies in class IV does not like Green. P studies in Class II. M likes Blue and does not study in class IV. The one who likes Yellow studies in class VI. S likes Pink and studies in class I. R does not study in class VI.

10. In which class does R study?
    (a) V (b) III
    (c) IV (d) Data inadequate
    (e) None of these

11. Which colour does R like?
    (a) Black (b) Yellow
    (c) Green (d) Data inadequate
    (e) None of these

12. Which colour does P like?
(a) Green (b) Yellow
(c) Red (d) Data inadequate
(e) None of these

13. Which of the following combinations is correct?
(a) P-II-Yellow (b) Q-III-Green
(c) S-I-Black (d) T-VI-Yellow
(e) None of these

14. In which class does M study?
(a) IV (b) III
(c) II (d) V
(e) None of these

Direction (Q. Nos. 15-19) *Read the following information carefully and then answer the questions given below it.* **IBPS (PO) 2014**

I. A, B, C, D, E and F are members of a club. Each of them plays a different game of Carrom, Chess, Cards, Table Tennis, Badminton and Volleyball.
II. D plays Chess and is married to B.
III. One out of two couples in the group plays Cards and Table Tennis.
IV. No lady plays either Badminton or Volleyball or Chess.
V. C plays Volleyball and F plays Badminton.
VI. A is the brother of F.

15. Who plays Table Tennis?
(a) C (b) D
(c) A (d) B
(e) None of these

16. How is F related to E?
(a) Brother
(b) Uncle
(c) Father
(d) Brother-in-law
(e) None of the above

17. Which game does B play?
(a) Table Tennis
(b) Chess
(c) Carrom
(d) Data inadequate
(e) None of the above

18. Which of the following pair is a couple?
(a) AE (b) BE
(c) BF (d) DE
(e) None of these

19. How many male members are there in the group?
(a) Two
(b) Three
(c) Four
(d) Data inadequate
(e) None of the above

Direction (Q. Nos. 20-25) *Read the following information and answer the questions that follow.* **NICL Assistant 2014**

Seven people namely A, B, C, D, E, F and G have a seminar on seven different days of the same week namely, Monday, Tuesday, Wednesday, Thursday, Friday , Saturday and Sunday but not necessarily in the same order. Each person also likes seven different colours namely, Green, Grey, White, Black, Orange, Pink and Blue but not necessarily in the same order. C likes Orange and has a seminar on Friday. Only one person has a seminar between C and the one who likes White. E has a seminar immediately before the one who likes White. Only three people have a seminar between E and D. B does not have a seminar on Wednesday. The one who likes Blue has a seminar immediately after B. Only three people have their seminars between the one who likes Blue and the one who likes Pink. The one who likes Black has a seminar immediately after the one who likes Grey. Neither G nor F likes Grey. F has a seminar on one of the days after G.

20. Four of the following five are alike in a certain way and so form a group as per the given arrangement. Which of the following does not belong to that group?
(a) F- Friday (b) G-Tuesday
(c) E-Thursday (d) C-Wednesday
(e) D-Saturday

21. Which of the following combinations is definitely correct?
(a) Monday-B-Black
(b) Monday-A-Grey
(c) Tuesday-B-Green
(d) Wednesday-A-Grey
(e) Tuesday-D-Green

22. Which of the following represents the day on which G has his seminar?
(a) Saturday (b) Wednesday
(c) Monday (d) Sunday
(e) Thursday

23. Based on the given arrangement, which of the following statements is true?
(a) A has a seminar on Monday
(b) D likes Green colour
(c) Only three people have a seminar between C and D
(d) None of the given statements is true
(e) The one who likes Pink colour has a seminar on Saturday

24. Which of the following colour does F like?
(a) Blue (b) Green
(c) Black (d) Pink
(e) White

25. Who amongst the following likes pink colour?
(a) E (b) G
(c) D (d) A
(e) F

Direction (Q. Nos. 26-30) *Study the following information carefully and answer the questions given below.* **SBI Asst. (Clerk) 2015**

P, Q, R, S, T, V and W are travelling in three buses A, B and C with atleast two of them in any of the buses. Each of them has a favorite (likes) cuisine *viz.* Punjabi, Rajasthani, Bengali, Maharashtrian, Gujarati, Kashmiri and Udipi not necessarily in the same order. Q is travelling in Bus B with T. T's favourite cuisine is Udipi. Those who travel in Bus A do not like Punjabi and Maharashtrian cuisines. The one who likes Rajasthani cuisine travels only with W in Bus C. The one whose favourite cuisine is Gujarati does not travel in the same bus with either T or W. P does not travel in Bus B P likes Kashmiri cuisine. S and V does not like Bengali cuisine. The one whose favourite cuisine is Maharashtrian doe not travel in Bus B

26. Which of the following combinations is correct?
(a) A-V Gujarati (b) B-S Bengali
(c) C-W Punjabi (d) B-Q Gujarati
(e) All are incorrect

27. Whose favourite cuisine is Rajasthani?
(a) Q (b) S (c) V (d) R
(e) Data inadequate

28. What is S's favourite cuisine?
(a) Maharashtrian (b) Bengali
(c) Rajasthani (d) Kashmiri
(e) None of these

29. What is Q's favourite cuisine?
(a) Kashmiri (b) Maharashtrian
(c) Punjabi (d) Data inadequate
(e) None of these

30. In which bus are three of them travelling?
(a) Only A (b) Only B
(c) A and B (d) Data inadequate
(e) None of these

Direction (Q. Nos. 31-35) *Study the following information carefully and answer the questions given below.* **Bank of India (PO) 2010**

A, B, C, D, E, F, G and H are eight persons working in three different departments viz, operations, sales and finance of an organisation with atleast two and not more than three in any department. They are in three different scales *viz,* I, II and III with atleast two in any one scale. Both the employees in operations department are in scale II. D works in sales department and belongs to scale I. A works in Finance department and belongs to Scale I. Two employees in Sales department belong to one scale. F works with only H in one of the departments. C works with E in one of the departments. B does not work with either C or A in the same department. G does not belong to Scale III. E does not belong to Scale I.

31. G belongs to which scale?
(a) II (b) III (c) I (d) I or II
(e) None of these

32. H belongs to which scale?
(a) I (b) II
(c) III (d) Data inadequate
(e) None of these

33. Which of the following combinations is correct?
(a) Operation - F - I
(b) Operation - H - III
(c) Scales - B - III
(d) Finance - E - III
(e) All are correct

34. C belongs to which scale?
(a) I (b) II (c) III (d) I or II
(e) None of these

35. Which of the following groups of employees work in sales department.
(a) DBE (b) DBC
(c) DBG (d) Data inadequate
(e) None of these

Direction (Q. Nos. 36-40) *Study the given information and answer the questions given below.*

There are four people sitting in a row : one each from India, Japan, USA and Germany but not in that order.

I. They are wearing caps of different colours green, yellow, red and white not necessarily in that order.
II. One is wearing a Kurta and one a T-shirt.
III. The Indian is wearing a green cap and a jacket.
IV. The American is not seated at either end.
V. The persons with Kurta and T-shirt are sitting next to each other.
VI. The person with Kurta wears a red cap and sits next to the Japanese.
VII. The Japanese wears a shirt and is not seated at either end.
VIII. The man with white cap wears T-shirt and is seated at one end.

36. Who wears the T-shirt?
(a) Indian (b) Japanese
(c) American (d) German

37. Who is wearing a Kurta?
(a) Indian (b) Japanese
(c) American (d) German

38. What is the colour of the cap worn by the Japanese?
(a) Red (b) Green
(c) Yellow (d) White

39. Who precedes the man wearing T-shirt?
(a) Indian (b) Japanese
(c) American (d) German

40. Who succedes the man wearing Jacket?
(a) Indian (b) German
(c) Japanese (d) Cannot say

Direction (Q. Nos. 41-45) *Study the following information carefully and answer the questions given below.*

A, B, C, D, E, F, G and H are eight employees of an organisation working in three departments *viz.* Personnel, Administration and Marketing with not more than three of them in any department. Each of them has a different choice of sports from football, cricket, volleyball, badminton, lawn tennis, basketball, hockey and table tennis not necessarily in the same order.

D works in Administration and does not like either football or cricket. F works in Personnel with only A who likes table tennis. E and H do not work in the same department as D. C likes hockey and does not work in Marketing. G does not work in Administration and does not like either cricket or badminton. One of those who work in Administration likes football. The one who likes volleyball works in personnel. None of those who work in Administration likes either badminton or lawn tennis. H does not like cricket.

41. Which of the following groups of employees work in Administration department?
(a) EGH
(b) AF
(c) BCD
(d) BGD
(e) Data inadequate

42. In which department does E work?
(a) Personnel
(b) Marketing
(c) Administration
(d) Data inadequate
(e) None of the above

43. What is E's favourite sport?
(a) Cricket
(b) Badminton
(c) Basketball
(d) Lawn Tennis
(e) None of the above

44. Which of the following combinations of employee-department-favourite sport is correct?
(a) E-Administration-Cricket
(b) F-Personnel-Lawn Tennis
(c) H-Marketing-Lawn Tennis
(d) B-Administration-Table Tennis
(e) None of the above

45. What is G's favourite sport?
(a) Cricket
(b) Badminton
(c) Basketball
(d) Lawn Tennis
(e) None of the above

Direction (Q. Nos. 46-48) *Study the information below to answer these questions.* **MAT 2012**

Delhi is known for speciality hospitals, where highly specialised doctors are available with modern technical medical gadgets aided by special computers. Patients with complicated ailments come from far and near for treatment. Some of these hospitals have performed extra ordinary surgical operations. As the cost of treatment and surgical operations are cheaper in India than in Western Countries, patients come to India for treatment.

A few seriously sick patients were asked to opt for hospitals they would like to be treated in their order of preferences was as follows

Patient A: Gangaram, AIIMS, Apollo and Escorts.

Patient B: Batra, Research and Referral (R and R), Apollo and Safdarjung.

Patient C: Holy Family, Apollo, AIIMS and Batra.

Patient D: R and R, Gangaram, Safdarjung and Escorts.

Patient E: Safdarjung, Holy Family, Batra and AIIMS.

46. Who does not like to go to Gangaram and Apollo but prefers AIIMS and Safdarjung Hospital?
(a) E (b) D
(c) C (d) B

47. Which pair is keen for Research and Referral (R and R) and Safdarjung but not for Holy Family and AIIMS?
(a) A and B (b) B and D
(c) C and E (d) D and E

48. Which pair prefers AIIMS and Apollo but not R and R and Safdarjung?
(a) B and C (b) C and D
(c) A and C (d) A and E

Direction (Q. Nos. 49-51) *Study the information below to answer these questions.* **MAT 2012**

Seven persons namely Prem, Tirkey, Madan, Jagan, Virendar, Raghubir and Waris are good friends and are studying in MBA, engineering and medical courses. Three are doing MBA course, two are in engineering course and another two are in medical course. Each of them has a very distinct and favourite colour choice ranging from blue, red, yellow, white, black, pink and brown but not necessarily in the same order. None doing MBA likes either red or black. Madan is doing engineering and he likes blue. Raghubir is doing medical and likes brown. Jagan is doing MBA and likes yellow. Prem, who does not like red, is in the same discipline of Raghubir. Tirkey is in the same discipline of Madan. Virendar does not like pink.

49. Which of the following groups is doing MBA?
(a) Jagan, Raghubir and Madan
(b) Virendar, Waris and Tirkey
(c) Jagan, Virendar and Waris
(d) Jagan, Prem and Raghubir

50. What is the colour combination choice of those, who are in medical discipline?
(a) Brown and pink
(b) Black and white
(c) Black and brown
(d) Yellow and black

51. Which colour does Virendar like?
(a) Yellow (b) Pink
(c) White (d) Brown

Direction (Q. Nos. 52-57) *Study the following information carefully and answer the given questions.*

Eight people A, B, C, D, E, F, G and H are sitting around a circular table facing towards the centre but not necessarily in the same order. All of them are at equidistant. Each one of them teaches different subjects *viz.* English, Hindi, Mathematics, Biology, Psychology, Physics, Chemistry and Accounts but not necessarily in the same order.

The person who teaches Accounts, sits third to the right of G. C is an immediate neighbour of G. The person who teaches Mathematics sits second to the left of C. B sits third to the right of H. H teaches neither Accounts nor Mathematics. Only two persons sit between C and the person who teaches Physics. A and F are immediate neighbours of each other. Neither A nor F teaches Accounts. The person who teaches English sits second to the right of A. Two persons sit between D and the person who teaches Hindi. D does not teach Accounts. The person who teaches Psychology is an immediate neighbour of the person who teaches Accounts. The person who teaches Physics sits second to the left of A. One of the immediate neighbours of G teaches Chemistry.

52. Who among the following teaches Chemistry?
(a) A (b) H
(c) D (e) G
(e) None of these

53. What is the position of B with repect to the person who teaches Psychology?
(a) Second to the left (b) Third to the right
(c) Third to the left (d) Second to the right
(e) None of these

54. Who among the following sits exactly between the person who teaches Biology and the person who teaches Physics?
(a) The person who teaches Mathematics
(b) E
(c) The person who teaches Accounts
(d) Cannot be determined
(e) These is no such person

55. Which of the following subjects does E teach?
(a) Chemistry
(b) Hindi
(c) Accounts
(d) English
(e) None of the above

56. Which of the following statement is true with regard to the given sitting arrangement?
(a) The person who teaches Hindi is an immediate neighbour of both H and D
(b) One of the immediate neighbours of F teaches Biology
(c) E is sitting exactly between B and the person who teaches Mathematics
(d) The person who teaches Chemistry is second to the right of E
(e) All are true

57. Four of the following five are alike in a certain way based on the given sitting arrangement and hence form a group. Which is the one that does not belong to the group?
IBPS (PO) 2014
(a) CF (b) GA (c) BD (d) EH
(e) BA

Direction (Q. Nos. 58-62) *Read the following information to answer the questions that follow.*
MAT 2014

Eight officers namely Anis, Buddha, Chaitanya, Dhyanchand, Erick, Fakir, Gyan and Harry have come using their own cars to attend a round table meeting. The following information is available regarding their seating arrangement and the cars they use.

I. Anis is sitting opposite to Chaitanya and owns an Ertiga Car.
II. Fakir is sitting between Erick and Buddha.
III. Dhyanchand is sitting opposite to Buddha.
IV. Gyan is not neighbour of Buddha or Dhyanchand.
V. Fakir uses Ritz and Harry uses jazz.
VI. Neighbours of Chaitanya use Splendor and Yuva.
VII. Users of Yuga and Yuva sit adjacent to each other.
VIII. Users of Yuga and Yuva sit adjacent to each other.
IX. Anis sits to the left of Dhyanchand.

58. Which information is not very useful to decide which seating position Chaitanya has occupied?
(a) Neighbour of Chaitanya use Splendor and Yuva
(b) Anis sits to the left of Dhyanchand
(c) Users of Yuga and Yuva sit adjacent to each other
(d) All are useful

59. Who among the following are not sitting adjacent to each other?
(a) Anis and Dhyanchand
(b) Dhyanchand and Gyan
(c) Buddha and Chaitanaya
(d) Erick and Anis

60. Who among the following use Yuga and Yuva?
(a) Chaitanya and Buddha
(b) Harry and Fakir
(c) Buddha and Dhyanchand
(d) Erick and Gyan

61. If Harry exchanges his seat with Erick, who will be his neighbours in the new position?
(a) Anis and Dhyanchand (b) Anis and Fakir
(c) Buddha and Chaitanaya (d) Erick and Anis

62. Who among the following uses Beat?
(a) Anis (b) Fakir
(c) Erick (d) Cannot be determined

Direction (Q. Nos. 63-69) *Study the following information carefully and answer the questions that follow.*

I. A, B, C, D, E, F, G and H are sitting around a circle facing the centre but not necessarily in the same order.
II. B sits second to left of H's husband. No female is an immediate neighbour of B.
III. D's daughter sits second to right of F. F is the sister of G. F is not an immediate neighbour of H's husband.
IV. Only one person sits between A and F. A is the father of G. H's brother D sits to the immediate left of H's mother. Only one person sits between H's mother and E.
V. Only one person sits between H and G. G is the mother of C. G is not an immediate neighbour of E.

63. What is position of A with respect to his mother-in-law?
(a) Immediate left (b) Third to the right
(c) Third to the left (d) Second to the right
(e) Fourth to the left

64. Who amongst the following is D's daughter?
(a) B (b) C
(c) E (d) G
(e) H

65. What is the position of A with respect to his Grandchild?
(a) Immediate right (b) Third to the right
(c) Third to the left (d) Second to the left
(e) Fourth to the left

66. How many people sit between G and her uncle?
(a) One (b) Two
(c) Three (d) Four
(e) More than four

67. Four of the following five are alike in a certain way based on the given information and so form a group. Which is the one that does not belong to that group?
(a) F (b) C
(c) E (d) H
(e) G

68. Which of the following is true with respect to the given seating arrangement?
(a) C is the cousin of E
(b) H and H's husband are immediate neighbours of each other
(c) No female is an immediate neighbour of C
(d) H sits third to left of her daughter
(e) B is the mother of H

69. Who sits to the immediate left of C?
(a) F's grandmother (b) G's son
(c) D's mother-in-law (d) A
(e) G

Direction (Q. Nos. 70-72) *Study the information carefully and answer the questions that follow.*
MAT 2011

Seven friends namely Anand, Deepak, Varun, Ujjawal, Pritam, Kadir and Jasmeet live in three different buildings namely Ashiana, Top-hill and Ridge. Each person is flying a kite of his choice with a different colour like red, green, blue, white, black, yellow and pink not necessarily in that order.

I. Kadir is flying a pink kite and lives in the same building, where Jasmeet stays, i.e. 'Ashiana'.
II. Varun is flying a black kite and does not live in Ridge building.
III. Ujjawal does not live in the same building, where Anand or Pritam are living and is flying a yellow coloured kite.
IV. Deepak lives in Ridge building with one more person and is flying a green kite.
V. None living in Top-hill building flies a white kite.
VI. Only two persons are staying in Ridge building while three of them are staying in Top-hill building.
VII. Pritam does not fly a blue kite and stays in Top-hill.

70. Who is flying the 'blue' kite?
(a) Anand (b) Pritam (c) Jasmeet (d) Deepak

71. Who are staying in Top-hill building?
(a) Anand, Varun and Pritam
(b) Varun, Jasmeet and Pritam
(c) Anand, Pritam and Deepak
(d) Anand and Pritam

72. Who are living in Ridge building?
(a) Deepak and Ujjawal
(b) Varun, Anand and Pritam
(c) Anand and Pritam
(d) Deepak, Anand and Pritam

Direction (Q. Nos. 73-77) *Read the information carefully and answer the questions that follow.*

I. Six friends Rahul, Kabeer, Anup, Raghu, Amit and Alok were engineering graduates. All six of them were placed in six different companies and were posted in six different locations, namely Tisco-Jamshedpur, Telco-Pune, Wipro-Bengaluru, HCL-Noida, Mecon- Ranchi and Usha Martin-Kolkata. Each of them has their personal e-mail id's with different e-mail providers i.e. Gmail, Indiatimes, Rediffmail, Yahoo, Hotmail, Sancharnet, though not necessarily in the same order.

II. The one having e-mail account with Sancharnet works in Noida and the one having an e-mail account with Indiatimes works for Tisco.

III. Amit does not stay in Bengaluru and does not work for Mecon, the one who works for Mecon has an e-mail id with Gmail.

IV. Rahul has an e-mail id with Rediffmail and works at Pune.

V. Alok does not work for Mecon and who works for Wipro does not have an e-mail account with Yahoo.

VI. Kabeer is posted in Kolkata and does not have an account with Hotmail.

VII. Neither Alok nor Raghu work in Noida.

VIII. The one who is posted in Ranchi has an e-mail id which is not an account of Rediffmail or Hotmail.

IX. Anup is posted in Jamshedpur.

73. The man who works in Wipro has an e-mail account with
(a) Sancharnet (b) Yahoo
(c) Rediffmail (d) None of these

74. Which of the following e-mail place of posting-person combination is correct?
(a) Kabeer-Kolkata-Rediffmail
(b) Alok-Bengaluru-Indiatimes
(c) Amit-Noida-Yahoo
(d) Raghu-Ranchi-Gmail

75. Which of the following is true?
(a) Amit is posted at Ranchi
(b) Raghu is posted at Jamshedpur
(c) Kabeer has an e-mail id with Yahoo
(d) Rahul has an e-mail id with Indiatimes

76. Which of the following sequences of location represent Alok, Kabeer, Anup, Rahul, Raghu and Amit in the same order?
(a) Bengaluru, Noida, Pune, Jamshedpur, Ranchi, Kolkata
(b) Bengaluru, Kolkata, Jamshedpur, Pune, Noida, Ranchi
(c) Kolkata, Bengaluru, Jamshedpur, Pune, Noida, Ranchi
(d) None of the above

77. People who have e-mail account with Indiatimes, Sancharnet and Yahoo work for which companies in the same sequence as the e-mail accounts mentioned?
(a) Usha Martin, HCL, Wipro
(b) Tisco, Wipro, Usha Martin
(c) HCL, Tisco, Wipro
(d) Tisco, HCL, Usha Martin

Advanced Level

Direction (Q. Nos. 1-4) *Read the following information carefully and answer the question that follow.*

Radhika, Neha, Rupa, Mahima, Sayali and Shobha joined six different renowned MBA institutes A, B, C, D, E and F and opted for six different specialisations in Management— Finance, IT, Operations, HR, Marketing and General management. Each of them has a different educational qualification out of BCA, B.Com., CA, BBM, B.Sc. and B. Tech.

The following information is available about them

I. Mahima joined institute B and did not take up marketing or IT and is not a B. Tech.

II. The persons who joined institute E opted for HR and is not a CA or a B.Sc.

III. The person, who is a BCA graduate, joined the institute D and took IT. Whereas, the person, who is B.Com graduate, took up General Management.

IV. Shobha is a CA and has taken Finance.

V. The person, who is a B.Tech, graduate has taken Operation Management and did not join institute A or C.

VI. Radhika joined institute F, Rupa is a BCA graduate and Neha took up HR.

1. What is the educational qualification of Mahima and what is the course she opted for?
(a) B. Sc. and Finance
(b) B. Com and General Management
(c) BBM and HR
(d) None of the above

2. Which institute did the B. Tech Graduate joint?
(a) F (b) D
(c) A (d) None of these

3. The educational qualification of Sayali is
(a) B. Sc. (b) BCA
(c) BBM (d) CA

4. If Shobha joined the institute C, then the student who joined the institute A opted for
(a) Finance
(b) Marketing
(c) General marketing
(d) HR

Direction (Q.Nos. 5-8) *Read the following information carefully and answer the question given below.*
CAT 2014

Five friends Amol, Mandar, Piya, Shashi and Reena attended Sagar's birthday party, where they partook of the sumptuous snacks and dinner. Each of the five friends gifted Sagar a different article— a fountain pen, a cellphone, a shirt, a jacket and an I-Pod and Sagar, in return, gifted each of them a different article a video game, a sweater, a perfume, a calculator and a pair of sunglases. The following is additional information about the gifts given by the friends and the gifts received from Sagar.

Amol gifted the shirt and received the video game in return. Shashi did not gift the I-Pod but received the perfume in return. Mandar did not gift an electronic item and received the calculator in return. The person who gifted the jacket received the sweater in return and Reena received the pair of sunglasses.

5. Who among the following gifted the jacket?
(a) Mandar (b) Shashi
(c) Reena (d) None of these

6. Which of the following statement is true?
(a) Two of the friends who did not gift electronic items, received electronic in return
(b) Piya gifted the jacket and Shashi gifted the I-Pod.
(c) Shashi neither gifted nor did she receive an electronic item
(d) The person who gifted the cellphone received the calculator in return

7. Which of the following is the correct combination of friends, article gifted and article received in return?
(a) Piya —Foundation Pen— Sunglasses
(b) Shashi —I-Pod—Perfume
(c) Reena —I-Pod—Sunglasses
(d) None of the above

8. Which of the following statement is false?
(a) Only one vowel, received an electronic item in return
(b) The friend whose name appears last in alphabetical order, gifted an electronic item and received a non-electronic item in return
(c) In alphabetical order, the friends who gifted the I-Pod appears before atleast two other friends
(d) The friend whose name in alphabetical order appears in the middle neither gifted nor received an electronic item

Direction (Q. Nos. 9-15) *Read the following information carefully and answer the questions that follow.*
MHT CET MBA 2012

Seven friends A, B, C, D, E, F and G are sitting around a circular table facing either the centre or outside. Each one of them belongs to a different department *viz.* Finance, Marketing, Sales, HR, Corporate Finance, Investment Banking and Operations but not necessarily in the same order.

C sits third to the right of G. G faces the centre. Only one person sits between C and the person working in the HR department. Immediate neighbours of C face outside. Only one person sits between F and D. Both F and D face the centre. D does not work in the HR department. A works in the investment banking department. A faces the centre. Two people sit between the persons, who work in investment banking and marketing departments. The person, who works in corporate finance sits to the immediate left of E. C faces same direction as E. The person, who works for sales department sits to the immediate left of the person, who works for operations department.

9. For which of the following departments does B work?
(a) Finance (b) Marketing
(c) HR (d) Corporate Finance
(e) Operations

10. What is position of B with respect to the person, who works for sales department?
(a) Immediate right (b) Third to the left
(c) Second to the right (d) Second to the left
(e) Fourth to the right

11. Who sits to the immediate right of E?
(a) The person who works for marketing department
(b) C
(c) B
(d) The person who works for HR department
(e) A

12. Who amongst the following sits exactly between C and the person who works for HR department?
(a) B
(b) The person who works for marketing department
(c) The person who works for operations department
(d) D
(e) G

13. Who amongst the following sit between the persons, who work for marketing and investment banking departments, when counted for the left hand side of the person working for marketing department?
(a) F and G (b) E and C (c) C and B (d) F and D
(e) B and D

14. How many people sit between the person, who works for operations department and A, when counted from the right hand side of A?
(a) One (b) Two
(c) Three (d) Four
(e) More than four

15. Four of the following five departments are alike in a certain way based on their positions in the given arrangement and so form a group. Which is the one that does not belong to that group?
(a) Sales (b) Investment Banking
(c) HR (d) Operations
(e) Corporate Finance

Direction (Q. Nos. 16-22) *Read the following information carefully and answer the questions that follow.* **MHT CET MBA 2012**

A hall is rented out for six different events in a week starting from Monday and ending on sunday of the same week. One of these days is an off-day, i.e. the hall is not rented out for any performance. These events are dance competition, singing competition, corporate conference, seminar, drama and a school's annual day but not necessarily in the same order.

There are three days between the corporate conference and the singing competition. Corporate conference is organised after singing competition. The school's annual day celebration is neither scheduled for the weekend (i.e. Saturday and Sunday) nor on a day immediately prior to or immediately after the singing competition.

There is one day between the school's annual day celebration and the seminar. Dance competition is held before the singing competition. There is one day between the annual day celebration and drama. Drama is not scheduled for Sunday.

16. On which of the following days is drama scheduled?
(a) Tuesday (b) Friday
(c) Thursday (d) Wednesday
(e) Cannot be determined

17. How many events are scheduled before the rest day?
(a) None (b) One (c) Two (d) Three
(e) Four

18. Which of the following events was organised on the day exactly between the school's annual day celebration and seminar?
(a) None as it is a rest day (b) Singing competition
(c) Drama (d) Dance competition
(e) Corporate conference

19. Which of the following is true with respect to the given schedule?
(a) Drama is organised on Saturday
(b) The off-day falls exactly between the days scheduled for drama and school's annual day celebration
(c) Corporate conference immediately follows the day scheduled for Seminar
(d) Singing competition is organised on Thursday
(e) Only four events are organised before seminar

20. Which of the following events was held on Friday?
(a) School's annual day celebration
(b) Corporate conference
(c) Drama
(d) Dance competition
(e) None as Friday is the rest day

21. Which of the following events was held on Sunday?
(a) None as it was a rest day
(b) Corporate conference
(c) Singing competition
(d) School's annual day celebration
(e) None of the above

22. Following the given schedule, Monday is related to drama in a certain way. Following the same way, Wednesday is related school's annual day celebration. To which of the following events is Thursday related to following the same logic?
(a) Seminar
(b) Dance competition
(c) Corporate conference
(d) Rest day
(e) Singing competition

Direction (Q. Nos. 23-27) *Study the following information carefully and answer the questions that follow.*

Seven Friends, Namely M, N, O, P, Q, R and S have an essay competition on seven different days of the same week namely, Monday, Tuesday, Wednesday, Thursday, Friday, Saturday and Sunday. Each friends also studies in a different standard namely first, second, third, fourth, fifth, sixth and seventh but not necessarily in the same order.

The one who studies in first standard has a competition on Saturday. S studies in second standard and has a competition on Wednesday. N has a competition immediately before Q. N does not have a competition on any of the day after S. The one who studies in seventh standard does not have a competition on any of the days after S. The one who studies in seventh standard does not have a competition on any of the days on or before Friday. The one who studies in third standard has a competition immediately after O. Q does not study in fifth standard. The one who studies in sixth standard does not have a competition immediately before or after S. R does not have a competition on Sunday and does not study in third standard. P does not have competition on any of the days before M.

23. Which of the following standards does R study in?
(a) Seventh
(b) Fifth
(c) First
(d) Second
(e) Fourth

24. Four of the following five form a group as per the given arrangement. Which of the following does not belong to that groups?
(a) O - Tuesday (b) M - Wednesday
(c) P - Saturday (d) S - Monday
(e) R - Thursday

25. Based on the given arrangement, which of the following statements is True?
(a) M has a competition on Saturday
(b) Q Studies in the sixth standard
(c) All the given statements are true
(d) Only two people have their competition between S and P
(e) R has a competition immediately after M

26. Which of the following combination is definitely correct?
(a) R- Friday- First
(b) O - Tuesday - Fourth
(c) M - Thursday - Third
(d) Q - Saturday - Fifth
(e) P - Sunday- Seventh

27. Which of the following represents the day on which N has his competition?
(a) Saturday
(b) Friday
(c) Sunday
(d) Tuesday
(e) Monday

Direction (Q. Nos. 28-36) *Study the information carefully and answer the questions that follow.*

UB Grameen Bank (PO) 2012

Nine people A, B, C, D, E, F, G, H and J stay in a building, not necessarily in the same order. The building has nine floors and only one person stays on one floor. All of them own one car each and each car is of a different colour, i.e. blue, grey, white, black, yellow, green, red, orange and pink not necessarily in the same order. The ground floor is numbered 1 , the floor above it number 2 and so on and the top most floor is numbered 9.

H owns, a black coloured car and stays on an even numbered floor. A stays on any even numbered floor below the floor on which H stays. The one who owns an orange coloured car stays on the fourth floor. E stays on the second floor and owns the white coloured car. The one who owns a pink coloured car stays on the third floor. A does not own a green coloured car. There are two floors between the floors on which the people owning the red and the black coloured cars stay. C owns a grey coloured car. There are three floors between the floors on which C and G stay. D stays on a floor immediately above J's floor. There is one floor between the floors on which F and G stay. F does not own the pink coloured car. The one who owns the blue car stays on the top most floor. F does not stay on the ground floor.

28. How many floors are there between the floor on which J stays and the floor on which C stays?
(a) One (b) Two
(c) None (d) Three
(e) More than three

29. Which of the following is true as per the given information?
(a) B stays on a floor immediately below the floor on which H stays
(b) G stays on a floor immediately above the floor on which A stays
(c) F stays on the eighth floor
(d) D owns the orange coloured car
(e) None is true

30. On which of the following floors does G stay?
(a) 1st (b) 6th
(c) 5th (d) 7th
(e) None of these

31. Who amongst the following stays on the top most floor?
(a) F
(b) G
(c) D
(d) C
(e) None of the above

32. A owns a car of which of the following colours?
(a) Orange (b) Pink
(c) Yellow (d) Blue
(e) None of these

33. Who stays on the floor, which is exactly between the floor on which H stays and the floor on which A stays?
(a) B (b) G
(c) C (d) F
(e) None of these

34. Who amongst the following owns the green coloured car?
(a) D (b) J
(c) G (d) F
(e) None of these

35. B is related to C in the same way as H is related to E as per the given information. Following the same pattern F is related to which of the following?
(a) J (b) D (c) A (d) G
(e) None of these

36. What is the colour of the car of the person, who stays on the ground floor?
(a) Red (b) Green (c) Yellow (d) Grey
(e) None of these

Direction (Q. Nos. 37-41) *Study the following information carefully and answer the questions that follow.* **SBI (Clerk) 2014**

Eight person A, B, C, D, E, F, G and H— are travelling in three different cars namely X, Y and Z but not necessarily in the same order. There are atleast two persons in each car and each car has persons of both the sexes. Out of eight persons three are females. All of them like different colours *viz*, Red, Green, Yellow, Blue, Black, White, Grey and Purple but not necessarily in the same order. One female does not like Grey or white colour. D is travelling with G in the car Z. G likes Black colour. The persons who like Red and Purple colours, are travelling in the same car. E does not like Purple colour and he is not travelling with H in the same car. A neither like purple nor Red colour. H is travelling in the car Y. B, C and H are females in the group. B likes Blue colour and travels with the person who likes Black colour. Red and Green colours are liked by female members. The person who is travelling with H, likes Grey colour. One of the persons travelling in car Z likes yellow colour.

37. In which of the following cars only two persons are travelling?

(a) Car X (b) Car Y
(c) Car Z (d) Cannot be determined
(e) None of these

38. The females member who is travelling in the car X likes which colour?

(a) Green (b) Blue
(c) Yellow (d) Red
(e) None of these

39. Who among the following likes yellow colour?

(a) D (b) E
(c) A (d) F
(e) None of these

40. Who among the following is/are travelling with female member C?

(a) E and G
(b) A and D
(c) E and F
(d) D and E
(e) F and G

41. Which of the following combinations of Person-Car- Colour is not correct?

(a) C—X— Red
(b) F— X— Purple
(c) G—Z—Black
(d) D—Z— Yellow
(e) E—Y—Grey

Direction (Q.Nos. 42-45) *Read the following passage carefully and answer the questions that follow.* **MHT CET MBA 2014**

Six friends Abhishek, Deepak, Maridul, Pritam, Rajan and Salil married within a year in the months of February, April, July, September, November and December and in the cities of Ahmedabad, Bengaluru, Chennai, Delhi, Mumbai and Kolkata but not necessarily following the above order. The brides' names were Geetika, Jasmine, Hema, Brinda, Ipsita and Veena, once again not following any order. The following are some facts about their weddings.

I. Mridul's wedding took place in Chennai, however, he was not married to Geetika or Veena.
II. Abhishek's wedding took place in Ahmedabad and Rajan's in Delhi, however neither of them was married to Jasmine or Brinda.
III. The wedding in Kolkata took place in February.
IV. Hema's wedding took place in April but not in Ahmedabad.
V. Geetika and Ispita got married in February and November and in chennai and Kolkata, but not following the above order.
VI. Pritam visited Bengaluru and Kolkata only after his marriage in December.
VII. Salil was married to Jasmine in September.

42. Hema's husband is

(a) Abhishek (b) Deepak
(c) Ranjan (d) Pritam
(e) Mridul

43. Deepak's wedding took place in

(a) Bengaluru
(b) Mumbai
(c) Kolkata
(d) Delhi
(e) Chennai

44. In Mumbai, the wedding of one of the friends took place in the month of

(a) April
(b) September
(c) November
(d) December
(e) July

45. Salil's wedding was held in

(a) Bengaluru
(b) Chennai
(c) Kolkata
(d) Delhi
(e) Mumbai

Direction (Q.Nos. 46-50) *Study the following information carefully and answer the questions that follow.* **IBPS (PO) 2013**

Seven people A, B, C, D, E, F and G have different hobbies, *viz.*, Travelling, Reading, Dancing, Painting, Sculpting, Singing and Pottery making but not necessarily in the same order. Each of them belongs to a different State, *viz.* Punjab, Odisha, Kerala, Rajasthan, Maharashtra, Gujarat and Karnataka but not necessarily in the same order. A belongs to Maharashtra. D likes Pottery making. The person who like sculpting is from the state of odisha. The person who like Dancing is from the state of Gujarat. F does not belongs to Gujarat, Odisha, Punjab or Rajasthan. F does not like Singing, Reading or Painting. B does not belong to Kerala, Odisha, Punjab or Rajasthan. B does not like Painting, Travelling, Reading or Singing. C does not like sculpting and he is not from Rajasthan or Punjab. Neither D nor G belongs to Punjab. A does not like Reading. The person from Kerala likes Singing.

46. Who among the following likes Singing?
(a) A
(b) C
(c) E
(d) G
(e) Cannot be determined

47. Which of the following combinations is true according to the given information?
(a) A – Travelling–Maharashtra
(b) C–Dancing–Gujarat
(c) E–Reading–Karanataka
(d) D–Pottey making–Rajasthan
(e) All are true

48. Who among the following belongs to the State of Karnataka?
(a) B
(b) D
(c) F
(d) E
(e) Cannot be determined

49. Which of the following combination is true about G?
(a) Sculpting– Odisha
(b) Pottery making– Karnataka
(c) Dancing–Gujarat
(d) Singing–Kerala
(e) Travelling–Karnataka

50. The person, who belongs to Punjab, likes
(a) Travelling
(b) Sculpting
(c) Painting
(d) Pottery making
(e) Reading

Direction (Q.Nos. 51-55) *These questions are based on the data given below.* **SNAP 2014**

There are two circular tables in a room. Six Americans - A1, A2, A3, A4, A5 and A6 are sitting at one table and six Germans -G1, G2, G3, G4, G5 and G6 are sitting at the other table. A1 and A4 are sitting opposite to each other. A2 and A5 are also sitting opposite to each other. A3 sits to be right of A4. A2 is the only person who can translate English to German language; A3 is the only person who can translate German language to English and none of them does the *vice-versa*, unless so stated. A5 and A6 sit adjacent to each other. Similarly, G1 sits opposite to G4; G6 sits opposite to G3 and G5 sits to the right of G6. G2 and G4 sit adjacent to G3. On the table, person can talk to another person, only as stated below. The only conversations that took place are as given below

A1 spoke to A2, A2 to G6, G6 to A3, G6 to G5, G5 to G4, G4 to G3, G2 to G1, G1 to G6, A3 to A4, A4 to A5, A6 to A1, G1 to G6 and A5 to A6.

The conversation are one sided i.e. A1 spoke to A2 implies that A1 is the speaker and A2 is the listener and not *vice-versa*.

51. If the person to the right of A1 wants to send a message to the person sitting to the left of G2, then the message has to pass through how many persons? (Excluding the first and the last)
(a) 7 (b) 5
(c) 6 (d) None of these

52. If A3 wants to send a message to G1, then how many person must the message pass through? (Excluding the first and the last)
(a) 6 (b) 4
(c) 10 (d) None of these

53. If the person sitting to the right of A2 wants to send a message to the person sitting two places to the left of A4, then what is the minimum number of people involved between them?(Excluding the two people)
(a) 6 (b) 10
(c) 4 (d) None of these

54. If every person is allowed to speak to the person who sits opposite to him directly, then what is the least number of person involved in passing a message from A3 to G1? (Excluding the two people)
(a) 3 (b) 6
(c) 7 (d) None of these

55. If the order of conveying messages is reversed at both the tables, i.e.'A1 speaks to A2 (now becomes 'A2 speaks to A1' and so on) and also A2 and A3 exchange their interpreting skills, then which of the following must be true?
(a) A1 can send a message to G5 involving only 2 persons
(b) The person sitting to the right of A6 can send a message to the person sitting to the lift of G2, by involving only five persons

(c) The person sitting to the right of A3, on the same table, can translate English to German language
(d) The maximum number of persons involved in the longest message in this new arrangement is more than in the previous arrangement

Direction (Q. Nos. 56-63) *Study the following information carefully and answer the questions that follow.* **MHT CET MBA 2012**

Eight people are sitting in two parallel rows containing four people each, in such a way that there is an equal distance between adjacent persons. In row- 1 A, B, C and D are seated and all of them are facing South. In row-2 E, F, G and H are seated and all of them are facing North. Therefore, in the given sitting arrangement each member seated in a row faces another of the other row. Each one of them also has a different profession, *viz.* Engineer, Doctor, Teacher, Pilot, Businessman, Banker, Lawyer and Builder but not necessarily in the same order.

B sits second to right of the Builder. G faces the immediate neighbour of the Builder. Only one person sits between G and the Pilot. Two people sit between H and the Lawyer. D faces the immediate neighbour of the Pilot. Only one person sits between the Teacher and C. Teacher does not sit at any of the extreme ends. Immediate neighbour of D faces the Doctor. E faces the Engineer. F is not the Banker.

56. Who amongst the following sit at extreme ends of the rows?
(a) B and the Pilot (b) C and the Builder
(c) The Builder and G (d) G and the Engineer
(e) G

57. Who amongst the following is the Banker?
(a) A (b) B
(c) C (d) E

58. Who is /are seated between the Lawyer and the Doctor?
(a) Pilot only
(b) G and the Businessman
(c) F, E
(d) Businessman and the Banker
(e) No one

59. Who amongst the following faces the Businessman?
(a) A (b) Doctor
(c) F (d) Teacher
(e) Builder

60. Which of the following is true regarding G?
(a) D faces G
(b) The pilot is an immediate neighbour of G
(c) G faces the person who is second to left of the Banker
(d) G is the Doctor
(e) G sits at one of the extreme ends of the line

61. F is related to Builder in the same way as H is related to Banker based on the given arrangement. To whom amongst the following is G related to, following the same pattern?
(a) Businessman (b) Teacher
(c) Pilot (d) Engineer

Direction (Q. Nos. 62-63) *Four of the following five are alike in a certain way based on the given sitting arrangement and thus form a group. Which is the one that does not belong to that group?*

62. (a) F (b) Banker
(c) Pilot (d) G
(e) Lawyer

63. (a) Lawyer (b) Banker
(c) Pilot (d) Businessman
(e) Doctor

Direction (Q. Nos. 64-68) *Read the given information carefully and answer the questions that follow.* **SBI (PO) 2014**

Ten people are sitting in two parallel rows, containing five people each in such a way that there is equal distance between adjacent persons. In row 1. J, K, L, M and N are seated and all of them are facing North and in row 2, P, Q, R, S and T are seated and are facing South (but not necessarily in the same order). Each person also likes a different cartoon character namely, Batman, Ben 10, Dexter, Donald Duck, Tom, Jerry, Noddy, Oswald, Superman and Spiderman (not necessarily in the same order).

N sits exactly in the centre of the row and faces the one who likes Tom. Only one person sits between S and the one who likes Tom. S faces one of the immediate neighbours of the one who likes Jerry. Only two people sit between K and the one who like Jerry. K faces the one who likes Oswald. P faces one of the immediate neighbours of L. P does not like Oswald. M is an immediate neighbour of L.

The one who likes Donald Duck is not an immediate neighbour of L. T is not an immediate neighbour of P and faces the one who likes Ben 10. R faces the one who likes Superman. The one who likes Spiderman faces North.

P does not face the one who likes Spiderman. The one who likes Batman sits to the immediate right of the person who likes Noddy. S does not like Batman.

64. Which of the following pairs represent the people sitting at the extreme end of the two rows?
(a) S, M (b) Q, L (c) P, N (d) Q, J
(e) R, L

65. Who amongst the following likes Donald Duck?
(a) S (b) P (c) T (d) R
(e) Q

66. Who amongst the followings is an immediate neighbour of the one who likes, Spiderman?
(a) The one who likes Jerry (b) The one who likes Noddy
(c) K (d) The one who likes Ben 10
(e) T

67. Which of the following cartoon character does T like?
(a) Batman (b) Tom
(c) Jerry (d) Noddy
(e) Oswald

68. Which of the following is definitely true as per the given arrangement?
(a) L faces R
(b) Q likes Oswald
(c) Q is an immediate neighbour of P
(d) The one who like Superman is an immediate neighbour of P
(e) The one who likes Dexter faces N.

Direction (Q. Nos. 69-71) *Read the passage carefully and answer the questions that follow.*

Note of the day long heavy queue in front of the Tarangabad Transport Department Office everyday for obtaining transport permits, the City Administration comes out with a 'Single Office Five Windows' system for facilitating the process. For simplicity, the windows are named as W1, W2, W3, W4 and W5, respectively. Office hours are from 8:00 am to 5:30 pm, barring saturday, when the office closes by 2:30 pm. To streamline the rush and reduce pressure on the employees, the working hours of the aforesaid windows are defined in the following manner:

I. W1 is open between 9:30 am and 2:30 pm on Monday and Wednesday between 8:00 am and 11:30 am on Tuesday and Thursday and between 3:00 pm and 5:00 pm on Friday.
II. W2 is open between 8:30 am and 11:30 am on Wednesday and Thursday between 8:00 am and 10:00 am on Friday, and between 12:30 pm and 2:30 pm on Monday and Saturday.
III. W3 is open between 10:00 am and 12:30 pm on Wednesday and Saturday between 10:00 am and 12:00 Noon on Friday and between 3:30 pm to 5:30 pm on Monday and Thursday.
IV. W4 is open between 11:30 am and 3:00 pm on Tuesday, between 12:30 pm and 3:00 pm on Thursday and Friday, between 8:00 am and 10:00 am on Saturday and between 3:30 pm to 5:30 pm on Wednesday.
V. W5 is open between 2:00 pm and 4:00 pm on Monday, 3:30 pm and 5:30 pm on Tuesday and Friday, between 8:00 am and 10:00 am Wednesday and between 10:30 am to 12:30 pm on Thursday.

69. On which of the following days, maximum number of windows is simultaneously open at 9:45 am?
(a) Monday (b) Wednesday
(c) Thursday (d) Friday

70. On which of the following days, not more than one window is open simultaneously at any given time during office hours?
(a) Monday (b) Wednesday
(c) Friday (d) Saturday

71. All windows of the transport permit office are closed for 1 h during the office hours on which of the following days?
(a) Wednesday (b) Monday
(c) Tuesday (d) Thursday

Direction (Q. Nos. 72-73) *Read the following information carefully and answer the questions that follow.*

Six persons– P, Q, R, S, T and U are sitting around a circular table facing towards the centre of the table in a restaurant. They have ordered for different items (rasgulla, strawberry, vanilla, mango, pastries and burfi) as their lunch.

They are wearing shirts of different colours, i.e. white, black, green, red, yellow and blue. Order of items for the lunch and colours of shirts are not necessarily according to the order of their names.

I. The persons who have ordered for rasgulla, vanilla and pasteries are neither in white shirt nor in black shirt.
II. The persons who are in green and yellow shirts have neither ordered for rasgulla nor for vanilla.
III. P is neither in white shirt nor on the immediate left of the person who has ordered for mango.
IV. The only person who is between T and U eats strawberry. The person who is on the left side of the person in white shirt does not eat burfi.
V. S has ordered for mango and the colour of his shirt is green. He is facing the person who has ordered for strawberry.
VI. One who has ordered for rasgulla is seated opposite to the person wearing blue shirt, while the person who wear shirt of green colour is on the left of the person who has ordered for pastries.
VII. One who has ordered for burfi is on the immediate right of the person in white shirt but on the immediate left of the person who has ordered for vanilla.
VIII. R has not ordered for vanilla, while U has not ordered for rasgulla.

72. Which of the following is not correctly matched?
(a) P-Yellow-Pastries
(b) S-Green-Mango
(c) U-Black-Burfi
(d) T-Red-Strawberry

73. The colour of the shirt of the person, who ordered for vanilla, is
(a) Blue
(b) Red
(c) Yellow
(d) Black

Direction (Q. Nos. 74-77) *Read the following passage and answer the questions that follow.* **IIFT 2014**

In an engineering college, five students from five different cities were elected as Secretaries by the students to perform different student activities. Each student studies in a different branch of engineering. Additionally, the following information is provided.

I. Abhishek does not stay in the Aravalli hostel, where the student from Nagpur stays.

II. The student, whose name is not Abhishek and does not study in Metallurgy, stays in Satpura hostel. He is the only student among the five to stay at Satpura hostel.

III. Hardeep neither belongs to Jodhpur nor does he study Mechanical Engineering.

IV. The student-in-charge of Cultural Activity stays in the Aravalli hostel where Civil Engineering student does not stay.

V. Sanjay and the student, who studies Metallurgy, both stay in the same hostel.

VI. The student who belong to Allahabad does not stay with the student-in-charge of the Sports activity staying at Aravalli hostel.

VII. Sanjay is not the student-in-charge of the Cultural activity.

VIII. Ravi, the student-in-charge of Mess activity, stays of Satpura hostel.

IX. The student from Patna and the student, who studies Mechanical Engineering, both stay at Aravalli hostel. They are the only two among the five students to stay at this hostel.

X. The student, who stays at Satpura hostel, studies Computer Sciences.

XI. Hemant, who does not belong to Kochi, studies Chemical Engineering. He is not the General Secretary of the Student Body.

XII. Sanjay does not belong to Allahabad.

XIII. The student from Kochi and the student-in-charge of Placement activity, both stay at the Vindhya Hostel

74. Which of the following statements is/are incorrect?

I. The Chemical Engineering student and the student-in-charge of Cultural activity, both stay in the same hostel.

II. The student-in-charge of Placement activity is studying Metallurgy.

III. The student who belongs to Nagpur is the student-in-charge of Sport's activity.

IV. Ravi belongs to Jodhpur.

(a) Only I
(b) I and II
(c) I, II and III
(d) None of the above

75. Which of the following statements is/are correct?

I. Sanjay and Abhishek stay at the same hostel.

II. The General Secretary of the student Body studies Mechanical Engineering.

III. The student who belongs to Patna is studying Metallurgy.

IV. The student who belongs to Kochi is studying Computer Science.

(a) Only I
(b) Only II
(c) Only III
(d) None of the above

76. The student who belongs to Allahabad is studying in

(a) Metallurgy
(b) Mechanical Engineering
(c) Civil Engineering
(d) None of the above

77. The General Secretary of the Student Body belongs to

(a) Patna
(b) Nagpur
(c) Kochi
(d) Jodhpur

Answers with Explanations

Intro Exercise 1

Solution (Q. Nos. 1-3) Following table can be drawn from the given information.

	Hockey	Volleyball	Tennis	Cricket	Football
Rajneesh	✓	✓	✓	✗	✗
Kavita	✓	✓	✗	✓	✗
Suresh	✓	✗	✓	✗	✓
Gambhir	✗	✓	✓	✓	✓
Mahesh	✗	✗	✓	✗	✓

1. (*c*) Kavita is good in hockey, volleyball and cricket.
2. (*d*) Gambhir is good in tennis, cricket, volleyball and football.
3. (*d*) Rajneesh is good in tennis, volleyball and hockey.

Solution (Q. Nos. 4-8) On the basis of given information, the arrangement can be drawn is as following

Friend	M	T	J	R	D	W	Q
Car	A	B	C	C	A	A	B
Sex	Male	Female	Male	Female	Male	Female	Male

4. (*b*) J travels in car C.
5. (*c*) Car A.
6. (*b*) D travels in car A.
7. (*e*) None of the given option is true.
8. (*e*) All are correct.

Solution (Q. Nos. 9-13) According to given conditions, we can make a table follow all conditions

Grandparents	Mohan (Engg) (Red)	Vanita (Teacher) (Orange)
Parents	Charan (CA)	Namita (White)
Children	Raman (Principal) (Black)	Sarita (Blue)

9. (*d*) Mohan is an Engineer.
10. (*d*) Namita's profession is not given.
11. (*b*) Pair of two couples are

    Vanita–Mohan

    Charan–Namita
12. (*b*) There are three ladies in the family.
13. (*d*) Charan is a CA and colour liked by him is not given.

Solution (Q. Nos. 14-18)

As per the statements

Course starts with Geography, i.e. on 12th December and 13th December will be Sunday. The course should end with the History, i.e. on 19th December. Political Science is after holiday, i.e. on 14th December and Sanskrit on 15th December.

Thus, we have

December	12th	13th	14th	15th	16th	17th	18th	19th
Course	Geography	Sunday	Political Science	Sanskrit	Music	English	Hindi	History

14. (*a*) From the above table, it is seen that English is followed by 'Music'.
15. (*a*) From the above table, it is clear that there is a one day gap between Music and Political Science.
16. (*d*) From the above table, it is clear that Hindi precedes History.
17. (*c*) As Sunday is on 13th December, therefore Tuesday will be on 15th December. So, Sanskrit will be on Tuesday.
18. (*c*) As per the above table, Political Science will start three days before the English subject.

Solution (Q. Nos. 19-23) On the basis of given information, the seating arrangement of eight people is shown below.

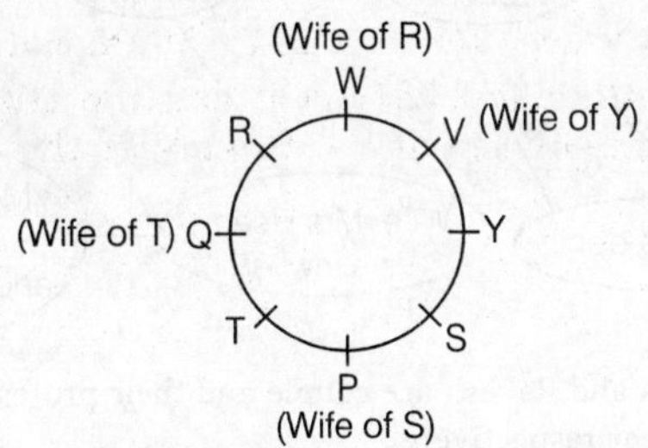

Person	Profession	Male/Female
P	–	Female
Q	–	Female
R	Engineer	Male
S	Editor	Male
T	Columnist	Male
V	–	Female
W	–	Female
Y	Teacher	Male

19. (*d*) Immediate left with respect to T.

20. (*a*) Third to the left of V.

21. (*b*) V is the wife of R is not true.

22. (*c*) Y, R are immediate neighbours.

23. (*c*) WVY does not belong to the group.

Solution (Q. Nos. 24-27) According to the information, the arrangement is as following

Persons	Subjects							Sports						
	Phy.	Chem.	Eng.	Bio.	His.	Geo.	Phil.	Football	Cricket	Hockey	Volly	Bad.	T.T.	Basket
P	✗	✗	✗	✓	✗	✗	✗	✗	✓	✗	✗	✗	✗	✗
Q	✗	✗	✗	✗	✓	✗	✗	✗	✗	✗	✗	✓	✗	✗
R	✗	✗	✗	✗	✗	✗	✓	✗	✗	✓	✗	✗	✗	✗
S	✗	✗	✗	✗	✗	✓	✗	✗	✗	✗	✗	✗	✗	✓
T	✗	✗	✓	✗	✗	✗	✗	✓	✗	✗	✗	✗	✗	✗
V	✓	✗	✗	✗	✗	✗	✗	✗	✗	✗	✗	✗	✓	✗
W	✗	✓	✗	✗	✗	✗	✗	✗	✗	✗	✓	✗	✗	✗

24. (*c*) Q likes History.

25. (*a*) S's favourite sport is Basketball.

26. (*e*) None of the option is true.

27. (*d*) Q's favourite sport is Badminton.

Solution (Q. Nos. 28-32) From the given information, we can draw the following figure.

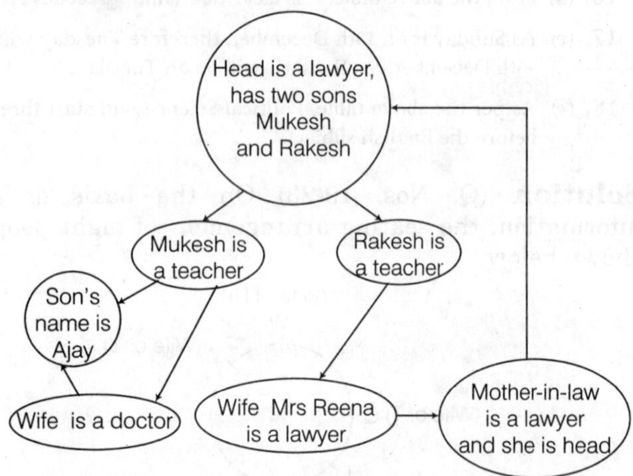

28. (*a*) Reena and Rakesh are couple and their professions are Lawyer and Teacher respectively .

29. (*c*) Rakesh's wife is Mrs Reena and she is a lawyer.

30. (*b*) There, are three male members- Mukesh, Rakesh and Ajay.

31. (*d*) No information is given about grandfather, so it cannot be determined.

32. (*d*) Profession of Ajay is not given, so it cannot be determined.

Solution (Q. Nos. 33-38) According to the given information, the seating arrangement is as following

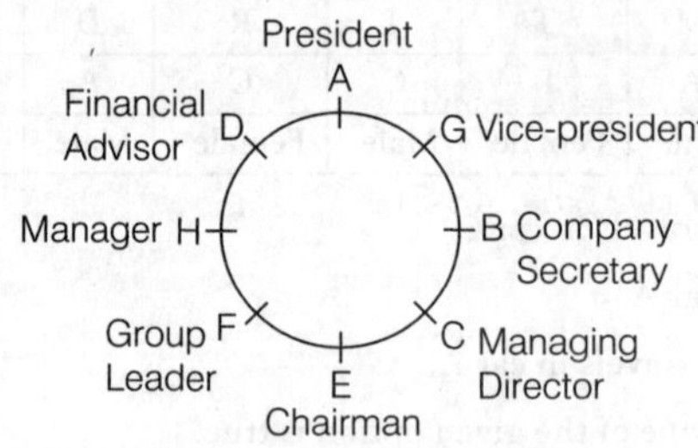

33. (*d*) D, the Financial Advisor sits third to the left of E.

34. (*e*) Except in B-Managing Director, in all others the first person is to the immediate left of the second person.

35. (*a*) A is the President of the Company.

36. (*d*) The Group Leader F is the immediate neighbour of H, the Manager or E, the Chairman. G sits second to the left of D.

The immediate neighbours of Group Leader, F are Chairman E and Manager H.

The Chairman E, is to the immediate left of Managing Director C. The Group Leader F sits second to the right of the Financial Advisor D.

37. (*c*) B is the Company Secretary of the Company.

38. (*e*) E, the Chairman and F, the Group Leader sit between C, the Managing Director and H, the Manager.

Solution (Q. Nos. 39-44) On the basis of given information, we get the following table.

Person	Expertise	Awards
A	P	Kalinga Award
B	Q	Gandhi Peace Prize
C	R/U	Vyas Samman/Saraswati Samman
D	S	Kabir Samman
E	T	Iqbal Samman
F	U/R	Saraswati Samman/Vyas Samman

39. (*d*) Vyas Samman has been won by either C or F.

40. (*c*) Winner of Saraswati Samman is an expert in the field of either R or U.

41. (*a*) D has expertise in the field of S.

42. (*b*) B is the winner of Gandhi Peace Prize.

43. (*e*) A is an expert in the field of P and he is the winner of Kalinga Award.

44. (*b*) A has expertise in the field of P and he is the winner of Kalinga Award.

Solution (Q. Nos. 45-47) Following table can be drawn from the given information.

Names	Home Towns					Specialist Slot				
	Sikandrabad	Panipat	Warangal	Banaras	Chennai	Spin	Pace bowler	Wicket-keeper	Bats man	Cap
Surinder	✗	✓	✗	✗	✗	✗	✗	✗	✗	✓
Prem	✗	✗	✓	✗	✗	✓	✗	✗	✗	✗
Wasim	✗	✗	✗	✗	✓	✗	✗	✗	✓	✗
Bishamber	✓	✗	✗	✗	✗	✗	✓	✗	✗	✗
Chauhan	✗	✗	✗	✓	✗	✗	✗	✓	✗	✗

45. (*c*) Chauhan is the wicket-keeper.

46. (*c*) Warangal is spinner's home town.

47. (*b*) Bishamber is the pace bowler.

Solution (Q. Nos. 48-50) On the basis of given information, we get the following table.

Student	Subject	Hobbies
Dinakaran	Psychology	Billiards and Chess
Sumit	Psychology	Weight Training and Chess
Tarun	Physics	Badminton and Chess
Amul	Commerce	Golf and Lawn Tennis

48. (*d*) Amul does not play Chess.

49. (*a*) Dinakaran studies Psychology and plays Billiards.

50. (*c*) 6 games are played and 3 subjects are studied by all the four students.

Solution (Q. Nos. 51-53) On the basis of given information, we get the following table.

P	Man	Hardware	
Q	Lady	Hardware	Marketing
R	Lady	Hardware	
S	Man		Marketing
T	Lady		
X	Man	Hardware	Marketing

51. (*a*) S is the male who knows marketing but not hardware.

52. (*d*) The female partner who knows hardware but not marketing is R.

53. (*c*) The female who knows neither hardware nor marketing is T.

54. (*d*) The given information can be summarised as

	A	B	C	D	E
Bank	✗	✗	✗	✓	✗
Cinema	✓	✗	✗	✗	✗
Pharma	✗	✓	✗	✗	✗
Sales	✗	✗	✗	✗	✓
Jewellery	✗	✗	✓	✗	✗

Clearly, A - Cinema, B-Pharma, C - Jewellery, D - Bank, E - Sales is correct.

Intro Exercise 2

Solution (Q. Nos. 1-5) Information given in the passage can be arranged in the tabular form like this

Days	Monday	Tuesday	Wednesday	Thursday	Friday
Subject	Statistics	History	English	Economics	Maths

1. (*d*) Statistics lecture is scheduled on Monday.
2. (*b*) From the table above, History is scheduled between Statistics and English.
3. (*c*) Mathematics lecture is scheduled on the last day of the week.
4. (*c*) English is scheduled on Wednesday.
5. (*a*) Economics is scheduled before the Mathematics lecture.

Solution (Q. Nos. 6-11) According to the given information, following table can be constructed.

Name	Flat	Game	Profession
Rohit	2nd	Football	Design Engineer
Manu	3rd	Cricket (Regional)	Mechanical Engineer
Amit	3rd	Chess, (Oldest)	Power Engineer
Ambrish	4th	Cricket (National-Youngest)	Mechanical Engineer
Tarun	5th	Tennis	Quality Inspector

6. (*a*) Ambrish stays in 4th flat.
7. (*d*) Tarun plays tennis.
8. (*c*) Rohit plays football.
9. (*d*) Agewise arrangement is as following

   Amit > Manu > Rohit > Tarun > Ambrish

   So, Rohit lies between Manu and Tarun and he is a design engineer.
10. (*c*) Amit and Manu stays in the same flat.
11. (*a*) The chess player is the power engineer.

Solution (Q. Nos. 12-17) On the basis of given information, we get the following arrangement.

Day	Lecture
Monday	Organisation Behaviour
Tuesday	Psychology
Wednesday	Statistics
Thursday	Computer Science
Friday	Research Methods
Saturday	–
Sunday	Economics

12. (*e*) Economics is the last lecture that is scheduled on Sunc y.
13. (*e*) If Wednesday is the 'off' day the code is 2-4. It means two days before Wednesday and 4 days after Wednesday are scheduled for different lectures.

    Similarly, if Thursday is the 'off' day the code is 3-3. It means three days before Thursday and three days after Thursday are scheduled for different lectures.

    Actually the 'off' day is Saturday. So, the code for this will be 5-1.
14. (*e*) Research Method is scheduled on Friday.
15. (*c*) Three lectures Statistics, Computer Science and Research Method are scheduled between Economics and Psychology.
16. (*c*) Computer Science is scheduled on Thursday.
17. (*e*) Saturday is the 'off' day.

Solution (Q. Nos. 18-22) On the basis of given information, we get the following arrangement.

Day	Date	Play
Monday	25th	A
Tuesday	26th	Z
Wednesday	27th	B
Thursday	28th	No play
Friday	29th	M
Saturday	30th	Q
Sunday	31th	X

18. (*e*) Play A was organised on Monday.
19. (*a*) Play Z was organised on Tuesday .
20. (*b*) 28th was a 'No play' day.
21. (*d*) First play was organised on 25th.
22. (*c*) Play Q was organised on Saturday.

Solution (Q. Nos. 23-27) According to the given information, following table can be constructed.

Countries	Sweden	Holland	Russia	America	France	Spain
Year	2005	2006	2007	2008	2009	2010
Cities	Athens	Dallas	Stockholm	Florence	Barcelona	Madrid

23. (*c*) Florence and Madrid were the two cities in which game was not held in two consecutive years.
24. (*b*) Barcelona - France - 2009 is correct.
25. (*b*) Holland tie just the year before Russia had won.
26. (*a*) Sweden and Holland won in two consecutive years.
27. (*b*) America and France won in Florence and Barcelona, respectively.

Solution (Q. Nos. 28-32) According to the given informations, four family members and their arrival order to the meeting place is tabulated as below

S. No.	Husband	Wife	Children
1	S	B	Two
2	R	D	Zero
3	Q	C	One
4	P	A	One

28. (*b*) C who arrived third.

29. (*c*) Q and C correct pair of husband and wife.

30. (*c*) P and Q daughters go to the same school.

31. (*b*) S has definitely more than one kid.

32. (*c*) R who arrived second.

Solution (Q. Nos. 33-35)

Persons	Days	Fruits
Amrinder	Tuesday	Cherries
	Wednesday	Apples
	Thursday	Pineapples
	Friday	Grapes
	Saturday	Mangoes
Bishamber	Tuesday	Mangoes
	Wednesday	Grapes
	Thursday	Apples
	Friday	Pineapples
	Saturday	Cherries

Persons	Days	Fruits
Chidambaram	Tuesday	Pineapples
	Wednesday	Cherries
	Thursday	Mangoes
	Friday	Apples
	Saturday	Grapes
Digamber	Tuesday	Apples
	Wednesday	Pineapples
	Thursday	Cherries
	Friday	Mangoes
	Saturday	Grapes

Persons	Days	Fruits
Inder	Tuesday	Grapes
	Wednesday	Mangoes
	Thursday	Apples
	Friday	Cherries
	Saturday	Pineapples

33. (*d*) Inder eat 'Mangoes' on Wednesday.

34. (*a*) Bishamber eats 'Mangoes' on Tuesday.

35. (*d*) Chidambaram eats 'Pineapples' on Tuesday.

Cumulative Exercises

Base Level

Solution (Q. Nos. 1-3) From the given information, the relation chart can be drawn as

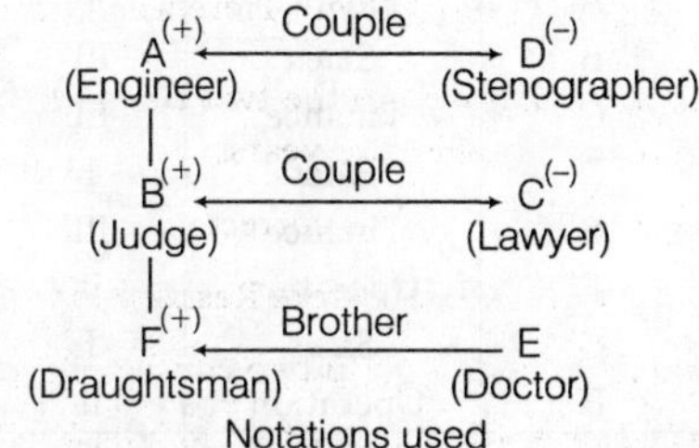

Here, (+) = Male, (–) = Female and ↔ = Married Couples

1. (*a*) From the above relation diagram, B is a Judge.

2. (*c*) Married couples are AD and BC.

3. (*b*) D is stenographer.

Solution (Q. Nos. 4-6) According to the given information, the arrangement can be drawn is as following

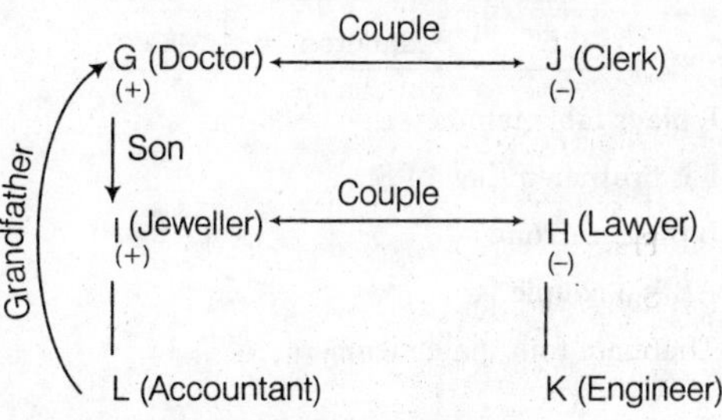

Here, (+) = Male and (–) = Female

4. (*c*) K's profession is Engineer.

5. (*d*) Cannot be determined as the gender of K and L not known.

6. (*d*) G is Grandfather of L.

Solution (Q. Nos. 7-9) According to the information, the arrangement is as following.

Important City	Industrial City	Port City	Hill Station	University
L	✓	✗	✗	✓
M	✓	✓	✗	✗
N	✗	✓	✗	✗
O	✗	✗	✓	✓
P	✓	✗	✗	✓

7. (*c*) City M has industries as well as port but does not has a university.
8. (*b*) City N has neither industries nor a university nor a hill station.
9. (*b*) Cities M and N have ports.

Solution (Q. Nos. 10-14) According to the information, the arrangement is as following

Person	Class	Colour
S	I	Pink
P	II	Green
Q	III	Black
R	IV	Red
M	V	Blue
T	VI	Yellow

10. (*c*) R studies in class IV.
11. (*e*) R likes red colour.
12. (*a*) P likes green colour.
13. (*d*) T-VI-yellow is correct.
14. (*d*) M studies in class V.

Solution (Q. Nos. 15-19) According to the information, the arrangement is as following

Person	Games	Gender
A	Cards	Male
B	Carrom	Female
C	Volleyball	Male
D	Chess	Male
E	Table Tennis	Female
F	Badminton	Male

15. (*e*) E plays table tennis.
16. (*d*) F is brother-in-law of E.
17. (*c*) B plays carrom.
18. (*a*) AE is a couple.
19. (*c*) There are four male members.

Solution (Q. Nos. 20-25) According to the information, the arrangement is as following

Person	Day	Colour
G	Thursday	Green
C	Friday	Orange
E	Sunday	Pink
F	Saturday	White
A	Monday	Grey
B	Tuesday	Black
D	Wednesday	Blue

20. (*e*) Except D-Saturday in all other option audition day is given before two days person's audition day.
21. (*b*) Monday-A-Grey is correct.
22. (*e*) G has his seminar on Thursday.
23. (*a*) A has a seminar on Monday.
24. (*e*) F likes white colour.
25. (*a*) E likes pink colour.

Solution (Q. Nos. 26- 30) According to the information, the arrangement is as following

Person	Bus	Favourite Cuisine
P	A	Kashmiri
Q	B	Punjabi
R	A	Gujarati
S	C	Maharashtian
T	B	Udipi
V	C	Rajasthani
W	C	Bengali

26. (*e*) All are incorrect.
27. (*c*) V's favourite cuisine is Rajasthani.
28. (*a*) S's favourite cuisine is Maharashtian.
29. (*c*) Q's favourite cuisine is Punjabi.
30. (*e*) None of the option is true.

Solution (Q. Nos. 31-35) From the given information, we get the following table.

Person	Department	Scale
A	Finance	I
B	Sales	III
C	Finance	III
D	Sales	I
E	Finance	III
F	Operation	II
G	Sales	I
H	Operation	II

31. (*c*) G belongs to scale I.
32. (*b*) H belongs to scale II.
33. (*d*) E works in Finance department and belongs to scale III.
34. (*c*) C belongs to scale III.
35. (*c*) D, B and G works in Sales department.

Solution (Q. Nos. 36-40) From the given information, we get the following table.

Nationality	Indian	Japanese	American	German
Clothing	Jacket	Shirt	Kurta	T-shirt
Colour of cap	Green	Yellow	Red	White

36. (*d*) German wears T-shirt.
37. (*c*) American is wearing Kurta.
38. (*c*) Japanese is wearing yellow cap.
39. (*c*) American precedes the German, who is wearing T-shirt.
40. (*c*) Japanese succeeds the Indian, who is wearing Jacket.

Solution (Q. Nos. 41-45) From the given information, we get the following table.

Person	Department	Sports
A	Personnel	Table Tennis
B	Administration	Football
C	Administration	Hockey
D	Administration	Basketball
E	Marketing	Cricket
F	Personnel	Volleyball
G	Marketing	Lawn Tennis
H	Marketing	Badminton

41. (*c*) B, C and D works in Administration department.
42. (*b*) E works in Marketing department.
43. (*a*) E's favourite sport is Cricket.
44. (*e*) None of the given combinations is correct.
45. (*d*) G's favourite sport is Lawn Tennis.

Solution (Q. Nos. 46-48) According to the information, the arrangement is as following

Patient	Hospitals							
	Gangaram	AIIMS	Apollo	Escorts	Batra	R and R	Safdarjung	Holy Family
A	✓	✓	✓	✓				
B			✓		✓	✓	✓	
C		✓	✓		✓			✓
D	✓			✓		✓	✓	
E		✓			✓		✓	✓

46. (*a*) E does not like to go Gangaram and Apollo but prefers AIIMS and Safdarjung Hospital.
47. (*b*) B and D pair is keen per Research and Referral (R and R) and Safdarjung but not for Holy family and AIIMS.
48. (*c*) A and C pair prefers AIIMS and Apollo but not Research and Referral and Safdarjung.

Solutions (Q. Nos. 49-51) According to the information, the arrangement is as following

Persons	Courses	Colours
Prem	Medical	Black
Trikey	Engineering	Red
Madan	Engineering	Blue
Jagan	MBA	Yellow
Virendar	MBA	White
Raghubir	Medical	Brown
Waris	MBA	Pink

49. (*c*) Jagan, Virendar and Waris groups are doing MBA.
50. (*c*) Medical persons choice of colours are black and brown.
51. (*c*) Virendar likes white colour.

Solution (Q. Nos. 52-57) According to the given information, the arrangement is a following

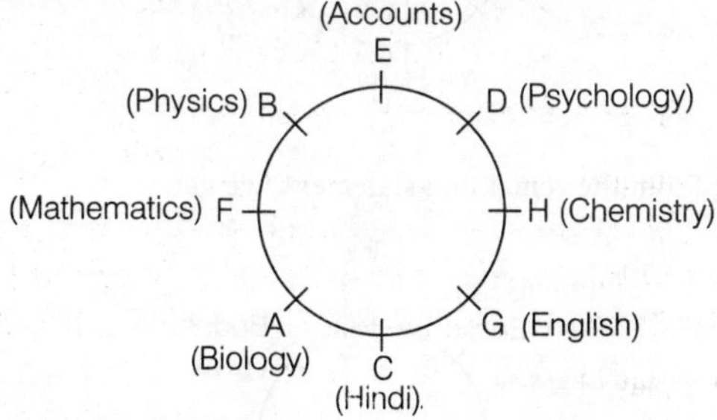

52. (*b*) H teaches Chemistry.
53. (*d*) D teaches Psychology. B is second to the right of D.
54. (*a*) A teaches Biology and B teaches Physics. F, who teaches Mathematics is exactly between A and B.

55. (*c*) E teaches Accounts.

56. (*b*) The person who teaches Hindi is C and C is an immediate neighbour of A and G.
Immediate neighbours of F are A and B. A teaches Biology.
E is sitting exactly between B and D, who teaches Psychology.
H teaches Chemistry and H is second to the left of E.

57. (*e*) Except in the pair BA, in all others the first person is second to the right of the second person. In BA, the first person is second to the left of the second person.

Solution (Q. Nos. 58-62) According to the given information, we have

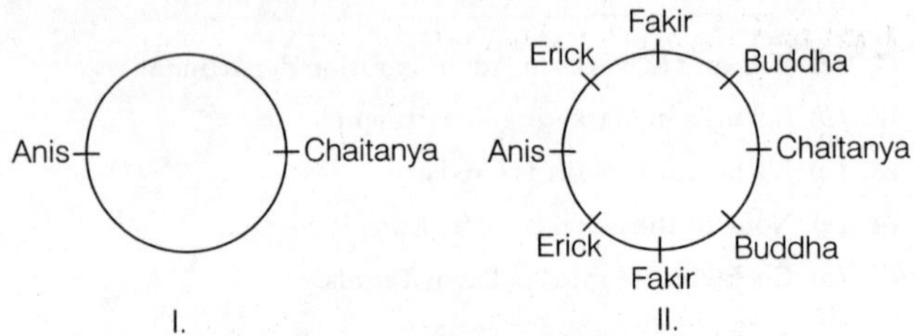

From Statements III and IX, we get

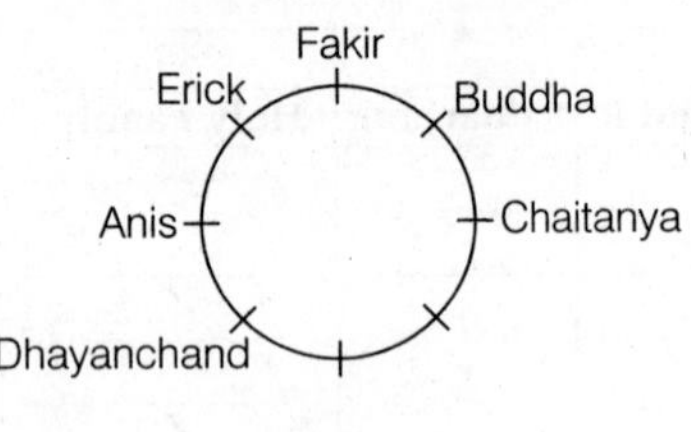

From Statement IV, we get

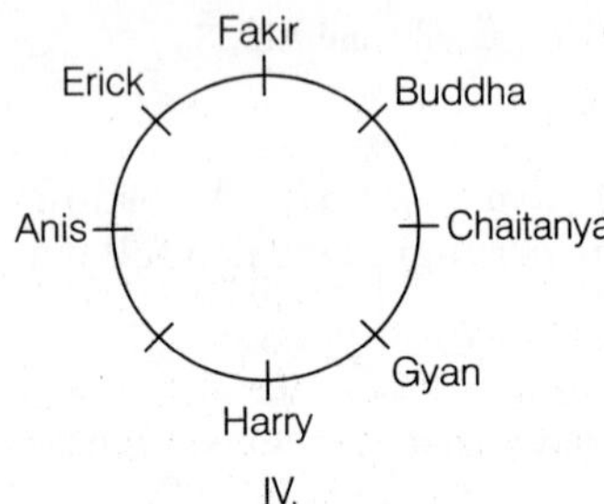

From the remaining statement, we get

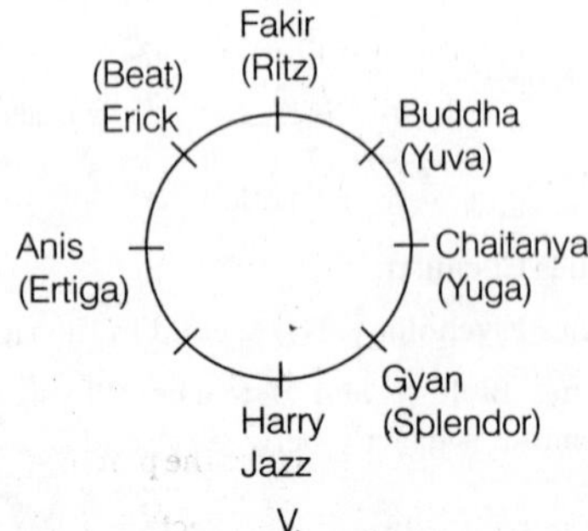

58. (*a*) Neighbour of Chaitanya use Splendor and Yuva.

59. (*b*) Dhayanchand and Gyan are not sitting adjacent to each other.

60. (*a*) Chaitanya and Buddha use Yuga and Yuva.

61. (*b*) Anis and Fakir will be his neighbours in the new position.

62. (*c*) Erick uses Beat.

Solution (Q. Nos. 63-69) According to the information of eight persons are as follow

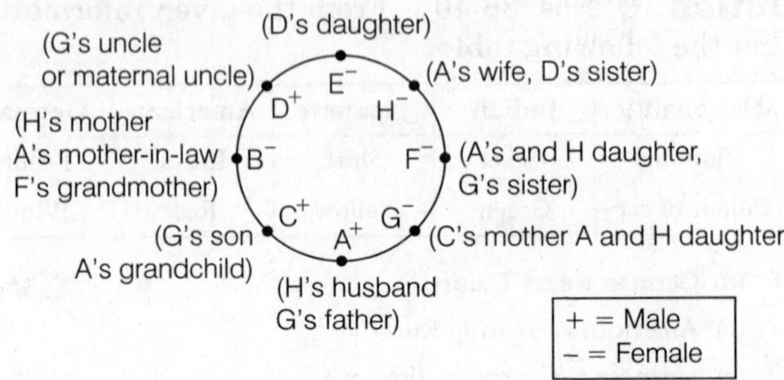

63. (*d*) A's mother-in-law is B and A is second to the right of B.

64. (*c*) D's daughter is E.

65. (*a*) A's grandchild is C and A is immediate right of C.

66. (*c*) G's uncle is D and three people (either clockwise or anti-clockwise) are sitting between G and her uncle.

67. (*b*) Except C, all others are women.

68. (*e*) B is the mother of H which is true with respect to the given seating arrangement.

69. (*a*) F's grandmother sits to the immediate left of C.

Solution (Q. Nos. 70-73) According to the information, the arrangement is as following

Friends	Building	Kite Colour
Anand	Top-hill	Blue
Deepak	Ridge	Green
Varun	Top-hill	Black
Ujjawal	Ridge	Yellow
Pritam	Top-hill	Red
Kadir	Ashiana	Pink
Jasmeet	Ashiana	White

70. (*a*) Anand is flying 'blue' kite.

71. (*a*) Anand, Varun and Pritam are staying in Top-hill building.

72. (*a*) Deepak and Ujjawal are living in Ridge building.

Solution (Q. Nos. 73-77) According to the information

From IX, Anup is placed in Tisco-Jamshedpur.

From IV, Rahul is placed in Telco-Pune and has Rediffmail id.

From VI, Kabeer is placed in Usha Martin-Kolkata.

From VII, Amit must have been placed in HCL-Noida.

From V, Raghu must have been placed in Mecon-Ranchi and Alok must have been placed in Wipro-Bengaluru.

From II, Amit has Sancharnet id and Anup has Indiatimes id.

From III, Mecon has G-mail id.

From VI, Alok has Hotmail id and Kabeer has Yahoo id.

So, the final table will be as following

Name	e-mail Provider	Company	City
Rahul	Rediffmail	Telco	Pune
Kabeer	Yahoo	Usha Martin	Kolkata
Anup	Indiatimes	Tisco	Jamshedpur
Raghu	Gmail	Mecon	Ranchi
Amit	Sancharnet	HCL	Noida
Alok	Hotmail	Wipro	Bengaluru

73. (*d*) Alok works in Wipro and he has an e-mail account with Hotmail.

74. (*d*) Raghu works at Ranchi and he has an e-mail account with Gmail.

75. (*c*) Kabeer has an e-mail id with Yahoo.

76. (*d*) The correct sequence of location of Alok, Kabeer, Anup, Rahul, Raghu and Amit is Bengaluru, Kolkata, Jamshedpur, Pune, Ranchi and Noida, respectively.

77. (*d*) People who have e-mail account with Indiatimes, Sancharnet and Yahoo are Anup, Amit and Kabeer respectively and they work in Tisco, HCL and Usha Martin, respectively.

Advance Level

Solution (Q. Nos. 1-4) According to the informtion, the arrangement is as following

	A	B	C	D	E	F	Finance	IT	Operations	HR	Marketing	General Management	BCA	B.Com	CA	BBM	B.Sc	B.Tech
Radhika	✗	✗	✗	✗	✗	✓	✗	✗	✓	✗	✗	✗	✗	✗	✗	✗	✗	✓
Neha	✗	✗	✗	✗	✓	✗	✗	✗	✗	✓	✗	✗	✗	✗	✗	✓	✗	✗
Rupa	✗	✗	✗	✓	✗	✗	✗	✓	✗	✗	✗	✗	✓	✓	✗	✗	✗	✗
Mahima	✗	✓	✗	✗	✗	✗	✗	✗	✗	✗	✗	✓	✗	✗	✗	✗	✗	✗
Sayali	—	✗	—	✗	✗	✗	✗	✗	✗	✗	✓	✗	✗	✗	✗	✗	✓	✗
Shobha	—	✗	—	✗	✗	✗	✓	✗	✗	✗	✗	✗	✗	✗	✓	✗	✗	✗

1. (*b*) The educational qualification of Mahima is B. Com and the course is General Management.

2. (*a*) F Institute

3. (*a*) The educational qualification of Sayali is B.Sc

4. (*b*) Marketing

Solution (Q.Nos. 5-8)

We know that Amol, Shashi, Mandar and Reena received the video game, perfume, calculator and sunglasses, respectively. This means that Piya received the sweater and we can, then conclude that gifted the jacket.

Since, Mandar did not gift an electronic item, he could have gifted the fountain pen, the shirt or the jacket. But we know that, the shirt and the jacket were gifted by Amol and Piya, respectively. So, Mandar must have gifted the fountain per.

We still need to figure out who gifted the cellphone and the I-Pod. Since, we know that Shashi did not gift the I-pod, Reena must have gifted the I-Pod and Shashi must have gifted the cellphone. We can now match the friends name with the gift given and the gift received as given in the table below.

Friends	Gifted to Sagar	Return gifts Sagar
Amol	Shirt	Video game
Mandar	Fountain Pen	Calculator
Piya	Jacket	Sweater
Shashi	Cellphone	Perfume
Reena	I-Pod	Pair of sunglasses

5. (*d*) Piya gifted the jacket.

6. (*a*) Amol and Mandar gifted the shirt and the fountain pen respectively (non-electronic items) and received the video game and the calculator, respectively (electronic items).

7. (*c*) Reena gifted the I-Pod and received the pair of sunglasses in return.

8. (*c*) Only Amol and Mandar received electronic items. So, option (a) is true. Shashi gifted the cellphone and received the perfume. So, option (b) is true. Reena gifted the I-Pod and in alphabetical order, she would not appear second last. So, option (c) is not true. In

alphabetical order, Piya appears in the middle and she gifted the jacket and received the sweater in return. So, option (d) is true.

Solutions (Q. Nos. 9-15) According to the given information, seating arrangement of all the seven friends is given below.

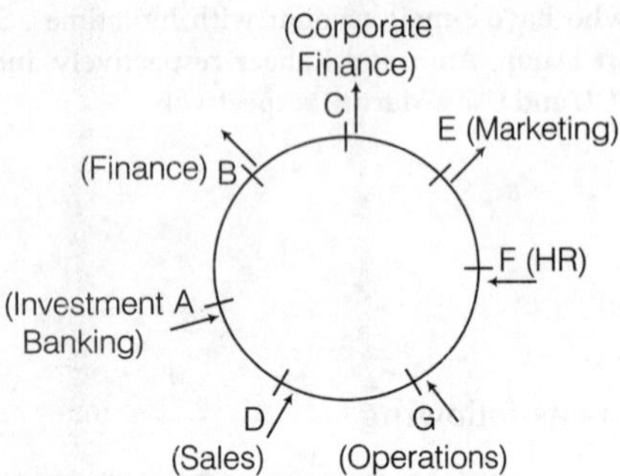

9. (*a*) B works in finance department.
10. (*d*) The person working in sales department is D and B is second to the left of D.
11. (*d*) The person who sits to the immediate right of E is F, who works in HR department.
12. (*b*) Clearly, E i.e. the person who works in marketing department sits between C and the person who works for HR department i.e. F.
13. (*c*) The persons who work in marketing and investment banking departments are E and A respectively and the persons who sit between them are C and B.
14. (*a*) The person who works for operations department is G. Therefore, number of persons who sit between G and A, when counted from right hand side of A, is one.
15. (*e*) In all the departments except corporate finance department, the persons sit facing inside while C who is in corporate finance department sits facing outside.

Solution (Q. Nos. 16-22) According to the given information events scheduled as follows

Monday	Dance competition
Tuesday	Singing competition
Wednesday	Drama
Thursday	Off-day
Friday	School's annual day
Saturday	Corporate conference
Sunday	Seminar

16. (*d*) Drama scheduled on Wednesday.
17. (*d*) Rest day was Thursday. Three events were scheduled before it.
18. (*e*) Between the school's annual day celebration and seminar, corporate conference was held.
19. (*b*) From the above schedule, it is clear that the off day falls exactly between the days scheduled for drama and school's annual day celebration.
20. (*a*) School's annual day was held on Friday.
21. (*e*) Seminar held on Sunday.
22. (*c*) As drama held after two days of Monday and school's annual day celebration held after two days of Wednesday, similarly corporate conference held after two days of Thursday.

Solution (Q. Nos. 23-27) The given information can be arranged as below.

Class	Friend	Day
I	R	Saturday
II	S	Wednesday
III	M	Friday
IV	Q	Tuesday
V	O	Thursday
VI	N	Monday
VII	P	Sunday

23. (*c*) R studies in class I.
24. (*c*) Except in option (c), in each combination, a student and the day which fall two days before the day of his competition are given.
25. (*e*) R has a competition (on Saturday) immediately after M. (M has his competition on Friday).
26. (*e*) Combination P - Sunday Seventh is definitely correct.
27. (*e*) N has his competition on Monday.

Solution (Q. Nos. 28-36) The given information can be arranged as below

People	Floor	Car (Colour)
B	9th	Blue
H	8th	Black
F	7th	Green
A	6th	Yellow
G	5th	Red
D	4th	Orange
J	3rd	Pink
E	2nd	White
C	1st	Grey

28. (*b*) Two (3rd, 1st) floors.
29. (*d*) D owns the orange coloured car.
30. (*c*) G stay's on 5th floor.
31. (*e*) B stay's on topmost floor.
32. (*c*) A owns yellow colour car.
33. (*d*) F stay's between H and A.
34. (*d*) F owns green colour car.
35. (*a*) As B is top most floor, C is lowest floor and H is second top most floor, E is second lowest floor. Similarly, F is third top most floor, J is third lowest floor.
36. (*d*) Grey colour car.

Solution (Q. Nos. 37-41) According to the information, the arrangement is as following

Person	Gender	Car	Colour
A	Male	Y	Grey
B	Female	Z	Blue
C	Female	X	Red
D	Male	Z	Yellow
E	Male	X	White
F	Male	X	Purple
G	Male	Z	Black
H	Female	Y	Green

37. (*b*) A and H are travelling in the car Y.

38. (*d*) C is the female member in the car X. She likes red colour.

39. (*a*) D likes yellow colour.

40. (*c*) E and F are travelling with C.

41. (*e*) The combination E-Y-grey is not correct.

E travels in car X and he likes white colour.

Solution (Q. Nos. 42-45) On the basis of information, we get the following results.

Months	February	April	July	September	November	December
Cities	Kolkata	Delhi	Ahmedabad	Bengaluru	Chennai	Mumbai
Friends	Deepak	Ranjan	Abhishek	Salil	Mridul	Pritam
Brides	Geetika	Hema	Veena	Jasmine	Ipsita	Brinda

42. (*c*) Ranjan is the husband of Hema.

43. (*c*) Deepak's wedding took place in Kolkata.

44. (*d*) In month of December, wedding of Pritam and Brinda took place in Mumbai.

45. (*a*) Salil's wedding was held in Bengaluru.

Solution (Q. Nos. 46-50) According to the given information, the arrangement is as following

Person	Hobby	State
A	Painting	Maharashtra
B	Dancing	Gujarat
C	Singing	Kerala
D	Pottery making	Rajasthan
E	Reading	Punjab
F	Travelling	Karnataka
G	Sculpting	Odisha

46. (*b*) C likes Singing.

47. (*d*) D–Pottery making– Rajasthan is true combination.

48. (*c*) F belongs to the State of Karnataka.

49. (*a*) Sculpting–Odisha combination is true about G.

50. (*e*) E belongs to Punjab, likes Reading.

Solution (Q. Nos. 51-55) The seating arrangement and pattern of conversation is as follow.

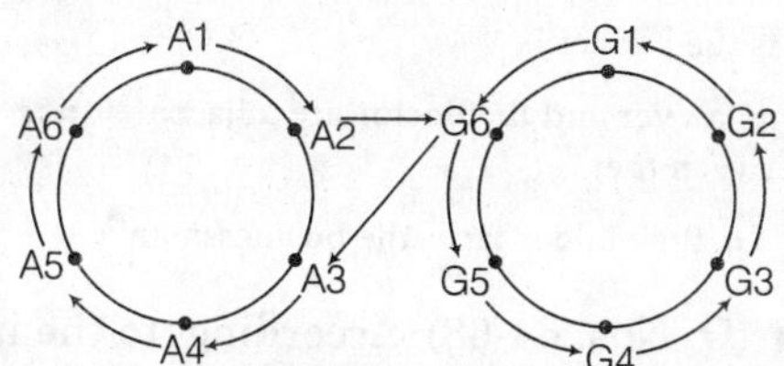

51. (*b*) A6 is the person to the right of A1 and G3 is the person sitting to the left of G2. So, route of send a message from A6 to G2 is as

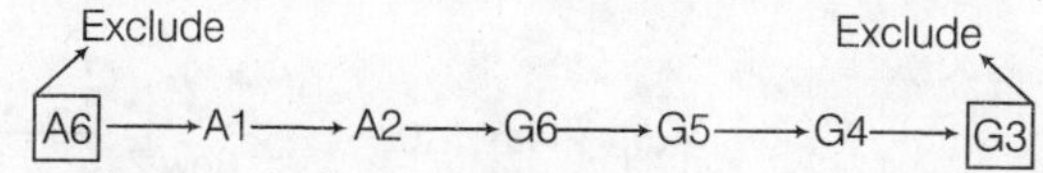

After excluding the first and last person i.e. A6 and G3, the message has to pass through 5 persons.

52. (*c*) Route of send a message from A3 to G1 is as

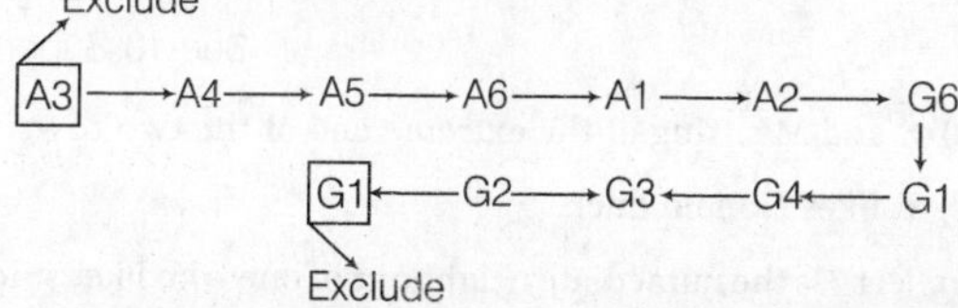

After excluding the first and last person, the message pass through 10 persons.

53. (*b*) A1 is the person sitting to the right of A2 and A6 is the person sitting two places to the left of A4.

So, the route of send a message from A1 to A6 is as

A1 → A2 → G6 → G5 → G4 → G3 → G3

A6 ← A5 ← A4 ← A3 ← G6 ← G1

As G6 comes two times, but we count only once. According to question, after excluding the two people, there are 10 minimum persons.

54. (*d*) According to the question, A3 direct speak to A6.

Now, the route of passing a message from A3 to G1 is as

A3 → A6 → A1 → A2 → G6 → G5 → G4

G1 ← G2 ← G3

After excluding the two people, there are 8 persons involved in passing a message from A3 to G1.

55. (*c*) A2 sitting to the right of A3 and from the question it is clear that, A2 is the only person who can translate English to German language.

Solution (Q. Nos. 56-63) According to the given information seating arrangement is given below.

Row 1: (Engineer) B, (Teacher) A, (Builder) D, (Banker) C — Facing South

Row 2: (Lawyer) E, (Doctor) G, (Business man) F, (Pilot) H — Facing North

56. (*a*) From the given options, only B and the Pilot (i.e. H) sit at the extreme end of the row.

57. (*c*) C is the banker.

58. (*e*) The lawyer and the doctor are adjacent sitters. So, no one sit between them.

59. (*e*) D, i.e. the builder faces the businessman.

60. (*d*) G is the doctor (from the arrangement).

61. (*b*) As F faces the builder and H faces the banker, similarly G faces the teacher.

62. (*b*) Except banker, all are sitting facing North.

63. (*b*) Except, banker all other are sitting in the same row.

Solution (Q. Nos. 64-68) According to the information, the arrangement is as following

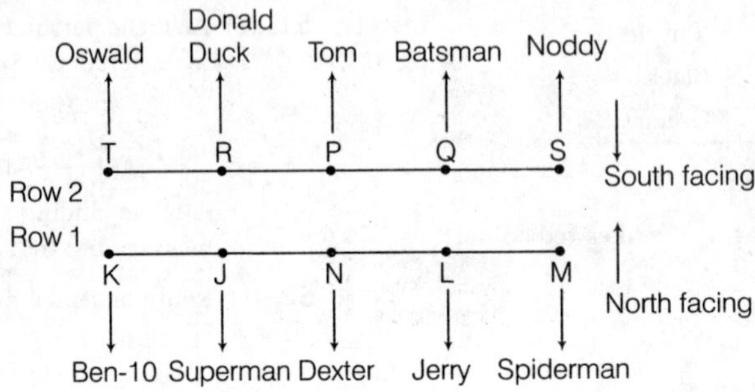

64. (*a*) S and M sitting at the extreme end of the two rows.

65. (*d*) R likes Donald duck.

66. (*a*) Jerry is the immediate neighbour of one who likes spiderman.

67. (*e*) T likes Oswald cartoon character.

68. (*c*) Q is an immediate neighbour of P.

Solution (Q. Nos 69-71) On the basis of given information, the arrangement as below

Days	Windows				
	W1	**W2**	**W3**	**W4**	**W5**
Monday	9:30 am to 2:30 am	12:30 pm to 2:30 pm	3:30 pm to 5:30 pm	8:00 am to 10:00 am	2:00 pm to 4:00 pm
Tuesday	8:00 am to 11:30 am	—	—	11:30 am to 3:00 pm	3:30 pm to 5:30 pm
Wednesday	9:30 am to 2:30 pm	8:30 am to 11:30 am	10:00 am to 12:30 pm	3:30 pm to 5:30 pm	8:00 am to 10:00 am
Thursday	8:00 am to 11:30 am	8:30 am to 11:30 am	3:30 pm to 5:30 pm	12:30 pm to 3:00 pm	10:30 am to 12:30 pm
Friday	3:00 pm to 5:00	8:00 pm to 10:00 am	10:00 am to 12:00 pm	12:30 pm to 3:00 pm	3:30 pm to 5:30 pm
Saturday	—	12:30 pm to 2:30 pm	10:00 am to 12:30 pm	8:00 am to 10:00 am	—

69. (*b*) On Wednesday, the maximum number of windows (W1, W2 and W5) is simultaneously open at 9:45 am.

70. (*d*) Only on Saturday, one window is open at any time.

71. (*a*) All windows are closed for one between 2:30 pm to 3:30 pm only on Wednesday.

Solution (Q. Nos. 72-73) On the basis of given information, the arrangement as below

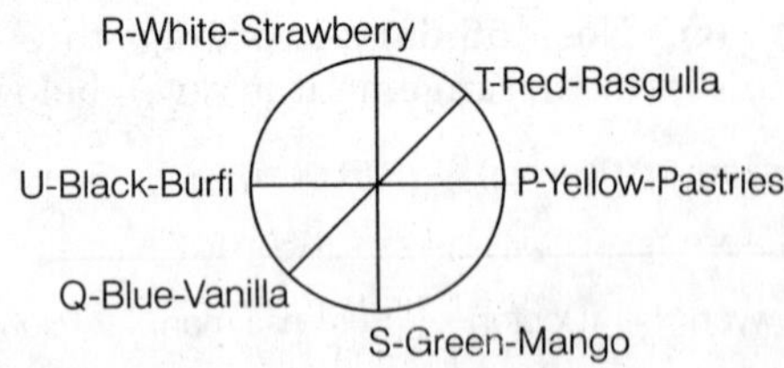

72. (*d*) Clearly, the person T eats rasgulla.

73. (*a*) Clearly, Q ordered for vanilla and wears blue colour shirt.

Solution (Q. Nos. 74-77) The given information can be tabulise as

Name	Activity	Hostel	Discipline	Cities
Ravi	Mess	Satpura	Computer Science	Jodhpur
Sanjay	Sports	Aravalli	Mechanical Engineering	Nagpur
Hardeep	Cultural	Aravalli	Metallurgy	Patna
Abhishek	Student Body	Vindhya	Civil Engineering	Kochi
Hemant	Placement	Vindhya	Chemical Engineering	Allahabad

74. (*b*) From the above table, we can see that the Chemical engineering student stays in Vindhya hostel while Cultural activity student stay in Aravalli hostel. So, Statement I is incorrect, Statement II is also incorrect because the student incharge of Placement activity is studying Chemical Engineering.

75. (*c*) From above table, it is clear that student belongs to Patna is studying Metallurgy.

76. (*d*) From above table, it is clear that the student from Allahabad is studying in Chemical Engineering.

77. (*c*) The General Secretary of the student body belongs to Kochi

3

Ranking and Time Sequence Test

In this chapter of Analytical Reasoning, we will come across questions based on comparison of different persons / objects (according to their height, weight, marks etc.) determining the position of a person / object in a row / queue and related to the time sequence test. Where the students are required to find out a particular day based on some given conditions.

Ranking

There are two types of Ranking test in Analytical Reasoning

1. **Sequential Order of Arrangement** In this type of questions, persons or objects are arranged based on the comparison of parameters such as age, height, marks, salary, weight, length, size etc. Generally, we compare the persons or objects using various notations such as greater than (>), less than (<), equal to (=), greater than or equal to (≥) and less than or equal to (≤)

For example

Umesh is taller than Satish, Suresh is shorter than Neeraj but taller than Umesh. Who is the tallest among them?

(a) Umesh (b) Suresh (c) Satish (d) Neeraj

Sol. (*d*) According to the question, Umesh > Satish

Neeraj > Suresh > Umesh

∴ Neeraj > Suresh > Umesh > Satish

So, Neeraj is tallest among them.

General Guidelines to Solve 'Sequential Order of Arrangement' Questions

Sometimes ranking of objects seems to be difficult when information given in the question is complicated and distorted. In that situation, establishing the relationship among ranks by using the symbols > (greater than) and < (less than) seems difficult. So, you are advised to follow some General Guidelines that may be useful while solving these types of questions.

***Guideline* 1.** Draw a straight line. Count the total number of objects in the question and mark as many points on the line. e.g. If there are six objects in the question, then you can mark them as following

|—|—|—|—|—|

Guideline 2. Now, if you are comparing heights, then you should assign the leftmost place to the shortest man and the rightmost place to the tallest man.

Guidelene 3. Similarly, while comparing of marks, the leftmost place should be assign to the student scoring the minimum marks and rightmost place to the student scoring maximum marks.

2. **Position Test** In this type of questions, either a total number of persons/objects in a row or the rank/position of a person (s) from either of the two ends of a row/queue is given. The students are asked to determine the total number of persons/objects in the row/queue or the rank of that person/object from the other end of the row/queue or the number of persons to the left/right (or above/below) of a particular person etc.

For example

In class of 45 students rank of Ayush is 15 from top, then the rank of Ayush from bottom is **SSC (multitasking) 2009**

(a) 30 (b) 32 (c) 31 (d) 35

Sol. (*c*) According to the question,

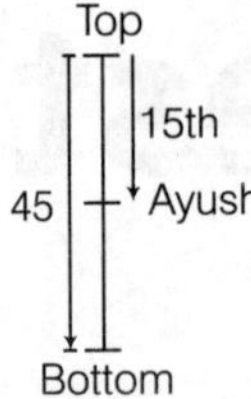

Ayush's rank from the bottom = Total number of students – Rank of Ayush from top $+1 = 45 - 15 + 1 = 31$

Some Important Formulae for Ranking Test

- Rank of a person from lower or right end = (Total number of persons in row) – (Rank of that person from upper or left end) +1

$$=(n-m)+1$$

e.g. If in a row of 26 boys, Ravi is at 17th position from left, then Ravi's position from right end

$$=(26-17)+1 \qquad (n=26,\ m=17)$$
$$=27-17=10\text{th}$$

- Rank of a person from upper or left end = (Total number of persons in row) – (Rank of that person from lower or right end) +1

$$=(n-m)+1$$

e.g. If in a row of 40 girls, Rashmi is 14th from the right end, then Rashmi's position from left end

$$=[40-14]+1 \qquad (n=40,\ m-14)$$
$$=26+1=27\text{th}$$

- Total number of persons in a row or class = (Rank of a person from upper end or left end) + (Rank of that person from lower or right end) –1

$$=(n+m)-1$$

e.g. If in a class of students, Sandeep is 25th from top and 32nd from bottom in a class, then total number of students in the class

$$=[25+32]-1 \qquad (n=25,\ m=32)$$
$$=57-1=56$$

- If in a row there are n persons, then the number of persons between mth person from left and pth person from right $= n-(m+p)$

e.g. If in a row of 13 persons, then the total number of persons between 5th person from left and 2nd person from right

$$=13-(5+2) \qquad (n=13,\ m=5,\ p=2)$$
$$=13-7=6 \text{ persons}$$

- If in a row there are n persons, then the position of the person exactly in the middle $=\left(\frac{n+1}{2}\right)$th, where n is always odd.

e.g. If in a row of 13 persons, then the position of the person exactly in the middle.

$$=\left(\frac{13+1}{2}\right)\text{th}=\frac{14}{2}\text{th}=7\text{th}$$

Types of Questions Generally Asked in Examinations

There are multiple types of questions which are asked from the chapter 'Comparison of Ranks', so it is quite difficult to predict exact type of questions that are asked but on the basis of Observation, Analysis and Experience, here we are giving different types of questions that are usually asked in the examination. Almost all the questions at this chapter can be categorised into these types. Also, this description of type will make your study easy and streamline.

Type 1 Direct Information Based

In this type, the questions are based on direct information in simple manner to answer the given question.

Examples Based on Type 1

Ex **1.** In a class, boys stand in a single line. One of the boys is nineteenth in order from both the ends. How many boys are there in the class?

(a) 27 (b) 37
(c) 38 (d) 29

Sol. (*b*) Total number of boys in a class = (Rank of a boy from top or left end) + (Rank of that boy from bottom or right end) − 1

∴ Total number of boys in the class = 19 + 19 − 1 = 38 − 1 = 37

So, there are 37 boys in the class.

Ex **2.** Sohan ranks 7th from the top and 26th from the bottom in a class. How many students are there in the class? **NIFT (UG) 2014, SSC (10+2) 2013**

(a) 31 (b) 32
(c) 33 (d) 34

Sol. (*b*) Total number of students in the class = (Rank of Sohan from the top) + (Rank of Sohan from the bottom) − 1

∴ Total number of students in the class = (7 + 26) − 1 = 32

So, there are 32 students in the class.

Ex **3.** In a class of 42 students Suresh's rank is 16th from the bottom. What is his rank from the top?

(a) 25th (b) 26th
(c) 24th (d) 27th

Sol. (*d*) Number of students ahead of suresh = 42 − 16 ⇒ 26

Now, Suresh's rank from the top = 26 + 1 = 27

So, Suresh's rank is 27th from the top.

or

Rank of a person from top or left end = (Total number of persons in row) − (Rank of that person from bottom or right end) + 1

∴ Suresh's rank from top = 42 − 16 + 1

= 26 + 1 = 27

Ex **4.** Among, P, Q, R, S and T each having a different height, Q is shorter than only T and S is shorter than P and Q. Who among them is the shortest? **Allahabad Bank (PO) 2010**

(a) R (b) S
(c) P (d) Data inadequate
(e) None of these

Sol. (*d*) Q is shorter than only T. It means that T is the tallest and Q is second tallest.

S is shorter than P and Q.

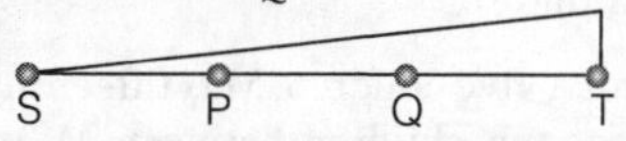

The position of R is not clear. So, either S or R is shortest.

Ex **5.** Suresh is five ranks below top student Samir in a class of forty students. What is Suresh's rank from the bottom in the class? **IBPS (PO) 2011**

(a) 34th (b) 36th (c) 33rd (d) 35th
(e) None of these

Sol. (*d*) Suresh's rank is 6th from the top.

Therefore, his rank from the bottom = 40 − 6 + 1 = 35th

Ex **6.** Keshav is taller than Vijay but shorter than Nitin, Nitin is taller than Kishan but shorter than Amar. If Vijay is taller than Kishan, then who is the shortest among them? **UPPSC (RO) 2014**

(a) Keshav (b) Vijay (c) Nitin (d) Kishan

Sol. (*d*) Let us deduce the orders of height as given in the question

Keshav is taller than Vijay but shorter than Nitin

Nitin > Keshav > Vijay

Nitin is taller than Kishan but shorter than Amar

Amar > Nitin > Kishan

and Vijay is taller than Kishan

Vijay > Kishan

Now, combining above orders interpreted from statements given in question, we have

Amar > Nitin > Keshav > Vijay > Kishan

Hence, Kishan is the shortest.

Ex **7.** K is more beautiful than B. B is not as beautiful as Y. J is not as beautiful as B or Y. Whose beauty is in the least degree? **SSC (LDC) 2014**

(a) B (b) J
(c) Y (d) K

Sol. (*b*) Here, K > B, Y > B, B, Y > J

K, Y > B > J. So, it is clearly shown that 'J' beauty is in the least degree.

Intro Exercise 1 (Based on Type 1)

1. Barun is taller than Sanjay. Bipul is taller than Barun. Krishna is also not as tall as Bipul but is taller than Barun. Who is the tallest? **SSC (10+2) 2013**
   (a) Barun (b) Bipul (c) Krishna (d) Sanjay

2. In a cricket team, Dhoni is taller than Virat but not as tall as Raina, Rohit is shorter than Dhoni but taller than Shikhar. Who among them is the shortest? **NIFT (UG) 2014**
   (a) Dhoni (b) Virat
   (c) Shikhar (d) Cannot be determined

3. Among A, B, C, D and E each having a different amount of money, C has more money than only E, B and A. Who among them has the highest amount of money? **BOI (PO) 2010**
   (a) C (b) D
   (c) E (d) Data inadequate
   (e) None of these

4. In a row of thirty five children, M is fifteenth from the right end and there are ten children between M and R. What is R's position from the left end of the row? **Corporation Bank (PO) 2009**
   (a) 15th (b) 5th
   (c) 30th (d) Data inadequate
   (e) None of these

5. Among five friends, Neelu is younger than Vibha but older than Puja. Puja is younger than Asha and Anupam. Asha is older than Vibha but younger than Anupam. Who is ranked fourth in the ascending order of the age?
   (a) Anupam (b) Asha
   (c) Neelu (d) Puja
   (e) None of these

6. D is taller than C and E. A is not as tall as E. C is taller than A. D is not as tall as B. Who among them is next to the tallest one?
   (a) A (b) D
   (c) B or D (d) Data inadequate
   (e) None of these

7. Five children were administered psychological tests to know their intellectual levels. In the report, psychologists pointed out that the child A is less intelligent than the child B. The child C is less intelligent than the child D. The child B is less intelligent than the child C and child A is more intelligent than child E. Which child is the most intelligent?
   (a) A (b) B
   (c) D (d) E
   (e) None of these

8. Lakshmi is elder than Meenu. Leela is elder than Meenu but younger than Lakshmi. Latha is younger than both Meenu and Hari but Hari is younger than Meenu. Who is the youngest? **SSC (10+2) 2013**
   (a) Lakshmi (b) Meenu
   (c) Leela (d) Latha

9. Priti scored more than Rahul. Yamuna scored as much as Divya. Lokita scored less than Manju. Rahul scored more than Yamuna. Manju scored less than Divya. Who scored the lowest?
   (a) Manju (b) Yamuna (c) Lokita (d) Rahul
   (e) None of these

10. In an examination, Raj got more marks than Mukesh but not as many as Priya. Priya got more marks than Gaurav and Kavita. Gaurav got less marks than Mukesh but his marks are not the lowest in the group. Who is second in the descending order of marks?
    (a) Priya (b) Kavita
    (c) Raj (d) Cannot be determined
    (e) None of these

11. In a row of children, Neeta is fifteenth from the left end of the row. If she is shifted towards the right end of the row by four places. She becomes eighth from the right end. How many children are there in the row? **MHT CET MBA 2009**
    (a) 27 (b) 26 (c) 28 (d) 24
    (e) None of these

12. In a row of twenty five children facing South R is 16th from the right end and B is 18th from the left end. How many children are there between R and B? **Punjab & Sind Bank (PO) 2010**
    (a) 2 (b) 3
    (c) 4 (d) Data inadequate
    (e) None of these

13. M earns more than X and less than T. V earns more than M and T. R earns more than only X. Who earns the least among the five of them? **IDBI (PO) 2009**
    (a) X (b) V
    (c) M (d) Cannot be determined
    (e) None of these

14. Among P, Q, R, S and T each having scored different marks, R scored more marks than P and T. Q scored less marks than T. S did not score the highest marks. Who among them scored the highest marks? **Syndicate Bank (PO) 2010**
    (a) P (b) T
    (c) R (d) Data inadequate
    (e) None of these

15. In a row of children facing North Ravi who is eighth from the left end of the row is sixth to the right of Sunil who is thirteenth from the right end of the row. How many children are there in the row? **IRMA 2009**
    (a) 15 (b) 16 (c) 14 (d) 17
    (e) None of these

16. Among A, B, C, D and E each having different weight, D is heavier than only A and C is lighter than B and E. Who among them is the heaviest? **SBI (PO) 2010**
    (a) B (b) E
    (c) C (d) Data inadequate
    (e) None of these

17. Rohan is taller than Hardik who is shorter than Susheel. Niza is taller than Harry but shorter than Hardik. Susheel is shorter than Rohan. Who is the tallest?
(a) Rohan (b) Susheel (c) Hardik (d) Harry
(e) Niza

18. Seema's younger brother Sohan is older than Seeta. Sweta is yonger than Deepti but elder than Seema. Who is the eldest? **SSC (10+2) 2013**
(a) Seema (b) Sweta (c) Seeta (d) Deepti

19. In a row of forty children, P is thirteenth from the left end and Q is ninth from the right end. How many children are there between P and R, if R is fourth to the left of Q? **NIFT (PG) 2015**
(a) 12 (b) 13 (c) 14 (d) 15

20. In a class of 35 children, Ameya's rank is sixth from the top. Annie is seven ranks below Ameya. What is Annie's rank from the bottom? **IBPS (PO) 2011**
(a) 22 (b) 20 (c) 19 (d) 23
(e) Cannot be determined

21. In a row at a bus stop, A is 9th from the right and B is 7th from the left. They both interchange their positions. If there are 20 people in the row, then what will be the new position of B from the left? **FMS 2010**
(a) 11th (b) 12th (c) 13th (d) 10th

22. Garima is taller than Sarita but not taller than Reena. Reena and Tanya are of the same height. Garima is shorter than Anu. Amongst all the girls, who is the shortest?
(a) Anu (b) Reena and Tanya
(c) Garima (d) Sarita
(e) None of these

23. Children are in pursuit of a dog whose leg has broken Krishnarajan is directly behind the dog. Rangarajan is behind Krishnarajan. Natrajan is behind Rangarajan, Premrajan is ahead of the dog walking down the street in the opposite direction. As the children and dog pass, Premrajan turns around and joins the pursuit. He runs in behind Rangarajan. Krishnarajan runs faster and is alongside the dog on the left. Rangarajan runs faster and is alongside the dog on the right. Which child is directly behind the dog? **XAT 2009**
(a) Krishnarajan (b) Rangarajan
(c) Natrajan (d) Premrajan
(e) None of these

24. In a row of letters, a letter is 5th from left end and 12th from the right end. How many letters are there in a row? **SSC (10+2) 2013**
(a) 15 (b) 16 (c) 17 (d) 18

25. Sunita is the 11th from either end of a row of girls. How many girls are there in that row? **SSC (10+2) 2013**
(a) 19 (b) 20 (c) 21 (d) 22

26. a row of girls, Veena is 12th from the start and 19th from the e. In another row of girls, Sunita is 14th from the start and 20th from the end. How may girls are there in both the rows together? **SSC (Multitasking) 2013**
(a) 72 (b) 65 (c) 63 (d) 61

27. If in a row, there are 23 persons, then find the position of the person exactly in the middle.
(a) 12th (b) 11th (c) 10th (d) 14th

28. 30 persons are sitting in a row. Find the number of persons sitting between 9th person from left and 16th person from right.
(a) 8 (b) 4 (c) 3 (d) 5

29. 40 persons are sitting in a row. How many persons are sitting between 31st person from left and 25th person from right?
(a) 18 (b) 14 (c) 20 (d) 9

30. In a row of 40 girls, when Komal was shifted to her left by 4 places her number from the left end of the row become 10. What was the number of Swati from the right end of the row, if Swati was three places to the right of Komal's original position? **SBI (PO) 2004**
(a) 22 (b) 24 (c) 27 (d) 26
(e) None of these

31. Amar is 16th from the left end in a row of boys and Vishal is 18th from the right end. Ganesh is 11th from Amar towards the right and 3rd from Vishal towards the right end. How many boys are there in the row?
(a) 45 (b) 26 (c) 39 (d) 41

32. In a row of girls, if Madhu, who is tenth from the left and Veena, who is ninth from the right interchange their places, Madhu becomes fifteenth from the left. How many girls are there in the row? **UPPSC (RO) 2014**
(a) 16 (b) 18 (c) 23 (d) 22

33. Gita is older than her cousin Mita. Mita's brother Bhanu is older than Gita. When Mita and Bhanu are visiting Gita, all three like to play a game of Monopoly. Mita wins more often than Gita does. **IIFT 2012**
(a) When he plays Monopoly with Mita and Gita, Bhanu often loses
(b) Of the three, Gita is the oldest
(c) Gita hates to lose at Monopoly
(d) Of the three, Mita is the youngest

34. There is a group of seven friends Rani, Neha, Mira, Juhi, Hema, Isha and Kuku. Mira is taller than Hema and Kuku. Rani is not the tallest but taller than Mira. Neha is shorter than Hema. Juhi is taller than Hema but shorter than Kuku. If they are ranked in the ascending order of their heights, then who will be ranked fifth?. **CMAT 2015**
(a) Kuku (b) Mira
(c) Isha (d) Juhi

35. Seven army recruits Laxman, Mahender, Narender, Omprakash, Preetam, Qutab and Raman are standing in a Column for physical inspection in order of height, shorter first. Omprakash is standing between Laxman and Qutab. Narender is taller than Laxman. Raman is shorter than Narender. Mahender and Preetam are not the two tallest. Preetam is two places ahead of Qutab. Which of the following is true? **CMAT 2015**
(a) Narender is the tallest
(b) Qutab is taller than Laxman
(c) Raman is ahead of Omprakash
(d) Mahender is the shortest

36. Pihu and Manu are ranked seventh and eleventh respectively from the top in a class of 31 students. What will be their respective ranks from the bottom in the class?
(a) 20th and 24th
(b) 24th and 20th
(c) 25th and 21st
(d) None of the above

37. In a shop, there were 4 dolls of different heights A, B, C and D. D is neither as tall as A nor as short as C.B is shorter than D but taller than C. If Nidhi wants to purchase the tallest doll, then which one should she purchase?
(a) A (b) D
(c) Either A or D (d) Either B or D
(e) None of these

Type 2 Jumbled Information Based

In this type of questions, some information is given in jumbled form or in the form of some statements that is followed by a set of 2-5 questions.

Examples Based on Type 2

Direction (Examples 1-3) *Read the following information carefully and answer the questions that follow.* **MAT 2006**

I. There is a group of five girls.
II. Kamini is second in height but younger than Rupa.
III. Pooja is taller than Monika but younger in age.
IV. Rupa and Monika are of the same age but Rupa is tallest between them.
V. Neelam is taller than Pooja and elder to Rupa.

Ex **1.** If they are arranged in the ascending order to height, then who will be in the third position?
(a) Monika (b) Monika or Rupa
(c) Rupa (d) None of these

Ex **2.** If they are arranged in descending order of their ages, then who will be in the fourth position?
(a) Monika or Rupa (b) Monika
(c) Kamini (d) None of these

Ex **3.** To answer the question, "Who is the youngest person in the group", which of the following statements is superfluous?
(a) Only I
(b) Only V
(c) Only II
(d) Either I or IV

SOLUTION (Examples 1-3) Descending order of heights and ages is as given below

Height	Rupa > Kamini > Neelam > Pooja > Monika
Age	Neelam > Rupa = Monika > Pooja > Kamini
or	Neelam > Rupa = Monika > Kamini > Pooja

Persons are arranged

1. (*d*) Neelam will be in the third position when the persons are arranged in ascending order of height.
2. (*d*) Fourth position cannot be determined, if they are arranged in descending order of their ages.
3. (*a*) Only Statement I is superfluous.

Direction (Examples 4-8) *Read the information given below and answer the questions. The age and height of six children in a class are as follows.*

I. Amit is taller and older than Tanu but shorter and younger than Shruti.
II. Bharat is taller than Chander who is not as tall as Tanu.
III. The oldest is the shortest.
IV. The youngest would be fourth if the children stood in a line according to their height and one started counting from the tallest.
V. Bharat is younger than Ritu but older than Chander who is older than Shruti.

Ex **4.** Who among them is the tallest?
(a) Tanu (b) Chander
(c) Shruti (d) Data inadequate
(e) None of these

Ex **5.** Who is older than Tanu but younger than Shruti?
(a) Ritu (b) Bharat
(c) Amit (d) Data inadequate
(e) None of these

Ex **6.** Which of the following statements is definitely true?
(a) Bharat is the most old person
(b) Tanu has the maximum height
(c) Amit is older than Bharat
(d) Ritu is the shortest
(e) None of the above

Ex **7.** Which of the following is the correct order of height in descending order?
(a) Amit, Shruti, Bharat, Tanu, Chander and Ritu
(b) Ritu, Bharat, Chander, Shruti, Amit and Tanu
(c) Bharat, Shruti, Amit, Tanu, Chander and Ritu
(d) Shruti, Bharat, Amit, Tanu, Chander and Ritu
(e) Data inadequate

Ex **8.** Whose rank in height cannot be positioned definitely?
(a) Tanu (b) Bharat (c) Shruti (d) Chander
(e) None of these

SOLUTION (Examples 4-8) The order of age is as following

Shruti > Amit > Tanu

Ritu > Bharat > Chander > Shruti

So, Ritu > Bharat > Chander > Shruti > Amit > Tanu

The order of height is as following

Shruti > Amit > Tanu > Chander > Ritu

Bharat

4. (*d*) Either Shruti or Bharat is tallest. So, the correct answer is (d).
5. (*c*) Amit is older than Tanu but younger than Shruti. So, the correct answer is (c).
6. (*d*) Ritu is the shortest. So, the correct answer is (d).
7. (*e*) Since, it is not determined that who is the tallest, so this question cannot be answered. So, the correct answer is (e).
8. (*b*) Bharat rank in height cannot be positioned definitely. So, the correct answer is (b).

Intro Exercise 2 (Based on Type 2)

Direction (Q. Nos. 1-2) *Answer the following questions based on the statements given below.* **CLAT 2013**

I. There are 3 poles on each side of the road.
II. These six poles are labelled A, B, C, D, E and F.
III. The poles are different colours namely - Golden, Silver, Metallic, Black, Bronze and White.
IV. The poles are of different heights.
V. E, the tallest pole, is exactly opposite to the golden coloured pole.
VI. The shortest pole is exactly opposite to the metallic coloured pole.
VII. F, the black coloured pole, is located between A and D.
VIII. C, the bronze coloured pole, is exactly opposite to A.
IX. B, the metallic coloured pole, is exactly opposite to F.
X. A, the white coloured pole, is taller than C but shorter than D and B.

1. Which is the second tallest pole?
(a) A (b) D
(c) B (d) None of these

2. Which is the colour of the tallest pole?
(a) Golden (b) Silver
(c) Bronze (d) None of these

Direction (Q. Nos. 3-6) *Read the following information carefully and answer the questions given below.*

In a study of the five brands of tooth pastes C, P, A, G and B the brands were tested and ranked against expensiveness per gram. The following results were obtained

I. P and G were equally expensive.
II. B was the least expensive brand among them.
III. C was more expensive than P.
IV. G was less expensive than A.
V. The expensiveness of A was more than that of P.

3. If the above statements are true, then which of the following must also be true?
(a) A was the most expensive among them
(b) C was more expensive than A
(c) G was somewhere in the middle when they were set in descending order in terms of expensiveness
(d) C was the most expensive among them
(e) None of the above

4. If a sixth brand F is tested and found to be more expensive than A, then which of the following must be true if the findings of the study are correct?
(a) Atleast four of the six brands are less expensive than F
(b) F is the most expensive than C
(c) F is more expensive than C
(d) F is less expensive than C
(e) None of the above

5. Which among the given informations is not necessary to find the relationship among them?
(a) Only V
(b) Only I
(c) I and III
(d) All are necessary
(e) None of the above

6. If same amount of G is more effective than C and B is less effective than G, then which of the following must be true for a consumer who wishes to buy a paste with the greatest effectiveness for the amount spent for the same quantity?
(a) B should be purchased instead of G
(b) C should be purchased instead of G
(c) G should be purchased instead of C
(d) G should be purchased instead of B
(e) None of the above

Direction (Q. Nos. 7-11) *Study the following information carefully and answer the question given below.* **RBI (Grade B) 2009**

I. A, B, C, D, E, F, G and H are eight students each having a different height.
II. D is shorter than A but taller than G.
III. E is taller than H but shorter than C.
IV. B is shorter than D but taller than F.
V. C is shorter than G.
VI. G is not as tall as F.

7. Which of the following is definitely false?
(a) G is shorter than F
(b) C is shorter than F
(c) F is taller than C
(d) B is taller than E
(e) None of the above

8. If another student J who is taller than E but shorter than G is added to the group, then which of the following will be definitely true?
(a) C and J are of same height (b) G is shorter than D
(c) G is shorter than H (d) G is taller than A
(e) None of these

9. Which of the following will definitely be the third from top when the eight students are arranged in descending order of height?
(a) B (b) F
(c) G (d) B or G
(e) Cannot be determined

10. How many of them are definitely shorter than F?
(a) Three (b) Four
(c) Five (d) Data inadequate
(e) None of these

11. Which of the following is redundant to answer all the above questions?
(a) Only II (b) II and III
(c) III and IV (d) II and V
(e) All are necessary

Direction (Q. Nos. 12-16) *Study the information given below and answer the questions that follow.*

I. A, B, C, D, E and F are six students in a class.
II. B and C are shorter than F but heavier than A.
III. D is heavier than B and taller than C.
IV. E is shorter than D but taller than F.
V. F is heavier than D.
VI. A is shorter than E but taller than F.

12. Who among them is the lightest?
(a) A (b) B
(c) C (d) B or C
(e) Data inadequate

13. Which of the following statements is true for F as regards height and weight?
(a) He is lighter than E and taller than E
(b) He is heavier than B and taller than E
(c) He is heavier than B and C but shorter than D
(d) He is lighter than E and also shorter than E
(e) He is lighter than B and C but taller than D

14. Who among them is the tallest?
(a) A (b) B
(c) D (d) E
(e) None of these

15. Who is third from the top when they are arranged in descending order of heights?
(a) A (b) B
(c) C (d) E
(e) None of these

16. Which of the following groups of friends is shorter than A?
(a) B and C (b) D, B and C
(c) E, B and C (d) F, B and C
(e) None of these

Direction (Q. Nos. 17-21) *Read the following passage to answer the questions given below it.*

Anita, Mahima, Rajan, Lata and Deepti are five cousins. Anita is twice as old as Mahima. Rajan is half the age of Mahima. Anita is half the age of Deepti and Rajan is twice the age of Lata.

17. Who is the youngest?
(a) Deepti (b) Rajan
(c) Lata (d) Anita

18. Who is the oldest?
(a) Deepti (b) Lata
(c) Anita (d) None of these

19. Which of the following pairs of persons are of the same age?
(a) Mahima and Lata (b) Anita and Mahima
(c) Mahima and Rajan (d) None of these

20. Anita is younger than
(a) Rajan (b) Mahima
(c) Deepti (d) None of these

21. If they are arranged in descending order of age, then who will be in the middle?
(a) Anita (b) Mahima
(c) Rajan (d) None of these

Direction (Q. Nos. 22-24) *Study the following information and answer the questions given below it.* **FMS 2010**

In a family picnic, Shikhar, Dolly, Snehal, Akash, Swarn and Amar were playing a game. Shikhar's father, mother and uncle were in the group. Group has only two females. Dolly, the mother of Shikhar got more points than Shikhar's father. Akash got more points in the game than Swarn but less than that of Amar. Niece of Swarn got the lowest points. Father of Shikhar got more points than Amar but could not win the game.

22. Who was the lady in the group besides Dolly?
(a) Snehal (b) Akash
(c) Swarn (d) None of these

23. Who stood second in the game?
(a) Shikhar (b) Dolly
(c) Snehal (d) None of these

24. Who won the game?
(a) Shikhar (b) Dolly
(c) Amar (d) Akash

Direction (Q. Nos. 25-30) *Study the following information and answer the questions given below it.*

A blacksmith have five iron articles A, B, C, D and E, each having a different weight.

I. A weight twice as much as B.
II. B weight four and a half time as much as C.
III. C weight half as much as D.
IV. D weight half as much as E.
V. E weight less than A but more than C.

25. Which of the above given statements is not necessary to determine the correct order of articles according to their weight?
(a) Only I (b) Only II
(c) Only III (d) Only IV
(e) Only V

26. Which of the following articles is the heaviest in weight?
(a) A (b) B
(c) C (d) D
(e) E

27. Which of the following represents the descending order of weight of the articles?
(a) A, B, E, D, C
(b) B, D, E, A, C
(c) E, C, D, A, B
(d) C, A, D, B, E
(e) A, B, D, E, C

28. Which of the following is the lightest in weight?
(a) A (b) B
(c) C (d) D
(e) E

29. E is lighter in weight than which of the other two articles?
(a) A, B (b) D, C
(c) A, C (d) D, B
(e) B, E

30. E is heavier than which of the following two articles?
(a) D, B (b) D, C (c) A, C (d) A, B
(e) None of these

Type 3 Time Sequence Test

In this type of questions, you are given a problem based on date and time. It is required to find out either date, number of days satisfying conditions in specific question.

Some Important Facts About Time Sequence Test

1. A normal year has 365 days.
2. A leap year is divisible by 4.
3. February in a leap year has 29 days.
4. The last day of a year is always the same as the first day.
5. A leap year has 366 days.

Examples Based on Type 3

***Ex* 1.** Sunita leaves her house at 20 min to seven in the morning, reaches Vineeta's house in 25 min, they finish their breakfast in another 15 min and leave for their office which takes another 35 min. At what time, did they leave Vineeta's house to reach their office?
(a) 7 : 40 am (b) 7 : 20 am
(c) 7 : 45 am (d) 8 : 15 am

Sol. (*b*) Sunita leaves her house at 6 : 40 am. She reaches Vineeta's house in 25 min, i.e. 6 : 00 + 40+ 0: 25 at 7 : 05 am. Both leaves for office, 15 min after 7 : 05 am, i.e. 7 : 05 + 0:15 at 7 : 20 am.

***Ex* 2.** If every alternate Saturdays and all Sundays are holidays in a 30 days month beginning on Saturday, then how many working days are there in that month?
(a) 20 (b) 21
(c) 22 (d) 23

Sol. (*d*) As the month begins on Saturday. So, 2nd, 9th, 16th, 23rd, 30th days are Sundays, while 8th and 22nd days are alternate Saturdays. Thus, there are 7 holidays in all.
∴ Number of working days = 30 − 7 = 23

***Ex* 3.** Praveen correctly remembers that his father's birthday is after 21st May but before 27th May whereas his sister correctly remembers that their father's birthday is after 24th May but before 30th May. On which day in May was definitely their father's birthday? **MAT 2012**
(a) 25th (b) 24th
(c) 26th (d) 25th or 26th

Sol. (*d*) According to Praveen, his father's birthday falls on one of the day among 22nd, 23rd, 24th, 25th, 26th. According to his sister, her father's birthday falls on one of the days among 25th, 26th, 27th, 28th and 29th. The day common to both the groups is 25th or 26th. So, Praveen's father's birthday falls on either 25th or 26th.

Intro Exercise 3 (Based on Time Sequence Test)

1. There are twenty people working in an office. The first group of five works between 8 : 00 am to 2 : 00 pm. The second group of ten works between 10 : 00 am to 4 : 00 pm and the third group of five works between 12 noon to 6 : 00 pm. There are three computers in the office which all the employees frequently use. During which of the following hours the computers are likely to be used most? **RRB (ASM) 2012**
   (a) 10 : 00 am - 12 noon
   (b) 12 noon - 4 : 00 pm
   (c) 1 : 00 pm - 3 : 00 pm
   (d) 2 : 00 pm - 4 : 00 pm

2. Sneha correctly remembers that her father's birthday is before 16th June but after 11th June whereas, her younger brother correctly remembers that their father's birthday is after 13th June but before 18th June and her elder brother correctly remembers that their father's birthday is on an even date. On what date, in June, is definitely their father's birthday? **Vijaya Bank (Clerk) 2010**
   (a) Sixteenth (b) Twelfth
   (c) Fourteenth (d) Data inadequate
   (e) None of these

3. Given that 25th February 2008 is Monday, what day is 2nd March of 2008? **SSC (LDC) 2012**
   (a) Tuesday (b) Saturday
   (c) Sunday (d) Monday

4. If the day before yesterday was Sunday, then what day will it be three days after the day after tomorrow? **SSC (CGL) 2010**
   (a) Sunday
   (b) Monday
   (c) Wednesday
   (d) Saturday

5. Satish read a book on Sunday. Sudha read that book one day prior to Anil but 4 days after Satish. On which day did Anil read the book?
   (a) Friday (b) Thursday
   (c) Tuesday (d) Saturday

6. Nitin correctly remembers that Nidhi's birthday is before Friday but after Tuesday. Deepak correctly remembers that Nidhi's birthday is after Wednesday but before Saturday. On which of the following days does Nidhi's birthday definitely fall? **PNB (Clerk) 2009**
   (a) Monday (b) Tuesday
   (c) Wednesday (d) Thursday
   (e) Cannot be determined

7. Vinay remembers that his brother Anupam's birthday is after 20th of August but before 28th of August, while Rita remembers that Anupam's birthday is before 22nd of August but after 12th of August. On which date does Anupam's birthday fall? **RRB (PO) 2010**
   (a) 20th August
   (b) 21th August
   (c) 22nd August
   (d) Cannot be determined
   (e) None of the above

8. Meena correctly remembers that her father's birthday is after 18th May but before 22nd May. Her brother correctly remembers that their father's birthday is before 24th May but after 20th May. On which date in May was definitely their father's birthday? **Andhra Bank (PO) 2010**
   (a) 20th (b) 19th
   (c) 18th (d) Cannot be determined
   (e) None of these

Cumulative Exercise

Base Level

1. In a row of forty children, R is eleventh from the right end and there are fifteen children between R and M. What is M's position from the left end of the row? **Allahabad Bank (PO) 2010**

(a) Fourteenth
(b) Fifteenth
(c) Thirteenth
(d) Cannot be determined
(e) None of the above

2. In a row of twenty students, R is fifth from the right end and T is fourth from the left end. How many students are there between R and T in the row? **BOI (PO) 2010**

(a) 11
(b) 12
(c) 10
(d) Cannot be determined
(e) None of the above

3. In a class of 20 students. Mridul's rank is 12th from the top and Veena's rank is 17th from the bottom. If Rohan's rank is exactly between Mridul and Veena rank, then what is Rohan's rank from the top? **IBPS (Clerk) 2011**

(a) 9th (b) 8th (c) 10th (d) 7th
(e) Cannot be determined

4. In a class of 20 students, Alisha's rank is 15th from the top. Manav is 4 ranks above Alisha. What is Manav's rank from the bottom? **OBC (PO) 2010**

(a) 10th (b) 11th (c) 9th (d) 12th
(e) None of these

5. In a class of 45 students, a boy is ranked 20th. When two boys joined, his rank was dropped by one. What is his new rank from the end? **UPSC CSAT 2013**

(a) 25th (b) 26th (c) 27th (d) 28th

6. There are 25 boys in a horizontal row. Rahul was shifted by three places towards his right side and he occupies the middle position in the row. What was his original position from the left end of the row? **CGPSC 2013**

(a) 15th (b) 16th
(c) 12th (d) 10th
(e) None of these

7. There are five friends Sachin, Kamal, Mohan, Arun and Ram. Sachin is shorter than Kamal but taller than Ram. Mohan is the tallest. Arun is little shorter than Kamal and a little taller than Sachin. Who is the second tallest? **SSC (CGL) 2014**

(a) Ram (b) Sachin (c) Kamal (d) Arun

8. In a row A is in the 11th position from the left and B is in the 10th position from the right. If A and B interchange, then A becomes 18th from the left. How many persons are there in the row other than A and B? **UPSC CSAT 2014**

(a) 27 (b) 26 (c) 25 (d) 24

9. Mohan is taller than Shyam but shorter than Ramesh. Ramesh is taller than Rajat but shorter than Gautam. If Shyam is taller than Rajat, then who is the shortest among all? **NCHMCT 2014**

(a) Gautam (b) Rajat
(c) Shyam (d) Ramesh

10. In a row at a bus stop, A is 7th from the left and B is 9th from the right. They both interchange their positions. Now, A becomes 11th from the left. How many people are there in the row? **SSC (CPO) 2013**

(a) 10 (b) 20
(c) 19 (d) 18

11. N is more intelligent than M. M is not as intelligent as Y. X is more intelligent than Y but not as good as N. Who is the most intelligent of all? **SSC (CGL) 2013**

(a) N (b) M
(c) X (d) Y

12. Five students participated in the scholarship examination. Sudha scored higher than Puja. Kavita scored lower than Suma but higher than Sudha. Mamta scored between Puja and Sudha. Who scored lowest in the examination? **MAT 2013**

(a) Kavita (b) Puja
(c) Mamta (d) Sudha

13. There are five books A, B, C, D and E. Book C lies above D, book E is below A, D is above A and B is below E. Which book is at the bottom? **MAT 2013**

(a) E (b) B
(c) A (d) C

14. Sita is older than Kanika. Ila is older than Kanika but younger than Sita, Shempa is younger than both Manas and Kanika, Kanika is older than Manas. Who is the youngest?
SSC (CPO) 2013
(a) Shempa (b) Manas
(c) Ila (d) Kanika

15. Among P, Q, R, S and T each having different weight, R is heavier than only P and S is lighter than Q and heavier than T. Who among them is the heaviest?
Corporation Bank (PO) 2010
(a) P (b) Q
(c) S (d) Data inadequate
(e) None of these

16. In a row of twenty five children facing North, W is fifth to the right of R, who is sixteenth from the right end of the row. What is W's position from the right end of the row?
Syndicate Bank (PO) 2010
(a) Eleventh (b) Tenth
(c) Twelfth (d) Data inadequate
(e) None of these

17. There are five friends Satish, Kishore, Mohan, Anil and Rajesh. Mohan is the tallest. Satish is shorter than Kishore but taller than Rajesh. Anil is little shorter than Kishore but little taller than Satish. Who is taller than Rajesh but shorter than Anil?
SSC (10+2) 2011
(a) Anil (b) Kishore (c) Rajesh (d) Satish

18. In an examination, Rahul got the 11th rank and he was 47th from the bottom among those who passed. 3 students could not appear for the exam. 1 student failed. What is the total number of students?
SSC (10+2) 2011
(a) 60 (b) 62 (c) 59 (d) 61

19. In a row of twenty five children facing North. Prakash, when shifted by four places towards his right, becomes tenth from the right end. What was his original position from the left end?
(a) 10th (b) 8th
(c) 11th (d) 9th
(e) None of the above

20. Twenty persons are sitting in a line facing the North. Rajiv is sitting at the eight position from the left. Five persons are sitting between Rajiv and Priya. Sharat is sitting exactly between Rajiv and Priya. What is the position of Priya?
LIC (ADO) 2013
(a) 14th from right (b) 8th from right
(c) 14th from left (d) 8th from left
(e) None of these

21. Among five weightlifters P, Q, R, S and T. Q lifts more weight than P but lifts less weight than T. Two of them can lift weight less than P. S does not lift minimum amount of weight. Who among them lifts the maximum weight?
LIC (ADO) 2013
(a) T (b) R (c) Q (d) S
(e) None of these

22. In a row of boys, Manish is 9th from the left and Suresh is 9th from the right. When they interchange their positions, Suresh becomes 18th from the right. What will be the Manish's new position from the left? **SSC (FCI) 2012**
(a) 9th (b) 16th
(c) 18th (d) 20th

23. Shailendra is shorter than Keshav but taller than Rakesh. Madhav is the tallest. Ashish is a little shorter than Keshav and little taller than Shailendra. If they stand in the order of increasing heights, then who will be the second?
SSC (FCI) 2012
(a) Ashish (b) Shailendra
(c) Rakesh (d) Madhav

24. If in a clock, 12 is replaced by 1, 11 by 2, 10 by 3 and so on, then what will be the time in that clock corresponding to 'twenty minutes past three in the usual clock'?
SBI (Clerk) 2012
(a) Twenty minutes past eleven
(b) Forty minutes past ten
(c) Forty minutes past eleven
(d) Twenty minutes past ten
(e) None of the above

25. In a group of five districts, Akbarpur is smaller than Fatehpur, Dhanbad is bigger than Palamu and Bara Banki is bigger than Fatehpur but not as big as Palamu. Which district is the biggest? **SSC (10+2) 2011**
(a) Akbarpur (b) Fatehpur
(c) Dhanbad (d) Palamu

26. 13 students are standing in a horizontal row from left to right. If all the odd numbered students in a row are shifted to the successive odd numbered positions, then what will be the position of a boy, who was seventh in the row initially?
IOC Exam 2012
(a) Fifth from left (b) Fifth from right
(c) Eighth from left (d) Ninth from right

27. In Ravi's clock shop, two clocks were brought for repairs. One clock has the cuckoo coming out every sixteen minutes, while the other one has the cuckoo coming out every eighteen minutes. Both cuckoos come out at 12 : 00 noon. When will they both come out together again?
SSC (CGL) 2011
(a) 2 : 06 pm (b) 2 : 08 pm
(c) 2 : 24 pm (d) 2 : 32 pm

28. Hari remembers that his father's birthday is between 13th and 16th of June, whereas his sister remembers that their father's birthday is between 14th and 18th of June. On which day is their father's birthday, which both agree?
SSC (CPO) 2011
(a) 14th June (b) 15th June (c) 16th June (d) 17th June

29. If the day before yesterday was Friday, then what day will two days after the day after tomorrow be?
SSC (10+2) 2011
(a) Saturday (b) Thursday (c) Friday (d) Sunday

30. Ram was born on 29th February. He celebrated his birthday falling on exactly 29th February 2008 for the fourth time. In which year he was born? **SSC (CGL) 2012**

(a) 1992 (b) 2004
(c) 2000 (d) 1996

31. The Chairman of the Selection Committee arrived at the Interview room for conducting an interview at 10 min to 12 : 30 h. He was earlier by twenty minutes than the other members of the board, who arrived late by 30 min. At what time were the interview scheduled?

(a) 12 : 10 (b) 12 : 20 (c) 12 : 30 (d) 12 : 40

32. A clock goes slow from midnight by 5 min at the end of the first hour, by 10 min at the end of the second hour, by 15 min at the end of the 3rd hours and so on. What will be the time by this clock after 6 h?

(a) 6 : 00 am (b) 5 : 30 am
(c) 6 : 30 am (d) 5 : 15 am

33. If the day before yesterday was Friday, then what will be the third day after the day-after-tomorrow?

(a) Thursday (b) Friday
(c) Saturday (d) Sunday

34. In a row of boys, Srinath is 7th from the left and Venkat is 12th from the right. If they interchange their positions, Srinath becomes 22nd from the left. How many boys are there in the row? **NICL (AO) 2013**

(a) 19 (b) 31
(c) 33 (d) 34

35. In a class of 60, where girls are twice that of boys, Kamal ranked seventeenth from the top. If there are 9 girls ahead of Kamal, then how many boys are after him in rank?

(a) 3 (b) 7 (c) 12 (d) 32

36. Sangeeta remembers that her father's birthday was certainly after eighth but before thirteenth of December. Her sister Natasha remembers that their father's birthday was definitely after ninth but before fourteenth of December. On which date of December was their father's birthday?

(a) 10th
(b) 11th
(c) 12th
(d) Data inadequate
(e) None of the above

37. The train for Lucknow leaves every two and a half hours from New Delhi Railway Station. An announcement was made at the station that the train for Lucknow had left 40 min ago and the next train will leave at 18:00 h. At what time was the announcement made?

(a) 15 : 30 h
(b) 17 : 10 h
(c) 15 : 50 h
(d) None of the above

38. Pratap correctly remembers that his mother's birthday is before 23rd April but after 19th April, whereas his sister correctly remembers that their mother's birthday is not on or after 22nd April. On which day in April is definitely their's mother's birthday? **Canara Bank (PO) 2010**

(a) 20th (b) 21st
(c) 20th or 21st (d) Cannot be determined
(e) None of these

39. Mohan correctly remembers that his father's birthday is before 20th January but after 16th January whereas his sister correctly remembers that their father's birthday is after 18th January but before 23rd January. On which date in January is definitely their father's birthday? **Syndicate Bank (PO) 2010**

(a) 18th (b) 19th
(c) 20th (d) Data inadequate
(e) None of these

40. Examine the following statements

1. Rama scored more than Rani.
2. Rani scored less than Ratna.
3. Ratna scored more than Rama.
4. Padma scored more than Rama but less than Ratna.

Who scored the highest? **UPSC (CSAT) 2012**

(a) Rama (b) Padma (c) Rani (d) Ratna

41. In a class boys stands in a single line. One of the boys is nineteenth in order from both the ends. How many boys are there in the class?

(a) 27 (b) 37
(c) 38 (d) 39

42. Aman is 16th from the left end in a row of boys and Vivek is 18th from the right end. Gagan is 11th from Aman towards the right and 3rd from Vivek towards the right end. How many boys are there in the row? **MAT 2014**

(a) 42 (b) 48
(c) 36 (d) None of these

43. Out of P, Q, R, S and T. S earns more than only R and T. P earns maximum. T earns ₹ 50000. Q earns less than only P. R earns less than Q. Q earns ₹ 80000. What does R earn?

(a) More than 40000
(b) More than 20000 and less than 40,000
(c) Less than 50000
(d) Cannot be determined

44. Priya is taller than Tiya and shorter than Siya. Riya is shorter than Siya and taller than Priya. Riya is taller than Diya, who is shorter than Tiya. Arrange them in order of descending heights. **IIFT 2012**

(a) Priya–Siya–Riya–Tiya–Diya
(b) Riya–Siya–Priya–Diya–Tiya
(c) Siya–Riya–Priya–Tiya–Diya
(d) Siya–Priya–Riya–Diya–Tiya

Advanced Level

1. In a queue, Mr X is fourteenth from the front and Mr Y is seventeenth from the end, while Mr Z is exactly in between Mr X and Mr Y. If Mr X is ahead of Mr Y and there are 48 persons in the queue, then how many persons are there between Mr X and Mr Z? **UPSC CSAT 2013**

(a) 6 (b) 7 (c) 8 (d) 9

Direction (Q. Nos. 2-5) *Read the following information carefully and answer the questions that follow.*

Among A, B, C, D and E, E is taller than D but not as fat as D. C is taller than A but shorter than B. A is fatter than D but not as fat as B. E is thinner than C who is thinner than D. E is shorter than A.

2. Who is the most thin person in the group?

(a) B (b) C (c) D (d) E
(e) Cannot be determined

3. Who is the tallest as well as having the highest weight in the group?

(a) A (b) B (c) C (d) D
(e) E

4. If all the persons stood in a line according to their height, then who would be in the middle?

(a) A (b) B (c) C (d) D
(e) E

5. Which person is taller than two but thinner than the remaining two?

(a) A (b) B (c) C (d) D
(e) E

Direction (Q. Nos. 6-10) *Read the following information carefully and answer the questions given below it*

- A,B, C, D and E are five friends.
- B is older to E but not as tall as C.
- C is younger to A and is taller to D and E.
- A is taller to D but younger than E.
- D is older to A but is shortest in the group.

6. Which of the following statements is correct about B?

I. B is not the tallest.
II. B is shorter to E.
III. When they are asked to stand in ascending order with respect to their heights, B is in the middle.

(a) Only I is correct (b) I and II are correct
(c) Only III is correct (d) All are incorrect
(e) None of these

7. If F, another friend, is taller than C, then how many of them will be between F and E according to their height?

(a) None (b) One
(c) Two (d) Three
(e) None of these

8. If a selection is to be made among them who would be relatively older and also taller, then who among them should be chosen?

(a) A (b) B
(c) C (d) D
(e) E

9. Who among the following is the oldest?

(a) A (b) B
(c) C (d) D
(e) None of these

10. Which of the following pairs of friends is older to D?

(a) BA (b) BC
(c) BE (d) EA
(e) None of these

Direction (Q. Nos. 11-14) *Read the following information and answer the questions.* **JMET 2011**

An ice-cream maker is experimenting with six chemical essences. U, V, W, X, Y and Z for developing a new flavour called 'SWEETER & HEALTHIER'. The details of these chemical essences are as follows

I. U is sweeter than V and healthier than Z.
II. V is sweeter than Y and less healthier than Z.
III. W is less sweeter than X and less healthier than U.
IV. X is less sweeter and healthier than Y.
V. Y is less sweeter and healthier than U.
VI. Z is sweeter than U and less healthier than W.

11. Which is the sweetest essence?

(a) U (b) W (c) X (d) Z

12. Which of the following essences is/are both sweeter and healthier than V?

(a) Only U (b) Only W (c) Only Z (d) U and Z

13. Which of the following essences is/are sweeter than Y and healthier than W?

(a) Only U (b) Only V (c) Only Z (d) U and V

14. Which is the least healthy essence?

(a) U (b) V (c) W (d) Y

Direction (Q. Nos. 15-18) *Read the following information carefully and answer the questions given below.*

There are seven persons A, B, C, D, E, F and G of varying heights. We have some information about them but not complete information.

I. Atleast four persons are shorter than A.
II. C is taller than B and there is nobody else in between.
III. D is neither the tallest nor the shortest.
IV. E is either the tallest or the shortest.
V. Atleast four persons are taller than F.

15. Which of the following may show them in the descending order of their heights?
(a) A, G, C, D, F, B, E
(b) C, B, A, D, G, F, E
(c) D, G, A, C, B, E, F
(d) E, A,G, C, D, B, G
(e) E, D, C, B, A, F, G

16. If G, D and A are in descending order of their heights without anybody in between, B is
(a) second tallest
(b) third tallest
(c) fourth tallest
(d) fifth tallest
(e) second shortest

17. If C is the tallest, who among the following could be in the middle when standing in a line according to height?
(a) A (b) B (c) D (d) E
(e) F

18. If F is the second shortest, C could be at any of the following positions (first being the tallest) except
(a) first (b) second (c) third (d) fourth
(e) fifth

Direction (Q. Nos. 19-21) *Read the following information carefully and answer the questions that follows.* **SNAP 2013**

Six students A, B, C, D, E and F participated in a dancing competition where in they won prizes 12000, 10000, 8000, 6000, 4000, 2000 according to the position secured. The following information is known to us

I. A won less money than B.
II. The difference between the winning of C and F was ₹2000.
III. The difference between the winning of D and F was atleast ₹ 4000.
IV. E won the ₹8000 prize.

19. Which of the following could be the ranking from first place to sixth place of students?
(a) A, D, E, B, F, C (b) B, A, E, C, F, D
(c) F, B, E, A, C, D (d) B, A, E, D, C, F

20. A bus for 'Chennai' leaves every 40 min from a bus stand. An enquiry clerk told a man that the bus had already left 10 min ago and the next bus will leave at 10 : 45 am. At what time this information was given to the man?
(a) 10:25 am (b) 9:55 am (c) 10:15 am (d) 10:35 am

21. Sushma has a dentist appointment at 7 : 20 in the evening. While entering the dentist's office, she saw reflection of the wall clock. The hands of clock read 4 :40. She knew that this being the reflection of the clock, the time she read is not the correct time. She is not on appointed time.
(a) She is 20 min late (b) She is 20 min before time
(c) She is on time (d) None of these

Direction (Q. Nos. 22-26) *Refer to the following statements and answer the questions.* **SNAP 2011**

Seven students Priya, Ankit, Raman, Sunil, Tony, Deepak and Vicky take a series of tests. No two students get similar marks. Vicky always scores more than Priya. Priya always scores more than Ankit. Each time either Raman scores the highest and Tony gets the least or alternatively Sunil scores the highest and Deepak or Ankit scores the least.

22. If Sunil is ranked sixth and Ankit is ranked fifth, then which of the following can be true?
(a) Vicky is ranked first or fourth
(b) Raman is ranked second or third
(c) Tony is ranked fourth or fifth
(d) Deepak is ranked third or fourth

23. If Raman gets the highest, then Vicky should be ranked not lower than
(a) second (b) third
(c) fourth (d) fifth

24. If Raman is ranked second and Ankit is ranked first, then which of the following must be true?
(a) Sunil is ranked third (b) Tony is ranked third
(c) Priya is ranked sixth (d) None of these

25. If Sunil is ranked second, then which of the following can be true?
(a) Deepak gets more than Vicky
(b) Vicky gets more than Sunil
(c) Priya gets more than Raman
(d) Priya gets more than Vicky

26. If Vicky is ranked fifth, then which of the following must be ture?
(a) Sunil scores the highest (b) Raman is ranked second
(c) Tony is ranked third (d) Ankit is ranked second

Direction (Q. Nos. 27-31) *Study the information below to answer these questions.*

I. Seven students Pradeep, Qadir, Rohit, Sushant, Tushar, Uday and Vikas write a test series.
II. Either Rohit or Sushant scores highest in each test.
III. Pradeep always scores less than Vikas.
IV. Qadir always scores less than Pradeep.
V. Each time either Rohit scores the highest and Tushar gets the least.
VI. Each time Sushant scores the highest, either Uday or Qadir scores the least.
VII. Each student scores marks different from each other.

27. In a particular test, if Sushant is ranked second, which of the following can be true?
(a) Uday gets more than Vikas
(b) Vikas is ranked fifth
(c) Tushar gets more than Qadir
(d) Pradeep is ranked third

28. In a particular test, if Sushant is ranked sixth and Qadir is ranked fifth, then which of the following can be true?
(a) Vikas is ranked first or fourth
(b) Rohit is ranked second or third
(c) Pradeep is ranked second or fifth
(d) Uday is ranked third or fourth

29. In a particular test, if Rohit gets the highest. Vikas should be ranked not lower than
(a) second (b) third (c) fourth (d) fifth

30. In a particular test, if Rohit is ranked second and Qadir is ranked fifth, which of the following connot be true?
(a) Tushar is ranked third
(b) Tushar is ranked sixth
(c) Pradeep is ranked sixth
(d) Vikas is ranked second

31. In a particular test, if Rohit is ranked second and Qadir is ranked fifth, which of the following must be true about Tushar's rank? **NIFT (UG) 2015**
(a) Fourth
(b) Third
(c) Seventh
(d) Sixth

Direction (Q. Nos. 32-34) *Read the information carefully and answer the questions.*

Each of the six poles P, Q, R, S, T and U has a different height. P is taller than only three poles. S is taller than T but shorter than U. U is shorter than P. Q is not the tallest. The second shortest pole is 2 ft tall. The third tallest pole is 5 ft tall.

32. Which of the following may be the possible height of the pole U?
(a) 7 ft (b) 2 ft (c) 5 ft (d) 3 ft
(e) 1 ft

33. The tallest pole is 11 ft taller than S which of the following may be the possible height of Q?
(a) 4 ft (b) 9 ft (c) 13 ft (d) 16 ft
(e) 17 ft

34. Which of the following is true with respect to the given information? **SBI (PO) 2014**
(a) Only two poles are shorter than Q
(b) Q's height is definitely less than 2 ft
(c) None of the given option is true
(d) S is the second tallest pole
(e) T is the shortest pole

Answers with Explanations

Intro Exercise 1

1. (*b*) The information given in the question may be arranged as follows
Bipul > Krishna > Barun > Sanjay
So, Bipul is the tallest.

2. (*d*) The data is inadequate because it is not given that who between Virat and Shikhar is taller. Hence, answer cannot be determined.

3. (*b*) C has more money than only E, B and A.
D > C > (E, B, A)
So, D has highest amount of money.

4. (*d*) R can be on the right or left of M. So, the position of R cannot be determined.

5. (*b*) Neelu is younger than vibha but older than Puja
Puja < Neelu < Vibha ...(i)
Puja is younger than Asha and Anupam
Puja < Asha Anupam ...(ii)
Asha is older than vibha but younger than Anupam.
Anupam > Asha > Vibha ...(iii)
From Eqs. (i), (ii) and (iii), we get
Anupam > Asha > Vibha > Neelu > Puja
Ascending order of ages is

Puja	Neelu	Vibha	Asha	Anupam
1	2	3	4	5

So, Asha is on 4th in ascending order of the age.

6. (*b*) D > (C, E); E > A; C > A
B > D; B > D > (C, E) > A
So, B is the tallest while D is next to tallest one.

7. (*c*) B > A; D > C; C > B; A > E
So, final order of intellectual level is E < A < B < C < D.
Hence, D is most intelligent.

8. (*d*) According to the question,
Lakshmi > Meenu; Lakshmi > Leela > Meenu
Latha < Meenu, Hari; Meenu > Hari
On arranging the above data, we get
Lakshmi > Leela > Meenu > Hari > Latha
Hence, Latha is the youngest.

9. (*c*) Priti > Rahul; Yamuna = Divya; Manju > Lokita
Rahul > Yamuna; Divya > Manju
So, the final order of marks is as following
Priti > Rahul > Yamuna = Divya > Manju > Lokita
Hence, Lokita got the lowest marks.

10. (*c*) Priya > Raj > Mukesh; Priya > (Gaurav, Kavita)
Mukesh > Gaurav
Gaurav's marks are not the lowest, so Kavita got the lowest marks.
So, the final order of marks is as following
Priya > Raj > Mukesh > Gaurav > Kavita
Hence, Raj is second in the descending order of marks.

11. (*b*) Total number of children = [(15 + 4 + 8) − 1]

= 27 − 1 = 26

12. (*e*) There are total 25 children.

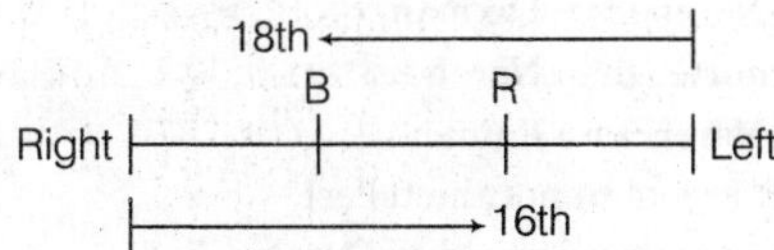

R is 16th from the right end.

B is 18th from the left end.

So, B is (25 − 18 + 1) = 8th from the right end.

Hence, there are total seven children between R and B.

13. (*a*) T > M > X; V > (M, T); R > X

So, V > T > M > R > X

So, X earns the least among the five of them.

Hence, R earns more than only X. It means that X earns the least while R earns second least.

14. (*c*) R > (P, T); T > Q

S did not score the highest marks.

So, R scored the highest marks.

15. (*c*) Ravi is 6th to the right of Sunil who is 13th from the right end.

So, Ravi is (13 − 6 = 7th) from the right end.

Ravi is 8th from the left end.

Thus, total number of children = 7 + 8 − 1 = 14

16. (*d*) D > A; (B, E) > C

D is heavier than only A.

So, the final order is as following (B, E) > C > D > A

Thus, either B or E is the heaviest.

17. (*a*) Rohan > Hardik < Susheel

Hardik > Niza > Harry

Rohan > Susheel

So, the final order is as following

Rohan > Susheel > Hardik > Niza > Harry

Hence, Rohan is the tallest.

18. (*d*) According to the question, sequence is as follows

Deepti > Sweta > Seema > Sohan > Seeta

So, Deepti is the eldest.

19. (*c*) Total number of children = 40

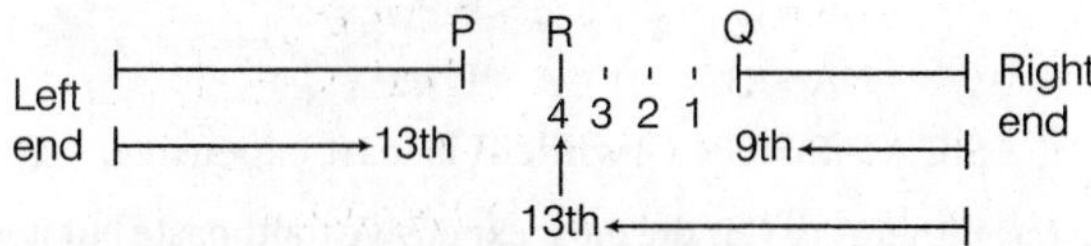

R is 4th to the left of Q and is 13th from the right end.

Number of children between P and R

⇒ 40 − (13 + 13)

⇒ 40 − 26 = 14

There are 14 person between P and R.

20. (*d*) Ameya's rank is 6th from the top.

Annie's rank from top is (6 + 7 = 13th)

So, Annie's rank from bottom is (35 − 13 + 1) = 23th

21. (*b*) Given B is 9th from the right end and A is 7th from the left end.

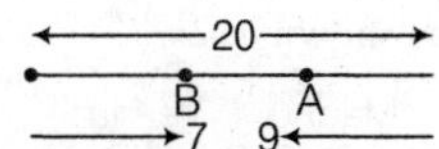

After interchange the position

A B

7 9

So, position of B from left end.

= (Total number of people − Position of B from right end) −1

= (20 − 9) + 1 = 11 + 1 = 12

So, position of B from left end is 12th.

22. (*d*) Reena > Garima > Sarita; Reena = Tanya

Anu > Garima

So, the final order of height is as following

(Reena = Tanya, Anu) > Garima > Sartia

Hence, Sarita is shortest.

23. (*e*) First time sequence is

Natrajan → Rangarajan → Krishnarajan → Dog ⟷ Premrajan

Again the sequence is

Natrajan or Premrajan → Krishnarajan Dog Rangarajan →

24. (*b*) Number of letters in the row = 5 + 12 − 1 = 16

25. (*c*) Total number of girls = 11 + 11 − 1 = 22 − 1 = 21

26. (*c*) In first row, Veena is 12th from start and 19th from end.

Then, total number of girls = (12 + 19 − 1) = 30

In second row, Sunita is 14th from start and 20th from the end.

Then, total number of girls = (14 + 20 − 1) = 33

Total number of girls = 30 + 33 = 63

27. (*a*) Required position $= \frac{23 + 1}{2} = 12\text{th}$

28. (*d*) Required number of persons = [30 − (9 + 16)] = 30 − 25 = 5

29. (*b*) 31st position from left = [(40 + 1) − 31]th position from right

= 10th position from right

25th position from right = [(40 − 25) + 1]

= 16th position from left

∴ Number of person between them

= [40 − (10 + 16)] = 40 − 26 = 14

30. (*b*) On shifting 4 places to the left Komal is 10th from the left end of the row. Thus, Komal's original position was 14th from left end.

Swati is 3 places to right of Komal's original position.

Clearly, Swati is 17th from the left end.

Number of girls to the right of Swati = (40 − 17) = 23

Thus, Swati is 23 + 1 = 24th from the right end of the row.

31. (*d*) Vishal is 18th from the right end and Ganesh is 3rd to the right of Vishal. So, Ganesh is15th from the right end.

Clearly, there are 15 boys to the left of Amar; 10 boys between Amar and Ganesh and 14 boys to the right of Ganesh.

Hence, total number of boys in the row

= (15 + 1 + 10 + 1 + 14) = 41

32. (*c*) Given that Madhu is 10th from the left and Veena is 9th from the right end as shown below

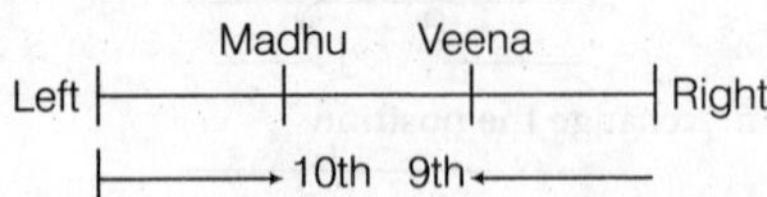

After interchanging position

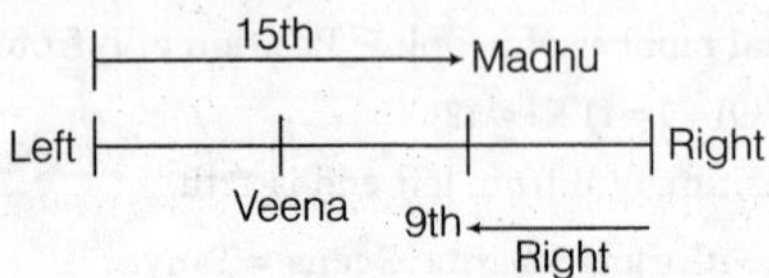

We see that interchanging the places ranking of Madhu changes 5 places than the previous ranks which implies Veena was at 15th position of the row and adding 8 to the ranking of Madhu will given the total number of girls in the row which is

$$15 + 8 = 23$$

33. (*d*) Gita > Mita; Bhanu > Gita

$\therefore$ Bhanu > Gita > Mita

So, it is clear that Mita is youngest.

34. (*b*) Mira is taller than Hema and Kuku

Mira > (Hema and Kuku) ...(i)

Rani is taller than Mira

Rani > Mira ...(ii)

Neha is shorter than Hema

Hema > Neha ...(iii)

Juhi is taller than Hema but shorter than Kuku

Kuku > Juhi > Hema ...(iv)

From Eqs. (i), (ii), (iii) and (iv) the ascending order of height is

$$\underset{1}{\text{Neha}} < \underset{2}{\text{Hema}} < \underset{3}{\text{Juhi}} < \underset{4}{\text{Kuku}} < \underset{5}{\text{Mira}} < \underset{6}{\text{Rani}} < \underset{7}{\text{Isha}}$$

Mira ranks 5th in the ascending order of heights.

35. (*a*) Omprakash is standing between Laxman and Qutab

Laxman Omprakash Qutab

Narender is taller than Laxman

Narender > Laxman

Raman is shorter than Narender

Narender > Raman

(Mahender, Preetam) not the tallest

Preetam is two places ahead of Qutab.

Preetam ——— Qutab
2 1

The order of height becomes

Narender > (Raman, Laxman)

So, the sequence of height becomes on the basis of shorter first.

$$\text{Preetam} < \text{Mahender} < \text{Qutab} < \text{Omprakash} < \text{Laxman} < \text{Raman} < \text{Narender}$$

Hence, Narender is the tallest.

36. (*c*) Number of students behind Pihu in rank $= 31 - 7 = 24$

So, Pihu is 25th from the bottom.

So, number of students behind Manu in rank $= 31 - 11 = 20$

$\therefore$ Manu is 21st from the bottom.

By using formula,

Pihu's rank from the bottom $= 31 - 7 + 1 = 24 + 1 = 25$th

Manu's rank from the bottom $= 31 - 11 + 1 = 20 + 1 = 21$st

Hence, the ranks of Pihu's and Manu's from the bottom in the class is 25th and 21st respectively.

37. (*a*) D is neither as tall as A nor as short as C. It means that A is taller than D and D is taller than C.

C D A or $C < D < A$

Now, B is shorter than D but taller than C. So, final ranking will be as following.

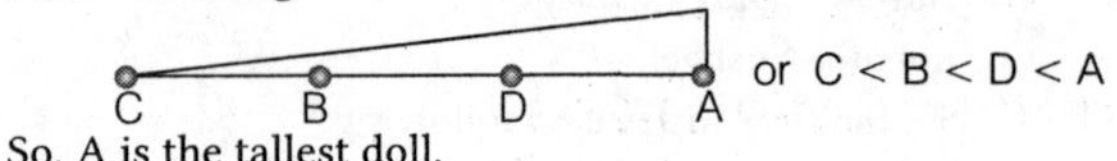

So, A is the tallest doll.

Intro Exercise 2

Solution (Q. Nos. 1-2) According to the question, the given information can be represented as

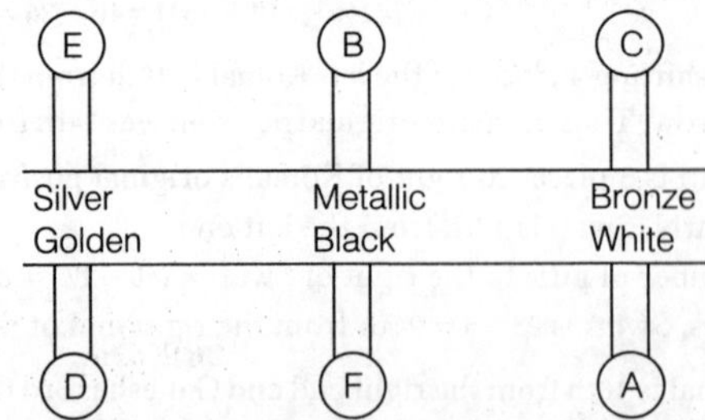

Arrangement as per height = E > D / B > A > C > F of poles.

1. (*d*) It cannot be established that which of the two poles B/D is taller but it is sure that either of B or D is the second tallest.
2. (*b*) The colour of tallest pole is silver.

Solution (Q. Nos. 3-6)

P = G C > P

A > G A > P

So, A > P = G < C, while B is least expensive.

3. (*c*) Either A or C is the most expensive toothpaste but it is not clear that which one is most expensive. So, (a), (b) and (d) are not true.

   G is somewhere in the middle of A or C and B.

4. (*a*) F is more expensive than A but it is not clear that it is more expensive than C or not. So, atleast four toothpaste A, P, G and B are less expensive than F.
5. (*a*) From I and II, it is clear that A is more expensive than P. So, V is not necessary.
6. (*d*) G is less expensive than C and it is more effective than C. So, G should be purchased instead of B.

Solution (Q. Nos. 7-11)

A > D > G; C > E > H; D > B > F

G > C; F > G

So, final order of height is as following

A > D > B > F > G > C > E > H

7. (e) None of these
8. (b) J must be placed between G and E with C but it is not clear that between C and J, who is taller. From the above arrangement G is shorter than D.
9. (a) B will be the third from top when they are arranged in descending order of height.
10. (b) G, C, E and H are shorter than F.
11. (e) All statements are necessary to answer the questions.

Solution (Q. Nos. 12-16) The order of height can be determined as following

F > (B, C); D > C; D > E > F; E > A > F

So, D > E > A > F > (B, C)

The order of weighs can be determined as following

(B, C) > A; D > B; F> D

So, F > D > B > A

12. (e) There is no idea about the position of E. So, either A or E is lightest.
13. (c) F is heavier than B and C but shorter than D.
14. (c) D is the tallest.
15. (a) A is third from the top when they are arranged in descending order of height.
16. (d) F, B and C are shorter than A.

Solution (Q. Nos. 17-21)

Let the age of Mahima be x year.

∴ Anita's age = 2x yr

Rajan's age = $\frac{x}{2}$ yr

Deepti's age = 4x yr

Lata's age = $\frac{x}{4}$ yr

So, the order of their age is as following

Deepti > Anita > Mahima > Rajan > Lata

17. (c) Lata is the youngest among them.
18. (a) Deepti is the oldest among them.
19. (d) From the above order, it is clear that none of the two person has same age.
20. (c) Anita is younger than Deepti.
21. (b) If they arranged in descending order of age, then Mahima will be in the middle.

Solution (Q. Nos. 22-24)

According to given information the arrangement in the descending order of points will be

Dolly > Shikhar's father > Amar > Akash > Swarn > Swarn's niece

So, Shikhar has to be Swarn's niece and Snehal has to be Shikhar's father.

∴ The final arrangement will be as following

Dolly > Snehal > Amar > Akash > Swarn > Shikhar

22. (d) Shikhar is the lady in the group besides Dolly.
23. (c) Snehal stood second in the game.
24. (b) Dolly won the game.

Solution (Q. Nos. 25-30)

Let the weight of C be x kg.

Then, B's weight = 4.5 x kg

A's weight = 9x kg

D's weight = 2x kg

E's weight = 4x kg

So, the order of their weight is,

A > B > E > D > C.

25. (e) It is clear that statement V is not required to determine the order of height.
26. (a) A is the heaviest in weight.
27. (a) The correct descending order is A, B, E, D and C.
28. (c) C is lightest in weight.
29. (a) E is lighter than A and B.
30. (b) E is heavier than D and C.

Intro Exercise 3

1. (b)

Twenty people	Shifts
First group of 5	8 : 00 am to 2 : 00 pm
Second group of 10	10 : 00 am to 4 : 00 pm
Third group of 5	12 noon to 6 : 00 pm

Here, timing 12 noon to 4 : 00 pm is commonly exist in all the shifts, so the computers are likely to be used most this time. Hence, option (b) is correct.

2. (c)

	Birth date
According to Sneha	12, 13, 14, 15
According to younger brother	14, 15, 16, 17
According to elder brother	14, 16

So, confirm date is fourteenth. Hence, option (c) is correct.

3. (*c*) Given, 25th February 2008 is Monday and 2008 was a leap year.

26th - Tuesday	27th - Wednesday
28th - Thursday	29th - Friday
1st - Saturday	2nd - Sunday

Hence, option (c) is correct.

4. (*a*) Day before yesterday was Sunday. Therefore, today is Tuesday. Day after tomorrow will be Thursday. Thursday + 3 days = Sunday. Hence, option (a) is correct.

5. (*a*) Sudha read the book 4 days after Sunday. It means Sudha read the book on Thursday. Hence, Anil will read the book on Friday.

6. (*d*)

According to	Nitin's Birthday
Nitin	Wednesday, Thursday
Deepak	Thursday, Friday

Here, Thursday is common to both. Hence, correct day is Thursday.

7. (*b*)

According to	Possibility of date
Vinay	21, 22, 23, 24, 25, 26, 27
Rita	13, 14, 15, 16, 17, 18, 19, 20, 21

Here, 21 is common to both.
Hence, the correct date is 21st August.

8. (*e*) Days according to Meena, 19th, 20th or 21st May.

Days according to her brother, 21st, 22nd or 23rd May.

Clearly, 21st May is common in both the groups and hence it is the required day.

Cumulative Exercise

Base Level

1. (*a*) Position of M from right end = 11 + 15 + 1 = 27th

So, the position of M from left end = 40 − 27 + 1 = 14th

2. (*a*) R is 5th from the right end. T is 4th from the left end.

Total number of student between = 20 − (5 + 4) = 11

3. (*b*)

17th
Veena
Mridul
Top or Left end
Right end or Bottom
12th
20

Total number of students = 20
Veena's rank from top = (20 − 17) + 1 = 3 + 1 = 4
Veena is at 4th rank from top.
Mridul rank from bottom = (20 − 12) + 1 = 8 + 1 = 9
Mridul is 9th from bottom.
Number of person between Veena and Mridul

= 20 − (4 + 9) = 20 − 13 = 7

There are 7 person in between Veena and Mridul

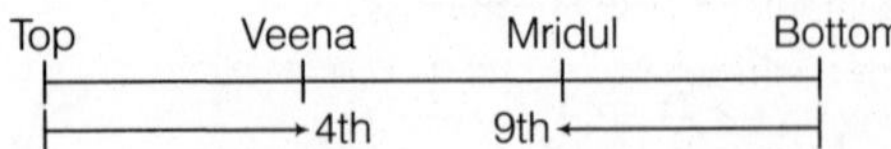

Position of person exactly in the middle between Veena and Mridul $= \frac{(n+1)}{2} = \frac{(7+1)}{2} = \frac{8}{2} = 4$

So, Rohan is at 8th rank from the top as Rohan is 4 places above Veena.

Hence, option (b) is the correct.

4. (*a*) Manav is (15 − 4) = 11th from the top.

There are 20 students.

So, Manav's rank from bottom = (20 − 11) + 1 = 10th.

5. (*a*) Total number of boys after 2 new boys joined = 47

Since, the rank of the boy dropped by 1, it become 21st from 20th.

∴ His new rank from the end = 47 − 21 + 1 = 27th

6. (*d*) When Rahul was shifted by three places towards his right side, then he occupies the middle position i.e. 13th position.

$= \frac{25+1}{2} = \frac{26}{2} = 13$

10th 13th

Thus, his original position from the left end of the row

= 13 − 3 = 10th

7. (*c*) Sachin is shorter than Kamal but taller than Ram

Kamal > Sachin

Sachin > Ram ...(i)

Mohan is tallest.

Arun is little shorter than Kamal and a little taller than Sachin

Kamal > Arun

Arun > Sachin ...(ii)

From above equations,

Mohan >	Kamal >	Arun >	Sachin >	Ram
1	2	3	4	5

Kamal is 2nd tallest in the above sequence.

8. (*c*) The arrangement is as shown

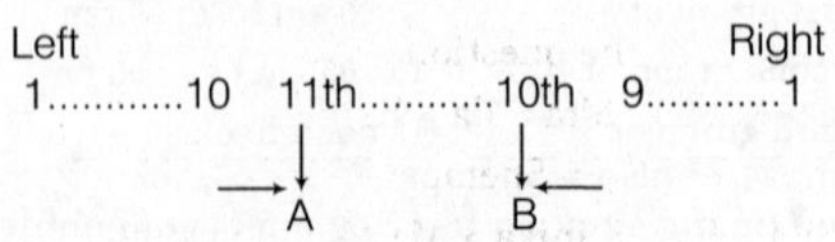

Now, they interchange their positions.

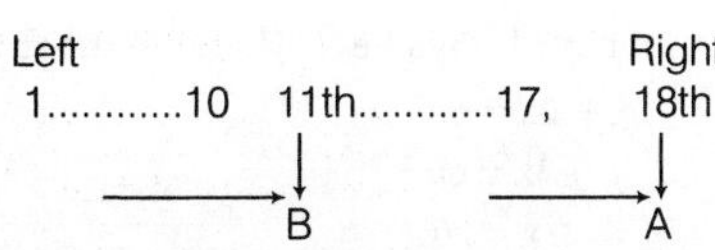

Now, total number of persons in row

$= 17 + 9 + 1 = 27$ persons

Now, total persons in a row other than A and B

$= 27 - 2 = 25$ persons

9. (*b*) From given information,

Ramesh > Mohan > Shyam ...(i)
Gautam > Ramesh > Rajat ...(ii)
Shyam > Rajat ...(iii)

Combining Eqs. (i), (ii) and (iii), we have

Gautam > Ramesh > Mohan > Shyam > Rajat

Hence, Rajat is the shortest among all.

10. (*c*)

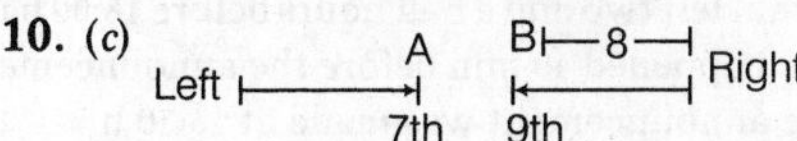

After interchanging the position A becomes 11th from left

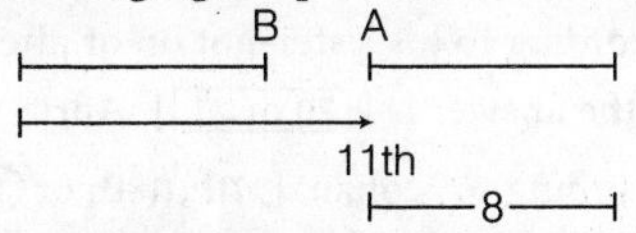

Total number of people in the row $= 11 + 8 = 19$

So, there are 19 persons in the row.

Hence, option (c) is the correct.

11. (*a*) According to the question, N > M; Y > M; N > X > Y

On arranging the above data, we get

∴ N > X > Y > M

So, N is the most intelligent among them.

12. (*b*) Total number of students = 5

Sudha scored higher than Puja.

Sudha > Puja ...(i)

Kavita scored lower than Suma but higher than Sudha

Kavita > Sudha

Suma > Kavita ...(ii)

Mamta scored between Puja and Sudha.

Sudha > Mamta > Puja. [From Eq. (i)] ...(iii)

From Eqs. (i), (ii) and (iii), we get

Suma > Kavita > Sudha > Mamta > Puja.

So, Puja scored lowest in the examination.

Hence, option (b) is correct.

13. (*b*) All the books are arranged as follows

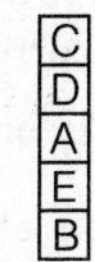

Hence, book at the bottom is B.

14. (*a*) According to the question,

Sita > Kanika; Sita > Ila > Kanika

Manas / Kanika > Shempa; Kanika > Manas

∴ Sita > Ila > Kanika > Manas > Shempa

So, Shempa is youngest among them.

15. (*b*) Q > S > T

R is heavier than only P. It means that P is the lightest and R is the second lightest.

So, final order of weight is

Q > S > T > R > P

Hence, Q is the heaviest.

16. (*a*) R is 16th from the right end.

W is 5th to the right of R.

∴ W's position from right end $= 16 - 5 = 11$th

17. (*d*) Kishore > Satish > Rajesh

Kishore > Anil > Satish

Now, Mohan > Kishore > Anil > Satish > Rajesh

So, it is clear that, Satish is taller than Rajesh but shorter than Anil.

18. (*d*) Number of successful candidates $= 11 + 47 - 1 = 57$

Total number of students $= 57 + 3 + 1 = 61$

19. (*e*)

P ||| P
14th 10th

Original position of Prakash from the left $= 25 - 14 + 1 = 12$th

20. (*c*)

8th
R || S || P || T 3

Priya is 14th from the left and 7th from the right.

Hence, option (c) is correct.

21. (*a*) T > Q > P; P > R , S; P > S > R

Now, T > Q > P > S > R

It is clearly shown that T lifts the maximum weight.

22. (*c*) Number of boys between Manish and Suresh

= Suresh's new position–Suresh's initial position–1

$= 18 - 9 - 1 = 8$

∴ Manish's new position $= 9 + 8 +$ Manish $= 18$th

23. (*b*) Shailendra is shorter than keshav but taller than Rakesh.

Keshav > Shailendra > Rakesh

Ashish is a little shorter than Keshav and little taller than Shailendra.

Keshav > Ashish > Shailendra

Madhav is the tallest.

The order of increasing heights.

Rakest < Shailendra < Ashish < Keahav < Madhav

1 2 3 4 5

So, Shailendra is 2nd among them.

Hence, option (b) is the correct.

24. (*e*)

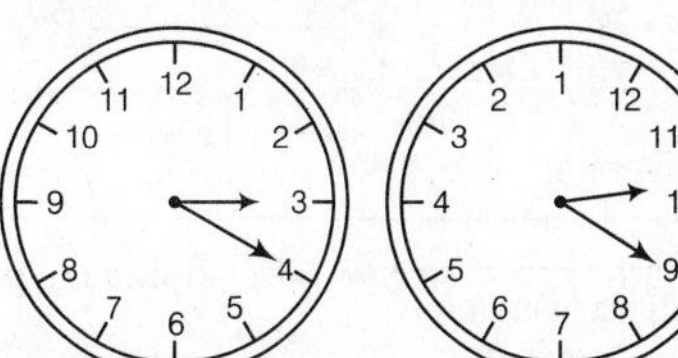

So, the time will be 'Forty five minute past nine'. There is no such option according to the answer.

25. (*c*) Akbarpur is smaller than Fatehpur

Fatehpur > Akbarpur ...(i)

Dhanbad is bigger than Palamu

Dhanbad > Palamu ...(ii)

Bara Banki is bigger than Fatehpur

Bara Banki > Fatehpur ...(iii)

Bara Banki is not as big as Palamu

Palamu > Bara Banki ...(iv)

From Eqs. (i), (ii), (iii) and (iv), we get

Dhanbad > Palamu > Bara Banki > Fatehpur > Akbarpur

Thus, Dhanbad district is biggest among them.

Hence, option (c) is the correct.

26. (*b*) 1 2 3 4 5 6 7 8 9 10 11 12 13

5th from right

Hence, option (b) is correct.

27. (*c*) LCM of 16 and 18 = $2 \times 8 \times 9 = 144$ = 2 h 24 min

Both cuckoos will come out together again at

12:00 h + 2h + 24 min = 2:24 min = 2:24 pm

28. (*b*) According to Hari, his father's birthday may be on 14th or 15th June.

According to Hari's sister their father's birthday may be on 15th, 16th or 17th June.

Common Date ⇒ 15th June

29. (*b*) Today's is Friday + 2 i.e. Sunday.

Tomorrow will be Monday. The day after tomorrow will be Tuesday and two days after Tuesday will be Thursday.

30. (*d*) Ram was born in a leap year. Ram celebrated his birthday for the third time in 2004.

Ram celebrated his birthday for the second time in 2000.

Therefore, he was born in the year 1996.

31. (*a*) The Chairman of the Selection Committee arrived at 12 : 20 h.

Other members arrived at 12 : 40 h.

Since, other members were 30 min late.

So, the scheduled time of the meeting was 12:40−30 min

= 12:10 min

32. (*b*) Time after 6 h after mid night = 6 : 00 am

Clock will go slow in 6 h = $6 \times 5 = 30$ min

∴ Time shown by the clock = 6 : 00 − 0:30 min = 5:30 am

33. (*b*) The day before yesterday was Friday. Therefore, today is Sunday.

The day after tomorrow will be friday

∴ Tuesday + 3 = Friday

34. (*c*)

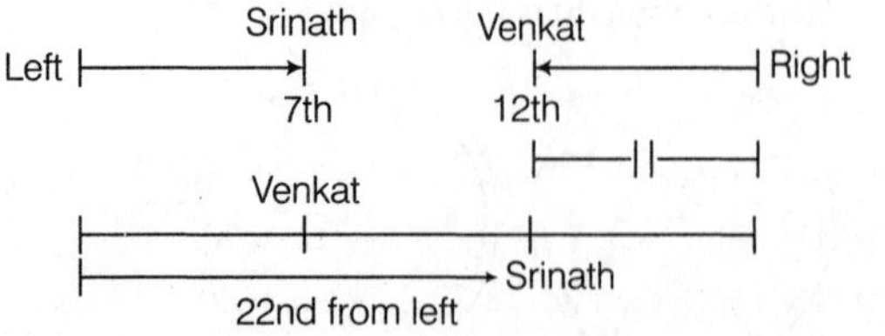

Left — Srinath 7th; Venkat 12th — Right

Venkat

Srinath

22nd from left

Total number of boys = 22 + 11 = 33

Hence, option (c) is correct.

35. (*c*) Let the number of boys be x. Then, number of girls = 2x.

∴ $x + 2x = 60$

⇒ $3x = 60$

⇒ $x = 20$

∴ Number of boys = 20 and number of girls = 40

Number of students behind Kamal in rank = (60 − 17) = 43

Number of girls ahead of Kamal in rank = 9

Number of girls behind Kamal in rank = 40 − 9 = 31

∴ Number of boys behind Kamal in rank = 43 − 31 = 12

36. (*d*) According to Sanbgeeta, the father's birthday falls on one of the days among 9th, 10th, 11th and 12th December. According to Natasha, the father's birthday falls on one of the day among 10th, 11th, 12th and 13th December. The days common to both the groups are 10th, 11th and 12th December. So, the father's birthday falls on any one of these days.

37. (*d*) Clearly, the last train left two and a half hours before 18:00 h i.e. at 15:30 h. But this happened 40 min before the announcement was made. So, the announcement was made at 16:10 h.

38. (*c*) Days according to Pratap – [20, 21 or 22] in April

Days according to his sister-not on or after 22 April

Clearly, the answer is [20 or 21] April

39. (*b*) Days according to Mohan, [17th, 18th or 19th] January.

Days according to sister, [19th, 20th, 21st or 22nd] January.

Required day is 19th January as it is common in both the groups.

40. (*d*) Rama scored more than Rani

Rama > Rani ...(i)

Rani scored less than Ratna

Ratna > Rani ...(ii)

Ratna scored more than Rama

Ratna > Rama ...(iii)

Padma scored more than Rama but less than Ratna.

Ratna > Padma > Rama ...(iv)

From above Eqs. (i), (ii), (iii) and (iv), we get

Ratna > Padma > Rama > Rani

Hence, Ratna scored highest marks.

41. (*b*)

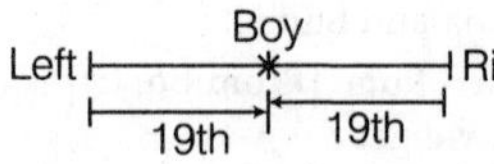

Boy

Left — Right

19th 19th

The boy is 19th from both the ends.

So, total number of boys in the row is

⇒ 18 + 18 + (1) boy

⇒ 36 + 1 = 37

There are 37 boys in the row.

Hence, option (b) is the correct.

42. (*d*) According to the given information the arrangement of boys will be like this

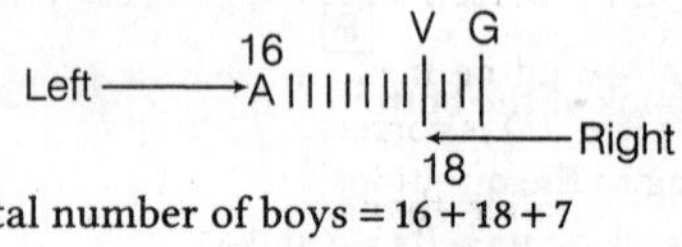

Left → 16 A | | | | | | | V | | G | ← Right 18

The total number of boys = 16 + 18 + 7

= 41

43. (*a*) We have, total 5 persons P, Q, R, S and T.

S > R and T ...(i)

P earns maximum

Q earns less than only P.

So, Q is second highest. ...(ii)

R earns less than Q.

Q > R ...(iii)

R → ₹ 50000

Q → ₹ 80000

From Eqs. (i), (ii) and (iii)

P > Q > S > R > T

Here, R is greater than T but less than S.

T earns 50000 so R earns more than T, so definitely R earns more than 40000.

Hence, option (a) is the correct.

44. (*c*) Given,

Siya > Priya >Tiya ...(i)

Siya > Riya >Priya ...(ii)

and Tiya > Riya > Diya ...(iii)

On combinning Eqs. (i), (ii) and (iii), we get

Siya > Riya > Priya > Tiya > Diya

Advanced Level

1. (*c*)

Front side ⊢—X—Y—⊣ Rear side; 14th from front to X, 17th from rear to Y

Total number of persons in queue = 48

Persons between X and Y = 48 − (14 + 17)

= 48 − 31 = 17

There are 17 persons between X and Y

Position of person in the middle of X and Y

$$= \left(\frac{17+1}{2}\right) = \frac{18}{2} = 9$$

So, Z is on 9th position between X and Y

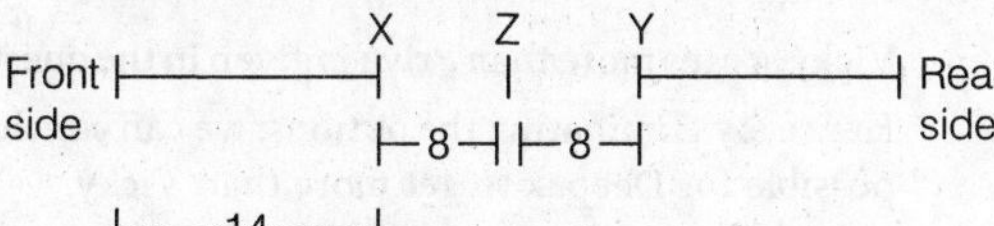

Now, position of Z from the front side or left

= 14 + 8 + 1 = 23 rd

Z is 23rd from the left side

There are 8 persons between X and Z.

Hence, option (c) is the correct.

Solution (Q. Nos. 2-5)

In this question two rankings- one related with height and other with figure of persons are given. On the basis of given information ranked in descending order as below

Height : B > C > A > E > D

Fat : B > A > D > C > E

2. (*d*) From the above, person E is the most thin person.

3. (*b*) B is the tallest person and possess the highest weight.

4. (*a*) Person A would be in the middle in order of the height. Hence, option (a) is correct.

5. (*c*) Person C is taller than A and E but thinner than the remaining two i.e. B and D.

Solution (Q. Nos. 6-10)

The order of age can be determined as following

B > E A > CE > A D > A

So, B > E > A > C and D > A

The order of height can be determined as following

C > B; C > (D,E)

A > D; E > D

6. (*a*) B is not the tallest as he is shorter than C.

B and E are shorter than C but is not known that B is shorter than E or not. So, II is not correct.

The definite order of height is not determined. So, Statement III is not correct. Only Statement I is correct.

7. (*e*) As the definite order of height is not determined, so it cannot be determined that how many persons will be between F and E.

8. (*b*) A and C are youngest. D is the shortest.

E is younger than B.

So, B should be selected as he is relatively older and also taller.

9. (*e*) Either B or D is the oldest.

10. (*e*) As the definite order of age is not determined, so it cannot be determined that who are older to D.

Solution (Q. Nos. 11-14)

According to given information, the order of sweetness is

Z > U > V > Y > X > W

and order of health is as following

X > Y > U > W > Z > V

11. (*d*) Z is the sweetest essence.

12. (*d*) U and Z are both sweeter and healthier than V.

13. (*a*) U is sweeter than Y and healtheir than W.

14. (*b*) V is the least healthy essence.

Solution (Q. Nos. 15-18)

If we arrange them in descending order or height, then tallest will be given number 1 while shortest will be given number 7.

So, A may be at number 1, 2 or 3 ...(i)
F may be at number 5, 6, 7 ...(ii)
C is immediately placed before B ...(iii)

15. (*b*) Options (a) and (d) are not correct because of the (iii) conclusion. Option (e) is not correct as A cannot be at number 5 one. Option (c) is not correct because D cannot be at number 1 or 7.

16. (*d*) If G, D and A are in descending order of height, then they should be placed at top positions.

Then, E will be at number 7.

C and B will be at number 4 and 5 respectively because F can be at only 6.

So, B will be 5th tallest.

17. (*c*) If C is at number 1, then B will at number 2 and A at number 3.E will be at number 7, F should be at 5 or 6. So, the middle position number 4 will go for D.

18. (*e*) If F is second shortest then he should be at number 6. So, C cannot be at number 5 because, if he is at number 5, then B must be at number 6 which is already given to F.

19. (*d*) Out of all the given options, only the ranking given in (d) satisfies the given conditions.

B-12000 (A won less money than B)
A-10000
E-8000 (E won ₹ 8000 prize)
D-6000
C-4000 and the difference between winning of C and F was ₹ 2000.
F-2000 and the difference between winning of D and F was atleast ₹4000.

20. (*c*) The gap between two buses is 40 min.

Next bus leave at 10:45

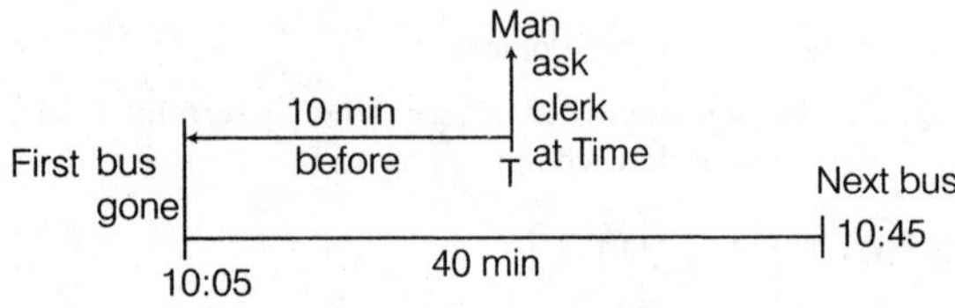

Man came 10 min after the bus gone and the gap between two buses is 40 min.

So, the time at which the first bus gone is 10:05 am.

Man came after 10 min, so 10:05 + 10 min = 10:15

Therefore, man came at 10:15 am.

Hence, option (c) is correct.

21. (*d*) What Sushma could see is the mirror image of clock and time seen is 4:40. It will resemble to time 8:20, hence Sushma is 1 h late.

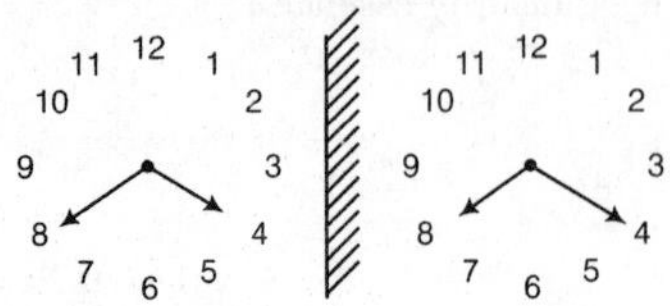

22. (*d*) The question states that Sunil is ranked 6th and Ankit is ranked 5th.

Thus, Raman is ranked 1st and Tony is ranked 7th.

So, the following situations are possible for ranks 2,3 and 4.

2 – Vicky, 3 – Priya, 4 – Deepak
or 2 – Vicky, 3 – Deepak, 4 – Priya
or 2 – Deepak, 3 – Vicky, 4 – Priya

Vicky can never be 1st, Raman will never be 2nd or 3rd, Tony is ranked 7th and hence cannot be 4th or 5th.

Deepak can be 3rd or 4th according to the above obtained conditions.

23. (*c*) If Raman gets the highest, he will be ranked 1st. Accordingly, Tony will be ranked 7th.

New, Priya and Ankit are always ranked numerically higher than Vicky.

Hence, Vicky can never be ranked lower than 4th as if he is ranked 5th, then there will not be enough positions to accommodate both Ankit and Priya.

24. (*d*) The question states that Ankit's rank is 1st.

This is not possible because he always scores less than Vicky and Priya.

25. (*a*) If Sunil's rank is 2nd, then Raman's rank is 1st and Tony's rank is 7th.

Vicky's lowest numerical rank will be 3rd, so he will always get less than Sunil.

Raman is ranked 1st so Priya will always get less than Raman.

Vicky scores more than Priya is given in the question data.

Hence, by eliminating the options, we can conclude that it is possible for Deepak to get more than Vicky.

26. (*a*) If Vicky's rank is 5th, then Priya's rank is 6th and Ankit's rank is 7th. Hence, Sunil's rank is highest or Sunil scores the highest.

Solution (Q. Nos. 27-31)

Total number of students = 7

Pradeep scores less than Vikas always.

Vikas > Pradeep

Qadir always scores less than Vikas

Vikas > Qadir

Condition

I. Either Rohit or Sushant scores highest in each test.
II. If Rohit scores the highest, then Tushar gets the least.
III. If Sushant scores the highest then either Uday or Qadir scores the least.

27. (*a*) If Sushant is ranked second then Rohit ranks first and Tushar gets the least. Now, Pradeep always scores less then Vikas and Qadir always scores less than Pradeep.

So, the rank of Vikas will be higher than fifth and also Pradeep can be at third. Now, it is clear that Uday gets more than Vikas.

28. (*d*) If Sushant is ranked sixth then Rohit is ranked first and Tushar ranked least. Now, Vikas scores more than Pradeep and Pradeep scores more than Qadir and the rank of Qadir is fifth. So, only the option (d) can be true i.e. Uday is ranked third or fourth.

29. (*c*) If Rohit gets the highest then Tushar gets the least. Now, the position of Sushant and Uday is not given in statements III and IV, so it is clear that the rank of Vikas should not be lower than fourth.

30. (*b*) If Rohit is ranked second then Sushant is ranked first and Qadir is ranked fifth then Uday is ranked seventh. Now, according to the statements III and IV the ranks of Vikas and Pradeep are third and fourth, respectively.

31. (*d*) If Rohit is ranked second, then Sushant is ranked first and Qadir is ranked fifth, then Uday is ranked seventh. Now, Tushar is ranked sixth according to the given statements.

Solution (Q. Nos. 32-34)

P is taller than only three poles.

S is taller than T but shorter than U.

$S > T$

$U > S$ ...(i)

U is shorter than P.

$P > U$ ...(ii)

Q is not the tallest

From the above Eqs. (i) and (ii), we get

$P > U > S > T$

We have total six poles and out of which Q is not the tallest, so R is the tallest pole.

$R > Q > P > U > S > T$

Here, P is taller than U, S and T only.

$R > Q > P > U > S > T$

1 2 3 4 5 6

So, S is second shortest pole, so S = 2 ft

and P is the third tallest pole, so P = 5 ft.

32. (*d*) Pole U is greater than pole S and pole U is less than pole P.

So, height of pole U is between 'S' an 'P'

$$U = \frac{S+P}{2} = \frac{2\text{ ft} + 5\text{ ft}}{2} = \frac{7}{2} = 3.5\text{ ft} \approx 3\text{ ft}$$

Hence, (U = 3 ft) option (c) is correct.

33. (*b*) Height of S = 2 ft

Tallest pole R is 11 ft taller than pole S.

So, height of pole R = 2 + 11 = 13 ft

Pole Q is less than pole R and greater than pole P.

Thus, height of pole $Q = \frac{R+P}{2}$

$$= \frac{13+5}{2} = \frac{18}{2} = 9\text{ ft}$$

Pole Q = 9 ft

Hence, option (b) is correct.

34. (*e*) In the above arrangement

$R > Q > P > U > S > T$

So, T is the shortest pole.

Hence, option (e) is correct.

4

Blood Relations

*Questions on **Blood Relations** involve analysis of certain blood relations and then inferring on the basis of the given informations. In the questions, a chain of relationships is given in the form of information and on the basis of which, relation between any two members of the chain is asked.*

A candidate's skill in solving the questions on blood relations depends upon his/her knowledge of blood relationships. The candidate should be able to find out a relationship between two people from the information given in the question. If the data given in the question is tabulated, it is very easy to find out the relationship between two people.

Some of the Common Relationships Given Below will Help You in Solving the Questions

- Mother's or Father's son → Brother
- Mother's or Father's daughter → Sister
- Mother's or Father's brother → Uncle
- Mother's or Father's sister → Aunt
- Mother's or Father's father → Grandfather
- Mother's or Father's mother → Grandmother
- Daughter's or Son's son → Grandson
- Daughter's or Son's daughter → Granddaughter
- Sister's or Brother's son → Nephew
- Sister's or Brother's daughter → Niece
- Aunt's or Uncle's son or daughter → Cousin
- Daughter's husband → Son-in-law
- Son's wife → Daughter-in-law
- Sister's husband → Brother-in-law
- Husband's or Wife's brother → Brother-in-law
- Brother's wife → Sister-in-law
- Husband's or Wife's sister → Sister-in-law
- Children of same parents → Siblings
- Husband or Wife's father → Father-in-law
- Husband's or Wife's mother → Mother-in-law

➘ Remember the word **'Spouse'**, which can be used for **'Husband'** or **'Wife'**.

Relationships from mother's side are prefixed by '**Maternal**' while relationships from father's side are prefixed by '**Paternal**'.

Additional Relationships

• Grandson's or granddaughter's daughter or son	Great granddaughter or son
• Paternal grandmother's or grandfather's only son	Father
• Paternal grandmother's or grandfather's only daughter-in-law	Mother
• Maternal grandmother's or grandfather's only daughter	Mother
• Maternal grandmother's or grandfather's only son-in-law	Father
• Paternal aunt's or uncle's only brother	Father
• Maternal aunt's or uncle's only sister	Mother

To develop blood relation some standard symbols are used to indicate the relationship among the family members.

S. No.	Symbolic instructions	Meaning
1.	□ or +	Male
2.	○ or –	Female
3.	□←→○	Husband-Wife
4.	○←→□	Wife-Husband
5.	□—□	Brother-Brother
6.	□—○	Brother-Sister
7.	○—○	Sister-Sister
8.	□ (above) │ □ (below)	Father-Son
9.	□ (above) │ ○ (below)	Father-Daughter
10.	○ (above) │ □ (below)	Mother-Son
11.	○ (above) │ ○ (below)	Mother-Daughter

Expert's Advice

The easiest and non-confusing way to solve these problems would be to draw a **family tree** and increase the levels of hierarchy according to the relation.
The above stages are made from the point of view of an individual person.

Relations from One Generation to Next

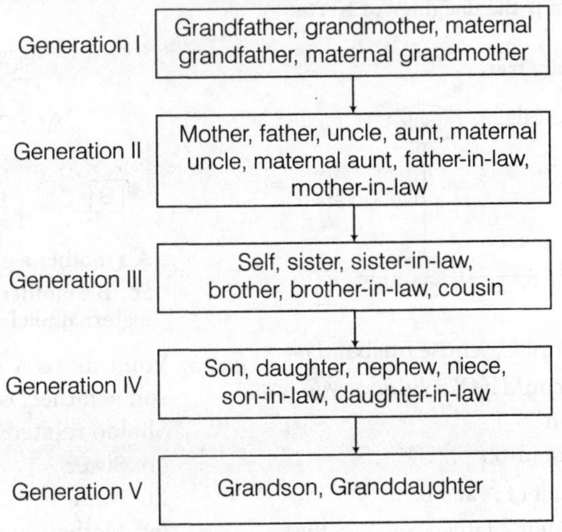

Types of Questions Generally Asked in Examinations

There are multiple types of questions which are asked from the chapter 'Blood Relations', so it is quite difficult to predict exact type of questions that are asked, but on the basis of **Observation, Analysis** and **Experience,** here we are giving different types of questions that are usually asked in the examination. Almost all the questions of this chapter can be categorised into these types. Also, this description of type will make your study easy and streamlined.

Type 1 Direct Information Based

In this type of questions, relationship between two people is given through a round about route of relating them through other people. The relationship can be in the form of a statement made by a person. Candidates have to go through the series of relationships and finally determine the relationship between the two people in the question.

Examples Based on Type 1

Ex 1. Introducing Asha to guests, Bhaskar said, "Her father is the only son of my father". How is Asha related to Bhaskar?
SSC (Multitasking) 2014

(a) Niece (b) Granddaughter
(c) Mother (d) Daughter

Sol. (*d*)

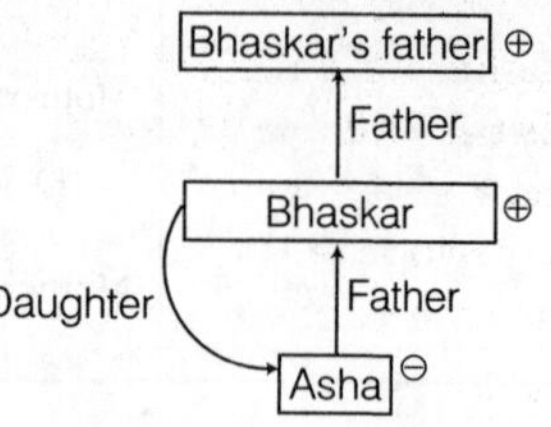

Only son of Bhaskar's father is Bhaskar himself. Therefore, Asha's father is Bhaskar. Hence, Asha is the daughter of Bhaskar.

Ex 2. Reeta has a son, named Arun. Ram is Reeta's brother. Neeta has a daughter, named Reena. Neeta is Ram's sister. How is Arun related to Reena?

(a) Brother (b) Nephew (c) Cousin (d) Father

Sol. (*c*) Reeta and Neeta are the sisters of Ram. So, they both are sisters. Arun is the son of Reeta while Reena is the daughter of Neeta. Hence, Arun and Reena are cousin.

This can be shown by following family tree.

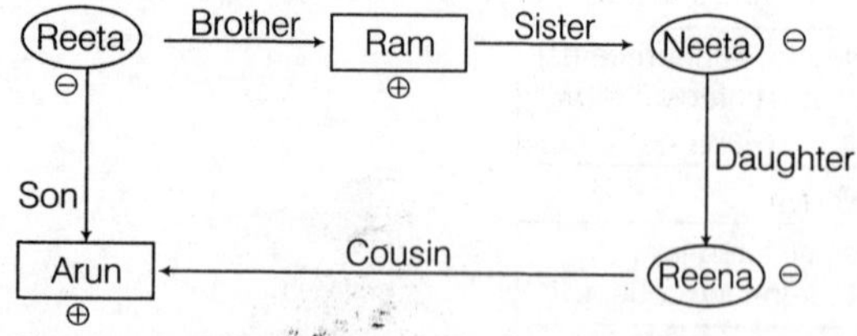

Ex 3. A's father has a son B who has an aunt C, whose husband is X. Y is the father-in-law of X. How could be Y related to A?

(a) Grandfather (b) Son
(c) Uncle (d) Grandson

Sol. (*a*) B is the brother of A. So, C is the aunt of A and B.

Aunt's husband's father-in-law is Aunt's father. So, Y is the father of C.

So, Y is the grandfather of A.

This can be shown by following family tree.

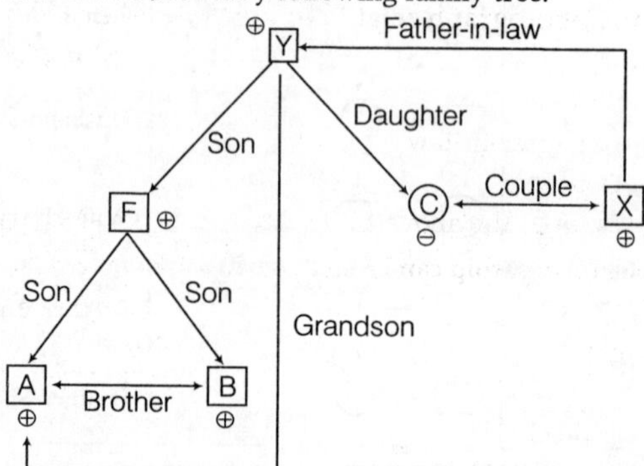

Ex 4. If B says that his mother is the only daughter of A's mother, then what is the relation of A with B? **UPPSC 2014**

(a) Son
(b) Father
(c) Uncle
(d) Brother

Sol. (*c*)

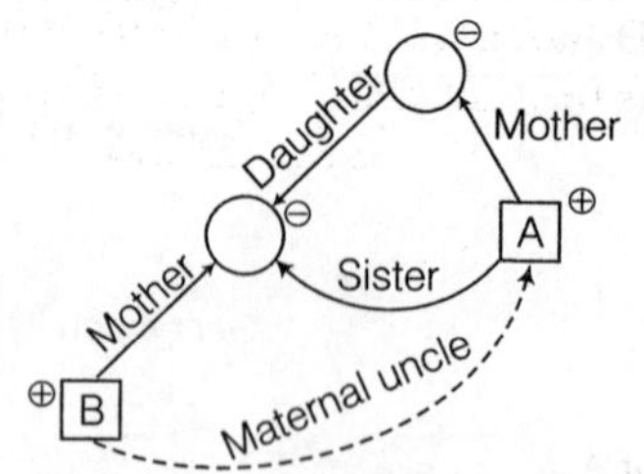

A's mother's only daughter is B's mother.

So, B's mother and A are brother and sister. Therefore, A is the maternal uncle of B.

Ex 5. Pointing to a lady in the photograph, Shaloo said, "Her son's father is the son-in-law of my mother". How is Shaloo related to the lady?

(a) Sister
(b) Aunt
(c) Mother
(d) Cousin

Sol. (*a*) Lady's son's father means lady's husband who is son-in-law of my mother means Shaloo's brother-in-law. So, the lady in the photograph is sister of Shaloo.

This can be shown by following family tree.

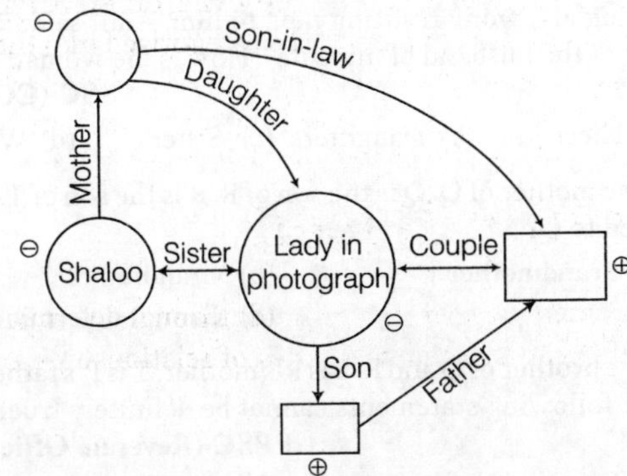

Ex 6. Pointing towards a photograph, Ram said, "She is the mother of my brother's son's wife's sister". How is the lady in the photograph related to Ram's brother's son?

SSC (CPO) 2012

(a) Sister
(b) Daughter-in-law
(c) Daughter
(d) None of the above

Sol. (*d*) The relationship can be shown by following family tree.

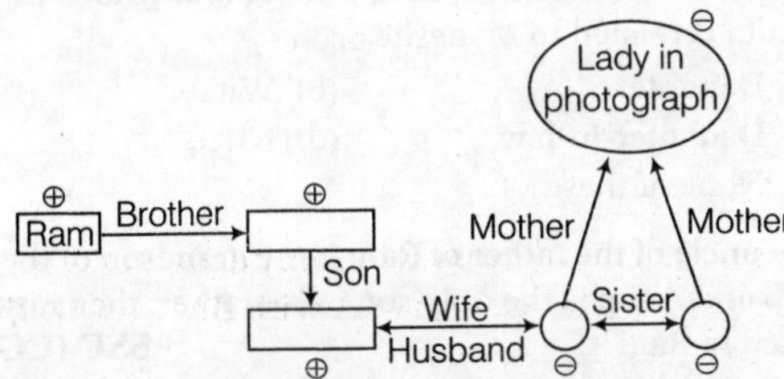

The lady in the photograph is the mother-in-law of Ram's brother's son and she is also the mother of Ram's brother's son's wife.

Ex 7. A is the mother of D and sister of B. B has a daughter C who is married to F. G is the husband of A. How is G related to D?

SSC (DEO & LDC) 2012

(a) Uncle
(b) Husband
(c) Son
(d) Father

Sol. (*d*) G is the husband of A.

A is the mother of D.

Hence, G is the father of D.

This can be shown by following family tree.

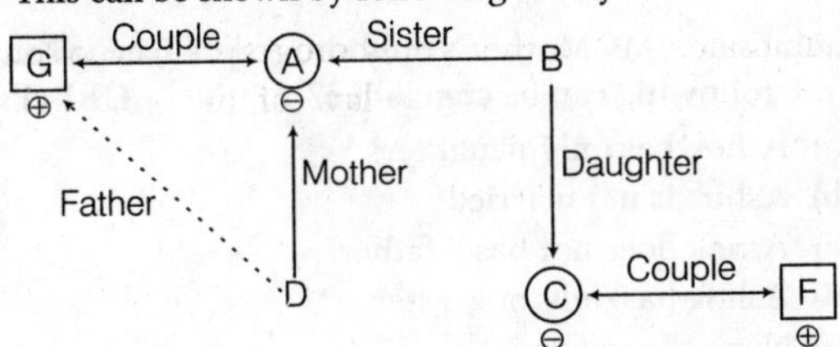

Ex 8. Nandani is the only daughter of Madan's sister Sangita's brother. How is Nandani related to Madan?

(a) Daughter
(b) Niece
(c) Cousin
(d) Niece/Daughter

Sol. (*d*) Madan is the brother of Sangita. If Sangita has only one brother Madan, Nandani is the daughter of Madan.

If Sangita has more than one brothers and Nandani is the daughter of Sangita's brother who is not Madan, Nandani is the niece of Madan.

So, Nandani is the daughter or niece of Madan.

This can be shown by following family tree.

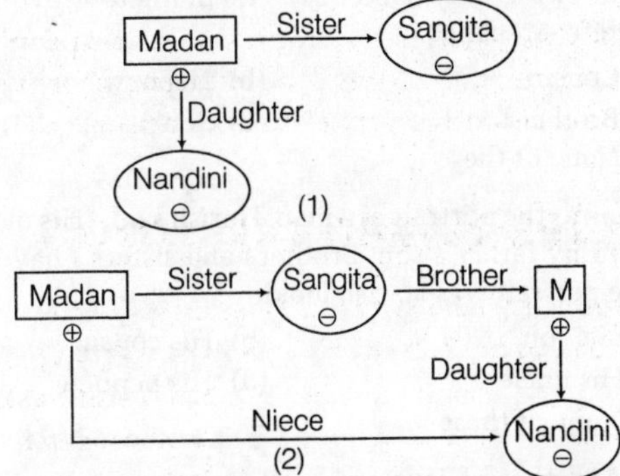

Ex 9. A, Q, Y and Z are different persons. Z is the father of Q, A is the daughter of Y and Y is the son of Z. If P is the son of Y and B is the brother of P, then **CGPSC 2011**

(a) B and Y are brothers
(b) A is the sister of B
(c) Z is the uncle of B
(d) Q and Y are brothers
(e) None of these

Sol. (*b*)

It is clear that A is the daughter of Y and P is the son of Y.

P and B are brothers, so B is also the brother of A.

In other words A is the sister of B.

Ex 10. Facing a man in the eye, Vasudev said, "Your son is my son's uncle". How is the man related to Vasdudev?

(a) Brother
(b) Father
(c) Grandfather
(d) Uncle
(e) None of these

Sol. (*b*)

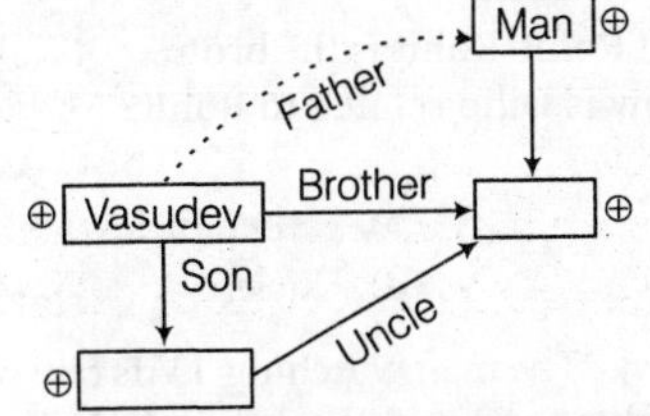

Vasudev's son's uncle → Vasudev's brother

The uncle of Vasudev's son is the brother of Vasudev.

Vasudev's brother's father is also Vasudev's father. So, it is clear from above that the man is the Vasudev's father.

Intro Exercise 1 (Based on Type 1)

1. If Kamal says, "Ravi's mother is the only daughter of my mother". How is Kamal related to Ravi?
   (a) Grandfather (b) Father
   (c) Brother (d) Cannot be determined
   (e) None of these

2. Pointing towards a man in the photograph, Archana said, "He is the son of the only son of my grandfather." How is that man related to Archana?
   (a) Cousin (b) Nephew
   (c) Brother (d) Son
   (e) None of these

3. Looking at the portrait of a man. Harish said, "His mother is the wife of my father's son. Brothers and sisters I have none". At whose portrait was Harish looking?
   (a) His son (b) His cousin
   (c) His uncle (d) His nephew
   (e) None of these

4. Mac is brother of Tina and brother-in-law of Tim. Sheron has two children and her son-in-law is Tim. Sheeba's grandmother is Sheron. Tina is Sheeba's aunt. Which of the following statements is true? **CMAT 2015**
   (a) Sheeba is daughter of Tim (b) Tina is Tim's sister-in-law
   (c) Sheeba is niece of Tim (d) Sheeba is niece of Mac

5. Sheela is Ravi's sister-in-law. Ram is Ravi's brother. Ram's wife is Sheela. Deepa is Ravi's sister. Deepa's mother is Shanthi. How is Sheela related to Shanthi? **SSC (LDC) 2012**
   (a) Mother-in-law (b) Daughter-in-law
   (c) Granddaughter (d) Daughter

6. Pointing to a gentleman, Deepak said, "His only brother is the father of my daughter's father." How is the gentleman related to Deepak?
   (a) Father (b) Grandfather
   (c) Brother-in-law (d) Uncle
   (e) None of these

7. Pointing to a lady Simon said, "She is the daughter of the only sister of my father." How is lady related to Simon? **SSC (10 + 2) 2013**
   (a) Mother (b) Aunt
   (c) Sister (d) Cousin

8. Tarun is the father of Rohit. Rohit is the brother of Kala. Kala is the wife of Dilip. How is Dilip related to Rohit? **SSC Asst. 2012**
   (a) Brother-in-law (b) Father-in-law
   (c) Son (d) Uncle

9. Sudeep said to Rajeev, "The man watching TV is one of the two brothers of the daughter of my father's wife". How the man watching TV is related to Sudeep? **NIFT (UG) 2015**
   (a) Brother (b) Brother-in-law
   (c) Cousin (d) Uncle

10. Looking at a woman sitting next to him, Amit said, "She is the sister of the husband of my wife". How is the woman related to Amit? **SSC (CGL) 2013**
    (a) Niece (b) Daughter (c) Sister (d) Wife

11. P is the mother of Q. Q is the son of R. R is the son of T. How is T related to Q?
    (a) Grandmother (b) Grandfather
    (c) Father (d) Cannot determined

12. P is the brother of Q and R. S is R's mother. T is P's father. Which of the following statements cannot be definitely true? **UPPSC (Revenue Officer) 2014**
    (a) T is Q's father (b) Q is T's husband
    (c) S is P's mother (d) T is S's husband

13. Pointing towards a woman in a photograph, Vijay said, "She is the daughter of the father of the sister of my brother." How is the lady in photograph related to Vijay?
    (a) Daughter (b) Wife
    (c) Mother (d) Grandmother
    (e) None of these

14. If Neha says, "Amruta's father Raj is the only son of my father-in-law Mahesh." Then, how Bindu, who is the sister of Amruta is related to Mahesh?
    (a) Daughter (b) Wife
    (c) Daughter-in-law (d) Niece
    (e) None of these

15. If the uncle of the father of Rani is the grandson of the father of Anup and Anup is the only son of his father, then how Anup is related to Rani? **SSC (CGL) 2015**
    (a) Grandfather (b) Uncle
    (c) Maternal Uncle (d) Great grandfather

16. Deepak said to Nitin, "That boy playing football is the younger of the two brothers of the daughter of my father's wife." How is the boy playing football related to Deepak?
    (a) Son (b) Brother
    (c) Cousin (d) Nephew
    (e) Brother-in-law

17. A girl introduced a boy as the son of the daughter of the father of her uncle. The boy is girl's **NICL (AO) 2013**
    (a) uncle
    (b) nephew
    (c) brother
    (d) son

18. Madhu said, "My Mother's only son Ashok has no son". Which of the following can be concluded? **CBI (PO) 2010**
    (a) Ashok has only daughters
    (b) Ashok is not married
    (c) Ashok does not has a father
    (d) Ashok has only one sister
    (e) None of the above

19. Arun said, "This girl is the wife of the grandson of my mother." How is Arun related to that girl?
(a) Father
(b) Grandfather
(c) Husband
(d) Father-in-law
(e) None of the above

20. A is the brother of B, B is the daughter of C and D is the father of A. Then, how is C related to D? **SSC (CGL) 2014**
(a) Husband
(b) Wife
(c) Granddaughter
(d) Grandfather

21. Pointing to a man in a photograph, a woman said, "His brother's father is the only son of my grandfather." How is the woman related to that man in the photograph?
(a) Mother
(b) Sister
(c) Aunt
(d) Daughter
(e) Grandmother

22. Rahul told Anand, "Yesterday I defeated the only brother of the daughter of my grandmother." Whom did Rahul defeat?
(a) Son
(b) Father
(c) Brother
(d) Father-in-law
(e) Cousin

23. Pinky, who is Victor's daughter, says to Lucy, "Your mother Rosy is the younger sister of my father, who is the third child of Joseph". How is Joseph related to Lucy? **CLAT 2014**
(a) Father-in-law
(b) Father
(c) Maternal uncle
(d) Grandfather

24. If 'A' and 'B' are brothers and 'C' is the sister of 'A', 'D' is the sister of 'E' while 'E' is the daughter of 'B'. Who is the uncle of 'D'? **MAT 2014**
(a) E (b) C
(c) A (d) B

25. Pointing out to lady, a girl said, "She is the daughter-in-law of the grandmother of my father's only son." How is the lady related to that girl?
(a) Sister-in-law
(b) Mother
(c) Aunt
(d) Mother-in-law
(e) Cousin

26. A is the brother of B. B is the brother of C. C is the husband of D. E is the father of A. D is related to E as **UGC NET 2014**
(a) daughter
(b) daughter-in-law
(c) sister-in-law
(d) sister

27. Pointing to the woman in the picture, Rajiv said, "Her mother has only one grandchild whose mother is my wife." How is the woman in the picture related to Rajiv?
(a) Cousin
(b) Wife
(c) Sister
(d) Data inadequate
(e) None of the above

28. A and B are brothers, C and D are sisters. A's son is D's brother. How is B related to C? **MAT 2014**
(a) Father
(b) Brother
(c) Grandfather
(d) Uncle

29. Pointing towards a man in the photograph, a lady said, "The father of his brother is the only son of my mother. How is the man related to that lady?
(a) Brother (b) Son
(c) Cousin (d) Grandson
(e) Nephew

30. A family consisted of a man, his wife, his three sons, their wives and three children in each son's family. How many members are there in the family? **SSC (10+2) 2014**
(a) 12 (b) 13
(c) 15 (d) 17

Type 2 Coded Information Based

In this type of questions, there are certain codes used to describe different relationships which are followed by a statement which relates people by using these codes. After analysing the codes, candidates have to find the relationship between the people.

Examples Based on Type 2

Ex 1. If 'P + Q' means 'P is the brother of Q', 'P × Q' means 'P is the mother of Q' and 'P ÷ Q' means 'P is the sister of Q', then which of the following would means 'R is the uncle of S'? **UPPSC (Revenue Officer) 2014**

(a) R× P+ S (b) R+ P× S (c) R× S+ S (d) R÷ P+ S

Sol. (*b*) In general, the best way of dealing with this type of questions is to take each answer choice and check out how the person given at the beginning of the statement is related to the person given at the end of the statement by going through the relationship with other persons given in between.

Here, take the option (a),

P + S means, P is the brother of S.

R × P means, R is the mother of P.

This can be represented as

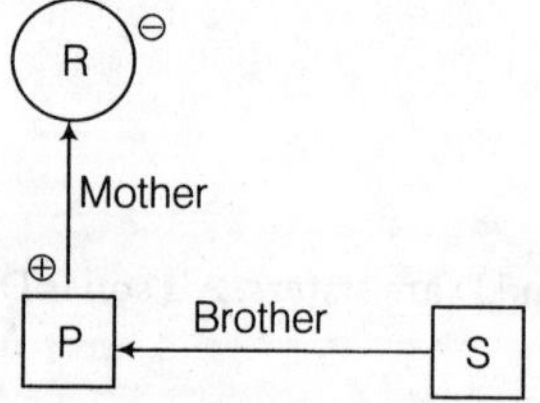

So, R is mother of P and S.

Now, take option (b),

P × S means, P is the mother of S.

R + P means, R is the brother of P.

This can be represented as

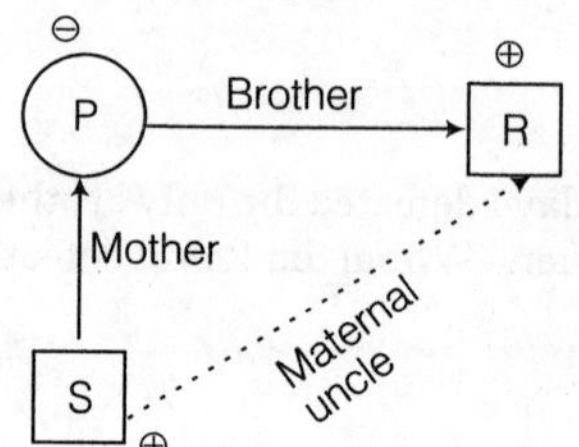

Hence, R is the uncle (maternal) of S.

Ex 2. If 'X + Y' means 'X is the daughter of Y'; 'X − Y' means 'X is the brother of Y'; 'X % Y' means 'X is the father of Y' and 'X × Y' means X is the sister of Y. Which of the following means 'I is the niece of J'?

(a) J − N % C × I (b) I × C − N % J (c) J + M × C % I (d) I × C + N − J

Sol. (*d*) Here, I × C → I is the sister of C, C + N → C is the daughter of N and N − J → N is the brother of J.

I is the daughter of J's brother N. Hence, I is niece of J.

This can be shown by following family tree.

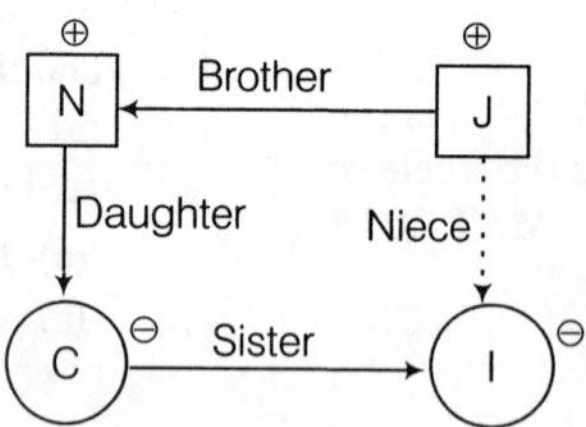

Here, gender of J is not define.

Intro Exercise 2 (Based on Type 2)

1. Read the given information and answer the following question.

(i) '$P + Q$' means 'P is the brother of Q'.
(ii) '$P \times Q$' means 'P is the mother of Q'.
(iii) '$P \div Q$' means 'P is the sister of Q'.

Which of hte following would mean R is the maternal uncle of S?

UPPSC (Revenue Officer) 2014

(a) $R \times P + S$ (b) $R + P \times S$
(c) $R \times S + P$ (d) $R \div P + S$

2. Read the given information and answer the following question.

(i) '$A + B$' means 'A is the sister of B'.
(ii) '$A - B$' means 'A is the brother of B'.
(iii) '$A \times B$' means 'A is the daughter of B'.

Which of the following shows the relation that E is the maternal uncle of D? **UPPSC (Revenue Officer) 2014**

(a) $D + F \times E$ (b) $D \times F + E$
(c) $D - F \times E$ (d) None of these

3. Read the information and answer the following question.

(i) '$X + Y$' means 'X is the mother of Y'.
(ii) '$X - Y$' means 'X is the brother of Y'.
(iii) '$X \% Y$' means 'X is the father of Y'.
(iv) '$X \times Y$' means 'X is the sister of Y'.

Which of the following shows P is the maternal uncle of Q?

SNAP 2014

(a) $Q - N + M \times P$ (b) $P + S \times N - Q$
(c) $P - M + N \times Q$ (d) $Q - S \% P$

Direction (Q. Nos. 4-7) *Following questions are based on the information given below.* **UII (AO) 2013**

(i) '$P \times Q$' means 'P is father of Q'.
(ii) '$P - Q$' means 'P is sister of Q'.
(iii) '$P + Q$' means 'P is the mother Q'.
(iv) '$P \div Q$' means 'P is brother of Q'.

4. In the expression $B + D \times M \div N$, how is M related to B?

(a) Grandfather
(b) Son
(c) Grandson
(d) Granddaughter or Grandson
(e) None of the above

5. Which of the follwing represents J is son of F?

(a) $J \div R - T \times F$ (b) $J + R - T \times F$
(c) $J \div M - N \times F$ (d) Cannot be determined
(e) None of these

6. Which of the following represents R is niece of M?

(a) $M \div K \times T - R$
(b) $M - J + R - N$
(c) $R - M \times T \div W$
(d) Cannot be determined
(e) None of the above

7. If $P - R \times Q$, which of the following statements is true?

(a) P is the sister of Q
(b) Q is the husband of P
(c) P is the sister-in-law of Q
(d) Q is the son of P
(e) None of the above

Direction (Q. Nos. 8-9) *Read the following information carefully and answer the questions that follow.* **NIACL (AO) 2015**

(i) If '$A \times B$' means 'A is the son of B'.
(ii) If '$A + B$' means 'A is the father of B'.
(iii) If '$A > B$' means 'A is the daughter of B'.
(iv) If '$A < B$' means 'A is the wife of B'.

8. Which of the following pairs of people represent first cousin with regard to the relations given in the expressions, if it is provided that A is the sister of J : '$L > V < J + P$' and '$S \times A < D + F < E + K$'?

(a) LP (b) SP
(c) SK (d) SF
(e) Cannot be determined

9. What will come in the place of the question mark (?), if it is provided that M is the grandmother of F in the expression '$F \times R < S ? M$'?

(a) $>$ (b) $<$
(c) $+$ (d) $\times$
(e) Cannot be determined

Direction (Q. Nos. 10-11) *Read the following information carefully and answer the questions that follow.* **IBPS (PO) 2011**

(i) If '$A \times B$' means 'A is son of B'.
(ii) If '$A + B$' means 'A is daughter of B.
(iii) If '$A \div B$' means 'A is wife of B'.
(iv) If '$A - B$' means 'A is father of B'.

10. What will come in the place of the question mark (?) to establish that Q is mother of N in the expression '$N + O - P ? Q$'?

(a) $+$
(b) $\times$
(c) $-$
(d) $\div$
(e) Either (a) or (b)

11. Which of the following relations are true based upon the relations given in the equation '$S \div T \times V - W + Y$'?

(a) T is brother of Y
(b) S is daughter-in-law of W
(c) S is daughter-in-law of Y
(d) Y is daughter of V
(e) None of the above

Direction (Q. Nos. 12-13) *Study the following information carefully and answer the questions given below.*

(i) 'P+Q' means 'P is father of Q.
(ii) 'P−Q' means 'P is mother of Q.
(iii) 'P×Q' means 'P is brother of Q.
(iv) 'P÷Q' means 'P is sister of Q.

12. Which of the following means 'M is niece of N'?
(a) M×R−N (b) N÷J+M÷D
(c) N÷J+M (d) N×J−M

13. How is M related to K in the expression 'B+K÷T×M'?
(a) Son (b) Daughter
(c) Son or daughter (d) Data inadequate

Direction (Q. Nos. 14-17) *Read the following information carefully and answer the questions that follow.*

(i) 'A + B' means 'A is son of B'.
(ii) 'A− B' means 'A is wife of B'.
(iii) 'A× B' means 'A is brother of B'.
(iv) 'A÷ B' means 'A is mother of B'.
(v) 'A= B' means 'A is the sister of B'.

14. What does P + R − Q mean?
(a) Q is the father of P (b) Q is the son of P
(c) Q is the uncle of P (d) Q is the brother of P

15. What does P×R÷Q mean?
(a) P is the brother of R (b) P is the father of Q
(c) P is the uncle of Q (d) P is the nephew of Q

16. What does P = R + Q mean?
(a) P is the aunt of Q (b) P is the daughter of Q
(c) P is the niece of Q (d) P is the sister of Q

17. What does P = R ÷ Q mean?
(a) P is the aunt of Q (b) P is the sister of Q
(c) Q is the niece of P (d) Q is the daughter of P

Direction (Q. Nos. 18-19) *Study the following information carefully and answer the questions that follow.* **Bank of India (PO) 2010**

(i) 'P×Q' means 'P is the mother of Q'.
(ii) 'P+Q' means 'P is the sister of Q'.
(iii) 'P÷Q' means 'P is the father of Q'.
(iv) 'P−Q' means 'P is the brother of Q'.

18. Which of the following means 'M is niece of R'?
(a) M − T÷J − R (b) R − T+M − K
(c) M − T÷J×R (d) R + T÷M + K
(e) None of these

19. Which of the following means 'J is paternal grandfather of W'?
(a) W÷T÷J (b) J÷T×W
(c) J×T×W (d) J×T÷W
(e) None of these

20. If 'P + Q' means 'P is the husband of Q'; 'P÷Q' means 'P is the sister of Q' and 'P×Q' means 'P is the son of Q', which of the following shows 'A is the daughter of B'?
(a) C×B÷A (b) B+C×A
(c) A÷D×B (d) None of these

21. If 'X+Y' means 'X is the mother Y' 'X−Y' means 'X is the brother of Y' 'X % Y' means 'X is the father of Y' and 'X×Y' means 'X is the sister of Y', then which of the following shows that 'P is the maternal uncle of Q'?
(a) Q−N+M×P (b) P+S×N−Q
(c) P−M+N×Q (d) None of these

22. 'S×T' means 'S is the mother of T', 'S + T' means 'S is the father of T', 'S−T' means 'S is the sister of T'. On the basis of this information, you have to select the option which shown that 'A is the grandfather of T'? **CMAT 2013**
(a) A + S + B − T (b) A× B + C − T
(c) A + B − C×T (d) A − C + B×T

Direction (Q. Nos. 23-27) *Read the following information carefully and answer the questions that follows.* **SBI & SBI Associates (Clerk) 2001, 2011**

(i) If 'P * Q' means 'P is the mother of Q'.
(ii) If 'P× Q' means 'P is the father of Q'.
(iii) If 'P+ Q' means 'P is the sister of Q'.
(iv) If 'P− Q' means 'P is the brother of Q'.
(v) If 'P> Q' means 'P is the son of Q'.
(vi) If 'P<Q' means 'P is the daughter of Q'.

23. In the expression 'A×B+R>S', how is S related to A?
(a) Daughter-in-law (b) Daughter
(c) Wife (d) Sister
(e) Cannot be determined

24. In the expression 'P+Q>A − B', how is P related to B?
(a) Daughter (b) Son
(c) Niece (d) Nephew
(e) Cannot be determined

25. In the expression 'W>X<Y * Z', how is W related to Z?
(a) Nephew (b) Uncle
(c) Son (d) Brother-in-law
(e) None of these

26. Which of the following means 'P is the father of S'?
(a) P×Q<R * S
(b) R×P<Q− S
(c) R+ S>Q+ P
(d) S+Q− R * P
(e) Cannot be determined

27. Which of the following means 'D is the aunt of C'?
(a) D>B * A * C
(b) D+ B− C * A
(c) D− B− A×C
(d) D+ B× A×C
(e) None of the above

Type 3 Hierarchical Structure Based

In this type of questions, candidates have to deal with hierarchical structure of a family which starts from grandparents and ends with grandchildren.

Expert's Advice To solve Hierarchical Structure Based questions, candidates are advised to establish the relationship within the family by drawing a family tree. It is not necessary that you should use symbols while solving the questions. You can make your own notations according to your own convenience.

Examples Based on Type 3

Direction (Examples 1-3) *Study the following information and answer the given questions.*

M is the mother of B. A is the father of N. N is the only brother of B. C is married to N. Q is the only child of C. N does not have any sister. J is the father of A.

SBI Associate (PO) 2014

***Ex* 1.** If A does not have any grandson, then how is Q related to B?

(a) Nephew (b) Sister-in-law
(c) Daughter-in-law (d) Niece
(e) Cannot be determined

***Ex* 2.** How is A related to C?

(a) Uncle
(b) Brother-in-law
(c) Father-in-law
(d) Nephew
(e) Cannot be determined

***Ex* 3.** How is B related to J?

(a) Father
(b) Nephew
(c) Brother-in-law
(d) Brother
(e) Grandson

SOLUTION (Examples 1-3) From the given information we can draw a family tree.

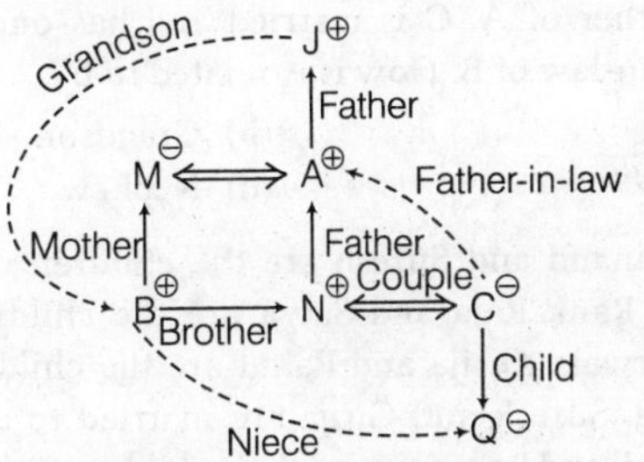

1. (*d*) If A does not have any grandson. So, we assume that Q is a baby girl. So, from above relation diagram it is clear that Q is the niece of B.
2. (*c*) From above relation diagram it is clear that, A is father-in-law of C.
3. (*e*) From above relation diagram it is clear that, B is grandson of J.

Intro Exercise 3 (Based on Type 3)

Direction (Q. Nos. 1-5) *Read the following information carefully and answer the questions given below it.*

In a family, there are six members A, B, C, D, E and F. A and B are a married couple, A being the male member. D is the only son of C, who is the brother of A. E is the sister of D. B is the daughter-in-law of F whose husband has died.

1. How is F related to A?

(a) Mother (b) Sister-in-law
(c) Sister (d) Mother-in-law
(e) None of these

2. How is E related to C?

(a) Sister (b) Daughter (c) Cousin (d) Aunt
(e) Mother

3. Who is C to B?

(a) Brother
(b) Brother-in-law
(c) Nephew
(d) Son-in-law
(e) None of the above

4. How many male members are three in the family?

(a) One (b) Two (c) Three (d) Four
(e) Five

5. How is F related to C?

(a) Mother-in-law
(b) Sister-in-law
(c) Mother
(d) Aunt
(e) Sister

Direction (Q. Nos. 6-8) *Read the following information carefully and answer the questions that follow.*

A, B and D meet their relations, C, E, F and G while visiting the trade fair. A is the brother of B and D is the father of A. F is the only son of C and E. E, who is the brother-in-law of G, is the father-in-law of B. **FMS 2009**

6. How many female members are there?
(a) 2 (b) 3 (c) 4 (d) 2 or 3

7. How is G related to A?
(a) Uncle
(b) Father-in-law
(c) Mother-in-law
(d) Cannot be determined

8. Who is the spouse of F?
(a) B (b) E (c) C (d) G

9. Mr A meets Mrs B. B is the mother of a son C and a daughter D. E is the mother of A. C is married and has one son, E is the daughter-in-law of B. How is A related to B? **UPPSC 2014**
(a) Uncle (b) Grandson
(c) Son (d) Nephew

10. Sita, Ramanand and Suresh are the children of Mr and Mrs Malhotra. Rani, Raja and Satya are the children of Mr and Mrs Aggarwals. Girija and Rahul are the children of Mr and Mrs Gupta. Suresh and Girija are married to each other and Rajni, Sushil and Ramayan are their children. Sita and Satya are also married to each other and Prem and Amar are their children. How is Suresh related to Rahul? **MAT 2014**
(a) Brother
(b) Cousin
(c) Uncle
(d) Brother-in-law

11. Javed's brother's sister's father's brother is Karim and Karim's daughter is Dolly. How is Javed related to Dolly?
UPPSC (Revenue Officer) 2014
(a) Brother (b) Cousin
(c) Sister (d) Uncle

Direction (Q. Nos. 12-13) *Read the following information carefully and answer the questions given below.* **UPPSC 2014**

There are six children playing football. These are A, B, C, D, E and F. A and E are brothers. F is the sister of E. C is the only son of A's uncle. B and D are the daughters of the brother of C's father?

12. How is C related to F?
(a) Cousin
(b) Brother
(c) Son
(d) Uncle

13. How many of the above football players are male?
(a) One (b) Two
(c) Three (d) Four

Direction (Q. Nos. 14-18) *These questions are based on the following data.*

All the six members of a family A, B, C, D, E and F are travelling together. B is the son of C but C is not the mother of B. A and C are a married couple. E is the brother of C. D is the daughter of A. F is the brother of B.

14. How many male members are there in the family?
(a) 1 (b) 2 (c) 3 (d) 4

15. Who is the mother of B?
(a) D (b) F (c) E (d) A

16. How many children does A have?
(a) One (b) Two (c) Three (d) Four

17. Who is the wife of E?
(a) A (b) F
(c) B (d) Cannot be determined

18. Which of the following is a pair of females?
(a) AE (b) BD (c) DF (d) AD

Direction (Q. Nos. 19-22) *These questions are based on the following data.*

Amit goes to the house of his sister Seema who is the neighbour of Gunjan. Gunjan has a daughter Meena. Meena studies in the first year of college. Anshu is the father of Amit and is married to Arti and has a sister who is Gunjan.

19. How is Gunjan related to Amit?
(a) Aunt (b) Mother (c) Cousin (d) Sister

20. How is Gunjan related to Arti?
(a) Sister (b) Sister-in-law
(c) Aunt (d) Mother

21. How is Meena related to Amit?
(a) Niece (b) Cousin (c) Uncle (d) Brother

22. How is Anshu related to Seema?
(a) Brother (b) Uncle (c) Cousin (d) Father

Direction (Q. Nos. 23-26) *Read the following information carefully to answer the questions that follow.*

There are six children taking part in an essay competition, namely A, B, C, D, E and F. A and E are brother. F and D are the sisters of E. C is the only son of A's uncle. B and D are the daughter of the brother of C's father. **MAT 2013**

23. How is D related to A?
(a) Uncle (b) Sister (c) Niece (d) Cousin

24. How many male competitors are there?
(a) 6 (b) 5 (c) 4 (d) 3

25. How many female competitors are there?
(a) 5 (b) 4 (c) 3 (d) 2

26. How is C related to F?
(a) Cousin (b) Brother
(c) Son (d) Uncle

Cumulative Exercise

Base Level

1. Pointing to a person, a man said to a women, "His mother is the only daughter of your father." How is the woman related to that person? **NCHMCT 2014**
(a) Wife (b) Daughter
(c) Sister (d) Mother

2. P's father Q is B's paternal uncle and A's husband M is P's paternal uncle. How is A related to B? **SBI (Clerk) 2014**
(a) Mother
(b) Sister
(c) Cousin
(d) Daughter
(e) None of the above

3. Introducing a man to her husband, a woman said, "His brother's father is the only son of my grandfather." How is the woman related to the man? **SBI (Clerk) 2014**
(a) Mother-in-law (b) Sister
(c) Daughter (d) Sister-in-law
(e) None of these

Direction (Q. Nos. 4-6) *Read the following information carefully and answer the questions that follow.* **IBPS (PO) 2011**

- If '$A \times B$' means 'A is the father of B'.
- If '$A + B$' means 'A is the wife of B'.
- If '$A \div B$' means 'A is the daughter of B'.
- If '$A - B$' means 'A is the son of B'.

4. How is L related to Q in the expression '$L \div M \times O - P \div Q$'?
(a) Granddaughter
(b) Niece
(c) Daughter-in-law
(d) Daughter
(e) Cannot be determined

5. What will come in the place of the question mark?, to establish that Q is the nephew of T in the expression '$Q ? R \div S \times T$'?
(a) + (b) × (c) − (d) ÷
(e) Either (c) or (a)

6. Which of the following relations are true based upon the relations given in the equation '$A - B \times C + D - E$'?
(a) C is mother of A
(b) E is wife of B
(c) D is brother of A
(d) E is mother-in-law of C
(e) None is true

7. R is uncle of A. R is grandfather of Q. Q's brother name is P, then what is relation of P to A? **Corporation Bank (PO) 2010**
(a) Brother
(b) Grandfather
(c) Father
(d) Uncle
(e) None of the above

8. Pointing to a boy, Sunita said, "He is the son of my grandfather's only son". How is the boy related to Sunita? **Indian Bank (PO) 2010**
(a) Son (b) Nephew
(c) Uncle (d) Data inadequate
(e) None of these

9. A is the father of C and D is the son of B. E is brother of A. If C is the sister of D, how is B related to E?
(a) Daughter
(b) Brother-in-law
(c) Husband
(d) Sister-in-law

10. Vinod introduces Vishal as the son of the only brother of his father's wife. How is Vinod related to Vishal? **NICL (GIC) AO 2013**
(a) Cousin (b) Brother
(c) Son (d) Uncle

11. Pointing to a person a man said to a woman' "His mother is the only daughter of your father". How as the woman related to that person?
(a) Aunt (b) Mother
(c) Wife (d) Daughter
(e) None of these

Direction (Q. Nos. 12-13) *Study the following information carefully and answer the questions given below it.*

'A+ B' means 'A is the mother-in-law of B'; 'A− B' means 'A is the daughter-in-law of B' and 'A * B' means 'A is the sister-in-law of B'. **FMS 2010**

12. P∗Q+R means
    (a) P is the mother-in-law of Q
    (b) P is the mother-in-law of R and Q
    (c) R is the daughter-in-law
    (d) None of the above

13. Given, X − Y + Z, which of the following is certainly true?
    (a) Y is the mother-in-law (b) X is the mother-in-law
    (c) Z is the mother-in-law (d) None of these

14. Pointing to a girl, Mihir said "She is the only daughter of my grandfather's only child". How is the girl related to Mihir? **Punjab & Sindh Bank (PO) 2010**
    (a) Daughter (b) Niece
    (c) Sister (d) Data inadequate
    (e) None of these

15. Pointing to a boy in a photograph Sudhir said, "He is the son of my maternal grandfather's only child". How is the boy related to Sudhir? **BOB (PO) 2010**
    (a) Self (b) Brother
    (c) Cousin brother (d) Data inadequate
    (e) None of these

16. Pointing to Kapil, Shilpa said, "His mother's brother is the father of my son Ashish". How is Kapil related to Shilpa?
    (a) Sister-in-law (b) Nephew
    (c) Niece (d) Aunt
    (e) None of these

Direction (Q. Nos. 17-18) *Study the following information and answer the questions given below.* **Syndicate Bank (PO) 2010**

(i) 'P÷ Q' means 'P is sister of Q'.
(ii) 'P×Q' means 'P is brother of Q'
(iii) 'P−Q' means 'P is mother of Q'.
(iv) 'P+Q' means 'P is father of Q'.

17. Which of the following means 'M is maternal uncle of T'?
    (a) M÷ K+ T
    (b) M× K+ T
    (c) M×K−T
    (d) M÷K−T
    (e) None of the above

18. Which of the following means 'H is maternal uncle of T'?
    (a) H+J+T
    (b) T×K+H
    (c) H+J×T
    (d) H−J+T
    (e) None of the above

19. Pointing to a girl, Subodh said, "She is the daughter of my mother's only brother. How is Subodh related to that girl? **Bank of India (PO) 2010**
    (a) Cousin (b) Maternal uncle
    (c) Brother (d) Data inadequate
    (e) None of these

20. Pointing to a woman, Nirmal said, "She is the daughter of my wife's grandfather's only child". How is the woman related to Nirmal? **RBI (Grade B) 2009**
    (a) Wife (b) Sister-in-law
    (c) Sister (d) Data inadequate
    (e) None of these

21. A man said to a lady, "Your mother's husband's sister is my aunt." How is the lady related to the man?
    (a) Daughter (b) Granddaughter
    (c) Mother (d) Sister
    (e) Aunt

22. Manish is Chitra's son, Chitra and Simran are sisters. Dibleen is Simran's mother. Sagar is the son of Dibleen. Which of the following statements is true? **FMS 2011**
    (a) Sagar and Manish are cousin
    (b) Sagar is the paternal uncle of Manish
    (c) Simran is Manish's grandmother
    (d) Chitra and Sagar are siblings

23. P is the brother of D, X is the sister of P. A is the brother of F. F is the daughter of D. M is the father of X. Who is the uncle of A?
    (a) X (b) P (c) F (d) M

24. Pointing to a girl, Nidhi said, "She is the daughter of my grandmother's only child". How is the girl related to Nidhi? **Syndicate Bank (PO) 2010**
    (a) Sister (b) Self
    (c) Cousin (d) Data inadequate
    (e) None of these

25. Pointing towards a girl Anurag says "this girl is the daughter of the only child of my father". What is the relation of Anurag's wife with the girl? **CGPSC 2012**
    (a) Sister (b) Aunt
    (c) Daughter (d) Mother
    (e) None of these

26. Savita introduced a boy as the son of the only daughter of the father of her maternal uncle. How is boy related to Savita? **SSC (FCI) 2012**
    (a) Brother (b) Son
    (c) Nephew (d) Son-in-law

27. Kusuma is the wife of Ravi. Govind and Prabhu are brothers. Govind is the brother of Ravi. Prabhu is Kusuma's **FCI Assistant Grade-II 2012**
    (a) Cousin
    (b) Brother
    (c) Brother-in-law
    (d) Uncle

28. Gopal said, pointing to Govind "His father is my father's only son". How is Gopal related to Govind? **SSC (FCI) 2012**

(a) Grandfather (b) Grandson
(c) Son (d) Father

29. Pointing to a lady on the stage, Bhumika said, 'She is the sister of the son of the wife of my husband'. How is the lady related to Bhumika? **CLAT 2014**

(a) Cousin (b) Sister-in-law
(c) Sister (d) Daughter

30. Pramod told Vinod, "Yesterday I defeated the only brother of the daughter of any grandmother". Whom did Pramod defeat? **CLAT 2014**

(a) Father (b) Son
(c) Father-in-law (d) Cousin

Direction (Q. Nos. 31-35) *Read the following information carefully and answer the questions.*
SBI & SBI Associates (Clerk) 2011

(i) If 'A + B' means 'A is the father of B'.
(ii) If 'A × B' means 'A is the sister of B'.
(iii) If 'A $ B' means 'A is the wife of B'.
(iv) If 'A % B' means 'A is the mother of B'.
(v) If 'A ÷ B' means 'A is the son of B'.

31. What should come in place of the question mark, to establish that J is the brother of T in the expression?

J ÷ P % H ? T % L

(a) × (b) ÷
(c) $ (d) Either ÷ or ×
(e) Either + or ÷

32. Which among the given expressions indicate that M is the daughter of D?

(a) L % R $ D + T × M (b) L + R $ D + M × T
(c) L % R % D + T ÷ M (d) D + L $ R + M × T
(e) L $ D ÷ R % M ÷ T

33. Which among the following options is true, if the expression 'I + T % J × L ÷ K' is definitely true?

(a) L is the daughter of T (b) K is the son-in-law of I
(c) I is the grandmother of L (d) T is the father of J
(e) J is the brother of L

34. Which among the following expressions is true, if Y is the son of X is definitely false?

(a) W % L × T × Y ÷ X
(b) W + L × T × Y ÷ X
(c) X + L × T × Y ÷ W
(d) W $ X + L + Y + T
(e) W % X + T × Y ÷ L

35. What should come in place of the question mark, to establish that T is the sister-in-law of Q in the expression?

R % T × P ? Q + V

(a) ÷ (b) %
(c) × (d) $
(e) Either $ or ×

Direction (Q. Nos. 36-38) *Following questions are based on the information given below.*
UIC (AO) 2005, 2013

(i) P × Q means P is father of Q.
(ii) P − Q means P is sister of Q.
(iii) P + Q means P is mother of Q.
(iv) P ÷ Q means P is brother of Q.

36. In the expression B + D × M ÷ N, how is M related to B?

(a) Granddaughter
(b) Son
(c) Grandson
(d) Granddaughter or grandson
(e) None of the above

37. Which of the following represents J is son of F?

(a) J ÷ R − T × F
(b) J + R − T × F
(c) J ÷ M − N × F
(d) Cannot be determined
(e) None of the above

38. Which of the following represents R is niece of M?

(a) M ÷ K × T − R
(b) M − J + R − N
(c) R − M × T ÷ W
(d) Cannot be determined
(e) None of the above

39. H is the father of J. J is the brother of L. N is the wife of L. K is the son of N. L and J are children of H. P is the wife of H. K and Z are grandchildren of P. Who is the uncle of K? **LIC (AAO) 2013**

(a) J (b) H
(c) Z (d) Cannot be determined
(e) None of these

40. Anil introduced Rohit as the son of the only brother of his father's wife. How is Rohit related to Anil? **NIFT (UG) 2014**

(a) Cousin (b) Son
(c) Uncle (d) Son-in-law

41. Introducing Amrita, Raj said "Her mother is the only daughter of my mother-in law." How is Raj related to Amrita? **CMAT 2014**

(a) Husband (b) Father
(c) Wife (d) Uncle

42. Z is maternal uncle of Y, X is maternal grandfather of Z. S is grandson of X. How is S related to Y? **CMAT 2013**

(a) Maternal grandfather (b) Maternal uncle
(c) Cousin brother (d) None of these

43. Pointing to a man in a photograph Pallavi said, "His mother's only daughter is my mother". How is Pallavi related to that man? **MAT 2014**

(a) Daughter
(b) Sister
(c) Brother
(d) None of the above

44. In a family there are seven persons comprising two married couples, T is the son of M and the grandson of K. M is a widower. M and R are brothers and W is the daughter-in-law of J, who is the mother of R and the grandmother of D. How is D related to M?

(a) Son
(b) Son-in-law
(c) Nephew or niece
(d) Brother

45. A girl introduced a boy as the son of the daughter of the father of her uncle. The boy is girl's **NICL (GIC) AO 2013**

(a) Uncle (b) Nephew (c) Cousin (d) Son

46. Pointing to a woman in a photograph a man says, "Her mother's mother is the mother of my father." How is the man related to the woman in the photograph? **MPPSC 2012**

(a) Uncle (b) Grandson
(c) Nephew (d) Maternal cousin

Advanced Level

Direction (Q. Nos. 1-3) *Read the following information carefully to answer the questions that follow.* **MAT 2013**

A family consists of six members P, Q, R, X, Y and Z. Q is the son of R but R is not the mother of Q. P and R are married couple. Y is the brother of R. X is the daughter of P and Z is the brother of P.

1. Who is the brother-in-law of R?

(a) P (b) Z (c) Y (d) X

2. How many female members are there in the family?

(a) One (b) Two (c) Three (d) Four

3. Which of these is a pair of brothers?

(a) P and X (b) P and Z (c) Q and X (d) R and Y

Direction (Q. Nos. 4-8) *These questions are based on the following information.* **JMET 2009**

Chandramohan and his wife Kamini have a family of three generations comprising thirteen members of whom six are female members'. Some of Chandramohan's children are married but none of his grandchildren are married.

Kamini has a daughter-in-law named Fullara and two sons-in-law, one being Eeshwaran.

Harihar's brother is Devesh, who has two nephews and two nieces-one being Leela.

Bandana, Devesh's sister has two children.

Fullara, who is sister-in-law of Devesh has four nephews and nieces.

Manohar who is married to Geeta in the family has a daughter Indira and a son.

Joy has a sister and two cousins, Akash and Indi a.

4. Amongst the following, which one is false?

(a) Bandana is Kamini's child
(b) Joy is Geeta's child
(c) Akash is Harihar's nephew
(d) Geeta has less than two nephews

5. Leela is the niece of

(a) Bandana (b) Eeshwaran
(c) Harihar (d) Kamini

6. Akash is the son of

(a) Geeta (b) Harihar
(c) Devesh (d) Bandana

7. Which of the following pairs is a brother and a sister?

(a) Manohar and Fullara (b) Devesh and Geeta
(c) Joy and Indira (d) Eeshwaran and Bandana

8. (i) Fullara is Harihar's wife.
(ii) Harihar's son's name is Akash.
(iii) Bandana is Leela's mother.

Based on the above facts, which of the following is true?

(a) (i) and (ii), but not (iii)
(b) (i) and (iii), but not (ii)
(c) (ii) and (iii), but not (i)
(d) All of the above

Direction (Q. Nos. 9-11) *Read the following information carefully to answer the questions that follow.* **FMS 2010**

Six directors of a private limited company named A,B,C,D,E and F are playing golf. A and E are brothers. F is the sister of E. C is the only son of A's uncle. B and D are the daughters of the brother of C's father.

9. How is C related to F?

(a) Cousin (b) Brother (c) Son (d) Uncle

10. How many male executives are there in the group?

(a) Two (b) Three (c) Four (d) One

11. How many of these executives are real brothers?

(a) Two
(b) Three
(c) Cannot be said
(d) None of the above

12. 'Ravi' and 'Dinesh' are the sons of Mr and Mrs Gupta. 'Ravi' has married to 'Surya' and this couple is blessed with 'Tarun', 'Vinni' and 'Minni'. 'Seema', is married to 'Tarun' and they are blessed with 'Zeena', a beautiful daughter. How is 'Dinesh' related to 'Tarun'? **CLAT 2014**
(a) Brother (b) Father
(c) Uncle (d) Brother-in-law

13. 'Arti' and 'Saurabh' are the children of Mr and Mrs Shah. 'Ritu' and 'Shakti' are the children of Mr and Mrs Mehra. 'Saurabh' and 'Ritu' are married to each other and two daughters 'Mukti' and 'Shruti' are born to them. 'Shakti' is married to 'Rina' and two children 'Subhash' and 'Reshma' are born to them. How is 'Arti' related to 'Shruti'? **MAT 2014**
(a) Mother (b) Mother-in-law
(c) Sister (d) Aunt

14. A's son B is married with C whose sister of D is married to E the brother of B. How is D related to A? **NICL (GIC) 2013**
(a) Sister (b) Daughter-in-law
(c) Sister-in-law (d) Cousin

15. Sanjay says, "I have as many sisters as brothers." Sarita says. "Each of us sisters has only half as many sisters as brothers." Assuming that Sanjay and Sarita are brother and sister, how many brothers and sisters are there in the family? **FMS 2010**
(a) 6 brothers and 4 sisters
(b) 4 brothers and 6 sisters
(c) 3 brothers and 4 sisters
(d) 4 brothers and 3 sisters

Direction (Q. Nos. 16-19) *Study the following information carefully and answer the questions given below it.* **FMS 2011**

Mohan is Rakesh's paternal uncle. Ritu is Rakesh's daughter. Madhav is Ritu's younger brother. Mukesh is Ritu's husband. John is Sunita's son. Tinu is Madhav's sister. Kulwant is Rakesh's father. Pushpa is Kulwant's sister. Kaushalaya is Mohan's wife. Gagan is Mohan's son. Sunita is Kulwant's daughter.

16. How is John related to Kulwant?
(a) Nephew
(b) Grandnephew
(c) Grandson
(d) Great grandson

17. Tinu is John's
(a) aunt (b) cousin
(c) sister (d) niece

18. Mukesh is Gagan's
(a) nephew
(b) brother
(c) brother-in-law
(d) nephew-in-law

19. From this data, which of the following statements can said to be correct?
(a) Mohan is younger than Kulwant
(b) Mukesh and Gagan do not share the same surname
(c) Madhav is younger than Rakesh
(d) Pushpa is younger than Mohan

Direction (Q. Nos. 20-22) *Study the following information carefully and answer the questions given below it.*

(i) A, B, C, D, E and F are six members of a family.
(ii) One couple has parents and their children in the family.
(iii) A is the son of C and E is the daughter of A.
(iv) D is the daughter of F who is the mother of E.

20. Who are the male members in the family?
(a) A and C (b) C and F
(c) A, B and D (d) Cannot be determined
(e) None of these

21. Which of the following pairs is the parents of the children?
(a) BC
(b) CF
(c) BF
(d) Cannot be determined
(e) None of the above

22. How many female members are there in the family?
(a) Two (b) Three
(c) Four (d) Cannot be determined
(e) None of these

Direction (Q. Nos. 23-25) *Study the following information carefully and answer the given questions.*

A family consists of six members P, Q, R, X, Y and Z. Q is the son of R but R is not mother of Q. P and R are a married couple. Y is the brother of R. X is the daughter of P. Z is the brother of P.

23. Who is the brother-in-law of R?
(a) P (b) Z (c) Y (d) X

24. Who is the father of Q?
(a) R (b) P
(c) Z (d) None of these

25. How many children does P have?
(a) One (b) Two
(c) Three (d) Four

26. In a joint family of seven persons F, E, N, J, P, M and L, there are two married couples. 'F' is a house-wife and her husband is 'E'. 'J' is the wife of 'N'. 'L' is the granddaughter of 'F'. 'E' is the father-in-law of 'J' and father of 'P'. 'M' is the son of 'N' and brother of 'L'. How is 'J' related to 'P'? **MAT 2014**
(a) Sister (b) Cousin
(c) Niece (d) Sister-in-law

Direction (Q. Nos. 27-29) *Study the given information carefully and answer the given questions.* **SBI Associates (Clerk) 2012**

A is the mother of B. B is the sister of C. D is the son of C. E is the brother of D. F is the mother of E. G is the granddaughter of A. H has only two children- B and C.

27. How is F related to H?
(a) Son-in-law (b) Daughter-in-law
(c) Father-in-law (d) Granddaughter
(e) Cannot be determined

28. How is C related to E?
(a) Father
(b) Son
(c) Mother
(d) Cousin
(e) Cannot be determined

29. Who is the mother of G?
(a) C
(b) B
(c) F
(d) Either B or F
(e) Either C of F

Direction (Q. Nos. 30-34) *Read the following information and answer the questions based on them.*

There are seven family members P, Q, R, S, T, U and V, four of them are females. The family runs into three generations. The family consists of two married couples, three daughters and two mothers. S is the brother of R. R is the mother of U, V is Q's son-in-law. P is the father of R.

30. Who is the husband of R?
(a) Q (b) U (c) V (d) T

31. Which of the following is not true?
(a) Q is the mother of R (b) T may be the sister of S
(c) V is the father of T (d) T and V are married

32. How many children does P have?
(a) 1 (b) 2
(c) 3 (d) Either (b) or (c)

33. How is Q related to U?
(a) Mother (b) Father
(c) Grandmother (d) Grandfather

34. T and U are
(a) sisters (b) aunt-niece
(c) uncle-niece (d) Either (a) or (b)

Answers with Explanations

Intro Exercise 1

1. (*e*)

Ravi is the son of Kamal's sister. So, Kamal becomes the maternal uncle of Ravi.

2. (*c*)

Archana's grandfather's only son is Archana's father.
Archana's father's son is the brother of Archana.
So, the man in the photograph is the brother of Archana.

3. (*a*) Harish is the only son of his father because he has no brother or sister. So, wife of Harish's father's son is Harish's wife. So, Harish was looking the portrait of his wife's son, i.e. his son.

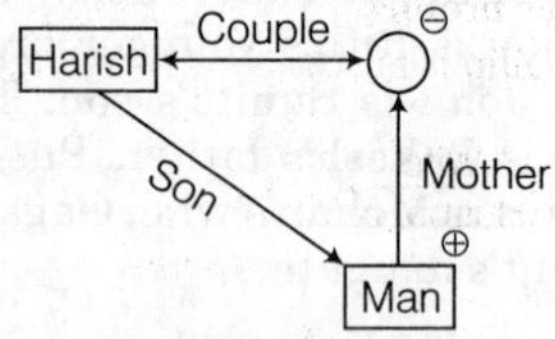

4. (*c*) Based on the given information we draw the following diagram.

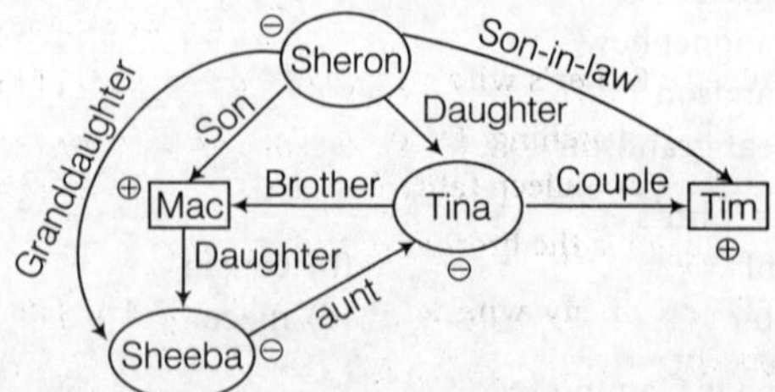

Mac is the brother of Tina and Tim is the son-in-law of Sheron. Sheron has only two children. So, Tina becomes the wife of Tim.

Tina is Sheeba's aunt and Sheron is Sheeba's grandmother, so Mac is the father of Sheeba and sheeba is niece of Tim.

5. (*b*)

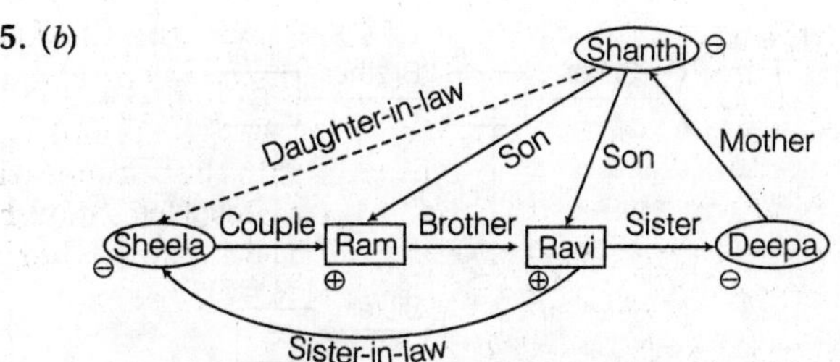

Shanthi is mother of Ravi and Sheela is the wife of Ram. Therefore, Sheela is the daughter-in-law of Shanthi.

6. (*d*)

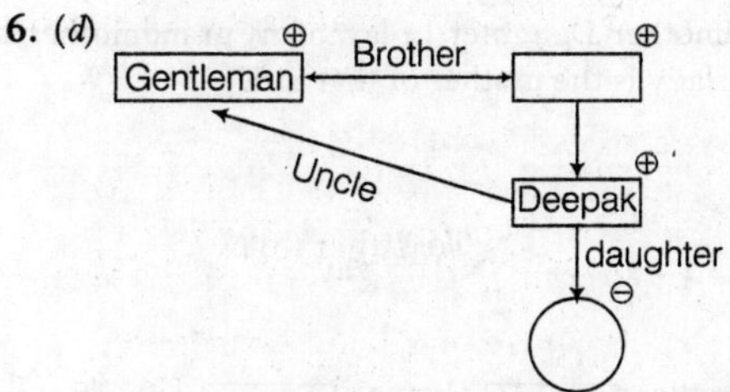

Father of Deepak's daughter's father is Deepak's father and Deepak's father's only brother is Deepak's uncle.

7. (*d*)

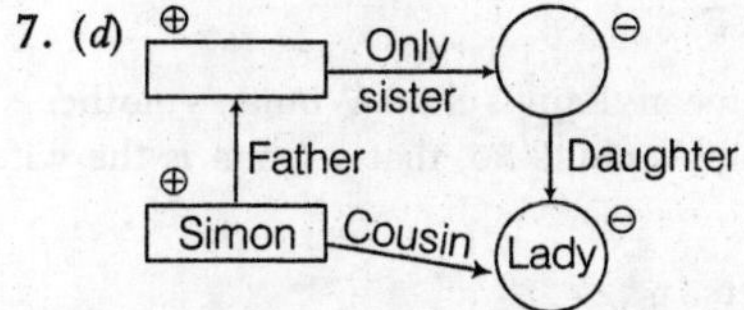

Aunt's daughter is cousin.

8. (*a*)

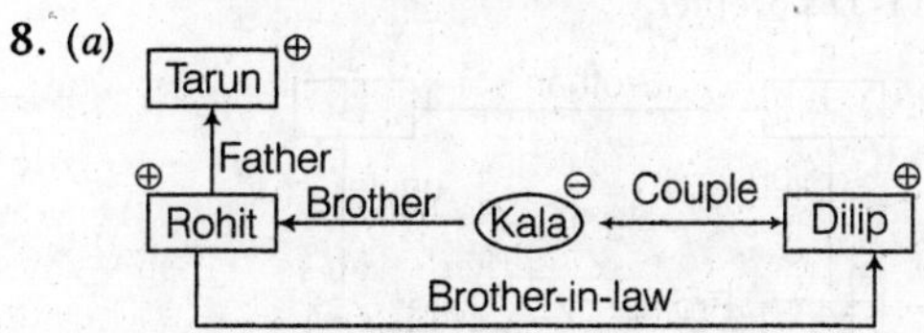

Rohit is the brother of Kala. Kala is the wife of Dilip. Therefore, Dilip is brother-in-law of Rohit.

9. (*a*)

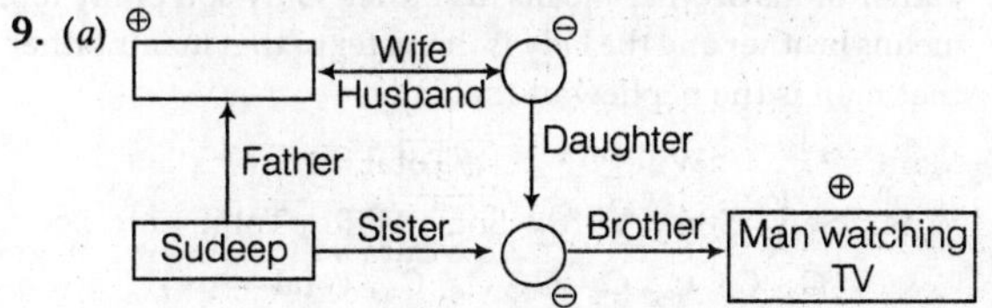

Sudeep's father's wife's daughter is the sister of Sudeep.

The man watching TV is one of the two brothers of the daughter of Sudeep father's wife.

So, Sudeep is the brother of the man watching the TV.

10. (*c*) Husband of my wife is myself. So, Amit is talking about himself.

Amit's wife's husband's sister is the sister of Amit.

So, the woman is the sister of Amit.

11. (*d*) P is the mother of Q and Q is the son of R. It means that P and R are couple. R is the son of T.

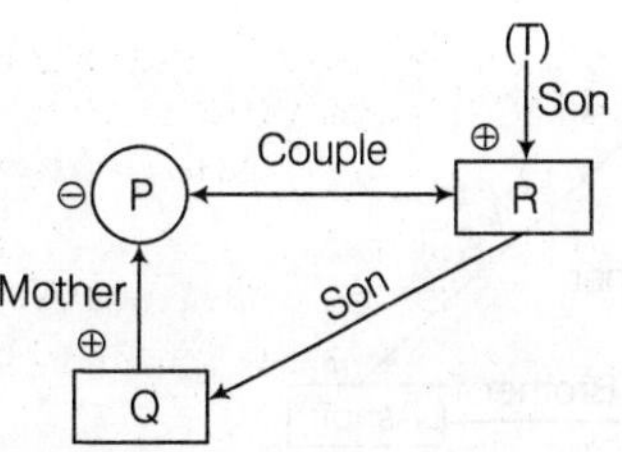

We cannot guess the gender of T, so we cannot determine whether T is grandfather or grandmother of Q.

12. (*b*)

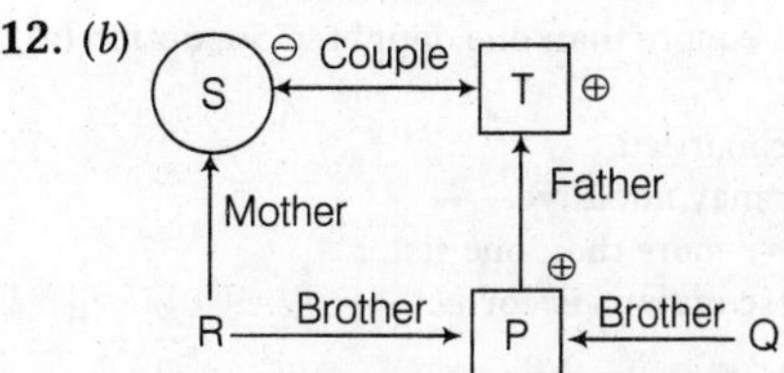

Here, the gender of R and Q is not determined.

In the above diagram it is clear that S is the wife of T.

So, statement (b) cannot be definitely true.

13. (*e*) Sister of Vijay's brother is Vijay's sister and father of his sister is Vijay's father. Daughter of Vijay's father is Vijay's sister. So, the woman in photograph is the sister of Vijay.

14. (*e*)

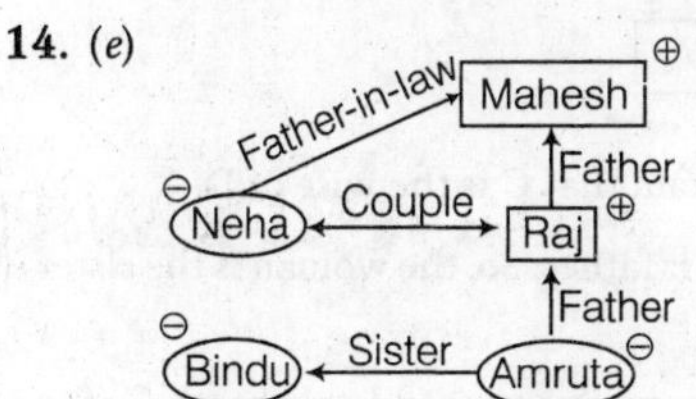

Only son of father-in-law is husband. So, Raj is the husband of Neha and Amruta is their daughters. So, Amruta and Bindu are granddaughters of Mahesh.

15. (*d*)

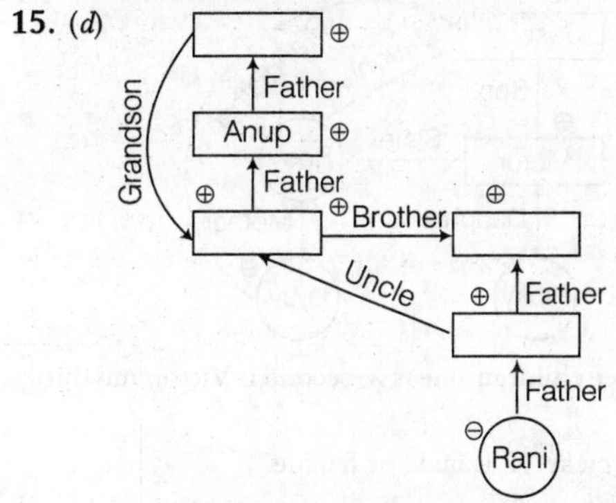

Anup's son's brother is also Anup's son, so Anup's son's son's daughter is Anup's great granddaughter.

Therefore, Anup is the great grandfather of Rani.

16. (*b*) Daughter of my father's wife is sister. So, that sister has two brothers, one is Deepak while the other who is playing football. So, Deepak is the brother of that boy who is playing football.

17. (*c*) The father of girl's uncle means the Grandfather of the girl. Daughter of the girl's grandfather is the aunt of the girl. Thus, the boy is the brother of that girl.

18. (*e*)

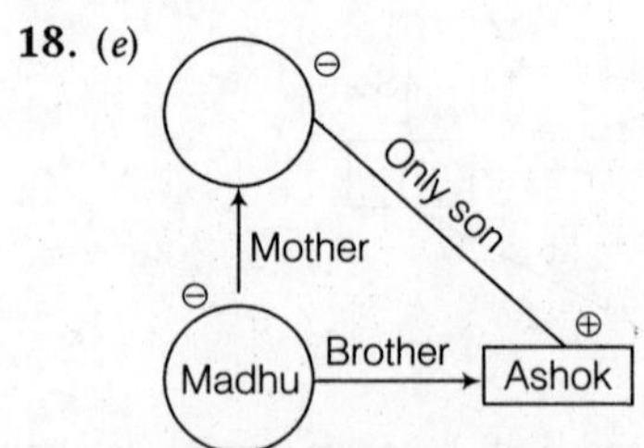

Madhu's mother's only son is the Madhu's brother.

(a) Ashok may have more than one daughter. So, option (a) is wrong.
(b) Ashok must be married.
(c) Ashok's father may not alive.
(d) Ashok may have more than one sister.
So, none of these options is correct.

19. (*d*) Grandson of mother means son. Wife of son is daughter-in-law. So, Arun is the father-in-law of that girl.

20. (*b*)

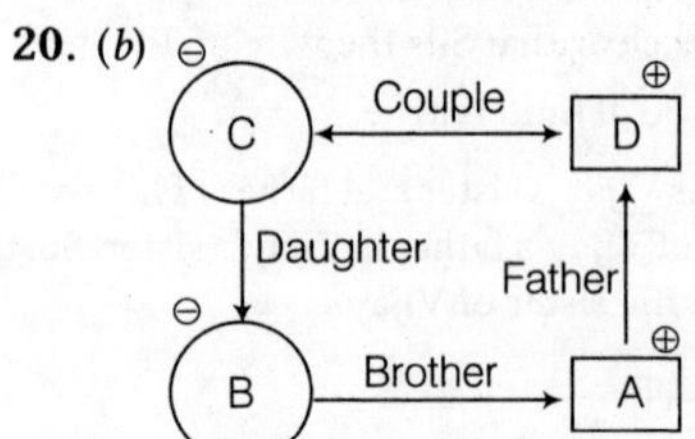

It is clear from the diagram that C is the wife of D.

21. (*b*) Only son of grandfather is father. So, the woman is the sister of that man in photograph.

22. (*b*) Daughter of grandmother means aunt and only brother of aunt means father. So, Rahul defeated his father.

23. (*d*) According to the given information, we make a relation tree.

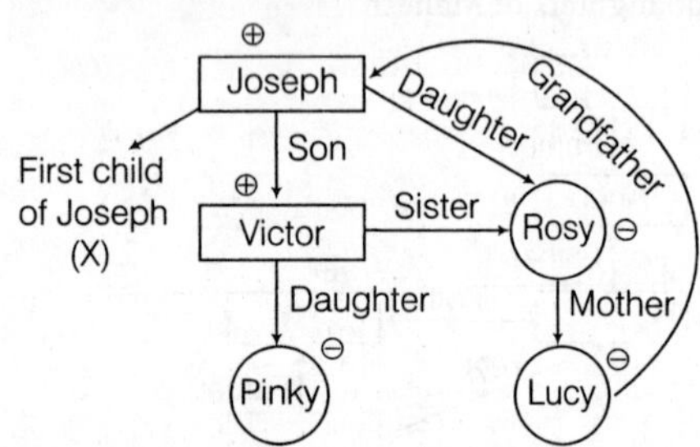

Joseph has three children, one is X, second is Victor and third is Rosy.

Here, it is not clear 'X' is male or female.

Rosy is the mother of Lucy.

So, Joseph is the grandfather of Lucy.

24. (*c*)

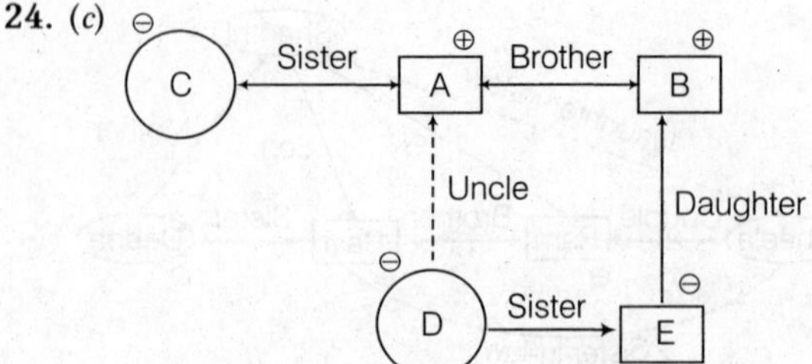

In the above diagram it is clear that A is the uncle of D.

25. (*b*) My father's son means my brother. My brother's grandmother is my grandmother. Daughter-in-law of my grandmother is my mother. So, lady is the mother of that girl.

26. (*b*)

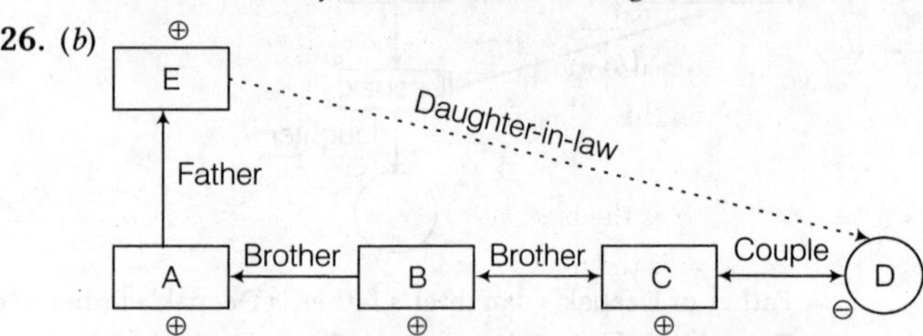

A, B and C are the son's of E. D is the wife of C, so it is the daughter-in-law of E.

27. (*b*) Rajiv's wife's child means Rajiv's child. Woman's mother is the grandmother of Rajiv's child. So, that woman is the wife of Rajiv.

28. (*d*) A and B are brothers.
C and D are sisters.
A's son is D's brother.

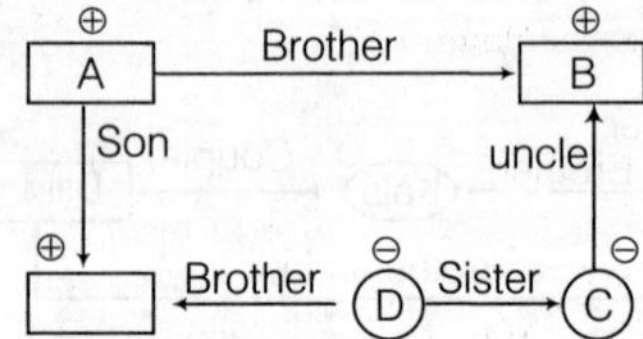

Hence, B is the uncle of C.

29. (*e*) Father of his brother means his father. Only son of my mother means brother and the lady is the sister of that man's father. So, that man is the nephew of that lady.

30. (*d*) Man Wife Total = 2

$Wife_1$ Son_1 Son_2 $Wife_2$ Son_3 $Wife_3$, Total = 6

C_1 C_2 C_3 C_4 C_5 C_6 C_7 C_8 C_9, Total = 9

So, total member of the family = 2 + 6 + 9 = 17

Intro Exercise 2

1. (*b*) In option (a),

R × P + S

R × P, R is the mother of P.

P + S, P is the brother of S.

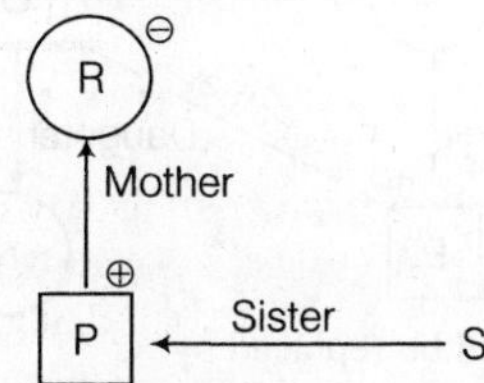

Here, R is also mother of S.

In option (b),

R + P × S

R + P, R is the brother of P.

P × S, P is the mother of S.

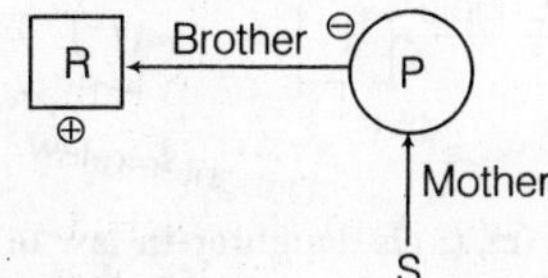

In the above diagram R is the maternal uncle of S.

2. (*d*) In option (a),

D + F × E

D + F, D is the sister of F.

F × E, F is the daughter of E.

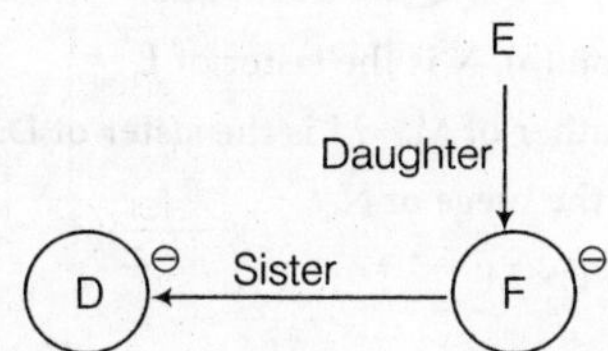

Here, E is either the mother of D or father of D.

In option (b),

D × F + E

D × F, D is the daughter of F.

F + E, F is the sister of E.

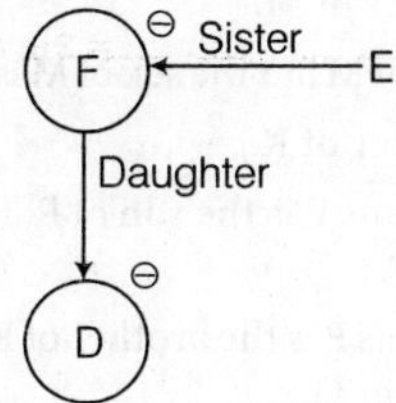

Here, gender of E is not define.

Similarly, option (c) does not show the relation that E is the maternal uncle of D.

3. (*c*) In option (a),

Q − N + M × P

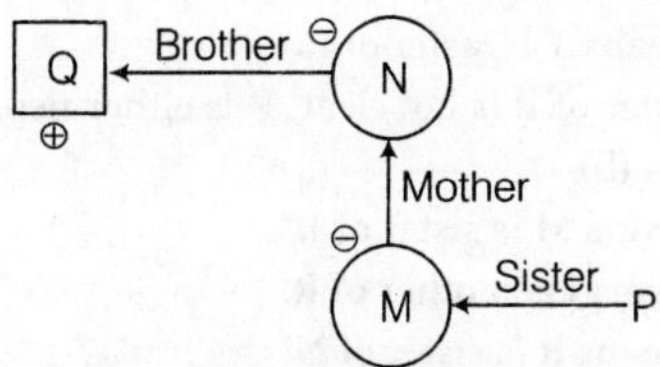

Here, Q is the maternal uncle of P.

In option (b), P + S × N − Q

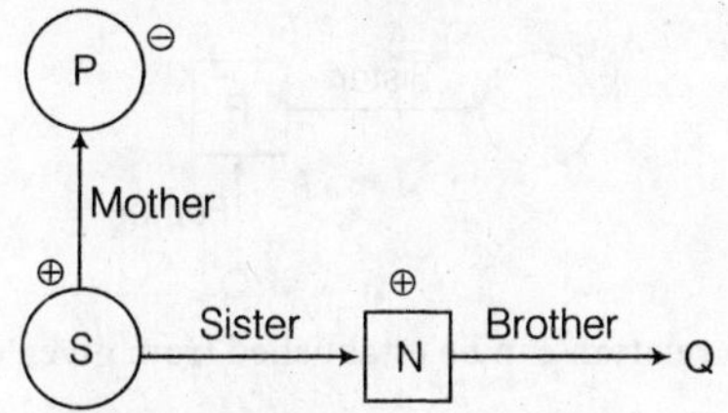

Here, P is the mother of Q.

In option (c),

P − M + N × Q

Here, P is the maternal uncle of Q.

4. (*c*) B + D means B is mother of D.

D × M means D is father of M.

M ÷ N means M is brother of N.

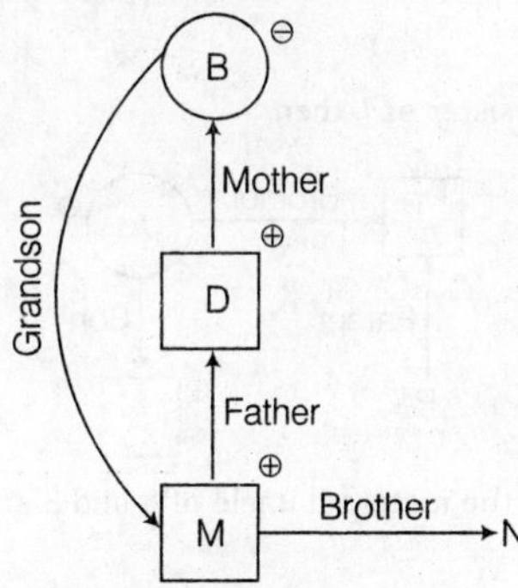

Therefore, M is grandson of B.

5. (*e*) In option (a), J ÷ R means J is brother of R.

R − T means R is sister of T.

T × F means T is father of F.

Therefore, J is uncle of F.

In option (b), J + R means J is mother of R.

J is female.

In option (c), J ÷ M means J is brother of M.

M − N means M is sister of N.

N × F means N is father of F.

Therefore, J is uncle of F.

6. (*b*) In option (a),

$M \div K$ means M is brother of K.

$K \times T$ means K is father of T.

$T - R$ means T is sister of R.

The gender of R is not clear. R is either nephew or niece of M.

In option (b),

$M - J$ means M is sister of J.

$J + R$ means J is mother of R.

$R - N$ means R is sister of N.

Therefore, R is niece of M.

7. (*e*) According to the given information,

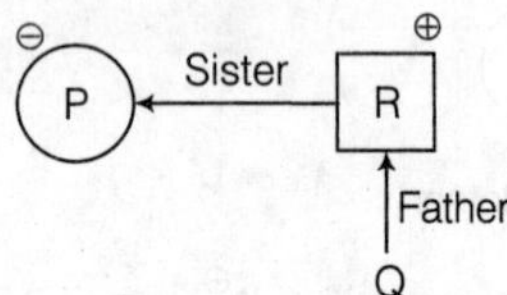

So, no relation can be established from given options.

8. (*b*) In $L > V < J + P$

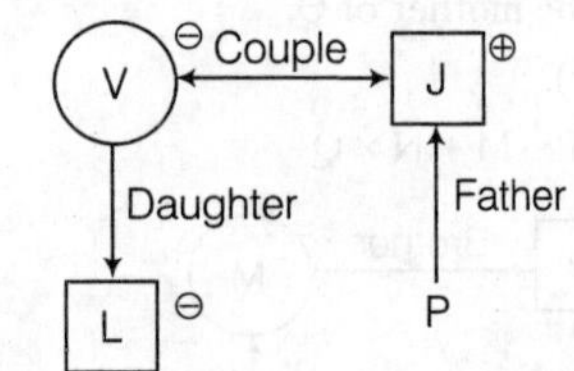

In $S \times A < D + F < E + K$

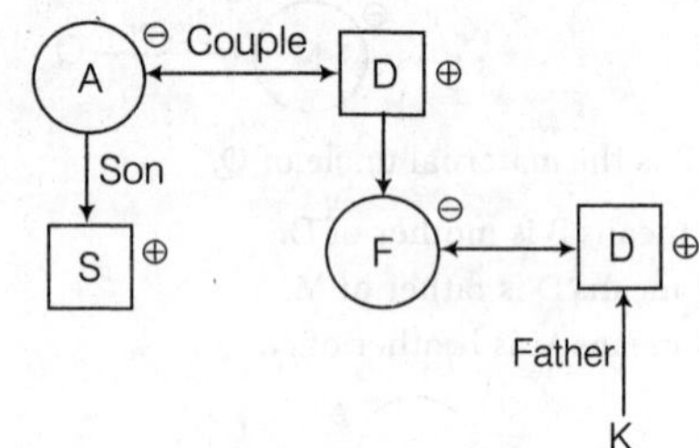

If A is the sister of J, then

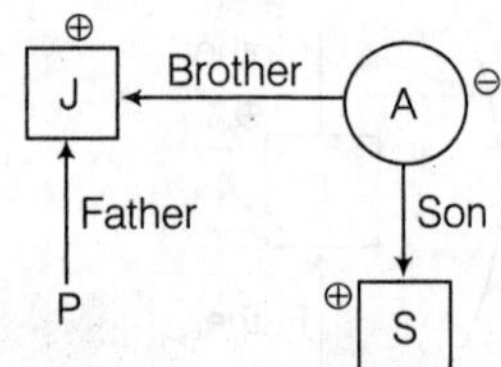

J becomes the maternal uncle of S and S and P becomes cousin.

9. (*d*) $F \times R < S ? M$

Given M is the grandmother of F.

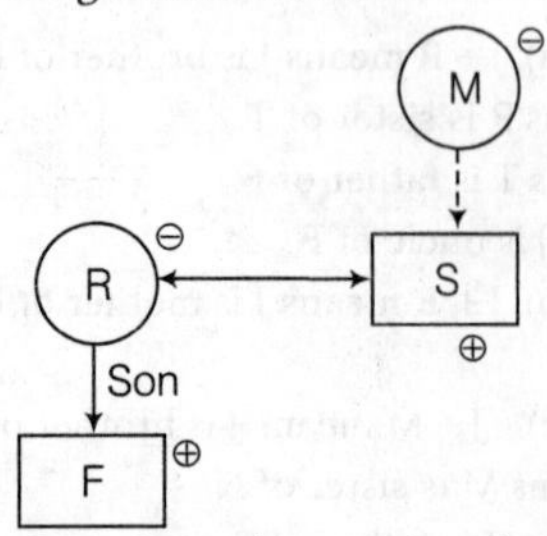

F is the son of S and M is the grandmother of S. So, definitely M is the mother of S.

$S \times M \rightarrow$ S is the son of M.

So, the expression becomes $F \times R < S \times M$

10. (*b*) $N + O - P$ means N is the daughter of O, O is the father of P. O is the father of N and P. If Q becomes the wife of O, Q will be mother of N.

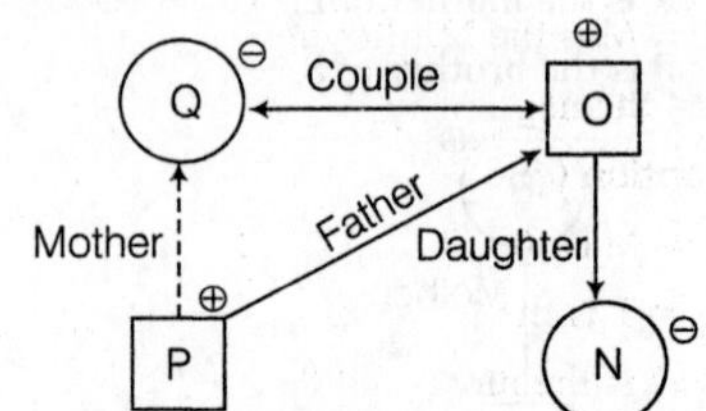

So, '?' should be replaced by ×.

11. (*c*) $S \div T \times V - W + Y$

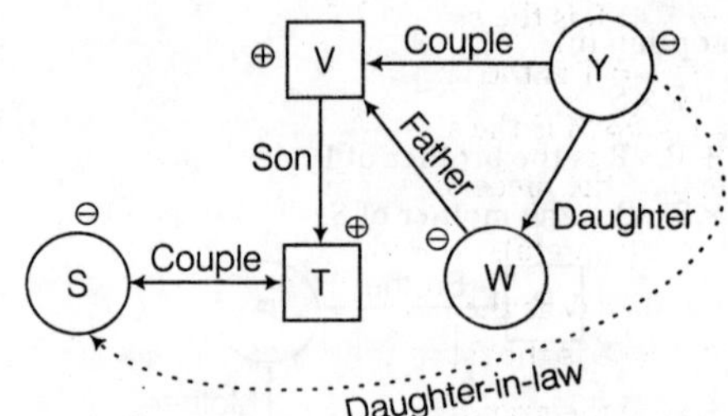

Hence, option (c), (S) is daughter-in-law of Y is correct.

12. (*b*) Go through options.

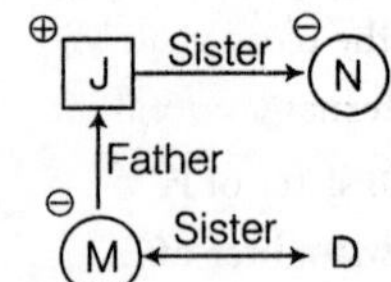

For option (b), N is the sister of J.

J is the father of M. M is the sister of D.

So, M is the niece of N.

13. (*d*) '$B + K \div T \times M$'

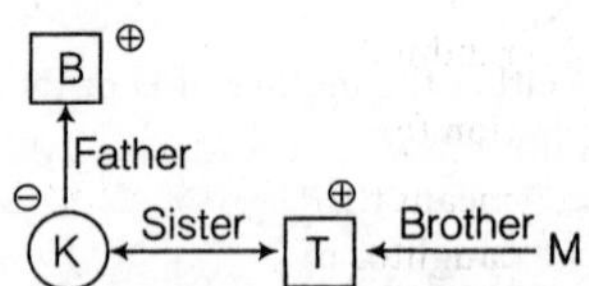

B is the father of K. K is the sister of T.

T is the brother of M.

K is the sister of M but the sex of M is not known, so M may be brother or sister of K.

14. (*a*) $P + R - Q$ means P is the son of R, R is the wife of Q. So, Q is the father of P.

15. (*c*) $P \times R \div Q$ means P is the brother of R, R is the mother of Q. So, P is the uncle of Q.

16. (*b*) $P = R + Q$ means, P is the sister of R, R is the son of Q. So, P is the daughter of Q.

17. (*a*) $P = R \div Q$ means, P is the sister of R, R is the mother of Q. So, P is the aunt of Q.

18. (*d*) From option (a),

$M - T \Rightarrow$ M is the brother of T.

$T \div J \Rightarrow$ T is the father of J.

J − R ⇒ J is the brother of R.

So, M is the uncle of R.

From option (b),

R − T ⇒ R is the brother of T.

T ÷ M ⇒ T is the father of M.

M − K ⇒ M is the brother of K.

So, M is the nephew of R.

From option (c),

M − T ⇒ M is the brother of T.

T ÷ M ⇒ T is the father of J.

J × R ⇒ J is the mother of R.

So, M is the maternal grandfather of R.

From option (d),

R + T ⇒ R is the sister of T.

T ÷ M ⇒ T is the father of M.

M + K ⇒ M is the sister of K.

So, M is the niece of R.

19. (*e*) From option (a),

W ÷ T ⇒ W is the father of T.

T ÷ J ⇒ T is the father of J.

So, W is the grandfather of J.

From option (b),

J ÷ T ⇒ J is the father of T.

T × W ⇒ T is the mother of W.

So, J is the maternal grandfather of W.

From option (c),

J × T ⇒ J is the mother of T.

T × W ⇒ T is the mother of W.

So, J is the maternal grandmother of W.

From option (d),

J × T ⇒ J is the mother of T.

T ÷ W ⇒ T is the mother of W.

So, J is the grandmother of W.

20. (*c*) Consider option (c),

A ÷ D × B, it means that A is the sister of D and D is the son of B.

So, A is the daughter of B.

21. (*c*) Let consider option (c), P − M + N × Q

From the given information

P − M ⇒ 'P is the brother of M'.

M + N ⇒ 'M is the mother of N'.

N × Q ⇒ 'N is the sister of Q'.

Therefore,

⊕ P ← Brother — M ⊖
Mother (N → M)
Q — Sister → N ⊖

So, 'P is the maternal uncle of Q'.

22. (*a*) In option (a), 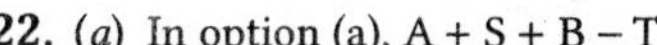 A + S + B − T

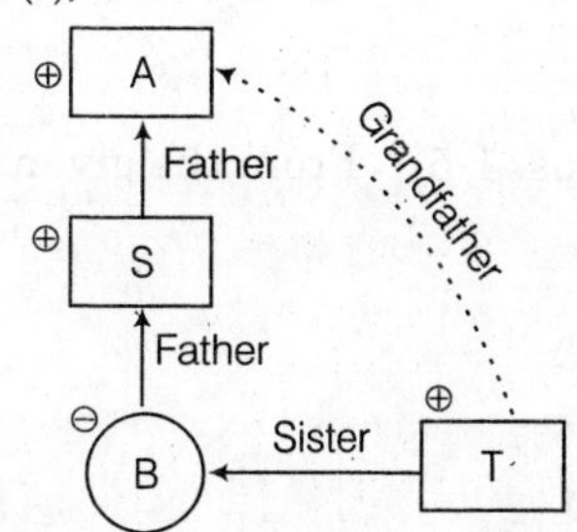

23. (*c*) A × B + R > S

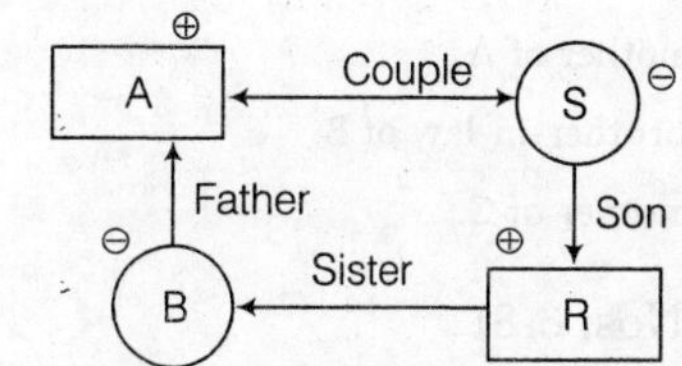

S is the wife of A. As, B is the daughter of A and R is the brother of B.

24. (*c*) P + Q > A − B

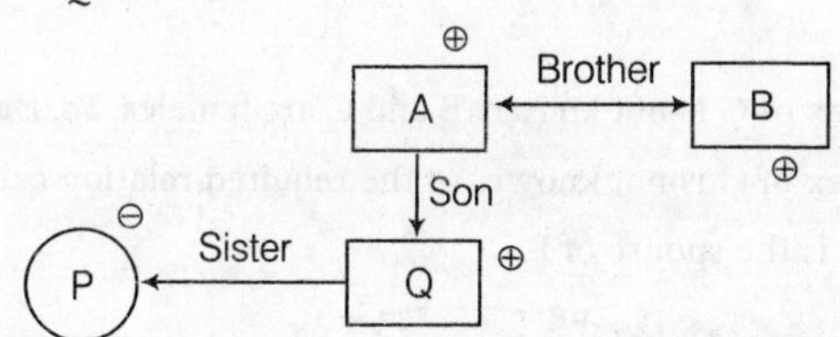

P is the sister of Q. So, it is also the daughter of A.

A is the brother of B and daughter of brother is called niece.

25. (*a*) W > X < Y ∗ Z

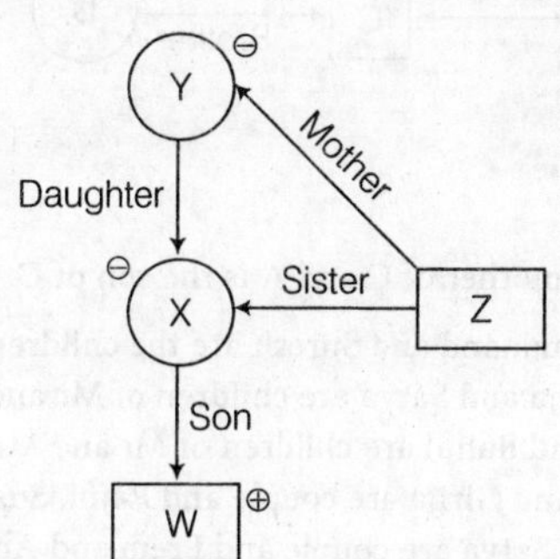

W is the nephew of Z.

26. (*a*) P × Q < R ∗ S

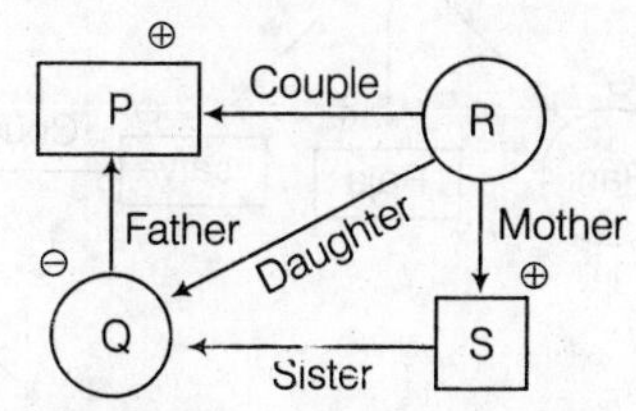

P is the father of S.

27. (*e*) None of the above

Intro Exercise 3

Solution (Q. Nos. 1-5) From the given information, we can draw the following family tree.

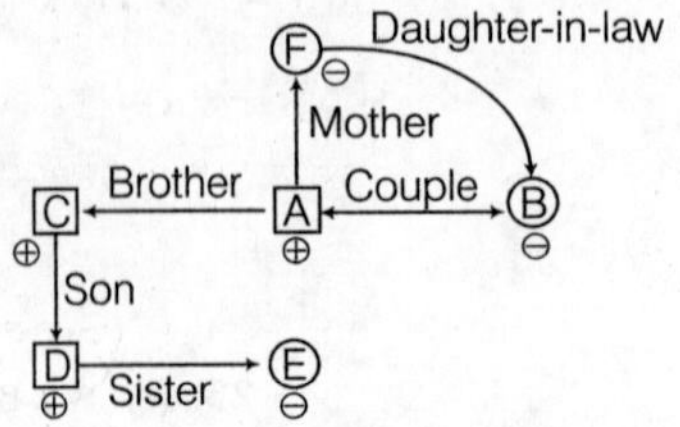

1. (*a*) F is the mother of A.
2. (*b*) E is the daughter of C.
3. (*b*) C is the brother-in-law of B.
4. (*c*) There are three male members, C, A and D.
5. (*c*) F is the mother of C.

Solution (Q. Nos. 6-8)

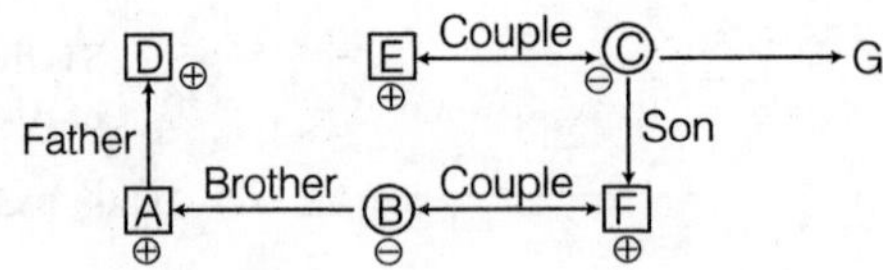

6. (*d*) Sex of G is not known. B and C are females. So, there are either 2 or 3 females.
7. (*d*) Sex of G is not known, so the required relation cannot be determined.
8. (*a*) B is the spouse of F.
9. (*b*)

B is the mother of C and A is the son of C. So, he is grandson of B.

10. (*d*) Sita, Ramanand and Suresh are the children of Mr and Mrs Malhotra.
Rani, Raja and Satya are children of Mr and Mrs Aggarwal.
Girija and Rahul are children of Mr and Mrs Gupta.
Suresh and Girija are couple and Rajni, Sushil and Ramayan are their children.
Sita and Satya are couple and Prem and Amar are their children.

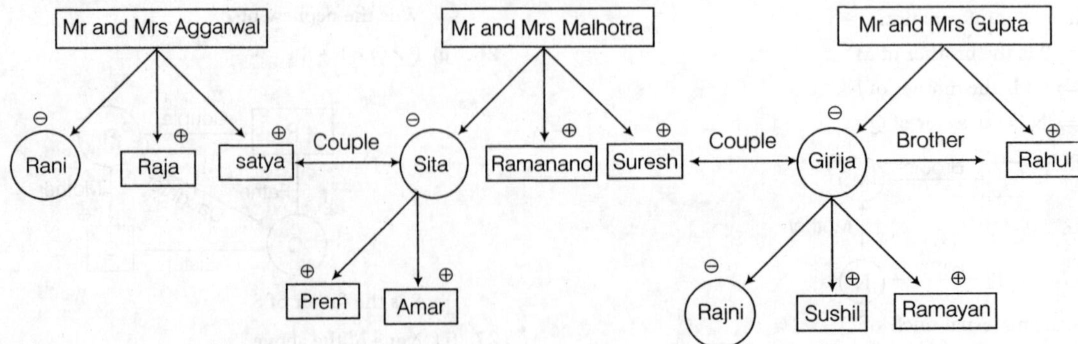

In the above diagram, Girija is the sister of Rahul and wife of Suresh.
Wife's brother is brother-in-law and sister's husband is also brother-in-law.
So, Suresh is brother-in-law of Rahul.

11. (*b*)

Brother
Karim
Father
Daughter
Javed
Brother
Sister
Dolly

Javed's brother's sister's father is the father of Javed.

Karim is Javed's uncle and Dolly is the daughter of Karim.

Therefore, Dolly is the cousin of Javed.

Solution (Q. Nos. 12-13) According to the given information, we can draw a family tree.

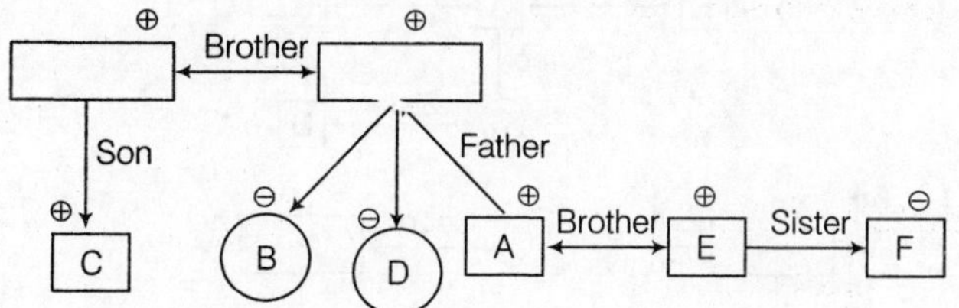

12. (*a*) C is the only son of A's uncle and F is the sister of A.

Therefore, C is the cousin of F.

13. (*c*) We have six children who play football in which C, A and E are male members.

Solution (Q. Nos. 14-18) From the given information we can draw a family tree.

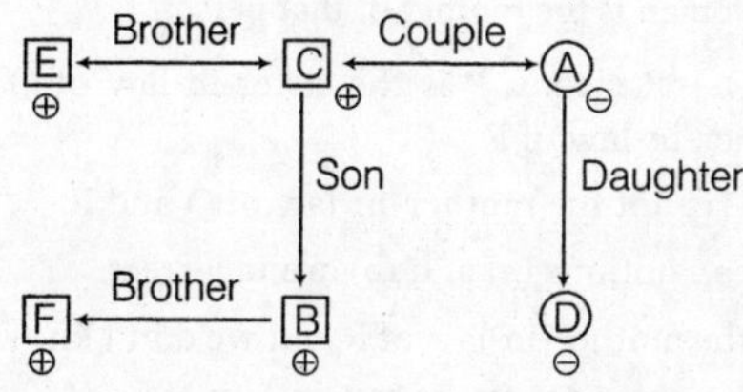

14. (*d*) There are 4 male members in the family.

15. (*d*) A is the mother of B.

16. (*c*) A has three children B, D and F.

17. (*d*) We cannot be determine E, as it is not mentioned in the given information.

18. (*d*) A and D is the pair of females.

Solution (Q. Nos. 19-22) From the given information we can draw a family tree.

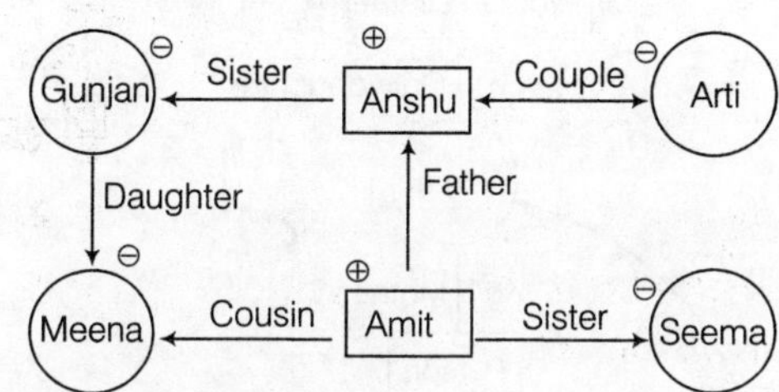

19. (*a*) Gunjan is the aunt of Amit.

20. (*b*) Gunjan is the sister-in-law of Arti.

21. (*b*) Meena is the cousin of Amit.

22. (*d*) Anshu is the father of Seema.

Solution (Q. Nos. 23-26) Let us draw the family diagram

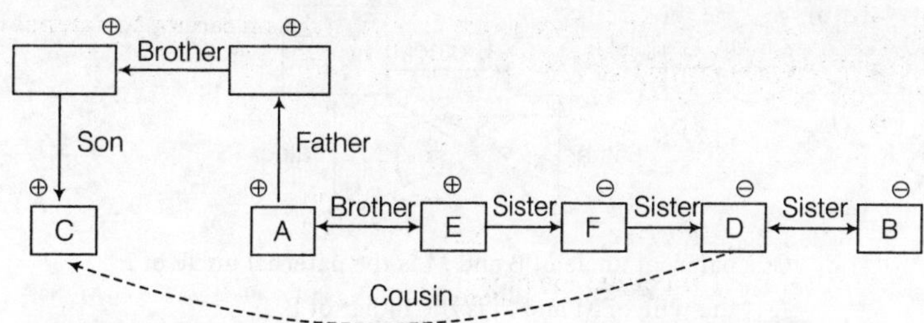

23. (*b*) D is A's sister.

24. (*d*) Males are A, E and C.

25. (*c*) Females are B, D and F.

26. (*a*) C is the cousin of F.

Cumulative Exercise

Base Level

1. (*d*)

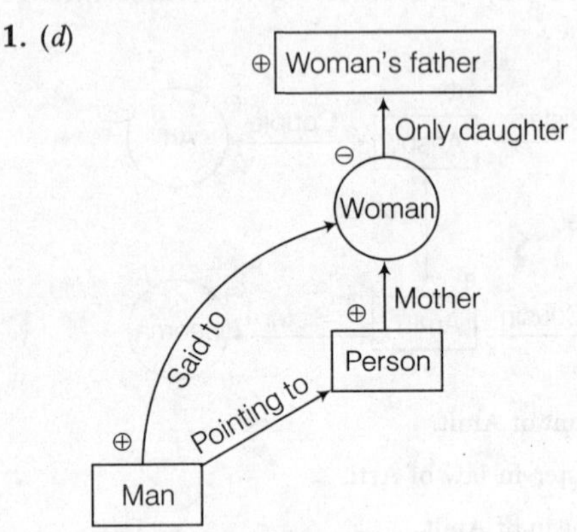

Man said to woman that the person's mother's is the only daughter of your father it means the woman itself.

So, the woman is the mother of person.

2. (*a*)

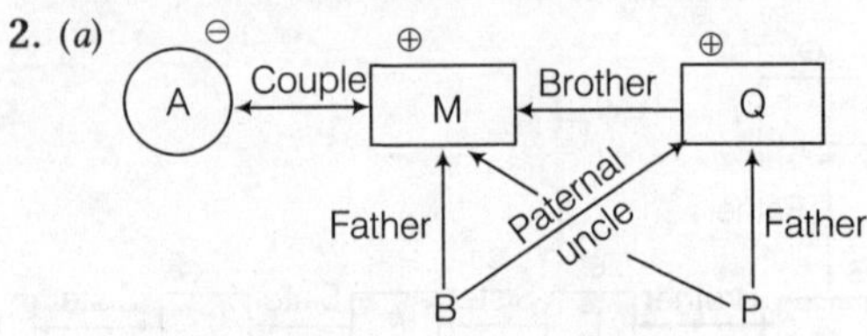

Q is paternal uncle of B and M is the paternal uncle of P.

A is the wife of M and M is the father of B.

Hence, A is the mother of B.

3. (*b*) The only son of woman's grandfather will be woman's father who is the father of man's brother and therefore of man also. Thus, the woman is the sister of that man.

4. (*a*) $L \div M \times O - P \div Q$ means L is the daughter of M, M is the father of O, O is the son of P, P is the daughter of Q. So, M is the husband of P, L and O are their children.

   So, L is the granddaughter of Q.

5. (*c*) $R \div S \times T$ means R is the daughter of S, S is the father of T. So, R and T are children of S. So, son of R is the nephew of T. So, '?' should be replaced by '–'.

6. (*e*) $A - B \times C + D - E$ means A is the son of B, B is the father of C, C is the wife of D, D is the son of E.

   So, C is the sister of A, B is a male person, D is the brother-in-law of A, gender of E is not define. So, none of the given options is correct.

7. (*e*)

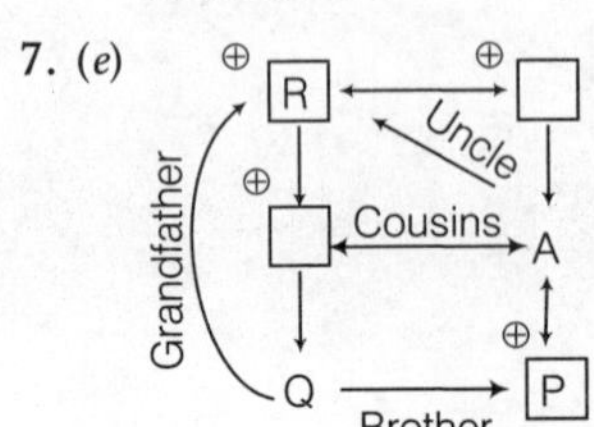

So, A can be uncle or aunt of P.

8. (*e*) Grandfather's only son is father. Son of father is brother. So, that boy is the brother of Sunita.

9. (*d*) A is the father of C and C is the sister of D. So, A is the father of D. D is the son of B, so B is the wife of A. E is the brother of A. B is the sister-in-law of E.

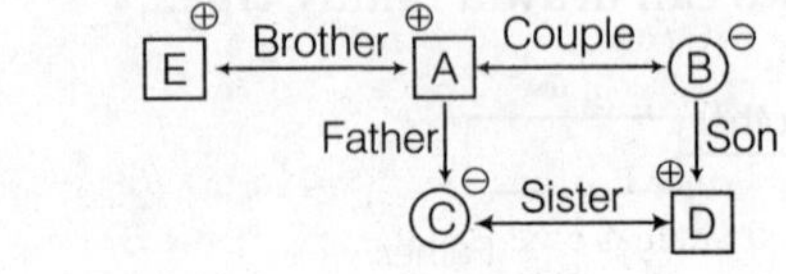

10. (*a*)

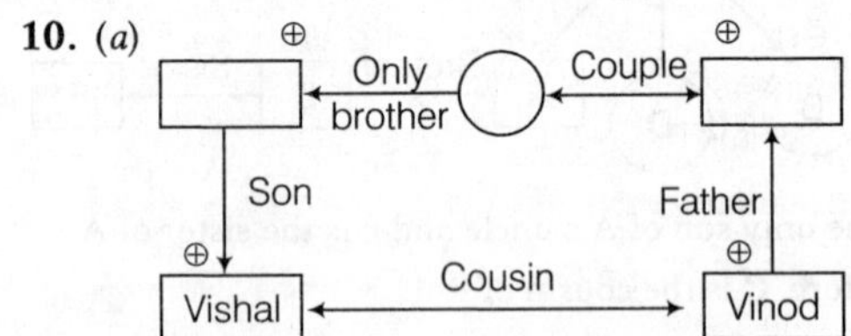

Vinod's father's wife's only brother is Vinod's maternal uncle.

Vishal is the son of Vinod's maternal uncle. So, Vishal is cousin of Vinod.

11. (*b*) Only daughter of woman's father means that woman herself. So, the woman is the mother of that person.

12. (*d*) $P * Q + R$ means, P is the sister-in-law of Q and Q is the mother-in-law of R.

    So, P is not the mother-in-law of Q and R.

    Hence, options (a) and (b) are incorrect.

    Q is the mother-in-law of R, but we don't know whether R is the daughter-in-law or son-in-law of Q.

13. (*a*) $X - Y + Z$ means, Y is the mother-in-law of Z and X is the daughter-in-law of Y.

    So, Y is definitely the mother-in-law.

14. (*c*) Only child of grandfather is mother or father. So, the daughter of that child, i.e. mother or father. So, that girl is the sister of Mihir.

15. (*d*) Maternal grandfather's only child means mother. Son of mother may be brother or Sudhir himself.

16. (*b*) Mother's brother is maternal uncle. So, Kapil's maternal uncle is the father of Shilpa's son. So, Shilpa is the maternal aunt of Kapil and Kapil is the nephew of Shilpa.

17. (*c*) From option (a), $M \div K + T$

    M is sister of K and K is father of T.

    So, M is the aunt of T.

    From option (b), $M \times K + T$

    M is brother of K and K is father of T.

    So, M is the uncle of T.

    From option (c), $M \times K - T$

    M is brother of K and K is mother of Q.

    So, M is maternal uncle of T.

18. (*e*) From option (a), $H+J+T$

H is father of J and J is father of T.

So, H is paternal grandfather of T.

From option (b), $T\times K+H$

T is brother of K and K is father of H.

So, T is the uncle of H.

From option (c), $H+J\times T$

H is father of J and J is brother of T.

So, H is the father of T.

From option (d), $H-J+T$

H is mother of J and J is father of T.

So, H is paternal grandmother of T.

Hence, none of the options follows.

19. (*a*) Mother's only brother means maternal uncle and daughter of maternal uncle is cousin sister. So, Subodh is the cousin of that girl.

Though sex of Subodh is not clear in the question but you can assume that Subodh is male.

20. (*d*) Wife's grandfather's only child means wife's father. Daughter of wife's father can be wife or sister-in-law.

21. (*d*) Mother's husband means father. Father's sister is aunt and she is also that man's aunt.

So, that lady is the sister of that man.

22. (*d*)

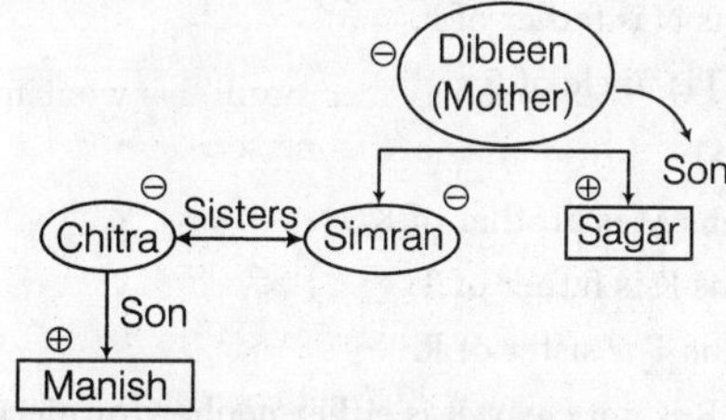

Sagar is Manish's maternal uncle.

So, options (a) and (b) are not true.

Simran is Manish's aunt. So, option (c) is not true.

Chitra is Sagar's sister. Option (d) is true.

23. (*b*) A is the brother of F and F is the daughters of D. So, A is the son of D. P is the brother of D. So, P is the uncle of A.

24. (*d*) Grandmother's only child means father or mother and daughter of that child means Nidhi herself or her sister.

25. (*d*) Anurag says that the girl is the daughter of only child of Anurag's father. So, the girl is the daughter of Anurag and Anurag's wife is the mother of that girl.

26. (*a*) Savita's maternal uncle's father's only daughter is the mother of Savita. Son of the Savita's mother is the brother of Savita.

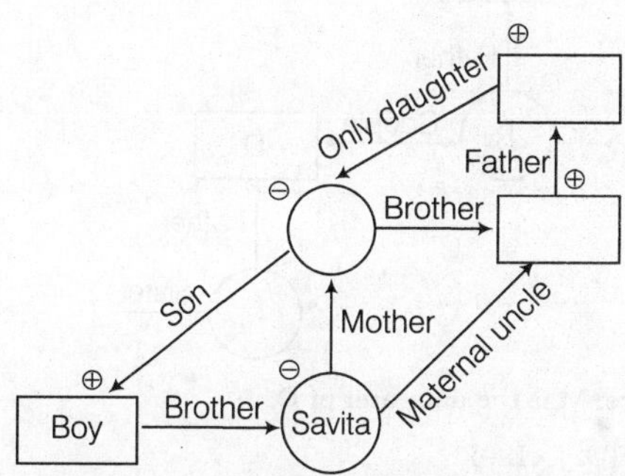

27. (*c*) Ravi is brother of Govind and Prabhu. Prabhu is brother-in-law of Kusuma.

28. (*d*) Gopal' s father only son means Gopal himself. Hence, Gopal is father of Govind.

29. (*d*) The relation may be analysed as follows

My husband's wife—Bhumika

Sister of the son—Daughter of Bhumika

So, the lady on the stage is the daughter of Bhumika.

30. (*a*) The relation may be analysed as follows

My grandmother's daughter - Aunt

My Aunt's only brother–Father

So, Pramod defeated his father.

31. (*a*) $J\div P\%H?T\%L$

Here, J is the son of P, P is the mother of H, T is the mother of L.

Given, J is the brother of T.

So, H, J and T are the childrens of P. So, $H\times T$ is the possible option for this expression.

32. (*b*) In option (a), $L\%R\$D+T\times M$

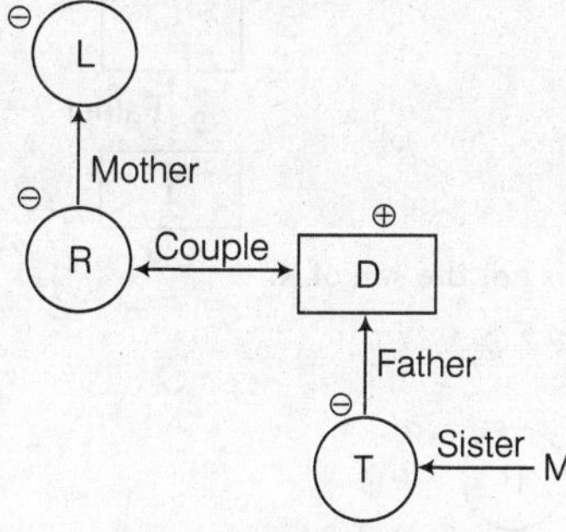

Here, M is not the daughter of D.

In option (b), $L+R\$D+M\times T$

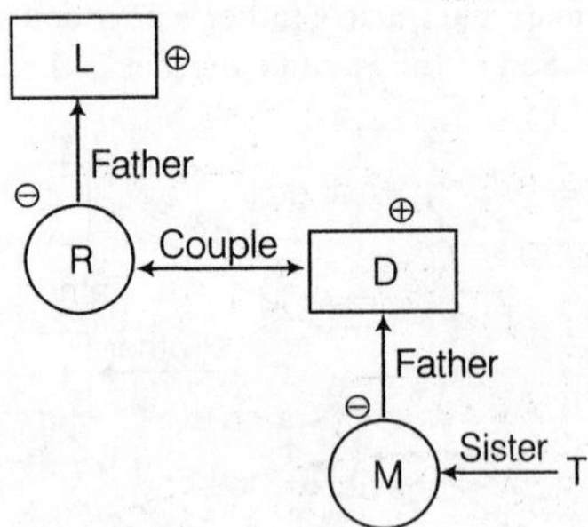

Here, M is the daughter of D.

33. (*b*) I + T % J × L ÷ K

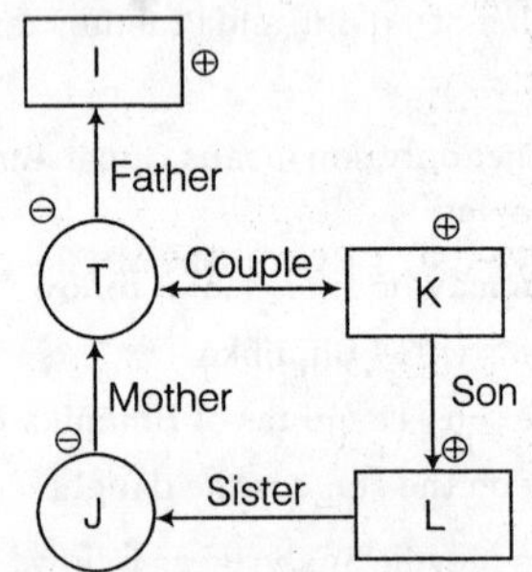

It is clear from the diagram that K is the son-in-law of I.

34. (*d*) Given, Y is the son of X is definitely false.

In expression W $ X + L + Y + T.

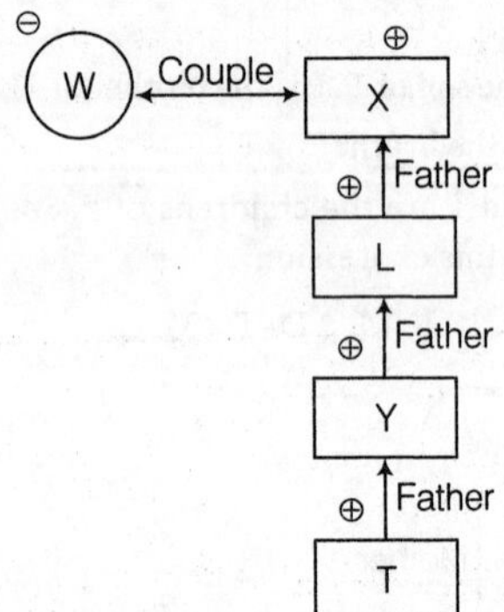

Here, Y is not the son of X.

35. (*d*) R % T × P ? Q+V

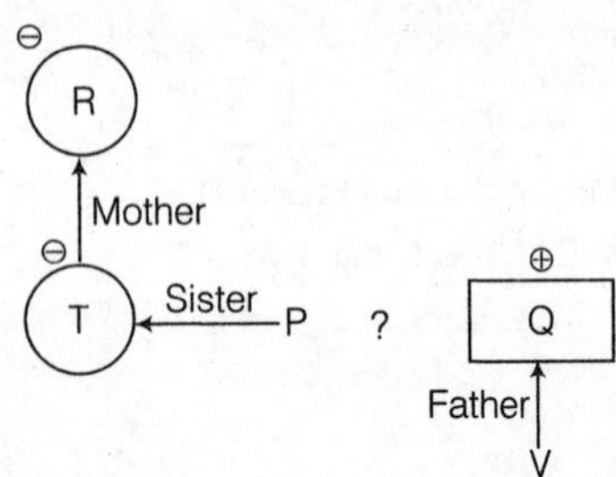

Given, T is the sister-in-law of Q we know that wife's sister is sister-in-law.

Therefore, when P becomes the wife of Q, then T becomes the sister-in-law of Q.

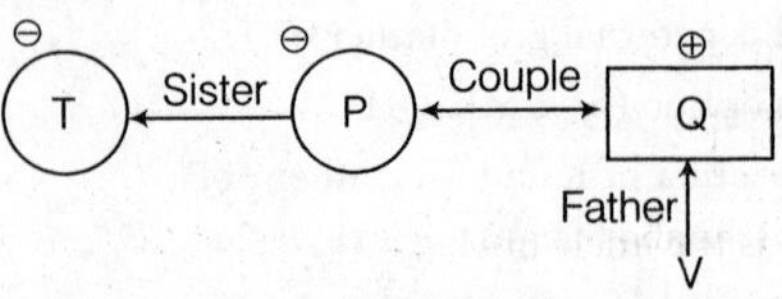

So, '?' should be replaced by $ sign.

36. (*c*) B+D means B is mother of D.

D × M means D is father of M.

M ÷ N means M is brother of N.

Therefore, M is grandson of B.

37. (*e*) In option (a),

J ÷ R means J is brother of R.

R – T means R is sister of T.

T × F means T is father of F.

Therefore, J is uncle of F.

In option (b),

J+R means J is mother of R.

J is a female.

In option (c),

J ÷ M means J is brother of M.

M – N means M is sister of N.

N × F means N is father of F.

Therefore, J is uncle of F.

38. (*b*) In option (a),

M ÷ K means M is brother of K.

K × T means K is father of T.

T – R means T is sister of R.

The sex of R is not clear. R is either nephew or niece of M.

In option (b),

M – J means M is sister of J.

J + R means J is mother of R.

R – N means R is sister of N.

Therefore, R is niece of M.

39. (*a*)

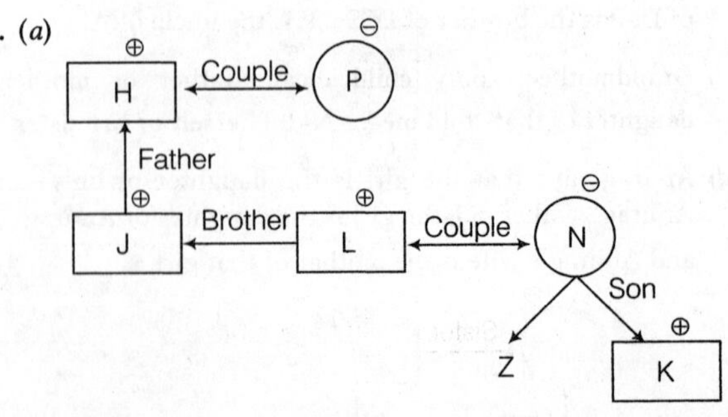

In the above diagram, L is the husband of N, so he is the father of Z and K. Now, J is the brother of L, then he is the uncle of K and Z.

40. (*a*)

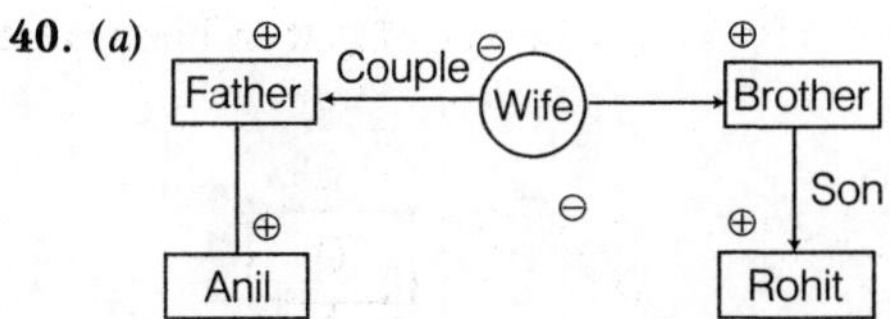

From the above figure, it is clear that Anil and Rohit are the cousin.

41. (*b*)

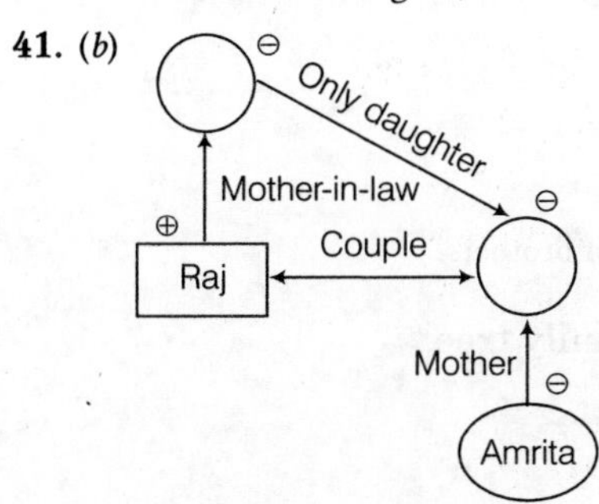

Raj is the father of Amritas, Raj's mother-in-law's only daughter is the wife of Raj.

42. (*b*) Z is maternal uncle of Y, X is maternal grandfather of Z. S is grandson of X.

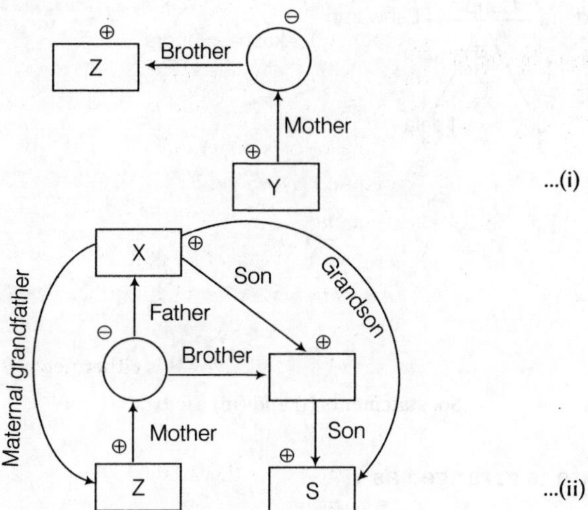

From diagrams (i) and (ii),

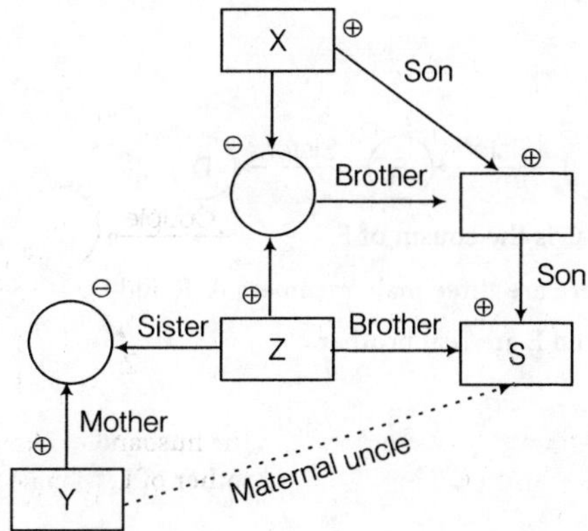

43. (*d*)

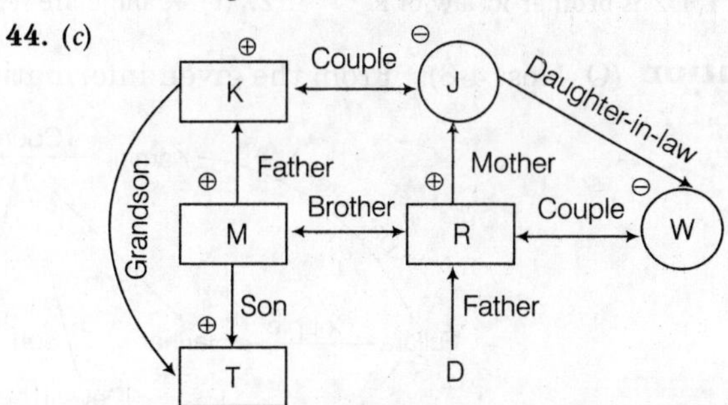

In the diagram, Pallavi becomes the niece of the man.

44. (*c*)

D is the nephew of M or niece of M. Hence, optoin (c) is the answer as the gender of D is not define in the information given in the question.

45. (*c*) The father of girl's uncle means the grandfather of the girl. Daughter of the girl's grandfather is the aunt of the girl. Thus, the boy is the cousin of that girl.

46. (*d*)

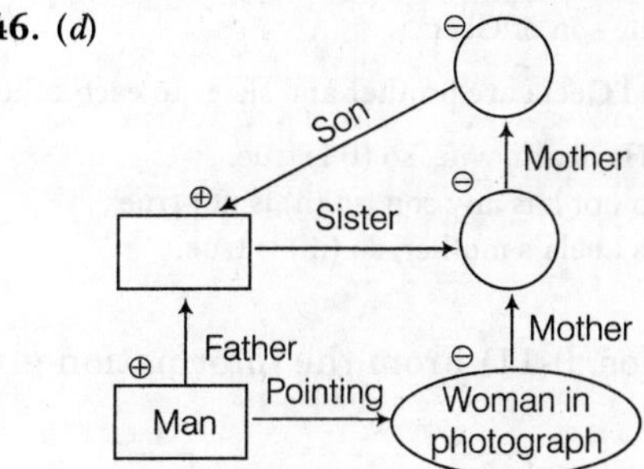

The mother of the woman in photograph is the sister of man's father. So, it becomes the maternal aunt of the man. Hence, the woman in photograph is the maternal cousin of the man.

Advanced Level

Solution (Q. Nos. 1-3) From the information given data is arranged as

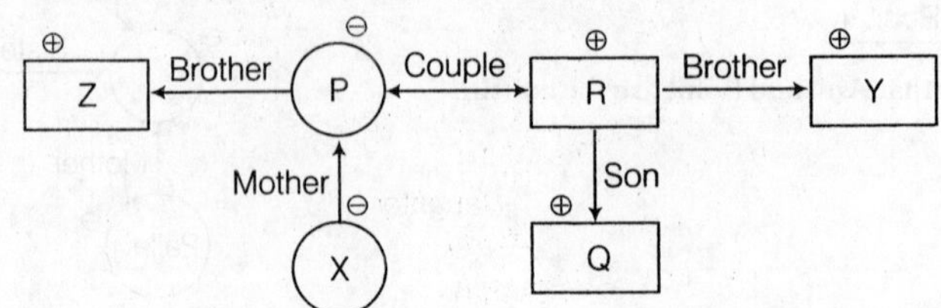

1. (*b*) Z is brother-in-law of R. **2.** (*b*) X and P are females. **3.** (*d*) R and Y is the pair of brothers.

Solution (Q. Nos. 4-8) From the given information, we can draw the following family tree.

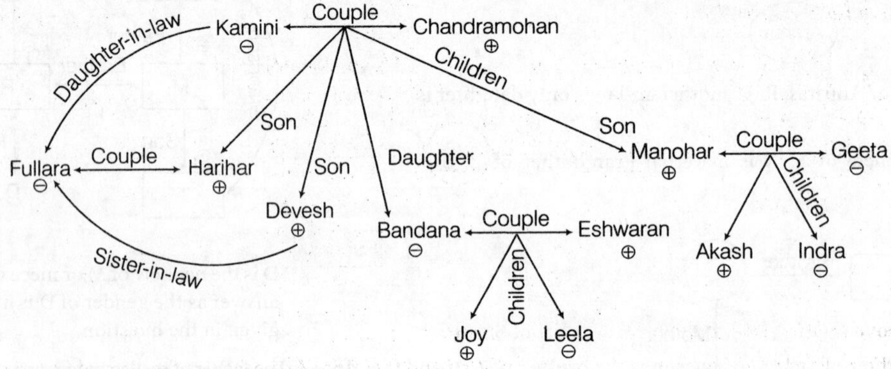

4. (*b*) Joy is the child of Bandana and Eshwaran.

5. (*c*) Leela is the niece of Harihar.

6. (*a*) Akash is the son of Geeta.

7. (*b*) Devesh and Geeta are brother and sister to each other.

8. (*b*) Fullara is Harihar's wife, so (i) is true.
Harihar do not has any son, so (ii) is not true.
Bandana is Leela's mother, so (iii) is true.
So, statements (i) and (iii) are true.

Solution (Q. Nos. 9-11) From the information given data is arranged as

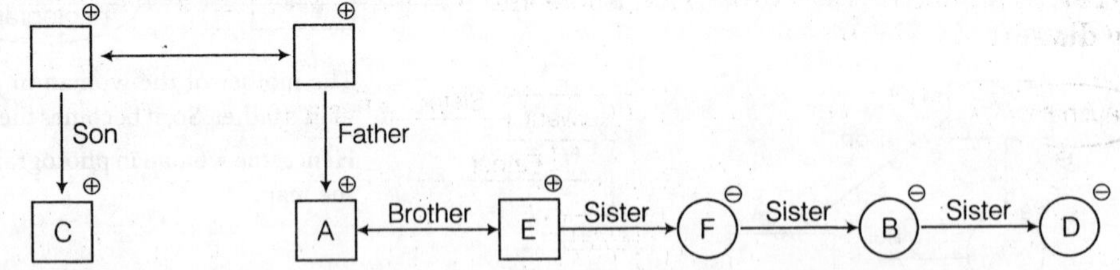

9. (*a*) F is the sister of E.
C is only son of A's uncle, i.e. C is A's cousin.
A is the brother of E and F.
So, C is the cousin of F.

10. (*b*) There are three male members A, E and C.

11. (*a*) A and E are real brothers.

12. (*c*) Making relation tree from given information,

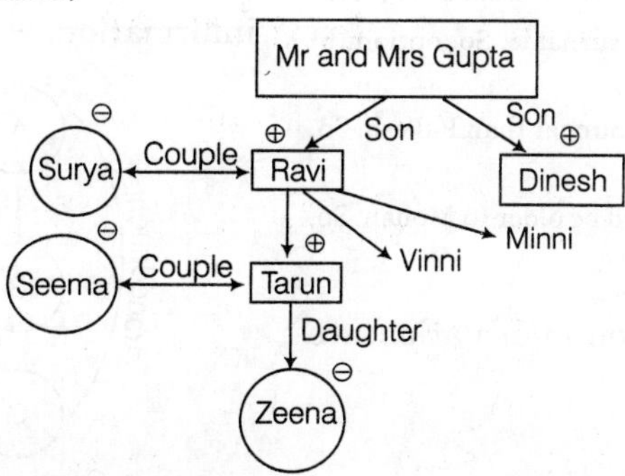

Ravi and Dinesh are brothers. So, Dinesh is uncle of Tarun.

The gender of Vinni and Minni is not specified. It is clear that from above relation tree that Dinesh is uncle of Tarun.

13. (*d*) Making relating tree from given information,

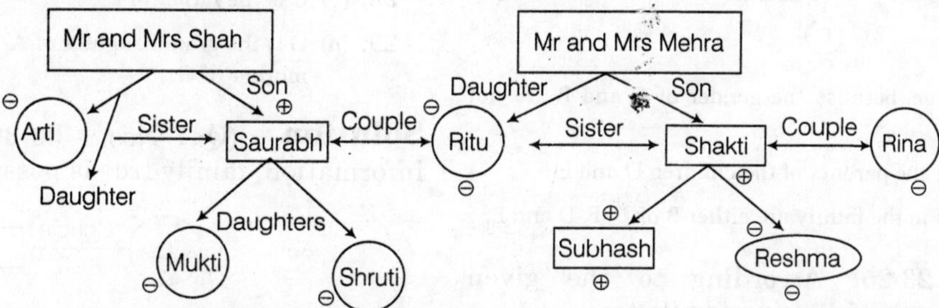

It is clear from above relation tree that Arti is the aunt of Shruti.

Shruti is the daughter of Saurabh. Saurabh is the brother of Arti and therefore Arti becomes the aunt of Shruti.

14. (*b*) A — Daughter-in-law — Son — B — Couple — C — Sister — D — Couple — E — Brother

B and E are brothers.

B and C are couple and D and E are also couple.

D is the wife of A's son, so D is the daughter-in-law of A.

15. (*d*) Let there are 'b' brothers and 's' sisters, then according to Sanjay

$$b - 1 = s \quad \text{...(i)}$$

According to Sarita, $b = 2(s - 1)$ ...(ii)

On solving Eqs. (i) and (ii) $b = 4$ and $s = 3$

Thus, there are 4 brothers and 3 sisters.

Solution (Q. Nos. 16-19) Mohan is Rakesh's paternal uncle and Kulwant is Rakesh's father. So, Mohan is the brother of Kulwant. The family diagram is as follows

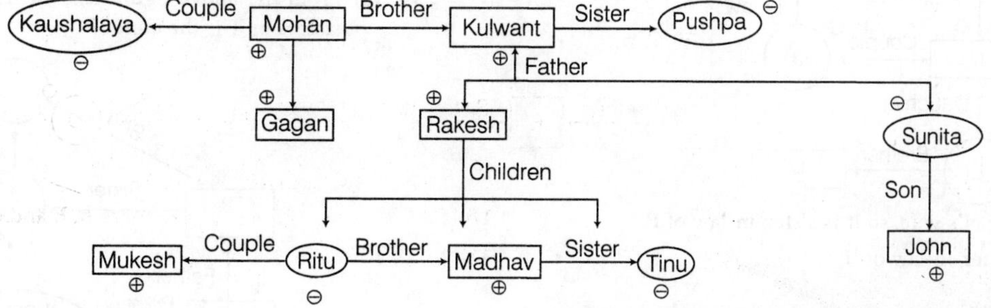

16. (*c*) From this, John is Kulwant's grandson.

17. (*b*) Tinu is John's cousin.

18. (*d*) Mukesh is Gagan's cousin's son-in- law.

So, Mukesh is Gagan's nephew-in-law.

19. (*c*) Mohan could be older than Kulwant. Option (a) cannot be correct.

Mukesh and Gagan may share the same surname. So, option (b) cannot be correct.

As, Madhav is Rakesh's son. Madhav is younger than Rakesh. So, option (c) is correct.

As, Pushpa is the Mohan's sister, she could be older to Mohan. So, option (d) cannot be correct.

Solution (Q. Nos. 20-22) From the given information, we can draw the following family tree.

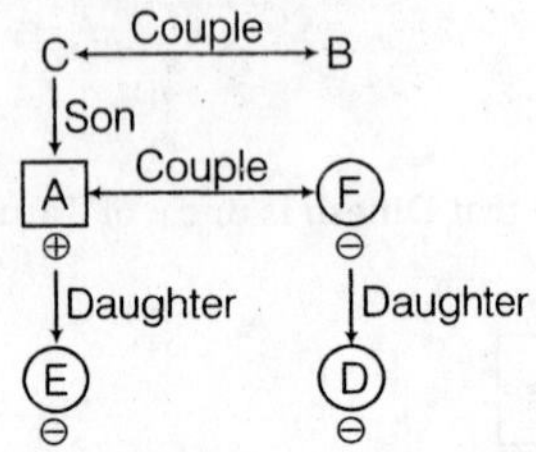

20. (*d*) We cannot determine, because the gender of C and B are not given.

21. (*e*) Clearly, A and F are the parents of the children D and E.

22. (*c*) Clearly, the females in the family are either B or C, F, D and E.

Solution (Q. Nos. 23-25) According to the given information, we can draw the following family tree.

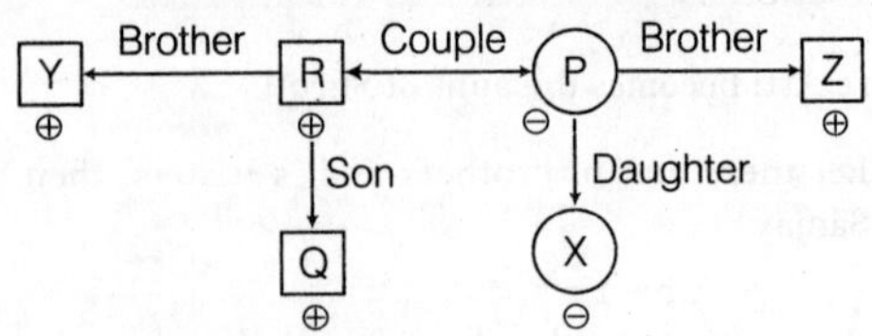

23. (*b*) Z is the brother-in-law of R.

24. (*a*) R is the father of Q.

25. (*b*) P has two children, i.e. Q and X.

26. (*d*) According to the given information in the question,

There are two married couples

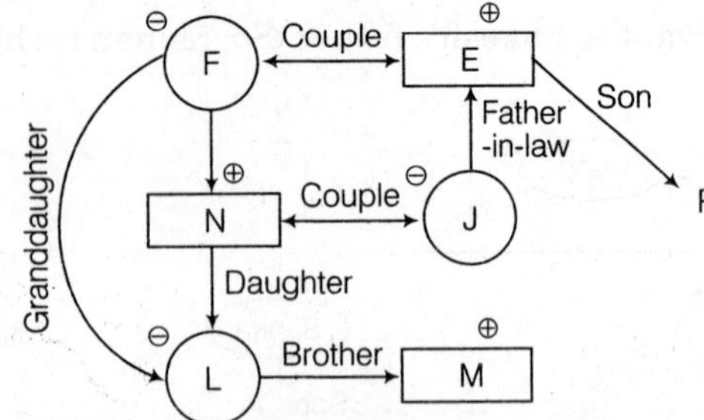

J is P's brother N's wife, so it is sister-in-law of P.

So 'J' is the sister-in-law of 'P'.

Solution (Q. Nos. 27-29) According to the given information, we can draw the following family tree.

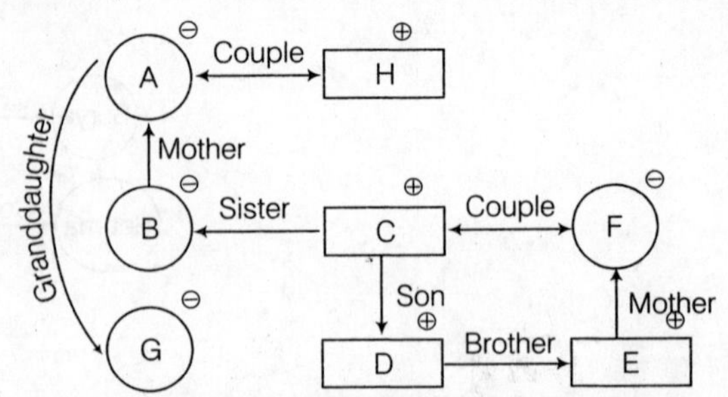

G is shown by doded lines is either daughter of B or sister of E.

27. (*b*) F is the daughter-in-law of H.

28. (*a*) C is the father of E.

29. (*d*) G is the granddaughter of A. Therefore, either B or F is the mother of G.

Solution (Q. Nos. 30-34) From the given information, family tree is possible.

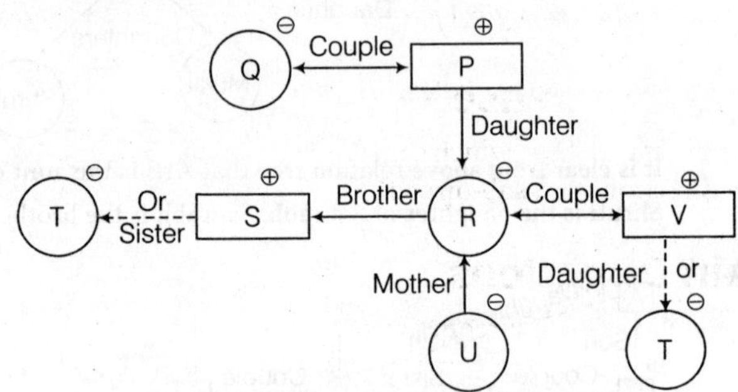

T may be either sister of S or daughter of V.

30. (*c*) V is the husband of R.

31. (*d*) T and V are not married because V is married to R.

32. (*d*) From the above figure, it is clear that, S and R are the children of P. T may or may not be the child of P. So, P has 2 or 3 children.

33. (*c*) Q is the grandmother of U.

34. (*d*) From the above figure it is clear that either T and U are sisters or T is the aunt of U.

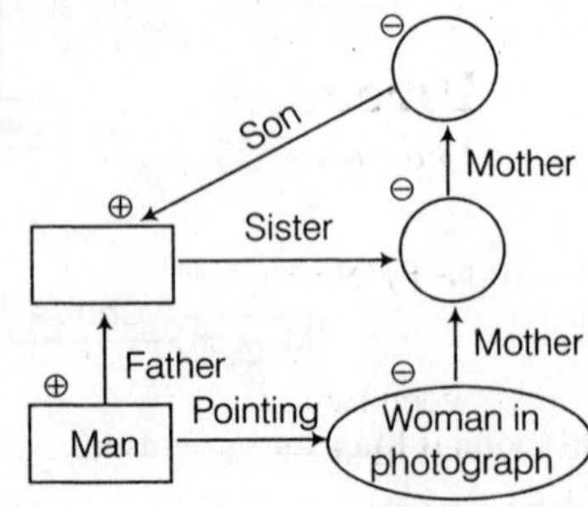

5

Direction Sense Test

*Questions on '**Direction Sense Test**' contains a set of directions, which need to be followed up in a successive manner to ascertain the final direction or the distance between the two points. This test is designed to judge the candidate's ability to trace and follow the logical path correctly and sense the direction correctly.*

Direction Sense Test

The position towards which someone or something moves or faces is known as direction. Directions can be classified as main directions and sub-directions.

Main Directions

There are four main directions East, West, North and South.

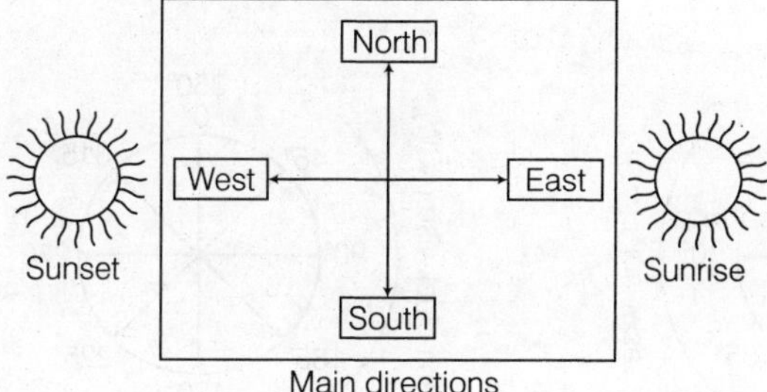

Main directions

East and West as well as North and South are opposite to each other as shown above. The Sun always rises in the East and sets in the West. To remember these four directions always remember the word 'NEWS'.

Sub/Cardinal Direction

A direction between two consecutive main directions is called sub or cardinal direction.

These are North-East (N–E), North-West (N–W), South-East (S–E) and South-West (S–W).

Here, angle formed between two consecutive main directions is 90° and angle formed between a cardinal direction and main direction is 45°.

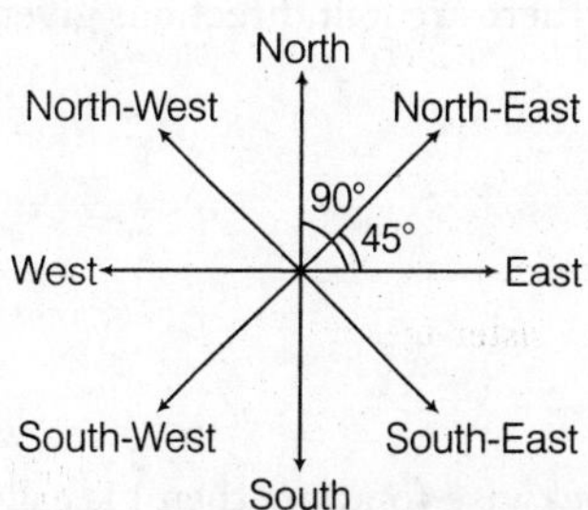

General Tip

If you are **facing East** direction, then your left hand is towards **North** while your **right hand** is towards **South** as shown below. Similarly, you can know the direction of your hands while you are facing or moving in any other three directions.

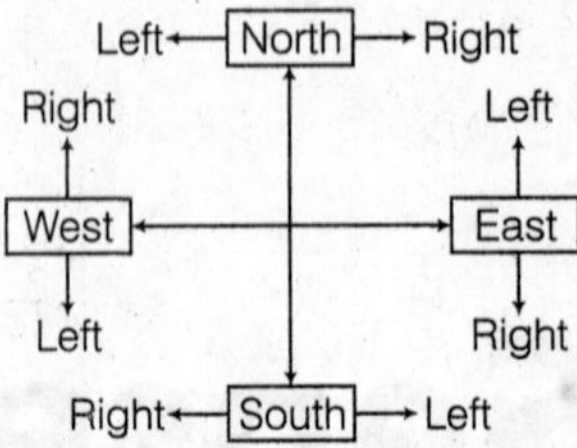

Concept of Turn (Movement)

(i) **Clockwise Turn** (Right turn) If a person turns in the direction of motion of hands of clock, then turning is called **clockwise turn.**

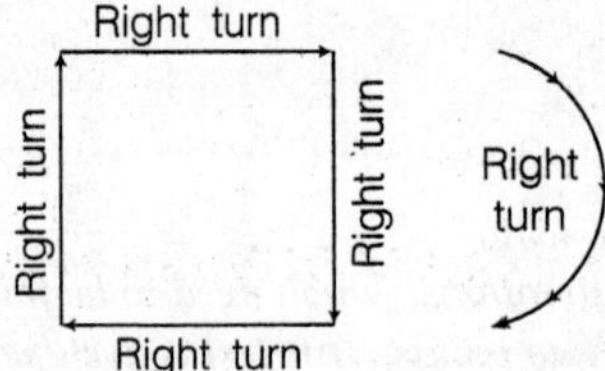

(ii) **Anti-clockwise Turn** (Left turn) If a person turns in the direction opposite to the motion of hands of clock, then turning is called **anti-clockwise turn.**

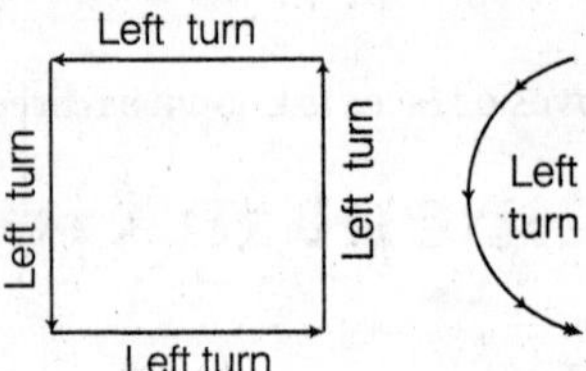

Concept of Degree

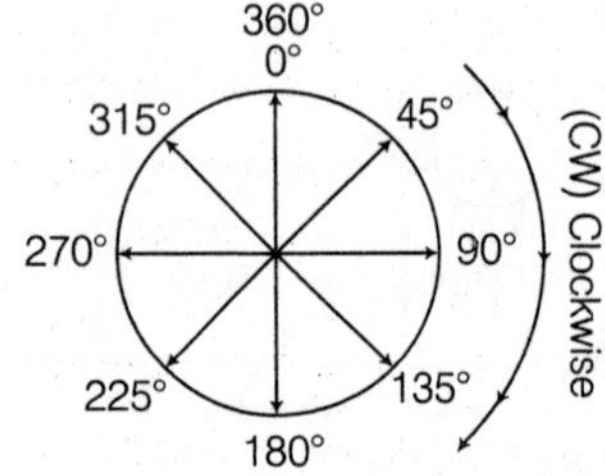

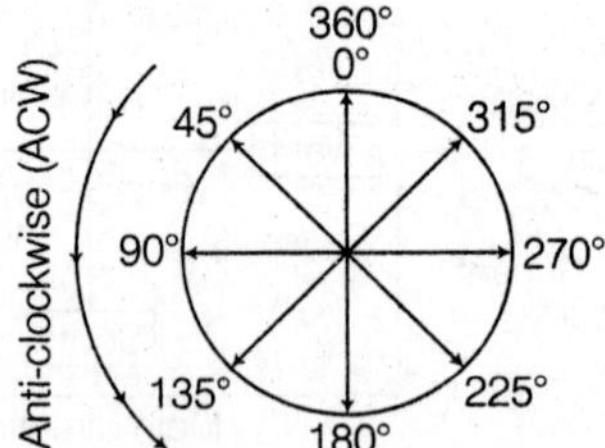

Rotation of Direction

Let us assume that there are four directions given as 1, 2, 3 and 4 and following movements take places in these directions.

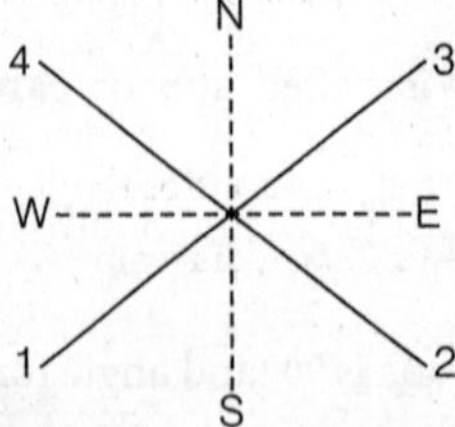

(i) **45° anti-clockwise rotation,** then 1 is called South direction, 2 is called East, 3 is called North and 4 is called West direction.

(ii) **135° clockwise rotation,** then 2 is called West direction, 1 is called North, 4 is called East and 3 is called South direction.

(iii) **90° clockwise rotation,** then 3 is called South-East direction, 2 is called South-West, 1 is called North-West and 4 is called North-East direction.

(iv) **45° anti-clockwise rotation,** then 4 is called West direction, 3 is called North, 2 is called East and 1 is called South direction.

Concept of Minimum Distance

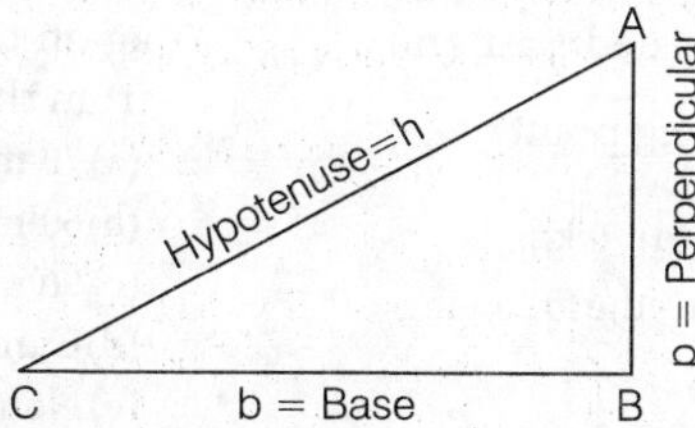

h = AC is the minimum distance to reach A to C or C to A, is calculated as

$$AC^2 = AB^2 + BC^2 \Rightarrow h^2 = p^2 + b^2.$$

The above formula is known as 'Pythagoras Theorem'.

Expert's Advice Around 1-3 questions are asked from this chapter. The best way of solving these questions is to follow the instructions given in the question and make a diagram accordingly, with the help of diagram you can solve the question easily.

Types of Questions Generally Asked in Examinations

There are multiple types of questions which are asked from the chapter 'Direction Sense Test', so it is quite difficult to predict exact type of questions that are asked, but on the basis of **Observation, Analysis and Experience**. Here, we are giving different types of questions that are usually asked in the examination. Almost all the questions in this chapter can be categorized into these types. Also, this description of type will make your study easy and streamline.

Type 1 Movement in Given Direction

These type of questions are pertaining to the movement of a person or a vehicle in a given direction. Using the sense of direction, you are required to determine the location of the object, after that object has covered a certain distance taking turns towards right or left. You should keep in mind the change in direction when a person or vehicle takes a right or left turn.

Initial direction	Direction in which the object will move after taking the turn	
	Right	**Left**
East	South	North
West	North	South
North	East	West
South	West	East

Examples Based on Type 1

Ex 1. A man starts from his house and walked straight for 10 m towards North and turned left and walked 25 m. He then turned right and walked 5 m and again turned right and walked 25 m. **FCI (Assist) 2012**

Which direction is he facing now?

(a) North (b) East (c) South (d) West

Sol. (*b*) According to the given information, we can draw the following diagram

According to the diagram, he is facing East.

Ex **2.** A man walked 2 km South, turned right and walked $\frac{1}{2}$ km, turned North and walked 5 km, then he turned East and walked $4\frac{1}{2}$ km. How far is he from the starting point?

(a) 3 km (b) 4 km (c) 5 km (d) 6 km

Sol. (*c*) According to the given information, we can draw the following diagram

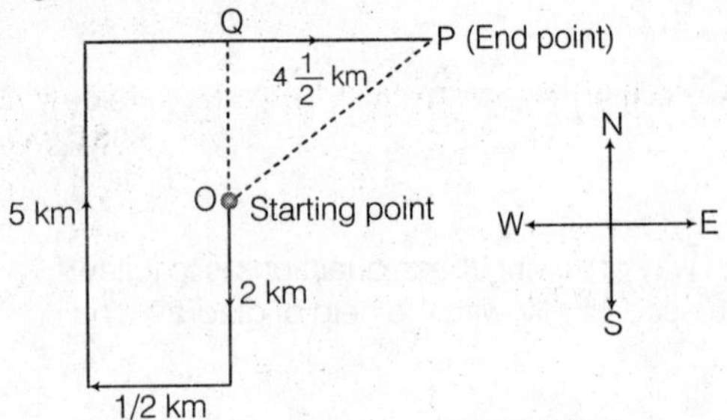

Now, required distance, $OP = \sqrt{OQ^2 + QP^2}$

$$= \sqrt{(5-2)^2 + \left(4\frac{1}{2} - \frac{1}{2}\right)^2} = \sqrt{3^2 + 4^2} = 5 \text{ km}$$

Ex **3.** Kartik start moving from a point, facing in East direction. After walking 10 m, he turned to his left and walked 20 m, before turning to his right. Then, he walked a distance of 15 m, then turned to his right and stop after walking further a distance of 20 m. Find how far Kartik is from his starting point. **CMAT 2015**

(a) 20 m (b) 30 m (c) 15 m (d) 25 m

Sol. (*d*) The direction map of Kartik's walk can be draw as

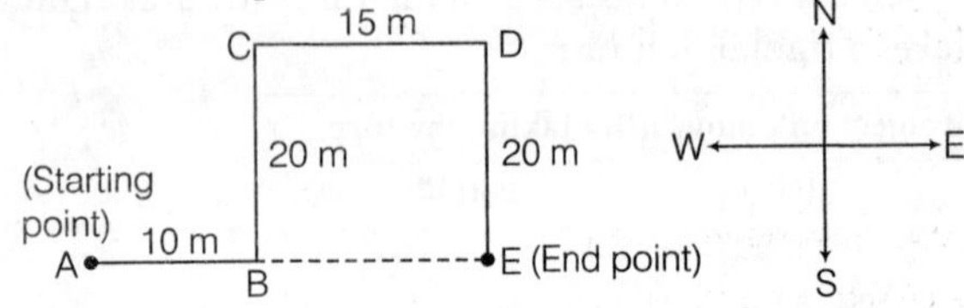

∴ The distance between the starting point and end point is

$$AB + BE = 10 + 15 = 25 \text{ m}$$

Ex **4.** Facing towards North, Ravi walks 30 m. He then turns left and walks 50 m. He again turns left and walks 30 m. How far is he from his original position and towards which direction?

(a) 30 m, North (b) 20 m, East
(c) 50 m, West (d) 20 m, South

Sol. (*c*) Movement of Ravi is shown in the figure

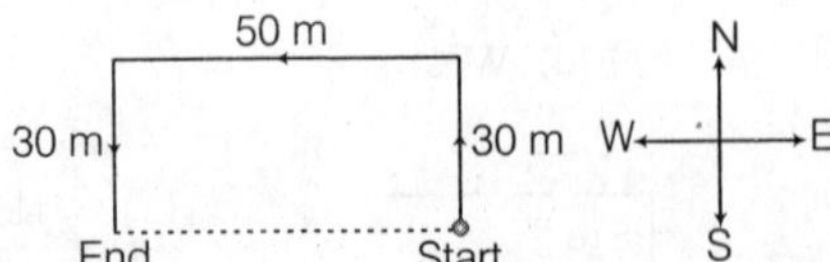

From the figure it is clear that, Ravi is 50 m away in West direction from his original position.

Ex **5.** A man walked 40 m towards West, took a left turn and walked 30 m. He then took a right turn and walked 20 m. He again took a right turn and walked 30 m. How far was he from the starting point? **Punjab & Sind Bank (PO) 2010**

(a) 70 m
(b) 60 m
(c) 90 m
(d) Cannot be determined
(e) None of the above

Sol. (*b*) Movement of W is shown in the figure

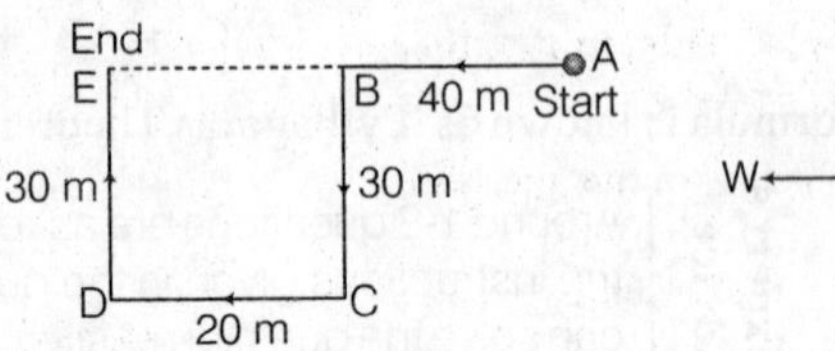

Required distance, AE = AB + BE
= 40 + 20
= 60 m

Ex **6.** A man is facing towards west and turns through 45° clockwise, again 180° clockwise and then turns through 270° anti-clockwise. In which direction is he facing now?

(a) West
(b) North-West
(c) South
(d) South-West

Sol. (*d*) As shown in figure, the man initially faces in the direction OA. On moving 45° clockwise, the man faces in the direction OB. On further moving 180° clockwise, he faces in the direction OC. Finally, on moving 270° anti-clockwise, he faces in the direction OD, which is South-west.

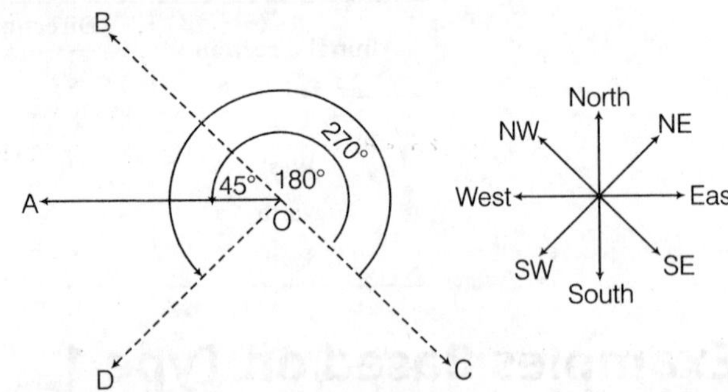

Ex **7.** In a clock, the time is 7:30 am. the clock is so placed that its hour-hand is facing North-West. In which direction will be minute hand facing?

(a) South
(b) East
(c) North-East
(d) West
(e) South-East

Sol. (*d*) When the time is 7:30, the minute hand is 45° behind the hour hand (see the diagram) thus the minute hand is facing West.

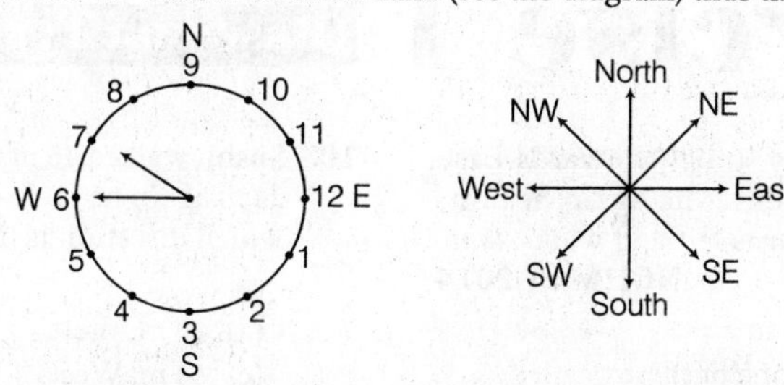

***Ex* 8.** One evening before Sunset, two friends Raman and Arjun were talking to each other face-to-face. If Raman's shadow was exactly to his left side, which direction was Arjun facing? **SSC (Steno) 2013**

(a) West (b) East (c) North (d) South

Sol. (*c*) According to the question,

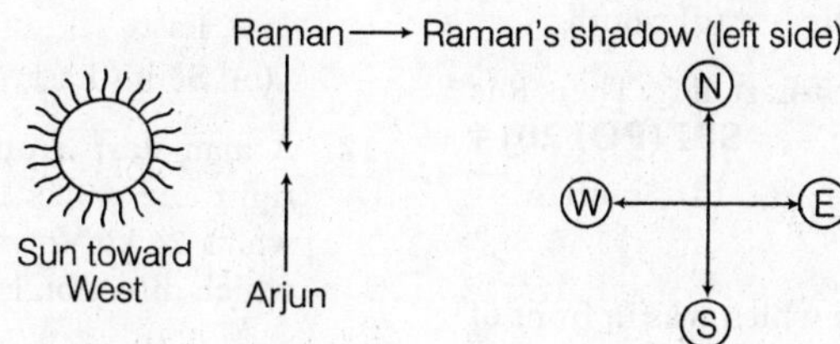

So, Arjun was facing North.

***Ex* 9.** If South-East becomes North and North-East becomes West and all the rest directions are changed in the same manner, what will be the direction for the West? **UPPSC (Pre) 2012**

(a) North-East (b) South (c) South-East (d) South-West

Sol. (*c*) According to the question, the direction diagram will be as follows

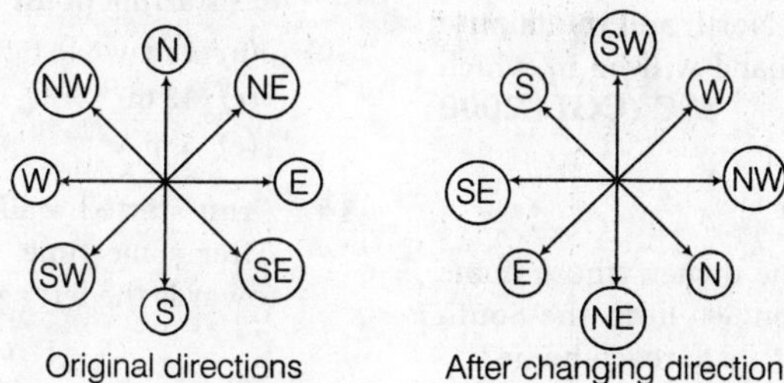

Now, from the above diagrams, it is clear that South-East will be the direction for West.

Intro Exercise 1 (Based on Type 1)

1. Ravi starts from his house and walks straight towards East. After walking 75 m, he turns left and walks 25 m. Again, he turns left and walks 25 m. Once again, he turns left and walks 25 m. How far is he now from his house? **NCHMCT 2014**
   (a) 0 m (b) 50 m
   (c) 150 m (d) None of these

2. One fine morning after Sunrise, Vikram and Sailesh were standing in a lawn with their back towards each other. Vikram's shadow fell exactly towards left hand side. Which direction was Sailesh facing?
   (a) East (b) West (c) North (d) South

3. P is 40 m South-West of Q, R is 40 m South-East of Q. Then, R is in which direction of P? **SBI (PO) 2014**
   (a) North (b) East (c) West (d) South
   (e) None of these

4. Postman was returning to the post office which was in front of him to the North. When the post office was 100 m away from him, he turned to the left and moved 50 m deliver the last letter at Vilashvilla. He then moved in the same direction for 40 m, turned to his right and moved 100 m. How many metres was he away from the post office?
   (a) 0 (b) 90 (c) 150 (d) 100

5. At 12:30 the hour hand of a clock faces North and the minute hand faces South. At 2:45 the minute hand will be in which direction? **SSC (CGL) 2000**
   (a) North-West (b) West
   (c) South-East (d) East

6. A dog is taken out every evening by the owner whose home faces East. They walk 200 m West, then 500 m in the South direction. Which direction should they take to reach home?
   (a) North-East (b) North
   (c) North-West (d) South-East

7. Pratap starts from school and walks 7 km towards East. He takes a left and walks 4 km, then takes a right and walks 2 km, again takes a right and walks 3 km. Which direction is he facing now?
   (a) South (b) North
   (c) East (d) West

8. A person rode his bicycle northwards, then turned left and rode 1 km and again turned left and rode 2 km. He found himself exactly 1 km West of his starting point. How far did he ride Northwards initially? **SBI (PO) 2014**
   (a) 1 km (b) 2 km
   (c) 3 km (d) 4 km
   (e) 5 km

9. Town D is towards East of town F. Town B is towards North of town D. Town H is towards South of town B. Towards which directions is town H from town F? **SBI (PO) 2010**
   (a) East (b) South-East
   (c) North-East (d) Cannot be determined
   (e) None of these

10. Sushil walked 15 m towards South, took a left turn and walked 20 m again he took a left turn and walked 15 m. How far and in which direction is he from the starting point? **BOB (PO) 2010**
    (a) 20 m, West (b) 20 m, East
    (c) 50 m, West (d) 50 m, East
    (e) Data inadequate

11. If South-East is called 'South', North-West is called North, 'South-West' is the called 'West' and so on, what will 'East' be called?
    (a) East (b) North-East
    (c) South-East (d) North

12. A man starts from a point, walks 8 km towards North, turns right and walks 12 km, turns left and walks 7 km, turns and walks 24 km towards South, turns right and walks 12 km. In which direction is he from the starting point? **NICL (GIC) AO 2013**
    (a) North (b) South
    (c) West (d) East

13. Anamika who is facing South walks 20 m, then she turns to her right and walks 15 m, then she turns to her right and walks 16 m, again she turns to her right and walks 12 m. How far is she from her starting point? **CGPSC (Pre) 2013**
    (a) 4 m (b) 16 m
    (c) 12 m (d) 7 m
    (e) 5 m

14. Arun started walking positioning his back towards the sun. After some time, he turned left, then turned right and then towards the left again. In which direction is he going now? **FMS 2010**
    (i) North (ii) West (iii) South (iv) East
    (a) (i) or (ii) (b) (i) or (iii)
    (c) (ii) or (iii) (d) (iii) or (iv)

15. P walked 20 m towards North, took a left turn and walked 10 m, then took a right turn and walked 20 m, again took a right turn and walked 10 m. How far is he from his starting point? **HGB (PO) 2009**
    (a) 50 m
    (b) 60 m
    (c) 40 m
    (d) Cannot be determined
    (e) None of the above

16. Two buses start from the opposite points of a main road, 150 km apart. The first bus runs for 25 km and takes a right turn and then runs for 15 km. It then turns left and for another 25 km and takes the direction back to reach the main road. In the Meantime due to a minor breakdown, the other bus has run only 35 km along the main road. What would be the distance between the two buses at this point? **CMAT 2013**
    (a) 65 km (b) 75 km
    (c) 80 km (d) 85 km

17. A person starts from a point A and travels 3 km Eastwards to B and then turns left and travels thrice that distance to reach C. He again turns left and travels five time the distance he covered between A and B and reaches his destination D. The shortest distance between the starting point and the destination is

(a) 12 km (b) 15 km (c) 16 km (d) 18 km

18. Manu goes 40 km North, turns right and goes 80 km, turns right again and goes 30 km. In the end, he turns right again and goes 80 km. How far is he from his starting point if he goes straight ahead another 50 km and turns left to go his last 10 km? **MAT 2014**

(a) 10 km (b) 30 km (c) 40 km (d) 50 km

19. Two ladies and two men are playing cards and are seated at North, East, South and West of a table. No lady is facing East. Persons sitting opposite to each other are not of the same sex. One man is facing South. Which directions are the ladies facing?

(a) East and West (b) South and East
(c) North and East (d) North and West

20. John's house is 100 m North of his uncle's office. His uncle's house is located 200 m West of his (uncle's) office. Kabir is the friend of John and he stays 100 m East of John's house. The office of Kabir is located 100 metres South of his house. Then, how far is his uncle's house from Kabir's office?

(a) 200 m (b) 300 m (c) 400 m (d) 500 m

21. Mohan walked 30 m towards South, took a left turn and walked 15 m. He then took a right turn and walked 20 m. He again took a right turn and walked 15 m. How far is he from the starting point? **SBI Associate Bank (PO) 2010**

(a) 95 m (b) 50 m
(c) 70 m (d) Cannot be determined
(e) None of these

22. Nikhil walked 30 m towards East, took a left turn and walked 20 m. He again took a left turn and walked 30 m. How far and in which direction is he from his starting point? **BOI (PO) 2010**

(a) 20 m, North (b) 80 m, North
(c) 20 m, South (d) 80 m, South
(e) Data inadequate

23. One evening, Raja started to walk towards the Sun. After walking a while, he turned to his right and again to his right. After walking a while, he again turned right. In which direction is he facing? **NICL (GIC) AO 2013**

(a) South (b) East
(c) West (d) North

24. A man walked 3 m towards North, turned West and walked 2 m, then turned North again and walked 1m and then turned East and walked 5 m. How far away is he from the starting point? **SSC (CGL) 2014**

(a) 1 m (b) 2 m (c) 3 m (d) 5 m

25. A child is looking for his father. He went 90 m in the East before turning to his right. He went 20 m before turning to his right again to look for his father at his uncle's place 30 m from this point. His father was not there. From here he went 100 m to the North before meeting his father in a street. How far did the son meet his father from the starting point? **MAT 2013**

(a) 80 m (b) 100 m (c) 140 m (d) 260 m

26. A start for his office and walks 3 km toward North. Then, he turns right and walks 2 and then again turns right and walks 5 km, then again turns right and walks 2 km and then again twin turns right and walks 2 km. Where is he now from the starting point? **GIC (Assist) 2013**

(a) 5 km (b) 10 km
(c) 20 km (d) in his own office

27. In a square-shaped field A, B, C, D persons are standing at the middle of each side. You have to bear in mind the directions to be followed as shown in the figure.

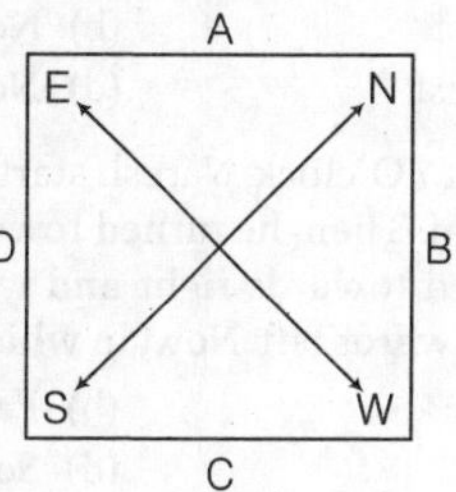

If A moves clockwise $2\frac{1}{2}$ sides and D moves anti-clockwise $2\frac{1}{2}$ sides they will be in **SSC (CPO) 2010**

(a) South and West region
(b) North and East region
(c) South and North region
(d) North and West region

28. John walks 20 m North. Then, he turns right and walks 30 m. Then, he turns right and walks 35 m. Then, he turns left and walks 15 m. Then, he again turns left and walks 15 m. In which direction and how many metres away is he from his original position?

(a) 15 m, West (b) 30 m, East
(c) 30 m, West (d) 45 m, East

29. A cyclist rides 40 km to the East, turns North and rides 20 km, again turns left and rides 20 km. How far is he from the starting point? **SSC (10+2) 2014**

(a) 0 km (b) 10 km
(c) $20\sqrt{2}$ km (d) 30 km

30. Rahul travelled from a point X straight to Y at a distance of 80 m. He turned right and walked 50 m, then again turned right and walked 70 m. Finally, he turned right and walked 50 m. How far is he from the starting point? **SSC (CGL) 2014**

(a) 10 m (b) 20 m
(c) 50 m (d) 70 m

31. Sanjeet walks 10 m towards the South. Turning to the left, he walks 20 m, then moves to his right. After moving a distance of 20 m , he turns to the right walks 20 m. Finally, he turns to the right and moves a distance of 10 m far, then in which direction is he from the starting point?

(a) 10 m, North (b) 20 m, South
(c) 20 m, North (d) 10 m, South

32. A watch reads 4:30. If the minute hand point East, in what direction will the hour hand point? **NIFT (UG) 2015**

(a) North-East (b) South-West
(c) North (d) South

33. I run along the sides of a square field ABCD, where C is to the North-East of A and D is to the South-East of B. Starting from A in anti-clockwise direction in which direction shall I be running after crossing B?

(a) East (b) West (c) North (d) South

34. The door of Ajay's house faces the East. From the back side of his house, he walks straight 50 m, then turns to the right and walks 50 m again. Finally, he turns towards left and stops after walking 25 m. Now, Ajay is in which direction from the starting point?

(a) South-East (b) North-East
(c) South-West (d) North-West

35. One morning at 7 O'clock, Naresh started walking with his back towards the Sun. Then, he turned towards left, walked straight and then turned towards right and walked straight. Then, he again turned towards left. Now, in which direction is he facing?

(a) North (b) East **SSC (10+2) 2013**
(c) West (d) South

36. Rani is facing North-West. She turns 90° in the clockwise direction and then 135° in the anti-clockwise direction. Which direction is she facing now?

(a) East (b) West (c) North (d) South

37. Shashank is facing East. He turns 100° in the clockwise direction and then 145° in the anti-clockwise direction. Which direction is he facing now?

(a) East (b) North-East
(c) North (d) South-West

38. While facing East you turn to your left and walk 10 yards. Then, turn to your left and walk 10 yards and now turn 45° to your right and go straight to cover 50 yards. Now, in what direction are you with respect to the starting point? **SNAP 2013**

(a) North-East (b) North
(c) South-East (d) North-West

39. Somesh is facing South. He turns 135° in the anti-clockwise direction and then 180° in the clockwise direction. Which direction is he facing now?

(a) North-East (b) North-West
(c) South-East (d) South-West

40. A is located to the West of B. C is located at North in between A and B. D is exactly to the South of B and also in line with B. In which direction to C is D located? **SSC (CGL) 2014**

(a) South (b) South-East
(c) West (d) South-West

41. Deepak walked 20 m towards North. He then turns left and walks 40 m. He again turns left and walks 20 m. Further he moves 20 m after turning to the right. How far is he from his original position? **SSC (CGL) 2014**

(a) 20 m (b) 60 m
(c) 50 m (d) 30 m

42. Ravi walks 8 km North-East and then 6 km South-East. How far is he from his starting point? **UPPSC (Revenue officer) 2014**

(a) 14 km (b) 7 km
(c) 9 km (d) 10 km

Type 2 Jumbled Information Based

In these type of questions, some information is given in jumbled form that is followed by a set of 2-5 questions while solving these type of questions, candidates are required to find out those points in the given information which are to be used in the set of questions.

Examples Based on Type 2

Direction (Examples 1-2) *Study the following information to answer the given questions.*

Point B is 12 m South of point A. Point C is 24 m East of point B. Point D is 8 m South of point C. Point D is 12 m East of point E and point F is 8 m North of point E.

OBC (PO) 2010

1. If a man has to travel to point E from point A (through these points by the shortest distance), which of the following points will he pass through first?

(a) Point C (b) Point D (c) Point F (d) Point B
(e) None of these

2. If a man is standing facing North at point C, how far and in which direction is point F?

(a) 12 m, West (b) 24 m, East
(c) 12 m, East (d) 24 m, West
(e) None of these

SOLUTION (Examples 1-2) First of all draw the following diagram.

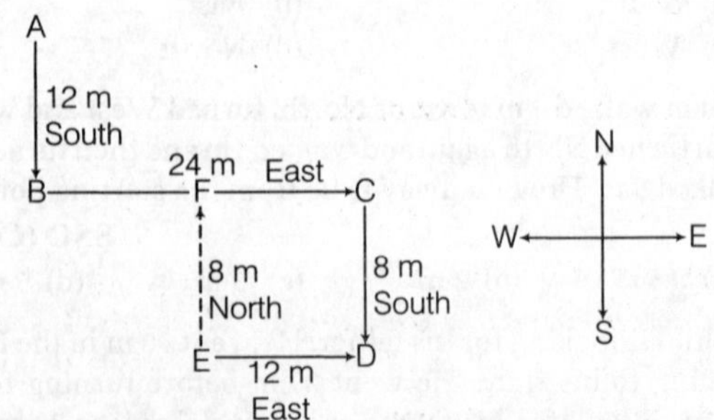

1. (*d*) While travelling to point E from point A, he will pass through point B first.

2. (*a*) Point F is 12 m West of point C.

Direction (Examples 3-5) These questions are based on the following information. **CSAT 2014**

Seven villages A, B, C, D, E, F and G are situated as follows :

- E is 2 km to the West of B.
- F is 2 km to the North of A.
- C is 1 km to the West of A.
- D is 2 km to the South of G.
- G is 2 km to the East of C.
- D is exactly in the middle of B and E.

3. A is in the middle of

(a) E and C (b) E and G (c) F and G (d) G and C

4. Which two villages are the farthest from one another?

(a) D and C (b) F and E (c) F and B (d) G and E

5. How far is E from F (in km) as the crow flies?

(a) 4 (b) $\sqrt{20}$ (c) 5 (d) $\sqrt{26}$

SOLUTION (Examples 3-5) The villages are situated as shown in the following figure

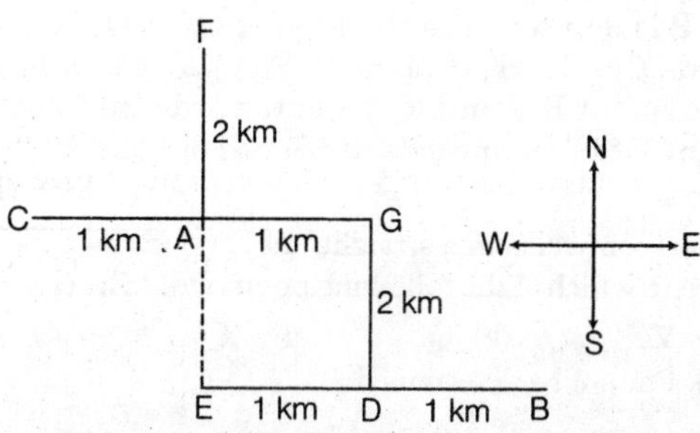

3. (*d*) From the figure, it is clear that A is between C and G.

4. (*c*) From the figure, it is clear that F and B are farthest from one another.

5. (*a*) Required distance, EF = EA + AF = 2 + 2 = 4 km

Intro Exercise 2 (Based on Type 2)

Direction (Q. Nos. 1-3) *Read the following information for answering the questions that follow.*
Oriental Insurance (AO) Exam 2010

On a playing ground A, B, C, D and E are standing as described below facing the North.

I. B is 50 m to the right of D.
II. A is 60 m to the South of B.
III. C is 40 m to the West to D.
IV. E is 80 m to the North of A.

1. If a boy walks from C, meets D followed by B, A and then E, how many metres has he walked if he has travelled the straight distance all through?

(a) 120 (b) 150
(c) 170 (d) 230

2. What is the minimum distance (in metre approximately) between C and E?

(a) 53 (b) 78
(c) 92 (d) 120

3. Who is to the South-East of the person who is to the left of D?

(a) A (b) B
(c) C (d) E

Direction (Q. Nos. 4-5) *Read the following information carefully and answer the questions which follow* **IBPS (Clerk) 2011**

Meghna started from point A, walked 7 m towards the West, took a left turn, walked 2 m and reached point C. She then took a right turn and walked 4 m to reach point D. She then took a right turn, walked 2 m before taking a final right turn and walking 3 m before stopping at point B.

4. How far and towards which direction is point A from Point B?

(a) 6 m towards West
(b) 8 m towards East
(c) 10 m towards East
(d) 10 m towards West
(e) Cannot be determined

5. If Meghna walks 2 m towards South from point A and reaches point E, which of the following points (including E) would fall in a straight line?

(a) A, B (b) A, D
(c) B, C (d) C, D
(e) None of these

Direction (Q. Nos. 6-8) *Study the information given below carefully and answer the questions that follow.*

If you start running from a point towards North and after covering 4 km you turn to your left and run 5 km, then again turn to your left and run 5 km and then turn to left again and run another 6 km and before finishing you take another left turn and run 1 km, then answer questions based on this information.

6. How many km are you from the place you started?

(a) 1 km (b) 2 km
(c) 3 km (d) 4 km

7. In which direction will you be running while finishing?

(a) East (b) West
(c) North (d) South

8. After taking the second turn, in which direction will you be running?

(a) East (b) West
(c) North (d) South

Direction (Q. Nos. 9-10) *Study the following information to answer the given questions.*

Point P is 9 m towards the East of point Q. Point R is 5 m towards the South of point P. Point S is 3 m towards the West of point R. Point T is 5 m towards the North of point S. Point V is 7 m towards the South of point S.

IBPS (PO) 2011

9. If a person walks in a straight line for 8 m towards West from point R, which of the following points would he cross the first?

(a) V (b) Q (c) T (d) S
(e) Cannot be determined

10. Which of the following points are in a straight line?

(a) P, R, V (b) S, T, Q (c) P, T, V (d) V, T, R
(e) S, V, T

Direction (Q. Nos. 11-13) *Study the following information carefully and answer the questions that follow.*

A, B, C, D, E, F, G, H and I are nine houses. C is 2 km East of B. A is 1 km North of B and H is 2 km South of A. G is 1 km West of H while D is 3 km East of G and F is 2 km North of G. I is situated just in middle of B and C while E is just in middle of H and D.

11. Distance between E and G is

(a) 1 km (b) 1.5 km (c) 2 km (d) 5 km

12. Distance between E and I is

(a) 1 km (b) 2 km (c) 3 km (d) 4 km

13. Distance between A and F is

(a) 1 km (b) 1.41 km (c) 2 km (d) 3 km

Direction (Q. Nos. 14-18) *Study the information given below carefully and answer the questions that follow.*

Ram walks 2 km towards North and turn to his right and walks 4 km more. He then turns to his right and walks 4 km and turns again to his right and walks another 4 km. Here, he meets Renu coming from the opposite direction. They both stop here.

14. After taking the first turn, in which direction was Ram going?

(a) South (b) North (c) West (d) East

15. If the starting point is marked 'A' and finishing point is marked 'E'. What will be the distance between points A and E?

(a) 10 km (b) 8 km (c) 6 km (d) 2 km

16. From which direction was Renu coming?

(a) South (b) North (c) South-East (d) West

17. After taking the second turn in which direction was Ram going?

(a) West (b) North (c) South-East (d) South

18. If Ram is again reach to the point from where he started in which direction he will have to go from where he's standing now?

(a) East (b) North
(c) South-East (d) North-East

Direction (Q. Nos. 19-20) *Read the following information carefully and answer the questions which follow.*

MHT CET MBA 2011

Jack starts from point A, walks 14 m towards the East, takes a left turn and walks 4 m. He then takes right turn, walks 2 m and stops.

Sam starts from the same point A, walks 14 m towards the South, takes a left turn and walks 20 m before stopping.

19. Jack walks 4 m from the point where he stopped in a straight line in the same direction which he faced when he stopped and reaches point B. How far would Sam have to travel from the point where he stopped and in which direction if he must meet Jack at point B?

(a) 12 m towards South (b) 14 m towards South
(c) 18 m towards South (d) 18 m towards North
(e) 16 m towards South

20. If Jack takes a right turn from the point where he stops walks 18 m and stops, how far would he be from the position where Sam stopped?

(a) 4 m (b) 2 m (c) 12 m (d) 18 m
(e) 14 m

Direction (Q. Nos. 21-24) *Study the information given below carefully and answer the questions that follow.*

A posse of four policemen A, B, C and D is combing a circular park, divided into sixteen plots P, Q, R and S are the offenders whom they have to catch after given moves. The figure below shows their positions.

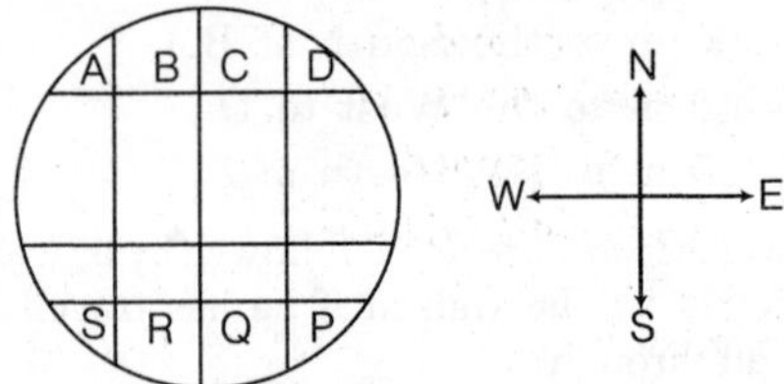

The by-lanes are North-South and East-West

21. Who two are positioned North-West, South-East?

(a) A, P (b) B, R (c) S, D (d) Q, C

22. If A, B, C and D were to move clockwise four plots and P, Q, R and S were to move anti-clockwise six-plots, then who two would be at North and South?

(a) P, A (b) Q, B (c) R, D (d) P, C

23. If both A, B, C and D and P, Q, R and S move clockwise three plots, then who would be positioned North-East, South-West?

(a) A, P (b) C, P
(c) D, Q (d) B, R

24. If A, B, C and D move clockwise two plots and P, Q, R and S move vertically up two plots, then which policeman will be able to catch whom?

(a) A, R (b) B, S
(c) C, P (d) D, Q

Cumulative Exercise

Base Level

1. A start and walks towards South, he then turns to his right and walks 5 km, then again turns left and walks 3 km and then again turns left and walks 5 km. In which direction is he from the starting point? **GIC (Asstistant) 2013**
(a) West (b) South (c) North (d) East

2. Vijay travelled 12 km Southward, then turned right and travelled 10 km, then turned right and travelled 12 km. How far was Vijay from the starting point? **SSC (CGL) 2013**
(a) 22 km (b) 44 km (c) 12 km (d) 10 km

3. One morning after sunrise, Suraj was standing facing a pole. The shadow of the pole fell exactly to his right. Which direction was Suraj facing? **CLAT 2014**
(a) West (b) South
(c) East (d) Data is inadequate

4. Ashok started walking towards South. After walking 50 m, he took a right turn and walked 30 m. He then took a right turn and walked 100 m. He again took a right turn and walked 30 m and stopped. How far and in which direction was he from the starting point? **SBI (PO) 2010**
(a) 50 m, South (b) 150 m, North
(c) 180 m, East (d) 50 m, North
(e) None of these

5. Arun travels 8 km towards the North, turns left and travels 3 km and then again truns right and cover another 4 km and then turns right and travels another 3 km. How far is he from the starting point? **GIC (Assist) 2013**
(a) 11 km (b) 12 km (c) 15 km (d) 18 km

6. Raju was to go to the planetarium. So,he walked 1.5 km towards East from the place and then turned to right and walked 2.5 km and then turned towards East walked 1 km and turned to South and walked 4 km and reached the place by walking 2.5 km towards West. What distance is he from the starting point? **SSC (10+2) 2012**
(a) 6.5 km (b) 9.5 km (c) 10 km (d) 9 km

7. Shobha moves towards South-East a distance of 7 km, then she moves towards West and covers 14 km. From here, she moves towards North-West a distance of 7 km and finally she moves a distance of 4 km toward East. How far is the starting point from the final point?
(a) 3 km (b) 4 km
(c) 10 km (d) 11 km
(e) None of these

8. Kishankant walks 10 km towards North. From there he walks 6 km towards South. Then he walks 3 km towards East. How far and in which direction is he from his starting point? **UPPSC (Revanue Officer) 2014**
(a) 5 km, North-East (b) 7 km, East
(c) 5 km, East (d) 7 km, West

9. A man is facing North-West. He turns 90° in the clockwise direction, then 180° in the anti-clockwise direction and then another 90° in the same direction. Which direction is he facing now?
(a) South
(b) South-West
(c) West
(d) South-East
(e) None of the above

10. Location of B is North of A and location of C is East of A. The distance AB and AC are 5 km and 12 km, respectively. The shortest distance (in km) between the locations B and C is **UPSC (CSAT) 2014**
(a) 60 (b) 13 (c) 17 (d) 7

11. A rat runs 20 ft towards East and turns to right, runs 10 ft and turns to right, runs 9 ft and again turns to left, runs 5 ft and then turns to left, runs 12 ft and finally turns to left and runs 6 ft. Now, which direction is the rat facing?
(a) East (b) West
(c) North (d) South
(e) None of these

12. Dilip walks 20 m North. Then, he turns right and walks 30 m, now he turns right and walks 35 m. Now turning left, he walks 15 m. Again, he turns left and moves 15 m. Finally, turning left, he again walks 15 m. In which direction and how many metres is he from his original position?
(a) 15 m, East
(b) 45 m, East
(c) 15 m, West
(d) 45 m, West

13. Kailash faces towards North. Turning to his right, he walks 25 m. He turns to his left and walks 30 m. Next, he moves 25 m to his right. He then turns to his right again and walks 55 m. Finally, he turns to the right and moves 40 m. In which direction he is now from his starting point?

MHT CET MBA 2013

(a) South-West (b) South
(c) North-West (d) South-East
(e) North

14. If South-East becomes North, North-East becomes West and so on, what will West become?

(a) North-East (b) North-West
(c) South-East (d) South-West
(e) South

15. A villager went to meet his uncle in another village situated 5 km away in the North-East direction of his own village. From there he came to meet his father-in-law living in a village situated 4 km in the South of his uncle's village. How far away and in what direction is he now?

(a) 3 km in the North (b) 3 km in the East
(c) 4 km in the East (d) 4 km in the West

16. The time on the watch is quarter to three. If the minute-hand points to North-East, in which direction does the hour hand point?

(a) South-West (b) South-East
(c) North-West (d) North-East

17. While facing East you turn not your left and walk 10 m then turn to your left and walk 10 m and now you turn 45° towards your right and go straight to cover 25 m. Now, in which direction are you from your starting point?

(a) North-East (b) South-West
(c) South-East (d) North-West
(e) East

18. A train runs 120 km in West direction, 30 km in South direction and then 80 km in East direction before reaching the station. In which direction is the station from the train's starting point? **MAT 2014**

(a) South-West (b) North-West
(c) South-East (d) South

19. A man drove his car 5 km towards East direction. He turned right went for 3 km, then he turned West and drove for 1 km. How far is he from the starting point.

GIC (Asstist) 2013

(a) 5 km (b) 6 km
(c) 10 km (d) 20 km

20. The time in a clock is quarter past twelve. If the hour hand points to the East, which is the direction opposite to the minute hand? **UPPSC 2013**

(a) South East
(b) South
(c) West
(d) North

21. Vinay starts walking towards East. After walking 35 miles, he turns to his right and walks another 40 miles. He then turns right and walks another 35 miles. Finally, he turns right and walks 20 miles. How far is he from the starting point and in which direction?

(a) 20 miles, North (b) 35 miles, South
(c) 20 milcs, South (d) 35 miles, North
(e) None of these

22. Raj is standing in the middle of a square field. He starts walking diagonally to North-East. Then, he turns right and reaches the far end of the field. Then, he turns right and starts walking. In the midway, he again turns right and starts walking. In halfway, he turns to his left and reaches a new far end. In what direction is Raj now? **SSC (CGL) 2013**

(a) North (b) South
(c) North-West (d) South-West

23. A direction pole was situated on the crossing. Due to an accident the pole turned in such a manner that the pointer which was showing East, started showing South. One traveller went to the wrong direction thinking it to be West. In what direction actually he was travelling?

SSC (CGL) 2013

(a) North (b) South (c) East (d) West

24. A man starts from his house and walked straight for 10 m towards North and turned left and walked 25 m. He then turned right and walked 5 m and again turned right and walked 25 m. Which direction is he facing now?

SSC (FCI) 2012

(a) North (b) East (c) South (d) West

25. Radhika went 50 m South from her house, then turned left and went 20 m, then turning to North she went 30 m. In which direction is her home from this point? **SSC (FCI) 2012**

(a) North (b) South-West
(c) East (d) North-West

26. A girl is facing North. She turns 180° in the anti- clockwise direction and then 225° in the clockwise direction. Which direction is she facing now? **CG PSC 2013**

(a) West (b) North-East
(c) South-West (d) East
(e) North-West

27. A man is facing West. He turns 45° in the clockwise direction and then another 180° in the same direction and then 270° in the anti-clockwise direction. Which direction is he facing now? **MAT 2013**

(a) South (b) North-West (c) West (d) South-West

28. Sumi ran a distance of 40 m towards the South. She then turned to the right and ran for about 15m, turned right again and ran 50m. Turning to right, then ran for 15 m. Finally she turned to the left an angle of 45° and ran. In which direction was she running finally? **SSC (10+2) 2013**

(a) South-East (b) South-West
(c) North-East (d) North-West

29. Veena walked 5 m towards North, took a left turn and walked 7 m. She took a left turn again and walked 8m before taking a left turn and walking 7 m. She then took a final left turn and walked 1m before stopping. How far is Veena from the starting point? **SBI (Asstist) 2012**
(a) 3 m (b) 6 m (c) 4 m (d) 2 m
(e) 7 m

30. Mahu goes 40 km North, turns right and goes 80 km, turns right again and goes 30 km in the end, he turns right again and goes 80 km. How far is he from his starting point if he goes straight ahead another 50 km and turns left to go his last 10 km? **MAT 2014**
(a) 20 km (b) 30 km (c) 40 km (d) 50 km

31. Immediately after leaving his house, Ritvik turned right and walked for 40 m. Then, he turned left and walked for 20 m. Then, he again took a left turn and walked for 30 m. There he met a friend and turned right to go to the coffee shop 20 m away. After having coffee, he walked back straight for 40 m in the direction he had come from. How far is he from his house? **IIFT 2012**
(a) 20 m (b) 0 m (c) 10 m (d) 40 m

32. The houses of A and B face each other on a road going North-South A's being on the western side, A comes out of his house, turns left, travels 5 km, turns right, travels 5 km to the front of D's house. B does exactly the same and reaches the front of C's house. In this context, which one of the following statements is correct? **UPSC (CSAT) 2014**
(a) C and D live on the same street
(b) C's house faces south
(c) The houses of C and D are less than 20 km apart
(d) None of the above

33. A boy was misdirected from his way while returning to his home from his school. In order to reach his home, he first moved 3 km in South direction and then turned to his left and moved 2 km in straight direction on the road leading to the East. From there he moved to his left and walked 3 km. After this, he again turned to his left and moved 1 km. Finally he reached his home. The home of the boy was in which direction from his school? **SSC (CGL) 2013**
(a) South (b) West
(c) North (d) East

Advanced Level

1. There are four towns P, Q, R and T. Q is to the South-West of P, R is the East of Q and South-East of P and T is to the North of R in line with QP. In which direction of P is T located?
(a) South-East (b) North
(c) North-East (d) East
(e) None of these

2. Sheela walks 2km from A to B. She turns right at 90° and goes 3 km up to C. She, then again turns right at 90° and goes 8 km up to D. Again, she takes right turn at 90° and goes 3 km upto K. From K she takes right turn at 90° again and reaches at F after covering 4 km. Find the distance between A and F. **MAT 2011**
(a) 2 km (b) 4 km (c) 6 km (d) 8 km

3. A school bus driver starts from the school, drives 2 km towards North, takes a left turn and drives for 5 km. He then takes a left turn and drives for 8 km before taking a left turn again and driving for further 5 km. The driver finally takes a left turn and drives 1 km before stopping. How far and towards which direction should the driver drive to reach the school again? **IBPS (PO) 2011**
(a) 3 km towards North (b) 7 km towards East
(c) 6 km towards South (d) 6 km towards West
(e) 5 km towards North

4. Hari travelled 17 km to the East, he turned left and went 15 km, he again turned left and went 17 km. How far is he from the starting point? **SSC (CPO) 2013**
(a) 32 km (b) 17 km
(c) 2 km (d) 15 km

5. Maya starts at point T, walks straight to point U which is 4 ft away. She turns left at 90° and walks to W which is 4 ft away, turns 90° right and goes 3 ft to P, turns 90° right and walks 1 ft to Q, turns left at 90° and goes to V, which is 1 ft away and once again turns 90° right and goes to R, 3 ft away. What is the distance between T and R?
(a) 4 ft (b) 5 ft (c) 7 ft (d) 8 ft

6. One day, Ravi left home and cycled 10 km Southwards turned right and cycled 5 km and turned right and cycled 10 km and turned left and cycled 10 km. How many kilometres will he now have to cycle in straight line to reach his home? **MAT 2013**
(a) 10 km (b) 15 km
(c) 20 km (d) 25 km

Direction (Q. Nos. 7-9) *These questions are based on the information given below.*

Eight persons A through H are standing in such a way that C is 20 m apart from B towards West, B is 30 m South with respect to A. A is 40 m towards West with respect to E. D is 50 m towards South with respect to E. F is 15 m apart from G towards North. H is 20 m towards East with respect to G. F is 40 m towards West with respect to D.

7. In which direction is B standing with respect to F?
(a) North-West
(b) North
(c) North-East
(d) Cannot be determined

8. If one more person I is standing towards South-West with respect to D, then in which direction is H, standing with respect to I?
(a) South-West (b) North-East
(c) North-West (d) Cannot be determined

9. What is the direction of C with respect to H?
(a) North-West (b) North
(c) West (d) Cannot be determined

10. A man faces North and covers 12 km, turns West and covers 6 km, then turns South and covers 3 km and turns West again and covers 6 km. How far is he from the starting point?
(a) 10 km (b) 12 km (c) 15 km (d) 18 km

11. A clock is so placed that at 12 noon its minute hand points towards North-East. In which direction does its hour hand point at 1:30 pm? **NIFT (UG) 2014**
(a) North (b) South (c) East (d) West

12. Rajnikanth left his home for office in car. He drove 15 km straight towards North and then turned Eastwards and covered 8 km. He, then turned to left and covered 1km. He again turned left and drove for 20 km and reached office. How far and in what direction is his office from the home? **IB (ACIO)2013**
(a) 21 km, West (b) 15 km, North-East
(c) 20 km, North-West (d) 26 Km, North-West

13. Starting from his office, Fernander drives his car towards the North for 40 km. He then takes a right turn and travels for 30 km to reach 'VXL Petrol Pump'. From there, he again drives North-West for a distance of 50 km, before travelling North for another 40 km. Finally, he turns and travels towards South-West for 50 km and stops. What is his direction now with respect to the starting point?
(a) South-West (b) North-East **JMET 2011**
(c) North-West (d) South-East

14. One evening before sunset two friends Sumit and Mohit were talking to each other face to face. If Mohit's shadow was exactly to his right side, which direction was Sumit facing?
(a) North (b) South
(c) West (d) Data inadequate
(e) None of these

15. Raju moves 40 km North, then he turns right and moves 50 km. Again, he turns right and moves 30 km. Finally, he turns right and reaches 50 km. How far is he from the starting point? **SSC (10+ 2) 2012**
(a) 10 km (b) 40 km (c) 20 km (d) 30 km

16. A boy starts from home in early morning and walks straight for 8 km facing the Sun. Then, he takes a right turn and walks for 3 km. Then, he turns right again and walks for 2 km and then turns left and walks for 1 km. Again he turned right and walked 1 km. Then, he turns right and travels for 4 km straight. How far is he from the starting point? **SSC (CGL) 2013**
(a) 5 km (b) 6 km (c) 2 km (d) 4 km

17. I am standing at the centre of a circular field. I go down South to the edge of the field and then turning left I walk along the boundary of the field equal to three-eighths of its length. Then, I turn West and go right across to the opposite point on the boundary. In which direction am I from the start?
(a) North-West (b) North
(c) South-West (d) West

Direction (Q. Nos. 18-20) *The following questions are based on the diagram given below.*

Showing four persons stationed at four corners (P, Q, R and T) of a square piece of plot as shown. There is a boundary around the plot.

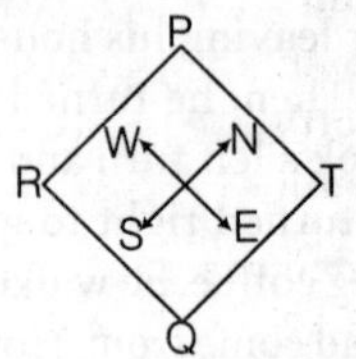

18. If the names of the corners designated as P and T are interchanged and then C starts walking along the boundary from T in the clockwise direction. After walking one and a half side, in which direction is C walking?
(a) South-West (b) West
(c) South (d) East

19. A starts walking from P towards Q along the shortest distance and midway he turns to his right and after covering half the distance, takes a 90° turn in the clockwise direction, which direction is he facing now?
(a) North-West (b) South-West
(c) South (d) North

20. After carrying out the changes as in Q. No. 19 in which direction is A standing?
(a) South (b) West
(c) South-East (d) None of these

Direction (Q. Nos. 21-22) *Read the following information carefully and answer the questions which follow.*

Amit was driving in new town, where all roads either North-South or East-West forming a grid. Roads were at a distance of 1 km from each other in parallel. **SNAP 2011**

21. Amit started at the intersection of streets number 7 and 8. He drove 3 km North, 3 km West and 4 km South. Which further route could bring him back to his starting point?
I. 3 km East, then 2 km South.
II. 1 km North, then 3 km East.
III. 1 km North, then 2 km West.
(a) Only I (b) Only II (c) I and II (d) II and III

22. After driving as stated in Q. No. 21 above, Amit did not return to his starting point but instead drove 4 km East and 1 km North. How far is he from his starting point?
(a) 5 km (b) 4 km (c) 1 km (d) 7 km

Direction (Q. Nos. 23-24) *Read the following information carefully and answer the questions which follow.* **MHT CET MBA 2012**

Ravi, who is facing North, starts from point A, walks 4 m towards the right. He then takes a left turn and walks 3 m before taking a right turn, walking 2 m and stopping at point B.

Seema starts from the same point A walks 2 m towards the South. She then takes a left turn and walks 4 m. She now takes a right turn, walks 2 m before taking a left turn, walking 2 m and stopping at point C.

23. How far and towards which direction must Ravi walk in order to reach point C?
(a) 5 m towards South (b) 8 m towards North
(c) 7 m towards North (d) 8 m towards South
(e) 7 m towards South

24. If Seema walks 4 m towards North from Point C, how far will she be from point A?
(a) 4 m (b) 2 m (c) 6 m (d) 8 m
(e) 7 m

25. Radhika moved a distance of 80 m towards North. She then turned to the left and after walking for another 20 m turned to the left again. She walked for another 80 m. Finally, she turned to the right at an angle of 45°. In which direction was she moving finally? **MAT 2011**
(a) South-East
(b) North-West
(c) North-East
(d) South-West

26. Raghubir drove 15 km Northwards by his car. He then turned towards West and drove for 10 km. He then drove towards South for 5 km and then turned towards East and drove for the next 8 km. Finally, he turned to the right and drove for the next 10 km. How far and in which direction is Raghubir from his starting point? **MAT 2011**
(a) 2 km West (b) 6 km South
(c) 5 km West (d) None of these

27. Krishna walks for 10 km towards North. From here he walks back 6 km towards South. Then, he walks 3 km towards East. How far and in which direction is he with reference to his starting point? **MAT 2011**
(a) 5 km East (b) 7 km West
(c) 7 km East (d) 5 km North-East

Direction (Q. Nos. 28-29) *Read the following information carefully and answer the questions which follow.* **NIACL 2014**

Point H is 6 m towards the East of point G. Point R is 8 m North of point G. Point Q is exactly midway between point R and point G. Point K is 10 m to the South of point Q. Point L is 3 m towards the East of point Q. Point S is exactly midway between point G and point H.

28. If a person walks 4 m towards the South from point L, takes a right turn and walks for another 3 m, which of the following points would he reach?
(a) Q (b) G (c) K (d) H
(e) Cannot be determined

29. If a person walks 8 m towards North from point S, which of the following points would he cross and how far will he be from point R?
(a) G, 4 m (b) H, 3 m (c) L, 6 m (d) L, 3 m
(e) G, 8 m

30. Mr. Raghav went in his car to meet his friend John. He drove 30 km towards North and then 40 km towards West. He then turned to South and covered 8 km. Further he turned to East and moved 26 km. Finally he turned right and drove 10 km and then turned left to travel 19 km. How far and in which direction is he from the starting point? **IIFT 2009**
(a) East of starting point, 5 km.
(b) East of starting point, 13 km.
(c) North-East of starting point, 13 km
(d) North-East of starting point, 5 km

Direction (Q. Nos. 31-32) *Study the information given below carefully and answer the questions that follow.* **IBPS (PO) 2011**

Point A is 5 m towards the West of point B. Point C is 2 m towards the North of point B. Point D is 3 m towards the East of point C. Point E is 2 m towards the South of point D.

31. If a person walks 2 m towards the North from point A takes a right turn and continues to walks, which of the following points would he reach the first?
(a) D (b) B (c) E (d) C
(e) Cannot be determined

32. Which of the following points are in a straight line?
(a) ABE (b) DCA (c) CED (d) BDA
(e) ACE

Direction (Q. Nos. 33-37) *These questions are based on the following diagram that shows four persons stationed at the square's four corners of a plot. Find the correct answer from among the alternatives given under each question.* **LIC (AAO) 2005**

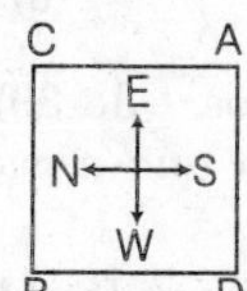

33. A starts crossing the field diagonally. After half the distance he turns right; walks some distance and turns left. Which direction is A facing now?
(a) North-East (b) North-West
(c) South-East (d) South-West

34. From the original position given in the diagram A and B move one arm length clockwise and then cross over to the corner diagonally opposite. C and D move one arm length anti-clockwise and cross over to the corner diagonally opposite. The original configuration ADBC has now changed to

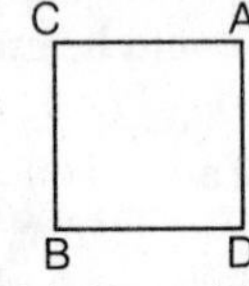

(a) CBDA (b) BDAC (c) DACB (d) ACBD

35. From the original position given in the diagram B and D move one and a half length of sides clockwise and anti-clockwise respectively. Which one of the following statements is true?

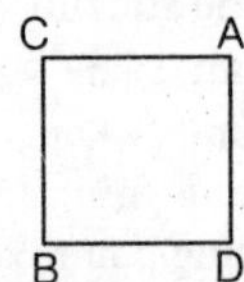

(a) B and D are both at the mid-points between A and C
(b) D is at the mid-point between A and C, and B at the corner originally occupied by A
(c) B and D are both at the mid-point between A and D
(d) B is at the mid-point between A and original position of D; and D, at the mid-point between original position of B and C

36. From the position in the diagram A and C move diagonally to opposite corners and then one side each clockwise and anti-clockwise respectively. D and B move two sides clockwise and anti-clockwise respectively, where is A now?

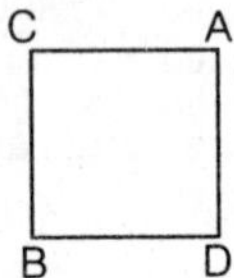

(a) At the North-West corner (b) At the North-East corner
(c) At the South-East corner (d) At the South-West corner

37. After the movements given in the above Q. No. 36, who is at the North-West corner?
(a) A (b) B
(c) C (d) None of these

Direction (Q. Nos. 38-39) *Read the following information carefully and answer the questions which follow.* **IBPS (Clerk) 2011**

Farhan started from point P walked 5m. South and then took a left turn, walked 2m and reached point Q. The then took a left turn walked 3m and then took a right turn and walked 1m to reach point R. The then took a left turn walked 2m and reached point S and took a final left turn walked 2m before stopping at point T.

38. If Farhan walks 2 m towards South from point T and takes a left turn, which point will he be facing?
(a) None (b) P (c) Q (d) R
(e) S

39. How far and in which direction is point T from point P ?
(a) 2 m towards East
(b) 1 m towards West
(c) 1 m towards East
(d) 2 m towards West
(e) Cannot be determined

Direction (Q. Nos. 40-41) *Study the given information and answer the given questions.* **IBPS (Clerk) 2013**

- Point A is 11 m North of point B.
- Point C is 11 m East of point B.
- Point D is 6 m North of point C.
- Point E is 7 m West of point D.
- Point F is 8 m North of point E.
- Point G is 4 m West of point F.

40. How far is point F from point A?
(a) 43 m (b) 4m
(c) 3 m (d) 7m
(e) 5m

41. How far and in which direction is point G from point A?
(a) 3 m, North
(b) 5 m, North
(c) 4 m, North
(d) 4 m, South
(e) 3m, South

Direction (Q. Nos. 42-43) *Read the following information carefully and answer the questions which follow.* **IBPS (Clerk) 2011**

Mehul starts from point A, walks 6 m towards South to reach point B. He then takes a right turn and walks 4 m, to reach point F before taking a right turn again and walking 6 m to reach point C. From point C he takes right turn again, walks 8 m and stops at point E.

42. If Mehul takes a right turn from point E and walks 6 m to reach point D, how far and towards which direction will point D be from point B?
(a) 4 towards West
(b) 8 m towards East
(c) 4 m towards East
(d) 6 m towards East
(e) Cannot be determined

43. Which of the following three points fall in a straight line?
(a) C, A, B
(b) F, B, A
(c) F, A, C
(d) E, A, B
(e) C, A, E

Answers with Explanations

Intro Exercise 1

1. (*b*)

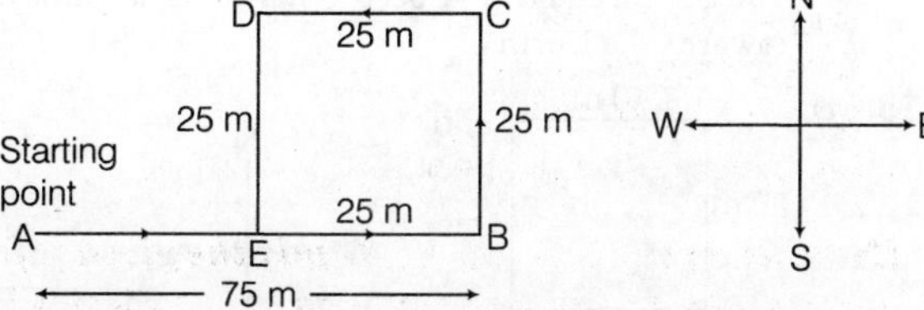

A is the starting point of Ravi and E is the end point

Distance between last and start point = AE

$= AB - BE$

$= 75 - 25 = 50$ m

2. (*d*) As Vikram's shadow fell towards left hand side, so he must be facing North. Sailesh is standing with his back towards Vikram, so he must be facing South.

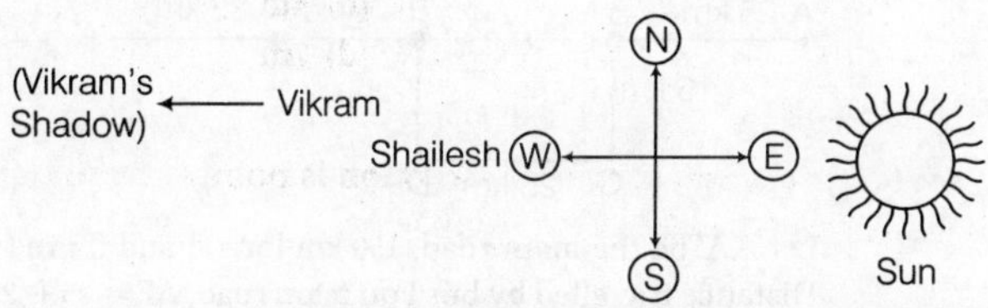

3. (*b*) According to the question, the points P, Q and R are situated as follow

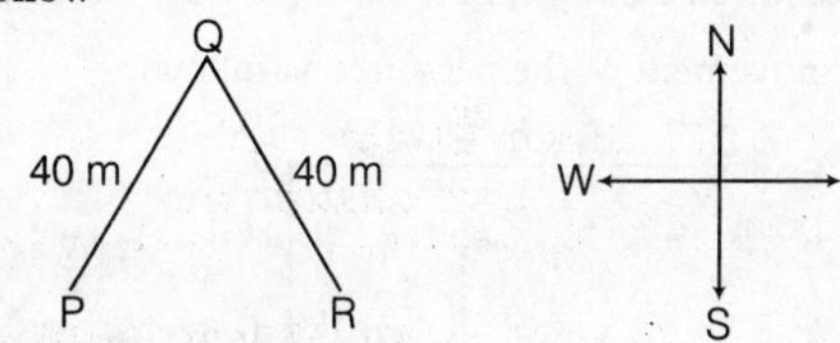

This R is in East of P.

Hence, option (b) is correct.

4. (*b*)

C
D
Post office
100 m
B
A
40 m Vilashvilla 50 m
N
W
E
S

$\therefore$ Requred distance (CD) $= 50 + 40$

$= 90$ m

5. (*b*)

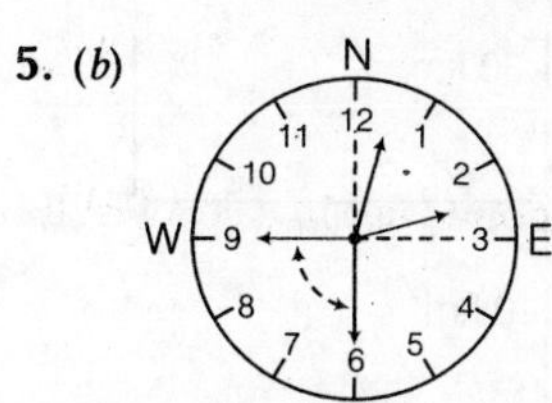

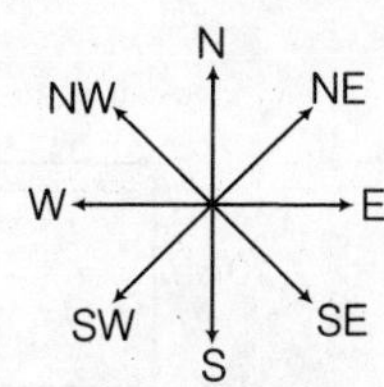

It is clear from the diagram that, minute hand will be in West direction.

6. (*a*)

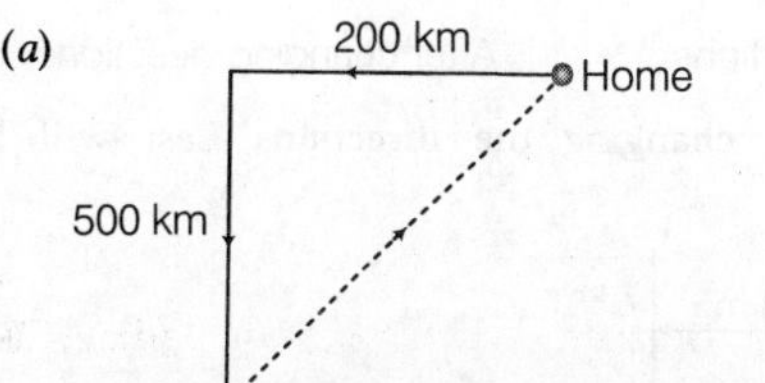

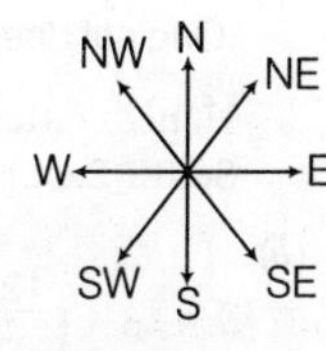

From the figure, it is clear that they should take North-East direction to reach home.

7. (*a*)

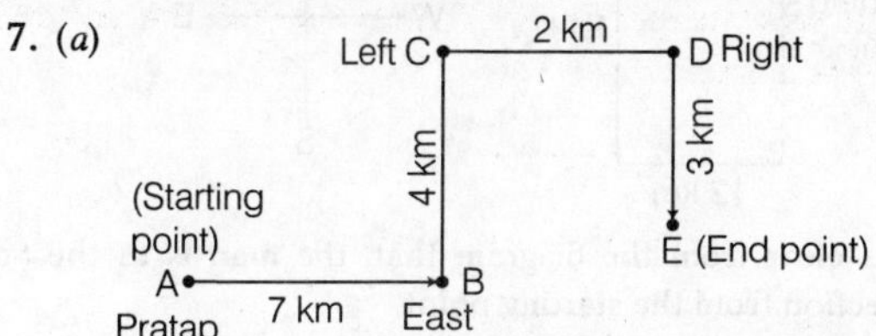

Pratap at point E is facing the South-direction.

8. (*b*) According to the question, way of riding of the person is as follow

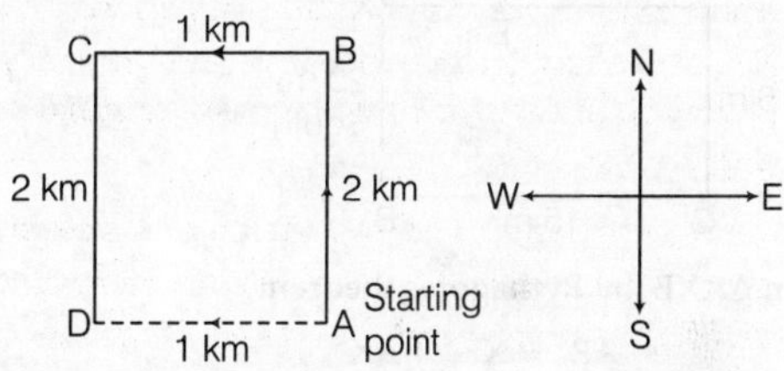

As per the question, D is 1 km West of A, therefore

$AB = DC = 2$ km

9. (*b*)

B
North
East
F
D
South
H

According to the question town H is to the South of Town B. The position of town H is to the South-East of Town F.

10. (*b*)

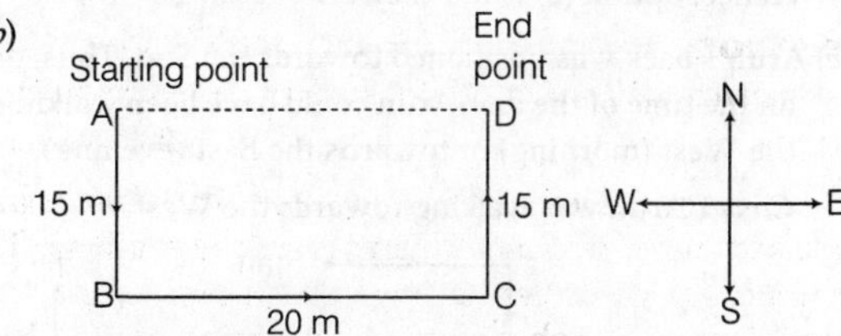

$\therefore$ Required distance, AD = 20 m and in East direction.

11. (*c*)

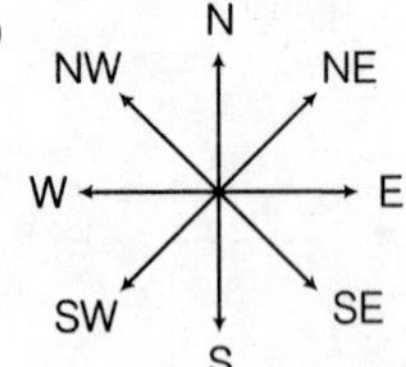

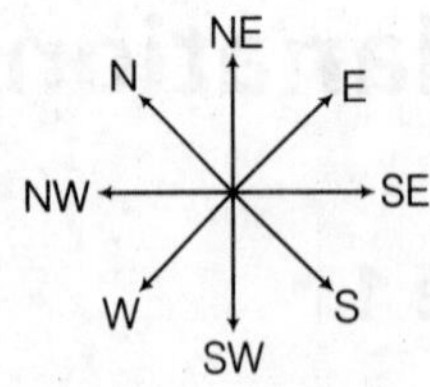

Hence, after changing the directions East will become South-East.

12. (*b*)

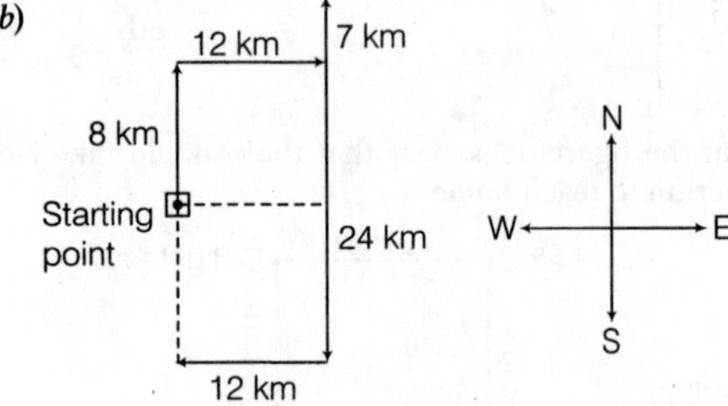

It is clear from the diagram that, the man is in the South direction from the starting point.

13. (*e*)

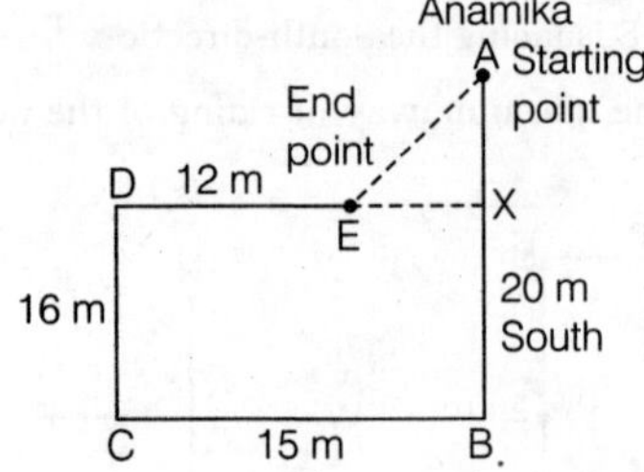

In ΔAXE, by Pythagoras theorem

$$AE^2 = XE^2 + AX^2$$

$$AE = ?$$

$$XE = DX - DE = 15 - 12 = 3 \text{ m}$$

$$AX = AB - BX = 20 - 16 = 4 \text{ m}$$

Putting values in the theorem, we get

$$AE^2 = XE^2 + AX^2$$

$$= (3)^2 + (4)^2 = 9 + 16 = 25$$

So, $AE^2 = 25$

$AE = \sqrt{25}$ (taking square root)

$= \sqrt{5 \times 5} = 5$

$\therefore \quad AE = 5$

The distance between the starting point and end point is 5 m. Hence, option (e) is the answer.

14. (*b*) Arun's back was positioned towards the Sun. Thus, depending on the time of the day, Arun could have been walking towards the West (morning) or towards the East (evening).

***Case* I** Arun was walking towards the West.

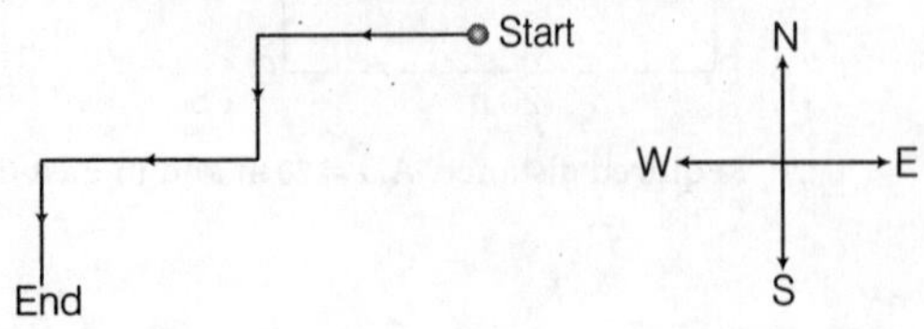

Thus, he finally faces the South.

***Case* II** Arun was walking towards the East.

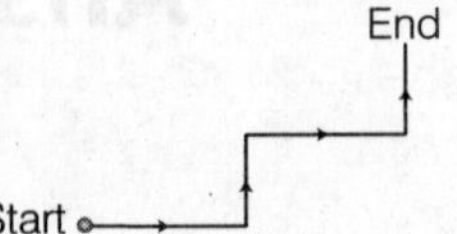

Thus, he finally faces the North.

Thus, Arun could have been going either towards the South or towards the North.

15. (*c*)

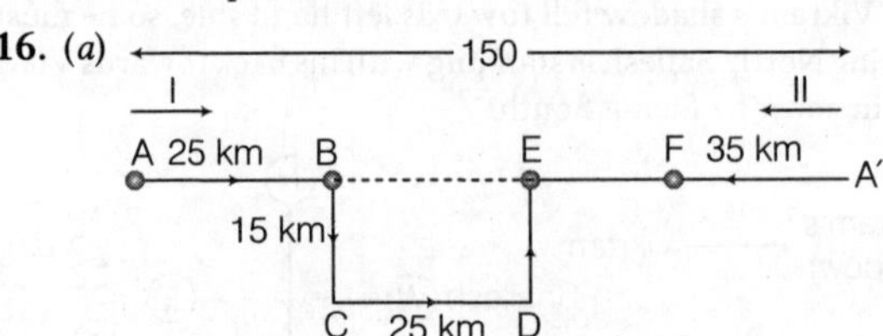

$\therefore$ Required distance $= 20 + 20 = 40$ m

16. (*a*)

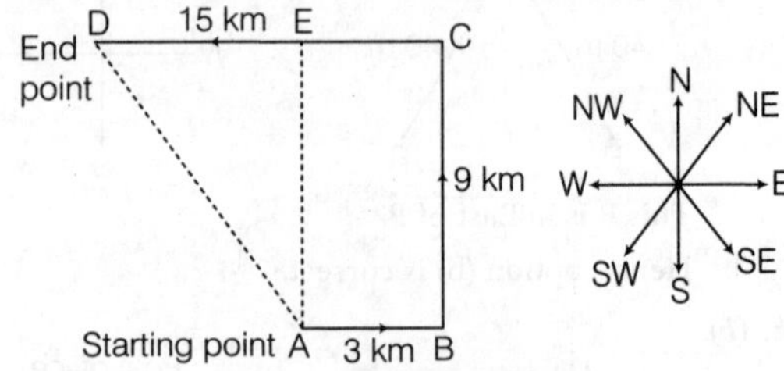

Let AA′ be the main road, 150 km long. I and II are two buses.

Distance travelled by bus I on main road, AE $= 25 + 25 = 50$ km.

Distance travelled by bus II on main road A′F $= 35$ km

$\therefore$ Required distance, EF $= 150 - (50 + 35) = 65$ km

17. (*b*) The movement of the person is as following

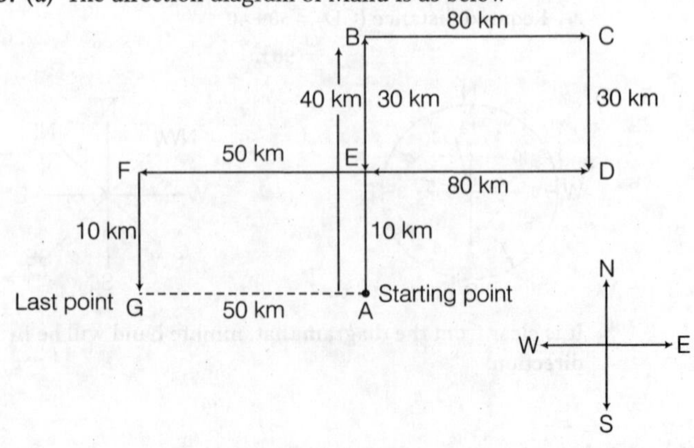

$\therefore$ Required distance, $AD = \sqrt{AE^2 + DE^2}$

$= \sqrt{9^2 + 12^2} = 15$ km

18. (*d*) The direction diagram of Manu is as below

Let A is the starting point of Manu and G is the last point of his journey.

Now, BC = ED = 80 km, FG = AE = 10 km

CD = BE = 30 km, AB = 40 km

EF = GA = 50 km

Clearly, from diagram atlast, distance between Manu's starting point and last point = GA = 50 km

19. (*d*) No lady is facing East, so one man is facing East and one woman is facing West. One man is facing South, so the other lady is facing North. So, the two ladies are facing North and West direction.

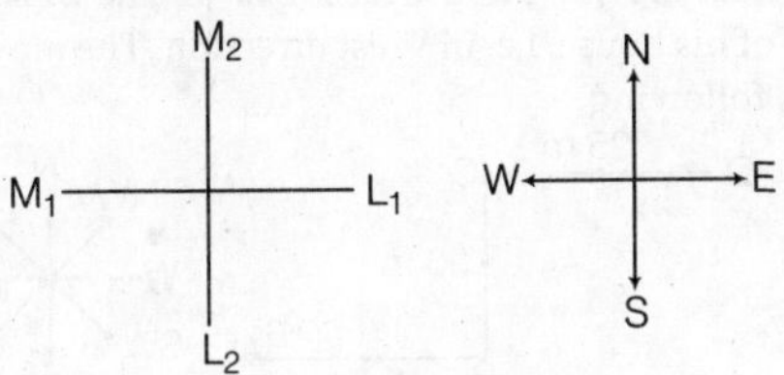

20. (*b*)

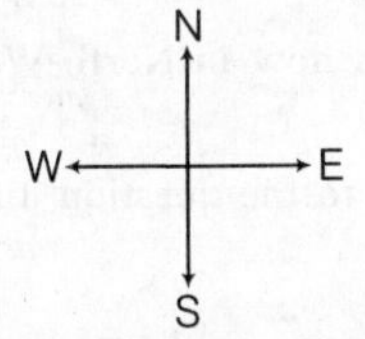

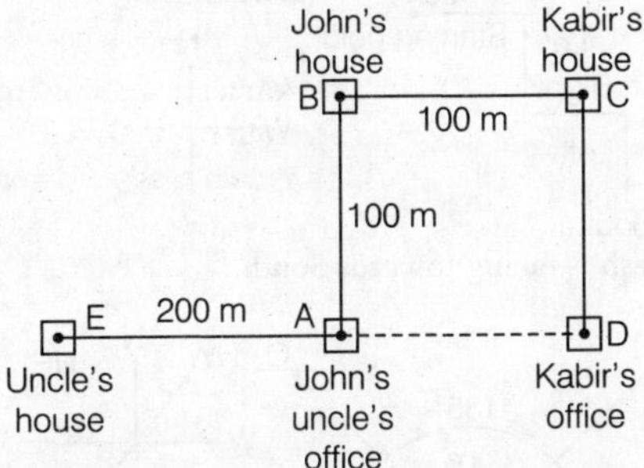

∴ Required distance = (200 + 100) = 300 m

21. (*b*)

A
30 m
B 15 m C
20 m
End point E 15 m D
N W E S

∴ Required distance, AE = (AB + BE) = (30 + 20) = 50 m

22. (*a*)

End point 30 m
20 m
Starting point 30 m
N W E S

From the figure, it is clear that Nikhil is 20 m North from the starting point.

23. (*a*) In the evening the Sun is seen in the West.

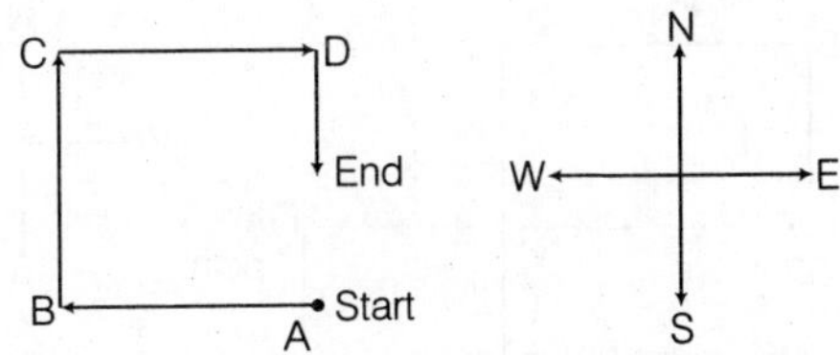

It is clear from the diagram that, he is facing towards South.

24. (*d*)

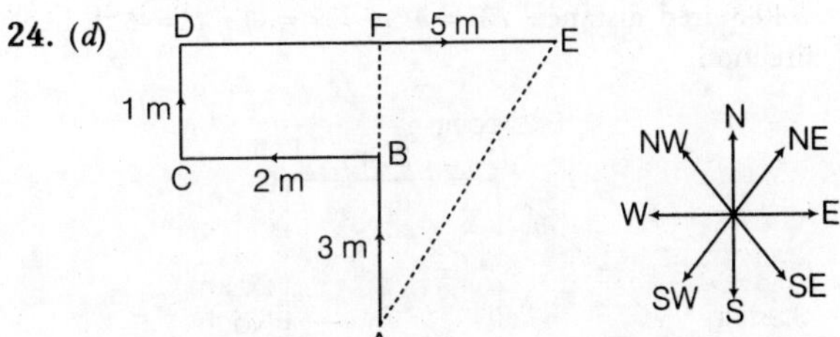

$$\therefore \text{Required distance, } AE = \sqrt{AF^2 + FE^2}$$

$$= \sqrt{4^2 + 3^2} = 5 \text{ m}$$

25. (*b*)

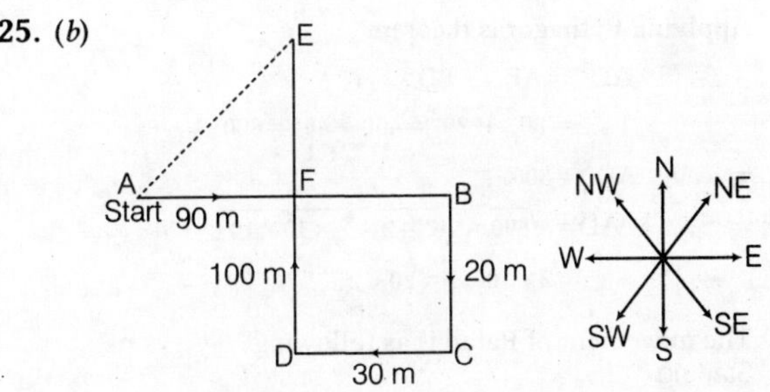

$$\therefore \text{Required distance, } AE = \sqrt{AF^2 + FE^2} = \sqrt{60^2 + 80^2} = 100 \text{ m}$$

26. (*d*)

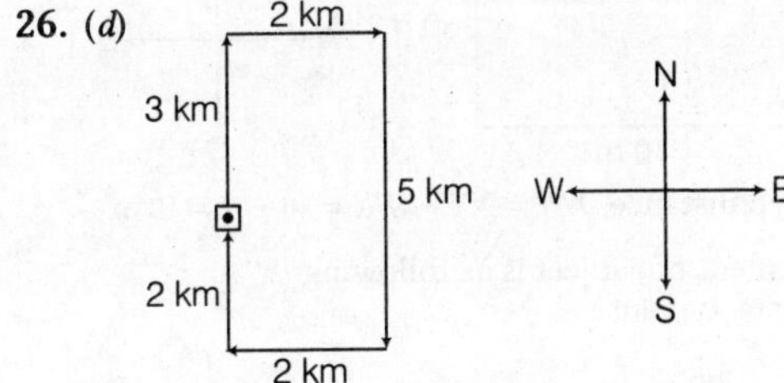

It is clear from the diagram that, A is in his own office.

27. (*c*)

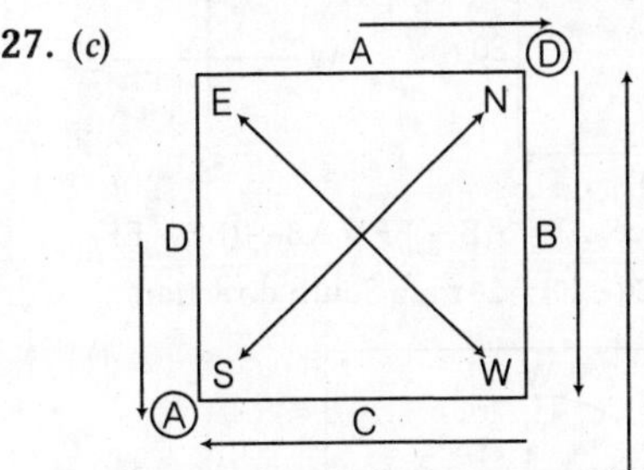

It is clearly shown that, A is in South and D is in the North region.

28. (*d*) The movement of John is as following

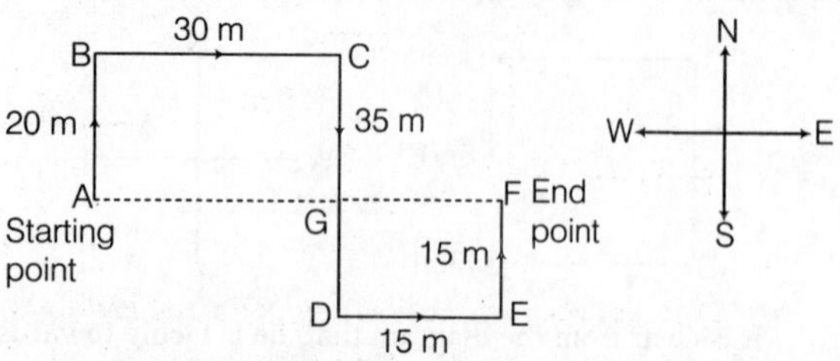

∴ Required distance, AF = AG + GF = 30 + 15 = 45 m in East direction.

29. (*c*)

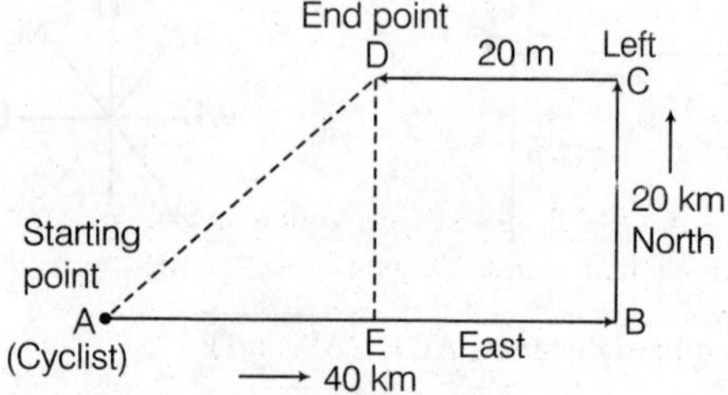

In ΔAED, AD = ?, AE = 20 and ED = 20

Applying Pythagoras theorem

$$AD^2 = AE^2 + ED^2$$

$$= 20^2 + 20^2 = 400 + 400 = 800$$

$$\Rightarrow \quad AD^2 = 800$$

$$\Rightarrow \quad AD = \sqrt{800} = \sqrt{2 \times 2 \times 2 \times 10 \times 10}$$

$$= 2 \times 10\sqrt{2} = 20\sqrt{2}$$

30. (*a*) The movement of Rahul is as following

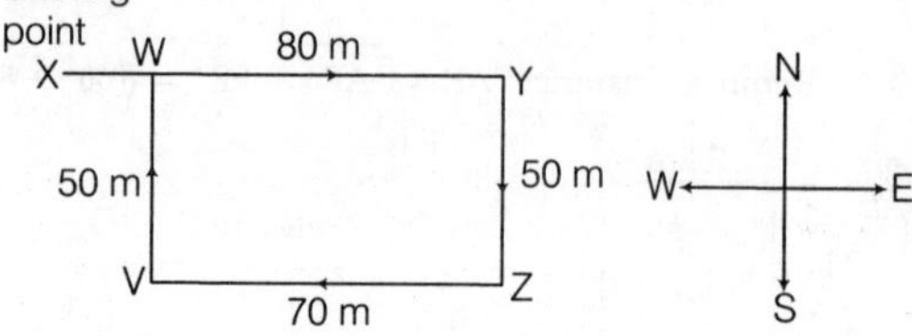

∴ Required distance, XW = XY − WY = 80 − 70 = 10 m

31. (*b*) The movement of Sanjeet is as following

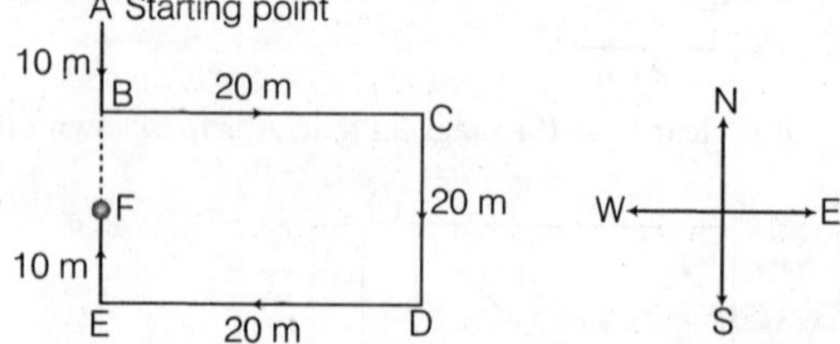

∴ Required distance, AF = AB + BF = AB + (BE − EF)

= 10 + (20 − 10) = 20 m in South direction

32. (*a*)

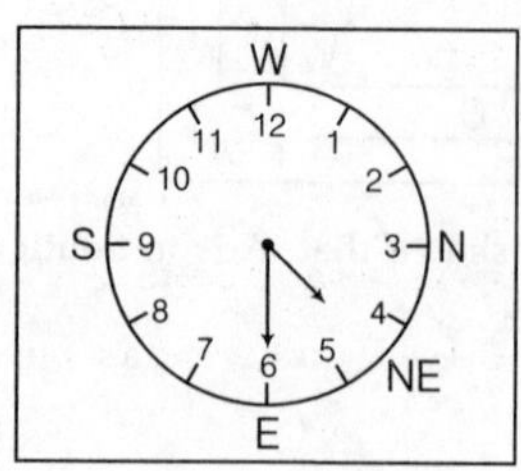

From the diagram at 4:30, the hour hand is 45° behind the minute hand, so moving 45° anti-clockwise from East, hour hand will point NE (North-East).

33. (*d*)

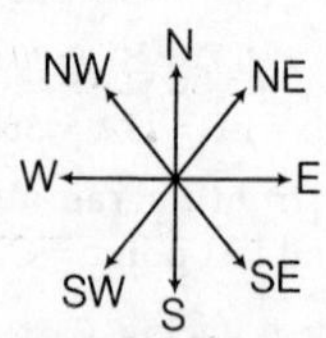

After crossing 'B' I will run towards A which is in South direction with respect of B.

34. (*d*) The door of Ajay's house faces East and he walks from the back side of his house, i.e. in West direction. The movement of Ajay is as following

So, Ajay is now in North-West direction from the starting point A.

35. (*d*) According to the question, the direction diagram will be as follows

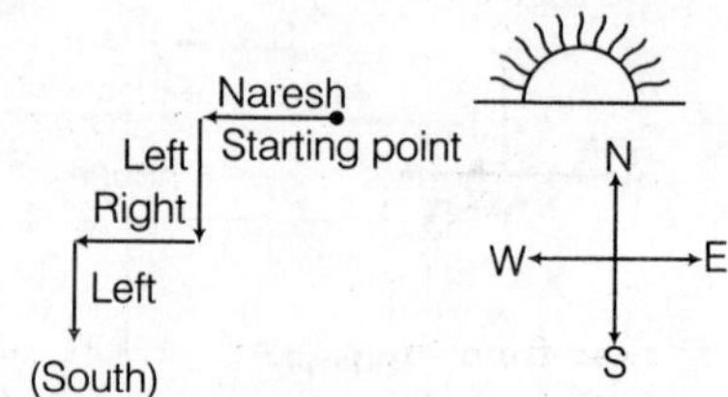

So, Naresh is facing towards South.

36. (*b*)

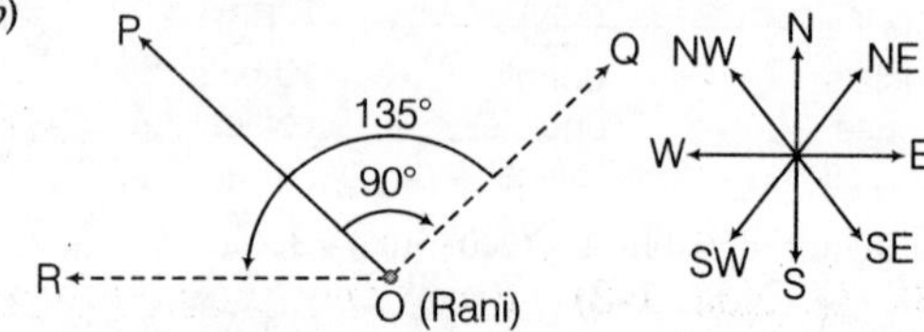

Rani initially faces in the direction OP. On moving 90° clockwise, she faces in the direction OQ. On further moving 135° anti-clockwise, she faces in the direction OR, which is West.

37. (*b*)

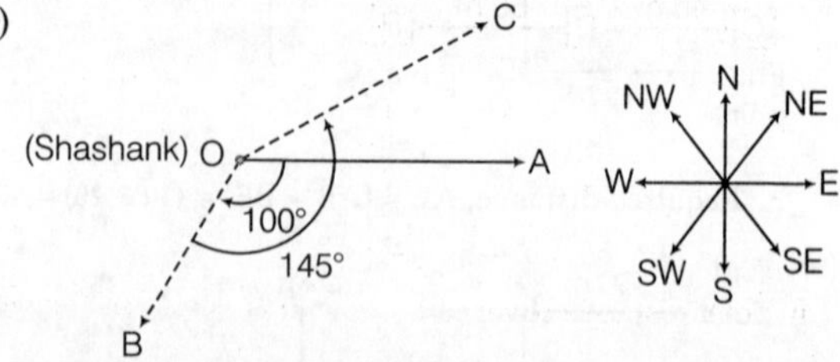

Shashank initially faces towards East i.e. in the direction OA. On moving 100° clockwise, he faces in the direction OB. On further moving 145° anti-clockwise, he faces in the direction OC. Clearly, OC makes an angle of (145° − 100°), i.e. 45° with OA and the direction of Shashank is North East.

38. (*d*) Let A be the initial position of the man. He initially faced East and then turned his left in the direction of North and walked 10 yards.

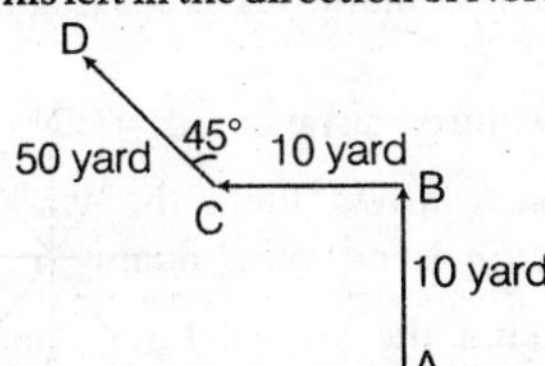

Then, turned his left in the direction of West and walked 10 yards. Now, he turned 45° to his right and walked 50 yards straight in the same direction. Now, the direction of the man will respect to his starting point is North-West.

39. (*d*)

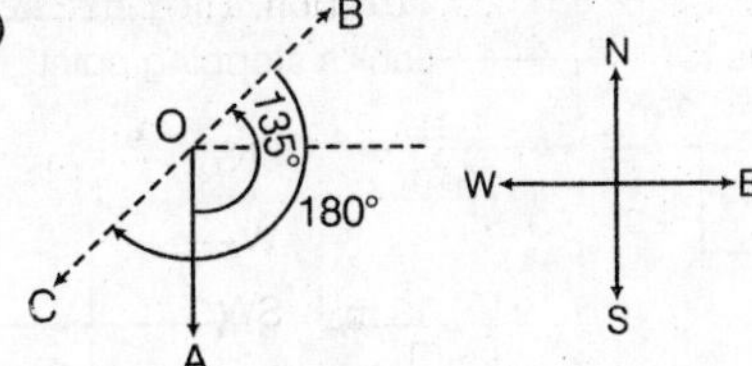

Somesh initially faces in the direction OA. On moving 135° anti-clockwise, he faces in the direction OB. On further moving 180° clockwise, he faces in the direction OC, which is South-West.

40. (*b*) The diagram is given below

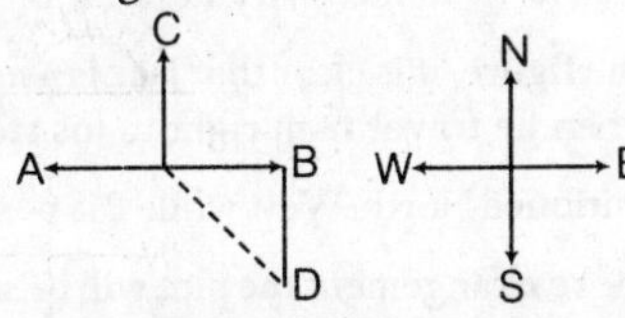

So, it is clear from the diagram that D is in the South-East direction of C.

41. (*b*) According to the question, diagram is as follows

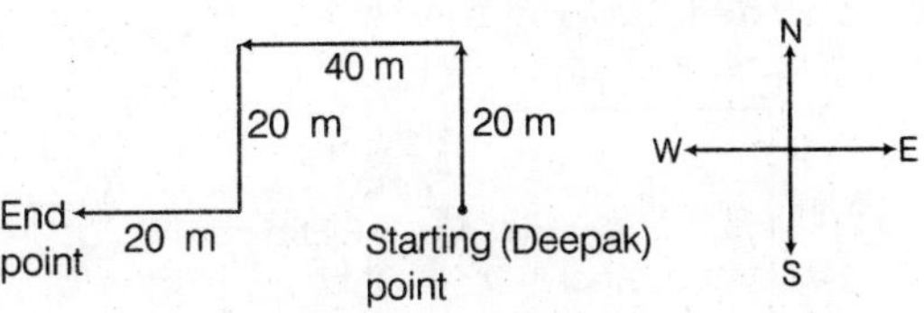

Distance between his starting point and ending point

$$= (40 + 20) = 60 \text{ m}$$

42. (*d*)

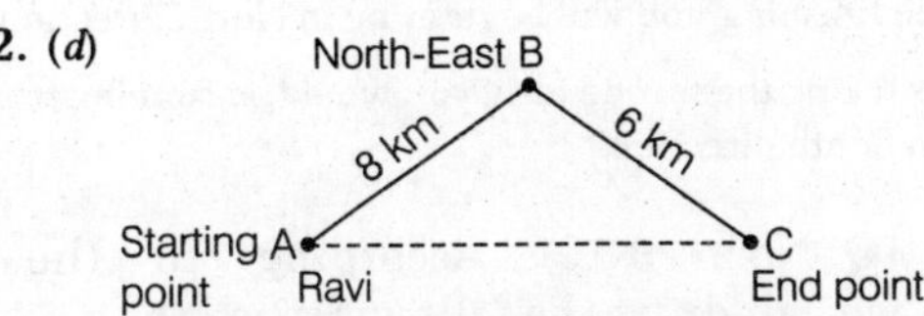

We have to find out the distance between point A (starting point) and point C (End point). ABC is a triangle and applying Pythagoras therem in it, we get

$$AC^2 = AB^2 + BC^2$$

Here, AB = 8 km, BC = 6 km and AC = ?

Putting values in above theorem, we get

$$AC^2 = (8)^2 + (6)^2$$
$$= 8 \times 8 + 6 \times 6 = 64 + 36 = 100$$

Now, $AC^2 = 100$

$\Rightarrow$ $AC = \sqrt{100}$ (taking square root)

$$= \sqrt{10 \times 10} = 10$$

$\therefore$ AC = 10 km

Therefore, Ravi is 10 km far away from his starting point.

Intro Exercise 2

Solution (Q. Nos. 1-3) From the given information we can draw the following figure

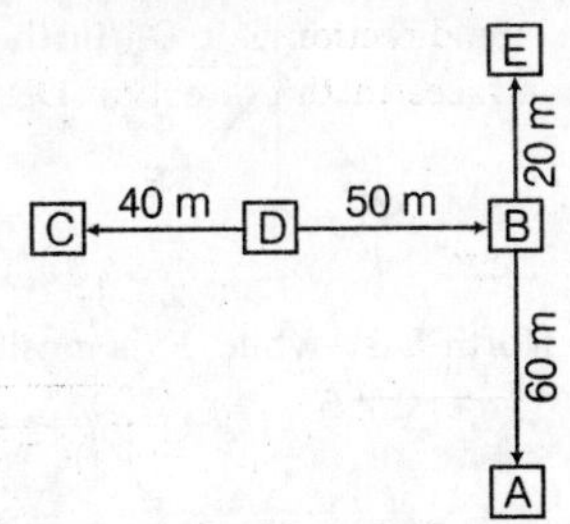

1. (*d*) Total distance covered by boy = (40 + 50 + 60 + 80) m = 230 m

2. (*c*)

E
20 m
C
90 m
B

By Pythagoras theorem,

$$(CE)^2 = (CB)^2 + (BE)^2$$

$\Rightarrow$ $CE = \sqrt{(90)^2 + (20)^2}$

$$= \sqrt{8100 + 400} = \sqrt{8500}$$
$$= 92.19 \text{ m} \approx 92 \text{ m}$$

3. (*a*) C is the left of D. A is to the South-East of C.

Solution (Q. Nos. 4-5)

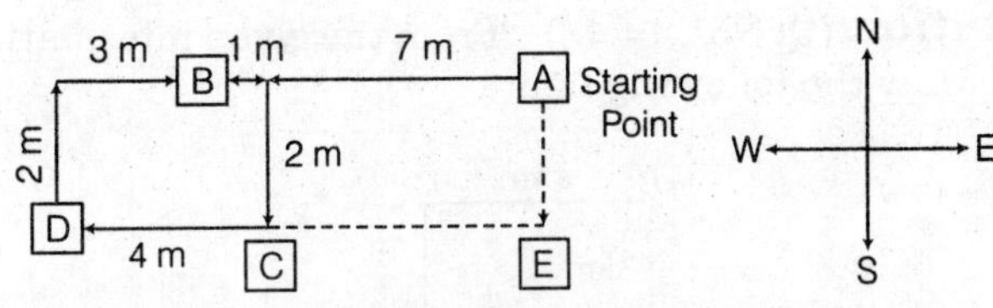

4. (*b*) Point A, is 8 m towards East.

5. (*d*) Points E, C and D will fall in a straight line.

Solution (Q. Nos. 6-8) From the given information we can draw the following figure

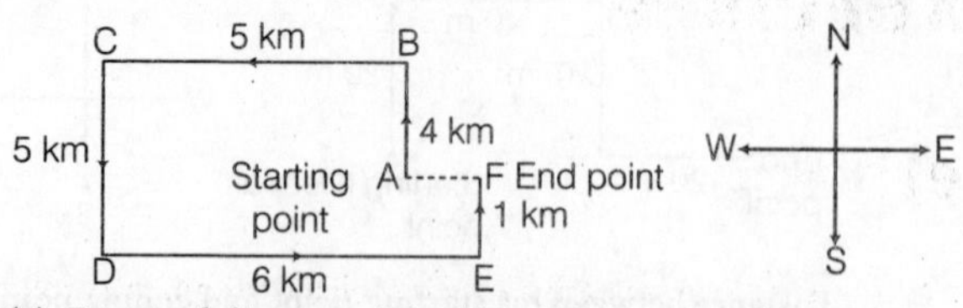

6. (*a*) Required distance, AF = DE − BC = 6 − 5 = 1 km

7. (*c*) While finishing you will be running in North direction.

8. (*d*) After taking the second turn, you would be running from C to D i.e. in South direction.

Solution (Q. Nos. 9-10) According to the given information, we can draw the following figure

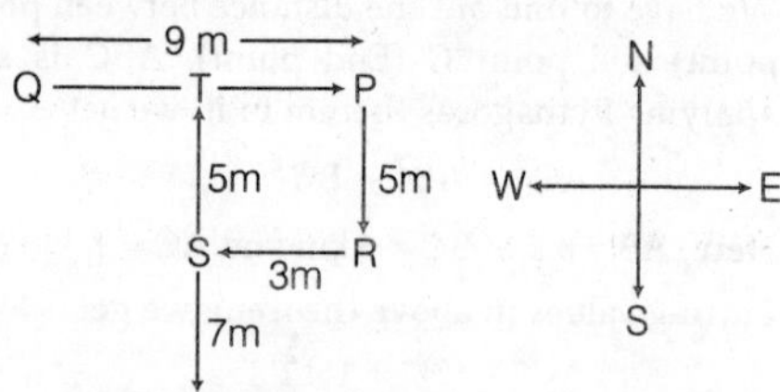

9. (*d*) If a person walks in a straight line for 8 m towards West from point R, then he would be cross 'S'. As shown below

5 m (S) 3 m R

8 m

10. (*e*) S, V, T are in straight line. As shown in the above figure.

Solution (Q. Nos. 11-13) Situation of houses is as shown in the figure given below

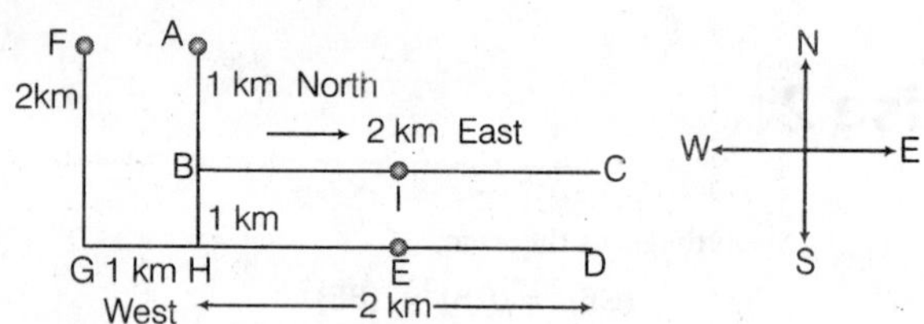

11. (*c*) E is in the middle of H and D.

So, $HE = \frac{1}{2} \times 2 = 1$ km

∴ Required distance, EG = EH + HG = 1 + 1 = 2 km

12. (*a*) Required distance, EI = HB = 1 km

13. (*a*) Required distance, AF = HG = 1 km

Solution (Q. Nos. 14-18) From the given information we can draw the following figure

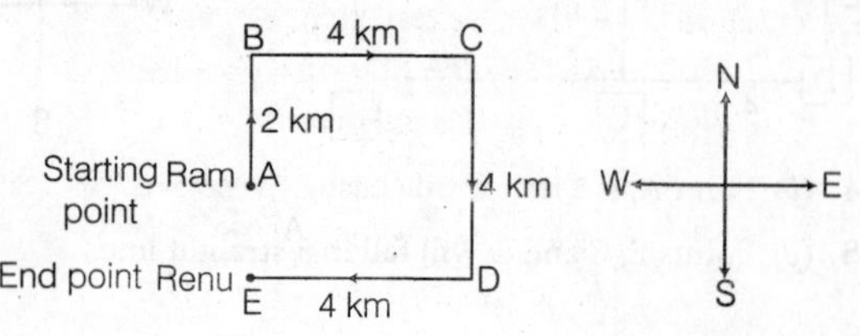

14. (*d*) After taking the first turn, Ram was going in East direction.

15. (*d*) Here, we have marked A as starting point and E as finishing point.

So, the required distance, AE = CD − AB = 4 − 2 = 2 km

16. (*d*) When Ram meets Renu, he was going towards West direction. So, Renu was comming from West direction.

17. (*d*) After taking the second turn, Ram was going in South direction.

18. (*b*) If Ram is to again reach the point from where he had started, he should go towards North direction.

Solution (Q. Nos. 19-20)

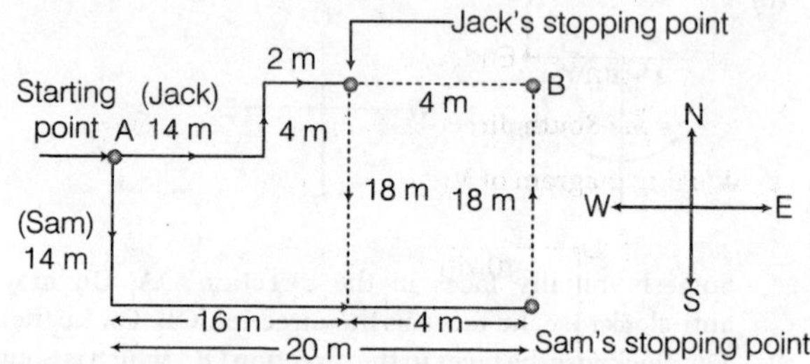

19. (*d*) From the figure, it is clear that Sam have to travel 18 m towards North to meet Jack at point B.

20. (*a*) From the figure, it is clear that Jack is 4 m distance away from Sam when he travel 18 m right to his stopping point.

21. (*a*) A is positioned North-West while P is positioned South-East.

22. (*c*) After the rearrangement the plot will be shown as following

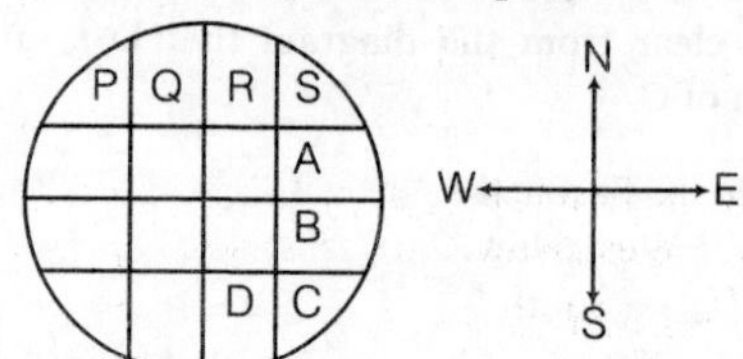

So, R is at North while D is at South direction.

23. (*a*)

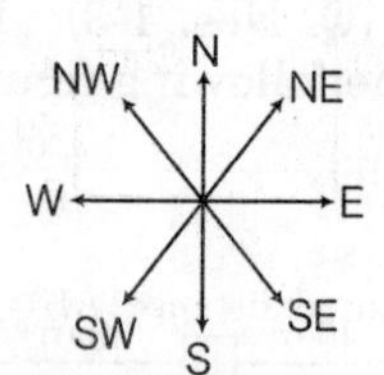

A is positioned at North-East while P is positioned at South-West.

24. (c)

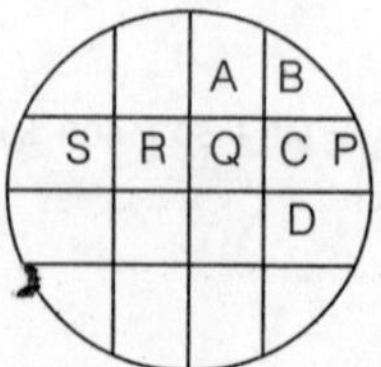

So, policeman C will be able to catch the offender P.

Cumulative Exercises

Base Level

1. (*b*)

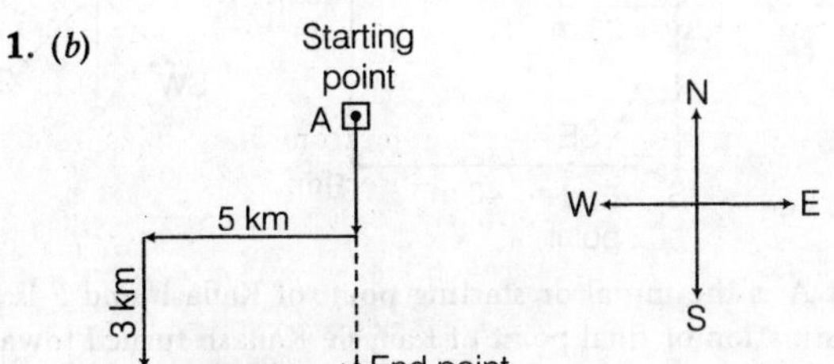

A is in the South direction from his starting point.

2. (*d*) Walking diagram of Vijay is as follow

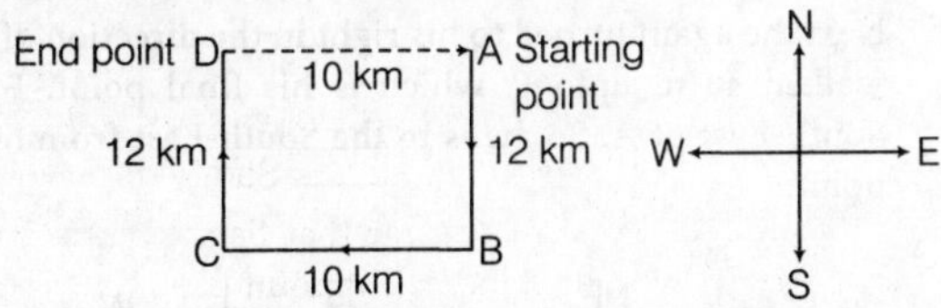

Point A is the starting point and D is ending point of Vijay. Now, Vijay's distance from starting point = AD = BC = 10 km

3. (*b*)

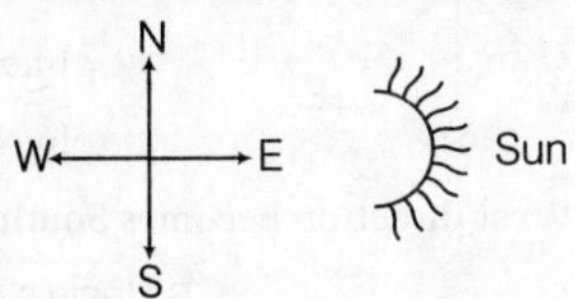

Sunrises in the East in the morning So, in morning the shadow falls towards the West. Now, Suraj's shadow falls to the right. So, he is standing facing South.

4. (*d*)

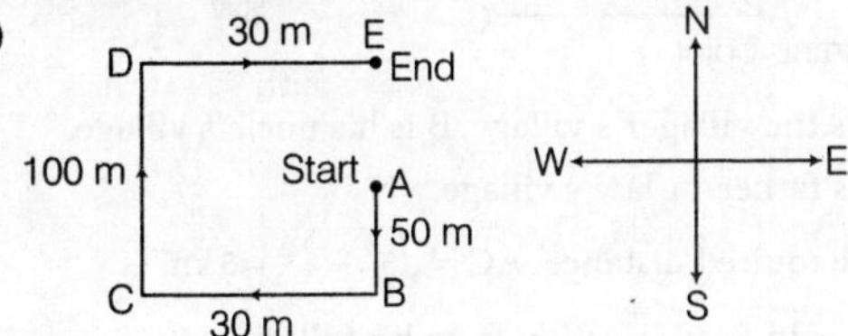

Required distance, AE = CD − AB = 100 − 50 = 50 m

[∵ CD = 100, AB = 50]

He is 50 m far away from starting point in North direction.

5. (*b*)

D 3 km E End point

4 km

C 3 km B

8 km

A Starting point

N W E S

∴ Required distance = AE = AB + BE = (8 + 4) = 12 km

(∵ BE = CD)

6. (*a*) The diagram of distance travelled by Raju is as follows

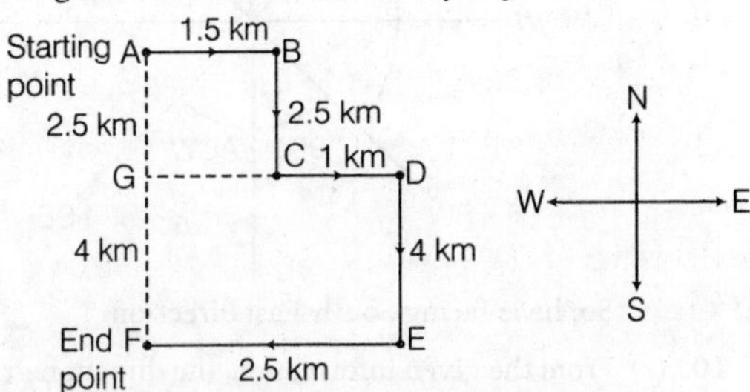

Let A is the starting point of Raju and F is the ending point.

Now, AG = BC = 2.5 km, GF = ED = 4 km

Now, distance of Raju from his starting point = AG + GF

= (2.5 + 4)

= 6.5 km

7. (*c*) The movement of Shobha is as following

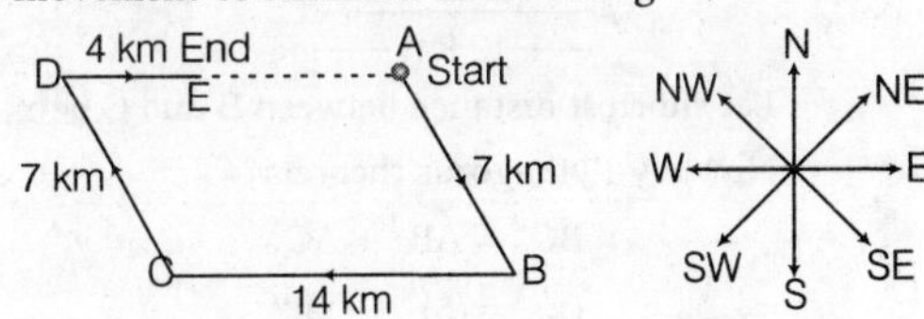

∴ Required distance, AD − ED = 14 − 4 = 10 km

8. (*a*)

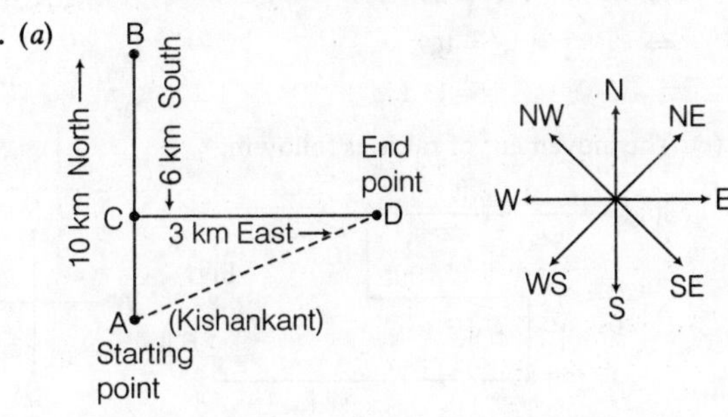

Kishankant goes 10 km North from point A towards point B. From point B he goes 6 km in South direction to point C. Now, from point C Kishankant travels 3 km in East direction. D is the end point of Kishankant.

We have to find out the direction of end point and distance of end point from starting point A.

So, in ΔACD applying Pythagoras theorem, we get

$$AD^2 = AC^2 + CD^2$$

Here, $AD = ?,\ CD = 3$ km

$AC = AB - BC = 10 - 6 = 4$ km

Putting values in the theorem, we get

$$AD^2 = AC^2 + CD^2 \Rightarrow AD^2 = (4)^2 + (3)^2$$

$$\Rightarrow \quad AD^2 = 16 + 9 \Rightarrow AD^2 = 25$$

$$\therefore \quad AD = \sqrt{25} = 5 \text{ km}$$

Point D is in the North-East direction from point A and it is 5 km far away from it.

9. (*d*) The movement of a man is as following

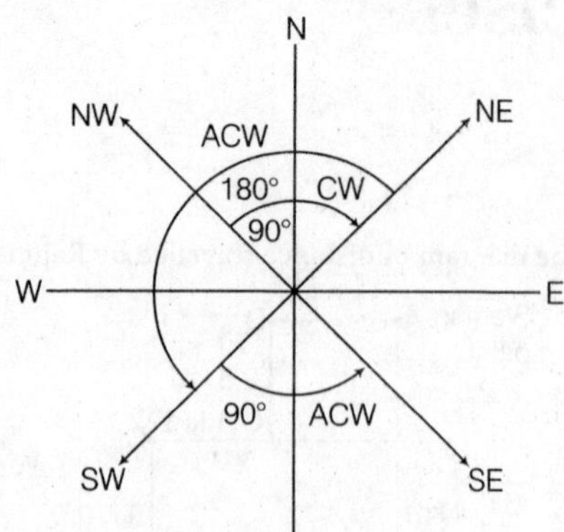

So, he is facing South-East direction.

10. (*b*) From the given information, the direction graph can be drawn as

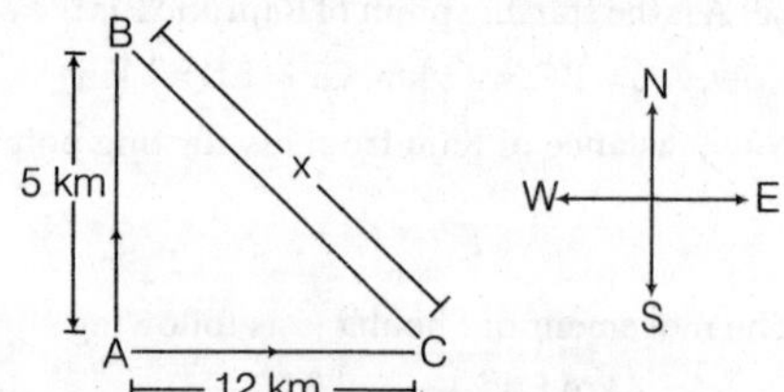

Let shortest distance between B and C be x km.

Now, by Pythagoras theorem

$$BC^2 = AB^2 + AC^2$$

$$\Rightarrow \quad (x)^2 = (5)^2 + (12)^{12}$$

$$\Rightarrow \quad x^2 = 25 + 144$$

$$\Rightarrow \quad x^2 = 169$$

$$\therefore \quad x = 13 \text{ km}$$

11. (*c*) The movement of rat is as following

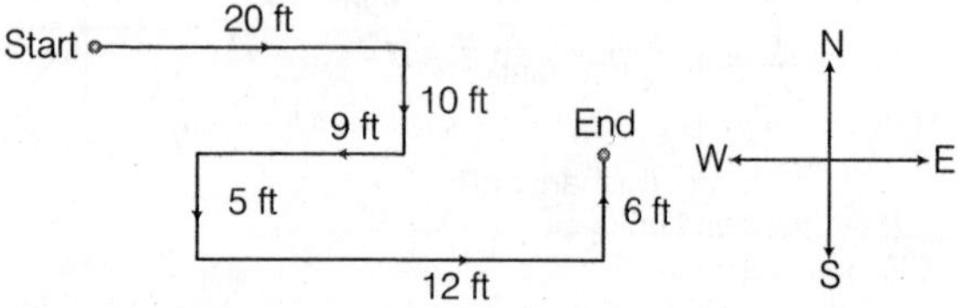

It is clear from the figure that, the rat is facing North direction.

12. (*b*) Required distance,

$$AF = 30 + 15 = 45 \text{ m}$$

The movement of Dilip is as following

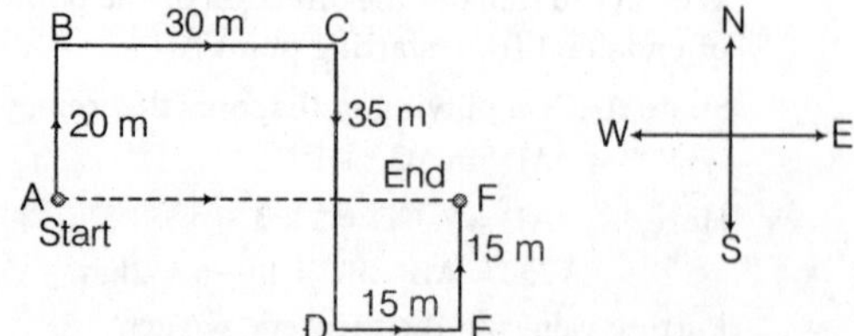

He is in East direction from starting point.

13. (*d*) The direction diagram of Kailash is are follows

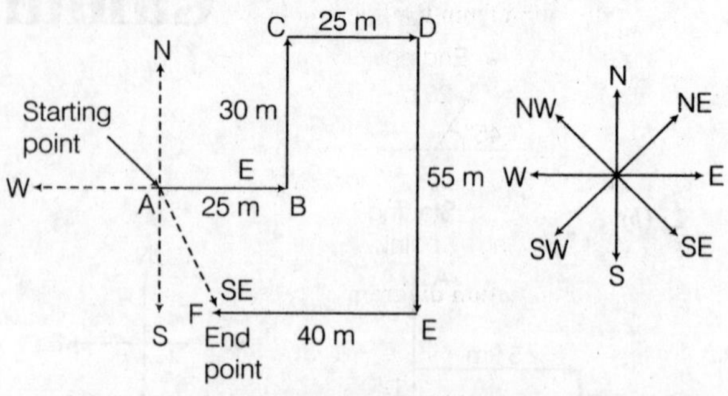

Let A is the initial or starting point of Kailash and F is the destination or final point of Kailash. Kailash turned towards right from North direction. He walked 25 m towards East upto B, turned left in the direction of North and walked 30 m upto C, turned right in the direction of East and walked 25 m upto D, turned right in the direction of South and walked 55 m upto E. Next, he again turned to his right in the direction of West and walked 40 m upto F, which is his final point. F is to the South-East of A. So, he is to the South-East from his starting point.

14. (*c*)

So, West direction becomes South-East.

15. (*b*)

A is the villager's village, B is his uncle's village. C is father-in-law's village.

$\therefore$ Required distance, $AC = \sqrt{5^2 - 4^2} = 3$ km

He is in East direction from his village.

16. (*a*) When the time is quarter to three, then hands of the watch are approximately diametrically opposite to each other.

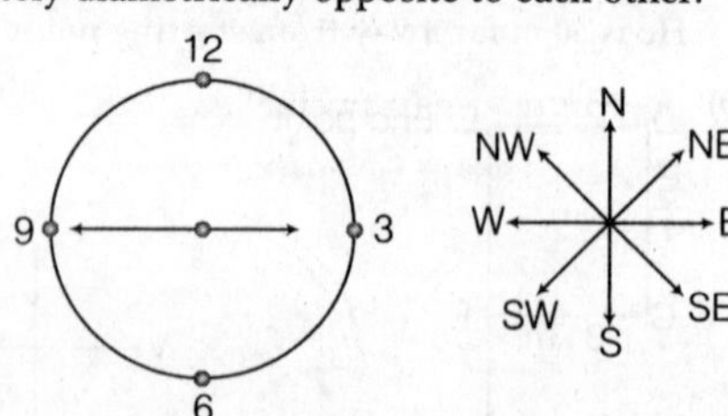

So, if minute hand points to North-East, then hour hand will point to South-West.

17. (*d*) From the figure, it is clear that you are in North-West direction from the starting point.

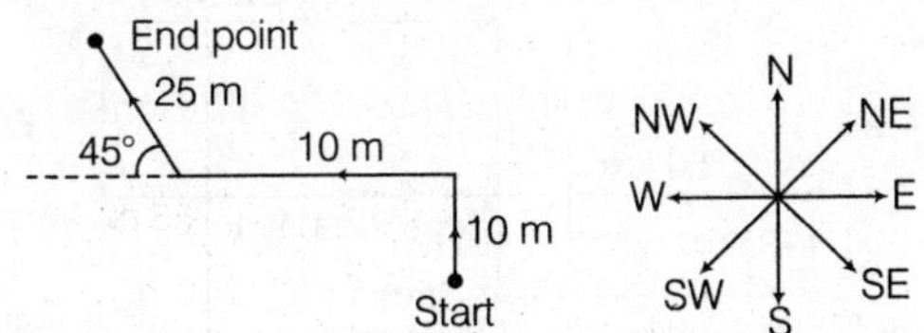

18. (*a*) The direction diagram of train is as below

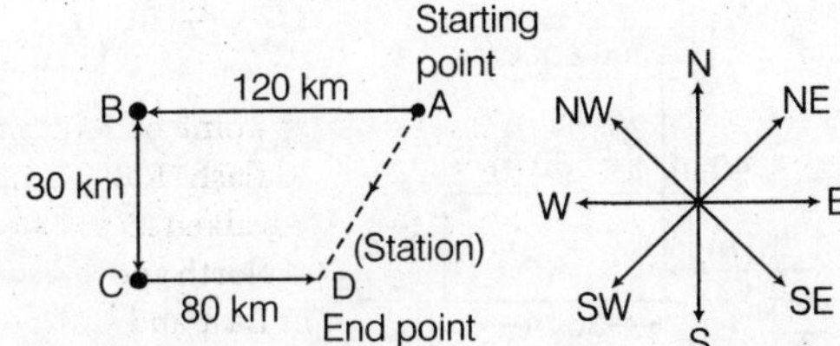

Let A is the starting point of train and D is the last point of train where it was stopped.

It is clear from the above diagram that the station is in South-West direction from the train's starting point.

19. (*a*)

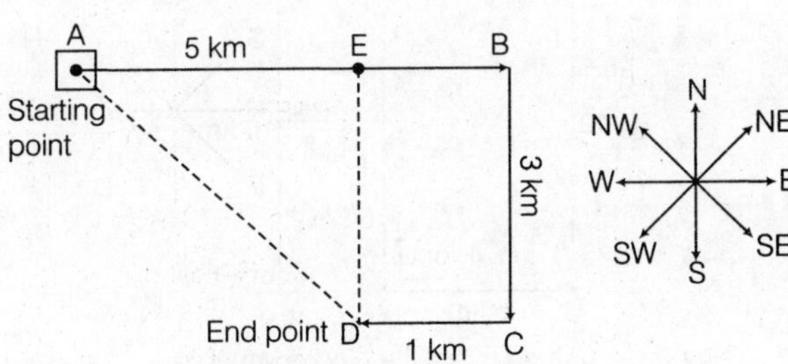

$AB = 5$ and $DC = 1$

So, $AE = BB - DC = 5 - 1$ $(CD = BE = 1 \text{ km})$

$AE = 4$ km

$BC = DE$

$BC = 3 = DE$

Now, $AD = \sqrt{(AE)^2 + (DE)^2}$

$= \sqrt{(4)^2 + (3)^2}$

$= \sqrt{16 + 9}$

$= \sqrt{25} = 5$ km

20. (*d*) Time quarter past twelve means that the time is 12 : 15.

Original position **After shifting**

Hence, when hour hand is pointing towards East, then the minute hand is pointing towards South.

So, the direction opposite to minute hand is North.

21. (*c*) The movements of Vinay is as following

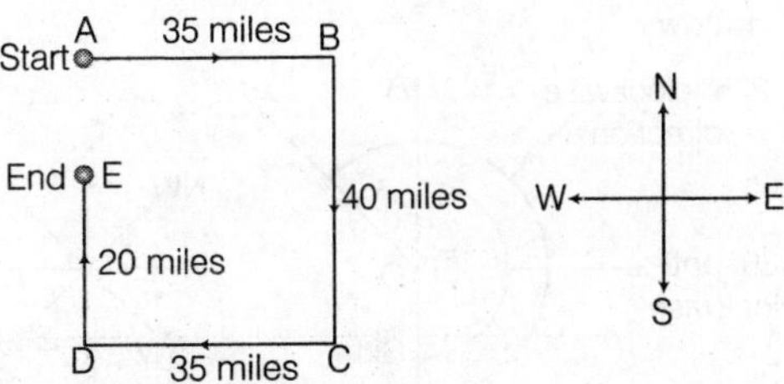

Here, $BC = AD = 40$ and $DE = 20$

$\therefore$ Required distance, $AE = AD - DE = 40 - 20 = 20$

So, Vinay is 20 miles away in South direction from his starting point.

22. (*d*) Path of Raj is as follows

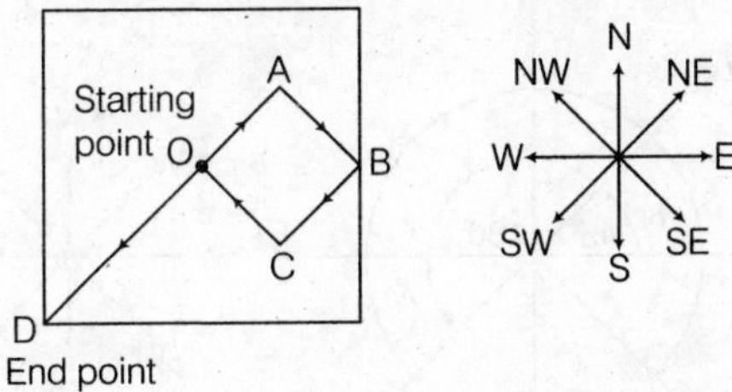

Here, O is starting point and D is the final point.

It is clear from the above figure that, now Raj is in South-West direction.

23. (*b*)

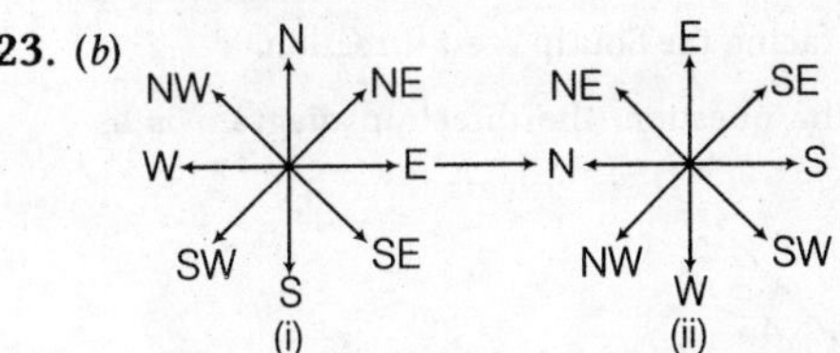

Fig. (i) is the original position and Fig (ii) is the position after the accident.

West direction shown by the pole in actual is South direction.

24. (*b*) Man's walking direction are as follows

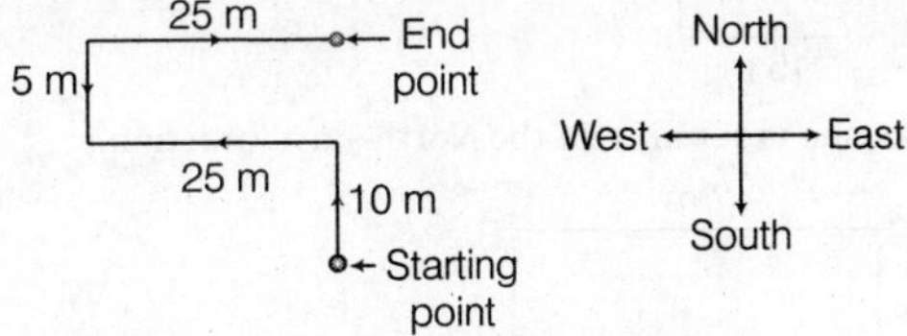

Hence, now man is facing East direction.

25. (*d*) Radhika's walking direction are as follows

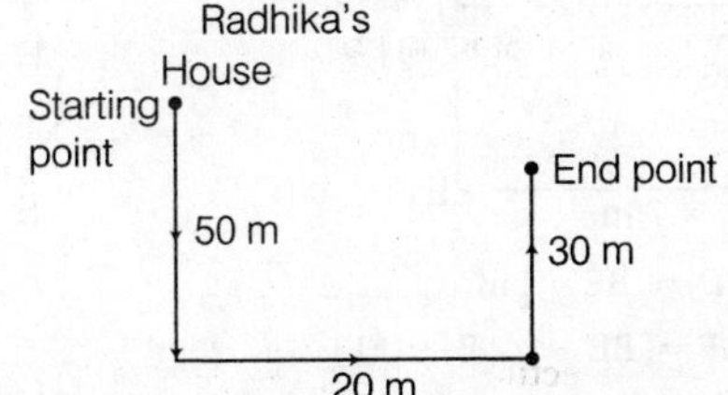

Hence, Radhika's house is in North-West direction from the end point.

26. (*b*) According to the question, the direction diagram will be as follows

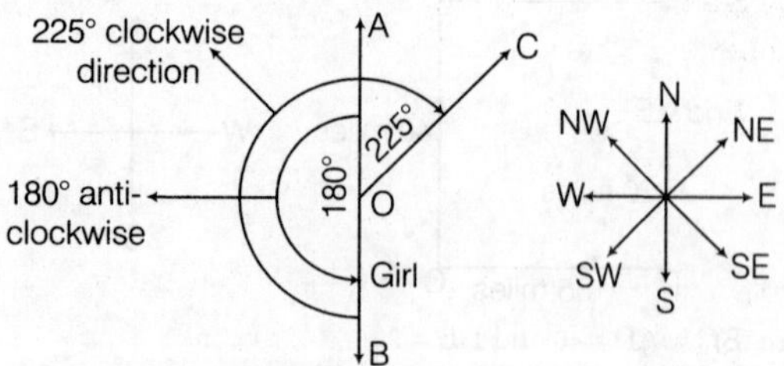

Clearly, the girl is facing North-East.

27. (*d*) According to the question, the direction diagram can be drawn as

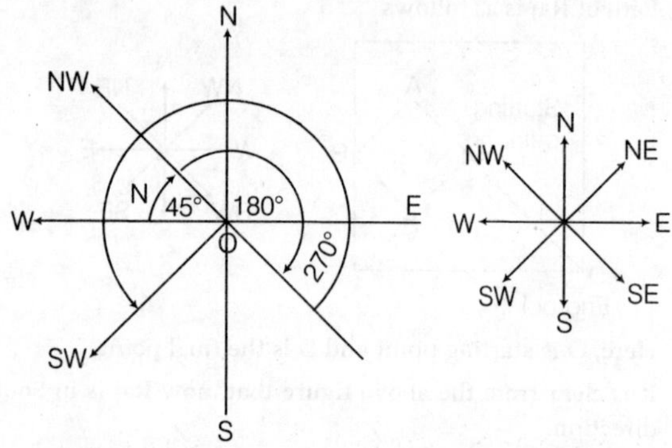

Finally, man is facing the South-West direction.

28. (*c*) According to the question, the direction diagram is as follows

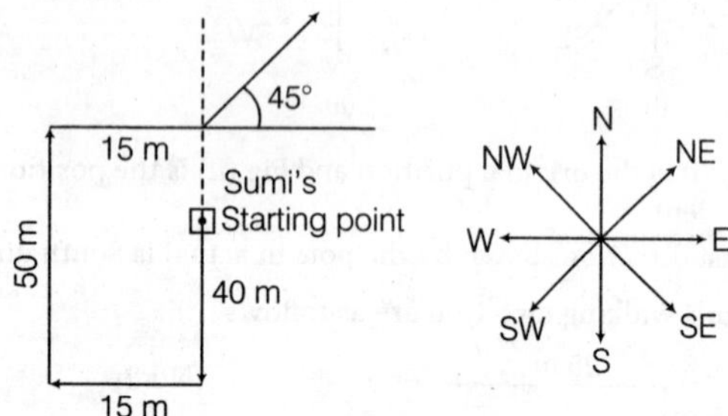

So, she is running in the North-East direction.

29. (*d*)

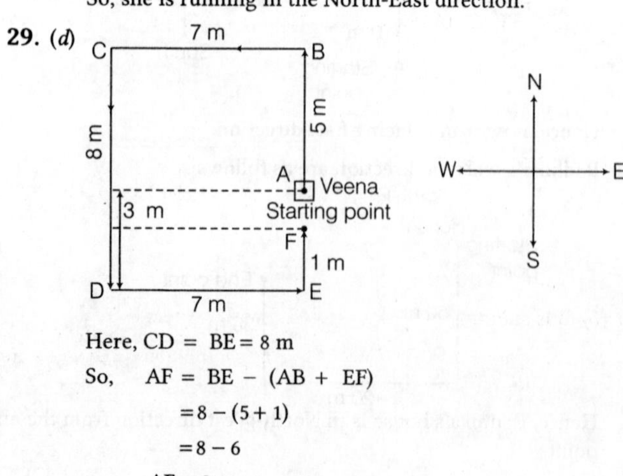

Here, CD = BE = 8 m

So, AF = BE − (AB + EF)

= 8 − (5 + 1)

= 8 − 6

∴ AF = 2 m

Hence, Veena is 2 m from the starting point.

30. (*d*) According to the question, the direction diagram is as follows

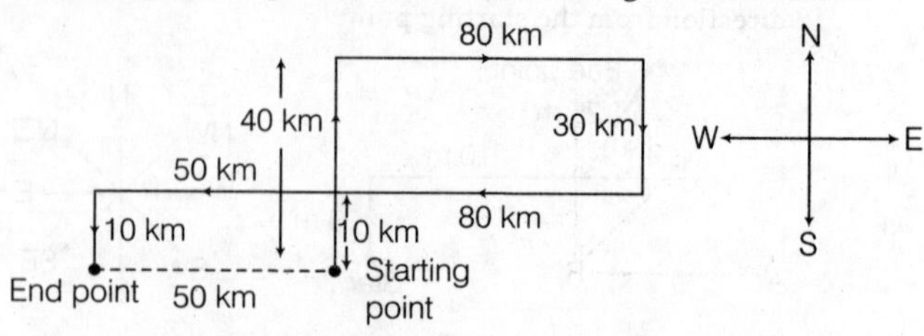

Clearly, he is 50 km far away from his starting point.

31. (*c*)

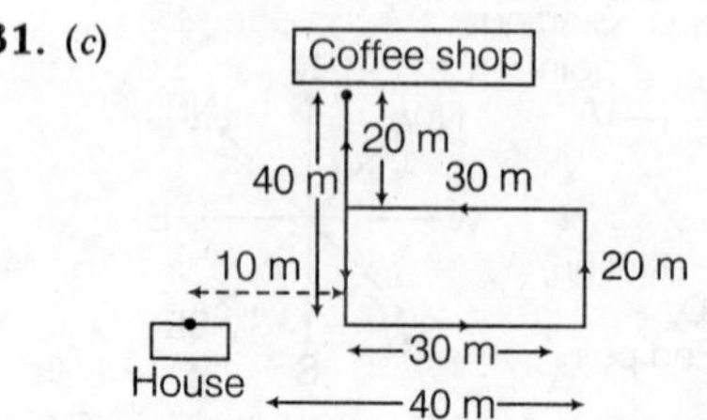

∴ Required distance = 40 − 30 = 10 m

32. (*c*) According to the question, the direction diagram will be as follows

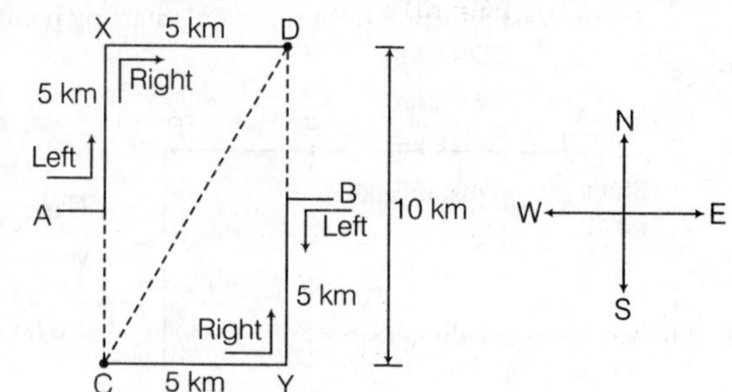

Now, AX = DB = BY = CA = 5 km

XD = CY = 5 km

XC = XA + AC

= 5 + 5 = 10 km

∴ Distance between C and D,

$$CD = \sqrt{(XD)^2 + (XC)^2} \quad \text{[by Pythagoras theorem]}$$

$$= \sqrt{5^2 + 10^2}$$

$$= \sqrt{25 + 100}$$

$$= \sqrt{125} = 5\sqrt{5}$$

$$= 5 \times 2.23$$

$$= 11.15 \text{ km}$$

So, it is clear from the figure that the houses of C and Dare less than 20 km apart.

33. (*d*) According to the question, the direction diagram is as follows

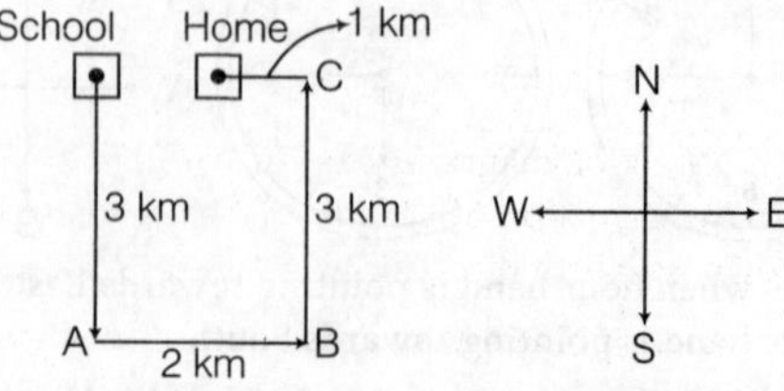

The home of the boy was in East direction from his school.

Advanced Level

1. (*c*)

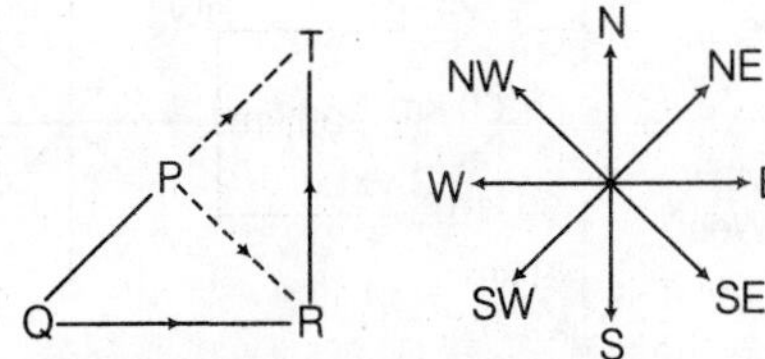

T is in the North-East of P.

2. (*a*) According to the question, the direction diagram will be as follows:

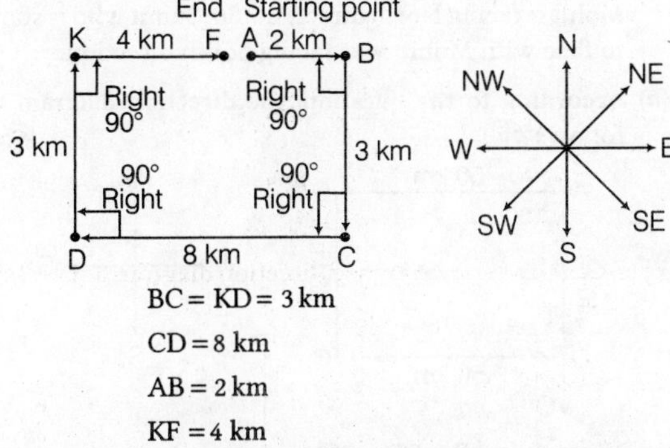

BC = KD = 3 km

CD = 8 km

AB = 2 km

KF = 4 km

∴ Required distance, AF = BK − (KF + AB)

= 8 − (4 + 2)

= 8 − 6 = 2 km

3. (*e*) According to the question, the direction diagram will be as follows:

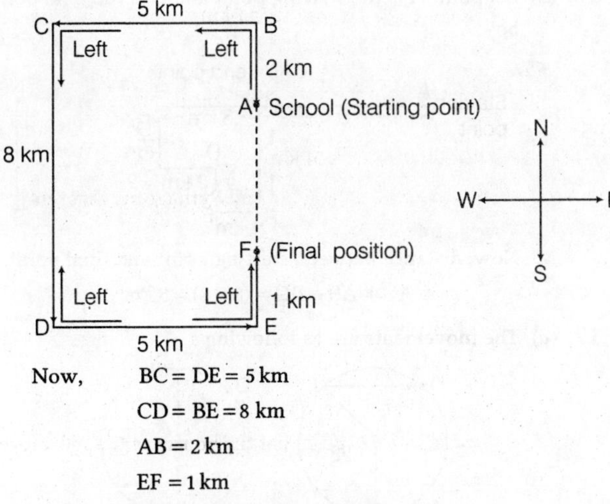

Now, BC = DE = 5 km

CD = BE = 8 km

AB = 2 km

EF = 1 km

∴ Required distance, AF = BE − (AB + EF)

= 8 − (2 + 1)

= 8 − 3 = 5 km

From the direction diagram, it is clear that the bus is present at in the South direction of school. So, the driver needs to drive 5 km towards North direction to reach the school.

4. (*d*) According to the question, the direction diagram will be as follows

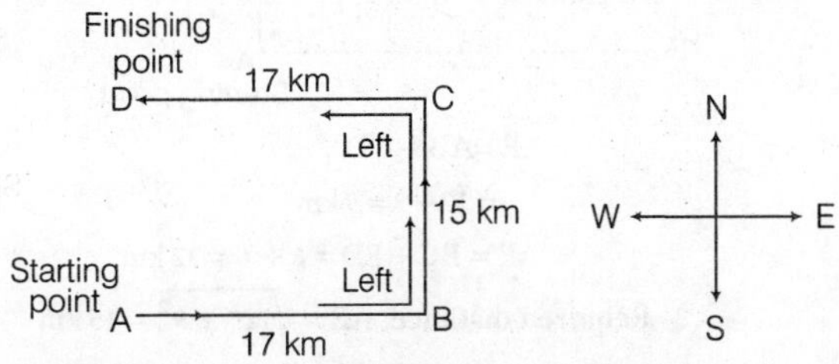

Now, AB = CD = 17 km and BC = AD = 15 km

∴ Required distance, AD = 15 km

5. (*d*) The movements of Maya are as following

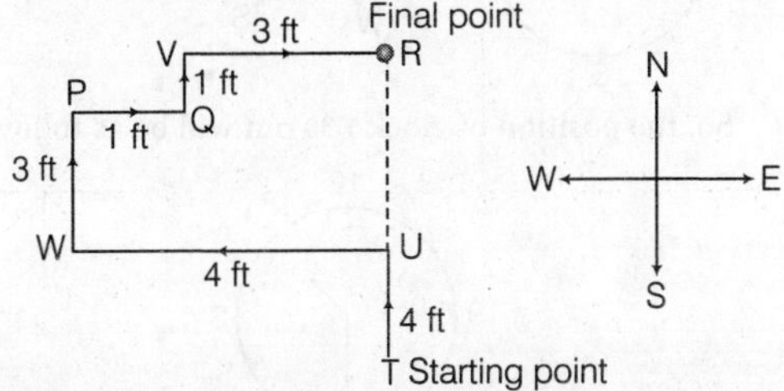

∴ Required distance, TR = 4 + 3 + 1 = 8 ft

6. (*b*) According to the question, the direction diagram will be as follows

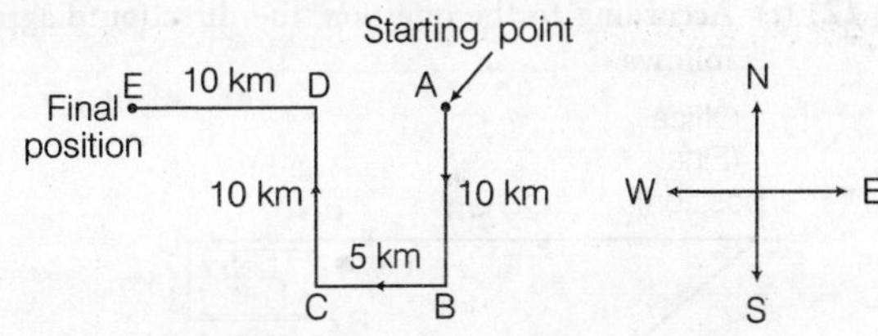

Now, AB = DC = 10 km, BC = DA = 5 km, ED = 10 km

∴ Required distance, EA = ED + DA = 10 + 5 = 15 km

Solution (Q. Nos. 7-9) According to the given information, the position of eight persons is as following

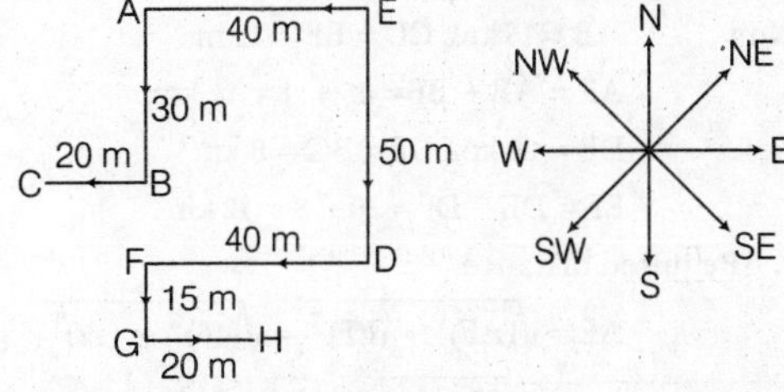

7. (*b*) B is standing in North direction with respect to F.

8. (*d*) As total distance between I and D is not given, so this question cannot be determined.

9. (*a*) C is in the North-West direction from H.

10. (*c*)

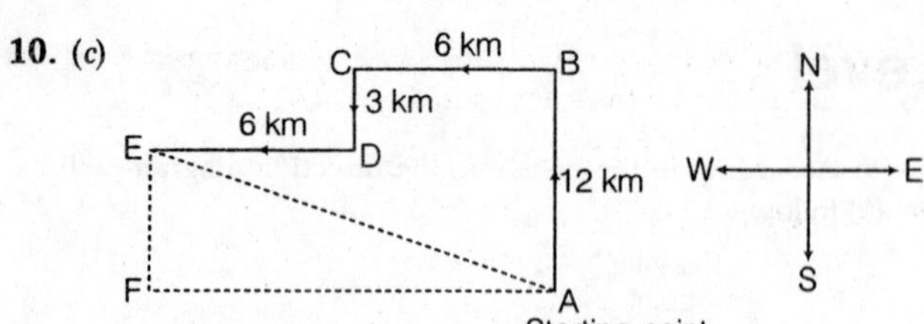

$$EF = AB - CD$$
$$= 12 - 3 = 9\text{ km}$$
$$AF = BC + ED = 6 + 6 = 12\text{ km}$$

$\therefore$ Required distance, $AE = \sqrt{12^2 + 9^2} = 15\text{ km}$

11. (*c*)

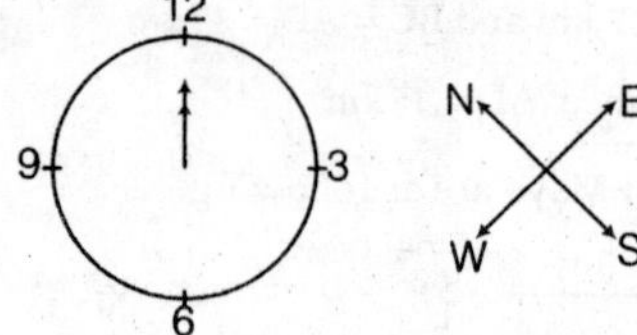

So, the position of clock 1:30 pm will be as following

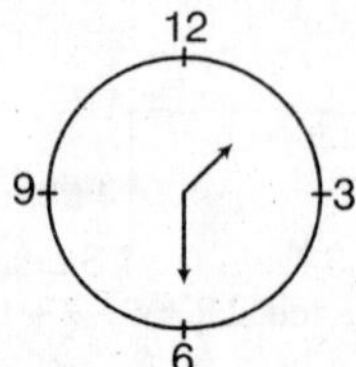

So, hour hand is pointing towards East.

12. (*c*) According to the question, the direction diagram will be as follows:

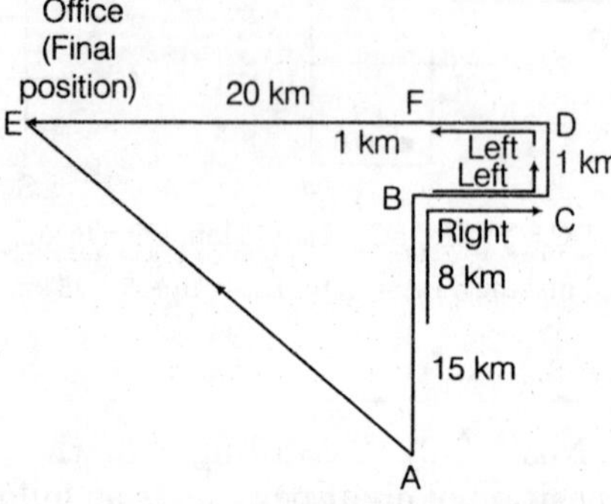

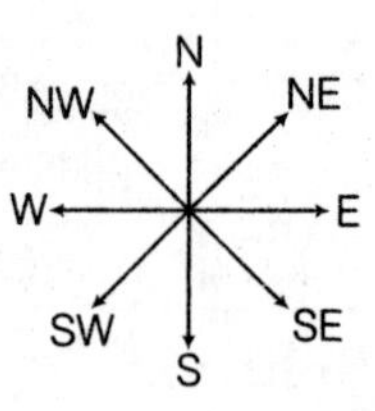

Now, $AB = 15\text{ km}, CD = BF = 1\text{ km}$

$AF = AB + BF = 15 + 1 = 16\text{ km}$

$DE = 20\text{ km}, DF = BC = 8\text{ km}$

$EF = DE - DF = 20 - 8 = 12\text{ km}$

$\therefore$ Required distance,

$$AE = \sqrt{(AF)^2 + (EF)^2} = \sqrt{(16)^2 + (12)^2}$$
$$= \sqrt{256 + 144} = \sqrt{400} = 20\text{ km}$$

So, his office is 20 km North-West.

13. (*c*)

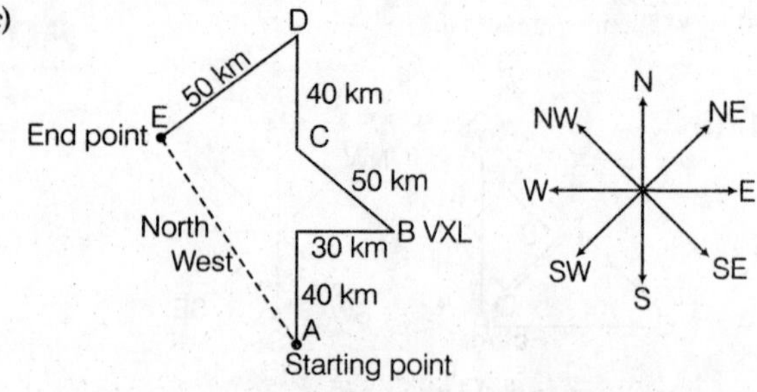

He is in the North-West direction from his starting point.

14. (*b*) In the evening, the sun is in West direction. So shadows fall in the East direction. As Mohit's shadow fall towards right. So, Mohit is facing North direction. So, Sumit who is standing face to face with Mohit, was facing South direction.

15. (*a*) According to the question, the direction diagram will be as follows

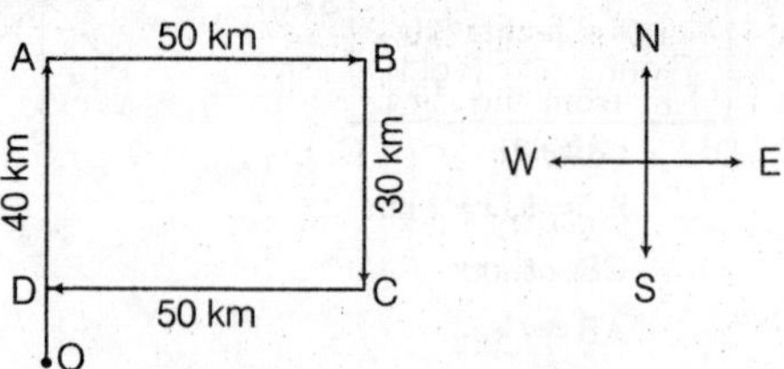

Now, $AB = CD = 50\text{ km}$

$OA = 40\text{ km}$

$AD = BC = 30$

$\therefore$ Required distance,

$$OD = OA - AD = 40 - 30 = 10\text{ km}$$

16. (*a*) Let point A is the starting point and G is the final point of the boy.

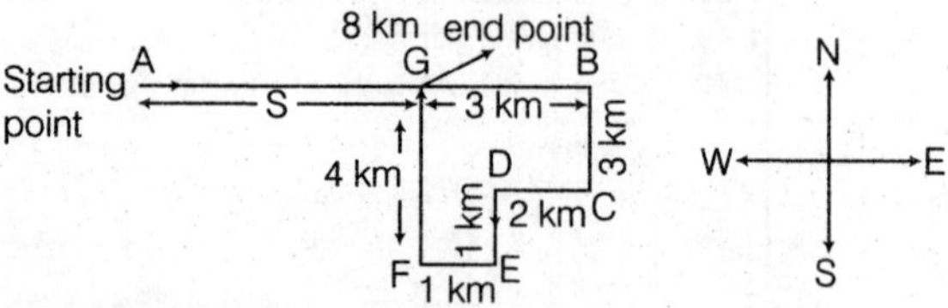

Now, distance between starting point and final point,

$$AG = AB - BG = (8 - 3) = 5\text{ km}$$

17. (*a*) The movements are as following

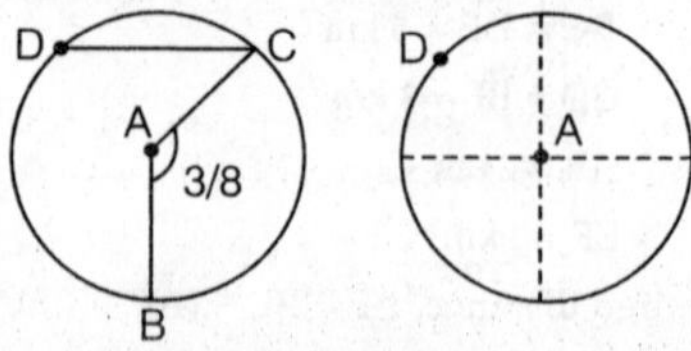

D is in North-West direction.

Final position is D which is in North-West direction from the starting point A.

18. (*c*) The movements are as following

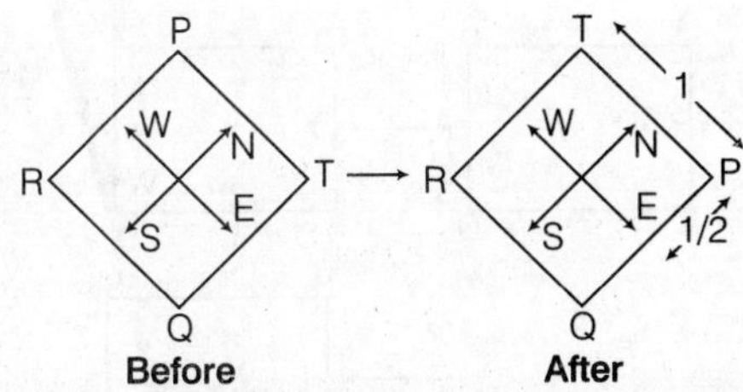

Now, as C is walking in clockwise direction, so he is walking from T to P i.e. in South direction.

19. (*a*) The movements of A is as following

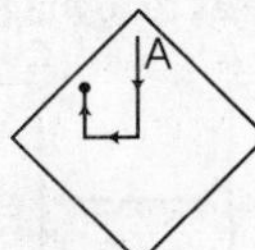

So, he is now facing North-West direction.

20. (*c*) It is clear from the above explanation that, A is standing in South-East direction.

21. (*b*) After driving 3 km North, 3 km West and 4 km South, Amit is 1 km to the South and 3 km to the West of his starting point.

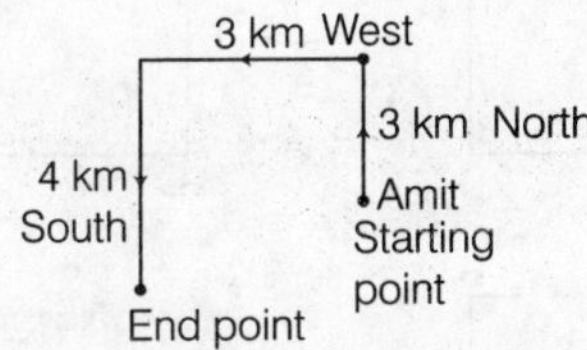

Hence, Amit will have to move 1 km North and 3 km East to reach the starting point.

22. (*c*) Driving as stated in the solution of Q. No. 21, Amit will reach the starting point, if he moves 1 km North and 3 km East. If he moves 1 km North and 4 km East, he will be 1 km West from his starting point.

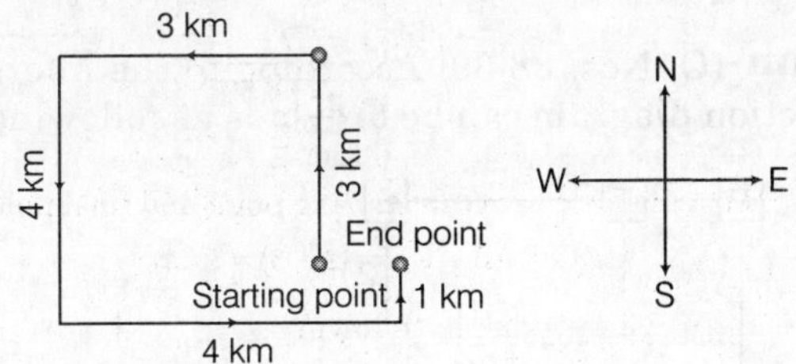

Solution (Q. Nos. 23-24) According to the given information, the direction can be drawn is as following

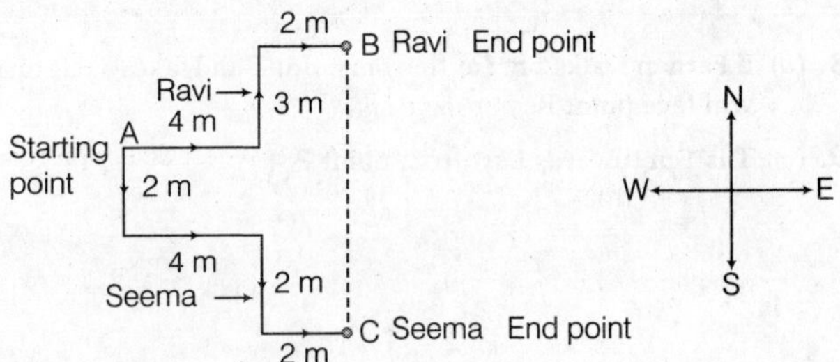

23. (*e*) From the figure, it is clear that Ravi has to cover the distance BC in the South direction to reach at C.

$$BC = (3+2+2) = 7 \text{ m}$$

24. (*c*) Starting point A, End point D

2 m, 4 m, 2 m, 2 m C, 4 m

$\therefore$ Required distance = AD = $(4+2) = 6$ m

25. (*b*) Radhika's walking directions are as follow

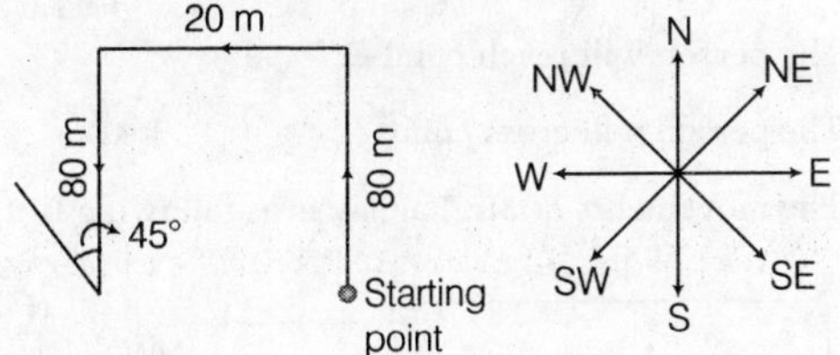

Hence, Radhika is finally moving in North-West direction.

26. (*a*) Raghubir's walking directions are as follow

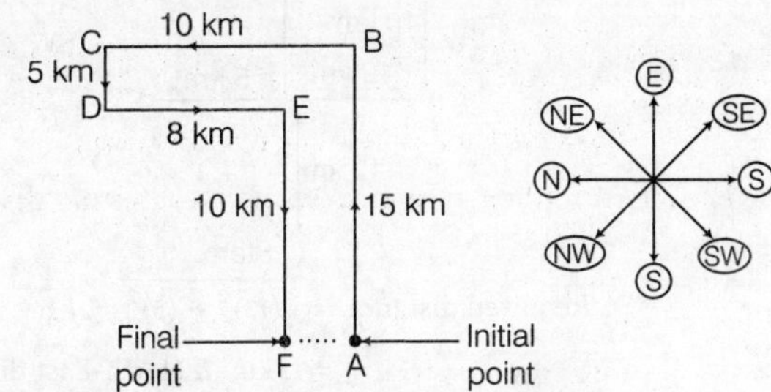

AB = 15 km, BC = 10 km, CD = 5 km, DE = 8 km,
EF = 10 km, AF = (10–8) = 2 km, West

Hence, Raghubir is 2 km in West direction from his initial point.

27. (*d*) Krishna's walking directions are as follow

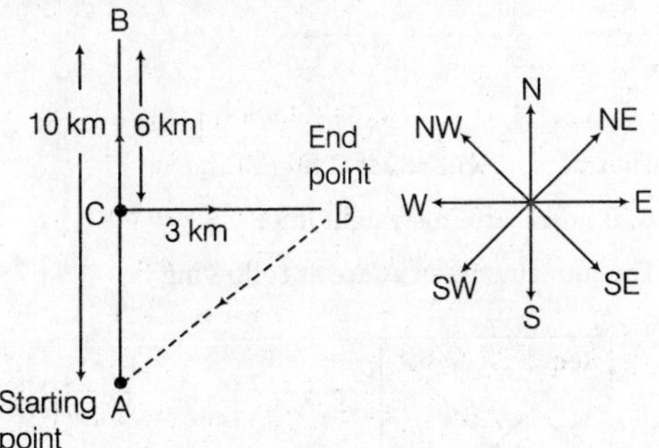

AB = 10 km, CD = 3 km, AC = AB – BC = 10 – 6 = 4 km

Required distance (AD) $= \sqrt{AC^2 + CD^2}$

$$= \sqrt{(4)^2 + (3)^2} = \sqrt{16+9} = \sqrt{25} = 5 \text{ km}$$

Hence, Krishna is 5 km North-East direction to his starting point.

Solution (Q. Nos. 28-29) According to the information the direction diagram can be drawn as following

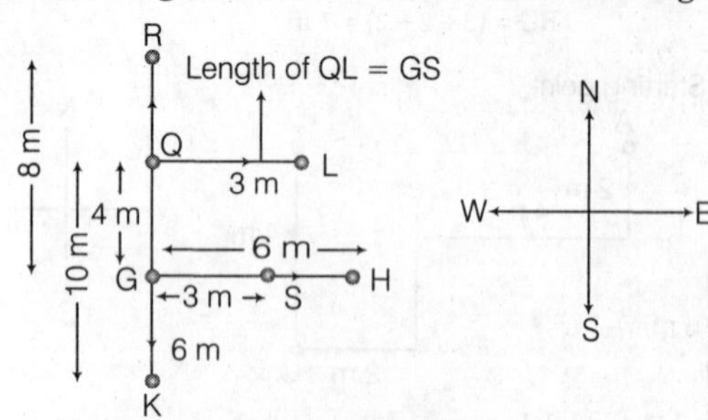

In the diagram QL lenth should be short.

GH = 6 m, GR = 8 m, GQ = 4 m, QK = 10 m, QL = 3 m, GS = 3 m

28. (*b*) The person will reach point G.

29. (*d*) The person will cross point.

30. (*c*) The movements of Mr. Raghav is as following L at a

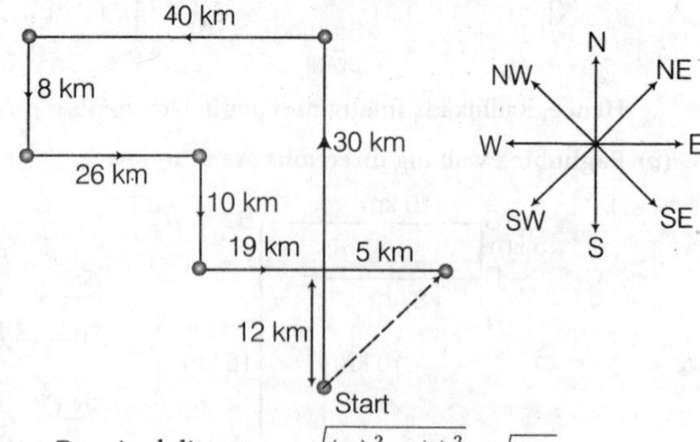

$\therefore$ Required distance $= \sqrt{(12)^2 + (5)^2} = \sqrt{169}$

$= 13$ km in North-East direction

Solution (Q. Nos. 31-32)

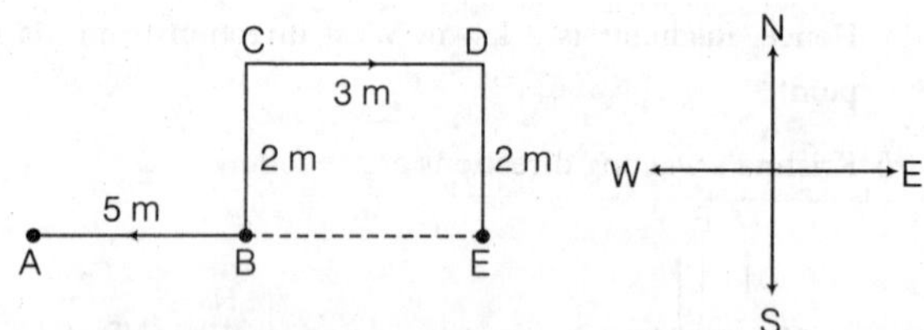

31. (*d*) That person will reach C first.

32. (*a*) A, B and E are in straight line.

33. (*b*) The movements of A are as following

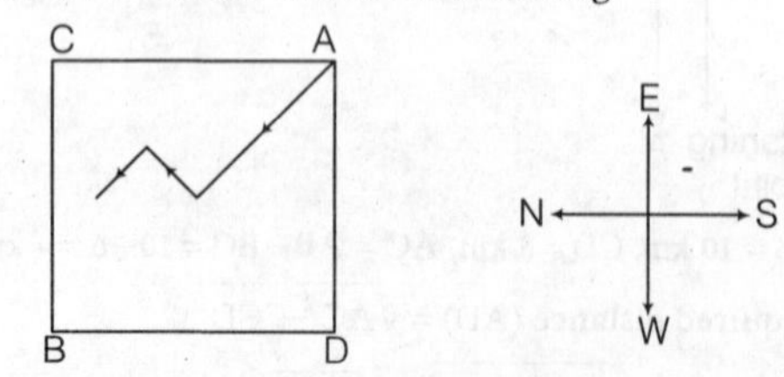

So, A is facing North-West direction.

34. (*a*) The movements are as following

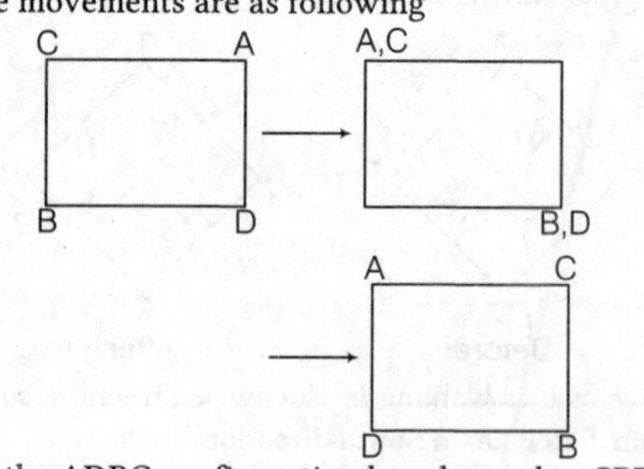

So, the ADBC configuration has changed to CBDA.

35. (*a*) The movements are as following

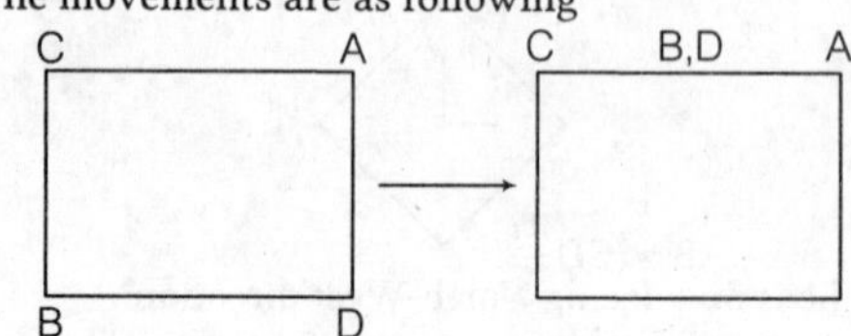

So, B and D both are at the mid-points between A and C.

36. (*d*) The movements are as following

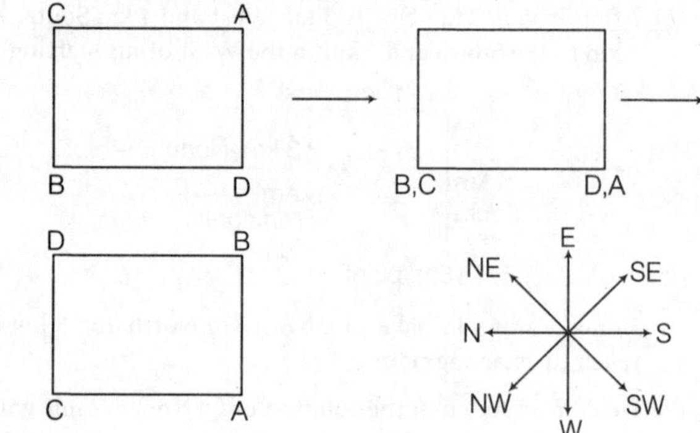

So, A is South-West corner.

37. (*c*) C is at the North-West corner.

Solution (Q. Nos. 38-39) According to the information, the direction diagram can be drawn is as following

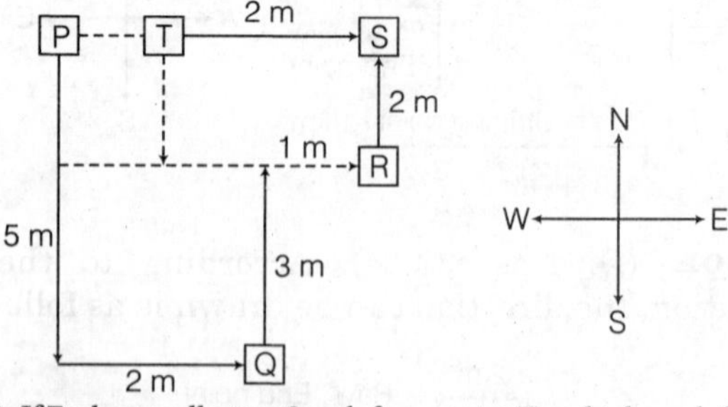

38. (*d*) If Farhan walks 2 m South from point T and takes a left turn, he will face point R.

39. (*c*) T is 1 m towards East from point P.

Solution (Q. Nos. 40-41) According to the question, the direction diagram can be drawn as

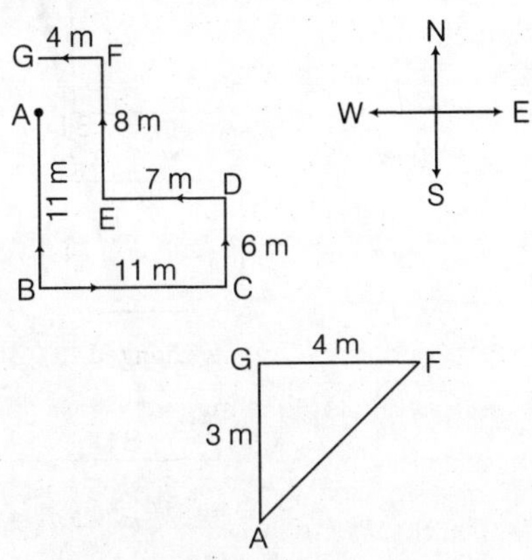

40. (*e*) $AG = BG - AB = (CD + EF) - (AB) = (6+8) - 11 = 3\text{ m}$

and $\quad GF = 4\text{ m}$

$\therefore \quad AF = \sqrt{AG^2 + GF^2}$ [by Pythagoras theorem]

$= \sqrt{9 + 16} = 5\text{ m}$

41. (*a*) Point G is in the North direction from point A and AG = 3 m [from above solution]

Solution (Q. Nos. 42-43) According to the information, the direction diagram can be drawn is as following

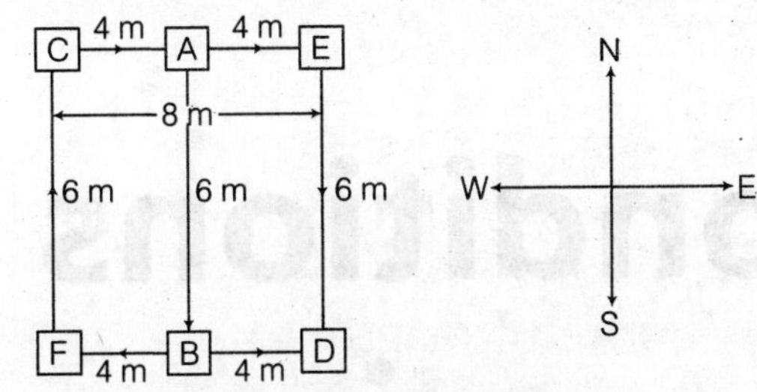

42. (*c*) Here, CE = 8 m (CAA = 4, AE = 4) FB = 4, so

$BD = CE - FB$

$= 8 - 4 = 4\text{ cm}$

Hence, point D would be 4 m from point B in the East direction.

43. (*e*) C, A and E fall in a straight line.

6

Conditions and Grouping

In this chapter, generally questions are asked to select, a small group of items or persons from a larger group satisfying some given conditions.

These given conditions will specify as to when a particular item or person can be selected or not in the required small group.

For example, the condition may specify that two particular persons should always be together or may specify that two particular persons should never be together.

Sometimes, the conditions given for selection or non-selection of items or persons may be based on logical connectivities like if-then, only-with, either-or, unless etc. So, you have to keep these conditions in mind and make the required selection as per the directions given in each questions.

Solved Examples

Direction (Examples 1-3) *Read the following information carefully and answer the questions that follow.*

There are six students J, K, L, M, N, and O. J and K belong to Priya Palace and the rest belong to Nisha Palace. M and O are tall while other students are short. J, L and M are identified by wearing jeans while other are wearing caps.

Ex **1.** Which two students are not wearing jeans and are short?
(a) L and N (b) K and N (c) J and N (d) K and O

Ex **2.** Which short student of Nisha Palace is wearing a cap?
(a) O (b) L (c) M (d) N

Ex **3.** Which tall student of Nisha palace is wearing jeans?
(a) O (b) N (c) M (d) L

SOLUTION (Q. Nos. 1-3) Following table can be drawn from the given information.

Students \ Requirement	Priya	Nisha	Tall	Short	Jeans	Caps
J	✓	✗	✗	✓	✓	✗
K	✓	✗	✗	✓	✗	✓
L	✗	✓	✗	✓	✓	✗
M	✗	✓	✓	✗	✓	✗
N	✗	✓	✗	✓	✗	✓
O	✗	✓	✓	✗	✗	✓

1. (*b*) From the above table, we see that the two students who are not wearing jeans and are short K and N.
2. (*d*) The short student of Nisha Palace and wearing a cap is N.
3. (*c*) The tall student from Nisha Palace who is wearing jeans is M.

Direction (Examples 4-5) *Read the following information carefully and answer the questions that follow.*

Seven people A, B, C, D, E, F and G are planning to enjoy boating. There are only two boats and the following conditions are to be kept in mind.

I. A will go in the same boat in which E is to go.
II. F cannot go in the boat in which C unless D is also accompanying.
III. Neither B nor C can be given the boat in which G is.
IV. The maximum number of persons in one boat can be four only.

Ex **4.** If F and B are in one boat, which of the following statements is true?

(a) G is in the other boat
(b) D is in the other boat
(c) C is in the other boat
(d) E is with F and B in one boat

Ex **5.** If E gets boat with F, which of the following is the complete and accurate list of the people who must be sitting in other boat?

(a) F and E (b) G and A (c) D and A (d) C, D and B

SOLUTION (Examples 4-5)

4. (*a*) According to the question and given conditions, the possible cases are as follows

Case I $\frac{\text{Boat 1}}{\text{B, C, D, F}} + \frac{\text{Boat 2}}{\text{A, E, G}}$

Case II $\frac{\text{Boat 1}}{\text{A, E, G}} + \frac{\text{Boat 2}}{\text{B, C, D, F}}$

Clearly, G is in other boat, if B, C, D and F are in the boat 1, then G is in boat 2 and if B, C, D and F are in boat 2, then G is in boat 1.

5. (*d*) According to the question and condition, the possible cases are as follows

Case I $\frac{\text{Boat 1}}{\text{E, F, A, G}} + \frac{\text{Boat 2}}{\text{C, D, B}}$

Case II $\frac{\text{Boat 1}}{\text{C, D, B}} + \frac{\text{Boat 2}}{\text{E, F, A, G}}$

Clearly, in either case, C, D and B are in other boat.

Direction (Examples 6-11) *Read the following information carefully and answer the questions based on them.*

The consumer complaint department of a firm employees exactly six people–G, H, I, J, K and L, who answer letters. Every complaint letter received by the department is classified as either red or blue.

The following procedures for answering the letters are used

(i) red letters are given first to G or H.
(ii) blue letters are given first of anyone of the following G, J or I.

If a letter raises a problem that cannot be resolved by the person to whom it is given, it must be forwarded until it reaches someone who can resolve the problem and answer the letter. A letter must be forwarded as follows

(i) by G to I, if the letter is red but to J, if the letter is blue.
(ii) by H to either G or I.
(iii) by I to J, if the letter is red but to K, if the letter is blue.
(iv) by J to either I or K whether the letter is red or blue.
(v) by K to L whether the letter is red or blue.
(vi) L answer every letter given to him.

Ex **6.** Any of the following can be true except

(a) G forwards a red letter to I
(b) H forwards a red letter to G
(c) H forwards a red letter to I
(d) I forwards a red letter to K
(e) J forwards a red letter to I

Ex **7.** A blue letter could reach L *via* which of the following sequences of people?

(a) G to H to K (b) H to I to J
(c) G to J to K (d) K to H to J
(e) H to G to J to K

Ex **8.** Any letter that reaches L must have been previously given to

(a) G (b) H
(c) I (d) J
(e) K

Ex **9.** Any letter that reaches L must have been given to a minimum of how many members of the consumer complaint department before reaching L?

(a) 1 (b) 2
(c) 3 (d) 4
(e) 5

Ex **10.** Which of the following could be given to each of the six members of the consumer complaint department in turn?

(a) A red letter that is first given to H
(b) A red letter that is first given to G
(c) A blue letter that is first given to G
(d) A blue letter that is first given to I
(e) A blue letter that is first given to J

***Ex* 11.** If a member of the consumer complaint department is given a letter that he or she had previously given to some other member of the department, the person who is given the letter a second time could be

(a) G (b) H (c) J (d) K
(e) L

SOLUTION (Examples 6-11)

6. (*d*) I forwards red letters to only J. So, option (d) cannot be true that 'I forwards a red letter to K'.
7. (*c*) Blue letters are given first by G, J or I. So, they should be the first person while forwarding a blue letter. So, option (b), (d) and (e) are ruled out.
   G may not forward a blue letter to H. So, option (a) is ruled out.
8. (*e*) Any letter that reaches L can have two sequence.
   (i) J to K to L (ii) I to K to L
   So, any letter that reaches L must have previously given to K.
9. (*b*) From the above explanation, it is clear that any letter that reaches L must have been given to a minimum number of two members.
10. (*a*) From the given information, it is clear that no one forward letters to H. Second, a blue letter can be given by either G, J or I. So, a blue letter cannot be given to each of the six members of consumer complaint department. The correct answer is (a) because a red letter first given to H, could be given to each member of the department in the sequence H to G to I to J to K to L.
11. (*c*) A red letter can reach to J second time *via* sequence H to I to J.

***Ex* 12.** Five friends A, B, C, D and E have different jobs. They work with either Bank or Cinema or Pharma or Sales or Jewellery. Pick the right job in which they are employed if B is neither concerned with Bank nor with Sales. E has nothing to do in Sales or Pharma. Cinema has not given a chance to B or D has nothing to do in Sales or Pharma. Cinema has not given a chance to B or D nor E is a bank employee. C is not in Sales nor B is in Jewellery.

Which of the following is correct? **SNAP 2014**

(a) A-Cinema; B-Sales; C-Jewellery; D-Pharma; E-Bank
(b) A-Cinema; B-Sales; C-Pharma; D-Bank; E-Jewellery
(c) A-Cinema; B-Sales; C-Jewellery; D-Bank; E-Pharma
(d) A-Cinema; B-Pharma; C-Jewellery; D-Bank; E-Sales

Sol. (*d*) The given information can be summerised as

Jobs	A	B	C	D	E
Bank	✗	✗	✗	✓	✗
Cinema	✓	✗	✗	✗	✗
Pharma	✗	✓	✗	✗	✗
Sales	✗	✗	✗	✗	✓
Jewellery	✗	✗	✓	✗	✗

***Ex* 13.** On a shelf six volumes are placed by side labelled A, B, C, D, E and F. Three volumes B. C and E have green covers while the other volumes have yellow covers. A, D and B are new volumes while the rest are old ones. A, C and B are law reports while the rest are gazetteers. Which of the following volumes is green convered, old and law report?

(a) A (b) B (c) C (d) D

Sol. (*c*)

	Green cover	Yellow cover	New	Old	Law report	Gazetteer
A	✗	✓	✓	✗	✓	✗
B	✓	✗	✓	✗	✓	✗
C	✓	✗	✗	✓	✓	✗
D	✗	✓	✓	✗	✗	✓
E	✓	✗	✗	✓	✗	✓
F	✗	✓	✗	✓	✗	✓

C is the book with green cover, old and law report.

***Ex* 14.** Mohsin is carrying 8 fruits (orange, mango, pineapple, strawberry, blueberry, apple and watermelon) to the farmhouse. However, he has only two boxes of equal weight and each will carry same number of fruits. Therefore, he has to ensure

A. orange and pineapple will be together, but not with watermelon.
B. mango and strawberry cannot be with pineapple.
C. blueberry will be in the same box with orange and guava but not with the apple. One more fruit will be with blueberry.

If apple and watermelon are in the same box which are the other two fruits in the same box? **CMAT 2015**

(a) Strawberry and pineapple
(b) Mango and guava
(c) Mango and strawberry
(d) Indeterminent

Sol. (*c*)

Box 1	Box 2
Guava	Apple
Blueberry	Strawberry
Pineapple	Mango
Orange	Watermelon

So, mango and strawberry are in the same box.

***Ex* 15.** In five flats, one above the other, live five professionals. The professor has to go up to meet his IAS officer friend. The doctor is equally friendly to all, and has to go up as frequently as go down. The engineer has to go up to meet his MLA friend above whose flat lives the professor's friend. **UPSC (CSAT) 2012**

From the ground floor to the top floor, in what order do the five professionals live?

(a) Engineer, Professor, Doctor, IAS officer, MLA
(b) Professor, Engineer, Doctor, IAS officer, MLA
(c) IAS officer, Engineer, Doctor, Professor, MLA
(d) Professor, Engineer, Doctor, MLA, IAS officer

Sol. (*d*) Information given in the paragraph can be arranged in the tabular form like this

Floor	Ground	Ist	2nd	3rd	4th
Professionals	Professor	Engineer	Doctor	MLA	IAS

So, from the table above, option (d) is correct.

Ex 16. Namita and Samita are brilliant and studious. Anita and Karabi are obedient and irregular. Babita and Namita are irregular but brilliant. Samita and Kabita are regular and obedient. Who among them is/are brilliant, obedient, regular and studious? **UGC NET 2014**

(a) Samita alone
(b) Namita and Samita
(c) Kamita alone
(d) Anita alone

Sol. (*a*)

	Brilliant	Obedient	Irregular	Studious	Regular
Namita	✓		✓	✓	
Samita	✓	✓		✓	✓
Anita		✓	✓		
Karabi		✓	✓		
Babita	✓		✓		
Kabita		✓			✓

Hence, Samita is brilliant, obedient, regular and studious among all of them.

Ex 17. In a group of six women, there are four dancers, four vocal musicians, one actress and three violinists.
Girija and Vanaja are among the violinists while Jalaja and Shailaja do not know how to play on the violin. Shailaja and Tanuja are all vocal musicians and two of them are also violinists. If Pooja is an actress, who among the following is certainly a dancer and a violinist?

(a) Jalaja (b) Pooja
(c) Shailaja (d) Tanuja

Sol. (*d*) From the given information the table can be drawn as

	Dancer	Vocal musicians	Actress	Violinists
Girija		✗	✗	✓
Vanaja		✓	✗	✓
Jalaja		✓	✗	✗
Shailaja	✓	✓	✗	✗
Tanuja	✓	✓	✗	✓
Pooja		✗	✓	✗

From the above table, Tanuja is certainly a dancer and a violinist.

Ex 18. Mr. Biswas is planning for 2 weeks holiday with his family to UK, Germany, France, Switzerland, Belgium, Italy, Norway and Austria. However, his family has imposed certain conditions for travel **CMAT 2015**

(i) will travel to Austria and Switzerland in different weeks.
(ii) Germany must be visited after Belgium in the same week.
(iii) Switzerland must be visited after France in the same week.
(iv) will travel to Germany and Norway in different weeks.
(v) will travel to UK and France in different weeks.
(vi) will travel to Austria and Belgium in the same weeks.
(vii) Italy must be visited in the 2nd week.
(viii) equal number of places must be visited in week 1 and 2.

Which places are visited in week 2, if all places are visited only once?

(a) Italy, UK, Switzerland, Norway
(b) Italy, France, Germany, Norway
(c) Italy, UK, Austria, Switzerland
(d) Italy, France, Switzerland, Norway

Sol. (*d*)

1st week visiting	2nd week visiting
UK	France
Austria	Swizerland
Belgium	Italy
Germany	Norway

France and Switzerland must be visited in same week. So, option (a) is eliminated, option (b) also eliminated on the same ground. Option (c) is also eliminated on the reason that Austria and Switzerland visited in different weeks. So, right option is (d).

Ex 19. Mohan has to revise 8 chapters -(A, B, C, D, E, F, G, H) two days before the board exams. Considering the complexity of different chapters, he has decided **MAT 2015**

(i) cannot revise A and G on the same day.
(ii) E must be revised after B on the same day.
(iii) G must be revised after C on the same day.
(iv) cannot revised D and F on the same day.
(v) cannot revise C and H on the same day.
(vi) D is revised on the 1st day.
(vii) D and E cannot be revised on the same day.
(viii) C is not revised on 1st day.
(ix) more chapters are revised on the 2nd day compared to 1st day.
(x) no chapters will be revised twiced.

Which are the chapters revised on the 2nd day?

(a) A, B, E, F, C, G
(b) B, E, A, C, G
(c) B, E, F, C, G
(d) Cannot be determined

Sol. (*c*)

1st day	2nd day
D	F
A	B
H	E
	C
	G

So, chapter revised on the 2nd day are F, B, E, C, and G. Considering all the given conditions.

***Ex* 20.** The music director of a film wants to select four persons to work on "different aspects of the composition of a piece of music. Seven persons are available for this work; they are Rohit, Tanya, Shobha, Kaushal, Kunal, Mukesh and Jaswant. Rohit and Tanya will not work together. Kunal and Shobha will not work together. Mukesh and Kunal want to work together. **UPSC (CSAT) 2013**

Which of the following is the most acceptable group of people that can be selected by the music director?

(a) Rohit, Shobha, Kunal and Kaushal
(b) Tanya, Kaushal, Shobha and Rohit
(c) Tanya, Mukesh, Kunal and Jaswant
(d) Shobha, Tanya, Rohit and Mukesh

Sol. (*c*) Rohit and Tanya cannot work together which means that options (b) and (d) are out. Kunal and Shobha will not work together and so option (a) is out. Hence, the right answer is (c) where no one has a problem working with another person of the group and Mukesh and Kunal are also working together.

***Ex* 21.** Examine the following statements.

(i) George attends Music classes on Monday.
(ii) He attends Mathematics classes on Wednesday.
(iii) His Literature classes are not on Friday.
(iv) He attends History classes on the day following the day of his Mathematics classes.
(v) On Tuesday, he attends his Sports classes.

If he attends just one subject in a day and his Sunday is free, then he is also free on

(a) Monday
(b) Thursday
(c) Saturday
(d) Friday

Sol. (*d*) From the given information, his week schedule can be concluded as

Monday	→	Music
Tuesday	→	Sport
Wednesday	→	Mathematics
Thursday	→	History
Friday	→	Free
Saturday	→	Literature
Sunday	→	Free

Apart from Sunday George is free on Friday.

Cumulative Exercise

Base Level

Direction (Q. Nos. 1-3) *Read the following passage and answer the questions that follows.*

A tennis coach is trying to put together a team of four players for the forthcoming tournament. For this, 7 players are available males A, B and C and females W, X, Y and Z. All players have equal capability and atleast 2 males will be there in the team. For a team of four, all players must be able to play with each other. But, B cannot play with W, C cannot play with Z and W cannot play with Y. **CSAT 2013**

1. If Y is selected and B is rejected, the team will consist of which one of the following groups?
(a) A, C, W and Y (b) A, C, X and Y
(c) A, C, Y and Z (d) A, W, Y and Z

2. If all the three males are selected, then how many combination of four member teams are possible?
(a) 1 (b) 2 (c) 3 (d) 4

3. If B is selected and Y is rejected, the team will consist of which one of the following groups?
(a) A, B, C, and W (b) A, B, C and Z
(c) A, B, C and X (d) A, W, Y and Z

Direction (Q. Nos. 4-8) *Study the following information carefully and answer the questions.*

P, Q, R, S, T and M are six students of a school, one each studies in class I-VI. Each of them has a favourite colour from Red, Black, Yellow, Pink, Blue and Green, not necessarily in the same order.

Q likes Black and does not study in class IV or V. The one who studies in class IV does not like Green. P studies in class II. M likes Blue and does not study in class IV. The one who likes Yellow studies in class VI. S likes Pink and studies in class I. R does not study in class VI.

4. In which class does R study?
(a) V (b) III
(c) IV (d) Data inadequate
(e) None of these

5. Which colour does R like?
(a) Black (b) Yellow (c) Green (d) Blue
(e) None of these

6. Which colour does P like?
(a) Green (b) Yellow
(c) Red (d) Data inadequate
(e) None of these

7. Which of the following combinations is correct?
(a) P-II-Yellow (b) Q-III-Green
(c) S-I-Black (d) T-VI-Yellow
(e) None of these

8. In which class does M study?
(a) IV (b) III
(c) II (d) V
(e) None of these

Direction (Q. Nos. 9-13) *These questions are based on the following data.*

A team consisting of five members has to be formed from among five boys P, Q, R, S, T and three girls U, V, W as per the following restrictions

(i) the team should have atleast three boys and atleast one girl.
(ii) if P is selected, R cannot be selected.
(iii) if S is selected, V cannot be selected.

9. If Q, R and V form three members of the team, then which of the following can be the other two members?
(a) U and W (b) S and W
(c) T and U (d) P and W

10. If P and Q are two boys selected to form the team and V is not selected for the team, then which of the following can be the possible team?
(a) P, Q, S, V, W (b) P, Q, T, U, W
(c) P, Q, S, R, W (d) P, Q, R, V, W

11. If P and S are the two boys selected, then in how many ways can the team be formed?
(a) 1 (b) 2
(c) 3 (d) 4

12. If four boys are selected for the team, then which of the following girl can never join the team?
(a) U (b) V
(c) W (d) Cannot be determined

13. Which of the following can never be a team consisting of the boys and the girls?
(a) P, Q, S, U, W
(b) P, Q, T, V, W
(c) P, Q, S, T, U
(d) P, Q, R, V, W

Direction (Q. Nos. 14-18) *Read the information given in the following paragraphs and then answer the questions based on them.*

There are 6 soccer teams A, B, C, D, E and F in the soccer league game. All the 6 teams play each Saturday during the season. Each team must play against each of the other teams once and only once during the seasons.

(i) Team A plays against team D first and team F second.
(ii) Team B plays against team E first and team C third.
(iii) Team C plays against team F first.

14. On the first Saturday, which of the following pairs of teams play against each other?
(a) A and B, C and F, D and E
(b) A and B, C and E, D and F
(c) A and C, B and E, D and F
(d) A and D, B and C, E and F
(e) None of the above

15. Which of the following team must B play second with?
(a) A
(b) C
(c) D
(d) Either E or A
(e) Either A or D

16. What is the total number of games that each team must play during the season?
(a) 1
(b) 2
(c) 3
(d) 4
(e) None of the above

17. If D wins 5 games, which of the following must be true?
(a) A loses 5 games
(b) A wins 4 games
(c) A wins its first game
(d) B loses atleast 1 game
(e) None of the above

18. The last set of games could be between
(a) A and B, C and F, D and E
(b) A and C, B and F, D and E
(c) A and D, B and C, E and F
(d) A and E, B and C, D and F
(e) None of the above

Direction (Q. Nos. 19-21) *Read the following information carefully to answer the questions that follow.*

Surinder, Prem, Wasim, Bishamber and Chauhan are five player of a college cricket team and their home towns are Sikandrabad, Panipat, Warangal, Banaras and Chennai (not in the order of their name). The five specialist slots of spinner, pace-bowler, wicket-keeper, batsman and captain are held by them (not in order of their names stated above). Their names, home town and specialities do not start with the same letter. Neither Prem nor Wasim is the captain and they do not belong to either Sikandrabad or Banaras. Panipat is not Bishamber's home town. The player who hails from Banaras is a wicket- keeper. The captain's home town is Panipat while the batsman does not hail from Warangal. Surinder is neither a wicket-keeper nor a batsman.

19. Who is the wicket-keeper?
(a) Wasim (b) Bishamber
(c) Chauhan (d) Surinder

20. The spinner's home town is
(a) Chennai (b) Banaras
(c) Warangal (d) Panipat

21. Who is the pace-bowler?
(a) Prem (b) Bishamber
(c) Surinder (d) Chauhan

Direction (Q. Nos. 22-26) *Read the following information carefully and answer the questions based on them.*

Ajay, Bony and Chetan are three persons who go to buy six items as P, Q, R, S, T and U. Each one of them buys two different items in such a way that if Ajay buys R, then Bony buys neither P nor S. If Bony buys Q, then Chetan buys neither U nor T.

22. If Ajay buys R and T, then Bony buys
(a) P and S (b) Q and U (c) P and Q (d) S and U

23. If Bony buys Q and S, then Ajay must buy
(a) P and R (b) T and U
(c) P and T (d) R and U

24. If Chetan has to buy P and S, then which of the following must be true?
(a) Ajay bought R (b) Bony bought Q
(c) Ajay bought T (d) None of these

25. If Ajay buys P and Bony buys Q,then which of the following is true?
(a) Chetan buys R and S
(b) Chetan can buy any two of P, R and S
(c) Chetan can buy any three of P, R, S and T
(d) Chetan can buy any two P, R, S, T and U

26. Which of the following is definitely true?
(a) Ajay buys R and Bony buys Q
(b) If Chetan buys T or U, then Bony buys Q and S
(c) If Ajay buys R, then Bony buys T
(d) If Ajay buys R and Bony buys Q, then Chetan buys P and S

Direction (Q. Nos. 27-28) *Read the following information carefully and answer the questions given below.* **FMS 2009**

Three men and three women are travelling in two cars (red and blue). Each car has exactly three persons. The cars cannot have all women or all men passengers. Mala, Ajit and Suman know how to drive a car. Mala and Sapna are women. Manjit and Sarat are not in the same car them. Ajit and Sarat are men.

27. If the red car can have either Manjit or Sarat but not both while Ajit drives it and Mala is driving the blue car, then which of the following can be true?
(a) Suman is a man
(b) Manjit is a woman
(c) Both (a) and (b) are correct
(d) (a) is correct but (b) is not

28. If Suman and Manjit are the two passengers in the red car, then who can be passengers of the blue car?
(a) Sapna and Sarat (b) Mala and Ajit
(c) Sapna and Ajit (d) Mala and Sarat

Direction (Q. Nos. 29-33) *Read the following information and answer the questions based on them.*

Seven friends T, N, P, M, R, F and K have to travel by car. Two cars are available.
(i) T must travel in the same car as R.
(ii) F cannot be in the same car as P unless M is also in the car.
(iii) Not more than 4 people can travel in a car.
(iv) Neither N nor P can be assigned to the same car as K.

29. If N travels in the same car as R and T, then who can be the fourth person in the car?
(a) Only P (b) Only M
(c) Either F or M (d) P or F or M

30. If F and P travel in the same car, then who else could be in the same car?
(a) T (b) R (c) K (d) N

31. Which of the following can be the combination of passengers in anyone car?
(a) T, K, R, M (b) F, P, M, K
(c) T, F, P, M (d) None of these

32. If car containing only 3 people has to include K, then which of the following persons cannot be present in that car?
(a) T
(b) F
(c) M
(d) All these can be present

33. If F and P are in the same car, then how many passengers can be present in that car?
(a) Only 3
(b) Only 4
(c) Either 3 or 4
(d) Insufficient data

Direction (Q. Nos. 34-35) *Read the following information and answer the questions.* **JMET 2011**

There are five teams, Paraguay, Qatar, Russia, Spain and Turkey playing in a tournament where each team plays against every other team only once. These are the following possibilities each match can result in a draw where each team scores two points or a team can win where it scores three points, while the losing team scores one point.

34. If Paraguay has won all the matches and Turkey has lost all the matches and all the remaining three teams score equal points, then how many points have each of the three remaining teams scored?
(a) 5 (b) 7 (c) 8 (d) 6

35. If all the five teams have an equal score, then what is the number of points scored by each team?
(a) 5 (b) 6
(c) 7 (d) 8

Direction (Q. Nos. 36-40) *Study the following information carefully and answer the questions that follow*

A team of five is to be selected from amongst five boys A, B, C, D and E and four girls P, Q, R and S. Some criteria for selection are as follows
(i) A and S have to be together.
(ii) P cannot be put with R.
(iii) D and Q cannot go together.
(iv) C and E have to be together.

Unless otherwise stated, these criteria are applicable to all the questions below.

36. If two of the members have to be boys, then the team will consist of
(a) A, B, S, P, Q (b) A, D, S, Q, R
(c) B, D, S, R, Q (d) C, E, S, P, Q

37. If R is one of the members, then the other members of the team are
(a) P, S, A, D (b) Q, S, A, D
(c) Q, S, C, E (d) S, A, C, E

38. If two of the members are girls and D is one of the members, then the members of the team other than D are
(a) P, Q, B, C (b) P, Q, C, E
(c) P, S, A, B (d) P, S, C, E

39. If A and C are members, then the other members of the team cannot be
(a) B, E, S (b) D, E, S
(c) E, S, P (d) P, Q, E

40. If including P atleast three members are girls, then the members of the team other than P are

(a) Q, S, A, B (b) Q, S, B, D
(c) Q, S, C, E (d) R, S, A, D

Direction (Q. Nos. 41-45) *Study the following information carefully and answer the questions given below.*

From amongst five doctors A, B, C, D and E, four engineers G, H, K and L and six teachers M, N, O, P, Q and R, some teams are to be selected. Of these, A, B, G, H, O, P and Q are females and the rest are males.

The formation of teams is subject to the following conditions

(i) Wherever there is a male doctor, there will be no female teacher.
(ii) Wherever there is a male engineer, there will be no female doctor.
(iii) There shall not be more than two male teachers in any team.

41. If the team consists of two doctors, then three female teachers and two engineers, the members of the team are

(a) A, B, O, P, Q, G, H (b) C, D, K, L, O, P, Q
(c) C, D, O, P, Q, G, H (d) D, E, G, H, O, P, Q

42. If the team consists of two doctors, then one engineer and four teachers, all the following teams are possible except

(a) A, B, G, M, N, O, P (b) A, B, H, M, O, P, Q
(c) A, B, H, M, R, P, Q (d) A, B, K, N,R, P, Q

43. If the team consists of two doctors, two female teachers and two engineers, the following teams are possible except

(a) A, B, G, H, O, Q (b) A, B, G, H, P, Q
(c) A, B, K, L, P, Q (d) O, P, G, H, A, B

44. If the team consists of three doctors, two male engineers and two teachers, the members of the team could be

(a) A, B, C, K, L, M, R (b) B, C, D, K, L, N, R
(c) C, D, E, K, L, M, N (d) C, D, E, K, L, P, R

45. If the team consists of two doctors, two engineers and two teachers, all of the following teams are possible except

(a) A, B, G, H, O, P (b) A, B, G, H, M, N
(c) C, E, K, L, N, R (d) C, D, K, L, O, P

Direction (Q. Nos. 46-50) *These questions are based on the following information.*

Amit, Bittu, Chintu, Dumpy, Falgun, Hitesh, Ronit, Purav and Saurav are nine players from among whom three teams consisting respectively of 4 members, 3 members and 2 members must be formed subject to the following conditions

(i) Chintu must have three more players with him while Dumpy must have only two more with him.
(ii) Chintu and Saurav cannot be in the same team.
(iii) Purav and Bittu cannot be in the same team.
(iv) Ronit and Hitesh must be in the same team.

46. If Dumpy, Falgun, Purav form the team of three members, then which of the following must be true?

(a) Hitesh must be in a team with Bittu
(b) Saurav must form a two member team with Amit or Chintu
(c) Saurav must form a two member team with Bittu or Amit
(d) Chintu should from a team of four members with Hitesh, Ronit and Amit

47. If Dumpy takes Amit as a part of his three-member team, which of the following must go into Chintu's team?

(a) Bittu and Hitesh (b) Hitesh and Ronit
(c) Purav and Ronit (d) Purav and Falgun

48. If Chintu and Falgun are together and Saurav is in the team of two members, then how many sets of different teams are possible?

(a) 4 (b) 3 (c) 2 (d) 1

49. If Chintu does not have Purav in his team and the two member team consists of Saurav and Amit, then Chintu should take

(a) Hitesh, Bittu and Ronit
(b) Bittu but not Ronit
(c) Bittu and Falgun
(d) Hitesh and Ronit

50. If Purav is in the same team as Chintu and Falgun, then Saurav must be in the same team as

(a) Bittu (b) Bittu and Amit
(c) Amit (d) Bittu and Dumpy

Direction (Q. Nos. 51-52) *These questions are based on the information given below.* **SNAP 2010**

Seven people A, B, C, D, E, F and G are planning to enjoy boating. There are only two boats and the following conditions are to be kept in mind.

(i) A will go in the same boat in which E is to go.
(ii) F cannot go in the boat in which C is, unless D is also accompanying.
(iii) Neither B nor C can be given the boat in which G is.
(iv) The maximum number of persons in one boat can be four only.

51. If F and B are in one boat, which of the following statements is true?

(a) G is in the other boat
(b) D is in the other boat
(c) C is in the other boat
(d) E is with F and B in one boat

52. If E gets boat with F, which of the following is the complete and accurate list of the people who must be sitting in other boat?

(a) F and E
(b) G and A
(c) D and A
(d) C, D and B

Direction (Q. Nos. 53-56) *Read the following information and answer the questions given below.*

JMET 2011

Every morning five friends Mahima, Nimisha, Omez, Parul and Quan go to the railway station and board a train that stops at six subsequent stations which are numbered 1 to 6. The train stops at station 1 and proceeds in numerical order to station 6.

(i) Mahima gets off either at station 1 or at station 2.
(ii) Omez always gets off one station before or one station after Quan's station.
(iii) Parul always gets off at station 3.
(iv) Quan always gets off at station 4, 5 or 6.
(v) No one re-boards the morning train after getting off.

53. On a morning, when no one gets off at station 5 or 6, which of the following must be true?
(a) Mahima gets off at station 2
(b) Nimisha gets off at station 2
(c) Omez gets off at station 4
(d) Omez and Parul gets off at the same station

54. On a morning, when Quan gets off at station 4 and no more than two of the friends get off at any one station. Which of the following must be true?
(a) If Nimisha gets off at station 2, Mahima gets off at station 1
(b) If Nimisha gets off at station 3, Omez gets off at station 5
(c) If Nimisha gets off at station 4, Omez gets off at station 5
(d) If Omez gets off at station 4, Nimisha gets off at station 2

55. At which amongst the following stations is it possible for Nimisha and Omez to be the only friends getting off the morning train?
(i) Station 3 (ii) Station 4 (iii) Station 5
(a) Only (i) (b) (ii) and (iii)
(c) Only (iii) (d) (i) and (ii)

56. On a morning, when no one gets off at station 1 and each of the five friends gets off at a different station which of following cannot be true?
(a) Nimisha gets off one station before Quan
(b) Parul gets off one station before Omez
(c) Mahima gets off at station 2
(d) Nimisha gets off at station 5

Direction (Q. Nos. 57-62) *Each question or group of questions is based on a passage or set of conditions. For each question, select the best answer choice given.*

Ms Jones is very fussy in watering her flower-pots. She waters pots A, B, C, D, E, F, G, H, I and J on every day of the week. In going from one pot to another, she strictly adheres to the following rules.

(i) The first two pots to be watered every day must be selected from C, D, E and F.
(ii) H cannot be watered before D, and J cannot be watered after I.
(iii) G can be watered only after B.
(iv) F must be watered before C.

57. If D is the fourth pot to be watered on a day, which of the following pots cannot be fifth on that day?
(a) C (b) F (c) E (d) H
(e) J

58. Which of the following is a possible arrangement for the watering of the first five pots?
(a) E, H, F, D, C (b) F, C, H, B, D
(c) C, D, E, B, H (d) C, J, E, D, A
(e) D, F, B, C, A

59. If D is to be watered immediately after J, then which of the following must be true?
(a) F is the first pot to be watered
(b) Of the first two pots to be watered, one is F
(c) H is the sixth pot to be watered
(d) H is either the sixth or seventh pot to be watered
(e) B is the fourth pot to be watered

60. If the given conditions are reversed, that is 'first' becomes 'last', 'before' becomes 'after' and so on, which of the following is a possible arrangement for watering the last four pots?
(a) G, D, B, H (b) H, F, C, E (c) F, B, C, E (d) C, B, E, F
(e) E, F, H, G

61. If D is the fourth pot to be watered and J the fifth, then which of the following can be the third pot to be watered?
(a) A (b) F (c) H (d) G
(e) I

62. If pot D breaks and only nine pots remain, which of the following must be true of the order of watering?
(a) F cannot be the second pot
(b) J cannot be the ninth pot
(c) E is the third pot
(d) I is the last pot
(e) G is the third pot

Direction (Q. Nos. 63-65) *Read the following information carefully and answer the questions that follow.*

In a cycling race, five participants from various nations—Chinese, Nepalese, Indian, Iraqi and English, take part. Track 1 is extreme left and Track 5 is extreme right. The following conditions exists. **FMS 2011**

(i) The Nepalese and the Englishman are not cycling adjacent to each other.
(ii) The Iraqi is not in one of the extreme tracks.
(iii) The Chinese is to the left of the Indian.

63. If the Nepalese is in track 3, the Chinese in track 1, then the Indian could be in
(a) track 4 (b) track 2
(c) track 2 or 4 (d) None of these

64. If the Nepalese is in track 4 and the Indian is in track 3, then the Englishman could be in
(a) track 1 (b) track 2
(c) track 1 or 2 (d) None of these

65. If the Iraqi is to the left of the Chinese, then the Iraqi could be in

(a) track 2 only (b) track 3 only
(c) track 2 or 3 (d) None of these

Direction (Q. Nos. 66-67) *Read the following passage and solve the question based on it.* **IIFT 2014**

Federation of Indian chamber of Commerce and Industries organised a business conclave on India's emerging electronic goods sector. CEOs and Managing Directors of four leading companies, namely, Klentech Industries, Andromeda Infotech, Zoomerang Technologies and Spearhead Unlimited were invited to deliver lectures on this occasion. The CEOs of the four companies were Mr Sethi, Mr D'Souza, Mr Puri and Mr Bisht respectively, while the Managing Directors were Mr Tandon, Mr Arora, Mr Karare and Mr Reddy in that order. The speeches were delivered subject to the condition that each of the Managing Directors delivered their speeches immediately after that of the CEOs of their company.

66. The first CEO to speak was Mr D'Souza and the next CEO to deliver his address was Mr Puri. If Mr Tandon is the third managing Director to deliver his address, which of the following statements must be true?

(a) Mr Bisht delivered his address sometime before Mr Sethi
(b) Mr Reddy delivered his address sometime before Mr Tandon
(c) Mr Puri delivered his address sometime before Mr Reddy
(d) Mr Karare delivered his address sometime before Mr Arora

67. If Mr Bisht was the second CEO to speak after Mr D'Souza, and two more Managing Directors speak after the address of the Managing Director of Spearhead Unlimited, then who is the last CEO to speak?

(a) Mr Sethi (b) Mr Puri
(c) Mr Tandon (d) Cannot be determined

Direction (Q. Nos. 71-72) *Read the data given below to answer the following questions.*

The director of a B-School wishes to select four members of a faculty-student committee as representatives to meet with the School's Board of Directors. The faculty-student committee consists of exactly four faculty members K, L, M and N and four students P, Q, R and S. The director can select any of the committee members as representatives as long as he observes the following restrictions.

(i) The group of four representatives must consists of exactly two faculty members and two students.
(ii) Either K or L must be one of the representatives but K and L both cannot be representatives.
(iii) If P is a representative, M must also be a representative.
(iv) If R is a representative, L cannot be a representative.

68. If L, N and Q are representatives, which of the following must also be a representative?

(a) M (b) S
(c) P (d) R

69. If P is a representative, which of the following cannot also be a representative?

(a) N (b) M (c) Q (d) R

70. If R is a representative and M is not a representative, the group of representatives would be completely determined, if it were also true that

(a) L is not a representative (b) S is not a representative
(c) P is not a representative (d) N is a representative

71. If neither Q nor S is a representative, which of the following is the pair of faculty members who must be representatives?

(a) K and M (b) K and N (c) L and M (d) L and N

72. If L is a representative, which of the following can be the other three representatives?

(a) N, S, P (b) M, Q, P
(c) M, Q, R (d) K, Q, S

Direction (Q. Nos. 73-78) *Read the following information carefully and answer the questions based on them.*

One wedding card, two graduation cards, three anniversary cards and four birthday cards are to be arranged in a triangular display with one card in the first row, two cards in the second row, three cards in the third row and four cards in the fourth row. The arrangement is subject to the following conditions.

(i) There is to be no birthday card in the fourth row.
(ii) There are to be no more than two cards of any type in any of the rows.
(iii) No birthday card is to be next to and in the same row as an anniversary card.

73. An acceptable arrangement can include which of the following?

(a) A birthday card in every row
(b) An anniversary card in the first; second and third rows
(c) All the birthday cards in the second and third rows
(d) Two anniversary cards in the third row

74. Which of the following must make up the second row?

(a) Two birthday cards
(b) Two anniversary cards
(c) A birthday and an anniversary card
(d) A wedding card and a graduation card

75. Which of the following can make up the third row?

(a) An anniversary card and two birthday cards
(b) A graduation card and two birthday cards
(c) A graduation card and two anniversary cards
(d) A wedding card, a birthday card and a graduation card

76. If all the birthday cards are in the second and third rows, which of these must be true?

(a) There is a wedding card between two birthday cards
(b) There is an anniversary card in the second row
(c) There is a graduation card next to and in the same row as an anniversary card in the fourth row
(d) There is a graduation card in the third row

77. If there is an anniversary card in the third row, which of the following can be true?
    (a) A birthday card next to and in the same row as a graduation card in the third row
    (b) A birthday card is in the middle of the third row
    (c) A birthday card is in the first row
    (d) Two birthday cards are in the second row

78. Which of the following is a complete and accurate list of the rows in which both graduation cards can be placed together?
    (a) The second (b) The third
    (c) The fourth (d) The third and the fourth

Direction (Q. Nos. 79-83) *Study the following information carefully and answer the questions given below.*

P, Q, R, S, T, V, W and Z are going to three destinations Delhi, Chennai and Hyderabad in three different vehicles- Honda City, Swift D' Zire and Ford Ikon. There are three females among them-one in each car. There are atleast two persons in each car. R is not travelling with Q and W. T, a male, is travelling with only Z and they are not going to Chennai. P is travelling in Honda City and is going to Hyderabad. S is the sister of P and is travelling by Ford Ikon. V and R are travelling together. W is not going to Chennai.

79. Member of which of the following cars are going to Chennai?
    (a) Honda City
    (b) Swift D' Zire
    (c) Ford Ikon
    (d) Either Swift D' Zire or Ford Ikon
    (e) None of the above

80. In which car are four members travelling?
    (a) None (b) Honda City
    (c) Swift D'Zire (d) Ford Ikon
    (e) Either Honda City or Ford Ikon

81. Which of the following combination represents the three female members?
    (a) Q, S, Z (b) W, S, Z
    (c) P, S, Z (d) Cannot be determined
    (e) None of these

82. Who is travelling with W?
    (a) Only Q (b) Only P
    (c) Both P and Q (d) Cannot be determined
    (e) None of these

83. Member of which of the following combination are travelling in Honda City?
    (a) P, R, S (b) P, Q, W
    (c) P, W, S (d) Data inadequate
    (e) None of these

Advanced Level

Direction (Q. Nos. 1-3) *Read the following information carefully and answer the questions that follow.*

There were four participants from Delhi, UP, Jharkhand and MP taking part in a beauty contest.

I. All the participants were sitting in a row.
II. All of them were wearing sarees of different colours i.e. blue, black, orange and red.
III. One who was wearing the black sarees won the contest.
IV. There was one runner up and she was sitting beside Miss MP. The runner up was wearing blue saree.
V. Miss Jharkhand was not seated on the extreme ends and was not the runner up.
VI. The winner and the runner up were not seated adjacent to each other.
VII. Miss MP was wearing the orange saree.
VIII. Miss Delhi was not wearing the blue saree.
IX. Participants wearing black saree and orange saree were seated at the extreme ends.

1. Who was the runner up ?
   (a) Miss Delhi (b) Miss MP
   (c) Miss UP (d) Miss Jharkhand

2. Which saree was worn by Miss Delhi?
   (a) Blue (b) Black (c) Orange (d) Red

3. Who was wearing the red saree?
   (a) Miss Jharkhand
   (b) Miss UP
   (c) Miss Delhi
   (d) Miss MP

Direction (Q. Nos. 4-8) *Read the following information carefully to answer the given questions.*

XYZ Ltd. presently has three accounts assistants—A, B and C and five account officers D, E, F, G and H. Its management is planning to open a new office in another city using three accounts officers and two accounts assistants from its present staff. The following guidelines have been established to set up the new office

I. A and C are constantly finding faults with each other and should not be sent as members of the same team.
II. C and E function well alone but not as a team. They should not be sent as members of the same team.
III. D and G do not enjoy good relations. They should not be sent as members of the same team.
IV. Since, D and F have been competing for a promotion, they should not be sent as members of the same team.

4. If C and F are moved to the new office, then what is the number of different teams that can be formed?
(a) 1 (b) 2 (c) 3 (d) 4

5. If C is sent to the new office, then which member of the staff cannot go with C?
(a) D (b) F (c) G (d) H

6. Under the guidelines developed, which of the following must go to the new office?
(a) B (b) D (c) E (d) G

7. Under the guidelines developed, which one of the following is the possible number different teams which can be sent to the new office?
(a) 6 (b) 8 (c) 12 (d) 15

8. If D goes to the new office, then which of the following is/are correct?
1. C cannot go. 2. A cannot go. 3. H must also go.
(a) Only 1 (b) Only 2
(c) 1 and 2 (d) 1 and 3

Direction (Q. Nos. 9-12) *Study the following information to answer the given questions.*

Six lecturers are scheduled in a week starting from Monday and ending on Sunday of the same week. Computer Science is not on Tuesday or Saturday. Psychology is immediately after Organisational Behaviour.

Statistics in not on Friday and there is one day gap between Statistics and Research Methods. One day prior to the schedule of Economics there is no lecture (as that day is the 'off' day and Monday is not the 'off' day).

9. Which of the following is the last lecture scheduled?
(a) Statistic
(b) Research methods
(c) Psychology
(d) Cannot be determined
(e) None of the above

10. How many lectures were scheduled between Economics and Psychology?
(a) One (b) Two
(c) Three (d) Cannot be determined
(e) None of these

11. Which day is Computer Science scheduled?
(a) Monday (b) Wednesday
(c) Cannot be determined (d) None of these

12. If Wednesday is the off day, the code would be 2-4. If Thursday was the off day, the code would be 3-3. Taking account the off day which of the following code is correct?
(a) 2 – 4
(b) 3 – 3
(c) 4 – 2
(d) Cannot be determined
(e) None of the above

Direction (Q. Nos. 13-15) *These are based on a set of conditions in answering some of the question, it may be useful to draw a rough diagram. Choose the response that most accurately and completely answer each question.*
XAT 2010

In a local pen store, seven puppies wait to be introduced to their new owners. The puppies named as Ashlen, Blackley, Custard, Daffy, Earl, Fala and Gabino are all kept in two available pen. Pen 1 holds three puppies and pen 2 holds four puppies.

I. If Gabino is kept in pen 1, then Daffy is not kept in pen 2.
II. If Daffy is not kept in pen 2, then Gabino is kept in pen 1.
III. If Ashlen is kept in pen 2, then Blackley is not kept in pen 2.
IV. If Blackley is kept in pen 1, then Ashlen is not kept in pen 1.

13. Which of the following group of puppies could be in pen?
(a) Gabino, Ashlen, Custard, Earl
(b) Blackley, Gabino, Ashlen, Daffy
(c) Ashlen, Gabino, Earl, Custard
(d) Blackley, Custard, Earl, Fala
(e) Gabino, Ashlen, Fala, Earl

14. If Earl Shares a pen with Fala, then which of the following must be true?
(a) Gabino is in pen 1 with Daffy
(b) Custard is in pen 2
(c) Blackley is in pen 2 and Fala is in pen1
(d) Earl is in pen 1
(e) Gabino shares a pen with Blackley

15. If Earl and Fala are in different pens, then which of the following must not be true?
(a) Fala shares a pen with Custard
(b) Gabino shares a pen with Ashlen
(c) Earl is in a higher numbered pen with Blackley
(d) Blackley shares pen 2 with Earl and Daffy
(e) Custard is in a highered numbered pen with Blackley

Direction (Q. Nos. 16-21) *Read the following information and answer the questions based on them.*

A five member committee is to be set up by and organisation for the wage revision negotiation with the finance ministry.

The committee must be composed of two representatives of management, two representatives of labour and one independent specialist in financial matters.

The management representatives must be chosen from among M, N and O.

The labour representatives must be chosen from among P, R and S.

Either J or K must be chosen as the independent specialist.

P cannot serve together with S.

O cannot serve together with P.

N cannot serve unless K serves at the same time.

16. Which of the following is a list of people who can serve together on the committee?
(a) J, M, N, R, S (b) J, N, O, R, S
(c) K, M, N, P, R (d) K, M, N, P, S

17. Which of the following persons must be chosen to serve on the committee?
(a) J (b) M (c) N (d) R

18. If P and R are chosen to be the labour representatives, which of the following statements must be true?
I. K is chosen to serve on the committee.
II. Both M and N are chosen to present the management.
III. J is chosen to serve on the committee.
(a) Only I (b) Only II (c) Only III (d) I and II

19. Which of the following is a list of four persons who can be chosen to serve together on the committee, if J has been chosen?
(a) M, N, P, R (b) M, N, R, S (c) M, O, P, R (d) M, O, R, S

20. If N, R and S have been chosen as three members of the committee, which of the following statements about the remaining two members of the committee is accurate?
(a) M and O are the only pair who can be chosen to complete the group
(b) K and O are the only pair who can be chosen to complete the group
(c) K and M are the only pair who can be chosen to complete the group
(d) Both the pair K and M and the pair K and O are possible choices for completing the group

21. If J must chosen to serve on the committee, which of the following persons cannot be chosen to serve on the committee?
(a) M (b) O
(c) P (d) R

Direction (Q. Nos. 22-25) *Read the following information and answer the questions based on them.*

XAT 2008

During a four-week period, each one of seven previously unadvertised products-G, H, J, K, L, M and O will be advertised. A different pair of these products will be advertised each week. Exactly one of the products will be a member of two of these four pairs. None of the other products gets repeated in any pair. Further, the following constraints must be observed
I. J is not advertised during a given week unless H is advertised during the immediately preceding week.
II. The product that is advertised twice is advertised during week 4 but is not advertised during week 3.
III. G is not advertised during a given week unless either J or O is also advertised that week.
IV. [illegible] is advertised during one of the first two weeks. O is one of the products advertised during week 3.

22. Which one of the following could be the schedule of the advertisements?
(a) Week 1 : G, J; week 2 : K, L; week 3 : O, M; week 4 : H, L
(b) Week 1 : H, K; week 2 : J, M; week 3 : O, L; week 4 : G, M
(c) Week 1 : K, M; week 2 : H, J; week 3 : O, G; week 4 : L, M
(d) Week 1 : H, L; week 2 : J, M; week 3 : O, G; week 4 : K, L
(e) Week 1 : H, K; week 2 : J, G; week 3 : O, L; week 4 : M, K.

23. If L is the product that is advertised during two of the weeks, which one of the following is a product that must be advertised during one of the weeks in which L is advertised?
(a) M (b) G (c) H (d) J
(e) K

24. Which one of the following is a product that could be advertised in any of the four weeks?
(a) H (b) J (c) K (d) L
(e) O

25. Which one of the following is a pair of products that could be advertised during the same week?
(a) M and O (b) G and H (c) H and J (d) H and O
(e) K and O

Direction (Q. Nos. 26-30) *Read the following information carefully and answer the questions given below.*

In a class, five out of eight subjects, *viz* Sanskrit, Economics, Physics, Chemistry, Biology, English, Hindi and History are taught daily. On anyone day, except for the first day of a month, only three of the subjects must be the ones that are taught on the previous day. The routine must also satisfy the following conditions
I. If Sanskrit is taught on a day, Hindi cannot be taught on that day.
II. If Economics is taught on a day, Biology must be one of the subjects taught after it on the same day.
III. If Physics is taught on a day, Hindi must be one of the subjects taught after it on the same day.
IV. The last subject taught on any day must be either Chemistry or English.

26. Which of the following could be subjects to be taught on the first day of a month?
(a) Hindi, Economics, Physics, Biology, Chemistry
(b) English, Economics, Chemistry, Biology, History
(c) Biology, English, Physics, Hindi, Sanskrit
(d) History, Chemistry, Physics, Hindi, English
(e) History, Sanskrit, Hindi, English, Chemistry

27. Which of the following is true of any day's routine?
(a) Sanskrit cannot be taught in the third period
(b) Economics cannot be taught in the third period
(c) Chemistry cannot be taught in the fourth period
(d) Biology cannot be taught in the fourth period
(e) None of the above

28. If Physics is taught in the third period, which of the following cannot be taught in the second period in that day?
(a) Economics (b) History
(c) Biology (d) Chemistry
(e) None of these

29. If Physics and History are taught on the first day, which of the following may be the other subjects to be taught on that day?
(a) Economics, Biology, Hindi
(b) Biology, Chemistry, Hindi
(c) Sanskrit, Biology, Hindi
(d) Economics, Chemistry, Hindi
(e) None of the above

30. If the routine of a day consists of Sanskrit, Economics, History, Biology, English, each of the following could be the next day's routine except
(a) History, Biology, English, Hindi, Chemistry
(b) History, Biology, Chemistry, Sanskrit, English
(c) History, Physics, Hindi, Biology, English
(d) Economics, Biology, Hindi, History, Chemistry
(e) Physics, Hindi, History, Biology, English

Direction (Q. Nos. 31-33) *Study the information carefully and answer the questions that follow.* **MAT 2012**

India is a multi-religion, multi-language and multi-cultural country, where people belonging to different religions join in celebrating the festivities together. The Indian Government declares such big occasions as public holidays to enable the citizens to enjoy and foster the feelings of brotherhood.

Five broad-minded persons belonging to different religions were asked to give their preferences of four such festivals which they would like to enjoy with like-minded brethren. Their options are

A. Holi, Dussehra, Diwali, Guru Nanak Birthday
B. Shivratri, Christmas, Onam, Eid
C. Holi, Shivratri, Christmas, Diwali
D. Holi, Dussehra, Guru Nanak Birthday, Eid
E. Christmas, Diwali, Onam, Guru Nanak Birthday

31. Which pair celebrates Christmas and Onam but not Dussehra and Holi?
(a) A and C (b) A and E
(c) B and D (d) B and E

32. Which pair does not participate in Eid and Onam but joins in Holi?
(a) A and B (b) A and C
(c) C and D (d) D and E

33. Who enjoys Holi and Eid but not Diwali and Christmas?
(a) B (b) C
(c) D (d) E

Direction (Q. Nos. 34-38) *These questions are based on the following information.*

From time-to-time, the Managing director of a company appoints planning committees, each consisting of exactly three members. Eligible for appointment are three executives from finance; B, C and D and three executives from Operations E, F and M.

Any given committee is subject to the following restrictions on appointments.

I. Atleast one member must be from finance and atleast one member must be from operations.
II. If B is appointed, C cannot be appointed.
III. Neither D nor F can be appointed unless the other is also appointed.
IV. If E is appointed, M must be appointed.

34. Which of the following is an acceptable committee?
(a) E, F and M
(b) D, E and F
(c) D, F and M
(d) B, D and M

35. If appointees from operations are in majority in a committee, that committee must include
(a) M (b) F
(e) E (d) C

36. If the restrictions on appointments apply also to a four member committee appointed from the same group of executives, which of the following will be true?
(a) If B is appointed, M must be appointed
(b) If F is appointed, C must be appointed
(c) If C is appointed, E must be appointed
(d) None of the above

37. If B is appointed to the same committee as M, which of the following will be true of that committee?
(a) E is not a committee member
(b) F is a committee member
(c) Appointees from finance are in majority
(d) Appointees from operations are in majority

38. If appointees from finance are in majority on a committee, that committee must include
(a) B (b) C
(c) F (d) M

Direction (Q. Nos. 39-42) *Read the following information and answer the questions based on them.*

The following are the nine options that are available for the Sleuth, a certain make of automobile, air conditioning, power brakes, power steering, power windows, a heavy-duty engine, heavy-duty shock absorbers, a hatchback, a sunroof, a tinted windshield. Because of certain manufacturing and safety considerations, the purchase of these options must conform to the following conditions.

I. If air conditioning is chosen, a heavy-duty engine, heavy-duty shock absorbers and a tinted windshield are also required.

II. If any of the power-assisted options (power brakes, power steering, power windows) are chosen, a heavy-duty engine is also required.

III. If a heavy-duty engine is chosen, power brakes are also required.

IV. If a hatchback is chosen, a sunroof cannot be chosen.

V. A tinted windshield can be chosen only for an automobile for which either a sunroof or air conditioning or both are chosen.

39. Of the following, which could be a completed selection of optional equipment that conforms to the conditions?

(a) Power steering, a sunroof

(b) A hatchback, a sunroof, a tinted windshield

(c) Power brakes, power steering, a heavy-duty engine, heavy-duty shock absorbers, a hatchback

(d) Air conditioning, power brakes, a heavy-duty engine, a hatchback, a tinted windshield

(e) Air conditioning, power brakes, a heavy-duty engine, heavy-duty shock absorbers, a hatchback

40. Which of the following must be true?

(a) A Sleuth equipped with air conditioning must also be equipped with power brakes

(b) A Sleuth equipped with a tinted windshield must also be equipped with a heavy-duty engine

(c) A Sleuth equipped with power brakes must also be equipped with power steering

(d) A Sleuth equipped with air conditioning must also be equipped with a sunroof

(e) A Sleuth equipped with a sunroof must also be equipped with a tinted windshield

41. Which of the following options can be chosen without the purchase of additional options?

(a) Heavy-duty shock absorbers (b) Power windows

(c) Power brakes (d) A heavy-duty engine

(e) A tinted windshield

42. A buyer, who does not want air conditioning but otherwise wants the maximum number of options for a Sleuth, cannot purchase

(a) power steering (b) power brakes

(c) power windows (d) a tinted windshield

(e) a hatchback

Direction (Q. Nos. 43-45) *These are based on a set of conditions. In answering some of the questions, it may be useful to draw a rough diagram. Choose the response that most accurately and completely answers each question.*

XAT 2010

Seven bands were scheduled to perform during the weeklong music festival at XLRI. The festival began on a Monday evening and ended on the Sunday evening. Each day only one band performed.

Each band performed only once. The organising committee had the task of scheduling the performances of the seven bands-Cactus, Axis, Enigma, Boom, Fish, Dhoom and Bodhi tree. The festival schedule followed the following conditions

The performance of Bodhi tree, the home band of XLRI, did not precede the performance of any other band. Among the visiting bands three were rock bands and the other three were fusion bands. All three bands of the same genre were not allowed to perform consecutively. Boom, which was a rock band, refused to perform immediately before or after Fish. Meet, who was a lead vocalist with a rock band, refused to perform after Angelina, the only female lead vocalist in the music fest besides Bony, was with the band Enigma. Angelina refused to perform after Thursday citing personal reason. Ali, who was the lead vocalist of a rock band, was not with the band Dhoom and did not perform on Saturday. Sid, the lead vocalist of the rock band Cactus, could perform only on Monday. Rupam, the only male among the lead vocalists of the fusion bands, was with Fish and performed on Wednesday. None of the bands performed in absence of their lead vocalist.

43. All of the following statements can be true except

(a) if Meet was the lead vocalist of Axis, then Ali was the lead vocalist of Boom

(b) if Meet was the lead vocalist of Dhoom, then Bony was the lead vocalist of Axis

(c) if Bony was the lead vocalist of Dhoom, then Meet was the lead vocalist of Axis

(d) if Ali was the lead vocalist of Boom, then Meet was the lead vocalist of Dhoom

(e) if Bony was the lead vocalist of Axis, then Meet was the lead vocalist of Boom

44. Which of the following must be true?

(a) Ali performed on Saturday and Enigma performed on Thursday

(b) Dhoom performed on Thursday and Angelina performed on Tuesday

(c) Boom performed on Friday and Meet performed on Tuesday

(d) Ali performed on Friday and Enigma performed on Tuesday

(e) Bony performed on Saturday and Axis performed on Thursday

45. Which of the following is a possible performance sequence?

(a) Cactus, Enigma, Fish, Dhoom, Boom, Axis

(b) Cactus, Dhoom, Fish, Boom, Enigma, Axis

(c) Cactus, Axis, Fish, Boom, Enigma, Dhoom

(d) Cactus, Axis, Fish, Engima, Boom, Dhoom

(e) Cactus, Boom, Fish, Axis, Enigma, Dhoom

Direction (Q. Nos. 46-50) *Read the following information and answer the questions based on them.*

A fabric designer is selecting colours for a striped pattern with a wide stripe, then a medium-width stripe, then three narrow stripes. Immediately after the narrow stripes, the pattern repeats, with the same colours as before.

The colours from among which the designer will choose are as follows

I. Light colours: lavender and white
II. Intermediate colours: red and orange
III. Dark colours: brown and green

Adjacent stripes in the fabric must be of different colours from each other. Adjacent stripes in the fabric must also be of different levels of darkness (light, intermediate or dark) from each other, except that the medium-width stripe and the narrow stripe adjacent to it can be of the same level as each other.

46. Which of the following, beginning with the wide stripe, is an order of colours that the designer can select?
(a) Lavender, white, red, brown, orange
(b) White, red, orange, brown, green
(c) Red, lavender, white, orange, brown
(d) Orange, green, white, red, orange
(e) Brown, white, brown, white, levender

47. Which of the following is true, if both lavender and white are used for the pattern?
(a) The two colours must each be used for a narrow stripe
(b) The two colours must be used, in either order, for the medium-width stripe and the narrow stripe adjacent to it
(c) If lavender is used for the middle of the three narrow stripes, white must be used for the medium-width stripe
(d) If white is used for any of the narrow stripe, lavender must be used for the wide stripe and can be used for another one of the remaining stripes as well
(e) If lavender is used for the wide stripe, white must be used for the narrow stripe adjacent to the medium-width stripe or for the middle of the three narrow stripes

48. Which of the following, beginning with the wide stripe, is an order of colours that the designer can select?
(a) Green, white, lavender, brown, orange
(b) Lavender, green, brown, orange, white
(c) Red, orange, green, brown, lavender
(d) Orange, white, green, lavender, red
(e) Brown, lavender, white, orange, green

49. If green is used for the middle of the three narrow stripes and for one other stripe and red and orange are the only other colours used, which of the following is true?
(a) The medium-width stripe must be green
(b) The medium-width stripe can be green but if it is, the two remaining narrow stripes must be of the same colour as each other
(c) The wide stripe must be green
(d) The wide stripe can be green but if it is, the two remaining narrow stripes must be of the same colour as each other
(e) The wide stripe can be green but if it is, the two remaining narrow stripes must be of different colours from each other

50. If atleast two of the stripes will be red and atleast two others will be white, which of the following is true?
(a) Lavender cannot be used for the wide stripe
(b) Brown cannot be used for the medium-width stripe
(c) Green cannot be used for the narrow stripe
(d) Orange can be used for the middle of the three narrow stripes
(e) Lavender can be used for the narrow stripe after which the pattern repeats

Direction (Q. Nos. 51-52) *Read the following paragraph and following conditions to answer the questions.* **IIFT 2011**

The Vice Chancellor of a University wants to select a team of five member organising committee for the next convocation of the University to be held in March 2012. The committee members are to be selected from five short listed professors (Prof. Ahuja, Prof. Banerjee, Prof. Chakravarty, Prof. Das and Prof. Equbal) and four short listed students (Prakash, Queen, Ravi and Sushil). Some conditions for selection of the committee members are given below.

I. Prof. Ahuja and Sushil have to be together.
II. Prakash cannot be put with Ravi.
III. Prof. Das and Queen cannot go together.
IV. Prof. Chakravarty and Prof. Equbal have to be selected.
V. Ravi cannot be selected with Prof. Banerjee.

51. If two members of the committee are students and Prof. Das is one of the member of the committee, who are the other committee members?
(a) Prof. Banerjee, Prof. Chakravarty, Prakash and Queen
(b) Prof. Ahuja, Prof. Banerjee, Sushil and Prakash
(c) Prof. Chakravarty, Prof. Equbal, Prakash and Sushil
(d) None of the above

52. In case Prof. Ahuja and Prof. Chakravarty are members, who are the other members who cannot be selected for the committee?
(a) Prof. Banerjee, Prof. Equbal and Sushil
(b) Prof. Equbal, Sushil and Prakash
(c) Prof. Equbal, Prakash and Queen
(d) None of the above

Direction (Q. Nos. 53-55) *Read the following information carefully and answer the questions given below it.*

Eight students A, B, C, D, E, F, G and H are planning to enjoy car racing. There are only two cars and following are the conditions

I. One car can accommodate maximum five and minimum four students.

II. A will it in the same car in which D is sitting but H is not in the same car.

III. B and C cannot sit in the same car in which D is sitting.

IV. F will sit in the car of four people only along with A and E but certainly not with G.

53. If H and G are sitting in the same car, who are other two students sitting in the same car?
(a) B and C (b) C and D (c) B and D (d) E and B
(e) None of these

54. If E and A are sitting in the same car, which of the following statements is true?
(a) Five students are sitting in the same car
(b) B is sitting in the same car
(c) F is not sitting in the same car
(d) G is not sitting in the same car
(e) None of the above

55. Which of the following statements is superfluous for the above sitting arrangements?
(a) Only I (b) Only II (c) Only III (d) Only IV
(e) None of these

Direction (Q. Nos. 56-59) *Read the following information and answer the questions based on them.* **FMS 2010**

In a club, combinations of five out of the eight songs P, Q, R, S, T, U, V and W are to be played by a DJ on a daily basis. On any day, except for the first day of a month, only three of the songs must be the ones that were played on the previous day. The song combinations must also satisfy the following conditions

I. If song P is to be played on a day, song V cannot be played.

II. If song Q is to be played on a day, T must be one of the songs to be played after Q.

III. If R is to be played on a day, V must be one of the songs to be played after R.

IV. The last song to be played on any day must be either S or U.

56. Which of the following could be the combination of songs to be played on the first day of a month?
(a) P, R, V, S, U (b) Q, S, R, V, U
(c) T, U, R, V, S (d) U, Q, S, T, W

57. If the songs R and W are to be played on the first day, which of the following could be the other songs to be played on that day?
(a) P, T, U (b) Q, S, V (c) T, S, V (d) Q, T,V

58. Which of the following is true of any day's valid combination of songs?
(a) P cannot be played at third place
(b) Q cannot be played at third place
(c) T cannot be played at third place
(d) None of the above

59. If song R is played at third place in a sequence, which of the following cannot be the second song to be played in that sequence?
(a) Q (b) S
(c) T (d) U

Direction (Q. Nos. 60-63) *Read the following information carefully to answer the given questions.*

A company wants to select a team of four call centres executives from its South Indian centre for transfer to North India where they are going to set up a new centre. The company is managed by professional managers and is very particular about human resources and personnel relations. There are seven team members of equal ability X, Y and Z (who are senior) and A, B, C and D (who are junior). The company requires that there should be two senior executives and two junior executives in the team. It is also necessary that all of the executives in a particular team are friendly with each other in order to have a real team spirit and avoid any personnel relations problem in the new centre being set up in the North.

Following is the situation of relations among the seven executives.

I. Y and A are not friendly.

II. Z and C are not friendly.

III. A and B are not friendly.

60. If A is on the team, then which other executives must be on the team as well?
(a) X, Y and D (b) X, Z and B
(c) X, Z and C (d) X, Z and D

61. Which statements must be false?
I. Y and C are never selected together.
II. Z and B are never selected together.
III. Z and D are never selected together.
(a) Only I (b) I and II
(c) I and III (d) I, II and III

62. If both Y and Z are selected, which of the executives must be on the team with them?
(a) Both B and A (b) Both B and D
(c) Both C and D (d) Only D

63. Which of the following statements is/are true for X?
I. X must be selected as one of the senior Executives on the team.
II. X must be selected, if C is selected.
III. X cannot be selected, if both A and C are rejected.
(a) Only I (b) Only II
(c) II and III (d) I, II and III

Direction (Q. No. 64) *Read the information carefully and answer the question that follows.*

The Bannerjees, the Sharmas and the Pattabhiramans each have a tradition of eating Sunday lunch as a family. Each family serves a special meal at a certain time of day. Each family has a particular set of chinaware used only for this meal. Use the clues below to answer the following question.

I. The Sharma family eats at noon.
II. The family that serves fried brinjal uses blue chinaware.
III. The Bannerjee family eats at 2 O'clock.
IV. The family that serves sambar does not use red chinaware.
V. The family that eats at 1 O'clock serves fried brinjal.
VI. The Pattabhiraman family does not use white chinaware.
VII. The family that eats last likes makka-ki-roti.

64. Which one of the following statements is true?
(a) The Bannerjees eat makka-ki-roti at 2 O'clock, the Sharmas eat fried brinjal at 12 O'clock and the Pattabhiramans eat sambar from red chinaware
(b) The Sharmas eat sambar served in white chinaware, the Pattabhiramans eat fried brinjal at 1 O'clock and the Bannerjees eat makka-ki-roti served in blue chinaware
(c) The Sharmas eat sambar at noon, the Pattabhiramans eat fried brinjal served in blue chinaware and the Bannerjees eat makka-ki-roti served in red chinaware
(d) The Bannerjees eat makka-ki-roti served in white chinaware, the Sharmas eat fried brinjal at 12 O'clock and the Pattabhiramans eat sambar from red chinaware

Direction (Q. Nos. 65-66) *Read the following passage and answer the questions that follow.*

An audit unearthed a financial scam in NWC corporation. One or more among the nine financial accountants of NWC corporation are suspected to have fudged the accounts. Following are the statements made by the nine suspects.

I. Shrinivas : Nagraj fudged the accounts.
II. Datta : Shrinivas did not fudge the accounts.
III. Nagraj : Datta is lying and I did not fudge accounts.
IV. Jose : Shrinivas is telling the truth.
V. Samuel : Exactly three of the suspects are telling the truth.
VI. Ejaz : Datta is lying and Shrinivas fudged the accounts.
VII. Chaudhary : Datta fudged the accounts.
VIII. Ganeshan : Datta is lying and Shrinivas is telling the truth.
IX. Panda : Samuel is lying.

65. If Samuel is telling the truth, which of the following statements is true?
(a) Chaudhary and Datta are telling the truth
(b) Nagraj fudged the accounts
(c) Chaudhary and Jose are telling the truth
(d) Shrinivas and Datta are telling the truth
(e) Shrinivas fudged the account

66. If Panda is lying, which of the following statements cannot be true?
(a) Nagraj, Ganeshan and Ejaz are all lying
(b) Datta fudged the accounts
(c) Shrinivas did not fudge the accounts
(d) Jose and Shrinivas are telling the truth
(e) Nagraj fudged the accounts

Direction (Q. Nos. 67-68) *Answer the questions based on the following information.*

Director of an institute wants to distribute teaching assignemnts of HRM, Psychology, Development Studies. Trade policy and Finance to five of six newly appointed faculty members. Prof. Fotedar does not want any assignment in Prof. Das gets one of the five. Prof. Chaudhury desires either HRM or Finance or no assignment. Prof. Banik opines that, if Prof. Das gets either Psychology or Trade Policy, then she must get the other one. Prof. Eswar insists on an assignment, if Prof. Acharya gets one.

67. Which of the following is a valid faculty-assignment combination, if all the faculty preferences are considered?
(a) Prof. Acharya-HRM, Prof. Banik-Psychology, Prof. Chaudhury-Development Studies, Prof. Das-Trade Policy, Prof. Eswar-Finance
(b) Prof. Chaudhury-HRM, Prof. Das-Psychology, Prof. Acharya Development Studies, Prof. Banik-Trade Policy, Prof. Eswar-Finance
(c) Prof. Acharya-HRM, Prof. Banik Psychology, Prof. Eswar-Development Studies, Prof. Das-Trade Policy, Prof. Fodetar-Finance
(d) Prof. Banik-HRM, Prof. Fotedar-Psychology, Prof. Eswar-Development Studies, Prof. Chaudhary-Trade Policy, Prof. Acharya-Finance

68. If Prof. Acharya gets HRM and Prof. Chaudhury gets Finance, then which of the following is not a correct faculty assignment combination assuming all faculty preferences are considered?
(a) Prof. Das-Development Studies, Prof. Banik-Trade Policy
(b) Prof. Fotedar-Development Studies, Prof. Banik-Trade Policy
(c) Prof. Banik-Development Studies, Prof. Eswar-Trade Policy
(d) Prof. Banik-Development Studies. Prof. Das-Trade Policy

Direction (Q. Nos. 69-71) *Go through the table that follows and pick up the best alternative to answer the questions.*

Teams A, B, C and D are participating in a cricket tournament. Team A has to pick up five batsmen out of the ten available. All batsmen have played 100 matches each in the past. Past data indicates that C beats A 8 out of 10 times. B beats A 5 out of 10 times and D beats A 1 out of 10 times. The conditions for series are likely to be normal and bowling strength of all teams is same. Manager of team A based on his past experience, feels that team should take high risk against stronger opponents and low risk against weaker opponents for maximising chances of wining the game.

The average score of the top 10 batsmen of team A is provided in the table given below.

Name of the batsmen	Average of batsmen based on past performance	Number of times dismissed below 20	Number of times dismissed around average	Number of times score more than a century
RD	40	20	70	3
ST	44	20	60	10
SG	41	25	50	10
VS	31	50	20	15
RU	28	55	25	12
YS	35	40	40	10
VV	35	35	50	5
MK	30	30	45	5
MT	36	45	30	10
MD	45	30	50	10

The average scores of the top 5 batsmen for each team playing in the tournament are, C (270); B (215); D (180) and A (215).

69. Team A is playing its first match with team C. Based on the statistics above, whom should the manager choose so that the team has maximum chances of winning?
(a) RD, ST, SG, MD, YS (b) VS, YS, RU, MD, MT
(c) RD, ST, SG, VS, MD (d) YS, RU, VS, MK, MD
(e) ST, VS, RU, MD, SG

70. Team A would play the second match with D. Based on the statistics above, whom should the manager choose so that A has maximum chances of winning?
(a) RD, ST, MD, VS, YS
(b) RD, ST, SG, VS, MD
(c) ST, RD, VV, SG, MD
(d) SG, RU, YS, MK, MD
(e) ST, RD, MK, MD, SG

71. Team A would play the third match with B. Based on the statistics above, whom should the manager choose so that A has maximum chances of winning?
(a) RD, RU, MK, VS, YS
(b) RD, VS, MT, RU, YS
(c) RD, VV, SG, VS, MD
(d) ST, RD, MK, MD, SG
(e) SG, RU, YS, MK, VV

Direction (Q. Nos. 72-75) *Answer the following questions based on the information given below.*

In a sports event, six teams (A, B, C, D, E and F) are competing against each other. Matches are scheduled in two stages. Each team plays three matches in stage 1 and two matches in stage 2. No team plays against the same team more than once in the event. No ties are permitted in any of the matches. The observations after the completion of stage 1 and stage 2 are as given below.

Stage 1

I. One team won all the three matches.
II. Two teams lost all the matches.
III. D lost to A but won against C and F.
IV. E lost to B but won against C and F.
V. B lost atleast one match.
VI. F did not play against the top team of stage I.

Stage 2

The leader of stage 1 lost the next two matches. Of the two teams at the bottom after stage 1, one team won both matches, while the other lost both matches.

3 one more team lost both matches in stage 2.

72. The two teams that defeated the leader of Stage 1 are
(a) F and D (b) E and F (c) B and D (d) E and D
(e) C and D

73. The only team(s) that won both matches in stage 2 is (are)
(a) B (b) E and F (c) A, E and F (d) B, E and F
(e) B and F

74. The teams that won exactly two matches in the event are
(a) A, D and F (b) D and E
(c) E and F (d) D, E and F
(e) D and F

75. The team(s) with the most wins in the event is (are)
(a) A (b) A and C
(c) F (d) E
(e) B and E

76. Mrs Ranga has three children and has difficulty remembering their ages and the months of their birth. The clues below may help her remembers.

I. The boy, who was born in June, is 7 yr old.
II. One of the children is 4 yr old but it is not Anshuman.
III. Vaibhav is older than Suprita.
IV. One of the children was born in September but it was not Vaibhav.
V. Suprita's birthday is in April.
VI. The youngest child is only 2 yr old.

Based on the above clues, which one of the following statements is true?
(a) Vaibhav is the oldest, followed by Anshuman who was born in September and the youngest is Suprita who was born in April
(b) Anshuman is the oldest being born in June, followed by Suprita who is 4 yr old and the youngest is Vaibhav who is 2 yr old

(c) Vaibhav is the oldest being 7 yr old, followed by Suprita who was born in April and the youngest is Anshuman who was born in September.

(d) Suprita is the oldest who was born in April, followed by Vaibhav who was born in June and Anshuman who was born in September.

Direction (Q. Nos. 77-80) *Refer to the data below and answer the questions that follow.*

3 coloured balls yellow, green and red each are to put in one of the there boxes numbered 1, 2 and 3 (not necessarily in the same order). 3 friends John, Jani and Janardhan make 2 statements about the arrangement of the balls in the boxes,one of which is true and the other is false.

Their statements are as follows.

I. John : The yellow ball is not in box 2 and the red ball is in box 1.

II. Jani : The yellow ball is not in box 3 and the green ball is in box 2.

III. Janardhan : The green ball is in box 3 and the red ball is not in box 1.

77. Box 1 contains the

(a) red ball (b) yellow ball
(c) green ball (d) Cannot be determined

78. The yellow ball is in

(a) box 1 (b) box 2
(c) box 3 (d) Either box 2 or box 3

79. In all of the friends, which one's both statements

(a) Only I (b) Only II
(c) Both I and II (d) None of these

80. If we ignore the second statements made by Jani and consider the first statements made by him to be true, then how many possible arrangements can we have following the remaining conditions?

(a) 3
(b) 4
(c) 5
(d) None of the above

Direction (Q. Nos. 81-84) *Read the following information carefully and answer the questions.*

Radhika, Neha, Rupa, Mahima, Sayali and Shobha joined six different renowned MBA institutes —A, B, C, D, E and F and opted for six different specialisations in Management—Finance, IT, Operations, HR, Marketing and General Management.

Each of them has a different educational qualification out of BCA, B. Com, CA, BBM, B.Sc and B. Tech.

The following information is available about them:

(i) Mahima joined institute B and did not take up marketing or IT and is not a B. Tech.

(ii) The person who joined institute E opted for HR and is not a CA or a B.Sc.

(iii) The person, who is a BCA graduate, joined the institute D and took IT.
Whereas, the person, who is B. Com graduate, took up General Management.

(iv) Radhika joined institute F, Rupa is a BCA graduate and Neha took up HR.

81. What is the educational qualification of Mahima and what is the course she opted for?

(a) B.Sc and Finance
(b) B. Com and General Management
(c) BBM and HR
(d) None of the above

82. Which institute did the B. Tech Graduate join?

(a) F (b) D
(c) A (d) None of these

83. The educational qualification of Sayali is

(a) B.Sc (b) BCA
(c) BBM (d) CA

84. If Shobha joined the institute C, then the student who joined the institute A opted for

(a) Finance
(b) Marketing
(c) General Marketing
(d) HR

Answers with Explanations

Base Level

Solution (Q. Nos. 1-3) From the given information, first we make a table of non-togetherness of players.

Males			Females			
A	B	C	W	X	Y	Z
	✓		✗			
		✓				✗
			✓		✗	

1. (*b*) From the question, it is clear that B is rejected. It means, from among males, A and C must be the part of team as it is given that atleast two males must be there in the team. Now, from the given table, it is clear that if C is selected Z must be rejected. So, Z must not be the part of team. It is also given in question that Y is selected W must be rejected. So, from females, X and Y will be the part of the teams. As a result, the team will consist of A, C, X and Y.

2. (*b*) If all the three males are selected, there are two possibilities of team formation i.e. ABCX and ABCY.

3. (*c*) Here, it is given that B is selected. It mean that W is rejected and also Y is rejected is given. Now, there are two possibilities of formation of team— ABXZ and ABCX. But from the option given ABCX will be the required team.

Solution (Q. Nos. 4-8)

Person	Class	Colour
S	I	Pink
P	II	Green
Q	III	Black
R	IV	Red
M	V	Blue
T	VI	Yellow

4. (*c*) 5. (*e*)
6. (*a*) 7. (*d*)

8. (*d*)

9. (*c*) If Q, R and V form three members of the team. Then, P and S cannot be related due to R and V, respectively. So, option (b) and (d) are ruled out. There should be atleast three boys. So, option (a) is ruled out. So the correct answer is (c) as T and U fulfil all the conditions.

10. (*b*) As V is not related for the team, so option (a) and (d) are ruled out. P and R cannot be related together, so option (c) rules out. So, option (b) is the correct answer.

11. (*d*) If P and S are two boys selected, then there are following possible combinations

    (i) P, S, Q, T, U (ii) P, S, Q, T, W
    (iii) P, S, Q, U, W (iv) P, S, T, U, W

    So, there are total four ways.

12. (*b*) From the above explanation, it is clear that, if four boys are selected, then girl V cannot be selected due to S.

13. (*d*) P and R cannot be selected together, so P Q R V W can never be a team.

14. (*e*) On the first Saturday,
    Team A plays against team D.
    Team B plays against team E.
    Team C plays against team F.
    So, none of the given option is correct.

15. (*e*) From (ii), team B cannot play its second game against team E and C.
    From (i), A plays its second game against F.
    So, B plays its second game against team A or D.

16. (*e*) From the given information, each team must play against each of the teams once and only once during the season. They are total 6 teams. So, each team has to play 5 games.

17. (*d*) If D wins 5 games, then it means that it has won all the games and all the other teams have lost atleast 1 game.

18. (*e*) No information is given for the condition.

Solution (Q. Nos. 19-21) Following table can be drawn from the given information.

Names	Home Towns					Specialist Slot				
	Sikandrabad	Panipat	Warangal	Banaras	Chennai	Spin	Pace-Bowler	Wicket-keeper	Batsman	Cap
Surinder	✗′	✓	✗	✗	✗	✗	✗	✗	✗	✓
Prem	✗	✗	✓	✗	✗	✓	✗	✗	✗	✗
Wasim	✗	✗	✗	✗	✓	✗	✗	✗	✓	✗
Bishamber	✓	✗	✗	✗	✗	✗	✓	✗	✗	✗
Chauhan	✗	✗	✗	✓	✗	✗	✗	✓	✗	✗

19. (*c*) Chauhan is the wicket-keeper.

20. (*c*) Warangal is spinner's home town.

21. (*b*) Bishamber is the pace-bowler.

22. (*b*) If Ajay buys R and T, then Bony cannot buys P or S. So, he buys Q and U.

23. (*b*) If Bony buys Q and S, then Chetan cannot buy U or T. So, he buys P and R and Ajay must buy T and U.

24. (*d*) If Chetan has to buy P and S, then Bony must not buy Q.

25. (*a*) If Bony buys Q, then Chetan cannot buy U or T. So, he can buy two out of P, R and S. Since Ajay buys P, so Chetan buys R and S.

26. (*d*) If Ajay buys R and Bony buys Q, then Chetan has to buy P and S.

27. (*c*) According to the given information Mala and Sapna are women and Ajit and Buman are men. So, if Suman is a man, then Manjit is a woman.

28. (*d*) If Manjit is in red car, then Sarat must be in blue car. In a car, one man or woman must be a driver. So, option (d) is correct because Mala knows driving.

29. (*d*) Any one from P, F or M can be the fourth person in the car.

30. (*d*) If F and P are travelling together, then M must be there. None F, P and M are in one car and T and R are in another car. Neither N nor P cannot be assigned to the same car as K. So, N must be with F, P and M.

31. (*a*) Option (b) is ruled out because P and K cannot be together.
Option (c) is ruled out because T and R must be together.
Option (a) is correct because it satisfies all the conditions.

32. (*d*) If K is in the car containing 3 people, then there are two possible combinations:
(i) K, T, R and N, P, F, M
(ii) K, F, M and N, P, T, R
So, T, F and M can be present with K.

33. (*b*) If F and P are in the same car, then M must be present with them. N and P cannot be with K. So, N must be present with F, P and M.
So that car contain 4 passengers only.

34. (*c*) Paraguay = Win all matches : Points = 12
Turkey = Loose all matches : Points = 4
Qatar, Russia and Spain = Win one match each, loose one match each and draw two matches each : Points = 8.

35. (*d*) If each country wins one match each loose one match each and draw two matches each, then the score will be 8.

36. (*a*) D and Q cannot be selected together, so option (b) and (c) are ruled out. A and S must be selected together, so option (d) is ruled out.
Option (a) is correct because it satisfies all the conditions.

37. (*d*) R and P cannot be selected together, so option (a) is ruled out. Q and D cannot be selected together, so option (b) is ruled out. S and A must be selected together, so option (c) is ruled out. Option (d) is correct because it satisfies all the conditions.

38. (*c*) D and Q cannot be selected together, so option (a) and (b) are ruled out. A and S must be together, so option (d) is ruled out.
Option (c) is correct because it satisfies all the conditions.

39. (*d*) If A and C are members then, S and E must be the members. So P, Q and E cannot be the other members of the team.

40. (*a*) A and S must be together, so option (b) and (c) are ruled out. P and R cannot be together, so option (d) is ruled out.
Option (a) is correct becaue it satisfies all the conditions.

41. (*a*) If female teachers are selected, then male doctors are not selected. So, two doctors that are selected A and B who are females. If female doctors are selected, then male engineers are not selected. So, two engineers that are selected are G and H who are females.
Three female teachers are O, P and Q.
So, the team members are A, B, O, P, Q, G and H.

42. (*d*) Four teachers are selected in the team. It means that atleast one female teacher is selected. So, male doctors C, D and E are not selected. Female doctors A and B are selected. So, male engineers K and L are not selected. Either G or H is selected.
So, team A, B, K, N, R, P, Q is not possible because K is not selected.

43. (*c*) If two female teacher are selected, then male doctors C, D and E are not selected. Two doctors A and B are selected, who are females. So, male engineers K and L are not selected. Two engineers G and H are selected.
So, team A, B, K, L, P and Q is not possible because K and L are not selected.

44. (*c*) Two male engineers are selected, so female doctors A and B are not selected. Three doctors C, D and E are selected who are male, so female teachers P, Q and R are not selected. Two teachers out of M, N and O are selected.
So, the possible team is C, D, E , K, L, M and N.

45. (*d*) C, D, K, L, O and P is not a possible team because C and D are male doctors who cannot be selected with female teachers O and P.

46. (*c*) If Dumpy, Falgun, Purav from the team of 3 members then, Saurav must be in two member team with Bittu or Amit because Hitesh and Ronit must be in the same team, so they will be in 4 member team.

47. (*b*) Chintu and Saurav cannot be in the same team and Purav and Bittu cannot be in the same team. So, Chintu team which is a 4 member team must have Hitesh and Ronit.

48. (*a*) If Chintu and Falgun are together and Saurav is in team of 2 members, then there are following possible teams.

Chintu	Dumpy	Saurav
Falgun	Bittu	Purav
Hitesh		
Rohit	Amit	

(i)

Chintu	Dumpy	Saurav
Falgun	Purav	Bittu
Hitesh	Amit	
Ronit		

(ii)

Chintu	Dumpy	Saurav
Falgun	Hitesh	Purav
Bittu	Ronit	
Amit		

(iii)

Chintu	Dumpty	Bittu
Falgun	Hitesh	
Purav	Ronit	
Amit		

(iv)

So, total four teams are possible.

49. (*a*) Chintu does not take Purav, so Purav should be in 3 member team and Bittu must be with Chintu in four member team. Ronit and Hitesh should be in same team, so they should be 4 member team with Chintu.

50. (*a*) If Purav is in the same team as Chintu and Falgun, then Ronit and Hitesh must be in 3 member team. Bittu will be in 2 member team with Purav.

51. (*a*) From condition (iii) B and G are in different boats.
So, if F and B are in one boat, G is, the other boat.

52. (*d*) From condition (iv), the maximum number of persons in one boat can be four only.
So, there must be atleast three people in the complete list of people who must be sitting in either boat.

53. (*d*)

Station	1	2	3	4	5	6
Friend			Parul, Omez	Quan	×	×

54. (*a*)

Station	1	2	3	4	5
Friend	Mahima	Nimisha	Parul	Quan	Omez

55. (*b*) At station 4 and 5, Nimisha and Omez get off.

56. (*d*) Nimisha cannot get off at station 5.

57. (*b*) F cannot be the fifth pot to be watered on a day because then C and E must be the first two pots to be watered. It means that C will be watered before F which violates condition (iv).

58. (*e*) Options (a) and (d) are ruled out because first two pots must be selected from C, D, E and F. Option (b) is ruled out because H cannot be watered before D. Option (c) is ruled out because F must be watered before C. Option (e) is correct because it satisfies all the given conditions.

59. (*b*) If D is watered immediately after J, then it cannot be among the first two pots to be watered. F must be watered before C. So, it must be the first two pots to be watered.

60. (*d*) According to the questions, the new conditions will be as following:
(i) The last two pots to be watered must be selected from C, D, E and F.
(ii) H cannot be watered after D and J cannot be watered before I.
(iii) G can be watered only before B.
(iv) F must be watered after C.
Now, option (a) and (e) are ruled out due to (i). Option (b) is ruled out due to (ii) and option (c) is ruled out due to (iv). Option (d) is correct as it satisfies all the conditions.

61. (*a*) If D is the fourth pot to be watered, then F must be among the first two pots to be watered. H cannot be watered before D. If I is watered at third, then J must be watered first or second which is not possible. G cannot be watered at third becasue G can be watered only after B.
So, A is watered at third and it satisfies all the conditions.

62. (*b*) J cannot be the ninth pot to be watered because it must be watered before I.

Solution (Q. Nos. 63-65) From the given information we get the following points.

(i) The Nepalese and the Englishman are not adjacent to each other.
(ii) The Iraqi is neither in track 1 nor in track 5.
(iii) The Chinese cannot be in track 5 and the Indian cannot be in track 1.

Chinese	–	Napalese	–	–
1	2	3	4	5

63. (*c*) From (i) the Englishman should be in track 5. The Indian and the Iraqi should be in track 2 and track 4 in any order.

64. (*d*)

–	–	Indian	Napalese	–
1	2	3	4	5

From (i), the Englishman should be in track 1 or track 2.
From (iii), the Chineses should be in track 1 or in track 2.
So, the Iraqi will be in track 5. But this violates condition (ii).

65. (*a*) It is given that the Iraqi is to the left of the Chinese. By (ii) the Iraqi can be in track 2 or track 3. Assuming that the Iraqi is in track 3, we get following arrangement:

–	–	Iraqi	Chinese	Indian
1	2	3	4	5

But, now the Napalese and the Englisman will be in adjacent track, which is against (i). So, the Iraqi should be in track 2.

Solution (Q. Nos. 66-67)

List of companies CEOs and Managing Director

Companies	CEOs	Managing Directors
Klentech Industries	Mr Sethi	Mr Tandon
Andromeda Infotech	Mr D'Souza	Mr Arora
Zoomerang Technologies	Mr Puri	Mr Karare
Spearhead Unlimited	Mr Bisht	Mr Reddy

66. (*c*) Mr Puri delivered his address sometime before Mr Reddy

67. (*d*) We cannot determined that who is the last CEO to speak.

68. (*b*) The committee must consists of exactly two faculty members and two students. L and N are faculty members, so we have to select a student. L and R cannot be selected together. P and M must be selected together and M is a faculty member. So, option (a), (c) and (d) are ruled out.

69. (*a*) If P is a representative, then M must also be a representative. Either K or L must be one of the representatives. So, N cannot be a representative because committee consist of only two faculty members.

70. (*b*) If R is a representative, then L cannot be a representative. M is not a representative, so K and N are representatives from faculty members. Either Q or S is the second representative from students. If S is not a representative then the group of representative would be completely determined.

71. (*a*) If neither Q nor S is a representative, then P and R are the representatives from students. If R is a representative, then L cannot be a representative, so K is a representative. If P is a representative, then M must be a representative.

72. (*b*) If L is a representative, then K cannot be a representative because only one of them can be a representative. So, option (d) is ruled out.
If L is a representative, then R cannot be a representative. So option (c) is ruled out.
If P is a representative, then M must also be a representative. So option (a) is ruled out.
So, option (b) is correct as it satisfies all the conditions.

73. (*c*) Option (a) violates condition (i)

Option (b) violates conditions (i) and (ii)

Option (d) violates condition (iii)

Option (c) is correct because it satisfies all the conditions.

74. (*a*) Since, anniversary card cannot come with birthday card and no more than two card of any type in any of the rows. So, second row must make up by two birthday cards.

75. (*b*) The third row can be make up by a graduation card and two birthday cards.

76. (*c*) If all the birthday cards are in the second an third rows and fourth row cannot contain more than two anniversary card, so two graduation cards can be placed in fourth row.

77. (*c*) A graduation card must be in the fourth row and it must be next to a anniversary card because fourth row must contain two anniversary card. So, a birthday card is in the first row.

78. (*c*) Both graduation cards can be placed in fourth row.

Solution (Q. Nos. 79-83) Following combinations can be formed from the given information

T, Z → Delhi → Swift D'zire
Q, P, W → Hyderabad → Honda City
S, R, V → Chennai → Ford Ikon.

79. (*c*) Members of Ford Ikon car are going to Chennai.

80. (*a*) None of the car has four members.

81. (*d*) S and Z are definitely females but nothing can be determined about the third female.

82. (*c*) Both P and Q are travelling with W.

83. (*b*) Clearly, P, Q and W are travelling in Honda City.

Advanced Level

Solution (Q. Nos. 1-3) Following table can be drawn from the given information.

States	Colour of Sarees			
	Blue	Black	Orange	Red
Delhi	✗	✓	✗	✗
UP	✓	✗	✗	✗
Jharkhand	✗	✗	✗	✓
MP	✗	✗	✓	✗

	Miss MP	(Runner up) Miss UP	(Winner) Miss Jharkhand	Miss Delhi
(Sarees)	Orange	Blue	Red	Black

1. (*c*) Miss UP was the runner UP.

2. (*b*) Black saree was won by Miss Delhi.

3. (*a*) Miss Jharkhand was wearing Red saree.

4. (*a*) C and A cannot be selected together. So, B must be selected.

C and E cannot be selected togehter. F and D cannot be selected. So, three account officers F, G and H are selected.

So, only one team is formed : B, C, F, G and H.

5. (*a*) If C is sent to the new office, then D cannot go with C because if D go with C, then neither F nor G can be selected. C and E cannot work together. So, three account officers F, G and H must be selected.

6. (*a*) Two account assistants must be selected. A and C cannot be selected together. So, A, B or B, C are selected.

So, B must go to the new office.

7. (*a*) Under the given guidelines, following teams are possible.

(i) A, B, D, E, H (ii) A, B, E, F, G
(iii) A, B, E, G, H (iv) A, B, E, F, H
(v) A,B, F, G, H (vi) B, C, F, G, H

8. (*d*) From the above explanation, it is clear that, if D is selected, then C cannot go with D and H must go with D.

Solution (Q. Nos. 9-12)

Day	Subject
Monday	Organisational Behaviour
Tuesday	Psychology
Wednesday	Statistics
Thursday	Computer Science
Friday	Research Methods
Saturday	Off day
Sunday	Economics

9. (*e*) Last lecture scheduled of Economics.

10. (*c*) Three lectures scheduled between Economics and Psychology.

11. (*c*) Computer Science is scheduled on Thursday.

12. (*d*) Cannot be determined.

Solution (Q. Nos. 13-15)

13. (*d*) Option (a) is incorrect as Gabino and Daffy must be in same pen.

Option (b) is incorrect is Blackley and Ashlen cannot be together in pen 2.

Option (c) is incorrect as Gabino and Daffy must be in same pen.

Option (d) is correct as it fulfils all the given conditions.

Option (e) is incorrect as Gabino and Daffy must be in same pen.

14. (*b*) According to question and given conditions, the possible arrangements are as below

I. Pen 1 : Earl, Fala, Ashlen
Pen 2 : Gabino, Daffy, Blackley, Custard

II. Pen 1 : Earl, Fala Blackley
Pen 2: Gabino Daffy, Ashlen, Custard

III. Pen 1 : Gabino, Daffy Blackley
Pen 2 : Earl, Fala, Ashlen, Custard

IV. Pen 1 : Gabino, Daffy, Ashlen
Pen 2 : Earl, Fala, Blackley, Custard
Clearly, in all cases custard is in pen 2.

15. (*e*) Possible arrangements are as follows
Pen 1 : Earl/Fala, Ashlen/Blackley and Custard
Pen 2 : Earl/Fala, Ashlen/Blackley Daffy and Gabino
Clearly, option (e) must not be true.

16. (*c*) Options (a) and (b) are ruled out because N and K should be together. Option (d) is ruled out because P and S cannot be together.
Option (c) is correct because it satisfies all the conditions.

17. (*d*) P cannot serve together with S. So, representatives of labour will have to be P, R or R, S. So, R is always chosen to serve on the committee.

18. (*d*) If P and R are chosen to be the labour representatives then O cannot be chosen. So, two representatives of management will be M and N. If N is chosen, then K must also be chosen. So, statements I and II are true.

19. (*d*) Options (a) and (b) are ruled out because N and K must be together. Option (c) is ruled out because O and P cannot be together.
Option (d) is correct becasue it satisfies all the cnditions.

20. (*d*) If N is chosen, then K has to be chosen. No condition is applicable on M and O, so they can also be chosen.

21. (*c*) If J must be chosen, then P cannot be chosen because if P is chosen, then O cannot be in the committee and it means that M and N has to be chosen but N and K cannot be chosen together.
So, P cannot be chosen.

22. (*e*) Option (a) is wrong because J cannot be advertised in week 1 (i.e. H than J). Option (b) is wrong because G is advertised with either J or O. Options (c) is wrong because J and H cannot be advertised together (i.e. H than J). Option (d) is wrong because K is advertised in either week 1 or week 2.

23. (*a*) Option (b) is wrong because G is advertised with either J or O.
Options (c) and (d) are wrong because H and J cannot be advertised in week 4.
Option (e) is wrong because K must be advertised in either week 1 or 2.

24. (*d*) Options (c) and (e) are wrong because K must be advertised in either week 1 or 2 whereas O must be advertised in week 3. Again, options (a) and (b) are wrong because J and H can be advertised in only three of the four weeks.

25. (*a*) Option (b) is wrong because G is advertised with either J or O.
Option (c) is wrong because H and J cannot be advertised together.
Options (d) and (e) are wrong because K and H cannot be advertised with O.

26. (*d*) Physics and Hindi must be taught on the same day, so option (a) is ruled out. Either Chemistry or English must be the last subject, so options (b) and (c) are ruled out.
Sanskrit and Hindi cannot be taught on the same day, so option (e) is ruled out.
Option (d) is correct because it satisfies all the conditions.

27. (*e*) None of the given option is true for any day's routine.

28. (*a*) If Physics is taught in third period, then Hindi must be taught in fouth period. Either Chemistry or English should be taught in fifth period. So, Economics cannot be taught in second period because from II no period will be vacant for Biology.

29. (*b*) If Physics and History are taught on the first day, then Hindi must be taught on that day. Either Chemistry or English should be taught in last period. One place is vacant which can be filled only by Biology.

30. (*b*) Option (b) is correct because four subjects cannot be repeated on the next day.

Solution (Q. Nos. 31-33)

Persons	Festivals							
	Holi	Dussehra	Diwali	Guru Nanak Birthday	Shivratri	Chris-tmas	Onam	Eid
A	✓	✓	✓	✓				
B					✓	✓	✓	✓
C	✓		✓		✓	✓		
D	✓	✓		✓				✓
E			✓	✓		✓	✓	✗

31. (*d*) B and E pair celebrates Christmas and Onam but not Dussehra and Holi.

32. (*b*) A and C pair does not participate in Eid and Onam but joins in Holi.

33. (*c*) D person enjoys Holi and Eid but not Diwali and Christmas.

34. (*c*) D and F should be appointed together, so options (a) and (d) are ruled out.
E and M must be appointed together, so option (b) is ruled out. Option (c) is correct because it satisfies all the conditions.

35. (*a*) This committee has two executives from operations and one executive from finance. Executives from operations are E, F and M. E and F cannot be selected because of IV. So, the committe must include M.

36. (*a*) Four member committee can be formed with B, D, F and M. So, option (a) is correct.

37. (*d*) If B and M are appointed, then cannot be appointed. D and F have to be appointed together. So, the third person appointed must be E. So, appointees from operations are in majority.

38. (*c*) If F is appointed, then D must be appointed. Thus, the appointees from Finance are in majority.

39. (*c*) If a power steering is chosen, then a heavy-duty engine is also required. So option (a) is ruled out. A run roof and a hatch book cannot be chosen together. So, option (b) is ruled out. Air conditioning should be chosen with heavy-duty shock absorbers and hinted windshield. So, option (d) and (e) are ruled out.

Option (c) is correct because it satisfies all the conditions.

40. (*a*) If air conditioning is chosen, then a heavy-duty engine is also required and heavy-duty engine required power breaks. So, a sleuth equipped with air conditioning must also be equipped with power brakes.

41. (*a*) Heavy-duty shock absorbers can be chosen without the purchase of additional options.

42. (*e*) If a hatchback is purchased, then sunroof cannot be chosen. Without sunroof, a timed windshield cannot be chosen. So for maximum options a buyer should not purchase a hatchback.

Solution (Q. Nos. 43-45) From the given information, we get the following results.

Days	Bands	Lead vacalists
Monday	Cactus (Rock)	Sid
Tuesday	(Rock)	Meet
Wednesday	Fish (Fusion)	Rupam (male)
Thursday	Engima (Fusion)	Angelina (Female)
Friday	Boom (Rock)	Ali
Saturday	(Fusion)	Bony (Female)
Sunday	Bodhi Tree	

43. (*e*) The Bony was the lead vocalist of Axis, then Meet could not be the lead vocalist of Boom.

44. (*c*) Boom performed on Friday and Meet performed on Tuesday.

45. (*d*) Cactus, Axis, Fish, Engima, Boom, Dhoom.

46. (*c*) As adjacent stripes in the fabric must be of different colours from each other and colour of adjacent stripes must be of different level. So, option (c) is correct because it satisfies all the conditions.

47. (*e*) If lavender is used for the wide stripe, white must be used for the narrow stripe adjacent to the medium width stripe or for the middle of the three narrow stripes.

48. (*a*) Green, white, lavender, brown, orange is the order of colours which the designer can select and this order satisfies all the conditions.

49. (*c*) If green is used for the middle of three narrow strips and for one other stripe. If red and orange are the only other colours used, then the wide strips must be green.

50. (*a*) If atleast two of the stripes will be read and atleast two others will be white, then lavender cannot be used for the wide stripe.

51. (*d*) According to condition IV, Prof. Chakravarty and Prof. Equbal have to be selected, therefore options (a) and (b) cannot be correct. Also, according to condition I, Prof. Ahuja and Sushil have to be together, option (c) cannot be correct.

52. (*d*) In the selection, Prof. Equbal always should be there. So, none of the first three options follow.

53. (*a*) If H and G are sitting in these same car, then B and C are also sitting in the same car.

54. (*d*) If E and A are sitting in the same car, then G is not sitting in the same car.

55. (*a*) Statement I is not necessary.

56. (*c*) We know that if song P is to be played on a day, song V cannot be played.

So, option (a) is incorrect.

If song Q is to be played on a day, T must be one of the songs to be played after Q.

Option (b) is not correct.

The last song to be played on any day must be either S or U. So, Option (d) is not correct.

Option (c) satisfies all the given conditions and hence can be a combination of songs to be played on the first day of the month.

57. (*c*) It is given that R and W are the songs to be played on the first day.

If R is to be played, V must be one of the songs to be played.

Option (a) is not correct.

If Q is one of the songs to be played, T must be one of the songs to be played after Q.

Option (b) is not correct.

The last song to be played on any day must be either S or U.

Option (d) is not correct.

Option (c) satisfies all the conditions and hence can be the combination of remaining songs to be played.

58. (*d*) If any one of the four given statements is true, that particular arrangement has to be invalid either for that day or for the subsequent day. Therefore, if the statement yields a valid combination for two consecutive days, the given statement becomes false. If song P is played at the third place,

Q, T, P, W and U can be one of the combination of songs played.

Then, on the next day R, V, Q, T and U can be the combination of songs played.

∴ Song P can be played at the third place.

∴ Option (a) is false.

If song Q is played at the third place, S, W, Q, T and U can be one of the combination of songs played.

Then, on the next day R, V, S, W and U can be the combination of songs played.

∴ Song Q can be the third place.

∴ Option (b) is false.

If song T is played at the third place, P, Q, T, U, S can be one of the combination of songs played.

On the next day R, V, Q, T and S can be the combination of songs played.

∴ Song T can be played at the third place.

∴ Option (c) is false.

∴ All the statements are false.

59. (*a*) If song R is to be played third in the sequence, then V must be the song to be played fourth and one of S or U must be the songs played fifth.

We know that, if Q is one of the songs to be played then T must be one of the songs to be played after Q.

∴ Q cannot be the second song to be played in that sequence.

60. (*d*) If A is on the team, Y and B cannot be selected as they are not friendly. So, two senior executives X and Z must be selected. As Z and C are not friendly, so the fourth executive must be D.

61. (*d*) Y and C can be selected with X and B. So, statement I is false. Z and B can be selected with X or Y. So, statement II is false, Z and D can be selected with X or Y. So, statement III is false. So, all the three statements are false.

62. (*b*) If Y and Z are selected, then A and C cannot be selected. So the junior executives B and D are selected with the team.

63. (*b*) Y, Z, B and D can form a team. So, statement I is false.

If C is selected, then Z cannot be selected. So, two senior executives X and Y must be selected. So, statement II is true.

If A and C are rejected, then two junior executives B and D can form a team by selecting only two senior executives from X, Y and Z. So, statement III is false.

64. (*c*) On the basis of the information given in the question we can find matching of family with lunch time and meal with the type of crockery as under

Family	Time		
	12:00	1:00	2:00
Sharma	✓	✗	✗
Bannerjee	✗	✗	✓
Pattabhiraman	✗	✓	✗

	Type of Crockery		
Recipe	Blue	White	Red
Brinjal	✓	✗	✗
Sambar	✗	✓	✗
Makkai	✗	✗	✓

Now, on the basis of above matching we conclude that family that eats at 10 O'clock serves fried brinjal, hence Pattabhiraman serves fried brinjal.

The family that eats last like makka-ki-roti, so Bannerjee like makka-ki-roti, hence Sharma eats with sambar. Thus, the matching of family with timing, recipe and crockery is given by

Sharma	12:00	Sambar	White
Pattabhiraman	1:00	Brinjal	Blue
Bannerjee	2:00	Makkai	Red

65. (*b*) If Samuel is telling the truth, then Nagraj fudged the accounts.

66. (*b*) If Panda is lying, then Datta did not fudged the accounts.

67. (*b*) Option (a) is wrong because chaudhury desires either HRM or Finance. Option (c) is wrong because Prof. Fotedar does not want any assignment, if Prof. Das gets one of the five Prof. Option (d) is wrong because Chaudhury desires either HRM or Finance.

68. (*b*) It is given that, if Prof. Banik get one Prof. Das must get other one and Prof. Fotedar does not want any assignment, if Prof. Das gets one of the five. So, Prof. Fotedar does not get any assignment, if Prof. Banik gets one of the five.

69. (*a*) The winning chances of

Option (a) = 653 points, option (b) = 617 points

Option (c) = 644 points, option (d) = 606 points

Option (e) = 631 points.

70. (*c*) The winning chances of option (a) = 643 points

Option (b) = 644 points, option (c) = 653 points

Option (d) = 616 points, option (e) = 638 points

71. (*d*) The winning chances of option (a) = 604 points

Option (b) = 615 points, option (c) = 635 points

Option (d) = 638 points, option (e) = 606 points

Solution (Q. Nos. 72-75)

Stage 1

Because A, B, D and E won atleast one match, hence C and F lost all the three matches.

Because B, D and E lost atleast one match, A won all the three matches in stage 1, there are a total of nine matches and a total of nine wins.

∴ B, D and E won two matches each.

Since, A (the top team of stage 1) did not play against F, A played a match against B, a match again C.

∴ The ninth match is between B and F.

So, the positions of nine matches that have taken place are as follows.

	I	II	III	IV	V	VI	VII	VIII	IX
WON	A	B	A	D	E	A	D	E	B
LOST	D	E	B	C	C	C	F	F	F

Stage 2

As each team played a total of five matches, the matches take place between the two teams as

(AE), (AF), (BC), (BD), (ED) and (CF)

It is given that is Stage 2, three teams lost all the two matches.

It is also given A lost the two matches.

∴ Each of E and F won the two matches.

This implies that C and D lost the two matches. Therefore, B also won the two matches.

72. (*b*) E and F defeated A (the top team in stage 1).

73. (*d*) Only B, E and F won the matches is stage 2.

74. (*e*) D and F won exactly two matches in the event.

75. (*e*) B and E won four matches each which is the highest.

76. (*c*) On the basis of information given, it is clear that there are three children namely Vaibhav, Suprita and Anshuman. From IV and V it is clear that Suprita was born in April, Anshuman in September and Vaibhav in June.

From I we conclude that Vaibhav is 7 yr old.

From II, III and VI it is very clear that Suprita is 4 yr old and Anshuman is the youngest one with age 2 yr.

Hence, option (c) refects the correct information.

Solution (Q. Nos. 77-80)

If we consider first statements made by John to the false, then the yellow ball is in box 2. Therefore, his statement II has to be false. So, the green ball is in box 3. Following this arrangement, we can see that Janardhan's statement I is true and the red ball is in box 1. Also, since the yellow ball is in box 2. Jani's statement I is true and so his second statements is true and statement I is false, which satisfies or required condition.

So, red in box 1, yellow in box 2 and green in box 3 is one probable arrangement.

Now, if we consider the statement I made by John to be true, then yellow ball can be in box 1 or box 3 and the red ball is in box 2 or box 3. This makes Janardhan's statement II true and statement I false, which means that the green ball is in box 2 or box 3. So, the possible combinations are

	Combination 1	Combination 2
Box 1	Yellow	Yellow
Box 2	Red	Green
Box 3	Green	Red

However, for combination 1 both of Janardhan's statements are true and for combination 2, both of Jani's statements are true, which is not possible. So, the only possible combination. is

Box 1	Red
Box 2	Yellow
Box 3	Green

77. (*a*) Box 1 contains the red ball.

78. (*b*) Yellow ball is in box 2.

79. (*c*) If we consider all three friends's statements, we will see that Jani's both statements are false.

80. (*d*) If we consider the I statement I made by Jani to be consider John's I statement I to be false, which mean yellow ball is in box 2 and red ball is in box 1 and green ball is in box 3. which makes Janardhan's I statement true and statement II false. So, this can be one of the combinations.

Now, if we consider John's I statement to be true, which means that yellow ball is in box 1 and red balls in in box 2 or box 3. This makes Janardhan's II statement true and so green ball is in box 2 and red ball in box 3, which is the II combination 2. So, there are two possible combination. Hence, option (d) is correct.

Solution (Q. Nos. 81-84)

	A	B	C	D	E	F	Fince	IT	Operations	Hr	Marketing	General Management	BCA	B.Com	CA	BBM	B.Sc	B. Tech
Radhika	✗	✗	✗	✗	✗	✓	✗	✗	✓	✗	✗	✗	✗	✗	✗	✗	✗	✓
Neha	✗	✗	✗	✗	✓	✗	✗	✗	✗	✓	✗	✗	✗	✗	✗	✓	✗	✗
Rupa	✗	✗	✗	✓	✗	✗	✗	✓	✗	✗	✗	✗	✓	✗	✗	✗	✗	✗
Mahima	✗	✓	✗	✗	✗	✗	✗	✗	✗	✗	✗	✓	✗	✓	✗	✗	✗	✗
Sayali	—	✗	—	✗	✗	✗	✗	✗	✗	✗	✗	✗	✗	✗	✗	✗	✓	✗
Shobha	—	✗	—	✗	✗	✗	✗	✗	✗	✗	✗	✗	✗	✗	✓	✗	✗	✗

81. (*b*) The educational qualification of Mahima is B.Com and the course is General Management.

82. (*a*)

83. (*a*)

84. (*b*)

7

Simple and Coded Inequality

To understand an 'inequality' you should first understand the word 'equality'.

We know that, $2 \times 3 = 6$. In other words, the result of a multiplication between 2 and 3 is equal to 6. Since, they are equal, so it is an equality.

Now, $2 \times 2 \neq 6$. Here, the product of 2 and 2 is not equal to 6. Since, they are not equal, so it is an inequality.

Now, if one thing is not equal to another then there can be only two possibilities that either one thing is greater than or less than the other thing. Mathematically 'greater than' is denoted by '>' and less than is denoted by '<'.

So, $2 \times 2 < 6$ and $3 \times 3 > 6$

Special Situation (Greater than or equal to' and 'Less than or equal to')

Sometimes you may face a situation where you cannot establish inequality between two numbers. e.g. Two numbers a and b are given and it is also given that 'a is not less than b'. In this case 'a' can be either equal to or greater than b. This situation can be represented by the symbol '≥'. Thus, we have '≥' meaning 'greater than or equal to and '≤' meaning less than or equal to

So, $a \geq b$ means *'a'* is either greater than or equal to *b*. $a \leq b$ means *'a'* is either less than or equal to *b*.

Chain of Inequalities

Sometimes you have to combine two or more inequalities to establish a new single inequality with three or more terms.

e.g. $a > b$ and $b > c$. Then, $a > b > c$

We can conclude that $a > c$.

1. Two inequality can be combined if and only if they have a common term. In the above example, 'b' is the common term.
2. Two inequalities can be combined if and only if the common term is greater than one and less than the other term. In the example, 'b' is greater than 'c' while less than 'a'.

Simple Inequality

In this type of inequality certain relations between different sets of elements are given in terms of 'less than', 'greater than' or 'equal to' using the real symbols. The candidate is required to analyse the given statements and then decide which of the relations given as alternatives follow(s) from those given in the statements.

Coded Inequality

Unlike the simple inequality, coded inequality has all the signs (>, <, =, ≥, ≤) in coded form, i.e. substituted symbols are used in place of real symbols, e.g. the sign of greater than (>) can be coded as ϕ/@/*/$ etc. The candidate is required to replace the codes with real signs and then solve the questions in the same way as the questions of simple inequality are solved.

Types of Questions Generally Asked in Examinations

There are multiple types of questions which are asked from this chapter, so it is quite difficult to predict exact type of questions that are asked but on the basis of Observation, Analysis and Experience, here we are giving different types of questions that are usually asked in the examination. Almost all the questions from this chapter can be categorised into these types. Also, this description of type will make your study easy and streamline.

Type 1 Two Conclusion Based

In this type of questions, either the four possible inequalities (>, ≥, ≤, <) and equality (=) between the elements are given directly or are defined by five different symbols taken a set of five questions is asked in which some inequalities are given which are followed by two conclusions. You have to determine which of the conclusion(s) is/are true.

Examples Based on Type 1

Direction (Examples 1-5) *In these questions, relationships between different elements is shown in the statement. The statement is followed by two conclusions. Study the conclusions based on the given statement and select the appropriate answer.* **MHT CET MBA 2014**

Ex 1. **Statements** $K > I \geq T \geq E; O < R < K$

Conclusions I. $R < E$

II. $O < T$

(a) Neither Conclusion I nor II follows
(b) Both Conclusions I and II follow
(c) Only Conclusion II follows
(d) Either Conclusion I or II follows
(e) Only Conclusion I follows

Ex 2. **Statements** $C < L < O = U = D \geq S > Y$

Conclusions I. $O > Y$

II. $D > C$ (because in Sol $C < D$ is given)

(a) Neither Conclusion I nor II follows
(b) Both Conclusions I and II follow
(c) Only Conclusion I follows
(d) Only Conclusion II follows
(e) Either Conclusion I or II follows

Ex 3. **Statements** $K \geq L > M \geq N$

Conclusions I. $N \leq K$

II. $N < K$

(a) Both Conclusions I and II follow
(b) Neither Conclusion I nor II follows
(c) Either Conclusion I or II follows
(d) Only Conclusion I follows
(e) Only Conclusion II follows

Ex 4. **Statements** $Z \geq Y = W \leq X$

Conclusions I. $W < Z$

II. $W = Z$

(a) Only Conclusion II follows
(b) Only Conclusion I follows
(c) Neither Conclusion I nor II follows
(d) Either Conclusion I or II follows
(e) Both Conclusions I and II follow

Ex 5. **Statements** $B > A > S < I > C > L > Y$

Conclusions I. $B > L$

II. $A > Y$

(a) Only Conclusion I follows
(b) Only Conclusion II follows
(c) Either Conclusion I or II follows
(d) Neither Conclusion I nor II follows
(e) Both Conclusions I and II follow

SOLUTION (Examples 1-5)

1. (*a*) **Statements** $K > I \geq T \geq E; O < R < K$

$\Rightarrow O < R < K > I \geq T \geq E$

Conclusions I. $R < E$ (False)

II. $O < T$ (False)

Thus, neither Conclusion I nor Conclusion II follows.

2. (*b*) **Statements** $C < L < O = U = D \geq S > Y$

Conclusions I. $O > Y$ (True)

II. $C < D$ (True)

Thus, both Conclusions I and II follow.

3. (*e*) **Statements** $K \geq L > M \geq N$

Conclusions I. $N \leq K$ (False)

II. $N < K$ (True)

Thus, only Conclusion II follows.

4. (*d*) **Statements** $Z \geq Y = W \leq X$
Conclusions I. $W < Z$ (may be true)
II. $W = Z$ (may be true)
Thus, either Conclusions I or II follows.

5. (*d*) **Statements** $B > A > S < I > C > L > Y$
Conclusions I. $B > L$ (False)
II. $A > Y$ (False)
Thus, neither Conclusions I nor II follows.

Direction (Examples 6-10) *In these questions symbols @, #, $, ★ and % are used with different meaning as follows.* **SBI (PO) 2008**

- 'A @ B' means 'A is not smaller than B'.
- 'A # B' means 'A is neither smaller than nor equal to B'.
- 'A $ B' means 'A is neither greater than nor smaller than B'.
- 'A ★ B' means 'A is not greater than B'.
- 'A % B' means 'A is neither greater than nor equal to B'.

In each of the following questions assuming the given statements to be true, find out which of the two Conclusions I and II given below them is/are definitely true.

Give answer
(a) if only Conclusion I is true
(b) if only Conclusion II is true
(c) if either Conclusion I or II is true
(d) if neither Conclusion I nor II is true
(e) if both Conclusions I and II are true

Ex 6. **Statements** N @ W, W # H, H % T
Conclusions I. H % N II. T # W

Ex 7. **Statements** F # R, H % R, L ★ H
Conclusions I. F # L
II. R @ L

Ex 8. **Statements** J @ K, K % M, M # T
Conclusions I. K % T
II. K @ T

Ex 9. **Statements** V ★ W, W $ H, H @ I
Conclusions I. V ★ I
II. I ★ W

Ex 10. **Statements** L ★ P, P % V, V # D
Conclusions I. L ★ V
II. L $ D

SOLUTION (Examples 6-10) First of all, you should abstract the meaning of given symbols.

A @ B $\Rightarrow A \geq B$
A # B $\Rightarrow A > B$
A $ B $\Rightarrow A = B$
A ★ B $\Rightarrow A \leq B$
A % B $\Rightarrow A < B$

6. (*a*) N @ W $\Rightarrow N \geq W$; W # H $\Rightarrow W > H$; H % T $\Rightarrow H < T$
$\therefore N \geq W > H < T$
Conclusions I. H % N $\Rightarrow H < N$ (True)
II. T # W $\Rightarrow T > W$ (False)
Only Conclusion I is true. So, the correct answer is (a).

7. (*a*) F # R $\Rightarrow F > R$; H % R $\Rightarrow H < R$; L ★ H $\Rightarrow L \leq H$
$\therefore F > R > H \geq L$
Conclusions I. F # L $\Rightarrow F > L$ (True)
II. R @ L $\Rightarrow R \geq L$ (False)
Only Conclusion I is true. So, the correct answer is (a).

8. (*c*) J @ K $\Rightarrow J \geq K$; K % M $\Rightarrow K < M$; M # T $\Rightarrow M > T$
$\therefore J \geq K < M > T$
Conclusions I. K % T $\Rightarrow K < T$ (may be true)
II. K @ T $\Rightarrow K \geq T$ (may be true)
Either I or II is true. So, the correct answer is (c).

9. (*b*) V ★ W $\Rightarrow V \leq W$; W $ H $\Rightarrow W = H$; H @ I $\Rightarrow H \geq I$
$\therefore V \leq W = H \geq I$
Conclusions I. V ★ I $\Rightarrow V \leq I$ (False)
II. I ★ W $\Rightarrow I \leq W$ (True)
Only Conclusion II is true. So, the correct answer is (b).

10. (*d*) L ★ P $\Rightarrow L \leq P$; P % V $\Rightarrow P < V$; V # D $\Rightarrow V > D$
$\therefore L \leq P < V > D$
Conclusions I. L ★ V $\Rightarrow L \leq V$ (False)
II. L $ D $\Rightarrow L = D$ (False)
Neither Conclusion I nor II is true.
So, the correct answer is (d).

Intro Exercise 1 (Based on Type 1)

Direction (Q. Nos. 1-5) *In the following questions, the symbols @, #, $, % and & are used with different meanings as follows.*

- 'P @ Q' means 'P is neither smaller than nor equal to Q'.
- 'P # Q' means 'P is not greater than Q'.
- 'P $ Q' means 'P is not smaller than Q'.
- 'P % Q' means 'P is neither greater than nor smaller than Q'.
- 'P & Q' means 'P is neither greater than nor equal to Q'.

In each of the following questions assuming the given statements to be true, find out which of the two Conclusions I and II given below is/are definitely true.

Give answer

(a) if only Conclusion I is true
(b) if only Conclusion II is true
(c) if either Conclusion I or II is true
(d) if neither Conclusion I nor II is true
(e) if both Conclusions I and II are true

1. Statements G # H, H $ K, K @ M
Conclusions I. M # G II. G & M

2. Statements F $ D, H # M, M % D
Conclusions I. F $ H II. F @ H

3. Statements R & M, M # L, L $ Q
Conclusions I. M % Q
II. M @ Q

4. Statements F # R, Q $ R, Q & M
Conclusions I. F # Q
II. R & M

5. Statements D & T, R # T, R $ M
Conclusions I. M & T
II. M % T

Direction (Q. Nos. 6-10) *In these questions, relationship between different elements is shown in the statements. These statements are followed by two conclusions. Study the conclusions based on the given statement and select the appropriate answer.*

Give answer **SBI Associate (PO) 2014**

(a) if only Conclusion I is true
(b) if only Conclusion II is true
(c) if neither Conclusion I nor II is true
(d) if either Conclusion I or II is true
(e) if both Conclusions I and II are true

6. Statements $A < B \le C = D, K \ge J > C$
Conclusions I. $C < K$
II. $B \le D$

7. Statements $A < B \le C = D, K \ge J > C$
Conclusions I. $A \ge J$
II. $K > B$

8. Statements $B \ge L > A \ge N < K$
Conclusions I. $B > N$
II. $K < B$

9. Statements $B \ge L > A \ge N < K$
Conclusions I. $L > N$
II. $L = N$

10. Statements $A > B > C \le D = E \le F$
Conclusions I. $C < F$
II. $C = F$

Direction (Q. Nos. 11-15) *In these questions, relationship between different elements is shown in the statements. These statements are followed by two conclusions.* **IBPS (PO) 2011**

Give answer

(a) if only Conclusion I follows
(b) if only Conclusion II follows
(c) if either Conclusion I or II follows
(d) if neither Conclusion I nor II follows
(e) if both Conclusions I and II follow

11. Statements $A = B \ge C < D = E \le F$
Conclusions I. $F > B$
II. $B \ge D$

12. Statements $P > M > Q, Q > Z > N$
Conclusions I. $M \ge Z$
II. $N < P$

13. Statements $X > Y, Y \ge Z, Z = V, V < W$
Conclusions I. $Y = V$ II. $Y > V$

14. Statements $D > B, C > K, K \le N, B < C, N < B$
Conclusions I. $D > N$
II. $C \ge K$

15. Statements $B < C, D > B, C > K, K \le N, N < B$
Conclusions I. $C > N$
II. $B > K$

Direction (Q. Nos. 16-20) *In the questions given below, certain symbols are used with the following meanings.*

- 'P $ Q' means 'P is neither equal to nor smaller than Q.'
- 'P © Q' means 'P is not smaller than Q.'
- 'P ★ Q' means 'P is neither greater nor smaller than Q.'
- 'P # Q' means 'P is neither greater than nor equal to Q.'
- 'P @ Q' means 'P is not greater than Q.'

Now, in each of the following questions, assuming the given statements to be true, find which of the two conclusions I and II given below them is/are definitely true

Give answer

(a) if only Conclusion I is true
(b) if only Conclusion II is true
(c) if either Conclusion I or II is true
(d) if neither Conclusion I nor II is true
(e) if both Conclusions I and II are true

16. Statements M # K, K ★ D, D @ P
Conclusions I. M @ P II. M ★ P

17. Statements W © T, T $ M, B # M
Conclusions I. W $ B II. M # W

18. Statements H ★ D, D # R, R © N
Conclusions I. N ★ H II. N $ H

19. Statements Z @ R, R © D, D # T
Conclusions I. D # Z II. Z # T

20. Statements Q # P, P @ F, F ★ M
Conclusions I. M $ P II. P ★ M

Direction (Q. Nos. 21-25) *In the questions given below, certain symbols are used with the followings.*

- 'A @ B' means 'A is greater than B.'
- 'A ★ B' means 'A is either greater than or equal to B.'
- 'A # B' means 'A is equal to B.'
- 'A $ B' means 'A is either smaller than or equal to B.'
- 'A + B' means 'A is smaller than B.'

Now, in each of the following questions, assuming the given statements to be true, find which of the two Conclusions I and II given below them is/are definitely true?

Give answer

(a) if only Conclusion I is true
(b) if only Conclusion II is true
(c) if either Conclusion I or II is true
(d) if neither Conclusion I nor II is true
(e) if both Conclusions I and II are true

21. Statements B + D; E $ T; T ★ P; P @ B
Conclusions I. P $ D II. P @ D

22. Statements E ★ F; G $ H; H # E; G @ K
Conclusions I. H @ K
II. H ★ F

23. Statements P $ Q; N # M; M @ R; R ★ P
Conclusions I. P + N
II. Q $ M

24. Statements D + T; E $ V; F ★ T; E @ D
Conclusions I. D $ V
II. D + F

25. Statements T ★ U; U $ W; V @ L; W + V
Conclusions I. V @ T
II. L # W

Direction (Q. Nos. 26-30) *In the following questions, the symbols ★, @, #, & and % are used with the following meaning as illustrated below.* **IBPS (Clerk) 2011**

- 'A @ B' means 'A is greater than B'.
- 'A % B' means 'A is equal to B'.
- 'A # B' means 'A is either equal to or smaller than B'.
- A & B means 'A is either equal to or greater than B.
- 'A ★ B' means 'A is smaller than B'.

Now, in each of the following questions assuming the given statements to be true. Find which of the two Conclusions I and II given below them is/are definitely true?

Give answer

(a) if only Conclusions I is true
(b) if only Conclusions II is true
(c) if either Conclusions I or II is true
(d) if neither Conclusions I nor II is true
(e) if both Conclusions I and II are true

26. Statements S % A, A & D, D ★ J
Conclusions I. D # S
II. A ★ J

27. Statements Q @ F, F % C, N ★ C
Conclusions I. Q @ C
II. F ★ N

28. Statements R & P, P ★ K, K ★ F
Conclusions I. R @ F
II. P ★ F

29. Statements M & F, F ★ C, C % K
Conclusions I. M @ C
II. F ★ K

30. Statements P & T, T ★ R, R # B
Conclusions I. P @ T
II. B & T

Direction (Q. Nos. 31-35) *In the following questions, the symbols ©, δ, $, ★ and % are used with the following meaning as illustrated below* **IBPS (Clerk) 2011**

- 'A δ B' means 'A is not greater than B'
- 'A © B' means 'A is neither greater than nor smaller than B'.
- 'A ★ B' means 'A is smaller than B'.
- 'A % B' means 'A is not smaller than B'
- 'A $ B' means 'A is greater than B'.

Now, in each of the following questions assuming the given statements to be true, find which of the two Conclusions I and II given below them is/are definitely true?

Give answer

(a) if only Conclusion I is true
(b) if only Conclusion II is true
(c) if either Conclusion I or II is true
(d) if neither Conclusion I nor II is true
(e) if both Conclusion I and II are true

31. Statements R $ J, J % M, M © K
Conclusions I. K © J II. K ★ J

32. Statements D δ R, M $ R, M © F
Conclusions I. F $ D II. F $ R

33. Statements H © F, F $ R, R ★ K
Conclusions I. R ★ H II. K $ F

34. Statements B % D, D ★ T, T δ R
Conclusions I. B $ T
II. R $ D

35. Statements M % N, N ★ A, A $ B
Conclusions I. B ★ N
II. A $ M

Type 2 Three/Four Conclusions Based

In this type of questions all the four possible inequalities (>, ≥, ≤, <) and equality (=) are defined by five different symbols, then a set of five questions is asked in which three or four inequalities are given which are followed by three or four conclusions. You have to determine that which of the conclusion(s) is/are true.

Examples Based on Type 2

Direction (Examples 1-5) *In the following questions, the symbols δ, #, %, @ and ★ are used with the following meaning as illustrated below* **RBI Officer Grade 2013**

- 'P # Q' means 'P is neither greater than nor smaller than Q'.
- 'P @ Q' means 'P is neither smaller than nor equal to Q'.
- 'P % Q' means 'P is neither greater than nor equal to Q'.
- 'P δ Q' means 'P is not smaller than Q'.
- 'P ★ Q' means 'P is not greater than Q'.

Now, in each of the following questions assuming the given statements to be true, find which of the three Conclusions I, II and III given below them is/are definitely true and give your answer accordingly.

Ex **1. Statements** D % F, F @ H, H ★ N
Conclusions I. N @ F II. D % N
III. H % D

(a) None is true
(b) Only I is true
(c) Only II is true
(d) Only III is true
(e) I and II are true

Ex **2. Statements** B δ D, D % T, T ★ M
Conclusions I. B @ T II. M @ D
III. B @ M

(a) Only I is true
(b) Only II is true
(c) Only III is true
(d) II and III are true
(e) None of these

Ex **3. Statements** K # W, M @ W, R δ M
Conclusions I. K % M II. W % R
III. R @ K

(a) I and II are true
(b) I and III are true
(c) II and III are true
(d) I, II and III are true
(e) None of these

Ex **4. Statements** M @ K, K δ T, T # J
Conclusions I. J # K II. M @ J
III. J % K

(a) Only I is true
(b) Only II is true
(c) Only III is true
(d) Either I or III is true
(e) Either I or III and II are true

Ex **5. Statements** R ★ N, N % B, B # T
Conclusions I. B @ R II. T @ N
III. R % T

(a) I and II are true
(b) I and III are true
(c) II and III are true
(d) I, II and III are true
(e) None of these

SOLUTION (Examples 1-5) *First of all, you should abstract the meaning of given symbols.*

$\# \Rightarrow =$	$\delta \Rightarrow \geq$	$@ \Rightarrow >$
$\bigstar \Rightarrow \leq$	$\% \Rightarrow <$	

1. (*a*) $D \% F \Rightarrow D < F$

$F @ H \Rightarrow F > H$

$H \bigstar N \Rightarrow H \leq N$

Therefore, $D < F > H \leq N$

Conclusions I. $N @ F \Rightarrow N > F$ (False)

II. $D \% N \Rightarrow D < N$ (False)

III. $H \% D \Rightarrow H < D$ (False)

None of conclusions true.

2. (*b*) $B \delta D \Rightarrow B \geq D$

$D \% T \Rightarrow D < T$

$T \bigstar M \Rightarrow T \leq M$

Therefore, $B \geq D < T \leq M$

Conclusions I. $B @ T \Rightarrow B > T$ (False)

II. $M @ D \Rightarrow M > D$ (True)

III. $B @ M \Rightarrow B > M$ (False)

Only Conclusion II is true.

3. (*d*) $K \# W \Rightarrow K = W$; $M @ W \Rightarrow M > W$; $R \delta M \Rightarrow R \geq M$

Therefore, $K = W < M \leq R$

Conclusions I. $K \% M \Rightarrow K < M$ (True)

II. $W \% R \Rightarrow W < R$ (True)

III. $R @ K \Rightarrow R > K$ (True)

All conclusions are true.

4. (*e*) $M @ K \Rightarrow M > K$

$K \delta T \Rightarrow K \geq T$

$T \# J \Rightarrow T = J$

Therefore, $M > K \geq T = J$

Conclusions I. $J \# K \Rightarrow J = K$ (may be true)

II. $M @ J \Rightarrow M > J$ (True)

III. $J \% K \Rightarrow J < K$ (may be true)

Therefore, either Conclusions I or III and II are true.

5. (*d*) $R \bigstar N \Rightarrow R \leq N$

$N \% B \Rightarrow N < B$

$B \# T \Rightarrow B = T$

Therefore, $R \leq N < B = T$

Conclusions I. $B @ R \Rightarrow B > R$ (True)

II. $T @ N \Rightarrow T > N$ (True)

III. $R \% T \Rightarrow R < T$ (True)

All Conclusions are true.

Intro Exercise 2 (Based on Type 2)

Direction (Q. Nos. 1-6) *In the following questions, the symbols δ, ★, %, @ and © are used with the following meaning as illustrated below.* **IOB (PO) 2010**

- 'P ★ Q' means 'P is not greater than Q'.
- 'P @ Q' means 'P is neither greater than nor equal to Q'.
- 'P © Q' means 'P is not smaller than Q'.
- 'P % Q' means 'P is neither smaller than nor greater than Q'.
- 'P δ Q' means 'P is neither smaller than nor equal to Q'.

Now, in each of the following questions assuming the given statements to be true, find which of the three Conclusions I, II and III given below them is/are definitely true and give your answer accordingly.

1. Statements R © K, K δ M, M ★ J

Conclusions I. J δ K II. M @ R

III. M % R

(a) None is true (b) Only I is true

(c) Only II is true (d) Either II or III is true

(e) Only III is true

2. Statements W © K, K δ R, R % N

Conclusions I. N @ K II. R @ W

III. W δ N

(a) I and II are true (b) Either II or III true

(c) II and III are true (d) I and III are true

(e) All of these

3. Statements D @ K, K % F, F © B

Conclusions I. F δ D II. B @ k

III. B % K

(a) Only I is true (b) Only II is true

(c) Only III is true (d) Either II or III is true

(e) Either II or III and I are true.

4. Statements R δ B, B © N, N @ T

Conclusions I. N @ R

II. T δ B

III. T δ R

(a) None is true (b) Only I is true

(c) Only II is true (d) Only III is true

(e) I and II are true

5. Statements H ★ W, W @ N, N % R

Conclusions I. R δ W

II. N δ W

III. H @ R

(a) I and II are true

(b) II and III are true

(c) I and III are true

(d) All of the above

(e) None of the above

6. **Statements** Z % M, M ★ F, F δ D
   Conclusions I. F % Z II. F δ Z
   III. D @ Z
   (a) Only I is true (b) Either I or II is true
   (c) Only II is true (d) Only III is true
   (e) None of these

Direction (Q. Nos. 7-11) *In the following questions, the symbols @, ©, #, $ and % are used with the following meanings.* **IRMA 2009**

- 'P @ Q' means 'P is neither smaller than nor equal to Q'.
- 'P © Q' means 'P is not greater than Q'.
- 'P # Q' means 'P is neither greater than nor equal to Q'.
- 'P $ Q' means 'P is neither greater than nor smaller than Q'.
- 'P % Q' means 'P is not smaller than Q'.

Now, in each of the following questions assuming the given statements to be true, find which of the three Conclusions I, II and III given below is/are definitely true and mark your answer accordingly.

7. **Statements** L @ W, M # W, M % J
   Conclusions I. M © L
   II. W % J
   III. L @ J
   (a) None follows (b) Only I follows
   (c) II and III follow (d) Only III follows
   (e) None of these

8. **Statements** N © B, B $ T, T # S
   Conclusions I. N # S
   II. S @ B
   III. T % N
   (a) None follows (b) I and II follow
   (c) I and III follow (d) II and III follow
   (e) All follow

9. **Statements** G @ H, H % K, K # D
   Conclusions I. D $ H
   II. D # H
   III. D % H
   (a) Only I follows (b) Only II follows
   (c) Either II or III follows (d) Only III follows
   (e) Neither II nor III follows

10. **Statements** F # D, D © K, R @ K
    Conclusions I. F # K II. R % D
    III. R @ F
    (a) I and II follow (b) I and either II or III follow
    (c) Either II or III follows (d) I and III follow
    (e) All of these

11. **Statements** H © B, B $ A, A # C
    Conclusions I. A % H II. C # H
    III. H # A
    (a) I and II follow (b) I and III follow
    (c) Either I or III follows (d) II and III follow
    (e) None of these

Direction (Q. Nos. 12-16) *In the following questions, the symbols @, ©, %, $ and ★ are used with the following meanings illustrated.* **Allahabad Bank (PO) 2010**

- 'P © Q' means 'P is not greater than Q'.
- 'P ★ Q' means 'P is not smaller than Q'.
- 'P % Q' means 'P is neither greater than nor equal to Q'.
- 'P $ Q' means 'P is neither smaller than nor equal to Q'.
- 'P @ Q' means 'P is neither greater than nor smaller than Q'.

Now, in each of the following questions assuming the given statements to be true, find out which of the three Conclusions I, II and III given below them is/are definitely true.

12. **Statements** J $ D, D © K, K % R
    Conclusions I. R $ J II. R $ D
    III. K $ J
    (a) None is true (b) Only I is true
    (c) Only II is true (d) Only III is true
    (e) II and III are true

13. **Statements** M ★ K, K @ R, R % N
    Conclusions I. R % M II. R @ M
    III. N $ K
    (a) Only I is true
    (b) Only II is true
    (c) Only III is true
    (d) Either I or II is true
    (e) Either I or II and III are true

14. **Statements** B % H, H $ J, J ★ M
    Conclusions I. B % J II. M % B
    III. H $ M
    (a) None is true
    (b) Only I is true
    (c) Only II is true
    (d) Only III is true
    (e) II and III are true

15. **Statements** Z © K, K % E, E @ R
    Conclusions I. R $ K
    II. Z % E
    III. R $ Z
    (a) Only I is true
    (b) I and II are true
    (c) I and III are true
    (d) II and III are true
    (e) I, II and III are true

16. **Statements** W @ M, M © R, R $ F
    Conclusions I. F % M
    II. R ★ W
    III. W % F
    (a) None is true
    (b) Only I is true
    (c) Only II is true
    (d) Only III is true
    (e) I and II are true

Direction (Q. Nos. 17-23) *In the following questions, the symbols @, $, %, © and ★ are used with the following meaning as illustrated below.*

Corporation Bank (PO) 2009

- 'P % Q' means 'P is neither greater than nor smaller than Q'.
- 'P $ Q' means 'P is neither smaller than nor equal to Q'.
- 'P © Q' means 'P is neither greater than nor equal to Q'.
- 'P ★ Q' means 'P is not greater than Q'.
- 'P @ Q' means 'P is not smaller than Q'.

Now, in each of the following questions assuming the given statements to be true, find which of the three Conclusions I, II and III given below is/are definitely true and give your answer accordingly.

17. Statements V © K, K @ B, B $ M

Conclusions I. V © B II. M © K III. M © V

(a) None is true (b) Only I is true (c) Only II is true (d) Only III is true (e) II and III are true

18. Statements D ★ R, R % F, F $ T

Conclusions I. F % D II. F $ D III. T © R

(a) Only I is true (b) Only II is true (c) Only III is true (d) Either I or II is true (e) Either I or II and III are true

19. Statements N @ D, D ★ K, K $ A

Conclusions I. K @ N II. A © D III. N $ A

(a) None is true (b) Only I is true (c) I and II are true (d) I and III are true (e) All are true

20. Statements K @ T, T $ N, N © R

Conclusions I. R $ K II. N ★ K III. K $ N

(a) None is true (b) Only I is true (c) Only II is true (d) Only III is true (e) All are true

21. Statements W % K, K © F, D $ F

Conclusions I. D $ K II. D $ W III. F @ W

(a) I and III are true (b) I and II are true (c) II and III are true (d) All are true (e) None of these

22. Statements B ★ K, K © F, F % R

Conclusions I. R $ K II. R $ B III. F $ B

(a) I and II are true (b) I and III are true (c) II and III are true (d) All are true (e) None of these

23. Statements H $ M, M % D, D @ K

Conclusions I. H $ D II. K ★ M III. K © H

(a) Only II is true (b) II and III are true (c) I and III are true (d) I and II are true (e) All are true

Direction (Q. Nos. 24-28) *In the following questions, the symbols δ, @, ©, % and ★ are used with the following meanings as illustrated below.*

SBI Associate (PO) 2010

- 'P © Q' means 'P is not smaller than Q.'
- 'P % Q' means 'P is neither smaller than nor equal to Q.'
- 'P ★ Q' means 'P is neither greater than nor equal to Q.'
- 'P δ Q' means 'P is not greater than Q.'
- 'P @ Q' means 'P is neither greater than nor smaller than Q.'

Now, in each of the following questions assuming the given statements to be true, find with of the four Conclusions I, II, III and IV given below them is/are definitely true and give your answer accordingly.

24. Statements D δ T, T @ R, R © M, M % K

Conclusions I. R @ D II. R % D III. K ★ T IV. M δ T

(a) Either I or II is true
(b) III and IV are true
(c) Either I or II and III are true
(d) Either I or II and IV are true
(e) Either I or II and III and IV are true

25. Statements J @ F, F δ N, N % H, H © G

Conclusions I. G ★ N II. N © J III. F ★ J IV. J δ G

(a) I and II are true (b) I, II and III are true (c) II, III and IV are true (d) All are true (e) None of these

26. Statements R ★ K, K % D, D @ V, V δ M

Conclusions I. R ★ D II. V ★ R III. D @ M IV. M % D

(a) None is true (b) Only III is true (c) Only IV is true (d) Either III or IV is true (e) Either III or IV and II are true

27. Statements B © T, T ★ R, R % F, F @ K

Conclusions I. B % R II. F ★ T III. R % K IV. K ★ T

(a) None is true (b) Only I is true (c) Only II is true (d) Only III is true (e) Only IV is true

28. Statements F % N, N © W, W δ Y, Y ★ T

Conclusions I. F % W II. T % N III. N % Y IV. T % W

(a) I and III are true (b) I and IV are true (c) I, II and IV are true (d) I, II and III are true (e) None of the above

Cumulative Exercise

Base Level

Direction (Q. Nos. 1-6) *In each of the following questions assuming the given statements to be true, find out which of the two conclusions I and II given below them is/are definitely true.*

New India Assurance Co. Ltd. (AO) 2015

Give answer

(a) if only Conclusion I is true
(b) if only Conclusion II is true
(c) if either Conclusion I or II is true
(d) if neither Conclusion I nor II is true
(e) if both Conclusions I and II are true

1. Statements $R \geq W, W < F, F = Z$
Conclusions I. $F < R$ II. $Z < W$

2. Statements $B > K, K \geq J, J < M$
Conclusions I. $J < B$ II. $M > B$

3. Statements $D = T, T \leq H, H > N$
Conclusions I. $H \leq D$ II. $H > D$

4. Statements $H \leq N, N < K, K \leq D$
Conclusions I. $D > N$ II. $H < K$

5. Statements $W \geq E, E > K, K = J$
Conclusions I. $J \leq E$ II. $W \geq K$

6. Statements $R < M, M = B, B \geq T$
Conclusions I. $R < T$
II. $T \leq M$

Direction (Q. Nos. 7-11) *In these questions, relationship between different elements is shown in the statements. The statements are followed by conclusions.*

Give answer **RGB (PO) 2011**

(a) if only Conclusion I is true
(b) if only Conclusion II is true
(c) if either Conclusion I or II is true
(d) if neither Conclusion I nor II is true
(e) if both Conclusions I and II are true

7. Statements $F \geq G = H; G > J \geq K$
Conclusions I. $F \geq K$
II. $K < H$

8. Statements $P < Q = R \geq S \geq T$
Conclusions I. $T \leq Q$ II. $R > P$

9. Statements $A \leq B < C; A \geq D; C \leq F$
Conclusions I. $D < C$ II. $F \geq D$

10. Statements $U > A = I \leq O < E$
Conclusions I. $I \leq E$ II. $O > U$

11. Statements $L = M \geq N; M > P; L < K$
Conclusions I. $K > P$ II. $N < K$

Direction (Q. Nos. 12-16) *In the following questions, the symbols δ, %, \$, # and @ are used with the following meaning as illustrated below.*

- 'P \$ Q' means 'P is not smaller than Q'.
- 'P @ Q' means 'P is not greater than Q'.
- 'P δ Q' means 'P is neither smaller than nor equal to Q'.
- 'P # Q' means 'P is neither greater than nor equal to Q'.
- 'P % Q' means 'P is neither smaller than nor greater than Q'.

Now, in each of the following questions, assuming the given statements to be true, find which of the two Conclusions I and II given below them is/are definitely true?

Give answer

(a) if only Conclusion I is true
(b) if only Conclusion II is true
(c) if either Conclusion I or II is true
(d) if neither Conclusion I nor II is true
(e) if both Conclusions I and II are true

12. Statements F @ N, N δ R, H @ R
Conclusions I. H δ N II. F # R

13. Statements M # T, T @ K, K \$ N
Conclusions I. M # N
II. K δ M

14. Statements T % H, H \$ W
Conclusions I. W # T
II. W % T

15. Statements N δ K, K # D, D % M
Conclusions I. M δ K
II. D δ N

16. Statements J \$ B, B % R, R δ F
Conclusions I. F # B
II. R @ J

Direction (Q. Nos. 17-21) *In these questions, relationship between different elements is shown in the **statements**. These statements are followed by two conclusions.* **CBI (Clerk) 2010**

Give answer
(a) if only Conclusion I follows
(b) if only Conclusion II follows
(c) if either Conclusion I or II follows
(d) if neither Conclusion I nor II follows
(e) if both Conclusions I and II follow

17. Statements $N = P, P \leq F, F \geq L, L = K$
Conclusions I. $F = K$
II. $F > K$

18. Statements $Z > T, T < M, M < J$
Conclusions I. $T < J$
II. $J < Z$

19. Statements $Q = Z, C \geq G, G \geq Q, Q \geq R, J \geq C$
Conclusions I. $G \geq Z$
II. $C \geq R$

20. Statements $A > B > C, D > E > F, D > C$
Conclusions I. $E > C$
II. $F > B$

21. Statements $K < L, K > M, M \geq N, N > O$
Conclusions I. $O < M$
II. $O < K$

Direction (Q. Nos. 22-26) *In the following questions, the symbols @, ©, \$, % and ★ are used with the following meanings as illustrated below.* **Andhra Bank (Clerk) 2009**

- 'P © Q' means 'P is not greater than Q'.
- 'P % Q' means 'P is not smaller than Q'.
- 'P ★ Q' means 'P is neither smaller than nor equal to Q'.
- 'P @ Q' means 'P is neither greater than nor equal to Q.'
- 'P \$ Q' means 'P is neither greater than nor smaller than Q'.

Now, in each of the following questions, assuming the given statements to be true, find which of the two Conclusions I and II given below them is /are definitely true.

Give answer
(a) if only Conclusion I is true
(b) if only Conclusion II is true
(c) if either Conclusion I or II is true
(d) if neither Conclusion I nor II is true
(e) if both Conclusions I and II are true

22. Statements K @ V, V © N, N % F
Conclusions I. F @ V II. K @ N

23. Statements H © W, W \$ M, M @ B
Conclusions I. B ★ H
II. M % H

24. Statements D % B, B ★ T, T \$ M
Conclusions I. T © D
II. M © D

25. Statements M ★ T, T @ K, K © N
Conclusions I. N ★ T
II. N ★ M

26. Statements R \$ J, J % D, D ★ F
Conclusions I. D \$ R
II. D @ R

Direction (Q. Nos. 27-33) *In these questions, relationship between different elements is shown in the statements. The statements are followed by conclusions.*

Give answer **MHT CET MBA 2012**
(a) if only Conclusion I is true
(b) if only Conclusion II is true
(c) if either Conclusion I or II is true
(d) if neither Conclusion I nor II is true
(e) if both Conclusions I and II are true

Statements (Q. Nos. 27-28)

$P \geq Q < T$
$R < Q \geq S$
$V \geq T$

27. Conclusions I. $R \leq P$
II. $S < V$

28. Conclusions I. $S \leq P$
II. $V > R$

Statements (Q. Nos. 29-33)

$H < I \leq J, R \geq I > A$

29. Conclusions I. $H < R$
II. $A > H$

30. Conclusions I. $J > R$
II. $J > A$

31. Statements $J = K \geq L \leq M, K < S, J > T$
Conclusions I. $L < S$
II. $M > T$

32. Statements $P < R \geq I = C, L > E \geq R$
Conclusions I. $E > C$
II. $C = E$

33. Statements $B \leq C = D > E, F > C$
Conclusions I. $F \geq B$
II. $C \geq E$

Direction (Q. Nos. 34-38) *In all the questions that follow, different symbols have been used with different meanings. For each set of questions you have to assume given statements to be true and then decide which of the two conclusions is/are definitely true.* **IOB (Clerk) 2010**

The symbols +, −, ×, ÷ and = are used with the following meanings :

- 'P + Q' means 'P is greater than Q'.
- 'P − Q' means 'P is greater than or equal to Q'.
- 'P × Q' means 'P is equal to Q'.
- 'P ÷ Q' means 'P is smaller than Q'.
- 'P = Q' means 'P is either smaller than or equal to Q'.

Give answer

(a) if only Conclusion I is true
(b) if only Conclusion II is true
(c) if either Conclusion I or II is true
(d) if both are true
(e) if neither Conclusion I nor II is true

34. Statements M × X, L ÷ O, N + M, L = X
Conclusions I. N + L II. X ÷ O

35. Statements S = F, K ÷ S, B × K, R + B
Conclusions I. F + K II. K ÷ R

36. Statements H = V, A × Z, H − Z, F + V
Conclusions I. A × H II. H + A

37. Statements I + O, R − I, Z × R, J ÷ Z
Conclusions I. Z × I II. Z + I

38. Statements Q ÷ R, C + D, F − R, D × F
Conclusions I. Q ÷ C II. C + F

Direction (Q. Nos. 39-43) *In the following questions, the symbols δ, %, ★, $ and © are used with the following meaning as illustrated below.*

- 'P % Q' means 'P is not smaller than Q'.
- 'P ★ Q' means 'P is neither greater than nor equal to Q'.
- 'P δ Q' means 'P is neither smaller than nor equal to Q'.
- 'P $ Q' means 'P is neither greater than nor smaller than Q'.
- 'P © Q' means 'P is not greater than Q'. **IBPS (Clerk) 2011**

Now, in each of the following questions assuming the given statements to be true, find which of the two Conclusions I and II given below them is/are definitely true?

Give answer

(a) if only Conclusion I is true
(b) if only Conclusion II is true
(c) if either Conclusion I or II is true
(d) if neither Conclusion I nor II is true
(e) if both Conclusions I and II are true

39. Statements D $ T, T % M, M ★ J
Conclusions I. J δ D II. M © D

40. Statements B ★ K, K $N, N % R
Conclusions I. R $ K
II. R ★ K

41. Statements H % F, F ★ W, W $ E
Conclusions I. E δ F II. H δ W

42. Statements Z δ D, D © K, K δ M
Conclusions I. M ★ D II. Z δ K

43. Statements W © B, N δ B, N © F
Conclusions I. F δ B II. W ★ N

Direction (Q. Nos. 44-46) *In each of the following questions, relationship between different elements is shown in the statements. These statements are followed by two conclusions.*

Give answer

(a) if only Conclusion I follows
(b) if only Conclusion II follows
(c) if either Conclusion I or II follows
(d) if neither Conclusion I nor II follows
(e) if both Conclusions I and II follow

44. Statements $P \geq Q = R, Q > S > T$
Conclusions I. $P \geq T$ II. $T < Q$

45. Statements $A \leq B = C, D > C = E$
Conclusions I. $E \geq A$ II. $A < D$

46. Statements $F \leq G = H, G > J \geq K$
Conclusions I. $F \geq K$ II. $K < H$

47. In which of the following expressions does the expression $M > R$ does not hold true?

(a) $M = P > Q > R$ (b) $M > P \geq Q = R$
(c) $R = P < Q < M$ (d) $R < Q \leq P = M$
(e) $M = P < Q = R$

48. Which of the following expression will be true if given expression $K \geq G > H \leq F$ is definitely true?

(a) $F \geq K$ (b) $H < K$ (c) $F < G$ (d) $K \geq H$
(e) None of these

Direction (Q. Nos. 49-51) *In each of these questions, relationship between different elements is shown in the statements. The statements are followed by two conclusions.* **IBPS (PO) 2012**

Give answer

(a) if only Conclusion I is true
(b) if only Conclusion II is true
(c) if either Conclusion I or II is true
(d) if neither Conclusion I nor II is true
(e) if both the Conclusions I and II are true

49. Statements $P > R, R < S \leq X, Y = X$
Conclusions I. $P < S$ II. $Y > R$

50. Statements $Z = C, B < A = N, C < B$
Conclusions I. $Z < B$ II. $N > Z$

51. Statements $T < V = W, X \geq Y, W > X$
Conclusions I. $V > Y$ II. $V < X$

Direction (Q. Nos. 52-55) *In each of these questions, relationship between different elements is shown in the statements. The statements are followed by two conclusions.* **IBPS (PO) 2012**

Give answer

(a) if only Conclusion I is true
(b) if only Conclusion II is true
(c) if either Conclusion I or II is true
(d) if neither Conclusion I nor II is true
(e) if both the Conclusions I and II are true

Statements (Q. Nos. 52-53)

$A > B = C, E = F, E \geq D > C$

52. Conclusions I. $B < E$ II. $F < B$

53. Conclusions I. $C < F$ II. $A > C$

Statements (Q. Nos. 54-55)

$I \leq J, K < L > M, J = K, G \geq H = I$

54. Conclusions I. $H < J$ II. $J < G$

55. Conclusions I. $L > J$ II. $J < M$

Advanced Level

Direction (Q. Nos. 1-5) *In the following questions, the symbols @, #, %, ★ and $ are used according to following meaning.*

- 'P @ Q' means 'P is not smaller than Q'.
- 'P # Q' means 'P is not greater than Q'.
- 'P % Q' means 'P is neither greater nor equal to Q'.
- 'P ★ Q' means 'P is neither smaller nor greater than Q'.
- 'P $ Q' means 'P is neither smaller nor equal to Q'.

Now, according to the following statement, if they are true, judge their Conclusion I, II and III follow definitely true.

1. Statements M % R, R # T, T ★ N

Conclusions I. N ★ R II. N $ R III. N $ M

(a) All are true
(b) Either I or II is true
(c) Either I or II and III are true
(d) Either I or III and II are true
(e) None of the above

2. Statements J # N, K @ N, T $ K

Conclusions I. J % T II. T $ N III. N @ J

(a) None is true
(b) I and II are true
(c) II and III are true
(d) I and III are true
(e) All are true

3. Statements B ★ D, D @ H, H % F

Conclusions I. B ★ F II. B $ F III. D $ F

(a) None is true
(b) Either I or II is true
(c) Either I or II and III are true
(d) Only III is true
(e) All are true

4. Statements T $ K, K # R, R ★ M

Conclusions I. M ★ K II. M % T III. M $ K

(a) All are true
(b) Either I or III is true
(c) Either I or II is true
(d) Either II or III is true
(e) None of these

5. Statements V @ M, A $ M, R # V

Conclusions I. R # A II. V @ A III. R $ M

(a) Only I is true
(b) Only II is true
(c) Only III is true
(d) None is true
(e) All are true

Direction (Q. Nos. 6-11) *In the following questions, the symbols @, © $, % and # are used with the following meaning as illustrated below.* **Syndicate Bank (PO) 2010**

- 'P $ Q' means 'P is not greater than Q'.
- 'P @ Q' means 'P is neither smaller than nor equal to Q'.
- 'P # Q' means 'P is not smaller than Q'.
- 'P © Q' means 'P is neither greater than nor equal to Q'.
- 'P % Q' means 'P is neither smaller than nor greater than Q'.

Now, in each of the following questions assuming the given statements not be true, find which of the three Conclusions I, II and III given below is/are definitely true and give your answer accordingly.

6. Statements D # K, K @ T, T $ M, M % J

Conclusions I. J @ T II. J % T III. D @ T

(a) Only I is true
(b) Only II is true
(c) Either I or II is true
(d) Only IV is true
(e) Either I or II and III are true

7. Statements R @ N, N © D, D $ J, J # B

Conclusions I. R @ J II. J @ N III. B @ D

(a) None is true
(b) Only I is true
(c) Only II is true
(d) Only III is true
(e) I and III are true

8. Statements W © B, B % V, V $ R, R @ K
Conclusions I. K © B
II. R # B
III. V @ W

(a) I and II are true (b) I and III are true
(c) II and III are true (d) I, II and III are true
(e) None of these

9. Statements H $ M, M # T, T @ D, D © R
Conclusions I. D © M
II. R @ M
III. H $ T

(a) None is true (b) Only I is true
(c) Only II is true (d) Only III is true
(e) I and II are true

10. Statements B % J, J @ K, K © T, T $ F
Conclusions I. F @ K
II. B @ K
III. B @ F

(a) I and II are true
(b) I and III are true
(c) II and III are true
(d) All of the above
(e) None of the above

11. Statements F # B, B $ M, M @ K, K © N
Conclusions I. N @ M
II. F $ M
III. K © B

(a) Only I is true (b) Only II is true
(c) Only III is true (d) II and III are true
(e) None of these

Direction (Q. Nos. 12-16) *In the following questions, the symbols ★ δ, %, @ and © are used with the following meaning as illustrated below.*

Punjab & Sind Bank (PO) 2010

- 'P % Q' means 'P is not smaller than Q'.
- 'P © Q' means 'P is neither smaller than nor equal to Q'.
- 'P ★ Q' means 'P is neither greater than nor equal to Q'.
- 'P δ Q' means 'P is not greater than Q'.
- 'P @ Q' means 'P is neither greater than nor smaller than Q'.

Now, in each of the following questions assuming the given statements to be true, find which of the three Conclusions I, II and III given below is/are definitely true and give your answer accordingly.

12. Statements R δ K, K ★ M, M @ J
Conclusions I. J © K
II. M © R
III. R ★ J

(a) I and II are true (b) II and III are true
(c) I and III are true (d) All are true
(e) None of these

13. Statements Z @ M, M © K, K ★ F
Conclusions I. F © Z
II. K ★ Z
III. F © M

(a) None is true (b) Only I is true
(c) Only II is true (d) Only III is true
(e) II and III are true

14. Statements B ★ JJ % W, W © M
Conclusions I. M ★ J
II. W ★ B
III. B © M

(a) None is true (b) Only I is true
(c) Only II is true (d) Only III is true
(e) I and III are true

15. Statements V% H, H @ F, F δ E
Conclusions I. F @ V
II. F ★ V
III. E % H

(a) Either I or II is true
(b) Only III is true
(c) I and II are true
(d) All of the above
(e) Either I or II and III are true

16. Statements W © T, T δ N, N % D
Conclusions I. D ★ T
II. W © N
III. D @ T

(a) None is true (b) Only I is true
(c) Only II is true (d) Only III is true
(e) I and II are true

Direction (Q. Nos. 17-20) *In the following questions, the symbols @, ©, %, ★ and $ are used with the following meaning as illustrated below.*

Corporation Bank (PO) 2010

- 'P © Q' means 'P is not greater than Q'.
- 'P $ Q' means 'P is not smaller than Q'.
- 'P @ Q' means 'P is neither smaller than nor greater than Q'.
- 'P ★ Q' means 'P is neither equal to nor greater than Q'.
- 'P % Q' means 'P is neither smaller than nor equal to Q'.

Now, in each of the following questions assuming the given statements to be true, find which of the three conclusions I, II and III given below them is/are definitely true and give your answer accordingly.

17. Statements D @ M, M $ B, B ★ R, R % T
Conclusions I. B ★ D
II. B @ D
III. T ★ M

(a) None is true (b) Only I is true
(c) Only II is true (d) Only III is true
(e) Either I or II is true

18. Statements W © F, F @ D, D ★ K, K $ J
Conclusions I. K % W
II. D $ W
III. F ★ K
(a) I and II are true (b) I and III are true
(c) II and III are true (d) All are true
(e) None of these

19. Statements R ★ K, K © M, M % T, T $ J
Conclusions I. J ★ M
II. R ★ M
III. K © J
(a) Only I is true (b) Only II is true
(c) I and II are true (d) All are true
(e) None of these

20. Statements R @ K, T © K, T $ M, M ★ W
Conclusions I. W % K
II. M © R
III. T © R
(a) Only I is true (b) Only II is true
(c) Only III is true (d) All are true
(e) None of these

Direction (Q. Nos. 21-25) *In the following questions, the symbols δ, ★, %, @ and # are used with the following meaning as illustrated below.* **BOI (PO) 2010**

- 'A % B' means 'A is neither greater than nor equal to B'.
- 'A # B' means 'A is neither smaller than nor equal to B'.
- 'A δ B' means 'A is neither smaller than nor greater than B'.
- 'A ★ B' means 'A is not smaller than B'.
- 'A @ B' means 'A is not greater than B'.

Now, in each of the following questions assuming the given statements to be true, find which of the three conclusions I, II and III given below them is/are definitely true and give your answer accordingly.

21. Statements P ★ D, D # Q, Q @ R
Conclusions I. Q % P II. R # D
III. P # D
(a) None is true (b) Only I is true
(c) Only II is true (d) Only III is true
(e) None of these

22. Statements M # R, R % P, P δ J
Conclusions I. M # P
II. J # R
III. J % M
(a) None is true (b) Only I is true
(c) Only II is true (d) Only III is true
(e) II and III are true

23. Statements F δ D, D ★ K, K # M
Conclusions I. M % D
II. K @ F
III. F # M
(a) I and II are true (b) I and III are true
(c) II and III are true (d) All are true
(e) None of these

24. Statements T % M, M @ K, K ★ F
Conclusions I. F % M II. F % T
III. K # T
(a) Only III is true (b) Only II is true
(c) Only I is true (d) II and III are true
(e) All are true

25. Statements H @ K, K δ N, N % T
Conclusions I. T # K
II. N δ H
III. H % N
(a) Only I is true (b) Only II is true
(c) Only III is true (d) Either II or III is true
(e) Either II or III and I are true

Direction (Q. Nos. 26-30) *In the following questions, the symbols □ %, $, # and @ are used with the following meaning as illustrated below.* **SBI (PO) 2014**

- 'P % Q' means 'P is neither smaller than nor equal to Q'.
- 'P □ Q' means 'P is not greater than Q'.
- 'P $ Q' means 'P is not smaller than Q'.
- 'P # Q' means 'P is neither greater than nor equal to Q'.
- 'P @ Q' means 'P is neither greater than nor smaller than Q'.

26. Statements D □ R, R # M, M @ K, K % F
Conclusions I. F $ M II. K @ R
III. K % R IV. D @ M
(a) None is true (b) Only I is true
(c) Only II is true (d) Only III is true
(e) Only IV is true

27. Statements R $ B, B @ A, A % K, K # M
Conclusions I. M % A II. K $ B
III. A % R IV. K # R
(a) Only IV is true (b) I and IV are true
(c) II and III are true (d) I, III and IV are true
(e) None of the above

28. Statements D # M, M $ R, R @ J, W % J
Conclusions I. W % R II. M $ J
III. R % D IV. W % M
(a) II and III are true
(b) I and IV are true
(c) I and II are true
(d) III and IV are true
(e) All of the above

29. Statements W @ T, T $ N, N # F, V % F
Conclusions I. V % N II. W $ N
III. T $ F IV. V @ N
(a) I and IV are true (b) I and II are true
(c) Only IV is true (d) II, III and IV are true
(e) III and IV are true

30. Statements B % K, K # D, D □ N, N @ T

Conclusions I. N % K II. T $ D

III. K # B IV. T % K

(a) I and II are true (b) II and III are true
(c) I, II and IV are true (d) III and IV are true
(e) All are true

Direction (Q. Nos. 31-35) *In the following questions the symbols @, $, ★, # and δ are used with the following meaning as illustrated below.* **SBI (PO) 2010**

- 'P $ Q' means 'P is not smaller than Q'.
- 'P @ Q' means 'P is neither smaller than nor equal to Q'.
- 'P # Q' means 'P is neither greater than nor equal to Q'.
- 'P δ Q' means 'P is neither greater than nor smaller than Q'.
- 'P ★ Q' means 'P is not greater than Q'.

Now, in each of the following questions assuming the given statements to be true, find which of the four Conclusions I, II, III and IV given below them is/are definitely true and give your answer accordingly.

31. Statements N δ B, B $ W, W # H, H ★ M

Conclusions I. M @ W II. H @ N

III. W δ N IV. W # N

(a) Only I is true
(b) Only III is true
(c) Only IV is true
(d) Either III or IV is true
(e) Either III or IV and I are true

32. Statements R ★ D, D $ J, J # M, M @ K

Conclusions I. K # J II. D @ M

III. R # M IV. D @ K

(a) None is true (b) Only I is true
(c) Only II is true (d) Only III is true
(e) Only IV is true

33. Statements H @ T, T # F, F δ E, E ★ V

Conclusions I. V $ F II. E @ T

III. H @ V IV. T # V

(a) I, II and III are true
(b) I, II and IV are true
(c) II, III and IV are true
(d) I, III and IV are true
(e) All of the above

34. Statements D $ R, R ★ K, K @ F, F $ J

Conclusions I. J # R II. J # K

III. R # F IV. K @ D

(a) I, II and III are true
(b) II, III and IV are true
(c) I, III and IV are true
(d) All of the above
(e) None of the above

35. Statements M $ K, K @ N, N ★ R, R # W

Conclusions I. W @ K II. M $ R

III. K @ W IV. M @ N

(a) I and II are true (b) I, II and III are true
(c) III and IV are true (d) II, III and IV are true
(e) None of these

Direction (Q. Nos. 36-40) *In the following questions, the symbols δ, ★, %, # and @ are used with the following meaning as illustrated below.* **BOB (PO) 2010**

- 'P % Q' means 'P is neither greater than nor equal to Q'.
- 'P δ Q' means 'P is neither smaller than nor equal to Q'.
- 'P @ Q' means 'P is not greater than Q'.
- 'P ★ Q' means 'P is not smaller than Q'.
- 'P # Q' means 'P is neither greater than nor smaller than Q'.

Now, in each of the following questions assuming the given statements to be true, find which of the four Conclusions I, II, III and IV given below them is/are definitely true and give your answer.

36. Statements R ★ T, T δ M, M % K, K @ V

Conclusions I. V δ M II. V δ T

III. M % R IV. K δ R

(a) I and II are true (b) I and III are true
(c) II and IV are true (d) I, III and IV are true
(e) None of these

37. Statements H δ J, J # N, N @ R, R δ W

Conclusions I. W % N II. W % H

III. R # J IV. R δ J

(a) Only I is true (b) Only II is true
(c) Only III is true (d) Only IV is true
(e) Either III or IV is true

38. Statements B @ D, D δ F, F % M, M ★ N

Conclusions I. B % F II. M δ D

III. N % F IV. D δ N

(a) None is true
(b) Only I is true
(c) Only II is true
(d) Only III is true
(e) Only IV is true

39. Statements F # Z, Z @ H, H % N, N δ B

Conclusions I. F @ H II. N δ Z

III. B % H IV. B % Z

(a) I and III are true
(b) II, III and IV are true
(c) I and II are true
(d) I, II and III are true
(e) None of the above

40. Statements M % K, K ★ W, W δ V, V @ N

Conclusions I. N ★ K II. M % W

III. K δ V IV. V % M

(a) None is true
(b) Only I is true
(c) Only II is true
(d) Only III is true
(e) Only IV is true

Direction (Q. Nos. 41-45) *In the following questions, the symbols @, $, #, © and % are used with the following meaning as illustrated below.* **IBPS (PO) 2012**

- 'P $ Q' means 'P is not smaller than Q'.
- 'P © Q' means 'P is neither greater than nor equal to Q'.
- 'P # Q' means 'P is neither smaller than nor equal to Q'.
- 'P % Q' means 'P is not greater than Q'.
- 'P @ Q' means 'P is neither greater than nor smaller than Q'.

Now, in each of the following questions assuming the given statements to be true, find which of the four Conclusions I, II, III and IV given below them is/are definitely true and give your answer accordingly.

41. Statements R # J, J $ D, D @ K, K % T

Conclusions I. T # D II. T @ D III. R # K IV. J $ T

(a) Either I or II is true
(b) Only III is true
(c) III and IV are true
(d) Either I or II and III are true
(e) None of the above

42. Statements T % R, R $ M, M @ D, D © H

Conclusions I. D % R II. H # R III. T © M IV. T % D

(a) Only I is true (b) I and IV are true
(c) I and II are true (d) II and IV are true
(e) None of these

43. Statements M @ B, B # N, N $ R, R © K

Conclusions I. K # B II. R © B III. M $ R IV. N © M

(a) I and III are true (b) I and II are true
(c) II and IV are true (d) II, III and IV are true
(e) None of these

44. Statements F # H, H @ M, M © E, E $ J

Conclusions I. J © M II. E # H III. M © F IV. F # E

(a) I and II are true (b) II and III are true
(c) I, II and III are true (d) II, III and IV are true
(e) None of these

45. Statements D % A, A @ B, B © K, K % M

Conclusions I. B $ D II. K # A III. M # B IV. A © M

(a) I, II and IV are true
(b) I, II and III are true
(c) II, III and IV are true
(d) I, III and IV are true
(e) All of the above

Direction (Q. Nos. 46-50) *In each of these questions, the symbols @, #, $, % and ★ are used with different meanings as follows.* **MHT CET MBA 2009**

- 'P @ Q' means 'P is not smaller than Q'.
- 'P # Q' means 'P is not greater than Q'.
- 'P $ Q' means 'P is neither smaller than nor greater than Q'.
- 'P % Q' means 'P is neither smaller than nor equal to Q'.
- 'P ★ Q' means 'P is neither greater than nor equal to Q'.

In each question, four statements showing relationships have been given, which are followed by four Conclusions I, II, III and IV. Assuming that the given statements are true, find out which conclusion(s) is/are definitely true.

46. Statements L # T, T ★ D, D @ H, H $ K

Conclusions I. K ★ D II. K # D III. L ★ D IV. K $ L

(a) I and III are true (b) II and III are true
(c) III and IV are true (d) I and II are true
(e) None of these

47. Statements E $ F, F @ I, I % K, L ★ K

Conclusions I. E @ I II. L ★ F III. F % K IV. E % K

(a) None is true (b) I and II are true
(c) II and III are true (d) I, II and III are true
(e) All are true

48. Statements R @ J, J ★ F, F # M, M % V

Conclusions I. J % V II. R @ M III. J # V IV. R ★ M

(a) Either I or III is true
(b) Either II or IV is true
(c) II and III are true
(d) Either I or III and either II or IV are true
(e) None of the above

49. Statements V % W, W # Z, Z @ T, T $ H

Conclusions I. Z % H II. V @ Z III. V ★ Z IV. W $ T

(a) Either II or III is true (b) Only I is true
(c) Only IV is true (d) I and II are true
(e) None of these

50. Statements H % L, L @ Q, Q ★ R, R # N

Conclusions I. H @ Q II. H % Q III. N @ Q IV. N % Q

(a) I and III are true
(b) II and III are true
(c) II and IV are true
(d) All of the above
(e) None of the above

Answers with **Explanations**

Intro Exercise 1

Solution (Q. Nos. 1-5)

$P @ Q \Rightarrow P > Q$
$P \# Q \Rightarrow P \leq Q$
$P \$ Q \Rightarrow P \geq Q$
$P \% Q \Rightarrow P = Q$
$P \& Q \Rightarrow P < Q$

1. (*d*) $G \# H \Rightarrow G \leq H$; $H \$ K \Rightarrow H \geq K$; $K @ M \Rightarrow K > M$

Form all above statements, $G \leq H \geq K > M$

Conclusions I. $M \# G \Rightarrow M \leq G$ (False)

II. $G \& M \Rightarrow G < M$ (False)

Neither I nor II is true.

2. (*a*) $F \$ D \Rightarrow F \geq D$; $H \# M \Rightarrow H \leq M$; $M \% D \Rightarrow M = D$

From all above statements, $F \geq D = M \geq H$

Conclusions I. $F \$ H \Rightarrow F \geq H$ (True)

II. $F @ H \Rightarrow F > H$ (False)

So, only I is true.

3. (*d*) $R \& M \Rightarrow R < M$; $M \# L \Rightarrow M \leq L$; $L \$ Q \Rightarrow L \geq Q$

From all above statements, $R < M \leq L \geq Q$

Conclusions I. $M \% Q \Rightarrow M = Q$ (False)

II. $M @ Q \Rightarrow M > Q$ (False)

So, neither I nor II is true.

4. (*e*) $F \# R \Rightarrow F \leq R$; $Q \$ R \Rightarrow Q \geq R$; $Q \& M \Rightarrow Q < M$

From all above statements,

$F \leq R \leq Q < M$

Conclusions I. $F \# Q \Rightarrow F \leq Q$ (True)

II. $R \& M \Rightarrow R < M$ (True)

So, both Conclusions I and II are true.

5. (*c*) $D \& T \Rightarrow D < T$; $R \# T$

$\Rightarrow R \leq T$; $R \$ M$

$\Rightarrow R \geq M$

From all above statements,

$D < T \geq R \geq M$

Conclusions I. $M \& T \Rightarrow M < T$ (may be true)

II. $M \% T \Rightarrow M = T$ (may be true)

Either I or II is true.

Solution (Q. Nos. 6-10)

6. (*e*) $A < B \leq C = D$

or $C = D \geq B > A$ ...(i)

$K \geq J > C$ ...(ii)

From Eqs. (i) and (ii), we get

$K \geq J > C = D \geq B > A$

Conclusions I. $C < K$ (True)

II. $B \leq D$ (True)

Both Conclusions I and II are true.

7. (*b*) $K \geq J > C = D \geq B > A$

Conclusions I. $A \geq J$ (False)

II. $K > B$ (True)

Only Conclusion II is true.

8. (*a*) $B \geq L > A \geq N < K$

Conclusions I. $B > N$ (True)

II. $L < K$ (False)

Only Conclusion I is true.

9. (*a*) $B \geq L > A \geq N < K$

Conclusions I. $L > N$ (True)

II. $L = N$ (False)

Only Conclusion I is true.

10. (*d*) $A > B > C \leq D = E \leq F$

Conclusions I. $C < F$ (True)

II. $C = F$ (True)

Either Conclusion I or II is true

Solution (Q. Nos. 11-15)

11. (*d*) **Conclusions** I. $F > B$ (False)

II. $B > D$ (False)

Neither Conclusion I nor II follows.

12. (*b*) **Conclusions** I. $M \geq Z$ (False)

II. $N < P$ (True)

Only Conclusion II follows.

13. (*c*) **Conclusions** I. $Y = V$ (may be true)

II. $Y > V$ (may be true)

Either Conclusion I or II follows.

14. (*a*) **Conclusions** I. $D > N$ (True)

II. $C \geq K$ (False)

Only Conclusion I is true.

15. (*b*) **Conclusions** I. $C > N$ (False)

II. $B > N$ (True)

Only Conclusion II follows.

Solution (Q. Nos. 16-20)

$P \$ Q \Rightarrow P > Q$
$P © Q \Rightarrow P \geq Q$
$P \bigstar Q \Rightarrow P = Q$
$P \# Q \Rightarrow P < Q$
$P @ Q \Rightarrow P \leq Q$

16. (*d*) $M \# K \Rightarrow M < K$

$K \bigstar D \Rightarrow K = D$

$D @ P \Rightarrow D \leq P$

So, $M < K = D \leq P$

Conclusions I. $M @ P \Rightarrow M \leq P$ (False)

II. $M \bigstar P \Rightarrow M = P$ (False)

So, neither I nor II is true.

17. (*e*) W © T ⇒ W ≥ T; T $ M ⇒ T > M; B # M ⇒ B < M
So, W ≥ T > M > B
Conclusions I. W $ B ⇒ W > B (True)
II. M # W ⇒ M < W (True)
So, both the conclusions are true.

18. (*d*) H ★ D ⇒ H = D; D # R ⇒ D < R; R © N ⇒ R ≥ N
So, H = D < R ≥ N
Conclusions I. N ★ H ⇒ N = H (False)
II. N $ H ⇒ N > H (False)
So, neither I nor II is true.

19. (*d*) Z @ R ⇒ Z ≤ R; R © D ⇒ R ≥ D; D # T ⇒ D < T
So, Z ≤ R ≥ D < T
Conclusions I. D # Z ⇒ D < Z (False)
II. Z # T ⇒ Z < T (False)
So, neither I nor II is true.

20. (*c*) Q # P ⇒ Q < P; P @ F ⇒ P ≤ F; F ★ M ⇒ F = M
So, Q < P ≤ F = M
Conclusions I. M $ P ⇒ M > P (may be true)
II. P ★ M ⇒ P = M (may be ture)
Either I or II is true.

Solution (Q. Nos. 21-25)

A @ B ⇒ A > B
A ★ B ⇒ A ≥ B
A # B ⇒ A = B
A $ B ⇒ A ≤ B
A + B ⇒ A < B

21. (*c*) B + D ⇒ B < D; E $ T ⇒ E ≤ T; T ★ P ⇒ T ≥ P; P @ B ⇒ P > B
So, E ≤ T ≥ P > B < D
Conclusions I. P $ D ⇒ P ≤ D (may be true)
II. P @ D ⇒ P > D (may be true)
Either I or II is true.

22. (*e*) E ★ F ⇒ E ≥ F; G $ H ⇒ G ≤ H; H # E ⇒ H = E
G @ K ⇒ G > K
So, K < G ≤ H = E ≥ F
Conclusions I. H @ K ⇒ H > K (True)
II. H ★ F ⇒ H ≥ F (True)
Both the conclusions are true.

23. (*a*) P $ Q ⇒ P ≤ Q; N # M ⇒ N = M; M @ R ⇒ M > R
R ★ P ⇒ R ≥ P
So, N = M > R ≥ P ≤ Q
Conclusions I. P + N ⇒ P < N (True)
II. Q $ M ⇒ Q ≤ M (False)
Only I is true.

24. (*b*) D + T ⇒ D < T; E $ V ⇒ E ≤ V; F ★ T ⇒ F ≥ T
E @ D ⇒ E > D
So, V ≥ E > D < T ≤ F
Conclusions I. D $ V ⇒ D ≤ V (False)
II. D + F ⇒ D < F (True)
So, only II is true.

25. (*d*) T ★ U ⇒ T ≥ U; U $ W ⇒ U ≤ W; V @ L ⇒ V > L
W + V ⇒ W < V
So, T ≥ U ≤ W < V > L
Conclusions I. V @ T ⇒ V > T (False)
II. L # W ⇒ L = W (False)
So, neither I nor II is true.

Solution (Q. Nos. 26-30)

@ ⇒ >	% ⇒ =	# ⇒ ≤
& ⇒ ≥	★ ⇒ <	

26. (*a*) S % A ⇒ S = A ⇒ A & D ⇒ A ≥ D ⇒ D ★ J ⇒ D < J
Therefore, S = A ≥ D < J
Conclusions I. D # S ⇒ D ≤ S (True)
II. A ★ J ⇒ A < J (False)
Only Conclusion I follows.

27. (*a*) Q @ F ⇒ Q > F ⇒ F % C ⇒ F = C ⇒ N ★ C ⇒ N < C
Therefore, Q > F = C > N
Conclusions I. Q @ C ⇒ Q > C (True)
II. F ★ N ⇒ F < N (False)
Only Conclusion I follows.

28. (*b*) R & P ⇒ R ≥ P, P ★ K ⇒ P < K, K ★ F ⇒ K < F
Therefore, R ≥ P < K < F
Conclusions I. R @ F ⇒ R > F (False)
II. P ★ F ⇒ P < F (True)
Only Conclusion II follows.

29. (*b*) M & F ⇒ M ≥ F; F ★ C ⇒ F < C; C % K ⇒ C = K
Therefore, M ≥ F < C = K
Conclusions I. M @ C ⇒ M > C (False)
II. F ★ K ⇒ F < K (True)
Only Conclusion II follows.

30. (*d*) P & T ⇒ P ≥ T, T ★ R ⇒ T < R, R # B ⇒ R ≤ B
Therefore, P ≥ T < R ≤ B
Conclusions I. P @ T ⇒ P > T (False)
II. B & T ⇒ B ≥ T (False)
Neither Conclusion I nor II follows.

Solution (Q. Nos. 31-35)

δ ⇒ ≤	% ⇒ ≥	© ⇒ =
$ ⇒ >	★ ⇒ <	

31. (*c*) R $ J ⇒ R > J; J % M ⇒ J ≥ M; M © K ⇒ M = K
Therefore, R > J ≥ M = K
Conclusions I. K © J ⇒ K = J (May be True)
II. K ★ J ⇒ K < J (May be True)
J ≥ K
Either Conclusion I or II is true.

32. (*e*) D δ R ⇒ D ≤ R; M $ R ⇒ M > R; M © F ⇒ M = F
Therefore, D ≤ R < M = F
Conclusions I. F $ D ⇒ F > D (True)
II. F $ R ⇒ F > R (True)
Both Conclusions are true.

33. (*a*) H © F ⇒ H = F; F $ R ⇒ F > R; R ★ K ⇒ R < K

Therefore, H = F > R < K

Conclusions I. R ★ H ⇒ R < H (True)

II. K $ F ⇒ K > F (False)

Only Conclusion I is true.

34. (*b*) B % D ⇒ B ≥ D; D ★ T ⇒ D < T; T δ R ⇒ T ≤ R

Therefore, B ≥ D < T ≤ R

Conclusions I. B $ T ⇒ B > T (False)

II. R $ D ⇒ R > D (True)

Only Conclusion II is true.

35. (*d*) M % N ⇒ M ≥ N; N ★ A ⇒ N < A; A $ B ⇒ A > B

Therefore, M ≥ N < A > B

Conclusions I. B ★ N ⇒ B < N (False)

II. A $ M ⇒ A > M (False)

Neither Conclusion I nor II is true.

Intro Exercise 2

Solution (Q. Nos. 1-6)

P ★ Q ⇒ P ≤ Q

P @ Q ⇒ P < Q

P © Q ⇒ P ≥ Q

P % Q ⇒ P = Q

P δ Q ⇒ P > Q

1. (*c*) R © K ⇒ R ≥ K

K δ M ⇒ K > M

M ★ J ⇒ M ≤ J

∴ R ≥ K > M ≤ J

Conclusions I. J δ K ⇒ J > K (False)

II. M @ R ⇒ M < R (True)

III. M % R ⇒ M = R (False)

So, only II is true.

2. (*e*) W © K ⇒ W ≥ K; K δ R ⇒ K > R; R % N ⇒ R = N

∴ W ≥ K > R = N

Conclusions I. N @ K ⇒ N < K (True)

II. R @ W ⇒ R < W (True)

III. W δ N ⇒ W > N (True)

All I, II and III are true.

3. (*e*) D @ K ⇒ D < K; K % F ⇒ K = F; F © B ⇒ F ≥ B

∴ D < K = F ≥ B

Conclusions I. F δ D ⇒ F > D (True)

II. B @ K ⇒ B < K (may be true)

III. B % K ⇒ B = K (may be true)

Either II or III and I are true.

4. (*b*) R δ B ⇒ R > B; B © N ⇒ B ≥ N; N @ T ⇒ N < T

∴ R > B ≥ N < T

Conclusions I. N @ R ⇒ N < R (True)

II. T δ B ⇒ T > B (False)

III. T δ R ⇒ T > R (False)

So, only I is true.

5. (*d*) H ★ W ⇒ H ≤ W; W @ N ⇒ W < N; N % R ⇒ N = R

∴ H ≤ W < N = R

Conclusions I. R δ W ⇒ R > W (True)

II. N δ W ⇒ N > W (True)

III. H @ R ⇒ H < R (True)

All I, II and III are true.

6. (*b*) Z % M ⇒ Z = M; M ★ F ⇒ M ≤ F; F δ D ⇒ F > D

∴ Z = M ≤ F > D

Conclusions I. F % Z ⇒ F = Z (may be true)

II. F δ Z ⇒ F > Z (may be true)

III. D @ Z ⇒ F < Z (False)

Either I or II is true.

Solution (Q. Nos. 7-11)

P @ Q ⇒ P > Q

P © Q ⇒ P ≤ Q

P # Q ⇒ P < Q

P $ Q ⇒ P = Q

P % Q ⇒ P ≥ Q

7. (*d*) L @ W ⇒ L > W; M % J ⇒ M ≥ J; M # W ⇒ M < W

So, L > W > M ≥ J

Conclusions I. M © L ⇒ M ≤ L (False)

II. W % J ⇒ W ≥ J (False)

III. L @ J ⇒ L > J (True)

So, only III is true

8. (*e*) N © B ⇒ N ≤ B

B $ T ⇒ B = T

T # S ⇒ T < S

So, N ≤ B = T < S

Conclusions I. N # S ⇒ N < S (True)

II. S @ B ⇒ S > B (True)

III. T % N ⇒ T ≥ N (True)

All follow.

9. (*c*) G @ H ⇒ G > H; H % K ⇒ H ≥ K; K # D ⇒ K < D

So, G > H ≥ K < D

Conclusions I. D $ H ⇒ D = H (False)

II. D # H ⇒ D < H (may be true)

III. D % H ⇒ D ≥ H (may be true)

Either II or III is true.

10. (*d*) F # D ⇒ F < D; D © K ⇒ D ≤ K; R @ K ⇒ R > K

So, F < D ≤ K < R

Conclusions I. F # K ⇒ F < K (True)

II. R % D ⇒ R ≥ D (False)

III. R @ F ⇒ R > F (True)

So, I and III follow.

11. (*e*) H © B ⇒ H ≤ B
B $ A ⇒ B = A
A # C ⇒ A < C
So, H ≤ B = A < C
Conclusions I. A % H ⇒ A ≥ H (True)
II. C # H ⇒ C < H (False)
III. H # A ⇒ H < A (False)
So, only I is true.

Solution (Q. Nos. 12-16)

P © Q ⇒ P ≤ Q
P ★ Q ⇒ P ≥ Q
P % Q ⇒ P < Q
P $ Q ⇒ P > Q
P @ Q ⇒ P = Q

12. (c) **Statements** J $ D ⇒ J > D
D © K ⇒ D ≤ K
K % R ⇒ K < R
∴ J > D ≤ K < R
Conclusions I. R $ J ⇒ R > J (False)
II. R $ D ⇒ R > D (True)
III. K $ J ⇒ K > J (False)
So, only II is true.

13. (*e*) **Statements** M ★ K ⇒ M ≥ K; K @ R ⇒ K = R; R % N ⇒ R < N
∴ M ≥ K = R < N
Conclusions I. R % M ⇒ R < M (may be true)
II. R @ M ⇒ R = M (may be true)
III. N $ K ⇒ N > K (True)
Either I or II and III are true.

14. (*d*) **Statements** B % H ⇒ B < H
H $ J ⇒ H > J
J ★ M ⇒ J ≥ M
∴ B < H > J ≥ M
Conclusions I. B % J ⇒ B < J (False)
II. M % B ⇒ M < B (False)
III. H $ M ⇒ H > M (True)
So, only III is true.

15. (*e*) **Statements** Z © K ⇒ Z ≤ K; K % E ⇒ K < E; E @ R ⇒ E = R
∴ Z ≤ K < E = R
Conclusions I. R $ K ⇒ R > K (True)
II. Z % E ⇒ Z < E (True)
III. R $ Z ⇒ R > Z (True)
All are true.

16. (c) **Statements** W @ M ⇒ W = M; M © R ⇒ M ≤ R
R $ F ⇒ R > F
∴ W = M ≤ R > F
Conclusions I. F % M ⇒ F < M (False)
II. R ★ W ⇒ R ≥ W (True)
III. W % F ⇒ W < F (False)
So, only II is true.

Solution (Q. Nos. 17-23)

P % Q ⇒ P = Q
P $ Q ⇒ P > Q
P © Q ⇒ P < Q
P ★ Q ⇒ P ≤ Q
P @ Q ⇒ P ≥ Q

17. (*c*) V © K ⇒ V < K; K @ B ⇒ K ≥ B; B $ M ⇒ B > M
So, V < K ≥ B > M
Conclusions I. V © B ⇒ V < B (False)
II. M © K ⇒ M < K (True)
III. M © V ⇒ M < V (False)
So, only II is true.

18. (*e*) D ★ R ⇒ D ≤ R; R % F ⇒ R = F; F $ T ⇒ F > T
So, D ≤ R = F > T
Conclusions I. F % D ⇒ F = D (may be true)
II. F $ D ⇒ F > D (may be true)
III. T © R ⇒ T < R (True)
Hence, either I or II and III are true.

19. (*a*) N @ D ⇒ N ≥ D
D ★ K ⇒ D ≤ K
K $ A ⇒ K > A
So, N ≥ D ≤ K > A
Conclusions I. K @ N ⇒ K ≥ N (False)
II. A © D ⇒ A < D (False)
III. N $ A ⇒ N > A (False)
So, none is true.

20. (*d*) K @ T ⇒ K ≥ T; T $ N ⇒ T > N; N © R ⇒ N < R
So, K ≥ T > N < R
Conclusions I. R $ K ⇒ R > K (False)
II. N ★ K ⇒ N ≤ K (False)
III. K $ N ⇒ K > N (True)
So, only III is true.

21. (*b*) W % K ⇒ W = K; K © F ⇒ K < F; D $ F ⇒ D > F
So, W = K < F < D
Conclusions I. D $ K ⇒ D > K (True)
II. D $ W ⇒ D > W (True)
III. F @ W ⇒ F ≥ W (False)
So, I and II are true.

22. (*d*) B ★ K ⇒ B ≤ K; K © F ⇒ K < F; F % R ⇒ F = R
So, B ≤ K < F = R
Conclusions I. R $ K ⇒ R > K (True)
II. R $ B ⇒ R > B (True)
III. F $ B ⇒ F > B (True)
So, all I, II and III are true.

23. (*e*) H $ M ⇒ H > M; M % D ⇒ M = D; D @ K ⇒ D ≥ K
So, H > M = D ≥ K
Conclusions I. H $ D ⇒ H > D (True)
II. K ★ M ⇒ K ≤ M (True)
III. K © H ⇒ K < H (True)
So, all I, II and III follow.

Solution (Q. Nos. 24-28)

$P © Q \Rightarrow P \geq Q$
$P \% Q \Rightarrow P > Q$
$P \bigstar Q \Rightarrow P < Q$
$P \delta Q \Rightarrow P \leq Q$
$P @ Q \Rightarrow P = Q$

24. (*e*) $D \delta T \Rightarrow D \leq T$
$T @ R \Rightarrow T = R$
$R © M \Rightarrow R \geq M$
$M \% K \Rightarrow M > K$
So, $D \leq T = R \geq M > K$

Conclusions I. $R @ D \Rightarrow R = D$ (may be true)
II. $R \% D \Rightarrow R > D$ (may be true)
III. $K \bigstar T \Rightarrow K < T$ (True)
IV. $M \delta T \Rightarrow M \leq T$ (True)

So, either I or II and III and IV are true.

25. (*a*) $J @ F \Rightarrow J = F$
$F \delta N \Rightarrow F \leq N$
$N \% H \Rightarrow N > H$
$H © G \Rightarrow H \geq G$
So, $J = F \leq N > H \geq G$

Conclusions I. $G \bigstar N \Rightarrow G < N$ (True)
II. $N © J \Rightarrow N \geq J$ (True)
III. $F \bigstar J \Rightarrow F < J$ (False)
IV. $J \delta G \Rightarrow J \leq G$ (False)

So, I and II are true.

26. (*d*) $R \bigstar K \Rightarrow R < K$; $K \% D \Rightarrow K > D$; $D @ V \Rightarrow D = V$
$V \delta M \Rightarrow V \leq M$
So, $R < K > D = V \leq M$

Conclusions I. $R \bigstar D \Rightarrow R < D$ (False)
II. $V \bigstar R \Rightarrow V < R$ (False)
III. $D @ M \Rightarrow D = M$ (may be true)
IV. $M \% D \Rightarrow M > D$ (may be true)

So, either III or IV is true.

27. (*d*) $B © T \Rightarrow B \geq T$
$T \bigstar R \Rightarrow T < R$
$R \% F \Rightarrow R > F$
$F @ K \Rightarrow F = K$
So, $B \geq T < R > F = K$

Conclusions I. $B \% R \Rightarrow B < R$ (False)
II. $F \bigstar T \Rightarrow F < T$ (False)
III. $R \% K \Rightarrow R > K$ (True)
IV. $K \bigstar T \Rightarrow K < T$ (False)

So, only III is true.

28. (*b*) $F \% N \Rightarrow F > N$; $N © W \Rightarrow N \geq W$
$W \delta Y \Rightarrow W \leq Y$; $Y \bigstar T \Rightarrow Y < T$
So, $F > N \geq W \leq Y < T$

Conclusions I. $F \% W \Rightarrow F > W$ (True)
II. $T \% N \Rightarrow T > N$ (False)
III. $N \% Y \Rightarrow N > Y$ (False)
IV. $T \% W \Rightarrow T > W$ (True)

So, I and IV are true.

Cumulative Exercises

Base Level

1. (*d*) **Statements** $R \geq W, W < F, F = Z$
From the statements, we get
$R \geq W < F = Z$

Conclusions I. $F < R$ (False)
II. $Z < W$ (False)

Conclusions I and II are false.

2. (*a*) **Statement** $B > K, K \geq J, J < M$
From the statements, we get
$B > K \geq J < M$

Conclusions I. $J < B$ (True)
II. $M > B$ (False)

Only Conclusion I is true.

3. (*b*) **Statements** $D = T, T \leq H, H > N$
From the statements, we get
$D = T \leq H > N$

Conclusions I. $H \leq D$ (False)
II. $H > D$ (True)

Only Conclusion II is true.

4. (*e*) **Statement** $H \leq N, N < K, K \leq D$
From the statements, we get
$H \leq N < K \leq D$

Conclusions I. $D > N$ (True)
II. $H < K$ (True)

Both Conclusions I and II are true.

5. (*d*) **Statements** $W \geq E, E > K, K = J$
From the statements, we get
$W \geq E > K = J$

Conclusions I. $J \leq E$ (False)
II. $W \geq K$ (False)

Both Conclusions I and II are false.

6. (*b*) **Statements** $R < M, M = B, B \geq T$

From the statements, we get

$R < M = B \geq T$

Conclusions I. $R < T$ (False)

II. $T \leq M$ (True)

Only Conclusion II is true.

7. (*b*) **Statements** $F \geq G = H; G > J \geq K$

From the statements, we get

$F \geq G = H > J \geq K$

Conclusions I. $F \geq K$ (False)

II. $K < H$ (True)

Hence, only Conclusion II is definitely true.

8. (*e*) **Statements** $P < Q = R \geq S \geq T$

Conclusions I. $T \leq Q$ (True)

II. $R > P$ (True)

Hence, both conclusions are definitely true.

9. (*a*) **Statements** $A \leq B < C; A \geq D; C \leq F$

From the statements, we get

$D \leq A \leq B < C \leq F$

Conclusions I. $D < C$ (True)

II. $F \geq D$ (False)

Hence, only Conclusion I is definitely true.

10. (*d*) **Statements** $U > A = I \leq O < E$

Conclusions I. $I \leq E$ (False)

II. $O > U$ (False)

Hence, neither Conclusion I nor II is definitely true.

11. (*e*) **Statements** $L = M \geq N; M > P; L < K$

Conclusions I. $K > P$ (True)

II. $N < K$ (True)

Hence, both Conclusions I and II are true.

Solution (Q. Nos. 12-16)

$P \$ Q \Rightarrow P \geq Q$

$P @ Q \Rightarrow P \leq Q$

$P \delta Q \Rightarrow P > Q$

$P \# Q \Rightarrow P < Q$

$P \% Q \Rightarrow P = Q$

12. (*d*) **Statements** $F @ N \Rightarrow F \leq N, N \delta R \Rightarrow N > R, H @ R \Rightarrow H \leq R$

$\therefore$ $F \leq N > R \geq H$

Conclusions I. $H \delta N \Rightarrow H > N$ (False)

II. $F \# R \Rightarrow F < R$ (False)

Neither Conclusion I nor II is true.

13. (*b*) **Statements** $M \# T \Rightarrow M < T; T @ K \Rightarrow T \leq K$

$K \$ N \Rightarrow K \geq N$

$\therefore$ $M < T \leq K > N$

Conclusions I. $M \# N \Rightarrow M < N$ (False)

II. $K \delta M \Rightarrow K > M$ (True)

Only Conclusion II is true.

14. (*c*) **Statements** $T \% H \Rightarrow T = H; H \$ W \Rightarrow H \geq W$

$\therefore$ $T = H \geq W$

Conclusions I. $W \# T \Rightarrow W < T$ (may be true)

II. $W \% T \Rightarrow W = T$ (may be true)

Either Conclusion I or II is true.

15. (*a*) **Statements** $N \delta K \Rightarrow N > K$

$K \# D \Rightarrow K < D$

$D \% M \Rightarrow D = M$

$\therefore$ $N > K < D = M$

Conclusions I. $M \delta K \Rightarrow M > K$ (True)

II. $D \delta N \Rightarrow D > N$ (False)

Only Conclusion I is true.

16. (*e*) **Statements** $J \$ B \Rightarrow J \geq B$

$B \% R \Rightarrow B = R$

$R \delta F \Rightarrow R > F$

$\therefore$ $J \geq B = R > F$

Conclusions I. $F \# B \Rightarrow F < B$ (True)

II. $R @ J \Rightarrow R \leq J$ (True)

Both Conclusions I and II are true.

17. (*c*) **Statements** $N = P, P \leq F, F \geq L$ and $L = K$

$\therefore N = P \leq F \geq L = K$

Conclusions I. $F = K$ (may be true)

II. $F > K$ (may be true)

Hence, either Conclusion I or II follows.

18. (*a*) **Statements** $Z > T, T < M, M < J$

$\therefore Z > T < M < J$

Conclusions I. $T < J$ (True)

II. $J < Z$ (False)

Hence, only Conclusion I follows.

19. (*e*) **Statements** $Q = Z, C \geq G, G \geq Q, Q \geq R, J \geq C$

$\therefore J \geq C \geq G \geq Q = Z \geq R$

Conclusions I. $G \geq Z$ (True)

II. $C \geq R$ (True)

So, both Conclusion I and II follow.

20. (*d*) **Statements** $A > B > C, D > E > F, D > C$

$\therefore A > B > C < D > E > F$

Conclusions I. $E > C$ (False)

II. $F > B$ (False)

Neither Conclusion I nor II follows.

21. (*e*) **Statements** $K < L, K > M, M \geq N, N > O$

$\therefore L > K > M \geq N > O$

Conclusions I. $O < M$ (True)

II. $O < K$ (True)

Hence, both Conclusions I and II follow.

Solution (Q. Nos. 22-26)

$P © Q \Rightarrow P \leq Q$; $P \% Q \Rightarrow P \geq Q$

$P \bigstar Q \Rightarrow P > Q$; $P @ Q \Rightarrow P < Q$

$P \$ Q \Rightarrow P = Q$

22. (*b*) $K @ V \Rightarrow K < V; V © N \Rightarrow V \leq N; N \% F \Rightarrow N \geq F$

$\therefore K < V \leq N \geq F$

Conclusions I. $F @ V \Rightarrow F < V$ (False)

II. $K @ N \Rightarrow K < N$ (True)

Only Conclusion II is true.

23. (*e*) $H \circledcirc W \Rightarrow H \le W$; $W \$ M \Rightarrow W = M$; $M @ B \Rightarrow M < B$

$\therefore H \le W = M < B$

Conclusions I. $B \bigstar H \Rightarrow B > H$ (True)

II. $M \% H \Rightarrow M \ge H$ (True)

So, both Conclusions I and II are true.

24. (*d*) $D \% B \Rightarrow D \ge B$; $B \bigstar T \Rightarrow B > T$; $T \$ M \Rightarrow T = M$

$\therefore D \ge B > T = M$

Conclusions I. $T \circledcirc D \Rightarrow T \le D$ (False)

II. $M \circledcirc D \Rightarrow M \le D$ (False)

Neither Conclusion I nor II is true.

25. (*a*) $M \bigstar T \Rightarrow M > T$; $T @ K \Rightarrow T < K$; $K \circledcirc N \Rightarrow K \le N$

$\therefore M > T < K \le N$

Conclusions I. $N \bigstar T \Rightarrow N > T$ (True)

II. $N \bigstar M \Rightarrow N > M$ (False)

Only Conclusion I is true.

26. (*c*) $R \$ J \Rightarrow R = J$; $J \% D \Rightarrow J \ge D$; $D \bigstar F \Rightarrow D > F$

$\therefore R = J \ge D > F$

Conclusions I. $D \$ R \Rightarrow D = R$ (may be true)

II. $D @ R \Rightarrow D = R$ (may be true)

Either I or II is true.

Solution (Q. Nos. 27-28)

The given statements are

$P \ge Q < T$, $R < Q \ge S$, $V \ge T$

27. (*b*) I. From given statement, $R < Q \le P \Rightarrow P > R$

$\therefore$ Conclusion I is not true.

II. From given statement, $S \le Q < T \le V \Rightarrow S < V$

$\therefore$ Conclusion II is true.

28. (*e*) I. From given statement, $P \ge Q \ge S \Rightarrow S \le P$

$\therefore$ Conclusion I is true.

II. From given statement, $V \ge T > Q > R \Rightarrow V > R$

$\therefore$ Conclusion II is true.

So, both Conclusions I and II are true.

Solution (Q. Nos. 29-33)

The given statements are $H < I \le J$, $R \ge I > A$

29. (*a*) I. From given statements, $H < I \le R \Rightarrow H < R$

$\therefore$ Conclusion I is true.

II. From given statements, $H < I > A$

$\therefore$ No relation can be found between H and A.

30. (*b*) I. From given statements, $R \ge I \le J$

$\therefore$ No relation can be established between J and R

II. From given statements $A < I \le J \Rightarrow J > A$

$\therefore$ Conclusion II is true.

31. (*a*) Given statements are $J = K \ge L \le M$, $K < S$, $J > T$

I. From given statements, $L \le K < S \Rightarrow L < S$

$\therefore$ Conclusion I is true.

II. From given statements, $T < J = K \ge L \le M$

$\therefore$ No relation can be established between M and T.

32. (*c*) Given statements are $P < R \ge I = C$, $L > E \ge R$

From given statements, $E \ge R \ge I = C$

$\Rightarrow$ $E > C$ (may be true)

$\Rightarrow$ $E = C$ (may be true)

$\therefore$ Either Conclusion I or II is true.

33. (*d*) Given statements are

$B \le C = D > E$, $F > C$

I. From given statements,

$B \le C < F \Rightarrow B \le F$

$\therefore$ Conclusion I is not true.

II. From given statements,

$C = D > E \Rightarrow C \ge E$

$\therefore$ Conclusion II is not true.

So, neither Conclusions I nor II are true.

Solution (Q. Nos. 34-38)

$+ \Rightarrow >$	$- \Rightarrow \ge$	$\times \Rightarrow =$
$\div \Rightarrow <$	$= \Rightarrow \le$	

34. (*a*) $M \times X \Rightarrow M = X$; $L \div O \Rightarrow L < O$

$N + M \Rightarrow N > M$; $L = X \Rightarrow L \le X$

Therefore, $N > M = X \ge L < O$

Conclusions I. $N + L \Rightarrow N > L$ (True)

II. $X \div O \Rightarrow X < O$ (False)

Only Conclusion I is true.

35. (*d*) $S = F \Rightarrow S \le F$, $K \div S \Rightarrow K < S$

$B \times K \Rightarrow B = K$, $R + B \Rightarrow R > B$

Therefore, $R > B = K < S \le F$

Conclusions I. $F + K \Rightarrow F > K$ (True)

II. $K \div R \Rightarrow K < R$ (True)

Both Conclusions I and II are true.

36. (*c*) $H = V \Rightarrow H \le V$

$A \times Z \Rightarrow A = Z$

$H - Z \Rightarrow H \ge Z$

$F + V \Rightarrow F > V$

Therefore, $F > V \ge H \ge Z = A$

Conclusions I. $A \times H \Rightarrow A = H$ (may be true)

II. $H + A \Rightarrow H > A$ (may be true)

Either Conclusion I or II is true.

37. (*c*) $I + O \Rightarrow I > O$; $R - I \Rightarrow R \ge I$

$Z \times R \Rightarrow Z = R$; $J \div Z \Rightarrow J < Z$

Therefore, $J < Z = R \ge I > O$

Conclusions I. $Z \times I \Rightarrow Z = I$ (may be true)

II. $Z + I \Rightarrow Z > I$ (may be true)

Either Conclusion I or II is true.

38. (*d*) $Q \div R \Rightarrow Q < R$; $C + D \Rightarrow C > D$

$F - R \Rightarrow F \ge R$; $D \times F \Rightarrow D = F$

Therefore, $C > D = F \ge R > Q$

Conclusions I. $Q \div C \Rightarrow Q < C$ (True)

II. $C + F \Rightarrow C > F$ (True)

Both Conclusions I and II are true.

Solution (Q. Nos. 39-43)

$P \% Q \Rightarrow P \geq Q$
$P \bigstar Q \Rightarrow P < Q$
$P \delta Q \Rightarrow P > Q$
$P \$ Q \Rightarrow P = Q$
$P © Q \Rightarrow P \leq Q$

39. (*b*) **Statements** $D \$ T \Rightarrow D = T, T \% M \Rightarrow T \geq M, M \bigstar J \Rightarrow M < J$

∴ $D = T \geq M < J$

Conclusions I. $J \delta D \Rightarrow J > D$ (False)

II. $M © D \Rightarrow M \leq D$ (True)

Only Conclusion II is true.

40. (*c*) **Statements** $B \bigstar K \Rightarrow B < K$,

$K \$ N \Rightarrow K = N, N \% R \Rightarrow N \geq R$

∴ $B < K = N \geq R$

Conclusions I. $R \$ K \Rightarrow R = K$ (may be true)

II. $R \bigstar K \Rightarrow R < K$ (may be true)

So, either Conclusion I or II is true.

41. (*a*) **Statements** $H \% F \Rightarrow H \geq F, F \bigstar W \Rightarrow F < W$,

$W \$ E \Rightarrow W = E$

∴ $H \geq F < W = E$

Conclusions I. $E \delta F \Rightarrow E > F$ (True)

II. $H \delta W \Rightarrow H > W$ (False)

Only Conclusion I is true.

42. (*d*) **Statements** $Z \delta D \Rightarrow Z > D$,

$D © K \Rightarrow D \leq K, K \delta M \Rightarrow K > M$

∴ $Z > D \leq K > M$

Conclusions I. $M \bigstar D \Rightarrow M < D$ (False)

II. $Z \delta K \Rightarrow Z > K$ (False)

Neither Conclusion I nor II is true.

43. (*e*) **Statements** $W © B \Rightarrow W \leq B$,

$N \delta B \Rightarrow N > B, N © F \Rightarrow N \leq F$

∴ $W \leq B < N \leq F$

Conclusions I. $F \delta B \Rightarrow F > B$ (True)

II. $W \bigstar N \Rightarrow W < N$ (True)

Both Conclusions I and II are true.

44. (*b*) On combining the two statements, we get

$P \geq Q = R > S > T$

Conclusions I. $P \geq T$ (False)

II. $T < Q$ (True)

So, only Conclusion II follows.

45. (*e*) On combining the two statements, we get

$A \leq B = C = E < D$

Conclusions I. $E \geq A$ (True)

II. $D > A$ (True)

So, both conclusions are follow.

46. (*b*) On combining the two statements, we get

$F \leq G = H > J \geq K$

Conclusions I. $F \geq K$ (False)

II. $K < H$ (True)

Only Conclusion II is true.

47. (*e*) We have to check the options one-by-one

(a) $M = P > Q > R \Rightarrow M > R$
So, expression $M > R$ holds true.

(b) $M > P \geq Q = R \Rightarrow M > R$
So, expression $M > R$ holds true.

(c) $R = P < Q < M \Rightarrow M > R$
So, expression $M > R$ holds true.

(d) $R < Q \leq P = M \Rightarrow R < M$
So, expression $M > R$ holds true.

(e) $M = P < Q = R \Rightarrow M < R$
So, expression $M > R$ does not holds true.

48. (*b*) Here, we will check options one-by-one

(a) $F \geq K$ (does not follow as no relation can be determined between F and K)

(b) $H < K$ (it follows)

(c) $F < G$ (does not follow as no relation can be found between F and G)

(d) $K \geq H$ (does not follow as K cannot equal to H)

49. (*b*) **Statements** $P > R, R < S \leq X, Y = X$ or $P > R < S \leq X = Y$

Conclusions I. $P < S$ (False)

II. $Y > R$ (True)

Hence, only Conclusion II is definitely true.

50. (*e*) **Statements** $Z = C, B < A = N, C < B$

or $Z = C < B < A = N$

Conclusions I. $Z < B$ (True)

II. $N > Z$ (True)

Hence, both conclusions are definitely true.

51. (*a*) **Statements** $T < V = W, X \geq Y, W > X$

or $T < V = W > X \geq Y$

Conclusions I. $V > Y$ (True)

II. $V < X$ (False)

Hence, only Conclusion I is definitely true.

Solution (Q. Nos. 52-53)

Statements $A > B = C, E = F, E \geq D > C$

or $A > B = C < D \leq E = F$

52. (*a*) **Conclusions** I. $B < E$ (True)

II. $F < B$ (False)

Hence, only Conclusion I is definitely true.

53. (*e*) **Conclusions** I. $C < F$ (True)

II. $A > C$ (True)

Hence, both conclusions are definitely true.

Solution (Q. Nos. 54-55)

Statements $I \leq J, K < L > M, J = K, G \geq H = I$

or $G \geq H = I \leq J = K < L > M$

54. (*d*) **Conclusions** I. $H < J$ (False)

II. $J < G$ (False)

Hence, neither Conclusion I nor II is definitely true.

55. (*a*) **Conclusions** I. $L > J$ (True)

II. $J < M$ (False)

Hence, only Conclusion I is definitely true.

Advanced Level

Solution (Q. Nos. 1-5)

$P @ Q \Rightarrow P \geq Q$
$P \# Q \Rightarrow P \leq Q$
$P \% Q \Rightarrow P < Q$
$P ★ Q \Rightarrow P = Q$
$P \$ Q \Rightarrow P > Q$

1. (*c*) **Statements** $M \% R \Rightarrow M < R$; $R \# T \Rightarrow R \leq T$; $T ★ N \Rightarrow T = N$
   So, $N = T \geq R > M$
   Conclusions I. $N ★ R \Rightarrow N = R$ (may be true)
   II. $N \$ R \Rightarrow N > R$ (may be true)
   III. $N \$ M \Rightarrow N > M$ (True)
   Either I or II and III are true.

2. (*e*) **Statements** $J \# N \Rightarrow J \leq N$; $K @ N \Rightarrow K \geq N$; $T \$ K \Rightarrow T > K$
   So, $T > K \geq N \geq J$
   Conclusions I. $J \% T \Rightarrow J < T$ (True)
   II. $T \$ N \Rightarrow T > N$ (True)
   III. $N @ J \Rightarrow N \geq J$ (True)
   All are true.

3. (*a*) **Statements** $B ★ D \Rightarrow B = D$; $D @ H \Rightarrow D \geq H$; $H \% F \Rightarrow H < F$
   So, $B = D \geq H < F$
   Conclusions I. $B ★ F \Rightarrow B = F$ (False)
   II. $B \$ F \Rightarrow B > F$ (False)
   III. $D \$ F \Rightarrow D > F$ (False)
   None is true.

4. (*b*) **Statements** $T \$ K \Rightarrow T > K$; $K \# R \Rightarrow K \leq R$; $R ★ M \Rightarrow R = M$
   So, $M = R \geq K < T$
   Conclusions I. $M ★ K \Rightarrow M = K$ (may be true)
   II. $M \% T \Rightarrow M < T$ (False)
   III. $M \$ K \Rightarrow M > K$ (may be true)
   Either I or III is true.

5. (*d*) **Statements** $V @ M \Rightarrow V \geq M$; $A \$ M \Rightarrow A > M$; $R \# V \Rightarrow R \leq V$
   So, $R \leq V \geq M < A$
   Conclusions I. $R \# A \Rightarrow R \leq A$ (False)
   II. $V @ A \Rightarrow V \geq A$ (False)
   III. $R \$ M \Rightarrow R > M$ (False)
   None is true.

Solution (Q. Nos. 6-11)

$P \$ Q \Rightarrow P \leq Q$
$P @ Q \Rightarrow P > Q$
$P \# Q \Rightarrow P \geq Q$
$P © Q \Rightarrow P < Q$
$P \% Q \Rightarrow P = Q$

6. (*e*) **Statements** $D \# K \Rightarrow D \geq K$
   $K @ T \Rightarrow K > T$
   $T \$ M \Rightarrow T \leq M$
   $M \% J \Rightarrow M = J$
   So, $D \geq K > T \leq M = J$
   Conclusions I. $J @ T \Rightarrow J > T$ (may be true)
   II. $J \% T \Rightarrow J = T$ (may be true)
   III. $D @ T \Rightarrow D > T$ (True)
   Only either I or II and III are true.

7. (*c*) **Statements** $R @ N \Rightarrow R > N$; $N © D \Rightarrow N < D$
   $D \$ J \Rightarrow D \leq J$; $J \# B \Rightarrow J \geq B$
   So, $R > N < D \leq J \geq B$
   Conclusions I. $R @ J \Rightarrow R > J$ (False)
   II. $J @ N \Rightarrow J > N$ (True)
   III. $B @ D \Rightarrow B > D$ (False)
   Only II is true.

8. (*c*) **Statements** $W © B \Rightarrow W < B$; $B \% V \Rightarrow B = V$
   $V \$ R \Rightarrow V \leq R$; $R @ K \Rightarrow R > K$
   So, $W < B = V \leq R > K$
   Conclusions I. $K © B \Rightarrow K < B$ (False)
   II. $R \# B \Rightarrow R \geq B$ (True)
   III. $V @ W \Rightarrow V > W$ (True)
   Both II and III are true.

9. (*b*) **Statements** $H \$ M \Rightarrow H \leq M$; $M \# T \Rightarrow M \geq T$
   $T @ D \Rightarrow T > D$; $D © R \Rightarrow D < R$
   So, $H \leq M \geq T > D < R$
   Conclusions I. $D © M \Rightarrow D < M$ (True)
   II. $R @ M \Rightarrow R > M$ (False)
   III. $H \$ T \Rightarrow H \leq T$ (False)
   Only I is true.

10. (*a*) **Statements** $B \% J \Rightarrow B = J$; $J @ K \Rightarrow J > K$
    $K © T \Rightarrow K < T$
    $T \$ F \Rightarrow T \leq F$
    So, $B = J > K < T \leq F$
    Conclusions I. $F @ K \Rightarrow F > K$ (True)
    II. $B @ K \Rightarrow B > K$ (True)
    III. $B @ F \Rightarrow B > F$ (False)
    Both I and II are true.

11. (*e*) **Statements** $F \# B \Rightarrow F \geq B$; $B \$ M \Rightarrow B \leq M$;
    $M @ K \Rightarrow M > K$; $K © N \Rightarrow K < N$
    So, $F \geq B \leq M > K < N$
    Conclusions I. $N @ M \Rightarrow N > M$ (False)
    II. $F \$ M \Rightarrow F \leq M$ (False)
    III. $K © B \Rightarrow K < B$ (False)
    None of the given conclusions is true.

Solution (Q. Nos. 12-16)

$P \% Q \Rightarrow P \geq Q$
$P © Q \Rightarrow P > Q$
$P ★ Q \Rightarrow P < Q$
$P \delta Q \Rightarrow P \leq Q$
$P @ Q \Rightarrow P = Q$

12. (*d*) **Statements** $R \delta K, K \bigstar M, M @ J;$
$R \le K, K < M, M = J; R \le K < M = J$
Conclusions I. $J © K = J > K$ (True)
II. $M © R = M > R$ (True)
III. $R \bigstar J = R < J$ (True)
All I, II and III are true.

13. (*c*) **Statements** $Z @ M, M © K, K \bigstar F;$
$Z = M, M > K, K < F; Z > M > K < F$
$\therefore Z = M > K < F$
Conclusions I. $F © Z \Rightarrow F > Z$ (False)
II. $K \bigstar Z \Rightarrow K < Z$ (True)
III. $F © M \Rightarrow F > M$ (False)
Only II is true.

14. (*b*) **Statements** $B \bigstar J, J \% W, W © M; B < J, J \ge W, W > M$
$B < J \ge W > M$
Conclusions I. $M \bigstar J \Rightarrow M < J$ (True)
II. $W \bigstar B \Rightarrow W < B$ (False)
III. $B © M \Rightarrow B > M$ (False)
Only I is true.

15. (*e*) **Statements** $V \% H, H @ F, F \delta E; V \ge H, H = F, F \le E$
$V \ge H = F \le E$
Conclusions I. $F @ V \Rightarrow F = V$ (may be true)
II. $F \bigstar V \Rightarrow F < V$ (may be true)
III. $E \% H \Rightarrow E \ge H$ (True)
Only either I or II and III are true.

16. (*a*) **Statements** $W © T, T \delta N, N \% D; W > T, T \le N, N \ge D$
$W > T \le N \ge D$
Conclusions I. $D \bigstar T \Rightarrow D < T$ (False)
II. $W © N \Rightarrow W > N$ (False)
III. $D @ T \Rightarrow D = T$ (False)
None is true.

Solution (Q. Nos. 17-20)

$P © Q \Rightarrow P \le Q; P \$ Q \Rightarrow P \ge Q;$ $P @ Q \Rightarrow P = Q$
$P \bigstar Q \Rightarrow P < Q; P \% Q \Rightarrow P > Q$

17. (*e*) **Statements** $D @ M \Rightarrow D = M; M \$ B \Rightarrow M \ge B;$
$B \bigstar R \Rightarrow B < R; R \% T \Rightarrow R > T$
So, $D = M \ge B < R > T$
Conclusions I. $B \bigstar D \Rightarrow B < D$ (may be true)
II. $B @ D \Rightarrow B = D$ (may be true)
III. $T \bigstar M \Rightarrow T < M$ (False)
Either I or II is true.

18. (*d*) **Statements** $W © F \Rightarrow W \le F; F @ D \Rightarrow F = D$
$D \bigstar K \Rightarrow D < K; K \$ J \Rightarrow K \ge J$
So, $W \le F = D < K \ge J$
Conclusions I. $K \% W \Rightarrow K > W$ (True)
II. $D \$ W \Rightarrow D \ge W$ (True)
III. $F \bigstar K \Rightarrow F < K$ (True)
All I, II and III are true.

19. (*c*) Statements $R \bigstar K \Rightarrow R < K; K © M \Rightarrow K \le M$
$M \% T \Rightarrow M > T; T \$ J \Rightarrow T \ge J$
So, $R < K \le M > T \ge J$
Conclusions I. $J \bigstar M \Rightarrow J < M$ (True)
II. $R \bigstar M \Rightarrow R < M$ (True)
III. $K © J \Rightarrow K \le J$ (False)
Both I and II are true.

20. (*e*) **Statements** $R @ K \Rightarrow R = K; T © K \Rightarrow T \le K$
$T \$ M \Rightarrow T \ge M; M \bigstar W \Rightarrow M < W$
So, $R = K \ge T \ge M < W$
Conclusions I. $W \% K \Rightarrow W > K$ (False)
II. $N © R \Rightarrow M \le R$ (True)
III. $T © R \Rightarrow T \le R$ (True)
Both II and III are true.

Solution (Q. Nos. 21-25)

$A \% B \Rightarrow A < B;$ $A \# B \Rightarrow A > B$
$A \delta B \Rightarrow A = B;$ $A \bigstar B \Rightarrow A \ge B$
$A @ B \Rightarrow A \le B$

21. (*b*) **Statements** $P \bigstar D \Rightarrow P \ge D$
$D \# Q \Rightarrow D > Q$
$Q @ R \Rightarrow Q \le R$
So, $P \ge D > Q \le R$
Conclusions I. $Q \% P \Rightarrow Q < P$ (True)
II. $R \# D \Rightarrow R > D$ (False)
III. $P \# D \Rightarrow P > D$ (False)
So, only I is true.

22. (*c*) **Statements** $M \# R \Rightarrow M > R$
$R \% P \Rightarrow R < P$
$P \delta J \Rightarrow P = J$
So, $M > R < P = J$
Conclusions I. $M \# P \Rightarrow M > P$ (False)
II. $J \# R \Rightarrow J > R$ (True)
III. $J \% M \Rightarrow J < M$ (False)
So, only II is true.

23. (*d*) **Statements** $F \delta D \Rightarrow F = D; D \bigstar K$
$\Rightarrow D \ge K; K \# M \Rightarrow K > M$
So, $F = D \ge K > M$
Conclusions I. $M \% D \Rightarrow M < D$ (True)
II. $K @ F \Rightarrow K \le F$ (True)
III. $F \# M \Rightarrow F > M$ (True)
So, all I, II and III are true.

24. (*a*) **Statements** $T \% M \Rightarrow T < M$
$M @ K \Rightarrow M \le K$
$K \bigstar F \Rightarrow K \ge F$
So, $T < M \le K \ge F$
Conclusions I. $F \% M \Rightarrow F < M$ (False)
II. $F \% T \Rightarrow F < T$ (False)
III. $K \# T \Rightarrow K > T$ (True)
So, only III is true.

25. (*e*) **Statements** $H @ K \Rightarrow H \le K$

$K \delta N \Rightarrow K = N$

$N \% T \Rightarrow N < T$

So, $H \le K = N < T$

Conclusions I. $T \# K \Rightarrow T > K$ (True)

II. $N \delta H \Rightarrow N = H$ (may be true)

III. $H \% N \Rightarrow H < N$ (may be true)

Either II or III and I are true.

Solution (Q. Nos. 26-30)

$P \% Q \Rightarrow P > Q$

$P \square Q \Rightarrow P \le Q$

$P \$ Q \Rightarrow P \ge Q$

$P \# Q \Rightarrow P < Q$

$P @ Q \Rightarrow P = Q$

$\% \Rightarrow >$	$\square \Rightarrow \le$	$\$ \Rightarrow \ge$
$\# \Rightarrow <$	$@ \Rightarrow =$	

26. (*d*) **Statements** $D \square R \Rightarrow D \le R$

$R \# M \Rightarrow R < M$

$M @ K \Rightarrow M = K$

$K \% F \Rightarrow K > F$

Therefore, $D \le R < M = K > F$

Conclusions I. $F \$ M \Rightarrow F \ge M$ (False)

II. $K @ R \Rightarrow K = R$ (False)

III. $K \% R \Rightarrow K > R$ (True)

IV. $D @ M \Rightarrow D = M$ (False)

Only III is true.

27. (*a*) **Statements** $R \$ B \Rightarrow R \ge B$

$B @ A \Rightarrow B = A$

$A \% K \Rightarrow A > K$

$K \# M \Rightarrow K < M$

Therefore, $R \ge B = A > K < M$

Conclusions I. $M \% A \Rightarrow M > A$ (False)

II. $K \$ B \Rightarrow K \ge B$ (False)

III. $A \% R \Rightarrow A > R$ (False)

IV. $K \# R \Rightarrow K < R$ (True)

Only IV is true.

28. (*c*) **Statements** $D \# M \Rightarrow D < M$, $M \$ R \Rightarrow M \ge R$

$R @ J \Rightarrow R = J$, $W \% J \Rightarrow W > J$

Therefore, $D < M \ge R = J > W$

$D < M \ge R = J < W$

Conclusions I. $W \% R \Rightarrow W > R$ (True)

II. $M \$ J \Rightarrow M \ge J$ (True)

III. $R \% D \Rightarrow R > D$ (False)

IV. $W \% M \Rightarrow W > M$ (False)

Both I and II are true.

29. (*b*) **Statements** $W @ T \Rightarrow W = T$

$T \$ N \Rightarrow T \ge N$

$N \# F \Rightarrow N < F$

$V \% F \Rightarrow V > F$

Therefore, $W = T \ge N < F < V$

Conclusions I. $V \% N \Rightarrow V > N$ (True)

II. $W \$ N \Rightarrow W \ge N$ (True)

III. $T \$ F \Rightarrow T \ge F$ (False)

IV. $V @ N \Rightarrow V = N$ (False)

Both I and II are true.

30. (*e*) **Statements** $B \% K \Rightarrow B > K$; $K \# D \Rightarrow K < D$

$D \square N \Rightarrow D \le N$; $N @ T \Rightarrow N = T$

Therefore, $B > K < D \le N = T$

Conclusions I. $N \% K \Rightarrow N > K$ (True)

II. $T \$ D \Rightarrow T \ge D$ (True)

III. $K \# B \Rightarrow K < B$ (True)

IV. $T \% K \Rightarrow T > K$ (True)

All are true.

Solution (Q. Nos. 31-35)

$P \$ Q \Rightarrow P \ge Q$

$P @ Q \Rightarrow P > Q$

$P \# Q \Rightarrow P < Q$

$P \delta Q \Rightarrow P = Q$

$P \bigstar Q \Rightarrow P \le Q$

31. (*e*) **Statements** $N \delta B \Rightarrow N = B$

$B \$ W \Rightarrow B \ge W$

$W \# H \Rightarrow W < H$

$H \bigstar M \Rightarrow H \le M$

So, $N = B \ge W < H \le M$

Conclusions I. $M @ W \Rightarrow M > W$ (True)

II. $H @ N \Rightarrow H > N$ (False)

III. $W \delta N \Rightarrow W = N$ } either III or IV

IV. $W \# N \Rightarrow W < N$ }

$\because$ $N \ge W$. So, either III or IV and I are true.

32. (*a*) **Statements** $R \bigstar D \Rightarrow R \le D$

$D \$ J \Rightarrow D \ge J$

$J \# M \Rightarrow J < M$

$M @ K \Rightarrow M > K$

So, $R \le D \ge J < M > K$

Conclusions I. $K \# J \Rightarrow K < J$ (False)

II. $D @ M \Rightarrow D > M$ (False)

III. $R \# M \Rightarrow R < M$ (False)

IV. $D @ K \Rightarrow D > K$ (False)

So, none is true.

33. (*b*) **Statements** $H @ T \Rightarrow H > T$, $T \# F \Rightarrow T < F$,

$F \delta E \Rightarrow F = E$, $E \bigstar V \Rightarrow E \le V$

So, $H > T < F = E \le V$

Conclusions I. $V \$ F \Rightarrow V \ge F$ (True)

II. $E @ T \Rightarrow E > T$ (True)

III. $H @ V \Rightarrow H > V$ (False)

IV. $T \# V \Rightarrow T < V$ (True)

So, I, II and IV are true.

34. (*e*) **Statements** D $ R ⇒ D < R, R ★ K ⇒ R ≤ K,
K @ F ⇒ K > F, F $ J ⇒ F ≥ J

So, D < R ≤ K > F ≥ J

Conclusions I. J # R ⇒ J < R (False)
II. J # K ⇒ J < K (True)
III. R # F ⇒ R < F (False)
IV. K @ D ⇒ K > D (True)

So, II and IV are true.

35. (*e*) **Statements** M $ K ⇒ M ≥ K, K @ N ⇒ K > N,
N ★ R ⇒ N ≤ R, R # W ⇒ R < W

So, M ≥ K > N ≤ R < W

Conclusions I. W @ K ⇒ W > K (False)
II. M $ R ⇒ M ≥ R (False)
III. K @ W ⇒ K > W (False)
IV. M @ N ⇒ M > N (True)

So, only IV is true.

Solution (Q. Nos. 36-40)

P % Q ⇒ P < Q
P δ Q ⇒ P > Q
P @ Q ⇒ P ≤ Q
P ★ Q ⇒ P ≥ Q
P # Q ⇒ P = Q

36. (*b*) **Statements** R★T⇒R≥T; TδM⇒T>M; M%K⇒M<K
K @ V ⇒ K ≤ V

So, R ≥ T > M < K ≤ V

Conclusions I. V δ M ⇒ V > M (True)
II. V δ T ⇒ V > T (False)
III. M % R ⇒ M < R (True)
IV. K δ R ⇒ K > R (False)

Both I and III are true.

37. (*e*) **Statements** H δ J ⇒ H > J
J # N ⇒ J = N
N @ R ⇒ N ≤ R
R δ W ⇒ R > W

So, H > J = N ≤ R > W

Conclusions I. W % N ⇒ W < N (False)
II. W % H ⇒ W < H (False)
III. R # J ⇒ R = J (may be true)
IV. R δ J ⇒ R > J (may be true)

Only either III or IV is true.

38. (*a*) **Statements** B@D⇒B≤D; DδF⇒D>F; F%M⇒F<M
M ★ N ⇒ M ≥ N

So, B ≤ D > F < M ≥ N

Conclusions I. B % F ⇒ B < F (False)
II. M δ D ⇒ M > D (False)
III. N % F ⇒ N < F (False)
III. D δ N ⇒ D > N (False)

So, none of the given conclusions is correct.

39. (*c*) **Statements** F # Z ⇒ F = Z; Z @ H ⇒ Z ≤ H;
H % N ⇒ H < N; N δ B ⇒ N > B

So, F = Z ≤ H < N > B

Conclusions I. F @ H ⇒ F ≤ H (True)
II. N δ Z ⇒ N > Z (True)
III. B % H ⇒ B < H (False)
IV. B % Z ⇒ B < Z (False)

Both I and II are true.

40. (*d*) **Statements** M % K ⇒ M < K; K ★ W ⇒ K ≥ W;
W δ V ⇒ W > V; V @ N ⇒ V ≤ N

So, M < K ≥ W > V ≤ N

Conclusions I. N ★ K ⇒ N ≥ K (False)
II. M % W ⇒ M < W (False)
III. K δ V ⇒ K > V (True)
IV. V % M ⇒ V < M (False)

Only III is true.

Solution (Q. Nos. 41-45)

P $ Q ⇒ P ≥ Q ⇒ P © Q ⇒ P < Q
P # Q ⇒ P > Q ⇒ P % Q ⇒ P ≤ Q
P @ Q ⇒ P = Q

41. (*d*) **Statements** R # J ⇒ R > J,
J $ D ⇒ J ≥ D,
D @ K ⇒ D = K,
K % T ⇒ K ≤ T

So, R > J ≥ D = K ≤ T

Conclusions I. T # D ⇒ T > D (True)
II. T @ D ⇒ T = D (True)
III. R # K ⇒ R > K (True)
IV. J $ T ⇒ J ≥ T (False)

Hence, either Conclusion I or II and III are definitely true.

42. (*a*) **Statements** T % R ⇒ T ≤ R, R $ M ⇒ R ≥ M,
M @ D ⇒ M = D, D © H ⇒ D < H

So, T ≤ R ≥ M = D < H

Conclusions I. D % R ⇒ D ≤ R (True)
II. H # R ⇒ H > R (False)
III. T © M ⇒ T < M (False)
IV. T % D ⇒ T ≤ D (False)

Hence, only Conclusion I is definitely true.

43. (*c*) **Statements** M @ B ⇒ M = B,
B # N ⇒ B > N,
N $ R ⇒ N ≥ R,
R © K ⇒ R < K

So, M = B > N ≥ R < K

Conclusions I. K # B ⇒ K > B (False)
II. R © B ⇒ R < B (True)
III. M $ R ⇒ M ≥ R (False)
IV. N © M ⇒ N < M (True)

Hence, Conclusions II and IV are definitely true.

44. (*b*) **Statements** $F \# H \Rightarrow F > H, H @ M \Rightarrow H = M,$

$M \copyright E \Rightarrow M < E, E \$ J \Rightarrow E \geq J$

So, $F > H = M < E \geq J$

Conclusions I. $J \copyright M \Rightarrow J < M$ (False)

II. $E \# H \Rightarrow E > H$ (True)

III. $M \copyright F \Rightarrow M < F$ (True)

IV. $F \# E \Rightarrow F > E$ (False)

Hence, Conclusions II and III are definitely true.

45. (*e*) **Statements** $D \% A \Rightarrow D \leq A,$

$A @ B \Rightarrow A = B,$

$B \copyright K \Rightarrow B < K,$

$K \% M \Rightarrow K \leq M$

So, $D \leq A = B < K \leq M$

Conclusions I. $B \$ D \Rightarrow B \geq D$ (True)

II. $K \# A \Rightarrow K > A$ (True)

III. $M \# B \Rightarrow M > B$ (True)

IV. $A \copyright M \Rightarrow A < M$ (True)

Hence, all Conclusions I, II, III and IV are definitely true.

Solution (Q. Nos. 46-50)

$P @ Q \Rightarrow P \geq Q$

$P \# Q \Rightarrow P \leq Q$

$P \$ Q \Rightarrow P = Q$

$P \% Q \Rightarrow P > Q$

$P \bigstar Q \Rightarrow P < Q$

46. (*b*) **Statements** $L \# T \Rightarrow L \leq T$

$T \bigstar D \Rightarrow T < D$

$D @ H \Rightarrow D \geq H$

$H \$ K \Rightarrow H = K$

So, $L \leq T < D \geq H = K$

Conclusions I. $K \bigstar D \Rightarrow K < D$ (False)

II. $K \# D \Rightarrow K \leq D$ (True)

III. $L \bigstar D \Rightarrow L < D$ (True)

IV. $K \$ L \Rightarrow K = L$ (False)

So, Conclusions II and III are true.

47. (*e*) **Statements** $E \$ F \Rightarrow E = F; F @ I \Rightarrow F \geq I$

$I \% K \Rightarrow I > K; L \bigstar K \Rightarrow L < K$

So, $E = F \geq I > K > L$

Conclusions I. $E @ I \Rightarrow E \geq I$ (True)

II. $L \bigstar F \Rightarrow L < F$ (True)

III. $F \% K \Rightarrow F > K$ (True)

IV. $E \% K \Rightarrow E > K$ (True)

So, all conclusions are true.

48. (*d*) **Statements** $R @ J \Rightarrow R \geq J; J \bigstar F \Rightarrow J < F;$

$F \# M \Rightarrow F \leq M; M \% V \Rightarrow M > V$

So, $R \geq J < F \leq M > V$

Conclusions I. $J \% V \Rightarrow J > V$

II. $R @ M \Rightarrow R \geq M$

III. $J \# V \Rightarrow J \leq V$

IV. $R \bigstar M \Rightarrow R < M$

Either I or III and either II and IV are true.

49. (*a*) **Statements** $V \% W \Rightarrow V > W; W \# Z \Rightarrow W \leq Z;$

$Z @ T \Rightarrow Z \geq T; T \$ H \Rightarrow T = H$

So, $V > W \leq Z \geq T = H$

Conclusions I. $Z \% H \Rightarrow Z > H$ (False)

II. $V @ Z \Rightarrow V \geq Z$

III. $V \bigstar Z \Rightarrow V < Z$

IV. $V \$ T \Rightarrow V = T$ (False)

Either II or III is true.

50. (*c*) **Statements** $H \% L \Rightarrow H > L$

$L @ Q \Rightarrow L \geq Q$

$Q \bigstar R \Rightarrow Q < R$

$R \# N \Rightarrow R \leq N$

So, $H > L \geq Q < R \leq N$

Conclusions I. $H @ Q \Rightarrow H \geq Q$ (False)

II. $H \% Q \Rightarrow H > Q$ (True)

III. $N @ Q \Rightarrow N \geq Q$ (False)

IV. $N \% Q \Rightarrow N > Q$ (True)

Conclusions II and IV are true.

LOGICAL REASONING

1

Syllogism

***Syllogism** is a Greek word which means **inference or deduction**. Syllogism is a logical argument where a quantified statement of a specific form (the conclusion) is inferred from two/or more quantified statements.*

Around 3-5 questions from this chapter are being asked in almost each and every competitive and entrance exam, so this is an important chapter of logical reasoning. Hence, a working knowledge of its rules is required on the part of the candidate. The questions of syllogism can be solved by using Venn diagrams and some rules devised with the help of analytical ability. Beside that, some basic concept and rules that are based on reasoning will be helpful.

Terms Used in Syllogism

To proceed further for the study of rules, we must first know some terminology used in syllogism.

Proposition

A proposition, also known as a premise, is a grammatical sentence which comprises a subject, a predicate and a copula. A **subject** is that about which something is said. **Predicate** is a term which states something about a subject and **copula** establishes relationship between subject and predicate.

e.g. (I) All $\underbrace{\text{Pens}}_{\text{Subject}}$ $\underbrace{\text{are}}_{\text{Copula}}$ $\underbrace{\text{Black}}_{\text{Predicate}}$

(II) No $\underbrace{\text{Car}}_{\text{Subject}}$ $\underbrace{\text{is}}_{\text{Copula}}$ $\underbrace{\text{Battery}}_{\text{Predicate}}$

(III) Some $\underbrace{\text{Doors}}_{\text{Subject}}$ $\underbrace{\text{are}}_{\text{Copula}}$ $\underbrace{\text{Windows}}_{\text{Predicate}}$

AEIO Relation

Proposition has been classified on the basis of its quality and quantity. Quality denotes whether the proposition is affirmative or negative. Quantity represents whether the proposition is universal or particular.

The four-fold classification of categorical proposition can be summarised as under

Symbol	Proposition	Quantity	Quality
A	All A are B	Universal	Affirmative
E	No A is B	Universal	Negative
I	Some A are B	Particular	Affirmative
O	Some A are not B	Particular	Negative

To draw valid inferences from the statement a student is required to have a clear understanding of A, E, I, O relationship.

Venn Diagram Representation of Four Propositions

1. **Universal Affirmative** (A) All S are P.

   There are two possible Venn diagram to represent the relation between S and P given by universal affirmative proposition "All S are P". This can also be understood by the theory of sets

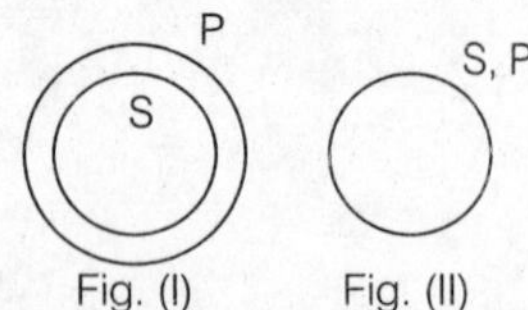

Fig. (I) Fig. (II)

Case I S = {a, b, c} P = {a, b, c, d}

Case II S = {a, b, c} P = {a, b, c}

Case I is represented by Fig. (I) and case II is represented by Fig. (II). In both these cases, we see that every element of set S is also the element of set P. Hence, we can definitely say that the above two figures show that "All S are P".

2. **Universal Negative** (E) No S is P.

   There is only one Venn diagram to represent the relation between S and P.

   S = {a, b, c}, P = {d, e, f}

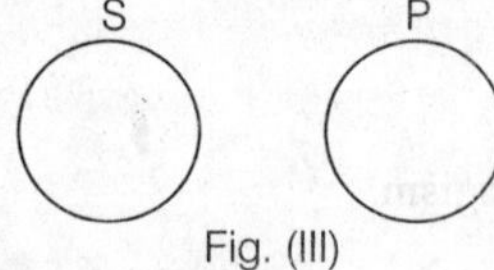

Fig. (III)

From the above two sets, it is clear that none of the elements of S is the element of set P.

3. **Particular Affirmative** (I) Some S are P.

   There are possible Venn diagram to represent the relation between S and P given by particular affirmative proposition, "Some S are P". This can be supported with the help of following sets.

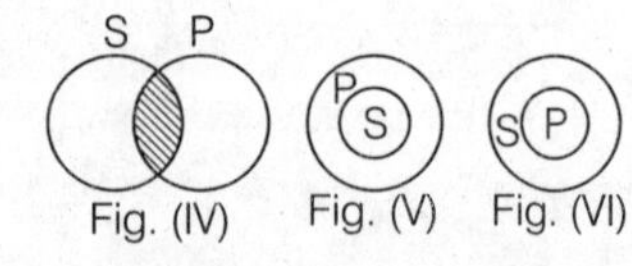

Fig. (IV) Fig. (V) Fig. (VI)

Case I S = {a, b, c, d} P = {c, d, e, f}

Case II S = {a, b} P = {a, b, c, d}

Case III S = {a, b, c, d} P = {a, b}

In all the three cases, we find that some of the elements of S are also the elements of set P.

4. **Particular Negative** (O) Some S are not P.

   There could be three possible Venn diagrams to represent the relation between S and P given by particular negative proposition, "Some S are not P".

   Venn diagram representations of the above propositions can be supported by way of following sets.

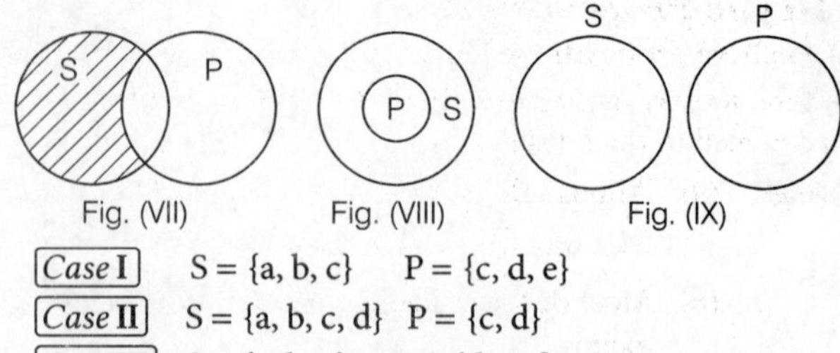

Fig. (VII) Fig. (VIII) Fig. (IX)

Case I S = {a, b, c} P = {c, d, e}

Case II S = {a, b, c, d} P = {c, d}

Case III S = {a, b, c} P = {d, e, f}

In all the three cases, we find that there are some elements in set S which are not elements of set P. Hence, all the cases along with the respective figures support the proposition "Some S are not P".

Hidden Proposition

The type of proposition we have discussed so far are of standard nature. But there are propositions which do not appear in standard format and yet can be classified under any of the four types. Let us now discuss the type of such propositions.

(I) A-Type Propositions

(i) **All positive propositions beginning with every, each, any are A-type propositions.**

e.g. (a) Every cot is mat.

⇒ All cots are mats.

(b) Each student of class V has passed.

⇒ All students of class V has passed.

(c) Anyone can do this job.

⇒ All (men) can do this job.

(ii) **A positive sentence with a particular person as its subject is always an A-type proposition.**

e.g. (a) He can qualify the CAT written test.

(b) Mahatma Gandhi is known as the father of the nation.

(II) E-Type Propositions

(i) **All negative sentences** beginning with **no one, none, not a single**, etc., are **E-type proposition.**

e.g. (a) Not a single student could answer the question.

(b) None can cross the English channel.

(ii) **A negative sentence** with a very definite **exception** is also of E-type proposition.

e.g. No student except Ram has failed.

(iii) When an **interrogative sentence** is used to make an **assertion**, this could be deduced to an **E-type proposition.**

e.g. Is there any person who can scale Mount Everest?

⇒ None can climb Mount Everest.

(III) I-Type Propositions

(i) **Positive propositions** beginning with words such as **most, a few, mostly, generally, almost, frequently, often** are to be deduced to the I-type.

e.g. (a) Almost all the fruits have been sold.
⇒ Some fruits have been sold.

(b) Most of the students will qualify the exams.
⇒ Some of the students will qualify the exams.

(c) Girls are frequently physically weak.
⇒ Some girls are physically weak.

(ii) **Negative propositions** beginning with words such as **few, seldom, hardly, scarcely, rarely, little** etc., are to be deduced to **I-type**.

e.g. (a) Seldom players do not take rest.
⇒ Some players take rest.

(b) Few priests do not tell a lie.
⇒ Some priests tell a lie.

(c) Rarely IT professionals get a good job.
⇒ Some IT professionals get a good job.

(iii) **A positive sentence** with an exception which is **not definite**, is deduced to **I-type** proposition.

e.g. (a) All students except three have passed.
⇒ Some students have passed.

(b) All innocents except a few are guilty.
⇒ Some innocents are guilty.

(IV) O-Type Propositions

(i) **All negative propositions** beginning with words such as **'all', 'every', 'any', 'each'** etc. are to be reduced to **O-type propositions**.

e.g. (a) All innocents are not guilty.
⇒ Some innocents are not guilty.

(b) All that glitters is not gold.
⇒ Some glittering objects are not gold.

(c) Everyone is not present.
⇒ Some are not present.

(ii) **Negative propositions** with words as **most, a few, mostly, generally, almost, frequently** are to be deduced to the **O-type propositions**.

e.g. (a) Girls are usually not physically weak.
⇒ Some girls are not physically weak.

(b) Priests are not frequently thief 's.
⇒ Some priests are not thief 's.

(c) Almost all the questions cannot be solved.
⇒ Some questions cannot be solved.

(iii) **Positive propositions** with starting words such as **few, seldom, hardly, scarcely, rarely, little**, etc. are to be deduced to the **O-type**.

e.g. (a) Few girls are intelligent.
⇒ Some girls are not intelligent.

(b) Seldom are innocent guilty.
⇒ Some innocent are not guilty.

(iv) **A negative sentence** with an exception, which is **not definite**, is to be deduced to the **O-type**.

e.g. (a) No students except Ram have passed.
⇒ Some students have not passed.

(b) No girls except a few are intelligent.
⇒ Some girls are not intelligent.

Term Term is defined as "a word or a set of words, which by itself can be used as a subject or predicate of a proposition."

Syllogism is concerned with three terms

1. **Major term** The major term is the term that occurs as the predicate of the conclusion.
2. **Minor term** The minor term is the term that occurs as the subject of the conclusion.
3. **Middle Term** The term that occurs in both premises, but not in the conclusion.

Example Premises I. All students are boys.
II. All girls are students.
Conclusion All girls are boys.

Here, 'boys' is the predicate of the conclusion. Therefore, it is the major term.

'Girls' is the subject of the conclusion. Therefore, it is the minor term. 'Students' is the term common to both the premises. Therefore, it is the middle term.

Major and Minor Premises The 'major premise' is that in which the middle term is the subject and the 'minor premise' is that in which the middle term is the predicate.

Example Premises I. Some lions are tigers.
II. No cats are lions.

Here, the first premise containing the middle term 'lions' as the subject. So, this premise is the major premise.

In premise II, the middle term 'lions' is the predicate. So, this premise is minor premise.

Type of Inferences

Inferences drawn from statements can be of two types:

1. **Immediate Inference** When inference is drawn from a single statement, then inference is known as immediate inference.

e.g. **Statement** All books are pages.
Conclusion Some pages are books.

In the above example, conclusion is drawn from a single statement and does not require the second statement to be referred, hence the inference is called an immediate inference.

2. **Mediate Inference** In mediate inference, conclusion has to be drawn from to propositions referred to as the 'Premises'. For example,

Statements All dogs are cats. All cats are black.

Conclusion All dogs are black.

In the above example, conclusion is drawn from the two statements or in other words, both the statements are required to draw the conclusion. Hence, the above conclusion is known as mediate inference.

Methods to Draw Immediate Inference

There are various methods to draw immediate inferences like conversion, obversion, contraposition, etc. Keeping in view, the nature of questions asked in competitive exams, we are required to study only two methods- implications and conversion.

1. Implications (of a given proposition)

In the following lines, we shall discuss the implications of all the four types of propositions.

While drawing conclusion through implication, subject remains the subject and predicate remains the predicate.

A-Type All boys are blue.

In A-type proposition, it is very clear that if all boys are blue, then some boys will definitely be blue because some is a part of all. Hence, from A-type proposition, we can draw A-type conclusion (through implication).

E-Type No cars are buses.

If no cars are buses, it clearly means that some cars are not buses. Hence, from E-type proposition, O-type conclusion (through implication) can be drawn.

I-Type Some chairs are tables.

From the I-type proposition, we cannot draw any valid conclusion (through implication).

O-Type Some S are not P.

From the O-type proposition, we cannot draw any valid inference (through implication). On first look, it appears that if some S are not P, then conclusion that some S are P must be true but the possibility of this conclusion being true can be overruled with the help of following example.

Case I S = {a, b, c} P = {d, e, f}

Case II S = {a, b, c} P = {b, c, d}

The above two cases show the relationship between S and P given by O-type proposition "Some S are not P".

Now, in case I, none of the elements of set S is the element of set P, hence conclusion "Some S are P" cannot be valid. However, in case (II), elements b and c are common to both sets S and P. Hence, here conclusion "Some S are P" is valid. But for any conclusion to be true, it should be true from all the cases. Hence, conclusion "Some S are P" is not a valid conclusion drawn from O-type proposition.

All the results derived for immediate inference through implication can be presented in the table as below

Type of proposition	Proposition	Type of inference	Inference
A	All S are P	I	Some S are P
E	No S is P	O	Some S are not P
I	Some S are P	—	—
O	Some S are not P	—	—

2. Conversion

In conversion, while drawing inference, subject and predicate of a proposition are interchanged, i.e. subject becomes the predicate and predicate becomes the subject but the quality of the proposition remains the same, i.e. the affirmative remains affirmative and the negative remains negative.

In conversion, A-type proposition is converted into I-type. E-type can be converted into E-type, I-type can be converted into I-type and O-type proposition cannot be converted.

e.g.

(I) **Statement** All lamps are mangoes. [A–type]
Conclusion Some mangoes are lamps. [I–type]

(II) **Statement** No men are wise. [E–type]
Conclusion No wise are men. [E–type]

(III) **Statement** Some chairs are tables. [I–type]
Conclusion Some tables are chairs. [I–type]

For the comprehension simplicity, we are combining and presenting the results of implication and conversion methods in the following table. This table will help students, in drawing immediate inferences from a given proposition quickly.

Type of proposition	Proposition	Valid inference	Type of inference	Method
A	All S are P	Some S are P	I	Implication
		Some P are S	I	Conversion
E	No S are P	Some S are not P	O	Implication
		No P is S	E	Conversion
I	Some A are B	Some B are A	I	Conversion
O	Some A are not B	No valid inference	—	—

It is important to note here, that only valid inferences given in the above table can be drawn from the four types of propositions. Hence, students are advised to make them familiar with the types of propositions (A, E, I, O) and to remember the results of immediate inferences as given above for solving questions quickly.

Venn Diagram Representation of Immediate Inference

Immediate inferences drawn from each type of propositions (A, E, I, O), as given in the above table, are based on the different rules (implication and conversion) as discussed in the foregoing paragraphs. The same inferences can also be drawn with the help of Venn diagrams but one of the important points to be noted while drawing inference from Venn diagrams is that all possibilities of Venn diagrams should be drawn. Let us now discuss each type of proposition in relation to the pictorial representation.

1. **A-Type** All S are P.

   It is clear from the A type of proposition that all S are contained in P. Therefore, circle representing S will be either inside or equal to circle representing P. However, in both the cases, conclusions (some P are S) and (Some S are P) are true. This case can be comprehended clearly by taking two sets in all possible ways.

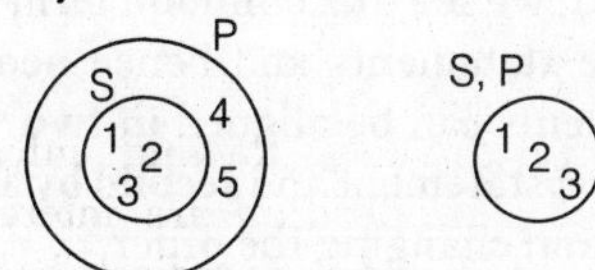

   (i) S = {1, 2, 3} P = {1, 2, 3, 4, 5}

   (ii) S = {1, 2, 3} P = {1, 2, 3}

   The above cases show the all possibilities of two sets S and P showing the relationship between each other as represented by the proposition. All S are P. Now, in both the cases we see that set {2, 3} is the part of set S and also of set P. Hence, it is clear that inference (some S are P) is true from this relationship.

   Likewise, set {2, 3} is the part of set P and also of set S. Therefore, it is also clear that inference (some P are S) is true. Inference (some P are not S) is not valid because it is true from case (i) but false from case (ii). Inference (all P are S) is not valid because it is true from case (ii) and false from case (i).

2. **E-Type** No S is P.

   There is only one possibility of Venn diagram representation of E-type proposition. The relationship can also be shown by two sets S = {1, 2, 3} and P = {4, 5, 6}. From these two sets, we see that set {2, 3} is the part of set S but not of set P.

   It implies that inference (some S are not P) is true. Similarly, set {5, 6} is the part of set P but not of set S. This means that inference (some P are not S) is true.

   Therefore, on the basis of E-type proposition, we can draw following immediate inferences.

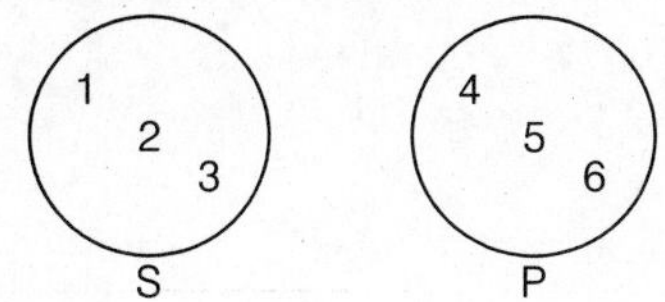

   (i) No P is S.

   (ii) Some S are not P.

   (iii) Some P are not S.

   Any other immediate inference drawn from E-type proposition is not valid.

3. **I-Type** Some S are P.

   This proposition gives rise to many possible representations of Venn diagrams and hence most of the inferences drawn therefore are invalid and doubtful. This relationship can be shown by following sets and respective Venn diagrams.

   (i) S = {1, 2, 3, 4}, P = {3, 4, 5, 6}

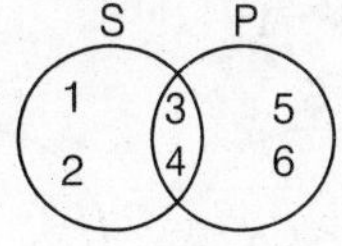

   Set {3, 4} is the part of set S as well as set P, hence some S are P.

   (ii) S = {1, 2, 3, 4}, P = {1,2}

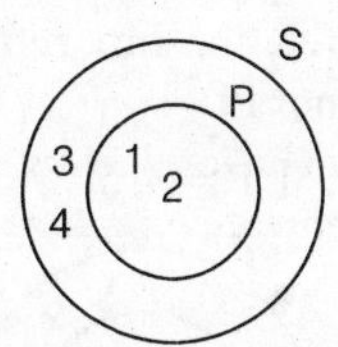

   Set {1, 2} is the part of set S as well as set P, hence some S are P.

   (iii) S = {1,2}, P = {1,2,3,4}

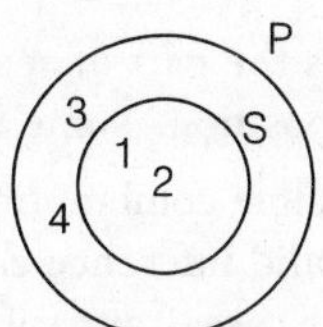

   Set {1} is the part of set S as well as set P, hence some S are P.

   (iv) S = {1,2}, P = {1,2,3}

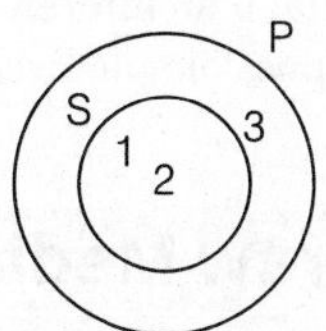

   Set {1, 2} is the part of set S as well as set P, hence, some S are P.

   The above four combinations of sets and respective diagrams show the relationship between S and P as represented by I-type proposition. From all the possible combinations it is clear that inference (some P are S) is true. Inference (some S are not P) is true from (i) and (ii) combinations. But it is not true from (iii) and (iv) combinations. Therefore, inference (some S are not P) is not a valid inference drawn from above proposition.

4. **O-Type** Some S are not P

From this proposition no immediate inference can be drawn. Let us discuss this proposition in the light of Venn diagram representation.

(i) S = {1, 2, 3, 4}, P = {3, 4, 5, 6}

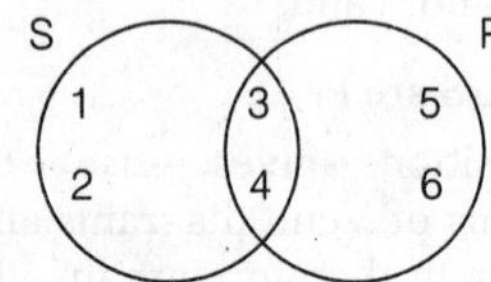

Set {1, 2} is the part of set S but not of set P, hence this shows the relationship represented by the proposition "some S are not P".

(ii) S = {1, 2, 3}, P = {4, 5, 6}

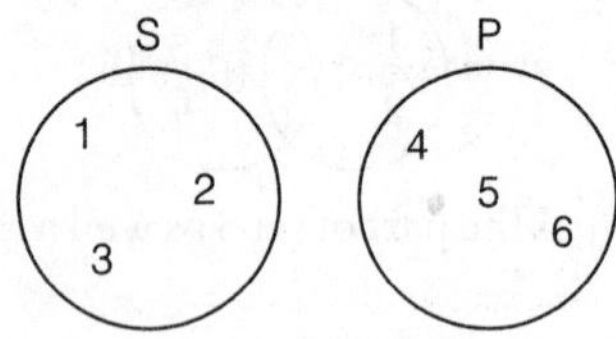

Set {2, 3} is the part of set S but not of set P, hence this shows the relationship represented by proposition 'some S are not P'.

(iii) S = {1, 2, 3, 4, 5}, P = {4, 5}

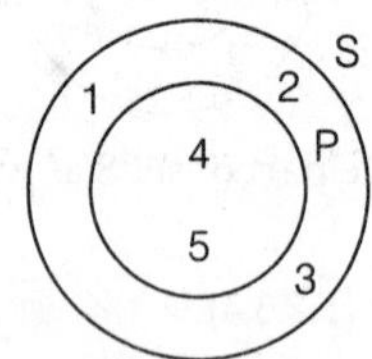

Set {1, 2, 3} is the part of set S but not of set P, hence denotes proposition "some S are not P".

On the basis of all possible combinations, showing relationship between S and P, no valid inference can be drawn. Inference – Some S are P is true from case (i) and (iii) but not true from case (ii) and hence it is an invalid inference. Inference – Some P are not S is true from case (i) and (ii) but not true from case (iii) and hence it is an invalid inference.

Students should note that if an inference is true, it has to comply with or follow all the possible pictorial representation of Venn diagrams.

Methods to Draw Mediate Inference

Like immediate inference, mediate inferences can also be drawn with the help of certain rules and Venn diagrams. We shall discuss each technique in the following paragraphs.

Steps for Mediate Inference

***Step* I** The first step in drawing **mediate inferences** is the alignment of statements. As we know, to draw mediate inference we need two statements having **one term common** to both the statements. By alignment, we mean that **predicate of the first statement** should be the **subject of the second statement.**

In other words, we can say that **common term is the predicate of the first statement and subject of second statement.** Alignment is required only when we find that common term is either subject in both the statements or predicate in both the statements. If the statements are already aligned then, we can move to the **step II.**

Following examples will make the concept of alignment more clear.

***Ex* 1.** **Statements** I. Some girls are boys.
II. All girls are black.

***Ex* 2.** **Statements** I. Some mangoes are baskets.
II. No tables are baskets.

In example 1, we see that **common term girls is subject** in both the statements and hence **needs alignment.** The statements can be aligned in **two ways : One by** aligning first statement and **second by** aligning second statement and changing the order.

***Case* I** **Statement** I. "Some girls are boys" can be converted into "Some boys are girls" using the rule of conversion already discussed in the previous paragraphs. After conversion of the first statement, both the statements are aligned as below

Statements I. Some boys are girls.
II. Some girls are boys.

***Case* II** **Statement** II. "All girls are black" can be converted into "Some black are girls." After converting the second statement and changing the orders of the statements, the statements are aligned as below

Statements I. Some black are girls.
II. All girls are black.

Likewise, the statements in example 2 can be aligned in two ways as below

***Case* I** **Statements** I. Some mangoes are baskets.
II. No baskets are tables.

***Case* II** **Statements** I. No tables are baskets.
II. Some baskets are mangoes.

Since, the statements in both the above **examples can be aligned in two ways,** hence it becomes important to **know that which alignment to consider.** In this connection, students may note that while aligning the **priority students be given in the following order**

$$\xrightarrow{\text{I E A}}$$

i.e. importance for conversion should be given first to I-type statement, then E-type statement and last A-type statement.

Using the above priority order in examples 1 and 2, we find that in example 1, Statement I is of I-type and Statement II is of A-type. Hence, Statement I should be aligned, being of I-type. Hence, alignment as per case I will have to be considered and not the alignment as per case II.

> *In example* 2, Statement I is of I type and Statement II is of E-type. Hence, Statement I should be aligned. As a result, proper alignment would be as per case II and 'not as per' case I.

***Step* II** After having aligned the statements, if required, inference can be drawn using the table as given below

Type of Ist statement		Type of IInd statement		Type of inference
A	+	A	=	A
A	+	E	=	E
E	+	A	=	O*
E	+	I	=	O*
I	+	A	=	I
I	+	E	=	O

The conclusion will follow the pattern in such a way that subject of the first statement is the subject of the inference and predicate of second statement is the predicate of the inference, except the cases (O* as shown in the table), where conclusion will follow the reverse pattern, i.e. subject of the first statement will be the predicate of inference and predicate of the second statement will be the subject of the inference.

The above table shows the combination of statements which produce definite and valid results. All other combinations will not produce definite inferences.

The following examples will make the concept more clear.

***Ex* 1.** **Statements** I. Some books are papers.

II. No copies are papers.

Sol. The statements are not aligned. Hence, first step will be to align the statements. Statement I is of I-type and hence will get the priority for alignment. After alignment and reordering, the statements will become

I. No copies are papers.

II. Some papers are books.

(E-type can be converted into E-type. Refer to conversion table.)

Now, using table for mediate inference, we find that

$$E + I = O^*$$

Hence, inference will be **"some books are not copies"**.

***Ex* 2.** **Statements** I. Some papers are white.

II. No black are papers.

Sol. In above statements, alignment is not required. Simply reordering the sentences will align the statements.

I. No black are papers.

II. Some papers are white.

$$E + I = O^*$$

Hence, inference will be "some white are not black."

Please note again that conclusion of the form O* will follow the reverse pattern, i.e. subject of the first statement will be the **predicate of the inference and predicate** of the second statement will be the subject of the inference.

***Ex* 3.** **Statements** I. All books are clocks.

II. All clocks are pens.

Sol. Both the statements are already aligned. Now, using table for mediate inference, we find that A + A = A. Hence, the valid inference will be "all books are pens".

It is important to note that table for mediate inference produce only one valid result from the above statements yet we can also convert the conclusion "All books are pens" as "some pens are books" according to rules for conversion. Hence, the conclusion "Some pens are books" is also valid.

Types of Questions Asked in Different Examinations

There are mainly two types of questions which may be asked under this

1. **When premises are in specified form** Here, premise is in the specified form. Here, mainly two propositions are given. Propositions may be particular to universal; universal to particular; particular to particular; universal to universal.
2. **When premises are in jumbled/mixed form** Here, atleast three or more than three propositions are given. Here, pair of two propositions out of them follow as, same as in specified form.

Type 1 Premises in Specified Forms

Case I The conclusion does not contain the middle term.

Ex 1. **Statements** All buses are cars.
All scooters are buses.

Conclusions I. No scooter is a bus.
II. All cars are buses.

(a) Only I follows (b) Only II follows
(c) Both I and II follow (d) Neither I nor II follows

Sol. (*d*)

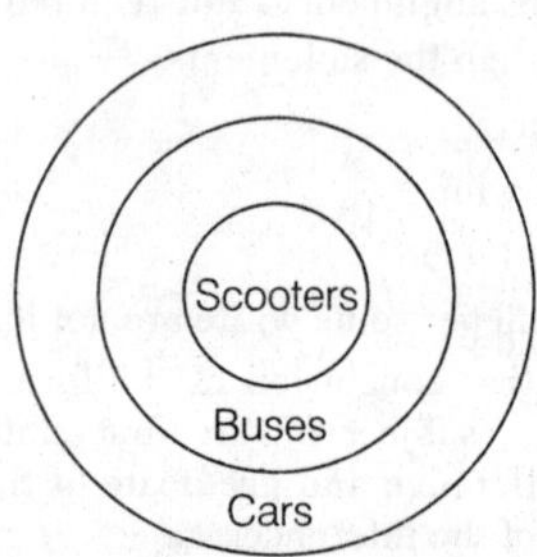

Conclusion I. No scooter is a bus. (false)

Conclusion II. All cars are buses. (false)

Hence, neither Conclusion I nor II follows.

Ex 2. **Statements** I. All mangoes are chairs.
II. Some chairs are tables.

SBI (Clerk) 2012

Conclusions I. All mangoes are tables.
II. Some tables are mangoes.
III. No mango is a table.

(a) Only I follows (b) Only II follows
(c) Only III follows (d) I and II follow
(e) None of these

Sol. (*e*) Here, the term chair is common to both the statements hence it is the middle term. Statement I is A-type proposition and in A-type proposition, only subject is distributed, hence chair being the predicate in the Statement I is not distributed in the second statement. Thus, none of the conclusions following statements is a valid inference.

Venn diagram representation All possible cases can be drawn as

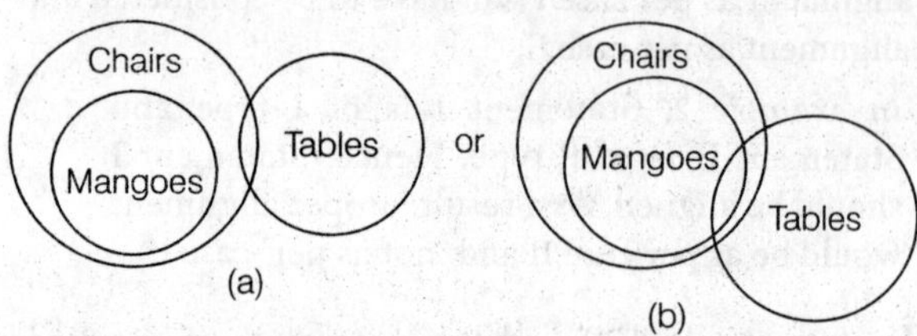

(i) All mangoes are table, this inference is definitely false, neither (a) nor (b) shows this conclusion.

(ii) Some tables are mangoes, this inference is uncertain or doubtful.

(iii) No mango is a table, this inference is also uncertain or doubtful. Though, it can be concluded from the above discussion that no valid inference can be drawn between mango and table.

Case II No term can be distributed in the conclusion unless it is distributed in the premises.

If case I is compiled by a pair of statements, it is confirmed that valid mediate inferences can be drawn from such pair of statements. But every mediate inference drawn cannot be valid. Therefore, case II is applied to check as to the conclusions drawn from a pair of statements in which middle term is distributed, is valid.

Ex 3. **Statements** I. Some boys are students.
II. All students are teenagers.

Conclusions I. All teenagers are students.
II. Some boys are teenagers.

(a) Only I follows
(b) Only II follows
(c) Both I and II follow
(d) Neither I nor II follows

Sol. (*b*) **Statement** I is an I-type proposition which distributes neither the subject nor the predicate. Statement II is an A-type proposition which distributes the subject 'students'. Conclusion I is an A-type proposition which distributes the subject 'teenagers' only.

Since, the term teenagers is distributed in Conclusion I without being distributed in the premises. So, Conclusion I cannot follow. In second conclusion, where it is asked that some boys are teenagers but from Statement I it is clear that some boys are not students. These boys may not be teenagers.

Venn diagram representation All possible cases can be drawn as follows :

We have given that all students are teenagers, so its reverse cannot be possible. Hence, Conclusion I is false. As, we are also given that some boys are students and all students are teenagers. So, some boys which are students must be teenagers. Hence, Conclusion II follows.

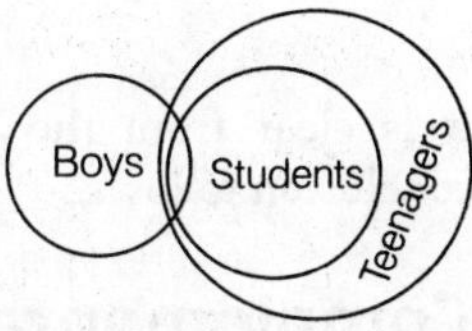

Case III If one premises is particular, conclusion is particular.

***Ex* 4.** **Statements** I. Some art works are paintings.
II. All paintings are master pieces.

General Insurance Corporation (AAO) Exam 2011

Conclusions I. All master pieces are paintings.
II. Some master pieces are art works.

(a) Only I follows (b) Only II follows
(c) Both I and II follow (d) Neither I nor II follows
(e) Either I or II follow

Sol. (*b*) Since, on premise is particular, the conclusion must be particular. So, Conclusion II follows but the Conclusion I does not follows.

Venn diagram representation

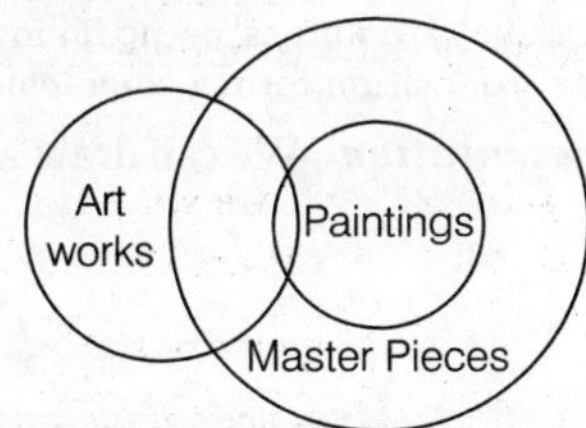

Here, Conclusion II follows but the Conclusion I does not follow.

Case IV If the middle term is distributed twice, the conclusion cannot be universal.

***Ex* 5.** **Statements** I. All Lotus are flowers.
II. No Lily is a Lotus.

Conclusions I. No Lily is a flower.
II. Some Lilies are flowers.

(a) Only I follows
(b) Only II follows
(c) Either I or II follows
(d) Neither I nor II follows

Sol. (*c*) Here, the first premise is an A-type proposition and so the middle term **'Lotus'** forming the **subject** is distributed.The second premise is an E proposition and so the middle term **'Lotus'** forming the **predicate** is distributed. Since, the middle term is distributed twice, so the conclusion cannot be universal.

Venn diagram representation All possible cases can be drawn as follows

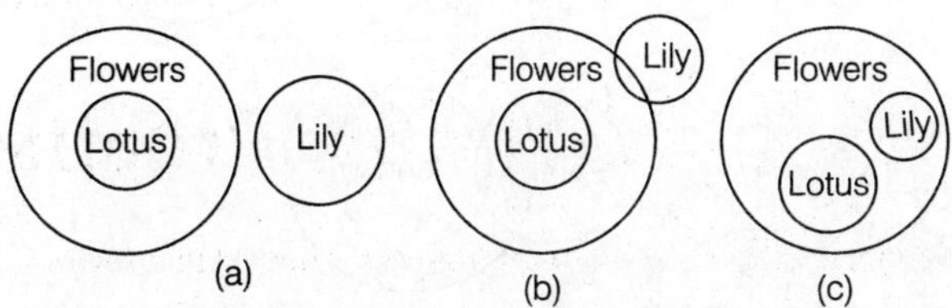

It is clear from the given Venn diagrams, either Conclusion I or II must be followed.

Case V If both the premises are affirmative, the conclusions must be affirmative.

***Ex* 6.** **Statements** I. All D's are A's.
II. All A's are C's.

Conclusions I. All D's are C's.
II. Some D's are not A's.

(a) Only I follows
(b) Only II follows
(c) Both I and II follow
(d) None follows

Sol. (*a*) All possible cases can be drawn as follows

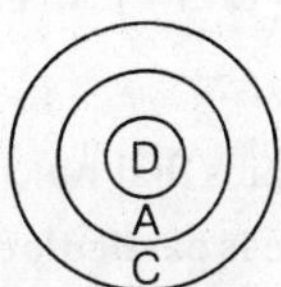

Now, taking Conclusion I, it is clear that all D's are also C's but taking Conclusion II, we cannot say that some D's are not A's because from Statement I it is clear that all D's are A's.

Hence, only Conclusion I follows.

Case VI No conclusion follows.

There are three types of such cases

(i) If both the premises are particular

***Ex* 7.** **Statements** I. Some eyes are ears.
II. Some ears are hands.

Conclusions I. No hand is an eye.
II. Some eyes are hands.

(a) Only I follows
(b) Only II follows
(c) Either I or II follows
(d) Neither I nor II follows

Sol. (*c*) Since, both the premises are particular affirmative (I-type). No conclusion follows from the two particular premises.

Conclusions I and II form complementary pair. Therefore, either Conclusion I or II follows.

Venn diagram representation All possible cases can be drawn as,

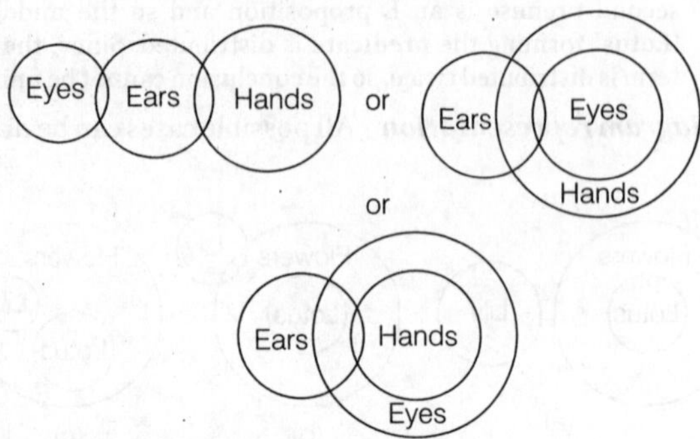

Hence, either I or II follows.

(ii) **If both the premises are negative**

Ex 8. **Statements** I. No flower is mango.
II. No mango is cherry. **SBI (PO) 2010**

Conclusions I. No flower is cherry.
II. Some cherries are mangoes.

(a) Only I follows (b) Only II follows
(c) Both I and II follow (d) Neither I nor II follows
(e) Either I or II follows

Sol. (*d*) Since, both the premises are negative, hence neither Conclusion I nor Conclusion II follows.

Venn diagram representation

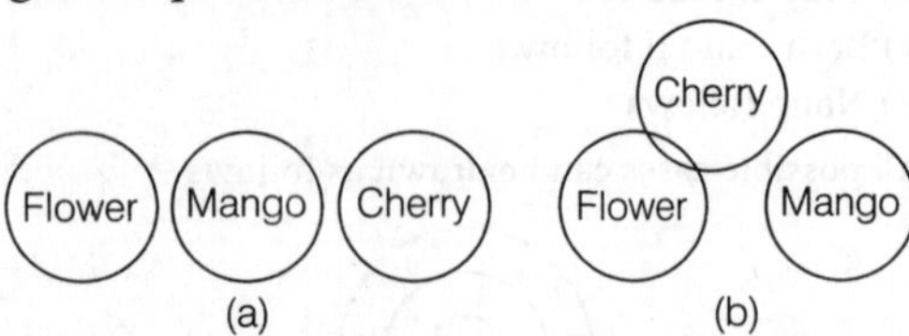

It is clear from Venn diagrams that no conclusion follows.

(iii) **If the major premise is particular and the minor premise is negative**

Major premise is the predicate of the conclusion and minor premise is the subject of the conclusion.

Ex 9. **Statements** I. Some pubs are cows.
II. No kitten are pubs.

Conclusions I. No pubs are kitten
II. Some cows are kitten.

(a) Only I follows (b) Only II follows
(c) Both I and II follow (d) None follows

Sol. (*d*) Here, the first premise containing the middle term 'Pubs' as the subject, is the major premise and the second premise containing the middle term 'Pubs' as the predicate, is the minor premise. Since, the major premise is particular and the minor premise is negative. So, no conclusion follows.

Venn diagram representation All possible cases are given

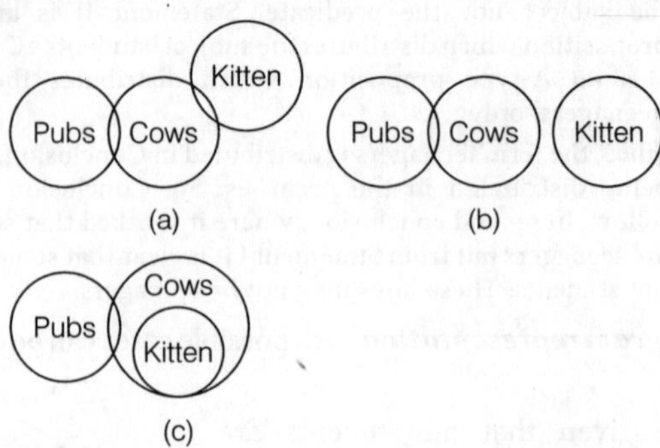

It is clear from the Venn diagram representation that, none conclusion follows.

Complementary Pair of Conclusions

In drawing mediate inferences from given statements, students are required to be **more attentive in selecting complementary pair of conclusion**, where neither of the conclusions is definitely true but a combination of both makes a complementary pair. As we have already discussed in case I that, in the statements, where middle term is not distributed, no valid mediate inference can be drawn but there still exists a possibility that a complementary pair of conclusions follows from the statements.

Ex 10. **Statements** I. Some cameras are radios.
II. Some statues are cameras.

Conclusions I. Some radios are statues.
II. No radio is statue.

(a) Only I follows
(b) Only II follows
(c) Either I or II follows
(d) None follows

Sol. (*c*) Either 'some radios are statues' or 'no radio is statue' follows, as I and E-types proposition form a complementary pair.

Venn diagram representation We can draw all possible cases as given below

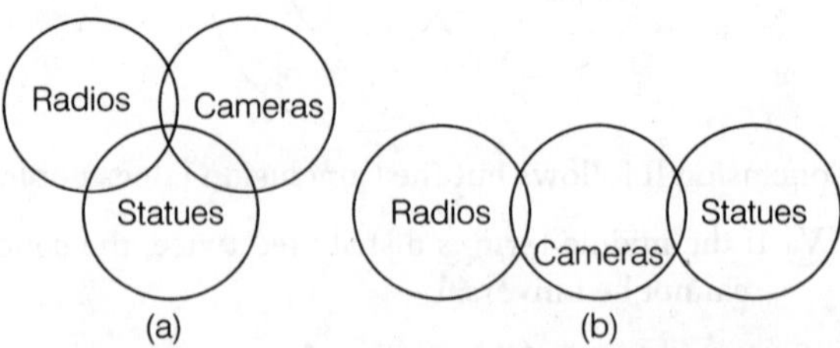

Hence, using both diagrammatical representations we can conclude either some radios are statues or 'no radio' is statue. Hence, atleast one of the conclusions must be true.

Works Only for Two Conclusions

Special cases

Combinations	Conclusion
A + E	Either I or II follows
E + I	Either I or II follows
I + O	Either I or II follows
E + O	Either I or II follows

***Ex* 11. Statements** I. All vegetables are green.
II. Some greens are fruits.

Conclusions I. Some fruits are vegetables.
II. No fruit is vegetable.

(a) Only I follows
(b) Only II follows
(c) Either I or II follows
(d) Neither I nor II follows

Sol. (*c*) Here, Conclusion I is particular affirmative and Conclusion II is universal negative proposition. Hence, either Conclusion I or Conclusion II follows.

Venn diagram representation We draw all possible cases as below

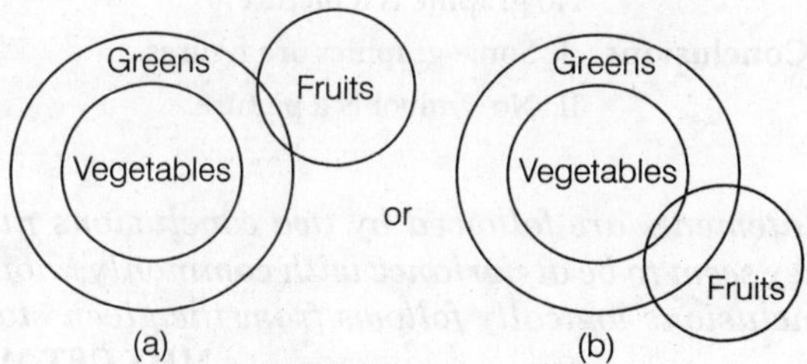

Conclusions If we follow Venn diagram (a), then we can say no fruit is vegetable (Conclusion II). But, if we follow Venn diagram (b), then we can say some fruits are vegetables (Conclusion I).

Here, either Venn diagram (a) or Venn diagram (b) is possible. Hence, either Conclusion I or Conclusion II must be followed.

Minimal Possibilities

- We can represent statements by keeping in mind our conclusions. If we follow that our two conclusions belong to special case, then either one of them is true.
- We can represent minimum possibilities as given directly in the statement, we don't need to think about parameters.

***Ex* 12. Statements** I. Some fruits are vegetables.
II. Some vegetables are junk food.
III. Some junk foods are snacks.

Conclusions I. Some junk foods are vegetables.
II. Some junk foods are fruits.

(a) Only I follows (b) Only II follows
(c) Both I and II follow (d) None follows

Sol. (*a*) **Minimum possibilities**

It is clear from the above diagrams that only Conclusion I follows.

Intro Exercise 1 (Based on Type 1)

Direction (Q. Nos. 1-6) *In each group of questions below are two/three statements followed by two conclusions numbered* I *and* II. *You have to take the given statements to be true even, if they seem to be at variance from commonly known facts and then decide which of the given conclusions logically follows from the two/three statements disregarding commonly known facts.*

Given answer

(a) if only Conclusion I follows
(b) if only Conclusion II follows
(c) if either Conclusion I or II follows
(d) if neither Conclusion I nor II follows
(e) if both Conclusions I and II follow

1. **Statements** Some exams are tests.
No exam is a question.
Conclusions I. No question is a test.
II. Some tests are definitely not exams.

Statements (Q. Nos. 2-3) *All forces are energies. All energies are powers. No power is heat.*

2. **Conclusions** I. Some forces are definitely not powers.
II. No heat is force.

3. **Conclusions** I. No energy is heat.
II. Some forces being heat is a possibility.

Statements (Q. Nos. 4-5) *No note is a coin. Some coins are metals. All plastics are notes.*

4. **Conclusions** I. No coin is a plastic.
II. All plastics being metals is a possibility

5. **Conclusions** I. No metal is plastic.
II. All notes are plastics.

6. **Statements** Some symbols are figures.
All symbols are graphics.
No graphic is a picture.
Conclusion I. Some graphics are figures.
II. No symbol is a picture.

Direction (Q. Nos. 7-8) *In each of the quesions given below statements are followed by two conclusions numbered* I *and* II. *You have to take the given statements to be true even if they seem to be at variance with commonly known facts. Read all the conclusions and then decide which of the given conclusions logically follows from the given statements disregarding commonly known facts.* **MHT CET MBA 2012**

Give answer

(a) if only Conclusion I follows
(b) if only Conclusion II follows
(c) if either Conclusion I or II follows
(d) if neither Conclusion I nor II follows
(e) if both Conclusions I and II follow

Statements (Q. Nos. 7-8) *All festivals are celebrations. Some celebrations are events.*

7. **Conclusions** I. All celebrations are festivals.
II. All events being festivals is a possibility.

8. **Conclusions** I. All those events if they are festivals are also celebrations.
II. Atleast some events are celebrations.

Direction (Q. Nos. 9-16) *In each of the questions given below statments are given followed by two conclusions numbered* I *and* II. *You have to take the given statements to be true even if they seem to be at variance with commonly known facts. Read all the conclusions and then decide which of the given conclusions logically follows from the given statements disregarding commonly known facts.*

Give answer

(a) if only Conclusion I follows
(b) if only Conclusion II follows
(c) if either Conclusion I or II follows
(d) if neither Conclusion I nor II follows
(e) if both Conclusions I and II follow

9. **Statements** Some papers are needles.
All needles are sharp.
Conclusions I. All papers are sharp.
II. All needles are papers.

10. **Statements** All cars are tables.
Some children are tables.
Conclusions I. Some cars are children.
II. Some children are cars.

11. Statements Some men are educated.
Educated persons prefer small families.
Conclusions I. All small families are educated.
II. Some men prefer small families.

12. Statements Some pots are belts.
No belt is white.
Conclusions I. Some pots are white.
II. Some pots are not white.

13. Statements Some cities are villages.
Some towns are villages.
Conclusions I. Some cities are towns.
II. No city is town.

14. Statements All windows are doors.
No door is a wall.
Conclusions I. No window is a wall.
II. No wall is a door.

15. Statements All lawyers are cheats.
Some women are lawyers.
Conclusions I. Some women are cheats.
II. All cheats are women.

16. Statements Some chairs are stools.
All tables are chairs.
Conclusions I. Some stools are chairs.
II. Table is not a stool.

Direction (Q. Nos. 17-18) *In the following questions statements are followed by conclusions. Choose the answer response that gives the correct conclusion which logically follows from the given statements. You have to take the given statements as true even if they seem at variance with commonly known facts.* **MPPSC 2014**

17. Statements Some scientists are literate.
No literate is intelligent.
Conclusions I. Some literates are scienctists.
II. Some intelligents are scientists.
III. Some scientists are not intelligent.
IV. All intelligents are scientists.

(a) I and II follow
(b) II and III follow
(c) III and IV follow
(d) I and III follow

18. Statements All dogs are vegetarians.
All blacks are white.
Some vegetarians are black.
Conclusions I. Some whites are dogs.
II. Some blacks are dogs.
III. Some whites are vegetarians.

(a) Only Conclusion I follows
(b) Only Conclusion II follows
(c) Only Conclusion III follows
(d) Both Conclusions II and III follow

Direction (Q. Nos. 19-24) *In each of the questions given below statements are given followed by two conclusions numbererd* I *and* II. *You have to take the given statements to be true even if they seem to be at variance with commonly known facts. Read all the conclusions and then decide which of the given conclusions logically follows from the given statements disregarding commonly known facts.*

Give answer
(a) if only Conclusion I follows
(b) if only Conclusion II follows
(c) if either Conclusion I or II follows
(d) if neither Conclusion I nor II follows
(e) if both Conclusions I and II follow

19. Statements All bags are boxes.
All boxes are utensils.
Some utensils are bowls.
Conclusions I. Some boxes are bowls.
II. All bags are utensils.

20. Statements Some phones are cells.
All cells are batteries.
Some batteries are tools.
Conclusions I. some tools are cells.
II. Some batteries are phones.

21. Statements All numbers are letters.
Some letters are words.
Some words are symbols.
Conclusions I. Some symbols are letters.
II. Some words are numbers.

22. Statements All keys are cards.
All cards are locks.
No keys are doors.
Conclusions I. No lock is door.
II. Some locks are doors.

23. Statements Some symbols are figures.
All symbols are graphics.
No graphic is a picture. **MHT CET MBA 2014**
Conclusions I. Some graphics are figures.
II. No symbol is a picture.

24. Statements All files are papers.
Some papers are books.
Some books are journals. **SSC CGL 2014**
Conclusions I. All files are journals.
II. All books are not journals.

Direction (Q. Nos. 25-29) *In these question two/three statements followed by two conclusions numbered I and II have been given. You have to take the given statements to be true even if they seem to be at variance from the commonly known facts and then decide which of the given conclusions logically follows the statements disregarding commonly known facts.* **SBI Associate (PO) 2014**

Give answer

(a) if either Conclusion I or II follows
(b) if both Conclusions I and II follows
(c) if neither Conclusion I nor II follows
(d) if only Conclusion II follows
(e) if only Conclusion I follows

25. Statements Some prices are costs.
Some costs are amounts.
All amounts are expenses.

Conclusions I. Atleast some amounts are prices.
II. All amounts being prices is a possibility.

26. Statements All invitations are rejections.
Some invitations are celebrations.
No rejection is an attraction.

Conclusions I. Some celebrations are rejections.
II. All celebrations are rejections.

27. Statements All grades are scales.
All scales are categories.

Conclusions I. All grades are categories.
II. All categories are scales.

28. Statements Some metals are papers.
All papers are alloys.
No alloy is a wood.

Conclusions I. All woods being metals is a possibility.
II. All metals being woods is a possibility.

29. Statements Some metals are papers.
All papers are alloys.
No alloy is a wood.

Conclusions I. No paper is a wood.
II. Atleast some metals are alloys.

Direction (Q. Nos. 30-32) *These questions having two statements followed by two Conclusions I and II. Decide which of the conclusions follows from the statements.*

Give answer

(a) if Conclusion I follows
(b) if Conclusion II follows
(c) if neither Conclusion I nor II follows
(d) if both Conclusions I and II follow

30. Statements A man must be wise to be a good wrangler.
Good wranglers are talkative and boring.

Conclusions I. All the wise persons are boring.
II. All the wise persons are good wranglers.

31. Statements All goods athletes win.
All good athletes eat well.

Conclusions I. All those who eat well are good athletes.
II. All those who win eat well.

32. Statements All roads are water.
Some water are boats.

Conclusions I. Some boats are roads.
II. All water are boats.

Direction (Q. Nos. 33-34) *Each question below are given two statements followed by two conclusions numbered I and II. You have to take the given statements to be true even if they seem to be at variance from commonly known facts and decide which of the given conclusions logically follows from the given statements, disregarding commonly known facts.* **CMAT 2014**

Give answer

(a) if only Conclusion I follows
(b) if only Conclusion II follows
(c) if either Conclusion I or II follows
(d) if neither Conclusion I nor II follows

33. Statements Some books are papers.
No copies are papers.

Conclusions I. Some books are not copies.
II. No books are copies.

34. Statements Some cups are plates.
Some plates are jugs.

Conclusions I. Some cups are jugs.
II. All cups are jugs.

Direction (Q. Nos. 35-42) *In the following questions, three statements followed by two conclusions numbered I and II have been given. You have to take the given statements to be true even if they seem to be at variance from the commonly known facts and then decide which of the given conclusions logically follows from the given statements disregarding commonly known facts.* **NIACL 2015**

Give answer

(a) if either Conclusion I or II is true
(b) if neither Conclusion I nor II is true
(c) if both Conclusions I and II are true
(d) if only Conclusion I is true
(e) if only Conclusion II is true

35. Statements All alphabets are letters.
All letters are digits.
No digit is a number.

Conclusions I. No alphabet is a digit.
II. All alphabets are digits.

36. **Statements** All fruits are flowers.
No flower is sweet.
Some sweets are deserts.

Conclusions I. Some deserts are flowers.
II. No desert is flower.

37. **Statements** Some planes are ships.
No ship is a radar.
All cars are radars.

Conclusions I. Some radars are ships.
II. All cars are planes.

38. **Statements** All locks are keys.
All keys are doors.
Some doors are windows.
Some windows are floors.

Conclusions I. Some keys are windows.
II. No floor is door.

39. **Statements** All rats are cats.
No cow is cat.
All dogs are cows.

Conclusions I. No dog is rat.
II. No dog is cat.

40. **Statements** Some towers are pillars.
Some pillars are buildings.
All buildings are flats.
No flat is house.

Conclusions I. No building is house.
II. Some towers are house.

41. **Statements** All cups are bowls.
All bowls are trays.
Some trays are plates.
No plate is spoon.

Conclusions I. Some bowls are plates.
II. Some cups are spoons.

42. **Statements** All books are pens.
Some pen are desks.
Some desks are chairs.
Some chairs are tables.

Conclusions I. Some tables are desks.
II. Some chairs are pens.

Type 2 Mixed/Jumbled Problems

In such type of problems, there is a constitution of mixed problems of universal and particular premises.

Direction (Examples 1-4) *In each of the questions given below there are three statements followed by three/four conclusions numbered* I, II *and* III, *you have to take the given statements to be true even, if they seem to be at variance from commonly known facts. Read all the conclusions and then decide which of the given conclusions logically follows from the given statements disregarding commonly known facts.*

Ex 1. **Statements** I. All baskets are poles.
II. Some poles are lamps.
III. All lamps are roads.

Conclusions I. Some lamps are baskets.
II. Some roads are poles.
III. Some lamps are roads.

(a) I and II follow
(b) I and III follow
(c) II and III follow
(d) All follow

Ex 2. **Statements** I. Some cards are pictures.
II. All pictures are paints.
III. Some paints are nail.

Conclusions I. Some paints are cards.
II. Some nails are cards.
III. Some nails are pictures.

(a) I follows
(b) Only II follows
(c) Only III follows
(d) All follow

Ex 3. **Statements** I. All tigers are lions.
II. All lions are horses.
III. No horses are monkeys.

Conclusions I. All tigers are horses.
II. No tigers are monkeys.
III. Some lions are tigers.
IV. Some monkeys are not tigers.

(a) All follow (b) I, II and III follow
(c) I, II and IV follow (d) II, III and IV follow

Ex 4. **Statements** I. Some shirts are pants.
II. All shoes are shirts.
III. All pants are gloves.

Conclusions I. Some shoes are gloves.
II. Some shirts are gloves.
III. No pants are shoes.
IV. All gloves are shirts.

(a) Only II follows
(b) Only IV follows
(c) I and III follow
(d) All follow

SOLUTION (Examples 1-4)

1. (*c*)

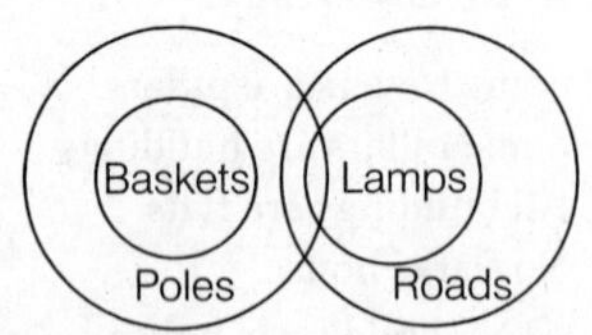

Conclusions I. ✗ II. ✓ III. ✓

Hence, II and III follow.

2. (*a*)

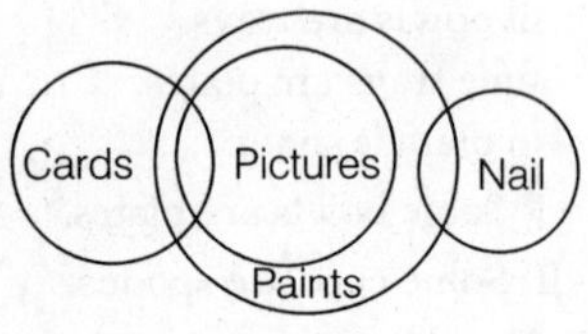

Conclusions I. ✓ II. ✗ III. ✗

Hence, only I follows.

3. (*a*)

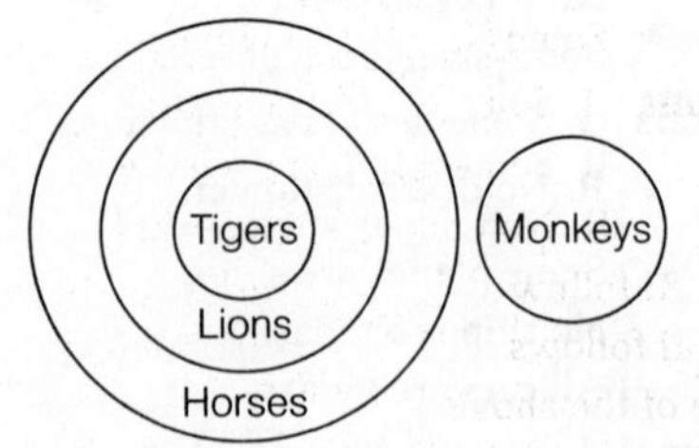

Conclusions I. ✓ II. ✓ III. ✓ IV. ✓

Hence, all follow.

4. (*a*)

Shirts, Pants, Shoes, Gloves or Shoes, Pants, Shirts, Gloves

Conclusions I. ✗ II. ✓ III. ✗ IV. ✗

Hence, Conclusion II follows.

Intro Exercise 2 (Based on Type 2)

Direction (Q. Nos. 1-10) *In each of the questions given below two or three statements are given followed by three conclusions numbered I, II and III. You have to take the given statements to be true even if they seem to be at variance with commonly known facts. Read all the conclusions and then decide which of the given conclusions logically follows from the given statements disregarding commonly known facts.* **IBPS (PO) 2013**

1. **Statements** All tables are boxes. Some boxes are windows.

   Conclusions I. Some tables are windows.
   II. All boxes are tables.
   III. No window is table.

   (a) None follows (b) Either I or III follows
   (c) Either II or III follows (d) I and II follows
   (e) None of these

2. **Statements** Some men are lions.
   All foxes are lions.

   Conclusions I. Some foxes are men.
   II. Some lions are men.
   III. All lions are foxes.

   (a) All follow (b) I and II follow
   (c) Only II follows (d) Only III follows
   (e) None follows

3. **Statements** All rats are bells.
   All bells are cars.

   Conclusions I. All bells are rats.
   II. Some cars are neither bells nor rats.
   III. No car is rat.

   (a) Only I (b) Only II (c) Only III (d) II and III
   (e) None follows

4. **Statements** Some hotels are bricks.
   All bananas are bricks.

   Conclusions I. Some bananas are hotels.
   II. Some bricks are hotels.
   III. No banana is hotel.

   (a) I and II (b) II and III
   (c) Only I follows (d) Either I or III and II follow
   (e) All follow

5. **Statements** Some fruits are stars.
   Some stars are rivers.
   All rivers are goats.

   Conclusions I. No goat is a fruit.
   II. Some goats are stars.
   III. No goat is a star.

   (a) None follows (b) Only II follows
   (c) Either II or III follows (d) Either I or II follows
   (e) All follow

6. **Statements** All snakes are trees.
   Some trees are roads.
   All roads are mountains.

   Conclusions I. Some mountains are snakes.
   II. Some roads are snakes.
   III. Some mountains are trees.

   (a) None follows (b) Only I follows
   (c) Only II follows (d) Only III follows
   (e) Both I and II follow

7. **Statements** Some doors are windows.
All chairs are tables.
Some chairs are windows.

Conclusions I. Some chairs are doors.
II. Some tables are windows.
III. No table is a window.

(a) I and III follow (b) II and III follow
(c) Only II follows (d) II and either I or III follow
(e) None of the above

8. **Statements** Some bottles are bags.
All cards are bottles.
All pens are bags.

Conclusions I. Some pens are cards.
II. Some cards are bottles.
III. Some pens are bottles.

(a) I and III follow (b) II and III follow
(c) Only II follows (d) Either I or III follows
(e) None follows

9. **Statements** Some cups are pots.
All pots are tubes.
All cups are bottles.

Conclusions I. Some bottles are tubes.
II. Some pots are bottles.
III. Some tubes are cups.

(a) I and II follow (b) II and III follow
(c) I and III follow (d) All follow
(e) None of these

10. **Statements** Some cards are files.
Some files are ink-pots.
Some ink-pots are pads. **MAT 2013**

Conclusions I. Some ink-pots are cards.
II. Some cards are pads.
III. Some pads are files.

(a) None follows (b) Only I follows
(c) Only II follows (d) Only III follows

Direction (Q. Nos. 11-15) *In each of the questions below are given three statements followed by three conclusions numbered* I, II *and* III. *You have to take the given statements to be true even if they seem to be at variance from commonly known facts. Read all the conclusions and then decide which of the given conclusions logically follows from the given statements disregarding commonly known facts.* **Punjab & Sind Bank (PO) 2010**

11. **Statements** Some carrots are brinjals.
Some brinjals are apples.
All apples are bananas.

Conclusions I. Some apples are carrots.
II. Some bananas are brinjals.
III. Some bananas are carrots.

(a) Only I follows (b) Only II follows
(c) Only III follows (d) Either II or III follows
(e) None of these

12. **Statements** All keys are locks.
All locks are bangles.
All bangles are cars.

Conclusions I. Some cars are locks.
II. Some bangles are keys.
III. Some cars are keys.

(a) Only I follows (b) I and II follow
(c) I and III follow (d) II and III follow
(e) All follow

13. **Statements** All fruits are leaves.
Some leaves are trees.
No tree is house.

Conclusions I. Some houses are fruits.
II. Some trees are fruits.
III. No house is fruit.

(a) Only I follows (b) Only II follows
(c) Only III follows (d) Only either I or III follows
(e) None follows

14. **Statements** All tables are mirrors.
Some mirrors are chairs.
All chairs are glasses.

Conclusions I. Some glasses are mirrors.
II. Some chairs are tables.
III. Some mirrors are tables.

(a) I and II follow (b) II and III follow
(c) I and III follow (d) All follow
(e) None of these

15. **Statements** All calculators are boxes.
All boxes are taps.
Some taps are machines.

Conclusions I. Some machines are boxes.
II. Some taps are calculators.
III. Some boxes are calculators.

(a) I and II follow (b) I and III follow
(c) II and III follow (d) All follow
(e) None of these

Direction (Q. Nos. 16-20) *In each of the questions below are given three statements followed by three conclusions numbered* I, II *and* III. *You have to take the given statements to be true even if they seem to be at variance from commonly known facts. Read all the conclusions and then decide which of the given conclusions logically follows from the given statements disregarding commonly known facts.* **IBPS (PO) 2011**

16. **Statements** All chairs are keys.
All keys are balloons.
Some balloons are mirrors.
Some mirrors are desks.

Conclusions I. Some desks are keys.
II. Some balloons are chairs.
III. Some mirrors are balloons.

(a) Only I follows (b) Only II follows
(c) Only III follows (d) Only II and III follow
(e) All, I, II and III follow

17. Statements Some drums are posters.
All posters are windows.
Some windows are tablets.
All tablets are books.

Conclusions I. Some windows are drums.
II. Some books are posters.
III. Some tablets are drums.

(a) None follows (b) Only I follows
(c) Only II follows (d) Only III follows
(e) Only I and II follow

18. Statements Some boxes are toys.
Some toys are nails.
Some nails are stores.
Some stores are shops.

Conclusions I. Some shops are nails.
II. Some nails are boxes.
III. No shop is toy.

(a) Only I follows (b) Only III follows
(c) Only either I or III follows (d) Only II follows
(e) None of the above

19. Statements All doors are windows.
No window is house.
Some houses are buildings.
All buildings are skies.

Conclusions I. Some skies are doors.
II. Some skies are houses.
III. Some buildings are doors.

(a) Only I follows (b) Only II follows
(c) Only III follows (d) II and III follow
(e) None of these

20. Statements All rivers are walls.
All walls are stones.
All stones are clothes.
All clothes are trees.

Conclusions I. Some trees are stones.
II. Some clothes are rivers.
III. All walls are clothes.

(a) Only I and II follow (b) Only I and III follow
(c) Only II and III follow (d) I, II and III follow
(e) None of these

Direction (Q. Nos. 21-24) *In each of the questions below are given three statements followed by three conclusions numbered* I, II *and* III. *You have to take the given statements to be true even if they seem to be at variance from commonly known facts. Read all the conclusions and then decide which of the given conclusions logically follows from the given statements disregarding commonly known facts.* **IOB (PO) 2009**

21. Statements All windows are doors.
All buildings are doors.
All doors are boats.

Conclusions I. All windows are boats.
II. All buildings are boats.
III. Some boats are doors.

(a) I and II follow (b) I and III follow
(c) II and III follow (d) All follow
(e) None of these

22. Statements Some desks are chairs.
Some chairs are pens.
Some pens are drawers.

Conclusions I. Some drawers are desks.
II. Some drawers are chairs.
III. No drawer is chair.

(a) None follows (b) Only II follows
(c) Only III follows (d) Either II or III follows
(e) I and either II or III follow

23. Statements All flowers are trees.
Some trees are houses.
All houses are wheels.

Conclusions I. Some wheels are trees.
II. Some trees are flowers.
III. Some wheels are flowers.

(a) I and II follow
(b) I and III follow
(c) II and III follow
(d) All follow
(e) None of the above

24. Statements Some radios are telephones.
All telephones are mirrors.
All mirrors are desks.

Conclusions I. Some radios are desks.
II. Some radios are mirrors.
III. Some desks are telephones.

(a) I and II follow
(b) I and III follow
(c) II and III follow
(d) All follow
(e) None of the above

Direction (Q. Nos. 25-27) *In each of the questions below are given four statements followed by three conclusions numbered* I, II *and* III. *You have to take the given statements to be true even if they seem to be at variance from commonly known facts. Read all the conclusions and then decide which of the given conclusions logically follows from the given statements disregarding commonly known facts.* **MAT 2014**

25. Statements All flowers are fruits.
No fruit is juice.
Some juices are proteins.
All proteins are vitamins.

Conclusions I. Some vitamins are fruits.
II. Some juices are vitamins.
III. No flower is juice.

(a) I and II follow (b) I and III follow
(c) All follow (d) II and III follow
(e) None of these

26. Statements Some bags are suits.
All suits are trousers.
Some trousers are shirts.
All shirts are coats.

Conclusions I. Some trousers are coats.
II. Some bags are trousers.
III. Some suits are coats.

(a) I and II follow (b) Only I follows
(c) II and III follow (d) All follow
(e) None of these

27. Statements All books are novels.
Some novels are poems.
Some poems are stories.
No story is a movie.

Conclusions I. Some books are poems.
II. Some movies are novels.
III. No movie is a novel.

(a) Only I follows (b) I and II follow
(c) Either II or III follows (d) None follows
(e) None of these

Direction (Q. Nos. 28-29) *Read all the conclusions and then decide which of the given conclusion(s) logically follow(s) from the given statements disregarding commonly known facts.* **CMAT 2013**

28. Statements Some dogs are rats.
All rats are trees.
Some trees are not dogs.

Conclusion I. Some trees are dogs.
II. All dogs are trees.
III. All rats are dogs.
IV. No tree is dog.

(a) None follows (b) Only I follows
(c) I and II follow (d) II and III follow

29. Statements Some uniforms are covers.
All covers are papers.
All papers are bags.

Conclusions I. All covers are bags.
II. Some bags are covers, papers and uniforms.
III. Some uniforms are not papers.

(a) Only I follow
(b) I and II follow
(c) Only III follow
(d) I, II and III follow

Direction (Q. Nos. 30-31) *In each of the questions below are given three statements followed by three conclusions numbered* I, II *and* III. *You have to take the given statements to be true even if they seem to be at variance from commonly known facts. Read all the conclusions and then decide which of the given conclusions logically follows from the given statements, disregarding commonly known facts.*

30. Statements All chickens are birds.
Some chickens are hens.
Female birds lay eggs. **IIFT 2012**

Conclusions I. All birds lay eggs.
II. Some hens are birds.
III. Some chickens are not hens.

(a) Only II
(b) II and III
(c) I, II and III
(d) None of the statements is a known fact

31. Statements Pictures can tell a story.
All story books have pictures.
Some story books have words.

Conclusions
I. Pictures can tell a story better than words can.
II. The stories in story books are very simple.
III. Some story books have both words and pictures.

(a) I and III
(b) Only II
(c) Only III
(d) None of the statements is a known fact

Direction (Q. Nos. 32-38) *In each of the questions below are given three statements followed by four conclusions numbered* I, II, III *and* IV. *You have to take the given statements to be true even if they seem to be at variance from commonly known facts. Read all the conclusions and then decide which of the given conclusions logically follows from the given statements, disregarding commonly known facts.*

32. Statements Some cups are utensils.
No utensil is a bucket.
All buckets are plates.

Conclusion I. Some cups are buckets.
II. Some utensils are plates.
III. No utensil is a plate.
IV. Some cups are plates.

(a) Only I follows
(b) Only III follows
(c) Either II or III follows
(d) Either III or IV follows
(e) None of the above

33. Statements All gates are flowers.
Some gates are fruits.
Some flowers are clips. **NIFT (UG) 2012**

Conclusions I. Some flowers are fruits.
II. Some clips are fruits.
III. Some clips are gates.
IV. No flower is fruit.

(a) Only I follows (b) I and IV follow
(c) II and IV follow (d) I and III follow
(e) None of these

34. Statements Some leaves are fruits.
All branches are fruits.
Some roots are branches.

Conclusions I. Some roots are fruits.
II. Some branches are leaves.
III. No leaf is branch.
IV. Some leaves are roots.

(a) Either II or III and I follow
(b) Only I follows
(c) Either II or III follows
(d) I and III follow
(e) None of the above

35. Statements All fans are tubelights.
No pen is a bulb.
Some bulbs are fans. **IBPS (PO) 2011**

Conclusions I. Some pens are tubelights.
II. No pens are tubelights.
III. Some tubelights are fans.
IV. All tubelights are fans.

(a) I and II follow
(b) I,II and III follow
(c) Either I or II and III follow
(d) III and IV follow
(e) None of the above

36. Statements No machine is a file.
Some file are colours.
All colours are sweets.

Conclusions I. Some machines are colours.
II. All sweets are colours.
III. Some sweets are files.
IV. No sweet is a machine.

(a) Either II or IV and III follow
(b) I and II follow
(c) Only IV follows
(d) Only III follows
(e) None of the above

37. Statements Some streets are roads.
Some roads are lanes.
Some lanes are highways.

Conclusions I. Some roads are not streets.
II. No highway is street.
III. Some streets are not roads.
IV. Some lanes are not roads.

(a) Only III follows (b) IV and III follow
(c) Either I or III follows (d) Both I and III follow
(e) None of these

38. Statements No table is fruit.
No fruit is window.
All windows are chairs. **PNB (PO) 2010**

Conclusions I. No window is table.
II. No chair is fruit.
III. No chair is table.
IV. All chairs are windows.

(a) None follows (b) All follow
(c) I and II follow (d) III and IV follow
(e) None of these

Direction (Q. Nos. 39-44) *In each of the questions below are given four statements followed by four conclusions numbered* I, II, III *and* IV. *You have to assume everything in the statements to be true even if they seem to be at variance from commonly known facts and then decide which of the four given conclusions logically follows from the statements disregarding commonly known facts and select the appropriate answer.* **IBPS (PO) 2013**

39. Statements Some numbers are digits.
All digits are alphabets.
No alphabet is a vowel.
All consonants are vowels.

Conclusions I. No digit is a vowel.
II. No alphabet is a consonant.
III. No vowel is a number.
IV. All vowels are numbers.

(a) I and III follow (b) II and IV follow
(c) I and II follow (d) I, II and III follow
(e) I, II and either III or IV follow

40. Statements All documents are files.
Some files are papers.
All papers are certificates.
No certificate is a manuscript.

Conclusions I. Atleast some documents are papers.
II. No manuscript is a document.
III. Atleast some certificate are files.
IV. No paper is a document.

(a) I, II and IV follow
(b) II and III follow
(c) I and IV follow
(d) Only III follows
(e) None of the above

41. Statements No group is people.
All people are animals.
All animals are plants.
All plants are roots.

Conclusions I. No group is a plant.
II. All people are plants.
III. Atleast some groups are plants.
IV. All plants are groups.

(a) Only II follows (b) I and IV follow
(c) II and III follow (d) III and IV follow
(e) None of these

42. Statements Some jobs are vacancies.
All jobs are works.
No work is a trade.
All professions are trades.

Conclusions I. Atleast some works are jobs.
II. No vacancy is a trade.
III. No profession is a work.
IV. Atleast some works are professions.

(a) I, II, III and IV follow (b) II, III and IV follow
(c) I and IV follow (d) None follows
(e) I and III follow

43. Statements All marks are grades.
No grade is a score.
All letters are scores.
All scores are characters.

Conclusions I. Atleast some letters are grades.
II. Atleast some scores are grades.
III. Atleast some characters are marks.
IV. Some characters are letters.

(a) II and IV follow (b) Only IV follows
(c) I and III follow (d) I, II, III and IV follow
(e) None follows

44. Statements All cricketers are football players.
Some hockey players are cricketers.
No football player is a basketball player.
No basketball player is a hockey player.

Conclusions I. Some hockey players are football players.
II. No basketball player is a cricketer.
III. Some hockey players are basketball players.
IV. Some football players are cricketers.

(a) Only I (b) I, II and IV (c) I and IV (d) I and II

Direction (Q. Nos. 45-49) *Some statements are given followed by some conclusions. You have to consider the statements to be true even if they seem to be at variance from commonly known facts. You have to decide which of the given conclusions if any, follows from the given statements.* **SBI (PO) 2014**

45. Statements Some pins are needles.
Some threads are needles.
All needles are nails.
All nails are hammers.

Conclusions I. Some pins are hammers.
II. Some threads are nails.
III. Some pins are threads.
IV. No pin is thread

(a) I, II and either III or IV follow
(b) III and IV follow
(c) I and II follow
(d) All follow
(e) None of the above

46. Statements All pens are clocks.
Some clocks are tyres.
Some tyres are wheels.
Some wheels are buses.

Conclusions I. Some buses are tyres.
II. Some wheels are clocks.
III. Some wheels are pens.
IV. Some buses are clocks.

(a) None follows (b) Only I follows
(c) Only II follows (d) Only III follows
(e) Only IV follows

47. Statements Some roses are flowers.
All flowers are buds.
All buds are leaves.
All leaves are plants.

Conclusions I. Some plants are flowers.
II. Some roses are buds.
III. All leaves are roses.
IV. No roses are buds.

(a) Only I follows (b) I and II follow
(c) I and either II or IV follow (d) Either II or IV follows
(e) None of these

48. Statements Some doctors are lawyers.
All teachers are lawyers.
Some engineers are lawyers.
All engineers are businessmen.

Conclusions I. Some teachers are doctors.
II. Some businessmen are lawyers.
III. Some businessmen are teachers.
IV. Some lawyers are teachers.

(a) None follows (b) Only II follows
(c) Only III follows (d) II and IV follow
(e) None of these

49. Statements Some sweets are chocolates.
Some chocolates are mint.
Some minsts are food.
Some food are diet.

Conclusion I. No sweets are diet.
II. No food is chocolates.
III. Some sweets are diet.
IV. Some sweets are food.

(a) None follows (b) Either I or III follows
(c) III and IV follow (d) II and III follow
(e) None of these

Direction (Q. Nos. 50-54) *In each of the questions below, are given four statements followed by four conclusions numbered* I, II, III *and* IV. *You have to take the given statements to be true even if they seem to be at variance from commonly known facts. Read all the conclusions and then decide which of the given conclusions logically follows from the given statements disregarding commonly known facts.*

50. Statements All plastics are glasses.
Some sponges are glasses.
All sponges are clothes.
All clothes are liquids.

Conclusions I. All liquids are sponges.
II. Some plastics are clothes.
III. All glasses are plastics.
IV. All liquids are clothes.

(a) None follows (b) Either II or IV follows
(c) Only IV follows (d) III and IV follow
(e) None of these

51. Statements All sands are beaches.
All shores are beaches.
Some beaches are trees.
All trees are hotels.

Conclusions I. Some shores are hotels.
II. All beaches are shores.
III. Some beaches are hotels.
IV. Some sands are trees.

(a) None follows (b) Only II follows
(c) Either I or III follows (d) Only IV follows
(e) None of these

52. Statements All parrots are pigeons.
Some crows are pigeons.
Some sparrows are crows.
All sparrows are koels.

Conclusions I. Some koels are crows.
II. Some parrots are crows.
III. Some sparrows are pigeons.
IV. No crow is a parrot.

(a) Only I follows (b) Only III follows
(c) I and either II or IV follow (d) Either I or III follows
(e) None of these

53. Statements All chairs are tables.
All tables are cushions.
Some cushions are trolleys.
All trolleys are lamps.

Conclusions I. Some lamps are tables.
II. Some trolleys are chairs.
III. Some cushions are lamps.
IV. All chairs are cushions.

(a) Only I follows (b) III and IV follow
(c) Either I or II follows (d) All follow
(e) None of these

54. Statements Some tools are radios.
Some radios are ponds.
Some ponds are mirrors.
All mirrors are chalks. **BOB (PO) 2010**

Conclusions I. Some mirrors are tools.
II. Some chalks are ponds.
III. Some ponds are tools.
IV. Some chalks are radios.

(a) None follows (b) Only I follows
(c) Only II follows (d) Only III follows
(e) Only IV follows

Direction (Q. Nos. 55-58) *In each of the questions below are given four statements followed by four conclusions numbered* I, II, III *and* IV. *You have to take the given statements to be true even if they seem to be at variance from commonly known facts. Read all the conclusions and then decide which of the given conclusions logically follows from the given statements disregarding commonly known facts.*

55. Statements All houses are rooms.
All rooms are baskets.
All baskets are tyres.
Some tyres are lanterns.

Conclusions I. Some lanterns are rooms.
II. Some tyres are houses.
III. Some tyres are rooms.
IV. All houses are baskets.

(a) I, II and III follow (b) II, III and IV follow
(c) I, III and IV follow (d) All follow
(e) None of these

56. Statements Some tractors are buses.
All buses are trains.
Some trains are boats.
All boats are ships.

Conclusions I. Some boats are buses.
II. Some ships are buses.
III. Some trains are tractors.
IV. Some ships are trains.

(a) I and II follow (b) I and III follow
(c) I and IV follow (d) II and IV follow
(e) None of these

57. Statements All chairs are sofas.
All sofas are books.
All books are nets.
All nets are gardens.

Conclusions I. Some nets are sofas.
II. Some gardens are books.
III. Some nets are chairs.
IV. All books are gardens.

(a) I, II and III follow (b) I, III and IV follow
(c) II, III and IV follow (d) All follow
(e) None of these

58. **Statements** All monkeys are parrots.
No parrot is crow.
Some crows are horses.
All horses are tigers.

Conclusions I. Some tigers are parrots.
II. Some crows are monkeys.
III. No tiger is parrot.
IV. Some horses are parrots.

(a) None follows (b) Only II follows
(c) Only III follows (d) Only I follows
(e) Either I or III follows

Direction (Q. Nos. 59-64) *In each of the questions below are given four statements followed by four conclusions numbered I, II, III and IV. You have to take the given statements to be true even if they seem to be at variance from commonly known facts. Read all the conclusions and then decide which of the given conclusions logically follows from the given statements disregarding commonly known facts.* **SBI (PO) 2013**

59. **Statements** All metals are silver.
All silver are diamonds.
Some diamonds are gold.
Some gold are marbles.

Conclusions I. Some gold are metals.
II. All metals are diamonds.
III. Some silver are marbles.
IV. Some gold are silver.

(a) Only I follows (b) Only II follows
(c) Only III follows (d) Only IV follows
(e) None follows

60. **Statements** Some carpets are books.
All books are pens.
Some pens are cartons.
All cartons are notebooks.

Conclusions I. Some cartons are carpets.
II. Some cartons are books.
III. Some pens are carpets.
IV. Some notebooks are pens.

(a) I and II follow
(b) II and III follow
(c) III and IV follow
(d) I and III follow
(e) None of the above

61. **Statements** Some paints are bottles.
Some bottles are brands.
Some brands are colours.
All colours are erasers.

Conclusions I. Some paints are brands.
II. Some erasers are bottles.
III. Some erasers are brands.
IV. Some bottles are colours.

(a) None follows (b) Only III follows
(c) II and IV follow (d) Only IV follows
(e) I, II and III follow

62. **Statements** Some boxes are triangles.
All spheres are triangles.
All circles are boxes.
All triangles are quadrilaterals.

Conclusions I. Some quadrilaterals are boxes.
II. Some quadrilaterals are triangles.
III. Some triangles are spheres.
IV. No circle is quadrilateral.

(a) Only I follows
(b) Only II follows
(c) I, II and III follow
(d) Only III follows
(e) All follow

63. **Statements** All plastics are trees.
Some trees are buildings.
Some buildings are windows.
Some windows are papers.

Conclusions I. Some papers are plastics.
II. Some buildings are papers.
III. No paper is tree.
IV. Some trees are windows.

(a) Only I follows
(b) Only II follows
(c) I and IV follow
(d) Only III follows
(e) None follows

64. **Statements** All rings are phones.
All phones are spoons.
Some phones are files.
All files are covers.

Conclusions I. Some files are rings.
II. Some covers are spoons.
III. Some spoons are phones.
IV. Some rings are covers.

(a) II and IV follow
(b) I, II and III follow
(c) I and II follow
(d) II and III follow
(e) None follows

Cumulative Exercise

Base Level

Direction (Q. Nos. 1-3) *Two statements are given below followed by two Conclusions I and II. You have to consider the two statements to be true even if they seem to be at variance with commonly known facts. You have to decide which of the conclusions, if any, follow from the given statements.*

1. Statements Some books are magazines.
Some magazines are novels.

Conclusions I. Some books are novels.
II. Some novels are magazines.

(a) Only I follows (b) Only II follows
(c) Both I and II follow (d) Neither I nor II follows

2. Statements All students like excursions.
Some students go for higher education.

Conclusions I. Students who go for higher education also like excursions.
II. Some students do not go for higher education, but like excursions.

(a) Only I follows (b) Only II follows
(c) Both I and II follow (d) Neither I nor II follows

3. Statements All good hockey players are in the Indian hockey team. 'X' is not a good hockey player.

Conclusions I. 'X' is not in the Indian Hockey team.
II. 'X' wants to be in the Indian Hockey team.

(a) Only I follows (b) Only II follows
(c) Both I and II follow (d) Neither I nor II follows

Direction (Q. Nos. 4-14) *In each question below are three statements (for a set of questions) followed by two conclusions numbered* I *and* II. *You have to take the given statements to be true even if they seem to be at variance from commonly known facts and then decide which of the given conclusions logically follows from the given statements disregarding commonly known facts.*

Give answer

(a) if only Conclusion I follows
(b) if only Conclusion II follows
(c) if either Conclusion I or II follows
(d) if neither Conclusion I nor II follows
(e) if both Conclusions I and II follow

Statements (Q. Nos. 4-5) *No shoe is glove. All gloves are caps. All caps are jackets.*

MHT CET MBA 2011

4. Conclusions I. Atleast some shoes are caps.
II. Atleast some jackets are gloves.

5. Conclusions I. No shoe is a jacket.
II. All gloves are jackets.

Statements (Q. Nos. 6-7) *All countries are streets. No street is flag. Some flags are avenues.*

MHT CET MBA 2011

6. Conclusions I. Some avenues being streets is a possibility.
II. Some countries are flags.

7. Conclusions I. No avenue is a country.
II. Some streets are flags.

Statements (Q. Nos. 8-9) *No paint is colour. All brushes are colours. No colour is varnish.*

8. Conclusions I. No brush is varnish.
II. No varnish is a paint.

9. Conclusions I. Some paints being brushes is a possibility.
II. Atleast some brushes are varnishes.

10. Statements All stones are pebbles.
All pebbles are rocks.

IBPS (Clerk) 2012

Conclusions I. All stones are rocks.
II. All rocks are pebbles.

11. Statements No auditorium is hall.
All theatres are halls.

Conclusions I. No auditorium is a theatre.
II. All halls are theatres.

12. Statements Some drugs are medicines.
No medicine is a treatment.

Conclusions I. All treatments being drugs is a possibility.
II. All drugs can never be treatments.

13. Statements Some cameras are photos.
All cameras are snaps.
Conclusions I. All snaps are photos.
II. Some snaps are photos.

14. Statements Some computers are tablets.
Some laptops are computers.
Conclusions I. No laptop is a tablet.
II. All tablets being computers is a possibility.

Direction (Q. Nos. 15-19) *In each of the following questions, one or two statements are given followed by two conclusions I and II. You have to consider the statements to be true, even if they seem to be at variance from commonly known facts. You have to decide which of the given conclusions definitely follows from the given statements.*

Given answer
(a) Only Conclusion I follows
(b) Only Conclusion II follows
(c) Both Conclusions I and II follow
(d) Neither Conclusion I nor II follows
(e) Either Conclusion I or II follows

15. Statements All students are boys.
No boy is dull.
Conclusions I. There are no girls in the class.
II. No students is dull.

16. Statements Some buses are four wheelers.
All four wheelers are vans.
Conclusions I. Some vans are buses.
II. Some buses are vans.

17. Statements Some soldiers are famous.
Some soldiers are intelligent.
Conclusions I. Some soldiers are either famous or intelligent.
II. Some soldiers are neither famous nor intelligent.

18. Statements All clerks are lazy.
Some men are clerks.
Conclusions I. All lazy are men.
II. Some men are lazy.

19. Statements Some aeroplanes are living beings.
Some non-living beings are ghosts.
Conclusions I. Some aeroplanes are ghosts.
II. Some aeroplanes are not ghosts.

Direction (Q. No. 20) *Two statements are given followed by two conclusions I and II. You have to consider the statements to be true even if they seem to be at variance from commonly known facts. You have to decide which of the given conclusions, if any, follows from the given statements. Indicate your answer.*
SSC (FCI) 2012

20. Statements All children are students.
All students are players.
Conclusions I. All students are children.
II. All children are players.
(a) Only Conclusion I follows
(b) Only Conclusion II follows
(c) Both Conclusions 1 and II follow
(d) Neither Conclusion I nor II follows

Direction (Q. No. 21) *Two statements are given followed by two Conclusions I and II. You have to consider the statements to be true even if they seem to be at variance from commonly known facts. You have to decide which of the given conclusions, if any, follows from the given statements. Indicate your answer.*

21. Statements Some food are sweet.
Some food are sour. **SSC (FCI) 2012**
Conclusions I. All food are either sweet or sour.
II. Some sweets are sour.
(a) Only Conclusion I follows
(b) Only Conclusion II follows
(c) Both Conclusions I and II follow
(d) Neither Conclusion I nor II follows

Directions (Q. Nos. 22-26) *In each question below, there are two statements followed by two conclusions numbered I and II. You have to take the given statements to be true even if they seem to be at variance from commonly known facts and then decide which of the given conclusions logically follows from the given statements disregarding commonly known facts.*
IBPS (Clerk) 2011

Give answer
(a) if only Conclusion I follows
(b) if only Conclusion II follows
(c) if either Conclusion I or II follows
(d) if neither Conclusion I nor II follows
(e) if both Conclusions I and II follow

22. Statements Some trees are bushes.
All flowers are bushes.
Conclusions I. Atleast some bushes are trees.
II. Atleast some flowers are trees.

23. Statements All colours are paints.
No paint is a brush.
Conclusions I. Atleast some brushes are colours.
II. No brush is a colour.

24. Statements Some chemicals are organics.
All organics are fertilisers.
Conclusions I. Atleast some fertilisers are chemicals.
II. All fertilisers are organics.

25. Statements No air is solid.
Some solids are liquids.
Conclusions I. No liquid is air.
II. Some airs are definitely not liquids.

26. Statement All gems are diamonds.
All diamonds are rocks.
Conclusions I. Atleast some rocks are gems.
II. All gems are rocks.

Direction (Q. Nos. 27-31) *In each question below are two statements followed by two conclusions numbered* I *and* II. *You have to take the given statements to be true even if they seem to be at variance from known facts and then decide which of the given conclusions logically commonly follows from the given statements disregarding commonly known facts.* **IBPS (Clerk) 2011**

Given answer
(a) if only Conclusion I follows
(b) if only Conclusion II follows
(c) if either Conclusion I or II follows
(d) if neither Conclusion I nor II follows
(e) if both Conclusions I and II follow

27. Statements Some gears are wheels.
All wheels are brakes.
Conclusions I. No brake is gear.
II. Atleast some gears are brakes.

28. Statements No month is a year.
No year is a second.
Conclusions I. All months are seconds.
II. No second is month.

29. Statements No plane is hill.
Some hills are towns.
Conclusions I. No town is plane.
II. Some towns are plane.

30. Statements All metals are liquids.
All liquids are gases.
Conclusions I. All metals are gases.
II. Atleast some gases are liquids.

31. Statements Some cities are towns.
Some villages are cities.
Conclusions I. Atleast some villages are towns.
II. No village is a town.

Direction (Q. Nos. 32-36) *In these questions two statements followed by two conclusions numbered* I *and* II *have been given. You have to take the given statements to be true even if they seem to be at variance from commonly known facts and then decide which of the given conclusions logically follows from the given statements disregarding commonly known facts.*

32. Statements No win is a loss.
All losses are victories.
Conclusions I. No victory is a win.
II. Some victories are wins.
(a) Both Conclusions I and II are true
(b) Neither Conclusion I nor II is true
(c) Only Conclusion I is true
(d) Only Conclusion II is true
(e) Either Conclusion I or II is true

33. Statements All sides are lengths.
No length is breadth.
Conclusions I. All lengths are sides.
II. No breadth is a side.
(a) Both Conclusions I and II are true
(b) Neither Conclusion I nor II is true
(c) Only Conclusion I is true
(d) Only Conclusion II is true
(e) Either Conclusion I or II is true

34. Statements No remark is a wish.
Some wishes are hopes.
Conclusions I. Atleast some remarks are hopes.
II. All hopes are wishes.
(a) Only Conclusion II is true
(b) Both Conclusions I and II are true
(c) Neither Conclusion I nor II is true
(d) Either Conclusion I or II is true
(e) Only Conclusion I is true

35. Statements Some pens are erasers.
All sharpeners are pens.
Conclusions I. All sharpeners being erasers is a possibility.
II. All erasers are pens.
(a) Neither Conclusion I nor II is true
(b) Either Conclusion I or II is true
(c) Only Conclusion II is true
(d) Both Conclusions I and II are true
(e) Only Conclusion I is true

36. **Statements** Some names are languages.
All languages are poems.
Conclusions I. Atleast some poems are names
II. Atleast some language are names.
(a) Both Conclusions I and II are true
(b) Only Conlusion II is true
(c) Only Conclusion I is true
(d) Either Conclusion I or II is true
(e) Neither Conclusion I nor II is true

Direction (Q. Nos. 37-41) *In each of the question sets below are two/three statements followed by two conclusions numbered I and II. You have to take the given statements to be true even if they seem to be at variance from commonly known facts and then decide which of the given conclusions logically follows from the given statements disregarding commonly known facts.*

Give answer
(a) if only Conclusion I follows
(b) if only Conclusion II follows
(c) if either Conclusion I or conclusion II follows
(d) if neither Conclusion I nor conclusion II follows
(e) if both Conclusion I and conclusion II follow

Statements (Q. Nos. 37-39) *All stars are bottles. Some bottles are paper. No paper is a calendar.*

37. **Conclusions** I. Atleast some calendars are bottles.
II. No calendar is a star.

38. **Conclusions** I. All stars being papers is a possibility.
II. No calendar is a bottle.

39. **Conclusions** I. All calendars being stars is a possibility.
II. Atleast some bottles are stars.

Statements (Q. Nos. 40-41) *Some pencils are blankets. All blankets are erasers.*

40. **Conclusions** I. Atleast some pencils are erasers.
II. All erasers being pencils is a possibility

41. **Conclusions** I. No eraser is a pencil.
II. All blankets being pencils is a possibility.

Direction (Q. Nos. 42-48) *In each question below are two or three statements followed by two conclusions numbered I and II. You have to take the given statements to be true even if they seem to be at variance from commonly known facts and then decide which of the given conclusions logically follows from the given statements disregarding commonly known facts.*

Give answer
(a) if only Conclusion I follows
(b) if only Conclusion II follows
(c) if either Conclusion I or II follows
(d) if neither Conclusion I nor II follows
(e) if both Conclusions I and II follow

42. **Statements** All computers are machines.
Some computers are calculators.
All calculators are objects.
Conclusions I. Atleast some objects are calculators.
II. Atleast some machines are computers.

43. **Conclusions** I. No object being a machine is possibility.
II. Atleast some calculators are machines.

44. **Statements** Some stars are planets.
No planet is Moon.
Conclusions I. Atleast some Moons are stars.
II. Atleast some planets are stars.

45. **Statements** Some whales are mammals.
No mammal is an insect.
All insects are kites.
Conclusions I. Atleast some kites are insects.
II. All mammals are kites.

46. **Statements** Some governors are directors.
All directors are managers.
Conclusions I. Some managers are governors.
II. Some directors are managers.

47. **Statements** Some pens are erasers.
No eraser is pencil.
All pencils are books.
Conclusions I. No book is eraser.
II. Some books are erasers.

48. **Conclusions** I. Some books are pens.
II. All pens can never be pencils.

Direction (Q. Nos. 49-53) *In each of the question sets below are two/three statements followed by two conclusions numbered I and II. You have to take the given statements to be true even if they seem to be at variance from commonly known facts and then decide which of the given conclusions logically follows from the given statements disregarding commonly known facts.*

Give answer
(a) if only Conclusion I follows
(b) if only Conclusion II follows
(c) if either Conclusion I or II follows
(d) if neither Conclusion I nor II follows

49. **Statements** All numbers are alphabets.
All alphabets are digits.
No digit is a letter.
Jharkhand Grameen Bank (PO) 2012
Conclusions I. No letter is a number.
II. Atleast some alphabets are letters.

50. **Statements** No mail is a post.
No post is a dispatch.
Conclusions I. No mail is a dispatch.
II. Atleast some dispatches are mails.

51. Statements Some symbols are figures.
All icons are figures.
Conclusions I. All symbols being icons is a possibility.
II. Atleast some icons are symbols.

Statements (Q. Nos. 52-53) *Some shields are trophies. All trophies are cups. No cup is a medal.*

52. Conclusions I. No trophy is a medal.
II. All shields being medals is a possibility.

53. Conclusions I. No medal is a shield.
II. Atleast some cups are shields.

Direction (Q. Nos. 54-59) *In each of the questions below are given three statements followed by two conclusions numbered I and II. You have to take the given statements to be true even if they seem to be at variance from commonly known facts. Read all the conclusions and then decide which of the given conclusions logically follows from the given statements disregarding commonly known facts.*

Give answer
(a) if only Conclusion I follows
(b) if only Conclusion II follows
(c) if either Conclusion I or II follows
(d) if neither Conclusion I nor II follows
(e) if both Conclusions I and II follow

54. Statements Some trees are forests.
Some forests are houses.
Some houses are tents.
Conclusions I. Some tents are forests.
II. Some houses are trees.

55. Statements All cards are boxes.
No box is slate.
Some slates are tiles.
Conclusions I. No slate is card.
II. Some tiles are boxes.

56. Statements Some papers are arrows.
All arrows are sticks.
Some sticks are boards.
Conclusions I. Some boards are papers.
II. No board is paper.

57. Statements All ropes are tiles.
Some tiles are bangles.
All bangles are nails.
Conclusions I. Some nails are ropes.
II. Some nails are tiles.

58. Statements Some days are nights.
All nights are stars.
All stars are clouds.
Conclusions I. Some clouds are days.
II. Some stars are days.

59. Statements All bells are hammers.
All hammers are dogs.
All dogs are packets.
Conclusions I. Some packets are hammers.
II. Some dogs are bells.

Direction (Q. Nos. 60-65) *In these questions, two/three statements followed by two conclusions numbered I and II have been given. You have to take the given statements to be true if they seem to be at variance from the commonly known facts and then decide which of the given conclusions logically follows from the given statements disregarding commonly known facts.*

SBI Associate (PO) 2014

Given answer
(a) if either Conclusion I or II is true
(b) if both Conclusions I and II are true
(c) if neither Conclusion I nor II is true
(d) if only Conclusion II is true
(e) if only Conclusion I is true

60. Statements All bugs are worms.
Some worms are moth.
No moth is a fly.
Conclusions I. No fly is a worm.
II. All moths being bugs is a possibility.

61. Statements Some stars are planets.
No planet is a Moon.
Conclusions I. No star is a Moon.
II. Some stars are Moons.

62. Statements No magic is a trick.
All charms are tricks.
All hoaxes are charms.
Conclusions I. No magic is a hoax.
II. No charm is a magic.

63. Statements All bugs are worms.
Some worms are moths.
No moth is a fly.
Conclusions I. All worms are bugs.
II. No bug is a fly.

64. Statements All watches are clocks.
Some clocks are towers.
All towers are poles.
Conclusions I. Atleast some poles are clocks.
II. All towers being watches is a possibility.

65. Statements No magic is a trick.
All charms are tricks.
All hoaxes are charms.
Conclusions I. All hoaxes are tricks.
II. All tricks are charms.

Direction (Q. Nos. 66-69) *In each of the questions below, two statements are given followed by two conclusions numbered* I *and* II. *You have to take the given statements to be true even if they seem to be at variance from the commonly known facts and then decide which of the given conclusions logically follows from the given statements disregarding the commonly known facts.*

Give answer
(a) if only Conclusion I follows
(b) if only Conclusion II follows
(c) if either Conclusion I or II follows
(d) if neither Conclusion I nor II follows
(e) if both Conclusions I and II follow

66. Statements All kings are rulers.
Some rulers are queens.
Conclusions I. Some kings are queens.
II. Atleast some queens are rulers.

67. Statements Some gardens are parks.
Some parks are areas.
Conclusions I. Atleast some areas are parks.
II. No garden is an area.

68. Statements No letter is a fax.
All messages are faxes.
Conclusions I. No message is a letter.
II. Atleast some faxes are messages.

69. Statements Some boards are plains.
No plain is a square.
Conclusions I. All squares are boards.
II. All plains are boards.

Direction (Q. Nos. 70-76) *In each question below are two statements followed by two conclusions numbered* I *and* II. *You have to take the two given statements to be true even if they seem to be at variance from commonly known facts and then decide which of the given conclusions logically follows from the given statements disregarding commonly known facts.*

Give answer
(a) if only Conclusion I follows
(b) if only Conclusion II follows
(c) if either Conclusion I or II follows
(d) if neither Conclusion I nor II follows
(e) if both Conclusions I and II follow

70. Statements Some windows are grills.
All glasses are grills.
Conclusions I. All grills are windows.
II. Atleast some grills are glasses.

71. Statements Some painters are artists.
Some dancers are painters.
Conclusions I. All artists are dancers.
II. All painters are dancers.

72. Statements All cabins are rooms.
All rooms are buildings.
Conclusions I. All buildings are rooms.
II. All cabins are buildings.

73. Statements All rings are necklaces.
No necklace is a bracelet.
Conclusions I. No ring is a bracelet.
II. All necklaces are rings.

74. Statements All hands are arms.
Some hands are muscles.
Conclusions I. Some muscles are arms.
II. All muscles are arms.

75. Statements All metals are plastics.
All plastics are fibres.
Conclusions I. Atleast some fibres are metals.
II. Some metals are not fibres.

76. Statements No leaf is a root.
All plants are roots.
Conclusions I. No leaf is a root.
II. Some plants are leaves.

Direction (Q. Nos. 77-81) *In these questions, there are three statements followed by two conclusions numbered* I *and* II. *You have to take the given statements to be true even if they seem to be at variance from commonly known facts and then decide which of the given conclusions logically follows from the given statements disregarding commonly known facts.*

77. Statements All railways are trains. No train is a station.
Some stations are platforms.
Conclusions I. All railways being platforms is a possibility.
II. No railway is a station.
(a) Only Conclusion I follows
(b) Only Conclusion II follows
(c) Both Conclusions I and II follow
(d) Either Conclusion I or II follows
(e) Neither Conclusion I nor II follows

78. Statements All erasers are sharpeners.
All sharpeners are pencils.
Some pencils are pens.
Conclusions I. No eraser is a pen.
II. All pencils are sharpeners.
(a) Only Conclusion I follows
(b) Only Conclusion II follows
(c) Either Conclusion I or II follows
(d) Neither Conclusion I nor II follows
(e) Both Conclusions I and II follow

79. Statements All winters are summers.
Some summers are springs.
No spring is an autumn.

Conclusions I. Atleast some winters are springs.
II. Some autumns being summer is a possibility.

(a) Either Conclusion I or II follows
(b) Both Conclusions I and II follow
(c) Only Conclusion I follows
(d) Neither Conclusion I nor II follows
(e) Only Conclusion II follows

80. Statements All erasers are sharpeners.
All sharpeners are pencils.
Some pencils are pens.

Conclusions I. Atleast some sharpeners are pens.
II. No sharpener is a pen.

(a) Either Conclusion I or II follows
(b) Only Conclusion II follows
(c) Neither Conclusion I nor II follows
(d) Only Conclusion I follows
(e) Both Conclusions I and II follow

81. Statements All winters are summers.
Some summers are springs.
No spring is an autumn.

Conclusions I. All summers can never be autumns.
II. Atleast some summers are winters.

(a) Either Conclusion I or II follows
(b) Both Conclusions I and II follow
(c) Neither Conclusion I nor II follows
(d) Only Conclusion I follows
(e) Only Conclusion II follows

Advanced Level

Direction (Q. Nos. 1-5) *In each of the questions below are given four statements followed by four conclusions numbered I, II, III and IV. You have to take the given statements to be true even if they seem to be at variance from commonly known facts. Read all the conclusions and then decide which of the given conclusions logically follows from the given statements known facts.*

SBI Management Executive Exam 2014

1. Statements All pens are books.
All books are chairs
Some chairs are desks.
Some desks are tables.

Conclusions I. Some tables are chairs.
II. Some desks are pens.
III. Some chairs are pens.
IV. All pens are chairs.

(a) I and II follow
(b) I and III follow
(c) I and IV follow
(d) III and IV follow
(e) None of these

2. Statements Some trains are buses.
Some buses are trucks.
Some trucks are boats.
Some boats are cars.

Conclusions I. Some trucks are trains.
II. Some cars are trucks.
III. Some boats are buses.
IV. Some boats are trains.

(a) None follows
(b) Only III follows
(c) Only II follows
(d) Only IV follows
(e) III and IV follow

3. Statements All hills are roads.
All roads are stones.
All stones are jungles.
All jungles are rivers.

Conclusions I. Some rivers are stones.
II. Some jungles are hills.
III. Some stones are hills.
IV. All rivers are jungles.

(a) I and II follow
(b) II and III follow
(c) I, II and III follow
(d) II, III and IV follow
(e) All follow

4. Statements Some books are pens.
Some pens are glasses.
Some glasses are plates.
Some plates are bottles.

Conclusions I. Some bottles are books.
II. Some glasses are books.
III. Some bottles are plates.
IV. Some plates are glasses.

(a) I and II follow
(b) Only III follows
(c) I, II and IV follow
(d) III and IV follow
(e) Only IV follows

5. Statements Some petals are flowers.
All flowers are desks.
Some desks are cards.
All cards are trains.

Conclusions I. Some desks are flowers.
II. Some desks are petals.
III. Some petals are cards.
IV. Some desks are trains.

(a) I and IV follow (b) II, III and IV follow
(c) III and IV follow (d) I, II and III follow
(e) I, II and IV follow

Direction (Q. Nos. 6-10) *In each of the questions below are given four statements followed by three conclusions numbered* I, II *and* III. *You have to take the given statements to be true even if they seem to be at variance from commonly known facts. Read all the conclusions and then decide which of the given conclusions logically follows from the given statements disregarding commonly known facts.*

6. Statements Some nails are plates. Some plates are disks. All disks are mirrors. All mirrors are tyres

Conclusions I. Some tyres are plates.
II. Some tyres are nails.
III. Some mirrors are plates.

(a) I and II follow (b) I and III follow
(c) II and III follow (d) All follow
(e) None of these

7. Statements Some windows are lakes.
Some lakes are forests.
Some forests are hills.
All hills are curtains.

Conclusions I. Some hill are windows.
II. Some curtains are lakes.
III. Some forests are windows.

(a) None follows (b) Only I follows
(c) Only II follows (d) Only III follows
(e) I and III follow

8. Statements All tapes are branches.
Some branches are roads.
All roads are fruits.
Some fruits are trees.

Conclusions I. Some trees are tapes.
II. Some fruits are tapes.
III. Some fruits are branches.

(a) None follows (b) Only I follows
(c) Only II follows (d) Only III follows
(e) II and III follow

9. Statements Some beads are chairs.
All chairs are trucks.
Some trucks are bricks.
All bricks are cars.

Conclusions I. Some cars are chairs.
II. Some cars are trucks.
III. Some trucks are beads.

(a) I and II follow (b) I and III follow
(c) II and III follow (d) All follow
(e) None of these

10. Statements All flowers are houses.
All houses are tigers.
All tigers are goats.
Some goats are bullocks.

Conclusions I. Some goats are flowers.
II. Some tigers are flowers.
III. Some bullocks are tigers.

(a) I and II follow (b) I and III follow
(c) II and III follow (d) All follow
(e) None of these

Direction (Q. Nos. 11-16) *In each of the questions below are given four statements followed by three conclusions numbered* I, II *and* III. *You have to take the given statements to be true even if they seem to be at variance from commonly known facts. Read all the conclusions and then decide which of the given conclusions logically follows from the given statements disregarding commonly known facts.* **BOI (PO) 2010**

11. Statements Some beads are rings.
Some rings are bangles.
All bangles are clothes.
All clothes are boxes.

Conclusions I. Some boxes are bangles.
II. Some clothes are rings.
III. Some bangles are beads.

(a) None follows (b) Only I follows
(c) Only II follows (d) Only III follows
(e) I and II follow

12. Statements All desks are pillars.
All pillars are circles.
Some circles are squares.
Some squares are rectangles.

Conclusions I. Some rectangles are pillars.
II. Some circles are desks.
III. Some squares are desks.

(a) None follows (b) Only I follows
(c) Only II follows (d) Only III follows
(e) I and II follow

13. Statements Some tyres are ropes.
Some ropes are tents.
Some tents are walls.
Some walls are buildings.

Conclusions I. Some buildings are ropes.
II. Some walls are ropes.
III. Some tents are tyres.

(a) None follows (b) Only I follows
(c) Only II follows (d) Only III follows
(e) I and II follow

14. Statements All chairs are fires. Some fires are winds.
All winds are nets. Some nets are clocks.

Conclusions I. Some clocks are winds.
II. Some nets are fires.
III. Some winds are chairs.

(a) None follows (b) Only I follows
(c) Only II follows (d) Only III follows
(e) II and III follow

15. Statements All sticks are hammers. No hammer is dress.
Some dresses are doors. All doors are cots.

Conclusions I. Some cots are hammers.
II. No cot is hammer.
III. Some dresses are sticks.

(a) Only I follows (b) Only II follows
(c) Only III follows (d) Either I or II follows
(e) Either I or II and III follow

16. Statements Some plates are knives.
All knives are chains.
Some chains are wheels.
All wheels are poles.

Conclusions I. Some poles are chains.
II. Some wheels are knives.
III. Some chains are plates.

(a) I and II follow (b) I and III follow
(c) II and III follow (d) All follow
(e) None of these

Direction (Q. Nos. 17-20) *In each of the questions below are given four statements followed by four conclusions numbered* I, II, III *and* IV. *You have to take the given statements to be true even if they seem to be at variance from commonly know facts. Read all the conclusions and then decide which of the given conclusions logically follows from the given statements disregarding commonly known facts.*

Allahabad Bank (Clerk) 2010

17. Statements Some pencils are windows.
All windows are roads.
Some roads are cups.
All cups are chains.

Conclusions I. Some chains are pencils.
II. Some cups are pencils.
III. Some chains are windows.
IV. Some roads are pencils.

(a) None follows (b) Only II follows
(c) Only IV follows (d) III and IV follow
(e) Only III follows

18. Statements Some beds are mirrors.
Some mirrors are dolls.
Some dolls are cheques.
Some cheques are pins.

Conclusions I. Some pins are dolls.
II. Some cheques are beds.
III. Some cheques are mirrors.
IV. Some dolls are beds.

(a) None follows (b) Only I follows
(c) Only II follows (d) Only III follows
(e) Only IV follows

19. Statements All chocolates are holders.
No holder is lamp.
Some lamps are desks.
All desks are pens.

Conclusions I. Some pens are holders.
II. Some desks are lamps.
III. No pen is holder .
IV. Some pens are chocolates.

(a) Only I follows (b) Only II follows
(c) Only III follows (d) Either I or III follows
(e) Either I or III and II follow

20. Statements All glasses are rooms.
Some rooms are planes.
All planes are ducks.
Some ducks are lanterns.

Conclusions I. Some lanterns are planes.
II. Some ducks are rooms.
III. Some rooms are glasses.
IV. Some ducks are glasses.

(a) I and II follow (b) II and III follow
(c) I, II and III follow (d) All follow
(e) None of these

Direction (Q. Nos. 21-26) *In each of the questions below are given four statements followed by four conclusions numbered* I, II, III *and* IV. *You have to take the statements to be true even, if they seem to be at variance from commonly logically facts. Read all the conclusions and then decide which of the given conclusions follows from the given statements disregarding logically common known facts.*

Corporation Bank (PO) 2010

21. Statements All rockets are poles.
Some poles are trams.
Some trams are ropes.
All ropes are tents.

Conclusions I. Some tents are trams.
II. Some ropes are rockets.
III. Some trams are rockets.
IV. Some poles are rockets.

(a) I and II follow
(b) I, II and III follow
(c) I and III follow
(d) I and IV follow
(e) None of the above

22. **Statements** All dials are mirrors.
All mirrors are spoons.
Some spoons are desks.
Some desks are chairs.

Conclusions I. Some desks are mirrors.
II. Some spoons are dials.
III. Some desks are dials.
IV. Some chairs are spoons.

(a) None follows (b) Only I follows
(c) Only II follows (d) Only III follows
(e) Only IV follows

23. **Statements** Some houses are forests.
All forests are trees.
Some trees are hills.
All hills are buses.

Conclusions I. Some buses are trees.
II. Some trees are houses.
III. Some hills are houses.
IV. Some buses are forests.

(a) I and II follow (b) I, II and IV follow
(c) I, II and III follow (d) All follow
(e) None of these

24. **Statements** Some ponds are rivers.
Some rivers are mountains.
Some mountains are books.
Some books are papers.

Conclusions I. Some books are rivers.
II. Some papers are ponds.
III. Some mountains are ponds.
IV. No paper is pond.

(a) None follows (b) Either II or IV follows
(c) Only II follows (d) Only IV follows
(e) Either II or IV and III follow

25. **Statements** Some tigers are horses.
All horses are goats.
All goats are dogs.
Some dogs are cats.

Conclusions I. Some cats are tigers.
II. Some dogs are horses.
III. Some goats are tigers.
IV. Some cats are horses.

(a) I and II follow
(b) I, II and III follow
(c) II and III follow
(d) II, III and IV follow
(e) None of the above

26. **Statements** All notebooks are pens.
No pen is table.
Some tables are desks.
All desks are tanks.

Conclusions I. Some tanks are pens.
II. Some desks are notebooks.
III. Some tanks are tables.
IV. No tank is pen.

(a) Only I follows (b) Only III follows
(c) Only IV follows (d) Either I or IV follows
(e) Either I or IV and III follow

Direction (Q. Nos. 27-29) *Answer the questions based on the following information, In each question below three statements (I, II and III) are given followed by four conclusions numbered I, II, III and IV. You have to take the given statements to be true even if they seem to be at variance with commonly known facts. Read all the conclusions and then decide which of the given conclusions logically follows from the given statements, disregarding commonly known facts. Choose the correct options presented below.* **IIFT 2008**

27. **Statements** Some drivers are technicians.
All technicians are engineers.
Some engineers are lecturers.

Conclusion I. Some technicians are lecturers.
II. Some lecturers are drivers.
III. All engineers are technicians.
IV. Some engineers are drivers.

(a) Only III follows
(b) Only IV follows
(c) III and IV follows
(d) None of the above

28. **Statements** Some barbers are fashion designers.
No fashion designers are businessmen.
Some businessmen are traders.

Conclusions I. No fashion designers are traders.
II. Some traders are not fashion designers.
III. Some fashion designers are traders.
IV. Some barbers are not businessmen.

(a) Either I or III, II and IV follow
(b) Either I and IV or III and IV follow
(c) Either I and II or III and II follow
(d) None of the above

29. **Statements** Some ropes are walls. Some walls are sticks.
All sticks are chairs. All chairs are tables.

Conclusions I. Some table are walls.
II. Some chairs are ropes.
III. Some sticks are ropes.

(a) None follows
(b) Only I follows
(c) Only II follows
(d) Only III follows
(e) II and III follow

Direction (Q. Nos. 30-34) *In each of the questions below are given four statements followed by four conclusions numbered I, II, III and IV. You hove to take the given statements to be true even if they seem to be at variance from commonly known facts. Read all the conclusions and then decide which of the given conclusions logically follows from the given statements disregarding commonly known facts.* **SBI Associates (PO) 2010**

30. Statements Some trains are cars.
All cars are branches.
All branches are nets.
Some nets are dresses.

Conclusions I. Some dresses are cars.
II. Some nets are trains.
III. Some branches are trains.
IV. Some dresses are trains.

(a) I and II follow (b) II and III follow
(c) I and IV follow (d) II, III and IV follow
(e) None of these

31. Statements All papers are clips.
Some clips are boards.
Some boards are lanes.
All lanes are roads.

Conclusions I. Some roads are boards.
II. Some lanes are clips.
III. Some boards are papers.
IV. Some roads are clips.

(a) I and II follow (b) I and III follow
(c) I, II and III follow (d) II, III and IV follow
(e) None of these

32. Statements Some pencils are kites.
Some kites are desks.
All desks are jungles.
All jungles are mountains.

Conclusions I. Some mountains are pencils.
II. Some jungles are pencils.
III. Some mountains are desks.
IV. Some jungles are kites.

(a) I and III follow
(b) I, II and III follow
(c) III and IV follow
(d) II, III and IV follow
(e) None of the above

33. Statements All stones are hammers.
No hammer is ring.
Some rings are doors.
All doors are windows.

Conclusions I. Some windows are stones.
II. Some windows are rings.
III. No window is stone.
IV. Some rings are stones.

(a) Only I follows (b) Only II follows
(c) Only III follows (d) Either I or III follows
(e) Either I or III and II follow

34. Statements All pens are clocks.
Some clocks are tyres.
Some tyres are wheels.
Some wheels are buses.

Conclusions I. Some buses are tyres.
II. Some wheels are clocks.
III. Some wheels are pens.
IV. Some buses are clocks.

(a) None follows
(b) Only I follows
(c) Only II follows
(d) Only III follows
(e) Only IV follows

Direction (Q. Nos. 35-39) *In each of the questions below are given four statements followed by three conclusions numbered I, II and III. You hove to take the given statements to be true even if they seem to be at variance from commonly known facts. Read all the conclusions and then decide which of the given conclusions logically follows from the given statements disregarding commonly known facts.* **BOI (PO) 2010**

35. Statements All cheques are notes.
All notes are tyres.
All tyres are books.
All books are rods.

Conclusions I. Some rods are notes.
II. Some books are tyres.
III. Some tyres are cheques.

(a) I and II follow (b) I and III follow
(c) II and III follow (d) All follow
(e) None of these

36. Statements Some pens are tables.
All tables are umbrellas.
Some umbrellas are sticks.
All sticks are caps.

Conclusions I. Some caps are umbrellas.
II. Some umbrellas are pens.
III. Some sticks are pens.

(a) I and II follow
(b) I and III follow
(c) II and III follow
(d) All follow
(e) None of the above

37. Statements Some lanes are poles.
All poles are skies.
Some skies are boxes.
No box is bottle.

Conclusions I. Some bottles are lanes.
II. Some boxes are poles.
III. No bottle is lane.

(a) None follows (b) Only I follows
(c) Only II follows (d) Only III follows
(e) Either I or III follows

38. Statements Some seeds are flowers.
All flowers are trees.
All trees are leaves.
Some leaves are branches.

Conclusions I. Some branches are flowers.
II. Some leaves are seeds.
III. Some leaves are flowers.

(a) I and II follow
(b) I and III follow
(c) II and III follow
(d) All follow
(e) None of the above

39. Statements All roads are buses.
Some buses are cars.
Some cars are days.
All days are nights.

Conclusions I. Some nights are buses.
II. Some nights are cars.
III. Some days are buses.

(a) None follows
(b) Only I follows
(c) Only II follows
(d) Only III follows
(e) I and II follow

Direction (Q. Nos. 40-44) *In each of the questions below are given four statements followed by four conclusions numbered* I, II, III *and* IV. *You have to take the given statements to be true even if they seem to be at variance from commonly known facts. Read all the conclusions and then decide which of the given conclusions logically follows from the given statements disregarding commonly known facts.* **SBI (PO) 2010**

40. Statements All cups are bottles.
Some bottles are jugs.
No jug is plate.
Some plates are tables.

Conclusions I. Some tables are bottles.
II. Some plates are cups
III. No table is bottle.
IV. Some jugs are cups.

(a) Only I follows
(b) Only II follows
(c) Only III follows
(d) Only IV follows
(e) Either I or III follows

41. Statements All birds are horses.
All horses are tigers.
Some tigers are lions.
Some lions are monkeys.

Conclusions I. Some tigers are horses.
II. Some monkeys are birds.
III. Some tigers are birds.
IV. Some monkeys are horses.

(a) I and III follow (b) I, II and III follow
(c) II, III and IV follow (d) All follow
(e) None of these

42. Statements Some chairs are handles.
All handles are pots.
All pots are mats.
Some mats are buses.

Conclusions I. Some buses are handles.
II. Some mats are chairs.
III. No bus is handle.
IV. Some mats are handles.

(a) I, II and IV follow
(b) II, III and IV follow
(c) Either I or III and II follow
(d) Either I or III and IV follow
(e) Either I or III and II and IV follow

43. Statements Some sticks are lamps.
Some flowers are lamps.
Some lamps are dresses.
All dresses are shirts.

Conclusions I. Some shirts are sticks.
II. Some shirts are flowers.
III. Some flowers are sticks.
IV. Some dresses are sticks.

(a) None follows
(b) Only I follows
(c) Only II follows
(d) Only III follows
(e) Only IV follows

44. Statements Some benches are walls.
All walls are houses.
Some houses are jungles.
All jungles are roads.

Conclusions I. Some roads are benches.
II. Some jungles are walls.
III. Some houses are benches.
IV. Some roads are houses.

(a) I and II follow
(b) I and III follow
(c) III and IV follow
(d) II, III and IV follow
(e) None of the above

Direction (Q. Nos. 45-49) *In each of the questions below are given four statements followed by four conclusions numbered I, II, III and IV. You have to take the given statements to be true even if they seem to be at variance from commonly known facts. Read all the conclusions and then decide which of the given conclusions logically follows from the given statements disregarding commonly known facts.* **MHT CET MBA 2009**

45. Statements Some computers are laptops.
Some laptops are notebooks.
All notebooks are papers.
All papers are phones.

Conclusions I. Some laptops are papers.
II. Some phônes are notebooks.
III. Some computers are notebooks.
IV. No computer is notebook.

(a) None follows
(b) I and II follow
(c) Either III or IV follows
(d) I, II and either III or IV follow
(e) None of the above

46. Statements Some keys are locks.
All locks are boards.
Some boards are cards.
All cards are papers.

Conclusions I. Some boards are papers.
II. Some boards are keys.
III. Some papers are cards.
IV. Some boards are locks.

(a) None follows (b) I and II follow
(c) II and III follow (d) I, II and III follow
(e) All follow

47. Statements All socks are shoes.
Some shoes are wallets.
Some wallets are bags.
No bag is purse.

Conclusions I. Some bags are socks.
II. Some wallets are socks.
III. No wallet is purse.
IV. Some purses are wallets.

(a) Either I or II follows (b) Either III or IV follows
(c) II and III follow (d) III and IV follow
(e) None of these

48. Statements Some walls are doors.
Some doors are grills.
No grill is window.
Some windows are roofs.

Conclusion I. No roof is grill.
II. No window is door.
III. Some windows are walls.
IV. Some roofs are walls.

(a) None follows
(b) I and II follow
(c) Either I or IV follows
(d) Either II or III follows
(e) All follow

49. Statements All letters are words.
Some words are poems.
All poems are plants.
Some plants are flowers.

Conclusions I. Some plants are words.
II. Some plants are letters.
III. Some flowers are poems.
IV. No flower is word.

(a) None follows
(b) Either III or IV follows
(c) Only I follows
(d) I and II follow
(e) All follow

Direction (Q. Nos. 50-54) *In each of the questions below are given four statements followed by four conclusions I, II, III and IV. You have to take the given statements to be true even if they seem to be at variance from commonly known facts. Read all conclusions and then decide which of the given conclusions logically follows from the given statements disregarding commonly known facts.*

50. Statements Some bags are trunks.
All trunks are shirts.
Some shirts are books.
All books are shops.

Conclusions I. All shops are bags.
II. Atleast some books are bags
III. Some shops being shirts is a possibility.
IV. No shirt is a bags.

(a) I and II follow (b) I and III follow
(c) III and IV follow (d) II and IV follow
(e) None of these

51. Statements All pens are chairs.
All flowers are chairs.
All chairs are trucks.
All trees are trucks.

Conclusions I. Some trucks are definitely pens.
II. All trucks are chairs.
III. All trees being pens is a possibility.
IV. Some trees are chairs.

(a) I and III follow
(b) I and II follow
(c) III and IV follow
(d) II and IV follow
(e) None of the above

52. **Statements** All desks are pillars.
Some pillars are towns.
All towns are benches.
Some benches are cars.

Conclusions I. No cars are towns.
II. Atleast some benches are desks.
III. All benches are not pillars.
IV. Some cars being pillars is not a possibility.

(a) None follows (b) Only I follows
(c) Only II follows (d) Only III follows
(e) Only IV follows

53. **Statements** All stations are houses.
No house is garden.
Some gardens are rivers.
All rivers are ponds.

Conclusions I. All ponds being gardens is a possibility.
II. Some ponds are stations.
III. Some ponds are definitely houses.
IV. No pond is station.

(a) Only I follows (b) Either II or IV follows
(c) I and II follow (d) I and IV follow
(e) None of these

54. **Statements** Some towers are lanes.
Some lanes are roads.
Some roads are rivers.
Some rivers are jungles.

Conclusions I. Some jungles are not roads.
II. All roads being lanes is a possibility.
III. Atleast some jungles are towers.
IV. Atleast some jungles are roads.

(a) Only I follows (b) Only II follows
(c) Either I or IV follows (d) Only I follows
(e) Either I or IV and II follow

Direction (Q. Nos. 55-56) *In each of the questions below starts with a few statements, followed by four conclusions numbered I, II, III and IV. You have to consider every given statement as true, even if it does not confirm to the accepted facts. Read the conclusions carefully and then decide which of the conclusion(s) logically follow(s) from the given statements, disregarding commonly known facts.* **IIFT 2011**

55. **Statements** Some boys are scholars.
Some teachers are boys.
All scholars are observers.

Conclusions I. Some scholars are boys.
II. Some scholars are not boys.
III. Some observers are boys.
IV. Some teachers are scholars.

(a) I and III follow (b) I, III, and IV follow
(c) Either I or II and III follow (d) None of these

56. **Statements** All teachers are professors.
All professors are researchers.
All researchers are consultants.

Conclusions I. Some consultants are teachers.
II. All professors are consultants.
III. Some researchers are teachers.
IV. All professors are teachers.

(a) I and II follow (b) I and III follow
(c) Either I or IV follow (d) None of these

Direction (Q. Nos. 57-66) *In each question, a set of six statements is given, followed by four answer choices. Each of the answer choices has a combination of three statements from the given set of six statements. You are required to identify the answer choice in which the statements are logically related.*

57. A. All green is blue.
B. All green is white.
C. All green is black.
D. All black is white.
E. All blue is yellow.
F. All blue is white.

(a) ABF (b) AEF (c) CDB (d) CBE

58. A. Pomfret is a fish.
B. Pomfret is not a fish.
C. Pomfret will not lay eggs.
D. Some fish lay eggs.
E. All fish lay eggs.
F. Pomfret may lay eggs.

(a) DFA (b) ADF (c) BDF (d) EBC

59. A. All copper is metal.
B. All bronze is non-metal.
C. Some metal is silver.
D. Some metal is not silver.
E. No copper is bronze.
F. Some silver is not metal.

(a) ABF (b) ACB (c) ABE (d) CDF

60. A. Actors know English.
B. He does not know English.
C. He is an actor.
D. He is not an actor.
E. He knows Hindi.
F. He should know English.

(a) ABD (b) AEF (c) DEA (d) ACF

61. A. All cows are goats.
B. All goats are dogs.
C. No goats are cows.
D. No goats are dogs.
E. All cows are dogs.
F. All dogs are cows.

(a) FAB (b) ABE
(c) AFB (d) ABF

62. A. Some pens are pencils.
B. Rubbers are sticky.
C. All pens are rubbers.
D. Pens must be sticky.
E. No pen is a rubber.
F. Some pens are rubbers.
(a) ACE (b) FCA (c) CBD (d) ABF

63. A. A is taller than B.
B. A and B play golf.
C. C is shorter than B but taller than D.
D. Golf and cricket are outdoor games.
E. C is the second shortest.
F. All outdoor games require energy.
(a) ABC (b) ACE (c) ADF (d) FBD

64. A. Birds like to fly.
B. Birds are in the sky.
C. All birds in the sky are free.
D. All birds in the sky like to fly.
E. Birds have a pair of wings.
F. Birds fly with each other.
(a) BDE (b) BDA
(c) FDB (d) BCD

65. A. All suns are white dwarfs.
B. A few suns are red giants.
C. Some red giants are suns.
D. All white dwarfs are red giants.
E. No red giant is a white dwarf.
F. No white dwarf is a sun.
(a) BEF (b) ADC
(c) AFC (d) CEF

66. A. Races are daces.
B. All daces are paces.
C. No daces are races.
D. No daces are paces.
E. All races are paces.
F. All paces are races. **NMAT 2009**
(a) ABE (b) FAB (c) AFE (d) DBE

Direction (Q. Nos. 67-68) *In each question four sets of three statements are given. You have to identify whether the three sentences in each of these sets are logically related.*

67. A. All plants are Moon.
All Moon are stars.
All stars are plants.
B. All men are thinkers.
All poets are thinkers.
All men write poetry.
C. Orange is a seasonal fruit.
Guava is a seasonal fruit.
Orange are guavas.
D. All tubes are handles.
All cups are handles.
Some cups may be tubes.
(a) D (b) A and B (c) C and B (d) B

68. A. All triangles are 12 sided.
This has 12 sides.
This is a triangle.
B. Some petals are peacocks.
No peacock is beautiful.
Some petals are beautiful.
C. Some pastries are salty.
Some fruits are salty.
Some pastries are fruits.
D. All roads are poles.
All poles are lamps.
Some lamps are roads.
(a) A (b) B (c) C (d) D

Direction (Q. Nos. 69-71) *In each question a main statement is followed by four statements A, B, C and D. Choose the ordered pair of statements where the first statement implies the second and the two statements are logically consistent with the main statement.* **CMAT 2014**

69. Vinod is either a poet or a doctor.
A. Vinod is a poet.
B. Vinod is a doctor.
C. Vinod is an engineer.
D. Vinod is not a poet.
(a) AB (b) CD (c) CA (d) DB

70. A is with B on Monday only, if X is not with Y.
A. A is with B on Wednesday.
B. Y is with X.
C. X is with Y.
D. A and B are not together on Monday.
(a) AB (b) AC (c) CD (d) CA

71. He has cold every time he plays.
A. He did not play.
B. He had cold.
C. He did not have cold.
D. He played.
(a) CA (b) BD
(c) AC (d) BA

Direction (Q. Nos. 72-74) *In each question, four sets of three statements are given. You have to identify whether the three sentences in each of these sets are logically related.* **JMET 2010**

72. A. Some plants are thorny.
Some plants are flowery.
Thorny are flowery.

B. All thorny are leafy.
All leafy are flowery.
Some flowers are thorny.

C. Bat is viviparous.
No mammal is a bird.
Bat is not a mammal.

D. Bat is viviparous.
Bat is a mammal.
Some mammals are viviparous.

(a) B and C (b) A and B (c) B only (d) B and D

73. A. All lamps are books.
No book is black.
No lamp is black.

B. All youngsters are open minded.
Open minded persons are not superstitious.
All non-superstitious persons are youngsters.

C. A is found in Z.
B is found in Z.
A is found in B.

D. No magazine is a monkey.
All monkeys are troops.
Some troops are magazines.

(a) A (b) B (c) D (d) C

74. A. Radha is fair.
Doctors marry only fair girls.
Radha is married to a doctor.

B. Milkha Singh is a sportsman.
Sportsmen are healthy.
Milkha Singh is healthy.

C. Rohan is honest.
All honest are boys.
Rohan is a boy.

D. Some ants are dinosaurs.
Some dinosaurs are carnivorous.
Some ants are carnivorous.

(a) B (b) D (c) B and C (d) A

Direction (Q. Nos. 75-77) *Each question contains four arguments of three statements each. Choose the set in which the third statement is a logical conclusion of the first two.* **CAT 2010**

75. A. Some Xs are Ps.
Some Ps are Ys.
Some Xs are Ys.

B. All Sonas are bright.
Some bright are crazy.
Some Sonas are crazy.

C. No faith is strong.
Only strong have biceps.
No faith has biceps.

D. All men are weak.
Some weak are strong.
Something are weak.

(a) A and D (b) C only
(c) Only D (d) None of these

76. A. Some icicles are cycles.
All cycles are men.
Some icicles are men.

B. All girls have teeth.
No teeth are yellow.
No girls are yellow.

C. No hand is foot.
Some feet are heads.
Some hands are heads.

D. Every man has a wife.
All wives are devoted.
No devoted has a husband.

(a) A, B and C (b) A and B
(c) C and B (d) A, B, C and D

77. All fish swim either in water tanks or in rivers.
A. Fishes swim in water tanks.
B. Fishes swim in river.
C. Fishes do not swim in river.
D. Fishes do not swim in water tanks.

(a) C and B (b) A and B (c) C and D (d) B and D

Direction (Q. Nos. 78-80) *Each question consists of five statements followed by options consisting of three statements put together in a specific order. Choose the option which indicates a valid argument, i.e. where the third statement is a conclusion drawn from the preceding two statements.* **CAT 2008**

78. A. All software companies employ knowledge workers.
B. Tata Tech employs knowledge workers.
C. Tata Tech is a software company.
D. Some software companies employ knowledge workers.
E. Tara Tech employs only knowledge workers.

(a) ABC (b) ACB (c) CDB (d) ACE

79. A. Apples are not sweets.
B. Some apples are sweet.
C. All sweets are tasty.
D. Some apples are not tasty.
E. No apple is tasty.

(a) CEA (b) BDC (c) CBD (d) EAC

80. A. Some towns in India are polluted.
B. All polluted towns should be destroyed.
C. Town Meghana should be destroyed.
D. Town Maghana is polluted.
E. Some towns in India should be destroyed.

(a) BDE (b) BAE (c) ADE (d) CDB

Answers with Explanations

Intro Exercise 1

1. (*d*) According to the statements, Venn diagram is

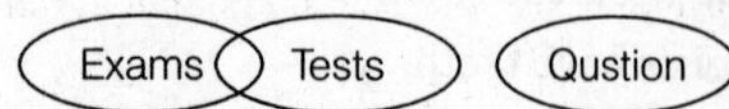

Conclusions I. ✗ II. ✓

Hence, neither conclusion I nor II follows.

Solution (Q. Nos. 2-3) According to the statements, Venn diagram is

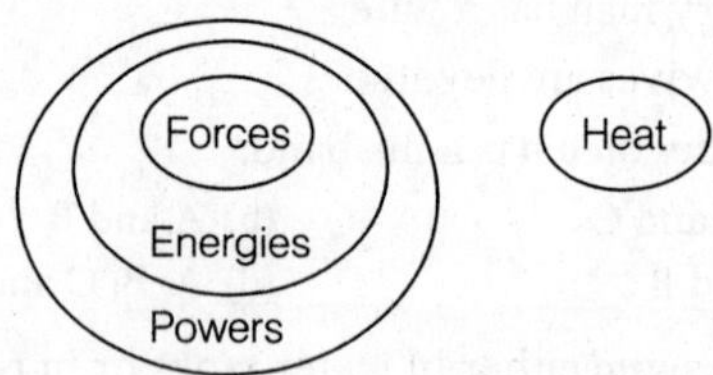

2. (*b*) **Conclusions** I. ✗ II. ✓

Hence, only Conclusion II follows from the given statements.

3. (*a*) **Conclusions** I. ✓ II. ✗

Hence, only Conclusion I follows from the given statements.

Solution (Q. Nos. 4-5) Accroding to the statements, Venn diagram is

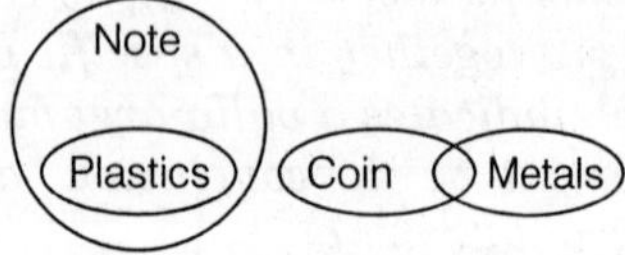

4. (*a*) **Conclusions** I. ✓ II. ✗
5. (*d*) **Conclusions** I. ✗ II. ✗

Hence, neither Conclusion I nor II follows.

6. (*e*) According to the statements, Venn diagram is

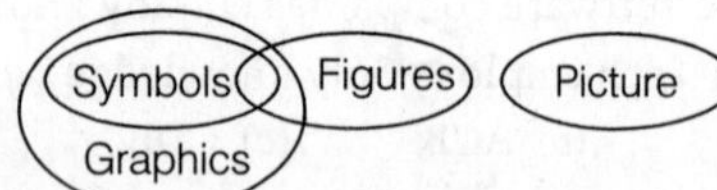

Conclusions I. ✓ II. ✓

Hence, both Conclusions I and II follow from the given stateaments.

Solution (Q. Nos. 7-8)

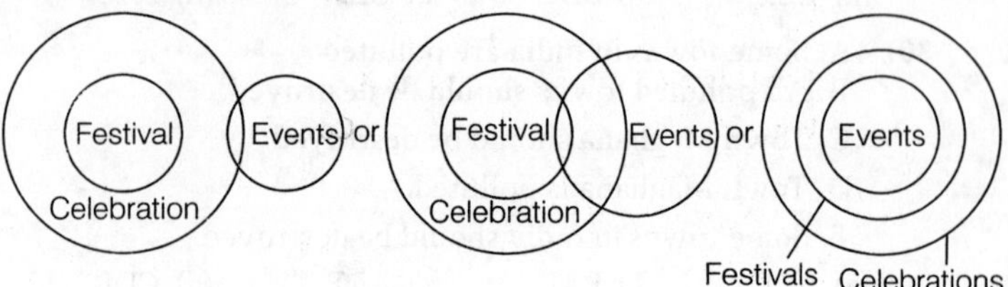

7. (*b*) **Conclusions** I. ✗ II. ✓

Hence, only Conclusion II follow.

8. (*e*) **Conclusions** I. ✓ II. ✓

Hence, both Conclusions I and II follow.

9. (*d*)

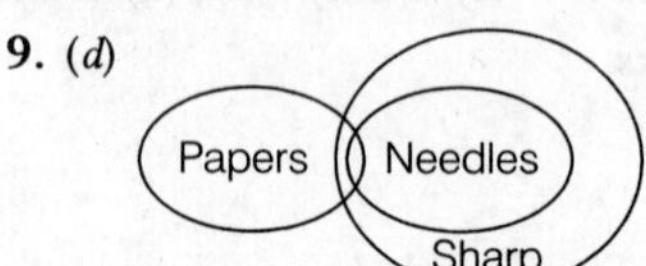

Conclusions I. ✗ II. ✗

So, neither I nor II follows.

10. (*d*)

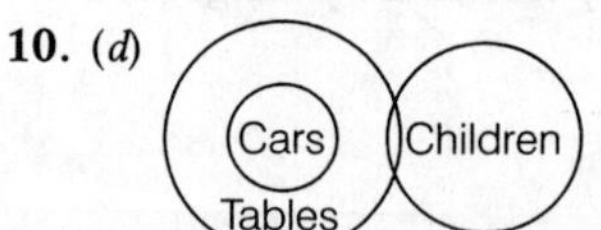

Conclusions I. ✗ II. ✗

So, neither I nor II follows.

11. (*b*)

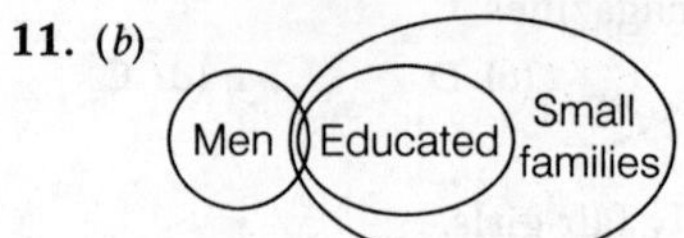

Conclusions I. ✗ II. ✗

So, only II follows.

12. (*c*)

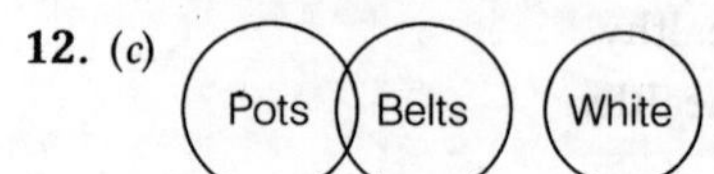

Conclusions I. ✗ II. ✓

So, either I or II follows.

13. (*c*)

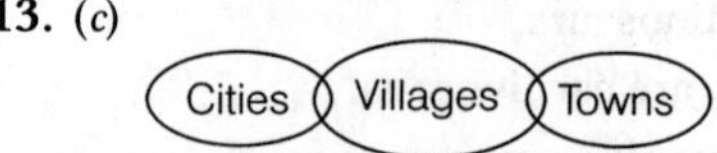

Conclusions

I.] Complementary
II.] pair

So, either I or II follows.

14. (*e*)

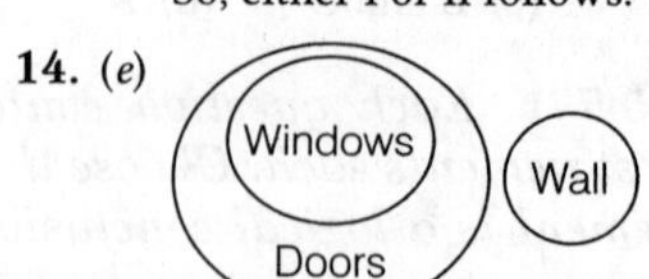

Conclusions I. ✓ II. ✓

So, both I and II follow.

15. (*a*)

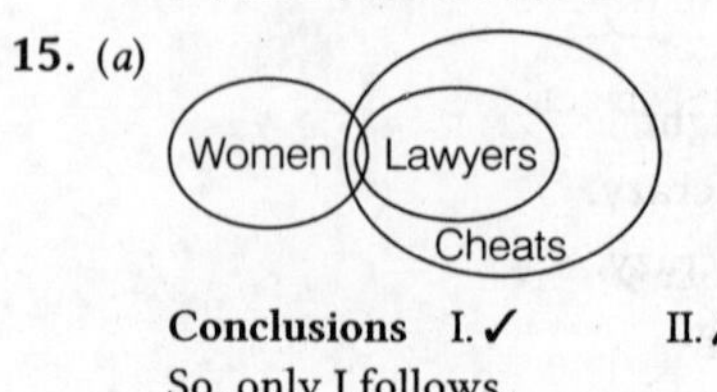

Conclusions I. ✓ II. ✗

So, only I follows.

16. (*a*)

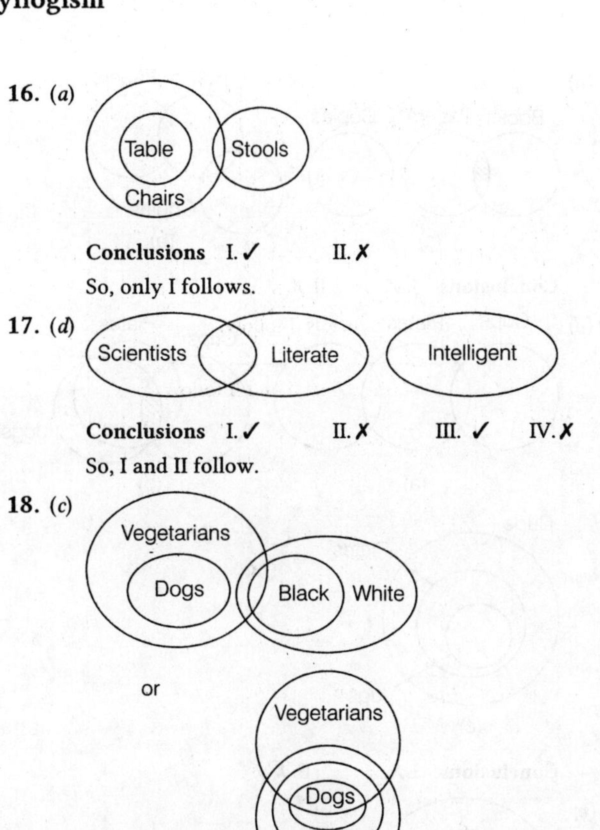

Conclusions I. ✓ II. ✗

So, only I follows.

17. (*d*)

Conclusions I. ✓ II. ✗ III. ✓ IV. ✗

So, I and II follow.

18. (*c*)

Conclusions I. ✗ II. ✗ III. ✓

So, only conclusion III follows.

Hence, only Conclusion I follows from the given statements.

19. (*b*)

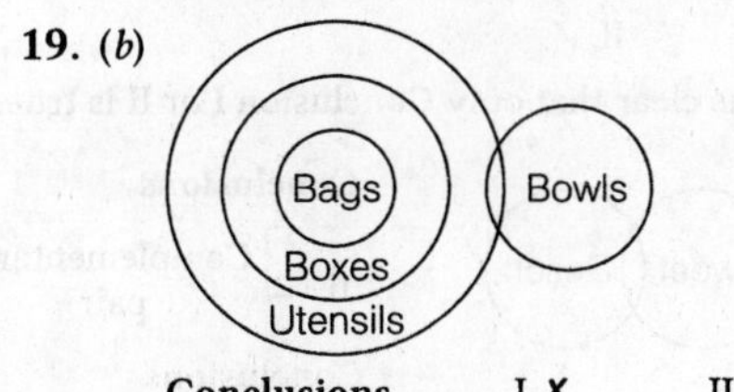

Conclusions I. ✗ II. ✓

So, only II follows.

20. (*b*)

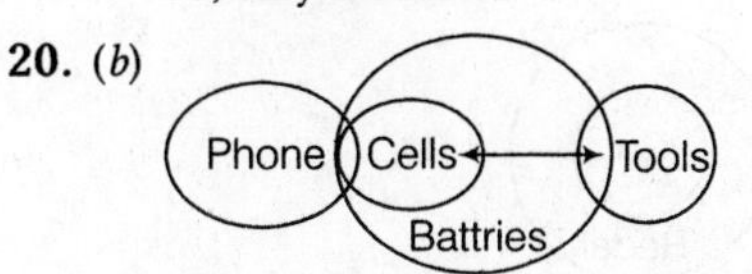

Conclusions I. ✗ II. ✓

So, only II follows.

21. (*d*)

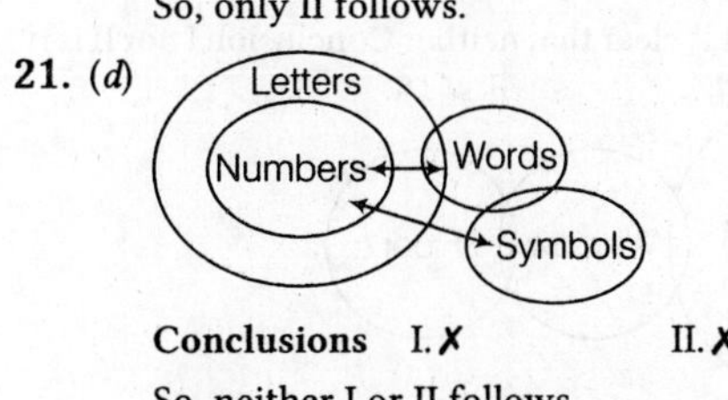

Conclusions I. ✗ II. ✗

So, neither I or II follows.

22. (*c*)

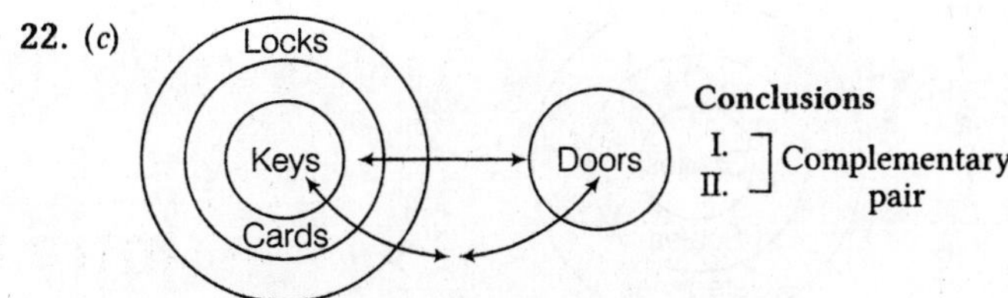

So, either I or II follows.

23. (*e*) According to the statements, Venn diagram is

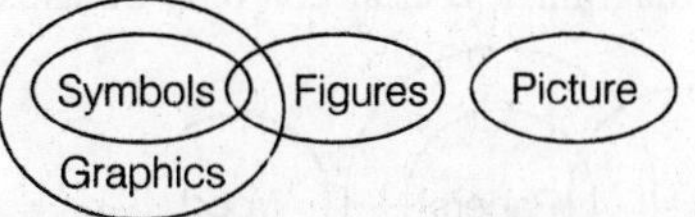

Conclusions I. ✓ II. ✓

Hence, both Conclusions I and II follow from the given statements.

24. (*d*)

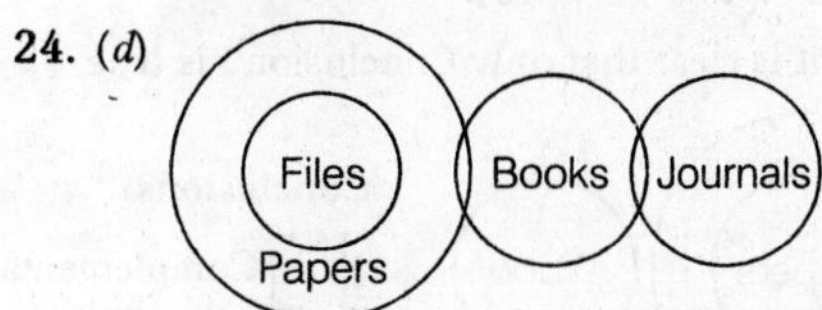

Conclusions I. ✗ II. ✗

Hence, neither conclusion I nor II follows.

25. (*d*)

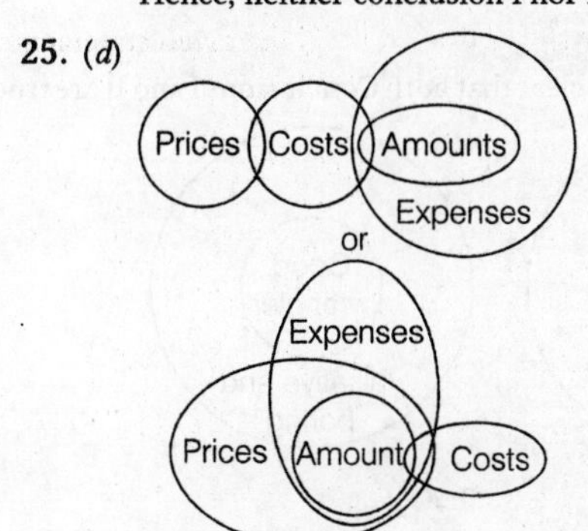

Conclusions I. ✗ II. ✓

From diagram, it is clear that only Conclusion I is true.

26. (*d*)

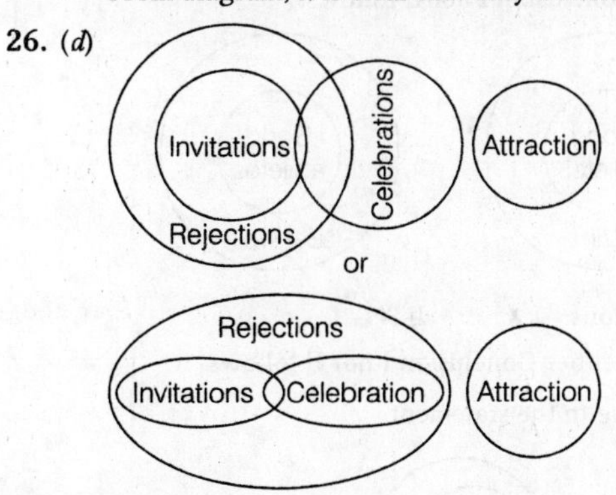

Conclusions I. ✓ II. ✗

From diagram, it is clear that only Conclusion I is true.

27. (*e*)

Grades
Scales
Categories

Conclusions I. ✓ II. ✗

From diagram, it is clear that only Conclusion I is true.

28. (*e*)

Metats Papers Wood
Alloys

Conclusions I. ✓ II. ✗

From diagram, it is clear that only Conclusion I is true.

29. (*b*)

Metats Papers Wood
Alloys

Conclusions
I.] Complementary
II.] pair

Conclusions I. ✓ II. ✓

From diagram, it is clear that both Conclusions I and II are true.

30. (*c*)

Good wrangler
Wise men
Good wrangler
Talkative and boring

Conclusions I. ✗ II. ✗

According to the statement, good wranglers are wise men. But it does not mean that, all wisemen are good wranglers. So, neither conclusion I nor II follows.

31. (*c*)

Good athletes
Win
Good athletes
Eat well

Conclusions I. ✗ II. ✗

Hence, neither Conclusion I nor II follows.

32. (*c*) According to the statement,

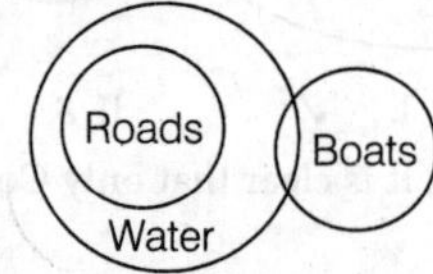

Conclusions I. ✗ II. ✗

Hence, neither Conclusion I nor II follows.

33. (*a*)

Books Papers Copies
(a)
Books Papers
Copies
(b)

Conclusions I. ✓ II. ✗

34. (*d*)

Cups Plates Jugs
(a)
Plates
Cups
Jugs
(b)
Cups
Plates
Jugs
(c)

Conclusions I. ✗ II. ✗

35. (*e*)

Alphabet
Letter
Digit
Number

Conclusions I. ✗ II. ✓

From diagram, it is clear that only Conclusion I or II is true.

36. (*a*)

Fruit
Flower
Sweet Desert

Conclusions
I.] Complementary
II.] pair

From diagram, it is clear that only conclusion II is true.

37. (*b*)

Plane Ship
Car
Radar

Conclusions I. ✗ II. ✗

From diagram, it is clear that neither Conclusion I nor II is true.

38. (*b*)

Lock
Key
Door
Window Floor

Conclusions I. ✗ II. ✗

From diagram, it is clear that neither I nor II is true.

39. (c)

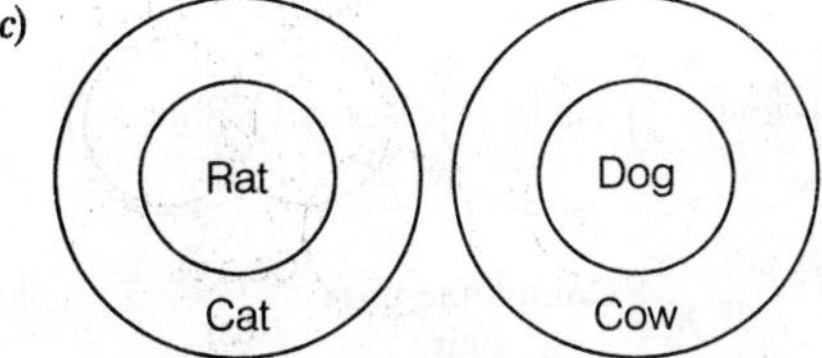

Conclusions I. ✓ II. ✓

From diagram, it is clear that both Conclusions I and II are true.

40. (d)

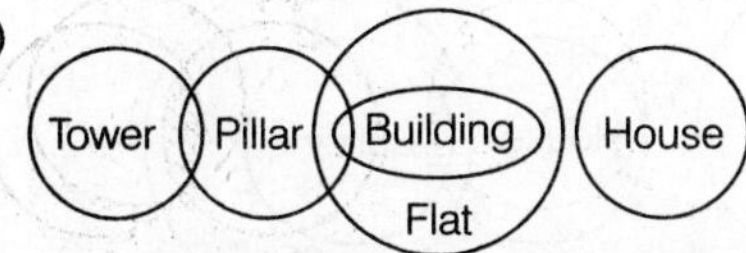

Conclusions I. ✓ II. ✗

From diagram, it is clear that only Conclusion I is true.

41. (b)

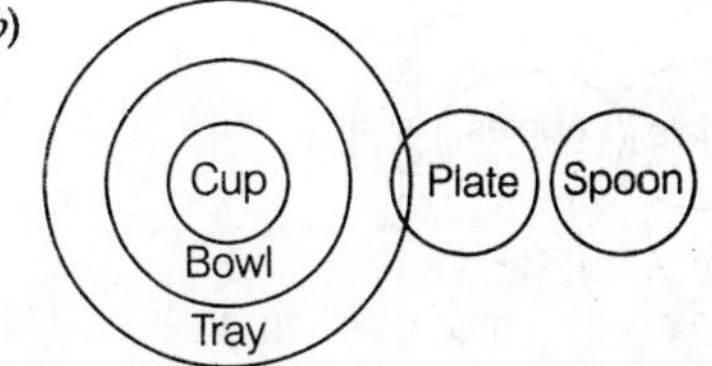

Conclusions I. ✓ II. ✗

From diagram, it is clear that neither Conclusion I nor II is true.

42. (b)

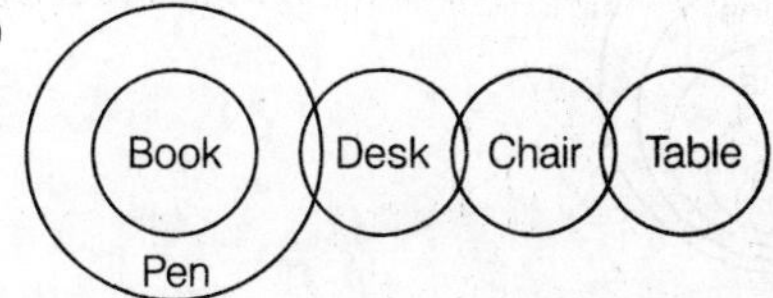

Conclusions I. ✗ II. ✗

From diagram, it is clear that neither I nor II is true.

Intro Exercise 2

1. (b)

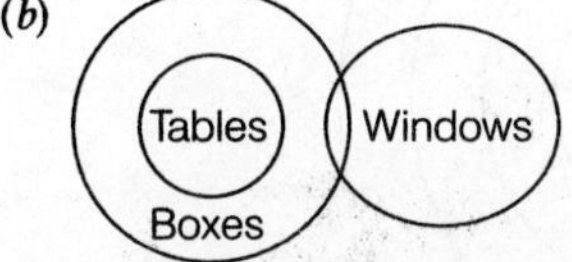

Conclusions

I. ⌉
II. ✗ | Complementary pair
III. ⌋

So, either I or III follows.

2. (c)

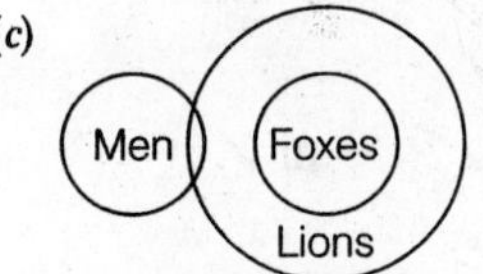

Conclusions I. ✗ II. ✓ III. ✗

So, only II follows.

3. (e)

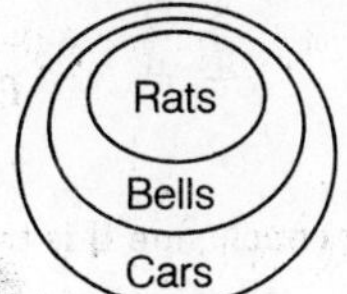

Conclusions I. ✗ II. ✗ III. ✗

So, none follows.

4. (d)

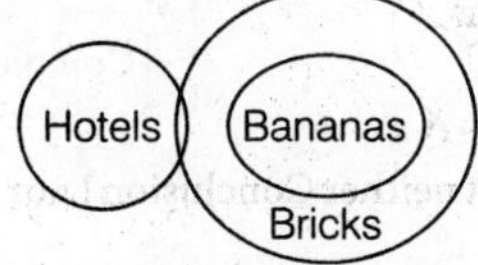

Conclusions

I. ⌉
II. | Complementary pair
III. ⌋

So, either I or III and II follows

5. (b)

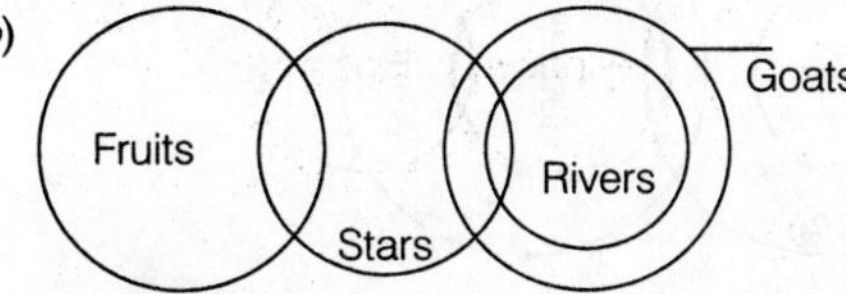

Conclusions I. ✗ II. ✓ III. ✗

So, only II follows.

6. (d)

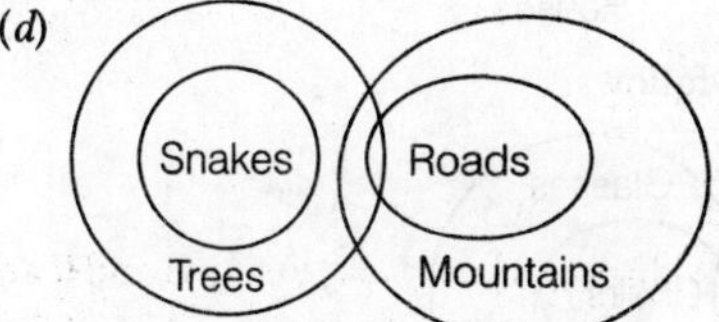

Conclusions I. ✗ II. ✗ III. ✓

So, only III follows.

7. (c)

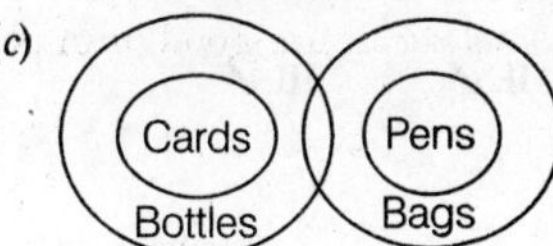

Conclusions I. ✗ II. ✓ III. ✗

So, only II follows.

8. (c)

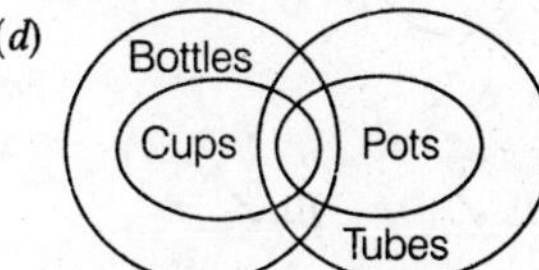

Conclusions I. ✗ II. ✓ III. ✗

So, only II follows.

9. (d)

Conclusions I. ✓ II. ✓ III. ✓

So, all follows.

10. (a)

Conclusions I. ✗ II. ✗ III. ✗

Hence, none follows.

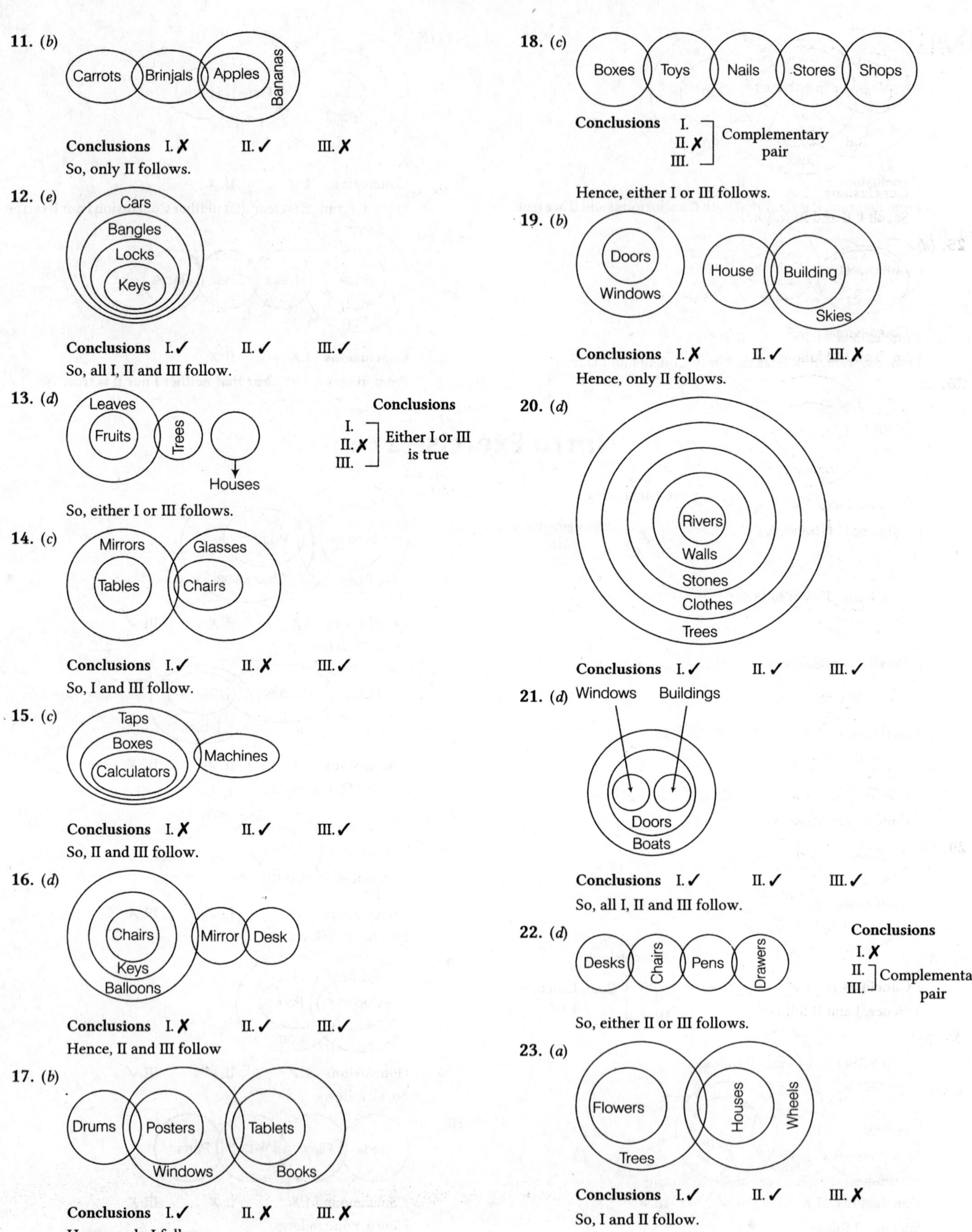
11. (b)
Carrots
Brinjals
Apples
Bananas
Conclusions I. ✗ II. ✓ III. ✗
So, only II follows.
12. (e)
Cars
Bangles
Locks
Keys
Conclusions I. ✓ II. ✓ III. ✓
So, all I, II and III follow.
13. (d)
Leaves
Fruits
Trees
Houses
Conclusions
I.] Either I or III
II. ✗ is true
III.
So, either I or III follows.
14. (c)
Mirrors
Glasses
Tables
Chairs
Conclusions I. ✓ II. ✗ III. ✓
So, I and III follow.
15. (c)
Taps
Boxes
Calculators
Machines
Conclusions I. ✗ II. ✓ III. ✓
So, II and III follow.
16. (d)
Chairs
Keys
Balloons
Mirror
Desk
Conclusions I. ✗ II. ✓ III. ✓
Hence, II and III follow
17. (b)
Drums
Posters
Windows
Tablets
Books
Conclusions I. ✓ II. ✗ III. ✗
Hence, only I follow.
18. (c)
Boxes
Toys
Nails
Stores
Shops
Conclusions I.] Complementary
II. ✗ pair
III.
Hence, either I or III follows.
19. (b)
Doors
Windows
House
Building
Skies
Conclusions I. ✗ II. ✓ III. ✗
Hence, only II follows.
20. (d)
Rivers
Walls
Stones
Clothes
Trees
Conclusions I. ✓ II. ✓ III. ✓
21. (d)
Windows
Buildings
Doors
Boats
Conclusions I. ✓ II. ✓ III. ✓
So, all I, II and III follow.
22. (d)
Desks
Chairs
Pens
Drawers
Conclusions
I. ✗
II.] Complementary
III. pair
So, either II or III follows.
23. (a)
Flowers
Trees
Houses
Wheels
Conclusions I. ✓ II. ✓ III. ✗
So, I and II follow.

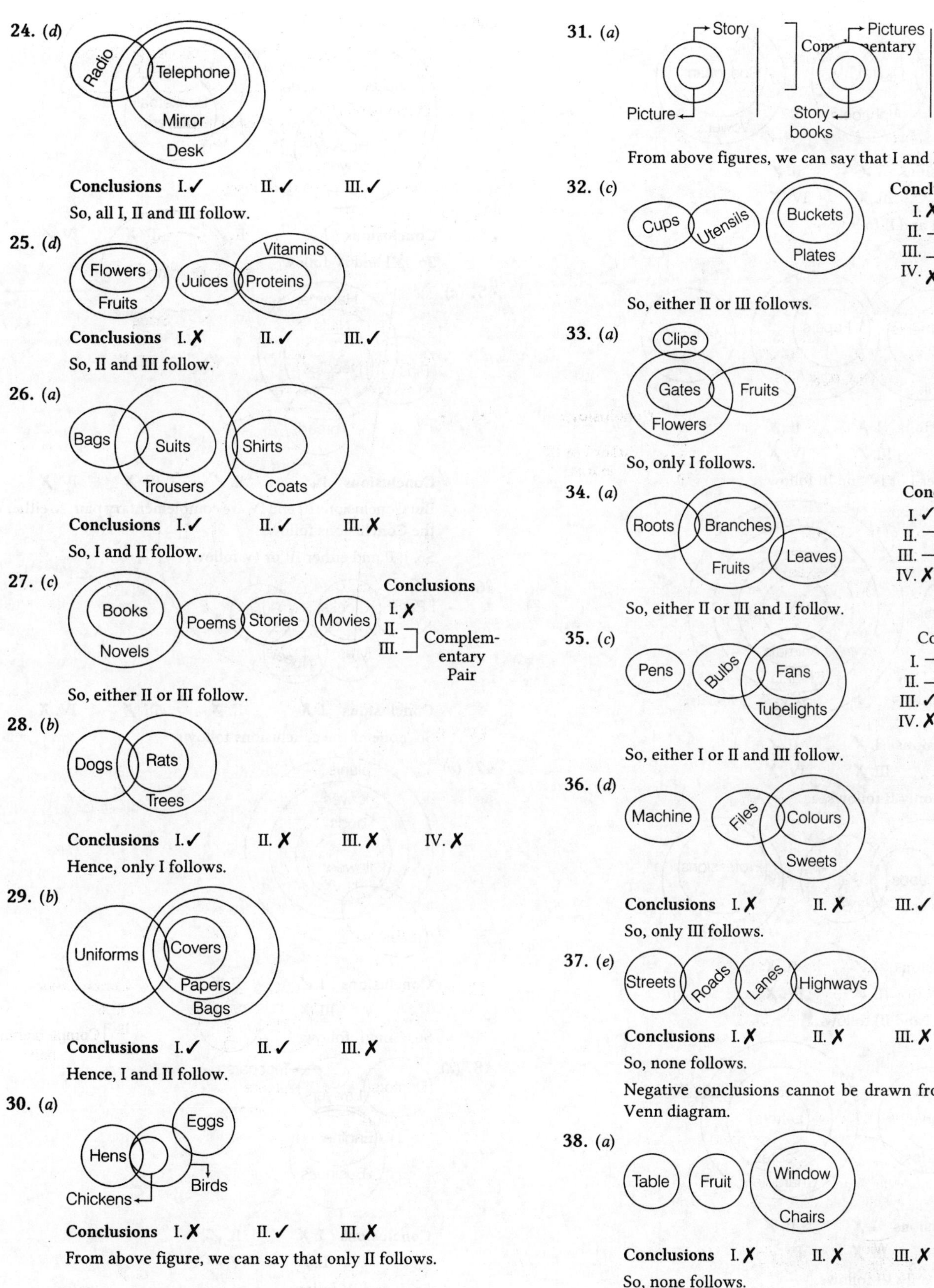

24. (*d*)

Conclusions I. ✓ II. ✓ III. ✓

So, all I, II and III follow.

25. (*d*)

Conclusions I. ✗ II. ✓ III. ✓

So, II and III follow.

26. (*a*)

Conclusions I. ✓ II. ✓ III. ✗

So, I and II follow.

27. (*c*)

Conclusions
I. ✗
II.] Complementary Pair
III.]

So, either II or III follow.

28. (*b*)

Conclusions I. ✓ II. ✗ III. ✗ IV. ✗

Hence, only I follows.

29. (*b*)

Conclusions I. ✓ II. ✓ III. ✗

Hence, I and II follow.

30. (*a*)

Conclusions I. ✗ II. ✓ III. ✗

From above figure, we can say that only II follows.

31. (*a*)

From above figures, we can say that I and III follow.

32. (*c*)

Conclusions
I. ✗
II.] Complementary pair
III.]
IV. ✗

So, either II or III follows.

33. (*a*)

Conclusions
I. ✓
II. ✗
III. ✗
IV. ✗

So, only I follows.

34. (*a*)

Conclusions
I. ✓
II.] Complementary pair
III.]
IV. ✗

So, either II or III and I follow.

35. (*c*)

Conclusions
I.] Complementary pair
II.]
III. ✓
IV. ✗

So, either I or II and III follow.

36. (*d*)

Conclusions I. ✗ II. ✗ III. ✓ IV. ✗

So, only III follows.

37. (*e*)

Conclusions I. ✗ II. ✗ III. ✗ IV. ✗

So, none follows.

Negative conclusions cannot be drawn from the above Venn diagram.

38. (*a*)

Conclusions I. ✗ II. ✗ III. ✗ IV. ✗

So, none follows.

39. (*c*)

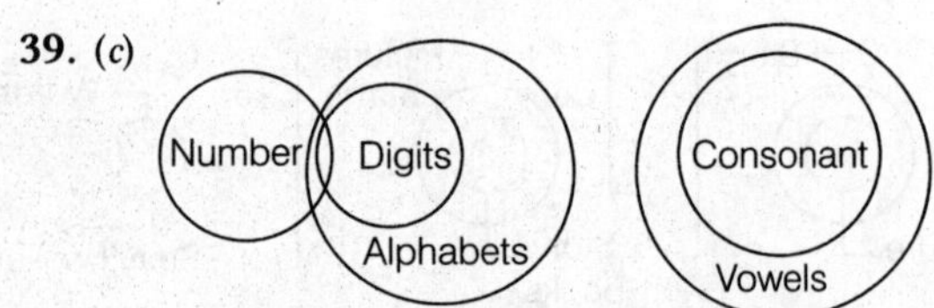

Conclusions I. ✓ II. ✓
III. ✗ IV. ✗

Hence, I and II follow.

40. (*e*)

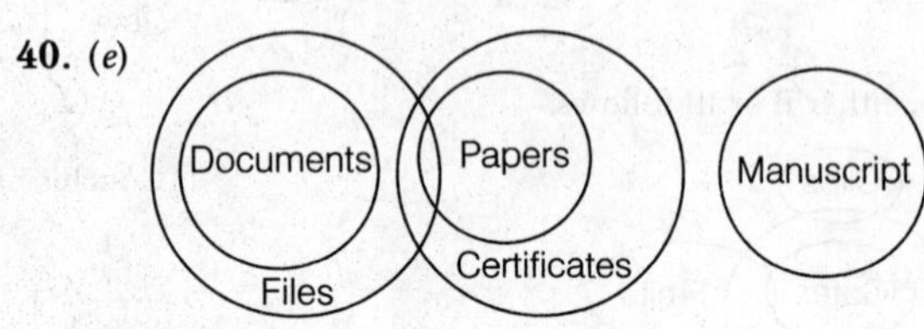

Conclusions I. ✗ II. ✗
III. ✓ IV. ✗

So, either I or IV and III follow.

41. (*a*)

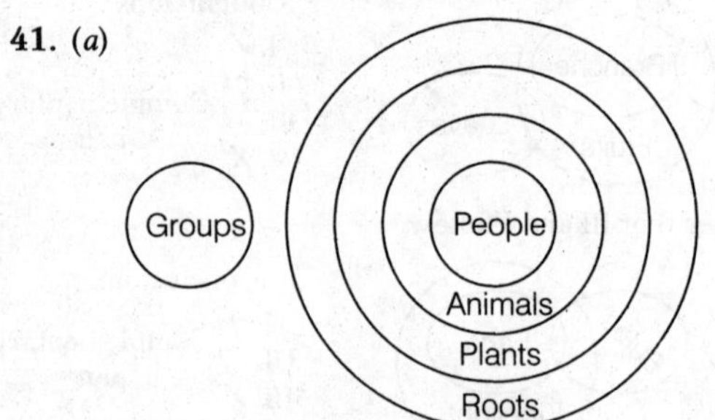

Conclusions I. ✗ II. ✓
III. ✗ IV. ✗

Hence, only II follows.

42. (*e*)

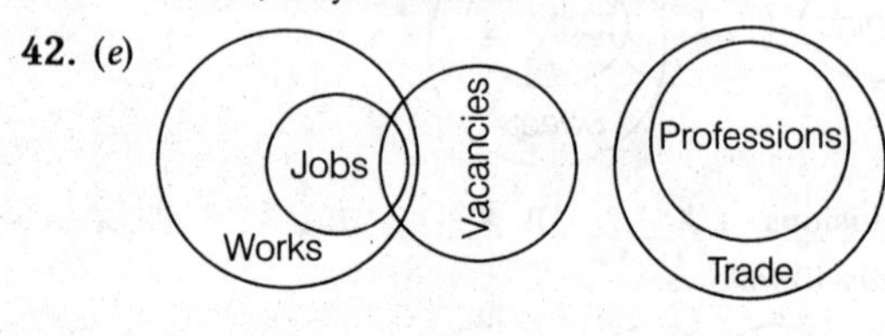

Conclusions I. ✓ II. ✗
III. ✓ IV. ✗

Hence, I and III follow.

43. (*b*)

Conclusions I. ✗ II. ✗
III. ✗ IV. ✓

Hence, only VI follows.

44. (*b*)

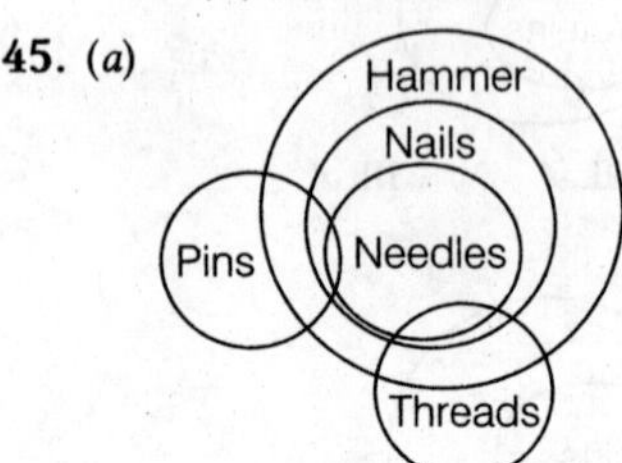

Conclusions I. ✓ II. ✓ III. ✗ IV. ✓

So, I, II and IV follow.

45. (*a*)

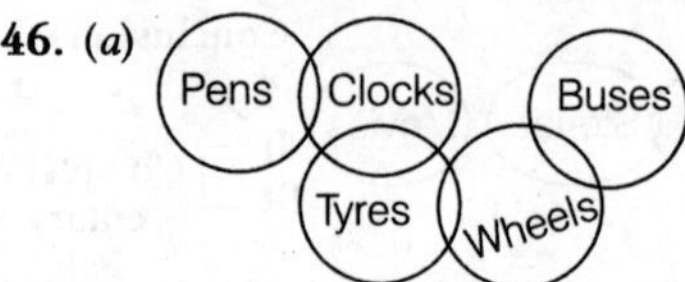

Conclusions I. ✓ II. ✓ III. ✗ IV. ✗

But Conclusions III and IV are complementary pair, so either of the Conclusions follows.

So, I, II and either III or IV follow.

46. (*a*)

Conclusions I. ✗ II. ✗ III. ✗ IV. ✗

So, none of the conclusions follows.

47. (*b*)

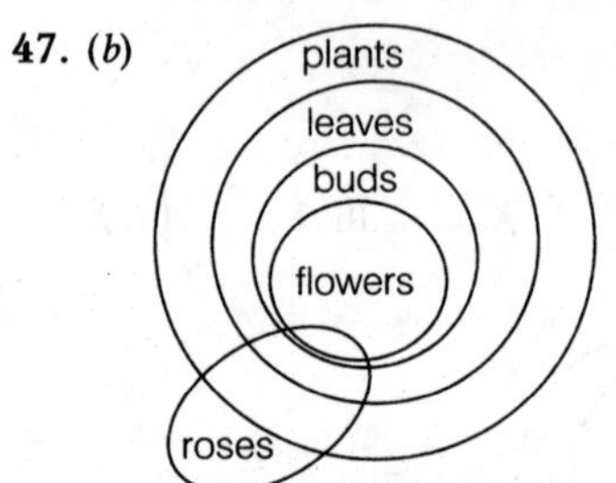

Conclusions I. ✓ II. ✓
III. ✗ IV. ✗

So, I and II follow.

48. (*d*)

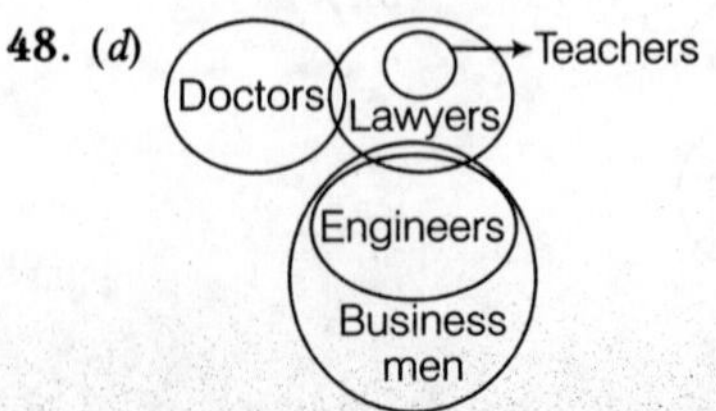

Conclusions I. ✗ II. ✓
III. ✗ IV. ✓

So, II and IV follow.

49. (*b*)

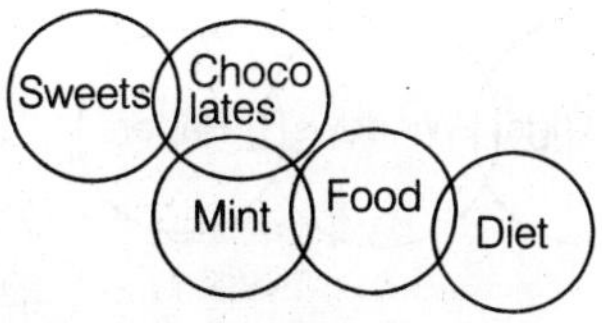

Conclusions I. ✗ II. ✗
III. ✗ IV. ✗

But Conclusions I and III are opposite or contradict each other so one has to follow.

So, either I or III follows.

50. (*a*)

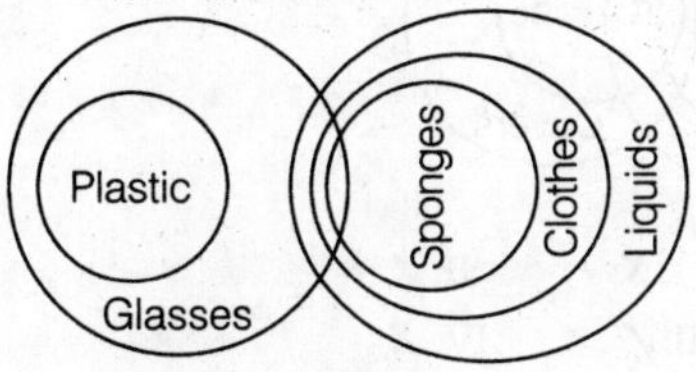

Conclusions I. ✗ II. ✗ III. ✗ IV. ✗

So, none follows.

51. (*e*)

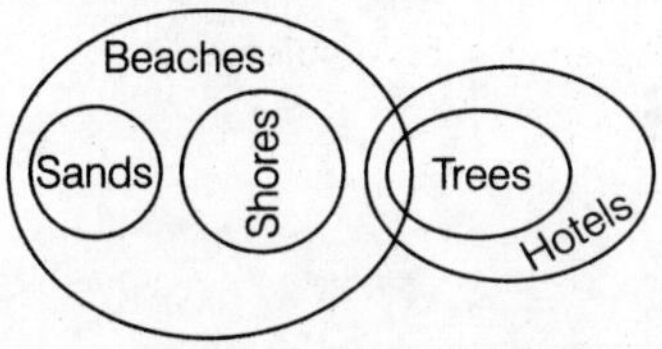

Conclusions I. ✗ II. ✗ III. ✓ IV. ✗

So, only III follows.

52. (*c*)

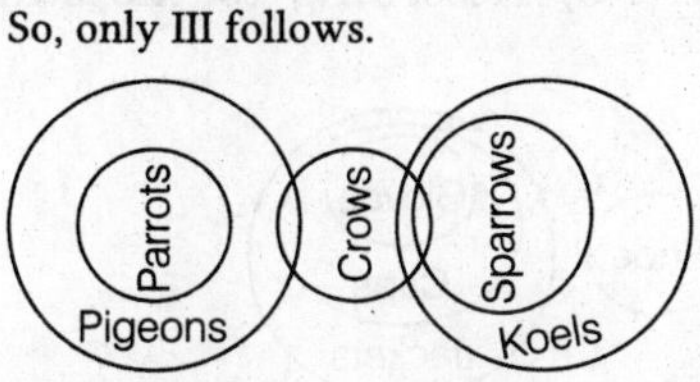

Conclusions I. ✓ II. ✗ III. ✗ IV. ✗

(II and IV: Complementary pair)

So, either II or IV and I follow.

53. (*b*)

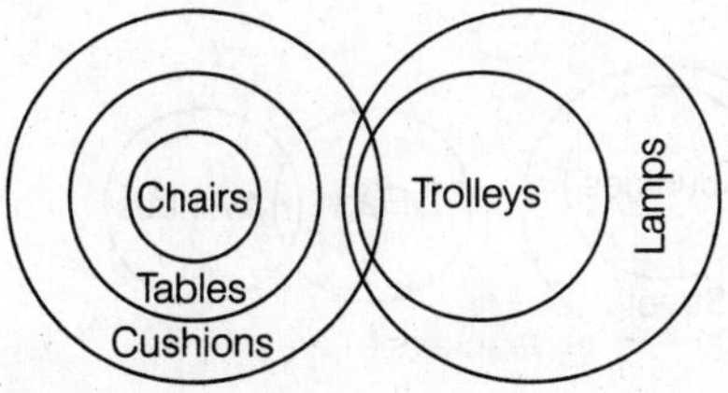

Conclusions I. ✗ II. ✗ III. ✓ IV. ✓

So, III and IV follow.

54. (*c*)

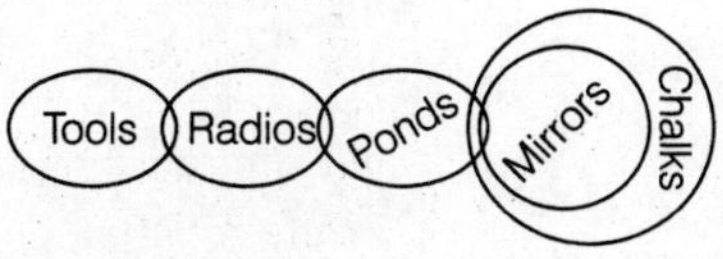

Conclusions I. ✗ II. ✓ III. ✗ IV. ✗

So, only II follows.

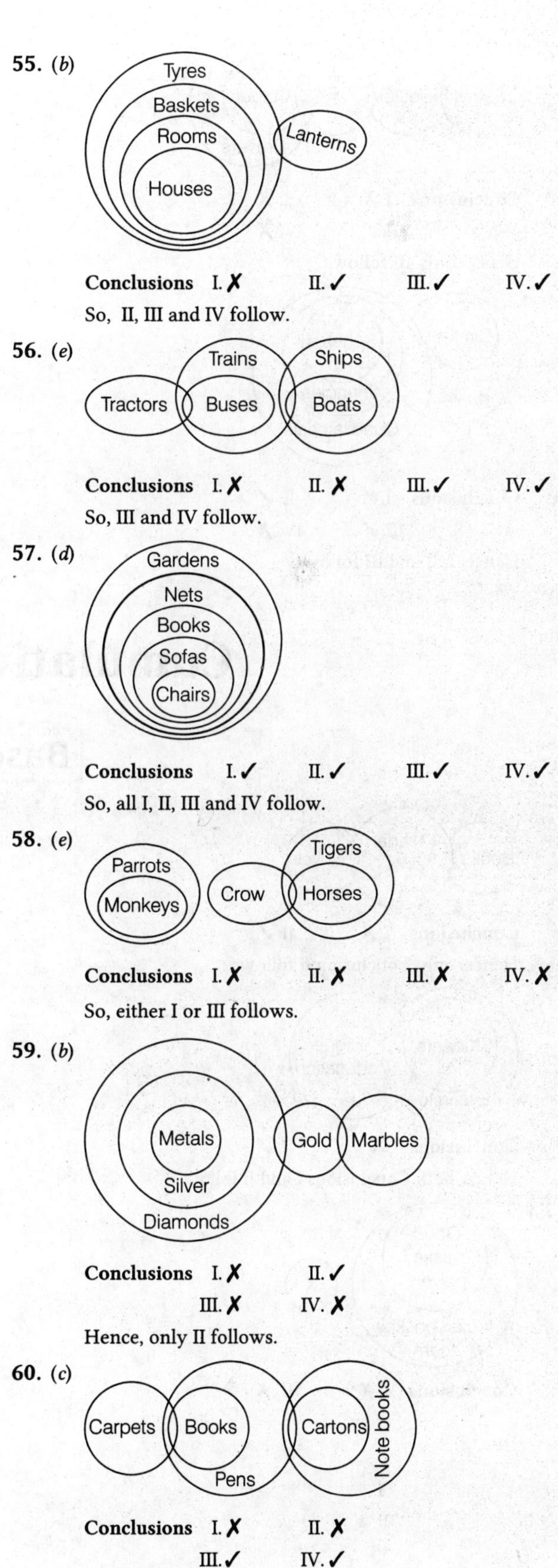

55. (*b*)

Conclusions I. ✗ II. ✓ III. ✓ IV. ✓

So, II, III and IV follow.

56. (*e*)

Conclusions I. ✗ II. ✗ III. ✓ IV. ✓

So, III and IV follow.

57. (*d*)

Conclusions I. ✓ II. ✓ III. ✓ IV. ✓

So, all I, II, III and IV follow.

58. (*e*)

Conclusions I. ✗ II. ✗ III. ✗ IV. ✗

So, either I or III follows.

59. (*b*)

Conclusions I. ✗ II. ✓
III. ✗ IV. ✗

Hence, only II follows.

60. (*c*)

Conclusions I. ✗ II. ✗
III. ✓ IV. ✓

Hence, III and IV follow.

61. (*d*)

Paints Bottles Brands Colours Erasers

Conclusions I. ✗ II. ✗
III. ✓ IV. ✗

Hence, only III follows.

62. (*c*)

Circles Boxes Spheres Triangles Quadilaterials

Conclusions I. ✓ II. ✓
III. ✓ IV. ✗

Hence, I, II and III follow.

63. (*e*)

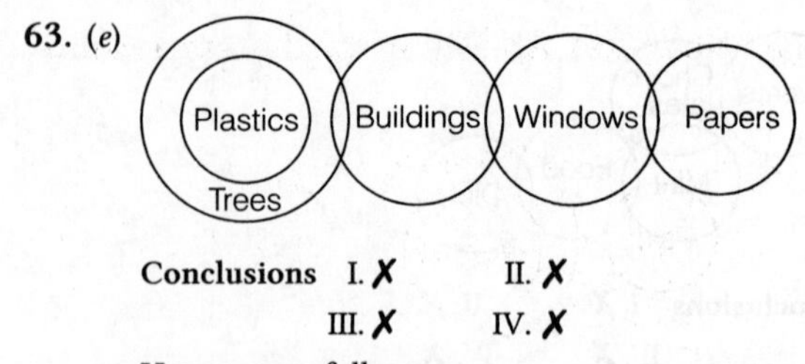

Conclusions I. ✗ II. ✗
III. ✗ IV. ✗

Hence, none follows.

64. (*d*)

Rings Phones Spoons Files Covers

Conclusions I. ✗ II. ✓
III. ✓ IV. ✗

Hence, II and III follow.

Cumulative Exercises

Base Level

1. (*b*)

Books Magazines Novels

Conclusions I. ✗ II. ✓

Hence, only Conclusion II follows.

2. (*c*)

Students Excursion Higher education

Conclusions I. ✓ II. ✓

Hence, both Conclusions I and II follow.

3. (*d*)

Conclusions I. ✗ II. ✗

Solution (Q. Nos. 4-5) According to the statements, Venn diagram is

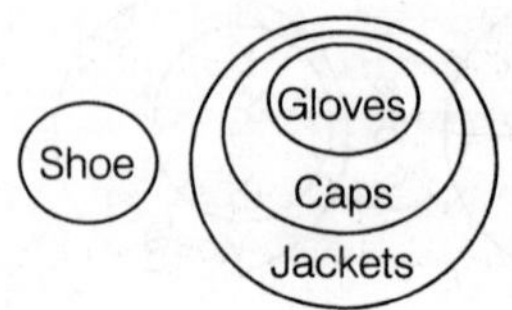

4. (*b*) **Conclusions** I. ✗ II. ✓

5. (*b*) **Conclusions** I. ✗ II. ✓

Solution (Q. Nos. 6-7) According to the statements, Venn-diagram is

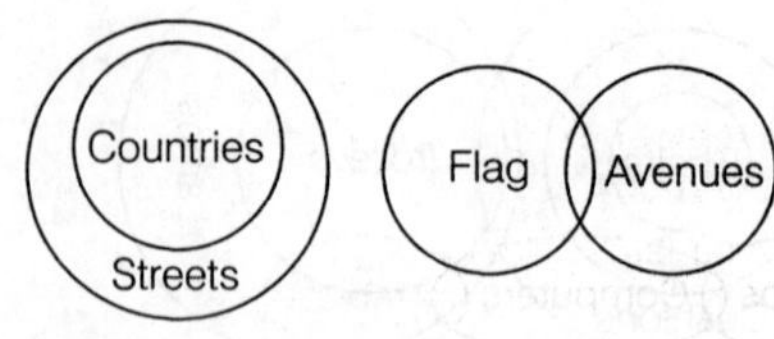

6. (*a*) **Conclusions** I. ✓ II. ✗

7. (*a*) **Conclusions** I. ✓ II. ✗

Solution (Q. Nos. 8-9) Accroding to the statements, Venn diagram is

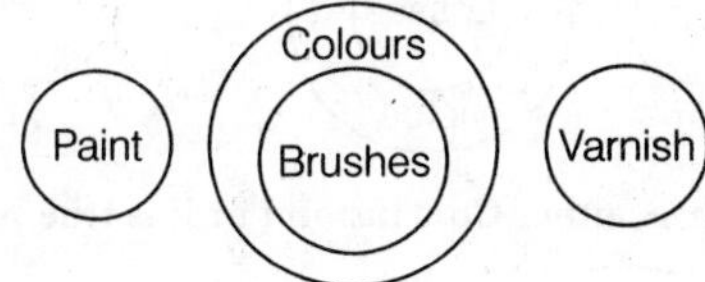

8. (*a*) **Conclusions** I. ✓ II. ✗

Hence only Conclusion I follows.

9. (*d*) **Conclusions** I. ✗ II. ✗

Hence, neither Conclusion I nor II follows.

10. (*a*)

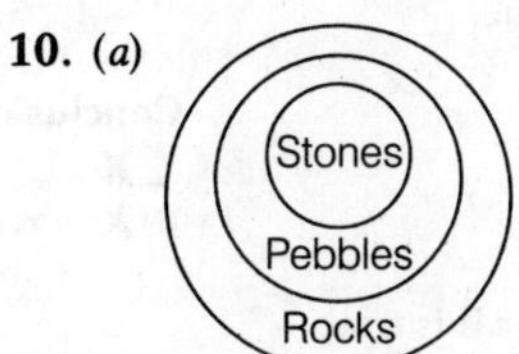

Conclusions I. ✓ II. ✗

Hence, only Conclusion I follows.

11. (*a*)

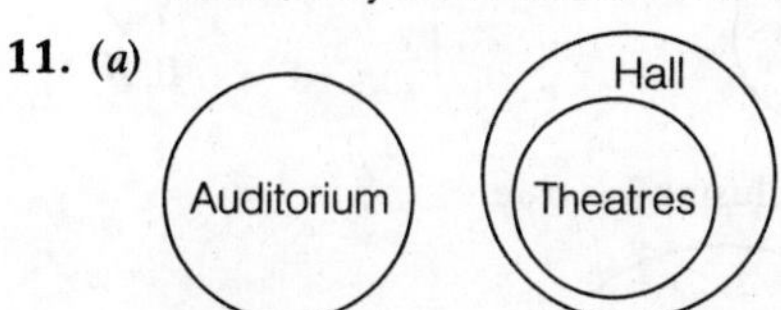

Conclusions I. ✓ II. ✗

So, only I follows.

12. (*e*)

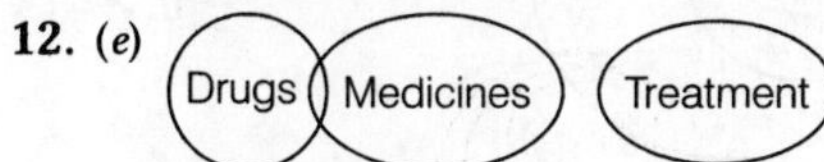

Conclusions I. ✓ II. ✓

Hence, both Conclusions I and II follow.

13. (*b*)

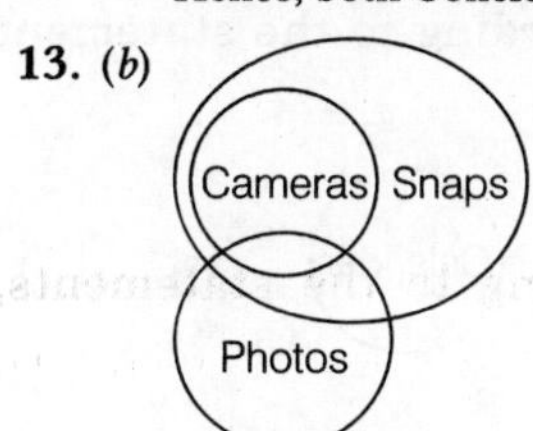

Conclusions I. ✗ II. ✓

So, only II follows.

14. (*b*)

Conclusions I. ✗ II. ✓

So, only II follows.

15. (*b*)

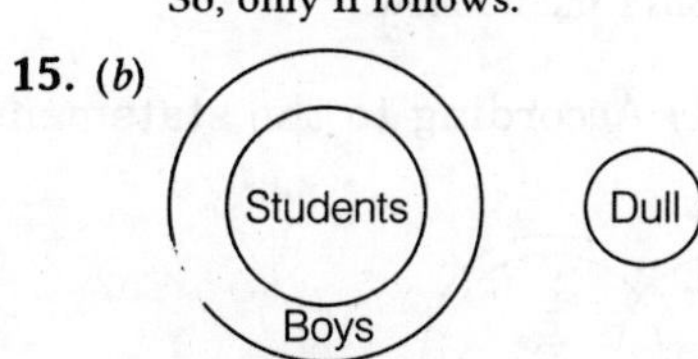

Conclusions I. ✗ II. ✓

Hence, only Conclusion II follows.

16. (*c*)

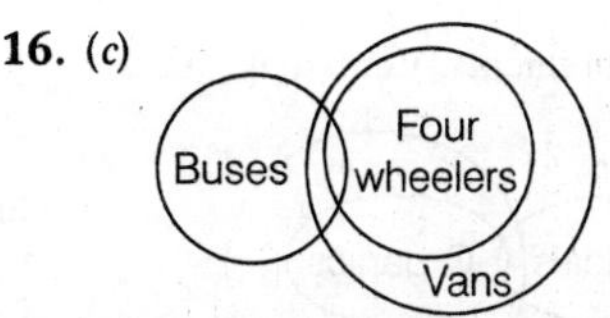

Conclusions I. ✓ II. ✓

Hence, both Conclusions I and II follow.

17. (*d*)

Intelligent Soldiers famous

Conclusions I. ✗ II. ✗

So, neither Conclusion I nor II follows.

18. (*b*)

Men Clerks Lazy

Conclusions I. ✗ II. ✓

So, only II follows.

19. (*e*)

Aeroplanes Living beings Non-living beings Ghosts

Conclusions

I.] Complementary
II.] Pair

So either I or II follows.

➘ No mediate inference can be drawn as there is no middle term. However, one of the conclusions must be true.

20. (*b*)

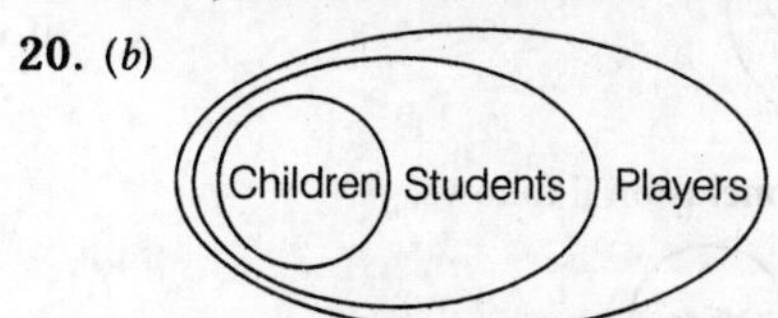

Conclusions I. ✗ II. ✓

So, only II follows.

21. (*d*) According to the statements, Venn diagram is

Conclusions
I. ✗
II. ✗

Hence, neither I nor II follows.

22. (*a*) According to the statements, Venn diagram is

Conclusions
I. ✓
II. ✗

Hence, only I follows.

23. (*b*) According to the statements, Venn diagram is

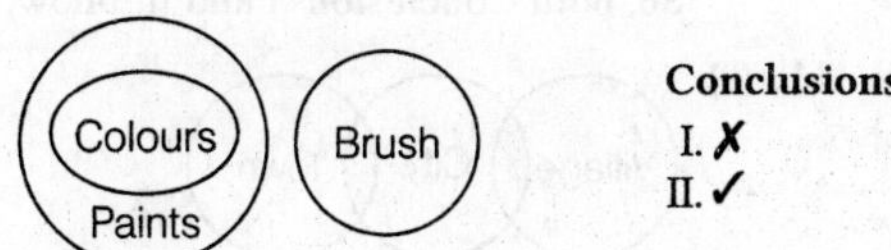

Conclusions
I. ✗
II. ✓

So, only II follows.

24. (*a*) According to the statements, Venn diagram is

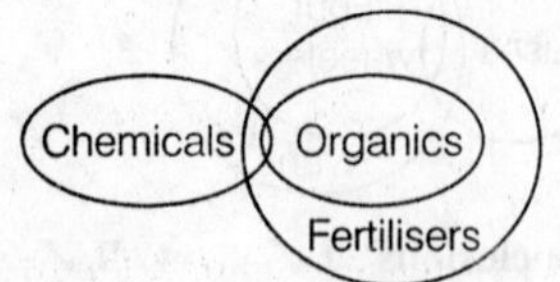

Conclusions
I. ✓
II. ✗

So, only I follows.

25. (*d*) According to the statements, Venn diagram is

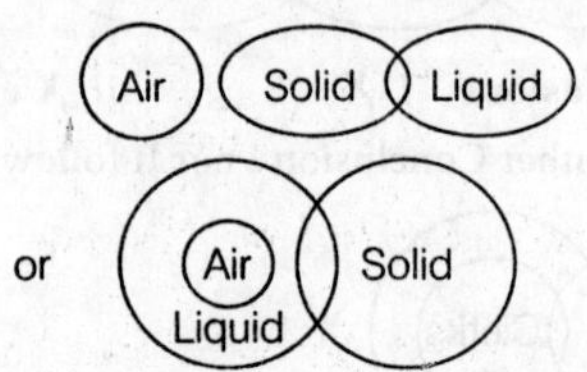

Conclusions
I. ✗
II. ✗

So, neither Conclusion I nor II follows.

26. (*e*) According to the statements Venn diagram is

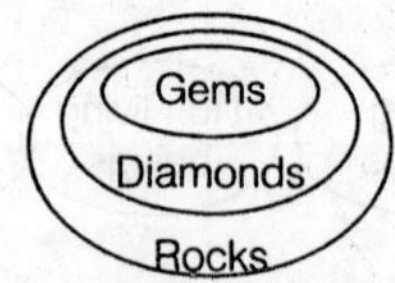

Conclusions
I. ✓
II. ✓

Hence, both conclusion I nor II follows.

27. (*b*)

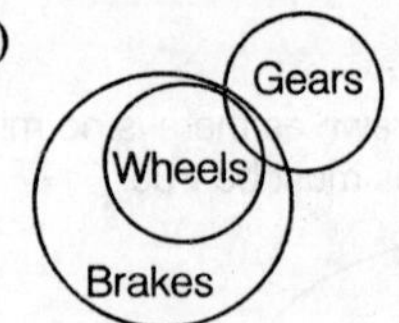

Conclusions
I. ✗
II. ✓

So, only Conclusion II follows.

28. (*d*)

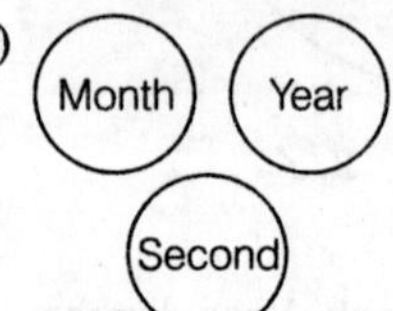

Conclusions I. ✗ II. ✗

So, neither Conclusion I nor II follows.

29. (*c*)

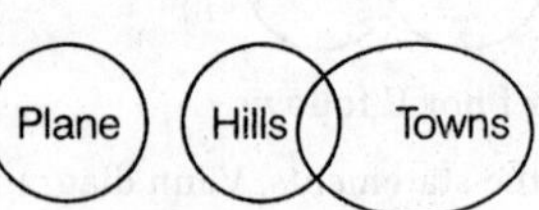

Conclusions
I.
II.] Complementary pair

So, either Conclusion I nor II follows.

30. (*e*)

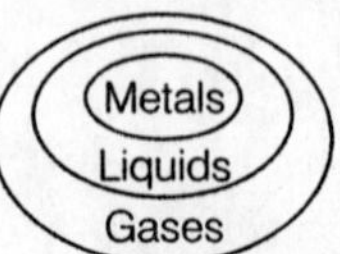

Conclusions
I. ✓
II. ✓

So, both Conclusions I and II follow.

31. (*c*)

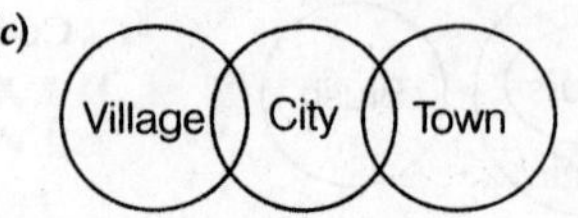

Conclusions
I.
II.] Complementary Pair

So, either Conclusion I or II follows.

32. (*e*)

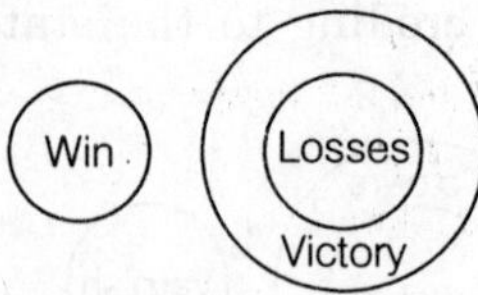

Conclusions
I.
II.] Complementary pair

Hence, either Conclusion I or II is true.

33. (*d*)

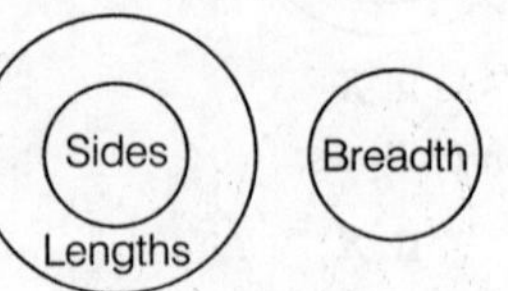

Conclusions
I. ✗
II. ✓

Hence, only Conclusion II is true.

34. (*c*)

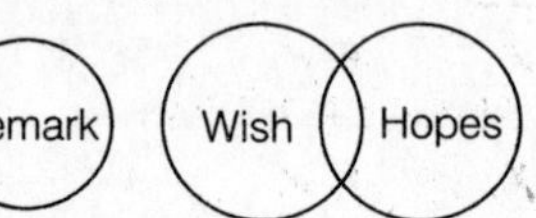

Conclusions
I. ✗
II. ✗

Hence, neither Conclusion I nor II is true.

35. (*e*)

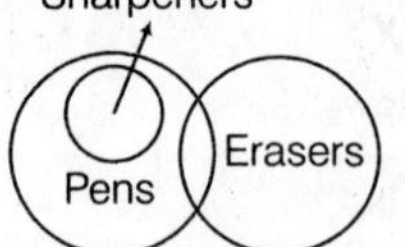

Conclusions
I. ✓
II. ✗

Hence, only Conclusion I is true.

36. (*a*)

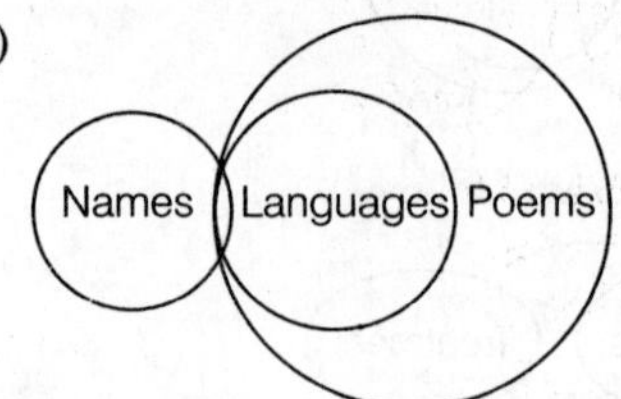

Conclusions
I. ✓
II. ✓

Hence, both Conclusions I and II are true.

Solution (Q. Nos. 37-39) According to the statements. Venn diagram is

37. (*d*) Conclusions I. ✗ II. ✗

Hence, neither Conclusion I nor II is true.

38. (*a*) Conclusions I. ✗ II. ✗

Hence, only Conclusion I follows.

39. (*e*) Conclusions I. ✓ II. ✓

Hence, both Conclusions I and II follow.

Solution (Q. Nos. 40-41) According to the statements, Venn diagram is

Pencils
Blandets
Erasers

40. (*e*) **Conclusions** I. ✓ II. ✓
Hence, both Conclusion I and II follow.

41. (*b*) **Conclusions** I. ✗ II. ✗
Hence, only Conclusion II follows.

Solution (Q. Nos. 42-43) according to the statements, Venn diagram is

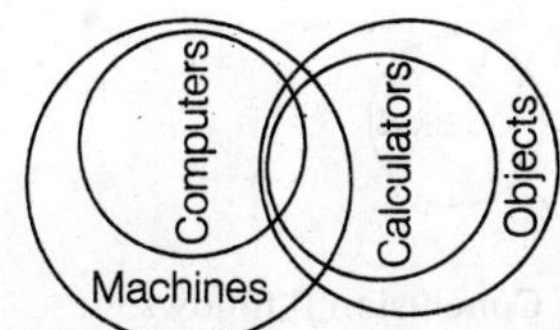

42. (*e*) **Conclusions** I. ✓ II. ✓
Hence, both Conclusions I and II follow.

43. (*b*) **Conclusions** I. ✗ II. ✓
Hence, only Conclusions II follows.

44. (*b*)

Stars Planets Moon

Conclusions
I. ✗
II. ✓

Hence, only Conclusion II follows.

45. (*a*)

Whales Mammals Insects Kites

Conclusions
I. ✓
II. ✗

Hence, only Conclusion I follows.

46. (*e*)

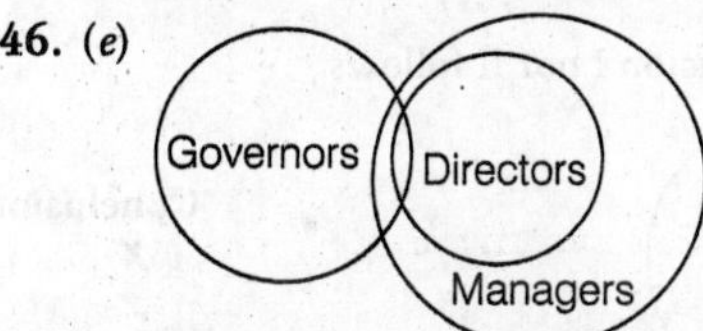

Conclusions
I. ✓
II. ✓

Hence, both Conclusions I and II follow.

Solution (Q. Nos. 47-48) According to the statements the Venn diagram is

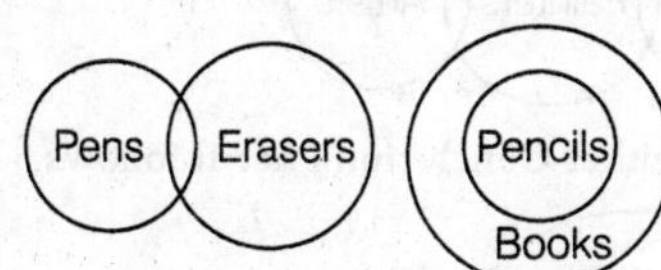

47. (*c*) **Conclusions** I.] II. Complementary pair
Hence, either Conclusion I or II follows.

48. (*b*) **Conclusions** I. ✗ II. ✓
Hence, only Conclusion II follows.

49. (*a*) According to the statements, Venn diagram is

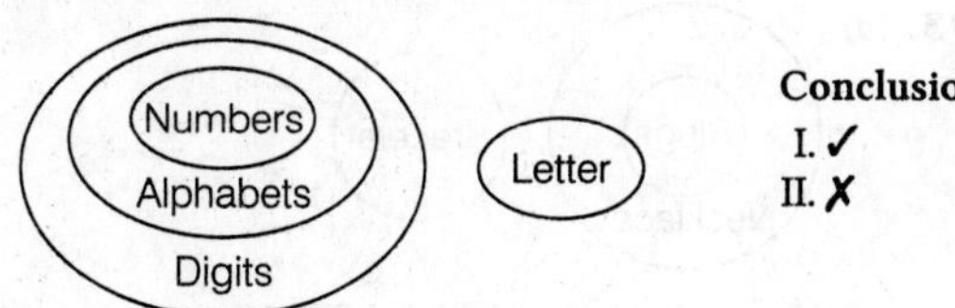

Conclusions
I. ✓
II. ✗

Hence, only Conclusion I follows.

50. (*c*) According to the statements, Venn diagram is

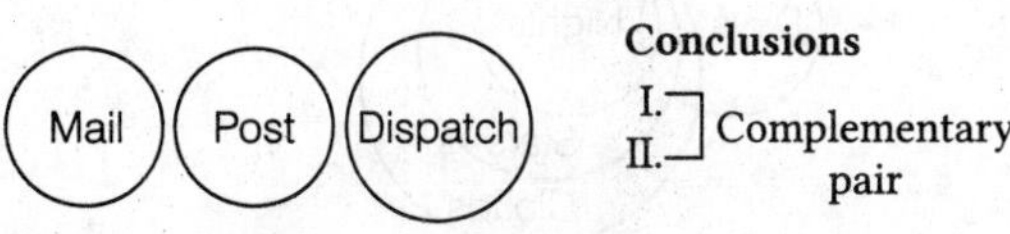

Conclusions
I.] II. Complementary pair

Hence, either Conclusion I or II follows.

51. (*d*) According to the statements, Venn diagram is

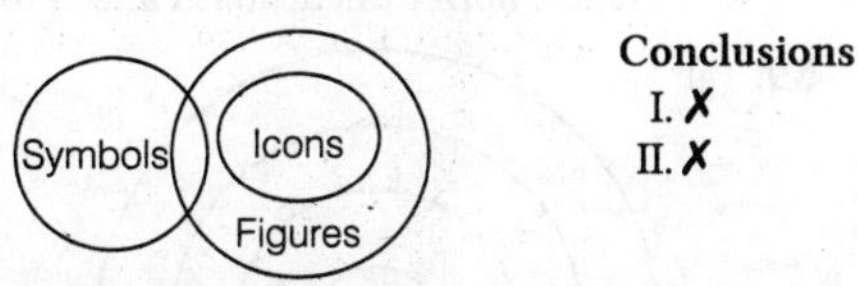

Conclusions
I. ✗
II. ✗

Hence, neither Conclusion I nor II follows.

Solution (Q. Nos. 52-53) According to the statements, Venn diagram is

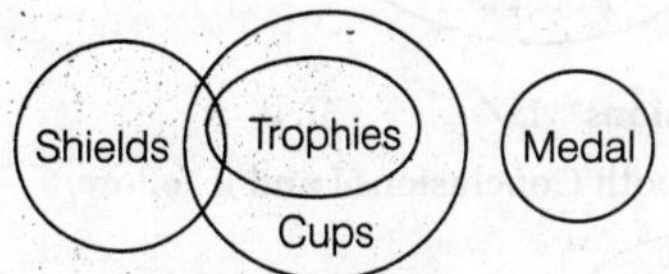

52. (*a*) **Conclusions** I. ✓ II. ✗
Hence, only Conclusion I follows.

53. (*b*) **Conclusions** I. ✗ II. ✓
Hence, only Conclusion II follows.

54. (*d*)

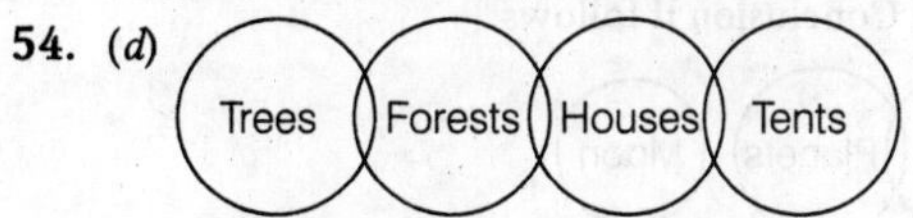

Conclusions I. ✗ II. ✗
Hence, neither I nor II follows.

55. (*a*)

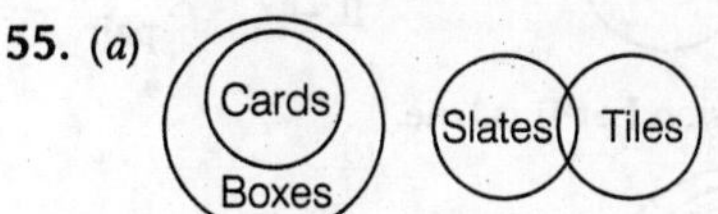

Conclusions I. ✓ II. ✗
Hence, only Conclusion I follows.

56. (*c*)

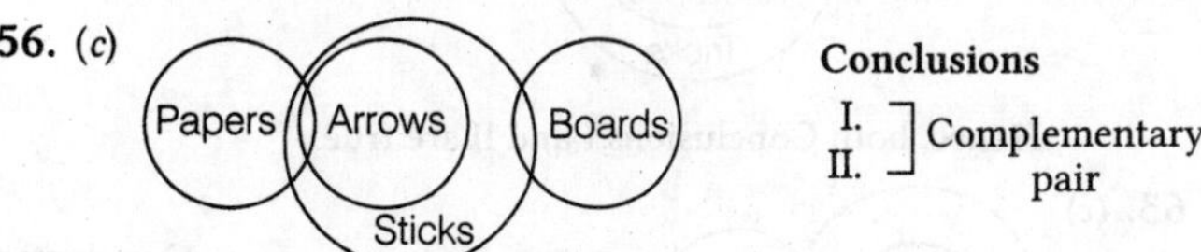

Conclusions
I.] II. Complementary pair

Hence, either Conclusion I or II follows.

57. (*b*)

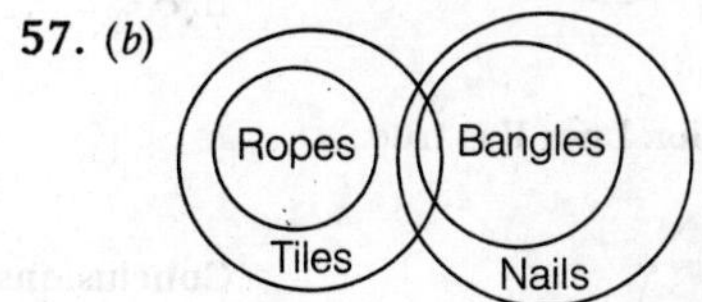

Conclusions I. ✗
II. ✓

Hence, only Conclusion II follows.

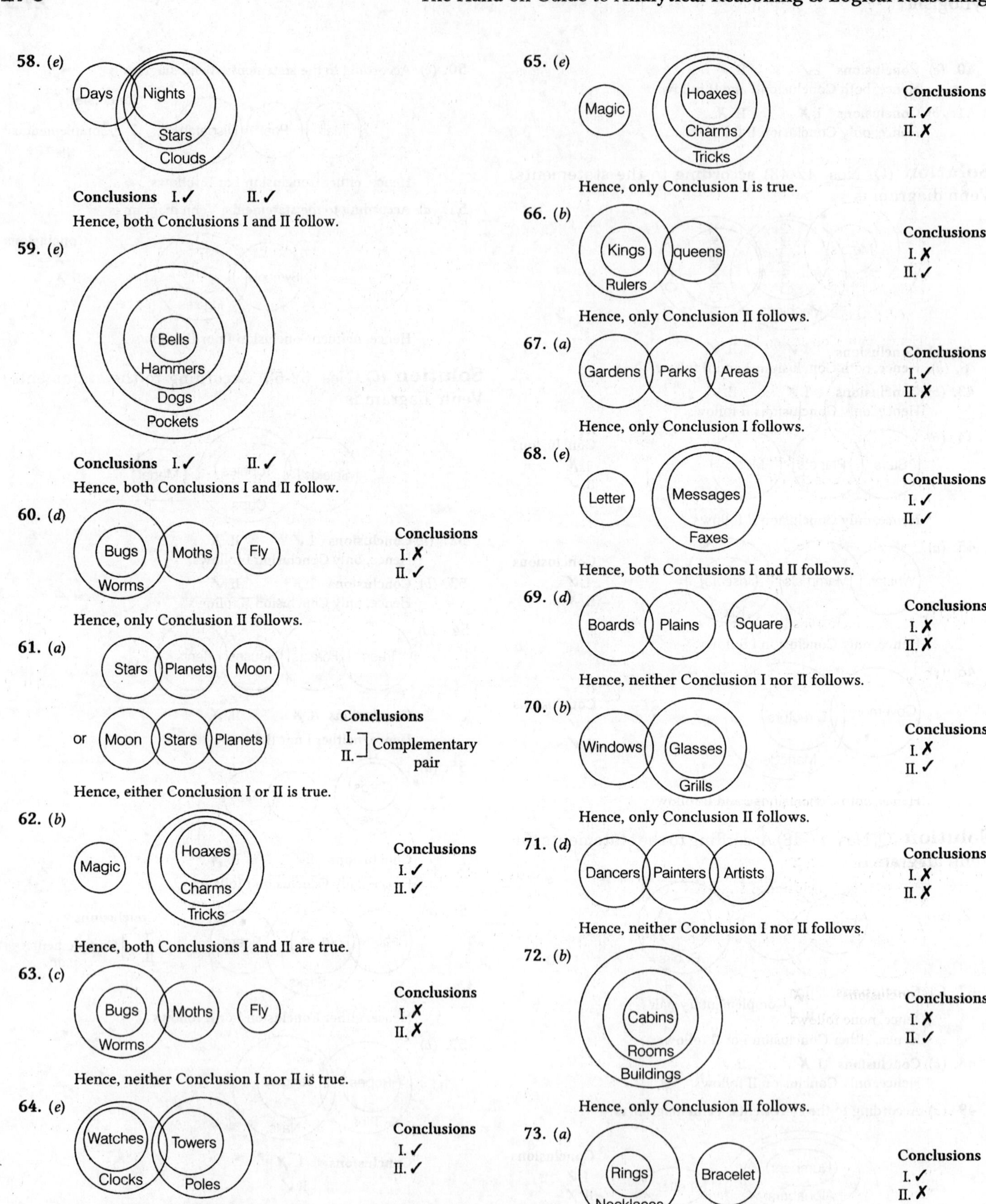

58. (*e*)

Conclusions I. ✓ II. ✓

Hence, both Conclusions I and II follow.

59. (*e*)

Conclusions I. ✓ II. ✓

Hence, both Conclusions I and II follow.

60. (*d*)

Conclusions I. ✗ II. ✓

Hence, only Conclusion II follows.

61. (*a*)

or

Conclusions I. II.] Complementary pair

Hence, either Conclusion I or II is true.

62. (*b*)

Conclusions I. ✓ II. ✓

Hence, both Conclusions I and II are true.

63. (*c*)

Conclusions I. ✗ II. ✗

Hence, neither Conclusion I nor II is true.

64. (*e*)

Conclusions I. ✓ II. ✓

Hence, only Conclusion I is true.

65. (*e*)

Conclusions I. ✓ II. ✗

Hence, only Conclusion I is true.

66. (*b*)

Conclusions I. ✗ II. ✓

Hence, only Conclusion II follows.

67. (*a*)

Conclusions I. ✓ II. ✗

Hence, only Conclusion I follows.

68. (*e*)

Conclusions I. ✓ II. ✓

Hence, both Conclusions I and II follows.

69. (*d*)

Conclusions I. ✗ II. ✗

Hence, neither Conclusion I nor II follows.

70. (*b*)

Conclusions I. ✗ II. ✓

Hence, only Conclusion II follows.

71. (*d*)

Conclusions I. ✗ II. ✗

Hence, neither Conclusion I nor II follows.

72. (*b*)

Conclusions I. ✗ II. ✓

Hence, only Conclusion II follows.

73. (*a*)

Conclusions I. ✓ II. ✗

Hence, only Conclusion I follows.

74. (*a*)

Conclusions
I. ✓
II. ✗

Hence, only Conclusion I follows.

75. (*a*)

Conclusions
I. ✓
II. ✗

Hence, only Conclusion I follows.

76. (*a*)

Conclusions
I. ✓
II. ✗

Hence, only Conclusion I follows.

77. (*c*)

Conclusions
I. ✓
II. ✓

Hence, Conclusions I and II follow.

78. (*a*)

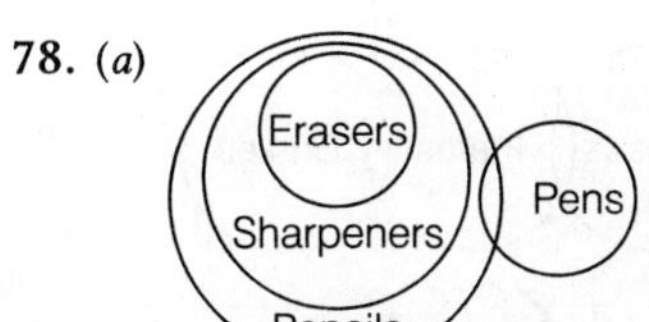

Conclusions
I. ✓
II. ✗

Hence, only Conclusion I follows.

79. (*e*)

Conclusions
I. ✗
II. ✓

Hence, only Conclusion II follows.

80. (*a*)

Conclusions
I.] Complementary
II.] pair

Hence, either Conclusion I or II follows.

81. (*b*)

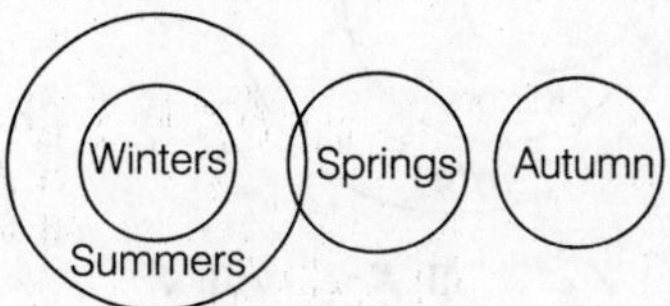

Conclusions
I. ✓
II. ✓

Hence, both Conclusions I and II follow.

Advanced Level

1. (*d*)

Conclusions I. ✗ II. ✗ III. ✓ IV. ✓

Hence, only Conclusions III and IV follow.

2. (*a*)

Conclusions I. ✗ II. ✗ III. ✗ IV. ✗

Hence, none follows.

3. (*c*)

Conclusions I. ✓ II. ✓ III. ✓ IV. ✗

Hence, I, II and III follow.

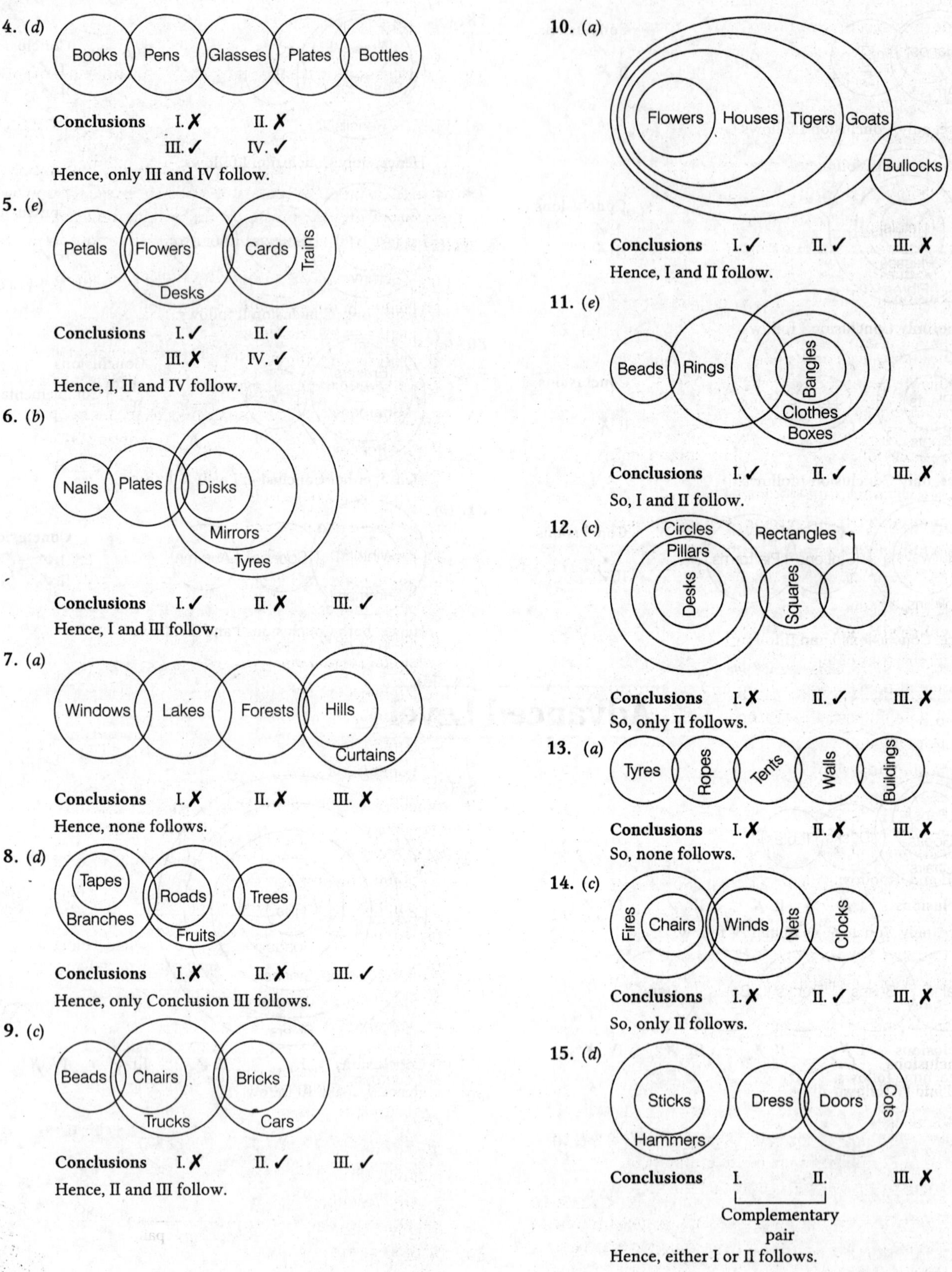
4. (d)
Books
Pens
Glasses
Plates
Bottles
Conclusions I. ✗ II. ✗
III. ✓ IV. ✓
Hence, only III and IV follow.
5. (e)
Petals
Flowers
Cards
Trains
Desks
Conclusions I. ✓ II. ✓
III. ✗ IV. ✓
Hence, I, II and IV follow.
6. (b)
Nails
Plates
Disks
Mirrors
Tyres
Conclusions I. ✓ II. ✗ III. ✓
Hence, I and III follow.
7. (a)
Windows
Lakes
Forests
Hills
Curtains
Conclusions I. ✗ II. ✗ III. ✗
Hence, none follows.
8. (d)
Tapes
Branches
Roads
Fruits
Trees
Conclusions I. ✗ II. ✗ III. ✓
Hence, only Conclusion III follows.
9. (c)
Beads
Chairs
Trucks
Bricks
Cars
Conclusions I. ✗ II. ✓ III. ✓
Hence, II and III follow.
10. (a)
Flowers
Houses
Tigers
Goats
Bullocks
Conclusions I. ✓ II. ✓ III. ✗
Hence, I and II follow.
11. (e)
Beads
Rings
Bangles
Clothes
Boxes
Conclusions I. ✓ II. ✓ III. ✗
So, I and II follow.
12. (c)
Circles
Pillars
Desks
Squares
Rectangles
Conclusions I. ✗ II. ✓ III. ✗
So, only II follows.
13. (a)
Tyres
Ropes
Tents
Walls
Buildings
Conclusions I. ✗ II. ✗ III. ✗
So, none follows.
14. (c)
Fires
Chairs
Winds
Nets
Clocks
Conclusions I. ✗ II. ✓ III. ✗
So, only II follows.
15. (d)
Sticks
Hammers
Dress
Doors
Cots
Conclusions I. II. III. ✗
Complementary pair
Hence, either I or II follows.

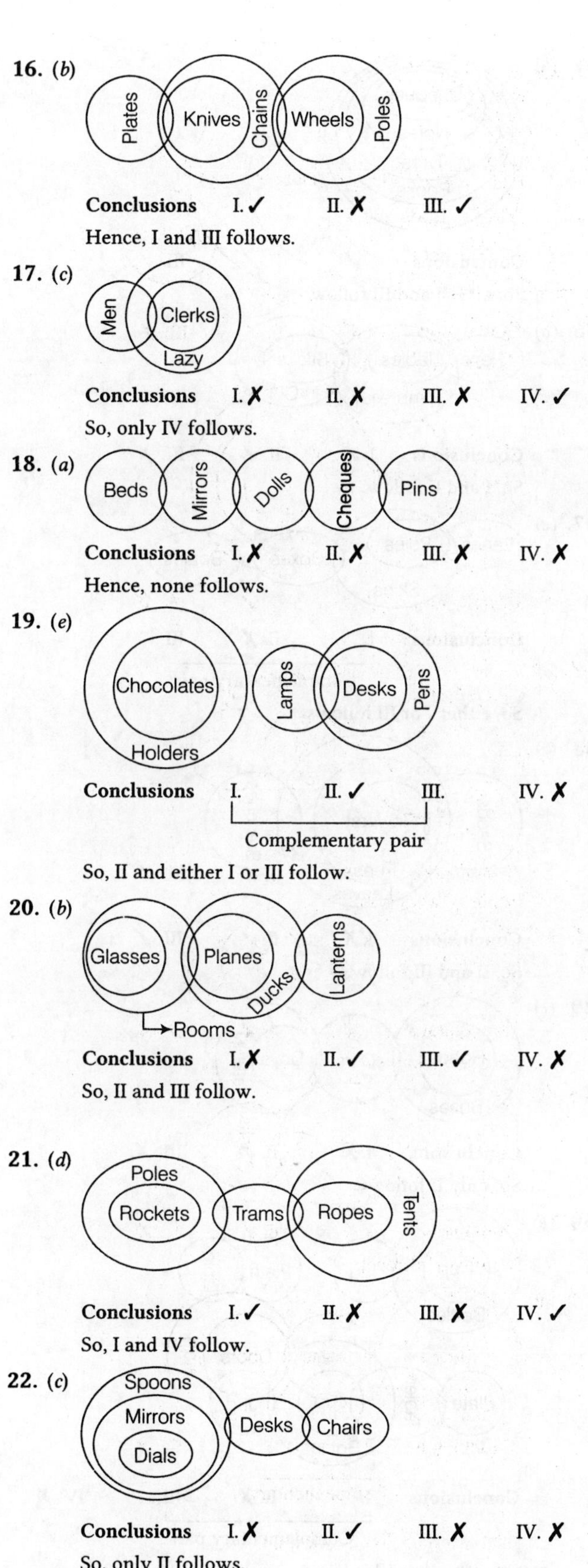

16. (*b*)

Conclusions I. ✓ II. ✗ III. ✓

Hence, I and III follows.

17. (*c*)

Conclusions I. ✗ II. ✗ III. ✗ IV. ✓

So, only IV follows.

18. (*a*)

Conclusions I. ✗ II. ✗ III. ✗ IV. ✗

Hence, none follows.

19. (*e*)

Conclusions I. II. ✓ III. IV. ✗

(I and III: Complementary pair)

So, II and either I or III follow.

20. (*b*)

Conclusions I. ✗ II. ✓ III. ✓ IV. ✗

So, II and III follow.

21. (*d*)

Conclusions I. ✓ II. ✗ III. ✗ IV. ✓

So, I and IV follow.

22. (*c*)

Conclusions I. ✗ II. ✓ III. ✗ IV. ✗

So, only II follows.

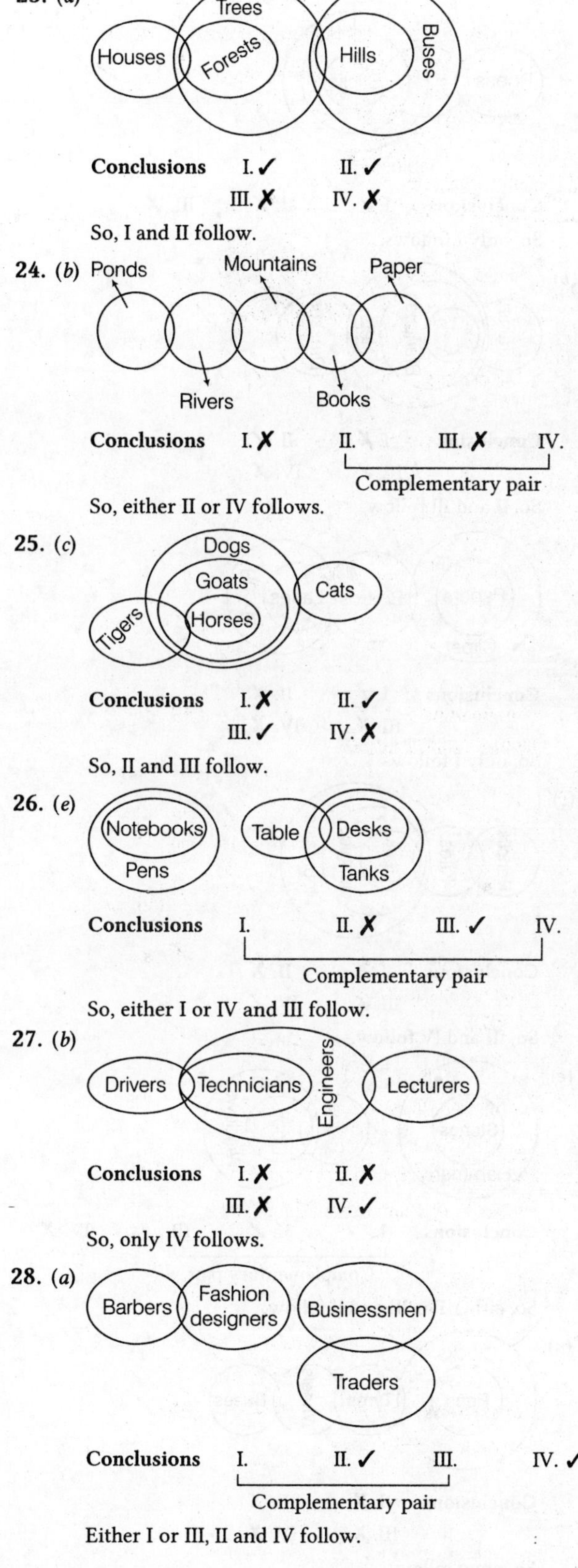

23. (*a*)

Conclusions I. ✓ II. ✓ III. ✗ IV. ✗

So, I and II follow.

24. (*b*)

Conclusions I. ✗ II. III. ✗ IV.

(II and IV: Complementary pair)

So, either II or IV follows.

25. (*c*)

Conclusions I. ✗ II. ✓ III. ✓ IV. ✗

So, II and III follow.

26. (*e*)

Conclusions I. II. ✗ III. ✓ IV.

(I and IV: Complementary pair)

So, either I or IV and III follow.

27. (*b*)

Conclusions I. ✗ II. ✗ III. ✗ IV. ✓

So, only IV follows.

28. (*a*)

Conclusions I. II. ✓ III. IV. ✓

(I and III: Complementary pair)

Either I or III, II and IV follow.

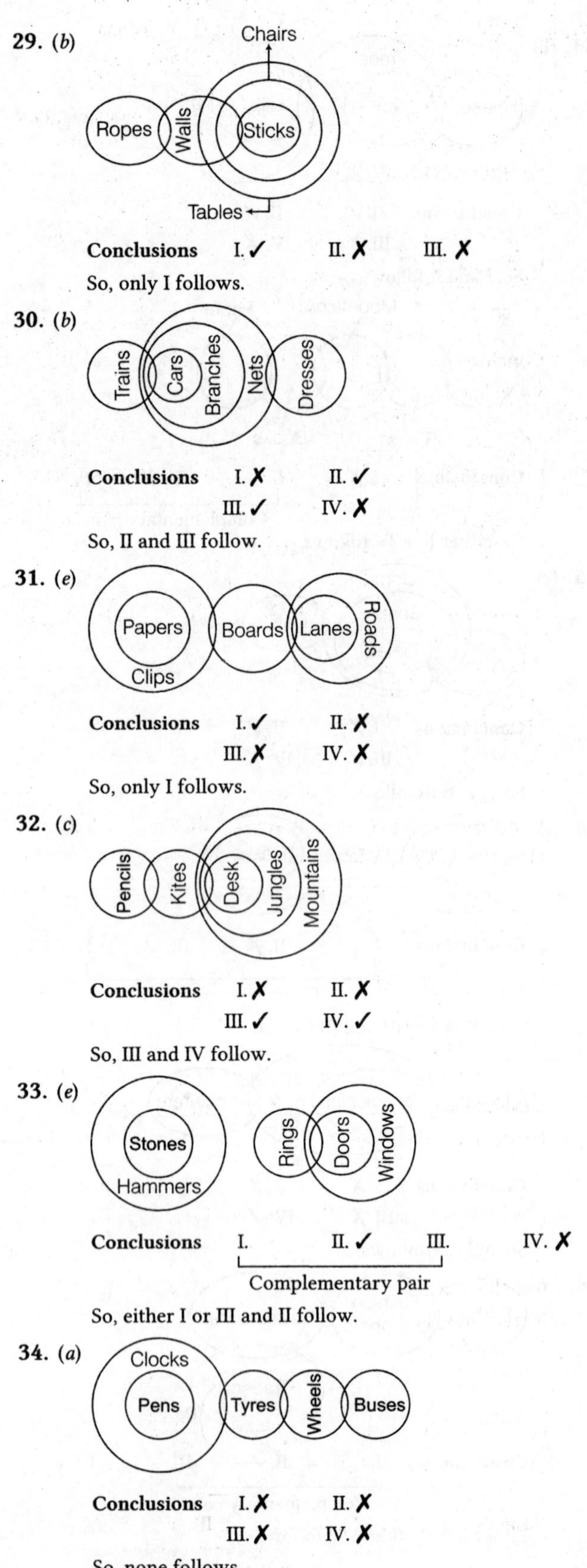

29. (*b*)

Conclusions I. ✓ II. ✗ III. ✗

So, only I follows.

30. (*b*)

Conclusions I. ✗ II. ✓ III. ✓ IV. ✗

So, II and III follow.

31. (*e*)

Conclusions I. ✓ II. ✗ III. ✗ IV. ✗

So, only I follows.

32. (*c*)

Conclusions I. ✗ II. ✗ III. ✓ IV. ✓

So, III and IV follow.

33. (*e*)

Conclusions I. II. ✓ III. IV. ✗

(I and III: Complementary pair)

So, either I or III and II follow.

34. (*a*)

Conclusions I. ✗ II. ✗ III. ✗ IV. ✗

So, none follows.

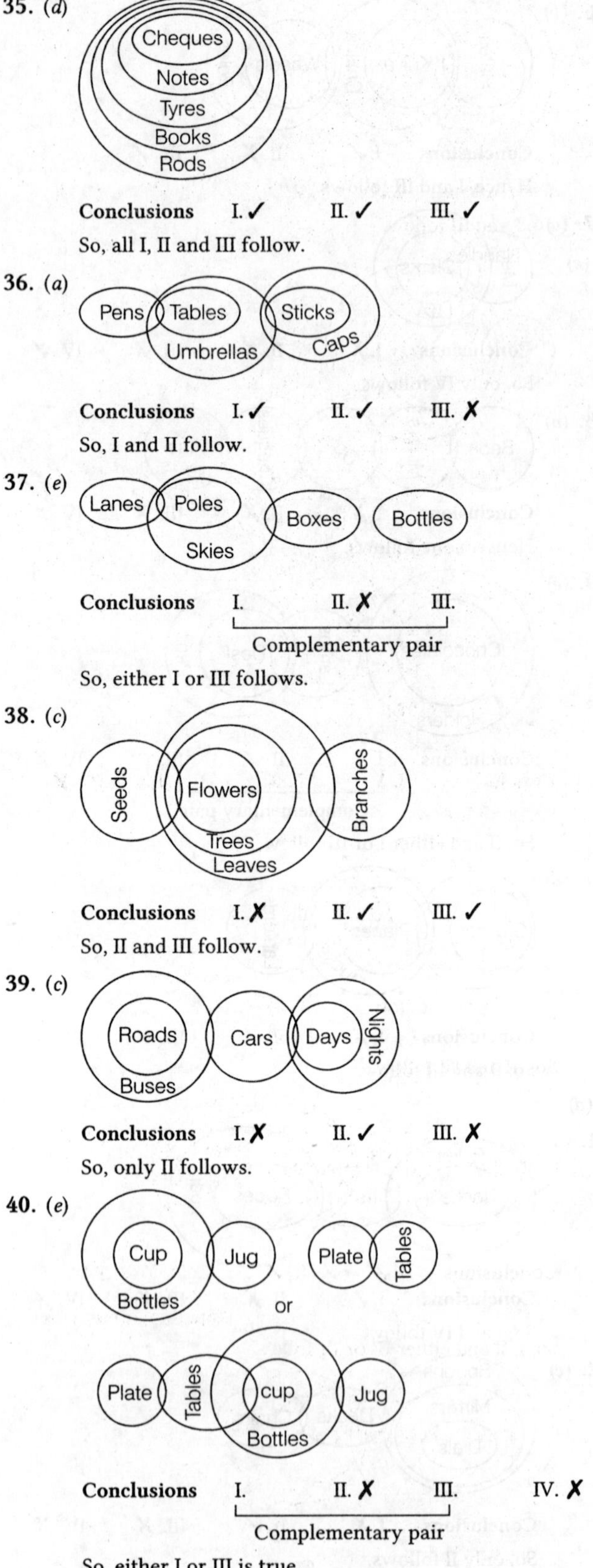

35. (*d*)

Conclusions I. ✓ II. ✓ III. ✓

So, all I, II and III follow.

36. (*a*)

Conclusions I. ✓ II. ✓ III. ✗

So, I and II follow.

37. (*e*)

Conclusions I. II. ✗ III.

(I and III: Complementary pair)

So, either I or III follows.

38. (*c*)

Conclusions I. ✗ II. ✓ III. ✓

So, II and III follow.

39. (*c*)

Conclusions I. ✗ II. ✓ III. ✗

So, only II follows.

40. (*e*)

Conclusions I. II. ✗ III. IV. ✗

(I and III: Complementary pair)

So, either I or III is true.

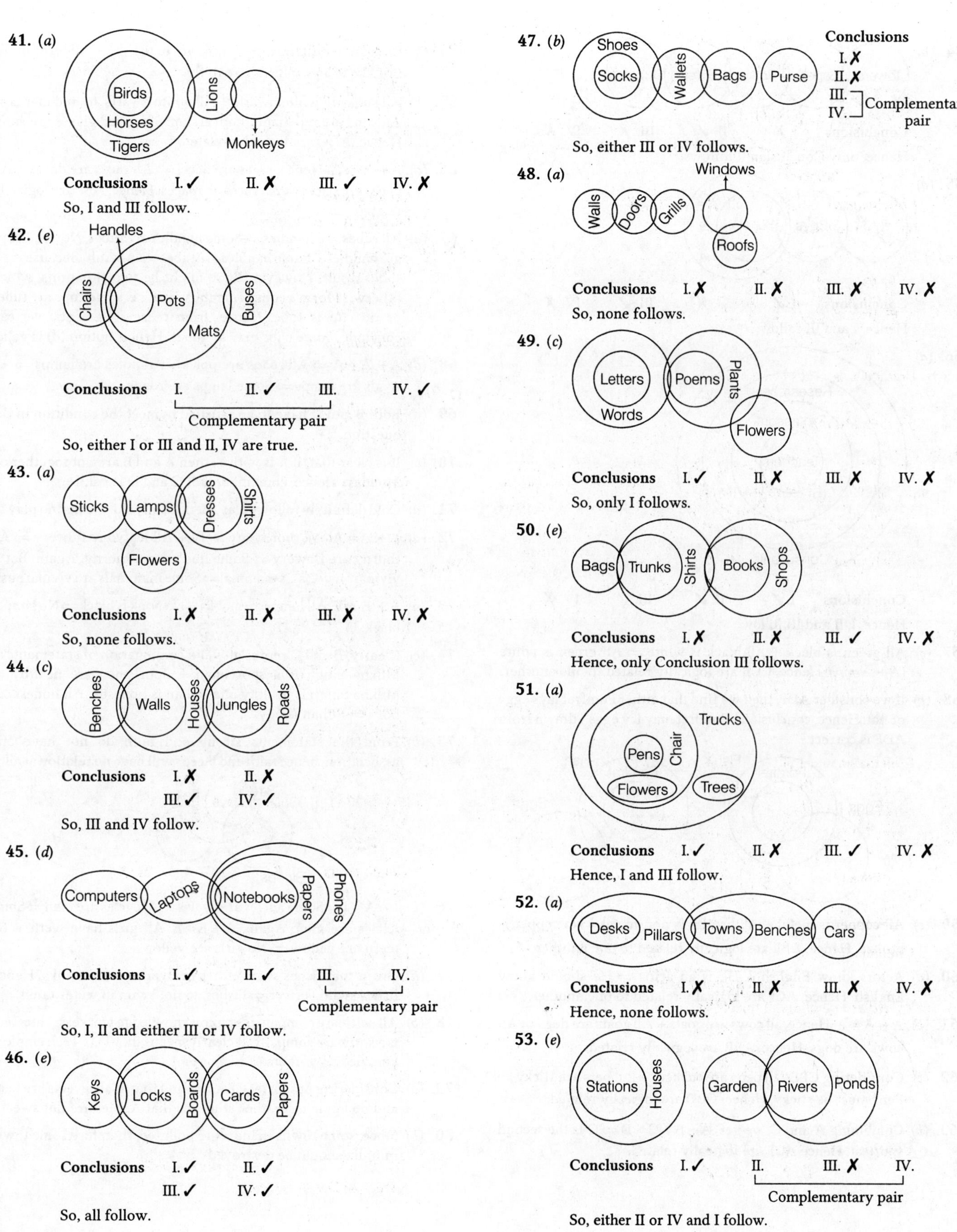

41. (*a*)

Conclusions I. ✓ II. ✗ III. ✓ IV. ✗

So, I and III follow.

42. (*e*)

Conclusions I. II. ✓ III. IV. ✓ (I, III: Complementary pair)

So, either I or III and II, IV are true.

43. (*a*)

Conclusions I. ✗ II. ✗ III. ✗ IV. ✗

So, none follows.

44. (*c*)

Conclusions I. ✗ II. ✗ III. ✓ IV. ✓

So, III and IV follow.

45. (*d*)

Conclusions I. ✓ II. ✓ III. IV. (III, IV: Complementary pair)

So, I, II and either III or IV follow.

46. (*e*)

Conclusions I. ✓ II. ✓ III. ✓ IV. ✓

So, all follow.

47. (*b*)

Conclusions I. ✗ II. ✗ III. IV. (III, IV: Complementary pair)

So, either III or IV follows.

48. (*a*)

Conclusions I. ✗ II. ✗ III. ✗ IV. ✗

So, none follows.

49. (*c*)

Conclusions I. ✓ II. ✗ III. ✗ IV. ✗

So, only I follows.

50. (*e*)

Conclusions I. ✗ II. ✗ III. ✓ IV. ✗

Hence, only Conclusion III follows.

51. (*a*)

Conclusions I. ✓ II. ✗ III. ✓ IV. ✗

Hence, I and III follow.

52. (*a*)

Conclusions I. ✗ II. ✗ III. ✗ IV. ✗

Hence, none follows.

53. (*e*)

Conclusions I. ✓ II. III. ✗ IV. (II, IV: Complementary pair)

So, either II or IV and I follow.

54. (*b*)

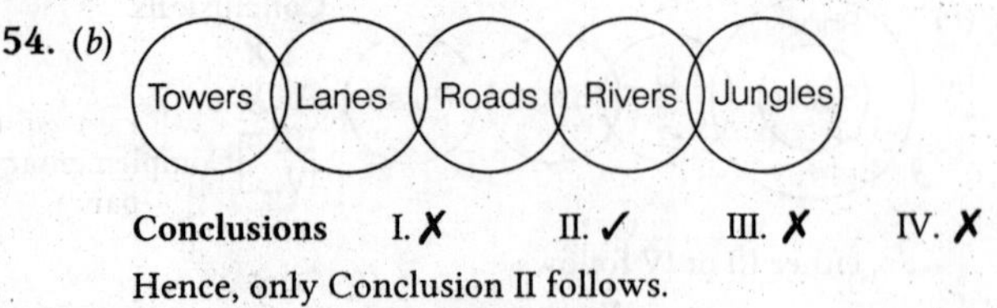

Conclusions I. ✗ II. ✓ III. ✗ IV. ✗

Hence, only Conclusion II follows.

55. (*a*)

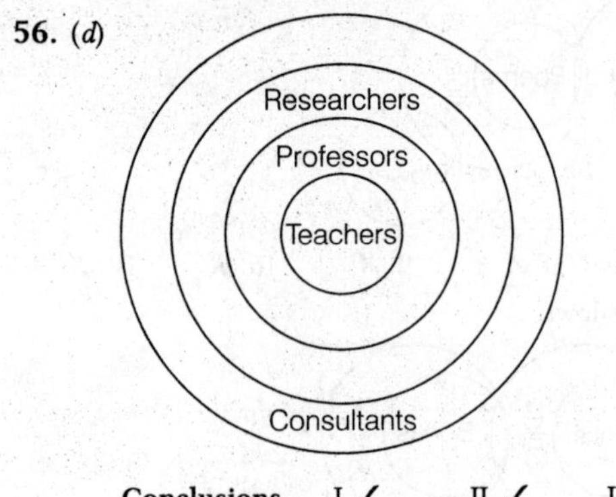

Conclusions I. ✓ II. ✗ III. ✓ IV. ✗

Hence, I and III follow.

56. (*d*)

Researchers

Professors

Teachers

Consultants

Conclusions I. ✓ II. ✓ III. ✓ IV. ✗

Hence, I, II and III follow.

57. (*c*) All green is black + All black is white ⇒ All green is white (A+ A= A). Hence, CDB are logically related to one another.

58. (*b*) If we consider ADF, then we find that either Pomfret lays eggs or not. Hence, conclusion "Pomfret may lay eggs" drawn from ADF is correct.

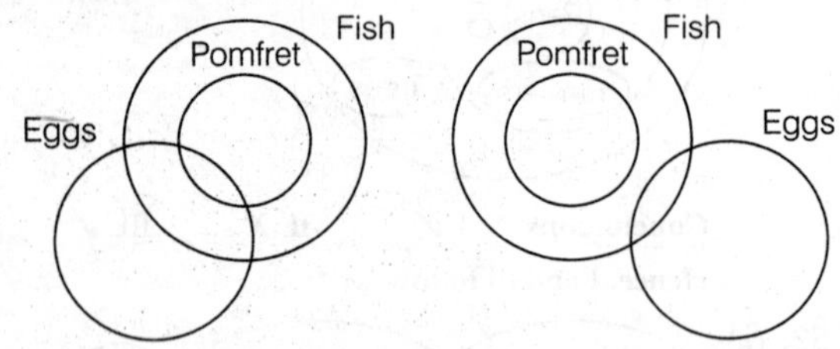

59. (*c*) All copper is metal + All bronze is non-metal = No copper is bronze. Hence, ABE are logically related to one another.

60. (*d*) Actors know English + He is an actor ⇒ He should know English. Hence, ACF are logically related to one another.

61. (*b*) A+ A= A. Hence, all cows are goats + All goats are dogs ⇒ All cows are dogs. Hence, ABE are logically related.

62. (*c*) Considering CBD, all pens are rubbers + Rubbers are sticky ⇒ Pens must be sticky. Hence, CBD are logically related.

63. (*b*) Combining A and C, we get A > B > C > D ⇒ C is the second shortest. Hence ACE are logically related.

64. (*b*) Considering BDA, we get birds are in the sky + All birds in the sky like to fly ⇒ Birds like to fly.

65. (*b*) All suns are white dwarfs + All white dwarfs are red giants ⇒ All suns are red giants, conversion. Some red giants are suns. Hence, ADC are logically related.

66. (*a*) A+ A⇒A. Hence, races are daces ⇒ All races are daces + All daces are paces ⇒ All races are paces. Hence, ABF are logically related.

67. (*a*) All tubes are handles ⇒ Some handles are tubes. Now, all cups are handles + Some handles are tubes = No result. Because A + I + No result. However, there might be two situations, which otherwise form a complementary pair, i.e. some cups are tubes or no cup is tube. Hence, from these statements, we can conclude. Some cups may be tubes. Hence, option (d) is valid.

68. (*d*) A+ A= A ⇒ All roads are poles + All poles are lamps ⇒ All roads are lamps ⇒ Some lamps are roads.

69. (*d*) Both B and D have to be satisfied to meet the condition in the question.

70. (*c*) It is clear that, if X is with Y, then A and B are not together on Monday. Hence, combination of C and D is valid.

71. (*a*) Cold definitely follows play. Hence, 'no cold' means 'no play'.

72. (*d*) A+ A= A. All thorny are leafy + All leafy are flowery ⇒ All thorny are flowery ⇒ Some flowers are thorny. Again, Bat is viviparous + Bat is mammal ⇒ Some mammals are viviparous.

73. (*a*) A+ E⇒E. All lamps are books + No book is black ⇒ No lamp is black.

74. (*c*) Clearly, B and C represent valid combination of statements as Milkha Singh is a sportsman + Sportsmen are healthy ⇒ Milkha Singh is healthy and Rohan is honest + All honest are boys ⇒ Rohan is boy.

75. (*b*) From the statements strong and faith do not have any association, hence faith and biceps will have no relation at all.

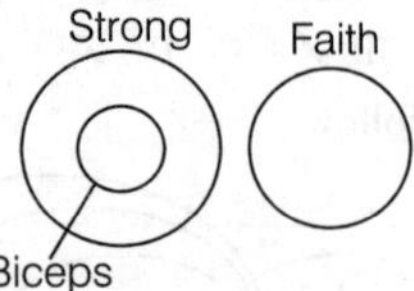

76. (*b*) I+ A= I ⇒ Some icicles are cycles + All cycles are men ⇒ Some icicles are men. Again, A + E = E. All girls have teeth + No teeth are yellow ⇒ No girls are yellow.

77. (*d*) Given that fishes swim either in river or water tanks. Hence, fishes swim is river ⇒ Fishes do not swim in water tanks.

78. (*b*) All software companies employ knowledge workers. Tata Tech is a software company. It clearly means that Tata Tech employs knowledge workers.

79. (*a*) Considering option (a) CEA, we find that, if all sweets are tasty and no apple tasty, then it means that Apples are not sweets.

80. (*b*) Since, some towns in India are polluted, therefore some towns in India should be destroyed.

2

Statement and Assumptions

An Assumption is something which is assumed, supported and taken for granted, i.e. an assumption is the logical support for the statement. It is a fact that can be supposed or assumed on the basis of a given statement.

When somebody says something, he does not put each and every aspect of his ideas into words. There are lots of things which remain unsaid. These unsaid things are defined as '**Assumption**'.

In another words, we can say that an assumption is the hidden part of an statement which is not said directly, but it is exposed indirectly.

An Illustration to Understand Assumption

To have a better concept about assumption just think over what we did in our school days while doing an arithmetical calculation. In fact, in those days we used to do such calculations with taking all possible steps. But when we do the same calculation today. We leave some steps and reach our answer very quickly.

Why do we leave some steps of calculation today? Only because of the following assumptions.

(a) The person who will see our calculation must be fully aware of the steps left.

(b) The person who will see our calculation must be assuming that we also know above steps left.

Hence, we can say that the steps left are the assumptions in some way.

To understand the above explanation. Let us do an arithmetical calculation of the following.

$$5\times 4+3\times 40\div 4-2=?$$

Case I (Childhood calculation)

$?=5\times 4+3\times 40\div 4-2$	Step I
$=5\times 4+3\times 10-2$	Step II
$=20+30-2$	Step III
$=50-2$	Step IV
$=48$	Step V

Case II (Today's calculation)

$?=5\times 4+3\times 40\div 4-2$	Step I
$=20+30-2$	Step II
$=48$	Step III

In management entrance exams like CAT, MAT and XAT 2-3 questions are asked from this chapter while in Bank PO examination a set of five questions is asked. In these types of questions, a statement is given which is followed by two or more assumptions. You have to assess the statement and following assumptions and decide which of the assumptions is implicit in the statement.

While solving these questions, you should remember some words like '**all**', '**every**', '**each**', '**only**' etc. which have a definite meaning in the sentence. Words like '**some**', '**few**', '**many**', '**more**' etc. do not have a definite meaning in the sentence. Therefore, you can easily differentiate between the implications, "All politicians are corrupt" and "Some politicians are corrupt".

Extracting the Assumption Hidden in the Statement

The task of determining the validity of an assumption from the statement is not very difficult. A statement may have more than one assumption. You can find out this by asking yourself the following facts.

***Fact* 1** **When talking of statements of an advertisement, it is taken for granted or assumed that**

- The advertisement would have an impact on its readers.
- Second, these readers would expect the 'qualities' in the 'subject' (of which the advertisement talks).

***Fact* 2** **Similarly, when talking of statements issued in public interest notices, it may be assumed that**

- The notice would be read by public and would make an impact.
- It is duty of related authorities to issue them.
- It is for the benefit of the people (generally public).

***Fact* 3** **For an appeal, it is assumed that**

- It would have some impact on the reader.
- It would have some reason for its existence.

***Fact* 4** **In case of an official notice, it is assumed that**

- It would have some impact on the staff.
- Its implementation would be good for the company.

***Fact* 5** **If the given statement has conjunctions like 'because', 'therefore', 'inspite of', 'so', 'despite', 'results', 'as a result of' between clause 1 and clause 2, then it means that it is assumed that clause 2 happens because of clause 1.**

e.g. He cried last night. The film must have had a tragic end.

The above statement assumes that tragic endings make people cry.

***Fact* 6** **It is obvious that anything that is being talked about as 'subject' in the given statement actually exists this is assumed.**

e.g. Saas Bahu serials are so boring. The first assumption that comes into picture is such serials like 'Saas Bahu' exists, because only then we can talk of them boring.

***Fact* 7** **If you have an adjective attached to the subject in the given statement, it is assumed that subject has that quality.**

e.g. The dramatic Saas Bahu serials are so boring. This means, Saas Bahu serials are dramatic.

***Fact* 8** **If the assumption shows no connection with the statement, it can immediately be discarded.**

e.g. **Statement** Hard labour is required to be perfect in Mathematics.

Invalid Assumption Hard labour is not required for subjects other than Mathematics.

Reason Nothing has been said in the statement about other subjects.

***Fact* 9** **If the statement is represented or said in different way, it is not assumption but remodelling of the statement.**

e.g. Since, several marriages are breaking up when in-laws interfere, the in-laws should be separated from the couple if interference cannot be stopped.

Here, the assumption is 'some marriages break up due to in-laws 'interference.'

***Fact* 10** **The same statement may be rewritten with subject and predicate negated. This is not an assumption but observed sentence or simply restating the same thing.**

e.g. "Drugs are injurious to health." Here "Not taking drugs promotes health" is restating the same fact, it is not an assumption.

***Fact* 11** **Some situations have similarity between themselves and another, thus the result would also be the same.**

e.g. Government school and public school students were given some English Grammar test. It was seen that public school students performed better. This shows that lower quality of education causes poor performance.

Here, it is assumed that public schools offer better quality education.

Difference between Implication and Assumptions

Implication and Assumptions both are different to each other. Sometimes implications are also treated as assumptions. Implications means something that is 'hidden' in the statement while assumptions is slightly different, it means something which is assumed, supposed and taken for granted.

For example "I am not going to call off the strike unless the government announces free education to every child of the area. Education is a basic right of every child and it is impossible for me to keep a blind eye when this right is being violated"—P, a political leader.

In the passage above, Mr P

I. Defines education as a basic right of every child.

II. Claims that this right is being violated.

III. Threatens to carry on the strike until the government announced free education.

From the I and II we define that "many children fail to get education." This is implied by Mr P's claim that the basic right of getting education is being violated. Finally in III, Mr P assumes that the threat of continuation of strike may lead to the government's acceptance of his demands." Thus one thing is implied here and the other is assumed.

To summarise, an assumption is something on which the statement is based, while an implication is something which is derived from the statement.

➘ A statement may have more than one assumption, but assumptions are never exclusive to each other. It means that if two assumptions are looking true then you can choose "Both assumptions are implicit" but it is very rare that the answer choice "Either of them is implicit" is correct for 'Statement-Assumption' questions.

Types of Questions Asked in Different Examinations

There are multiple types of questions which are asked from the chapter 'Statement and Assumptions', so it is quite difficult to predict exact type of questions that are asked, but on the basis of Observation, Analysis and Experience, here we are giving you different types of questions that are usually asked in the examination. Almost all the questions in this chapter can be categorized into two types. Also, this description of type will make your study easy and streamline.

Type 1 Two Assumptions Based

In these types of questions, a statement is given that is followed by two assumptions. Candidates are required to assess the given statement and decide which of these assumptions is implicit in the statement.

Examples Based on Type 1

Direction (Examples 1-5) *In each question below is given a statement followed by two assumptions numbered* I *and* II. *An assumption is something supposed or taken for granted. You have to consider the statement and the following assumptions and decide which of those is/are implicit in the statement.*

Give answer

(a) if only I is implicit
(b) if only II is implicit
(c) if either I or II is implicit
(d) if neither I nor II is implicit
(e) if both I and II are implicit

Ex 1. **Statement** Whenever you have any doubt on this subject, you may refer to the book written by XYZ.

Assumptions

I. The book written by XYZ is available.

II. There is no other book on this subject.

Ex 2. **Statement** "Though the candidates have been instructed to bring pencils, yet provide some pencils with each invigilator"– An instruction to test administration staff.

Assumptions **UIIC (AO) 2012**

I. Pencils are in short supply.

II. All the candidates will bring the pencil.

Ex 3. **Statement** Let us change the eligibility criteria to reduce the number of applicants.

Assumptions

I. The present eligibility criteria are very low.

II. Large number of applications are not desirable.

Ex 4. **Statement** 'Do not enter-avoid the risk of getting infected with the ABC disease'- written outside the quarantine ward number 2 (meant only for ABC disease) of a hospital.

Assumptions **IBPS (PO) 2011**

I. Disease 'ABC' is contagious.

II. All the patients in ward number 2 suffer from disease ABC.

Ex 5. **Statement** "We need to appoint more teachers"- Principal informs the school staff.

Assumptions **UIIC (AO) 2012**

I. Teachers are available.

II. Present teachers are not good.

SOLUTION (Examples 1-5)

1. (*a*) The recommendation of the book written by XYZ implies that it is available. So, Assumption I is implicit. From the statement it seems that the book is a good one, but this does not mean that no other books are available on this subject. So, Assumption II is not implicit.
2. (*d*) Assumption I is not appropriate. Pencils are provided to each invigilator for emergency. It does not imply that pencils are in short supply.
   Any instruction is given assuming that some people will follow that instruction. Therefore, as Assumption II is also not appropriate. The use of term 'all' makes unsuitable.
   So, neither I nor II is implicit.
3. (*d*) From the statement it can be concluded that eligibility criteria is low but the word 'very' in Assumption I makes it not implicit. Assumption II does not show the status of the applicants. So, Assumption II is also not implicit.
4. (*e*) From the statement, it is clear that 'ABC' is a contagious disease and all the patients in ward number 2 suffer from disease ABC. Hence, both the assumptions are implicit in the statement.
5. (*a*) Only Assumption I is implicit in the statement. One can appoint teachers only when teachers are available.
   Assumption II is not implicit as the statement is not talking about the quality of teachers.

Direction (Examples 6-11) *In each question below is given a statement followed by two assumptions numbered* I *and* II. *An assumption is something supposed or taken for granted. You have to consider the statement and the following assumptions and decide which of those is/are implicit in the statement.*

Give answer

(a) if only I is implicit
(b) if only II is implicit
(c) if either I or II is implicit
(d) if both I and II are implicit

Ex 6. **Statement** If people are intelligent they should be creative.

Assumptions **SSC (CGL) 2013**

I. Creativity and intelligence are related.

II. Creative people are intelligent.

Ex 7. **Statement** In city Z, people prefer to buy Car X instead of Car Y as Car X has German technology which is very advanced.

Assumptions

I. Cars with German technology are perceived to be better than other cars in city Z.

II. Had German technology been present in Car Y also, its sales would have crossed car X's sales.

Ex 8. **Statement** Railway does not provide concession to any one for travelling to certain holiday destinations.

Assumptions

I. Railway services are available for travelling to these holiday destinations.

II. Railway provides concession to certain persons for travelling to places other than these holiday destinations.

Ex 9. **Statement** "Travellers with a ticket for the second class, if found travelling in the first class compartments would be penalized"- Notice in the compartments of a train.

Assumptions

I. Travellers with a ticket for the first class are also not allowed to travel in the second class compartments.

II. Inspections are carried out in the train to check the tickets.

Ex 10. **Statement** The prices of petrol and diesel have remained unchanged only in Nigeria since the past three years.

Assumptions

I. Petrol and diesel prices have changed elsewhere in the world during these three years.

II. Before this three years period, petrol and diesel were available at a price different from the present rates.

Ex 11. **Statement** "Ensure a good night's sleep for your family with safe and effective XYZ mosquito coil". An advertisement.

Assumptions

I. XYZ mosquito coil is better than many other mosquito coils.

II. A good night's sleep is desirable.

SOLUTION (Examples 6-11)

6. (*a*) Only Assumption I is valid. It is clear that creativity and intelligence are related. Assumption II is not an assumption at all. It is mere restatement of the given statement.
7. (*a*) From the statement, it is clear that people in city Z prefer to German technology car. Hence, only Assumption I is implicit in the statement.
8. (*b*) From the statement, we clearly say that Railway provides concession to certain persons for travelling to places other than these holiday destinations so Assumption II is implicit.
9. (*b*) From the statement, we clearly say that inspections are carried out in the train to check the tickets.
   Hence, only Assumption II is implicit in the statement. Nothing is said about first class ticket.
10. (*d*) From the statement, it is clear that except Nigeria in all other countries petrol and diesel prices have changed in the past three years and also before this three years period, petrol and diesel were available at a price different from the present rates. Hence, both the assumptions are implicit in the statement.
11. (*d*) The advertisement suggests that if you need good sleep for your family, you must use XYZ mosquito coil. It may be assumed that it may be better than many other mosquito coils and a good sleep is always desirable. So, both the assumptions implicit.

Intro Exercise 1 (Based on Type 1)

Direction (Q. Nos. 1-4) *In each question below is given a statement followed by two assumptions numbered* I and II. An assumption is something supposed or taken for granted. You have to consider the statement and the following assumption and decide which of the assumption is implicit in the statement.

Give answer

(a) if only Assumption I is implicit
(b) if only Assumption II is implicit
(c) if neither I nor II is implicit
(d) if both I and II are implicit

1. Statement Postal rates have been increased to meet the deficit.

Assumptions **NIFT (UG) 2013**

I. The preser.. rates are very low.

II. If the rates ..re not increased, then deficit cannot be met.

2. Statement Most people who stop smoking gain weight.

Assumptions **NIFT (UG) 2013**

I. If one stops smoking, then one will gain weight.

II. If one does not stop smoking, then one will not gain weight.

3. Statement Many institutions have adopted on-line method of conducting their examinations.

Assumptions **MPPSC (Pre) 2013**

I. It is possible that candidates from all parts of the country are adapt at computers.

II. The on-line method of examination helps to recruit more qualified people.

4. Statement "You are hereby appointed as a programmer with a probation period of one year and your performance will be received at the end of the period for confirmation."

A line is an appointment letter.

Assumptions **SSC (10+2) 2014**

I. The performance of an individual generally is not known at the time of appointment offer.

II. Generally an individual tries to prove his worth in probation period.

Direction (Q. Nos. 5-54) *In each question below is given a statement followed by two assumptions numbered* I and II. An assumption is something suppos d or taken for granted. You have to consider the statem..nt and the following assumption and decide which f the assumption is implicit in the statement.

Give answer

(a) if only assumption I is implicit
(b) if only assumption II is implicit
(c) if either I or II is implicit
(d) if neither I nor II is implicit
(e) if both I and II are implicit

5. Statement Many people fell ill after consuming meal at a wedding reception and were rushed to the nearby government and private hospitals.

Assumptions **MHT CET MBA 2010**

I. The relatives of the affected people may refuse to take them to the government hospitals.

II. The nearby hospitals may be able to attend to all the affected people.

6. Statement The government has recently announced an incentive package for setting up new business ventures in the rural areas and promised uninterrupted power supply to all the units.

Assumptions **MHT CET MBA 2010**

I. The government may be able to supply adequate power to all such units.

II. People living in the rural areas may welcome the government decision.

7. Statement The municipal authority blocked movement of traffic in and around the temple on the main festival day.

Assumptions **MHT CET MBA 2009**

I. Very large number of devotees may visit the temple on the main festival day.

II. People travelling to the areas near the temple may postpone their journey by a day unless they have very urgent work in the areas.

8. Statement The government has instructed all the private schools in the city to maintain the current fees for atleast two more years.

Assumptions **MHT CET MBA 2008**

I. The authorities of private schools may not follow the government instruction as they are not dependent on government funds.

II. The parents of the students of private schools of the city may still be eager to pay higher fees.

9. Statement The municipal authority has decided to demolish the old bridge on a bus road for constructing a new flyover.

Assumptions **MHT CET MBA 2008**

I. The traffic department may be able to divert movement of vehicles through alternate roads.

II. The people travelling in the nearby areas may demonstrate to protest against the authority's decision.

10. Statement Warning: Smoking is injurious to health.

Assumptions

I. Non-smoking promotes health.

II. Really, this warning is not necessary.

11. Statement Patient's condition would improve after operation.

Assumptions

I. The patient can be operated upon in this condition.

II. The patient cannot be operated upon in this condition.

12. **Statement** Travelling by trains rather than cabs is more convenient and economical in Paris.

Assumptions **IBPS (PO) 2011**

I. Paris is an expensive city.

II. Train services are reasonably good in Paris.

13. **Statement** He continues to be busy as he was while handling the premier investigating agency.

Assumptions

I. Nowadays he is busy writing books.

II. The speaker is talking about the ex-CBI chief.

14. **Statement** Use our medicine to fight the problem of obesity.

Assumptions **IBPS (PO) 2011**

I. Other slimming medicines available in the market do not reduce weight.

II. Obesity cannot be controlled without medicines.

15. **Statement** The Municipal Corporation has informed the people that to avoid water borne diseases they should boil water before drinking.

Assumptions

I. People will still drink water without boiling.

II. People generally overlook such advisories issued by the Municipal Corporation.

16. **Statement** A nationalized bank gave an advertisement in a national daily that eligible candidates may apply for 120 posts of Chartered Accountant.

Assumptions **IBPS (PO) 2011**

I. Eligible Chartered Accountants will reply to this advertisement.

II. There will be enough eligible Chartered Accountants who want to work in the nationalized bank.

17. **Statement** In order to attract people the city transport corporation has introduced air conditioned buses on various routes for those who go to their work place in own vehicles. This will help in reducing traffic on roads.

Assumptions

I. Most of the people will prefer to go to their work places in their own vehicles.

II. Many people will now choose the options of these buses to travel to their work place.

18. **Statement** The new educational policy envisages major modifications in the education system.

Assumptions

I. Present educational system is inconsistent with national needs.

II. Present educational system needs changes.

19. **Statement** The credit cooperative society has decided to increase the upper limit of loan to ₹ 3 lakh.

Assumptions **IRMA 2008**

I. There may be demands from the members to take loan up to ₹ 3 lakh.

II. The credit cooperative society may have enough money to disburse such loans.

20. **Statement** Lack of stimulation in the four or five years of life can have adverse consequences.

Assumptions

I. A great part of the development of observed intelligence occurs on the earliest years of life.

II. 50% of the measurable intelligence at 17 is predictable by the age of four.

21. **Statement** Farmers must immediately switch over to organic fertilisers from chemical fertilisers for better yield.

Assumptions **IBPS (PO) 2011**

I. All the farmers use only chemical fertilisers.

II. Organic fertilisers are readily available to the farmers.

22. **Statement** Though the Indians have returned from a disastrous tour, they should not be written off.

Assumptions

I. In past, Indians had excellent tour.

II. In future, Indians may perform excellently as they did in past.

23. **Statement** This book is for those who are interested to know more about 'Indian History'.

Assumptions

I. People, who are interested to know about the author may read the book.

II. Every book may attract some reader.

24. **Statement** A good executive has to be task-oriented as well as people-oriented.

Assumptions

I. Some executives are people-oriented.

II. Some executives are not people-oriented.

25. **Statement** Although he has done MBA through a correspondence course, he is as smart as a person from college X.

Assumptions **IBPS (PO) 2011**

I. Students from college X are known for their smartness.

II. Students should do MBA through correspondence in order to become smart.

26. **Statement** Subodh wrote to his brother at Bengaluru to collect personally the application form from the university for the post-graduation course in Mathematics.

Assumptions

I. The university may issue application forms to a person other than the prospective student.

II. Subodh's brother may receive the letter well before the last date of collecting application form.

27. **Statement** "Develop a strategic plan for Internet adoption. Do not treat the Internet any differently that you would treat any other crucial business decision."—A Manager, IBM India.

Assumptions

I. All crucial businesses need a strategic plan to succeed.

II. Internet is the need of the hour.

28. Statement Government should deploy army to rehabilitate the people displaced due to earthquake.

Assumptions

I. Army can be used for purposes other than war also.

II. Only army can rehabilitate the displaced victims of earthquake.

29. Statement Why don't you invite Anthony for the Christmas party this year?

Assumptions

I. Anthony is not from the same city.

II. Unless invited, Anthony will not attend the party.

30. Statement Unless the officials do their duty honestly and with the spirit to serve the nation, the constitution of any number of safety boards amounts to nothing but paper work.

Assumptions

I. Safety boards are useless.

II. Employees of the department can prevent accidents.

31. Statement It is not always true that adoption of sophisticated technology increases production and efficiency.

Assumptions

I. Adoption of sophisticated technology is not a difficult thing to achieve.

II. Production and efficiency can be increased by getting rid of sophisticated technology.

32. Statement For members at IIC, seek out those who have topped the civil exams, distinguished themselves in graduate studies or have made a mark at an early age in the arts or the media.

Assumptions

I. The present selection process for membership has lack of transparancy.

II. Present members of IIC are not up to the expectations of the IIC.

33. Statement The state government has asked the management of all the private schools to take consent of the parents before increasing the school fees.

Assumptions

I. The management of majority of the private schools may call the parents for discussion regarding fee hike.

II. Majority of the parents may not agree for any hike of school fees.

34. Statement Government has made huge security arrangement during the Olympic torch relay within the country in view of nationwide protests by some group of people.

Assumptions

I. The protestors may still disrupt the relay of Olympic torch within the country.

II. The relay of Olympic torch may pass peacefully during its journey within the country.

35. Statement The state government has instructed all its employees interacting with public to be patient and compassionate in their dealings.

Assumptions

I. The general public may otherwise be bullied by the Government officials.

II. Majority of the Government officials may follow the Government directives.

36. Statement Mohan invited about 200 people on the occasion of his daughter's marriage and made food arrangement of about 200 people in a nearby hotel.

Assumptions

I. Many people invited by Mohan may not turn upon the day of the occasion.

II. Most of the people invited by Mohan may attend the wedding ceremony.

37. Statement Local administration made elaborate security arrangement and alerted the local hospitals to be in readiness during the ensuing festival days.

Assumptions

I. A very large number of devotees may assemble in the city during the festival days.

II. Security personnel may not be able to control the crowd.

38. Statement "Traffic police will be provided with alcometers to identify drunken drivers." —Police chief.

Assumptions

I. So, many accidents take place everyday because of drunken drivers.

II. Alcometers is a machine which can identify the drunken persons easily.

39. Statement The income tax rules need to be amended so that there is more incentive for the people to declare there actual wealth.

Assumptions

I. The income tax rules are not proper.

II. Some people do not declare their actual wealth.

40. Statement If you lose after competing hard that's fine. If you lose without trying hard, that's what disappoints me.

Assumptions

I. Losing after trying hard is excusable.

II. Losing without effort is regrettable.

41. Statement A Government advertisement in public interest—For a child's better mental health, admit him/ her to a school only after five years of age.

Assumptions **IBPS (PO) 2011**

I. A child cannot learn before he/she turns five.

II. Some school admit children who are below five years of age.

42. Statement Conveyance facility provided by organisation helps employees report to work on time.

Assumptions **IBPS (PO) 2011**

I. The conveyance facility which is provide by the organisation always reaches on time.

II. It is not possible to report to work on time unless conveyance facility is provided by the organisation.

43. **Statement** "Best way to solve this problem of workers' dissatisfaction is to offer them cash rewards. If this type of incentive can solve the problem in HUDCO company, then why not here".– A Personnel Manager tells the Chairman of a Company.

Assumptions **UIIC (AO) 2012**

I. The reason for workers's dissatisfaction in both the companies was similar.

II. Monetary incentives have universal appeal.

44. **Statement** If a doctor's degree is your ambition, then the choice of a good guidance institution is half the job done.

Assumptions

I. Without proper guidance, it is very hard to be a doctor.

II. Institute alone can't help a student in his success.

45. **Statement** Government has recently allowed the private medical colleges to increase the fees by about 30% over the previous year's fees.

Assumptions **IRMA 2009**

I. The private medical colleges may not agree with 30% increase and demand for more hike.

II. The guardians of the students may disagree with the Government's decision and boycott the admission process.

46. **Statement** A management institute has decided to admit in its post-graduate programme students having work experience of atleast three years.

Assumptions **IRMA 2008**

I. There may be adequate number of students having work experience of atleast three years who are desirous of joining the institute.

II. The management institute may dilute the condition if it does not receive adequate number of applications.

47. **Statement** The High Court located in the city has ordered the municipal corporation to repair all the roads within the next fortnight.

Assumptions **IRMA 2008**

I. The municipal corporation has the capability of carrying out the repair work within the next fortnight.

II. The vehicle owners may start an agitation against the municipal corporation.

48. **Statement** In view of the increase in fares announced by different airlines, Mahesh decided to travel by train to attend his friend's wedding in Delhi.

Assumptions **IRMA 2008**

I. Railways also may increase fares in near future.

II. Mahesh may be able to get reservation in a suitable train to Delhi before the wedding date.

49. **Statement** If parking space is not available in office, park your vehicles in the mall and walk to the office.

Assumptions **IBPS (PO) 2011**

I. The mall is at a walkable distance from the office.

II. The office does not allow visitor's vehicles in its premises.

50. **Statement** An advertisement by bank X—'Our interest rates for education loans are lower than any other bank'.

Assumptions **IBPS (PO) 2011**

I. Some other banks also provide education loans.

II. Interest rates charged on education loans are different for different banks.

51. **Statement** For any kind of problem with your mobile phone, contact our help desk immediately.

Assumptions **IBPS (PO) 2011**

I. Help desk has a solution to all kinds of problems related to mobile phones or will guide accordingly.

II. Unless the problem is reported immediately, it cannot be solved.

52. **Statement** Thick milk does not mean high-quality milk—Issued in public interest by a reputed milk company.

Assumptions

I. There is misconception among the people that thick milk is good.

II. Some companies are producing adulterated thick milk.

53. **Statement** "There is concern about the health of the arrested VIPs but not about the harm they have done to the nation's health"—A journalist.

Assumptions

I. The VIPs are not more important than the nation.

II. The practice of being concerned over the health of the VIPs should be stopped.

54. **Statement** "Please drop this letter in the letter box"- An Officer tells his Assistant.

Assumptions **UIIC (AO) 2012**

I. The Assistant knows the address where the letter is to be sent.

II. The Assistant would follow the instructions.

Type 2 Three Assumptions Based

In this type of questions, a statement is given that is followed by three assumptions. Candidates are required to choose the group of assumptions which is implicit in context of the given statement.

Examples Based on Type 2

Ex 1. Consider the following statements :

Statement "The situation in this area still continuous to be tense and out of control.

People are requested to remain in their homes only.

Assumptions **UPPSC (Pre) 2014**

I. There has been some serious incidents.

II. People will not go to offices.

III. Normalcy will be restored shortly.

(a) Only I is implicit
(b) I and II are implicit
(c) I and III are implicit
(d) None of the assumptions is implicit

Sol. (*b*) There had been some serious incidents so that the situation in the area is out of control and tense. So, assumption I is implicit. The message is delivered to the people to remain in their homes because they will not go to their work to avoid any mishappening.

So, assumption II is also implicit in the statement. But nothing is said in the statement about the situation, that when will it be under control.

So, assumption III does not implicit.

Ex 2. **Statement** "The prices should fall after March. By that time the demand of foodgrains starts dropping." -An economist

Assumptions

I. Price may not fall before March.

II. The economist has good links with farmers.

III. A drop in demand of foodgrains will result a drop in supply of foodgrains.

(a) Only I is implicit
(b) Only II is implicit
(c) Only III is implicit
(d) I and II are implicit
(e) I and III are implicit

Sol. (*a*) According to economist the price should fall after March because then demand starts dropping. Till then demand remains heavy and price may not fall before March. So, Assumption I is implicit. Assumptions II and III have nothing to do with the statement so they do not implicit.

Ex 3. **Statement** "Today I am rejecting your proposal to play a cricket match against your team because of absence of Mr Z but tomorrow I am ready to play against your team at any cost." —Mr X says to Mr Y.

Assumptions

I. Mr Z will be available tomorrow.

II. Match will be played tomorrow irrespective of availability of Mr Z.

III. Mr Y will be ready to play a match against Mr X tomorrow.

(a) All of these
(b) Either I or II and III
(c) II and III
(d) I and III
(e) None of these

Sol. (*c*) From the statement it is clear that match will be played on tomorrow, irrespective of availability of Z. So, Assumption II is implicit but Assumption I is not implicit. Mr Y is ready to play against Mr X. So, Assumption III is implicit.

The word 'at any cost' makes it clear.

Ex 4. **Statement** Mandatory verification of identity before acquiring a prepaid cellular connection is taking a toll on numbers. —CEO of a cellular company.

Assumptions

I. Lesser subscribers have joined due to decrease in subscription rate.

II. Unnecessary delay as well as red-tapism discourages consumer's appetite.

III. Holders of cellulars do not want to reveal their identity.

(a) I and II
(b) II and III
(c) I and III
(d) All of these
(e) None of these

Sol. (*b*) Assumption I is not related to the statement, so it is not implicit. Due to mandatory verification numbers are decreasing. It may be due to unnecessary delay and subscribers do not want to reveal their identity. So, Assumptions II and III implicit.

Ex 5. **Statement** "The Prime Minister is expected to announce an expansion in his Ministry shortly."- A newspaper report. **SNAP 2014**

Assumptions

I. The newspaper has quoted authentic sources.

II. The newspaper has reliable sources for the news.

III. The Prime Minister has the power to expand his cabinet.

(a) I and II
(b) II and III
(c) I and III
(d) All are implicit

Sol. (*b*) The newspaper has not quoted authentic sources, so Assumption I is not implicit. The newspaper has reliable sources that's why it has published the news so Assumption II is implicit. The announcement from PM shows that PM has such power. So, Assumption III is implicit.

Intro Exercise 2 (Based on Type 2)

Direction (Q. Nos. 1-18) *In each question below is given a statement followed by three assumptions numbered* I, II and III. *An assumption is something supposed or taken for granted. You have to consider the statement and the assumptions and decide which of the assumptions is implicit in the statement. Then decide which of the answers (a), (b), (c), (d) and (e) is the correct answer.*

1. **Statement** "If you want best training in computers, join our classes." — An advertisement.

Assumptions **IBPS (PO) 2014**

I. People want training related with Computers.
II. People read advertisements.
III. People want quality training.

(a) Only I is implicit
(b) All are implicit
(c) I and III are implicit
(d) II and III are implicit
(e) I and II are implicit

2. **Statement** A group of friends decided to go for a picnic to Avon during the next holiday season to avoid crowd of people.

Assumptions **IBPS (PO) 2014**

I. Generally many people do not go to Avon.
II. People prefer other spots to Avon.
III. Many people do not know about Avon.

(a) All are implicit
(b) Only II is implicit
(c) I and II are implicit
(d) I and III are implicit
(e) None of the above

3. **Statement** Prabodh wrote a second letter to his mother after a month when he did not receive any reply to the first letter.

Assumptions

I. Prabodh's mother did not receive the letter.
II. The letter generally reaches within a fortnight.
III. His mother promptly sends reply to his letters.

(a) II and III are implicit (b) I and II are implicit
(c) Only III is implicit (d) I and III are implicit
(e) None of these

4. **Statement** Despite strong opposition, the controversial Prohibition of Forcible Conversion of Religion Bill was passed by the Tamil Nadu Assembly. —A news

Assumptions

I. Conversions create resentment among several sections and also inflame religious passions, leading to communal clashes.
II. Conversions only lead to the isolation of the converted.
III. Strong opposition puts hindrance before a bill in taking final shape.

(a) All are implicit (b) I and II
(c) I and III (d) II and III
(e) None of these

5. **Statement** The State Government has unilaterally increased octroi by five percent on all commodities entering into the State without seeking approval of the Central Government .

Assumptions

I. The State Government may be able to implement its decision.
II. The Central Government may agree to support the State Government's decision.
III. The State Government may be able to earn considerable amount through the additional octroi.

(a) All are implicit (b) I and II are implicit
(c) I and III are implicit (d) II and III are implicit
(e) None of these

6. **Statement** "Bar Council of India (BCI) has decided to go on a hunger strike to protest the implementation of the Legal Services Authority (Amendment) Act." —Chairman of BCI

Assumptions

I. The amendment has several loopholes and is bound to hurt the litigants' interests.
II. All the members of BCI will welcome the decision.
III. The hunger strike held in front of the court will put a pressure on the respective authority.

(a) Only I (b) I and II (c) I and III (d) All of these
(e) None of these

7. **Statement** "Look at her audacity, Madhu has not replied to my letter" —A tells B.

Assumptions

I. Madhu received his letter.
II. Madhu did not receive his letter.
III. The letter was sent by post.

(a) Only I is implicit (b) Only II is implicit
(c) Only III is implicit (d) All are implicit
(e) None is implicit

8. **Statement** "Every successful person who claims to have come from a village has achieved success after he or she left the village." —A leader of party X

Assumptions

I. The average Indian village is a place with little capital, low technology and limited market access.
II. Opportunity for growth is more in metro cities.
III. Opportunities for growth are scarce in villages.

(a) All of these (b) I and III
(c) Only II (d) Only III
(e) None of these

9. **Statement** State Council for Teacher Education (SCTE) has laid down guidelines in respect of minimum qualification for a person to be employed as a teacher in universities or in recognised institutions.

Assumptions

I. The authorities will now appoint only qualified teachers.
II. Only qualified people will apply for the teaching post.
III. SCTE decides all the norms of educational qualification for teaching faculty.

(a) All are implicit (b) None is implicit
(c) Only I is implicit (d) I and II are implicit
(e) I and II are implicit

10. **Statement** "You should be very careful so that the society does not adversely comment on the police leadership." —A statement made by a CBI officer to the newly recruited young officers.

Assumptions

I. The society always indulge in adverse comments.
II. People's trust in the police force is not up to the desired level.
III. Society has the efficiency to judge accurately about the police leadership.

(a) Only I (b) Only II
(c) I and III (d) II and III
(e) None of these

11. **Statement** The company has recently announced series of incentives to the employees who are punctual and sincere.

Assumptions

I. Those who are not punctual at present may get motivated by the announcement.
II. The productivity of the company may increase.
III. The profit earned by the company may be more than the amount to be spent for the incentive programmes.

(a) I and III are implicit (b) All are implicit
(c) II and III are implicit (d) I and II are implicit
(e) None of these

12. **Statement** "If you did not have a mobile connection of MTNL you will feel a jolt when you come to know about a unique, free facility from 10:00 pm to 8:00 am, without any condition, for any network." —X tells Y

Assumptions

I. X knows about the facilities provided by other mobile services.
II. X wants Y to be a subscriber of MTNL mobile services.
III. People like free facilities without any condition.

(a) Only I (b) I and II
(c) II and III (d) I and III
(e) All are implicit

13. **Statement** In view of the recent spurt in sugar prices in the open market, the Government has asked the dealers to release vast quantity of imported sugar in the open market.

Assumptions

I. The dealers will follow the government directive.
II. The sugar prices will come down.
III. The price of indigenous sugar will remain unchanged.

(a) None is implicit (b) I and II are implicit
(c) I and III are implicit (d) All are implicit
(e) II and III are implicit

14. **Statement** For the third time in a row this week, the Indira Gandhi International Airport was put on a full alert today after Air India received an anonymous message that two terrorists laden with explosives were aboard its Mumbai-Delhi-Hong Kong flight. —An authority of Indira Gandhi International Airport.

Assumptions

I. Anonymous message is not likely to be hoax call.
II. Anonymous message is likely to be a hoax call.
III. Alertness might be helpful in reducing the menace.

(a) I and III (b) II and III
(c) Either I or II and III (d) Only III
(e) None of these

15. **Statement** In the recently held All India Commerce Conference, the session on 'Management of Service Sector in India' surprisingly attracted large number of participants and also received a very good media coverage in the leading newspapers.

Assumptions

I. People were not expecting such an encouraging response for service sector.
II. Service sector is not managed properly in India.
III. Media is always very positive towards service sector.

(a) Only I is implicit (b) All are implicit
(c) None is implicit (d) Either I or III is implicit
(e) II and III are implicit

16. **Statement** "A rare opportunity to be a millionaire while being in middle class or lower middle class." —An advertisement by a company named "Fortune India"

Assumptions

I. The base of Fortune India is growing at a fast speed.
II. There are some people who belong either to middle class or to lower middle class but have a dream to become a millionaire.
III. Being a millionaire is not impossible despite belonging to lower middle class.

(a) I and II (b) II and III
(c) I and III (d) All of these
(e) None of these

17. **Statement** "Put a notice on the board that all the employees should come in time to office." —An officer tells his assistant.

Assumptions

I. All the employees come late.
II. Employees read such notice on the board.
III. Employees will follow the instructions.

(a) I and II are implicit
(b) III is implicit
(c) I and III are implicit
(d) II and III are implicit
(e) All are implicit

18. Statement The High Court has ordered state X to submit the case papers of the hit-and-run accident involving actor Mr Y and directed the police not to allow the actor or his family members and friends to meet witnesses or victims.

Assumptions

I. The kith and kin of an accused are likely to make an effort to tamper with the evidence or create a nuisance to help acquit the accused.

II. The capacity of the wrongdoer cannot be a yardstick for deciding punishment for a crime.

III. The court's immediate concern is the grievance of the victims which needs redressal.

(a) Only I (b) I and II (c) I and III (d) All of these
(e) None of these

Direction (Q. Nos. 19-20) *In the following questions, a statement is given followed by three assumptions* I, II and III. *In the context of the questions, an assumption is something to be taken for granted. You have to consider the statement and the assumptions, and decide which of the assumptions is implicit in the statement, then decide which one of the answer is correct.*

19. Statement Prakash decided to get his railway reservation done in the month of May for the journey he wants to undertake in July to Mumbai.

Assumptions **JMET 2011**

I. The railways open reservation two months in advance.

II. There is more than one train to Mumbai.

III. There will be a vacancy in the desired class.

(a) II and III
(b) Only I
(c) I and II
(d) Only III

20. Statement In a recently held all-India conference, the session on Brand Management in India surprisingly attracted a large number of participants and also received excellent media coverage in the leading newspapers.

Assumptions **JMET 2011**

I. Nobody expected such an encouraging response to Brand Management.

II. Brands are not managed properly in India.

III. The Media is always very positive towards Brands.

(a) Only I
(b) I and II
(c) I and III
(d) I, II and III

Direction (Q. No. 21) *A statement followed by four assumptions numbered* I, II, III *and* IV *is given. An assumption is something supposed or taken for granted. You have to consider the statement and the following assumptions and decide which of the assumptions is implicit in the statement, then decide which of the answers (a), (b), (c) and (d) is correct.*

21. Statement The companies that showed relatively high import orientation in India were not the ones that benefitted the most from government interventions during the heydays of import substitution.

Assumptions **JMET 2009**

I. High import companies do not need government support.

II. Low import companies received more government support.

III. Import oriented companies are affected by government policies.

IV. Exporting of goods get affected by government policies.

(a) Only I (b) Only III
(c) II and IV (d) All of these

Direction (Q. Nos. 22-34) *A statement followed by four assumptions numbered* I, II and III *is given. An assumption is something supposed or taken for granted. You have to consider the statement and the following assumptions and decide which of the assumptions is implicit in the statement, then decide which of the answers (a), (b), (c), (d) and (e) is correct.*

22. Statement The company has decided to increase the price of all its products to tackle the precarious financial position.

Assumptions

I. The company may be able to wipe out the entire losses incurred earlier by this decision.

II. The buyer may continue to buy its products even after the increase.

III. The company has adequate resources to continue production for few more months.

(a) I and II are implicit (b) II and III are implicit
(c) I and III are implicit (d) Only II is implicit
(e) None of these

23. Statement After weekend holidays, a person should be fresh and active.

Assumptions

I. Look, today is Monday. Ask Ravindra to take up the new project and execute it by Wednesday evening.

II. Since it is Monday, office atmosphere is relaxed. After lunch, some work will begin.

III. It's Friday afternoon. Can you give it to me on Monday morning? I will finish it by lunch.

(a) I and II (b) Only II (c) I and III (d) Only III
(e) None of these

24. Statement "Let us enter into a deal with company Y to come out of our financial crisis." —Company X

Assumptions

I. Company Y can bail company X out of its financial crisis.

II. Two companies can enter into a deal.

III. Company Y is financially sound.

(a) II and III (b) Only II (c) I and III (d) Only III
(e) None of these

25. Statement Hurdles in restoring security in travelling through train will be removed by the railway ministry and travelling by train will once again be perceived as safe.

Assumptions

I. The railway ministry has created hurdles in travellers' security.

II. Today travelling by train is not considered safe.

III. It is possible to make train journey safe.

(a) I and II (b) II and III (c) I and III (d) All of these
(e) None of these

26. Statement Dogs are trainable.

Assumptions

I. Dogs prefer human contact.

II. Most household dogs are emotionally stable.

III. Dog show is an important item in any circus.

(a) Only I is implicit (b) Only II is implicit
(c) Only III is implicit (d) I and III are implicit
(e) All of these

27. Statement "A court can convict an accused solely on the basis of a dying declaration but such a declaration should be free from any doubt and the victim making the statement should be mentally fit." —Supreme Court

Assumptions

I. One who is not mentally fit always makes statements untrustworthy in nature.

II. Declaration made by the dying person is likely to be true.

III. It is possible to distinguish whether a declaration is dubious or not.

(a) Only I is implicit (b) I and II are implicit
(c) II and III are implicit (d) Only III is implicit
(e) None of these

28. Statement The Telephone company informed the subscribers through a notification that those, who do not pay their bills by the due date, will be charged penalty for every defaulting day.

Assumptions

I. Majority of the people may pay their bills by the due date to avoid penalty.

II. The money collected as penalty may set off the losses due to delayed payment.

III. People generally pay heed to such notices.

(a) I and II implicit (b) I and III are implicit
(c) Only II is implicit (d) II and III are implicit
(e) None of these

29. Statement "An asteroid which burned up in the earth's atmosphere in June could have triggered a mistaken nuclear war between India and Pakistan had it detonated over South Asia." —Statement of Mr X in a report in the New York Times.

Assumptions

I. India and Pakistan are equipped with nuclear weapons.

II. Neither India nor Pakistan had the sophisticated sensors that could determine the difference between a natural NEO (near-earth object) impact and a nuclear detonation.

III. India and Pakistan have no good relationship with each other.

(a) Only I (b) I and II (c) II and III (d) I and III
(e) All of these

30. Statement Considering the tickets sold during the last seven days, the circus authorities decided to continue the show for another fortnight which includes two weekends.

Assumptions

I. People may not turn up on week days.

II. The average number of people who will be visiting circus will be more or less same as that of the last seven days.

III. There may not be enough response at other places.

(a) Only I is implicit (b) Only II is implicit
(c) I and II are implicit (d) All are implicit
(e) None of these

31. Statement Training must be given to all the employees for increasing productivity and profitability.

Assumptions

I. Training is an essential component of productivity.

II. Employee can't function effectively without proper training.

III. Profitability and Productivity are supplementary to each 1other.

(a) None is implicit (b) All are implicit
(c) Only III is implicit (d) I and II are implicit
(e) I and III are implicit

32. Statement "Addictive 'gutkha' and 'paan masala' with or without tobacco has been banned from Aug 1, 2010 in Delhi, where even school and college students were increasingly becoming their consumers. " —A court notice.

Assumptions

I. Some of the 'gutkha' manufacturers may not abide by the court's directions.

II. School children and college students are vulnerable to gutkha.

III. Consumers as well as manufacturers of 'gutkha' will abide by the court's directions.

(a) Only II is implicit
(b) Either I or III and II are implicit
(c) Either I or III is implicit
(d) II and III are implicit
(e) None of the above

33. Statement "X-Chocolate is ideal as a gift for someone you love". —An advertisement

Assumptions

I. People generally give gifts to loved one.

II. Such advertisements generally influence people.

III. Chocolate can be considered as a gift item.

(a) I and II are implicit (b) I and III are implicit
(c) All are implicit (d) II and III are implicit
(e) None of these

34. **Statement** For realising a 9% GDP growth rate, we would need our gross investments to increase to 28-30 per cent. This is not a tall order.

Assumptions

I. GDP growth rate seems to be a far cry.
II. The more you invest, the better the GDP growth.
III. The GDP growth rate is the indicator of a nation's development.

(a) Only I is implicit (b) I, II and III are implicit
(c) Only II is implicit (d) II and III are implicit
(e) Only III is implicit

Direction (Q. Nos. 35-38) *In the question below, a statement is followed by three assumptions numbered* I, II *and* III. *An assumption is something supposed or taken for granted. You have to consider the statement and the following assumptions and decide which assumptions are implicit in the statement.*

35. **Statement** It is believed by many economists that to realise a 7% GDP growth rate in India, which is very much attainable, the gross fixed capital formation in the country must increase to 30% of GDP from the present level of 28%.

Assumptions **IIFT 2014**

I. The target of 7% GDP growth is not feasible.
II. GDP growth rate is directly related to capital formation rate.
III. The GDP growth rate in a country is the only indicator of country's economic development.

(a) I and II are implicit (b) II and III are implicit
(c) III and I are implicit (d) None of these

36. **Statement** "We believe that the adjustment that has already taken place in the value of the rupee is adequate. There is no ground for a further weakening of the rupee." —RBI governor

Assumptions

I. The value of the rupee has depreciated recently.
II. Dollar-buying has been on the rise.
III. Currencies do not fall after a certain level.

(a) None is implicit (b) Only III is implicit
(c) I and III are implicit (d) Only II is implicit
(e) I and II are implicit

37. **Statement** "Buy 'Y' TV for better sound quality." —An advertisement.

Assumptions

I. 'Y' TV is the only TV in the market.
II. 'Y' TV is the costliest.
III. People generally ignore such advertisement.

(a) Only I is implicit (b) Only II is implicit
(c) Only III is implicit (d) All are implicit
(e) None of the above is implicit

38. **Statement** "In our report published last week, the name of the author was mis-spelt. We regret the error"—A magazine editor.

Assumptions **IBPS (PO) 2013**

I. The name of the author was not easy to spell.
II. Publishing correct names of authors is not as important as the quality of the article.
III. Publishing correct names of authors is desirable.

(a) Only I is implicit
(b) Only II is implicit
(c) Only III is implicit
(d) I and III are implicit
(e) II and III are implicit

39. **Statement** The Government has decided to auction construction of highways to private entities in several blocks across the country on build-operate-transfer basis.

Which of the following assumption(s) is/are implicit in the above statement?

Assumptions **SBI Associate (PO) 2010**

I. An adequate number of private entities may not respond to the Government's auction notification.
II. Many private entities in the country are capable of constructing highways within reasonable time.
III. The Government's proposal of build operate-transfer may financially benefit the private entities.

(a) I and II are implicit
(b) II and III are implicit
(c) Only II is implicit
(d) I and III are implicit
(e) None of the above

40. **Statement** Government has urged all the citizens to use electronic media for carrying out their daily activities, whenever possible, instead of using paper as the manufacture of paper requires the cutting down of a large number of trees causing severe damage to the ecosystem.

Which of the following assumption(s) is/are implicit in the above statement?

Assumptions

I. Most people may be capable of using electronic media to carry out various routines.
II. Most people may have access to electronic media for carrying out their daily routine activities.
III. People at large may reject the Governments' appeal and continue using paper as before.

(a) Only I is implicit
(b) Only II is implicit
(c) I and II are implicit
(d) Only III is implicit
(e) None of the above

41. Statement The apex body controlling universities in the country has decided to revise the syllabus of all the technical courses to make them focused towards the present needs of the industry thereby making the technical graduates more employable than they are at present.

Which of the following assumption(s) is/are implicit in the above statement?

Assumptions

I. Technical colleges affiliated to different universities may not welcome the apex body's decision and may continue with the same syllabus as at present.

II. The industry may welcome the decision of the apex body and scale up their hiring from these colleges.

III. The Government may not allow the apex body to implement its decision in all the colleges as it may lead to chaos.

(a) None is implicit (b) Only I is implicit
(c) Only II is implicit (d) Only III is implicit
(e) I and II are implicit

42. Statement Police authority cordoned off the entire locality for the entire day and stopped all vehicular movement for the visit of a top functionary of the government in view of the threat perception and advised all the residents in the area to limit their movement outside their dwellings.

Which of the following assumption(s) is/are implicit in the above statement?

Assumptions

I. Police personnel may not be able to control the vehicular movement in the locality and may seek help from the armed forces.

II. People living in the locality may move out of their houses for the day to avoid inconvenience.

III. The Government functionary may request the police authority to lift the ban on movement residents of the locality outside their dwellings.

(a) None is implicit
(b) Only I is implicit
(c) Only II is implicit
(d) Only III is implicit
(e) II and III are implicit

43. Statement The airlines have requested all their bona fide passengers to check the status of flight operations before leaving their homes as heavy fog is causing immense problems to normal flight operations.

Which of the following assumption(s) is/are implicit in the above statement?

Assumptions

I. The majority of the air passengers may check the flight status before starting their journey to the airport.

II. The Government may take serious objection to the notice issued by the airline company.

III. Majority of the passengers may cancel their tickets and postpone their journey till the situation becomes normal.

(a) None is implicit
(b) Only I is implicit
(c) Only II is implicit
(d) Only III is implicit
(e) I and III are implicit

Cumulative Exercise

Base Level

Direction (Q. Nos. 1-28) *In each question below is given a statement followed by two assumptions numbered* I *and* II. *An assumption is something supposed or taken for granted. You have to consider the statement and the following assumptions and decide which of the assumptions is/are implicit in the statement.*

Give answer

(a) if only Assumption I is implicit
(b) if only Assumption II is implicit
(c) if either Assumption I or II is implicit
(d) if neither Assumption I nor II is implicit
(e) if both Assumptions I and II are implicit

1. **Statement** "If you want timely completion of work-provide independent cabins"– An employee tells to the Director of a Company.

   Assumptions **UIIC (AO) 2012**

   I. There are not enough cabins.
   II. Others' presence hinders timely completion of work.

2. **Statement** The address of the principal to the students, "Dear students, if you want a healthy mind, listen to music".

   Assumptions

   I. Normally student like to follow good advice.
   II. It is desirable to develop a healthy mind.

3. **Statement** Let the secretary prepare Power Point presentation for Ashish.

   Assumptions **IBPS (PO) 2013**

   I. Ashish is incapable for preparing a Power Point presentation himself.
   II. The secretary is well versed with operations of Power Point.

4. **Statement** Many employees of the organisation applied for special sabbatical leave of two years to pursue higher education.

   Assumptions **IOB (PO) 2009**

   I. The management of the organisation may not grant leave to most of these employees.
   II. These employees may be able to complete their education during the sabbatical leave.

5. **Statement** Most of the private companies have decided against awarding annual increase in the salaries of their employees for the previous year due to current economic situations.

   Assumptions **IOB (PO) 2009**

   I. Majority of the employees may leave their job to protest against the decision.
   II. These companies may announce hike in salaries next year.

6. **Statement** The college administration has instructed all the students to stop using cell phones within the college premises.

   Assumptions **IOB (PO) 2009**

   I. The students may stop using cell phones in the college premises.
   II. The students may continue to use cell phones in the college premises.

7. **Statement** The government has decided to levy congestion tax to passengers travelling by air to and from the metro cities.

   Assumptions **IOB (PO) 2009**

   I. The tax so collected may be adequate to meet part of the expenses for providing additional resources to handle huge traffic.
   II. Passengers travelling by air to and from these cities may be able to pay extra amount by way of congestion tax.

8. **Statement** The local citizens group submitted a memorandum to the civic authority for allowing them to convert the vacant plot in the locality into a garden at their own cost.

   Assumptions **IOB (PO) 2009**

   I. The local citizen group may be able to gather enough funds to develop the garden.
   II. The civic authority may not accede to the request of the local citizen group.

9. **Statement** Please use public transport to avoid traffic congestion during the Trade Fair.

Assumptions **OBC (PO) 2010**

I. Only private vehicles cause traffic congestion.

II. Many people posses private vehicles.

10. **Statement** For better health have fruits instead of vitamin supplementing tablets.

Assumptions **OBC (PO) 2010**

I. Vitamins are essential for good health.

II. Vitamins supplementing tablets do not help at all in attaining good health.

11. **Statement** As the day for result declaration for board exams closes by, the students awaiting their result started feeling the heat.

Assumptions **OBC (PO) 2010**

I. Anxiety levels are more during board exams than any other exam.

II. Some students are more anxious than other students.

12. **Statement** Only first class science graduates are eligible for the job.

Assumptions **OBC (PO) 2010**

I. Students with graduation in fields other than science are not as intellectual.

II. Courses other than science are available at the graduation level.

13. **Statement** Any one found smoking in the 'non-smoking' area would be penalized.

Assumptions **OBC (PO) 2010**

I. There are separate smoking and non-smoking areas.

II. There are some people who do not smoke.

14. **Statement** A very large number of people stood in the queue for buying tickets for the one-day international cricket match scheduled to be played in the city on the next day.

Assumptions **Punjab & Sind Bank (PO) 2010**

I. No other one-day international cricket match may be played in the city for the next six months.

II. Majority of those who stood in the queue may be able to get ticket for the one-day international cricket match.

15. **Statement** The highway police authority put up large boards at regular intervals indicating the speed limit and dangers of over-speeding on the highways.

Assumptions **Punjab & Sind Bank (PO) 2010**

I. Most of the motorists may drive their vehicles within the speed limit on the highways.

II. Motorists generally ignore such cautions and over-speed on the highways.

16. **Statement** The employees' association urged its members to stay away from the annual function as many of their demands were not met by the management.

Assumptions **Punjab & Sind Bank (PO) 2010**

I. Majority of the members of the association may not attend the function.

II. The management may cancel the annual function.

17. **Statement** The sarpanch of the village called a meeting of all the heads of the families to discuss the problem of acute shortage of drinking water in the village.

Assumptions **Punjab & Sind Bank (PO) 2010**

I. The sarpanch had earlier called such meetings to discuss about various problems.

II. Most of the heads of families may attend the meeting called by the sarpanch.

18. **Statement** The municipal corporation advised all the people living in the shanties along the beaches to move to higher places during monsoon.

Assumptions **Punjab & Sind Bank (PO) 2010**

I. Many people living in the shanties may leave the city and relocate themselves elsewhere in the state.

II. Majority of the people living in the shanties along the beach may try to relocate to higher places during monsoon.

19. **Statement** India must earn a lot of foreign exchange to achieve its target of economic development.

Assumptions

I. India desires to achieve the target of economic development.

II. It is possible for India to earn more foreign exchange.

20. **Statement** "If the Indian men play to potential, they have a good chance to make the grade this time in Thomas cup."–The coach of Indian badminton team.

Assumptions

I. Indian men have the potential to win the trophy.

II. Indian men have the potential but they do not want to perform good.

21. **Statement** "We are in talks with Japanese Bank for International Cooperation (JBIC) for the second loan of ₹ 1600 crore" –Delhi Metro Rail Corporation (DMRC) Chairman.

Assumptions

I. DMRC has already received the first loan from JBIC.

II. Talks for receiving the first loan have been finalised.

22. **Statement** KLM Company has decided to issue debentures to mop up resources.

Assumptions

I. KLM Company has already explored other sources to collect resources.

II. There are very few competitors in the market for the product of KLM Company.

23. **Statement** "Students are not allowed to wear western dresses in the university campus". –VC of a reputed university.

Assumptions

I. It looks vulgar and encourages more eve teasing.

II. If the girls will come to the college in Indian dresses, then they will concentrate more on studies.

24. **Statement** India is suffering because citizens have given and taken votes based on caste/religion and not on principles.

Assumptions

I. The days of value-based voting are numbered in India.

II. The voting based on principles has the potential to multiply the problems created by the politics of caste and religion.

25. **Statement** The net has a lot of useless sites floating around and www.com is one of them, the difference being that it admits to being a big waste of time.

Assumptions

I. Most of the websites claim to be useful even when they are not so.

II. The net has no mechanism to distinguish useless sites from useful ones.

26. **Statement** The state government 'X' is committed to restrict smoke level on the roads of the metropolis as per the desired parameters.

Assumptions

I. It is possible to determine the smoke level.

II. A committed government can carry forward welfare for its people.

27. **Statement** Unemployment has increased inspite of the Indian economy growing well.

Assumptions

I. Economic growth is supposed to create more job opportunities.

II. There are certain factors other than economic growth which influence employment.

28. **Statement** Ideas have always been more potent than the actual protagonists who act them out.

Assumptions

I. Famous protagonist can make any idea famous despite their less importance.

II. Both ideas and protagonists have the same importance in any play.

Direction (Q. Nos. 29-33) *In the following questions, one statement and two assumptions have been given. You have to go through both statement and assumptions and find out which assumption(s) is/are implicit in the given statement.*

29. **Statement** The journey from Bengaluru to Delhi can be completed in less time.

Assumptions **SSC (CGL) 2012**

I. Bengaluru and Delhi are connected by air route.

II. There is no other facility to transport from Bengaluru to Delhi.

(a) Only I is implicit (b) Only II is implicit
(c) I and II both are implicit (d) Neither I nor II is implicit

30. **Statement** If you laugh, then the whole world will laugh with you.

Assumptions **SSC (CGL) 2009**

I. Generally, people laugh.

II. Laughter gives us happiness.

(a) Only I is implicit (b) Only II is implicit
(c) I and II both are implicit (d) Neither I nor II is implicit

31. **Statement** The teachers work for best, have right to get reward.

Assumptions **SSC (CGL) 2009**

I. All teachers work hard.

II. Reward is given only for best work.

(a) Only I is implicit (b) Only II is implicit
(c) I and II both are implicit (d) Neither I nor II is implicit

32. **Statement** Values of life for educated people are different form those who are uneducated.

Assumptions **SSC (CGL) 2010**

I. Education has an impact on the values of life of a person.

II. An uneducated person is worthless.

(a) I and II both are implicit
(b) Only I is implicit
(c) Only II is implicit
(d) Neither I nor II is implicit

33. **Statement** Send employee XYZ for a training in UK to gain more insight into the project which he is handling at present.

Assumptions **SBI Associate (PO) 2014**

I. Some similar training programmes are available in the employee's own country as well.

II. With the present skill sets, employee XYZ is incapable of handling the project.

(a) Only I is implicit (b) Either I or II is implicit
(c) Only II is implicit (d) I and II both are implicit
(e) Neither I nor II is implicit

Direction (Q. Nos. 34-53) *In each question given below a statement is given that is followed by three assumptions numbered* I, II *and* III. *An assumption is something supposed or taken for granted. You have to consider the statement and the following assumptions and decide which of the assumptions is/are implicit in the statement.*

34. **Statement** "Move into the upper echelons without paying steep price. Book a luxurious flat with us". –Advertisement of a construction company.

Assumptions

I. It is possible to join the selected brand of rich people by hard work.

II. Staying in luxury without paying steep price is the criterion of upper crust of society.

III. Booking a luxurious flat is very easy now.

(a) Only II (b) Only III
(c) II and III (d) Only I
(e) None of these

35. Statement "City 'X' should have more women driving public transport because most of them do not like to speed unnecessarily, prefer not to talk on mobiles while driving, do not listen to blaring music and rarely skip red lights." – A minister of state X.

Assumptions

I. More women driving buses and autos will create more job opportunities for women.

II. Women are more disciplined than men on the roads.

III. If women start driving buses and autos it would increase chances of safety for commuters.

(a) I and II (b) II and III
(c) I and III (d) All of these
(e) None of these

36. Statement In the recently held All India Commerce Conference the session on 'Management of Service Sector in India' surprisingly attracted large number of participants and also received a very good media coverage in the leading newspapers.

Assumptions

I. People were not expecting such an encouraging response for service sector.

II. Service sector is not managed properly in India.

III. Media is always very positive towards service sector.

(a) None is implicit (b) Only I is implicit
(c) All are implicit (d) II and III are implicit
(e) Either I or III is implicit

37. Statement "Tender specification will not be issued to the firms where there is 25% or more default in supplies against earlier purchase orders placed on them". -Condition of a company X inviting tenders for the purchase of materials.

Assumptions

I. The company X will be watching the quality of performance of its suppliers.

II. This time the firms should keep the percentage of default as less as possible.

III. The company X expects quality and professional approach from its suppliers.

(a) Only I is implicit (b) Only II is implicit
(c) Either II or III is implicit (d) Only III is implicit
(e) None of these

38. Statement "The employees association has appealed to the managers of company 'S' to introduce written examination for clerical cadre recruitment to prevent selection of incompetent persons".

Assumptions

I. So far, the company 'S' used to select candidates without conducting a written examination.

II. A written exam can help to identify competent persons.

III. At higher level, written examination may not be of much use.

(a) I and II (b) Only I (c) Only III (d) All of these
(e) None of these

39. Statement "Several labour and industrial courts in this state have no proper premises. Vacancies of judges and stenos are kept pending". – A statement of a retired judge of state X.

Assumptions

I. Adequate number of staff and judges helps in the smooth functioning of the industrial and labour courts.

II. The state is not bothered about the condition of the labour and industrial courts.

III. Physical facilities of an office help in increasing efficiency of its employees.

(a) I and III are implicit (b) Only II is implicit
(c) II and III are implicit (d) All are implicit
(e) None of these

40. Statement "Performing complex mental tasks while driving is dangerous" – A psychologist

Assumptions

I. Thinking too much reduces the ability to spot potential problems and react to them safely.

II. Handsfree phone conversations are as safe or as risky as talking to a passenger, depending upon the demands of conversation.

III. Insecurity of humans is a man-made problem.

(a) I and II (b) II and III
(c) I and III (d) All of these
(e) None of these

41. Statement "We have the distinction of being the only company in India as well as the second in the world to have won an ISO 9002 certification in our line of business". – Statement of company X's chairman.

Assumptions

I. There were not many companies in the line of business of company X.

II. Getting ISO 9002 in the line of business of company X is not easy.

III. The company X desires to expand its business.

(a) Only I is implicit
(b) Only II is implicit
(c) Only III is implicit
(d) II and III are implicit
(e) None of the above

42. Statement "Z-TV, the only TV which gives the viewers a chance to watch two programmes simultaneously"– An advertisement.

Assumptions

I. Sale of Z-TV will increase because of the advertisement.

II. Some people may be influenced by the advertisement and buy Z-TV.

III. The sale of Z-TV may be on the downward trend.

(a) Only I is implicit (b) All are implicit
(c) I and II are implicit (d) II and III are implicit
(e) None of these

43. Statement Use 'X' brand shoes. These are durable and available in all sizes. An advertisement in the newspaper A.

Assumptions

I. Normally people like durable shoes.

II. Very few people read advertisement in a newspaper.

III. Very few people read the newspaper A.

(a) Only I is implicit
(b) I and II are implicit
(c) I and either II or III are implicit
(d) All are implicit
(e) None of the above

44. Statement "Why are only high profile people considered to be adventurous? The villagers in India, who have no buses, walk barefoot for miles on dusty, untarred roads Isn't that more adventurous than rafting or gliding ?" – View of a person.

Assumptions

I. It is a Herculean task to walk barefoot for miles on dusty untarred roads.

II. Rafting and gliding are considered adventurous by the people.

III. Walking barefoot for miles on dusty untarred roads is not considered adventurous by the people.

(a) I and II (b) II and III (c) I and III (d) All of these
(e) None of these

45. Statement "The simplest and the most cost effective way to upgrade your home–Exchange your old furniture and get 25% to 33% off on the new furniture". – An advertisement of a furniture company.

Assumptions

I. Now-a-days, there is no demand for furniture products unless some attractive scheme is offered.

II. Some customers always desire to have best quality and do not bother either for cost or for convenience.

III. Some customers want to keep their home up-to-date with reasonable cost and with less hassles.

(a) Only I is implicit (b) Only II is implicit
(c) Only III is implicit (d) I and II are implicit
(e) None of these

46. Statement The situation of this area still continues to be tense and out of control. People are requested to be in their homes only.

Assumptions

I. There had been some serious incidents.

II. People will not go to the office.

III. Normally will be restored shortly.

(a) Only I is implicit (b) I and II are implicit
(c) None is implicit (d) I and III are implicit
(e) All are implicit

47. Statement "Buy pure and natural honey of company X". – An advertisement in a newspaper.

Assumptions

I. Artificial honey can be prepared.

II. People do not mind paying more for pure and natural honey.

III. No other company supplies pure honey.

(a) Only I is implicit (b) I and II are implicit
(c) I and III are implicit (d) All are implicit
(e) None of these

48. Statement "If we really want to reduce the menace of smoking, we need to reflect our intention through our deeds, our creations such as movies, in which incidence of smoking is shown much higher than the actual cigarette consumption among the Indian population". –View of Mr X.

Assumptions

I. There is a strong link between films and viewers behaviour.

II. Smoking shown in movies results in corresponding increase in smoking among the public.

III. Menace of smoking can be reduced by proper planning followed by appropriate efforts.

(a) Only I (b) Only II
(c) II and III (d) I and III
(e) All of these

49. Statement There is big boom in drug business and a number of jhuggi-jhopari dwellers in Delhi can be seen pedaling with small pouches of smack and brown sugar.

Assumptions

I. Drug addiction is increasing in the country, specially in the capital.

II. All the big dons involved in the smuggling of drugs live in jhuggi-jhopari areas.

III. Most of the jhuggi-jhopari dwellers would do anything for money.

(a) Only I is implicit
(b) Only II is implicit
(c) Only III is implicit
(d) I and III are implicit
(e) Either I or III is implicit

50. Statement A state government suspended two additional district judges.

Assumptions

I. They were negligent in discharging duties.

II. There was a charge of misconduct against them.

III. The government officials were biased against them.

(a) None is implicit
(b) Either I or II is implicit
(c) Any one of the three is implicit
(d) I and III are implicit
(e) Either I or III is implicit

51. Statement The X passenger car manufacturing company announced a reduction in the prices of its luxury cars.

Assumptions

I. There will be an increase in the sale of luxury cars of company.

II. The other such car manufactures may also reduce their prices.

III. The competitor companies may not reduce their prices.

(a) Only I is implicit (b) I and II are implicit
(c) Only II is implicit (d) I and III are implicit
(e) None of these

52. Statement "You should publish the names of the ten worst colleges or institutions which will lead to an overall improvement of Indian institutes".— Request of a reader to the editor of a weekly magazine.

Assumptions

I. The management and administrators of the respective institutes will come under pressure and will be compelled to improve the condition of the institutes if the names of the institutes are published in the weekly magazine.

II. The move will be helpful for admission seekers from being a victim of degraded standard of the institutions.

III. The editor may concede the request and take positive steps in this regard.

(a) I and II are implicit
(b) II and III are implicit
(c) I and III are implicit
(d) All of these
(e) None of the above

53. Statement "Do not lean out of the moving train". – A warning in the railway compartment.

Assumptions

I. Such warnings will have some effect.

II. Leaning out of a moving train is dangerous.

III. It is the duty of railway authorities to take care of passengers safety.

(a) I and II are implicit (b) II and III are implicit
(c) Only II is implicit (d) I and III are implicit
(e) All are implicit

Advanced Level

Direction (Q. Nos. 1-32) *In each question below is given a statement followed by two assumptions numbered* I *and* II. *An assumption is something supposed or taken for granted. You have to consider the statement and the following assumptions and decide which of the assumptions is/are implicit in the statement.*

Give answer

(a) if only Assumption I is implicit
(b) if only Assumption II is implicit
(c) if either Assumption I or II is implicit
(d) if neither Assumption I nor II is implicit
(e) if both Assumptions I and II are implicit

1. Statement Minute traces of nitrate sometimes present in cattle fodder B may be responsible for the poor health of the cattle therefore use fodder G to ensure that your cattle remain healthy.

Assumptions **SBI Associates (PO) 2014**

I. Cattle fodder G does not contain nitrate.

II. Nitrate is toxic to all living beings.

2. Statement The city transport corporation has introduced air-conditioned buses on various routes to attract people travelling to their work places by car and hence reduce congestion on the roads.

Assumptions

I. Majority of the people may still prefer to travel to their work places in their own cars.

II. Many people may now opt for these buses for travelling to their work places.

3. Statement The state government has announced an amnesty scheme for all the housing societies defaulting on payment of municipal taxes asking these societies to pay upfront six per cent of the dues and regularize their status without any penalty.

Assumptions

I. Most of the defaulting housing societies may now opt for amnesty scheme and pay up their dues.

II. Other housing societies which have been paying their taxes regularly may file case against the government for discriminatory practice.

4. Statement Mr X started at 9:00 am from his residence to attend a meeting scheduled to be held at 11:00 am and instructed his assistant to meet him at the venue of the meeting and hand over the relevant documents.

Assumptions

I. Mr X may arrive at the meeting place before 11:00 am.

II. Mr X's assistant may be able to arrive at the venue before commencement of the meeting.

5. Statement "If you are a first class graduate with good communication skills and also have work experience of atleast two years in the sales related activities, you are welcomed in our organisation."– An employment advertisement.

Assumptions

I. Many with good communication skills may not respond to the advertisement.

II. All the first class graduates may possess good communication skills.

6. **Statement** There are many instances of dacoity and looting in passenger trains every now and then in our country.

Assumptions

I. The railway authorities should immediately deploy policeman in all the trains.

II. The passengers travelling by train should be given training on how to deal with dacoits and looters.

7. **Statement** The railway authority has announced suspension of movements of trains on the main track within the city limit for carrying out major repair works during Saturday and Sunday and advised the commuters to plan their journey accordingly.

Assumptions **UBI (PO) 2009**

I. The commuters may protest against the decision of the railway authority and may disrupt other transport services.

II. The municipal authority may be able to deploy additional buses during Saturday and Sunday to help the commuters.

8. **Statement** The biggest private airline decided to increase the number of flights between cities A and B to 10 flights everyday.

Assumptions **Haryana Grameen Bank (PO) 2009**

I. Other private airlines may also increase the frequency of daily flights between cities A and B.

II. There may be adequate passenger load on all the bigger private airline even after this increase.

9. **Statement** Majority of the employees of the organisation decided to join with their family the overnight picnic funded by the organisation.

Assumptions **Haryana Grameen Bank (PO) 2009**

I. The management of the organisation may not welcome the employees enthusiasm.

II. The management of the organisation may provide adequate funds for the picnic.

10. **Statement** The reputed management institute in the city increased the fees by 300 % from the last academic year.

Assumptions **Haryana Grameen Bank (PO) 2009**

I. The institute may still attract good number of students for all its courses.

II. Many students may now opt for other institutes in the city which charge less fees.

11. **Statement** Many residents of the locality decided not to attend the cultural function organized by the local club to protest against the club's limited invitations.

Assumptions **Haryana Grameen Bank (PO) 2009**

I. The local club may cancel the cultural function.

II. The local club may stop all its activities.

12. **Statement** Government has announced a relief package for all the drought hit farmers in the country and advised the state governments to put in a mechanism for disbursement.

Assumptions **Haryana Grameen Bank (PO) 2009**

I. The state governments may be able to put in place the system for disbursement of government relief to the affected farmers.

II. Government may be able to identify all the farmers affected by drought in the country.

13. **Statement** The civic body put up a huge notice board on the beach located at an isolated part of the city as "Many picknicker died while swimming in the sea during the past few months".

Assumptions **BOI (PO) 2010**

I. Picknickers may ignore the notice and continue venturing into the sea.

II. Picknickers may read and be careful while venturing into the sea.

14. **Statement** The government has recently advised all the public sector banks to reduce rate of interest on home loans upto ₹ 25 lakh.

Assumptions **BOI (PO) 2010**

I. The public sector banks may reduce the interest on all home loans upto ₹ 25 lakh.

II. People may take undue advantage of the government's decision.

15. **Statement** The local hospital put up a notice board at the main entrance stating that the hospital will carry out free check up for detecting cancer for the people staying in the locality.

Assumptions **BOI (PO) 2010**

I. Large number of people living in the locality may avail the free check up facility offered by the hospital.

II. Hospital staff deployed for the purpose may be able to cope up with the rush of people for check up.

16. **Statement** The government has decided to distribute 3 kg of foodgrains to every family living below poverty line for the next three months at a nominal price of ₹ 5 per kg.

Assumptions **BOB (PO) 2010**

I. To government has enough stock to distribute foodgrains for that period.

II. Families living below poverty line may be able to afford to buy foodgrains at ₹ 5 per kg.

17. Statement The cricketing body decided to hold the final match of the tournament in the biggest stadium of the country which can accommodate above one lakh spectators.

Assumptions **BOI (PO) 2010**

I. Most of the tickets may be sold resulting into huge income for the cricketing body.

II. Most of the spectators may prefer to watch the match on TV at their homes rather than going to the stadium.

18. Statement The driver of the huge truck pulled the emergency brakes to avoid hitting the auto rickshaw which suddenly came in front of the truck.

Assumptions **Allahabad Bank (PO) 2010**

I. The auto rickshaw driver may be able to steer his vehicle away from the oncoming truck.

II. The truck driver may be able to stop the truck before it hits the auto rickshaw.

19. Statement The doctor warned the patient against any further consumption of alcohol, if he desired to get cured from the ailment and live a longer life.

Assumptions **Allahabad Bank (PO) 2010**

I. The patient may follow the doctor's advice and stop consuming alcohol.

II. The doctor may be able to cure the patient from the ailment, if the patient stops consuming alcohol.

20. Statement The Chairman of the company urged all the employees to refrain from making long personal calls during working hours in order to boost productivity.

Assumptions **Allahabad Bank (PO) 2010**

I. Majority of the employees may respond positively to the Chairman's appeal.

II. Most of the employees may continue to make long personal calls during working hours.

21. Statement The lock cultural club decided to organise a musical event to raise money for the construction of the club building.

Assumptions **Allahabad Bank (PO) 2010**

I. The local residents may not allow the club to organise the musical event in the locality.

II. The money collected by organising the musical event may be substantial enough for the club to start construction.

22. Statement The traffic police department has put huge notice boards at all the major junctions of the city warning drivers to refrain from using cell phones while driving or else their licences will be impounded.

Assumptions **Allahabad Bank (PO) 2010**

I. The drivers of the vehicles may ignore the warning and continue using cell phones while driving.

II. The traffic police department may be able to nab most of the offenders and impound their licences.

23. Statement The Municipal Corporation has announced 50% reduction in water supply till monsoon arrives in the city.

Assumptions **BOB (PO) 2010**

I. People may protest against the unilateral decision of the Municipal Corporation.

II. Municipal Corporation may reduce its taxes from the residents as it failed to provide adequate water.

24. Statement Many people were caught by the railway police while they were trying to cross the railway tracks and imposed heavy penalty before releasing them.

Assumptions **BOB (PO) 2010**

I. People may refrain from crossing railway tracks in future.

II. People may continue crossing railway tracks and pay hefty penalty.

25. Statement The government has recently announced additional food for work programmes for all the drought affected regions in the country.

Assumptions **BOB (PO) 2010**

I. The government has adequate funds to run these programmes.

II. Affected people may be able to get atleast one meal a day due to these programmes.

26. Statement Most of the engineering colleges in the state applied to the regulatory body for sanctioning more number of seats for the next academic session.

Assumptions **BOB (PO) 2010**

I. The regulatory body may grant additional seats sought the engineering colleges of the state.

II. The engineering colleges of the state may get adequate number of applications to fill in the additional seats.

27. Statement In view of the severe heat wave passing through the state, the government has asked all the schools to remain closed for the next fortnight with immediate effect.

Assumptions **BOB (PO) 2010**

I. The heat wave may not continue beyond a fortnight.

II. The parents of the students may not allow their wards to attend school even after a fortnight.

28. Statement The largest domestic airlines corporation has announced new summer schedules in which more number of flights in trunk routes are introduced.

Assumptions **Corporation Bank (PO) 2010**

I. More number of passengers may travel by this airlines corporation during summer months in trunk routes.

II. Other airlines companies may also increase the number of flights in all the sectors.

29. Statement The chairman of the company decided to hold a grand function to celebrate silver jubilee during the next weekend and invited a large number of guests.

Assumptions **Corporation Bank (PO) 2010**

I. The company officials may be able to make all the necessary preparations for the silver jubilee celebration.

II. Majority of the guests invited by the Chairman may attend the function.

30. Statement The largest computer manufacturing company slashed the prices of most of the desktop models by about 15% with immediate effect.

Assumptions **Corporation Bank (PO) 2010**

I. The company may incur heavy losses due to reduction in prices of the desktop.

II. The sales of desktop manufactured by the company increase substantially in the near future.

31. Statement The school authority decided to rent out the school premises during weekends and holidays for organising various functions to augment its resources to meet the growing needs of the school.

Assumptions **Corporation Bank (PO) 2010**

I. The parents of the school students may protest against the decision of the school authority.

II. There may not be enough demand for hiring the school premises for organising functions.

32. Statement The local civic body has urged all the residents to voluntarily reduce consumption of potable water by about 30 per cent to tide over the water crisis.

Assumptions **Corporation Bank (PO) 2010**

I. Many residents may reduce consumption of potable water.

II. Many activity may welcome the civic body's move and spread awareness among residents.

Direction (Q. Nos. 33-45) *In each question below is given a statement followed by three assumptions numbered* I, II *and* III. *You have to consider the statement and the giving assumptions, decide which of the assumptions is/are implicit in the statement and choose your answer accordingly.*

33. Statement "I think that she has gone mad. Last night I saw her barking like a dog."– A tells B about Madhu.

Assumptions **SNAP 2014**

I. Madhu is a friend of A.

II. B knows Madhu.

III. Some people do not bark like dogs.

(a) I and II are implicit (b) II and III are implicit
(c) I and III are implicit (d) All are implicit

34. Statement This book is so prepared that even a layman can study science in the absence of a teacher.

Assumptions

I. A layman wishes to study science without a teacher.

II. A teacher may not always be available to teach science.

III. A layman generally finds it difficult to learn science on its own.

(a) I and II are implicit (b) II and III are implicit
(c) I and III are implicit (d) All are implicit
(e) None of these

35. Statement The professor announced in the class that the next periodical examination will be held on 15th of the next month.

Assumptions

I. All the students may appear in the examination.

II. The college will remain open on 15th of the next month.

III. The students can study till 15th of the next month to pass examination.

(a) I and II are implicit (b) Only II is implicit
(c) II and III are implicit (d) Only III is implicit
(e) None of these

36. Statement An advertisement : Now you can own a new car in just ₹ 1999 per month.

Assumptions

I. People aspire for owning a car.

II. People do not want to buy used cars.

III. Most people can afford to pay ₹ 1999 per month for a new car.

(a) I and II are implicit (b) II and III are implicit
(c) I and III are implicit (d) All are implicit
(e) None of these

37. Statement An advertisement of Bank X – "Want to open a bank account ! Just dial our 'home service' and we will come at your doorsteps."

Assumptions

I. No, other bank makes available service at the doorstep of the customer.

II. People may choose bank X for their financial transactions.

III. Now, a days banking has become very competitive.

(a) I and II are implicit (b) II and III are implicit
(c) I and III are implicit (d) All are implicit
(e) None of these

38. Statement The civic authority has decided that all the factories located inside the city limits be shifted outside to reduce the level of environmental pollution in the city.

Assumptions

I. The pollution level in the city in future may reduce after these factories are shifted outside the city limit.

II. Enough usable land is available outside the city limit for these factories.

III. Many of these factories may shift to some other smaller towns to remain profitable.

(a) Only I is implicit (b) I and II are implicit
(c) Only II is implicit (d) II and III are implicit
(e) None of these

39. **Statement** "If you are a mechanical engineer, we want you as our supervisor."— an advertisement by company X.

Assumptions

I. Mechanical engineers are expected to be better performers by company X.

II. The company X needs supervisors.

III. Mechanical engineers may get attracted and apply to company X.

(a) I and II are implicit (b) II and III are implicit
(c) I and III are implicit (d) All are implicit
(e) None of these

40. **Statement** "We do not want you to see our product on newspaper, visit our shop to get a full view". – An advertisement.

Assumptions

I. People generally decide to purchase any product after seeing the name in the advertisement.

II. Uncommon appeal may attract the customers.

III. People may come to see the product.

(a) I and III are implicit (b) I and II are implicit
(c) II and III are implicit (d) All are implicit
(e) None of these

41. **Statement** Keeping in view the financial constraints, the management institution has decided to charge at the time of providing employment in various organisations, a placement fee of ₹ 25000 from the organisations in which the student will be provided the employment.

Assumptions

I. It will help in increasing the demand of the students belonging to the management institution.

II. The amount collected in this way will be purposeful.

III. It may be possible that the organisation providing employment may select less number of students in future.

(a) Only II is implicit (b) Only I is implicit
(c) I and II are implicit (d) II and III are implicit
(e) None of these

42. **Statement** Many engineering and medical graduate are taking up jobs in administrative services and banks and thus wasting the application of knowledge earned during these courses.

Assumptions **MAT 2014**

I. All the professionals should be advised to refrain from taking up such jobs.

II. The government should appoint a committee to find out the reasons for these professionals taking up such jobs and to suggest the remedial measures.

(a) Only I is implicit
(b) Neither Assumption I or II is implicit
(c) Only II is implicit
(d) None of the above

43. **Statement** Rabindranath Tagore wrote many poems. Every poet has aesthetic knowledge, aesthetic is a part of axiological study.

Assumptions **SSC (10+2) 2014**

I. Rabindranath Tagore did different axiological study

II. He followed the base of logic and ethics.

(a) Only I is implicit
(b) Only II is implicit
(c) Either Assumption I or II is implicit
(d) Neither Assumption I nor II is implicit

44. **Statement** At present 10% of our villages receive 24 h electricity. In the next two years, the state government would strive to add 16% more villages to the list.

Assumptions **SBI Associate (PO) 2014**

I. At present 60% villages in the state have no access to electricity at all.

II. Even after couple of years more than that of the villages may lack assess to 24 h electricity.

(a) Only I is implicit
(b) Only II is implicit
(c) Either Assumption I or II is implicit
(d) Neither Assumption I nor II is implicit
(e) Both Assumptions I and II are implicit

45. **Statement** The new educational policy envisages major modifications in the education system.

Assumptions

I. Present educational system is inconsistent with national needs.

II. Present educational system needs changes.

(a) Only I is implicit
(b) Only II is implicit
(c) Either Assumption I or II is implicit
(d) Neither Assumption I nor II is implicit
(e) Both Assumptions I and II are implicit

Answers with Explanations

Intro Exercise 1

1. (*c*) On the basis of statement, it is not certain that present rates are very low. We cannot say that increasing the rates is the only way to meet the deficit. Hence, none of the assumptions is implicit.

2. (*c*) Most of the people who stop smoking have gained weight, that does not mean that if one quits smoking, he/she will surely gain weight or non-smokers cannot gain weight. So, neither Assumption I nor II is implicit.

3. (*d*) Both the assumptions are implicit because the institutions that adopted the on-line method of conducting their examinations assumed that candidates from all parts of the country are adapt at computers and this method of the examination will help to recruit more qualified people.

4. (*c*) Assumption I is not implicit as it is said that performance is reviewed after one year. Assumption II is also not implicit on the basis of the statement.

5. (*b*) In such cases of illness, the patient is rushed to hospital, irrespective of how the relatives of patients may behave. So, Assumption I is not implicit. Assumption II is implicit because affected people were rushed to the nearby hospitals, that means nearby hospitals may be able to attend all the affected people.

6. (*e*) A promise is made only after assuming that it would be fulfilled. So, Assumption I is implicit. As the new business ventures are to be set up in rural areas, so the people of these areas may welcome the Government decision. So, Assumption II is also implicit.

7. (*e*) It is expected that a large number of devotees may visit the temple on main festival day. So, municipal authority is blocking the movement of traffic in that area. So, Assumption I is implicit. People travelling to that areas may postpone their journey because of blocked movement. So, Assumption II is also implicit.

8. (*d*) The Government has taken that decision after analysing many facts and parents never want to pay more fees. So, neither Assumption I nor II is implicit.

9. (*a*) Assumption I is implicit because diversion would be necessary when the construction is going on. Assumption II is not implicit as negative reactions are not assumed.

10. (*a*) Smoking is injurious to health means that non-smoking promotes health and yes, this warning is necessary for various public places, therefore Assumption I is implicit.

11. (*a*) In the statement it is given that patient's condition would improve after operation. That means that patient can be operated upon in this condition. So, Assumption I is implicit while Assumption II is not implicit.

12. (*b*) On the basis of transportation we cannot say that Paris is an expensive city. So, Assumption I is not implicit. In the statement it is given that train services are convenient and economical in Paris. So Assumption II is implicit.

13. (*d*) Neither the name of department nor the post held by him can be assumed from the statement. What he is doing at present cannot be assumed from the statement. So, neither Assumption I nor II is implicit.

14. (*d*) The given medicine are not the only medicine to reduce the weight and weight can be reduced without medicines. So, neither Assumption I nor II is implicit.

15. (*b*) The advisories is issued with the assumption that people will overlook it. So, only assumption II is implicit.

16. (*e*) Both the assumption are implicit because the advertisement is published. So that the enough eligible Chartered Accountants will reply.

17. (*b*) Many people will choose to travel in air conditioned buses, therefore the city transport corporation has introduced air conditioned buses on various routes. So, only assumption II is implicit.

18. (*e*) Modifications in the education system in a major part imply that the present educational system was not proper and needs modification or changes.

So, both the assumptions are implicit in the statement.

19. (*e*) The credit cooperative society has decided to increase the upper limit of loan to ₹ 3 lakh. It was after assuming that there may be demands from the members to take loan upto ₹ 3 lakh. So, Assumption I is implicit. Assumption II is also implicit because any authority provide facilities with in their capacity.

20. (*a*) Assumption I is implicit because a great part of observed intelligence occurs on the earliest years of life i.e. at the age of four or five. Assumption II has intelligence measure at the age of 17 which is not related to the statement, so it is not implicit.

21. (*b*) The words 'all' and 'only' does not make Assumption I implicit. In the statement it is said that farmers must immediately switch over to organic fertilisers. That means organic fertilisers are readily available to the farmers. So,

Assumption II is implicit.

22. (*d*) Both the assumptions are not related to the statement. So, neither assumption is implicit.

23. (*d*) Both the assumptions are not related to the statement. So, neither assumption is implicit.

24. (*d*) The statement advises that an executive should be task-oriented as well as people-oriented. It is based on the assumptions that some executives are only people-oriented and some executives are only task-oriented. Hence, none of the assumptions follows.

25. (*a*) In the statement it is clear that the person is as smart as a person from college X. That means the students of college X are smart. So, Assumption I is implicit. If a person became smart after doing MBA through a correspondence course then it does not mean that all other students can become smart by doing so. So, Assumption II is not implicit.

26. (*e*) Subodh has written a letter to his brother to collect the application form from the university. He wrote the letter after assuming that university may issue application forms to a person other than the prospective student. It is supposed that Subodh's brother may receive the letter well before the last date of collecting application form. So, both Assumptions I and II are implicit.

27. (*b*) Assumption I is not related to the given statement and it is not given that how all crucial business will succeed. So, Assumption I is not implicit. Assumption II is implicit because Internet is the need of the hour and thats why a strategic plan need to be developed for Internet adoption.

28. (*a*) In the statement it is given that army should be deployed to rehabilitate the people displaced due to earthquake. It means that army can be used for purposes other than war also. So, Assumption I is implicit. Assumption II is not implicit because the world 'only' is making it baseless as there may be some other measures which can rehabilitate the displaced victims of earthquake.

29. (*b*) It is not clear from the statement that Anthony is not from the same city or from the same city. So, Assumption I is not implicit. Assumption II is implicit because Anthony will not attend that party as invitation has been emphasised in the statement.

30. (*b*) If employees do their duty honestly than they can prevent accidents. Safety boards are not useless but they have a little role in preventing accident. So, Assumption I is not implicit but II is implicit.

31. (*d*) Assumption I is not related to the statement. It is clear from the statement that sometimes adoption of sophisticated technology increases production and efficiency. So, neither Assumption I nor II is implicit.

32. (*b*) In the statement, any information about transparency is not given. So, Assumption I is not implicit. Present members of IIC are not up to the expectations of the IIC thats why they are seeking for those who have topped the civil exams. So, Assumption II is implicit.

33. (*a*) For taking the consent of parents, management of many private schools may call the parents for discussion regarding fee hike. So, Assumption I is implicit. The word 'any hike' is making Assumption II weak, so it is not implicit.

34. (*b*) Government has made huge security arrangement, so protestors cannot disrupt the relay of Olympic torch within the country. So, Assumption I is not implicit. Due to huge security arrangement the relay of Olympic torch may pass peacefully during its journey within the country. So, Assumption II is implicit.

35. (*e*) Both the assumptions are implicit because general public may otherwise be bullied by the government officials and majority of the government officials may follow the government directives.

36. (*b*) Mohan has invited 200 people and made food arrangement of about 200 people. So, most of the people invited by Mohan may attend the wedding ceremony. So, Assumption II is implicit. And Assumption I is not implicit.

37. (*a*) During the festival days, a large number of devotees may assemble in the city for which local administration is making appropriate security arrangement. So, Assumption I is implicit. Security person are able to control the crowd. So, Assumptions II is not implicit.

38. (*e*) The move to make traffic police equipped with alcometers must have been necessitated because of many accidents taken place every day because of drunken drivers. Alcometers is a machine which can identify the drunken persons easily. So, Assumption I and II both are implicit.

39. (*b*) In the statement it is given that income tax rules need to be amended so that people will declare their actual wealth because at present some people do not declare their actual wealth. It does not mean that income tax rules are not proper. So, Assumption I is not implicit while Assumption II is implicit.

40. (*d*) Both Assumptions I and II are sort of restatements of the given statement. So, neither of these is implicit.

41. (*b*) A child can learn before he/she turns five. So, Assumption I is not implicit. Some school admit children who are below five years of age, so government gives that advertisement. So, Assumption II is implicit.

42. (*d*) The word 'always' in Assumption I and 'not possible' in Assumption II are making them baseless. So, neither Assumption is implicit.

43. (*a*) If similar solution is being applied then it implies that the nature of problem is also same. Therefore, Assumption I is implicit in the statement. The use of term 'universal' in the second assumption makes it unsuitable.

44. (*e*) The phrase 'half the job done' is helpful in assuming both the assumptions. Assumption I is implicit because half work is done by having proper guidance and institute alone can not help a student in his success, it only helps a half and the rest half is hard labour of student. So, Assumption II is also implicit.

45. (*d*) When decisions are taken, the assumptions are positive. It is assumed that every person would respect the Govt. decision. So, neither Assumption I nor II is implicit.

46. (*a*) Assumption I is implicit because if there is not adequate number of such students then such type of conditions will not be introduced. As it is Assumed that there may be adequate number of students, so Assumption II is not implicit.

47. (*a*) Assumption I is implicit because the High Court has ordered the municipal corporation after assuming its capability of carrying out the repair work in next fortnight. Assumption II is not related to the statement and also it is baseless.

48. (*b*) Assumption I is not related to the statement, so it is not implicit. Mahesh has decided to travel by train, so he may be able to get reservation in a suitable train to Delhi before the wedding date. So, Assumption II is implicit.

49. (*a*) Assumption I is implicit because, the phrase 'walk to the office' defines that the mall is at a walkable distance from the office. Office allows all type of vehicles till the parking space is available. So, Assumption II is not implicit.

50. (*e*) Bank X is comparing its interest rates for education loans to other banks. That means other banks are also providing education loans and interest rates are different for different banks. So, both Assumptions I and II are implicit.

51. (*a*) Assumption I is implicit because help desk has a solution to all kinds of problems related to mobile phones, so you should contact help desk for mobile phone problems. Problem will be solved though it is not reported immediately. If not by help desk, some other desk may solve that problem. So, Assumption II is not implicit.

52. (*a*) The milk company wants to dispel the misconception among the people that thick milk is good. So, Assumption I is implicit. There is a difference between low quality milk and adulterated milk. So, Assumption II is not implicit.

53. (*d*) None of the assumptions is implicit because both the assumptions do not have any direct relation with the statement.

54. (*e*) Clearly, both the assumptions are implicit in the statement. The letter is given to Assistant to drop it, it may be assumed that he does know the address. The Assistant will follow the instructions given by Officer.

Intro Exercise 2

1. (*b*) It is assumed in the statement that people want quality training in Computers. Secondly, it is an advertisement. Hence, people read advertisements. Hence, all the assumptions are implicit.

2. (*c*) It is given in the statement that friends have decided to go for picnic to avoid crowd. This implies that many people do not go to Avon. Hence, Assumptions I and II are implicit. Now, we cannot say that reason for the Avon being non-crowdy is people's unacquaintence with this spot. It may be due to other reasons also.

3. (*c*) Prabodh wrote the second letter to his mother after a month when he did not receive any reply from his mother. This can be assumed that his mother promptly sends reply to his letters. So, Assumption III is implicit. Prabodh's mother may or may not receive the first letter and it is not given in the statement that in what time letters generally reaches. So, Assumptions I and II are not implicit.

4. (*e*) The phrase 'despite strong opposition' indicates that a strong opposition puts hindrance before a bill in taking final shape. So, Assumption III is implicit. Assumptions I and II are not related to the statement so they are not implicit.

5. (*a*) The state government increased octroi by five per cent after assuming that it may be able to implement its decision. The state government may get the consent of central government on this issue. After the hike, the state government may be able to earn considerable amount. So, all assumptions are implicit.

6. (*e*) It is not clear from the statement that the given act will hurt the litigants interest or the lawyers interest. So, Assumption I is not implicit. Assumption II is not implicit because of the word 'all'. The venue is not given in the statement, so Assumption III is also not implicit.

7. (*a*) A has categorically stated that Madhu has not replied to his letter, it means that Madhu has received his letter. So, Assumption I is implicit and Assumption II is not implicit. Assumption III is not related to the statement, so it is not implicit.

8. (*d*) Assumption I is not implicit because it goes two much deep (specific). Assumption II is not implicit because leaving the village does not necessarily mean migrating to the metro cities. Assumption III is implicit because opportunities for growth are scare in villages and thats why people are leaving villages.

9. (*a*) All the assumptions are implicit as only qualified people will apply for the teaching post and the authorities will now appoint only qualified teachers. From the statement it is clear that SCTE decides all the norms of educational qualification for teaching faculty.

10. (*b*) Assumption I is not implicit due to the word 'always.' Assumption II is implicit because it is lack of trust that leads to adverse comments. Assumption III is not implicit due to the word 'accurately'.

11. (*d*) Incentive is an award for punctuality and sincerity and this will work as a motivational force for those who are not punctual. This will increase the productivity of the company. So, Assumptions I and II are implicit. Assumption III is not implicit because profit of a company cannot be predicted as depends on several factors.

12. (*e*) All the assumptions are implicit as X knows the facilities provided by other mobile services. X tells Y about this because he wants Y to be a subscriber of MTNL and it is true that people like free facilities without any condition.

13. (*b*) Government has asked the dealers to release vast quantity of imported sugar then dealers will follow it because government directions are not taken in a negative way. By this sugar prices will come down. So, Assumptions I and II are 'implicit.' Assumption III is not implicit because it is not related to the statement.

14. (*a*) Airport was put on a full alert, so the anonymous message is not likely to be hoax call. So, Assumption I is implicit while II is not. Assumption III is implicit because alertness might be helpful in reducing the menace.

15. (*a*) The word 'surprisingly' in the statement clearly implies that people were not expecting such an encouraging response for service sector. So, Assumption I is implicit. Assumption II is not related to the statement so it is not implicit. Assumption III is not implicit due to the word 'always'.

16. (*b*) Assumption I is not related to the statement so it is not implicit. Assumptions II and III are implicit because there are some people whose income is low but have a dream to become a millionaire and it is not impossible though you have a lower income.

17. (*d*) Assumption I is not implicit due to the word 'all.' Assumptions II and III are implicit because that notice is to be displayed on a notice board. These type of notices are issued after assuming that employees will take them in a positive manner.

18. (*a*) Assumption I is implicit because kith and kin of accused are likely to make an effort to tamper with the evidence or create a nuisance to help acquit the accused. Assumption II is not related to the statement, so it is not implicit. Assumption III is not implicit due to the word 'immediate'.

19. (*b*) Prakash wants to go Mumbai in July, while he get his railway reservation done in May. It means that railways open reservation two months in advance. So, Assumption I is implicit. Assumptions II and III are not related to statement, so they are not, implicit.

20. (*a*) The word 'surprisingly' in the statement clearly implies that nobody expected such an encouraging response to Brand Management. So, Assumption I is implicit. Assumption II is not related to the statement, so it is not implicit. Assumption III is not implicit due to the word 'always'.

21. (*b*) It is clear from the statement that import oriented companies are affected by government policies. So, Assumption III is implicit. Assumptions I, II and IV are not related to the statement, so they are not implicit.

22. (*e*) Assumption I is not implicit due to the word 'entire.' In the statement, we do not have any information about Assumptions II and III so they are also not implicit.

23. (*c*) In Assumptions I and III, it is shown that work, if carried out on Monday, can be executed efficiently. Both the assumptions are related to the statement that after weekend holidays, a person should be fresh and active. So, both these assumptions are implicit.

24. (*e*) Since company X talks of entring into a deal, it must be assumed that two companies can enter into a deal. From the statement it is clear that company Y can bail company X out of its financial crisis and it can be possible when company Y is financially sound. So, all the three assumptions are implicit.

25. (*b*) If railway ministry has an initiative to remove the hurdles in travellers' security then it does not mean that railway ministry has created these hurdles. So, Assumption I does not implicit. Indicate Assumption II is implicit because it the problem for which railway ministry has an initiative.

If initiative is taken then it is possible to make train journey safe. So, Assumption III is also implicit.

26. (*c*) Assumptions I and II are not related to the statement, so they are not implicit. Assumption III is implicit because for a dog show, dogs are need to be trained.

27. (*c*) Assumption I is not implicit due to the word 'always'. From the statement it is clear that a person can be convicted on the basis of 'dying declaration.' So, Assumption II is implicit. It is possible to distinguish whether a statement is doubtful or not. So, Assumption III is also implicit.

28. (*b*) These type of notices have a positive impact on people, so Assumption I is implicit. It cannot be definitely said that for what purpose the money collected as penalty may be used. So, Assumption II is not implicit. Assumption III is implicit because people generally pay heed to such notices.

29. (*e*) The phrase 'nuclear war' used in the statement indicates that India and Pakistan are equipped with nuclear weapons. The word 'mistaken' implies that these two countries do not have the sophisticated sensors that could determine the difference between a natural NEO and a nuclear detonation. The possibility of war is only possible when these two countries do not have good relationship with each other. So, all the three assumptions are implicit.

30. (*b*) The response of the public to the circus shows during the last seven days is considerably good. So, it can be assumed that the similar response may be expected in the extended days. So, Assumption II is implicit. Assumptions I and III are not related to the statement, so they are not implicit.

31. (*d*) It is clear from the statement that training given to employees is essential for increasing productivity and profitability. So, Assumptions I and II are implicit. Assumption III is not related to the statement, so it is not implicit.

32. (*d*) This court notice is given after assuming that people will follow this notice. So, Assumption I is not implicit while III is implicit. While describing this problem, school children and college students are mentioned. So, Assumption II is implicit.

33. (*c*) The statement implies that gifts are given to loved ones. It is assumed that such advertisements generally influence people. In the advertisement, chocolate has been recommended as gift. So, all the three assumptions are implicit.

34. (*c*) Assumption I is the contrary of the given statement. So, it is not implicit. Assumption II is implicit because more investment means better GDP growth. Assumption III is not related to the statement, so it is not implicit.

35. (*d*) To attain the target of 7% of GDP the gross fixed capital formation has to increase. So, it is not implicit.

The economist believe to attain that growth level, so their is no direct relation of growth rate with capital formation. So, Assumption II is not implicit. The word 'only indicator' is not correct, so Assumption III is not implicit.

36. (*c*) The RBI Governor said that there would not be 'further weakening' of rupee. It means that rupee has weakened in the recent past. So, Assumption I is implicit. Assumption II is not related to the statement, so it is not implicit. The word 'adequate' implies that currencies do not fall after a certain level. So, Assumption III is implicit.

37. (*e*) It is clear that none of the assumption is implicit.

38. (*c*) It is only said in the statement that the name was miss-spelt and that is regretted. It would not be proper to draw assumptions such as I or II. Only Assumption III is implicit. If it were not desirable, then the name would be spelt correctly.

39. (*c*) Only Assumption II is implicit because government as decided means private entities are capable of constructing highways within reasonable time. Assumptions I and III are not implicit.

40. (*c*) Assumptions I and II are implicit because if government has urged all the citizens and as a result people will try to save ecosystem.

41. (*c*) Only Assumption II is implicit.

42. (*a*) None is implicit.

43. (*b*) Only Assumption I is implicit.

Cumulative Exercises

Base Level

1. (*e*) There are not enough cabins that is why employee is telling the Director to provide cabins, so Assumption I is implicit. There is no cabin so others' presence certainly hinders work, so Assumption II is also implicit.

2. (*e*) Student follow the advice which is good so assumption I is implicit.

   Healthy mind has to be developed by students.

   So, assumption II is implicit.

   Hence, both the Assumption I and II are implicit.

3. (*b*) Assumption I is not implicit because there may be other cause for Ashish not preparing presentation. Secretary preparing the presentation shows that he is certainly well versed in presentation, so Assumption II is implicit.

4. (*b*) Assumption I is not implicit to the word 'most.' Employees have applied for special sabbatical leave of two years after assuming that they may be able to complete their education during the sabbatical leave. So, Assumption II is implicit.

5. (*d*) Assumption I is not implicit because in economic slowdown employees did not leave their job though their salaries are not increased. We cannot predict about future, so Assumption II is also not implicit.

6. (*a*) The college administration has given instruction after assuming that students will follow this instruction. So, Assumption I is implicit but II is not.

7. (*e*) Both the assumptions are implicit because tax so collected may be adequate to meet part of the expenses of air traffic and these passengers may be able to pay extra tax.

8. (*a*) Assumption I is implicit because the local citizens group has submitted the memorandum after assuming that it may be able to gather enough funds to develop the garden. Assumption II is not implicit.

9. (*b*) Assumption II is implicit because most of people have private vehicles and they are using it frequently.

   Assumption I is not implicit because of the word 'only'.

10. (*a*) For better health fruits are advisable because fruits are rich source of vitamin and fibres and vitamins are essential for good health. So, Assumption I is implicit and II is not implicit.

11. (*e*) Both assumptions are implicit. Anxiety levels are more during board exams result because it is the first bigger achievement and exam of life and normally students are of younger age. Also, anxiety level is more in some students rather than other students.

12. (*b*) Assumption II is implicit because the statement is 'Only first class Science graduates are eligible for the job'.

13. (*a*) Assumption I is implicit because anyone would be penalized in the non-smoking area means smoking and non-smoking areas are separated for convenience of people.

14. (*b*) Assumption I is not related to the statement so it is not implicit. Assumption II is implicit because people are standing in the queue hoping that they will get the ticket.

15. (*e*) Both the assumptions are implicit because many motorist drive their vehicles within the speed limit and many drive over-speed on the highways. Traffic police authority put up boards telling about the dangers of over-speeding on the highways for those who ignore the speed limit.

16. (*a*) Assumption I is implicit because members of the association may not attend the function because they follow their association urge. Assumption II is not implicit because management can still organise the annual function by having its members and those employees who are not following their associative urge.

17. (*e*) Both the assumptions are implicit because people will take part in meeting to solve this problem.

18. (*b*) Assumption II is implicit because people living in the shanties along the beaches may follow the advice of the municipal corporation.

19. (*e*) Both the assumptions are implicit as India desires to achieve the target of economic development and India has put a target because it is possible to achieve that target.

20. (*a*) Assumption I is implicit since the coach has given that statement that India men have potential to win the trophy. Assumption II is not implicit because if one has a potential then one always wants to perform good.

21. (*c*) Either Assumption I or II is implicit.

22. (*a*) Assumption I is implicit because debentures are issued when other sources are already used. Assumption II is not directly related to the statement, so it is not implicit.

23. (*a*) Assumption I is implicit because western dresses looks vulgar and encourage more eve teasing. Dresses are not related to concentration on studies. So, Assumption II is not implicit.

24. (*d*) None of the assumptions is implicit.

25. (*a*) Assumption I is implicit because most websites claim to be useful but infact they are not. Assumption II is not implicit because the net has a mechanism that distinguish useless sites from useful ones.

26. (*e*) Both the assumptions are implicit because a commitment is made by assuming that it will be fulfilled. So, smoke level can be determined and restricted. It means that government is committed for the welfare of its people.

27. (*e*) Both the assumptions are implicit because economic growth is supposed to create more job opportunities. If unemployment is increased inspite of economic growth then it means that there are certain other factors which influence employment.

28. (*d*) Both the assumptions are not implicit because they are not directly related to the statement.

29. (*a*) If a journey from Bengaluru to Delhi is possible by plane, then it is obvious that the two cities are connected by air route. Hence, Assumption I is implicit. Assumption II is not implicit as the other mode of transport has not been discussed in the given statement.

30. (*b*) Assumption I is not implicit as it is not connected with the given statement. Assumption II is implicit because if we laugh, then it is a sign of happiness.

31. (*b*) Assumption II is a clear assumption as it is hidden in the given statement. But Assumption I is irrelevant because of the word 'All'.

32. (*b*) Assumption I is obvious as if it is said that the values of life is different for educated, uneducated persons, then it is obvious that education has its impact on the values of life of a person. Assumption II is not connected with the given statement.

33. (*d*) From given statement, it is clear that at present skill sets, employee XYZ is feeling uncomfortable of handling the project and similar training programme are available in his own country as well but it is also possible that this training programme is not related to his present project. So, we can say for the given statement both Assumptions I and II are implicit.

34. (*b*) Assumptions I and II are not directly related to the statement, so they are not implicit. Assumption III is implicit because from the advertisement of the company it is clear that booking a luxuries flat is very easy now.

35. (*b*) Assumption I is not implicit because job opportunities for women is not the perspective of the minister. Assumptions II and III are implicit because from the statement it can be assumed that women are more disciplined than men on the roads and this will increase chances of safety for commuters.

36. (*b*) Assumption I is implicit because people were surprised to see large number of participants which was not expected. Assumptions II and III are not implicit because they are not directly related to the statement.

37. (*e*) All the three assumptions are implicit. Company X wants to invite tender from those firms which were less defaulter. This time it wants percentage of default lesser and it expects quality and professional approach from its suppliers, so it is watching the quality of performance of its suppliers.

38. (*a*) From the statement, it is clear that at present company 'S' is selecting candidates without conducting a written examination. A written exam can help to identify competent persons. So, Assumptions I and II are implicit. Assumption III is not implicit as it is going against the statement.

39. (*d*) Statement is concerned about the inadequate number of staff and lack of physical facilities in the industrial and labour courts. When a office has good physical facilities then the efficiency of its employees is increased. So, all the three assumptions are implicit.

40. (*e*) Assumption I is implicit because thinking too much reduces the ability to spot potential problems and react to them safely. Assumptions II and III are not implicit because they are not correlated to the statement.

41. (*d*) From the statement it is clear that only two companies in the world are ISO 9002 certified in the line of business of company X. So, getting ISO 9002 in the line of business of company X is not easy and company X has reached up so high because it desires to expand its business. So, Assumptions II and III are implicit. Assumption I is not implicit because it is not clear from the statement that how many companies are there in the line of business of company X.

42. (*d*) From the statement it is clear that advertisement can influence people and some people will buy Z-T.V. It can be assumed that the sale of Z-T.V. may be on downward trend that is why its owner advertise their new product. So, Assumptions II and III are implicit. Assumption I is not implicit because it cannot be said surely that the sale of Z-T.V. will increase.

43. (*a*) Assumption I is implicit because normally people like durable shoes and that is why that advertisement was given. Advertisement was given in newspaper A, it means that many people read the newspaper A and people who read newspaper also read advertisements in it. So, Assumptions II and III are not implicit.

44. (*d*) From the tone of the statement, it is clear that walking barefoot for miles on dirty roads should be considered adventurous. The comparison is made between walking barefoot and rafting or glinding. So, all the three assumptions are implicit.

45. (*c*) The exchange offer on furniture does not mean that there is no demand for furniture products. So, Assumption I is not implicit. The given advertisement is 'simplest' and 'cost effective', so Assumption II is also not implicit. Assumption III is implicit because some customers want to keep their home upto-date with reasonable cost and with less hassles and that is why that advertisement was given.

46. (*b*) From the statement, it is clear that there had been some serious incidents in that area, so the situation become tense and out of control. If people remain in their home then they cannot go to their offices. So, Assumptions I and II are implicit. It cannot be said that when it will be normal. So, Assumption III is not implicit.

47. (*a*) The word 'natural' in the statement means that artificial honey can be prepared. So, Assumption I is implicit. Assumptions II and III are not correlated to the statement, so they are not implicit.

48. (*e*) Menace of smoking cannot be reduced till the smoking is shown in movies. Smoking in movies results in corresponding increase in smoking among the public. Menace of smoking can be reduced by proper planning followed by appropriate efforts. So, all the three assumptions are implicit.

49. (*d*) From the statement it is clear that drug addiction is increasing in the capital. So, Assumption I is implicit. Jhuggi-jhopari dwellers in Delhi can be seen pedaling with small pouches of smack and brown sugar. This means that they would do anything for money. So, Assumption III is implicit. Assumption II is not implicit because nothing is given about this in the statement.

50. (*b*) Either Assumption I or II is implicit because judges were suspended because they were negligent in discharging their duties or a charge of misconduct was against them. Assumption III is not correlated to the statement, so it is not implicit.

51. (*e*) When a price of a product is decreased, its sale is increased. So, Assumption I is implicit. Other companies may or may not reduce their prices. So, either Assumption II or III is implicit.

52. (*c*) The request was made to improve Indian institutes. A request is made after assuming its positive response. So, Assumptions I and III are implicit. Assumption II is not implicit because it does not correlate with the statement.

53. (*e*) The warning was made because leaning out of a moving train is dangerous. Warning are made because they have some positive effect. Passengers' safety is the duty of railway authorities. So, all the three assumptions are implicit.

Advance Level

1. (*b*) From given statement, it is clear that by using fodder G cattle will remain healthy, but it is not clear that cattle fodder G does not contain nitrate.
It is true that nitrate is toxic to all living beings.
So, only Assumption II is implicit.

2. (*c*) People may travel to their work places by their own cars or they can go by newly introduced air-conditioned buses. So, either Assumption I or II is implicit.

3. (*a*) After this amnesty scheme many defaulting housing societies may now opt for amnesty scheme and pay up their dues. So, Assumption I is implicit but Assumption II is not implicit because it is not correlated with the statement.

4. (*e*) Mr X started at 9:00 am from his residence after assuming that he may be able to reach the meeting place before 11:00 am. He has given instructions to his assistant so his assistant may be able to arrive at the venue before commencement of the meeting. So, both the assumptions are implicit.

5. (*d*) Assumption I is going against the statement, so it is not implicit. Assumption II is also not implicit due to the word 'all'.

6. (*a*) Instances of dacoity and looting can be controlled by deploying policeman, so Assumption I is implicit.
Training passengers is not implicit as everyday the passengers will going to be changed.
Hence, only Assumption I is implicit.

7. (*b*) The railway authority made the announcement in advance, so commuters will be ready for that and they will not protest as the problem is genuine. So, Assumption I is not implicit. To help the commuters, municipal authority may deploy some additional buses. So, Assumption II is implicit.

8. (*e*) After the biggest private airline increases the number of flight between cities A and B, some other private airlines may also follow this step. There may be enough load on all the bigger private airlines even after this increase. So, both the assumptions are implicit.

9. (*b*) As the picnic is funded by the organisation, so management of the organisation may provide adequate funds for the picnic, so Assumption II is implicit. Assumption I is not implicit because it is going against the statement.

10. (*c*) After the 300 % increase in fees, the institute may still attract many students or due to the increase in fees many students may opt for the institutes in the city which charge less fees. So, either Assumption I or II is implicit.

11. (*d*) None of the given assumption is implicit.

12. (*a*) Assumption I is implicit because the state governments may be able to put in place the system for disbursement of government relief to the affected farmers. Assumption II is not implicit due to he word 'all the farmers.'

13. (*b*) The civic body put the huge notice board after assuming that picknickers may read this and they will be careful while venturing into the sea. So, Assumption II is implicit while Assumption I is not implicit because it is going against the statement.

14. (*a*) The public sector banks may reduce the interest on all home loans upto ₹ 25 lakh as they have to follow the government decision. So, Assumption I is implicit. Assumption II is not implicit because it is not a decision of which undue advantage can be taken.

15. (*e*) Both the assumptions are implicit because large number of people living in that locality may avail this free check up facility. The hospital has put that board after assuming that its staff may be able to cope up with the rush of people for check up.

16. (*e*) The government has taken the decision to distribute food grains at nominal price because it has enough stock to distribute for that period. The price is decided so that people living below poverty line may afford that. So, both the assumptions are implicit.

17. (*d*) Both the assumptions are not correlated with the statement, so both are not implicit.

18. (*e*) Both the assumptions are implicit because after pulling emergency brakes the truck driver may be able to stop the truck before it hits the auto rickshaw. As the truck may stop, the auto rickshaw driver may be able to steer his vehicle away.

19. (*e*) Both the assumptions are implicit because the patient may follow the doctor's advice and if he stops consuming alcohol then the doctor may be able to cure the patient.

20. (*a*) As employees cannot neglect the chairman's appeal, so majority of employees will stop making long personal calls. So, Assumption I is implicit but II is not.

21. (*b*) Assumption II is implicit because the money collected by organising the musical event may be substantial enough for the club to start construction. Assumption I is not implicit because it is going against the statement.

22. (*b*) Assumption I is not implicit because the notice board was put after assuming its positive response. Assumption II is implicit because the traffic police department may be able to nab most of the offenders and impound their licences.

23. (*d*) None of the assumptions is implicit because before the monsoon, municipal corporation may have shortage of water. Assumption II is not correlated with the statement.

24. (*a*) After seeing that heavy penalty was imposed on those who were trying to cross the railway track, people may refrain from crossing railway track in future. So, assumption I is implicit while II is not because no one wants to pay hefty penalty.

25. (*e*) The government has made that announcement because it has adequate funds to run these programmes. By these programmes, affected people may be able to get atleast one meal a day. So, both the assumptions are implicit.

26. (*d*) None of the assumptions is implicit because seats can be increased when there is enough infrastructure and these type of decisions generally take enough time.

27. (*a*) Assumption I is implicit because government assumes that heatwaves may not continue beyond a fortnight. Assumption II is not correlated with the statement, so it is not implicit.

28. (*a*) The largest domestic airlines corporation has made the announcement that more number of flights in trunks routes are introduced because it assumes that more number of passengers may travel in trunk routes. So, Assumption I is implicit. Assumption II is not implicit because no information is given about other routes.

29. (*e*) Both the assumptions are implicit because company officials may be able to make all the necessary preparations for the silver jubilee celebrations and majority of guest invited by the chairman may attend the function.

30. (*b*) By decreasing the price of a product, its sale can be increased. So, Assumption II is implicit. Assumption I is not correlated with the statement, so it is not implicit.

31. (*d*) None of the assumptions is implicit.

32. (*e*) Both the assumptions are implicit because after this appeal many residents may reduce consumption of potable water and many activities may welcome this move.

33. (*a*) From the given statement, it is clear that Madhu is a friend of A, because A tells B about Madhu. So, it is clear that B knows Madhu.

Therefore, Statements I and II are implicit.

34. (*b*) The statements tells the importance of the book. The wishes of laymen is not included in the statement. So, Assumption I is not implicit. Assumptions II and III are implicit due to the words 'not always' and 'difficult' respectively.

35. (*c*) Assumption I is not implicit due to the word 'all.' Assumption II is implicit because the college will remain open on the date of examination. Assumption III is also implicit because students can study till the date of examination.

36. (*d*) That advertisement is giving after knowing that people aspire for owning a car. The words 'new car' in the statement implies that people do not want to buy used cars. The words 'just ₹ 1999 per month' means that most people can afford to pay ₹ 1999 per month for a new car. So, all the three assumptions are implicit.

37. (*b*) Assumption I is not implicit due to the words 'no other bank.' People may choose bank X for their financial transactions because it is providing 'home service' to open a bank account. When a bank account is opened they will do their financial transaction in it. From the advertisement it is clear that nowadays banking has become very competitive. So, Assumptions II and III are implicit.

38. (*b*) When the factories will be shifted outside the city then the pollution level in the city in future may reduce. As it is planned to shift them outside the city, it means that enough usable land is available there. So, Assumptions I and II are implicit. Statement is not talking about profit so Assumption III is not implicit.

39. (*d*) It is clear that according to company X, mechanical engineers are better performers. That advertisement was given because company X needs supervisors. That advertisement was given to attract mechanical engineers. So, all the three assumptions are implicit.

40. (*c*) It is clear from the statement that people like to see a product before buying. So, Assumption I is not implicit. This is an uncommon advertisement and people may attract and come to see the product. So, Assumptions II and III are implicit.

41. (*d*) Assumption I is not correlated with the statement, so it is not implicit. The management institution is charging ₹ 25000 for financial constraints to it will be purposefully. It is possible that organisation providing employment may select less number of students in future. So, Assumptions II and III are implicit.

42. (*b*) The word refrain does not relate with information in the statement hence Assumption I is not implicit.

Government appointing a committee is also not relate to statement, hence Assumption II is not implicit.

43. (*a*) Rabindranath Tagore was a poet and every poet has aesthetic knowledge which is a part of axiological study. So, Assumption I is implicit.

Assumption II is not implicit as the word base of logic and ethics does not relate the statement.

44. (*e*) At present 10% of villages in the state receive 24 h electricity so 90% villages have either no electricity or less than 24 h of electricity.

Next year government will add 16% more villages to the list. So, Assumption I is implicit.

Assumption II is also implilcit as the government has failed to provide electricity to all the villages for the whole day at present and in future.

45. (*e*) Modifications in the education system in a major part imply that the present educational system was not proper and needed modification or changes.

So, both the assumptions are implicit in the statement.

3 Statement and Arguments

Argument *is a sequence of two or more phrases/clauses/sentences that includes a claim or conclusion. We arrive at such conclusion with the help of one or more than one statements which may be called premise or proposition.*

Arguments are generally based on certain premises, assumptions and conclusions. An argument can be in favour or against the statement. You have to check the strength of the argument. You should not be confused that only favourable arguments are considerable. So, it is irrelevant that an argument is favourable or against the statement.

One will have a better idea about argument with following example:

> e.g. If one says that 'Sachin Tendulkar is a great batsman', then he will have to put some evidences to support and prove his point of view. But someone else may have opposite point of view i.e. 'Tendulkar is not a great batsman'. In this case, the person opposing the greatness of Tendulkar too, will put some evidences in support of his negation. Therefore, we can firmly say that an argument may be either in favour of or against a certain subject.

Now, we can divide the given statement into three parts

(i) **Premise** Virat Kohli is the most attacking batsman in today's cricket.

(ii) **Assumption** (Hidden premise), An attacking batsman is able to score 50 runs in 4 overs.

(iii) **Conclusion** India will score required 50 runs in 4 overs.

Hence, it is clear that an argument is a substantial proof that we put forward to support over a point of view on a particular matter.

A Strong Argument is that which is important and touches the practical and real aspect of the situation as described in the statement.

A Weak Argument is that which is less important and superfluous.

Points to be Taken Into Consideration while Choosing a Strong Argument

- A strong argument should give the realistic diagnosis of the situation described in the statement.
- A strong argument should give the deep analysis of the topic dealt within the statement.
- A strong argument should relate with the statement and be supported up by facts or established notions.
- There should be consistency and conformity in arguments with the prevailing ideas and truth.
- A strong argument should not be mere reiteration of the situation given in the statement.
- Arguments should not be based on assumption.
- The argument should be specific, not generalised.
- The argument should not be ambiguous.
- There should not be material fallacy in the argument i.e. there should not be a fallacy of composition, division, equivocation or amphibology uncritical analogy.

Basic Method to Check Argumentation

Some of the basic methods are given below to find out the 'Strong Argument'

1. **Identify the conclusion in the argument**
   The conclusion can be anywhere in the given passage. Conclusions generally use phrases like 'so', 'therefore', 'hence', 'thus', 'consequently', 'as a result', 'it follows that,' 'which proves' etc., before conclusion.
2. **Find out what is being assumed**
   It is not necessary that we always have assumptions.
3. **Understand what logic is being used for arguing**
   For instance, you may try proving some points by giving example of similar situations.

Ex. This dog may become dangerous to men folk, if he regularly feeds on dead bodies in adjacent graveyard. Dogs who fed on dead in Tsunami hit areas became man-eaters and attacked the remaining people.

Sol. Though this seems to be good reason. It is not necessary that all dogs turn into man-hunters. Usually, arguments based on examples are either weak or fallacious.

Suggested Rules for Analysis of an Argument

These questions need more logic (brain work) and hence, more of practice. They have no fixed rules for reaching the solution, at the most you can work on the following rules.

***Rule* 1.** They help you in locating the 'strong argument'

(i) The argument should not be ambiguous, it should be clear in its meaning.

(ii) Look, if the argument is assumption; it assumes something but is not a fact, the argument is not strong.

(iii) The argument should not be factually incorrect. Factually incorrect one is definitely weak.

(iv) The words and phrases used in statements and arguments should be used in the same sense.

(v) The arguments that are too simple should outrightly be rejected.

(vi) Arguments may simply state "both conditions have its pros and cons" are superfluous, do not go into heart of the matter. These should be rejected for strong argument.

***Rule* 2.** If the argument is strong, then check the statements for whether the argument actually leads to the result. For this check, if the

(i) Argument should be logically feasible and must also have the probability of satisfying the statement in question.

(ii) Argument is an established fact (i.e. universally accepted or scientifically proves)

(iii) Argument taken up should be connected or linked properly to the statement.

(iv) Argument should not 'prove' something using/quoting previous examples.

Questions based on statement and argument have a statement which is followed by two or more arguments. Candidates are required to assess the statement and following arguments and then distinguish between strong and weak argument.

Flow chart for the analysis of an argument

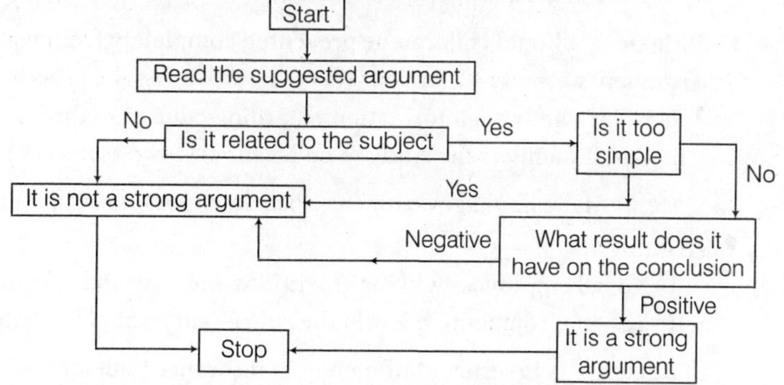

Different Cases of Hypothetical Statements

An important part of all this discussion is reasoning. We should have strong reasoning power for argumentation. The most confusing are hypothetical statements, the statements that have choices, **if-then, either-or, neither-nor**. Consider the following cases

Case I If A, then B (Hypothetical)
- Now, if A is true, B would be true.
- But if A is false, B is not necessarily false.
- If B is true, does not mean A would be true.
- If B is false, does not necessarily mean that A is false too.

Case II Either A or B (Disjunctive)
- If A is false, B is true.
- If A is true, does not mean B is necessarily false.
- If B is true, does not mean A is false.
- If B is false, A is true.

Types of Questions Asked in Different Examinations

There are multiple types of questions which are asked from the chapter 'Statement and Arguments', so it is quite difficult to predict exact type of questions that are asked but on the basis of Observation, Analysis and Experience, here we are giving different types of questions that are usually asked in the examination. Almost all the questions at this chapter can be categorised into these types. Also, this description of type will make your study easy and streamline.

Type 1 Two Arguments Based

In these types of questions, a statement is given that is followed by two arguments. Candidates are required to assess the given statement and decide which of the arguments is/are strong?

Examples Based on Type 1

Direction (Examples 1-7) ***In making decisions about important questions, it is desirable to be able to distinguish between 'strong' arguments and 'weak' arguments. 'Strong' arguments are those which are important and directly related to the question. 'Weak' arguments are those which are of minor importance and also may not be directly related to the question or may be related to a trivial aspect of the question. Each question below is followed by two arguments numbered I and II. You have to decide which of the arguments is a strong argument and which is a weak argument.***

Give answer
(a) if only Argument I is strong
(b) if only Argument II is strong
(c) if both Arguments I and II are strong
(d) if neither Argument I nor II is strong

Ex 1. **Statement** Should children be prevented completely from watching the television? **NIFT (UG) 2013**

Arguments

I. No, we get vital information regarding education through television.
II. Yes, it hampers the study of children.

Ex 2. **Statements** Should government close down loss-making public sector enterprises? **MAT 2012**

Arguments

I. No, all employees will lose their jobs, security and earning; what would they do?
II. Yes, in a competitive world the rule is 'survival of the fittest'.

Ex 3. **Statement** Is investment of money in insurance policies a wise step?

Arguments

I. Yes, it ensures security and covers risks.
II. No, by the time the policy matures, the value of money falls down considerably.

Ex **4. Statement** Should the tution fees in all post- graduate courses be hiked considerably?

Arguments

I. Yes, this will bring in some sense of seriousness among the students and will improve the quality.

II. No, this will force the meritorious poor students to stay away from post-graduate courses.

Ex **5. Statement** Keeping in consideration the longevity of life in India, should the age limit for retirement in government jobs be increased?

Arguments

I. Yes, other countries have decided so long before.

II. Yes, it is the actual demand of lakhs of employees.

Ex **6. Statement** Are educational institutions responsible for unrest among the youth?

Arguments

I. Yes, there is no discipline in educational institutions.

II. No, there is no disciplinary problem in educational institutions.

Ex **7. Statement** Should the organisations like the UNO be abolished?

Arguments

I. The cold war **is going to an end** so there is no role of such organisations.

II. No, in the absence of these organisations, there may be a world war.

SOLUTION (Examples 1-7)

1. (*a*) Television provides vital information of the surrounding world and current events that are taking place around us. Basically, it is helping the children in gaining knowledge of the outside world.
2. (*a*) Argument I is strong because a large section of employees cannot be ignored. Argument II is not strong because, it does not give any reason behind it.
3. (*a*) Insurance is meant to cover the risk of life and property and it also promotes savings. So, argument I is strong. Argument II is weak because it lacks of clear logic.
4. (*b*) Argument I is irrelevant because hike in tution fees cannot bring seriousness among students. So, this argument is weak. Argument II is strong because poor and deserving students will be affected by the hike in fees.
5. (*b*) Argument I is not strong because different countries have different culture, economy and various other factor. So, some implementations are successful in one country while failure in other country. Argument II is strong because it is the demand of lakhs of employees.
6. (*d*) Neither Argument I nor II is strong because none of them logically supports the statements.
7. (*c*) Argument I is strong because the role of UNO is to ensure friendly relation among various countries. Now, all countries. living friendly, so there is no role of UNO. Argument II is also strong because in the absence of UNO, there may be a world war.

Direction (Examples 8-9) *In making decisions about important questions, it is desirable to be able to distinguish between 'strong' arguments and 'weak' arguments. 'Strong' arguments are those which are important and directly related to the question. 'Weak' arguments are those which are of minor importance and also may not be directly related to the question or may be related to a trivial aspect of the question. Each question below is followed by two arguments numbered I and II. You have to decide which of the arguments is a strong argument and which is a weak argument.*

Give answer

(a) if only Argument I is strong
(b) if only Argument II is strong
(c) if both Arguments I and II are strong
(d) if neither Argument I nor II is strong
(e) None of the above

Ex **8. Statement** Should Indian scientists working abroad be called back to India?

Arguments **IBPS (Clerk) 2012**

I. Yes, they must serve the motherland first and forget about discoveries, honours facilities and all.

II. No, we have enough talent let them stay where they want.

Ex **9. Statement** Should higher qualification be the only criteria for internal promotions in any organisation.

Arguments **IBPS (Clerk) 2014**

I. Yes, why not? Infect only higher qualification is more important than other factors.

II. No, quality of performance and other factors are more important than mere higher qualification in case of internal promotion.

SOLUTION (Examples 8-9)

8. (*d*) Neither of the arguments is strong because I is not logical and II is more than the scope of the statement.
9. (*d*) It is a well known fact that higher qualification could not be only criteria for any kind of promotion in an organisation. Other factors are also equally important. It is very difficult to judge the higher qualification and other factors on the same scale. Therefore, neither of the arguments is strong.

Intro Exercise 1 (Based on Type 1)

Direction (Q. Nos. 1-34) *In making decisions about important questions, it is desirable to be able to distinguish between 'strong' arguments and 'weak' arguments. 'Strong' arguments are those which are important and directly related to the question. 'Weak' arguments are those which are of minor importance and also may not be directly related to the question or may be related to a trivial aspect of the question. Each question below is followed by two arguments numbered I and II. You have to decide which of the arguments is a strong argument and which is a weak argument.*

Give answer

(a) if only Argument I is strong
(b) if only Argument II is strong
(c) if either Argument I or II is strong
(d) if neither Argument I nor II is strong
(e) if both Argument I and II are strong

1. **Statement** Should the government immediately stop registration of new cars for private use throughout the country with immediate effect?

Arguments **MAT 2014**

I. No, the government does not have authority to do so.
II. Yes, this is the only way to decongest the roads of big cities in India.

2. **Statement** Should restrictions on rickshaw-pullers and prisoners for donation of blood be removed?

Arguments

I. Yes, by putting these restrictions, a large section of public are not able to donate their blood even to their own relatives in emergencies.
II. No, blood donation is meant to save people's life; if fingers are pointed towards someone's eligibility as a donor owing to possibility of non-suitable or erroneous blood, then such persons must be restricted from doing so.

3. **Statement** Should subsidy on domestic LPG cylinders be stopped?

Arguments **MAT 2012**

I. Yes, it leads to misuse of LPG by housewives who over-cook their food.
II. No, any subsidy cannot be stopped in a country committed to social welfare.

4. **Statement** Should cricket teams of smaller countries who have no long history in cricket be allowed to play in World Cup cricket matches?

Arguments **MAT 2015**

I. Yes, this will help the globalisation of cricket gentleman's game.
II. No, this will upset the records established in tougher, more challenging situations.

5. **Statement** Should we impart sex education in schools?

Arguments

I. Yes, all the progressive nations do so.
II. No, we cannot impart it in coeducational school.

6. **Statement** Should the provision to dissolve the assembly prematurely be amended?

Arguments

I. Yes, on many occasions the provision has been used by ruling governments to fulfil their vested interests.
II. No, to fulfil the constitutional obligations and norms, it sometimes becomes the need of the hour to dissolve the assembly prematurely.

7. **Statement** Should only reputed NGO's be authorised to distribute the commodities to the public under the programme of Public Distribution System (PDS)?

Arguments **NIFT (UG) 2013**

I. Yes, the move will be helpful to implement the programme more effectively and will keep a tab on various problems like black marketing of the commodities supplied under PDS.
II. Yes, NGO's have helped government on many occasions.

8. **Statement** Should the government sell major part of its stake in all the profit making public sector undertakings?

Arguments **CMAT 2014**

I. No, government should not give up its control of these undertaking as these are profit making organisations.
II. Yes, this will help government reduce the quantum of huge budgetary deficit and argument its resources.

9. **Statement** Should the private companies be allowed to operate passenger train services in India?

Arguments

I. Yes, this will improve the quality of service in Indian Railways as it will have to face severe competition.
II. No, the private companies may not agree to operate in the non-profitable sectors.

10. **Statement** Should all the electricity state boards be privatised in India?

Arguments **CMAT 2012**

I. No, this will increase the grievances of the people.
II. Yes, it will check the growing menace of power theft which has resulted in annual pilferage of a huge amount.

11. **Statement** Should voting be made compulsory for all adults?

Arguments **MAT 2013**

I. Yes, the candidates then elected would be far more representational.
II. No, the citizens would thereby loss the right to not choose a representative.

12. **Statement** Should India send its troops to a foreign country, for constructive purposes, without a UN resolution?

Arguments **NIFT (PG) 2013**

I. Yes, it will bring accolades from all over the world and will strengthen the claim for candidature for permanent membership of the UN.

II. No, India is already facing many troubles.

13. **Statement** Should students be allowed to work while they are studying?

Arguments

I. Yes, economic background of every individual does not allow them to pursue education; such allowing therefore makes it feasible to fulfil one's dream.

II. Yes, vocational education plays an important role to make a person self-sufficient. Besides, this practical knowledge becomes necessary to make studies meaningful.

14. **Statement** Should the sole evidence of a rape victim be supposed enough to prove the guilt?

Arguments

I. Yes, rape is a heinous offence.

II. No, the move will increase the chances of conviction of innocent persons.

15. **Statement** Should banks be allowed to offer different interest rates in India?

Arguments

I. Yes, this is the only way to eventually lower interest rates in the country.

II. No, this will discourage the customers and they might be compelled to switch over from one bank to another.

16. **Statement** Should the NCERT withdraw its directive for deletion of passages from History books in the CBSE curriculum?

Arguments **IIFT 2013**

I. Yes, it will adversely affect school children.

II. No, History should not be taught to school children in a one-sided manner and any distortions would have to be rectified.

17. **Statement** Should Indian government allow the neighbouring country X to dump huge quantities of vanaspati ghee into India at a price which is cheaper than market price?

Arguments **IRMA 2008**

I. No, it is a violation of the fundamental right of the farmer to grow crops and that of the industry to operate with a level playing field.

II. Yes, it is essential for India to provide shelter to all the industries of X at all costs because it is a neighbouring country.

18. **Statement** Should India stop participating in Olympic games?

Arguments

I. Yes, India has been unsuccessful in winning medals in Olympic games in spite of competing in so many events.

II. No, participation in Olympic games will help the sports persons improve their performance standards.

19. **Statement** Should there be equivalent salary structure for different states and central government employees?

Arguments **CMAT 2013**

I. No, state government has limited resources available at their disposal and hence these employees may be paid less than the central government employees.

II. Yes, all are government employees and they go out similar functions and hence there should be equivalent salaries.

20. **Statement** Should the state level taxes on goods be abolished?

Arguments

I. Yes, instead there should be a consolidated central tax on all commodities.

II. No, the states will incur huge loss due to less collection of taxes.

21. **Statement** Should the maintenance of all the roads in the big cities be handed over to private organisations against a fixed amount to be paid by the residents?

Arguments **MAT 2012**

I. No, this is not at all practicable.

II. Yes, this practice is adopted in many foreign countries.

22. **Statement** Should the graduate doctors be made to work in rural areas for atleast two years before they are given licence for practice?

Arguments

I. Yes, otherwise the rural areas will always have shortage of qualified medical practitioners.

II. No, the choice should be given to the graduate doctors to decide their place of work.

23. **Statement** Should military training of 3 years be made compulsory to all able-bodied youths in India?

Arguments **NIFT (UG) 2012**

I. Yes, similar practice is being followed in some developed countries.

II. No, compulsion spoils the best in everything.

24. **Statement** Should all the utility services be immediately brought under essential services to avoid frequent agitation and strikes by the employees?

Arguments **CMAT 2012**

I. No, otherwise how the employees may voice their grievances and demands?

II. Yes, the employees are becoming more and more greedy and they take the general public for ride by striking work.

25. **Statement** Do children adopted from poor families love their new rich parents like their own poor ones?

Arguments

I. Yes, because they are loved, cared for and provided with comforts of life.

II. No, because in the criminal world, they become selfish and hard-boiled.

26. Statement Should schools invite IIT students to give practical tips on science subjects?

Arguments

I. Yes, IIT students can be a boon to the careers of science students by giving them proper guidance that they certainly require at the stage of their schooling.

II. No, IIT students have more vital responsibilities to carry out for which they have been prepared.

27. Statement Should jobs be declined with academic degrees and diplomas?

Arguments

I. No, a very large number of persons with meagre academic qualification will apply.

II. No, importance of higher education will be diminished.

28. Statement Should women be exempted from wearing helmets?

Arguments

I. Yes, it doesn't look good on women.

II. No, it compromises on their safety.

29. Statement Should state police or central police be banned from firing indiscriminately on the rampant mob in a trouble-torn area?

Arguments

I. Yes, humans should always be treated in a humanitarian way.

II. No, this is the only way to restrict the rampant mob from indulging in illegal activities.

30. Statement Should competitive examinations for selecting candidates for job consist thorough objective test only?

Arguments

I. Yes, the assessment of objective test is reliable.

II. No, the number of questions to be answered is always very large.

31. Statement Should corruption-free services from the bureaucrats be made a fundamental right for the citizens of India?

Arguments

I. Yes, the move will eliminate corruption from the bureaucracy and bring happiness to the citizen.

II. No, this will give a free hand to citizens to intervene in the work of bureaucracy and discourage the bureaucrats.

32. Statement Should Indian players, who have played for India on International level, be allowed to work as coach for the team of other countries?

Arguments

I. Yes, that experience which does not harm one's nation must be used to benefit others.

II. No, this will put the prestige of the country in danger because these coaches will reveal our team's weaknesses to other teams.

33. Statement Should the pension schemes in government services be abolished?

Arguments

I. Yes, this will reduce the number of aspiring candidates to a great extent and it will be easy for the common man to get into government services.

II. No, this will destroy the very purpose of providing financial help to the employee so that they can sustain themselves in old age.

34. Statement Should bomb disposal squads be given cooperation by the public?

Arguments

I. Yes, they are necessary to rescue people's lives.

II. No, they are a nuisance to day-to-day life.

Direction (Q. Nos. 35-40) *In making decisions about important questions, it is desirable to be able to distinguish between 'strong' arguments and 'weak' arguments. 'Strong' arguments are those which are important and directly related to the question. 'Weak' arguments are those which are of minor importance and also may not be directly related to the question or may be related to a trivial aspect of the question. Each question below is followed by two arguments numbered I and II. You have to decide which of the arguments is a strong argument and which is a weak argument.*

Give answer

(a) if only Argument I is strong
(b) if only Argument II is strong
(c) if either Argument I or II is strong
(d) if neither Argument I nor II is strong
(e) if both Arguments I and II are strong

35. Statement Should the railways in India be privatised in a phased manner like other public sector enterprises?

Arguments **IBPS (Clerk) 2014**

I. Yes, this is the only way to bring in competitiveness and provide better service to the public.

II. No, this will pose a threat to national security of our country as multinationals will enter into the fray.

36. Statement Can education be ensured as a fundamental right without tackling the problem of child labour in India?

Arguments

I. Yes, the root cause of child labour lies in the problem of depriving the child of education.

II. No, the root causes which makes a child deprived of education are the compulsion of its family and the circumstances which force a child to resort to child labour.

37. Statement Should MLA's and MPs be allowed to change parties?

Arguments

I. Yes, every individual in democratic set up is free to leave or join any party any time.

II. No, they should remain faithful to the party which nominated them as its candidate.

38. Statement Should an electricity-surplus state at one end of the country supply electricity to an electricity deficient state at the other end?

Arguments

I. Yes, such a move will benefit both the states —one will get the money, the other the electricity.

II. No, a cross-country transfer of electricity will involve huge transmission losses.

39. Statement Should there be complete ban on manufacture of fire-crackers in India?

Arguments

I. No, this will render thousands of workers jobless.

II. Yes, the fire-cracker manufacturers use child labour to a large extent.

40. Statement Should doctors and engineers be banned from civil services examination?

Arguments

I. No, banning engineers and medicos from joining civil services means denying the best talent in the land to work for the welfare of the society.

II. Yes, taxpayers money is being used to finance the studies of doctors and engineers, particularly in government institutes. The money spent on them goes down the drain once a medico or engineer shifts tracks to civil services.

Type 2 More than Two Arguments

In this type of questions, a statement is given that is followed by more than two arguments. Candidates are required to choose the group of arguments which are strong in context of the given statement.

Examples Based on Type 2

Ex **1. Statement** Should the institutes of higher learnings in India like IITs and IIMs be made totally free from government control?

Arguments **IBPS (PO) 2013**

I. Yes, such institutes in the developed countries are run by non-government agencies.

II. No, government needs to regulate functions of these institutes for national interest.

III. No, these institutes are not capable to take policy decisions for smooth functioning.

(a) Only I is strong (b) Only II is strong
(c) Only III is strong (d) I and III are strong
(e) None of these

Sol. (*b*) Argument I is not strong because it is like an example. Argument II is strong because government control makes it work in national interest Argument III is not a logical argument.

Ex **2. Statement** Is it necessary that education should be job oriented?

Arguments **SSC (CGL) 2011**

I. Yes, the aim of education is to prepare persons for earning.

II. Yes, educated person should stand on his own feet after completion of education.

III. No, education should be for sake of knowledge only.

IV. No, one may take up agriculture where education is not necessary.

(a) I and II are strong (b) III and IV are strong
(c) Only I is strong (d) I and III are strong

Sol. (*a*) Arguments I and II are strong. Education is meant for job, so that one should stand on his own feet after completion of education. The word 'only' makes the Argument III week and Argument IV is not relevant.

Ex **3. Statement** Should there be reservation of jobs in the organisations in the private sector also as in the public sector undertakings in India?

Arguments

I. Yes, this would give more opportunities of development to the weaker sections of the society and thus help reduce the gap between the affluent and the downtrodden in India.

II. No, the private sector does not get any government assistance and therefore, they should not be saddled with such policies.

III. No, now where else in the world such a practice is being followed.

IV. No, the management of the private sector undertaking would not agree to such compulsions.

(a) Only I is strong (b) I and II are strong
(c) I, II and IV are strng (d) I and IV are strong
(e) All are strong

Sol. (*a*) Argument I is strong because it gives more opportunities for the weaker section to grow and reduces the gap between the affluent and the downtrodden. Arguments II, III and IV are vague or they are not strong to support the statement.

Intro Exercise 2 (Based on Type 2)

Direction (Q. Nos. 1-12) *Each question below is followed by three arguments numbered I, II and III. You have to decide which of the arguments is 'strong' and which is 'weak'.*

1. **Statement** Should there be a common pay structure of the central government and all state government employees in the country?

Arguments **IBPS RRB (PO) 2014**

I. No, each state government should have the freedom to decide the pay structure of its employees.

II. No, the workload and responsibilities of central government and state government employees differ and hence there should be different pay structure.

III. Yes, all are government employees fall in similar category and hence they should be treated equally irrespective of their working with central government or any state government.

(a) Only I is strong
(b) I and III are strong
(c) Only III is strong
(d) II and III are strong
(e) None of the above

2. **Statement** Should there be a complete ban on genetically modified imported seeds?

Arguments

I. Yes, this will boost the demand of domestically developed seeds.

II. No, this is the only way to increase production substantially.

III. Yes, genetically modified products will adversely affect the health of those who consume these products.

(a) I and II are strong
(b) Only II is strong
(c) II and III are strong
(d) I and III are strong
(e) All are strong

3. **Statement** Should there be only few banks in place of numerous smaller banks in India?

Arguments **NMAT 2012**

I. Yes, this will help to secure the investor's money as these big banks will be able to withstand intermittent market related shocks.

II. No, a large number of people will lose their jobs as after the merger many employees will be redundant.

III. Yes, this will help consolidate the entire banking industry and will lead to healthy competition.

(a) None is strong
(b) I and II are strong
(c) II and III are strong
(d) I and III are strong

4. **Statement** Should there be a complete ban on Indian professionals seeking jobs elsewhere after getting their education in India?

Arguments **NMAT 2012**

I. Yes, this is the only way to sustain present rate of technological development in India.

II. No, the Indians settled abroad send huge amount of foreign exchange and this constitutes a significant part of foreign exchange reserve.

III. No, the practical knowledge gained by Indians by working in other countries help India to develop its economy.

(a) None is strong (b) All are strong
(c) I and II are strong (d) Only III is strong

5. **Statement** Should the government take over all the private passenger transport companies across the country.

Arguments **CMAT 2014**

I. Yes, this should be done as the government runs the railways.

II. No, governments does not have expertise to handle such operations.

III. Yes, this way general public can be taken out of the clutches of the private transport companies.

(a) Only I is strong
(b) I and II are strong
(c) II and III are strong
(d) None of the above

6. **Statement** Should the parliamentary elections in India be held every three years as against five years at present?

Arguments

I. No, this will enhance wastage of money and resources.

II. Yes, this will help the voters to change non-performing representatives without much delay.

III. No, the elected representatives will not have enough time to settle and concentrate on developmental activities.

(a) None is strong (b) I and II are strong
(c) II and III are strong (d) I and III are strong
(e) All are strong

7. **Statement** Should 'literacy' be the minimum criterion for becoming a voter in India?

Arguments

I. No, mere literacy is no guarantee of political maturity of an individual.

II. Yes, illiterate people are less likely to make politically wiser decisions of voting for a right candidate or party.

III. No, voting is the constitutional right of every citizen.

(a) None is strong (b) I and II are strong
(c) III is strong (d) II and III are strong
(e) All are strong

8. Statement Should the public sector undertakings be followed to adopt hire and fire policy?

Arguments **NMAT 2011**

I. Yes, this will help the public sector undertakings to get rid of non-performing employees and reward the performing employees.

II. No, this will give an unjust handle to the management and they may use it indiscriminately.

III. Yes, this will help increase the level of efficiency of these organisation and these will become profitable establishments.

(a) None is strong (b) I and II are strong
(c) II and III are strong (d) I and III are strong

9. Statement Should administrative officers be transferred after one or two years?

Arguments

I. Yes, they get friendly with local people and are manipulated by them.

II. No, by the time their policies and schemes start taking shape, they have to leave.

III. No, this will create a lot of administrative hassles and cause a lot of inconvenience to the officers.

(a) Only II is strong (b) I and II are strong
(c) II and III are strong (d) I and III are strong
(e) All are strong

10. Statement Should all the students graduating in any discipline desirous of pursuing post graduation of the subjects of their choice be allowed to enroll in the post graduate courses?

Arguments **SNAP 2010**

I. Yes, the students are the best judge of their capabilities and there should not be restrictions for joining post graduate courses.

II. No, the students need to study relevant subjects in graduate courses to enroll in post graduate courses and the students must fulfill such conditions.

III. No, there are not enough institutes offering post graduate courses which can accommodate all the graduates desirous of seeking post graduate education of their own choice.

(a) All are strong (b) I and II are strong
(c) II and III are strong (d) None of these

11. Statement Should admission to all professional courses be made on the basis of past academic performance rather than through entrance tests?

Arguments

I. Yes, it will be beneficial for those candidates who are unable to bear the expenses of entrance tests.

II. Yes, many deserving candidates securing high marks in their qualifying academic examinations do not perform well on such entrance tests.

III. No, the standard of examinations and assessment conducted by different boards and universities are not comparable and hence there is a need to conduct entrance tests to calibrate them on a common yardstick.

(a) I and II are strong (b) II and III are strong
(c) I and III are strong (d) Only III is strong
(e) All are strong

12. Statement Should there be only one university throughout India?

Arguments

I. Yes, this is the only way to bring about uniformity in the educational standards.

II. No, this is administratively very tough task.

III. Yes, this will make the degrees procured by students, comparable for offering jobs.

(a) None is strong (b) I and II are strong
(c) II and III are strong (d) I and III are strong
(e) All are strong

Direction (Q. Nos. 13-17) *Each question below is followed by three arguments numbered I, II and III. You have to decide which of the arguments is a 'strong' argument and which is a 'weak' argument.*

13. Statement Should there be complete ban on setting up of thermal power plants in India?

Arguments **SBI (PO) 2010**

I. Yes, this is the only way to arrest further addition to environmental pollution.

II. No, there is a huge shortage of electricity in most parts of the country and hence generation of electricity needs to be augmented.

III. No, many developed countries continue to set up thermal power plants in their countries.

(a) None is strong (b) Only I is strong
(c) Only II is strong (d) Only III is strong
(e) Either I or II is strong

14. Statement Should road repair work in big cities be carried out only late at night?

Arguments

I. No, this way the work will never get completed.

II. No, there will be unnecessary use of electricity.

III. Yes, the commuters will face a lot of problems due to repair work during the day.

(a) None is strong (b) Only I is strong
(c) Only III is strong (d) II and III are strong
(e) I and II are strong

15. Statement Should all the deemed universities be derecognized and attached to any of the central or state universities in India?

Arguments

I. Yes, many of these deemed universities do not conform to there required standards of a full-fledged university and hence the level of education is compromised.

II. No, these deemed universities have been able to introduce innovative courses suitable to the requirement of various industries as they are free from strict government controls.

III. Yes, many such universities are basically money spinning activities and education takes a backseat in these institutions.

(a) I and II are strong (b) II and III are strong
(c) I and III are strong (d) All are strong
(e) None of these

16. Statement Should there be a cap on drawing groundwater for irrigation purposes in India?

Arguments

I. No, irrigation is of prime importance for food production in India and it is heavily dependent on groundwater in many parts of the country.

II. Yes, water levels have gone down to a alarmingly low levels in some parts of the country where irrigation is primarily dependent on groundwater, which may lead to serious environmental consequences.

III. Yes, India just cannot afford to draw groundwater any further as the international agencies have cautioned India against it.

(a) I and II are strong
(b) II and III are strong
(c) I and III are strong
(d) All are strong
(e) None of the above

17. Statement Should there be a restriction on the construction of high rise buildings in big cities in India?

Arguments

I. No, big cities in India do not have adequate open land plots to accommodate the growing population.

II. Yes, only the builders and developers benefit from the construction of high rise buildings.

III. Yes, the government should first provide adequate infrastructural facilities to existing buildings before allowing the construction of new high rise buildings.

(a) Only II is strong (b) Only III is strong
(c) I and III are strong (d) Only I is strong
(e) None of these

Direction (Q. Nos. 18-22) *Each question below is followed by three/four arguments numbered* I, II, III *and* IV. *You have to decide which of the arguments is a 'strong' argument and which is a 'weak' argument.*

18. Statement Should the rule of wearing helmet for both driver and pillion rider while driving a motorbike be enforced strictly?

Arguments

I. Yes, it is a rule and should be followed strictly by all.

II. No, each individual knows how to protect his own life and it should be left to his discretion.

III. No, it does not ensure safety as only the head is protected and rest of the body is not.

IV. Yes, it is a necessity as head, being the most sensitive organ, is protected by the helmet.

(a) None is strong (b) I and III are strong
(c) I and IV are strong (d) II and IV are strong
(e) All are strong

19. Statement Should the income generated out of agricultural activities be taxed?

Arguments

I. No, farmers are otherwise suffering from natural calamities and low yield coupled with low procurement price and their income should not be taxed.

II. Yes, majority of the population is dependent on agriculture and hence their income should be taxed to augment the resources.

III. Yes, many big farmers earn much more than the majority of the service earners and they should be teased to remove the disparity.

(a) All are strong (b) I and II are strong
(c) II and III are strong (d) All are strong
(e) None of these

20. Statement Should all the indirect taxes in India be combined into a single tax on all commodities?

Arguments

I. Yes, this will considerably simplify the tax collection mechanism and the cost of collecting tax will also reduce.

II. Yes, the manufacturers and traders will be benefited by this which in turn will boost tax collection.

III. No, no other country has adopted such system.

(a) None is strong (b) I and III are strong
(c) Only II is strong (d) II and III are strong
(e) None of these

21. Statement Should all the management institutes in the country be brought under government control?

Arguments

I. No, the government does not have adequate resources to run such institutes effectively.

II. No, each institute should be given freedom to function on its own.

III. Yes, this will enable to have standardized education for all the students.

IV. Yes, only then the quality of education would be improved.

(a) None is strong
(b) I, II and III are strong
(c) I and II are strong
(d) All are strong
(e) Only III is strong

22. Statement Should the consumption of aerated drinks be banned in India?

Arguments

I. Yes, this is the only way to reduce the risk of exposing people to some diseases.

II. No, each individual should have right to choose what he wants.

III. No, there is no confirmed evidence that such products have adverse effects on human body.

IV. Yes, it is banned in many other countries also.

(a) Only I is strong
(b) I and II are strong
(c) Only III is strong
(d) I and IV are strong
(e) All are strong

Cumulative Exercise

Base Level

Direction (Q. Nos. 1-15) *In making decisions about important questions, it is desirable to be able to distinguish between "Strong" arguments and "Weak" arguments insofar as they relate to the question. "Strong" arguments are those which are both important and directly related to the questions. "Weak" arguments are those which are of minor importance and also may not be directly related to the questions or may be related to a trivial aspect of the questions.*

Give answer

(a) if only Argument I is strong
(b) if only Argument II is strong
(c) if either Argument I or II is strong
(d) if neither Argument I nor II is strong
(e) if both Arguments I and II are strong

1. Statement Should young entrepreneurs be encouraged?

Arguments **NIFT (PG) 2013**

I. Yes, they will help in the industrial development in the country.

II. Yes, they will reduce the burden on the employment market.

2. Statement Should there be a complete ban on use of pesticides in agricultural sector?

Arguments **MAT 2014**

I. Yes, this the only way to save the underground water from getting polluted with such dangerous chemicals.

II. No this will adversely affect the agricultural production and the pests will damage the crops.

3. Statement Should all the criminals convicted for committing murder be awarded capital punishment?

Arguments **IIFT 2012**

I. Yes, this will be a significant step towards reducing cases of murder in future.

II. No, nobody has the right to take any person's life irrespective of the acts of such individuals.

4. Statement Should India support all the international policies of United States of America?

Arguments **MAT 2013**

I. No, many other powerful countries do not support the same.

II. Yes, this is the only way to gain access to USA developmental funds.

5. Statement Should government standardize rent for rented houses in big cities in India?

Arguments **NIFT (UG) 2012**

I. No, it is an interference in the relationship between landlord and tenant.

II. Yes, government can do it, provided it has political will to do it.

6. Statement Should India carry out free tests of nuclear weapons?

Arguments **MAT 2013**

I. Yes, this will send a stern message to the whole world that India is serious to defend herself by any means from aggression.

II. No, the international community will isolate India and this will bring a set back to Indian economy.

7. Statement Should the subsidy on kerosene be immediately increased further?

Arguments **MAT 2012**

I. Yes, this will bring considerable relief to the poorer section of the society as they will be the major beneficiary.

II. No, our economy is otherwise in a difficult stage and it will not be able to with stand any further burden on it.

8. Statement Should all the rivers of India be brought under Central Water Commission?

Arguments **MAT 2013**

I. Yes, it will ensure equal distribution of water to the states.

II. No, because it will be contrary to the geographical conditions in the states.

9. Statement Should all the drugs patented and manufactured in western countries be first tried out on sample basis before giving licence for sale to general public in India?

Arguments **NIFT (PG) 2013**

I. Yes, many such drugs require different doses and duration for Indian population and hence, it is necessary.

II. No, this is just not feasible and hence, cannot be implemented.

10. Statement Should the system of paying minimum purchase price for farmers for wheat, rice and the like be scrapped in India?

Arguments **SNAP 2013**

I. No, farmers who produce our staple food must get decent return on their investment and labour in a welfare state like India.

II. Yes, it is an outdated practice which we must discard.

11. Statement Should the practice of transfers of clerical cadress employees from one city to another government offices be stopped?

Arguments **CMAT 2013**

I. No, transfer of employees is a routine administrative matter and we must continue it.

II. Yes,it involves lot of governmental expenditure and inconvenience to many compared to the benefits it yields.

12. Statement Should all the foreign banks immediately be asked to close down their operations in India?

Arguments **CMAT 2011**

I. No, this will have an adverse impact on Indian economy.

II. Yes , this is the only way to make the Indian banks survive and prosper.

13. Statement Should the government open more medical colleges in the country?

Arguments **IIFT 2012**

I. No, because the government should ensure quality education in the existing Medical colleges as majority of the colleges lack necessary infrastructure.

II. Yes, because there is urgent need of qualified doctors and the ratio between doctors and citizens is the lowest in India.

14. Statement Should there be compulsory medical examination of both the man and the woman before they marry each other?

Arguments **MAT 2011**

I. No, this is an intrusion into the privacy of an individual and hence cannot be tolerated.

II. Yes, this will substantially reduce the risk of giving birth to children with serious ailments.

15. Statement Should there be capital punishment for those who are found guilty of rape charges?

Arguments **IIFT 2011**

I. Yes, this is the only way to eliminate such atrocities on women.

II. No, this will lead to more violence as culprits may even kill the rape victims.

Direction (Q. Nos. 16-35) *In making decisions about important questions, it is desirable to be able to distinguish between "Strong" arguments and "Weak" arguments in sofar as they relate to the question. "Strong" arguments are those which are both important and directly related to the questions. "Weak" arguments are those which are of minor importance and also may not be directly related to the questions or may be related to a trivial aspect of the questions.*

Give answer

(a) if only Argument I is strong
(b) if only Argument II is strong
(c) if either Argument I or II is strong
(d) if neither Argument I nor II is strong
(e) if both Arguments I and II are strong

16. Statement Should there be a maximum ceiling imposed on the earnings of an individual in an organisation?

Arguments

I. Yes, this will help equitable distribution of earnings to all the employees.

II. No, the organisation should have free hand to decide the pay package of its employees.

17. Statement Should government-dependent loss-making academic institutes like universities/ colleges be closed down in India?

Arguments

I. Yes, they are only creating batches of unemployable young graduates.

II. Yes, none of the developed countries support universities by such massive financing.

18. Statement Should schemes of voluntary retirement be introduced in all sick public sector units in India?

Arguments

I. Yes, excess and inefficient staff is one of the reasons of sickness of public sector organisation.

II. Yes, this is what private and multinational companies do in developed countries.

19. Statement Should there be only one rate of interest for term deposits of varying durations in banks?

Arguments

I. No, people will refrain from keeping money for longer duration resulting into reduction of liquidity level of banks.

II. Yes, this will be much simple for the common people and they may be encouraged to keep more money in banks.

20. Statement Should all students passing out from the government run colleges and desirous of settling abroad be asked to pay back the cost of their education to the government?

Arguments **SBI (PO) 2014**

I. Yes, such students who study on the resources of the exchequer should be discouraged to leave the country.

II. No every citizen has the right to select their place of further study or work and therefore such as condition is unjustified.

21. Statement Do scientists believe in religion?

Arguments

I. Yes, because science as a profession does not come in the way of faith.

II. No, because religion and science do not go together.

22. Statement Are nuclear families better than joint families?

Arguments

I. No, joints families ensure greater security.

II. Yes, nuclear families ensure greater freedom.

23. Statement Should the parents of those children who do not send their wards to school be fined?

Arguments

I. Yes, this is the only way to eradicate illiteracy.

II. No, why should the parents be fined?

24. Statement Should India become a permanent member of UN's Security Council?

Arguments

I. Yes, India has emerged as a country which loves peace and amity.

II. No, let us first solve problems of our own people like poverty, malnutrition.

25. Statement Should persons convicted of criminal offences in the past be allowed to contest elections in India?

Arguments

I. No, such persons cannot serve the cause of the people and the country.

II. Yes, it is democracy–let people decide whom to vote.

26. Statement Should 'computer knowledge' be made a compulsory subject for all students at secondary school certificate (SSC) examination in India?

Arguments

I. No, our need is 'bread' for everyone, we cannot follow western models.

II. Yes, we cannot enter the year 2020 without equipping our children with computers.

27. Statement Should all the non-performing employees in the public sector be compulsorily retrenched from service?

Arguments

I. No, this will give an unjust handle to the management and they may use indiscriminately.

II. Yes, this will help increase the level of efficiency of these organisations and these organisations will be come profitable establishments.

28. Statement Should India engage into a dialogue with neighbouring countries to stop cross-border terrorism?

Arguments

I. Yes, this is the only way to reduce cross-border terrorism and stop loss of innocent lives.

II. No, neighbouring countries cannot be relied upon in such matters; they may still engage in subversive activities.

29. Statement Should labour reforms be immediately introduced in India?

Arguments **IBPS (Clerk) 2013**

I. Yes, this will help increase the productivity in all the sectors in general and in the public sector in particular.

II. No, many other countries have not implemented this so far.

30. Statement Should the subsidy on petroleum products be further reduced?

Arguments

I. Yes, the present subsidy is a drain on national resources; let the consumer share the burden.

II. No, this will have a cascading effect and the prices of all the commodities will sharply increase, creating higher rate of inflation.

31. Statement Should government 'freeze' pay-scales and salary of all private and public sectors and its own employees to contains inflation?

Arguments

I. Yes, all over the world this is considered as a sure way to contain information.

II. No, the government should control market forces to keep check on the prices.

32. Statement Should postal services be privatised in India.

Arguments

I. Yes, it will make life easy for the citizens of India.

II. No, privatisation is not a panacea for all the problems, even private service can be equally bad.

33. Statement Should there be more than one High Court in each State in India?

Arguments

I. No, this will be a sheer wastage of taxpayer money.

II. Yes, this will help reduce the backlog of cases pending for a very long time.

34. Statement Should all the youngsters below 21 years of age be disallowed from going to bar.

Arguments

I. No, it is not correct to prevent matured youngsters above 18 year of age who can vote from having fun.

II. Yes, this will help in preventing youngsters from getting into bad company and imbibing bad habits.

35. Statement Should old and poorly maintained petrol/diesel vehicle like autorickshaws and taxis which generate heavy pollution be banned for public services in big cities?

Arguments

I. Yes, it will reduce pollution level in these cities which will enhance health of citizen.

II. No, what will the poor autorickshaw/taxi drivers do for their survival?

Advanced Level

Direction (Q. Nos. 1-11) *In making decisions about important questions, it is desirable to distinguish between 'strong' argument and weak argument. A strong argument must be 'both' important and directly relate to the question. A weak argument may not be related to the trivial aspect of the question. Each question below is followed by three arguments, numbered I, II and III. You have to decide which of the arguments is 'strong' and which is 'weak'.*

1. Statement Should religion be taught in our schools?

Arguments

I. No, ours is a secular state.

II. Yes, teaching religion helps inculcate moral values among children.

III. No, how can one dream of such a step when we want the young generation to fulfill its role in the 21st century.

(a) All are strong
(b) None is strong
(c) Only I is strong
(d) Only II is strong
(e) I and III are strong

2. Statement Should the parliament elections in India be held on a single day throughout the country?

Arguments **CMAT 2014**

I. Yes, this is the only way to handle such elections.

II. Yes, this will help the commission to concentrate on a single day for election related issues.

III. No, some other countries hold such elections spread over several days.

(a) None is strong
(b) Only I is strong
(c) Only II is strong
(d) Only III is strong

3. Statement Should there be a total ban on tobacco product and smoking in India?

Arguments

I. Yes, it is wrong to smoke away millions of money?

II. No, it will throw thousands of workers in the tobacco industry out of employment.

III. No, the government will loose huge amount of money as it will not care by way of taxes on these products.

(a) None is strong
(b) I and II are strong
(c) Only II is strong
(d) II and III are strong
(e) All are strong

4. Statement Should the government ban all forms of protests including strikes and precessions?

Arguments

I. Yes, this is the only way to teach discipline to the employees.

II. No, government cannot deprive its citizens of their basic rights.

III. Yes, this is the only way to ensure maximum productivity without disruption of work.

(a) Only II is strong
(b) I and II are strong
(c) Only III is strong
(d) I and III are strong
(e) All are strong

5. Statement Should India acquire/manufacture the latest nuclear weapons?

Arguments

I. Yes, the enemies of India are improving their weapons continuously and it becomes imperative to protect the sovereignty and integrity of the country.

II. No, instead the money should be diverted to development activities.

III. No, the international community will isolate Indians and this will bring a setback to India economy.

(a) Only I is strong
(b) I and III are strong
(c) I and II are strong
(d) All are strong
(e) None of these

6. Statement Should the system of Lok Adalats and mobile courts be encouraged in India?

Arguments

I. Yes, it helps to grant speedy justice to the masses.

II. Yes, the dispensing of minor cases at this level would reduce the burden on the higher courts.

III. No, these courts are usually partial in justice.

(a) I and II are strong
(b) II and III are strong
(c) I and III are strong
(d) All are strong
(e) Only I is strong

7. **Statement** Should seniority be the only criterion for the promotion?

Arguments

I. No, it would be an injustice to those juniors who are more deserving and suitable for higher positions than their senior counterparts.

II. Yes, otherwise senior employees do feel humiliated.

III. Yes, senior employees are more experienced and must be rewarded for the same.

(a) None is strong (b) Only I is strong
(c) I and III are strong (d) I and II are strong
(e) All are strong

8. **Statement** Is caste-based reservation policy in professional colleges justified?

Arguments **MHT CET MBA 2011**

I. Yes, the step is a must to bring the underprivileged at par with the privileged ones.

II. No, it obstructs the establishment of a classless society.

III. Yes, this will help the backward castes and classes of people to come out of the oppression of upper caste people.

(a) I and II are strong (b) Only II is strong
(c) II and III are strong (d) I and III are strong
(e) None of these

9. **Statement** Should government established higher level Institutes of Technology (IIT's) be privatised?

Arguments

I. Yes, privatisation will make these institutes financially healthy, competitive and quality conscious.

II. Yes, privatisation is the key of the new era can we survive without it?

III. No, standard of education of these institutes will fall.

(a) None is strong (b) All are strong
(c) Only I is strong (d) I and III are strong
(e) II and III are strong

10. **Statement** Should India immediately stop digging coal from its mines?

Arguments

I. Yes, the present stock of coal will not last long if we continue mining at the present rate.

II. No, we do not have alternate energy source of sufficient quantity.

III. No, this will put millions of people at a disadvantage and their lives will get adversely affected and also the industry.

(a) I and II are strong (b) II and III are strong
(c) I and III are strong (d) All are strong
(e) None is strong

11. **Statement** Should woman be given equal opportunity in the matter of employment in every felid?

Arguments **SNAP 2012**

I. Yes, they are equally capable.

II. No, they have to shoulder household responsibilities.

III. Yes, they should also go into the outside world.

(a) Only I is strong (b) I and II are strong
(c) II and III are strong (d) I and III are strong

Direction (Q. Nos. 12-16) *In making decisions important questions it is desirable to be able distinguish between strong arguments and weak arguments. A strong arguments must be both importance and directly related to the question. Weak arguments may not be directly related to the question and may be minor importance or may be related to the trivial as of the question. Each question below is followed by there arguments numbered I, II and III. You have to decide which of the argument (s) is/are strong and indicate your answer accordingly.*

12. **Statement** Should the government restrict use of electricity for each household depending upon the requirement?

Arguments **SNAP 2013**

I. Yes, this will help government tide 'cause the problem of inadequate generation at electricity'.

II. No, every citizen has right to consume electricity as per their requirement as they pay for using electricity.

III. No, the government does not have the machinery to put such a restriction on use of electricity.

(a) Only I is strong (b) Only II is strong
(c) I and II are strong (d) II and III are strong

13. **Statement** Should the government order closure of all educational institutions for a month to avoid fast spreading of the contagious viral infection?

Arguments

I. No, closure of educational institution alone is not the solution for curbing spread of viral infection.

II. No, students will visit crowded places like malls, markets, playgrounds etc., in more numbers and spread the disease, as they will have lot of spare time at their disposal.

III. Yes, young persons are more prone to get affected by the viral infection and hence they should remain in doors.

(a) None is strong (b) Only I is strong
(c) Only III is strong (d) I and II are strong
(e) All are strong

14. **Statement** Should the government ban export of all types of foodgrains for the next one year to tide over the unpredicted drought situation in the country?

Arguments **RBI (Clerk) 2009**

I. Yes, there is no other way to provide food its citizen during the year.

II. No, the government does not have its jurisdiction over private exporters for banning exporters.

III. Yes, the government should not allow the exporters to export foodgrains and procure all the foodgrains held by such exporters and make it available for home consumption.

(a) I and II are strong (b) II and III are strong
(c) I and III are strong (d) All are strong
(e) None of these

15. Statement Should there be a common syllabus for all subjects in graduate courses in all the universities across the country?

Arguments

I. Yes, this is the only way to spring in uniformity in the education system in the country.
II. Yes, it will help standardize the quality of graduation certificates being given by different universities in the country.
III. No, each university should have the autonomy to decide its syllabus based on the specific requirement of the university.

(a) None is strong (b) Only I is strong
(c) Only II is strong (d) I and II are strong
(e) II and III are strong

16. Statement Should all those students who failed in one or two subjects in HSC be allowed to take admission in degree courses and continue their study subject to their successfully passing in the supplementary examination?

Arguments **NMAT 2011**

I. Yes, this will help the students to complete their education without a break of one year.
II. Yes, this is a forward looking strategy to help the students and motivate them for higher studies.
III. No, such students do not choose to continue their studies without having passed in all the subjects in HSC.

(a) Only I is strong (b) Only II is strong
(c) Only III is strong (d) None of these

Direction (Q. Nos. 17-20) *In making decisions about important questions, it is desirable to distinguish between a 'strong' argument and a 'weak' argument. A 'strong' argument must be both important and directly related to the question. A 'weak' argument may not be directly related to the question and may be of minor importance or may be related to the trivial aspect of the question. Each question below is followed by four arguments numbered* I, II, III *and* IV. *You have to decide which of the arguments is 'strong' and which is 'weak'.*

17. Statement Should all the school teachers be debarred from giving private tuitions?

Arguments **Syndicate Bank (PO) 2009**

I. No, the needy students will be deprived of the expertise of these teachers.
II. Yes, this is an injustice to the unemployed educated people who can earn their living by giving tuitions.
III. Yes, only then the quality of teaching in schools will improve.
IV. Yes, now salary of these teachers is reasonable.

(a) I and III are strong (b) I, II and III are strong
(c) III and IV are strong (d) II, III and IV are strong
(e) None of these

18. Statement Should people with educational qualification higher than the optimum requirements be debarred from seeking jobs?

Arguments **PNB (PO) 2006**

I. No, it will further aggravate the problem of educated unemployment.
II. Yes, it creates complexes among employees and affects the work adversely.
III. No, this goes against the basic rights of the individuals.
IV. Yes, this will increase productivity.

(a) I and III are strong (b) All are strong
(c) II and IV are strong (d) Only III is strong
(e) None of these

19. Statement Should class IV children have Board examination?

Arguments **Allahabad Bank (PO) 2004**

I. Yes, this will motivate the children to study and get higher marks and thus more knowledge can be imbibed at a younger age.
II. No, the children will be forced to study and won't enjoy the process.
III. Yes, in today's competitive world the children need to be prepared right from the beginning to face such difficult examinations.
IV. No, this will add pressure on tender aged children and leave very little time for them to play.

(a) All are strong (b) I, II and IV are strong
(c) II, III and IV are strong (d) I and III are strong
(e) I and IV are strong

20. Statement It has been reported in a recent study that in take of moderate quantity of milk chocolate reduces the risk of suffering from central nervous system related illnesses.

Which of the following would weaken the findings of the study reported in the above statement? **IBPS (PO) 2012**

(a) People generally prefer to eat chocolate when they are young
(b) Majority of those not diagnosed with diseases related to central nervous system have stayed away from eating chocolates in their lives
(c) Chocolates contain certain elements which strengthen the functions of the central nervous system
(d) Majority of those suffering from central nervous system related diseases are middle aged
(e) Many of those who suffer from diabetes also suffer from other major ailments

Answers with Explanations

Intro Exercise 1

1. (*d*) Argument I is not strong as the statement is wrong because the government has authority to do so. Argument II is also not strong because of the word 'only'.

2. (*e*) Both the Arguments I and II are strong because by putting restrictions, rickshaw pullers and prisoners are not able to donate their blood to their own relatives. Restricting non-suitable persons is a precautionary step.

3. (*d*) Argument I does not related to statement. Any subsidy which is for social welfare should be stopped when it is misused on a large scale. So, neither Argument I nor II is strong.

4. (*e*) Argument I is strong because allowing teams from smaller countries will help the globalisation of cricket. Argument II is also strong because sometimes records established in tougher and challenging situations are broken against these teams.

5. (*d*) What other progressive nations are doing, we should not follow that blindly. So, Argument I is not strong. Argument II is absurd, so it is not strong.

6. (*c*) Either Argument I or II is strong because many times ruling government misuse it while sometimes dissolving the assembly becomes the need of the hour.

7. (*a*) Argument I is strong because it will reduce the problem of black marketing of commodities supplied under PDS. Argument II is not strong because it is not directly related with the statement.

8. (*a*) Argument I is strong because the organisations are profit making and it will boost government financially. Argument II is not strong because the organisations are profit making so there is no question of budgetary deficit.

9. (*a*) Argument I is strong because competition increases the quality of service. From the statement it is not clear that railways is a non-profitable sector and private companies are also operating in non-profitable sectors. So, Argument II is not strong.

10. (*b*) Argument I is not strong because it does not tell that why the grievances of people will increase. Argument II is strong because it will reduce the power theft which has resulted a huge amount.

11. (*a*) Argument I is strong because by this a better candidate can be selected. Argument II is not strong because, if citizen do not want to choose a candidate, they should vote against him.

12. (*d*) Neither Argument I nor II is strong because it is not a proper way to claim permanent membership of the UN.

13. (*a*) Argument I is strong because it will help economically weak students to earn something. Argument II is not strong because it means 'learning while earning' while the statement is talking about 'earning while learning'.

14. (*c*) Either Argument I or II is strong because rape is a heinous offence but innocent person should not be punished.

15. (*d*) Argument I is not strong due to the word 'only'. Different interest rates encourage the customers to switch the banks. So, Argument II is also not strong.

16. (*b*) Argument I is not strong because it is not directly related with the statement. Argument II is strong because History should not be taught to school children in a one sided manner and any distortions would have to be rectified.

17. (*a*) Argument I is strong because when huge quantity of cheaper vanaspati ghee will enter in the market, then it will affect the interest of farmers and industries. Argument II is absurd so it is not strong.

18. (*b*) Argument I is not strong because we cannot stop our strive on the basis of unsuccess.Argument II is strong because our experiences will help us to improve ourselves.

19. (*b*) Argument II is strong because of similarly of work, functions and positions.

20. (*b*) Argument II is strong, if state level taxes on goods be abolished, there will be huge reduction in tax collections and this will adversely affect the development work funded by state government.

21. (*d*) Argument I is not strong because of lack of explanations and Argument II is not strong because there is no space for example and analogy in argumentations.

22. (*b*) Because in a democratic country every one can hear his will.

23. (*d*) Argument I is not strong because conditions in India are different from other developed countries. Argument II is also not strong because it series away from being specific.

24. (*e*) Argument I is strong because the need aries for the employees to voice their demands. Argument II is also strong because the employees are abusing their right.

25. (*a*) Argument I is strong because adopted children are loved, cared for and provided with comforts of life by new parents. Argument II is not strong because it is not related with the statement.

26. (*a*) Argument I is strong because a proper guidance is required at the stage of schooling. Going to school does not mean that other vital responsibilities will left behind. So, Argument II is not strong.

27. (*b*) Argument I is not strong because it not logically linked with the statement. Argument II is strong because by this importance of higher education will be diminished.

28. (*b*) Argument I is absurd so it is not strong. Argument II is strong because exempting women from wearing helmets is the compromise on their safety.

29. (*a*) Argument I is strong because humans should always be treated in a humanitarian way. Argument II is not strong due to the word 'only way'.

30. (*a*) Argument I is strong because assessment of objective test is reliable. Argument II is not strong due to the phrase 'always very large'.

31. (*a*) Argument I is strong because this fundamental right of citizens will eliminate corruption from the bureaucracy and bring happiness to the citizen. Argument II is not strong because it may remain tough to intervene in the work of bureaucracy.

32. (*a*) Argument I is strong because it shows the true sportsman spirit. Argument II is not strong because a former player cannot know the weakness of the present team.

33. (*b*) Argument I is absurd so it is not strong. Argument II is strong because pension provides financial help to retired employees so that they can sustain themselves in old age.

34. (*a*) Argument I is strong because public security is necessary. Argument II is not strong because bomb disposal squads are not nuisance to day-to-day life.

35. (*d*) The use of the word 'only' in the Argument I makes it invalid. The policy of open market advocates privatisation. Each country is opening its market for foreign investors. How, privatisation will pose a threat to national security? Both Arguments I and II are not strong.

36. (*e*) Both the arguments are strong because there may be some family problems due to which a child leaves his education and became a labourer.

37. (*e*) Both the arguments are strong because both are supported by a valid logic.

38. (*e*) Both the arguments are strong because both the states will get benefit as one state which has surplus electricity will get money while the other state which is electricity deficient will get electricity. A cross-country transfer of electricity will involve huge transmission losses.

39. (*e*) Argument I is strong because implementing complete ban on manufacture of fire-crackers will render thousands of workers jobless. Argument II is also strong because child labour is used in this industry.

40. (*e*) Both the arguments are strong because doctors and engineers are considered as the best talent but taxpayers money is spent on their studies which goes into the drain when they joined civil services.

Intro Exercise 2

1. (*c*) Argument I is not strong because the pay structure should be according to work. Argument II is not strong as work load cannot be the criteria of pay. Argument III is strong as for similar work same pay is logical.

2. (*d*) If there is a complete ban on genetically modified seeds, it will boost the demand of domestically developed seeds. So, Argument I is strong. Argument II is not strong due to the word 'only'. Argument III is strong because genetically modified products will adversely affect the health of those who consume these products.

3. (*a*) None of the given argument is strong because the security of investor's money is not related with the size of bank and employees will not lose their jobs as their duties will remain same. Healthy competition is there where there are many players.

4. (*a*) None of the given argument is strong.

5. (*d*) Argument I is not strong as running railways does not mean to run private passenger transport. Argument II is illogical. Argument III is not relevant as it is not true.

6. (*d*) Holding elections after short intervals will leads to wastage of money and resources. So, Argument I is strong. Three years can be considered as a short time against five years, so Argument III is strong but Argument II is not.

7. (*e*) It cannot be said that a literate person has sound knowledge of politics. So, Argument I is strong. Illiterate person can easily be misled on various factors but voting is also a constitutional right of every citizen. So, Arguments II and III are also strong.

8. (*d*) In 'hire and fire' policy performing employees are rewarded while non-performing employees are shown the door. This increases the level of efficiency and profitability. So, Arguments I and III are strong while II is not.

9. (*c*) Administrative officers should remain friendly with local people. So, Argument I is absurd and not strong. Arguments II and III are strong because administrative officer require some time to implement their schemes and policies. Transfer after a short period create a lot of inconvenience to the officers.

10. (*d*) Students should take subjects of their interest at graduate level. At post graduate level only interest is not the factor to take subjects. So, Argument I is not strong but Argument II is strong because at post graduate level, students must fulfill the essential conditions.

Argument III is not strong because the seats at post graduate level will remain same even if students seek subjects of their choice.

11. (*d*) Only Argument III is strong because same knowledge level of students get different marks in different boards and universities. An entrance test can judge their knowledge level.

12. (*c*) Argument I is not strong due to the word 'only'. Argument II is strong because administratively this is a very tough task that there be only one university throughout India. Argument III is strong because this move will make the degrees procured by students, comparable for offering jobs because at present different universities have different grading method for providing marks to students.

13. (*c*) Argument I is not strong due to the word 'only'. Argument II is strong because there is a huge shortage of electricity in most part of the country. Argument III is not strong because what other countries are doing. We should not follow that blindly.

14. (c) Argument I is not strong due to the word 'never'. If work is done at night, it cannot be said that there is unnecessary use of electricity as it is very essential. Arguments III is strong because at day time commuters will face a lot of problems.

15. (c) Arguments I and III are strong because many deemed universities are not performing to the required standard, so level of education is decreasing and these universities are basically money oriented.

16. (a) Arguments I and II are strong because our country is based on irrigation and it is dependent on ground water. Due to heavy use of ground water for irrigation. Water level has gone to a alarming level. International agencies are not the concerned authority to give advice to India. So, Argument III is not strong.

17. (d) Argument I is strong because big cities in India does not provide adequate open space of residential colonies. So, the solution is high rise buildings to accommodate the growing population. less Argument II is not strong because concerned development authority and some other people are benefitted by it. Argument III is not strong because providing adequate infrastuctural facilities is the prime responsibility of the builders and developers.

18. (c) Arguments I and IV are strong because the rule of wearing helmet for both driver and pillion rider while driving a motorbike should be followed strictly by all. It protects our head which is the most sensitive organ of human body.

19. (c) Arguments II and III are strong because many farmers earn more money than service class people and a huge amount of tax can be collected if income tax is implemented on farmers.

20. (e) Arguments I and II are strong because a single tax will simply the tax collection mechanism and manufacturers and traders will be benefited by it. What other countries are doing, we should not adopt that blindly. So, Argument III is not strong.

21. (a) Clearly, none of the argument is strong.

22. (c) Argument I is not strong due to the word 'only'. There are some law which stop an individual to do wrong acts which he wants. So, Argument II is not strong. Argument III is strong because there is no confirmed evidence that such products have adverse effects on human body. What other countries are doing. We should not follow that blindly. So, Argument IV is not strong.

Cumulative Exercises

Base Level

1. (e) Young entrepreneurs should be encouraged as they have fresh mind and relatively more active than old ones, so they will help in industrial development and will reduce the burden on the employment market. Therefore, both argument holds strong.

2. (b) Argument I is not correct because of the word 'only' used in the argument. Hence, Argument I is not strong. Argument II is strong because adverse impact on agriculture will break the backbone of the economy.

3. (e) Both the arguments are strong because I will reduce the number of cases of murder while II is strong on humanitarian ground.

4. (d) Argument I is not strong because India should take its stand according to its need. Argument II is not strong due to the word 'only'.

5. (d) Neither Argument I nor II is strong because there must be a standard rent and Argument II deviates from the question. The question is why the government should do it not whether it can do it.

6. (b) Argument I is not strong because fresh tests of nuclear weapons will be termed as an exhibition of nuclear weapons. Present nuclear weapons are enough to defend by any means. Argument II is strong because it divulges the bad effects if India carries out fresh terms of nuclear weapons.

7. (e) Both the Arguments I and II are strong. Argument I is strong on the basis of its benefit to the real beneficiary. Argument II is strong because of the adverse impact of subsidy on the economy of the country.

8. (d) Neither Argument I nor II is strong.

9. (a) Argument I is strong because it is an established fact. Argument II is not strong because it can be implemented.

10. (a) Argument I is strong because of the welfare state theory. Argument II is not strong because it does not give a proper reason.

11. (b) Argument I is not strong as a routine practice is not logical. Argument II is strong as it will ease the problem of inconvenience.

12. (a) Argument I is strong because it is not desirable that the Indian Economy be lead into trouble . Argument II is not strong due to the word 'only'.

13. (c) Argument I is strong because if existing medical colleges lack necessary infrastructure, then opening new medical colleges will not be an appropriate step. Argument II is also strong because there is urgent need of qualified doctors.

14. (b) Argument I is not strong because it gives importance to the privacy of the individual more than health care. Argument II is strong because it is desirable.

15. (b) Argument I is not strong due to the word 'only'. Argument II is strong because it is a correct logical thinking.

16. (d) Argument I is not strong because maximum ceiling will reduce the scope of getting higher salary for those who work hard and contribute very much in an organisation's profit. Argument II is also not strong because there should be some restrictions on organisations to decide the salaries of its employees.

17. (*d*) Argument I is not strong due to the word 'only'. What other countries are doing, we should not follow that blindly because there are different situations in different countries. So, Argument II is also not strong.

18. (*a*) Argument I is strong because this move may improve the situation of sick public sector units. There is different culture in public rector units and private companies. So, it is tough to follow each-other steps. So, Argument II is not strong.

19. (*a*) Higher rate of interest attracts people to deposit money for longer duration. If higher rate of interest is available for short duration, then people will refrain from keeping money for longer duration. So, Argument I is strong while II is not.

20. (*e*) Both the Arguments I and II are strong. Argument I is strong because optimum use of the resources of the exchequer is desirable. Discouraging such people will lessen the problem of brain drain. Argument II is strong on the basis of the power equipped by the constitution to the citizens.

21. (*a*) Argument I is strong as profession and religion are different and Aargument II is not strong.

22. (*e*) The joint family has several members to help you or support you which ensure more security. In nuclear family you have less member, so more freedom is enjoyed by its member.

Hence, both Arguments I and II are strong.

23. (*d*) Argument I is not strong due to the word 'only'. Argument II is not strong because such parents are increasing illiteracy, so they should be fined.

24. (*a*) Argument I is strong because it mentions the indispensable requirement in support of its claim. Argument II is not strong because after becoming a permanent member of UN's Security Council. India can solve its other problems.

25. (*b*) Argument I is not strong due to the word 'cannot'. Argument II is strong because the choice of the people should be given supremacy.

26. (*b*) Argument I is not strong because bread and education are two different things. Argument II is strong because in this hi-tech world when India is thinking about to be a developed country by 2020, we cannot enter in that year without equipping our children with computers.

27. (*e*) Argument I is strong because management may misuse its powers. Argument II is strong because it will increase the level of efficiency. So, productivity will increased.

28. (*b*) Argument I is not strong due to the word 'only'. Argument II is strong because it go into reason that our neighboring countries are engaged in subversive activities.

29. (*a*) Argument I is strong. No doubt, labour reforms will encourage the labour to work more efficiently, which will be helpful in increasing the productivity. Argument II is not strong because it is not a right way of arguing. Basic needs of India may be different from those of other countries.

30. (*e*) Argument I is strong because consumers should also share some burden. Argument II is also strong because increase in the price of petroleum products will increase the price of many other commodities.

31. (*a*) Since, India is a part of world, so whatever is true for all over the world is also true for India. So, argument I is strong. Argument II is not strong because it provides an alternative instead of going into the reason.

32. (*b*) Argument I is not strong because it is not providing any reason behind it. Argument II is strong because private service can be equally bad.

33. (*b*) Argument I is not strong because it does not give any reason behind it. Argument II is strong because a large number of cases are pending for a very long time.

34. (*e*) Argument I is strong as if states genuine reason against such ban. Argument II is also strong as the youngsters may fall into bad company. Both Arguments I and II are strong.

35. (*a*) Argument I is strong because health and pollution level cannot be neglected. Argument II is not strong because it is a cry of desperation.

Advance Level

1. (*d*) Secular state does not mean neglecting religion and religion value. So, argument I is not strong. Argument II is strong because teaching religion will help to inculcate moral values among children. Teaching religion to young generation will be helpful to fulfill their role in 21st century. So, argument III is not strong.

2. (*a*) Argument I is weak because of the word only. Argument II is also weak as helding election in a day will create more problem. Argument III is also not strong as no country should copy other country.

3. (*b*) Argument I is strong because millions of money is spent on tobacco products and smoking and that should be saved. It is also true that complete ban on tobacco products and smoking will throw out thousands of workers in these industries out of work. So, Argument II is strong. Argument III is not strong because the heath of people should not be compromised to earn money through taxes.

4. (*a*) Arguments I and III are not strong due to the word 'only'. Argument II is strong because strike is a basic right of employees and government should not deprive it.

5. (*d*) If enemies of India are improving their weapons then India should also develop the latest nuclear weapons. India is a developing country and a huge amount will spent to acquire the latest nuclear weapons, so that money should be diverted to development activities. International Community may also isolate Indians and that may be a setback to Indian Economy. So, all the three arguments are strong.

6. (*a*) The system of Lok Adalats and mobile courts will be helpful to grant speedy justice to the masses. At present lakhs of cases are pending in different courts of India. Many of them are for minor causes. So, these cases should be dispensed in these Lok Adalats and mobile courts. So, Arguments I and II are strong. Argument III is not strong because it is not providing proper reasons behind it.

7. (*b*) Productivity and profitability are most important factors for an organisation. This can be done by promoting deserving Candidate irrespective of seniority. So, Argument I is strong but Argument II and III are not strong.

8. (*b*) Arguments I and III are not strong due to the words 'must' and 'oppression', respectively. We are talking about professional level, so caste should not come in this matter. So, Argument II is strong.

9. (*a*) From the statement, it is not clear that IITs are facing any problem. At present many private run institutes or far behind them. So, privatisation will not be helpful. So, Arguments I and II are not strong. It is not clear that why standard of education will fall when IIT's are privatised. So, Argument III is also not strong.

10. (*b*) Stock of coal is limited, then it does not mean that its production should be stopped. So, Argument I is not strong. Arguments II and III are strong, because alternate energy source are available in limited quantity and a large number of people are dependent on coal, so they will be affected.

11. (*d*) Arguments I and III are strong because women are equally capable as men and they should also get into the outside world for self development and self dependent. Argument II is not strong because they should not be confined to only household responsibilities.

12. (*c*) Argument I is strong because, if saving is going on, then it will reduce the power problem. Argument II is also strong because people needed the electricity and power and for that they are paying enough. Argument III is not strong because government can make rules and regulation to reduce the consumption.

13. (*b*) Argument I is strong but II is not strong because to close the school one cannot stop infections and virals.

14. (*e*) Argument I is weak, II is also weak but Argument III is strong.

15. (*e*) Argument I became weak because of the word 'only' used but Arguments II and III are strong.

16. (*d*) Argument I is strong because one previous year of students will save. If this move is implemented, then it is possible that students might not concentrate on HSC exams because they think that they will be promoted, weather they pass HSC or not but it will motivate those students who failed in one or two subjects by a small margin. So, either Argument II or III follows.

17. (*e*) None of the argument stated provides the strong and convincing reason to support or to oppose the statement given.

18. (*d*) Only Argument III is strong because we can seek any job for which we qualify and stopping an individual from doing this will go against the basic rights of the individual.

19. (*c*) Argument I is not strong as board exams do not provide any criterion to gain more knowledge but they certainly provide a competitive environment to prepare a child to face such exams. Also, it would add an extra burden and pressure on tender aged children and will leave them with less time to play and enjoy. So, Arguments II, III and IV are strong.

20. (*b*) The study reported that chocolate reduces the risk of suffering from central nervous system is weaker by the statement (b) which says that "Majority of these not diagnosed with diseases related to central nervous system have stayed away from eating chocolates in their lines."

4 Passage and Conclusion

In these type of questions an unseen passage is given that is followed by some 'Inferences'. On the basis of the information given in the passage, you have to check the truthfulness or falsity of the given statement (inference). An inference is a conclusion drawn on the basis of knowledge and facts available.

Unlike previous chapters like Statement-Argument, Statement-Assumption and Syllogism, where there was no scope of truthfulness and falsity of the conclusions, in this chapter the conclusions have probability of both. So, the conclusion drawn may be probably true or probably false.

For solving these questions you must possess logical skills, comprehension capacity and ability for interpretation. This will help you to comprehend the full implications of the passage. You should acquire as much knowledge as possible of phrasal verbs, vocabulary and nuances of English language.

Solved Example

In these type of questions, a passage is given on any topic followed by conclusions in the form of statements. A candidate is required to mark the answer in the following way

(i) Mark (a) if the conclusion is definitely true.

(ii) Mark (b) if the conclusion is probably true, though not definitely true.

(iii) Mark (c) if the conclusion is neither true nor false because the data given in the passage are inadequate.

(iv) Mark (d) if the conclusion is probably false, though not definitely false.

(v) Mark (e) if the conclusion is definitely false.

➘ A student must note that all these conclusions are to be arrived at, in the light of what has been discussed in the passage.

In the following passage, the methodology will be discussed as to how to opt for right option– (a, b, c, d and e) which a student is expected to select for a given conclusion.

For the sake of the convenience of the students, each option mentioned above will be discussed and analysed in detail in the light of the passages given below.

Passage

"Now the question of the freedom of the press becomes an important question in view of the fact that the press has vast potentialities for both good and evil. The press is as much a passion rouser as it is a peace maker. In the days of discords and dissensions, it bars the door to reconciliation or atleast the quarrel is prolonged beyond its limits. Knowledge is not always good and sometimes ignorance is bliss."

Option (a) Definitely True – If the conclusion directly follows the statement or group of statements given in the passage, we can arrive at option (a) because the conclusion is definitely true.

It is important to note that in such cases the conclusion is the direct result of the statement and no indirect inference is derived from the given statement.

Let us analyse the conclusions which are definitely true in the light of this rule.

***Conclusion* 1** Press has multi-dimensional potentialities.

Analysis It is very clearly mentioned in the passage that press possesses vast potentialities and can play different roles during work and peace time.

***Conclusion* 2** Press can rouse the passions of the public.

Analysis The author has described the press as a passion rouser as well as peace maker.

Since both the conclusions drawn from the passage can directly be derived from the passage, hence both are definitely true. We have not relied on any indirect inference.

Option (b) Probably True The word 'probable' means that there are chances of occurring or not occurring of an event. This option is available for testing a conclusion when it is not definitely true. In other words, it does not follow the statement directly.

It is to be noted here that a conclusion is not definitely true because there exists little chance for its being wrong as well.

Therefore, there is every possibility of its swing towards truthfulness.

***Conclusion* 3** It is a folly to be wise where ignorance is bliss.

Analysis In the last line of the paragraph, it is mentioned that knowledge is not always good and sometimes ignorance is bliss.

It is to be noted that we cannot infer anything definite from this line because the words 'always' and 'sometimes' reduce the chance of the conclusion being definitely true or false.

In the light of the rule under consideration, the conclusion has derived greater swing towards probability of being true than being false.

Hence, the conclusion is probably true.

Option (c) Data Inadequate In such option the candidates do not have relevant information to arrive at the conclusion. In other words, data contained in the passage are inadequate. As such the option (c) – data inadequate, is required to be opted for the candidate.

***Conclusion* 4** "Salary of journalists should be increased to suppress their resentment".

Analysis This conclusion speaks of salary of journalists. Nothing about salary of journalists has been discussed in the passage. Additional data, therefore are required to arrive a conclusion. Hence, we opt for option (c) – data inadequate.

Option (d) Probably False The criterion to opt for this option is similar to the one applied in the case of option (b) – Probably true. Whenever the conclusion is not definitely false, it is so because there exists little chance of its being true. In such cases, the conclusion is said to be probably false.

Here, the swing seems to be towards falsity and the conclusion is termed probably false.

***Conclusion* 5** Knowledge is good.

Analysis Though the conclusion contradicts the statement of the passage that knowledge is not always good, yet the conclusion cannot be taken for as definitely false.

All the same, the use of word 'always' in the statement reduces the chance of the conclusion being definitely true and there is an apparent swing towards falsity.

Hence , the option (d) – probably false is correct.

Option (e) Definitely False The student arrives at this option when direct definite information is available to prove that the conclusion is totally contrary to the information given in the passage.

***Conclusion* 6** The question about the freedom of press is not a significant one.

Analysis Now, if we analyse the conclusion in the light of the information available in the passage, it will be observed that the conclusion contradicts the first line in the passage which reads "The question of freedom of press becomes an important question".

Therefore, the conclusion is definitely false.

General Guidelines to Solve 'Passage and Conclusion' Questions

Guideline **1** In order to evaluate an inference, first of all check whether it can be evaluated with the help of passage directly. Check, if this inference is **directly supported** or **contradicted** by something in the passage.

Guideline **2** You can also evaluate an inference with the help of some **key words** used in the passage.

Guideline **3** To avoid confusion between the answers **'definitely true'** and **'probably true'** you should check, if the extra assumption you have made to evaluate the inference is **universally true**. The same funda can be employed to avoid a confusion between the answer **'definitely false'** and **'probably false.'**

Guideline **4** To avoid confusion between the answers **'probably true'** and **'data inadequate'**, check if it is possible to make an extra assumption to take the inference as **'probably true'**. If you can make a reasonable extra assumption the answer would be **'probably true'**. The same funda could be used to avoid confusion between the answer **'probably false'** and **'data inadequate'**.

Examples Based on Passage and Conclusion

Direction (Examples 1-2) *The given below passages are followed by several possible inferences which can be drawn from the facts states in the passage. You have to examine each inference separately in the context of the passage and decide upon its degree of truth or falsity.*

Give answer

(a) if the inference is 'definitely true', i.e. it properly follows from the statement of facts given
(b) if the inference is 'probably true', though not 'definitely true' in the light of the facts given
(c) if the 'data are inadequate', i.e. from the facts given you cannot say whether the inference is likely to be true or false
(d) if the inference if 'probably false', though not 'definitely false' in the light of the facts given
(e) if the inference is 'definitely false', i.e. it cannot possibly be drawn from the facts given or it contradicts the given facts

Passage 1

The water resources of our country are very much underutilised. The main reason of this underutilisation is the lack of capital and technology. A large portion of our water resources is wasted due to floods unwise use of water for irrigation as well as domestic purposes. We can make full use of our water resources by building dams on river and by adopting policy of awareness among people not to waste water. **CGPSC 2013**

1. Conservation of water resources is possible through wise use of water.
2. Technology does not have any effect on uses of water utilisation.

SOLUTION (Examples 1-2)

1. (*a*) It has been reported in the passage that conservation of water resources is possible through wise use of water, so the inference is definitely true.
2. (*e*) In the given passage, technology, is considered crucial for water utilsation. So, the inference technology does not have any effect on uses of water utilisation is definitely false.

Cumulative Exercise

Base Level

Direction (Q. Nos. 1-91) *The given below passages are followed by several possible inferences which can be drawn from the facts states in the passage. You have to examine each inference separately in the context of the passage and decide upon its degree of truth or falsity.*

Give answer

(a) if the inference is 'definitely true', i.e. it properly follows from the statement of facts given
(b) if the inference is 'probably true', though not 'definitely true' in the light of the facts given
(c) if the 'data are inadequate', i.e. from the facts given you cannot say whether the inference is likely to be true or false
(d) if the inference if 'probably false', though not 'definitely false' in the light of the facts given
(e) if the inference is 'definitely false', i.e. it cannot possibly be drawn from the facts given or it contradicts the given facts

Passage 1

The deterioration in the overall asset quality of banks-gross Non-Performing Assets (NPAs) are reportedly 27% higher at the end of December 2009 than at the end of December 2008– is not surprising. Any slowdown in growth is bound to trigger a rise in NPAs as more and more companies default on loan repayments. The effect would be pronounced when the slowdown coincides with the severe global recession. But for the restructuring of loans permitted by the Central Bank on fairly generous terms, NPAs would have been still higher. Prudent Banks that took care while sanctioning loans and then monitored the post-sanction disbursement diligently should be able to weather the crisis. But it is one thing to have NPAs rise because of a cyclical downturn, it is quite another to have NPAs rise because of policy errors that are entirely within the realm of policymakers. And this is what we need to guard against. Excessively low interest rates skew the risk-reward equation by making projects that are actually not viable, appear viable-till interest rates reverse and the same projects cease to be viable! It is now well established that long periods of unduly low interest rates encourage banks to take more risks. A low interest rate regime driven by an easy money policy rather than macroeconomic fundamentals leads to excessive expansion of credit. It incentivizes banks to take on more risk in search of higher returns and to misprice risk. **SBI Associates (PO) 2010**

1. Low interest rate on credit reduces the capacity to absorb various unaccounted risk factors.
2. Banks' NPAs occur only due to economic factors.
3. The Central Bank always allows banks to restructure their loans in the event of rise in NPAs.
4. Lower interest rate cycle projects commercially unviable projects as viable.
5. Higher NPAs indicate shortcomings in disbursement and follow-up of credit given by banks.

Passage 2

Even after India has become home to 16.7% of the world's population with just 2.4% of world's land area one cannot see a conscious effort on the government's part to tackle the problem facing by the country. Instead, the attention is being focused on trivialities with the sole aim of winning the next election. The government and its policymakers have no clue as to how to act to avert a major disaster waiting to happen. The problem is not because of a dearth of ideas but the extreme reluctance of the government to take action to implement these ideas, making use of available resources. Even when action is taken in the name of family welfare and population stablisation, it is either halfhearted or devoid of any understanding of ground realities.

6. The present government and the policy-makers are not concerned with the gravity of the situation created by the extraordinary growth of India's population.
7. Analysis, planning and administration of population stabilisation programmes must be from the panchayats.
8. India has adopted democratic means to stabilise population.
9. Not only campaign of family welfare and population stabilisation be launched but effective machinery should also be brought in.

Passage 3

The development of a country is primarily determined by the quality of its human resources, which depends on the level of knowledge, skills and attitudes. The role of higher education is crucial in the development of knowledge.

In most of the institutes and universities (in the business management courses too) in India, the curriculum is highly theoretical. When the teachers themselves are not fully equipped to handle industry related situations, one cannot expect much from the students. In the absence of practical exposure, students fail to apply theories in real life. An academician is not only a teacher, but also should be capable of updating his knowledge through research.

10. Most of the skilled human resources in USA are Indians.
11. The knowledge of a teacher plays an important role in shaping up the skills and attitudes of his student.
12. Professionals with practical knowledge can be good teachers.
13. A student cannot have as much knowledge as his teacher has.
14. There are some other sources to determine the development of a country.
15. IITs have teachers with academic and professional knowledge; that is why students from IITs are successful in real life.

Passage 4

In the context of computers, the hardware specialities like the tendency of research connected with human factors, the design of the workstations, keyboards, visual display etc., are being concentrated through the literature connected with interface and software problems, has recently been on the increase. There are two reasons for it. The first reason in the light of the increasing powers of computers is that the designers have got an opportunity to select and organise that technique which the user follows in communicating the message. The second is that the human factors research organisations have deviated from physical specialities of self-improving work-system and gone to the repeated live psychological dimensions of the man-machine interaction.

16. In the field of computers, a change has taken place in the approach of the human factors research organisations.
17. The human factors research organisations do not help in designing the software system. They help only in the evaluation of ultimate production.
18. The physical specialities of work area are less important than their psychological dimension.
19. There has been a systematic progress in the basic computer technique.
20. How the user communicates message through computer hardware, is supposed to be the hardware area of human research.
21. The tools and methods of human research organisations have also undergone a change.
22. The human research organisations in the field of computers, had been started two decades ago.

Passage 5

The first time I saw *The Wizard of Oz*, the story bewitched me. The second time I saw *The Wizard of Oz*, the special effects amazed me. The third time I saw *The Wizard of Oz*, the photography dazzled me. Have you ever seen a movie twice, three times? You notice subtleties and hear sounds you completely missed the first time around.

It's the same on the phone. Because your business conversations are more consequential than movies, you should listen to them two, may be three times. Often we have no clear idea of what really happened in our phone conversation until we hear it again. You'll find shadings more significant than the colour of Toto's collar– and more scarecrows than you imagined who 'have n't got a brain.

How do you listen to your important business conversations again? Simply legally and ethically tape record them. I call the technique of recording and analyzing your business conversations for subtleties instant replay.

CBI (PO) 2010

23. The movie *'The Wizard of Oz'* will help improve business conversation.

24. For most, if they watch a movie more than once, different aspects in different order, like special effects, photography, story, music etc., would impress in a better way.

25. The tips are given for understanding business conversation.

26. The advice is being given to the sales team.

27. The author watches most movies more than twice.

Passage 6

A worrying feature of Indian urbanisation has been its tendency to increase pressure on the inner cities. The first results of the 1991 census suggest that the density of population in urban areas is within manageable limits, with most cities, including Greater Bombay, being well below the 23000 per square kilometre, mark set by Calcutta, but within several of the older cities, the walled areas have high densities which exert pressure on the outdated amenities in these area, a pressure that is accentuated by the poor maintenance of housing as well as other assets in the inner cities. The inner cities were designed for a pattern of urban life far removed from what exists today. The makers of narrow winding lanes could hardly have anticipated modern transportation.

28. The density of population in the inner city of Greater Bombay is the highest in India.
29. At the time of planning the cities in the past, the use of bigger roads was envisaged by the planners.
30. The pace of Indian urbanisation is much slower by international standards.
31. The rate of growth in density of population in the inner cities has been more than that in surrounding areas.
32. The increase in density of population in urban areas has outgrown the increase in amenities.

Passage 7

History has shown that modern economic growth has been inspired by a rapid and persistent upgradation of technology and scientific knowledge. It is estimated that from one-third to one-half of the growth experienced by the industrially advanced countries has come from technological progress.

Thus, technology has emerged as the principal driving force for long-term economic growth. Economic growth results both from slow and steady improvements in technology as well as from the 'breakthrough' inventions. Breakthrough inventions are, however, unpredictable and such inventions change almost the direction of the entire industrial structure.

33. Economic growth and technological progress depend on each other.
34. The invention of computer can be listed in 'breakthrough' inventions.
35. There are some other causes on which economic growth depends.
36. With growth in economy, technology advancement can be speed up.
37. It requires a lot of money for improving the technology.

Passage 8

Indians are now moving faster towards value-added rich diet. From consuming cereals in large quantities in the past, Indian's over the next two decades, would move towards milk and milk products in large quantities followed by fruits, vegetables, meat and fish. India now ranks as the world's largest milk-producing country followed by US and Russia. Moreover, milk has been a part of the traditional Indian diet. In the last 38 years, Indians have already touched the WTO norms of daily milk consumption of 220 g of milk per persons from 111 m in 1973. Consumption of cereals has been declining across several states in India barring Kerala, Paschim Banga and Odisha. The consumption of non-cereal food such as milk, eggs, meat, fruits and vegetables has been highest in the State of Punjab and Haryana.

38. In India milk and milk products are likely to witness the highest growth by 2030 from the present consumption in comparison to other diets.

39. Milk and its variants are at the top of the diet charts of Indians owing to the large availability and adopting it as a traditional diet.

40. Income levels of Indians are witnessing descending trends and this is likely to continue in the coming years.

41. To meet the demand of non-cereal consumption the policy on agriculture needs to facilitate diversification and release of land from rice and wheat crops.

42. Milk consumptions per person in Russia and US are less than that in India.

Passage 9

Cinema's obsession with violence is growing. Most films have a liberal dose of it, and what is even worse is that much of it could have been edited out or not shot at all in the first place. Frames of brutality – cold-blooded murder or sadistic rape – mix and run along with perfect love stories or pleasing family dramas or pure children's fare. With the increasing tendency among our directors and producers to allow their heroes/heroines to act out evil, if only to justify the end, the line between good and bad is disappearing. For teenagers and even those younger, this can cause moral confusion, leaving them to often grapple with this dilemma by arguing that their favourite stars can do no wrong . If they kill, they had to. If they drank, drove and ran over someone, they had no other choice.

43. The teenagers and youngsters watch movies more frequently than older people.

44. Nowadays all sections of viewers watch violence in cinema.

45. Cinema is the most popular means of entertainment.

46. The filmstars leave much influence on the viewers.

47. The taste of film varies from generation to generation.

Passage 10

The IMD forecast of a normal monsoon this year comes as the icing on the cake for the Indian Economy. The forescast removes clouds, if any, over the prospects for a strong economic performance this year. The economy appears poised for high growth with moderate inflation. A good monsoon was a key assumption in the finance ministry targeting a growth of nine per cent or more in this year's budget and in the predictions of similar high growth rates by the RBI. A normal monsoon for the country as a whole, as was the case last year, is not a guarantee against drought.

Structural changes in the Indian economy such as decontrol of the manufacturing sector and reduction in import tariffs, have narrowed the differences between domestic and international inflation. The average inflation in India during the last half-a-decade has been about six per cent.

48. Monsoon is a deciding factor for Indian economy.

49. A normal monsoon shows that there will be moderate inflation.

50. Finance ministry has assumed a good monsoon.

51. A normal monsoon never gives a guarantee against drought.

52. For the last half a decade the inflation of 6% is a bad sign.

Passage 11

There has been considerable debate in Indian regarding the privatisation of higher education. In this debate, there is generally an implicit assumption that privatisation is essentially the same as corporatisation i.e. private investment comes due to the potential of returns. In the higher education field, privatisation and corporatisation are actually quite different. Privatisation is regarding who controls the educational institute and the role of government in the management and funding of the institute, while corporatisation is about making profits in India, there is no doubt that private not-for-profit universities need to be encouraged to increase educational opportunities and the fact that there is no other alternative as the government simply cannot create enough public universities to satisfy the demand. However, guidelinès for private not-for-profit universities should be made clear, simple and transparent to ensure that they are truly not for profit and offer a level playing field to all those who might want to set up a private university. **Allahabad Bank (PO) 2010**

53. Privatisation of higher education has yet to take proper shape in India.

54. Expansion of higher education opportunities in India is needed to meet the increasing demand.

55. Corporatisation of higher education has benefitted the students in the developed countries.

56. Privatisation of higher education will lead to commercialisation of education in India.

57. India does not have any extant guidelines for setting up higher educational institutions by private entities.

Passage 12

A radical new surgery procedure launched at, not long ago in India, is holding out fresh hope for patients of cardiac myopathy or enlargement of the heart. The technique now in India, allows patients to go home two weeks after the operation to lead a near-normal sedantary life. Cardiac myopathy is a condition that has a variety of causative factors. An attack from one of the 20 identified viruses, parasite infection, long-term alcohol abuse and blood pressure could bring it on and in rare cases, it could follow child birth and is even known to run in families. The condition is marked by an increase in the size of heart's chambers and a decrease in the efficiency of pumping.

58. The cardiac myopathy slows down the heart beat.

59. Cardiac myopathy is hereditary.

60. Earlier the patients suffering from cardiac myopathy were required to travel abroad for such operation.

61. The new technique was never tried in India in the past.

62. The efficiency of the heart is inversely proportional to the size of the heart.

Passage 13

Sunday clears away the rust of the whole week. The working man has always looked forward to Sunday, when he could get away from it all. In the office on Saturday afternoon , the eye often steals a furtive glance at the clock and the evening is blissful, in anticipation of a full day of leisure and fun. The five-day week made Friday evenings special, and then there were two wonderful days to look forward to. But there is no unmixed blessing in life and Sunday night blues continues to haunt us as ever. Once again, there is the hurry to get into bed early because one has to rise early and face the same old drill. There is also a feeling of dissatisfaction that Sunday was not really as good as anticipated. Perhaps a bit too much is expected of Sundays.

63. For non-working men all days of the week are like Sunday.

64. It is not necessary that every Sunday will pass in fun.

65. Holidays are necessary to enhance the productivity of the company.

66. Holidays provide freshness to the working man.

67. Working people usually work half-heartedly on Saturday.

Passage 14

India ranks 120th among the group of 122 countries evaluated for water quality by the United Nations. India also ranks 133rd out of 180 countries for its poor water availability. It is well-known that 70 to 80% of all illnesses in India are related to water contamination, with women and children particularly susceptible. Despite huge amounts of money being spent by government on increasing water supply and installing water treatment plants, the quality and availability of water is fast deteriorating. Faulty management compounds the problems. Farmers are using more than 100 to 200 times the pesticides and insecticides stipulated by the government and other agencies. The dangerous trace elements, due to their bio-accumulative character, find their way into vegetables and the metabolisms of cattle and chicken as well.

68. One of the reasons for the lack of clean drinking water is the pervasive contamination of the country's surface and ground water supply.

69. Food items like meat, milk and eggs are also contaminated.

70. Better water management by the government and the community cannot help in conserving water.

71. Through strict implementation of the government's water treatment programme, water can be rendered safe for drinking.

72. The ranking of the India, regarding quality and availability, are based on the findings which came close on the heels of discovery of more than tolerable level of pesticides in the country's bottled water.

Passage 15

India constitutes 2% of world's geographical area. It has only 1% of the world's forest cover and 0.5% of the world's pasture land. However, it has to support 18% of the world's human population and 15% of the global population of livestock. The productivity of India's forests is among the lowest— 0.7 cubic metre per hectare as compared to the world average of 2.1 cubic metres.

73. India is not very densely populated.

74. The productivity of world's forests is thrice that of India's forests.

75. More than half of India is under forest cover.

76. The number of livestock population in India exceeds that of human population.

77. In terms of livestock population, India is one of the six largest countries in the world.

Passage 16

Even as the economy is back on track and consumer confidence up, the number of credit cards in the system continues to dip. In the last one year, the total number of credit cards in use has dipped by almost 50 lakh. According to the latest data released, the number of credit cards dipped to about 2 crore as of end February 2010 from around 2.5 crore a year ago. The data also indicate that average monthly card spends both in terms of value as well as volume has still not touched the precrisis levels. Average monthly spend in FY'10 has fallen to ₹ 5100 crore against ₹ 5400 crore in FY, 09, while average monthly volumes in the current years has been just 1.94 crore a month compared to 2.16 crore a month in FY' 09. Even peak festival spending through cards in the current fiscal is less than the previous year's levels.

BOB (PO) 2010

78. Credit card usage in the current year has substantially decreasing from FY 09.

79. People are not using credit cards in the current year due to rampant credit card related fraud.

80. There has been a drop of about 40% in use of credit card in the current year from the previous year.

81. There has been a drop of about 10% in the number of credit card transactions in the current year from the previous year.

82. The drop in usage of credit cards in India is less than that in many other countries.

Passage 17

Of late, studies in the phenomenon of rural migration have acquired great relevance and the observations of broad spectrum of impact have been exceedingly tantalising even at the penultimate phase. The labourers of Bihar are migrating in large numbers every year due to lamentable prospect of industrial development and absence of an ideal condition for agriculture. Various problems ensure out of it. Summarily, it has adversely affected the economy of the state.

83. Unemployment in rural Bihar induces people to migrate to earn their livelihood.

84. To stop migration and provide people engagement in their local areas, the only way is to improve the standard of life of villagers.

85. Industries will face shortage of labourers in the years to come in Bihar.

Punjab & Sind Bank (PO) 2010

Passage 18

Internationally, tourism occupies a very important place in the economies of several countries . It has today achieved the status of an industry Governments all over the world are competing with each other in selling "tourism and travel" concept, its history,culture, sunshine, snow and sands to people all over the world, It is the world's largest industry which is forecasted to grow 4 % annually till 2020. At present it generates 4494 billion dollars in economic activity, contributes about 11. 6% to the global GDP and employs about 9.4% of the global labor force. International tourist arrivals reached 699 million in 2010, almost 50 million more than in 2009. What is heartening about this industry is the fact that despite a number of conflicts all over the world, in the last 50 years, it had never seen as single year of decline.

However, in India, the industry has largely remained ignored, performing well below its potential,despite the fact that India has a unique heritage and culture and a wide gamut of tourist attractions, Tourism economy in India accounts for 5.6% of the GDP, supports 5.8% of the total employment in the country and generates 10.8% of the total exports from the country, wath just 2.4 million arrivals. India accounted for only 0.4% of the world tourist arrivals in the year 2010.

In spite of the fact that there are some of the most exquisite sites and locales and some of the best monuments to see, we rank a poor 43rd in the world. Smaller countries like France, Spain Hungary and Poland are way ahead of India. Even a small country like Sri Lanka, despite ethnic strife for the last 12 years, is ahead of India with about 4 million international arrivals.

86. Smaller countries have more attractive history, culture, sunshine, snow and sands than bigger countries.

87. Tourism industry is the second largest net foreign exchange earner in India.

88. Poor infrastructure facilities are responsible for the dismal performance of tourism sector in India.

89. Tourism in India is an industry with a huge potential.

90. There has been phenomenal growth in tourism all over the world.

91. Tourism industry cannot be affected badly by prolonged world conflict.

Direction (Q. Nos. 92-101) *Each of these questions has a statement based on the preceding passage. Evaluate each statement.*

Give answer

(a) if the statement is a Major Objective in making the decision; one of the goals sought by the decision maker

(b) if the statement is a Major Factor in making the decision; an aspect of the problem, specifically mentioned in the passage, which fundamentally affects and/or determines the decision

(c) if the statement is a Minor Factor in making the decision; a less important element bearing on or affecting a Major Factor, rather than a Major Objective directly

(d) if the statement is a Major Assumption in making the decision; a projection or supposition arrived at by the decision maker before considering the factor and alternative

Passage 19

The railroads was not the first institution to impose regularity on society or to draw attenion to the importance of precise time keeping. For as long as merchants have set out their wars at day break and communal festivities have been celebrated, people have been in rough agreement with their neighbours as to the time of day. The value of tradition is today more apparent than ever. Were it not for public acceptance of a single yardstick of time, social life would be unbearably chaotic. The massive daily transfer of goods. Services and information would proceed in fits and starts, the very fabric of modern society would begin to unravel. **NIFT (PG) 2014**

92. An accepted way of measuring time is essential for the smooth functioning of society.

93. In modern society we must make more time for our neighbour's.

94. Society judges people by the time at which they conduct certain activities.

95. The Phrase 'this tradition' in the passage refers to people's agreement on the measurement of time.

96. Railroad supports precise time keeping.

Passage 20

A slowing economy, rising fuel prices and high taxes hit Indian aviation in 2012. Strikes at Air India and a bleeding Kingfisher added to the heat because foreign airlines would not pick up stakes in cash-strapped Indian carriers unless steps are taken to stem high costs of aviation operations in India, International Air Transport Association (IATA) chief Tony Tyler said, No, I don't think it (allowing foreign airlines to invest in Indian carriers) is a game changer but it is a good thing, said Tyler in but it will not solve the problems of Indian aviation.

It is a step in the right direction but not the panacea that some believe it is', 'As long as high taxes prevail, high airport costs and congestion and poorly developed air navigation (services) means more congestion, high cost of operations exist, you are not going to get a lot of people to invest in airlines,' the director-general and CEO of IATA said. Observing that there were restrictions on investing in airlines around the world, which was 'a problem for the industry', Tyler said "any move that we see in liberalising is a good thing. But unless conditions in India are improved for airlines, you are not going to see a flood of foreign carriers coming into the industry. Because foreign capital needs a return just as anywhere else." he added. **NIFT (PG) 2013**

97. Foreign capital should be invested in Indian aviation.

98. There is a slowing Indian economy.

99. There were strikes at Air India.

100. Foreign airlines would pick up stakes in Indian carriers.

101. There is a poorly developed air navigation leading to more congestion.

Direction (Q. Nos. 102-106) *The given below passages are followed by several possible inferences which can be drawn from the facts states in the passage. You have to examine each inference separately in the context of the passage and decide upon its degree of truth of falsity.*

Give answer

(a) if the inference is 'definitely true', i.e. it properly follows from the statement of facts given
(b) if the inference is 'probably true', though not 'definitely true' in the light of the facts given
(c) if the 'data are inadequate', i.e. from the facts given you cannot say whether the inference is likely to be true or false
(d) if the inference if 'probably false', though not 'definitely false' in the light of the facts given
(e) if the inference is 'definitely false', i.e. it cannot possibly be drawn from the facts given or it contradicts the given facts

Passage 21

A study conducted by a committee, titled "World Class in India", found the Indian bicycle industry to be globally competitive. It projected the demand to grow from 117.2 lakh units in 2010-11 to 129.5 lakh units in 2012-13. However, all this has changed drastically post-imposition of excise duty. According to All India Cycle Manufacturers' Association (AICMA), the production figure would be in the vicinity of 100 lakh units. It says that against the net gain of excise duty of ₹ 50 crore, the government has lost 29 lakh bicycles. Even if one assumes that the production is less by 29 lakh units, the government will lose ₹ 122 per bicycle, which is the excise duty paid actually on inputs by manufacturers. Thus, the government has lost ₹ 35 crore. Not to forget the losses in terms of 2% Central Sales Tax (CST) and the state taxes which vary from 4-8%. Assuming an average of 6% states tax and 2% CST, the government has lost another ₹ 25 crore.

102. In the total bargain it seems that there will be a net loss of ₹ 10 crore to the government.

103. There will be no decline in domestic demand of bicycle in this current year.

104. AICMA acts as a liaisoning body with the government to highlight the industry's problem.

105. The reason for India's export success in the past is the large home base of the black cycle.

106. Imposition of excise duty has unnerved the Indian bicycle industry.

Advanced Level

Direction (Q. Nos. 1-25) *Passages are followed by several possible inferences which can be drawn from the facts stated in the passages. You have to examine each inference separately in the context of the passage and decide upon its degree of truth or falsity.*

Give answer

(a) if the inference is 'definitely true', i.e. it properly follows from the statement of facts given
(b) if the inferences is 'probably true' though not 'definitely true' in the light of the facts given
(c) if the 'data inadequate' i.e. from the facts given you can not say whether the inference is likely to be true or false
(d) if the inference is 'probably false', though not 'definitely false' in the light of the facts given
(e) if the inference is 'definitely false', i.e. it cannot possibly be drawn from the facts given or it contradicts the given facts

Passage 1

Asia has become the growth center of the world economy in recent years. Within the region, India and South Korea are the third and fourth largest economies after China and Japan. Though the Asian growth stories mainly revolve around India and China, South Korea has remained a key player for these countries as one of their major trading and investment partners. South Korea adopted outward oriented economic policies with the beginning of its first five year economic development plan in 1962. Which resulted in high growth and the integration of the Korean economy with the rest of the world. Subsequently, high and consistent economic growth made South Korea one of the high-income economies in Asia. Korea is still growing at a faster rate compared to other developed economies. India on the other hand, adopted an import substitution policy since its independence until the early 90s. Since, then India has introduced wide-ranging economic policy reforms and is moving towards market-driven economy. This has resulted in consistent high economic growth over the last one-and-a half decade. **Corporation Bank (PO) 2010**

1. Only Korean economy is considered as robust by the international community.

2. Japan's economic growth over the last decade is the highest in Asia.

3. The Korean economy is traditionally different than the Indian economy in its approach.
4. The economic growth of India prior to1990s was much higher than the present growth rate.
5. India and China together are considered the driving force of Asian economy.

Passage 2

Sub-saharan Africa whose GDP grew at less than 3% a year through entire 1990, grew 5.1% in 2009 and at 5.2% in 2010 and is projected to grow at 5.6% in the fiscal year ending 2011. In other words, India is growing about 1.5% per year faster than sub-saharan Africa. If India is merely doing somewhat better than the worst preforming region in the world, there is no reason to get euphoric. Why is the world economy faring so well that even the worst historical performers are suddenly looking good? Africans who are the fragments of the former Soviet union, are patting themselves on the back for reforming and becoming efficient . He world economy has hit a gold patch, even most pitiful ones, India has benefited from the rising tide like all other. But it is illusory to think that policies Remove Full stop from here and project will always keep improving. **IOB (PO) 2010**

6. India's projected economic growth for the current fiscal year is around 7%.
7. India's economy is way above the perennially low performing countries in the world.
8. Indian economy may be above to sustain present rate of growth in the coming years without major changes in its economic policies.
9. In the past economy has never grown at the present rate.
10. Average economic growth of breakaway Soviet Republics is about 6% at present.

Passage 3

Privatisation is no panacea when it comes to education nor can high-cost intervention at the tertiary stage produce quality talent. The backbone of quality education is primary hooling and improving that is not just a question of funding. The government has taken some steps to improve the situation by increasing the percentage of allocation in the budget. But it has done precious little to increase the efficacy of public spend in education. For that is political and administrative task. Teachers who do not turn unto teach at real schools (absenteeism is about 30% according to one estimate) and teachers who are not equipped or motivated to teach but continue is their services with challenge are part of India's socio-political reality.

11. Quality of education is ensured in all the privately run educational institutions in India.
12. Motivating the primary school teachers and improving attendance of these teachers are major challenges in India.
13. The Indian Government has not done enough to improve the quality of secondary education.
14. Allocation of more funds in the budget for primary education will substantially improve the quality of education.
15. Government has been unsuccessful in achieving the desired result in education.

Passage 4

The cotton textile industry is facing a major shortage of good quality cotton with very little contamination . At present, the weakest link in cotton production is the lack of home-grown Extra Long Staple (ELS) cotton. This has been the traditional problem with the Indian industry since independence, which has been partially overcome but growing demand is setting the industry back India produces about 5.3 lakh bales of ELS cotton as against the requirement of 8 lakh bales. So, the need of the hour is to see that India's dependence on imported cotton is reduced by improving the quality of domestic ELS cotton. The demand of ELS cotton is likely to increase to 10 lakh bales due to a rise in spinning capacity and also due to under-spinning of ELS coton due to its shortage.

16. India regularly imports ELS cotton to meet its requirement.
17. India at present does not have extra spinning capacity.
18. The quality of ELS cotton produced in India is superior to that of other countries.
19. India produces about two-third of its requirement of ELS than cotton.
20. There may be more than thirty per cent increase in the demand of ELS cotton in future.

Passage 5

Coal and power are the mainstay of India's energy sector. Coal is the country's backbone of energy supply and is likely to continue playing a significant role in meeting energy demands it accounts for over 50% of the commercial energy requirements of the country. Despite raported figures of a relatively large coal resource compared with other fossil fuels, it should be capital the country has been facing shortages from time to time. Projections for time to time by various study groups show an increasing gap between the demand and supply of domestic coal, which may result in increased imports. Moreover, the country's resources are often overstated as assessment process does not consider the quality, technical feasibility and economic viability of coal mining and exploration. **BOI (PO) 2010**

21. The coal mines of the developed countries generate more profits than those in India.

22. India's coal mines and mining activities are commercially viable.

23. India's dependence on coal for generating energy will continue in the times to come.

24. India's coal reserves are much more than it's requirement.

25. Assessment process of coal reserves is not capable of identifying coal reserves accurately.

Direction (Q. Nos. 26-50) *Each of these questions has a statement based on the preceding passage. Evaluate each statement.*

Give answer

(a) if the statement is a Major Objective in making the decision; one of the goals sought by the decision maker

(b) if the statement is a Major Factor in making the decision; an aspect of the problem, specifically mentioned in the passage, which fundamentally affects and/or determines the decision

(c) if the statement is a Minor Factor in making the decision; a less important element bearing on or affecting a Major Factor, rather than a Major Objective directly

(d) if the statement is a Major Assumption in making the decision; a projection or supposition arrived at by the decision maker before considering the factor and alternative

Passage 6

Morgan Stanley on Monday became the second large global giant to exit India's crowded and barely profitable mutual fund industry when it agreed to sell its business to HDFC, the country's biggest mutual fund manager. HDFC Mutual Fund (MF), with assets of ₹ 1.03 lakh crore, agreed to buy all eight schemes of Morgan Stanley with combined assets of ₹ 3290 crore.

The purchase is expected to help the fund widen the gap with Reliance, the second biggest mutual fund house and consolidate its position at the top of the industry. Reliance has assets worth ₹ 93249 crore. Morgan was the first global giant to launch a mutual fund in India in 1994 after liberalisation but its performance in the country has been rather lacklustre.

Its asset size is small by international and Indian standards and like Fidelity it has been unable to keep pace with the growth of Indian mutual funds such as HDFC MF, Reliance MF, ICICI Pru, UTI MF and Birla Sunlife which between them control over 50% of the industry's size. The fund posted losses in both 2011 and 2012. The mutual fund and insurance industry must go through consolidation. Small funds are not viable and more people are beginning to sense that.

The opportunity cropped up as Morgan Stanley approached us, Chairman HDFC told. Tough business conditions are forcing many Asset Management Companies (AMCs) to either rope in strategic partners or exit the business completely. India has about 44 mutual fund houses with numerous schemes and they compete for investors money in the main cities of Mumbai and Delhi.

The proportion of small savers investing in these schemes is not very high and the funds depend upon cash rich companies and high net worth individuals for a bulk of their investments. The consolidation in the industry is likely to continue as industry faces tough times we believe only those companies can survive which have a strong distribution reach, said CEO of mutual fund AMC who did not want to be identified. **NIFT (PG) 2014**

26. The purchase is expected to help the fund widen the gap with Reliance.

27. The asset size of Morgan Stanley is small by international and Indian Standards.

28. Small funds are not viable and more and more people are beginning to sense that.

29. Only those companies can survive which have a strong distribution reach.

30. Asset management companies are facing tough business conditions.

Passage 7

ING Groep NV, the biggest Dutch financial services company, is said to be seeking a buyer for its 43% stake in, ING Vysya Bank, as the prospects of limited purpose banking in India and tough competition in retail market make it rethink its local strategy, five people familiar with the thinking said. ING, which has been selling assets across the Asian region and some in Europe itself to repay the Dutch Government for bailing it out from the 2008 credit crisis, may exit the domestic banking business comprising retail, corporate and treasury, to focus on corporate banking. they said.

The group, which also has to bolster capital to meet the Basel III regulations, may get atleast $ 600 million at current market prices or even more for the stake depending on the transaction. There is no certainty that a deal will happen.

Although ING Vysya may be an attractive asset for every private sector bank because of its clean books, 575 branches and loyal customer. Kotak Mahindra Bank seems to be best placed to benefit from the acquisition of ING Vysya, say analysis. It is a very good business and it (ING Vysya) provides Kotak the opportunity to scale up, said chief mentor BMR and Associates, an advisory firm.

Although Kotak's market value is about six times that of ING Vysya, Kotak's loan assets is about ₹ 50539 crore, compared with ING's ₹ 33575 crore regulatory filings show ING's ₹ 40000 crore of deposits, of which a third is low cost and its customer loyalty may be the most attractive part. But Kotak said it is not negotiating for a takeover. 'We have not been approached for purchase of shares of ING Group in ING, Vysya Bank, said a Kotak Mahindra Group spokesman in an e-mail response.

'We have had no negotiations with officials of ING, Vysya Bank on this matter.' For Kotak, it might make sense to go for a stock-swap deal, since it could achieve twin objectives of the management, said one of the persons familiar with the thinking. There will be no cash outflow and at the same time help founder Uday Kotak to reduce his stake in the bank to meet regulations.

The Reserve Bank of India last June directed Uday Kotak to lower his stake in the bank to 10% over the next eight years. It is at 44% now, filings show International banks in India are redrawing their strategy as the industry goes through tough capital requirements after the credit crisis. Institutions such as JP Morgan Chase and Co have decided to remain a corporate and investment banking company in India and others such as Barclays are moving toward that, shedding retail, the Reserve Bank of India's decision to possibly mandate local incorporation many lead to further changes. **NIFT (PG) 2014**

31. ING Groep NV, the biggest Dutch financial services company perceives that there is tough competition in retail market.

32. ING will focus on corporate banking.

33. The group may get atleast $ 600 million at current market price.

34. ING Vysya has 575 branches.

35. The industry in India is going through tough requirements after the credit crisis.

Passage 8

McLeod Russel India Ltd. (MRIL) is keen to make further acquisitions in Rwanda where it already has a presence. "Rwanda is on our scanner now", sources said. MRIL, which had bought into a Government-owned tea oufit in the African country in 2010, has so far had a good experience, according to sources. Following a privatisation drive in Rwanda, the Government had divested 60% of its stake in this estate while retaining 30%. The remaining 10% has been given to a workers, cooperative. "This is as per the divestment policy of the Government." At present, two more tea estates-Mulundi and Saggasa have been put on the block for which bids have been invited by the Government.

MRIL may bid for these two estates after getting a nod from its board. The Gisovu tea estate in Rwanda, which was bought earlier this year, contributed 2 million kg out of the 23 million kg tea crop that McLeod Russel reaped out of its overseas estates in Vietnam, Rwanda and Uganda. "Production increases were recorded from our tea estates in all these three countries," say sources.

The company's overseas foray started with acquisition of the Phu Ben Tea Company in Vietnam in 2008-09. From a production level of 4.5 million kg, Phu Ben now produces around 5 million kg.

The B M Khaitan group company believes that the only way to grow is through acquisition and since 2005 it has made quite a few acquisitions within the country. In 2010, it completed its acquisition of the Ugandan tea company, Rwenzi Tea Investments Ltd, from James Finlay International Holdings Ltd. of the UK through its wholly-owned subsidiary Borelli Tea Holdings (UK), the outfit through which McLeod Russel makes its overseas acquisitions. MRIL, which makes its acquisitions through a mix of debt and internal accruals, currently has reserves of around ₹ 900 crore. "Our debts are set to decline to ₹ 260 crore by 31 March, 2012, from ₹ 316 crore at end-March 2011 and we have enough liquidity to fund any future acquisition," sources said. **NIFT (PG) 2012**

36. The privatisation drive by the Government of Rwanda.

37. The company's belief that the only way to grow is through acquisitions.

38. The debts of MRIL are set to decline in the coming months.

39. The board of MRIL, will give its permission to bid for two more tea estates in Rwanda.

40. Making further acquisitions in Rwanda.

Passage 9

Wipro Consumer Care and Lighting, part of Wipro, plans to enter body lotions and shampoo categories with its flagship brand Santoor. "While the category is highly competitive, there is a lot of headroom to grow as penetration level is significantly lower in India compared to other markets," according to the president at Wipro Consumer Care. The company started test marketing, the hair care and body lotion products recently. Wipro Consumer, which recorded a 17% increase in its revenues in the third quarter and ended December at ₹ 1028 crore, also expects hall of its total sales to come from international business with the addition of Singapore-based FMCG firm LD Waxsons.

At present international operations contribute 40-45% to its revenues, Wipro Consumer acquired LD Waxsons for about $144 million (approx ₹ 775 crore). During the third quarter, its Indonesia and Vietnam businesses grew 26% and 24%, respectively, while China and middle East grew by 32%.The Santoor brand has been growing over 20% in the last few quarters. It is the third largest soap brand in the country after Hindustan Unilever's Lifeboy and Lux and has market leadership in South and Western India. Last month, it became the top brand in states such as Maharashtra , Karnataka and Gujarat.

However, it's a huge task for Wipro to replicate a similar feat in the ₹ 4500 crore shampoo market, where HUL is by far the leader with over 50% market share. Also, margins have moderated in the past on account of promotions and ad spends, says a recent report by JP Morgan. Hence, companies such as Proctor and Gamble and L'Oreal are introducing various premium products like hair treatments, serums, hair masks, hair conditioners to help support margin profile for their hair care portfolio. **NIFT (PG) 2013**

41. Expanding in the body lotion and shampoo category is easier due to low penetration levels in India.

42. Santoor is an established brand in certain markets and hence, it will be easier to grow.

43. Margins in the shampoo market decreasing due to increasing promotion and ad spends.

44. Ensuring growth in international markets through the Waxsons acquisition.

45. Significant growth in the international businesses of the company.

Passage 10

The Union Commerce and Industry Minister on Friday unveiled a new corporate logo for the National Textile Corporation (NTC), reflecting the new face of the state-owned enterprise as part of the plans to make it a world-class textile company. "The Government is committed to making NTC a world-class eco-friendly integrated textile company and flag bearer of the sector. The ongoing revival-cum-modernisation programme and new corporate and brand identity launch by NTC is aimed at achieving this goal", he said at a function organised for the purpose.

He said NTC was a key player in the textile sector and its recent moves would definitely transform it into an integrated company capable of addressing the needs of the nation. NTC had made a turn-around within a short span to emerge as a debt-free company with a highly competitive revival strategy, he added. He also launched two new look retail stores of NTC-one in Delhi and another in Coimbatore, Tamil Nadu via satellite link up. This is a part of revamping of NTC's 93 stores to reflect the company's new face across the country.

Speaking on the occasion, the Textile Secretary said the revamp and modernisation steps taken by NTC in the recent past in view of the changing times and consumer aspirations of modern India would help in instilling confidence in the minds of all stakeholders. The NTC Chairman and Managing Director said the new corporate logo reflected the new face of NTC to the world. It had been designed as free flowing fabric, indicating the new aspirations and changing aspirations of India.

Apart from re-branding, NTC had developed a new marketing and corporate strategy that included revamping of all NTC stores and setting up of new stores, he said. The internal marketing programme to employees and key customers includes undertaking a complete programme to bring the new vision and culture to its employees. Respective mill managers would be conducting a smaller unveiling ceremony of the new logo along with the NTC anthom at all the mills. Besides, all the employees would be given a small commemorative badge of the new logo. **NIFT (PO) 2012**

46. Making NTC a world-class integrated textile company and the leader of the Indian textile industry.

47. The new corporate logo of NTC reflects its new face to the world.

48. The highly competitive revival strategy that helped make NTC debt-free.

49. The recent modernisation steps taken by NTC would instill confidence in the minds of all stakeholders.

50. Implementing a programme to bring the new vision and culture to the employees of NTC.

Direction (Q. Nos. 51-53) *Study the following information carefully and answer the questions given below.* **SBI (PO) 2010**

The centre reportedly wants to continue providing subsidies to consumers for cooking gas and kerosene for five more years. This is no-good news form the point of view of in the fiscal deficit. Mounting subventions for subsidies means diversion of savings by the government from investment to consumption, raising the cost of capital in the process. The government must cut expenditure on subsidies to create more fiscal space for investments in both physical and social infrastructure. It should outline a plan for comprehensive reform in major subsidies including petroleum, food and fertilisers and set goal posts.

51. Which of the following is a conclusion which can be drawn from the fact stated in the given paragraph?
 (a) Subsidy provided by the government under various heads to the citizen increases the cost of capital
 (b) Government is unable to withdraw subsidies provided to various items
 (c) Government subsidy on kerosene is purely a political decision
 (d) Government does not have enough resources to continue providing subsidy on petroleum products
 (e) None of the above

52. Which of the following is an assumption which is implicit in the facts stated in the given paragraph?
 (a) People in India may not be able to pay more of petroleum products
 (b) Many people in India are rich enough to buy petroleum products at market cost
 (c) Government may not be able to create more infrastructure facilities if the present level of subsidy continues for a longer time
 (d) Government of India has sought assistance from international financial organisations for its infrastructural projects
 (e) None of the above

53. Which of the following is an inference which can be made from the facts stated in the given paragraph?
 (a) India's fiscal deficit is negligible in comparison to other emerging economies in the world
 (b) Subsidy on food and fertilisers are essential for the growth of Indian economy
 (c) Reform in financial sector will weaken India's position in the international arena
 (d) Gradual withdrawl of subsidy is essential for effectively managing fiscal deficit in India
 (e) None of the above

54. During the SARS days, about 23500 doctors who had treated SARS sufferers died and about 23670 doctors who had not engaged in treatment for SARS sufferers died. On the basis of those figures, it can be concluded that it was not much more dangerous to participate in SARS treatment during the SARS day than it was not to participate in SARS treatment.
 Which of the following would reveal most clearly the absurdity of the conclusion drawn above? **MHT CET MBA 2014**
 (a) Counting deaths among doctors who had participated in SARS treatment in addition to deaths among doctors who had not participated is SARS treatment
 (b) Expressing the difference between the numbers of deaths among doctors who had treated SARS sufferers and doctors who had treated SARS sufferers and doctors who had not treated SARS suffers as a percentage of the total number of deaths
 (c) Separating deaths caused by accidents during the treatment to SARS suffers from deaths caused by infect of SARS suffers
 (d) Comparing darth rates per thousand members of each group rather than comparing total numbers of deaths
 (e) None of the above

Direction (Q. Nos. 55-57) *Study the following information carefully and answer the questions that follow.*

Poverty measurement is an unsettled issue, both conceptual and methodological. Since, poverty is a process as well as an outcome; many come out of it while others may be falling into it. The net effect of these two parallel processes is a proportion commonly identified as the 'head count ratio' but these ratios hide the fundamental dynamism that characterises poverty in practice.

The most recent poverty reestimates by an expert group has also missed the crucial dynamism. In a study conducted on 13000 households which represented the entire country in 1993-94 and again on 2004-05, it was found that in the ten-year period 18.2% rural population moved out of poverty whereas another 22.1% fell into it over this period. This net increase of about four percentage points was seen to have a considerable variation across states and regions.

55. Which of the following is an assumption which is implicit in the facts stated in the above paragraph?
(a) It may not be possible to have an accurate poverty measurement in India
(b) Level of poverty in India is static over the years
(c) Researchers avoid making conclusions on poverty measurement data in India
(d) Government of India has a mechanism to measure level of poverty effectively and accurately
(e) None of the above

56. Which of the following is a conclusion which can be drawn from the facts stated in the above paragraph?
(a) Accurate estimates of number of people living below poverty line in India is possible to be made
(b) Many expert groups in India are not interested to measure poverty objectively
(c) Process of poverty measurement needs to take into account various factors to tackle its dynamic nature
(d) People living below poverty line remain in that position for a very long time
(e) None of the above

57. Which of the following is an inference which can be made from the facts stated in the above paragraph?
(a) Poverty measurement tools in India are outdated
(b) Increase in number of persons falling into poverty varies considerably across the country over a period of time
(c) Government of India has stopped measuring poverty related studies
(d) People living in rural areas are more susceptible to fall into poverty over the time
(e) None of the above

Direction (Q. No. 58) *Read the following paragraph and answer the questions which follows.*

MHT CET MBA 2011

Trucks carrying load of more than 10 tonnes are not allowed to run on the city roads from 8 am to 10 pm. These trucks can run on the highways which are outside city limits. Taking highways rather than city roads, however, means that these trucks have to travel a minimum of 10 km extra as compared to city roads.

58. Which of the following can be inferred from the given paragraph?
(a) After 10 pm, there are more trucks than cars on the city roads
(b) Cars are not allowed to run on the highways between 8 am to 10 pm
(c) Trucks carrying more than 10 tonnes of weight cause more traffic inconvenience than the ones carrying lesser load
(d) It is as convenient for the trucks to run on highways as on the city roads
(e) Most truck drivers would prefer to drive on the highways rather than city roads as the highways do not have regular city traffic such as cars and buses

Direction (Q. No. 59) *Read the following paragraph carefully and answer the question which follows.*

MHT CET MBA 2011

The price of a TV in Bangkok is 65% less than the price of the same TV in India. Even after adding custom duty and transportation charges, it is still 65% cheaper to import a TV from Bangkok to India than to buy it from India. The reason for this difference in price can be attributed to high wholesale price in India set by the manufacturing company.

59. Which of the following can be inferred/concluded form the given facts?
(a) All electronic items are cheaper in Bangkok than in India
(b) The custom duty on a TV bought from Bangkok is less than 65% of the price of the same TV bought in India
(c) 65% of the price of the TV bought in India is equal to the custom duty and the tarrif charges paid by a person in Bangkok
(d) TV dealers in India earn 65% more profit than a dealer in Bangkok
(e) Custom duty on export of TVs imposed by India is far higher than that imposed by Thailand (Bangkok)

Direction (Q. No. 60) *Read the following paragraph carefully and answer the question which follows.*

XAT 2010

Dr Puneet worried about the test results of his patient, Ms Benita. Ms Benita was an old rich window with no potentially fatal Lymphanigioleiomyomatosis (LAM) disease. LAM is rare and difficult to diagnose. People with LAM often need oxygen and lung transplants as the disease continues its course. According to the test results, Ms Benita might have got it.

Dr Puneet explained the situation to Ms Benita carefully. Without naming the disease, he explained that the disease was progressive and would need treatment using drugs which were still at the experimental stage. Even, then the chance of success was not too bright. If the treatment was unsuccessful, then they would have to get ready for a lung transplant. The lung transplant itself was a risky course of treatment. Even if successful, she would require constant medical support and treatment.

Ms Benita looked blank. She asks Dr Puneet for his advice about the course of action. He nods gravely, 'I'm afraid, Ms Benita, I think there is only one course we can take.

60. What should be Dr Puneet's advice?
(a) Tell Ms Benita the details of the disease
(b) Conduct another test to confirm the diagnosis
(c) Leave the matter; anyway the outcome cannot be changed
(d) Treat Ms Benita without telling her about the disease
(e) Propose that Ms Benita go ahead with the experimental drugs

61. Find the best conclusion of the passage.

Now-a-days, people are so busy in their work that they do not take care of their health. A lot of diseases like diabetes, arthritis, heart attack, blood pressure are increasing due to unhealthy lifestyle. People do not find time to exercise. Stress is continuously increasing. The fast food is quick, easy and tastes better but it is not healthy. Habits like smoking and drinking alcohol have many side effects. Polluted city environment has also negative impact on the health of citizens. To live happy and healthy life; it is important to take care of oneself. **SNAP 2014**

(a) Now-a-days everybody smokes and drinks
(b) Diseases are increasing only because of pollution
(c) People are happy and stress free because their life is too busy
(d) Current city environment, life style and habits are affecting health of citizens

Direction (Q. Nos. 62-65) *Read the following information and the five statements given below it carefully and answer the questions which follow.*

MHT CET MBA 2011

India and China make competing plans for the river Brahmaputra's precious waters. The dams and hydropower projects planned are stated to have a potential of about 20000 MW. There is, however, apprehension in the Indian water and power ministries that China's similar dam construction programmes on the same river could adversely affect this potential.

(a) Brahmaputra river passes through both the countries
(b) India should take the lead and begin construction of dams for hydropower projects before China does
(c) Building cascades of dams at multiple locations in the river would have massive environmental impacts
(d) A dam built by China on river Xang, close to Indian border, led to severe floods in India and some parts of China last year
(e) Similar dams built on the river Xang which passes through both the countries did not affect the power generating capacity of either dams

62. Which of the statements A, B, C, D and E mentioned above represents an assumption implicit in the given paragraph or an inference which can be drawn from it?

(a) Only A (b) Only B (c) Only C (d) Only D
(e) Both A and C

63. Which of the statements A, B, C, D and E mentioned above would weaken the case for both the countries to build dams on the river?

(a) Only A (b) Only B (c) Only C (d) Only D
(e) Both C and D

64. Which of the statements A, B, C, D and E mentioned above would ease India's apprehensions regarding China's similar dam construction projects?

(a) A (b) B (c) C (d) D
(e) E

65. Which of the statements A, B, C, D and E mentioned above would best represent a course of action which can be taken by the Indian government to counter China's competing plans?

(a) A (b) B
(c) C (d) D
(e) E

66. Read the following passage and find best conclusions.

Diwali is a festival of lights; which signifies that good will always be better than evil. In the present day, many people have developed a lot of negativity in their minds and hearts, which has led to high corruption and higher crime rates. Value based education is the need of the day to eliminate darkness of cruelty, selfishness and greed and bring the light of wisdom, peace, kindness, truthfulness, right attitude, hard work and cooperation. Mahatma Gandhi also said that we should eradicate sins from hearts not the sinners. If a society has people with good heart, it will definitely flourish **SNAP 2014**

(a) Now-a-days nobody is good
(b) Now-a-days everybody is corrupt and criminal
(c) Value based education can save the society from crime and corruption
(d) It is not possible to fight against corruption as everybody is corrupt

67. The enrolment of first-time graduate students from India has registered a 16% decline in comparison to last year while that of China has increased by the same level, says a latest report. 'First time enrolment of students increased by 16% from China and by 22% from the Middle East. However, there was a 26% decline from India and 13% decline from South Korea', the Council of Graduate Schools (CGS) has said in its report. India sends one of the largest numbers of international students to the US for higher studies along with China and South Korea and the sharp drop of 16%, follows two years of modest decline, 2% in 2008 and 8% in 2007. The report also pointed that there was no growth in first time enrolment of international students in the US graduate schools from 2008 to 2009. **NIFT (PG) 2014**

(a) The overall number of first time enrolment of international students in US graduate schools has remained static with the Middle East showing growth and Asian Countries reflecting a mixed trend
(b) India and South Korea are gradually veering away from sending its students to the US for higher studies, whereas China, North Korea and the Middle East are sending higher numbers thereby even out the overall numbers
(c) The CGS has published a report to assess the trends in first time enrolment of international student populations in graduate schools in the US
(d) India, China and South Korea together account for a sizeable contingent of international students enrolling in US graduate schools for the first time, and help to keep the overall numbers stable even it there is a decline in number from other countries

68. The $ 300 pair of designer jeans is now, courtesy of the recession, the $ 200 pair of designer jeans. 'It was all just a fad', said Jeff Rudes, a founder of the hot denim label J Brand Jeans and an astute observer of the suspiciously inflated prices of fashion's most eternally reinvented staple. Like and commodity that becomes over-priced, there eventually comes a market correction. And denim's day of reckoning was long overdue **NIFT (PG) 2014**

(a) Jeff Rudes had been wary of the suspiciously inflated prices of jeans and had naticipated their fall owing to the recession

(b) As in the case of any product that becomes over-priced, recession brought about a correction in the 'prices of designer jeans that are now priced at a reasonable $ 200 a pair

(c) The fad of designer jeans at $ 300 a pair has been corrected by the recession and jeans are now available for just $ 200

(d) Recession or no recession, branded jeans continue to sell earlier at $ 300 a pair but now at a recession-reduced $ 200 a pair

69. A photochromic lens automatically adjusts, to the brightness of the Sun. Silver particles embedded in the lens material are triggered by UV light to darken when solar radiation increase and lighter when sunlight fades. The result is that your glasses have a much wider range of application into lower light conditions overcast, fog, morning and early evening. This process adjusts quickly and never wears out. If you go out and use it in a wide variety of light conditions with the same pair of glasses, photochromicity is highly desirable. **NIFT (PG) 2014**

(a) For someone who is exposed to different light conditions with the same pair of glasses, photochromic lenses are desirable, as they automatically adjust to the various light conditions

(b) Be it in the brightness of the Sun or in lower light conditions such as overcast, fog, morning and early evening, photochromic glasses are the best for your eyes

(c) Photochromic glasses are essential for healthy eyes as they protect them from UV rays by darkening in bright sunlight

(d) In order to have a much wide range of application into brighter or lower light conditions, it is essential to use photochromic lenses in your glasses

70. The Internet is about to get more accessible for millions worldwide with the imminent approval of a new multilingual address system that uses Asian and Arabic scripts, a global regulator said on Monday. The Internet Corporation for Assigned Names and Numbers (ICANN) said it would declare an end to the exclusive use of Latin characters for website addresses on Friday the final day of its six day conference in Seoul. 'This is the biggest change technically to the Internet, since it was invented 40 years ago', Peter Dengate Thrush, Chairman of the ICANN board in charge of reviewing the change told a press conference

(a) The ICANN board has plans to abolish exclusive use of Latin characters in the addresses and introduce both Arabic and Asian scripts to make Internet more broad based

(b) Multilingual Internet addresses with Chinese, Arabic, Korean and Japanese characters would soon be a reality as the ICANN board has approved this move

(c) Exclusive use of Latin American characters, in Internet addresses over the last 40 years has hindered the growth of Internet in Asian and Arabic countries

(d) Internet is to get more accessible soon with the move by global regulator ICANN to introduce a multi-lingual address system that uses Asian and Arabic scripts, instead of just Latin characters

71. In what can be seen as a positive impact of global warming, large bloom's of tiny marine plants called 'phytoplankton', that can absorb carbon dioxide from the atmosphere, are flourishing in the area opened up by massive ice melting in Antarctica. Without ice cover, the water gets exposed to light and circulation of nutrients that help the plants move in and take up extra amounts of carbon dioxide, becoming what scientists call a carbon sink. This is really massive—it's like having a new forest the size of Wales, said Professor Llyod Peck, a near-shore marine biologist from the British Antarctic Survey **NIFT (PG) 2014**

(a) An exciting fallout of the melting of ice in Antarctica due to global warming is the creation of 'carbon sinks' by blooming marine plants

(b) The melting of ice in the Antarctic region due to global warming has resulted in the blooming of tiny marine plants called phytoplankton that absorb massive quantities of carbon dioxide

(c) Global warming has resulted in some benefits as well, in the form of growth of vegetation in the hitherto barren Antarctic region

(d) The discovery of phytoplankton blooms in the Antarctic waters has got the scientists excited because it is a positive fallout of global warming

72. Study the following passage and find out which statement is best supported by this passage

"The school has always been the most important means of transferring the wealth of tradition from one generation to the next. This applies today in an even higher degree than informer times for, through the modern development of economy, the family as bearer of tradition and education has been weeked." **Uttarakhand PSC(Pre) 2012**

(a) There are means other than schools for transfer of traditions

(b) Several different sources must be tried

(c) Economic development plays a crucial role

(d) Family as ever is the most popular means

Answers with Explanations

Base Level

1. (*e*) From the passage it is clear that low interest rate encourage banks to take more risks. So, the inference is definitely false.
2. (*c*) In the passage, it is not given that NPAs occur by which factor. So, data are inadequate.
3. (*a*) This inference is definitely true.
4. (*d*) This inference is probably false.
5. (*b*) From the passage, it can be assumed that higher NPAs indicate shortcomings in disbursement and follow up of credit given by banks. So, it is probably true.
6. (*a*) From the passage it is clear that present Government and its to policy makers are not making any conscious effort to tackle the problem created by the extraordinary growth of India's population. So, the inference is definitely true.
7. (*c*) Roles of panchayats are not given in the passage.
8. (*d*) This inference is probably false.
9. (*b*) It can be assumed from the passage that effective machinery should also be brought in with family welfare and population Stabilisation programmes. So, this inference is probably true.
10. (*c*) It is not given in the passage that most of the skilled human resources in USA are Indians.
11. (*a*) From last couple of sentences of the passage, it is clear that the knowledge of a teacher plays an important role in shaping up the skills and attitudes of his student.
12. (*b*) From the passage, it can be assumed that professionals with practical knowledge can be good teachers. This inference is probably true.
13. (*c*) In the passage, the knowledge level of a student and his teacher is not compared.
14. (*a*) The word 'primarily' in the first line of the passage confirms that there are some other sources to determine the development of a country.
15. (*c*) In the passage, there is no information about IITs, its teachers and its students.
16. (*a*) In the opening lines of passage, it is clear that, in the field of computers, a change has taken place in the approach of the human factor research organisations.
17. (*e*) From the last sentence of passage, its clear that this inference is definitely false.
18. (*b*) From the last sentence of passage, it can be assumed that the physical specialities of work area are less important than their psychological dimension.
19. (*c*) No information is given in this regard.
20. (*b*) From the first couple of lines of the passage, this inference is probably true.
21. (*c*) No information is given in this regard.
22. (*c*) No information is given in this regard.
23. (*e*) The movie *'The Wizard of Oz'* is an example and an example cannot support any inference. So, this inference is definitely false.
24. (*b*) From the passage, it can be assumed that some aspects of movie like special effect, photography, story, music, etc., requires to watch the movie more than once. So, this inference is probably true but not definitely true because one can also understand these aspects in first time.
25. (*a*) From the passage, it is clear that the tips are given for understanding business conversation. So, the inference is definitely true.
26. (*d*) The advice is given to business purposes. This inference is probably false because in sales direct conversations is required while this is a telephonic conversation advice.
27. (*c*) It is not given in the passage that author watch movies how many times.
28. (*d*) In the passage, it is given that the density of population of Greater Bombay was within manageable limits. So, the inference is probably false.
29. (*e*) From the last sentence of passage it is clear that this inference is definitely false.
30. (*c*) No information is given in this regard.
31. (*b*) From the opening lines of passage it can be assumed that the rate of growth in density of population in the inner cities has been more than that in surrounding areas. So, this inference is probably true.
32. (*a*) From the passage it is clear that this inference is definitely true.
33. (*b*) From the first couple of lines it is clear that economic growth depends upon technological progress. But it is not clear that technological progress depends upon economic growth.
34. (*b*) From the last sentence of the passage, the inference is probably true.
35. (*a*) From the passage it is clear that there are some other causes beside technological progress on which economic growth depends. So, the inference is definitely true.
36. (*c*) No information is given in this regard.
37. (*c*) No information is given in this regard.
38. (*b*) From the second sentence of the passage, it is given that Indians, over the next two decades would move towards milk and milk products in large quantity. But the growth in these product is highest or not is not given. So, the inference is probably true.

39. (*d*) This inference is probably false because at present cereals are assumed to be at top position.

40. (*d*) Indians are moving faster towards value-added rich diet. So, income level of Indians may be increasing. So, this inference is probably false.

41. (*c*) No information is given in this regard.

42. (*c*) No information is given in this regard.

43. (*c*) No information is given in this regard.

44. (*a*) From the passage it is clear that all sections of viewers watch violence in cinema. So, this inference is definitely true.

45. (*c*) In the passage cinema is not compared with other sources of entertainment.

46. (*b*) From the passage it is clear that favourate stars influence teenagers. So, the inference is probably true.

47. (*b*) From the opening lines of passage, it can be assumed that violence was not the taste of viewers. But at present all sections of viewers are watching violence. So, the inference is probably true.

48. (*a*) From the first couple of lines of passage it is clear that monsoon is a deciding factor for Indian Economy. So, this inference is definitely true.

49. (*d*) From the second paragraph it can be assumed that inflation is dependent on international factors and not on monsoon. So, this inference is probably false.

50. (*a*) From the passage it is clear that finance ministry is assuming a good monsoon. So, this inference is definitely true.

51. (*b*) From the last sentence of first paragraph, it can be assumed that a normal monsoon never gives a guarantee against drought. This inference is probably true due to the word 'never'.

52. (*c*) It is not clear from the passage that the inflation of 6% is a bad sign on not.

53. (*b*) From the passage it can be assumed that privatisation is increasing in higher education but yet to take proper shape in India. So, the inference is probably true.

54. (*a*) To meet the increasing demand, expansion of higher education opportunities is needed. So, the inference is definitely true.

55. (*c*) No information is given in this regard.

56. (*e*) From the passage it is clear that private not-for-profit universities should be encouraged. So, inference is definitely false.

57. (*d*) This inference is probably false.

58. (*b*) Inference is probably true because it is given in the last line that cardiac myopathy is a result of enlargement of heart's chamber and decrease in the efficiency of pumping.

59. (*a*) Inference is definitely true as it is given in the passage that cardiac myopathy could follow child birth.

60. (*c*) Data given in the passage are inadequate to analyse this conclusion as nothing has been given regarding the facility available for this disease earlier in India.

61. (*a*) Opening line of the passage reads "A radical new surgery procedure launched not long ago is holding fresh hopes." This implies that this surgery has not been used in India earlier.

62. (*a*) Inference is definitely true from the last line of the passage that the condition is marked by an increase in the size of heart's chamber and a decrease in efficiency of pumping.

63. (*b*) Sunday makes a difference to working man because Sunday is a non-working day. So, it can be assumed that for non-working man all days of the week are like Sunday. So, the inference is probably true.

64. (*a*) From the last couple of lines "Sunday was not really as good as anticipated" it is clear that inference is definitely true.

65. (*c*) This inference cannot be concluded from the given information in the passage.

66. (*a*) From the first line of passage, it is clear that holidays provide freshness to the working man. So, the inference is definitely true.

67. (*c*) No information is given in this regard.

68. (*b*) From the passage it can be assumed that the perversive contamination of the country's surface and ground water supply is one of the reason for the lack of clean drinking water. So, the inference is probably true.

69. (*a*) From the last sentence of the passage, it is clear that meat, milk and eggs are also contaminated.

70. (*e*) From the passage it is clear that better water management by the government and the community can ensure for quality and availability of water and it can help in conserving water. So, the inference is definitely false.

71. (*b*) This inference is probably true.

72. (*c*) No information is given in this regard.

73. (*e*) 18% of world's human population lives in 2% of world's geographical area. It means that India is densely populated.
Density = Mass/Volume

74. (*a*) From the last sentence of the passage, it is clear that productivity of world's forests is thrice that of India's forests.

75. (*e*) From the passage, it is clear that this inference is definitely false.

76. (*c*) No information is given in this regard. So, data is inadequate.

77. (*a*) It is given that 18% of world's population lives in India. Remaining 82% population can be divided atmost five other countries, each country having population around the population of India. So, the inference is definitely true.

78. (*a*) It is clear from the last two lines of the passage that inference is true.

79. (*e*) Inference is false because it is not given in the passage.

80. (*c*) There is no such fact in the passage which showed 40% downfall.

81. (*b*) Approximately it is true but not definitely true.

82. (*e*) There is no such facts between the usages of cards in India and rest of all countries.

83. (*a*) In the passage it is given that labourers of Bihar are migrating in large numbers every year due to lamentable prospect of industrial development and absence of an ideal condition for agriculture.

84. (*c*) No information is given in this regard.

85. (*b*) If labourers migrate in large numbers then it can be assumed that industries will face shortage of labourers in the comming years.

86. (*d*) In the passage it is given that smaller countries are ahead of India, in terms of international arrival while it cannot be said that they have more attractive history, culture, sunshine, snow and sand than bigger countries. So, the inference is probably false.

87. (*c*) No information is given in this regard.

88. (*b*) From the passage, it can be assumed that poor infrastructure facilities are responsible for the dismal performance of tourism sector in India. So, the inference is probably true.

89. (*a*) From the passage, it is clear that tourism industry has huge potential in India. So, the inference is definitely true.

90. (*b*) From the passage, it can be assumed that there has been phenomenal growth in tourism all over the world, as around. So, million tourist were increased from year 2009 to 2010.

91. (*d*) This inference is probably false.

92. (*a*) Statement is a major objective in making the decision one of the goals sought by the decision maker.

93. (*c*) Statement is a minor factor in making the decision, a less important element bearing on or affecting a major factor rather than a major objective directly.

94. (*c*) This statement is minor factor in making the decision.

95. (*a*) The phrase, this tradition, refers to the preceding clause 'people have been in rough agreement with their neighbours as to the time of day' means people don't have enough time for social activities.

96. (*d*) This statement is major assumption made in the passage.

97. (*a*) It is the major objective as foregin capital will help the Indian aviation to come out of the crisis, that it is facing right know.

98. (*b*) The slowing down of the economy is a major factor for decision maker to make the decision, an aspect of the problem.

99. (*b*) Strikes at Air India is also a major factor for the decision maker to reach to the decision an important aspect of the problem.

100. (*c*) It is a minor factor that foreign airlines would pick up states in Indian carries as compared to others, it will help the Indian aviation to grow but other factors are more important.

101. (*d*) Poorly developed air navigation leading to more congestion is the major assumption as, this is the primary problem before which any factors or objective is considered. This has played a major role for the current situation of the Indian aviation.

102. (*a*) Net gain on excise duty = ₹ 50 crore
Due to reduction in production,
Loss in exise duty = ₹ 35 crore
Loss of CST and state tax = ₹ 25 crore.
Total loss = 35+25 = 60 crore
Net loss = 60 − 50 = 10
So, inference is definitely true.

103. (*d*) After imposition the excise duty it can be assumed that there will be a decline in domestic demand of bicycle in this current year. So, the inference is probably false.

104. (*c*) In the passage, the roles of AICMA are not given.

105. (*c*) The reason for India's export success in past is not given in the passage.

106. (*b*) The inference is probably true as it can be assumed from the passage.

Advanced Level

1. (*d*) This inference is probably false because economies of China, India and Japan are also booming.

2. (*e*) This inference is definitely false because Japan's economic growth is not the highest in Asia. It may be of China.

3. (*b*) From the passage, it can be assumed that the Korean Economy is traditionally different from the Indian Economy in its approach. So, the inference is probably true.

4. (*c*) No information is given in this regard. So, data are inadequate.

5. (*a*) From the passage it is clear that India and China together are considered the driving force of Asian Economy. So, the inference is definitely true.

6. (*a*) India is at present growing at the rate of 6.7% (1.5% faster than Africa). So, projected growth might be in the vicinity of that.

7. (*e*) Definitely false because Indian economy is only 1.5% above the other countries.

8. (*d*) The last sentence of the passage expresses doubt about India's policies and projects.

9. (*c*) Though the world economy is growing at present phenomenally, information regarding past things are not clear.

10. (*b*) Africa has been called the fragment of Soviet Union and if the fragment is growing by over 5%, the given proposition could be true.

11. (*d*) Inference is probably false because in the passage The backbone of quality education is primary schooling has been written.

12. (*b*) From the passage, it can be assumed that primary school teachers need to be motivated and their attendence should be improved. So, the inference is probably true.

13. (*c*) In the passage nothing has been mentioned about secondary education. So, data is inadequate to take decision.

14. (*e*) Inference is definitely false because in the passage it is given that improving the quality is not only about funding.

15. (*a*) From the passage it is clear that Government is taking some steps to improve the level of education. So, the inference is definitely true.

16. (*b*) Though the passage talks about India's dependence on imported cotton, whether India imports ELS cotton regularly cannot be ascertained confirmedly.

17. (*e*) There is a reference of present requirement of 8 lakh bales as against fulfilled 5.3 lakh bales. As also there is reference of under spinning.

18. (*d*) The passage take about improving the quality of domestic ELS cotton to reduce dependence on imported one.

19. (*a*) 5.3 lakh bales as against the required 8 lakh bales.

20. (*e*) At present it is 8 lakh bales likely to go to 10 lakh bales. So, increase is only 25%.

21. (*c*) No information is given in this regard.

22. (*a*) From the second and third line of the passage, it is clear that India's coal mines and mining activities are commercially viable. So, the inference is definitely true.

23. (*b*) From the first three lines of the passage, it can be assumed that India's dependence on coal for generating energy will continue in the time to come. So, the inference is probably true.

24. (*d*) From the passage, gap between demand and supply of domestic coal is increasing. So, the inference is probably false.

25. (*a*) From the last line of the passage, it is clear that assessment process of coal reserves is not capable of identifying coal reserves accurately.

26. (*c*) Statement is a minor factor in making the decision as it is not mentioned further in the passage any where.

27. (*b*) Statement is a major factor in making the decision as it shows a causal dependency with the consequence.

28. (*b*) Statement is a major factor in making the decision as it is mentioned in passage.

29. (*d*) Statement is a major assumption in making the decision as it includes the personal view.

30. (*b*) Statement is a major factor in making decision as it is mentioned in passage with facts and figures.

31. (*d*) Statement is major assumption in making the decision as it is not firmly presented paragraph anywhere.

32. (*a*) Statement is a major objective in making the decision as it is clear in passage.

33. (*d*) Sentence is a major assumption in making the decision as it based on future prospects.

34. (*b*) Sentence is a major factor in making the decision as its aspect is clearly depicted in passage.

35. (*b*) Sentence is a major factor in making the decision as it is clearly mentioned in passage.

36. (*a*) The decision is major decision that drove the Government of Rawanda towards disinvestment of 60%.

37. (*d*) The belief of a company is an assumption. It has assumed that, through acquisition only, we can achieve the growth and development.

38. (*d*) The assumption of decline in debt of MRIL has been made.

39. (*a*) It is a major decision as the company is increasing it's production.

40. (*c*) A statement is a minor factor in making decisions as the current acquisitions are enough to further invest and is a economically feasible event.

41. (*d*) Expanding in the body lotion and shampoo category is easier due to low pentration level in India is a major assumption for the decision maker before considering any aspect.

42. (*a*) It is the major objective because the ultimate aim is to grow and as it has already established brand of santoor, which will help it to grow.

43. (*c*) It is a minor factor for the decision maker, as if its market grows, then he can spend easily on ads etc.

44. (*b*) As the decision maker has ensured its growth in international market, so it is a major factor for the decision maker to reach to that decision to expand it business in India.

45. (*b*) Significant growth in international market is also a major factor for the decision maker to reach that decision to expand its business in India in other producs and aspects.

46. (*a*) This is because the NTC to be made worldclass is a goal that will change the view of textile industry.

47. (*d*) This is because when the new logo of NTC was formulated it was assumed that some targets will be achieved through this step.

48. (*a*) Because the review of competitive strategy helped them to achieve the goal of making the industry debt free.

49. (*d*) The steps are taken assuming the future results to be achieved.

50. (*d*) The programme has been implemented assuming the new vision will be coming with cultural innovations that will benefit the employees of NTC.

51. (*a*) From the passage, it can be concluded that subsidy provided by the government under various heads to the citizen increases the cost of capital.

52. (*c*) From the passage, it can be assumed that government may not be able to create more infrastructure facilities if the present level of subsidy continue for a longer time.

53. (*d*) From the passage, it is clear that gradual withdrawl of subsidy is essential for effectively managing fiscal deficit in India.

54. (*d*) Most logically such comparison should reveal mortality rate per thousand doctors indulged in SARS treatment and not indulged in treatment.

55. (*a*) From the passage, it is clear that accurate poverty measurement is not possible in India.

56. (*c*) From the passage it can be concluded that to tackle the dynamic nature of poverty, process of its measurement needs to be taken into account.

57. (*b*) From the passage it can be concluded that the increase in number of persons falling into poverty varies considerably across the country over a period of time.

58. (*c*) From the passage it can be concluded that the trucks carrying more than 10 tonnes of weight cause more traffic inconvenience than the ones carrying lesser load.

59. (*c*) From the passage it can be concluded that 65% of the price of the TV bought in India is equal to the custom duty and the tarffic charges paid by a person in Bangkok.

60. (*a*) Dr Puneet should tell Mr Benita about the details of the disease because the drugs which would be used for treatment may be useful even if they are at the experimental stage.

61. (*d*) The conclusion that can be drawn from the paragraph most appropriately and correct is option (d).

62. (*a*) An inference can be drawn from the given paragraph is that the 'Brahmaputra river passes through both the countries.'

63. (*c*) The weaken statement for both the countries to build dams on the river is that the 'Building cascades of dams at multiple locations in the river would have massive environmental impacts.'

64. (*e*) The statement would case India's apprehensions regarding China's similar dam construction projects in that the 'similar dams guilt on the river Xang which passes through both the countries did not affect the power generating capacity of either dams.'

65. (*b*) A course of action taken by the Indian government to counter China's competing plans is that the 'India should take the lead and begin construction of dams for hydro power projects before China does.'

66. (*c*) By reading the paragraph, we can clearly conclude that value based education can save the society. So, option (c) is best choice.

67. (*c*) The motto of the passage is that the CGS has published a report to assess the trends in first-time enrolment of international student populations in graduate schools in the US.

68. (*b*) There is no prominent effect of the recession on the sales of jeans. If is evident from the first two lines. So, option (b) which says, if a product is over-priced, then market correction in the price is brought about.

69. (*a*) The passage clearly suggests that people who are exposed to different light conditions with the same pair of glasses, photo chromic lenses are desirable, as they automatically adjust to the various light conditions.

70. (*d*) The passage suggests that 'Internet is to get more accessible soon with the move by global regulator ICANN to introduce a multi-lingual address system that used Asian and Arabic scripts, instead of Just Latin characters'.

71. (*b*) As the passage suggests that the melting of ice in the Antarctic region due to global warming has resulted in the blooming of tiny marine plants called phytoplankton the absorb massive quantities of CO_2.

72. (*a*) The words "most important means" states that their are several other means than schools for transfer of traditions. So, option (a) is definitely true.

5

Statement and Course of Action

***A course of action** is a step (after an administrative decision) taken in a given situation and circumstance to improve or solve the situation. In such questions, a situation is presented in a statement and some courses of action are suggested in the context of that situation.*

Questions based on statement and courses of action are designed to test the ability of candidates to judge a problem correctly and determine the cause of the problem and then prescribe a suitable course of action by which the problem can be solved.

Such problems have two parts

(i) **Statement** It presents a problem.

(ii) **Courses of action** It suggests step to solve or minimise that particular problem which is presented through the given statement.

Deciding the Course of Action

Here, the question has a statement followed by two courses of action. The candidate is required to analyse the statement (situation) and finally decide on which course of action is correct and logically follows. **There are no set rules to decide what should be the course of action. It is only logic that should be used.**

> *For example*
>
> **Statement** An IAS officer has been killed in Paschimbanga by violent mob. It is being suspected that the police played a deliberately inert role during the incident.
>
> **Courses of action** All IAS officers in Paschimbanga should be given tight security and a committee must be setup to enquire about, if police was really inert in this case.

Therefore, the above example makes it clear that the statement presents the problem of insecurity of IAS officers in Paschimbanga and inactive police while the course of action suggests the solution to prevent such happenings in future.

General Guidelines to Find a Suitable Course of Action

***Guideline* 1** Don't let your personal perception come into play while suggesting a course of action.

***Guideline* 2** While suggesting the action to the given situation (statement), make sure your course of action is not creating some other problems.

***Guideline* 3** The obvious approach is to first decide if the action would actually improve the situation in any way. The course of action can improve situation only, if

- it is universally acknowledged fact or Particular kind of action has previously improved a similar situation.
- finally, if you do not have universally accepted solution or examples of such situation then use logic.

Important points, always to be remembered while deciding 'Course of Action'.

1. The course of action either solve or lesser the problem.
2. The course of action should be practical.
3. The course of action should be directly related with the statement.
4. Negative course of action should not be taken.
5. Simple problem must have simple course of action, because complex course of action may create another problem.
6. The course of action should independently be able to solve the problem and it should not be dependent on other conditions.
7. In case you are having difficulty in deciding whether a suggested course of action will really improve a situation, ask yourself these questions.
   a. Is it an established fact? b. Do experiences predict so? c. Does logic predict so?
8. In case you are having difficulty in deciding whether a suggested course of action is practical or not, ask yourself these questions.
   a. Will the suggested course of action create any new problems?
   b. Are the given situation and suggested course of action properly related?

Types of Questions Asked in Different Examinations

There are multiple types of questions which are asked from the chapter 'Statement and Courses of Action', so it is quite difficult to predict exact type of questions that are asked, but on the basis of Observation, Analysis and Experience, here we are giving different types of questions that are usually asked in the examination. Almost all the questions of this chapter can be categorized into these types. Also, this description of type will make your study easy and streamline.

Type 1 Based on Two Courses of Action

In these type of questions, a statement is given that is followed by two courses of action. Candidates are required to assess the given statement and decide which of the course(s) of action follow(s).

Examples Based on Type 1

Direction (Examples 1-6) *In each question below is given a statement followed by two courses of action numbered I and II. A course of action is a step or administrative decision to be taken for improvement, follow up of further action in regard to the problem, policy, etc. On the basis of the information given in the statement, you have to assume everything in the statement to be true, then decide which of the suggested course(s) of action logically follow (s) for pursuing.*

Give answer

(a) if only I follows (b) if only II follows (c) if either I or II follows (d) if neither I nor II follows
(e) if both I and II follow

Ex 1. **Statement** The police department has come under a cloth with recent revelations that atleast two senior police official are suspected to have been involved in the illegal sale of a large quantity of weapons from the state police armoury.

Courses of action **SBI (PO) 2014**

I. A through investigation should be ordered by the State Government to bring out all those who are involved in the illegal sales of arm.
II. State police armoury should be kept under Central Government's control.

Ex 2. **Statement** The condition of most of the arterial roads in the city have deteriorated following heavy downpour during the past fortnight due to bad quality of bitumen and other material.

Courses of action **IRMA 2008**

I. Government should immediately suspend the officials responsible for maintenance of the city roads.
II. Government should evolve a mechanism to monitor the quality of all the roads throughout the year.

Ex 3. **Statement** There has been sudden increase in the number of migrants from rural areas to big cities in the recent past causing extensive pressure on the meager resources of the civic amenities.

Course of action **IRMA 2008**

I. The concerned civic authority should immediately put a complete ban on entry of migrant population.

II. The government should immediately set up a task force with a mandate to find ways to reduce the influx of migrant population in the big cities.

Ex 4. **Statement** There is an exodus of good students from the vernacular medium schools to the nearby English medium schools in the locality.

Course of action **IRMA 2008**

I. The management of the vernacular medium schools should immediately set up a joint action committee to find out the reason for the exodus and find ways to reverse the tend.

II. The management of the English medium schools should immediately set up a joint action committee to regulate the exodus to accommodate the next/students as per their capacity.

Ex 5. **Statement** The private utility company has decided to increase the power tariff by about 40% with immediate effect though the state owned power company has increased by only 10%.

Course of action **IRMA 2008**

I. The government should instruct the private utility company to increase the tariff by only 10%.

II. The government should penalise the private utility company for announcing such high increase.

Ex 6. **Statement** The cost of raw materials required for manufacturing passenger cars have increased considerably resulting into reduction in demand for mid-sized passenger cars.

Course of action **IRMA 2008**

I. The government should provide tax rebate to the manufacturers to bring down the price level.

II. The passenger car manufacturing companies should rationalise pricing of passenger cars of different segment to boost sales in near future.

SOLUTION (Examples 1-6)

1. (*a*) Course of action I is advisable because it is Judicious step. But course of action II is irrelevant to the given statement.
2. (*b*) Course of action I does not follow because of the word 'immediately.' Course of action II follows because government should evolve a mechanism to monitor the quality of all the roads, throughout the year.
3. (*b*) Course of action I does not follow because of the phrase 'immediately' put a complete ban. Course of action II follows because government should find ways to reduce the influx of migrant population in big cities.

   ➘ Course of action II follows even it has word 'immediately' because it is used for a positive step.
4. (*e*) Both the courses of action follow because reason should be find out for the exodus and some ways should be find to revolve the trend. Exodus should be regulated to accommodate the students as per their capacity.
5. (*d*) None of the course of action follows because government rarely instruct private utility companies.
6. (*a*) As the price of raw materials have increased considerably, now government should provide some tax rebate. So, course of action I follows. The price of cars of different segment should be rationalised.

Intro Exercise 1 (Based on Type 1)

Direction (Q. Nos. 1-41) *In each question below a statement is given followed by two courses of action numbered* I *and* II. *A course of action is a practicable and feasible step or administrative decision to be taken for follow-up, improvement, or further action in regard to the problem, policy etc. On the basis of the information given in the statement, you have to assume everything in the statement to be true and decide which of the suggested courses of action logically follow(s) for pursuing.*

Give answer

(a) if only I follows (b) if only II follows (c) if either I or II follows
(d) if neither I nor II follows (e) if both I and II follow

1. Statement Majority of the students fell ill after consuming the mid-day meal provided by the school.

Courses of action **IRMA 2010**

I. The people who cooked the mid-day meal should immediately be suspended.

II. The affected students should immediately be admitted to nearby hospitals for treatment.

2. Statement Jaundice and typhoid are on the rise in ABC city.

Course of action

I. Government must increase medical facilities as soon as possible.

II. Government must take steps to clean the city.

3. Statement The hygienic condition of the city X is not good. Polythenes and garbage are littered all over.

Course of action

I. The hygienic condition of the city 'X' is a problem which has been persisting over a long time and can't be improved immediately.

II. NGOs and Nagar Nigam should start a cleanliness movement.

4. Statement Over the years there has been increasing use of money power in elections.

Course of action

I. Candidates found indulging in such malpractices should be banned from contesting elections for life.

II. Tax should be imposed on the amount of advertisement expenditure incurred in excess of certain limits.

5. Statement A large number of manhole covers (lids) are disappearing in the city X.

Course of action

I. Street vigilance by the authority concerned should be strengthened in the city.

II. Residents of the areas concerned should be fined.

6. Statement Zee Telefilms has terminated its contract with an actor without any proper notice.

Course of action

I. The actor should file a case against Zee Telefilms.

II. The other actors should not sign the contract with Zee Telefilms for that program.

7. Statement The mafia is running a parallel government in State X.

Course of action

I. Government must take strict action against the mafia group.

II. People of the state should be provided with weapons for self-defence.

8. Statement Valuable time of our parliament is wasted through din and ruckus.

Course of action

I. The members responsible for the chaos should be restricted and their salaries should be chopped off.

II. The disputed matters should be sorted out outside the house.

9. Statement Primary teachers are on indefinite strike.

Course of action

I. Alternative arrangement should be made with teachers on daily wages.

II. Government should meet the demands of the teachers.

10. Statement A major part of North India is facing load-shedding.

Course of action

I. People of this region must develop the habit of using less electricity.

II. Government must generate more electricity to meet the demand in this region.

11. Statement The salaried class feels highly disappointed at the recent budget proposals.

Course of action

I. The Finance Minister should reconsider the budget proposal.

II. The tax rate on different slabs of salary should be brought down.

12. Statement People see tax as a burden and thus devise ways to underpay or avoid it altogether.

Course of action **IBPS (PO) 2011**

I. Government should educate and inform citizens about the ways in which taxes help in development of the nation.

II. Tax rates should be increased so that the under recovery in collection is compensated.

13. **Statement** Illinois has become the first state in the US to ban *bidis*, which are imported from India.

Course of action

I. India should cut off all its business with the US.

II. *Bidi* producers should be given compensation by the Indian Government.

14. **Statement** PTV, Pakistan's official television, is posing threat to the viewership of DD, India's official television.

Course of action

I. The threat should be ignored as both countries are not comparable when it comes to democracy and individual freedom the two are not comparable in quality and professionalism.

II. Doordarshan network should be expanded and efforts should be made to make it more professional.

15. **Statement** Proliferating computer graveyards have become a major threat for human health.

Course of action

I. Major computer firms should be requested to create a common facility to collect and recycle e-waste.

II. Efforts should be made to follow the guidelines issued by the government in reprocessing of computer waste.

16. **Statement** Many fake passes have been issued by some unidentified staffs of a state-owned transport corporation.

Course of action

I. The authorities must take action against the staff who are caught involved in this nefarious game.

II. The police must arrest the passengers who travel with fake passes.

17. **Statement** There is no motivation among today's generation to join the armed forced owing to frequent transfers to risky areas. Perhaps they are not aware of the good side of it.

Course of action

I. Short term internship should be introduced at high school level to give students a peek into the adventurous life of the forces and provide a more realistic job purview.

II. The salary levels of the defence forces should be increased with immediate effect.

18. **Statement** A plethora of bodies with no single one which can be held accountable for city's development is the key reason behind its rather stagnant state.

Course of action

I. Each body should be give a set of duties and there should be no duplication in such allocation.

II. An umbrella committee should be appointed with powers to regulate actions of all other bodies.

19. **Statement** Number of hospital beds per 1000 people in India, which is a key indicator of healthcare infrastructure, is much lower than many other nations which are thought to be poorer than India.

Course of action

I. The expenditure of importing costly medicines should be borne by the State.

II. Incentives should be given to encourage entry of private players into building of healthcare infrastructure.

20. **Statement** As per the provisions of the Master Plan, 2001, state government 'A' has to start construction work for the beautification in and around state 'A' by this year.

Course of action

I. Government should give notice to the slum-dwellors to vacate their slums by the end of this year.

II. Government should demolish all the illegal constructions by the end of this year.

21. **Statement** State government 'X' has announced its Right of Way (RoW) policy and agreement to provide a communication backbone for encouraging distance education through IT tools and to take internet to the rural areas.

Course of action

I. Other state government should follows the same policy in their states.

II. The related officials should issue guidelines for issuing permissions to infrastructure providers desirous of implementing optical fibre projects in the state.

22. **Statement** There have been sporadic cases of stone throwing and damaging vehicles in the locality during the day following altercation between two local youth clubs last night.

Course of action **Corporation Bank (PO) 2010**

I. The local police administration should arrest all those whose are caught committing these acts.

II. The local police administration should call a meeting of office bearers of both the clubs of the locality to bring the situation under control.

23. **Statement** A huge truck overturned on the middle of the main road and blocked most part of the road causing a huge traffic jam.

Course of action **Corporation Bank (PO) 2010**

I. The traffic department should immediately deploy its personnel to divert traffic through other roads.

II. The traffic department should immediately send mean and equipment to move the truck and clear the road.

24. **Statement** Some workers of the company making diamond jewellery were caught while they were leaving the premises as they were trying to smuggle small pieces of diamonds hidden in their purses.

Course of action **Corporation Bank (PO) 2010**

I. The management of the company should be immediately put on hold all activities in the premises till a fool proof security system is in place.

II. The belongings of all the workers should be thoroughly searched before they leave the premises of the company.

25. **Statement** A huge tidal wave swept away many fishing boats and hutments of the fishermen living along the coast line.

Course of action **Corporation Bank (PO) 2010**

I. The fishermen should henceforth be restrained from constructing their huts along the coast line.

II. The local administration should send a team of officials to assess the extent of damage and suggest remedial measures.

26. Statement A large number of invitees who attended the marriage function fell ill due to food poisoning and were rushed to various hospitals located in the area.

Course of action **Corporation Bank (PO) 2010**

I. The government should ban such marriage functions till further notice.

II. The local hospitals should be advised by the government to provide best services to the affected people.

27. Statement There is great fear among people that a neighbouring country X will drop an atom bomb on India within 24 h.

Course of action

I. India should take initiative, drop atom bombs and destory the atomic centres of country X.

II. The president of India should talk to his counterpart of country X.

28. Statement Taking advantage of loopholes in service rules and protection from political authorities, a large number of government employees have been doing a 'disappearing act' by remaining absent from work for prolonged periods after availing simple leave for a brief period.

Course of action

I. All such employees should be shown the door immediately.

II. All such employees should be deprived of pension and other such benefits.

29. Statement There are repeated complaints by tourists of misbehaviour by CISF (Central Industrial Security Force) men deployed at heritage sites like Taj Mahal in the name of ticket-checking, etc.

Course of action

I. A letter should be issued instructing the DG of CISF to tell his men to avoid any direct contact with the tourists during duty.

II. The responsibility to check tickets etc. should be entrusted to the men of ASI (Archaeological Survey of India).

30. Statement Fake currency is being supplied to India through the bus service that comes from Pakistan.

Course of action

I. Indian government should stop this bus service.

II. Indian police should check the bus properly and keep proper vigilance in the bus.

31. Statement Nothing can be crueller than getting children addicted to an evil. Tobacco manufacturers are now targetting boys and girls as young as 12, hoping that they would grow up into being slaved of nicotine.

Course of action

I. Tobacco manufacturing units should be closed down by the government.

II. If children below 12 are found using narcotics, they should be punished.

32. Statement Violence took place in most of the places during election.

Course of action

I. Election should be banned in the country.

II. Government should deploy adequate number of police so that no violence takes place.

33. Statement Unauthorised construction goes on unabated in the city even after High Court orders for maintaining status quote.

Course of action

I. Action should be taken against engineers and officials in whose jurisdiction such constructions are taking place.

II. The municipal corporation should approach the courts for vacating the stay order in each such case with the request that as the owners of the building have violated the Court orders, it be permitted to demolish the unauthorised construction.

34. Statement Reports of a reputed news channel has claimed that the question paper for a written test of Bank PO, which was held recently, were leaked.

Course of action

I. An enquiry committee should be formed to look into the matter.

II. The concerned authorities should be questioned and punished, if found guilty.

35. Statement Rajdhani Express was derailed while crossing a bridge near city Y. This resulted in loss of life and property.

Course of action

I. An investigation committee should be set upto look into the matter related to the accident.

II. Proper action should be taken against the accused.

36. Statement According to a claim made by an NGO, carbonated drinks sold by MNCs have toxic 'pesticide residues' 35 times the globally accepted level.

Course of action

I. Licences of all the companies associated with the drinks should be cancelled.

II. Since, the basic problem lies with ground water, the companies should be allowed to continue.

37. Statement Many customers complained to the manager of the local branch of the bank against the highhandedness of the bank employees while dealing with the customers.

Course of action **BOI (PO) 2010**

I. The bank management should immediately suspend all the employees of the branch and deploy a different set of employees.

II. The bank management should ask for a report from the manager of the branch for taking necessary steps.

38. Statement Two persons while on their daily walks in the jogger's park were killed by unidentified miscreants early in the morning.

Course of action **BOI (PO) 2010**

I. The police authority should deploy police constables near the jogger's park to prevent such criminal acts in future.

II. The citizens of the locality should go for early morning walks in groups to avoid such attacks.

39. Statement Many school children died in few accidents caused due to poor maintenance of school buses during the last few months.

Course of action **BOI (PO) 2010**

I. The government should set up an expert group to inspect the condition of school buses to avoid such accidents.

II. The government should suspend the licence of all the school buses till these buses are properly checked.

40. Statement A very large number of recently recruited officers left the Bank after attending the training programme on branch Banking operations conducted by the Bank.

Course of action **BOI (PO) 2010**

I. The bank should take a bond of atleast two years from each newly recruited officers before putting them into the training programme.

II. The bank should conduct the training programme atleast one year after the newly recruited officers joined the bank.

41. Statement A huge oil tanker overturned on the highway leading to the state capital and blocked most part of the highway from vehicular traffic.

Course of action **BOI (PO) 2010**

I. The government should immediately constitute a high level enquiry committee to look into the matter.

II. The driver of the oil tanker should immediately be arrested.

Direction (Q. Nos. 42-46) *In each question below is given a statement followed by two courses of action numbered* I *and* II. *A course of action is a step or administrative decision to be taken for improvement, follow-up or further action in regard to the problem, policy, etc. On the basis of the information given in the statement, you have assume everything in the statement to be true, then decide which of the suggested courses of action logically follows for pursuing.*

Give answer

(a) if only I follows
(b) if only II follows
(c) if either I or II follows
(d) None of these

42. Statement Many people are caught stealing foodgrains from the government storehouses.

Courses of action

I. Security personnel should be deployed round the clock around these government storehouses.

II. People living around the government storehouses should be warned against such thefts.

43. Statement Five people are killed in an accident between a tempo and a running train at an unmanned level crossing.

Courses of action

I. The railway authority should immediately put permanent barricades on either side of the tracks at the crossing so that no vehicle can cross the tracks.

II. The railway authority should immediately post an employee at the crossing round the clock to avoid such accidents.

44. Statement Many footpath dwellers are found to be spoiling the beautiful promenade at the sea front.

Courses of action

I. The civic administration should deploy its staff to patrol the promenade area.

II. Those footpath dwellers who are caught dirtying the promenade should be arrested and put behind bars.

45. Statement Large part of the low lying areas in 'the city are inundated due to the heavy downpour during the last few days'.

Courses of action

I. The local administration should immediately make necessary arrangements to move the affected people to safer places.

II. The local administration should deploy fire brigade personnel in these areas to save the affected people.

46. Statement Expensive clothes and accessories are becoming a growing need among college going teenage children of middle-income group.

Courses of action **CMAT 2014**

I. Colleges should introduce dress code.

II. Children should be counselled emphasizing the importance of many other things.

Type 2 Based on More than Two Courses of Action

In these type of questions, a statement is given that is followed by more than two courses of action. Candidates are required to choose the group of course of actions that follow in the context of given statement.

Examples Based on Type 2

Ex 1. **Statement** The prices of vegetables and other food articles have decreased in the recent months raising hope among policy planners that the RBI's (Reserve Bank of India) tight grip on supply of liquid money in the market for controlling inflation may be eased. **IBPS (SO) 2012**

Which of the following may be a possible action of the above situation?

(a) The Reserve Bank of India may not reduce its key interest rates in near future
(b) The government may step in and make certain concessions to the common people on various issues
(c) The Reserve Bank of India may consider lowering certain rates to bring in more liquidity in the market
(d) The RBI may wait for atleast another year before taking any step
(e) The RBI may collect more data from the market and wait for another four months to ensure that they take the correct step

Sol. (*e*) From the given statement, the RBI may collect more data from the market and wait for another four months to ensure that they take the correct step for controlling inflation.

Ex 2. **Statement** A severe cyclonic storm hit the Eastern coastline last month resulting in huge loss of life and property on the entire East coast and the government had to disburse a considerable amount for relief activities through the district administration machineries. **IBPS (SO) 2012**

Which of the following may possibly be a follow up measure to be taken up by the government?

(a) The government may setup a task force to review the post relief scenario in all districts and also to confirm proper and user receipt of the relief supplies
(b) The government may setup a committee for proper disbursement of relief supplies in future
(c) The government may empower the District Magistrates to make all future disbursements of relief
(d) The government may send relief supplies to the affected people in future only after proper assessment of the damage caused by such calamities
(e) The government may not need to activate any follow up measure

Sol. (*c*) For relief of people who are affected by cyclonic hit the correct measure taken by the government may empower the District Magistrates to make all future disbursements of relief.

Ex 3. **Statement** Many teachers of the local school have rendered their resignation to the Principal to protest the management's decision for not implementing revised pay scales. **CMAT 2013**

Courses of action

I. The school management should accept the resignations and appoint new teachers.
II. The school management should persuade the teachers to continue with an assurance of considering the pay hike issue.
III. The school management should approach the government for guidelines.

(a) Only I follows (b) Only II follows
(c) Only III follows (d) II and III follows

Sol. (*d*) Actions II and III are the right course of actions as II will solve the problem immediately and III will solve it permanently.

Ex 4. **Statement** Read the following information carefully and answer the question which follows. **SBI Associate (PO) 2014**

Most students from Sate X prefer to move base to other States for higher education. The government of the State is concerned about this problem as these student might not come back even after completing their education.

Which of the following statements may be a **course of action** to deal with this problem?

(a) The government should set-up well equipped State of the art universities which will provide quality education.
(b) The government should not give much importance to this problem as there is high density of population per square km in the State
(c) Scholarships should be declared for those students who perform well in tenth and twelfth standard examinations
(d) All the colleges and universities should be asked to emphasise the importance of higher education and benefits of studying in their institute should also be highlighted
(e) The government should make education free for all people of the State

Sol. (*d*) When the students know the benefits of studying in college and universities of their own state, then they think twice before going outside the state for higher education.

Hence, option (d) action is the right one.

Intro Exercise 2 (Based on Type 2)

Direction (Q. Nos. 1-28) *In each question given below a statement is followed by three courses of action numbered, I, II and III. A course of action is a step or administrative decision to be taken for improvement, follow-up or further action in regard to the problem, policy. On the basis of the information given in the statement. You have to assume everything in the statement to be true, then decide which of the three given/suggested courses of action logically follow (s) for pursuing and then decide the answer.*

1. Statement As a result of communal tensions in the city, everyday activity has come to a halt and there is a fear on the face of every individual.

Course of action

I. The government should employ additional security in highly sensitive areas.

II. Efforts should be made to stop rumours from spreading

III. Extremist religious leaders of both the communities should be jailed.

(a) All follow (b) I and III follow
(c) I and II follow (d) II and III follows
(e) None of these

2. Statement Higher disposal costs encourage those who produce waste to look for cheaper ways to get rid of it.

Course of action

I. The disposal costs should be made higher.

II. The disposal costs should be brought down.

III. A committee should be set up to study the details in this respect.

(a) Only I follows (b) Only II follows
(c) Either I or II follows (d) II and III follow
(e) All follow

3. Statement There was a spurt in criminal activities in the city during the recent festival season.

Course of action

I. The police should immediately investigate into the causes of this increase.

II. In future the police should take adequate precaution to avoid recurrence of such situation during festival.

III. The known criminals should be arrested before any such season.

(a) I and III follow (b) I and II follow
(c) II and III follow (d) All follow
(e) None of these

4. Statement Suicides are on the rise among youths, particularly due to unemployment.

Course of action

I. A committee should be made to find out the main cause of the rise in cases of suicide.

II. People should be discouraged from indulging in love affairs and encouraged to get self-employed.

III. Parents of wards should be instructed to nurse their wards if they observe that their wards are facing critical circumstances.

(a) All of these (b) I and II
(c) I and III (d) II and III
(e) None of these

5. Statement Over 27000 bonded labourers identified and freed are still awaiting rehabilitation.

Course of action

I. More cases of bonded labourers should be identified.

II. Till the proper rehabilitation facilities are available, the bonded labourers should not be freed.

III. The impediments in the way of speedy and proper rehabilitation of bounded labourers should be removed.

(a) None follows (b) Only I follows
(c) Only II follows (d) III follows
(e) II and III follow

6. Statement Many people living in the slums of western part of the town are diagnosed to be suffering from malaria.

Course of action **IBPS (PO) 2013**

I. The municipal corporation should immediately make necessary arrangements to spray mosquito repellent in the affected area.

II. The municipal authority should immediately make necessary arrangements to provide quick medical help to the affected people.

III. The municipal authority should take steps to shift all the people staying in the slums of western part of the town to other areas.

(a) Only I follows
(b) Only II follows
(c) I and II follow
(d) All I, II and III follow
(e) None of the above

7. Statement Without the active cooperation between the proprietor and the employees of the mill, it cannot remain a profitable concern for long.

Course of action

I. The mill should be closed down.

II. The workers should be asked to cooperate with the owners.

III. The owners should be asked to cooperate with the employees.

(a) Only I (b) I and II follow
(c) All follow (d) II and III follow
(e) None of these

8. **Statement** It has been reported that water level is declining rapidly in many cities and causing water crisis.

Course of action

I. Misuse of water should be banned in these cities.

II. An awareness drive should be launched to make the people aware of the problem.

III. Alternative methods should be explored to store rain-water.

(a) All follow (b) II and III follow
(c) Only II follows (d) Only III follows
(e) None of these

9. **Statement** Country X has decided to put a ban on entry of Indian software engineers.

Course of action

I. Indian software engineers should give up the idea of going abroad.

II. Indian government should immediately make a delegation for a trip to country X to sort out the issue.

III. Indian software engineers should prove their miracles either in India or seek opportunities in other countries.

(a) Either II or III follows (b) I and II follow
(c) All follow (d) I and III follow
(e) None of these

10. **Statement** Prices of oil and gas are likely to rise in India owing to the rising tension in the gulf due to the US attack on Iraq, a major source of oil.

Course of action

I. India should tap new oil sources.

II. At least a month's stock of oil and its products should be stored.

III. A fortnight's supply of oil is generally in transit on the high seas, hence there is nothing to worry about.

(a) Only I (b) I and II
(c) Only III (d) Either II or III
(e) None of these

11. **Statement** Trees are being cut in metropolitan cities in the name of construction of underground rail services under the cut-and-cover method and adding to ecological degradation.

Course of action

I. Tunneling method should replace cut-and-cover method.

II. Effort should be made to transplant the removed trees if feasible.

III. Compensatory afforestation scheme should be launched.

(a) Only III (b) I and III (c) I and II (d) II and III
(e) All of these

12. **Statement** Some strains of mosquito have become resistant to chloroquine, the widely used medicine for malaria patients.

Course of action

I. Selling of chloroquine should be stopped.

II. Researchers should develop a new medicine for patients affected by such mosquitoes.

III. All the patients suffering from malaria should be checked for identification of casual mosquito.

(a) I and III follow (b) I and II follow
(c) II and III follow (d) All follow
(e) None of these

13. **Statement** State X has decided to provide auto- rickshaws to all unemployed youth of the state in the coming year.

Course of action

I. Material, managerial and other resources will have to be in fine tune to maintain production schedule.

II. A special allotment for this provision should be made in the budget of the state in the coming year.

III. Authorities concerned should be informed to collect applications from the youth.

(a) Only I follows (b) I and III follow
(c) All follow (d) I and II follow
(e) None of these

14. **Statement** There is a considerable increase in the number of persons affected by water-borne diseases during monsoon period.

Course of action

I. The question should be raised in the Legislative Assembly.

II. The Government should disseminate adequate information regarding the pure drinking water to people.

III. All the hospitals in the city should be equipped properly for the treatment of patients during monsoon period.

(a) All follow (b) I and II follow
(c) II and III follow (d) I and III follow
(e) None follows

15. **Statement** Indian Railways is absolutely dependent on government subsidies and lack concentration on transportation activities.

Course of action

I. A committee should be constituted to look into the matter.

II. Railways should explore new areas to generate revenues.

III. Railways should concentrate on hiving off non-core activities such as design and manufacture of rolling stock, construction, housing etc. to private sectors.

(a) Only I follows (b) I and II follow
(c) II and III follow (d) All follow
(e) None of these

16. **Statement** The weather bureau has through a recent bulletin forecast heavy rainfall during the next week which may cause water logging in several parts of the city.

Course of action **JMET 2011**

I. The bulletin should be given wide publicity through the mass media.

II. The civic authority should keep in readiness the pumping system for removal of water from these parts.

III. The people should be advised to stay indoors during the period.

(a) Only I follows (b) I and II follow
(c) Only II follows (d) II and III follow
(e) None of these

17. Statement Lack of coordination between the university, its colleges and various authorities has resulted in students ousted from one college seeking migration to another.

Course of action **JMET 2011**

I. If a student is ousted from a college, the information should be sent to all the other colleges of the university.

II. The admissions to all the colleges of the university should be handled by the university directly.

III. A separate section should be made for taking strict action against students indulging in anti-social activities.

(a) Only I follows (b) Only II follows
(c) Only III follow (d) I and III follow
(e) II and III follow

18. Statement The condition of all the major roads in the city has deteriorated due to incessant rain during the last two months.

Course of action

I. The city civic authority should deploy additional traffic staff to regulate the vehicular movement.

II. The city civic authority should immediately make arrangements for repairs of the damaged roads.

III. Motorists should be alerted at various places by putting up sign boards about the bad patches of the roads to enable them to plan their journey accordingly.

(a) I and II follow (b) II and III follow
(c) I and III follow (d) All follow
(e) None of these

19. Statement India's national bird does not have a safe sanctuary in the nation's capital itself. Last week about a dozen of them were brutally killed in some parts of the city and such killing have been going on for last couple of months.

Course of action

I. Killing of national bird should be declared as treason.

II. Poachers should be banned from entering forests.

III. Nation's interest should be kept above all and no action should be taken towards such trivial issues.

(a) I and II follow (b) Only I follows
(c) Only III follows (d) Only II follows
(e) None of these

20. Statement A blast was triggered off, injuring many, when the night shift workers at an ordinance factory were handling 'fox signalling explosive'.

Course of action

I. The factory management should train its staff as regards to the safety aspects of handing such explosive materials.

II. The service of the supervisor incharge of the night shift should be terminated.

III. The factory should immediately stop carrying out such exercises at night.

(a) Only II follows (b) All follow
(c) Only I follows (d) I and II follow
(e) None of these

21. Statement The day time temperatures in this summer have been four to five degree Celsius above the normal temperature across the country.

Course of action

I. All the district headquarters should be alerted to send prompt reports of death due to heat waves in their jurisdiction.

II. The government machinery should be put on high alert and provided with necessary equipments to prevent any untoward incident.

III. The government should make necessary arrangements to provide drinking water in all the areas affected due to extreme heat waves.

(a) Only I follows (b) I and II follow
(c) All follow (d) Only II follows
(e) II and III follow

22. Statement Many private sector banks have reduced interest rate on housing loans in comparison to public sector banks.

Course of action

I. The case should be raised before the regulatory authority for investigation by the public sector banks as they cannot follow such reduction.

II. Public sector banks must adopt such policy to remain in competition.

III. The public sector banks should advertise their special feature repeatedly so that they do not lose their future customers.

(a) All follow
(b) I and II follow
(c) I and III follow
(d) Either II or III follows
(e) None of the above

23. Statement Residents from Model Colony coming under North Ward of City have complained to the Ward Officer that for last three days the tap water in the ward is contaminated and no action is being initiated by municipal staff.

Course of action

I. The Ward Officer of North Ward should initiate action against residents who have lodged complaints against municipal staff.

II. The Ward Officer should ask his junior officer to visit Model Colony to assess the actual condition of water with his staff and to get samples of water tested from laboratories.

III. The Ward Officer should ask Ward Engineer to check water installations and pipelines in the Model Colony area.

(a) I and II follow
(b) II and III follow
(c) I and III follow
(d) Either I or III and II follow
(e) None of the above

24. Statement It has been reported by one of the TV channels that the answer paper of Board examination of one state are evaluated by students studying in the same standard with the help of model answers as instructed by the examiners.

Course of action

I. All such examiners should be suspended from the official positions.

II. All such papers evaluated by the students should be immediately confiscated and got evaluated by qualified teachers.

III. The Board should explore possibilities even though they are remote of getting the answer papers of this examination evaluated by computerized machines.

(a) Only I follows (b) Only II follows
(c) Only III follows (d) Only I and II follow
(e) All follow

25. Statement 'X' state government stopped supply of free power to farmers. The decision came as a major setback to the farmers and gave rise to resentment among them.

Course of action

I. The government of state 'X' should withdraw its decision in order to placate the farmers.

II. The government of state 'X' should assure the farmers that if there is an improvement in the fiscal situation of the electricity supply board, free power supply to farmers will be resumed.

III. Opposition parties of state 'X' should start demonstrations as well as persuading people that the steps taken by the ruling government is a total betrayal of the farming community of the state.

(a) Only I follows (b) Only II follows
(c) Only II and III follow (d) All follow
(e) None of these

26. Statement Every year thousands of eligible students do not get admission in colleges, both in urban and rural areas, after passing their school leaving certificate exams.

Course of action

I. More colleges should be set up in both urban and rural areas.

II. The number of schools in both urban and rural areas should be reduced.

III. No school should offer vocational courses to equip students for taking up their vocation after completing their school education.

(a) Only I follows (b) II and III follow
(c) All follow (d) I and III follow
(e) None of these

27. Statement Drinking water supply to Navi Mumbai has been suspended till further orders from Maharashtra Pollution Control Board following pollution of Patalganga river, caused by discharge of effluents from some chemical industries.

Course of action

I. The industries responsible for discharging effluents into the river should be asked to close down immediately.

II. The river water should immediately be treated chemically before resuming supply.

III. The Pollution Control Board should check the nature of effluents being discharged into the river by industries at regular intervals.

(a) Only I follows (b) II and III follow
(c) Only III follows (d) All follow
(e) None of these

28. Statement The company X has rejected first lot of valves supplied by company A and has cancelled its entire huge order quoting use of inferior quality material and poor craftsmanship.

Course of action

I. The company A needs to investigate functioning of its purchase, production and quality control departments.

II. The company A should inspect all the valves rejected by company X.

III. The company A should inform company X that steps have been taken for improvement and renegotiate schedule of supply.

(a) Only I follows (b) Only II follows
(c) Only III follows (d) All follow
(e) None follows

Direction (Q. Nos. 29-31) *In each question below is given a statement followed by three courses of action numbered I, II and III. A course of action is a step or administrative decision to be taken for improvement, follow up or further action in regard to the problem, policy etc. On the basis of the information given in the statement, you have to assume everything in the statement to be true, then decide which of the suggested courses of action logically follow(s) for pursuing.*

29. Statement Many political activists have decided to stage demonstrations and traffic movement in the city during peak hours to protest against the steep rise in prices of essential commodities.

Course of action

I. The government should immediately ban all forms of agitations in the country.

II. The police authority of the city should deploy additional forces all over the city to help traffic movement in the city.

III. The state administration should carry out preventive arrests of the known criminals staying in the city.

(a) Only I (b) Only II (c) Only III (d) I and II
(e) None of these

30. Statement The school dropout rate in many districts in the state has increased sharply during the last few years as the parents of these children make them work in the fields owned by others to earn enough for them to get at least one meal a day.

Course of action **SNAP 2013**

I. The government should put up a mechanism to provide foodgrains to the poor people in these districts through public distribution system to encourage the parents to send their wards to school.

II. The government should close down some of these schools in the district and deploy the teachers of these schools to nearby schools and also ask remaining students to join these schools.

III. The government should issue arrest warrants for all the parents who force their children to work in fields instead of attending classes.

(a) Only I
(b) Only II
(c) Only III
(d) I and II

31. Statement A large private bank has decided to retrench one-third of its employees in view of the huge losses incurred by it during the past three quarters.

Course of action

I. The government should issue a notification to general public to immediately stop all transactions with the bank.

II. The government should direct the bank to refrain from retrenching its employees.

III. The government should ask the central bank of the country to initiate an enquiry into the bank's activities and submit its report.

(a) None
(b) Only I
(c) Only II
(d) Only III
(e) I and III

Direction (Q. Nos. 32-33) *In each question given below, statement is followed by three courses of action numbered I, II and III. You have to assume everything in the statement to be true, and then decide which of the three suggested courses of action logically follow (s).*

IIFT 2011

32. Statement School dropout rate is very high in the rural areas as children support their parents in income earning activities.

Course of action

I. Public awareness programme on primary education should be expanded immediately to educate parents.

II. Compensation should be given to those parents whose children are in the school.

III. Law on universal education and ban on child labour should be made rigorous.

(a) I and II follow (b) II and III follow
(c) I and III follow (d) All follow

33. Statement In a recent bulletin the Meteorological Department of India has forecasted severe drought in next cropping season which may cause failure of crops.

Course of action

I. The forecast should be widely published in media.

II. The drought relief team should be ready for relief work.

III. The people should be advised to go for drought resistant variety.

(a) I and II follow (b) Only II follow
(c) II and III follow (d) None of these

Cumulative Exercise

Base Level

1. Study the following statement and courses of action and decide which course(s) of action is (are) logical.

Statement The sale of shoes has gone down. Considerably causing great concern to the company.

Course of action **MPPSC 2012**

I. The price of shoes should be reduced.

II. The company should make a study carefully about other brands of shoes in the market.

(a) If only I follows
(b) If only II follows
(c) If either I or II follows
(d) If neither I nor II follows

Direction (Q. Nos. 2-49) *In each question below a statement is given followed by two courses of action numbered I and II. A course of action is a practicable and feasible step or administrative decision to be taken for follow-up improvement, or further action in regard to the problem, policy etc. On the basis of the information given in the statement, you have to assume everything in the statement to be true and decide which of the suggested courses of action logically follow(s) for pursuing.*

Give answer

(a) if only I follows
(b) if only II follows
(c) if either I or II follows
(d) if neither I nor II follows
(e) if both I and II follow

2. **Statement** It is reported that vitamins and minerals in vegetables and fruits are beneficial for human body. Medicines do not have the same effect on human body.

Course of action **CGPSC 2012**

I. People should be encouraged to take fresh fruits and vegetables to meet human body's requirement of vitamins and iminerals.

II. The sale of medicines of vitamins and minerals should be banned.

3. **Statement** Travelling on metro roads might become a nightmare due to urban congestion.

Course of action

I. One of the ways of reducing urban congestion is making car purchase very expensive.

II. Encroachment along roadsides should be demolished.

4. **Statement** Indian Airlines is running in loss.

Course of action

I. It should be privatized.

II. It must curb the expenditure by removing concessions in the fare to MPs, bureaucrats and airline officers.

5. **Statement** Party 'A' was overthrown in DUSU polls and its rival party 'B' made a clean sweep.

Course of action

I. Party 'A' should not contest election for the next two or three years.

II. Party 'A' should dismiss its president.

6. **Statement** Three girls in a prestigious university campus were molested by a group of people.

Course of action

I. Police must catch them and put them behind bars.

II. The university authority should provide security on the campus for the safety of the students.

7. **Statement** Some of India's greatest musicians and folk artists are struggling to make both ends meet.

Course of action

I. The folk artists should be advised to leave their traditional profession and adopt any other profession to earn their living.

II. The government should give financial aids to these artists.

8. **Statement** Despite good economic progress of country, significant number of under nourished children has been observed in the rural parts of the country.

Courses of action

I. Government should increase wealth tax and income tax and use that money for upliftment of the deprived class.

II. Government should introduce schemes like free meals in primary schools and make primary education compulsory.

9. **Statement** Many complaints have been registered lately by commuters regarding unavailability of railway tickets during the peak travelling season.

Course of action **OBC (PO) 2010**

I. The commuters should be advised to defer their travel plans till the peak season gets over.

II. Railways should try to accommodate as many commuters as possible by adding extra coaches to the trains.

10. **Statement** Leader of a tribal community residing near a proposed highway project has given an application expressing his community's opposition for construction of the highway through their residential area.

Course of action

I. Government should convince the tribal community stating the fact that building of the highway would bring development in their area.

II. Government should immediately stall the highway project in response to the resistance faced by the tribal community.

11. **Statement** More and more farmers have been shifting to cultivation of export quality rice rather than the rice eaten daily by people as export quality rice helps them earn more profit.

Course of action

I. Strict action should be taken against the farmers growing only export quality rice in their fields.

II. Procurement price of other qualities of rice should be increased so as to make their cultivation a profitable venture as well.

12. **Statement** According to a recent report, almost 90% students from a premier college in India end up settling in foreign countries for nearly thrice the salary drawn in India.

Course of action

I. Indian organizations should pay salaries to students from this college which are at par with the foreign organizations.

II. Signing of a bond which prevents them from taking a job in any foreign country should be made mandatory by the government.

13. **Statement** The police reported that two armed terrorists had entered the city a couple of days ago.

Course of action

I. Police should immediately circulate the photographs of the terrorists using electronic and print media in order to take public's helps in nabbing them.

II. Public should be informed to stay indoors until the terrorists are arrested.

14. **Statement** In the people's magazine's annual list Pamela Anderson has topped among the well-dressed women around the world.

Course of action

I. Other women should follow the dress sense of Pamela Anderson.

II. Pamela Anderson should start dressing- schools all over the world.

15. **Statement** A phone was received at the district control office from an anonymous person that there was a deadly bomb in the secretariat.

Course of action

I. Bomb defusing squad should be sent immediately.

II. The authority should not give any heed to this type of hoax.

16. **Statement** There has been more than one accident on each day of the tenure of railway minister X. 60 % of accidents have been caused by human error and 20% due to inadequate expansion of railway lines.

Course of action

I. New trains should not be introduced in an overburdened system.

II. New technology should be introduced and provision for this should be made in the budget in this regard.

17. **Statement** It is expected that India will cross 1.5 billion in population by 2020 and it will account for one-sixth of the world population.

Course of action

I. More fertilizers and advanced agricultural implements should be used to enhance the productivity of crops to meet requirement of increasing population.

II. Awareness of the benefits of family planning should be extended to the masses.

18. **Statement** In a 'No Tobacco Day' function, it was observed that the number of smokers is increasing rapidly.

Course of action

I. Government should highlight through media the harms due to tobacco.

II. Government should ban smoking.

19. **Statement** Drinking water supply to many parts of the town has been disrupted due to loss of water because of leakage in pipes supplying water.

Course of action **MHT CET MBA 2008**

I. The Government should order an enquiry into the matter.

II. The civic body should set up a fact-finding team to assess the damage and take effective steps.

20. **Statement** There is an alarming increase in the number of people suffering from malaria in many parts of the city.

Course of action

I. The municipal corporation has advised all the government hospitals to store adequate supply of malaria drugs.

II. The municipal corporation has urged people to use mosquito repellants and keep their premises clean.

21. **Statement** Many people have encroached upon the government property and built their houses and business establishments.

Course of action

I. The government should take immediate steps to remove all unauthorised constructions on government land.

II. All the encroachers should immediately be put behind bars and also be slapped with a hefty fine.

22. **Statement** The meteorological department has predicted normal rainfall throughout the country during the current monsoon.

Course of action

I. The government should reduce the procurement price of foodgrains for the current year.

II. The government should reduce subsidy on fertilizers for the current year.

23. **Statement** The number of dropouts in government schools has significantly increased in the urban areas over the past few years.

Course of action

I. The government should immediately close down all such schools in the urban area where the dropout goes beyond 20%.

II. The parents of all the students who dropped out of the government schools in urban areas should be punished.

24. **Statement** Majority of the students have failed in one paper in the first semester examination.

Courses of action

I. All those student who failed should be asked to drop out of the course.

II. The faculty teaching the paper should be asked to resign.

25. **Statement** The rate of inflation has reached its highest in last twenty years and there is no sign of its softening in the coming months.

Courses of action

I. The Government should initiate steps like reducing Government taxes on essential commodities with immediate effect.

II. Farmers should be asked by the government to sell their products at lower prices.

26. **Statement** An increasing number of graduates produced by Indian universities are unemployable.

Course of action **OBC (PO) 2009**

I. Colleges and institutes of higher learning should be given greater autonomy to decide course content.

II. World class foreign universities should be encouraged to set up campuses in India.

27. **Statement** Heavy rains hit the state during October, just the State Assembly elections and caused heavy damage to standing crops in most parts of the state.

Course of action

I. Elections should be postponed to give candidates the opportunity to campaign.

II. The Government should announce a relief package for those who are affected.

28. **Statement** Cell phone users have found that tariff plans are not as attractive as promoted by telecom companies and complained to regulatory authority about the same.

Course of action

I. The regulatory authority should direct telecom companies to be transparent on the traiff structure of all plans.

II. The government should restrict the number of telecom companies operating in the country.

29. **Statement** More number of students passing SSC examinations has resulted into frustration among children for not getting admissions into colleges of their choice.

Course of action

I. Government should permit the colleges to increase the number of seats.

II. Children and their parents should be counselled for being flexible on the choice of college.

30. **Statement** The dolphin population in India has been decreasing sharply over the past few years.

Course of action **MHT CET MBA 2009**

I. Dolphins should be declared an endangered species and be bred in aquariums or protected areas.

II. Locals should be enlisted to protect dolphins.

31. **Statement** Employees of the organizations gave a call for strike in protest against certain decisions taken by the management.

Course of action

I. The management should call a joint meeting of management and union leaders to listen to the employees grievances.

II. The management should appeal to the employees to withdraw the call for strike assuring them the decisions will be considered for review.

32. **Statement** The Bus Transport Company received a phone call alerting bomb scare in the bus on one of its route.

Course of action

I. The Bus Transport Company should alert all the buses on that route advising them to vacate and take precautionary measures.

II. The Bus Transport Company should call for the help from the Bomb squad.

33. **Statement** Twenty five children in the school were reported to be suffering from diarrhoea after having midday meals.

Course of action

I. Parents of the children should be advised to give home made meals to the children.

II. Schools should arrange for immediate medical help to all the affected children.

34. **Statement** Terrorist activities in the city have been continuously increasing since last few years.

Course of action

I. The Government should alert the police department to deploy more security checks at all the entries into the city.

II. Public should be cautioned and advised not to go out in late night hours.

35. **Statement** A huge rally was organized by the people in the locality on a religious occasion and the police was informed accordingly.

Course of action **IBPS (PO) 2011**

I. Adequate police force should be deployed to oversee the procession of the rally.

II. Vehicles on the road should be advised a diversion to avoid traffic congestion.

36. **Statement** The sales of ball-point pens manufacture by company lixus have gone down considerably even, since the same company introduced a gel-ink pen in the market.

Course of action

I. Ball-point pens should not be manufactured by lixus any more.

II. Lixus should immediately withdraw all gel-ink pen from the market so, as to force people to buy ball-point pens.

37. **Statement** Nearly 26 per cent of all engineering graduated have been left unemployed owing to severe recession worldwide.

Course of action

I. All the unemployed students should be advised to take up jobs in foreign countries.

II. The unemployed students should be advised to take up jobs only after the recession is over.

38. **Statement** The government airline has been making huge losses even as private airliners continue to prosper and make substantial profit.

Course of action

I. All the private airlines should be banned from their operation in the country.

II. The government airline should be instructed to increase passenger fare significantly in order to increase its profit.

39. **Statement** Many private schools have been violating government directives and have been charging more fees than the specified limits.

Course of action

I. The government should identify such schools and take stringent actions against them.

II. The government should not limit school fees and keep it flexible for the schools to decide.

40. **Statement** A large number of patients admitted in a particular hospital have been diagnosed with a serious contagious disease.

Course of action

I. These patients should be immediately evicted from the hospital for fear of spread of the disease.

II. The hospital should make appropriate quarantine arrangements to control the spread of disease.

41. **Statement** The number of students suffering from depression during examination days is increasing every year.

Course of action

I. The schools and colleges should set up counselling centres within the campus to provide psychological support.

II. Efforts should be made to minimize the pressure from parents and society.

42. **Statement** Computers have become a part of life and getting a job without computer knowledge has become very difficult.

Course of action

I. Computer related subjects should be made compulsory at college level for the disciplines.

II. Students should be advised to join computer coaching classes, simultaneously while pursuing college education.

43. **Statement** With the change in value system, money assumed topmost importance now a days, ultimately leading to criminal activities.

Course of action

I. Social service organizations should make special efforts to propagate the importance of ethical values over money.

II. Print and electronic media should be advised by the government to give special emphasis on the importance of ethics and value systems.

44. **Statement** With improving financial status of the urban parents, majority of the children are pampered and find it difficult to struggle when faced with adverse situations.

Course of action

I. Parents should prepare themselves to orient their children to face difficult situations in their formative years.

II. Parents should encourage their children to manage all their affairs on their own.

45. Statement Many sportspersons today are more attracted by the glamour than by the sport they pursue.

Course of action

I. Sportspersons should not be permitted to act as model/ or brand ambassadors.

II. Sportpersons should be paid higher compensation for their achievements in sports.

46. Statement Misuse of subsidies offered to the farmers was observed and brought to the notice of the concerned authorities.

Course of action

I. Government should issue orders to the concerned officials to be stricter and more careful while verifying the required documents while granting subsidy.

II. Government should take stringent action against those making false claim of subsidy.

47. Statement Expensive clothes and accessories are becoming a growing need among college going teenage children of middle income group.

Course of action

I. Colleges should introduce a dress code.

II. Children should be counseled emphasising the importance of many other things.

48. Statement People in the locality were agitated as more than thirty people died in a building collapse.

Course of action

I. Government should immediately announce compensations for the affected families.

II. Authorities should take a stringent action against builders tending to compromise over quality of material used.

49. Statement With the onset of monsoon all the hospitals are getting increased number of patients due to various epidemics.

Course of action

I. Civic authorities should educate the public the need for observing minimum required hygiene.

II. Civic authorities should make arrangements to equip the hospitals with required medicines and other facilities.

Direction (Q. Nos. 50-54) *In each question below is given a statement followed by two courses of actions numbered I and II. A course of action is a step or administrative decision to be taken for improvement, follow-up or further action in regard to the problem, policy, etc. On the basis of the information given in the statement, you have to assume everything in the statement to be true, then decide which of the suggested courses of action logically follow(s) for pursuing.*

Give answer

(a) if only I follows (b) if only II follows (c) if either I or II follows (d) if neither I nor II follows
(e) if both I and II follow

50. Statement Many dilapidated buildings in the city collapsed during monsoon in the city killing many residents.

Courses of action

I. The residents of all the remaining dilapidated buildings should be immediately shifted to other buildings located nearby.

II. The residents of all the buildings in bad condition should be served notices to vacate these buildings immediately.

51. Statement Even after more than fifty eight years of independence people living below poverty line is still a cause for concern in India.

Courses of action

I. The Government should revamp the public distribution system for providing adequate food to all its citizens.

II. The Government should make sincere efforts to generate employment in the rural areas to improve the economic condition of the poor.

52. Statement People residing in the locality have complained against the high handedness of the police officers of the local police station in dealing with people approaching the police station with grievances.

Courses of action

I. All the officers of the local police station should immediately be transferred to another police station.

II. The administration should immediately investigate into the complaint and take action against erring officers.

53. Statement Majority of students of class IX of the vernacular medium schools have scored very less marks in Mathematics in the final examination.

Courses of action

I. The school authority should immediately suspend all the Mathematics teachers of the school.

II. All these students should be transferred to other English medium schools.

54. Statement It has been observed that rate of divorce is higher in the cases when both husband and wife are having regular jobs.

Courses of action

I. The working couples should regularly consult the counsellors to save their marriage.

II. One member of the couple should be discouraged to take up a regular job.

Advanced Level

Direction (Q. Nos. 1-18) *In each question below is given a statement followed by three courses of action numbered I, II and III. A course of action is a step or administrative decision to be taken for improvement, follow up or further action in regard to the problem, policy etc. On the basis of the information given in the statement, you have to assume everything in the statement to be true, then decide which of the suggested course of action logically follow(s) for pursuing.*

1. **Statement** Nuclear power cannot make a country secure.

Courses of action **UKPSC 2014**

I. We should stop further increasing our nuclear power.
II. We should destroy our nuclear capability.
III. We should focus on improving diplomatic relations.

(a) Only I follows (b) Only II follows
(c) Only III follows (d) I and II follow

2. **Statement** A sudden cloud burst over the island city resulted into unpredicted rainfall causing flood like situation in the entire area. Large number of people were caught unaware and were stranded on the road.

Course of action

I. The local administration should immediately put in place an action plan for avoiding such situation in future.
II. The local administration should immediately deploy personnel to help the stranded people to move to safer places.
III. The local administration should advise all the citizens not to venture out on the road till situation improves.

(a) Only I follows
(b) Only II follows
(c) Only III follows
(d) II and III follow
(e) All of the above follow

3. **Statement** The prices of essential commodities have gone up substantially during the past few weeks.

Courses of action

I. The government should set up an expert committee to study the trend of prices.
II. The government should immediately abolish taxes on essential commodities.
III. The government should advise the general public to refrain from purchasing essential commodities for few days.

(a) None follows
(b) Only I follows
(c) Only II follows
(d) Only III follows
(e) I and II follow

4. **Statement** The members belonging to two local clubs occasionally fight with each other on the main road and block traffic movement.

Course of action **RBI (Grade B) 2009**

I. The local police station should immediately deploy police personnel round the clock on the main road.
II. Those involved in fighting should be identified and put behind bars.
III. The local administration should disband the management of the two clubs with immediate effect.

(a) I and II follow (b) II and III follow
(c) I and III follow (d) All follow
(e) None of these

5. **Statement** Many students of the local school fell ill for the fourth time in a row in the last six months after consuming food prepared by the school canteen.

Course of action

I. The school management should immediately terminate the contract of the canteen and ask for compensation.
II. The school management should advice all the students not to eat food articles from the canteen.
III. The owner of the canteen should immediately be arrested for negligence.

(a) None follows (b) Only II follows
(c) Only III follows (d) I and II follow
(e) II and III follow

6. **Statement** Many school buses have fitted CNG kit without observing the safety guidelines properly. This results into some instances of these buses catching fire due to short circuit and endangering the lives of the school children.

Course of action

I. The regional transport authority should immediately carry out checks of all the school buses fitted with CNG kit.
II. The management of all the schools should stop hiring buses fitted with CNG kit.
III. The government should issue a notification banning school buses for use of CNG kit.

(a) Only I follows (b) Only II follows
(c) Only III follows (d) I and III follow
(e) None of these

7. **Statement** The migration from villages to cities is detrimental to both.

Courses of action **UKPSC 2014**

I. Rural postings should be mandatory.
II. Employment opportunities be created in villages.
III. There should be trains lining villages to cities.

(a) Only I follows
(b) Only II follows
(c) Only III follows
(d) I and II follow

8. **Statement** It is reported that during the last fortnight there has been three cases of near miss situation involving two aircrafts over the busy city airport. In all these cases both the aircrafts came perilously close to each other and could avoid collision as the pilots acted just in time.

Course of action

I. The pilots of all the six aircrafts involved in these incidents should immediately be de-rostered.

II. Some flights should be diverted to other airports for the next few months to decongest the sky over the city airport.

III. Air traffic controllers of the city airport should be sent for refresher courses in batches to prepare themselves to handle such pressure situation.

(a) Only I follows
(b) Only II follows
(c) Only III follows
(d) Only II and III follows
(e) None of the above

9. **Statement** A final year student of the department of fine arts has complained to the VC of the university 'X' that the students of the department are being harassed by their teachers.

Course of action

I. A case should be registered against those teachers in the nearest police station.

II. University authorities should constitute a probe panel to look into the teacher's misconduct.

III. Records of charges against those person should be made available to the probe panel.

(a) Only I follows (b) Only II follows
(c) I and II follow (d) None follows
(e) None of these

10. **Statement** There are more than 200 villages in the hill area of Uttarakhand which are severely damaged due to cyclone and it causes and extra burden of ₹ 200 crore on State Government for relief and rehabilitation work.

Course of action

I. People of hill area should be shifted to other safer places.

II. State Government should ask more financial support from Central Government.

III. Government should levy relief tax to the corporate sector to ease the additional burden.

(a) None follows (b) I and II follow
(c) II and III follow (d) I and III follow
(e) None of these

11. **Statement** Cases of self-medication are on the rise. It leads to severe side-effects which may turn out to be even deadly.

Course of action

I. People should be made aware and persuaded not to play doctor themselves.

II. People should be advised to consult the doctor immediately in case of illness.

III. All the chemists should be instructed not to provide drugs to those who lack prescription from a renowned doctor.

(a) All I, II and III (b) I and II
(c) II and III (d) Only III
(e) None of these

12. **Statement** The city council of *Brownwood City* has decided to install a plant of mineral water to provide the citizens mineral water bottles at $ 1 per bottle as against bottles costing $ 1.5 being sold by local private players.

Course of action **IIFT 2014**

I. All the local private companies selling bottled water in *Brownwood City* will have to close their operations.

II. The city council of *Brownwood City* will have to provide for the losses from this project in its budget.

III. The normal tap water supply of *Brownwood City* will have no taker and that will have to be discontinued.

(a) None of I, II or III follow
(b) Only II follows
(c) II and III follw
(d) All I, II and III follw

13. **Statement** Smuggling of valuable idols has increased and stealing of idols from the temples has become a common feature.

Course of action

I. Government should provide security for all the temples.

II. A special task force should be constituted to nab the persons involved in it.

III. With the help of different NGOs people's participation should be increased to save idols.

(a) II and III follow
(b) I and III follow
(c) All follow
(d) None follows
(e) None of the above

14. **Statement** Poverty is increasing because the people, who are deciding how to tackle it, know absolutely nothing about the poor.

Course of action

I. The decision makers should go to the grass root levels.

II. The decision makers should come from the poorer sections of the society.

III. A new set of decisions makers should replace the existing one.

(a) Only I follows
(b) Only II follows
(c) Either I or III follows
(d) All follow
(e) None of the above

15. Statement Land near border is being used by security forces without acquiring it or paying rent for it and has become cause for resentment for the land-owners of the state X.

Course of action

I. The security forces should be ordered to vacate the land immediately.

II. Defence ministry should acquire the land.

III. Defence ministry should pay the rent for the land.

(a) Only I
(b) Only I and II
(c) Either II or III
(d) All I, II and III
(e) None of these

16. Statement A mass mortality of shrimps in ponds on entire Andhra coast has recently been reported due to the presence of a virus.

Course of action

I. The water of the ponds affected should immediately be treated for identifying the nature of the virus.

II. The catching of shrimps from the ponds should temporarily be stopped.

III. The fisherman should be asked to watch for the onset of such phenomenon in nature.

(a) Only I follows
(b) I and II follow
(c) All follow
(d) II and III follow
(e) None of these

17. Statement In the recent elections held in country X, a large number of eunuch succeeded in becoming members of Parliament.

Course of action

I. Eunuchs should be banned from contesting elections.

II. People should be encouraged to vote for efficient persons.

III. All the parties should be directed not to distribute tickets to eunuchs.

(a) Only I follows
(b) I and II follow
(c) All follows
(d) None follows
(e) None of these

18. Statement A large number of students who have passed their XII Std. terminal examination in the country could not get admission to colleges as the number of seats available are grossly inadequate.

Course of action

I. The evaluation system of XII Std. terminal examination should be made more tough so that fewer students pass the examination.

II. The Government should encourage the private sector to open new colleges by providing them land at cheaper rate.

III. The rich people should be asked to send their wards to foreign countries for higher studies enabling the needy students to get admission in colleges within the country.

(a) Only I follows
(b) Only II follows
(c) I and II follow
(d) II and III follow
(e) None of these

Answers with Explanations

Intro Exercise 1

1. (*b*) Because of mid-day meal provided by the school majority of the students fell ill so they should immediately be taken to the nearby hospitals for treatment. Hence, only course of action II follows.

2. (*e*) Both the actions follow because government should increase medical facilities and take steps to clean the city. It will be helpful for those people who are suffering from jaundice and typhoid.

3. (*b*) Action I does not follow because a good course of action can never be negative. Action II follows because NGO' s and Nagar Nigam should start a cleanliness movement in city 'X'.

4. (*d*) Banning for life is too harsh. So, action I does not follow. Candidates cannot spend beyond the limit set by election commission (atleast on paper). Tax is calculated on the amount that is spent on paper. So, action II does not follow.

5. (*a*) Action I follows because concerned authorities should keep a close watch on this issue and caught the culprits. Action II does not follow because resident of that area should not be punished for the crime which they did not commit.

6. (*a*) If the actor thinks that his termination was wrong, then he should file a case against Zee Telefilms. So, action I follows but II does not follow because it is possible that actor was not performing well or there may be some genuine reason behind his termination.

7. (*a*) Action I will help government to curb the mafia. Action II is not feasible. Hence, only action I is the right course of action.

8. (*d*) Salary of members is not compariable to the valuable time of parliament. Parliament is made for sorting out matters wheather it is disputed or not. So, neither action I nor II follows.

9. (*a*) If regular teachers are on strike then alternative arrangement should be made with teachers on daily wages so that studies should not be affected. So, action I follows but II does not follow because demands of teachers may or may not be feasible.

10. (*b*) This situation can not be compromised, so action I does not follow. Action II follows because Government must generate more electricity to meet the demand of North India.

11. (*e*) As the salaried class is highly disappointed, so the Finance Minister should reconsider the budget proposal and for the relief of salaried class, the tax rate on different slabs of salary should be brought down. So, both action I and II follow.

12. (*a*) Statement points out that people see tax as burden, hence, government should educate and inform citizens about the ways in which taxes help in development of the nation. Hence, only action I is the right course of action.

13. (*d*) It does not mean that if one state of US ban bidis, imported from India then India should cut off all its business with the US. Its also does not mean that business of bidi producers is dependent on only one state of US. So, neither action I nor II follows.

14. (*b*) Action I does not follow because no threat should be ignored. Action II follows because by this action viewership of DD may increased.

15. (*e*) Both the actions follow because major computer firms can create a comn on facility to collect and recycle e-waste. Major computer firms should follow the guidelines issued by the government in reprocessing of computer waste.

16. (*a*) Culprits should be punished not the innocent. So, the authorities must take action against the staff who are involved in this game. So, action I follows but II does not follow.

17. (*a*) For the motivation among today's generation to join armed forces, the right action is that the short term internship should be introduced at high school level to give students a peek into the adventurous life of the armed forces. Hence, only action I is the right course of action.

18. (*b*) For accountability of plethora of bodied, an umbrella committee should be appointed with powers to regulate action of these bodies. Hence, only action II is the right course of action.

19. (*b*) For improvement of Healthcare infrastructure of India. incentives should be given to private players. Hence, only action II is the right course of action.

20. (*a*) Action I follows because for beautification slums should be removed. So, government should give notice to the slum dwellors to vacate that place and government should provide them some alternate place. Action II does not follow due to the word 'all'.

21. (*b*) Action I does not follow because what one state is doing, it is not considered by other states. Action II follows because distance education and taking internet to rural areas requires proper infrastructure and optical fibre projects.

22. (*e*) Both the actions follow because local police administration should current all those who are caught committing the act like stone throwing and damaging vehicles. A meeting should be called in which officers of both the clubs and police officers should present.

23. (*e*) Both the actions follow because after a huge traffic jam traffic department should immediately send its staff on the spot to divert traffic through other roads and try to remove the truck from the road.

24. (*b*) Action I does not follow because all activities can not be put on hold due to the act of some workers. Action II follows because belongings of workers should be thoroughly searched before they leave the premises of the company.

25. (*c*) Either action I or II follows because if fisherman did not construct their huts along the coast line then the loss due to huge tidal waves may be less. But in present situation, the local administration should send a team of officials to assess the extent of damage and suggest remedical measures.

26. (*d*) Failure of one function does not mean that all other functions should be banned. Government does not give advice on these type of issues to local hospital. It always gives order to the concerned authorities. So, neither action I nor II follows.

27. (*d*) Fear among people does not mean that what they are thinking is going to be true, so action I does not follow. Action II also does not follow because it is a very high level talk and it should be placed when there is a surety of fear.

28. (*d*) Neither action I nor II follows because of the word 'all,' as there may be some employees who are on leave for genuine reasons.

29. (*d*) Safety of heritage sites like Taj Mahal is the duty of CISF. For this they may have to check each and every person visiting these sites. So, action I does not follow action II also does not follow because checking tickets is not the duty of ASI.

30. (*b*) Stopping the bus service is not the solution of the problem. So, action I does not follow. To stop the supply of fake currency. Indian police should check the bus properly and keep proper vigilance in the bus. So, action II follow.

31. (*d*) Closing tobacoo manufacturing units is not the solution of the problem and punishing children below 12 is not feasible. So, neither action I nor II follows.

32. (*d*) Elections are very important activity of a country, so they should not be banned. There is no sense of deploying police after the elections. So, neither action I nor II follows.

33. (*a*) Action I follows because strict action should be taken against engineers and officials in whose jurisdiction the unauthorized constructions were done. Action II does not follow because no information is given about stay orders.

34. (*e*) As the new channel is reputed, so the news might be true. So, an enquiry committee should be formed to look into the matter and the concerned anthorities should be questioned and punished, if found guilty. So, both actions I and II follow.

35. (*e*) Due to the accident, there was a loss of life and property. It is a big fault, so an investigation committee should be set up to look into the matter and proper action should be taken against the accused. So, both actions I and II follow.

36. (*d*) Action I does not follow due to the word 'all.' As the level of pesticide resides, is 35 times the global accepted level to the companies should not be allowed to continue. So, action II also does not follow.

37. (*b*) Action I does not follow because it is a very hard step and the complaint may not be against some employees. Action II follows as the bank management should ask for a report from the branch manager for taking necessary steps.

38. (*e*) Both actions I and II follow as police constables should be deployed near that park and citizens should go in group for early morning walks.

39. (*a*) Action I follows because government should set up an expert group to impact the conditions of school buses to avoid such Accidents. Action II does not follow due to the word 'all'.

40. (*c*) Either action I or II follows because it is the best way to retain its employees. After one year if officers left the bank then it may not be a loss for bank as they did not have attended any training program.

41. (*d*) Neither action I nor II follows due to the word immediately. In that situation, the priority should be to clean the road for smooth traffic.

42. (*d*) Both courses of actions are correct as both will help in the action. Hence, both follow.

43. (*b*) Only II is the correct course of action because it will minimise the number of accidents. Hence, only II follows.

44. (*a*) Only I course of action is correct because by deploying the staff the dwellers will minimise spoiling the beauty of the sea front. Hence, only I follows.

45. (*a*) The local administration should immediately make necessary arrangements to move the affected people to safer places. Hence, only course of action I follows.

46. (*a*) Action I is correct course of action because it will bring not only similarity among students but also save their money. II is not a good action.

Intro Exercise 2

1. (*c*) Action I and II follow because additional security should be employed in highly sensitive areas and rumours should be stopped from spreading. Action III does not follow because it is an extreme step and create another problem.

2. (*d*) If disposal costs be made higher then the situation becomes worse. So, action I does not follow. Action II and III follow because disposal costs should be brought down and study should be done in this respect.

3. (*b*) Investigation should be done and precautions should be taken to avoid the criminal activities in the city during the recent festival season.So, action I and II follow. Action III is not advisable.

4. (*e*) Action I does not follow because the main cause is already mentioned in the statement. Action II is not related with the statement so it does not follow. Action III follows because parents should keep close look when they observe that their wards are facing critical circumstances.

5. (*d*) From the statement, it is clear that there are some problems in rehabilitation of bonded labourers. These problems must be solved quickly. So, action III follows.

6. (*c*) I and II are right actions as they will ease the action III is impractical.

7. (*d*) Negative actions are not expected, so action I does not follow. The owners and workers should cooperate with each other. So, action II and III follow.

8. (*b*) Misuse of water cannot be define and determined and thats it cannot be banned. An awareness drive may be helpful and storing rain water can solve the problem to some extent. So, action II and III follow.

9. (*e*) Action II follows because this a big issue and Indian government should sort out this issue with country X. Actions I and III are not directly related with the statement, so they do not follow.

10. (*b*) Action I follows because India should reach new sources of oil. This will take care our demands and reduces the dependency on other countries. Action II also follows because if situation become worse then it will be helpful. Action III does not follows because a fortnight is not an enough time.

11. (*d*) Action I does not follow because no information is given about the nature of soil and the area underconstruction, which is required for tunneling method. Efforts should be made to transplant the removed trees and new trees should be planted in the neighbouring areas. So, action II and III follow.

12. (*c*) Chloroquine may be used for some other purposes. So, stop the selling of chloroquine is absurd. As it is clear from the statement that chloroquine become ineffective for malaria patients, so researchers should develop a new medicine for the patients suffering from malaria and they should be checked for identification of casual mosquito.

13. (*c*) Providing auto-rickshaw need resources to implement such programmes. So, action I and II follow. It is necessary to know, who need auto-rickshaw, so action III also follows.

14. (*c*) Action I is not directly related with the statement, so it does not follow. Health can be maintained by prevention and treatment. So, action II and III follow.

15. (*d*) All the courses of action follow because for income of Indian Railways, a committee should be constituted to get New ideas and railways should explore new areas to generate revenues. Some non-core activities should be given to the expert of that field.

16. (*d*) Action I does not follow because this bulletin does not require wide publicity. The civic authority should be ready for removal of water from that area and people should be advised to remain at home to avoid any problem. So, action II and III follow.

17. (*a*) Action I follows because if a student is ousted from a college, then this information should be sent to all the other colleges of the university. The issue stated in the statement is not related with the admission and anti-social activities. So, action II and III do not follow.

18. (*d*) All the actions follow because vehicular movement should be regulated, road should be repaired and motorists should be alerted by putting the condition of roads on sign boards.

19. (*e*) Action I does not follow became it is an extreme step. It is very difficult to identify who is poacher or not, so action II does not follow. Action III is a negative action which is not admirable.

20. (*c*) Action I follows because training to staff on the safety aspects of handling explosive materials will reduce the chance of such accidents in future. Termination of supervisor incharge is an extreme step. An enquiry should be done against him and if found guilty then he can be terminated. Action III is not advisable as it is a negative action.

21. (*e*) Action I is of no use to provide relief for people, so it does not follows. Government should provide necessary equipments and drinking water to cope up with extreme hot weather. So, action II and III follow.

22. (*d*) Private sector banks have reduced interest rate to attract new customers which is not a wrong move. So, action I does not follow. To remain in competition, public sector banks should reduce their interest rate or they should advertise their special features for the customers. So, either action II or III follows.

23. (*b*) Action I is saving the culprits and punishing innocents. So, it does not follow. Water samples should be checked in laboratories and ward engineer should check water installations and pipelines in the Model Colony area. So, action II and III follow.

24. (*d*) It is a very serious offence and the examiners who are playing with the future of students should be punished. All those papers which were evaluated by the students should be rechecked by qualified teachers. So, action I and II follow while III does not follow.

25. (*b*) Action I does not follows because this move may make the respective department financially weak. Action II follows because it will help in reducing the resentment among the farmers. Action III is not a proper way of protest, so it does not follow.

26. (*a*) Action I follows because more colleges should be set up in both urban and rural areas. So, that every student gets admissition in college after passing the school exams. Action II and III are negative in nature, so they do not follow.

27. (*b*) Action I is an extreme action. Industries responsible for this should be warned, not closed. So, action I does not follow. Action II and III follow because water should be treated chemically before resuming water supply. Effluents being discharged into the river should be checked.

28. (*a*) Course of action I follows.

29. (*b*) Statement followed by course of action II only solves the traffic problems.

30. (*a*) Course of action I logically follows.

31. (*d*) Course of action III logically follows, because government controls banking system with the help of Central Bank.

32. (*d*) All the course of action follow.

33. (*c*) Publishing the forecast in media should not be the course of action while relief team should be ready if drought occurs as in course of action II. Also, course of action III is good because by using drought resistant variety, drought may be lesser.

Cumulative Exercise

Base Level

1. (*b*) Only the course of action II follow because a study about other brands can be helpful to find out the reasons behind the problem. Course of action I does not follow because we can not definately say that the price is the reason of sale.

2. (*a*) It is not possible to ban the sale of medicines of vitamins and minerals, so the people should be encouraged to take fruits and vegetables.

Hence, only the course of action I follows.

3. (*d*) Neither action I nor II follows.

4. (*b*) Reasons should be detected for the loss. Privatization of Indian Airlines is not a guarantee of making it a profitable organization. So, action I does not follow but action II follows, because it must curb its expenditure.

5. (*d*) Neither action I nor II follows because action I will make party 'A' more weak while II is not the solution of the problem.

6. (*e*) Both the actions follow because such type of culprits should put them behind bars and the university authority should provide security in campus, so that such incidents should not be repeated.

7. (*b*) Action I does not follow because there will be a negative impact on India's greatest musicians and folk artists. Action II follows because the government should give financial aid to these artists.

8. (*c*) Course of action I is advisable because providing nourishment to children for the upliftment of deprived class need money. Course of Action II is also advisable because it will be helpful in providing nourishment.

9. (*b*) Course of action I does not follow because for many people peak season is convenient to travel. Course of action II follows as extra coaches should be added to train, so that more people can travel.

10. (*a*) Course of action I follows because highway would bring development in their area. Course of action II does not follow due to the word 'immediately'.

11. (*b*) Eatable rice should also produce. Otherwise, it will either create inflation or starvation or both. So, government should provide increase procurement price of other qualities.

12. (*a*) Course of action I follows. No body should stop to earn high. Instead of course of action II, government should take high fee from those who are rich and should arrange educational loan to whom are poor. It will be practical decision.

13. (*a*) Course of action I follows because circulating the photographs of terrorists in electronic and print media will be helpful in nabbing them. Course of action II does not follow because it is not feasible and a coward step.

14. (*d*) It is impractical to follow what toppers are doing. So, action I does not follow. Action II does not follow because opening schools all over the world is not an easy task.

15. (*a*) Secretariat is a very important place, so such type of calls cannot be taken lightly and bomb defusing squad should be sent immediately. So, I follows but II does not.

16. (*e*) Course of action I follows, because if new trains are introduced then number of accidents may increase. Action II also follows, because upgradation and new technology will ensure more safety to the passengers.

17. (*b*) Action I is not directly related with the statement, so it does not follows. Action II follows as awareness of the benefits of family planning should be extended to the masses.

18. (*a*) Government should advise the people not to smoke Government should not force to impose upon. So, action I follows while II does not.

19. (*b*) The first course of action does not match the scale of the problem. The problem is not so big as to merit a government enquiry. It is enough that the civic body takes action and hence, II follows.

20. (*e*) Course of action I will help in cure while II will help in prevention.

21. (*a*) II is a very extreme action and hence, does not follow. I is a proper course of action. Note that taking immediate steps is not the same as immediate removal of the constructions, which may again have been considered to be an extreme course of action.

22. (*d*) If the rainfall is normal, it does not mean we would deprive the farmer of his due. The actions may be deemed to be correct only if we know that they are the reversal of policies which had been frames during the years of crisis.

23. (*d*) Both are extreme courses of action.

24. (*d*) Course of action I is not the correct action to be taken as there can be a lack of teaching faculty.

Course of action II is also not the correct action to be taken as faculty teaching the particular subject may be asked to change their way of teaching. So, none of the courses of actions follows.

25. (*d*) Going for I and II will create other problems. Hence, none follows.

26. (*e*) From the statement, it is clear that graduates produced by Indian universities are unemployable. So, world class foreign universities should be encouraged to set up campuses in India. Providing autonomy to colleges and institutes may also improve the situation. So, both the courses of action follow.

27. (*b*) Due to heavy damage to standing crops, government should announce a relief package for those who are affected. So, course of action II follows but I does not follow as it is not directly related with the statement.

28. (*a*) From the statement, it is clear that telecom companies are not transparent on the tariff plans. So, regulatory authority should direct them. So, course of action I follows but II does not follow.

29. (*b*) Course of action I may prove to be counter-productive. There is a risk that the increase may be at the cost of quality. Hence, it does not follow. Course of action II follows.

30. (*e*) Since, the population of dolphin has been decreasing, so it should be declared an endangered species and be bred in protected areas. Some locals should be enlisted to protect dolphins. So, both the courses of action follow.

31. (*e*) Both the actions follow as a meeting should be needed between the management and union leaders, and management should appeal to the employees to withdraw the call for strike assuring them the decisions will be considered for review.

32. (*e*) Action I is advisable in the view of precautionary measures and action II is helpful in controlling the damage. So, both the actions follow.

33. (*b*) Action I does not follow because mid-day meal is also good and this incident is not so big. Action II follows because school should arrange for medical help to all the affected children.

34. (*a*) Action I follows because policeman should be deployed at security checks at all the entries into the city.

35. (*e*) Both the actions follow because adequate police force should be deployed and vehicles on the road should be advised a diversion to avoid traffic congestion.

36. (*d*) Company should do research for causes of decline of sales.

37. (*d*) Neither the students should advice go abroad nor to try job after recession.

38. (*b*) To increase profit, fare should be increased.

39. (*a*) Government has made rule, so it must be followed by schools otherwise government should identify such schools and take proper actions against them.

40. (*b*) The hospital should make proper arrangement for those patients.

41. (*a*) Only I follows, society and parents are not our control, so we cannot minimize pressure.

42. (*c*) Either the students can study at college or they join coaching classes.

43. (*e*) Both the statements will help in educating people about value system.

44. (*e*) Both the statements can help the yung people to acquire their responsibility.

45. (*d*) Players should be encouraged to concentrate on their sport.

46. (*a*) Second course of action is very stricit, so only first course of action will help subsidies to be put to proper use.

47. (*b*) Course of action I does not make sense as any kind of imposition because of negative effect. Course of action II is likely to help things improve.

48. (*e*) Course of action I is desirable on the basis of humanity. Course of action II will help for long time means helpful for future.

49. (*e*) While the course of action I helps in prevention of disease, the II helps in cure.

50. (*b*) Course I does not sound very feasible.

51. (*e*) Both the course will come in good aid to people below poverty line.

52. (*b*) Course I is neither practical nor sane. Only course of action II follows.

53. (*d*) In fact, Mathematics teaching process and faculty in vernacular schools should be updated.

54. (*a*) Only course of action I is feasible.

Advanced Level

1. (*c*) Diplomatic relations are helpful to promote peace, development and progress with all the other nations in the international community. So, only the course of action III follows.

2. (*e*) Proper planning should be made, so that such incidents can be prevented in future. Beside that the local administration should deploy personal for help and people should be advised to remain at home till the situation improve. So, all the course of action I , II and III follow.

3. (*a*) None follows as I is a long time activity. II will adversely affect government income. III is illogical.

4. (*a*) As the members of two clubs fight with each other on main road which block traffic movement. So, police personnel should be deployed in that area and those involved in fighting should be identified and put behind bars. So, courses of action I and II follow. Course of action III is too Harsh, so, it does not follow.

5. (*d*) As the incident is repeated again and again, so the contract of the canteen should be terminated and compensation should be asked. Students should be advised not to eat food articles from the canteen. So, courses of action I and II follow. Course of action III is too harsh, so it does not follow.

6. (*a*) As safety guidelines are not observed by many school buses, so regional transport authority should carry out checks of all the buses fitted with CNG kit. So, course of action I follows. CNG is a pollution free fuel and its sources are more than petrol and diesel. So, it should be encouraged but with safety norms. So, course of action II and III do not follow.

7. (*b*) Employment in villages will ensure the stability and fullfill the other human needs. So, only course of action II follows.

8. (*c*) Collision of aircrafts were avoided because pilots acted just in time. So, course of action I does not follow. Course of action II does not follow because it is not feasible, since many passengers have to travel to that city. Course of action III follows because it was the mistake of air traffic controllers, so they should be sent for refreshed courses.

9. (*e*) Course of action I does not follow because a case in police station should not be registered without verifying the charges against the teachers. Course of actions II and III follow, because a probe panel should look into teachers misconduct and all records should be made available to the probe panel.

10. (*b*) As the villages in the hill area are severly damaged due to cyclone. So, people of that area should be shifted to other safer places. As relief and rehabilitation work is causing burden on State Government, so it should ask Central Government for help. Implementing additional taxes for this cause is not a solution. So, courses of action I and II follow while III does not.

11. (*b*) Awareness of people and immediate consultation with doctor, in case of sudden illness will be helpful in minimising the cases of self medication. So courses of action I and II follow. Action III does not follow due to the word 'renowned'.

12. (*a*) Action I does not follow as all companies have to close their operations which lead to problem. Action II also does not follows as it is talking about losses from the project. Action III also does not relate to the situation. So, none of the action I, II and III follows.

13. (*a*) Providing security to all the temples is impractical. So course of action I does not follow. A special task force should be constituted to nab the culprits helpful. So, people's participation will certainly be helpful. So courses of action II and III follow.

14. (*c*) From the statement, it is clear that decision makers do not know anything about the poor, so either they should go to the grass root levels or a new set of decision makers should replace them. So, either I or III follows.

15. (*c*) Course of action I does not follow due to the word 'immediately'. Defence Ministry should either acquire the land or pay the rent for the land. So, either II or III follows.

16. (*a*) The present and most urgent need is to identify the nature of virus and then treat the water of pond accordingly. So, course of action I follows.

17. (*e*) Eunuchs becoming member of Parliament is not undemocratic. So, courses of action I and III do not follow. Course of action II follows, because people should be encouraged to vote for efficient persons.

18. (*b*) Courses of action I and III do not follow because they are not the proper solution of this problem. Course of action II follows because government should encourage the private sector to open new colleges by providing them land at cheaper rate.

6

Decision Making

Decision-making is a process in which a final outcome is derived by evaluating and analysing the given information. In these type of questions, you are required to decide that a candidate is selected or not for a certain job, in an organisation or admission in a college, by going through his bio-data, that is given in the question.

Questions from this chapter are designed to judge the decision-making capability of a candidate. The importance of this chapter can be assumed by this, that 5-15 questions are asked in Bank PO, IBPS CWE for PO and 3-10 questions are asked in management exams like XAT, IIFT, SNAP, NMAT and MHA CET MBA.

There are two types of informations given in such questions. First is the **basic conditions** and second is the **additional conditions.**

➘ While solving these questions, you must strictly adhere to the given conditions and nothing should be assumed.

Difference between Data Inadequate and Data Not to be Selected

It is important, to know that the difference between data **Inadequate and Data not to be selected data because students make mistake in this criteria.**

If the details given about any candidate give no information as required by the basic conditions (or the additional conditions), then this case would be called **Inadequacy of data.**

If the details given about any candidate give **less information** as required by the basic conditions (or the additional conditions), then this case would be called **not to be selected data.**

Types of Questions Asked in Different Examinations

There are multiple types of questions which are asked from the chapter 'Decision Making', so it is quite difficult to predict exact type of questions that are asked. Here, we are giving different types of questions that are usually asked in the examination. Almost all the questions at this chapter can be categorised into these types. Also, this description of type will make your study easy and streamline.

Type 1 Eligibility Test

In these type of questions, a set of necessary conditions and qualifications required to be fulfilled by the candidate for a certain vacancy in job/ promotion / admission in a college, along with the biodata of certain candidates who have applied for the same is given. You are required to evaluate and assess a candidate's eligibility and thereby decide upon the appropriate course of action to taken from among the given alternatives.

Examples Based on Type 1

Direction (Examples 1-4) *Read the given information carefully and answer the questions given below.* **IIFT 2014**

The management of the national daily newspaper *Tomorrow Digest* decides to enhance its subscriber base through major changes in the style, layout, design and content of the paper. In order to make to content more amenable to the mindset of the growing younger population of the country, the paper decides to appoint a number of young and promising Associate Editors.

For facilitating the appointment process, several selection criteria were finalised and provided to the selection panel, which are noted in the following. It was noted that in order to get selected, the candidates are required to fulfil, in addition to I, at least three of the following conditions:

I. The age of the candidates must not be lower than 25 yr, but should not cross 30 yr.

II. The candidate has secured 60% and above at her/his graduation level.

III. The candidate has obtained a post graduate diploma in journalism with atleast 55% marks.

IV. The candidate has gained working experience of a minimum period of 2 yr in a daily newspaper with responsibility of regular writing assignments.

V. The candidate has been awarded at state-level for her/his articles published in state-level English daily.

If, however it is observed that some candidates fulfill only two conditions from II-V, but does not fulfill

A. V above, but he/she has already gathered an experience of 5 yr in a news agency, the case of the candidate will be referred to the Managing Editor of *Tomorrow Digest.*

B. II above, but he/she holds a PG Diploma in journalism with 80% marks, the case of the candidate will be referred to the chairman of *Tomorrow Digest.*

C. III above, but he/she has completed graduation with 70% marks, the case of the candidate will be referred to the Editor *Tomorrow Digest.*

All the information about a few candidates applying for the Associate Editor position provided in the following are dated on August 31, 2014. Based on the information furnished, decide in each case, which of the following course of action the selection panel should adopt, from the available options. You are not to assume any information.

Ex **1.** Sarangsh Malhotra has graduated from Agra University with 66% marks and later has completed PG Diploma in Journalism from Indian Institute of Mass Communication, New Delhi with 71%. After completion of the PG Diploma programme, she joined Galaxy News at Jaipur on Christmas Eve in 2006.

She received an award from the hands of the Governor of Rajasthan for her series of investigative articles on January 26, 2008, a day which coincided with her 25th birthday. During June next year, she joined in a corporate house and is working there since then.

(a) The candidate is to be selected
(b) The candidate is not to be selected
(c) The case of the candidate is to be referred to the Managing Editor
(d) The case of the candidate is to be referred to the Chairman

Ex **2.** Nalin Saxena graduated in Sociology Honours from Bengaluru University with 61% marks, after which he joined an NGO for social work. After two years, he took migration and joined Mumbai University for the PG Diploma in Journalism Programme and he secured 59% in the exam.

He subsequently joined *Ahmadabad Weekly* magazine, which is published in English, in July 18, 2011, to write regular features on city life. He was born in June 1986, in the midst of the FIFA World Cup.

(a) The candidate is to be selected
(b) The candidate is not to be selected
(c) The case of the candidate is to be referred to the Chairman
(d) The case of the candidate is to be referred to the Editor

Ex 3. Geetika Arora is working as a reporter on issues pertaining to international news events in the Indore-based English news daily *The New Dawn* since September 20, 2012. She was awarded by the Madhya Pradesh Newspapers Guild in 2013 for her series of articles on global climate change concerns.

Geetika had graduated in Political Science from Udaipur University in 2010 with 58% marks. After graduation, she immediately joined Allahabad University and earned her Gold Medal in PG Diploma in Journalism by securing 82% marks two years later. While studying at Allahabad, she celebrated her 24th birthday.

(a) The candidate is to be selected
(b) The candidate is not to be selected
(c) The case of the candidate is to be referred to the Chairman
(d) The case of the candidate is to be referred to the Editor

Ex 4. Manjeet Tyagi was born on September 5, 1988 and completed his graduation in Economics from Garhwal University with 68% marks in 2009. He subsequently completed his PG Diploma in Journalism from Punjab University in July 2010, but his marks dropped by ten percentage points *vis-a-vis* his graduation results.

After completing PG degree, Manjeet immediately joined in a data analytics firm and worked there for one and half years as business analyst, after which he joined the Delhi-based English daily *Financial Standard* as a trade and industry expert for writing regular columns on these areas.

(a) The candidate is to be selected
(b) The candidate is not to be selected
(c) The case of the candidate is to be referred to the Managing Editor
(d) The case of the candidate is to be referred to the Editor

SOLUTION (Examples 1-4)

1. (*b*) Because age of Sarangsh Malhotra on January 26, 2008 was 25 yr. So, her age on January 26, 2014 will be 31 yr. Therefore, she did not fulfill the first condition. Hence, the candidate is not to be selected.
2. (*b*) Nalin Saxena is working in a weekly newspaper. He is not working in daily newspaper. He also does not fulfill three conditions, in addition to Condition I. Hence, the candidate is not to be selected.
3. (*c*) The candidate satisfies the Conditions I, III and V. Since, Geetika did not fulfill condition II, but fulfill condition A. So, her case will be referred to the Chairman.
4. (*a*) In addition to condition I, candidate fulfill three conditions i.e. II, III and IV. So, he will be selected.

Direction (Examples 5-9) *Following are the conditions for selection of IT Officers in an organisation. The candidate must*

I. be an engineer in IT/Computers/Electronics or an MCA with Ist class securing a minimum of 65% marks.
II. have an experience of working in the related area at least for two years after acquiring the desired qualification.
III. have passed the selection test with at least 60% marks.
IV. be not less than 21 yr and not more than 30 yr of age as on 1.2.2012.

However, if a candidate fulfills all the above criteria except

(i) at (II) above, but has an experience of one year and has obtained atleast 70% marks at the degree examination, the case may be referred to the Chairman and Managing Director of the organization.
(ii) at (IV) above, but less than 32 yr of age and has minimum 5 yr post qualification experience of working in the related area, the case may be referred to the Divisional Head of the organization.

In each question below, detailed information of candidate is provided. You have to read the information provided, carefully and decide which of the following courses of actions you will adopt, as regarding status of the candidate, based on the conditions stated above. You are not to assume anything other than the information provided in each question. All these cases are given to you as on 1.2.2012. You have to indicate your decision by marking answers to each question as follows

Give answer

(a) if the candidate is to be selected
(b) if the candidate is not to be selected
(c) if the data is not adequate to take the decision
(d) if the case is to be referred to the Divisional Head
(e) if the case to be referred to the Chairman and Management Director

Ex 5. Sujata Bhatt is an IT engineer, passed out in 2005 with 72% marks. She is working as a software engineer since June 2006. Her date of birth is 23rd December 1981. She has cleared the selection test with 65% marks.

Ex 6. Nisha Chavan has passed MCA with 68% marks in the year 2009 and has passed the selection test with 62% marks. She has been working as clerk-cum-cashier in a co-operative bank since 2009. Her date of birth is 16th July, 1989.

Ex 7. Aditya Joshi is an electronics engineer passed with 72% marks in 2008 and is MBA-Finance passed in 2010 with 70% marks. He started working as a software manager in May 2010, immediately after completing MBA. He was born on 23rd October, 1985. He has secured 66% marks in the selection test.

Ex 8. Ravi Verma is a computer engineer passed with 70% marks in 2007 and thereafter, he is working as a software engineer. He has cleared the selection test with 68% marks. His date of birth is 5th October, 1984.

Ex 9. Nilesh Zaveri has passed engineering examination in 2007 with 72% marks and thereafter, passed MCA in 2009. He has been working for the last two years since September 2009. He has recently completed 25 yr of age.

SOLUTION (Examples 5-9)

5. (*d*) Age of sujata is more than the required age, but she has more than 5 yr of post qualification experience, so her case is to be referred to the Divisional Head of the organisation.
6. (*b*) Nisha Chavan does not have the experience in the field of IT or computers, so she is not to be selected.
7. (*e*) Aditya Joshi has the experience as a software manager, not as a software engineer, but he has more than 70% marks in degree examination, so his case is to be referred to the Chairman and Managing Director of the company.
8. (*a*) Ravi Verma fulfills all the given conditions, so he is to be selected.
9. (*c*) Marks obtained by Nilesh Zaveri in the selection test are not given. So, no decision can be taken in this case.

Direction (Examples 10-19) *Study the following information carefully and answer the questions given below.*

Following are the conditions for granting advance of ₹10 lakh to the farmers for purchasing a tractor by a Gramin Bank. The farmer must

I. have atleast five acres of cultivable land.
II. be able to produce collateral of atleast ₹ 8 lakh.
III. not be more than 50 yr as on 1.12.2010.
IV. not have any outstanding unpaid loan from any bank.
V. be able to produce a recommendation letter from the Panchayat Pradhan.

In the case of farmer who satisfies all other criteria except

A. at (i) above, but is able to cultivate more than one crop in each piece of land, the case is to be referred to Chairman of the bank.
B. at (iv) above, but has fixed deposits of at least ₹ 4 lakh with the bank, the case is to be referred to the General Manager of the bank.

In each question below, detailed information of each farmer is given. You have to carefully study the information provided, in each case, and take one of the following courses of actions, based on the information and the conditions given above You are not to assume anything other than the information provided in each question. All these cases are given to you as on 1.12.2010.

You have to indicate your decision by marking answers to each question as follows

Give answer

(a) if the advance is not be granted
(b) if the case is to be referred to the General Manager of the bank
(c) if the data provided is not adequate, to take a decision
(d) if the advance is to be granted
(e) if the case is to be referred to the Chairman of the bank

Ex 10. Mohan Sadukhan was born on 2nd February, 1961. He has six acres of cultivable land. He has submitted a recommendation letter issued by the Panchayat Pradhan. He can pledge collateral of more than ₹ 8 lakh. He does not have any unpaid loan from the bank.

Ex 11. Sudhir Maiti has seven acres of cultivable land. He has obtained a recommendation letter from the Panchayat Pradhan. He does not have any unpaid loan from the bank. He grows two crops in the entire land. He can produce collateral of more than ₹ 6 lakh.

Ex 12. Prabhakar Awale has obtained a recommendation letter from the Panchayat Pradhan. He has seven acres of cultivable land and can produce collateral of ₹ 8 lakh. He was born on 4th July, 1960. He does not have any outstanding loan from the bank.

Ex 13. Akhilesh Mazumdar was born on 8th June, 1962. He has obtained a recommendation letter from the Panchayat Pradhan. He has eight acres of cultivable land and can pledge collateral of ₹ 8 lakh in addition to his fixed deposits of ₹ 6 lakh. He has an outstanding loan of ₹ 4 lakh.

Ex 14. Sukhchand Mahato was born on 8th October, 1961. He has obtained a recommendation letter from the Panchayat Pradhan. He has four acres of cultivable land with two crops in each piece of land. He can pledge ₹ 8 lakh as collateral. He has no outstanding loan from the bank.
So, his case is to be referred to the Chairman of the bank.

Ex 15. Vikram Singh has six acres of cultivable land and he does not have any outstanding loan from the bank. He can produce a recommendation letter from the Panchayat Pradhan. He can produce collateral of ₹ 9 lakh. He was born on 8th January, 1962

Ex 16. Ketan Sharma was born on 17th July, 1961. He has nine acres of cultivable land. He can produce a recommendation letter from the Panchayat Pradhan. He can give collateral of more than ₹ 8 lakh. He grows two crops on half of his total land.

Ex 17. Suren Hembross was born on 12th August, 1963 and he has three acres of cultivable land. He can produce a recommendation letter from the Panchayat Pradhan. He can give collateral of ₹ 9 lakh and does not have any outstanding loan from the bank. He grows two crops in each piece of his land.

Ex 18. Vikram Sibal can produce a recommendation letter from the Panchayat Pradhan. He can produce collateral of ₹ 8 lakh. He has outstanding loan of ₹ 5 lakh from the bank and also has fixed deposit of ₹ 3 lakh with the bank. He was born on 9th May, 1962.

Ex 19. Avik Khetrapal was born on 8th March 1961 and he can produce a recommendation letter from the Panchayat Pradhan. He does not have any outstanding loan. He has a fixed deposit of ₹ 5 lakh in addition to his collateral of ₹ 8 lakh. He has four acres of cultivable land with only one crop.

SOLUTION (Examples 10-19)

10. (*d*) Mohan Sadukhan fulfills all the given conditions, so the advance is to be granted.

11. (*c*) Age of Sudhir Maiti is not given and it is also not given how much amount of collateral can he produce. So, no decision can be taken in this case.

12. (*a*) Age of Prabhakar Awale is more than the required 50 yr. So, the advance is not to be granted.

13. (*b*) Akhilesh Mazumdar has an outstanding loan, but he has fixed deposit of ₹ 6 lakh. So, his case is to be referred to the General Manager of the bank.

14. (*e*) Sukhchand Mahato does not have five acres of cultivable land but he can cultivate two crops in each piece of land.

15. (*d*) Vikram Singh fulfills all the given conditions, so the advance is to be granted.

16. (*c*) It is not given that Ketan Sharma has any outstanding unpaid loan or not. So, no decision can be taken in this case.

17. (*e*) Suren Hembross does not have five acres of cultivable of land but he can cultivate two crops in each piece of land. So, his case is to be referred to the Chairman of the bank.

18. (*a*) Vikram Sibal has an outstanding loan and he does not have fixed deposit of at least ₹ 4 lakh. So, the advance is not to be granted.

19. (*a*) Avik Khetrapal does not have five acres of cultivable land and he can not cultivate more than one crop. So, the advance is not to be granted.

Type 2 Passage Based Decision Making

In such type of questions, generally a paragraph or a group of statements is given followed by some question and a candidate is required to read the data carefully and decide accordingly that which option follows from the data.

Direction (Examples 1-3) *Answer the questions on the basis of information given in the following case.* **XAT 2015**

Mr. Dipangshu Barua, a young IT professional, came early to office to assist his boss in the preparation for an important client presentation. When he switched on his computer, he saw an e-mail from Mr. Patel. The e-mail was as follows:

January 2, 2015

Dear Mr. Barua,

This e-mail serves as a follow-up of my conversation with you on December 1, 2014. I have already conveyed need for improvement in your behaviour as desired by your project leader and colleagues. They are yet to notice any visible improvements. I am apprehensive that your failure to act may warrant further action leading to dismissal.

I will continue to monitor and assess your performance over the next three months to determine whether improvements meet the expectations. At the same time, I would like to re-affirm that you are very valuable for our organisation.

Best Wishes,

Mr. A Patel

HR Director

Ex 1. Initially, the e-mail distracted Dipangshu but he decided to focus on the job. Which of the following options might best explain his decision to do so?

(a) Mr. Patel would soon be transferred to another department
(b) Last week, Mr. Dipangshu has been assigned to a new team in the same project
(c) Three days back, Mr. Dipangshu has been assigned a new project similar to his final year engineering project
(d) His friend has been hospitalised for the last three months
(e) Failing to perform in the client meeting might further complicate things

(e) Failure to perform the duty would lead to further complications. This is the least that he can do at this juncture and this is the only thing that can be controlled by Dipangshu to avoid further negative consequence. 'We can only control the controllable'. Hence, option (e) is the best option.

Ex **2.** The scheduled presentation went off smoothly. Back in his cabin, Dipangshu read Mr. Patel's e-mail once more and pondered over it. During the last meeting he tried hard to put forward his explanation but Mr. Patel had not allowed him to speak.

Dipangshu was thinking of meeting Mr. Patel once again but was doubtful whether that would help. Incidentally, he had a job offer from a start-up with a comparable salary.

If Dipangshu was to join the new job, he had to accept the offer within the next two weeks. However, he cannot think of a life without a job. Dipangshu was confused!

Which of the following options would be the best move for Dipangshu?

(a) Talk to Mr. Patel and highlight the initiatives he has taken but at the same time start applying for other jobs
(b) Reject the offer from the start-up. Use the next three months to find a better job, but continue in the present job
(c) Resign from this organisation right now
(d) Accept the offer, only if the start-up gives a salary hike, else keep prospecting
(e) Accept the offer with a request to give him a 10% salary hike

Ex **3.** After a couple of weeks, Mr. Patel came to know that Dipangshu's project leader Mr. John, a very competent senior executive, may have wilfully influenced his team members to file a wrong complaint against Dipangshu.

Mr. John may have done it because Dipangshu has refused to tow John's line. Mr. Patel also came to know that Dipangshu was thinking of quitting this job. He felt regretful about his letter to Dipangshu. He wanted to resolve the complicated situation. He was contemplating following five actions in his mind.

I. Talk to Mr. John about Dipangshu and convey to him that losing a bright employee would cost the organisation dearly.
II. Catch up with Mr. John during coffee break and convey that Dipangshu has a very good track record.
III. Chat with Dipangshu-during coffee break.
IV. Catch up with Dipangshu during coffee break and convey that the organisation values him.
V. Arrange a meeting among Mr. John, Dipangshu and himself to sort out the differences.

Which of the following is the best sequence of actions for resolving the problem?

(a) I, III, V (b) II, III, V (c) I, II, IV (d) I, IV, V
(e) III, IV, V

SOLUTION (Examples 1-3)

1. (*e*) Failure to perform the duty would lead to further complications. This is the least that he can do at this juncture and this is the only thing that can be controlled by Dipangshu to avoid further negative consequence. 'We can only control the controllable'. Hence, option (e) is the best option.

2. (*e*) Option (e) is a the best option. This is the safest option with comparable salary and if he gets a salary hike then it would be win-win for him and it would be better than option (d). However, if the start up doesn't honour his request, then it would be equivalent to option (c).

3. (*d*) The intention of HR Director is to retain Dipangshu (as it is good for organisation as well as because organisation does not lose a competent employee), by bring three together to amicably sort out the issues. Thus, one statement has to be picked from Statements III and IV. Statement V is a must as no solution can be found without three of them coming together.

Out of Statements III and IV, Statement IV is a better option as Statement III does not specify an action. Hence, Statements IV and V should be part of the correct option along with either Statement I or II. So, from the available choices, option (d) is the best answer.

Direction (Examples 4-5) *Answer the questions on the basis of information given in the following case.*

XAT 2015

MBA entrance examination comprises two types of problems: formula-based problems and application-based problems. From the analysis of past data, Interesting School of Management (ISM) observes that students good at solving application-based problems are entrepreneurial in nature.

Coaching institutes for MBA entrance exams train them to spot formula-based problems and answer them correctly, so as to obtain the required overall cut-off percentile. Thus students, in general, shy away from application-based problems and even those with entrepreneurial mind-set target formula-based problems.

Half of a mark is deducted for every wrong answer.

Ex **4.** ISM wants more students with entrepreneurial mind-set in the next batch. To achieve this, ISM is considering following proposals.

I. Preparing a question paper of two parts, Part A and Part B of duration of one hour each. Part A and Part B would consist of formula-based problems and application- based problems, respectively. After taking away Part A, Part B would be distributed. The qualifying cut-off percentile would be calculated on the combined scores of two parts.
II. Preparing a question paper comprising Part A and Part B. While Part A would comprise formula-based problems, part B would comprise application-based problems, each having a separate qualifying cut-off percentile.
III. Assigning one mark for formula-based problems and two marks for application-based problems as an incentive for attempting application-based problems.
IV. Allotting one mark for formula -based problems and three marks for application-based problems, without mentioning this in the question paper.

Which of the following proposal (or combination of proposals) is likely to identify students with best entrepreneurial mind-set?

(a) II (b) I and II
(c) I and III (d) II and III
(e) I and IV

Ex 5. ISM conducts a common entrance examination every year. This year, the question paper would comprise 60 questions with an equal mix of formula-based problems and application-based problems. All questions would carry equal marks. Balaji is appearing for the examination. Before, appearing for the examination he gets the following information from coaching institutes.

I. Application-oriented problems take more time to solve in an examination hall.
II. Chances of silly mistakes would be low in application-based problems.
III. ISM would assist the students with bank loans to start a new venture.
IV. Options are generally confusing for formula-based problems.
V. 'Practice makes a man perfect' can apply only to formula-based problems.
VI. Students get very good campus jobs.

Based on above information, which of the following options would help him to be better prepared for the examination?

(a) I and II
(b) I, III and V
(c) II, III and V
(d) IV, V and VI
(e) I, II, IV and V

SOLUTION (Examples 4-5)

4. (*d*) **Proposal I** indicates that cut off would be based on combined score and hence students might maximise their sure by attempting 'formula-based problems'.

Proposal II indicates that both would have separate cut offs and hence, most likely students would be forced to attempt questions from both the sections. But in extreme cases, all students can choose to attempt very few (or zero) questions from 'application-based problems'.

Proposal III gives additional incentive to attempt 'application-based problems'. In a way, it might avoid the extreme outcomes of proposal II (as mentioned above).

Proposal IV is not 'fair' to the students as they have no idea about the evaluation.

Combining proposals II and III is best option among the four proposals mentioned above. Hence, option (d) is the best answer.

5. (*e*) Statements III and VI are not related to the examination and relate to post examination stages of candidate's life. Information provided on these dimensions would not be helpful 'to be better prepared for the exam', whereas, all other information are relevant.

So, option (e) is the correct answer as it excludes both III and VI.

Direction (Example 6) *Answer the question on the basis of information given in the following case.*

Ex 6. Innovative Institute of Business (IIB) has decided to be the first green campus in India. IIB Administration has advised all campus residents to reduce carbon footprints. IIB faculty members did a brainstorming and came up with the following suggestions:

I. Replacing electricity source for street lights with solar panels.
II. Replacing the existing buildings with environment friendly buildings.
III. Organising a seminar on 'Towards a Sustainable Future' involving all students, staff, and experts from around the country.
IV. Introducing a compulsory course on sustainability to increase awareness among students.
V. Conducting an initial energy audit to explore where IIB can reduce carbon footprints.

Which of the following options would be the most preferred sequence of actions to reduce carbon footprints on campus?

(a) II, IV, V
(b) IV, V, III
(c) V, I, II
(d) V, I, III
(e) V, III, I

Sol. (*c*) To have maximum impact, there should be concrete changes/actions, which can be initiated after a fact finding (which starts from suggestion V). Hence option (a) and option (b) are not correct. Option (d) is also not correct as 'III' should not come after I. Option (e) as well as (c) are both logically sequenced.

Next issue is reduction of carbon footprints. Option (e) talks about seminar. Seminar might reduce carbon footprints indirectly by increasing awareness.

Administration has already conveyed this to campus residents. organising a seminar would have only incremental benefit, at best. Which of the options can reduce maximum amount of carbon footprints? Option (c) is the best answer as it contains concrete actions.

Direction (Examples 7-10) *Answer the questions on the basis of information given in the following case.*
XAT 2015

The Disciplinary Committee of National Political Party (NPP) is meeting today to decide on the future of two of their party members, Mr Loyal and his son Mr Prodigal.

Mr Prodigal is the prime accused in the brutal murder of Mr Victim, an opposition party leader. Mr Prodigal is in police custody and his appeal for bail has got rejected. Mr Loyal claims that his son is innocent and Mr Victim's death was the result of internal rivalry in the opposition party. Though
Mr. Loyal is not accused in this case, his weakness for his son is well known. The media is blaming him for influencing key witnesses to protect his son. Severe criticism of this father-son duo, both by the media and some social activists, is damaging the image of the party.

However, Mr Loyal has significant followers within the party and is considered an asset to the party. Any harsh decision against Mr Loyal would adversely affect the future of NPP and could even lead to a split in the party. This would benefit the opposition.

Ex 7. Which of the following actions would adversely affect both NPP and Mr. Loyal, the most?
(a) Take no action against Mr. Loyal
(b) Suspend Mr. Prodigal from the party with immediate effect
(c) Expel Mr. Loyal from the party with immediate effect
(d) Ban Mr. Loyal from entering party premises till completion of the court proceedings
(e) Initiate an internal inquiry to find the truth

Ex 8. At the Disciplinary Committee meeting, members came up with the following suggestions. Which of the following suggestions would harm the party, the least?
(a) Maintain status-quo
(b) Expel Mr Prodigal from the party with immediate effect to maintain party's clean image
(c) Initiate an internal inquiry to find the truth
(d) Suspend Mr Prodigal from the party with immediate effect but announce that he will be taken back if the court declares him innocent
(e) Suspend both Mr Loyal and Mr. Prodigal from the party with immediate effect

Ex 9. Mr. Opportunist, a veteran member of NPP, stakes his claims to be nominated as an NPP candidate in the upcoming election, Mr. Opportunist presented the following arguments in favour of his candidature to the NPP Executive Committee
I. Mr. Loyal's candidature in the upcoming election will adversely impact NPP's chances. Hence, the party should not nominate him.
II. The party should call a press conference to disown Mr. Loyal. This would enhance the party's image.
III. The party would not be able to take any strong disciplinary action against Mr. Loyal, if he gets re-elected.
IV. I have a lot of goodwill and significant followers in the constituency.
V. None of my close relatives are into active politics.

Which of the following combinations would best strengthen the claim of Mr. Opportunist?
(a) I and III (b) I and IV
(c) II and III (d) III and V
(e) IV and V

Ex 10. The Disciplinary Committee has decided to suspend Mr. Loyal from the party because they felt he was influencing the judicial process. However, Mr. Loyal feels that the committee is biased and he is being framed. Now, election has been announced.

The last time, Mr. Loyal had won with a majority on account of his good work. Which of the following options is most likely to resurrect Mr. Loyal's immediate political career?
(a) The main opposition party has invited Mr. Loyal to join the party and contest the election. Chance of winning is high
(b) Not participating in the campaign and instructing his followers to stay away from the campaigning process
(c) Ask his followers to support the NPP nominated candidate and display his loyalty to NPP
(d) Mr. Loyal should contest as an independent candidate. But because of a split in votes, his chances of winning would be low
(e) Influence the nomination process through his followers within NPP, to get one of his close associates nominated

---

SOLUTION (Examples 7-10)

7. (*c*) Here, it is important to note: Any action against Mr. Prodigal would affect Mr. Loyal which in turn may affect the party. Similarly, any direct action against Mr. Loyal may again affect the party. In other words, any direct or indirect action against Mr. Loyal may affect the party.
Expelling Mr. Loyal for something that Mr. Prodigal has done may be unfair, unless charges are proved. Further, expelling Mr. Loyal from the party would alienate him.
It is the worst action that can be taken against him and it might lead to a split within the party (as mentioned in the passage). Expelling indicates that chances of Mr. Loyal coming back to the party would be very low. Hence, option (c) is the correct answer since this is not good for both of them.

8. (*d*) Option (d) gives fair chance to Mr. Prodigal and indirectly to Mr. Loyal as well. Furthermore, this would ensure a good image among public and media that party adheres to the decision of the court. And at the same time it conveys a message that party is not unfair to the members during crisis time and would boost the morale of the party members.

9. (*b*) Statement I directly conveys that Mr. Loyal might not have high chance of winning and Statement IV says how opportunist can be ideal replacement of Loyal in terms of trustworthy followers.
So, combination of I and IV (option (b)) would be the correct answer. This option is having both anti-Loyal and pro-opportunist arguments.

10. (*a*) Option (a) gives him chance to stay afloat 'chance of winning is high' (as mentioned in the option). Hence, it is better than option (d) and this is the correct option. There are no obvious benefits from option (b).
Options (c) and (e) for his immediate political career. There might be beneficial (except option (b)) in the long run but not in near future. In case of option (e) there is no guarantee that his close associate will remain loyal to him.
Option (d) is a viable strategy but chances of winning is low and hence this option is less likely than option (a).

Direction (Examples 11-13) *On the basis of the information given in the following case, answer the questions that follow.* **XAT 2012**

Tina, a blast furnace expert, who works as a technology trouble shooter stays in Jamshedpur. She has got an important assignment in Delhi, which requires six hours to complete. The work is so critical that she has to start working the moment she reaches the client's premises.

She is considering various options for her onward and return journey between Jamshedpur to Delhi.

A quick search revealed that ticket from Jamshedpur to Delhi is available in two trains. Trains 12801 and 12443 depart from Jamshedpur station at 06 : 45 h and 15 : 55 h and reach Delhi next day at 04 : 50 h and 10 : 35 h, respectively. Trains 12444 and 12802 start from Delhi at 17 : 20 h and 22 : 20 h and reach Jamshedpur next day at 10 : 35 h and 20 : 05 h, respectively.

Another option is to reach Ranchi by a three hour road trip and take a flight to Delhi from Ranchi. The distance between Ranchi and Delhi is covered in 105 min both ways by any of the scheduled flights. Air India operates two flights, AI 9810 and AI 810, which depart Ranchi at 8 : 00 h and 15 : 25 h respectively.

Flight number IT-3348 operated by Kingfisher Airlines departs Ranchi at 19 : 20 h. Return flights operated by Air India, AI 9809 and AI 809, depart Delhi at 5 : 50 h and 11 : 00 h respectively. Flight number IT-3347 operated by Kingfisher Airlines departs Delhi at 17 : 10 h.

From Tina's home, Jamshedpur railway station is five minutes drive and her destination at Delhi is 90 min and 30 min, drive from airport and railway station, respectively. One has to reach the airport atleast one hour before the scheduled departure to complete the boarding procedure. At every railway station she loses five minutes in navigating through the crowd.

Ex **11.** Tina gets a message that her work has to be completed between 9 : 00 h and 17 : 00 h. If she wants minimize the total time out of Jamshedpur, the best option, from the options given below, for her among the following is to go by

(a) train 12443 and returns by train 12444
(b) train 12801 and return by train 12802
(c) AI 9810 and return by AI 9809
(d) AI 810 and return by AI 9809
(e) IT 3348 and return by IT 3347

Ex **12.** Tina has to appear for an exam on 8th of January in Jamshedpur and she can start from her residence in Jamshedpur only after 16 : 00 h of the same day. Choose the option, from the options given below, that will help her to minimize the total time out of Jamshedpur.

(a) go by train 12443 and return by train 12444
(b) go by train 12443 and return by AI 9809
(c) go by IT 3348 and return by train 12801
(d) go by AI 810 and return by train 12801
(e) go by AI 9810 and return by AI 9809

Ex **13.** Tina has to appear for an exam on 8th of January in Jamshedpur and she can start from her residence in Jamshedpur only after 16 : 00 h of the same day. Choose the option, from the options given below, that will help her to minimize the total time out of Jamshedpur.

(a) go by train 12443 and return by train 12444
(b) go by train 12443 and return by AI 9809
(c) go by IT 3348 and return by train 12801
(d) go by AI 810 and return by train 12801
(e) go by AI 9810 and return by AI 9809

SOLUTION (Examples 11-13)

11. (*e*) Note that in this question, the work needs to be completed any time between 9 : 00 h and 17 : 00 h. It does not mean that the work has to be commenced and completed between the 9 : 00 h and 17 : 00 h.

Now, let us consider each option one-by-one.

Option (a)

Since, there are 2 train journeys.

Travel time = (2 × 10) + (2 × 35) + Actual travel time in 12443 + Actual travel time in 12444

= 20 + 70 + 1120 + 1035

= 2245 min

Work time = 360 min

If she goes by train 12443, she will arrive at the work site at 11 : 10 h and finish the work at 17 : 10 h which does not follow the condition of the question.

So, she will have to wait till 03 : 00 h on the next day to begin the work so that she can complete the work at 09 : 00 h. This is a stay of 950 min.

Once she completes the work at 09 : 00 h, she will have to wait till 16 : 45 h on that day to catch train 12444. This is a waiting time of 465 min.

Total waiting time = 950 + 465

= 1415 min

So, total time = 2245 + 360 + 1415

= 4020 min

Hence, option (a) can be rejected.

Option (b)

Since, there are 2 train journeys,

Travel time = (2 × 10) + (2 × 35) + Actual travel time in 12801 + Actual travel time in 12802

= 20 + 70 + 1325 + 1305

= 2720 min

Work time = 360 min

If she goes by train 12801, she will reach the work site at 05 : 25 h, start immediately and finish the work at 11 : 25 h which meets the condition of the question.

Once she completes the work at 11 : 25 h, she will have to wait till 21 : 45 h on that day to catch train 12802. This is a waiting time of 620 min. So, total time = 2720 + 360 + 620

= 3700 min

Hence, option (b) can be rejected.

Option (c)

Since, there are 2 flight journeys.

Travel time = 435 × 2 = 870 min

Work time = 360 min

If she goes by Air India 9810, she will reach the work site at 11 : 15 h and finish the work at 17 : 15 h which breaks the condition of the question.

So, she will have to wait till 03 : 00 h on the next day to start the work so that she can complete the work at 09 : 00 h. This is a wait of 945 min.

Once she completes the work at 09 : 00 h, she will have to wait till 03 : 20 h on the next day to catch AI 9809. This is a waiting time of 1100 min.

Total waiting time = 945 + 1100
= 2045 min

So, total time = 870 + 360 + 2045
= 3275 min

Hence, option (c) can be rejected.

Option (d)

Since, there are 2 flight journeys.

Travel time = 435 × 2
= 870 min

Work time = 360 min

If she goes by AI 810, she will arrive at the work site at 18 : 40 h and complete the work at 00 : 40 h which violates the condition of the question.

So, she will have to wait till 03 : 00 h on the next day to begin the work so that she can complete the work at 09 : 00 h. This is a wait of 500 min.

Once she complete the work at 09 : 00 h, she will have to wait till 03 : 20 h on the next day to catch AI 9809. This is a waiting time of 1100 min.

Total waiting time = 500 + 1100
= 1600 min

So, total time = 870 + 360 + 1600
= 2830 min

Hence, option (d) can be rejected.

Option (e)

Since, there are 2 flight journeys.

Travel time = 435 × 2
= 870 min

Work Time = 360 min

If she goes by IT 3348, she will get to the work site at 22 : 35 h and finish the work at 04 : 35 h which breaks the condition of the question.

So, she will have to wait till 03 : 00 h on the next day to start the work so that she can complete the work at 09 : 00 h. This is a wait of 265 min.

Once she completes the work at 09 : 00 h, she will have to wait till 14 : 40 h on the same day to catch IT-3347. This is a waiting time of 340 min.

Total waiting time = 265 + 340 = 605 min

So, total time = 870 + 360 + 605
= 1835 min

12. (*e*) Tina cannot leave before 16:00 h on 8th January. So, if any of the travel modes necessitate departure before 16:00 h, she will have to begin the journey on 9th January. However, consider that the 'time out of Jamshedpur' is to be minimized. So, the time that she spends in Jamshedpur till her departure on 9th January cannot be considered 'waiting time'.

Now, let us consider each option one-by-one.

Option (a)

Since, there are 2 train journeys.

Travel time = (2 × 10) + (2 × 35) + Actual travel time in 12443 + Actual travel time in 12444
= 20 + 70 + 1120 + 1035
= 2245 min

Work time = 360 min

If she goes by train 12443, she will leave on 9th January, reach the work site at 11 : 10 h on 10th and finish the work at 17 : 10 h. Because train 12444 departs at 17 : 20 h, she will miss it and will have to catch it on 11th January. It means a waiting time till 16 : 45 h of 11th January i.e., 1415 min.

So, total time = 2245 + 360 + 1415
= 4020 min

Hence, option (a) can be rejected.

Option (b)

She goes by train and comes back by flight.

Travel time = Time from home to Jamshedpur station + Actual time in train travel + Time from Delhi railway station to work site + Flight time
= 10 + 1120 + 35 + 435
= 1600 min

Work time = 360 min

If she goes by train 12443, she will leave on 9th January, reach the work site at 11 : 10 h on 10th and finish the work at 17 : 10 h. Flight AI 9809 departs at 05 : 50 h on 11th January. So, she will have to wait till 03 : 20 h of 11th January i.e., a waiting time of 610 min.

So, total time = 1600 + 360 + 610
= 2570 min

Hence, option (a) can be rejected.

Observe that options (c) and (d) can straightaway be rejected as they mention a return journey by train 12801, which is not feasible as that train travels from Jamshedpur to Delhi and not the other way round.

Hence, options (c) and (d) can be rejected.

Option (e)

She travels both ways by flight.

Travel time = 435 × 2
= 870 min

Work time = 360 min

If she goes by AI 9810, she departs on 9th January, arrives the work site at 11 : 15 h on 9th and complete the work at 17 : 15 h. Flight AI 9809 departs at 05 : 50 h on 10th January. So, she will have to wait till 03 : 20 h of 10th January i.e., a waiting time of 605 min.

So, total time = 870 + 360 + 605
= 1835 min

Hence, option (e) can be rejected.

13. (*e*) Tina cannot leave before 16:00 h on 8th January. So, if any of the travel modes necessitate departure before 16:00 h, she will have to begin the journey on 9th January. However, consider that the 'time out of Jamshedpur' is to be minimized. So, the time that she spends in Jamshedpur till her departure on 9th January cannot be considered 'waiting time'.

Now, let us consider each option one-by-one.

Option (a)

Since, there are 2 train journeys.

Travel time = (2 × 10) + (2 × 35) + Actual travel time in 12443 + Actual travel time in 12444

= 20 + 70 + 1120 + 1035

= 2245 min

Work time = 360 min

If she goes by train 12443, she will leave on 9th January, reach the work site at 11 : 10 h on 10th and finish the work at 17 : 10 h. Because train 12444 departs at 17 : 20 h, she will miss it and will have to catch it on 11th January. It means a waiting time till 16 : 45 h of 11th January i.e., 1415 min.

So, total time = 2245 + 360 + 1415 = 4020 min

Hence, option (a) can be rejected.

Option (b)

She goes by train and comes back by flight.

Travel time = Time from home to Jamshedpur station + Actual time in train travel

+ Time from Delhi railway station to work site + Flight time

= 10 + 1120 + 35 + 435

= 1600 min

Work time = 360 min

If she goes by train 12443, she will leave on 9th January, reach the work site at 11 : 10 h on 10th and finish the work at 17 : 10 h. Flight AI 9809 departs at 05 : 50 h on 11th January. So, she will have to wait till 03 : 20 h of 11th January i.e., a waiting time of 610 min.

So, total time = 1600 + 360 + 610

= 2570 min

Hence, option (a) can be rejected.

Observe that options (c) and (d) can straightaway be rejected as they mention a return journey by train 12801, which is not feasible as that train travels from Jamshedpur to Delhi and not the other way round.

Hence, options (c) and (d) can be rejected.

Option (e)

She travels both ways by flight.

Travel time = 435 × 2

= 870 min

Work time = 360 min

If she goes by AI 9810, she departs on 9th January, arrives the work site at 11 : 15 h on 9th and complete the work at 17 : 15 h. Flight AI 9809 departs at 05 : 50 h on 10th January. So, she will have to wait till 03 : 20 h of 10th January i.e., a waiting time of 605 min.

So, total time = 870 + 360 + 605

= 1835 min

Hence, option (e) can be rejected.

Cumulative Exercise

Base Level

Direction (Q. Nos. 1-5) *Study the following information carefully and answer the questions given below.*

Following are the conditions for selecting Management Trainee in an organization **Indian Bank (PO) 2010**

The candidate must

I. be a graduate with at least 60 per cent marks.
II. be not less than 21 yr and not more than 28 yr as on 1.1.2010.
III. be ready to pay ₹ 50000 as security deposit.
IV. have secured at least 40 per cent marks in the selection examination.
V. have secured at least 50 per cent marks in personal interview.

In the case of a candidate who has satisfied all the above conditions except

1. at (i) above, but has secured at least 65 per cent marks in the post graduation, the case is to be referred to GM-personnel.
2. at (iii) above, but is ready to sign a bond for one year, the case is to be referred to ED-personnel.

In each question below, are given details of one candidate. You have to take one of the following courses of actions, based on the information provided and the conditions and sub conditions given above, and mark the number of that course of action as your answer. You are not to assume anything other than the information provided in each question. All these cases are given to you as on 1.1.2010.

Give answer

(a) if the data provided is not adequate to take a decision
(b) if the candidate is to be selected
(c) if the candidate is not to be selected
(d) if the case is to be referred to the GM-Personnel
(e) if the case is to be referred to the ED-personnel

1. Abhinav Ghosal has secured 52% marks in the personal interview and 40% marks in the selection examination. He can pay ₹ 25000 as security deposit. Alternatively, he can sign a bond of one year. He was born on 3rd December, 1984. He has secured 63% marks in graduation.

2. Sohan Awasthi was born on 8th June, 1987. He has secured 55% marks in both the selection examination and the personal interviews. He can pay the security deposit of ₹ 50000. He has secured 68% marks in post graduation and 59% marks in graduation.

3. Namita Jaiswal has secured 62% marks in graduation and 52% marks in the personal interview. She was born on 12th July, 1983. She is ready to pay the security deposit of ₹ 50000. She has secured 46% marks in the selection examination.

4. Seema Biswas was born on 15th May, 1985. She has secured 65% marks in graduation and 70% marks in post graduation. She is ready to pay ₹ 50000 as security deposit. She has also secured 45% marks in the selection examination.

5. Anuj Soren was born on 15th march, 1984. He has secured 58% marks in graduation and 63% marks in post graduation. He has secured 50% marks in both selection examination and personal interview. He is ready to pay security deposit of ₹ 50000.

Direction (Q. Nos. 6-14) *Study the following information carefully and answer the questions that follow.*

Applications are invited form citizen of India for the post of Charge man GD II at Ordnance Factory in city X. The recruitment board has laid down the following criteria. The candidate

(i) should have a diploma (3 yr full time) in Computer Science/Technology recognised by AICTE or should have passed 'A' level course in computer Application recognised by department of Electronics, or should be MCA/Engineering Graduate in Computer Science/Technology from any government recognised University.

(ii) should have atleast 2 yr's experience in the following areas

- Operating system
- MS office suite
- Programming in dBase/Fox Pro/MS Access/C/C^{++} (at least one of these languages)
- Local area Networking
- Internet applications

(iii) should have knowledge of programming in Oracle/Informix and knowledge of computer hardware.

(iv) should be between 18 and 27 yr (General)as on 01-07-2012. It the candidate belongs to either SC/ST or OBC categories he/she should be between 18 and 32 yr and 18 and 30 yr respectively as on 01-07-2012, a female candidate should be given relaxation of 1 yr in upper age limit as compared to general male candidate.

➘ No two or more benefits (related with age) be given any candidate.

However, if the candidate fulfils, all the criteria except

1. at (iii) above but is ready to sign a bond of 10 yr service in the company,his case should be referred to MD of the factory.
2. at (iv) above but appears in a test conducted by the company and gets one of the top five positions in the test, his case should be referred to vice-president of the factory.

Based on the above criteria and the information given in each of the following questions.You have to take a decision in regard to each of the following question, you have to take a decision in regard to each case. You are not to assume anything. These cases are given to you as on 1 st July 2012.

Give answer

(a) if the application of the candidate is to be accepted
(b) if the application of the candidate is not to be accepted
(c) if the case of the candidate is to be referred to the managing Director
(d) if the case of the candidate is to be referred to the Vice-president
(e) if the given data are not adequate

6. Rajiv Sharma is an engineering graduate in computer science from a recognised university. He has 2 yr experience in the following areas: Operating system, MS office suite, Local Area Networking and internet applications. He lacks in knowledge of programming in Oracle/Informix and knowledge of computer hardware. He is ready to sign a contract of 10 yr according to the given conditions. He is 26 yr old as on 1 July, 2012.

7. Chandrashekhar Azad is a male candidate of the OBC category. His date of birth is 1 November,1983. He has knowledge of programming in Oracle/Informix and knowledge of computer hardware. He has experience of 3 yr in the required areas. He has passed 'A' level course in computer applications, recognised by the department of electronics.

8. Suman is a female candidate of the ST category. She has not appeared in the test conducted by the authority of the factory. Her date of birth is 1 July, 1979. She has a diploma (3 yr full time) in computer science, recognised by AICTE. She has two years experience in the required areas.

9. Krishan Semwal is an ST candidate. His date of birth is 18 March, 1975. He got the fourth rank in the test conducted. He has the required experience in required areas. He has passed 'A' level course recognised by department of electronics. He enjoys good knowledge of programming in Oracle/Informix and knowledge of computer hardware.

10. Awadh Taneja has passed 'A' level course in computer application recognised by the department of electronics. He has the required experience in the stipulated areas. His date of birth is 1 August, 1987.

11. Vinod Shah is a male candidate of the SC category. He has done graduation in computer science from a renowned university which still lacks government recognition. He has an experience of two years in the required areas. He is ready to give a bond to provide service to the company for 10 years. His date of birth is 04 July 1984. He has no knowledge of computer hardware.

12. Rina Kulkarni is a female of excellent personality. She has a certificate of 3 year diploma (full time) in computer science which enjoys recognition of AICTE. She has experience of two and a half years in the required areas. She has knowledge of programming in Oracle/ Informix as well as knowledge of computer hardware. Her date of birth is 01 July, 1983.

13. Punam Jaiswal is a candidate belonging to the general category. Her date of birth is the same as that of Rina Kulkarni. She has appeared in the test organized by the board of the factory and secured first position. Despite belonging to a family of hardware engineers, she lacks the knowledge of computer hardware. She has passed 'A' level course in computer applications recognized by the department of electronics. She has 2 yr experience in the required areas.

14. Hemant Nehra has no knowledge of programming in Oracle/Informix. But he knows the required basics of computer hardware. He is ready to sign a bond for service of 10 yr. He has the required experience of 2 yr in all the given areas but he knows programming in d-Base only. He has done MCA from a university recognized by the government. He is 25 yr old as on 01-07-2012.

Direction (Q. Nos. 15-21) *IT Pharma, a joint venture company in collaboration with a Swiss multinational, requires performers who desire to make a career in pharmaceutical selling and wish to go up the ladder on a fast track. The candidate must*

(i) have completed 26 yr of age but be less than 28 as on 1.8.2012.
(ii) have a degree in Science Pharmacy.
(iii) have a minimum of 2 yr experience as a manager in a reputed company.
(iv) possess leadership qualities, e.g. taking independent decisions, motivating and developing representatives.

However, if a candidate fulfils all the criteria except.

1. at (ii) but possesses excellent communication skills in English, he should be referred to HRD.
2. at (iii) but has an experience of at least two years in pharmaceuticals selling, he should be referred to the Vice-President of the company.
3. at (i) but is less than 32 yr old and has 4 yr experience as a manager in a reputed company, he should be referred to the President of the company.

All the information are being given to you on 1.8.2012. Now, based on the above criteria and the information given below, you have to take a decision in regards to each case. You are not to assume any information. No further information is available.

Give answer

(a) if the candidate is to be rejected
(b) if the candidate is to be selected
(c) if the candidate is to be referred to HRD
(d) if the candidate is to be referred to the Vice-President
(e) if the candidate is to be referred to the President

15. Vishnu Nagar was born on 1st June, 1982. Though poor in English, he is good at medicine and is an M. Pharma. A born leader, he has been the manager of a reputed company for the last six years.

16. TCA Raghavan has three years experience as a manager in a reputed company. Though lacking in leadership qualities, he has excellent communication skills. The 26 yr old is a graduate in Agriculture.

17. Mohan Rakesh has three years experience in pharmaceutical selling. When he did his B. Pharma in 2007, he was only 22 yr of age. Though gifted with leadership qualities, he has only one year's experience as a manager in a reputed company.

18. 30 yr old Chhapra Sanyal was an able leader but has become irritating for the past two years. He is a B. Pharma and two years of experience in selling pharmaceuticals and two years as a manager in a reputed company.

19. Achala Bhaumik has three-year experience in pharmaceutical selling. The 27 yr old did her B.Sc. in Physics and has worked for four years as a manager in a reputed company. She is good at decision-making and motivating her team.

20. Hemwati Sachdev is known for her ability to take independent decisions and enthusiastically guiding her team. At the age of 34, she has four years experience as a manager in a reputed company. She did her M.Sc. in Zoology.

21. Krishna Prasad, who was born on 1 October, 1987 is an M Pharma. He has exactly two years experience in pharmaceutical selling. As far as leadership qualities are concerned, he is an amply gifted person.

Direction (Q. Nos. 22-26) *Study the following information carefully and answer the questions given below.*

Following are the conditions for selecting Senior Manager-Credit in a bank. The candidate must **SBI (PO) 2010**

(i) be a graduate in any discipline with at least 60% marks.
(ii) have post qualification work experience of atleast 10 yr in the Advances section of a bank.
(iii) be atleast 30 yr and not more than 40 yr as on 1.4.2010.
(iv) have secured atleast 40% marks in the group discussion.
(v) have secured atleast 50% marks in interview.

In the case of a candidate who satisfies all the conditions except

1. at (i) above but has secured at least 50% marks in graduation and at least 60% marks in post graduation, the case is to be referred to the General Manager-Advances.
2. at (ii) above but has total post qualification work experience of atleast 7 yr, out of which, atleast 3 yr as Manager-Credit in a bank, the case is to be referred to the Executive Director.

In each question below, details of one candidate is given. You have to take one of the following courses of action based on the information provided, and the conditions and sub-conditions given above and mark the number of that course of action as your answer. You are not to assume anything other than the information provided in each question. All these cases are given to you as on 01.04.2010.

Give answer

(a) if the case is to be referred to the Executive Director
(b) if the case is to be referred to the General Manager-Advances
(c) if the data is inadequate to take a decision
(d) if the candidate is not to be selected
(e) if the candidate is to be selected

22. Prakash Gokhale was born on 4th August, 1977. He has secured 65% marks in post graduation and 58% marks in graduation. He has been working for the past ten years in the Advances Department of a bank after completing his post graduation. He has secured 45% marks in the group discussion and 50% marks in the interview.

23. Amit Narayan was born on 28th May, 1974. He has been working in the Advances Department of a bank for the past eleven years after completing his B.Sc. degree with 65% marks. He has secured 55% marks in the group discussion and 50% marks in the interview.

24. Shobha Gupta has secured 50% marks in the interview and 40% marks in the group discussion. She has been working for the past eight years, out of which four years as Manager-Credit in a bank after completing her BA degree with 60% marks. She was born on 12th September, 1978.

25. Rohan Maskare was born on 8th March, 1974. He has been working in a bank for the past twelve years after completing his B. Com degree with 70% marks. He has secured 50% marks in both the group discussion and the interview.

26. Sudha Mehrotra has been working in the Advances Department of a bank for the past twelve years after completing her B. Com. degree with 60% marks. She has secured 50% marks in the group discussion and 40% marks in the interview. She was born on 15th February, 1972.

Direction (Q. Nos. 27-33) *Read the following information carefully and answer the questions given below it.*

Following are the criteria set up by the UNO for setting up a UN task force for keeping peace and rehabilitation worldwide. It will take the armed men from the countries, which satisfy the following criteria.

(i) The army strength of that country should not be less than 3 lakh.
(ii) The government of that country must be elected by a democratic process.
(iii) The defence budget of that country should not be less than $ 50 b.
(iv) The army of that country has, atleast, the experience of a war having lasted a month.

However, if a country fulfils all the criteria except

1. at (i) above, but the country has nuclear power, the case may be referred to the Secretary, UNO.
2. at (iv) above, but the army of that country has the experience of at least five joint defence exercises with another country, which has acquired nuclear power, the case may be referred to Secretary-General, UNO. Based on the above criteria and the information given in each of the following questions, you have to take a decision with regard to each case. You are not to assume anything.

Give answer

(a) if the army of that country can be selected
(b) if the army of that country can't be selected
(c) if data is inadequate
(d) if the case is to be referred to the Secretary, UNO
(e) if the case is to be referred to the Secretary- General, UNO

27. India has acquired nuclear power and the army strength of the country is more than 7 lakh. In the recent budget India has allocated $ 70 b to its defence sector. The Indian army has experienced three wars and many proxy wars having lasted more than a month.

28. Australia has only 2 lakh army personnel but expense on its defence budget is $ 60 b. It has acquired the nuclear power. Its army performs 5-6 joint exercises every year with different nuclear-power nations. Australia has a democratic government.

29. France has a democratic government. It has 4.5 lakh defence personnel. The defence budget of the country is more than $ 50 b. The army of the country has witnessed four wars, all lasting a month, in recent years.

30. Israel has the strongest army in the world. The strength of the army in Israel is 4 lakh. It has a democratic government. Its defence budget is $ 50 b.

31. China has the largest population in the world. 10% of the total population of the country is in army. China has a democratic government. China spends $ 100 b on its defence sector. China has nuclear power and its army has experience of two wars with Russia, each having lasted for a month.

32. Germany has one of the most advanced defence forces. The country spends 30% of its total budget expenses in defence sector. army has conducted many joint defence exercises with most of the countries in the world. Germany has a democratic government It has 5 lakh defence personnel. The total budget of the country is $ 300 b.

33. Pakistan had a democratic government but recently the army chief of the country has sacked the government and overpowered the throne. It has 3 lakh army personnel and a defence budget, of $ 50 b. Pakistan has witnessed three unsuccessful wars having lasted more than a month with India.

Direction (Q. Nos. 34-43) *Study the following information carefully and answer the questions which follow.*

IDBI Executive (PO) 2009

A bank is disbursing educational loans to meritorious students. Loans will be made available to applicants who possess the following criteria.

The candidate must

(i) be a citizen of India.

(ii) have secured admission to a post graduate course (Masters or PG Diploma) offered by an Indian or a foreign university in India.

(iii) have secured 60% marks in the entrance examination for the course.

(iv) have security (property/LIC policy) equivalent to the loan amount.

However, if the applicant fulfils the above mentioned criteria except

1. at (ii) above the case may be referred to the loan committee.
2. at (iv) above guarantee of a third party who has an account with the bank may be obtained.

Give answer

(a) if the loan is to be sanctioned

(b) if the loan is to be rejected

(c) if the loan is to be referred to the loan committee

(d) if a guarantee from an account holder is needed

(e) if the data provided is inadequate to take a decision

34. Shruti has secured admission to MNV University in Chennai for a post graduate degree in Management. She obtained 65% in the entrance test for the course. She has an Indian passport.

35. Milind has applied and secured admission for a post graduate degree in Advertising at MIC University, Ahmedabad. He has an LIC policy equivalent to the loan amount. He secured 70% in his graduation and is an Indian citizen.

36. Prakash has applied for a post graduate course in IT and Animation which will commence from January in Kolkata. He has secured admission to the course, having obtained 60% in the written entrance test. His uncle who has an account with the bank is willing to stand as guarantor.

37. Anil is an Indian Science graduate who has secured admission for a Masters degree in Computer Science from a prestigious Indian University. He stood first in the entrance test with 82% marks. His family is willing to use their house, which is equivalent in value to the loan amount, as security. He will stay with his uncle in Dubai during the course.

38. Nikhil's part time PG Diploma in Management will begin in December. He secured 65% in the All India entrance exam and has secured admission to a college in Mumbai. He has requested a transfer for the duration of the course. He has an LIC policy equivalent to the loan amount. Nikhil holds an Indian passport.

39. Maria secured 75% in the entrance exam to NVT College Pune and has obtained admission. An Indian national, she has the necessary property to offer as security for the loan amount. The duration of her undergraduate degree course in Computer Applications is 3 yr.

40. Deepa obtained 70% in her engineering entrance exam for her Masters and has secured admission to the college of her choice. She has an LIC policy equivalent in value to the loan amount. Her interview to obtain a visa for her course in the US is on November 25. She is an Indian citizen.

41. Sudhir has applied for a postgraduate degree in Pharmacy at All India Institute at New Delhi. He is an Indian citizen and having secured 60% in the entrance exam, he has been granted admission. He does not have any property to use as security. His father who has an account with the bank is willing to guarantee the loan.

42. Anandi has secured admission for a PG Diploma in Management at a University in Allahabad with 72% in the entrance examination. She has an LIC policy amounting to the loan amount. She is an Indian citizen.

43. Ravi has obtained admission to the Indian Institute of Research at Chandigarh for a Masters in Mathematics offered only to Indian citizens. He secured 68% the entrance test. He does not have any security against the loan. However his employer who has an account with the bank, is willing to guarantee the loan.

Direction (Q. Nos. 44-48) *Study the following information carefully to answer these questions.* **IRMA 2009**

A public sector organization has stipulated following criteria for recruitment of Marketing Officers. To be eligible for selection, the candidate must

I. be a graduate in any discipline with atleast 60% marks.
II. have done MBA with specialization in Marketing with at least 65% marks.
III. obtained at least 50% marks in the interview and 55% marks in the selection test.
IV. be not more than 28 yr of age as on 1.5.2006.

However, if a candidate fulfils all the above mentioned criteria except

1. at (I) above but has secured 60% marks in interview, the case may be referred to the external committee of experts.
2. at (II) above but is an MBA with specialization in Marketing with atleast 55% marks and is having atleast 2 yr experience of working as an officer, the case may be referred to the Executive Director (ED) of the Bank.

In each question below, information about one candidate is given. You have to study the information provided with reference to the criteria and conditions given above and take one of the following courses of actions. You are not to assume anything other than the information provided in each question. All these cases are given to you as on 1.5.2006.

Give answer

(a) if the case is to be referred to the ED
(b) if the case is to be referred to external committee of experts
(c) if the candidate is to be selected
(d) if the candidate is not to be selected
(e) if the information is not sufficient to take a decision

44. Ashok Sardesai is an Engineering graduate with 63% marks, passed out in 2003 at the age of 22 yr. Thereafter, he has done MBA in Marketing securing 68% marks. He has scored 66% marks in the interview as well as in selection test, Presently, he is working as a software engineer in a private company since last 6 months.

45. Shashikala is a commerce graduate with 59% marks and an MBA Marketing with 69% marks. She has scored 66% marks in interview and 56% marks in the selection test. Her date of birth is 27.3.1982.

46. Rajshekhar is a Science graduate with 73% marks and passed out in 2000 at the age of 21 yr. Thereafter, he did MBA with specialization in Marketing with 57% marks. He appeared for selection test and interview, cleared with 60% and 62% marks respectively. He is working as a marketing officer since December, 2005.

47. Lalita passed Electronics Engineering degree with 66% marks and MBA Marketing with 68% marks. She has secured 58% marks in the selection Test as well as in the interview.

48. Himanshu is a 23 yr old boy, passed B. Com with 72% marks in 2004 and joined MBA with Marketing, immediately after graduation. He will complete his MBA in June 2006 and is expecting to score an overall percentage of 75. He appeared for the the selection test and scored 70% marks and scored 58% marks in the interview.

Direction (Q. Nos. 49-54) *Read the given information carefully and answer the questions given below.*

A leading English daily of India, ABC News, invites applications for the post of sub-editors in the company. The candidates are required to fulfil, apart from (i) atleast three of the following conditions for his/her selection.

(i) He/she must be between 21-30 yr.
(ii) He/she has first a class degree in his/her graduation.
(iii) He/she has a diploma in journalism with atleast 55% marks.
(iv) He/she has an experience of at least 2 yr in a newspaper.
(v) He/she has won a prize at state level for his/her articles published in state-level English daily.

If however, he/she does fulfil all conditions except

1. (v) above, but he/she has 5 yr experience in a news agency, then refer to the editor of the ABC News.
2. (ii) above, but he/she has diploma in journalism with 75%, then refer to the chairman of the ABC News.
3. (iii) above, but he/she has completed graduation with 75%, then refer to the managing director of ABC News. All the information are given to you on 01-10-2010.

Now, you have to take a decision in regard to each case given below. You are not to assume any information.

Give answer

(a) if the candidate is not to be selected
(b) if the candidate is to be selected
(c) if the candidate is to be referred to the chairman
(d) if the candidate is to be referred to the managing director
(e) if the candidate is to be referred to the editor

49. Niharika Chawla, 26-yr-old graduate from Delhi University with 66% marks, has also done her diploma in journalism from Jamia with 75% marks. She has been working with *The Hindu*, Delhi for the last 3 yr.

50. Swatika Gupta is an English Hons graduate from Bangaluru University with 63% marks. She also holds diploma in journalism from the same university with 56% marks. Her date of birth is 22-09-81. She has been working with *The Economic Times*, Bangaluru for the last one year.

51. Amisha Patel holds both BSc and diploma in journalism with 64% and 60% marks respectively from the University of Ahmedabad. She is working with *The Tribune*, Ahmedabad for the last 7 yr and she has won many prizes at state level for her articles. She is a very hardworking professional.

52. Shreya Singh, a first class graduate from Patna University, has done diploma in journalism from the same university with 72% marks. She has won several prizes for her articles at state level and has been working with *The Hindustan Times*, Patna from 20.07.2008.

53. Akanksha Mathur, who hails from Mumbai, is a graduate from University of Mumbai with 50% marks. She also holds a degree in journalism with 76% marks. She has been working with *Mid-Day*, Mumbai for the last 4 yr. Her date of birth is 29-07-86.

54. Rohit Sen has won many awards for his articles at state level and he has been working with *The Telegraph*, kolkata since 2005. He did his B. Com. with 77% marks from the University of Kolkata and after that, he finished his diploma in journalism from Jadavpur University with 53%. His date of birth is 15-10-84.

Direction (Q. Nos. 55-64) *Study the following information carefully and answer the questions given below.*

Following are the conditions for selecting Chief Manager-Marketing in an organization **Allahabad Bank (PO) 2010**

The candidate must

(i) be atleast 35 yr old as on 01.02.2010.
(ii) have secured atleast 55% marks in graduation.
(iii) have secured atleast 60% marks in post graduate degree/diploma in Marketing Management.
(iv) have post qualification work experience of atleast ten years in the marketing division of an organization.
(v) have secured atleast 50% marks in the selection process.

In the case of a candidate who satisfies all the above conditions except

1. at (iv) above but has post qualification work experience of atleast six years as Manager-Marketing, the case is to be referred to the Head-Marketing Division.
2. at (ii) above but has secured atleast 65% marks in post graduate degree/diploma in Marketing Management, the case is to be referred to the GM-Marketing.

In each question below, are given the details of one candidate. You have to take one of the following courses of action based on the information provided and the conditions and sub-conditions given above and mark the number of that course of action as your answer. You are not to assume anything other than the information provided in each question. All these cases are given to you as on 01.02.2010.

Give answer

(a) if the candidate is to be selected
(b) if the case is to be referred to the Head-Marketing Division
(c) if the case is to be referred to the GM-Marketing
(d) if the candidate is not be selected
(e) if the data provided is inadequate to take a decision

55. Arnab Behera has secured 65% marks in PG degree in Marketing-Management and 58% marks in graduation. He has been working in the marketing division of an organization for the past eleven years after completing his post graduate degree. He has secured 55% marks in the selection process. He was born on 8th July, 1970.

56. Neeta Ghosal was born on 4th May, 1974. She has been working in the marketing division of an organization for the past twelve years after completing her post graduate in diploma in Management with 70% marks. She has obtained 60% marks in graduation and 50% marks in the selection process.

57. Sudesh Sarkar was born on 15th June, 1974. He has secured 55% marks in the selection process and 50% marks in graduation. He has been working in the marketing division of an organization for the past twelve years after completing post graduate degree in Marketing Management with 75% marks.

58. Sudha Naik was born on 14th April, 1973. She has been working in the marketing division of an organization for the past fourteen years after completing her post graduate diploma in Marketing-Management with 70% marks. She has secured 50% marks in the selection process and 52% marks in graduation.

59. Sunita Jaiswal was born on 5th July, 1976. She has secured 55% marks in graduation and 58% marks in the selection process. She has been working in the marketing division of an organization for the past ten years after completing post graduate degree in Marketing-Management with 57% marks.

60. Nayan Dastur was born on 8th October, 1968. He has secured 55% marks in both graduation and the selection process. He has been working in the marketing division of an organization for the past ten years after completing post graduate diploma in Marketing-Management with 65% marks.

61. Sunil Kamath has secured 58% marks in graduation. He was born on 24th May, 1974. He has been working in the marketing division of an organization for the past seven years as Manager-Marketing after completing post graduate degree in Marketing-Management with 65% marks. He has secured 50% marks in the selection process.

62. Md.Yusuf was born on 29th January, 1975. He has secured 55% marks in graduation and 52% marks in the selection process. He has also secured 68% marks in post graduate diploma in Marketing-Management. He has been working for the past twelve years in the marketing division of an organization.

63. Navind Ghosh was born on 12th December, 1973. He has been working in the marketing division of an organization for the past ten years after completing his post graduate degree in Marketing-Management with 63% marks. He has secured 54% marks in graduation and 45% marks in the selection process.

64. Avinash Sargota has been working for the past eight years, out of which for six years as Manager-Marketing in an organization, after completing his post graduate degree in Marketing-Management with 62% marks. He has secured 58% marks in graduation and 52% marks in the selection process. He was born on 14th February, 1972.

Direction (Q. Nos. 65-74) *Study the following information carefully and answer the questions given below.*

Following are the conditions for selecting Trainee Officers in an organization. **BOI (PO) 2010**

The candidate must

I. be a graduate in any discipline with at least 55 per cent marks.
II. have secured atleast 60% marks in the examination class XII standard.
III. be at least 22 yr and not more than 29 yr as on 1.1.2010.
IV. have secured atleast 40% marks in the selection examination.
V. have secured atleast 50% marks in the interview.
VI. be ready to sign a bond for two years.

In the case of candidate who satisfies all the conditions except

1. at (i) above, but is a qualified Accountant/ Chartered Accountant, the case is to be referred to the ED.
2. at (v) above, but has secured at least 60% marks in the selection examination, the case is to be referred to the Chairman.

In each question below are given details of one candidate. You have to take one of the courses of actions based on the information provided and the conditions and sub-conditions given above and mark the number of the course of action as your answer. You are not to assume anything other than the information provided in each question. All these cases are given to you as on 1.1.2010.

Give answer

(a) if the candidate is to be selected
(b) if the candidate is not to be selected
(c) if the case is to be referred to ED
(d) if the case is to be referred to Chairman
(e) if the data provided is not adequate to take a decision

65. Susan D'Souza has secured 62% marks in Xll standard, and 59% marks in BA. She was born on 15th July 1984. She has secured 50% marks in both the selection examination and the personal interview. She is ready to sign the bond for two years.

66. Archana Sahu was born on 8th May, 1986. She has secured 60% marks in both XII standard and B. Sc. She is ready to sign bond for two years. She has secured 40% marks in the personal interview and 50% in the selection examination.

67. Atul Garg was born on 2nd December, 1980. He has secured 56% marks in B. Sc. and 63% marks in XII Std. He has also secured 55% marks in both the selection examination and personal interview. He is ready to sign the bond for two years.

68. Meena Gogoi was born on 14th March, 1985. She has secured 62% marks in XII standard and 65% marks in the selection examination. She has also secured 58% marks in graduation and 48% marks in personal interview. She is ready to sign the bond for two years.

69. Sudhakar Bagchi was born on 4th November, 1982. He has secured 67% marks in XII standard and 50 per cent marks in graduation. He has also successfully qualified as a Chartered Accountant. He has secured 50% marks, in both the selection examination and the personal interview. He is ready to sign the bond for two years.

70. Ashok Pradhan has secured 56% marks in graduation and 63% marks in XII standard. He was born on 12th December, 1986. He has secured 45 per cent marks in the selection examination and 55% marks in the personal interview.

71. Antara Ghosh was born on 2nd December, 1981. She has secured 60% marks in both the selection examination and the personal interview. She has secured 62% marks in XII standard and 57% marks in B. Sc. She is ready to sign the bond for two years.

72. Navin Malhotra was born on 3rd August, 1987. He has secured 68% marks in XII standard and 50% marks in BA. He has secured 50 per cent marks in the personal interview and 40% marks in the selection examination. He is qualified Cost Accountant. He is ready to sign the bond for two years.

73. Abhinav Shukla has secured 70% marks in XII standard and 58% marks in B. Com. He was born on 15th September, 1984. He has secured 65% marks in the selection examination and 48% marks in the personal interview. He is ready to sign the bond for two years.

74. Suresh Das is ready to sign bond for two years. He is first class graduate in science. He was secured 50% marks in personal interview and 40 per cent marks in the selection examination. He was born on 25th April, 1982. He got 10% more marks than his friend in XII standard.

Direction (Q. Nos. 75-79) *Study the following information carefully and answer the questions that following*.

Following are the conditions for selecting senior Manager General Banking in a bank **SBI Associate (PO) 2010**

The candidate must

I. have secured atleast 60% marks in Std. XII.
II. have secured atleast 55% marks in Graduation in any discipline.
III. have secured atleast 60% marks in Post-Graduate Degree/Diploma in Management /Economics/Statics.
IV. be atleast 25 yr and not be more than 35 yr as on 1.3.2010.
V. have post qualification work experience of atleast 2 yr as General Banking Officer in a bank.
VI. have secured atleast 50% marks in written examination.
VII. have secured atleast 40% marks in personal interview.

In the case of a candidate who satisfies all the above conditions except

1. at (iii) above, but has secured atleast 60 per cent marks in CA or ICWA, the case is to be referred to VP-Recruitment.
2. at (vii) above, but have secured atleast 65 per cent marks in the written examination and atleast 35% marks in the personal interview, the case is to be referred to President Recruitment.

In each question below are given details of one candidate. You have to take one of the following courses of actions based on the information provided and the conditions and sub-conditions given above and mark the number of that course of action as your answer. You are not to assume anything other than the information provided in each question. All these cases are given to you as on 1.3.2010.

Give answer

(a) if the data provided are inadequate to take a decision
(b) if the case is to be referred to VP-Recruitment
(c) if the case is to be referred to President- Recruitment
(d) if the candidate is to be selected
(e) if the candidate is not be selected

75. Sohan Majhi has secured 65% marks in B. Sc. and 70% marks in MSc Statistics. He has been working in a bank as generalist officer for the past three years after completing his Post-Graduation. He has secured 55% marks in the written examination and 50% marks in the personal interview. He was born on 8th July, 1982.

76. Neeta Jaiswal was born on 2nd June, 1980. She has been working in a bank as generalist officer for the past three years after completing her Post-Graduate degree in Economics with 60 per cent marks. She has secured 68 per cent marks in HSC and 58% marks in B. Com. She has also secured 50% marks in both the written examination and personal interview.

77. Arindam Ghosh has been working in a bank as generalist officer for the past four years after completing his Post-Graduate Diploma in management with 60% marks. He has secured 50% marks in the written examination and 40% marks in the personal interview. He has also secured 70% marks in Std XII. He was born on 25th February, 1975.

78. Keshav Vora was born on 8th November, 1978. He has secured 65 per cent marks in Std XII and 60 per cent marks in Graduation. He has secured 58 per cent marks in MA. Economics and 60 per cent marks in ICWA. He has been working in a bank as generalist officer for the past two years after completing his education. He has also secured 50% marks in the written examination and 45% marks in personal interview.

79. Neha Salve has been working in a bank as generalist officer for the past four year after completing her Post-Graduate degree in Economics with 60% marks. She has secured 60% marks in both graduation and Std. XII. She was born on 24th August, 1979. She was secured 70% marks in the written examination and 38% marks in the personal interview.

Direction (Q. Nos. 80-84) *Study the following information carefully and answer the questions given below.*

Following are the conditions for selecting Marketing-Manager in an organization **UBI (PO) 2009**

The candidate must

(i) be atleast 30 yr old as on 1.3.2009.
(ii) have secured atleast 55% marks in graduation.
(iii) have secured atleast 60% marks in Post Graduate degree/diploma in Marketing.
(iv) have post qualification work experience of atleast five years in the Marketing Division of an organization.
(v) have secured atleast 45% marks in the selection process.

In the case of a candidates who satisfies all above conditions except

1. at (iv) above, but has post qualification work experience of at least two years as Deputy Marketing Manager, the case is to be referred to GM-Marketing.
2. at (ii) above, but has secured at least 65% marks in Post Graduate Degree/Diploma in Marketing-Management, the case is to be referred to Vice President-Marketing.

In each question below is given details of one candidate. You have to take one of the following courses of action based on the information provided and the conditions and sub-conditions given above and mark your anwser accordingly. You are not to assume anything other than the information provided in each question. All these cases are given to you as on 1.3.2009.

Give answer

(a) if the candidate is not to be selected
(b) if the candidate is to be selected
(c) if the data are inadequate to take decision
(d) if the case is to be referred to Vice President-Marketing
(e) if the case is to be referred to GM-Marketing

80. Suresh Mehta has secured 58% marks in Graduation. He was born on 19th May, 1975. He has secured 50% marks in the selection process. He has been working for the past seven years in the Marketing division of an organization after completing his Post Graduation with 62 per cent marks.

81. Sudha Gopalan has secured 50% marks in both selection process and Graduation. She has been working for the past six years in the Marketing division of an organization after completing her Post Graduate diploma in Marketing with 70% marks. She was born on 14th October, 1978.

82. Divya Kohli has been working for the past five years in Marketing division of an organization after completing her Post Graduate diploma in Marketing with 65% marks. She has secured 55% marks in Graduation and 50 per cent marks in the selection process. She was born on 2nd April, 1979.

83. Navin Marathe was born on 8th April, 1975. He secured 60% marks in both Graduation and Post Graduate in Marketing. He has been working for the past six years in the Marketing division of an organization after completing his PG Degree in Marketing. He as secured 50% marks in the selection process.

84. Varun Malhotra was born on 3rd July, 1976. He been working as Deputy Marketing-Manager in an organization for the past three years after completing his Post Graduate degree in Marketing with 65% marks. He secured 55% marks in both Graduation and selection process.

Direction (Q. Nos. 85-94) *Following are the criteria laid down for the selection of Junior Executives in an organization.* **Dena Bank (PO) 2008**

The candidate must

(i) Have scored atleast 70% marks in SSC examination.
(ii) Have obtained Graduation degree in any discipline with at least 65% marks and first class.
(iii) Have cleared the selection test with atleast 55% marks.
(iv) Have cleared the interview with atleast 50% marks.
(v) Be not less than 21 yr of age and not more than 28 yr of age as on 1.9.2008.
(vi) have completed atleast a certificate/diploma course in computers.

However, if a candidate satisfies all the above mentioned critieria except

1. at (ii) above, but has completed Post- Graduation in any discipline, the case may be referred to the Vice-President of the company.
2. at (iii) above, but has secured at least 50% marks in selection test and at least 60% marks in interview, the case may be referred to the General Manager (Recruitment) of the company.

In each of the questions below, information of one candidate is given. You have to take one of the following five decisions based on the information provided and the criteria and conditions given above. You are not to assume anything other than the information provided in each question. All these cases are given to you as on 1.09.2008. You have to indicate your decision by marking answers to each question as follows

Give answer

(a) if the candidate is to be selected
(b) if the candidate is not to be selected
(c) if the data is inadequate to take a decision
(d) if the case is to be referred to the Vice President of the company
(e) if the case is to be referred to the General Manager (Recruitment) of the company

85. Shamika is a Science graduate passed in first class with 69% marks. She had passed SSC exam securing 83% marks. She has cleared selection test with 53% marks and interview with 63% marks. Her date of birth is 1.8.1983. She has completed a six months certificate course in computers.

86. Abhijit is a Graduate with 60% marks and a Post Graduate with 65% marks. He has completed one year diploma course in computers. He had scored 85% marks in SSC. He has cleared the selection test and interview with 58% and 56% marks respectively. His date of birth is 17.5.1986.

87. Ankita is a Commerce Graduate passed in first class with 68% marks. She has completed a two years diploma course in computers after Graduation. Her SSC score was 85%. She has cleared the selection test with 64% marks and interview with 58% marks. Her date of birth is 27.8.1985.

88. Manisha has scored 73% marks in SSC and 62% marks in Graduation. After Graduation she is working in a private firm. She has cleared the selection test with 58% marks and interview with 62% marks. Her date of birth is 11.5.1983. She has completed a certificate course in computers.

89. Nikita is a Graduate in Engineering passed in first class with 72% marks. She has cleared the selection test and interview with 63% and 65% marks respectively. She has done one year diploma course in computers. Her date of birth is 16.7.1984.

90. Rajesh Chavan is an Arts Graduate passed in first class with 61% marks. He has also completed MA in English with 62% marks. His SSC score was 78%. He has cleared the selection test with 56% and interview with 54% marks. His date of birth is 25.3.1984. He has completed a diploma course in computers.

91. Jyotika Basu is B. Sc. passed out in 2004, in first class with 68% marks. She scored 67% marks in SSC. She is pursuing M. Sc. at present. She has cleared the selection test and interview with 56% and 53% marks respectively. She has completed a certificate course in computers. Her date of birth is 15.5.1985.

92. Sujay Chaudhary has passed SSC with distinction and 81% marks and B Com in first class with 68% marks. He has completed a certificate course in computers. He has cleared the selection test with 51% marks and interview with 61% marks. He has completed 23 yr of age on 21.2.2008.

93. Vivek is presently pursuing Post Graduation in Economics. He has passed Graduation in first class with 72% marks. He had scored 78% marks in SSC. His date of birth is 21.8.1985. He has secured 58% marks in selection test and 62% marks in interview. He has passed a 6 months diploma course in computers.

94. Nandan Savla is a B. Com. passed in first class with 66% marks. He has secured 75% marks in HSC. He has completed 25 yr of age on 25th July, 2008. He has cleared selection test and interview each with 56% marks. He has completed one year certificate course in computers in grade 'A'.

Direction (Q. Nos. 95-104) *Following are the criteria for selection of officers in an organization.* **BOB (PO) 2008**

The candidate must

(i) have passed HSC examination in first class with at least 60% marks.
(ii) have passed Graduation degree in any discipline with at least 55% marks.
(iii) have completed a Certificate/Diploma/Degree course in Computer Science.
(iv) be not less than 21 yr and not more than 30 yr of age as on 1.7.2008.

If a candidate satisfies all the above mentioned criteria except

1. at (ii) above but is a Post Graduate, case may be referred to the Executive Direction (ED).
2. at (iii) above but has studied Computer Science as one of subjects of curriculum, case may be referred to the Vice-President (VP).

In each of the questions below, information of one candidate is given. You have to take one of the following five decisions based on the information provided and the criteria and conditions given above. You are not to assume anything other than the information provided in each question. All these cases are given to you as on 01.07.2008. You have to indicate your decision by marking answers to each question as follows

Give answer

(a) if the case is to be referred to ED
(b) if the case is to be referred to VP
(c) if the candidate is to be selected
(d) if the information is inadequate to take a decision
(e) if the candidate is not to be selected

95. Ashutosh is a Commerce Graduate passed in first class with 67% marks. He had secured 73% marks in HSC. He has studied Computer Science as one of the subjects at HSC. His date of birth is 22.9.1982.

96. Rajni has passed BMS degree examination in second class with 58% marks and HSC in first class with 65% marks. She has completed a diploma in Computer Science. She has completed 25 yr of age in November 2007.

97. Raj Grover has passed HSC exam in first class with 89% marks. Thereafter he did a 6 months certificate course in Computer Science and presently is pursuing final year of Engineering degree examination. His date of birth is 28.12.1980.

98. Shamika Gupta is a Science Graduate passed in 2006 with 47% at the age of 22 yr. She had scored 64% marks in HSC. She has also passed M. Sc. with 58% marks. She has done a certificate course in Computers.

99. Jasmine is a Post-Graduate in Computer Science passed in first class with 62% marks. She had scored 81% marks in HSC. Her date of birth is 17.6.1979.

100. Shyamala is a BA passed in first class with 63% marks. She had passed HSC examination in first class with 69% marks. She has also completed a certificate course in Computer Science with 'A' grade. Her date of birth is 23.9.1984.

101. Anubhav Gokhale is a B. Sc. with Computer Science passed in second class with 58% marks. He had passed HSC in first class with 76% marks. He has completed 25 yr of age in December 2007.

102. Manish Chaudhary passed HSC examination in first class with 83% marks and B. Com. in second class with 57% marks. He has completed a computer certificate course very recently. His date of birth is 26.4.1982.

103. Harish Vora passed HSC examination in 2003 with 85% marks and B. Sc. degree examination in 2006 with 69% marks. He has studied Computer Science as one of the subject at B. Sc. His date of birth is 17.9.1984.

104. Vandana Bhave is B. Com. Graduate passed in second class with 56% marks. She had passed HSC in second class with 59% marks. She has also completed a Computer diploma with 56% marks. Her date of birth is 11.5.1982.

Direction (Q. Nos. 105-109) *A marketing firm wants to recruit trainee officers. Following is the criteria for selection.*

MHT CET MBA 2009

The candidate must

(i) be a Graduate in any discipline with atleast 55% marks.
(ii) have completed Post-Graduate degree/diploma in Marketing-Management with atleast 65% marks.
(iii) have cleared the selection test with at test 50% marks.
(iv) have cleared the interview with atleast 55% marks.
(v) be willing to sign a bond for 2 yr.
(vi) be not less than 21 yr and not more than 26 yr of age as on 1.2.2009.

However, if a candidate satisfies all the above criteria except

1. At (ii) above but has working experience in the Marketing department for atleast one year and has a Post-Graduate degree/diploma with any specialization, the case is to be referred to the Vice-President.
2. At (v) above but is willing to pay an amount of ₹ 1 lakh in case if the candidate leaves the case is to be referred to the head of Marketing department.

In each of the questions below, information of one candidate is given. You have to take one of the following five decisions based on the information provided and the criteria and conditions given above. You are not to assume anything other than the information provided in each question. All these cases are given to you as on 1.2.2009. You haves to indicate your decision by marking answers to each question as follows

Give answer

(a) if the case is to be referred to Vice-President
(b) if the case is to be referred to head of marketing department
(c) if the data is inadequate to take a decision
(d) if the candidate is to be selected
(e) if the candidate is not to be selected

105. Meenal Soni is an Arts Graduate passed with 58% marks. She has done MBA-HR with 64% Marks in August 2004 and is working in the Marketing department of a bank since January 2005. She has completed 24 yr of age in November 2008. She is willing to sign the bond for 2 yr. She has cleared the selection test with 58% marks and interview with 56% marks.

106. Avinash Chavan is a Post-Graduate in Management with specialization in Marketing, passed with 67% marks. He is working as a Junior. Officer in the Marketing department of a private company. He is not willing to sign the bond but is wiling to pay ₹ 1 lakh in case if he leaves. He has cleared the selection test with 52% marks and interview with 59% marks. His date of birth is 17.6.1983.

107. Sujay has passed BE with 67% marks and MBA Marketing with 69% marks. He has scored 56% in selection test and 63% marks in interview. He has recently celebrated his 25th birthday on 17th September, 2008. He does not want to sign a bond but is willing to pay ₹ 1 lakh if he leaves.

108. Rohan Bhalla is 24 yr old Science Graduate passed with 58% marks and MBA in Marketing with 68% marks. He has secured 53% marks in selection test as well as in interview. He is willing to sign the bond for 2 yr.

109. Nandita Sharma is a B. Com. Graduate passed in first class with 62% marks and has passed Post-Graduate diploma in Marketing management with 72% marks. She has cleared selection test and interview with 56% and 58% marks respectively. Her date of birth is 21.12.1985. She is willing to sign the bond for 2 years.

Direction (Q. Nos. 110-114) *XYZ Ltd. Company wants to recruit Junior Executives in its Marketing department. Following criteria are laid down by the company.*

NMAT 2008

The candidate must

I. be a Graduate in any discipline with atleast 65% marks.
II. have passed Post-Graduate degree/diploma in Marketing-Management or public relations with at least 60% marks.
III. have cleared the selection test with atleast 55% marks.
IV. be not less than 21 yr and not more that 26 yr of age as on 1.12.2008.
V. have cleared the interview with atleast 50% marks.

However, if a candidate satisfies all the above mentioned criteria except

1. at (i) above but has secured at least 70% marks in Post-Graduate degree/diploma in Marketing Management, the case is to be referred to the Vice-President of the company.
2. at (iii) above but has secured atleast 50% marks in selection test and atleast 55% marks in interview the case may be referred to the Managing Director.

Give answer

(a) if candidate is to be selected

(b) if candidate is not to be selected

(c) if the data is inadequate to take a decision

(d) if the case is to be referred to the Vice-President

(e) if the case is to be referred to the Managing Director

110. Abhishek Neve is a B. Com. passed in first class with 63% marks and has a Post-Graduate degree in Marketing-Management with 72% marks. His date of birth is 1.7.1985. He has cleared the selection test and interview with 56% and 58% marks respectively.

111. Mangesh is an Arts Graduate passed with 66% marks and a Post-Graduate in Computer Management with 72% marks. He has cleared the selection test as well as interview with 58% marks. He has completed 24 yr of age on 12th August, 2008.

112. Leela Mehra is a Science Graduate passed with 69% marks in first class and has done Post-Graduate diploma in Marketing Management with 73% marks. She was cleared the selection test with 52% marks and interview with 59% marks. Her date of birth is 23rd September, 1983.

113. Manjusha Salve is an Engineering Graduate with 67% marks and has done Post-Graduation in Management with 64% marks. She has cleared the selection test with 62% marks and interview with 60% marks. Her date of birth is 25.1.1984.

114. Niranjan, is a Science Graduate with 68% marks and has a Post-Graduate diploma in Public Relations with 65% marks. He has completed 23 yr of age in November 2008. He has cleared the selection test with 58% marks and interview with 53% marks.

Direction (Q. Nos. 115-119) *Study the following information carefully and answer the questions given below.*

Following are the conditions for selecting Accounts Officer in an organization. **IBPS CWE 2011**

The candidate must

(i) be atleast 21 yr and not more than 26 yr as on 1.11.2011.

(ii) be a commerce graduate (B.Com.) with atleast 55% aggregate marks.

(iii) have work experience of atleast 2 yr in the Accounts Department of an organization.

(iv) have secured atleast 50% marks in the Selection Process.

In the case of a candidate who fulfils all the conditions except

1. at (i) above, but atleast 21 yr old and not more than 28 yr old and has work experience of 5 yr as Accounts Assistant in an organization, his/her case is to be referred to GM-Accounts.
2. at (ii) above but has secured atleast 50% aggregate marks in graduation and has secured atleast 55% marks in the selection process, his/her case is to be referred to VP Accounts.

In each question below, details of one candidate are provided. You have to take one of the following courses of actions based on the conditions given above and the information provided in each question and mark the number of that course of action as your answer. You are not to assume anything other than the information provided in each question. All these cases are given to you as on 1.11.2011.

Give answer

(a) if the case is to be referred to GM-Accounts

(b) if the case is to be referred to VP-Accounts

(c) if the candidate is to be selected

(d) if the candidate is not to be selected

(e) if the data provided are inadequate to take a decision

Now, read the information provided in each question and mark your answer accordingly.

115. Umesh Choksi was born on 25th November, 1989. He has secured 60% aggregate marks in B.Com. and 65% marks in the Selection Process. He has been working in the Accounts Department of an organization for the past 3 yr.

116. Pratibha Kale was born on 6th June, 1988. She has secured 60% aggregate marks in B.Com. and 49% marks in the Selection Process. She has been working in the Accounts Department of an organization for the past 3 yr.

117. Arun Patil has secured 55% aggregate marks in graduation. He has been working for past 4 yr in the Accounts Department of an organization. He has secured 50% marks in the Selection Process. He was born on 12th July, 1988.

118. Prabha Dixit was born on 18th April, 1985. She has been working as Accounts Assistant in an organization for the past 5 yr. She has secured 60% aggregate marks in B.Com and 55% marks in the Selection Process.

119. Amul Verma has secured 50% aggregate marks in B. Com. and 60% marks in the Selection Process. He has been working in the Accounts Department of an organization for past 4 yr. He was born on 2nd January, 1987.

Advanced Level

Direction (Q. Nos. 1-3) *Answer the questions on the basis of information given in the following case.* **XAT 2015**

Bright Engineering College (BEC) has listed 20 elective courses for the next term and students have to choose any 7 of them. Simran, a student of BEC, notices that there are three categories of electives: Job-oriented (J), Quantitative-oriented (Q) and Grade-oriented (G). Among these 20 electives, some electives are both Job and Grade-oriented but are not Quantitative-oriented (JG type).

QJ type electives are both Job and Quantitative-oriented but are not Grade-oriented and QG type electives are both Quantitative and Grade-oriented but are not Job-oriented. Simran also notes that the total number of QJ type electives is 2 less than QG type electives. Similarly, the total number of QG type electives is 2 less than JG type and there is only I common elective (JQG) across three categories.

Furthermore, the number of only Quantitative-oriented electives is same as only Job-oriented electives, but less than the number of only Grade-oriented electives. Each elective has at least one registration and there is at least one elective in each category, or combinations of categories.

1. On her way back Simran met her friend Raj and shared the above information. Raj is preparing for XAT and is only interested in Grade-oriented (G) electives. He wanted to know the number of G-type elective being offered. Simran replied, "You have all the information. Calculate the number of G-type electives yourself. It would help your XAT preparation". Raj calculates correctly and says that there can be ______ possible answers.

   Which of the following options would best fit the blank above?

   (a) 3 (b) 5 (c) 8 (d) 9
   (e) 11

2. Simran prefers J-type electives and wants to avoid Q-type electives. She noted that the number of only J-type electives is 3. Raj's preference is G-type electives followed by Q-type electives. However, they want to take as many common electives as possible. What is the maximum number of electives that can be common between them, without compromising their preferences?

   (a) 3 (b) 4 (c) 5 (d) 7
   (e) None of these.

3. Vijay and Raj want to avoid each other. Vijay is interested in J-type electives and wants to avoid Q-type elective. Raj's preference is G-type electives followed by Q-type electives. Raj noted that the number of only G-type electives is 2. Is there a possibility that they would not share any common electives?

   (a) Yes. There is a possibility
   (b) No. They would meet in one elective
   (c) No. They would not be able to avoid in two electives
   (d) No. They would meet in five electives
   (e) Cannot be solved with the information given

Direction (Q. Nos. 4-6) *Answer the questions on the basis of information given in the following case.* **XAT 2015**

A few years back Mr. Arbit and Mr. Boring started an oil refinery business. Their annual earning is currently just 50000 million rupees. They are now exploring various options to improve the business. Mr. Xanadu, a salesperson from Innovative Technology Solutions (ITS), is trying to sell a new oil refinery technology to Mr. Arbit and Mr. Boring.

This technology could potentially enhance their annual earning to 150000 million rupees within a year. But they have to make one-time investment of 100000 million rupees to implement the technology. If the technology is not successful, the investment would be lost. Mr. Arbit and Mr. Boring are discussing about possible risks of the investment.

4. Mr. Arbit is enthusiastic about this investment idea but Mr. Boring is a little sceptical. This impasse makes them approach a consultant. The consultant makes some observations. Which of the following observations, made by the consultant, might reduce Mr. Arbit's enthusiasm for the new investment idea?

   (a) Investment is warranted only when benefits outweigh costs
   (b) Technology investments give higher earnings in future
   (c) Investment in technology leads to reduction of costs in the long run
   (d) Technology risks can be controlled
   (e) Business is all about taking risky decisions

5. In order to sell the technology to Mr. Arbit and Mr. Boring, Mr. Xanadu is thinking of five possible sales pitches. Which of the following sales pitches would reduce uncertainties the most for Mr. Arbit and Mr. Boring?

   (a) All other competitors are aggressively investing in risky technologies
   (b) If the technology succeeds, the annual earnings would grow 3 times from the next financial year and they would be able to recover the invested money within 1 year
   (c) Preliminary studies indicate that success rate of the technology is 85%
   (d) The R & D team of ITS is working to counter any possible downside of the technology
   (e) Business is all about taking risky decisions

6. Mr. Arbit and Mr. Boring did not invest in the new technology, but the new technology is a big success. Repentant, they are now estimating the additional amount they would have earned (i.e. forgone earnings) had they invested in the new technology. However, the two owners differed on expected lifespan of the new technology. Mr. Arbit expected lifespan to be 5 yr, whereas, Mr. Boring expected it to be 2 yr. After the technology gets out-dated, the earnings from the business would drop back to 50000 million rupees.

What would be the difference between two expected foregone earnings after 5 yr of the technology investment, if yearly earnings are deposited in a bank @ 10%, compounded annually?

Forgone Earnings
= (Earnings from business with new technology)
− (Earnings from business without new technology)

(a) 231200 million rupees (b) 331000 million rupees
(c) 400510 million rupees (d) 431000 million rupees
(e) 464100 million rupees

Direction (Q. Nos. 7-10) *Answer the questions on the basis of information given in the following case.*

XAT 2015

Life Saving Pharmaceuticals (LSP) is an India-based pharmaceutical company. Their business mostly revolves around a couple of generic drugs and a few patented drugs. LSP operates in 30 odd countries and more than 50% of their sales volume is from outside India.

7. If more than 50% of their sales volume is from generic drugs, which of the following options is definitely correct?

All percentages figures are with respect to total sales volume.

(a) If sales volume of patented drugs in India is 43%, the sales volume of generic drugs in India will be less than 43%
(b) If the sales volume of generic drugs in foreign countries is at least 24%, the sales volume of patented drugs in India will be above 24%
(c) If the sales volume of patented drugs in India is 54%, the sales volume of generic drugs in foreign countries will be above 54%
(d) If the sales volume of patented drugs in India is 29%, the sales volume of generic drugs in foreign countries will be above 29%
(e) If the sales volume of generic drugs in India is at least 60%, the sales volume of patented drugs in foreign countries will be above 60%

8. Mr. Sinha, a senior executive of LSP, observes that their business in India is not vibrant. LSP faces stiff competition from Indian and global players, except in rural areas. Interestingly, most of their sales in the rural areas are from cough syrup, used as sedatives by teenagers. Mr. Sinha is planning the following actions to improve business in the long run.

I. Invest in development of new drugs.
II. Increase sales of cough syrup in the rural markets.
III. Try and cut costs.
IV. Recruit more medical representatives in the rural areas.

Which of the following sequences is best arranged in the descending order of appropriateness?

(a) I, III, II (b) II, I, III (c) II, III, I (d) IV, II, III
(e) IV, III, I

9. Mr. Rastogi, HR head of LSP, is contemplating of transferring Mr. Jose, from India to their Luxembourg office. Mr. Jose's wife is also with the HR department of LSP. The couple is expecting their first child within next four months and hence they want to be together. Mr. Rastogi is wondering whether Mr. Jose would accept the transfer. If he doesn't, Mr. Rastogi would have to send a less competent person for this job as early as possible. The office in Luxembourg is very important for the company's future. It is at its nascent stage and does not yet have an HR department. Hence, it is not possible to transfer Mrs. Jose to Luxembourg.

Which of the following options would be most appropriate, from the organisation's perspective, to resolve the issue?

(a) Giving a salary hike to Mr. Jose with a promise to transfer Mrs. Jose to Luxembourg in the near future
(b) Giving Mrs. Jose option to work from home while in Luxembourg so that she can be with Mr. Jose
(c) Giving Mr. Jose option to work from India for the time being, so that he can be with Mrs Jose in India
(d) Giving a salary hike to Mr Jose to compensate for Mrs. Jose's salary so that she can join Mr. Jose at Luxembourg even with loss of pay
(e) Asking Mr. Jose to accept the offer right now but give him up to six months to join Luxembourg office

10. Mr. Khan used to work as the Vice President of LSP India. However, he had resigned from LSP India for a better job in New York. In the meantime, his wife was promoted to head the HR of LSP India. Mrs. Khan had struggled hard to reach this position and was quite popular and respected within the organisation. Mrs. Khan was contemplating whether she should give up her career and join him in New York. Mrs. Khan is considering the following actions.

I. Take a break for the time being and focus on personal life. Given her reputation, she can always get back to the same job, if required.
II. Go to New York, on leave without pay for two months to help Mr. Khan settle down. After that she can come back and resume her responsibility in LSP India.
III. Request Mr. Khan to look for an equivalent job in India.
IV. Resign from LSP India, join Mr. Khan in New York, and look for a similar job there.
V. Request LSP India for a similar position in LSP, USA and follow Mr. Khan to New York.

Which of the following sequence of actions can be immediately taken by Mrs. Khan to maintain her work-life balance?

(a) I and II (b) I and III (c) I and IV (d) II and V
(e) III and V

Direction (Q. Nos. 11-13) *Answer the question on the basis of information given in the following case.* **XAT 2015**

Mohan's was a popular fast-food joint at Connaught Place, Delhi. Initially Mohan handled his business alone. His sons, Ram and Kishan, joined the business after graduating from college. Ram was entrepreneurial in nature. Subsequently, another branch of Mohan's was opened in Panipat.

Mohan had chosen Ram to head the Panipat branch. Though Ram increased sales in a short time, he had stopped using premium quality organic vegetables, the speciality of Mohan's. Mohan and Kishan were not happy with his way of doing business.

Now, the foremost challenge for Mohan was to sort out this issue with Ram. Mohan knew that replacing Ram with Kishan was difficult as Kishan did not want to leave Delhi. However, giving a freehand to Ram might have long term negative consequences. Mohan was confused about the future course of actions.

11. Mohan sought the help of five consultants, who gave the following opinions:

I. Organic vegetables might be a big success at Connaught place but awareness about organic vegetables is low among Panipat customers.

II. The Connaught place model can be implemented in Panipat provided the business is prepared to face the consequences.

III. Many high end restaurants in Panipat use organic vegetables. So, using organic vegetables will not be a differentiating factor.

IV. Selling prices of their dishes in Panipat are significantly lower. Using organic vegetables will bring down profits.

V. Premium quality organic vegetables are not easily available in Panipat.

Which of the following set of options would support Ram's argument of not using organic vegetables?

(a) I, III, IV (b) II, IV, V
(c) I, III, IV, V (d) II, III, IV, V
(e) All of these

12. Mohan sought feedback from a few of his businessmen friends, who were familiar with both the branches. Here is what they said:

Businessman 1 Customers of Connaught place and Panipat are very different.

Businessman 2 Customers in Panipat are extremely happy with Ram's behaviour.

Businessman 3 Panipat branch does not use the same quality of ingredients but maintains good hygiene and taste.

Businessman 4 Who knows, tomorrow the customers of Panipat might also appreciate what Connaught place customers appreciate today!

If Mohan thinks all these are valid concerns, which of the following actions would be best for the business?

(a) Training Kishan to replace Ram in a few months
(b) Not worrying about ingredients as long as business grows
(c) Bringing Ram to Connaught place branch
(d) Naming the Panipat branch as 'Ram's', and changing it back to Mohan's, when needed
(e) Asking Kishan to run the Panipat branch

13. After discussing with a few customers, Mohan realised that compromising on the quality of ingredients at Panipat branch may not be a good idea but at the same time he also realised that Panipat branch had grown fast. He was contemplating following five actions. Which of the following actions would be the best for the future of his business?

(a) Creating awareness campaign for organic vegetables in Panipat
(b) Mohan himself should look after the Panipat branch
(c) Close down the Panipat branch
(d) Send Kishan to Panipat branch and bring Ram to Connaught place permanently
(e) Hire a new person to run the Panipat branch

Direction (Q. Nos. 14-23) *Study the following information carefully and answer the questions given below.*

Following are the conditions for selecting Assistant General Manager-HR in an organization. **Syndicate Bank (PO) 2010**

The candidate must

(i) be atleast 40 yr and not more than 50 yr old as on 01.05.2010.
(ii) be Post Graduate in Personnel Management/ HR with atleast 60% marks.
(iii) have post qualification work experience of atleast fifteen years out of which at least five years as senior Manager-HR in an organization.
(iv) have successfully implemented HR system in his/her organization some time during the past three years.
(v) have secured atleast 45% marks in the selection process.

In the case of a candidate who satisfies all the above conditions except

1. at (ii) above but has secured atleast 50 per cent marks in Post Graduation and atleast 65% marks in the selection process, the case is to be referred to Executive Director.
2. at (iii) above but has atleast twelve years post qualification work experience out of which atleast eight years as Senior Manger-HR in an organization, the case is to be referred to Chairman.

In each question below details of one candidate are given. You have to take one of the courses of action based on the information provided and the conditions and sub-conditions given above and mark the number of that course of action as your answer. You are not to assume anything other than the information provided in each question. All these cases are given to you as one 01.05.2010.

Give answer

(a) if the candidate is to be selected
(b) if the candidate is not to be selected
(c) if the data provided are not adequate to take a decision
(d) if the case is to be referred to Executive Director
(e) if the case is to be referred to Chairman

14. Pranab Ghosh was born on 8th March, 1968. He has been working for the past eighteen years in an organization out of which last seven years as Senior Manager-HR after completing his Post Graduation in HR with 68% marks. He had successfully implemented HR system last year in his organization. He has secured 50% marks in the selection process.

15. Sheetal Jha has been working in an organization for the past twenty years out of which ten years as Senior Manager-HR after completing her Post Graduation in Personnel Management with 70% marks. She was born on 2nd December, 1965. She has secured 45% marks in the selection process.

16. Prabir Sengupta was born on 8th May, 1963. He has secured 65% marks in the selection process. He has been working for the past fifteen years in an organization out of which twelve years as Senior Manager-HR after completing his Post Graduation in HR with 55% marks. He has successfully implemented HR system in his organization during the last two years.

17. Shailesh Kumar has been working in an organization for the past thirteen years out of which nine years as Senior Manager-HR after completing his Post Graduation in HR with 68% marks. He was born on 15th September, 1968. He has secured 48% marks in the selection process. He has successfully implemented HR system in his organization two years back.

18. Navin Chopra was born on 12th June, 1967. He has been working for the past sixteen years out of which seven years as Senior Manager-HR after completing his Post Graduation in Personal Management with 75% marks. He has secured 44% marks in the selection process. He has successfully implemented HR system in his organization last year.

19. Meera Kulkarni has been working for the past seventeen years out of which eight years as Senior Manager-HR after completing her Post Graduation in Personnel Management with 66% marks. She has successfully implemented HR system in her organization during the last two years. She has secured 49% marks in the selection process. She was born on 14th December, 1971.

20. Akash Shastri was born on 12th April, 1967. He has been working for the past sixteen years out of which six years as Senior Manager-HR in an organization after completing his Post Graduationin HR with 58% marks. He has successfully implemented HR system in his organization last year. He has secured 65% marks in the selection process.

21. Shekhar Jena has been working for the past fifteen years out of which last seven years as Senior Manager-HR in an organization after completing his Post Graduation in HR with 68 per cent marks. He has secured 60% marks in the selection process. He was born on 16th August, 1965. He has successfully implemented HR system in his organization in past three years.

22. Sunetra Govil was born on 5th April, 1964. She has been working for the past seventeen years out of which nine years as Senior Manager HR in an organization. She has secured 48% marks in the selection process. She has also secured 69 per cent marks in her Post Graduation in Personnel Management. She has successfully implemented HR system in her organization last year.

23. Mohit Saxena was born on 27th July, 1963. He has been working for the past thirteen years out of which nine years as Senior Manager-HR after completing his Post Graduation in HR with 67% marks. He has secured 49% marks in the selection process. He has successfully implemented HR system in his organization during the past three years.

Direction (Q. Nos. 24-26) *Answer the questions based on the following information.* **IIFT 2008**

For selection of films produced before December 2007 for the national film festival of India, following criteria are given.

(i) The film must be submitted to the National Film Development Corporation (NFDC) by 31.10.2007.
(ii) The production cost of the film should not exceed rupees five crores.
(iii) The director of the film should have passed a three years course either from the Film and Television Institute of India (FTII) or from Satyajit Ray Film and Television Institute.
(iv) The length of the film should not exceed 150 min.
(v) The film must have been approved by the film Censor Board of India.

However, if the film fulfils all the above criteria except

1. criteria (ii) above, it must be sent to the Finance Secretary.
2. criteria (iii) above, the director has done atleast a one year course from FTII or Satyajit Ray Film and Television Institute, the film is kept as a stand-bye.

On the basis of the above information and information provided below, decide the course of action in each case. No further information is available. You are not to assume anything.

Give answer

(a) if the film is to be selected
(b) if the film is not be selected
(c) if the film should be sent to the finance secretary
(d) if the film should be kept as a stand-bye
(e) if the data given about the film are not adequate to make a decision

24. Film *Dainandini* was produced at the cost of ₹ 2.5 crore. It was submitted to the NFDC on 29th September, 2007. The director of the film Govind Chadha passed a 3 yr course from FTII. Length of film was 120 min and has been approved by the Censor Board of India.

25. *Bhadrasalam* is a 135 min film directed by Katyani, who was a student of Satyajit Ray Film and Television Institute from 1996 to 1999. The cost of producing the film was ₹ 2.3 crore and it was submitted to NFDC on 24th July, 2007. The film has been approved by the Censor Board of India.

26. Rakesh Mohan, the director of film *Ek Bar Achanak*, has successfully completed a 2 yr course at Satyajit Ray Film and Television Institute. The 150 min film was produced at ₹ 4.85 crore. It has been approved by the Censor Board of India and submitted to NFDC on 30th, November 2007.

Direction (Q. Nos. 27-28) *Answer the questions based on the following information.* **IIFT 2008**

To get admission in a management course at Dadhichi Institute of Management (DIM) following criteria are given.
A candidate must

(i) be a Graduate from a recognized university with minimum 54% marks.
(ii) not be more than 33 yr of age as on 1.4.2008.
(iii) have secured 60% or more marks in the entrance test.
(iv) pay one-time deposite fee of ₹ 200000 at time of admission.
(v) pay tution fee of ₹ 4000 per month.

1. Any candidate who fails to fulfil the condition (iv) at above, he/she may be referred to the chairman admission.
2. Any candidate who has scored 80% mark in the entrance test but does not fulfil the condition (i) at above, he/she may be referred to the director.
3. Any candidate having work experience of atleast 10 yr in supervisory cadre and does not satisfy the condition (ii) at above, he/she may be admitted under sponsored quota.

Given the above information and condition in each of the following questions, you have to decide which of the following course of action should be taken. You should not assume anything in case of any of the candidates.

Give answer

(a) if the candidate is admitted
(b) if the candidate is not admitted
(c) if the candidate is referred to the director
(d) if the candidate is referred to the chairman- admission
(e) if the candidate is admitted under sponsor quota

27. Kamaljeet secured 60% marks in Graduation and was born on 15th April, 1976. He scored 56% marks in the entrance test. He can pay one-time deposit of ₹ 200000 and monthly tution fee of ₹ 4000.

28. Gaurav is a first-class Science Graduate who obtained 81% marks in entrance test. He has 12 yr of work experience in supervisory cadre. He can pay the stipulated one-time deposit and monthly tution fees. His date of birth is 20th October, 1970.

Direction (Q. Nos. 29-38) *Study the following information carefully and answer the questions given below.*

Following are the conditions for selecting Marketing Manager in an organization. **Corporation Bank (PO) 2010**

The candidate must

(i) be a Graduate in any discipline with atleast 55% marks.
(ii) have a Post Graduate degree/diploma in Marketing-Management with atleast 60% marks.
(iii) have post qualification work experience of atleast five years in the Marketing division of an organization.
(iv) have secured atleast 45% marks in the selection examination.
(v) have secured atleast 40% marks in the selection interview.

In the case of a candidate who satisfies all the conditions except

1. at (iii) above, but has post qualification work experience of atleast three years as Deputy Marketing Manager, the case is to be referred to GM-Marketing.
2. at (v) above, but has secured atleast 60% marks in the selection examination, the case is to be referred to VP-Marketing.

In each question below, details of one candidate are given. You have to take one of the following courses of actions based on the information provided and the conditions and sub-conditions given above and marks the number of that course of action as your answer. You are not to assume anything other than the information provided in each question. All these cases are given to you as on 01.05.2010.

Give answer

(a) if the candidate is to be selected
(b) if the candidate is not to be selected
(c) if the case is to be referred to GM-Marketing
(d) if the case is to be referred to VP-Marketing
(e) if the data provided not adequate to take a decision

29. Nidhi Agarwal has secured 60% marks in the selection interview and 40% marks in the selection examination. She has been working in the Marketing division of an organization for the past eight years after completing her Post Graduate degree in Marketing-Management with 65% marks. She has secured 59% marks in B. Sc.

30. Navin Desai has secured 56% marks in BA. He has been working in the Marketing division of an organization for the past seven years after completing his Post Graduate degree in Marketing with 62% marks. He has secured 62% marks in the selection examination and 38% marks in the selection interview.

31. Sabina Handa has been working for the past four years as Deputy Marketing Manager in an organization after completing her Post Graduate diploma in Marketing-Management with 65% marks. She has secured 45% marks in both selection examination and selection interview. She has also secured 58% marks in B. Com.

32. Manoj Malhotra has secured 65% marks in B. Sc. and 60% marks in Post Graduate degree in Marketing- Management. He has also secured 50% marks in both selection examination and selection interview. He has been working in the Marketing division of an organization for the past six years after completing his Post Graduation in Marketing.

33. Varsha Akolkar has secured 59% marks in BA. She has secured 42% marks in the selection interview and 48% marks in the selection examination. She has been working in the Marketing division of an organization for the past seven years after completing her Post Graduation in Marketing-Management with 57% marks.

34. Utpal Goswami has been working in the Marketing division of an organization for the past five years after completing his Post Graduate diploma in Marketing-Management with 65% marks. He is a first class Science Graduate with 60% marks. He has secured 45% marks in the selection examination and 40% marks in the selection interview.

35. Anindita Ghosh has been working for the past eight years in an organization after completing her Post Graduate degree in Marketing-Management with 70% marks. She has secured 56% marks in BA. She has also secured 50% marks in the selection examination and 45% marks in the selection interview.

36. Samir Phukan has been working in the Marketing division of an organization for the past five years after completing his Post Graduate diploma in Management with 65% marks. He has secured 60% marks in B. Com. He has also secured 50% marks in both selection examination and selection interview.

37. Nimisha Patil has secured 59% marks in B. Com. She has also secured 50% marks in both selection examination and the selection interview. She has been working as Deputy Marketing-Manager in an organization for the past three years after completing her Post Management degree in Marketing-Management with 63% marks.

38. Sadashiv Ghatge has secured 60% marks in B. Com. He has been working for the past five years in the Marketing division of an organization after completing his Post Graduate degree in Marketing-Management with 68% marks. He has secured 35% marks in the selection interview and 62% marks in the selection examination.

Direction (Q. Nos. 39-48) *Study the following information carefully and answer the questions given below.*

Following are the conditions for selecting personnel manager in an organization **MHT CET MBA 2008**

The candidate must

(i) be a Graduate with atleast 50% marks.
(ii) have a Post Graduate degree/diploma in Personnel Management/HR with atleast 60% marks.
(iii) not be more than 35 yr as on 1.6.2009.
(iv) have Post-qualification work experience of atleast five years in the Personnel/HR Division of an organization.
(v) have secured atleast 45% marks in the selection process.

In the case of a candidate who satisfies all the conditions except

1. at (iii) above, but has Post-qualification work experience of atleast ten years, the case is to be referred to the Director-Personnel.
2. at (iv) above, but has Post-qualification work experience as Deputy Personnel Manager of atleast three years, the case is to be referred to President-Personnel.

In each question below are given details of one candidate. You have to take one of the following courses of action based on the information provided and the conditions and sub-conditions given above and mark the number of that course of action as your answer. You are not to assume anything other than the information provided in each question. All these cases are given to you as on 1.6.2009.

Give answer

(a) if the candidate is to be selected
(b) if the candidate is not to be selected
(c) if the information provided is inadequate to take a decision
(d) if the case is to be referred to the Director-Personnel
(e) if the case is to be referred to the President-Personnel

39. Meena Srivastava was born on 6th March, 1978. She has been working as Deputy Personnel Manager in an organization for the past four years after completing her Post Graduate diploma in HR with 68% marks. She has secured 50% marks in both Graduation and selection process.

40. Ketan Desai was born on 5th January, 1976. He has been working for the past five years in the Personnel department of an organization after completing his Post Graduate diploma in Personnel Management with 64% marks. He has secured 40% marks in the selection process and 52% marks in Graduation.

41. Anant Joshi has been working in the personnel department or an organization for the past six years. He was born on 7th November, 1977. He has secured 60% marks in Post Graduate degree in Personnel Management. He has also secured 55 per cent marks in both Graduation and selection process.

42. Mohan Bajpai was born on 10th April, 1975. He has secured 55% marks in Graduation and 65% marks in Post Graduate diploma in Personnel Management. He has been working in the HR department, of an organization for the past six years after completing his Post Graduate diploma.

43. Gopal Sharma has been working for the past five years in the HR department of an organization after completing his Post Graduate diploma in HR with 62% marks. He has secured 50% marks in both graduation and selection process. He was born on 29th May, 1974.

44. Arun Vohra has secured 55% marks in Graduation. He has been working in the Personnel Department of an organization for the past eleven years after completing his Post Graduate degree in Personnel Management with 65 per cent marks. He has secured 50 per cent marks in the selection process. He was born on 12th August, 1972.

45. Asha Dhar has secured 52% marks in Graduation and 62% marks in Post Graduate degree in Personnel Management. She has also secured 48% marks in the selection process. She has been working for the past seven years in the Personnel Department. of an organisation after completing her Post Graduate degree. She was born on 8th June, 1974.

46. Sudha Ghosal was born on 20th October, 1976. She has been working as Deputy Personnel Manager for the past four years in an organization after completing her Post Graduate degree in HR with 67% marks. She has secured 60 per cent marks in Graduation and 45% marks in the selection process.

47. Amit Saxena was born on 25th July, 1973. He has been working in the Personnel department of an organization for the past eleven years after completing his Post Graduate diploma in HR with 70% marks. He has secured 60% marks in both Graduation and selection process.

48. Navin Das was born on 14th April, 1978. He has been working in the Personnel Department of an organization for the past six years after completing his Post Graduate diploma in HR with 65% marks. He has secured 45% marks in both Graduation and selection process.

Direction (Q. Nos. 49-53) *Study the following information carefully and answer the questions given below.*

Following are the conditions for selecting Manager-Marketing in an organization. **BOB (PO) 2010**

The candidate must

(i) be atleast 25 yr and not more than 30 yr as on 01.05.2010.
(ii) be a Graduate in any discipline with atleast 55 per cent marks.
(iii) have completed Post Graduate degree/diploma in Marketing-Management with atleast 60% marks .
(iv) have Post qualification work experience of atleast three years in the Marketing division in an organization.
(v) have secured atleast 45% marks in the selection process.

In the case of a candidate who satisfies all the conditions except

1. at (ii) above but has secured atleast 65% marks in Post graduation degree/diploma in Marketing. Management, the case is to be referred to GM-Marketing.
2. at (iv) above but has Post qualification work experience of atleast one year as Deputy Marketing-Manager in an organization, the case is to be referred to CGM-Marketing.

In each question below details of one candidate are given. You have to take one of the following courses of actions based on the information provided and the conditions and sub-conditions given above and mark the number of that course of action as your answer. You are not to assume anything other than the information provided in each question. All these cases are given to you as on 01.05.2010.

Give answer

(a) if the data provided is not adequate to take a decision
(b) the candidate is to be selected
(c) if the candidate is not to be selected
(d) if the case is to be referred to GM-Marketing
(e) if the case is to be referred to CGM-Marketing

49. Shreyas Ingle was born on 12th July, 1983. He has secured 57% marks in B. Com. He has been working in the Marketing division of an organization for the past four years after completing his Post Graduate diploma in Marketing- Management with 67% marks. He has secured 48% marks in the selection process.

50. Archit Pradhan has been working in the Marketing division of an organization for the past five years. He has secured 60% marks in both B. Sc. and Post Graduate degree in Marketing-Management. He was born on 8th May, 1984. He has secured 46% marks in the selection process.

51. Nisha Awasthi was born on 29th April, 1981. She has been working in the Marketing division of an organization for the past five years after completing her Post graduate degree in Marketing-Management with 67% marks. She has secured 50% marks in the selection process and 53% marks in B. Com.

52. Ankita Bhave has been working in the Marketing division of an organization for the past four years after completing her Post Graduate diploma in Marketing-Management with 62% marks. She was born on 11th August, 1982. She has secured 52% marks in B. Sc. She has secured 48% marks in the selection process.

53. Subodh Saxena was born on 15th November, 1982. He has been working as Deputy Marketing Manager in an organization for the past two years after completing his Post Graduate degree in Marketing-Management with 68 pre cent marks. He has secured 56% marks in B. Com. and 50% marks in the selection process.

Direction (Q. Nos. 54-63) *Read the following information carefully and answer the questions given below.*

Directorate-General Border Security Force invites applications from male candidates for the Post of Head Constable (Radio Operator). The following criteria are needed for a candidate to be selected. The candidate

(i) should have passed Matric or equivalent with 60% marks.
(ii) should have a two-years ITI certificate in Radio and TV/Electronics.
(iii) should be between 18 yr and 23 yr as on 1 August, 2012 in case of a candidate belonging to general category. Upper age limit shall be relaxable in respect of SC/ST candidates by 5 yr and OBC candidates by 3 yr.
(iv) should fulfil the following physical and medical criteria
 (a) He should have a height of atleast 170 cm, 168 cm, 169 cm and 165 cm if he belongs to North, South, East and West region respectively.
 (b) He should have minimum distant vision of 6/6 and 6/9 in both eyes without correction, *i.e.*, without wearing glasses. He must pass high-grade colour vision test.
 (c) He must not have knock knee, flat feet or squint in eyes.

However, if a candidate fulfils all these criteria except

1. at (i) above but has passed 10 + 2 examination with atleast 50% marks, then his case may be referred to back-up file and considered later for appointment.
2. at (ii) above but has a three-year diploma certificate in Radio and TV/Electronics, then his case should be mentioned in priority list.
3. at (iii) above but is an ex-serviceman not more than 35 yr, he should be selected.

On the basis of the above criteria and information provided below, decide the course of action in each case. Please note that you are not to assume any data other than those described. However, you may treat the candidate as 'General Category' if his category is not explicitly mentioned as SC/ST/OBC. Only male candidates have sent applications. These cases are given to you as on 1st May, 2012.

Give answer

(a) if the candidate is to be selected but not from the priority list
(b) if the candidate is not to be selected
(c) if the candidate is selected according to the priority list
(d) if the candidate is to be considered later for appointment
(e) if the data given about the candidate are inadequate to make a decision

54. Satyaprakash is an ex-serviceman. He is 30 yr old. He has a two-years ITI certificates in relevant field. He belong to North region and his height is 170 cm. He fulfils the other required medical and physical criteria. He is an intelligent student and has gotten 62% marks in matriculation.

55. Rakesh K Yadav has done a three-year diploma in electronic engineering. He has secured 69% marks in matriculation. His date of birth is 1st August, 1993. He has no ITI certificates. His height is 168 cm. He belongs to West region. He has the required minimum distant vision without correction. He fulfils the other required medical and physical criteria.

56. Amresh Kumar has succeeded to get more than 59% marks in matriculation and same percentage of marks in 10+2 examination. He is an ST candidate. H is date of birth is 2 August, 1984. He certificate of ITI in the required fields. He belongs to West region and his height is 169 cm. He fulfils other physical and medical criteria.

57. Abhishek Gupta is 20 yr old. He has a two-years ITI certificate in Radio and TV. He has gotten 60% marks in matriculation. His height is 168 cm. He has minimum distant vision of 6/6 and 6/9 in both eyes without correction. He has passed high-grade colour vision test. He is not suffering from problems such as knock knee, flat feet or squint in eyes.

58. Bhavesh Kr Jha is 24 yr old. He is an OBC candidate. He has a two-year certificate of ITI. He secured 67% marks in matric. He is 168 cm tall. He belongs to North region. He fulfils other required physical and medical criteria.

59. Himanshu Rajoria has a good academy record. He has done a three-year diploma course in electronic engineering after passing 10+2 and matriculation with 60% and 65% respectively. He has no physical and medical disability. He is an ST candidate. His date of birth is 7 August, 1984.

60. Prabhat Ranjan has done matriculation and 10 + 2 with 75% marks. His date of birth is 31 December, 1990. He has done a three-year diploma course in Radio and TV engineering. He belongs to North region and has the height according to stipulated norms. He is not suffering from any physical disorder. He is medically fit for the job.

61. Bhuvan Chandra failed to get even 55% marks in matriculation but succeeded in getting the same percentage of marks in 10 + 2 and 10 + 2 + 3 level. He has done a three-year diploma course too in electronic engineering. His date of birth is 11 July, 1989. He is physically fit for the job and fulfils the stipulated medical norms.

62. Vishal Choudhary is a candidate of over twenty years. His academic record is exemplary because of full marks in each subject and in each examination. Last year when he finished his three-year diploma course in electronic engineering he was very pleased because he repeated the same performance as the previous one in matriculation. He is confident of being selected for the Post because he fulfils physical and medical norms regarding height, feet, knee and eye.

63. Bankim Anand got less marks in matriculation than Vishal Choudhary. He is 22 yr old. He fulfils all the required physical and medical norms.

Direction (Q. Nos. 64-66) *Read the following instructions and answer the questions.* **IIFT 2011**

After the discussion at a high level meeting of Government officers, the criteria for issuing of import / export licence to eligible business firms for the year 2011-12 were finalized as follows. The firms must

I. Have a Grade - 'A' certified unit for any products.
II. Not have any legal dispute case against it.
III. Possess minimum asset worth ₹ 40 lakhs.
IV. Submit an environment clearance certificate issued by the Pollution Control Board (PCB) of the state, where the firm is located.
V. Deposit the margin money of ₹ 1 lakh.

VI. Arrange for three guarantors with their personal identity cards (IDs).

However, if the firm satisfies all the above mentioned criteria except

(a) Criteria (I) but is a traditional handloom production unit, then the case may be referred to Development Commissioner, Handloom (DCH) of the state.

(b) Criteria (IV) but is a local employment provider / thread (input) supplier / cloth supplier, the case may be referred to the Director, Department of Industry of the state.

(c) Criteria (V) but can deposit atleast ₹ 50000, the firm will be given import licence only and the case may be referred to the Deputy Director, Department of Industry of the state.

Based on the above criteria and information provided on each of the firms in the questions below, you have to decide which course of action should be taken against each firm. Without assuming anything regarding any applicant firm, the decision should be based on the information provided.

64. Mahalaxmi Weaving Center is a traditional handloom production unit. It has property worth more than ₹ 1 crore. It managed to get three guarantors with their personal IDs. No legal case is there against it. There is no problem submitting an environmental clearance, as the same is already issued to it by the State Pollution Control Board. It is also ready to deposit ₹ 1 lakh.

(a) Licence can be issued
(b) Licence not to be issued
(c) May be referred to the Development Commissioner Handloom
(d) May be referred to the Director of Industry

65. Ramayan Enterprise is a textiles firm which possesses assets worth ₹ 50 lakhs and is located in Surat, where no firm having any legal dispute is permitted to operate. The firm agreed to deposit ₹ 1 lakh and give details of three guarantors with their personal details as required. It has got grade A certificate and can submit an environment clearance certificate issued by the Pollution Control Board of the state.

(a) Licence can be issued
(b) Licence not to be issued
(c) May be referred to the Development Commissioner Handloom
(d) May be referred to Deputy Director of Industry

66. Hirabhai Handlooms is a Vadodara based traditional Gujarati handloom firm keen to get an export licence. It is ready to pay the required security amount and possesses assets of ₹ 55 lakhs. Hirabhai Chamanlal is the owner of the firm as well as the President of State Handloom Association. Hence, getting more than three guarantors with their IDs is not a problem. The firm possesses the environmental clearance certificate from the State Pollution Control Board after it was made mandatory for all handloom firms in the state.

(a) Licence can be issued.
(b) Licence not to be issued.
(c) May be referred to the Development Commissioner Handloom.
(d) May be referred to the Director of Industry.

Direction (Q. Nos. 67-71) *Study the following information carefully and answer the questions given below.*

Following are the conditions for selecting Manager HR in an organization. **IBPS (SO) 2012**

The candidate must

(i) be atleast 30 yr and not more than 35 yr as on 1.3.2012.
(ii) have secured atleast 60% marks in graduation in any discipline.
(iii) have secured atleast 65% marks in the Post Graduate Degree/Diploma in Personnel Management/HR.
(iv) have post qualification work experience of atleast five years in the Personnel/ HR Department of an organization.
(v) have secured atleast 50% marks in the selection process.

In the case of a candidate who satisfies all the above conditions except.

1. at (ii) above but has secured atleast 55% marks in Graduation in any discipline and atleast 70% marks in Post Graduate Degree/Diploma in Personnel Management/HR, the case is to be referred to GM-HR.
2. at (iv) above but has post qualification work experience of atleast four years out of which atleast two years as Deputy Manager HR, the case is to be referred to President HR.

In each question below are given details of one candidate. You have to take one of the following courses of actions based on the information provided and the conditions and sub-conditions given above and mark the number of that course of action as your answer. You are not to assume anything other than the information provided in each question. All these cases are given to you as on 1.3.2012.

Give answer

(a) if the candidate is not to be selected
(b) if the data provided are not adequate to take a decision
(c) if the case is to be referred to President HR
(d) if the case is to be referred to GM-HR
(e) if the candidate is to be selected

67. Rita Bhatt was born on 25th July, 1978. She has secured 62% marks in Graduation and 65% marks in Post Graduate Diploma in Management. She has been working for the past six years in the Personnel Department of an organization after completing her Post Graduation. She has secured 55% marks in the selection process.

68. Ashok Pradhan was born on 8th August, 1980. He has been working in the Personnel Department of an organization for the past four years after completing his Post Graduate Degree in Personnel Management with 67%. Out of his entire experience, he has been working for the past two years as Deputy Manager HR. He has secured 62% marks in Graduation and 58% marks in the selection process.

69. Alok Verma was born on 4th March, 1976. He has been working in the Personnel Department of an organization for the past six years after completing his Post Graduate Diploma in Personnel Management with 66% marks. He has secured 57% marks in the selection process and 63% marks in Graduation.

70. Swapan Ghosh has been working in the Personnel Department of an organization for the past five years after completing his Post Graduate Degree in HR with 72% marks. He has secured 56% marks in Graduation. He was born on 12th May, 1977. He has secured 58% marks in the selection process.

71. Seema Behl has been working in the Personnel Department of an organization for the past seven years after completing her Post Graduate Diploma in Personnel Management with 70% marks, 'She was born on 5th July, 1979. She has secured 65% marks in Graduation and 50% marks in the selection process.

Direction (Q. Nos. 72-76) *Read the following caselet carefully and answer the questions that follow.* **XAT 2013**

Head of a nation in the Nordic region was struggling with the slowing economy on one hand and restless citizens on the other. In addition, his opponents were doing everything possible to discredit his Government. As a famous saying goes, 'There is no smoke without a fire', it cannot be said that the incumbent Government was doing all the right things. There were reports of acts of omission and commission coming out every other day.

Distribution of public resources for private businesses and for private consumption had created a lot of problems for the Government. It was being alleged that the Government has given the right to exploit these public resources at throw away prices to some private companies. Some of the citizens were questioning the Government policies in the Supreme Court of the country as well as in the media. In the midst of all this, the head of the nation called his cabinet colleagues for a meeting on the recent happenings in the country.

He asked his minister of water resources about the bidding process for allocation of rights to set up mini hydel power plants. To this, the minister replied that his ministry had followed the laid out policies of the Government. Water resources were allocated to those private companies that bid the highest and were technically competent. The minister continued that later on some new companies had shown interest and they were allowed to enter the sector as per the guidelines of the Government.

This the minister added, would facilitate proper utilisation of water resources and provide better services to the citizens. The new companies were allocated the rights at the price set by the highest bidders in the previous round of bidding. After hearing this, the head of the nation replied that one would expect the later allocations to be done after a fresh round of bidding. The minister of water resources replied that his ministry had taken permissions from the concerned ministries before allocating the resources to the new companies.

72. Media reports suggested that the minister of water resources had deliberately allocated the water resources at old prices to the new companies and in return some received kickbacks. However, the minister denied these charges. His counter argument was that he followed the stated policies of the Government and it is very difficult to price a scarce resource. He also said that the loss that the media is talking about is national and in reality the Government and the citizens have gained by the entry of new players.

Which of the following is the most appropriate inference?

(a) If benefit to the citizens is higher than national losses, then it is not unethical
(b) If benefit to the citizens is lower than national losses, then it is unethical
(c) If benefit to the citizens is higher than actual losses, then it is not unethical
(d) If benefit to the citizens is lower than actual losses, then it is unethical
(e) All of the above are inappropriate

73. Subsequently, the minister questioned the role of the media in the whole affair. He said that the media cannot act like a reporter, prosecutor and judge at the same time. Mr Swamy, an independent observer, was asked about appropriateness of the minister's opinion. What should be Mr Swamy's reply?

(a) Media has been rightly accused by the minister
(b) Minister's statement may be factually incorrect
(c) Media has rightly accused the minister
(d) Media has wrongly accused the minister
(e) None of the above

74. Looking at the public unrest and discontent, the Government's anti-corruption branch was entrusted with the task of investigating the matter. Within a week's time the branch charge sheeted top corporate managers and the minister for wrong doings. Mr Swamy was again asked to identify the guilty. Who should Mr Swamy pick?
(a) Only corporate managers (b) Only the minister
(c) Only the head of the nation (d) All of these
(e) None of the above

75. Over the last five year, Bank of Bharat has seen the number of its retail customer accounts drop by over 40%. Over the same period, the share price of Bank of Bharat has increased by more than 80%. This amazed a few investors, who believe that a bank's share price should drop, if its number of customers drops.
Which of the following, if true over the last five year, best accounts for the observed movement in the price of Bank of Bharat's equity shares?
(a) Two year ago, Securities and Exchange Board started an investigation on the bank for accounting irregularities but last year the company was cleared of all charges
(b) The bank recently implemented a highly publicised programme for free home loans
(c) The bank has been switching its customer base from retail customers to commercial customers, which now accounts for over 75% of the bank's revenues
(d) There have been many new banks, which have entered retail banking business over the last five years
(e) The bank is known to be the best paymaster in the industry

76. Gastric bypass surgery has been shown to be effective at helping extremely obese people lose weight. Some patients have lost as much as 300 pounds after undergoing the surgery, thereby substantially prolonging their lives. Despite the success of the treatment, most doctors have not embraced the surgery.
Which of the following statements, if true, best accounts for the lukewarm reaction of the medical community to gastric bypass surgery?
(a) Gastric bypass surgery carries a high risk of serious complications, including death
(b) Obesity is one of the leading contributors to heart disease and hypertension two leading causes of death
(c) Incidences of obesity among the Indian urban middle class population have been increasing consistently for the last three decades
(d) Many patients report that losing weight through diets is ineffective, since they usually gain the weight back within six months
(e) Most health insurance plans will cover the cost of gastric bypass surgery for morbidly obese patients at high risk of heart disease

Direction (Q. Nos. 77-80) *Read the following caselet carefully and answer the questions that follow.* **XAT 2013**

A teacher wanted to administer a multiple choice (each question having six choices) based quiz of high difficulty level to a class of sixty students. The quiz had sixty questions. The probability of selecting the correct answer for a good student and a brilliant student was 0.2 and 0.25, respectively. The poor students had no learning advantage. The teacher did not want students to cheat but does not have time and resources to monitor. All students were seated serially in 10 rows and 6 columns.

77. Is it possible for the teacher to detect cheating without monitoring? Choose the statement that best describes your opinion.
(a) It is not at all possible, teacher will have to introduce technology, if there is no human support
(b) It is always possible but teacher has to calculate the exact answer
(c) It is possible when many students sitting next to each other have the same incorrect answers for multiple questions. However, there can be a small error in judgment
(d) It is possible when many student sitting next to each other have the same correct answers for multiple questions. However, there can be a small error in judgement
(e) It is possible only for poor students but not for good and brilliant students. However, there can be a small error in judgement

78. Three good students were seated next to each other. What is the probability of them having the same incorrect choice for four consecutive questions?
(a) 256/390625 (b) 256/3125 (c) 4/3125 (d) 1/3125
(e) Cannot be determined

79. Students from four sections of a class accompanied by respective class teachers planned to go for a field trip. There were nineteen people in all. However, on the scheduled day one of the four teachers and a few students could not join the rest. Given, below are some statements about the group of people who ultimately left for the trip.
I. Section A had the largest contingent.
II. Section B had fewer students than section A.
III. Section C's contingent was smaller than section B.
IV. Section D had the smallest contingent.
V. The product of the number of student from each section is a multiple of 10.
VI. The number of students from section C is more than 2.
VII. The product of the number of students from each section is a multiple of 24.
VIII. The largest contingent has more than 4 students.
IX. Each section contributed different number of students.

The statements that taken together can give us the exact number of students from each section

(a) I, II, III, IV, VI
(b) I, VI, VIII, IX
(c) I, II, III, IV, V, VI
(d) I, II, III, IV, VI, VII
(e) I, IV, VI, VII, IX

80. There is a lot of interest in the first five ranks for Class XI students. One student guessed the rank order as Ankita, Bhagyashree, Chanchal, Devroopa and Esha. Later upon announcement of the results, it was found that not only did he get each student out off her true position, none of the students in his ranking correctly followed her immediate predecessor. Another student guessed Devroopa, Ankita, Esha, Chanchal and Bhagyashree. Even his guess was wrong. It was found that he had got two positions correct and two students in his ranking correctly followed their immediate predecessors.

Which of the following is true about the correct rank order?

(a) Ankita got the third position
(b) Bhagyashree got the fourth position
(c) Chanchal got the second position
(d) Devroopa stood first

Direction (Q. Nos. 81-82) *Read the following caselet carefully and answer the questions that follow.* **XAT 2013**

Island of Growth was witnessing a rapid increase in GDP. Its citizens had become wealthier in recent times and there had been a considerable improvement in the standards of living. However, this rapid growth had increased corruption and nepotism in the Island. In the recent times, a fear had gripped the population that corruption would destroy the inclusive nature of the society and hinder economic progress. However, most citizens had kept quiet because

(i) they had benefitted from the corruption indirectly, if not directly
(ii) they did not have the time and energy to protest
(iii) they did not have courage to rise against the established power centres

There was a need to remove corruption but no one was willing to stick his neck out. Many politicians, bureaucrats and private organisations were corrupt. Media and intellectuals kept quiet, as they benefitted indirectly from corruption. The common man was scared of state's retribution and the youngsters feared insecure future.

Against this background, an old, unmarried and illiterate gentleman of high moral and ethical authority, Shambhu, decided to take on the issue of corruption. He sat on a hunger strike in the heart of the capital city of the Island. Shambhu demanded that the Government should constitute new laws to punish the corrupt across all walks of life. Media and the citizens of the Island gave massive support to Shambhu. Buckling under the pressure, the Government promised to accept Shambhu's demands. He ended the hunger strike immediately following the Government's announcement. Shambhu became the darling of the media. He used this opportunity as a platform to spread the message that only citizens with an unblemished character should be allowed to hold a public office. A few months later, it was found that the Government had not fulfilled any of its promises made to Shambhu. Infuriated, he was thinking of launching another Island-wide protest. However, this time, he sensed that not many people and media persons were willing to support him.

81. Read the following statements

I. People's latent anger against corruption.
II. Shambhu's moral courage.
III. Hungry media looking to raise issues.
IV. Rising income level.

In your opinion, which combination of the above statements is the most unlikely reason for Shambhu's initial success?

(a) I, II and IV
(b) III and IV
(c) I and III
(d) I, III and IV
(e) All of the above

82. Which of the following could be the most likely reason for decline in public support for Shambhu?

(a) The common man had become sick and tired of Government's inaction against rising corruption
(b) Shambhu was old and he lacked the energy to garner the same support that he enjoyed from the media and the public in the initial stages
(c) The general public may have realised that Shambhu was focusing too much on 'indirect involvement' in past incidences of corruption. Common men found it difficult to live up to the high standards set by Shambhu
(d) Shambhu's colleagues were misleading him
(e) Shambhu came from a village, while most of his supporters were city dwellers

Direction (Q. Nos. 83-85) *Read the following caselet carefully and answer the questions that follow.* **XAT 2013**

It was the end of performance review cycle for the year 2012, when you asked your subordinates about any problems they were facing. Natrajan told you that an important member of his team, Vardarajan, who had also won the best performance award for the year 2011, was not taking interest in work. Despite Natrajan's counseling, no change was noticed in Vardarajan, rather his attitude deteriorated.

You had also received such information from other employees. You had not interfered hoping that Natrajan, an experienced hand, would be able to solve the problem. But, now that Natrajan himself brought this to your notice, you decided to call Vardarajan and counsel him.

83. Which of the following could be the most unlikely reason for Vardarajan's declining involvement in the workplace?

(a) Vardarajan does not find the work challenging enough as he has already achieved the best performance award
(b) Others in the organisation have been trying to pull him down, since he was declared best performer
(c) Vardarajan was not promoted after his superlative performance, while another colleague, Sundararajan, was promoted although he was not as good a performer as Vardarajan
(d) After putting in lots of effort for the superlative performance, Vardarajan felt burnt out
(e) Vardarajan was appreciated by his bosses for his achievement last year

84. Vardarajan did not find his work challenging enough, given below are some steps that could be taken to motivate him.

I. Give Vardarajan a more challenging assignment.
II. Transfer Vardarajan from projects department to training department.
III. Ask him to take a vacation for two months
IV. Send him for further training on decision making under stress.

Which of the following combinations would be the most appropriate?

(a) I, II and III
(b) I, III and IV
(c) I and IV
(d) II, III and IV
(e) I, II, III and IV

85. You overheard a conversation between Vardarajan and his colleague over an official dinner. He expressed his unhappiness about the fact that good performers were not given their due credit while poor performers were promoted faster. If Vardarajan is right, which of the following steps would help in creating a better organisation?

(a) Promote Vardarajan with immediate effect
(b) Ensure that performance is objectively and transparently assessed
(c) Give another assignment to Vardarajan
(d) Give higher salary to Vardarajan
(e) Fire Vardarajan

Direction (Q. Nos. 86-89) *Read the following caselet carefully and answer the questions that follow.* **XAT 2013**

Professor Vijya, the chairperson of the Faculty Academic Committee (FAC), was trying to understand the implications of decisions taken by the Student Placement Committee (SPC) on placement issues.

It was alleged that Biswajit, a final year student, inflated his grades in his biodata that was sent to the recruiters. The President of SPC requested the FAC to debar Biswajit from the campus recruitment process. When the matter was brought up for discussion in FAC, one of the professors remarked that Biswajit too should be allowed to defend himself. When Biswajit arrived for the meeting the situation became even more challenging.

Biswajit raised the issue that many other students who had misrepresented grades to get coveted jobs had gone scot-free. He alleged that these students were close to the President of SPC and therefore no action was taken against them. He stated that somebody has deliberately manipulated his grades in the biodata. This allegation confused the members and it was decided to adjourn the meeting. Vijya was to decide on the next course of action.

86. If you were Vijya, what in your opinion would be the most appropriate action?

(a) Debar Biswajit and the President of SPC from the placement process as they have failed to uphold the rules of the SPC
(b) Suspend Biswajit and the President of SPC
(c) Constitute a fact finding committee to investigate the matter and ask them to submit a report to you within a week's time
(d) Apprise the corporate recruiters of the situation and assure them that corrective actions will be taken
(e) Both (c) and (d)

87. It was found that a large section of the students have been indulging in such practices. Unfortunately, the HR Manager of a much coveted campus recruiter, who is an alumnus of the college came to know about this. Considering yourself in the position of that HR Manager. What would be your reaction?

(a) Express your displeasure and stop any further recruitment from the college
(b) Talk to your contact in the college and try to find out the truth
(c) Do not change anything and continue the process as, if nothing has happened

(d) Ask the college to send a fresh set of bio data as you wanted verified grades of the students
(e) Ask the SPC to resend the details of the short listed students including their verified grades

88. As a potential entrant you are having an informal facebook chat with one of the college seniors. You wanted to know about the pay packages of the graduating students. The senior replied that one will be able to understand this only after joining the college. He did not reveal any information but suggested that it is not very difficult to get a high salary job as you have already started networking. He also cautioned that you should not believe any rumors and you should directly contact the student body for any further information. What will be your most appropriate choice for seeking further information about placements?
(a) This conversation will increase your interest and you will network more with the students of the college for increasing your chances of getting a high salary job
(b) You will contact the college authorities to get more insights about the placement process
(c) You will start networking with the HR Managers to understand their requirements
(d) You will try to contact the President of SPC.
(e) You will contact your other facebook friends to find out about the placement activities at the college

89. Vijya found that there were many such cases of grade inflation. She was giving final touches to the report when her attention was diverted by a phone call on her personal cell phone. It was from an unlisted number. The caller conveyed to her that it will be in her interest as well as in the interest of the college, if the report is not presented to the director. The caller also told her these findings will change nothing only result in bad publicity for the college. The caller identified himself as a well-wisher of the college before hanging up. Consider yourself in Vijya's position and choose an appropriate decision from the following choices.
(a) Disregard the phone call and do not share its details with others
(b) Understand the implications of the phone call and apply for a leave
(c) Call up the director, tell him about the phone call and excuse yourself from the responsibility
(d) Talk to the director and seek his opinion
(e) Constitute a different committee to investigate the 'phone call' and carry on with normal activities

Direction (Q. Nos. 90-93) *Read the following caselet carefully and answer the questions that follow.* **XAT 2014**

Krishna Reddy was the head of a pharmaceutical company that was trying to develop a new product. Reddy, along with his friend Prabhakar Rao, assessed that such products had mixed success, Reddy and Rao realised that if a new product (a drug) was a success/it may result in sales of 100 crore but if it is unsuccessful, the sales may be only 20 crore. They further assessed that a new drug was likely to be successful 50% of times.

Cost of launching the new drug was likely to be 50 crore. Now, Reddy and Rao were in a quandary whether the company should go ahead and market the drug. They contacted Raj Adduri, a common friend for advice. Adduri was of the opinion that given the risky nature of launch, it may be a better idea to test the market.

Rao and Reddy realised test marketing would cost 10 crore. Adduri told them the previous test meeting results have been unfavorable 70% of times and success rate of products favorably tested was 80%. Further, when test marketing results were unfavorable; the products have been successful 30% of the times.

90. How much profit can the company expect to earn, if it, launches the new drug (suppose there are no additional (costs)?
(a) 12 crore
(b) 10 crore
(c) 10.5 crore
(d) 11crore
(e) 11.5 crore

91. How much profit can the company expect to make, if the product is launched after favourable test marketing results (assume there are no additional costs)?
(a) 11.5 crore
(b) 10 crore
(c) 8.5 crore
(d) 13.8 crore
(e) 24 crore

92. What is the probability of product failure, if Reddy and Rao decides to test market?
(a) 0.21
(b) 0.35
(c) 0.14
(d) 0.28
(e) Cannot be computed

93. If Rao and Reddy decides to launch the product despite unfavorable test marketing, how much profit/loss can the company expect to earn?
(a) 13.2crore profit
(b) 36.8 crore profit
(c) 46.8 crore loss
(d) 16 crore loss
(e) 10 crore loss

Direction (Q. Nos. 94-96) *Read the following caselet carefully and answer the questions that follow.* **XAT 2014**

Ms Banerjee, class teacher for 12th standard, wants to send teams (based on past performance) of three students each to District, State, National and International competition in Mathematics. Till now, every student of the class has appeared in 100 school level tests. The students had following distribution of of marks in the tests, in terms of 'average' and 'number of times a student scored cent per cent marks'.

Student	Average	Number of times a student scores cent-per cent
1	70	7
2	60	15
3	65	8
4	70	1
5	65	6
6	65	10
7	65	4
8	60	12
9	65	3
10	60	8
11	70	1
12	65	6
13	70	2
14	60	20
15	65	5

Ms Banerjee has carefully studied chances of her school winning each of the competitions. Based on in depth calculations, she realised that her school is quite likely to win district level competition but has low chances of winning the international competition. She listed down the following probabilities of wins for different competitions, Prize was highest for international competition and lowest for district level, competition (in that order).

Competition	District	State	National	International
Probability of win	0.95	0.6	0.1	0.05

All the students are studying in the school for last 12 yr. She wanted to select the best team for all four competitions (Ms Banerjee had no other information to select students).

94. Which of three members should form the team for the international competition?
(a) 4, 11, 14 (b) 2, 8, 14 (c) 1, 6, 1.2 (d) 13, 14, 15
(e) 1, 3, 4

95. Which of the following members should constitute the team for the district level competition?
(a) 4, 11, 14 (b) 1, 4, 11 (c) 4,5, 6 (d) 4, 11, 13
(e) Any team can win the competition

96. Ms Banerjee has to select the team for national competition after she has selected the team for international competition. A student selected for international competition can not be a part of national competition.
Which is the best team for the national competition?
(a) 1, 7, 4 (b) 8, 9, 10
(c) 2, 8, 14 (d) 3, 6, 1
(e) Any of remaining students, as it would not matter

Direction (Q. Nos. 97-99) *Read the following caselet carefully and answer the questions that follow.* **XAT 2014**

97. The main issues of interpretation arising from the work of professionally trained anthropologists are that they are late in colonial/post-colonial trajectories, because professional training shapes their interpretations. However, within field of interest and training, their works are most thorough and systematic. The best, conclusion drawn from the above paragraph is analogous to
(a) Heisenberg uncertainty principle, which states that speed and position cannot be determined simultaneously
(b) cultural relativism, which states that two or more than two cultures cannot be compared
(c) personal relativism, which states that one should not study anthropological phenomenon for personal gains
(d) conclusive relativism, which states that anthropologists should not **knowingly colour their findings**
(e) communicative relativism, which states that Anthropologists should not be selective in communicating their findings

98. Consider merit pay for teachers. Schools face constant pressure to change their management approaches to improve performance, which is usually assessed by standardised reading, Maths and Science scores. In most schools, teachers' pay is determined by seniority, years of total teaching experience and credentials. Pay is rarely based on performance, which is contrary to the belief among parents and private sector. Parents and business leaders lament that there are no carrots/sticks used to motivate teachers. Consequently, there has been greater push to implement some form of merit pay to improve motivation.

Which of the following statements will disprove the claim of the parents and business leaders?

(a) A recent study suggested that teachers are self-motivated,
(b) Teachers are largely motivated, by financial incentives; so pay for performance will induce, greater and more effective effort
(c) Learning cannot be measured reliably and accurately hy a test given once a year
(d) Teaching is a solo-activity, there is a little interdependence with other co-curricular and extra curricular activities in school
(e) To error is human and hence stick should be used to reduce errors

99. Read the following newspaper report

In a new study by Harvard School of Public Health (HSPH), researchers explored how caffeine can serve us a "mild anti-depressant". They concluded that "drinking several cups of coffee daily appears to reduce the risk of suicide". Data pulled in from three large studies in the US showed that the suicide risk of those who drank two to four cups of caffeinated coffee a day was about half of those who drank decaffeinated coffee or very little or no coffee.

In the studies, a respondent's caffeine consumption was assessed every four years through a questionnaire. The respondents were all adults and the study was published online. The authors, however, cautioned the public from increasing coffee intake as it could result in 'unpleasant side effects', 'Overall, our results suggest that there is little further benefit for consumption above two to three cups/day or 400 mg of caffeine/day/ wrote the researchers. The authors observed that there was no major difference in sucide risk for adults who drank two to three cups a day from those who drank four cups or more.

Which of the following shaped graph would best capture the above paragraph (X-axis represents 'coffee intake' and Y-axis represents 'coffee intake' and Y-axis represents 'suicidal tendency')?

(a) A straight line
(b) Saw tooth curve
(c) S shaped curve
(d) U shaped curve
(e) L shaped curve

Answers with Explanations

Base Level

1. (*e*) Abhinav Ghosal does not satisfy condition (iii) but satisfies condition (2).

2. (*d*) Sohan Awasthi does not satisfy condition (i) but he has secured 68% marks in PG, so his case is to be referred to the GM-personnel.

3. (*b*) Namita Jaiswal satisfies all conditions, So she is to be selected.

4. (*a*) Is not clear about personal interview, So data is insufficient to take a decision.

5. (*c*) Anuj Soren does not satisfy condition (i) and his marks are also less than 65% in PG. So, he is not selected.

6. (*c*) Rajiv Sharma does not satisfy condition (iii) as he lacks in knowledge of programming. So, his application is referred to Managing Director.

7. (*a*) Chandrashekhar Azad satisfies all the given conditions, so his application is to be accepted.

8. (*b*) Suman does not satisfy condition (iv) as her age is more than the required 32 yr and she has not appeared in the test conducted by the authority of factory which is mandatory for those who does not satisfy condition (iv). So, her application is not to be accepted.

9. (*d*) Krishan Semwal does not satisfy condition (iv) but satisfies condition (2), so his case is to be referred to the Vice President of factory.

10. (*e*) No information is given about condition (iii).

11. (*b*) Vinod Shah does not satisfy condition (i), which is very important, so his application is not to be accepted.

12. (*b*) Rina Kulkarni does not satisfy condition (iv) as her age is more than the required 28 yr. So, her application is not to be accepted.

13. (*b*) Punam Jaiswal does not satisfy condition (iii), so her application is not to be accepted.

14. (*c*) Hemant Nehra does not satisfy condition (iii) but satisfies condition (1), so his case is to referred to the Managing Director of the factory.

15. (*e*) Vishnu Nagar does not satisfy condition (i) but satisfies condition (3), so his case is referred to the President of the company.

16. (*a*) TCA Raghavan does not satisfy condition (iv), so he is to be rejected.

17. (*d*) Mohan Rakesh does not satisfy condition (iii) but satisfies condition (b), so he should be referred to the Vice-President of the company.

18. (*a*) Chhapra Sanyal does not satisfy condition (i) and (3), so he is to be rejected.

19. (*b*) Achala Bhaumik satisfies all the given conditions, so she is to be selected.

20. (*a*) Hemwati Sachdev does not satisfy condition (i), so she is to be rejected.

21. (*a*) Krishna Prasad has not completed 26 yr of age as required in condition (i), so he is to be rejected.

22. (*b*) Prakash has less than 60% in graduation but more than 60% in PG. So, his case is to be referred to the GM-Advances.

23. (*e*) Amit Narayan fulfils all requirements, so he is to be selected.

24. (*a*) Shobha Gupta does not fulfil condition (ii) but fulfils condition (2). So his case referred to Executive Director.

25. (*c*) Data insufficient (experience in advances department is not clear).

26. (*d*) Sudha Mehrotra has less than 50% marks in the interview. So, she is not to be selected.

27. (*c*) No information is given about condition (ii), so no decision can be taken in this case.

28. (*b*) Australia does not satisfy condition (iv), so its army cannot be selected.

29. (*a*) France satisfies all the given conditions, so its army is to be selected.

30. (*c*) No information is given about condition (iv), so no decision can be taken in this case.

31. (*d*) No information is given about the army strength of China, which is condition (ii) but satisfies alternative condition (i), so its case should be referred to the Secretary, UNO.

32. (*c*) No information is given about condition (iv) and alternative condition (2) is not clear, as it is not given that how many joint defence exercises were conducted with other countries, which has acquired nuclear power. So, no decision can be taken in this case.

33. (*b*) Pakistan does not satisfy condition (ii), so its army cannot be selected.

Solution (Q. Nos. 34-43)

Students	Conditions			
	(i)	(ii) or (A)	(iii)	(iv) or (B)
Shruti	✓	✓	✓	✗
Milind	✓	✓	✗	✓
Prakash	✗	✓	✓	✓
Anil	✓	✓	✓	✓
Nikhil	✓	✗	✓	✓
Maria	✓	✗	✓	✓
Deepa	✓	✓	✓	✓
Sudhir	✓	✓	✓	✓
Anandi	✓	✓	✓	✓
Ravi	✓	✓	✓	✓

34. (*e*) Condition (iv) missing.

35. (*e*) Nothing is given about the entrance examination marks. So, data is inadequate to take a decision.

36. (*e*) **37.** (*a*)

38. (*b*) Nikhil does not fulfil condition (ii) because he has done part time course.

39. (*e*) **40.** (*a*)

41.(*d*) **42.** (*a*)

43. (*d*)

44. (*c*) Ashok Sardesai satisfies all the given conditions, so he is to be selected.

45. (*b*) Shashikala does not satisfy condition (i), so her case is be referred to the external committee of experts.

46. (*c*) Rajshekar does not satisfy condition (ii)and(2), so he is not to be selected.

47. (*e*) No information is given about the age of Lalita which is condition (iv), so no decision can be taken in this case.

48. (*d*) Himanshu has not completed his MBA till 01-05-2006, so he is not to be selected.

49. (*b*) Niharika Chawla satisfies all the conditions except (v), so she is to be selected.

50. (*a*) Swatika Gupta does not satisfy condition (iv) and (v), so she is not to be selected.

51. (*a*) Age of Amisha Patel is not given, which is very essential, so she is not to be selected.

52. (*a*) Age of Shreya Singh is not given, which is very essential, so she is not to be selected.

53. (*c*) Akansha Mathur does not satisfy condition (ii) but she satisfies condition (2), so her case is referred to the Chairman.

54. (*b*) Rohit Sen satisfies all the given conditions, so he is to be selected.

Solution (Q. Nos. 55-64)

Candidates	Conditions						
	(i)	(ii) or (b)		(iii)	(iv) or (a)		(v)
Arnab Behera	✓	✓	–	✓	✓	–	✓
Neeta Ghosal	✓	✓	–	✗	✓	–	✓
Sudesh Sarkar	✓	✗	✓	✓	✓	–	✓
Sudha Naik	✓	✗	✓	✓	✓	–	✓
Sunita Jaiswal	✗	✓	–	✓	✓	–	✓
Nayan Dastur	✓	✓	–	✓	✓	–	✓
Sunil Kamath	✓	✓	–	✓	✗	✓	✓
Md. Yusuf	✓	✓	–	✓	✓	–	✓
Navind Ghosh	✓	✗	–	✓	✓	–	✗
Avinash Sargota	✓	✓	–	✓	✗	✓	✓

55. (*a*) Arnab Behera fulfils all conditions, so he is to be selected.

56. (*e*) Neeta Ghosal has done PG in management but stream is not clear (either in finance or marketing etc.) So, given data is insufficient.

57. (*c*) Sudesh Sarkar does not fulfil condition (ii) but fulfils (2) So, his case is to be referred to the GM-Marketing.

58. (*c*) Sudha Naik does not fulfil condition (ii) but she follows(2). So, her case is to be referred to the GM-Marketing.

59. (*d*) Sunita Jaiswal does not fulfil condition (i) so, she is not to be selected.

60. (*a*) Nayan Dastur fulfils all the conditions, so he is to be selected.

61. (*b*) Sunil Kamath does not fulfil condition (iv) or fulfils (1). so his case is to be referred to the Head-marketing division.

62. (*a*) Md. Yusful fulfils all conditions, so he is to be selected.

63. (*d*) Navind Ghosh does not fulfil condition (ii) and (v), so he is not to be selected.

64. (*b*) Avinash Sargota does not fulfil condition (iv)) Fulfils so (1) his case is to be referred to Head-marketing division.

Solution (Q. Nos. 65-74)

Candidates	Conditions							
	(i) or (a)		(ii)	(iii)	(iv)	(v) or (b)		(vi)
Susan D'Souza	✓	–	✓	✓	✓	✓	–	✓
Archana Sahu	✓	–	✓	✓	✓	✗	–	✓
Atual Garg	✓	–	✓	✗	✓	✓	–	✓
Meena Gogoi	✓	–	✓	✓	✓	–	✓	✓
Sudhakar Bagchi	–	✓	✓	✓	✓	✓	–	✓
Ashok Pradhan	✓	–	✓	✓	✓	✓	–	NG
Antara Ghosh	✓	–	✓	✓	✓	✓	–	✓
Naveen Malhotra	–	✓	✓	✓	✓	✓	–	✓
Abhinav Shukla	✓	–	✓	✓	✓	–	✓	✓
Suresh Das	✓	–	NG	✓	✓	✓	–	✓

Here, NG means data not given.

65. (*a*) Susan D'Souza fulfils all conditions, so she is to be selected.

66. (*b*) Archana Sahu does not fulfil condition (v) or (2), so she is not to be selected.

67. (*b*) Atul Garg does not fulfil condition (iii) so he is not to be selected.

68. (*d*) Meena Gogoi fulfils condition (2) instead of (v), so her case is to be referred to the Chairman.

69. (*c*) Sudhakar Bagchi fulfils condition (1), so his case is to referred to the ED.

70. (*e*) Ashok Pradhan's condition (vi) is not clear, so data is insufficient.

71. (*a*) Antara Ghosh fulfils all conditions, so she is to be selected.

72. (*c*) Navin Malhotra fulfils condition (1), so his case is to be referred to the ED.

73. (*d*) Abhinav Shukla fulfils condition (2), so his case is to be referred to the Chairman.

74. (*e*) Suresh Das' XII class marks are not clear. So, data is insufficient.

Solution (Q. Nos. 75-79)

Candidates	Conditions								
	(i)	(ii)	(iii) or (1)		(iv)	(v)	(vi)	(vii) or (2)	
Sohan	NG	✓	✓	–	✓	✓	✓	✓	–
Neeta	✓	✓	✓	–	✓	✓	✓	✓	–
Arindam	✓	NG	✓	–	✓	✓	✓	✓	–
Keshav	✓	✓	–	✓	✓	✓	✓	✓	–
Neha	✓	✓	✓	–	✓	✓	✓	–	✓

Here, NG means data not given.

75. (*a*) Condition (i) is not cleared, so data inadequate.

76. (*d*) Neeta Jaiswal fulfils all conditions, so she is to be selected.

77. (*a*) Arindam Ghosh's condition (ii) is not cleared, so data is insufficient.

78. (*b*) Keshav Vora fulfils conditions (1), so his case is to be referred to VP-Recruitment.

79. (*c*) Neha Salve fulfils condition (2), so her case is to be referred to President Recruitment.

Solution (Q. Nos. 80-84)

Candidates	Conditions						
	(i)	(ii) or (2)		(iii)	(iv) or (1)		(v)
Suresh	✓	✓	–	NG	✓	–	✓
Sudha	✓	–	✓	✓	✓	–	✓
Divya	✗	✓	–	✓	✓	–	✓
Navin	✓	✓	–	✓	✓	–	✓
Varun	✓	✓	–	✓	–	✓	✓

Here, NG means data not given.

80. (*c*) Suresh Mehta's condition (iii) is not given, so data is insufficient to take decision.

81. (*d*) Sudha Gopalan fulfils condition (2) instead of condition (ii), so her case is to be referred to Vice President- Marketing.

82. (*a*) Divya Kohli does not fulfil condition (i), so she is not to be selected.

83. (*b*) Navin Marathe fulfils all conditions, so he is to be selected.

84. (*e*) Varun Malhotra fulfils condition (1) instead of (iv), so his case is to be referred to GM-Marketing.

Solution (Q. Nos. 85-94)

Candidates	Conditions							
	(i)	(ii) or (1)		(iii) or (2)		(iv)	(v)	(vi)
Shamika	✓	✓	–	–	✓	✓	✓	✓
Abhijit	✓	–	✓	✓	–	✓	✓	✓
Ankita	✓	✓	–	✓	–	✓	✓	✓
Manisha	✓	✗	–	✓	–	✓	✓	✓
Nikita	NG	✓	–	✓	–	✓	✓	✓
Rajesh	✓	–	✓	✓	–	✓	✓	✓
Jyotika	✗	✓	–	✓	–	✓	✓	✓
Sujay	✓	✓	–	–	✓	✓	✓	✓
Vivek	✓	✓	–	✓	–	✓	✓	✓
Nandan	NG	✓	–	✓	–	✓	✓	✓

Here, NG means data not given.

85. (*e*) Shamika fulfils condition (2) instead of (iii), so her case may be referred to the General Manager (Recruitment) of the company.

86. (*d*) Abhijit fulfils condition (1) instead of (ii), so his case may be referred to the Vice-President of the company.

87. (*a*) Ankita fulfils all conditions, so she is to be selected.

88. (*b*) Manisha does not fulfil condition (ii) so, she is not to be selected.

89. (*c*) Nikita's SSC examination and percentage is not given, so data is inadequate to take a decision.

90. (*d*) Rajesh Chavan fulfils condition (1) instead of (ii), so his case may be referred to the Vice-President of the company.

91. (*b*) Jyotika Basu does not fulfil condition (i), so she is not to be selected.

92. (*e*) Sujay Chaudhary fulfils condition (2) instead of (iii), so his case is to be referred to the General Manager (Recruitment) of the company.

93. (*a*) Vivek fulfils all conditions, so he is to be selected.

94. (*c*) Nandan Salva's information about SSC is not given, so data is inadequate to take a decision.

Solution (Q. Nos. 95-104)

Candidates	Conditions					
	(i)	(ii) or (1)		(ii) or (2)		(iv)
Ashutosh	✓	✓	–	–	✓	✓
Rajni	✓	✓	–	✓	–	✓
Raj Grover	✓	✗	–	✓	–	✓
Shamika	✓	–	✓	✓	–	✓
Jasmine	✓	–	✓	NG	✓	✓
Shyamala	✓	✓	–	✓	–	✓
Anubhav	✓	✓	–	✓	–	✓
Manish	✓	✓	–	✓	–	✓
Harish	✓	✓	–	–	✓	✓
Vandana	✗	✓	–	✓	–	✓

Here, NG means data not given.

95. (*b*) Ashutosh fulfils condition (2) instead of (iii) so his case may be referred to the Vice-President (VP).

96. (*c*) Rajni fulfils all conditions, so she is to be selected.

97. (*e*) Raj Grover does not fulfil condition (ii) or (1), so he is not to be selected.

98. (*a*) Shamika Gupta fulfils condition (1) instead of (ii), so her case may be referred to the Executive Director (ED).

99. (*d*) Data insufficient.

100. (*c*) Shyamala fulfils all conditions, so she is to be selected.

101. (*c*) Anubhav Gokhale fulfils all conditions, so he is to be selected.

102. (*c*) Manish Chaudhary fulfils all conditions so he is to be selected.

103. (*b*) Harish Vora fulfils condition (2) instead of (iii), so his case may be referred to the VP.

104. (*e*) Vandana Bhave does not fulfil condition (i), so she is not to be selected.

Solution (Q. Nos. 105-109)

Candidates	Conditions							
	(i)	(ii) or (1)		(iii)	(iv)	(v) or (2)		(vi)
Meenal	✓	✗	–	✓	✓	✓	–	✓
Avinash	–	✓	–	✓	✓	✗	✓	✓
Sanjay	✓	✓	–	✓	✓	–	✓	✓
Rohan	✓	✓	–	✓	✗	✓	–	✓
Nandita	✓	✓	–	✓	✓	✓	–	✓

105. (*e*) Meenal Soni does not fulfil condition (ii), so she is not to be selected.

106. (*c*) Marks of Avinash Chavan at graduate level is not given. So, no decision can be taken in this case.

107. (*b*) Sujay does not fulfil condition (v) but fulfil condition (2), so his case is to be referred to the head of Marketing department.

108. (*e*) Rohan Bhalla does not fulfil conditions (iv), so she is not to be selected.

109. (*d*) Nandita Sharma fulfils all the given conditions, so she is to be selected.

Solution (Q. Nos. 110-119)

Candidates	Conditions						
	(i) or (1)		(ii)	(iii) or (2)		(iv)	(v)
Abhishek	–	✓	✓	✓	–	✓	✓
Mangesh	✓	–	✗	✓	–	✓	✓
Leela	✓	–	✓	–	✓	✓	✓
Manjusha	✓	–	NG	✓	–	✓	✓
Niranjan	✓	–	✓	✓	–	✓	✓

Here, NG means data not given.

110. (*d*) Abhishek Neve does not fulfil condition (i) but he fulfils condition (i), so his case is to be referred to the Vice President of the company.

111. (*b*) Mangesh does not fulfil condition (ii), so he is not to be selected.

112. (*e*) Leela Mehra does not fulfil condition (iii), but fulfill condition (2), so his case is to be referred to the Managing Director.

113. (*c*) It is not given that Manjusha has done her Post Graduation in Marketing-Management or Public Relations. So, no decision can be taken in this case.

114. (*a*) Nirajan fulfils all the given conditions. So, he is to be selected.

115. (*c*) Umesh Choksi,

(i) Age (on 1.11.2011)—21 yr 11 months and 2 days
(ii) Marks in Graduation (B.Com.) — 55%
(iii) Experience in Account Department— 3 yr
(iv) Marks in Selection Process — 65%
So,Umesh Choksi is to be selected.

116. (*d*) Pratibha Kale

(i) Age (on 1.11.2011)—23 yr 4 months and 25 days
(ii) Marks in graduation (B.Com.)— 60%
(iii) Experience in Account Department— 3 yr
(iv) Marks in Selection Process— 49%
So, Pratibha Kale is not to be selected.

117. (*c*) Arun Patil,

(i) Age (on 1.11.2011)— 23 yr 3 months and 19 days
(ii) Marks in Graduation (B.Com.) — 55%
(iii) Experience in Account Department— 4 yr
(iv) Marks in Selection Process — 50%
So, Arun Patil is to be selected.

118. (*a*) Prabha Dixit,

(i) Age (on 1.11.2011)— 26 yr 6 months and 13 days
(ii) Marks in Graduation (B.Com.)— 60%
(iii) Experience in Account Department— 5 yr
(iv) Marks in Selection Process— 55%
So, the case is to be referred to GM-Accounts.

119. (*b*) Amul Verma,

(i) Age (on 1.11.2011)—24 yr 9 months and 29 days
(ii) Marks in Graduation (B.Com.)—50%
(iii) Experience in Account Department—4 yr
(iv) Marks in Selection Process—60%

So, in case is to be referred to VP-Accounts.

Advanced Level

1. (*b*) There are 6 possible answers for G type courses (i.e. Only G + QG + JG + QJG) but Scenario 2 as well as scenario 6 gives the same value (15). Thus, possible answer for G-type electives would be 5.
   So, the correct option would be (b).

2. (*c*) Based on their preferences, Simran should take 5JG and 2 only J-type courses and Raj would take 5 JG and 2 only G-type courses. They would have 5 common courses.
   Hence, the correct option would be (c).

3. (*a*) Vijay can take a combination of 7 courses from JG and only J-type 2 only G-type courses and 5QG type courses. So, they can completely avoid each other.
   So, option (a) would be the correct answer.

4. (*a*) Only option (a) reduces Arbit's enthusiasm all others clearly favour his decision to go ahead with the investment decision.
   Statement (b) is in favour of Mr. Arbit, as technology investments give better results → green signal.
   Statement (c) is also in favour of Mr. Arbit technology invest reduces cost → green signal.
   Statements (d) and (e) also are in favour of Mr. Arbit 'risk controlled/risks have to be taken'- green signal.

5. (*c*) Option (c) is the only answer which strongly hints about the potential success of this technology and low chances of failure (roughly 1 out of 6 cases, i.e. 15%)

6. (*b*)

Year	Forgone earnings of Arbit	Forgone earnings of Boring	Difference	Amount at the end of five years
1.	100000	100000	0	0
2.	100000	100000	0	0
3.	100000	0	100000	$100000 \times (1.1)^2$
4.	100000	0	100000	$100000 \times (1.1)$
5.	100000	0	100000	100000
			Total	331000

7. (*d*) Main passage

	Patented < 50%	Generic > 50%
India < 50%	Patented India	Generic India
Foreign > 50%	Patented Foreign	Generic Foreign

Option (a) Not possible

	Patented < 50%	Generic > 50%
India < 50%	43% (given)	< 7%
Foreign > 50%	< 7%	> 43%

Option (b) Not possible

	Patented < 50%	Generic > 50%
India < 50%	< 24%	≥ 50% generic (foreign)
Foreign > 50%	> 50% - generic (foreign)	> 24% (given)

Option (c) Patented drugs in India must be < 50% (as total sales in India is < 50%).

Option (d)

	Patented < 50%	Generic > 50%
India < 50%	29%(given)	< 21%
Foreign > 50%	< 21%	> 29%

Option (e) Generic drugs in India must be < 50% (as total sales in India is < 50%).

Hence, option (d) is the correct answer.

8. (*a*) Statement I is the best option if we consider the long term prospect of the business. Statement II is clearly unethical actions might have some short term benefits but are least appropriate for long term.
   Statement III can boost performance in the near future. Statement IV might also have a negative connotation if we assume that LSP is recruiting more employees to sell cough syrup in the rural areas.
   Thus, Statement I should come first if we consider 'to improve business in the long run'. Moreover, Statement II should not come before Statement I as well as III from the long run perspective. Hence, option (a) is the correct answer from the available choices.

9. (*b*) Option (b) is the correct answer as it is suitable to all stakeholders. Organisation gets the work done. Mr. Jose and Mrs. Jose stay together and Mrs. Jose does not lose her job.

10. (*e*) Statement III is a valid option as she is requesting Mr. Khan to find a job in India. If he agrees and is able to find a suitable job, they can stay together without Mrs. Khan sacrificing her career. Thus, work life balance might be maintained (this can be immediately requested by Mrs. Khan).
    Statement V is a valid action as she can always make a request, if it is granted the couple would be together. Thus, work life balance can be maintained like Statement III. Further it would be viable follow up (sequential) action, if Statement III does not work.
    Hence, option (e) (which combine III and V) is the best possible sequential option.

11. (*c*) Statement I states that awareness is low and hence it conveys that using organic vegetables in Panipat might be a premature step.

Statement III says that a few restaurants are already using organic vegetables but the argument here is that using organic vegetables is not going to be the unique selling point for them. Hence, they might not get any advantage by using organic vegetables. Why change something that is already doing well?

Statement IV implicitly indicates that Panipat customers might not accept high prices of dishes (due to uses of organic vegetables). Use of organic vegetables might reduce the projects.

Statement V states that if premium vegetables are not available then it might not be convenient to procure them on a regular basis. This is increase the complexity.

Hence option (c) is the best answer.

12. (*d*) First businessman says that customers are very different. That indicates business at Panipat should be somehow different from Cannaught place.

Second business says that customers are happy with Ram, which means identity of business in Panipat should be ideally tied with 'Ram'.

Third businessman says that ingredients at Panipat are not same as Cannaught place but taste is good. It indicates both business have their own advantages and should be treated differently.

Fourth businessman says that in future customers at both the places might have similar tastes. In other words, it suggests that in future the two business models might be alike.

Options (a) and (e) may not be viable as Kishan is not interested to go to Panipat (as mentioned in passage).

Option (b) is not the correct answer (as per passage 'giving a freehand to Ram might have long term negative consequences').

Option (c) may not be best as Panipat customers like Ram (businessman 2).

Option (d) is the only answer that can satisfy the opinions expressed by all four businessman.

13. (*b*) Option (b) is the best option because Mohan can derive Panipat branch and probably Kishan can handle Delhi branch or, Ram can join Kishan.

Solution (Q. Nos. 14-28)

Candidates	Conditions						
	(i)	(ii) or (1)		(iii) or (2)		(iv)	(v)
Pranab	✓	✓	–	✓	–	✓	✓
Sheetal	✓	✓	–	✓	–	NG	✓
Prabir	✓	–	✓	✓	–	✓	✓
Shailesh	✓	✓	–	–	✓	✓	✓
Navin	✓	✓	–	✓	–	✓	✗
Meera	✗	✓	–	✓	–	✓	✓
Akash	✓	–	✓	✓	–	✓	✓
Shekhar	✓	✓	–	✓	–	✓	✓
Sunetra	✓	✓	–	✓	–	✓	✓
Mohit	✓	✓	–	–	✓	✓	✓

Here, NG means data not given.

14. (*a*) Pranab Ghosh fulfils all the conditions, so he is to be selected.

15. (*c*) Nothing is said for Sheetal Jha about the condition (iv), So, the data provided is not adequate to take decision.

16. (*d*) Prabir Sengupta does not satisfy the condition (ii) but he fulfils the condition (1). So, his case is to be referred to Executive Director.

17. (*e*) Shailesh Kumar does not satisfy the condition (iii) but he fulfils the condition (2). So, his case is to be referred to Chairman.

18. (*b*) Navin Chopra does not satisfy the condition (v) Hence, he is not to be selected.

19. (*b*) Meera Kulkarani is younger than 40 yr. Hence, she is not to be selected.

20. (*d*) Akash Shastri does not satisfy the condition (ii) but he fulfils the condition (1). So, his case is to be referred to Executive Director.

21. (*a*) Shekhar Jena fulfils all the conditions, so he is to be selected.

22. (*a*) Sunetra Govil fulfils all the conditions, so she is to be selected.

23. (*e*) Mohit Saxena does not satisfy the condition (iii) but he fulfils the condition(2). So, his case is to be referred to Chairman.

24. (a) Film 'Dainandini' fulfils all the given conditions, so it is to be selected.

25. (*d*) Director of the film 'Bhadrasalam' was a student of Satyajit Ray Film and Television Institute for 3 yr, but it not clear that the had completed the course of 3 yr or not, but it can be assumed that he had completed at least 1 yr course. So, the film is to be kept stand-bye.

26. (*b*) The film 'Ek Bar Achanak' was submitted to NFDC after the last date, so it is not be selected.

27. (*b*) Kamaljeet does not fulfil criteria 3 and there is no any alternative of this criteria. So, Kamlajeet is not admitted.

28. (*d*) Gaurav satisfies all the conditions except condition no. 2 but he fulfils the alternative of this condition i.e., experience of 10 yr. So, Gaurav is referred to the chairman-admission.

Solution (Q. Nos. 29-38)

Candidates	Conditions						
	(i)	(ii)	(iii) or (1)		(iv)	(v) or (2)	
Nidhi	✓	✓	✓	–	✗	✓	–
Navin	✓	✓	✓	–	✓	–	✓
Sabina	✓	✓	–	✓	✓	✓	–
Manoj	✓	✓	✓	–	✓	✓	–
Varsha	✓	✗	✓	–	✓	✓	–
Utpal	✓	✓	✓	–	✓	✓	–
Anindita	✓	✓	NG	–	✓	✓	–
Samir	✓	✓	✓	–	✓	✓	–
Nimisha	✓	✓	–	✓	✓	✓	–
Sadashiv	✓	✓	✓	–	✓	–	✓

Here, NG means data not given.

29. (*b*) Nidhi Agarwal does not fulfil condition (iv), so she is not to be selected.

30. (*d*) Navin Desai fulfils condition (2) instead of condition (v), so his case is to be referred to VP-Marketing.

31. (*c*) Sabina Handa fulfils condition (1) instead of condition (iii), so her case is to be referred to GM-Marketing.

32. (*a*) Manoj Malhotra fulfils all the given conditions, so he is to be selected.

33. (*b*) Varsha Akolkar does not fulfil condition (ii), so she is not to be selected.

34. (*a*) Utpal Goswami fulfill all the given conditions, so he is to be selected.

35. (*e*) It is not clear that the experience of Anindita Ghosh is in Marketing division or not. So, no decision can be taken in this case.

36. (*a*) Samir Phukan fulfils all the given conditions, so he is to be selected.

37. (*c*) Nimisha Patel fulfils condition (1) instead of condition (iii), so her case is to be referred to GM-Marketing.

38. (*d*) Sadashiv Ghatge fulfils condition (2) instead of condition (v), so his case is to be referred to VP-Marketing.

Solutions (Q. Nos. 39-48)

Candidates	Conditions						
	(i)	(ii)	(iii) or (1)		(iv) or (2)		(v)
Meena	✓	✓	✓	–	–	✓	✓
Ketan	✓	✓	✓	–	✓	–	✗
Anant	✓	✓	✓	–	✓	–	✓
Mohan	✓	✓	✓	–	✓	–	NG
Gopal	✓	✓	✗	–	✓	–	✓
Arun	✓	✓	–	✓	✓	–	✓
Asha	✓	✓	✓	–	✓	–	✓
Sudha	✓	✓	✓	–	–	✓	✓
Amit	✓	✓	–	✓	✓	–	✓
Navin	✗	✓	–	✓	✓	–	✓

Here, NG means data not given.

39. (*e*) Meena Srivastava fulfils condition (2) instead of condition (iv), so her case is to be referred to the President-Personnel.

40. (*b*) Ketan Desai does not fulfils condition (v), so he is not to be selected.

41. (*a*) Anant Joshi fulfils all the given conditions, so he is to be selected.

42. (*c*) Marks of Mohan Bajpai in selection process is not given, so no decision can be taken in this case.

43. (*b*) Gopal Sharma does not fulfil condition (iii), so he is not to be selected.

44. (*d*) Arun Vohra fulfils condition (1) instead of condition (iii), so his case is to be referred to the Director-Personnel.

45. (*a*) Asha Dhar fulfils all the given conditions, so she is to be selected.

46. (*e*) Sudha Ghosal fulfils condition (2) instead of condition (iv), so her case is to be referred to the President-Personnel.

47. (*d*) Amit Saxena fulfils condition (1) instead of condition (iii), so his case is to be referred to the Director-Personnel.

48. (*b*) Navin Das does not fulfil condition (i), so he is not to be selected.

Solutions (Q. Nos. 49-53)

Candidates	Conditions						
	(i)	(ii) or (1)		(iii)	(iv) or (2)		(v)
Shreyas	✓	✓	–	✓	✓	–	✓
Archit	✓	✓	–	✓	✓	–	✓
Nisha	✓	–	✓	✓	✓	–	✓
Ankita	✓	✗	–	✓	✓	–	✓
Subodh	✓	✓	–	✓	–	✓	✓

39. (*b*) Shreyas Ingle fulfils all the conditions, so he is to be selected.

50. (*b*) Archit Pradhan fulfils all the conditions, so he is to be selected.

51. (*d*) Nisha Awasthi does not fulfil condition (ii) but she fulfils condition (1) (67% in Post Graduate in Marketing-Management), so her case is to be referred to GM-Marketing.

52. (*c*) Ankita Bhave does not fulfil condition (ii) (less than 55% marks in Graduation). So, her case is not to be selected.

53. (*e*) Subodh Saxena has worked as DMM, so his case is to be referred to CGM-Marketing.

Solution (Q. Nos. 54-63)

Candidates	Conditions								
	(i) or (1)		(ii) or (2)		(iii) or (3)		(iv) (a)	(iv) (b)	(iv) (c)
Satyaprakash	✓	–	✓	–	–	✓	✓	✓	✓
Rakesh	✓	–	–	✓	✓	–	✓	✓	✓
Amresh	–	✓	✓	–	✓	–	✓	✓	✓
Abhishek	✓	–	✓	–	✓	–	NG	✓	✓
Bhavesh	✓	–	✓	–	✓	–	✗	✓	✓
Himanshu	✓	–	–	✓	✓	–	✓	✓	✓
Prabhat	✓	–	–	✓	✓	–	✓	✓	✓
Bhuvan	–	✓	–	✓	✗	–	✓	✓	✓
Vishal	✓	–	–	✓	NG	–	✓	✓	✓
Bankim	NG	–	NG	–	✓	–	✓	✓	✓

Here, NG means data not given.

54. (*a*) Satyaprakash is an ex-serviceman. He fulfils all the other conditions except age. So, he is to be selected but not from the priority list.

55. (*c*) Rakesh K Yadav fulfils condition (2) instead of condition (ii), so he should be selected from the priority list.

56. (*d*) Amresh Kumar fulfils condition (1) instead of condition (i), so he is to be considered later for appointment.

57. (*e*) The region of Abhishek Gupta is not given, so no decision can be taken in this case.

58. (*b*) Bhavesh Kr Jha does not fulfils condition (iv) (a), so he is not to be selected.

59. (*c*) Himanshu Rajoria fulfils condition (2) instead of condition (ii), so he should be selected from the priority list.

60. (*c*) Prabhat Ranjan fulfill condition (2) instead of condition (ii), so he should be selected from the priority list.

61. (*b*) Bhuvan Chandra does not fulfil condition (iii) and he is not an ex-serviceman, so he is not to be selected.

62. (*e*) Age of Vishal Choudhary is not given, so no decision can be taken in this case.

63. (*e*) Marks of Bankim Anand in matric is not given and it is also not given that he has a two year ITI certificate in Radio and TV/Electronics or not. So, no decision can be taken in this case.

Solution (Q. Nos. 64-66)

64. (*c*) Mahalaxmi Weaving centre satisfies all the mentioned criteria except but is a traditional handloom production unit. So, it may be referred to the Development commission Handloom.

65. (*a*) Since, Ramayana Enterprise satisfies all the mentioned criteria, so licence can be issued to it.

66. (*b*) Since, Hirabhai Handlooms does not have Grade A certificate, so licence not to be issued to it.

Solution (Q. Nos. 67-71)

Candidate	Conditions						
	(i)	(ii) or (a)		(iiii)	(iv) or (b)		(v)
Rita Bhatt	✓	✓	–	✓	✓	–	✓
Ashok Pradhan	✓	✓	–	✓	✗	✓	✓
Alok Verma	✗	✓	–	✓	✓	–	✓
Swapan Ghosh	✓	✗	✓	✓	✓	–	✓
Seema Behl	✓	✓	–	✓	✓	–	✓

67. (*e*) Rita Bhatt fulfills all the conditions. Hence, she is to be selected.

68. (*c*) Ashok Pradhan is not fulfill the condition (iv) but he fulfill the condition (b), Hence, his case is to be referred to President HR.

69. (*a*) Alok Verma is not fulfill the condition (i). Hence, he is not to be selected.

70. (*d*) Swapan Ghosh is not fulfill the condition (ii) but he fulfill the condition (a). Hence, his case is to be referred to GM-HR.

71. (*e*) Seema Behl fulfills all the conditions. Hence, she is to be selected.

72. (*a*) It is inferred from the passage that the bidding has been done according to government policies and in the benefit of the citizens. According to the minister, the loss that the media is talking about is national.

73. (*a*) According to the minister's view, it is correct to say that media should not act as a reporter, prosecutor and judge at the same time, as it may affect the goodwill and policies of the Government.

74. (*d*) Corporate managers, the minister and the head of the nation all are responsible for the issue, as the one who disburses the responsibility is held equally responsible to the one who is fulfilling it.

75. (*c*) Option (c) seems to be the only possible reason because both the instances happenned over the same period of time.

76. (*b*) Option (b) seems to be the correct answer in the last lines of the statement. It is mentioned "Despite the success of the treatment, most doctors have not embraced the surgery." This means that there is definitely some risk of life that's why doctors might not easily suggest Gastric bypass surgery and obesity is one of the leading contributors to heart disease and hypertion because from the starting line we can understand that it usually happens with obese people.

77. (*c*) To best describe the opinion, it is possible when many students sitting next to each other have the some incorrect answers for multiple choice. However, there can be small error in judgement.

78. (*c*) Among the six options only one is correct. So, rest five are wrong.

If they all mark same option at a time then probability of wrong answer is $\frac{1}{5}$.

As they all can mark 5 wrong choices,

Then, probability of same wrong answer

$$= \frac{1}{5} \times \frac{1}{5} \times \frac{1}{5} \times \frac{1}{5} \times \frac{1}{5} = \frac{1}{3125}$$

∴ Probability for same wrong answer for 4 consecutive questions $= 4 \times \frac{1}{3125} = \frac{4}{3125}$

79. (*c*) Statements numbered from I to VI are only necessary statements which, if taken together can give us the exact number of students from each sections.

80. (*d*) If we consider the condition or ranking given by second student, then he has got two ranks to be correct and two student correctly followed by their predecessor.

So, two positions are fixed among the five also they cannot follow the ranking given by first student. Then ranking can be Devroopa, Ankita, Bhagyashree, Chanchal and Esha.

So, Devroopa stood first in all.

81. (*a*) Only option (c) is the reason for the initial success of Shambu's hunger strike and rest I, II, IV are not responsible for Shambu's success, as it is clear from the passage that many people benefitted from corruption as the income lend of people was rising directly or indirectly i.e., the people were not very upset, only the media caught the opportunity to make the news.

82. (*b*) As, it is already described in the passage that Shambu was an old and illiterate man, therefore he was only able to use hunger strike as a weapon but for next time the same method failed.

83. (*a*) Vardarajan was not finding the work challenging enough as he has already achieved the best performance award.

84. (*c*) By giving Vardarajan a more challenging assignment he can be rejuvenated and start taking more interest in his work. Or by sending him for further training on decision making under-stress.

85. (*b*) If we considered that Vardarajan is right then the officers of the organisation should ensure that every member of the organisation is promoted objectively and with full transperancy.

86. (*e*) Both (c) and (d) options are correct, committee should be constituted for the investigation and appropriate action should be taken.

87. (*e*) Ask the SPC to resend the details of the short-listed students including their verified grades.

88. (*b*) To contact the college authorities to get the more information is the best choice because the accurate and detailed information can be only obtained from college only neither from any facebook friend or president of SPC.

89. (*d*) If I were in position of Vijaya, I will talk to the director and seek his opinion as it's the director who has given the responsibility to Vijaya for preparing report.

90. (*b*) Launching cost of the product = 50 crore

Expected sale when there is 50% probability of product being successful = 50% of sale on successful + 50% of sale being unsuccessful

$$= \frac{50}{100} \times 100 + \frac{50}{100} \times 20 = 50 + 10 = 60 \text{ crore}$$

∴ Total sale = 60 crore

Now, Profit = Sale – Launching cost = 60 – 50 = 10 crore

91. (*e*) After favourable test result

Success rate = 80%

∴ Unsuccessful rate = 100 – 80 = 20%

Now, total cost of product after test = 50 + 10 = 60 crore

∴ Total sale after test result = 80% sale on successful + 20% sale on unsuccessful

$$= \frac{80}{100} \times 100 + \frac{20}{100} \times 20 = 80 + 4 = 84 \text{ crore}$$

∴ Profit = Total sale – Total cost = 84 – 60 = 24 crore

92. (*b*) P (Product failure) = *P* (Product failure when test was favourable) + P (Product failure when test was unfavourable)

$$= [0.7 \times (1 - 0.8)] + [(1 - 0.7) \times (1 - 0.3)]$$
$$= (0.7 \times 0.2) + (0.3 \times 0.7) = 0.14 + 0.21 = 0.35$$

93. (*d*) Cost of product = 50 + 10 = 60 crore

Now, when unfavourable, the success rate is 30% and failure rate is 70% = 30% of 100 + 70% of 20

$$= \frac{30}{100} \times 100 + \frac{70}{100} \times 20 = 30 + 14 = 44 \text{ crore}$$

∴ Profit = 44 – 60 = – 16 crore (negative sign indicates loss)

94. (*b*) Since, the probability of winning at international level is minimum, so the best team would be the team having maximum of cent-per cent scores. There students scoring cent-per cent scores maximum number of times are 2, 6, 8, 14.

Now, looking at the option (b) 2, 8, 14 would from a team for international competition.

95. (*d*) Since, the probability of wining at district level is maximum i.e., 0.95, so the best team would be the team having maximum average but minimum of cent-per cent scores.

Hence 4, 11 and 13 would form a team for district level competition.

96. (*d*) Since, the probability of winning at national level is less so the students having maximum number of cent-per cent score will form a team other than those students who are already in team for international competition. Therefore, team for national competition contains 3, 6, and 1 students.

97. (*a*) In the given lines, the issue deals with the interpretation of works of anthropologists and the Heisenberg uncertainly principle is for predicting the position of electrons.

98. (*a*) Passage clearly suggests that money is a great motivator.

So, disproving is lying in option (a).

99. (*e*)

7

Assertion and Reason

***'Assertion'** means stating or claiming something forcefully and that of Reason is fact. So, a statement made with a strong belief on a **strong reason** is called an 'Assertion'.*

Questions on 'Assertion and Reason' are designed to judge the candidate's knowledge and ability to reason out correctly. Each question contains a statement called Assertion and an explanation called Reason. The candidate has to establish whether the reason is an opt explanation of the assertion. The statement or assertion can be from the field of History, Geography, Science, Information Technology or any latest development from major streams. Following examples will describe the type of these questions.

Solved Examples

Direction (Examples 1-5) *In each of the questions given below, there are two statements labelled as Assertion (A) and Reason (R).*

Give answer

(a) if both (A) and (R) are true and (R) is the correct explanation of (A)
(b) if both (A) and (R) are true but (R) is not the correct explanation of (A)
(c) if both (A) and (R) are false
(d) if (A) is false but (R) is true

Ex 1. **Assertion (A)** Tamil Nadu gets most of the rainfall in winter. **NIFT (PG) 2014**
Reason (R) Tamil Nadu gets rainfall from retreating monsoons.

Ex 2. **Assertion (A)** DDT has now-a-days lost its use as an insecticide.
Reason (R) DDT is harmful to man.

Ex 3. **Assertion (A)** Carbon monoxide when inhaled causes death. **NIFT (PG) 2014**
Reason (R) Carbon monoxide combines with haemoglobin.

Ex 4. **Assertion (A)** A person with blood group O is considered a universal recipient.
Reason (R) Blood group 'O' does not contain any antigens.

Ex 5. **Assertion (A)** We feel comfortable in hot and humid climate.
Reason (R) Sweat evaporates faster in humid climate.

SOLUTION (Examples 1-5)

1. (*a*) Both (A) and (R) are true and (R) is the correct explanation of (A).
   Justification Rainfall in Tamil Nadu is caused by the retreating monsoons which occur in winter.
2. (*b*) Both (A) and (R) are true but (R) is not the correct explanation of (A), because now-a-days insects become resistant to DDT and DDT has no effect on them.
3. (*a*) Carbon monoxide when inhaled causes death because it combines with haemoglobin. So, the transport of oxygen in body stopped. So, both (A) and (R) are true and (R) is the correct explanation of (A).
4. (*d*) A person with blood group O is considered a universal donor. So, (A) is false and (R) is true because blood group O does not contain any antigens.
5. (*c*) We feel uncomfortable in hot and humid climate. In humid climate there is a moisture in atmosphere. So, sweat evaporates slowly in humid climate. So, both (A) and (R) are false.

Direction (Examples 6-8) *For the Assertion (A) and Reason (R) below, choose the correct alternative from the following.*

Give answer

(a) if (A) is true but (R) is false
(b) if both (A) and (R) are true but (R) is not the correct explanation of (A)
(c) if both (R) and (R) are true and (R) is the correct explanation of (A)
(d) if (A) is false but (R) is true

Ex 6. **Assertion (A)** In the ordinary fire extinguisher, carbon dioxide is generated by the chemical reaction of sodium bicarbonate and dilute sulphuric acid. **MAT 2011**

Reason (R) Carbon dioxide can be used to extinguish fire.

Ex 7. **Assertion (A)** All machines suffer a loss of efficiency due to the frictional force acting on any moving member of that machine.

Reason (R) The frictional force can be reduced by providing a thin film of lubricant between any two mating parts.

Ex 8. **Assertion (A)** The escape velocity from the surface of the Moon is less than that from the Earth's surface.

Reason (R) The Moon has no atmosphere.

SOLUTION (Examples 6-8)

6. (*c*) Carbon dioxide is good for putting out fires because it displaces air (oxygen). Therefore, both (A) and (R) are true and (R) is the correct explanation of (A).
7. (*b*) Frictional force is always act in the direction opposite to the applied force, so all the machines suffer a loss of efficiency. Therefore, both (A) and (R) are true but (R) is not the correct explanation of (A).
8. (*b*) We know that the escape velocity depends on the value of G (universal gravitational constant) and M (mass of the body). The escape valocity from the surface of the Moon is less than from the Earth is surface because the value of G and M of Moon are less than that of Earth. So, both (A) and (R) are true but (R) is not the correct explanation of (A).

Cumulative Exercise

Base Level

Direction (Q. Nos. 1-28) *Each of these question has an assertion (A) and a reason (R).*

Give Answer

(a) if both (A) and (R) are true and (R) is the correct explanation of (A)
(b) if both (A) and (R) are true but (R) is not the correct explanation of (A)
(c) if (A) is true but (R) is false
(d) if (A) is false but (R) is true

1. **Assertion (A)** Rajiv Gandhi was Prime Minister of India for many years.
   Reason (R) Rajiv Gandhi was the grandson of Pandit Nehru.
2. **Assertion (A)** India has a number of states.
   Reason (R) India follows a 'unitary' system of government.
3. **Assertion (A)** Aluminium is used for transmission of electricity. **MAT 2014**
   Reason (R) Aluminium is a good conductor of electricity.
4. **Assertion (A)** Spectacles are used for correction of vision. **MAT 2014**
   Reason (R) Lenses have the 'property' of refraction.
5. **Assertion (A)** There is rainbow in the sky only after rains. **MAT 2013**
   Reason (R) Water drops suspended in the air breakup Sun's rays into seven colours.
6. **Assertion (A)** An iron ball floats on mercury but gets immersed in water.
   Reason (R) The specific gravity of iron is more than mercury.
7. **Assertion (A)** Prices can be brought down by increasing production. **MAT 2013**
   Reason (R) It is so because supply of the goods is made more than its demand.
8. **Assertion (A)** Diamond dazzles in dark.
   Reason (R) It has low refractive index.
9. **Assertion (A)** In the upper course, the main work of the river is erosion.
   Reason (R) River flows swiftly in the upper course.
10. **Assertion (A)** Most of the ancient civilisation grew near the rivers.
    Reason (R) The main occupation of man was agriculture.
11. **Assertion (A)** The use of chlorofluorocarbons is banned throughout the world now-a-days.
    Reason (R) These chemicals cause skin cancer.
12. **Assertion (A)** Inside the Earth, metals are present in molten state. **NIFT (UG) 2014**
    Reason (R) Earth absorbs the Sun's rays.
13. **Assertion (A)** Photosynthesis takes place in all green plants.
    Reason (R) Chlorophyll is essential for photosynthesis.
14. **Assertion (A)** Baking soda creates acidity in the stomach.
    Reason (R) Baking soda is alkaline.
15. **Assertion (A)** For the production of aluminium cheap electricity is essential.
    Reason (R) Extraction of aluminium from its ore requires abundant supply of electricity.
16. **Assertion (A)** In the solar system Earth moves in West to East direction.
    Reason (R) The rotation of the Earth takes place in 365 days.
17. **Assertion (A)** Plaster of paris is used by doctors for setting fractured bones.
    Reason (R) When plaster of paris is mixed with water and applied around the fractured limbs, it sets into a hard mass.
18. **Assertion (A)** Pressure cookers are fitted with ebonite handles.
    Reason (R) Ebonite is strong.
19. **Assertion (A)** Water kept in earthen pots gets cooled in summer.
    Reason (R) Evaporation causes cooling.

20. **Assertion (A)** Leaves of plants are green.

    Reason (R) Plants contain chromoplasts, the green pigment.

21. **Assertion (A)** Clothes are not washed properly in hard water. **NIFT (PG) 2014**

    Reason (R) Hard water contains many minerals.

22. **Assertion (A)** Buddha preached four noble truths.

    Reason (R) He wanted to remove desire, which is the cause of human sorrow and misery.

23. **Assertion (A)** Winds are deflected to their right in Northern Hemisphere and to the left in Southern Hemisphere.

    Reason (R) Rotation of Earth causes the change in wind direction.

24. **Assertion (A)** India is a 'sovereign' country.

    Reason (R) Policies of India are decided by USA.

25. **Assertion (A)** Mahatma Gandhi is considered as 'Father of the nation' in India.

    Reason (R) Mahatma Gandhi was the first Governor General of Independent India.

26. **Assertion (A)** 'DNA' Finger Printing has become an important test to establish paternity and identify of criminal of rape cases.

    Reason (R) Small samples such as hair, dried blood and semen are adequate for DNA analysis.

27. **Assertion (A)** The common value of all religion should be taught to the children in our schools. **MAT 2014**

    Reason (R) Yes, it will help in inculcating moral values amongst the children of our country.

28. **Assertion (A)** The data in disk drives can be accessed faster than the data in magnetic tapes.

    Reason (R) The disk drives have random access, therefore they are faster than magnetic tapes which have serial access.

29. In the following question, there are two statements labelled as Assertion (A) and Reason (R).

    Assertion (A) Autism is a development disability. **SSC (CGL) 2014**

    Reason (R) Heredity and lower development of brain are the causes of the Autism.

    (a) (A) is false and (R) is true (b) Both (A) and (R) are false
    (c) Both (A) and R are true (d) (A) is true and (R) is false

Advance Level

Direction (Q. Nos. 1-11) *Each of these questions has an Assertion (A) and Reason (R).*

Give answer

(a) if both (A) and (R) are true and (R) is the correct explanation of (A)
(b) if both (A) and (R) are true but (R) is not the correct explanation of (A)
(c) if (A) is true but (R) is false
(d) if (A) is false but (R) is true

1. **Assertion (A)** The steam engine was invented by James Watt. **NIFT (PG) 2014**

   Reason (R) There was a problem of taking out water from flooded mines.

2. **Assertion (A)** In India, the judiciary is independent of the executive.

   Reason (R) Judiciary favours, the government and helps in the implementation of its plans.

3. **Assertion (A)** Increase in carbon dioxide would melt polar ice.

   Reason (R) Global temperature would rise.

4. **Assertion (A)** Graphite is slippery and used as a lubricant. **NIFT (PG) 2014**

   Reason (R) Graphite has free electrons.

5. **Assertion (A)** Hot air balloon rises up in sky, because hot air is less dense than cold air.

   Reason (R) Volume of a gas increases on heating.

6. **Assertion (A)** Mercury is the farthest planet from the Sun. **NIFT (PG) 2013**

   Reason (R) Mercury is the smallest planet in the entire solar system.

7. **Assertion (A)** The British sovereignty continued to exist in free India.

   Reason (R) The British sovereign appointed the last Governor-General of free India.

8. **Assertion (A)** The filament in an electric bulb does not burn up although its temperature is about 2700°C when it glows. **NIFT (UG) 2013**

   Reason (R) Bulb filament is made up of tungsten.

9. **Assertion (A)** When a gold laden ship is emptied into the sea, then the ship rises with respect to the sea water. **NIFT (UG) 2013**

   Reason (R) The volume of water displaced by the loaded ship is more than the empty ship.

10. **Assertion (A)** Interpersonal behaviour is mostly pushed by internal needs. **UPPSC (Pre) 2014**

Reason (R) People pull behaviours from each other too.

11. **Assertion (A)** Regulative rules of communication tell us what we should and should not do. **UPPSC (Pre) 2014**

Reason (R) In communication it is essential to structure and coordinate interactions.

Direction (Q. Nos. 12-30) *In each of the questions given below, there are two statements labelled as Assertion (A) and Reason (R).*

Give answer

(a) if both (A) and (R) are true and (R) is the correct explanation of (A)
(b) if both (A) and (R) are true but (R) is not correct explanation of (A)
(c) if (A) is true but (R) is false
(d) None of the above

12. **Assertion (A)** Interpersonal roles relate to a person's behaviour that focuses on interpersonal contact. **UPPSC (Pre) 2012**

Reason (R) Such roles are derived directly from the authority and status.

13. **Assertion (A)** We prefer to wear white clothes in winter. **Uttarakhand PSC (Pre) 2012**

Reason (R) White clothes are good reflectors of heat.

14. **Assertion (A)** Roughage prevents constipation.

Reason (R) Roughage adds bulk to the food.

15. **Assertion (A)** Alcohol rather than mercury is used in a thermometer to measure a temperature of −60°C.

Reason (R) Alcohol has a lower freezing point than mercury.

16. **Assertion (A)** There is no vaccine for AIDS.

Reason (R) The AIDS virus changes its genetic code.

17. **Assertion (A)** The body of the fish is streamlined.

Reason (R) The streamlined body helps the fish to cut its way through the water.

18. **Assertion (A)** Milk production in India is low as compared to other countries of the world.

Reason (R) The animal rearers in India are poor.

19. **Assertion (A)** An electric bulb makes a 'bang' when it is broken.

Reason (R) The air inside the bulb rushes out immediately on breaking.

20. **Assertion (A)** Salt is added to cook food at higher altitudes. **Uttarakhand PSC (Pre) 2012**

Reason (R) Temperature is lower at higher altitudes.

21. **Assertion (A)** Red green colour blindness occurs with more frequency in males than in females.

Reason (R) Females have two chromosomes and males have one.

22. **Assertion (A)** Forest cutting is undesirable from the point of view of soil erosion. **MAT 2008**

Reason (R) Cutting of forests reduces the interception of rain water.

23. **Assertion (A)** Moon cannot be used as a satellite for communication.

Reason (R) Moon does not move in the equatorial plane of the earth.

24. **Assertion (A)** Ventilators are provided near the roof.

Reason (R) Conduction takes place better near the roof.

25. **Assertion (A)** Telephone wires sag more in summer.

Reason (R) They expand due to summer heat.

26. **Assertion (A)** Food materials should not be soaked in water for a long time.

Reason (R) Washing leads to loss of Vitamin A and Vitamin D from the foodstuff.

27. **Assertion (A)** Earthworms are not good for agriculture.

Reason (R) Earthworms break down the soil into fine particles and make it soft.

28. **Assertion (A)** Areas near the Equator receive rainfall throughout the year.

Reason (R) High temperatures and high humidity cause convectional rainfall in most afternoons near the Equator.

29. **Assertion (A)** Sprouting should not be done before consuming the grains.

Reason (R) Sprouting kills many vital vitamins.

30. **Assertion (A)** We feel colder on mountains than on plains. **NIFT (UG) 2014**

Reason (R) Temperature decreases with altitude.

31. **Statement** The State Government granted special status to the seminar on the importance of protecting the environment around us organized by the local academic body to create awareness among the citizens. **IBPS (SO) 2012**

Which of the following may be a probable reason for the State Government's decision?

(a) The Central Government has accorded highest priority to issues related to protection of environment, over all other issues
(b) In the past the State Government had granted special status to such seminars
(c) The State Government has failed to implement measures for protecting the environment
(d) The local academic body made a fervent appeal for the special status
(e) None of the above

32. **Statement** Most car manufacturers have marginally reduced the price of their products despite higher input costs and increased Government duties and have promised to keep the prices at the present level for atleast the next couple of months. **IBPS (Clerk) 2012**

Which of the following can be a best possible reason for the above step by car manufacturers?

(a) Car manufacturers have not been able to meet their sales target for the current year so far
(b) The Government is planning to review taxes on the raw materials for manufacturing cars
(c) The car sales market is going through a jubilant phase as the volume of sales has picked up considerably in the recent past and profit per car has also gone up
(d) Car buyers are still hesitant to make their purchases and may postpone for another few months
(e) Oil marketing companies are contemplating reviewing the petrol and diesel prices in order to decide future market prices

Direction (Q. Nos. 33-36) *Each of these questions has an Assertion (A) and a Reason (R).* **MAT 2012**

Give answer

(a) if both (A) and (R) are true and (R) is the correct explanation of (A)
(b) if both (A) and (R) are true but (R) is not the correct explanation of (A)
(c) if (A) is true but (R) is false
(d) if (A) is false but (R) is true

33. **Assertion (A)** Too much work causes stress.

Reason (R) It disturbs the body balance between its capacity and the demand.

34. **Assertion (A)** Good performance at work causes satisfaction.

Reason (R) Job satisfaction results in good performance.

35. **Assertion (A)** Social integration at workplace is necessary.

Reason (R) There are many backward classes in society.

36. **Assertion (A)** Parliament means the Lok Sabha, Rajya Sabha and the President.

Reason (R) President is directly elected by the people of India.

Direction (Q. Nos. 37-40) *Each of these questions has an Assertion (A) and a Reason (R).* **MAT 2011**

Give answer

(a) if (A) is true but (R) is false
(b) if both (A) and (R) are true but R is not the correct explanation of (A)
(c) if both (A) and (R) are true and (R) is the correct explanation of (A)
(d) if (A) is false but (R) is true

37. **Assertion (A)** A person jumping out of the moving train falls forward because his feet suddenly come to rest, while his body is in motion with the train.

Reason (R) This is based on Newton's first law of motion, which states that a body continues to be in its state of rest or of uniform motion in a straight line unless compelled by an external force to change that state.

38. **Assertion (A)** Gandhiji withdrew the non-cooperation movement against British rule in India for sometime.

Reason (R) Gandhiji believed in non-violence but the protestations by people against the British rule at Chauri-Chaura turned violent. This event disappointed Gandhiji.

39. **Assertion (A)** A parachute enables a person to descend safely from a height in case of an accident.

Reason (R) A parachute is made of a fabric with limited air permeability and has a very large frontal area. When it falls through air, it experiences heavy air resistance. The forces of lift and drag due to air flow balance the weight of the parachutist, so that one descends at a constantly slow speed.

40. **Assertion (A)** It is difficult to cook food on the hills.

Reason (R) The atmospheric pressure on the hills is quite low because of which water starts boiling at a higher temperature and therefore, it takes longer to cook food on the hills.

Answers with **Explanations**

Base Level

1. (*b*) It is true that Rajiv Gandhi was Prime Minister of India for many years and he was the grandson of Pandit Nehru.

So, both (A) and (R) are true but (R) is not the correct explanation of (A).

2. (*a*) It is true that India has a number of states and India follows a 'unitary' system of government.

So, both (A) and (R) are true and (R) is the correct explanation of (A).

3. (*a*) It is true that aluminium is used for transmission of electricity and aluminium is a good conductor of electricity.

So, both (A) and (R) are true and (R) is the correct explanation of (A).

4. (*b*) It is true that spectacles are used for correction of vision and lenses have the 'property' of refraction.

So, both (A) and (R) are true but (R) is not the correct explanation of (A).

5. (*a*) Assertion is true because water droplets act like prisms and form rainbow.

Reason is also true as the water droplets suspended in the air breakup Sun rays into seven colours due to dispersion.

Hence, (A) and (R) are true and (R) is the correct explanation of (A).

6. (*c*) Iron floats in the mercury but immersed in the water because the specific gravity of iron is less than mercury, but more than that of water.

Hence, (A) is true but (R) is false.

7. (*a*) Increasing production will surely help in bringing down prices by increasing the supply.

Hence, option (a) is correct.

8. (*c*) Diamond has high refractive index and small critical angle.

So, total internal reflection occurs in diamond and it dazzles in dark.

Hence, (A) is true but (R) is false.

9. (*a*) In the upper course, the river rushes down a steep slope, so it flows swiftly and it causes erosion. So, both (A) and (R) are true and (R) is the correct explanation of (A).

10. (*a*) Most of the ancient civilisation grew near the rivers due to easy availability of water for his occupation as agriculture. (R) is also true and correctly explain the assertion.

11. (*c*) Chloroflurocarbon is the main cause behind the hole in ozone layer which protects us harmful ultraviolet rays of the Sun. So, it is banned throughout the world. So, (A) is true while (R) is false.

12. (*c*) Inside the Earth, metals are present in molten state due to the high temperature and high pressure. The Earth does not absorbs the Sun's rays as it reflects them. So, (A) is true while (R) is false.

13. (*a*) Chlorophyll is a green pigment which is essential for photosynthesis and this process takes place in all green plants. So, (A) and (R) are true and (R) is the correct explanation of (A).

14. (*d*) Baking soda neutralizes the acidity in the stomach because it is alkaline. So, (A) is false while (R) is true.

15. (*a*) Aluminum is produced from its ore and its extraction from ore requires abundant supply of electricity. So, both (A) and (R) are true and (R) is the correct explanation of (A).

16. (*c*) Rotation of the Earth occur in 24 h and revolution of Earth take place in 365 days. (A) is true and (R) is false.

17. (*a*) When plaster of paris sets into a hard mass, it keeps the fractured bones in a fixed position which helps them to rejoin. So, it is used by doctors. Both (A) and (R) are true and (R) is the correct explanation of (A).

18. (*c*) Pressure cookers are fitted with ebonite handles because ebonite is a bad conductor of heat, so it does not heats up with pressure cooker, so hands don't get burn while handling it. So, (A) is true while (R) is false.

19. (*a*) Earthen pots have pores through which evaporation takes place which causes cooling. So, both (A) and (R) are true and (R) is the correct explanation of (A).

20. (*c*) Leaves of plants are green because they contain chlorophyll which is a green pigment. Plants contains chromoplasts which is not a green pigment. So, (A) is true while (R) is false.

21. (*b*) Clothes are not washed properly in hard water because it does not form lather with soap. However, it is true that hard water contains many minerals. Both (A) and (R) are true but (R) is not the correct explanation of (A).

22. (*a*) Buddha preached four noble truths because he wanted to remove desire, which is the cause of human sorrow and misery. So, both (A) and (R) are true and (R) is the correct explanation of (A).

23. (*a*) Rotation of Earth causes the winds to deflect to their right in Northern Hemisphere and to the left in Southern Hemisphere. Here, both (A) and (R) are true and (R) is the correct explanation of (A).

24. (*c*) As, India is a 'sovereign' country, policies of India are not decided by USA. (A) is true and (R) is false.

25. (*c*) As, Mahatma Gandhi is considered as 'Father of the nation' in India but he was not the first Governor General of independent India. (A) is true and (R) is false.

26. (*a*) Both (A) and (R) are true and (R) is the correct explanation of (A).

27. (*a*) Both (A) and (R) are true and (R) is the correct explanation of (A).

28. (*a*) Disk drive means hard disk is faster than magnetic tapes both of them are storage device. Floppy disk are magnetic tapes.
Both (A) and (R) are true and (R) is the correct explanation of (A).

29. (*c*) Both (A) and (R) are true.

Advanced Level

1. (*a*) Both (A) and (R) are true and (R) is the correct explanation of (A).
Justification The problem of pumping out water from the flooded mines provided the need of a self-working engine, which led James Watt to invent the same.

2. (*c*) (A) is true but (R) is false.
Justification In India, the judiciary is completely independent of the executive. It has no interference in the judicial affairs.

3. (*a*) Both (A) and (R) are true and (R) is the correct explanation of (A).
Justification The carbon dioxide envelope in Earth's atmosphere traps the heat. Which is increase in the proportion of carbon dioxide, therefore the global temperature would rise, thus causing the polar ice to melt.

4. (*b*) Both (A) and (R) are true but (R) is not the correct explanation of (A).
Justification Graphite has a layered structure with two successive layers held by weak force and able to slide over one another. So, graphite is slippery and this property finds its use as a lubricant. But in graphite, each carbon atom is linked to three carbon atoms while one electron in the carbon atom is delocalised.
So, graphite has free electrons.

5. (*a*) According to charle's law volume of a gas increases on heating and its density (mass/volume) decreases. Since, hot air is less dense than cold air, so hot air inside the balloon is lighter than cold atmospheric air. Due to this hot air, balloon rises up by displacing the atmospheric air.
Hence, option (a) is correct.

6. (*d*) According to IAU.
Now, Neptune is the farthest planet of solar system. So, assertion is false but reason is true as mercury is the smallest planet of the solar system.
Hence, option (d) is the answer.

7. (*d*) Assertion is false because India has its own constitution and government. But reason is true as the last Governor General of free India was appointed by the British sovereign.
Hence, option (d) is true.

8. (*b*) It is true that the filament in a bulb does not get burnt due to the absence of oxygen as the bulb is first evacuated and then filled with an inert gas like helium or argon.
It is also true that bulb filament is made up of tungsten but it is not correct explanation of (A).
Hence, option (b) is correct.

9. (*a*) When a gold laden ship is emptied into the sea, then the ship rises with respect to sea water because volume of the water displaced by the loaded ship is more than that by the empty ship.
Hence, option (a) is correct.

10. (*a*) Given assertion is correct and reason explains clearly the aspect of human learning from society around them. Be it any environment, i.e. work, home, public gathering, etc.
Hence, option (a) is correct.

11. (*a*) Regulative rules of communication are required to make communication in a manner that it does not create controversy, public anger and fallacy. Hence, assertion is correct and reason explains vividly that regulative rules are result of structuring and coordinated interactions.
Hence, option (a) is correct.

12. (*a*) Assertion (A) is true and Reason (R) is the correct explanation of (A). Because interpersonal roles are directly derived from authority and status hence, shaping the way a person communicate.

13. (*d*) Here, assertion is wrong while reason is true that white clothes are good reflectors of heat. But it cannot be correct explanation of the Assertion.

14. (*a*) Both (A) and (R) are true and (R) is the correct explanation of (A).

15. (*a*) Alcohol is used in thermometer to measure a temperature of $-60°C$ because mercury freezes at $-39°C$ while Alcohol freezes at around $-119°C$. So, (R) is the correct explanation of (A).

16. (*a*) Both (A) and (R) are true and (R) is the correct explanation of (A).

17. (*a*) The body of fish is streamlined which helps it to cut its way through the water. So, both (A) and (R) are true and (R) is the correct explanation of (A).

18. (*c*) Other countries are producing more milk than India because their animals are of good breed. It cannot be said that the animal rearers in India are poor. So, (A) is true but (R) is false.

19. (*c*) An electric bulb has vaccum inside it, so when it is broken, air from atmosphere rushes to fill the vaccum, so it makes a bang. So, (A) is true while (R) is false.

20. (*b*) At higher altitudes, water boils before 100°C, so salt is added which increases the boiling point of water. Temperature is lower at higher altitudes. So, (R) is not the correct explanation of (A).

21. (*a*) Both (A) and (R) are true and (R) is the correct explanation of (A).

22. (*a*) Both (A) and (R) are true and (R) is the correct explanation of (A).

23. (*a*) Both (A) and (R) are true and (R) is the correct explanation of (A).

24. (*c*) Ventilators are provided near the roof because hot air is light and remain upper than the cool air. So, hot air can be easily out through the ventilators. So, (A) is true but (R) is false.

25. (*a*) Telephone wires sag more in summer because they expand due to summer heat. So, (R) is the correct explanation of (A).

26. (*c*) Food materials should not be soked in water for a long time because it leads to loss of Vitamin B and Vitamin C from the foodstuff because these Vitamins are soluable in water. So, (A) is true while (R) is false.

27. (*d*) Earthworms are good for agriculture because they break down the soil into fine particles and make it soft. So, (A) is false while (R) is true.

28. (*a*) Both (A) and (R) are true and (R) is the correct explanation of (A).

29. (*d*) Sprouting grains has more nutrients, so both (A) and (R) are false.

30. (*a*) We feel colder on mountains than on plains because temperature decreases with altitude. So, (R) is the correct explanation of (A).

31. (*b*) The probable reason behind the State Government decision to granted special status to seminar of local academic body because in the past, the State Government had granted special status to such seminars, which are related to environment awareness.

32. (*c*) The best possible reason behind the car manufactures companies have marginally reduced the price of their products because, "The car sales market is going through a jubilant phase as the volume of sales has picked up considerably in the recent past and profit per car has also gone up".

33. (*a*) Too much work causes stress because it disturbs the body balance between its capacity and the demand. Hence, both (A) and (R) are true and (R) is the correct explanation of (A).

34. (*c*) Good performance at work causes satisfaction is definitely true but job satisfaction results in good performance, is not true because level of satisfaction are variable from person to person and work place environment, (A) is true but (R) is false.

35. (*b*) Social integration at workplace is necessary, is definitely true but its reason is not correct explanation for this social integration. Hence, both (A) and (R) are true but (R) is not the correct explanation of (A).

36. (*c*) Assertion is true and reason is false.

President of India is elected by a electroal college which consist of elected member of Lok Sabha and Rajya Sabha and elected member of legislative assembly.

Hence, option (c) is answer.

37. (c) Both (A) and (R) are true and (R) is the correct explanation of (A).

38. (*c*) Gandhiji withdrew the non-cooperation movement because of the violence in the Chauri-Chaura.

Hence, both (A) and (R) are true and (R) is the correct explanation of (A).

39. (*c*) A parachute enables a person to descend safely from a height because of a parachute is made of a fabric with limited air permeability and has a very large frontal area.

Hence, both (A) and (R) are true and (R) is the correct explanation of (A).

40. (*c*) It is difficult to cook on the hills because of the atmospheric pressure on the hills is quite low.

Hence, both (A) and (R) are true and (R) is the correct explanation of (A).

8

Cause and Effect

Cause means logical or scientific reason of an event. **In other words we can say that the strong points behind any reason are known as 'cause' and the impact of the cause is known as 'effect'.**

In the questions of 'cause and effect' candidates are asked to determine that a given event is a cause or a effect. Candidates should always remember that 'cause' always occur before the 'effect' and the effect happens at the same point of time after the cause. The questions of 'cause and effect' are designed to test the ability of candidate to analyse a pair of given statements (events) and then correlate them as cause and effect.

General Guidelines to Solve 'Cause and Effect' Questions

Guideline **1.** The cause will always occur before the effect. Hence, if two events are given, then the effect that is chronologically antecedent to the other can only be regarded as a possible cause.

Guideline **2.** A necessary condition for the occurrence of a specified event is a circumstance in whose absence the event cannot occur.

Guideline **3.** A sufficient condition for the occurrence of an event is a circumstance in whose presence the event must occur.

Guideline **4.** Both the events express generalised results that may not be backed by any specific cause but may influence certain other factors.

Guideline **5.** The effects in both the given statements may be caused or triggered by a third unmentioned event which may thus be called the common cause of the given events.

Besides these rules you should remember the word '**principal cause**' & '**immediate cause**' which are the most important factors behind the occurrence of an effect. Sometimes an event is caused by various factors but one of them is the most dominant factor without which the event may not have occurred.

Principal Cause

This is major condition that governs occurrence or non-occurrence of an event. Though only its presence does not gurantee happening of that event (as event might need some more occurrences too) but its absence would definitely lead to non-occurrence of this event.

Immediate Cause

This is the condition that triggers the event so it is an important cause that has just happened before occurrence of an event and caused the event to happen.

Difference between Principle Cause and Immediate Cause

Generally, examinations have questions to find principal and immediate cause. Although they sound similar but there is a difference between principle and immediate cause. The **principle cause** is the main and most important reason for the effect, while **immediate cause** is the most proximate in time to the effect.

e.g. If you have read Indian history you may appreciate that the principle cause for the mutiny of 1857 was the Doctrine of Lapse and other repressive policies of Lord Dalhousie but the immediate cause was the fact that sepoys were made to bite cartridge that had fat of sacred animals such as cows.

Strategy to Solve Cause and Effect Questions

In the examinations, we are usually asked to find out if a cause is immediate as well as principal. It means that the said cause must be the principal reason of the given effect and it should be also be fairly proximate time to the said effect. We can follow the steps given below to eliminate obviously wrong choices.

***Step* I.** Check, if both the events are atleast related.

***Step* II.** Next, if one event preceeds other it means the one that happened earlier might be the cause as the cause always occur before only, then can we see its effects.

***Step* III.** However, if both the events are in Present Perfect Tense you would not be able to decide which occurred earlier, here most probably one is not the cause of the other but this may not always be true. In this cause, use your knowledge and logic.

Expert's Advice

If you are not following it easy to solve the questions, inspite of study all the concerned facts given in the chapter, you can still use your common-sense to get the answer. Ask these simple question from yourself.

***Que* 1.** Can Ist event lead the IInd event or *vice-versa.*

***Que* 2.** If yes, then Ist is most important cause behind IInd or IInd is the most important cause behind Ist? You can read self upon these simple questions, you will get the right answer.

Solved Examples

Direction (Examples 1-3) *In the following questions, two statements have been given, which bear a cause and effect relationship.* **NIFT (PG) 2015**

Given answer

(a) if Statement I is the cause and the Statement II is its effect
(b) if Statement II is the cause and the Statement I is its effect
(c) if both the Statements I and II are effects of a common cause
(d) if both Statements I and II are effects of independent causes

***Ex* 1.** I. The Times of India has reported today that water of Ganga at Varanasi contains level of pollutant much higher than the permissible limit.

II. The people living in the area are to be shifted to another area to avoid a catastrophic situation.

***Ex* 2.** I. The Government has planned to make arrangements for supply of safe drinking water from Tehri Dam.

II. The Ganga water at Kanpur is not even fit for bathing as it contains very high level of pollutants.

***Ex* 3.** I. The internet users of the country have been advised to stay alert while using internet till the hackers are caught.

II. The Government machinery will make an all out effort to catch those who are responsible for hacking and put in place a sound internet security system for all its websites.

SOLUTION (Examples 1-3)

1. (*c*) Both are the effects of common cause i.e. water of Ganga at Varanasi contains higher level of pollutant.
2. (*b*) Statement II is the cause i.e. water of Ganga is not even fit for bathing and Statement I is its effect because Government is taking necessary action for the occurred problem.
3. (*c*) Both the statements are the effects of common cause i.e. hackers are active.

Ex **4.** In this question, there are two Statements I and II. These may either be independent causes or effects of independent causes or a common cause. One these statements may be the effect of the other statement. Read both the statements carefully and decide which of the following answer choices correctly depicts the relationship between these two statements?

I. As per the statistics, there has been a rise in the number of electric cars in country 'Y' this year.

II. The oil prices have fallen strongly in country. 'Y' this year and are estimated to stay low for at least two years for now and not decrease further.

New India Assurance Company Ltd (AO) 2015

(a) Statement I is the cause and Statement II, is its effect
(b) Both Statements I and II are effects of independent causes
(c) Statement II is the cause and Statement I is its effect
(d) Both Statements I and II are independent causes
(e) Both Statements I and II are effects of some common cause

Sol. (*b*) Electric cars does not depend on the prices of oil, so both the Statements I and II are effects of independent causes.

Direction (Examples 5-7) *In the following questions, two statements have been given, which bear a cause and effect relationship.* **NIFT (PG) 2015**

Given answer

(a) if Statement I is the cause and the Statement II is its effect
(b) if Statement II is the cause and the Statement I is its effect
(c) if both the Statements I and II are effects of a common cause
(d) if both Statements I and II are effects of independent causes

Ex **5.** I. Many villages in the district are marooned as the river overflowed the banks and many people have managed to survive on the tree tops and which ever place they could find above water.

II. The district administration has sent relief teams to the affected villages to rescue the stranded villagers and have sent supplies of food and water to the nearby villages.

IRMA 2006

Ex **6.** I. The Reserve Bank of India has recently put restrictions on few small banks in the country.

II. The small banks in the private and cooperative sector in India are not in a position to withstand the competitions of the bigger in the public sector.

Ex **7.** I. India is ranked fifth most powerful country in the world, next to US, China, Russia and Japan, in the hierarchy of top 50 nations, identified on the basis of their GDP, as per national security index.

II. The assessment is based on defence capability, economic strength, effective population, technological capability and energy security of top 50 countries. **MAT 2012**

SOLUTION (Examples 5-7)

5. (*a*) As the river overflowed the banks and it is like a position of flood, so the district administration has sent relief teams to the affected villages. So, Statement I is the cause and Statement II is its effect.

6. (*b*) The inability of the small banks to compete with the bigger ones shall not ensure security and good service to the customers, which is an essential concomitant that has to be looked into by the RBI. It seems to be a remedial step for the same.

7. (*b*) Statement (II) is the cause and Statement (I) is its effect because India's rank as the fifth most powerful county is based on its defence capability, economic strength, effective population, technological capability and energy security among top 50 countries.

Cumulative Exercise

Base Level

Direction (Q. Nos. 1-8) *Below in each question are given two Statements* I *and* II. *These statements may be either independent causes or may be effects of independent causes or a common cause. One of these statements may be the effect of the other statement. Read both the statements and decide which of the following answer choice correctly depicts the relationship between these two statements.*

Give answer

(a) if Statement I is the cause and Statement II is its effect
(b) if Statement II is the cause and Statement I is its effect
(c) if both the Statements I and II are effects of independent causes
(d) if both Statements I and II are effects of some common cause

1. I. The prices of petroleum products dropped marginally last week.

II. The State Government reduced the tax on petroleum products last week. **MAT 2013**

2. I. Many people visited the religious place during the weekend.

II. Few people visited the religious place during the week days. **MAT 2013**

3. I. School education has been made free for children of poor families.

II. Literacy rate among poor is steadily growing.

NIFT (PG) 2012

4. I. Hallmarking of gold jewellery has been made compulsory.

II. Many persons do not prefer to buy hall marked jewellery.

NIFT (PG) 2012

5. I. Many vegetarians are suffering stomach ailments.

II. Many dead fish were found near the lake shor.

NIFT (PG) 2012

6. I. This year the cut-off percentages for admission to junior colleges have increased over the last year.

II. This year's performance of students in Xth final exam was considerably higher than the previous year.

MAT 2014

7. I. The conditions of most of the national highways are very bad.

II. Government has now sanctioned a huge amount of money to maintain the national highways. **MAT 2014**

8. I. Rain and thunder showers lashed the city during the past three days.

II. Many people stayed indoors during the past three days.

MAT 2014

Direction (Q. Nos. 9-21) *Below in each question are given two Statements* I *and* II. *These statements may be either independent causes or may be effects of independent causes or a common cause. One of these statements may be the effect of the other statement. Read both the statements and decide which of the following answer choice correctly depicts the relationship between these two statements.*

Give answer

(a) if Statement I is the cause and Statement II is its effect
(b) if Statement II is the cause and Statement I is its effect
(c) if both the Statements I and II are independent causes
(d) if both the Statements I and II are effects of independent causes
(e) if both the Statements I and II are effects of some common causes

9. I. Many seats in the private engineering colleges in the state have remained vacant this year.

II. The government engineering colleges in the state could not accommodate all the students who sought admission this year. **IBPS (PO) 2011**

10. I. Most of the steel manufacturing companies in the country have made considerable profit during the last fiscal year.

II. Many Asian countries have been importing huge quantities of steel from India. **IBPS (PO) 2011**

11. I. The State Government has now decided to increase the stamp duty on house purchased with immediate effect.

II. The real estate prices have decreased considerably during the last few months. **IBPS (PO) 2011**

12. I. Three top players of the Indian cricket missed all the matches of the five match tournament due to injury.

II. India lost the cricket tournament to the visitors with a 2 : 3 margin. **BOI (PO) 2010**

13. I. The prices of foodgrains have increased by about 20% over the same period last year.

II. The prices of vegetables have substantially decreased during the past few weeks.

14. I. A huge explosion rocked the housing complex as a cooking gas cylinder exploded in one of the flats in the complex.

II. Residents of the housing complex came running out of their houses and assembled in the open courtyard. **BOI (PO) 2010**

15. I. Majority of the students of the school passed in Mathematics in the annual examination.

II. Majority of the students of the school failed in English in the annual examination.

16. I. The municipal authority advised all the schools in the city to close down for the next two days.

II. A huge storm is likely to hit the city during the next two days.

17. I. State Government has ordered immediate ban on airing of certain movie channels on television.

II. A few social activists have come together and demanded ban on telecasting 'Adult' movies on television.

18. I. Employment scenario in the country has remarkably improved recently.

II. The number of prospective job-seekers going abroad has increased recently. **IBPS (PO) 2011**

19. I. Government has tightened security checks at all important places and also at various public places.

II. Incidences of terrorist attacks are increasing day-by-day.

20. I. This high court has fixed a time limit for repairing all the roads in the city.

II. Road development authorities in the city are carrying out road repair work on an urgent basis. **IBPS (PO) 2011**

21. I. There is an outbreak of several epidemics in the country.

II. There was a worst flood situation ever experienced in the past in most parts of the country.

Direction (Q. Nos. 22-33) *Below in each question are given two Statements I and II. These statements may be either independent causes or may be effects of independent causes or a common cause. One of these statements may be the effect of the other statement. Read both the statements and decide which of the following answer choice correctly depicts the relationship between these two statements.*

Give answer

(a) if Statement I is the effect and Statement II is its immediate cause

(b) if Statement I is the immediate cause and Statement II is its effect

(c) if Statement I is the effect but Statement II is not its immediate cause

(d) if Statement II is the effect but Statement I is not its immediate cause

(e) if both the Statements I and II are independent cause

22. I. The attack by militants on Parliament in December 2001 haunts our parliamentarians whenever militants attack any target in the country.

II. New parking labels have been introduced for the members of Parliament, aiming at strengthening the security of the Indian Parliament and the parliamentarians.

23. I. The people of state X have claimed that vegetables like parwal and kakora as treated with malachite green to make them look fresh.

II. The officials of Food Adulteration Department has started collecting samples of vegetables from suspicious places in state X.

24. I. Cricketer 'A' has denied to talk with media persons.

II. BCCI special commissioner Rajiv Shukla has quizzed cricketer 'A' for nearly six hours for his role in betting and match-fixing scam.

25. I. Transporters have threatened to go on strike in protest against the hike in diesel prices.

II. The talks between the government and agitating transporters have failed.

26. I. Mr X resigned from the post of coach of Indian cricket team.

II. BCCI is looking for a foreign coach for Indian cricket team.

27. I. The National Human Rights Commission has ordered ₹ 1 lakh interim compensation to be paid to the legal heirs of the deceased in Delhi.

II. A few hawkers in Delhi were driven to commit suicide due to humiliation by the police.

28. I. Recently the government has established a bamboo innovation studio and allied workshops in Agartala.

II. There has been witnessed a radical change in the choices of people using bamboo as an alternative to timber and steel.

29. I. The Bar Council of India (BCI) has ordered all evening law colleges in the country to close down from the coming academic session.

II. The standard of education in evening law colleges was found in the state of deterioration.

30. I. Usha Mangeshkar has been awarded Kavi Pradeep Shikhar Samman for her excellence in the field of playback singing.

II. Usha Mangeshkar is a very dedicated playback singer.

31. I. DTTDC recorded an all-time high liquor sale on this Holi eve.

II. Dry days increased liquor sales.

32. I. Recently Supreme Court has directed banning smoking in public places.

II. The railways have decided to ban smoking in trains, railway stations and all railway offices saying any violation would attract a fine of ₹ 100.

33. I. The finance ministry has imposed additional taxation.

II. The fiscal deficit of the country has been reduced.

Direction (Q. Nos. 34-37) *Below in each question are given two Statements* I *and* II. *These statements may be either independent causes or may be effects of independent causes or a common cause. One of these statements may be the effect of the other statement. Read both the statements and decide which of the following answer choice correctly depicts the relationship between these two statements.* **MAT 2013**

Give answer

(a) if Statement I is the cause and Statement II is its effect
(b) if Statement II is the cause and Statement I is its effect
(c) if both the Statements I and II are independent causes
(d) if both the Statements I and II are effects of independent causes

34. I. Large number of people living in the low-lying areas have been evacuated during the last few days to safer places.

II. The government has rushed in relief supplies to the people living in the affected areas.

35. I. International Agency for Research on Cancer (IARC)—an arm of the World Health Organisation (WHO)—will meet in France to take a call on bitumen, the black, oily material used to make roads to be banned as probably carcenogenic, i.e. causing cancer to humans.

II. IARC has asked experts from across the globe to submit data from their research studies conducted on bitumen so as to help it to come to some conclusion.

36. I. In a survey conducted recently in America, almost 70% of Americans said they find it easier to care for their cars than their personal health. 40% of them said they would be more likely to address their issues with their car than their health.

II. Base on the above survey, the national campaign network for men's health launched this awareness through Abbott Laboratories to encourage men to visit their doctors more often to enjoy better health.

37. I. The local cooperative credit society has decided to stop giving loans to farmers with immediate effect.

II. A large number of credit society members have withdrawn major parts of their deposits from the credit society.

Direction (Q. Nos. 38-53) *Below in each question are given two Statements* I *and* II. *These statements may be either independent causes or may be effects of independent causes or a common cause. One of these statements may be the effect of the other statement. Read both the statements and decide which of the following answer choice correctly depicts the relationship between these two statements.*

Give answer

(a) if Statement I is the cause and Statement II is its effect
(b) if Statement II is the cause and Statement I is its effect
(c) if both the Statements I and II are independent causes
(d) if both the Statements I and II are effects of independent causes
(e) if both the Statements I and II are effects of some common causes

38. I. There has been mass recruitment of IT professionals by Indian IT companies.

II. Many developed countries are increasingly outsourcing IT related functions to India and China. **IDBI Executive 2009**

39. I. The government has marginally increased the procurement price of wheat for the current crop.

II. The current wheat crop is expected to be twenty per cent more than the previous wheat crop.

Syndicate Bank (PO) 2010

40. I. The braking system of the tourist bus carrying 40 passengers failed while negotiating a stiff climb on a hilly road.

II. The tourist bus fell into the gorge killing atleast ten passengers and seriously injuring all the remaining.
Syndicate Bank (PO) 2010

41. I. The State government has decided to boost English language education in all the schools from the next academic year.

II. The level of English language of the school students of the state is comparatively lower than that of the neighbouring states.

42. I. The municipal authority demolished the tea stall located on the footpath on the busy road.

II. Large number of people have been taking their evening tea at the tea stall located on the footpath on the main road blocking pedestrian movement.

43. I. Majority of three students left the local school as the school building was in a dilapidated condition.

II. The school authority decided to close down the school immediately and shift the remaining students to a make-shift school. **Syndicate Bank (PO) 2010**

44. I. All the airlines companies in India have increased the airfares in all routes with immediate effect.

II. There has been substantial reduction in aviation fuel prices in India during the past few weeks. **IOB (PO) 2009**

45. I. There has been continuous increase in average temperature during winter in many parts of the country over the past few years.

II. There has been significant changes in the wind pattern across the country over the last few years.

46. I. The conditions of all the major roads in the city have deteriorated causing hardship to motorists.

II. The municipal authority has sanctioned significant amount to repair all the major roads in the city.

47. I. The BPO sector has laid off a large number of employees in the recent months.

II. Very few projects are now being outsourced to BPO sector.
IOB (PO) 2009

48. I. There has been sharp decline in sales of passenger cars during the last few months.

II. Many finance companies have announced attractive schemes of car loans with moderate interest rate.

49. I. There have been sporadic events of stone pelting throughout the day in the affected areas of the city.

II. Many wounded people were brought to the nearby hospitals from the affected areas of the city. **UBI (PO) 2009**

50. I. Many people left from the city for their native places during the summer months.

II. Many tourists gathered in city during summer months.

51. I. All the schools declared holiday on the next day of the major festival.

II. All the colleges declared holiday on the next day of the major festival.

52. I. The residents reported of increased criminal activities in the area to the local police station.

II. Many criminals were arrested by searching the residence of the suspected individuals.

53. I. Government has awarded a high stake reward scheme for such persons who may provide any information about the suspect.

II. Four members of a family were brutally murdered by unidentified gunmen. **UBI (PO) 2009**

Direction (Q. Nos. 54-64) *Below in each question are given two Statements I and II. These statements may be either independent causes or may be effects of independent causes or a common cause. One of these statements may be the effect of the other statement. Read both the statements and decide which of the following answer choice correctly depicts the relationship between these two statements.*

Give answer

(a) if Statement I is the cause and Statement II is its effect
(b) if Statement II is the cause and Statement I is its effect
(c) if both the Statements I and II are independent causes
(d) if both the Statements I and II are effects of independent causes
(e) if both the Statements I and II are effects of some common causes

54. I. The government has increased number of buses running between Mumbai and Surat.

II. The government has allowed private bus owners to operate between Mumbai and Surat. **IBPS (PO) 2011**

55. I. The association of management colleges conducted a combined admission exam for all the institutes this year.

II. As the dates for entrance exam for many management colleges clashed last year, many candidates complained that they could not appear for a number of entrance exams.

56. I. The departmental store owner put cameras for surveillance of the store.

II. Many products were reported missing by the staff working in the departmental store.

57. I. Asthma cases in the city are on a continuous rise since last year.

II. The number of commonly found animals such as sparrows, squirrels and pigeons in the city has continuously dwindled since last year. **OBC (PO) 2010**

58. I. Prices of foodgrains in India has increased substantially.

II. Lakhs of farmers have quit farming owing to the lack of governmental support in the form of subsidies.

59. I. The university decided to postpone the final exams for course X by a month.

II. Nearly twenty five students out of sixty students in course X failed to pass the final exams last year.

60. I. Worldwide recession has created uncertainity in the job market.

II. Many people are opting for change from private sector to public sector. **MHT CET MBA 2009**

61. I. A large number of employees could not report to the duty on time.

II. Police had laid down barricades on the road to trap the miscreants.

62. I. There was a huge crowd of buyers at various shopping outlets in the city.

II. Prices of most of the commodities have gone up substantially in the recent past.

63. I. There has been constant rise in the number of immigrants to the metropolis for last many years.

II. The infrastructure of the metropolis is struggling to take care of its increasing population. **MHT CET MBA 2009**

64. I. Earnings of all the government employees have gone up with the revision of pay scales.

II. Salaries of employees in the private companies are being revised from time to time.

Advanced Level

Direction (Q. Nos. 1-4) *In each question, two Statements I and II are provided. These may have a cause and effect relationship or may have independent causes or be the effects of independent causes. Read the statements carefully and firm mark your answer as*

(a) if Statement I is the cause and Statement II is its effect
(b) if Statement II is the cause and Statement I is its effect
(c) if both the Statements I and II are effects of independent causes
(d) if both the Statements I and II are effects of some common cause

1. I. The capital city is facing a huge crisis of drinking water.

II. The Chief Minister of Delhi has ordered the Delhi Jal Board to increase the number of tankers to curb the problem of drinking water.

2. I. The NGT (National Green Tribunal) has banned diesel vehicles more than 10 years old in Delhi.

II. The air of Delhi is highly polluted.

3. I. The Prime Minister of India is focussing on the 'Make in India' Mission to Increase Employment.

II. The people of India are highly educated but have no jobs related to their education.

4. I. The fast food among the children is very common that's why we see the problem of obesity among them.

II. The childrens also facing the problem of blood pressure, Diabeties in the small age.

Direction (Q. Nos. 5-11) *In each of these questions, two statements numbered as I and II are provided. These may have a cause and effect relationship or may have independent causes or be the effects of independent causes. Read the statements and mark answer as* **MAT 2011**

(a) if both the Statements I and II are effects of independent causes
(b) if Statement II is the cause and Statement I is its effect
(c) if Statement I is the cause and Statement II is its effect
(d) if both the statements are effects of some common cause

5. I. Most of the private schools have increased the tuition fees in Delhi this year to meet their expenses.

II. The tuition fees in Government-run schools have not been hiked inspite of the unexpected price rise witnessed this year.

6. I. The results of the students of science stream of class XII in the Kendriya Vidyalayas this year were excellent.

II. Many teachers of Kendriya Vidyalayas have left these schools and joined private schools.

7. I. If we incorporate fruits as part of our meals, we avoid excess calories in our daily in take. Fruits are wholesome and have a very high water content.

II. Many fruits like watermelon or cucumber are calorie burners as digesting them burns more calories than eating them.

8. I. World Health Organisation believes that one in 10 hospital admissions leads to an adverse event and one in 300 admissions in death. Unintended medical errors are a big threat to patient safety.

II. American Medical Association claims and quantifies that there are nearly 2000 deaths due to unnecessary surgery. 7000 deaths from medication errors, 8000 deaths from infections and nearly 16000 deaths due to adverse effects of medicines.

9. I. A bone ossification test conducted by AIIMS doctors has led to the release of a man, who spent 11 yr behind bars on charges of murder despite being a juvenile at the time of offence.

II. As per the calculation done by High Court Judge, Farooq must have been not more than 17 yr, when he committed the crime and should have been tried as per the Juvenile Justice Act and should not have been imprisoned for over 3 yr for crimes including murder.

10. According to a survey innumerable diseases and unhealthy habits from the recent pandemic to cancer, AIDS and obesity have plagued the mankind.

Which of the following may be the most possible cause of the situation given in the above statements? **IBPS (PO) 2013**

(a) The lifestyle and food habits of people are responsible for this state
(b) Environmental degradation has led to the present situation
(c) The people remain ignorant above their health
(d) Technological advancement and fast pace of life are contributing to the spread of diseases
(e) None of the above

11. I. There has been heavy rains in the catchment area of the lakes supplying drinking water to the city.

II. The Municipal authority has suspended the proposed cut in water supply to the city. **OBC (PO) 2008**

Direction (Q. Nos. 12-16) *Below in each question are given two Statements I and II. These statements may be either independent causes or may be effects of independent causes or a common cause. One of these statements may be the effect of the other statement. Read both the statements and decide which of the following answer choice correctly depicts the relationship between these two statements.*

Given answer

(a) if Statement I is the effect and Statement II is its immediate cause
(b) if Statement I is the immediate cause and statement II is its effect
(c) if Statement I is the effect but Statement II is not its immediate cause
(d) if Statement II is the effect but Statement I is not its immediate cause
(e) if both the Statements I and II are independent cause

12. I. In the world's biggest conference on AIDS in Bacelona, officials in their declaration called for $ 10 billion per year to be donated to the global AIDS fund and for atleast two million people with HIV in developing countries to receive anti-retroviral treatment by 2012.

II. According to recent UN report, about 70 million people will die of AIDS over the next two decades in the 45 worst affected countries.

13. I. 500000 people were forced to flee to Rwanda from the Eastern Congo town of Goma.

II. Fires burned out of control in the Eastern Congo town of Goma, after a nearby volcano sent 100 foot-wide rivers of lava flowing through the centre of the town and into Lake Kivu.

14. I. In a significant move, cabinet of State X has approved a proposal by the State commercial tax department to issue tax payer identification number to all businessmen registered under the value-added tax system.

II. The Railway Ministry has enhanced the allocation from ₹ 3119 crore to ₹ 3995 crore in the current budget for rolling stock procurement to meet the next year's passenger and freight traffic targets.

15. I. For the last couple of weeks commuters in city X have been facing a lot of problems because of lack of transportation facilities.

II. In a landmark decision recently, the court has put a ban on the plying of thousands of diesel buses in city X that have not converted to CNG.

16. I. All India Confederation of Scheduled Castes and Tribes Organisation Chairman Udit Raj today resigned from the Government and floated the 'Justice Party'.

II. Next month assembly elections will be held in Gujarat.

Direction (Q. Nos. 17-20) *In each question, two Statements I and II are provided. These may have a cause and effect relationship or may have independent causes.* **MAT 2012**

Given answer

(a) if Statement I is the cause and Statement II is its effect
(b) if both the Statement I and II are effect of independent cause
(c) if Statement II is the immediate cause and Statement I is its effect
(d) if both the Statements I and II are effects of some common cause

17. I. Sri Lankan skipper Kumar Sangakara justified his decision to step down from the captaincy of the ODI and T20 teams by saying, I will be 37 by the next World Cup and I cannot be sure of my place in the team. It is better that Sri Lanka is now led by a player who will be at the peak of his career during that tournament'.

II. Remarkably, unlike most skippers whose individual performance drops drops after assuming the leadership role, Sangakara has actually batted better as captain in all three formats of the game.

18. I. The prices of 'silver' have gone up from ₹ 27000 per kg to ₹ 50000 per kg in almost a year's time.

II. Indian jewellers are receiving a lot of demand for the silver ornaments from American and European clients.

19. I. There is an alarming increase in the number of young unemployed MBA's this year in comparison to the last year's figures.

II. Nearly one lakh applications were received against a recruitment call given by a private bank for only ten vacant posts.

20. I. Many people visit the religious places on week days and weekends to pray to Mother Durga in Navratras.

II. Many religious people go on fasting during Navratras to seek the blessings of Mother Durga.

21. **Effect** The prices of food grains and vegetables have increased by about 30% in the past three months. Which of the following can be a probable cause of the above effect? **CGPSC 2013**

(a) The farmers have decided to change their farming style
(b) The prices of other products have increased more than 30%
(c) The number of farmers has reduced
(d) Occupation of farming has not been viewed as a repuited work
(e) None of the above

22. **Effect** Majority of the employees of the ailing organisation opted for voluntary retirement scheme and left the organisation with all their retirement benefits within a fortnight of launching the scheme.

Which of the following can be a probable cause of the above effect? **IOB (PO) 2010**

(a) The company has been making huge losses for the past 5 yr and is unable to pay salary to its employees in time
(b) The management of the company made huge personal gains through unlawful activities
(c) One of the competitions of the company went bankrupt last year
(d) The company owns large tracts of land in the state which will fetch huge sum of its owners
(e) None of the above

23. **Effect** The temple at the religious site wears a deserted look will with the number of devotees trickling down.

Which of the following can be a possible cause of the above effect? **PNB (PO) 2010**

(a) A structural engineer had visited the temple a month back and had declared the structure unsafe
(b) The temple is facing a drastic depletion of its funds which had accumulate over the years due to offerings made by devotees
(c) The local corporation decided to donate a huge amount of money to the temple for its renovations
(d) The village housing the religious site has qualified priests to perform religious ceremonies
(e) A famous actor recently visited the temple and paid his respects to the deity

24. **Cause** The income tax authorities carried out raids at three different business houses in the city last week.

Which of the following can be a possible effect of the above statement?

(a) The three business houses are regular defaulters in payment of their income tax
(b) The income tax department had received a tip off about the illegal activities going on in the three business houses
(c) The government decided to look into the matter and has appointed an inquiry committee
(d) The government houses took immediate action to clear off all their income tax dues, in order to avoid a raid on their establishments
(e) The authorities intend to conduct raids in several other business houses in the vicinity

25. **Effect** As a step to regulate private hospitals, the state health department is framing rules to ensure all such hospitals are registered with it.

Which of the following can be a possible cause of the above statement?

(a) The department realised that private hospitals charge much less for treatment as compared to government hospitals
(b) Government run hospitals do not maintain the same standards as private hospitals
(c) The department realised that several hospitals were rejecting cases stating lack of infrastructure
(d) Apart from the number of doctors, nurses and beds, the kind of procedure a hospital can carry out based on its infrastructure will also be registered and detailed
(e) Private hospitals not registering with the department shall be forced to do so and will have to pay hefty penalties

Direction (Q. Nos. 26-35) *Read the given statements carefully and answer the questions which follow.*
IBPS (PO) 2011

26. **Effect** After the government announced a compensatory policy for farmers in return for the acquisition of their land, the farmers demanded a written proof of the policy.

Which of the following could possibly be a cause for demanding the written proof?
(a) The farmers were unable to contest the inadequate compensation for their land in earlier such policies
(b) The compensation promised in the policy was grossly inadequate
(c) The farmers were unwilling to surrender their lands to the government
(d) The farmers demand a certain percentage of share out of the revenue generated by the government off their lands
(e) The only option to enforce the government official to frame a compensatory policy for the farmers was to demand a proof

27. **Effect** The number of cases cancerning a non-contagious chemical poisoning is on the rise among local villagers.

Which of the following could possibly be a cause of the statement given above?
(a) The government has ordered an immediate enquiry into the matter
(b) Unless timely treatment is provided to the patients, the poisoning can prove to be fatal
(c) Many factories surrounding the village do not dispose off their wastes appropriately
(d) The only hospital in the areas is not equipped to treat chemical poisoning related ailments
(e) A study done a couple of years ago had reported that a large number of farmers had stopped using chemical fertilizers owing to their ill-effects on health

28. **Cause** In a government initiative, which started a couple of years ago, school teachers of a particular state were engaged in teaching the illiterate every evening after the regular school hours.

Which of the following can be an effect of the statement given above?
(a) A report given to the State government a couple of years ago stated a high percentage of illiterate population as compared to some other states
(b) Many teachers were motivated to join the scheme started by the government as the remuneration provided to them was attractive
(c) Lack of accessibility to schools and extreme poverty were major causes of illiteracy in the state
(d) Evening classes help individuals working as daily wagers attend classes after work
(e) The literacy rate in the state has improved significantly this year

29. **Cause** Small grocery shop owners have gone on a day's strike in order to protest against the entry of a foreign retail store chain in the city.

Which of the following statement can be an effect of the statement given above?
(a) The small grocery shop owners perceive the big retail giants as sharks, trying to dominate the available market space
(b) Foreign investment retail has shown a tremendous growth in India since a couple of years
(c) There have been several countries in which retail chain giants have totally wiped out small scale grocery shops
(d) The government agreed to take all political steps required to safeguard the interests of small scale retailers.
(e) A recent survey indicated that a large number of people prefer to buy their daily grocery items from the nearby grocery stores than big retail chain store

30. **Cause** It has been reported by some important news papers that current year monsoon can be lower than desired level as in so many part of the country its not raining as it is required.

Which of the following can be a possible effect of above mentioned situation? **IBPS (PO) 2011**
(a) People from less rain affected area can be displaced towards urban area
(b) Government can help the farmers of these areas with money package
(c) Government can declare these areas as drought regions
(d) People can blame government for this situation and they can protest for not getting sufficient water for agriculture
(e) None of the above

31. **Effect** It has been reported in recent years that so many seats remain vacant in the engineering colleges of the country, at the end of admission session.

Which of the following can be a possible effect mentioned above? **IBPS (PO) 2011**
(a) Because of the bad state of economy in the recent years, there has been dearth of jobs for engineering graduates
(b) Students have always given a priority to 3 yr engineering course in stead of 4 yr
(c) Government has decided to give professional training to all qualified engineering graduates on Government expenditure
(d) The success rate of engineering graduates has always been very poor
(e) None of the above

32. **Statement** The State Government granted special status to the seminar on the importance of protecting the environment around us, organised by the local academic body to create awareness among the citizens.

Which of the following may be a probable reason for the State Government's decision? **IBPS (SO) 2012**
(a) The Central Government has accorded highest priority to issues related to protection of environment overall other issues

(b) In the past, the State Government had granted special status to such seminars
(c) The State Government has failed to implement measures for protecting the environment.
(d) The local academic body made a fervent appeal for the special status
(e) None of the above

33. Statement Most car manufacturers have marginally reduced the price of their products despite higher input cost and increased government duties and have promised to keep the prices at the present level for atleast the next couple of months.

Which of the following can be the best possible reason for the above step by the car manufacturers?
(a) Car manufacturers have not been able to meet their sales target for the current year so far
(b) The government is planning to review taxes on the raw materials for manufacturing cars
(c) The car sales market is going through a jubilant phase as the volume of sales has picked up considerably in the recent past and profit per car has also gone up
(d) Car buyers are still hesitant making purchases and may postpone for another few months
(e) Oil marketing companies are contemplating reviewing the petrol and diesel prices in order to decide future market prices

34. Statement The college has finally received accreditation and has gained the status of a deemed university.

Which of the following can be a possible effect of the above statement? **PNB (PO) 2010**
(a) The principal of the college will now have to be a retired government official
(b) Number of students seeking admission to this college in the next academic year would drop significantly
(c) The college will charge lesser fees from all its students despite not getting a grant from the government
(d) The college will reduce the number of courses that runs by a significant margin
(e) The reputation of the college amongst the study population in general has improved

35. Cause The government has recently increased its taxes on petrol and diesel by about 10%.

Which of the following can be a possible effect of the above cause?
(a) The petroleum companies will reduce the prices of petrol and diesel by about 10%
(b) The petroleum companies will increase the prices of petrol and diesel by about 10%
(c) The petroleum companies will increase the prices of petrol and diesel by about 5%
(d) The petrol pumps will stop selling petrol and diesel till the taxes are rolled back by the government
(e) None of the above

Answers with Explanations

Base Level

1. (*b*) State Government reduced the tax on petroleum products last week, that is why the price of petroleum products dropped marginally, so Statement II is the cause and Statement I is the effect.

2. (*c*) Both statements are effects of independent causes.

3. (*a*) Statement II is the effect of Statement I.

4. (*b*) Since, many people have reservations about buying hallmarked jewellery, therefore it has been made compulsory.
So, Statement II is the cause and Statement I is its effect.

5. (*c*) Statements I and II are not related to each other and seem to be effects of different causes.

6. (*b*) Statement II is the cause and Statement I is its effect.

7. (*a*) Statement I is the cause and Statement II is its effect.

8. (*a*) Statement I is the cause and Statement II is its effect.

9. (*c*) Both are the effects of independent causes.

10. (*b*) Statement II will be the cause for considerable profit of steel manufacturing companies. So, statement II is cause and Statement I is its effect.

11. (*b*) Statement II is the cause for increasing stamp duty.
So, Statement II is cause and Statement I is its effect.

12. (*a*) India lost the cricket tournament because its top three players were injured. So, Statement I is the cause and Statement II is its effect.

13. (*c*) Both the Statements I and II are effects of independent causes.

14. (*a*) Statements I is the cause and II is its effect.

15. (*c*) Both the Statements I and II are effect of independent causes.

16. (*b*) The municipal authority advised all the schools in the city to close down for the next two days because a huge storm is likely to hit the city during the next two days. So, Statement II is the cause and Statement I is its effect.

17. (*b*) The pressure of social activists has led to the baning of channels. So, Statement II is cause and Statement I is its effect.

18. (*d*) The two statements are contradictory, so they are effects of independent causes.

19. (*b*) The large number of terrorist attacks has led to tightened security checks. So, Statement II is cause and Statement I is its effect.

20. (*a*) The high court order has led to road repair work on urgent basis. So, Statement I is cause and Statement II is its effect.

21. (*b*) The flood has caused outbreaking of epidemics. So, Statement II is cause and Statement I is its effect.

22. (*d*) New parking levels are not introduced because of the attack on parliament but due to strengthening the security of the Indian Parliament and the parliamentarian. So, Statement II is the effect but Statement I is not its cause.

23. (*b*) The officials of Food Adulteration Department has started collecting samples of vegetables from suspicions places in state X because in that state people have claimed that vegetables are treated with malachite green. So, Statement II is the cause and Statement I is its effect.

24. (*c*) Cricketer 'A' has denied to talk with media persons. So, Statement I is the effect but Statement II is not the cause because there may be some other reason for that.

25. (*c*) Statement I is the effect but Statement II is not the principal cause for it because the cause is hike in diesel prices.

26. (*e*) Both I and II are independent causes.

27. (*a*) Driven to commit suicide due to humiliation is violation of human rights. So, the National Human Rights Commission is giving ₹ 1 lakh as interim compensation to the legal heirs who commit suicide. So, Statement II is the cause and Statement I is its immediate effect.

28. (*a*) Statement II is the cause and Statement I is its immediate effect.

29. (*a*) The Bar Council of India (BCI) has ordered evening law colleges to close down because the standard of education in evening law colleges was decreasing. So, Statement II is the cause and Statement I is its effect.

30. (*c*) Statement I is the effect but Statement II is not the principal cause of it.

31. (*a*) The sale of liquor was high due to the Holi which is a dry day. So, Statement II is the cause and Statement I is its effect.

32. (*b*) Statement I is the cause and Statement II is its effect.

33. (*b*) The fiscal deficit of the country has decreased because the finance ministry has imposed additional taxation. So,

Statement I is the cause and Statement II is its effect.

34. (*d*) Both statements are effects of some common cause as these are measures taken by Government.

35. (*d*) Since, both Statements I and II are effects of some common cause i.e. bitumen causing cancer to humans.

36. (*a*) Here, Statement I is the cause and Statement II is its effect, i.e. after the survey is conducted, then based on that survey, national compaign network for men's health launched its awareness.

37. (*b*) Here, Statement II is the cause and Statement I is its effect i.e. since a large number of members have withdrawn major amount of deposits from the credit society, so the credit society has decided to stop giving loans to farmers with immediate effect.

38. (*b*) The mass recruitment of IT professionals by Indian IT companies is due to the work companies are getting from the developed countries. So, Statement II is the cause while Statement I is its effect.

39. (*e*) Both Statements I and II are effects of some common causes.

40. (*a*) Statement I is the cause while Statement II is its effects.

41. (*b*) The State government has decided to implement English language education in all the schools because the level of English language of the school students is lower when compared with the neighbouring states. So, this move will all help in improving the level of English language. So, Statement II is the cause while Statement I is its effect.

42. (*c*) Both Statements I and II are independent causes.

43. (*a*) Statement I is the cause while Statement II is its effect.

44. (*d*) Both Statements I and II are effects of independent causes.

45. (*e*) Both Statements I and II are effects of some common causes

46. (*a*) Statement I is the cause while Statement II is its effect.

47. (*b*) As few projects are outsourced to BPO sector, so large number of employees working in this sector are fined. So, Statement II is the cause while Statement I is its effect.

48. (*c*) Both Statements I and II are independent causes.

49. (*a*) Statement I is the cause while Statement II is its effect.

50. (*d*) Both Statements I and II are effects of independent causes.

51. (*e*) Both Statements I and II are effects of some common causes.

52. (*a*) Statement I is the cause while Statement II is its effect.

53. (*b*) Statement II is the cause while Statement I is its effect.

54. (*e*) Both Statements I and II are effect of some common cause.

55. (*b*) The association of management colleges conducted a combined admission exam for all the institutes this year because last year date of entrance exams of many management colleges clashed and many student could appear for a number of entrance exams. So, Statement II is the cause and Statement I is its effect.

56. (*b*) The departmental store owner put cameras for surveillance of the store because many products were reported missing by the staff of that store. So, Statement II is the cause and Statement I is its effect.

57. (*d*) Both statements are effects of independent causes. Asthma cases are not responsible for dwindling of birds and animals.

58. (*b*) If Statement II is the cause then definitely due to less production, Statement I is the effect.

59. (*d*) Both are effects of independent causes. The University decide to postpone the final exams for course X by a month due to some administrative problems.

60. (*a*) Many people are opting for change from private sector to public sector because worldwide recession has created uncertainty in the job market. It is considered that public sector jobs are more certain than the private sector jobs. So, Statement I is the cause while Statement II is the effect.

61. (*b*) A large number of employees could not report to the duty on time because police had laid down barricades on the road to drop the miscreants. So, Statement II is the cause while Statement I is its effect.

62. (*c*) Both Statements I and II are independent causes.

63. (*d*) Both Statements I and II are effects of independent causes.

64. (*e*) Both the Statements I and II are effects of some common causes.

Advanced Level

1. (*a*) The people of capital are facing problem of acute shortage of water, so the chief minister takes the decision to supply more tankers.

   Statement I is cause and II is the effect.

2. (*b*) The air quality is decreasing day-by-day in Delhi that is why NGT takes the decision to ban diesel vehicles.

   So, Statement II is the cause and I is the effect.

3. (*d*) Both the statements are effects of the common cause that people are unemployed and needs job.

4. (*d*) Both the statements are based on the problem of obesity and its effects .

5. (*d*) Both statements are effects of some common cause which is inflation.

6. (*a*) Both statements are effects of independent causes, because the results of the students were excellent and teachers left Kendriya Vidyalayas are different causes.

7. (*b*) Statement II is the cause and Statement I is its effect because in Statement II, it is clearly say that many fruits like watermelon or cucumber are calorie burners as digesting them burns more calories than eating them.

8. (*a*) Both statements are effects of independent causes.

9. (*c*) Statement I is the cause and Statement II is its effect.

10. (*a*) The word in survey 'on healthy habits' signifies that life style and food habits are responsible.

    So, option (a) is the cause.

11. (*c*) Heavy rains in the catchment area of lakes supplying drinking water force the municipal authority to take the decision.

    So, I is the cause and II is the effect.

12. (*e*) Both Statements I and II are independent causes.

13. (*a*) Statement II is the cause and Statements I is its effect.

14. (*e*) Both Statements I and II are indentendent causes.

15. (*a*) Commuters are facing lots of problems because thousands of diesel buses are not running on roads. So, Statement II is the cause and Statements I is its effect.

16. (*e*) Both Statements I and II are independent causes.

17. (*b*) Both statements are effects of independent causes.

18. (*c*) The prices of 'silver' going up from ₹ 27000 per kg to over ₹ 50000 per kg and Indian jewellers receiving a lot of demand for the silver ornaments from American and European clients.

    So, Statement II is immidiate cause and Statement I is its effect.

19. (*a*) Statement I is the cause and Statement II is its effect.

20. (*d*) 'Blessing of Mother Durga' is a common cause between two statements. Hence, both the statements are effects of some common cause.

21. (*b*) The prices of foodgrains and vegetables have increased by about 30% due to increase of more than 30% in the price of other products, because farmers will need 30% more funding for purchasing other products.

22. (*a*) Option (a) should be the obvious cause for the given effect.

23. (*a*) The main cause for number of devotees trickling down at the religious site because of a structural engineer had visited the temple a month back and had declared the structure unsafe.

24. (*d*) Income tax authorities carried out raids due to non-payment of tax or illegal money so as an effect business houses took immediate action to clear off all their income tax dues in order to avoid raid.

25. (*e*) The rule is going to frame for compulsory registration else charging fine.

26. (*a*) Due to early bad experience, farmers demanded a written proof of the policy.

27. (*c*) Due to not disposing off wastes, non-contagious chemical poisoning is on the rise among local villagers.

28. (*e*) Due to evening classes, the literacy rate in the state has improved significantly.

29. (*d*) The main effect of small grocery owners a day's strike will be that the government agreed to take all political steps required to safeguard the interest of small scale retailers.

30. (*c*) Option (c) is also possible but its possibility can only be after declaring the areas as drought region.

31. (*a*) Option (a) is the obvious possible cause.

32. (*a*) Central Government's priority has made State Government to grant special status to the seminar.

33. (*a*) The sales target has become unachievable that is why the companies are not increasing the price.

34. (*e*) Accreditation improves reputation of the college.

35. (*b*) As petroleum companies are deciding the price of petrol, so they may increase the price of petrol and diesel by about 10%.

9

Input-Output

In general parlance, Input is a group of words, numbers or data that is fed into the system or expended in its operation to achieve output or a result, while Output means an artifact of the arrangement that has been created by someone or some process.

Input-Output questions are based on a given input of line of words or numbers or words and numbers that are organised step-by-step following a specific rule to arrive at the final step. Candidates are required to be conversant with the rule of arrangement of words or numbers or words and numbers. They are required to observe the change in order of words or numbers in each step sequentially to specify the rule of arrangement of words and numbers.

Generally, each set of questions on Input-Output based on a particular rule. The different sets of questions involve different rules of arrangement of words or numbers. Thus, there is no fixed number of rules of arrangement of words or numbers. However, most common type of questions on input involves arrangement of words as per dictionary or in alphabetical order or arrangement of numbers in ascending or descending order. Generally, one word or number is arranged in every step and procedure is continued until all the words or numbers get arranged according to a specific rule.

Types of Questions

There are mainly four types of questions that are asked from Input-Output, i.e. Shifting, Arranging, Arithmetic Operations, Miscellaneous.

1. **Shifting** In this type of questions, the given words of the Input are Shifted as per a certain pattern.
2. **Arranging** In this type of questions, the numbers or the words are arranged as per a given order. The given order can be Alphabetical order in case of words and Ascending or Descending order in case of numbers.
3. **Arithmetic Operations** In this type of questions, the Input has some numbers. Different steps are obtained by taking the numbers of the input and different arithmetic operations are performed after that.
4. **Miscellaneous** This type of questions cover miscellaneous questions. This input can be anything and machine perform set of random operations on this.

Identifying the Types of Problem

***Step* I First, check for Arrangement**

First of all check that, if there is any arrangement. In case of Arrangement, words would be arranged in alphabetical order and the numbers would be arranged in increasing or decreasing order. To check it, just look at the first two-three steps, if an arrangement is found, then the problem is arrangement based problem.

***Step* II Next, check for Shifting**

If the given problem is not arrangement based, then check whether Shifting is taking place. Just check the first two-three steps, if the words from a particular position are moving to another particular position and that is being repeated, then the given problem is Shifting Problem.

***Step* III Check for Arithmetic Operations**

Arithmetic Operations is possible if and only if the Input has only the numbers. If the input has numbers and the chances of Arrangement & Shifting are not there, then the problem is based on Arithmetic Operations for sure.

If none of the above is applicable, then you can be sure that the given problem is of miscellaneous type.

Expert's Advice

Here are some tips, which you can use to some **Input-Output** based questions.

1. First of all, observe the given input line of words or numbers and the last step of rearrangement, so that candidate may get an idea about the changes effected in various steps of rearrangement.
2. In order to know what changes have been made in each step, observe two consecutive steps carefully.
3. Now, correlate the input, the last step and anyone of the middle steps. This will enable you to identify the rule of arrangement.

Solved Examples

Direction (Examples 1-2) *A word arrangement machine, when given a particular input, rearranges it following a particular rule upto step 4. The following is the illustration of the input and the steps of the arrangement. Study the inherent logic and answer the following questions.* **IIFT 2014**

Input be the change you wish to see in this world
Step I the be you change to wish in see world this
Step II you be the change to world in see wish this
Step III you see the this to world in be wish change
Step IV see you this the world to be in change wish

***Ex* 1.** If the input is, 'don't cry because it's over smile since it actually happened', then Step 4 will be

(a) it's since actually happened cry smile don't it over because
(b) since cry it's happened actually smile it don't because over
(c) since it's actually cry happened smile don't it because over
(d) since it's cry actually happened don't smile it over because

***Ex* 2.** If Step IV generates, 'dog sea school star ice moon flower home rock ball', then the input was

(a) flower star rock sea ball moon dog home school ice
(b) rock flower sea ball dog star moon school home ice
(c) flower ball star sea rock dog moon ice home school
(d) star moon rock sea home flower ice ball dog school

SOLUTION (Examples 1-2)

Input	be	the	change	you	wish	to	see	in	this	world
	1	2	3	4	5	6	7	8	9	10
Step I	2	1	4	3	6	5	8	7	10	9
Step II	4	1	2	3	6	10	8	7	5	9
Step III	4	7	2	9	6	10	8	1	5	3
Step IV	7	4	9	2	10	6	1	8	3	5

1. (c)

Given,	Input :	don't	cry	because	it's	over	smile	since	it	actually	happened
		1	2	3	4	5	6	7	8	9	10

Step I Cry don't it's because smile over it since happened actually
Step II it's don't cry because smile happened it since over actually
Step III it's since, cry actually smile happened it don't over because
Step IV since, it's actually cry happened smile don't it because over

2. (*a*)

Step IV	dog	sea	school	star	ice	moon	flower	home	rock	ball
	7	4	9	2	10	6	1	8	3	5
Input	1	2	3	4	5	6	7	8	9	10
	flower	star	rock	sea	ball	moon	dog	home	school	ice

Direction (Examples. 3-8) *Study the given information and answer the questions.* **SBI (PO) 2014**

When a word and number arrangement machine is given an input line of words and numbers, it arranges them by following a particular rule. The following is an illustration of input and rearrangement :

(All the numbers are two-digit numbers)

Input initiators 32 67 of 40 the company 21 are 18 96 humble

Step I 21 initiators 32 67 of 40 the company are 96 humble 18

Step II company 21 initiators 32 67 of 40 the 96 humble 18 are

Step III 40 company 21 initiators 67 of the 96 humble 18 are 32

Step IV initiators 40 company 21 67 of the 96 18 are 32 humble

Step V 96 initiators 40 company 21 of the 18 are 32 humble 67

Step VI the 96 initiators 40 company 21 18 are 32 humble 67 of

Step VI is the last step of the above arrangement as the intended arrangement is obtained.

As per the rules followed in the given steps, find out the appropriate steps for the given input.

Input parenting 16 36 and raising 44 children 21 is 89 very 95 demanding 72 job 65.

Ex 3. In which step are the elements '95 job 16 and' found in the same order?

(a) The given order of elements is not found in any step
(b) Fifth
(c) Fourth
(d) Second
(e) Third

Ex 4. What is the position of the '72' from the right end in the fourth step?

(a) Fifth
(b) Eight
(c) Ninth
(d) Seventh
(e) Sixth

Ex 5. Which element is fifth to the left of the element which is tenth from the left end of the third step?

(a) Raising (b) Parenting
(c) Is (d) 72
(e) job

Ex 6. How many steps will be required to complete the given arrangement based on the given input?

(a) Ten (b) Eight (c) Six (d) Nine
(e) Seven

Ex 7. Which element is exactly between 'parenting' and 'raising' in the second step of the given arrangement?

(a) 36 (b) 16 (c) 44 (d) 21
(e) 95

Ex 8. Which of the following is the third last step of the arrangement based on the given input

(a) 72 44 21 parenting is raising children 89 very 95 and job demanding 16 36 65
(b) 72 parenting 44 is 21 children raising 89 very 95 and 16 demanding 36 job 65
(c) parenting 72 is 44 children 21 raising 89 very 95 16 and 36 demanding 65 job
(d) parenting job is demanding children raising 89 very 95 16 and 36 21 44 65 72
(e) parenting is 72 44 children raising 21 89 very 95 16 and 36 65 demanding job

SOLUTION (Examples 3-8)

Input parenting 16 36 and raising 44 children 21 is 89 very 95 demanding 72 job 65

Step I 21 parenting 36 and raising 44 children is 89 very 95 demanding 72 job 65 16

Step II Children 21 parenting 36 raising 44 is 89 very 95 demanding 72 job 65 16 and

Step III 44 children 21 parenting raising is 89 very 95 demanding 72 job 65 16 and 36

Step IV is 44 children 21 parenting raising 89 very 95 72 job 65 16 and 36 demanding

Step V 72 is 44 children 21 parenting raising 89 very 95 job 16 and 36 demanding 65

Step VI parenting 72 is 44 children 21 raising 89 very 95 16 and 36 demanding 65 job

Step VII 95 parenting 72 is 44 children 21 raising very 16 and 36 demanding 65 job 89

Step VIII very 95 parenting 72 is 44 children 21 16 and 36 demanding 65 job 89 raising

3. (*b*) Order of element '95 job 16 and' found is step V.
4. (*d*) Position of 72 is seventh from the right end in fourth step.
5. (*a*) Raising
6. (*b*) Eight
7. (*a*) 36
8. (*c*) parenting 72 is 44 children 21 raising 89 very 95 16 and 36 demanding 65 job.

Direction (Examples 9-13) *Study the following information carefully and answer the given questions.* **BOI (PO) 2010**

A word and number arrangement machine when given an input line of words and numbers rearranges them following a particular rule in each step. The following is an illustration of input and rearrangement.

Input rose petal 29 32 86 goal 41 toll
Step I 29 rose petal 32 86 goal 41 toll
Step II 29 toll rose petal 32 86 goal 41
Step III 29 toll 32 rose petal 86 goal 41
Step IV 29 toll 32 rose 41 petal 86 goal
Step IV is the last step of the rearrangement.

Ex **9. Step III** of an input is 15 yes 24 80 today never go 59, which of the following will definitely be the input?
(a) 24 80 today never go 59 15 yes
(b) 24 80 today yes never go 59 15
(c) 24 15 yes 80 today never go 59
(d) Cannot be determined
(e) None of the above

Ex **10. Input** man 79 over 63 like 43 joy 15. How many steps will be required to complete the rearrangement?
(a) Six (b) Seven (c) Eight (d) Nine
(e) None of these

Ex **11. Step III** of an input is 18 tower 38 basket 82 76 hall new, which of the following will be step VII?
(a) 18 tower 38 hall 76 new basket 82
(b) 18 tower 38 new 76 hall 82 basket
(c) 18 tower 38 hall 76 new 82 basket
(d) There will be no such step
(e) None of the above

Ex **12. Input** 94 join for 81 style home 32 48, which of the following step will be the last?
(a) VI (b) V (c) VII (d) IX
(e) None of these

Ex **13. Step II** of an input is 27 world go 57 48 stem 35 kite. How many more steps will be required to complete the rearrangement?
(a) Five
(b) Four
(c) Three
(d) Six
(e) None of the above

SOLUTION (Examples 9-13)

9. (*d*) **Input** Cannot be determined.

10. (*e*) **Input** man 79 over 63 like 43 joy 15
Step I 15 man 79 over 63 like 43 joy
Step II 15 over man 79 63 like 43 joy
Step III 15 over 43 man 79 63 like joy
Step IV 15 over 43 man 63 79 like joy
Step V 15 over 43 man 63 like 79 joy

11. (*b*) **Step III** 18 tower 38 basket 82 76 hall new
Step IV 18 tower 38 new basket 82 76 hall
Step V 18 tower 38 new 76 basket 82 hall
Step VI 18 tower 38 new 76 hall basket 82
Step VII 18 tower 38 new 76 hall 82 basket

12. (*a*) **Input** 94 join for 81 style home 32 48
Step I 32 94 join for 81 style home 48
Step II 32 style 94 join for 81 home 48
Step III 32 style 48 94 join for 81 home
Step IV 32 style 48 join 94 for 81 home
Step V 32 style 48 join 81 94 for home
Step VI 32 style 48 join 81 home 94 for
So, last step is step VI.

13. (*a*) **Step II** 27 world go 57 48 stem 35 kite
Step III 27 world 35 go 57 48 stem kite
Step IV 27 world 35 stem go 57 48 kite
Step V 27 world 35 stem 48 go 57 kite
Step VI 27 world 35 stem 48 kite go 57
Step VII 27 world 35 stem 48 kite 57 go

Direction (Examples 14-19) *An electronic device, when fed with the numbers, rearranges them in a particular order following certain rules. The following is a step by step process of rearrangements for the given input of numbers.*

Input	5	28	12	74	3	11	31	42
Step I	74	5	28	12	3	11	31	42
Step II	74	3	5	28	12	11	31	42
Step III	74	3	42	5	28	12	11	31
Step IV	74	3	42	5	28	11	12	31

For the given input, Step IV is the last step.

Ex **14.** Which of the following will be the Step III for the following input?
Input 89 24 44 25 9 14 5 2
(a) 44 5 14 25 89 9 2 24
(b) 44 5 14 9 24 2 89 25
(c) 44 5 24 9 85 25 14 2
(d) 44 5 89 24 25 9 4 2
(e) None of the above

Ex **15.** Which step would be the last step for the following input?
Input 89 24 44 25 9 14 5 2
(a) Step IV (b) Step III (c) Step VI (d) Step VII
(e) Step VIII

Ex **16.** If the Step IV is as given below, which of the following will be the input?
Step IV 48 03 22 7 12 25
(a) 03 25 12 48 22 07 (b) 03 25 48 12 22 07
(c) 03 48 25 12 22 07 (d) None of these
(e) Cannot be determined

Ex **17.** Which of the following will be the Step III for the following input?
Input 03 25 12 48 22 07
(a) 48 03 22 25 12 07 (b) 48 03 25 12 22 07
(c) 48 03 22 07 12 25 (d) 48 03 22 07 25 12
(e) None of these

Ex **18.** Which of the following will be the last step for the following input?
Input 05 27 50 14 24 9
(a) III (b) IV (c) VI (d) VII
(e) None of these

Ex **19.** Which of the following will be the Step III for the following input ?
Input 25 08 35 11 88 67 24 78
(a) 88 11 78 25 24 08 35 67
(b) 88 11 78 25 08 35 67 24
(c) 88 25 08 35 11 67 24 78
(d) 88 11 25 08 35 67 24 78
(e) None of the above

SOLUTION (Examples 14-19)

Pattern of the arrangement of steps of given input suggests that given input is split into two sections—one for even numbers and other for odd numbers. Then, arrange these numbers in such a way that even numbers are arranged in descending order and odd numbers are arranged in ascending order.

14. (*e*)

Input	89	24	44	25	09	14	5	2
Step I	44	89	24	25	09	14	5	2
Step II	44	05	89	24	25	09	14	2
Step III	44	05	24	89	25	09	14	2

Since, none of the options contains the correct input as shown by Step III. Hence, the correct answer is option (e).

15. (*d*) If we keep arranging the steps from Step III onward as in the previous question, we get the final arrangement of the input in Step VII as shown below:
Step VII 44 05 24 09 14 25 2 89

16. (*e*) We cannot determine the input for the given step because exact placement of the numbers in input cannot be known. As a result, option (a) and (b) both reflect the probable input.

17. (*d*)

Input	03	25	12	48	22	07
Step I	48	03	25	12	22	07
Step II	48	03	22	25	12	07
Step III	48	03	22	07	25	12

18. (*b*)

Input	05	27	50	14	24	09
Step I	50	05	27	14	24	09
Step II	50	05	24	27	14	09
Step III	50	05	24	09	27	14
Step IV	50	05	24	09	14	27

Step IV is the last step for the given input as it arranges the input completely.

19. (*b*)

Input	25	08	35	11	88	67	24	78
Step I	88	25	08	35	11	67	24	78
Step II	88	11	25	08	35	67	24	78
Step III	88	11	78	25	08	35	67	24

Cumulative Exercise

Base Level

Direction (Q. Nos. 1-5) *Study the following information to answer the given questions.*

A word and number arrangement machine when given an input line of words and numbers rearranges them by following a particular rule. The following is an illustration of input and rearrangement.

Input 52 peak 91 snow freeze 46 cold 15 high 31 73 trek
Step I 15 52 peak snow freeze 46 cold high 31 73 trek 91
Step II 15 31 52 peak snow freeze 46 cold high trek 73 91
Step III 15 31 46 peak snow freeze cold high trek 52 73 91
Step IV 15 31 46 cold peak snow freeze high trek 52 73 91
Step V 15 31 46 cold freeze peak snow high trek 52 73 91
Step VI 15 31 46 cold freeze high peak snow trek 52 73 91

Step VI is the last step of the rearrangement. As per the rules followed in the above steps, find out in each of the following questions the appropriate steps for the given input.

Input 67 hot sun 19 best 83 ice 49 ace 77 cut 37

IBPS (PO) 2011

1. How many steps would be needed to complete the arrangement?
(a) X (b) VIII (c) IX (d) VII
(e) None of these

2. Which step number would be the following output?
19 37 49 ace best hot sun ice cut 67 77 83
(a) II (b) VI (c) V (d) IV
(e) None of these

3. Which of the following would be the Step I?
(a) 19 37 49 hot sun best ice ace cut 67 77 83
(b) 83 67 hot sun best ice 49 ace 77 cut 37 19
(c) 19 67 ace best hot sun ice 49 77 cut 37 19
(d) 19 67 hot sun best ice 49 ace 77 cut 37 83
(e) None of the above

4. Which of the following would be the final arrangement?
(a) 67 77 83 ace best cut hot ice sun 19 37 49
(b) 19 37 49 ace best cut hot ice sun 67 77 83
(c) 19 37 49 67 77 83 ace best cut hot ice sun
(d) 19 37 49 ace ice best cut hot sun 67 77 83
(e) None of the above

5. In Step IV, which of the following word/number would be on 7th position (from the right)?
(a) sun (b) best
(c) 67 (d) cut
(e) None of these

Direction (Q. Nos. 6-11) *Study the following information carefully and answer the given questions.*

Syndicate Bank (PO) 2010

A word and number arrangement machine when given an input line of words and numbers rearranges them by following a particular rule in each step. The following is an illustration of input and rearrangement.

Input sale data 18 23 for 95 then 38
Step I data sale 18 23 for 95 then 38
Step II data 95 sale 18 23 for then 38
Step III data 95 for sale 18 23 then 38
Step IV data 95 for 38 sale 18 23 then
Step V data 95 for 38 sale 23 18 then
Step VI data 95 for 38 sale 23 then 18

Step VI is the last step of the rearrangement of the above input.

As per the rules followed in the above steps, find out in each of the following questions the appropriate step for the given input.

6. **Input** year 39 stake 47 house full 94 55
How many steps will be required to complete the rearrangement?
(a) Five
(b) Six
(c) Four
(d) Seven
(e) None of the above

7. **Step II** of an input is car 83 lost ever 32 46 74 now
How many more steps will be required to complete the rearrangement?
(a) Three
(b) Four
(c) Five
(d) Six
(e) None of the above

8. Step III of an input is and 79 code 27 18 new goal 34

Which of the following will definitely be the input?

(a) code and 79 27 18 new goal 34
(b) code 27 18 new goal 34 and 79
(c) code 27 and 18 79 new goal 34
(d) Cannot be determined
(e) None of the above

9. Input water full never 35 78 16 height 28

Which of the following step will be the last?

(a) VI (b) VII
(c) VIII (d) IX
(e) None of these

10. Step II of an input is high 69 store pay 36 43 15 there

Which of the following will be step VI?

(a) high 69 pay 43 store 36 there 15
(b) high 69 pay 43 store 36 15 there
(c) high 69 pay 36 43 store 15 there
(d) there will be no such step
(e) None of the above

11. Input train more 29 53 fast gear 37 84

Which of the following steps will be the last but one?

(a) IX (b) VIII
(c) VII (d) VI
(e) None of these

Direction (Q. Nos. 12-17) *Read the following information carefully and answer the questions given below* **SBI (PO) 2001**

A word-number arrangement machine when given an input as set of word-numbers rearranges them by following a particular rule and generates stepwise outputs till the rearrangement is complete following that rule.

Following is an illustration of input and steps of rearrangement till the last step.

Input pour ask 57 dear 39 fight 17 28
Step I ask pour 57 dear 39 fight 17 28
Step II ask 57 pour dear 39 fight 17 28
Step III ask 57 dear pour 39 fight 17 28
Step IV ask 57 dear 39 pour fight 17 28
Step V ask 57 dear 39 fight pour 17 28
Step VI ask 57 dear 39 fight 28 pour 17
and Step VI is the last output.

As per the rule followed in the given steps find out the answer to each of the following questions:

12. If Step II of an input is "cut 97 38 end for 29 46 down", which of the following will be the last step?

(a) V (b) IV
(c) VI (d) VII
(e) None of these

13. If the IVth step of an input is "ago 85 elite 79 exile fat 26 41" which of the following will definitely the IInd step of the input?

(a) ago 85 79 elite fat 41 26 exile
(b) ago 85 exile elite 41 26 fat 79
(c) ago 85 26 exile 41 elite 79 fat
(d) Cannot be determined
(e) None of the above

14. If the Ist step of an input is "car 17 vas tiger 92 87 like 52" which of the following will be the IVth step?

(a) car 92 like 87 tiger 52 17 vas
(b) car 92 like 87 17 vas tiger 52
(c) car 92 like 87 tiger 17 vas 52
(d) car 92 like 17 vas tiger 87 52
(e) None of the above

15. Input zeal for 49 31 high 22 track 12

Which of the following will be the IIIrd step ?

(a) for 49 high 31 track 22 zeal 12
(b) for 49 high 31 zeal 22 track 12
(c) for 49 high zeal 31 22 track 12
(d) for 49 high 31 track zeal 22 12
(e) None of the above

16. Input 19 feat 34 28 dog bag take 43

Which of the following steps would be "bag 43 dog 19 feat 34 28 take"?

(a) IInd (b) IVth
(c) Ist (d) Cannot be determined
(e) None of these

17. In Step III position of 34 from the left end?

(a) Fifth (b) Sixth
(c) Third (d) Cannot be determined
(e) None of these

Direction (Q. Nos. 18-23) *A word and number arrangement machine when given an input line of words and numbers rearranges them by following a particular rule in each step. The following is an illustration of input and rearrangement.*

RBI (Grade B) 2009

Input but 32 71 glory fair south 65 84
Step I south but 32 71 glory fair 65 84
Step II south 84 but 32 71 glory fair 65
Step III south 84 glory but 32 71 fair 65
Step IV south 84 glory 71 but 32 fair 65
Step V south 84 glory 71 fair but 32 65
Step VI south 84 glory 71 fair 65 but 32
and step VI is the last step of the rearrangement.

As per the rules followed in the above steps, find out in each of the following questions the appropriate step for the given input.

18. Step III of an input is year 92 ultra 15 23 strive house 39.

How many more steps will be required to complete the rearrangement?

(a) Three (b) Four
(c) Two (d) Five
(e) None of these

19. Input any how 49 24 far wide 34 69

Which of the following steps will be the last but one?

(a) VI (b) VII
(c) V (d) VIII
(e) None of these

20. Step II of an input is town 74 pair 15 31 nice job 42

Which of the following is definitely the input?

(a) pair 15 31 town nice job 42 74
(b) pair 15 town 31 74 nice job 42
(c) pair 15 town 74 31 nice job 42
(d) Cannot be determined
(e) None of the above

21. Input play over 49 37 12 match now 81

Which of the following will be step IV?

(a) play 81 over 49 39 match now
(b) play 81 over 49 37 12 match now
(c) play 81 over 49 now 37 match 12
(d) there will be no such step
(e) None of the above

22. Step II of an input is war 58 box cart 33 49 star 24

Which of the following step will be the last?

(a) V (b) VI
(c) IV (d) VII
(e) None of these

23. Input shower fall water 34 51 67 98 goal

How many steps will be required to complete the rearrangement?

(a) Three
(b) Four
(c) Six
(d) Five
(e) None of the above

Direction (Q. Nos. 24-27) *A word arrangement, when rearranged by given input follow a particular logic behind it. Study that logic and apply on given problems.*

Input heater and sun rays helps in winter
Step I winter heater and sun rays helps in
Step II winter sun heater and rays helps in
Step III winter sun rays heater and helps in
Step IV winter sun rays in heater and helps
Step V winter sun rays in helps heater and

Now, words are fully arranged and we finish the process here.

24. Which of the following will be step III for the given input?

Input life become bore without success

(a) bore life become success without
(b) without life become bore success
(c) without success life bore become
(d) Data insufficient/Cannot be determined
(e) None of the above

25. If the following result is IInd for input, then what will be the fourth step?

Step II the success my is outcome of diligence

(a) my success is outcome of the diligence
(b) the my success is outcome of diligence
(c) success is the outcome of my diligence
(d) the success outcome of my is diligence
(e) None of the above

26. Which of the following will be the last step of given input?

Input an invitation to a most exclusive evening

(a) an invitation to exclusive a most evening
(b) to a most exclusive evening an invitation
(c) invitation to a most an exclusive evening
(d) Cannot be determined
(e) None of the above

27. How many step will be required to get the final output from given input?

Input never break your elders trust

(a) I (b) VI (c) III (d) II
(e) None of these

Direction (Q. Nos. 28-32) *Read the information carefully and answer the questions given below. A word arrangement machine, when given an input line of words, rearranges them by following a particular rule in each step. The following is the illustration of the input and the steps of arrangement.*

Input Dhoni cannot but feel sorry for him
Step I but cannot Dhoni sorry feel him for
Step II cannot but feel sorry Dhoni for him
Step III but cannot sorry feel him for Dhoni
Step IV sorry cannot but him feel Dhoni for

and so on for subsequent steps. You have to find out the logic and answer the questions given below.

28. If Step V read weeks of tepid slothful and weak ideas, then what would Step IV read?

(a) ideas weeks and tepid of weak slothful
(b) of weeks and slothful tepid ideas weak
(c) of tepid slothful ideas weak and weeks
(d) ideas and tepid weeks of weak slothful
(e) None of the above

29. If Step I read it was the name bestowed upon him, then what would be the arrangement for Step VII?

(a) bestowed it was the name upon him
(b) him it name bestowed the was upon
(c) it was him the name bestowed upon
(d) upon the him was it bestowed name
(e) None of the above

30. If Step VI reads workers must take a stand against working, then what will be the last word of Step III?

(a) workers (b) must
(c) take (d) a
(e) None of these

31. If Step III reads the best way of promoting our sports, then what will be the arrangement of the input?
(a) best the sports way of our promoting
(b) our promoting the best sports way of
(c) sports best the of way our promoting
(d) of our best the way sports promoting
(e) None of the above

32. If the given input is it is good approach with care, then what will be Step IV?
(a) with approach it is a good care
(b) approach is a care good it with
(c) a good approach it is with care
(d) care with a good approach is it
(e) None of the above

Direction (Q. Nos. 33-37) *Study the following information carefully and answer the given questions.*

A word and number arrangement machine when given an input line of words and numbers rearranges them by following a particular rule in each step. The following is an illustration of input and rearrangement.

Input base 35 or gone 62 49 87 ahead
Step I 87 base 35 or gone 62 49 ahead
Step II 87 ahead base 35 or gone 62 49
Step III 87 ahead 62 base 35 or gone 49
Step IV 87 ahead 62 base 49 35 or gone
Step V 87 ahead 62 base 49 gone 35 or

and Step V is the last step of the rearrangement. As per the rules followed in the above steps, find out in each of the following questions the appropriate step for the given input.

33. Input how was your stay 56 25 36 64
Which of the following will be step VI?
(a) 64 how 56 was your stay 25 36
(b) 64 how 56 stay 36 was 25 your
(c) 64 how 56 stay 36 was your 25
(d) there will be no such step
(e) None of the above

34. Input power fail now 52 24 75 gate 34
Which of the following steps will be the last but one?
(a) IV (b) V (c) VI (d) VII
(e) None of these

35. Step III of an input is 91 car 85 14 27 few new house
Which of the following is definitely the input?
(a) 85 14 91 car 27 few new house
(b) car 91 85 14 27 few new house
(c) car 85 14 27 few new house 91
(d) Cannot be determined
(e) None of the above

36. Step II of an input is 75 down 16 24 farm eager 62 sky
How many more steps will be required to complete the rearrangement?
(a) Four (b) Five (c) Six (d) Seven
(e) None of these

37. Input 14 35 when they came 61 48 home
How many steps will be required to complete the rearrangement?
(a) Four (b) Five
(c) Six (d) Seven
(e) None of these

Direction (Q. Nos. 38-43) *Study the following information carefully and answer the given questions.*
UBI (PO) 2009

A word and number arrangement machine when given an input line of words and numbers rearranges them following a particular rule in each step. The following is an illustration of input and rearrangement.

Input shop 17 table 20 53 oven desk 39
Step I 17 shop table 20 53 oven desk 39
Step II 17 table shop 20 53 oven desk 39
Step III 17 table 20 shop 53 oven desk 39
Step IV 17 table 20 shop 39 53 oven desk
Step V 17 table 20 shop 39 oven 53 desk

and step V is the last step of the rearrangement.
As per the rules followed in the above steps, find out in each of the following questions that appropriate step for the given input.

38. Step II of an input is 15 yes 62 51 48 talk now gone
Which of the following will be step VI?
(a) 15 yes 48 talk 51 now gone 62
(b) 15 yes 48 talk 51 62 now gone
(c) 15 yes 48 talk 51 now 62 gone
(d) there will be no such step
(e) None of the above

39. Step III of an input is 21 victory 30 joint 64 47 all gone
How many more steps will be required to complete the rearrangement?
(a) Three (b) Four
(c) Five (d) Five
(e) None of these

40. Input 89 bind 32 goal house 61 12 joy
How many steps will be required to complete the arrangement?
(a) Four (b) Five
(c) Six (d) Seven
(e) None of these

41. Input save 21 43 78 them early 36 for
Which of the following steps will be the last but one?
(a) VI
(b) VII
(c) VIII
(d) V
(e) None of the above

42. **Input** desire 59 63 all few 38 46 zone
How many steps will be required to complete the rearrangement?
(a) Four (b) Five (c) Six (d) Seven
(e) None of these

43. **Input** win 92 task 73 59 house range 34
Which of the following will be step IV of the above input?
(a) 34 win 59 task 73 range 92 house
(b) 34 win 92 59 task 73 house range
(c) 34 win 92 task 73 59 house range
(d) there will be no such step
(e) None of the above

Direction (Q. Nos. 44-48) *Given an input line, the machine rearranges them step by step as per the illustration given below.* **Dena Bank (PO) 2008**

Input	show must 73 85 go 69 on 32
Step I	32 show must 73 85 go 69 on
Step II	32 go show must 73 85 69 on
Step III	32 go 69 show must 73 85 on
Step IV	32 go 69 must show 73 85 on
Step V	32 go 69 must 73 show 85 on
Step VI	32 go 69 must 73 on show 85
Step VII	32 go 69 must 73 on 85 show

Step VII is the last step and the arrangement in step VII is the final arrangement. As per the rules followed in the above steps, find out in each of the following questions the appropriate step for the given input.

44. **Step III** of an input is 14 but 26 not just 63 fundamental 47
Which of the following is definitely the input?
(a) 26 14 but not just 63 fundamental 47
(b) 63 26 but 14 not just 63 fundamental 47
(c) fundamental 26 14 but not just 63 47
(d) Cannot be determined
(e) None of the above

45. **Step I** of an input is 34 fire dress well 63 43 prime 52
Which of the following steps will be the last but one?
(a) IV (b) III (c) VI (d) VII
(e) V

46. What will be the fourth step for the following input?
Input just in time for 36 48 14 59
(a) 14 for 36 in just time 48 59
(b) 14 for 36 just in time 48 59
(c) 14 for 36 in 48 just time 59
(d) Cannot be determined
(e) None of the above

47. **Step II** of an input is 23 fine 49 sixty rely 38 56 next, how many more steps will be required to complete the arrangement?
(a) Two (b) Five (c) Six (d) Four
(e) None of these

48. **Step II** of an input is 17 do foreign 95 74 heights mountain 29, what will be the fifth step?
(a) 17 do 29 foreign heights 74 95 mountain
(b) 17 do 29 foreign 74 mountain heights 95
(c) 17 do 29 foreign 74 heights 95 mountain
(d) there will be no such step
(e) None of the above

Direction (Q. Nos. 49-55) *Study the following information carefully and answer the given questions.* **Andhra Bank (PO) 2007**

A word and number arrangement machine when given an input line of words and numbers rearranges them by following a particular rule in each step. The following is an illustration of input and rearrangement.

Input	day case 20 13 now for 49 56
Step I	13 day case 20 now for 49 56
Step II	13 now day case 20 for 49 56
Step III	13 now 20 day case for 49 56
Step IV	13 now 20 for day case 49 56
Step V	13 now 20 for 49 day case 56
Step VI	13 now 20 for 49 day 56 case

and Step VI is the last step.

As per the rules followed in the above steps, find out in each of the following questions the appropriate step for the given input.

49. **Input** yes 21 far 32 17 12 wide goal
Which of the following will be Step V of the above input?
(a) 12 yes 21 wide 32 far 17 goal
(b) 12 yes 21 wide far 32 17 goal
(c) 12 yes 21 far 32 17 wide goal
(d) there will be no such step
(e) None of the above

50. **Step IV** of an input is 17 hotel 29 father 83 76 door eye
Which of the following will be Step VII?
(a) 17 hotel 29 father 76 door 83 age
(b) 17 hotel 29 father 76 age 83 door
(c) 17 hotel 29 father 76 83 door age
(d) there will be no such step
(e) None of the above

51. **Step III** of an input is 25 win 32 85 73 tax break home
How many more steps will be required to complete the rearrangement?
(a) Five (b) Four
(c) Six (d) Seven
(e) None of these

52. **Step III** of an input is 37 yellow 42 61 53 violet green red.
How many more steps will be required to complete the rearrangement?
(a) Three (b) Four
(c) Five (d) Six
(e) None of these

53. **Input** can you go there 22 36 13 46
How many steps will be required to complete the rearrangement?
(a) Seven (b) Eight (c) Six (d) Five
(e) None of these

54. **Input** 42 36 go and come back 20 15
Which of the following steps will be the last but one?
(a) IV (b) V (c) VII (d) VIII
(d) None of these

55. **Step II** of an **input is** 39 sure 72 63 height over 42 lamp
Which of the following is definitely the input?
(a) height 39 sure 72 63 over 42 lamp
(b) 72 63 39 sure height over 42 lamp
(c) 63 39 sure 72 height over 42 lamp
(d) Cannot be determined
(e) None of the above

Direction (Q. Nos. 56-60) *Given an input, a coding machine generates pass-code for six batches every day as follows* **Andhra Bank (PO) 2007**

Input the shopkeeper offered discount to customers.
Pass-code for
Batch I customer the shopkeeper offered discount to
Batch II customer discount the shopkeeper offered to
Batch III customer discount offered the shopkeeper to

and so on until the arrangement is completed. After the arrangement is completed the next batch gets the same code as that for batch I.

Duration of each batch is 1 h. There is a break of one hour after the fourth batch. Sixth batch is the last batch. Now, answer the following questions.

56. If the pass-code for the second batch is do lean window out of not, what will be the pass-code for the fourth batch?
(a) do lean of not out window
(b) do lean of out not window
(c) do lean not out window of
(d) do lean not of window out
(e) None of the above

57. If the input is please do not delay the matter, what will be the pass-code for third batch?
(a) do please not delay the matter
(b) delay do matter please not the
(c) delay do matter not please the
(d) delay do matter not the please
(e) None of the above

58. If the pass-code for third batch is brisk every for morning go walk, what will definitely be the input?
(a) morning brisk go walk for every
(b) morning go brisk walk for every
(c) morning go walk brisk for every
(d) Cannot be determined
(e) None of the above

59. If the pass-code for the second batch is children for not is good watching television, what will be the pass-code for the fifth batch?
(a) children for good not is watching television
(b) children for good is not watching television
(c) children good for is not television watching
(d) Cannot be determined
(e) None of the above

60. If the input is necessary arrangements have already been made
How many batches are required to complete the rearrangement?
(a) Three (b) Four (c) Five (d) Six
(e) None of these

Direction (Q. Nos. 61-65) *Given an input line the machine arranges the words and numbers in steps in a systematic manner as illustrated below.*

Input 56 dress fine shine 32 66 72 offer
Step I 72 56 dress fine shine 32 66 offer
Step II 72 shine 56 dress fine 32 66 offer
Step III 72 shine 66 56 dress fine 32 offer
Step IV 72 shine 66 offer 56 dress fine 32
Step V 72 shine 66 offer 56 fine dress 32
Step VI 72 shine 66 offer 56 fine 32 dress

Step VI is the last step and the output in Step VI is the final output.

As per the rules followed in the above steps, find out in each of the following questions the appropriate step for the given input.

61. **Step IV** of an input is 62 sound 56 sleep roam present 33 49.
What will be the input definitely?
(a) sound 62 sleep 56 roam present 33 49
(b) sleep sound 62 56 roam present 33 49
(c) 62 sound sleep 56 roam present 33 49
(d) Cannot be determined
(e) None of the above

62. Which of the following will be the third step for input jockey firm 36 43 growth chart 22 45?
(a) 45 jockey 43 growth firm 36 chart 22
(b) 45 jockey 43 firm growth 36 chart 22
(c) 45 jockey 43 growth 36 firm chart 22
(d) 45 jockey 43 firm 36 growth chart 22
(e) None of the above

63. **Step II** of an input is 53 window 42 50 door lock key 36. How many more steps will be required to complete the rearrangement?
(a) Three
(b) Four
(c) Five
(d) Six
(e) None of the above

64. What will be the fifth step of an input whose first step is 85 journey train 36 54 daily 28 mansion?
(a) 85 train 54 mansion 28 journey daily 36
(b) 85 train 54 mansion journey 36 daily 28
(c) 85 train 54 mansion 36 journey daily 28
(d) there is no such step
(e) None of the above

65. Which step will be the last step for an input whose second step is 63 sour 18 56 grapes healthy 32 rise?
(a) IV
(b) V
(c) VIII
(d) VII
(e) None of the above

Advanced Level

Direction (Q. Nos. 1-5) *Study the following information to answer the given questions.*

A word arrangement machine when given an input line of words rearranges them by following a particular rule. The following is an illustration of input and rearrangement.

Input age road own wire tire ink pen uni dice eat
Step I uni age road own wire tire ink pen eat dice
Step II uni own age road wire tire ink eat pen dice
Step III uni own ink age wire tire eat road pen dice
Step IV uni own ink eat age wire tire road pen dice

And Step IV is the last step of the rearrangement.

As per the rules followed in the above steps, find out in each of the following questions the appropriate steps for the given input.

Input for the questions

Input gem stat ace cast omit fan rate uncut era input

1. Which of the following would be the final arrangement?
(a) cast gam fan rate stat uncut omit input era ace
(b) uncut omit input era ace cast fan gem rate stat
(c) uncut omit input era ace stat rate gem fan cast
(d) uncut omit input era ace stat fan gem rate cast
(e) None of the above

2. In Step III, which of the following word would be at sixth position from the left?
(a) rate (b) ace
(c) stat (d) gem
(e) None of these

3. Which step number would be the following output? uncut omit gem stat ace rate era input fan cast
(a) II (b) III (c) V (d) IV
(e) None of these

4. In Step IV of the rearrangement, if 'omit' is related 'era' and 'rate' is related to 'fan' in a certain way, to which of the following would 'ace' be related to, following the same pattern?
(a) rate (b) input (c) stat (d) gem
(e) None of these

5. Which of the following would be Step VII?
(a) uncut omit input era ace stat rate gem fan cast
(b) uncut omit input era ace rate stat fan gem cast
(c) uncut omit input era ace cast fan gem rate stat
(d) uncut omit input era stat ace rate gem fan cast
(e) There will be no such step as the input gets rearranged before step VII

Direction (Q. Nos. 6-9) *Study the following information carefully and answer the given questions:*

IBPS (PO) 2012

A word and number arrangement machine when given an input line of words and numbers rearranges them by following a particular rule in each step. The following is an illustration of input and rearrangement. (All the numbers are two-digit numbers).

Input tall 48 13 rise alt 99 76 32 wise jar high 28 56 barn
Step I 13 tall 48 rise 99 76 32 wise jar high 28 56 barn alt
Step II 28 13 tall 48 rise 99 76 32 wise jar high 56 alt barn
Step III 32 28 13 tall 48 rise 99 76 wise jar 56 alt barn high
Step IV 48 32 28 13 tall rise 99 76 wise 56 alt barn high jar
Step V 56 48 32 28 13 tall 99 76 wise alt barn high jar rise
Step VI 76 56 48 32 28 13 99 wise alt barn high jar rise tall
Step VII 99 76 56 48 32 28 13 alt barn high jar rise tall wise

Step VII is the last step of the above input, as the desired arrangement is obtained.

As per the rule followed in the above steps, find out in each of the following questions the appropriate step for the given input.

Input 84 why sit 14 32 not best ink feet 51 27 vain 68 92 (All the numbers are two-digit numbers).

6. Which step number is the following output?
32 27 14 84 why sit not 51 vain 92 68 feet best ink
(a) Step V (b) Step VI (c) Step IV (d) Step III
(e) There is no such step

7. Which word/number would be at 5th position from the right in Step V?
(a) 14 (b) 92
(c) feet (d) best
(e) why

8. How many elements (words or numbers) are there between 'feet' and '32' as they appear in the last step of the output?
(a) One
(b) Three
(c) Four
(d) Five
(e) Seven

9. Which of the following represents the position of 'why' in the fourth step?
(a) Eighth from the left
(b) Fifth from the right
(c) Sixth from the left
(d) Fifth from the left
(e) Seventh from the left

Direction (Q. Nos. 10-14) *Study the following information and answer the questions given below it.*

When a word and number arrangement machine is given an input line of words and numbers, it arranges them by following a particular rule. The following is an illustration of input and rearrangement

Input 25 93 as hill stamp bolt 45 34 63 total 13 alter rise
Step I alter 25 93 as hill stamp bolt 45 34 63 total rise 13
Step II alter as 93 hill stamp bolt 45 34 63 total rise 25 13
Step III alter as bolt 93 hill stamp 45 63 total rise 34 25 13
Step IV alter as bolt hill 93 stamp 63 total rise 45 34 25 13
Step V alter as bolt hill rise 93 stamp total 63 45 34 25 13
Step VI alter as bolt hill rise stamp total 93 63 45 34 25 13

Step VI is the last step of the above arrangement as the intended arrangement is obtained. As per the rules followed in the above steps, find out in each of the following questions, the appropriate steps for the given input.

Input ropes 12 33 strong 35 19 in blue ample kite 47 77 57

10. What is the position of '47' in Step III?
(a) fifth from the left end
(b) seventh from the left end
(c) sixth from the left end
(d) sixth from the right end
(e) seventh from the right end

11. Which of the following is fifth from the left end of Step V in the above arrangement?
(a) kite
(b) ropes
(c) strong
(d) 35
(e) None of these

12. What is the position of 'in' in Step IV?
(a) fourth from the left end
(b) third from the right end
(c) second from the left and
(d) third from the left end
(e) fifth from the left end

13. Which of the following is the last step (final output) of the given input?
(a) ample blue in kite strong ropes 77 57 47 35 33 19 12
(b) ample blue in kite ropes strong 12 19 33 35 47 57 77
(c) strong ropes kite in blue ample 77 57 47 35 33 19 12
(d) ample blue in kite ropes strong 57 77 47 35 33 19 12
(e) None of the above

14. How many steps are needed to complete this arrangement?
(a) Five
(b) Three
(c) Four
(d) Six
(e) None of these

Direction (Q. Nos. 15-19) *Study the following information carefully and answer the questions given below:* **IBPS (PO) 2013**

A word and number arrangement machine when given an input line of words and numbers rearranges them by following a particular rule in each step. The following is an illustation of input and various steps rearrangement. (All the numbers are two-digit numbers).

Input 11 day 34 night 93 pace 27 easy 44 joy
Step I 93 11 day 34 night pace 27 easy 44 joy
Step II 93 11 34 night pace 27 easy 44 joy day
Step III 93 44 11 34 night pace 27 easy joy day
Step IV 93 44 11 34 night pace 27 joy day easy
Step V 93 44 34 11 night pace 27 joy day easy
Step VI 93 44 34 11 night pace 27 day easy joy
Step VII 93 44 34 27 11 night pace day easy joy
Step VIII 93 44 34 27 11 pace day easy joy night
Step IX 93 44 34 27 11 day easy joy night pace

and Step IX is the last step of the rearrangement as the desired arrangement is obtained. As per rules followed in the above steps, find out in each of the questions the appropriate step for the given input.

Input class 25 war 15 race 73 heap 58 just 88 take 38

15. What is the positon of 'war' in the Step VII?
(a) Seventh from the left end
(b) Eighth from the right end
(c) Fifth from the left end
(d) Fifth from the right end
(e) Sixth from the left end

16. Which of the following is the ninth from the right in Step VI?
(a) race
(b) 38
(c) war
(d) 58
(e) 15

17. What is the position of 15 in the Step IX?
(a) Seventh from the left end
(b) Eighth from the left end
(c) Fifth from the right end
(d) Seventh from the right end
(e) Eighth from the right end

18. How many Steps are required to complete this arrangement?
(a) Eleven
(b) Twelve
(c) Ten
(d) Nine
(e) None of these

19. Which of the following represents the Step X?
(a) 88 73 58 38 25 war 15 race take class heap just
(b) 88 73 58 38 25 15 class heap just race take war
(c) 88 73 58 38 25 15 war class heap just race take
(d) 88 73 58 38 25 15 war take class heap just race
(e) There is no such Step

Direction (Q. Nos. 20-24) *Study the following information to answer the given questions*

IBPS (PO/MT) 2011

A word and number arrangement machine when given an 'input line of words and numbers rearranges them by following a particular rule. The following is an illustration of input and rearrangement, (All the numbers are two-digit numbers.)

Input sine 88 71 cos theta 14 56 gamma delta 26
Step I cos sine 71 theta 14 56 gamma delta 26 88
Step II delta cos sine theta 14 56 gamma 26 88 71
Step III gamma delta cos sine theta 14 26 88 71 56
Step IV sine gamma delta cos theta 14 88 71 56 26
Step V theta sine gamma delta cos 88 71 56 26 14

and Step V is the last step of the arrangement of the above input as the intended arrangement is obtained.

As per the rules followed in the above steps, find out in each of the following questions the appropriate steps for the given input.

Input for 52 all 96 25 jam road 15 hut 73 bus stop 38 46 (All the numbers given in the arrangement are two-digit numbers)

20. Which word/number would be at the 6th position from the left in Step V?
(a) 25 (b) stop
(c) jam (d) all
(e) road

21. Which of the following would be the Step III?
(a) hut for bus all 25 jam road 15 stop 38 96 73 52 46
(b) for us all 25 jam road 15 hut 38 stop 96 46 73 52
(c) hut for bus all jam road 15 stop 38 96 73 52 46 25
(d) for bus all 25 jam road 15 hut stop 38 46 96 73 52
(e) None of the above

22. Which word/number would be at 8th position from the right in Step IV?
(a) 15 (b) road
(c) hut (d) jam
(e) stop

23. Which of the following would be Step VII?
(a) stop road jam hut for bus all 15 96 73 52 46 38 25
(b) road jam hut for bus all stop 15 25 38 46 52 73 96
(c) stop road jam hut for bus all 96 73 52 46 38 25 15
(d) jam hut for bus all 25 road stop 15 96 73 52 46 38
(e) There will be no such step as the arrangement gets established at Step VI

24. Which step number would be the following output?
bus all for 52 25 jam road 15 hut stop 38 46 96 73
(a) There will be no such step
(b) III
(c) II
(d) V
(e) VI

Direction (Q. Nos. 25-27) *Study the following information to answer the given questions.* **IBPS (PO) 2013**

A word and number arrangement machine when given an input line of words and numbers rearranges them by following a particular rule. The following is an illustration of input and rearrangement.

(All numbers in these questions are two-digit numbers)

Input 16 today 32 waiting 21 are 11 people 46 bus 66 long
Step I 16 today 32 waiting 21 11 people 46 bus 66 long
Step II 16 today 32 waiting 21 people 46 bus 66 long 11 are
Step III 16 today 32 waiting 21 people 46 66 long bus 11 are
Step IV today 32 waiting 21 people 46 66 long 16 bus 11 are
Step V today 32 waiting people 46 66 21 long 16 bus 11 are
Step VI today waiting 46 66 32 people 21 long 16 bus 11 are
Step VII waiting 46 66 today 32 people 21 long 16 bus 11 are
Step VIII waiting 66 46 today 32 people 21 long 16 bus 11 are
Step IX 66 waiting 46 today 32 people 21 long 16 bus 11 are

Step IX is the last step of the arrangement of the above input as the intended arrangement is obtained.

Now, answer the questions based on the following input :
Input 23 you 13 wake 81 me 43 before 72 go 34 up

25. Which of these words/numbers would be fourth (from left side) in Step IV for the input?
(a) me (b) 43 (c) 81 (d) wake
(e) None of these

26. The following stands for which step of the rearrangement ?
you wake 81 43 72 34 up me 23 go 13 before
(a) Step IX (b) Step IV (c) Step VI (d) Step V
(e) None of these

27. Which of the following would be Step II for the above input ?
(a) 23 you wake 81 me 43 72 34 up go 13 before
(b) 23 you 13 wake 81 me 43 72 go 34 up before
(c) 23 you wake 81 me 43 72 go 34 up before 13
(d) 23 you wake 81 me 43 72 go 34 up 13 before
(e) None of the above

Direction (Q. Nos. 28-33) *Study the following information carefully and answer the given questions.*

Corporation Bank (PO) 2010

A word and number arrangement machine, when given an input line of words and numbers rearranges them by following a particular rule in each step. The following is an illustration of input and rearrangement.

Input gone 93 over 46 84 now for 31
Step I 31 gone 93 over 46 84 now for
Step II 31 over gone 93 46 84 now for
Step III 31 over 46 gone 93 84 now for
Step IV 31 over 46 now gone 93 84 for
Step V 31 over 46 now 84 gone 93 for

and step V is the last step of the rearrangement of the above input.

As per the rules followed in the above steps, find out in each of the following questions the appropriates step for the given input.

28. **Step III** of an Input is 15 window 29 93 86 sail tower buy. Which of the following will be Step VI?
(a) 15 window 29 tower 86 sail 93 buy
(b) 15 window 29 tower 86 93 sail buy
(c) 15 window 29 tower 93 86 sail buy
(d) There will be no such step
(e) None of the above

29. **Input** station hurry 39 67 all men 86 59
How many steps will be required to complete the rearrangement?
(a) Four (b) Five (c) Six (d) Three
(e) None of these

30. **Step II** of an Input is 49 zone car battery 56 87 71 down
Which of the following is definitely the input?
(a) car 49 battery zone 56 87 71 down
(b) zone 49 car battery 56 87 71 down
(c) battery car 49 zone 56 87 71 down
(d) Cannot be determined
(e) None of the above

31. **Input** news 79 53 glory for 46 29 task
Which of the following will be Step IV?
(a) 29 task 46 news 53 glory 79 for
(b) 29 task 46 news 53 79 glory for
(c) 29 task 46 news 79 53 glory for
(d) 29 news 79 53 glory for 46 task
(e) None of the above

32. **Step III** of an Input is 27 tube 34 gas chamber row 74 53
Which of the following steps will be the last but one?
(a) VI (b) VII (c) VIII (d) V
(e) None of these

33. **Step II** of an Input is 19 year 85 74 near gone 26 store
How many more steps will be required to complete the rearrangement?
(a) Three (b) Four (c) Two (d) Five
(e) None of these

Direction (Q. Nos. 34-38) *Study the following information carefully and answer the given questions.*

A word and number arrangement machine, when given an input line of words and numbers rearranges them by following a particular rule in each step. The following is an illustration of an input and rearrangement.

Input 17 put show on 39 27 85 gold
Step I show 17 put on 39 27 85 gold
Step II show 85 17 put on 39 27 gold
Step III show 85 put 17 on 39 27 gold
Step IV show 85 put 39 17 on 27 gold
Step V show 85 put 39 on 17 27 gold
Step VI show 85 put 39 on 27 17 gold
Step VII show 85 put 39 on 27 gold 17

and Step VII is the last step of the rearrangement of the above input.

As per the rules followed in the above steps, find out in each of the following questions the appropriate step for the given input.

34. **Input** glass full 15 37 water now 85 67
Which of the following will be Step VI of the above input?
(a) water 85 now 67 full glass 15 37
(b) water 85 now 67 glass full 15 37
(c) water 85 now 67 glass 37 full 15
(d) There will be no such step
(e) None of the above

35. **Step II** of an input is ultra 73 12 16 mail sort 39 kite
Which of the following steps will be the last but one?
(a) VIII (b) IX (c) VII (d) VI
(e) None of these

36. **Step III** of an input is win 75 voice 15 39 store gap 26
Which of the following is definitely the input?
(a) voice 15 win 75 39 store gap 26
(b) voice win 75 15 39 store gap 26
(c) 15 75 win voice store gap 26
(d) Cannot be determined
(e) None of the above

37. **Step II** of an input is tube 83 49 34 garden flower rat 56
How many steps will be required to complete the rearrangement?
(a) Four (b) Five (c) Six (d) Three
(e) None of these

38. **Input** hunt for 94 37 good 29 48 book
How many steps will be required to complete the rearrangement?
(a) Four (b) Five
(e) Six (e) Seven
(e) None of these

Direction (Q. Nos. 39-42) *The following questions are based on grammatical rules.*

Input cigarette smoking is injurious to health.
Rule I follows smoking of rule
Rule II cigarette when smoked
Rule III due to
Rule IV in any form etc.

Solve the problems by using above rules.

A grammar teacher instructs her students with the following inputs for restatement as per given rules.

Input cigarette smoking is injurious to health.
Rule I smoking of cigarette is injurious to health
Rule II cigarette when smoked injurious health
Rule III health is injured due to smoking
Rule IV smoking in any form is injurious to health

As per rules dictated by the teacher, find out (as a student), the relevant step or the input, as asked in the given problems.

39. **Input** tobacco chewing is harmful for teeth
Which of the following rule is chewing of tobacco is harmful for teeth?
(a) II
(b) III
(c) I
(d) IV
(e) None of the above

40. Students are benefited due to coachings, is which rule of given input?
(a) I
(b) III
(c) II
(d) Data inadequate
(e) None of the above

41. Rule IV on an input is coachings in any form are beneficial for the students; what would be Rule I for the input?
(a) taking of coachings is beneficial to the students
(b) coaching when taken, benefit the student
(c) students are benefited due to coachings
(d) Data inadequate
(e) None of the above

42. **Input** given by a teacher is excessive weightlifting is harmful for joints, which of the following will be Rule III of the input?
(a) weights are harmful for joints
(b) excessive weights, when lifted harm joints
(c) weightlifting in any form harm joints
(d) joints are harmed due to excessive weightlifting
(e) Data inadequate

Answers with **Explanations**

Base Level

Solution (Q. Nos. 1-5) There are six numbers and six words in the input.

The three numbers are placed in the beginning and the remaining three numbers are placed in the last. The numbers are rearranged in ascending order. The six words are rearranged in alphabetical order in the middle.

Input	67 hot sun 19 best 83 ice 49 ace 77 cut 37
Step I	19 67 hot sun best ice 49 ace 77 cut 37 83
Step II	19 37 67 hot sun best ice 49 ace cut 77 83
Step III	19 37 49 hot sun best ice ace cut 67 77 83
Step IV	19 37 49 ace hot sun best ice cut 67 77 83
Step V	19 37 49 ace best hot sun ice cut 67 77 83
Step VI	19 37 49 ace best cut hot sun ice 67 77 83
Step VII	19 37 49 ace best cut hot ice sun 67 77 83

1. (*d*) Seven steps are needed to complete the arrangement.
2. (*c*) It is Step V.
3. (*d*) Option (d) is Step I.
4. (*b*) Option (b) is the final arrangement.
5. (*a*) In Step IV 'sun' would be seventh from the right.
6. (*b*)

Input	year 39 stake 47 house full 94 55
Step I	full year 39 stake 47 house 94 55
Step II	full 94 year 39 stake 47 house 55
Step III	full 94 house year 39 stake 47 55
Step IV	full 94 house 55 year 39 stake 47
Step V	full 94 house 55 stake year 39 47
Step VI	full 94 house 55 stake 47 year 39

7. (*b*)

Step II	car 83 lost ever 32 46 74 now
Step III	car 83 ever lost 32 46 74 now
Step IV	car 83 ever 74 lost 32 46 now
Step V	car 83 ever 74 lost 46 32 now
Step VI	car 83 ever 74 lost 46 now 32

8. (*d*) **Input** cannot be determined

9. (*a*)

Input	water full never 35 78 16 height 28
Step I	full water never 35 78 16 height 28
Step II	full 78 water never 35 16 height 28
Step III	full 78 height water never 35 16 28
Step IV	full 78 height 35 water never 16 28
Step V	full 78 height 35 never water 16 28
Step VI	full 78 height 35 never 28 water 16

10. (*d*)

Step II	high 69 store pay 36 43 15 there
Step III	high 69 pay store 36 43 15 there
Step IV	high 69 pay 43 store 36 15 there
Step V	high 69 pay 43 store 36 there 15
Step VI	will not exist

11. (*e*)

Input	train more 29 53 fast gear 37 84
Step I	fast train more 29 53 gear 37 84
Step II	fast 84 train more 29 53 gear 37
Step III	fast 84 gear train more 29 53 37
Step IV	fast 84 gear 53 train more 29 37
Step V	fast 84 gear 53 more train 29 37
Step VI	fast 84 gear 53 more 37 train 29

Solution (Q. Nos. 12-17) After careful analysis of the given input and various steps of rearrangement it is evident that in the first step one word is arranged in alphabetical order and in the second step one number, which is the highest among the given numbers, is placed after the first word. In the final step all the words get arranged in alphabetical order while the numbers are arranged in descending order alternately.

12. (*a*) **Step II** cut 97 38 end for 29 46 down
Step III cut 97 down 38 end for 29 46
Step IV cut 97 down 46 38 end for 29
Step V cut 97 down 46 end 38 for 29
This is the last step.

13. (*d*) It is not possible to determine the previous step.

14. (*b*) **Step I** car 17 vas tiger 92 87 like 52
Step II car 92 17 vas tiger 87 like 52
Step III car 92 like 17 vas tiger 87 52
Step IV car 92 like 87 17 vas tiger 52

15. (*c*) **Input** zeal for 49 31 high 22 track 12
Step I for zeal 49 31 high 22 track 12
Step II for 49 zeal 31 high 22 track 12
Step III for 49 high zeal 31 22 track 12

16. (*e*) **Input** 19 feat 34 28 dog bag take 43
Step I bag 19 feat 34 28 dog take 43
Step II bag 43 19 feat 34 28 dog take
Step III bag 43 dog 19 feat 34 28 take

17. (*b*) 34 is at 6th position in Step III
Hence, option (b) is correct.

18. (*b*) **Step III** year 92 ultra 15 23 strive house 39
Step IV year 92 ultra 39 15 23 strive house
Step V year 92 ultra 39 strive 15 23 house
Step VI year 92 ultra 39 strive 23 15 house
Step VII year 92 ultra 39 strive 23 house 15
So, four more steps are required.

19. (*c*) **Input** any how 49 24 for wide 34 69
Step I wide any how 49 24 for 34 69
Step II wide 69 any how 49 24 for 34
Step III wide 69 how any 49 24 for 34
Step IV wide 69 how 49 any 24 for 34
Step V wide 69 how 49 for any 24 34
Step VI wide 69 how 49 for 34 any 24
So, Step V is first step from last.

20. (*d*) **Step II** town 74 pair 15 31 nice job 42
Input cannot be determined.

21. (*d*) **Input** play over 49 37 12 match now 81
Step I play 81 over 49 37 12 match now
Step II play 81 over 49 now 37 12 match
Step III play 81 over 49 now 37 match 12
So, Step IV cannot be determined.

22. (*b*) **Step II** war 58 box cart 33 49 star 24
Step III war 58 star box cart 33 49 24
Step IV war 58 star 49 box cart 33 24
Step V war 58 star 49 cart box 33 24
Step VI war 58 star 49 cart 33 box 24
So, last step is Step VI.

23. (*d*) **Input** shower fall water 34 51 67 98 goal
Step I water shower fall 34 51 67 98 goal
Step II water 98 shower fall 34 51 67 goal
Step III water 98 shower 67 fall 34 51 goal
Step IV water 98 shower 67 goal fall 34 51
Step V water 98 shower 67 goal 51 fall 34
Five steps required to complete the rearrangement.

Solution (Q. Nos. 24-27) These questions are based on alphabetical reverse order like Z Y X W V U ... reverse order will follow.

24. (*c*) **Input** life become bore without success
Step I without life become bore success
Step II without success life become bore
Step III without success life bore become

25. (*d*) **Step II** the success my is outcome of diligence
Step III the success outcome my is of diligence
Step IV the success outcome of my is diligence

26. (*e*) In such type of problems direct rule follows that is to arrange the input in descending order.
Input an invitation to a most exclusive evening
Last result will be to most invitation exclusive evening an a.

27. (*c*) **Input** never break your elders trust
Step I your never break elders trust
Step II your trust never break elders
Step III your trust never elders break

Solution (Q. Nos. 28-32) Let reference chart be

Dhoni = 1 cannot = 2
but = 3 feel = 4
sorry = 5 for = 6
him = 7

Input	1	2	3	4	5	6	7
Step I	3	2	1	5	4	7	6
Step II	2	3	4	5	1	6	7
Step III	3	2	5	4	7	6	1
Step IV	5	2	3	7	4	1	6
Step V	2	5	4	7	3	6	1
Step VI	5	2	7	4	1	6	3
Step VII	7	2	5	1	4	3	6

28. (*b*) Given,

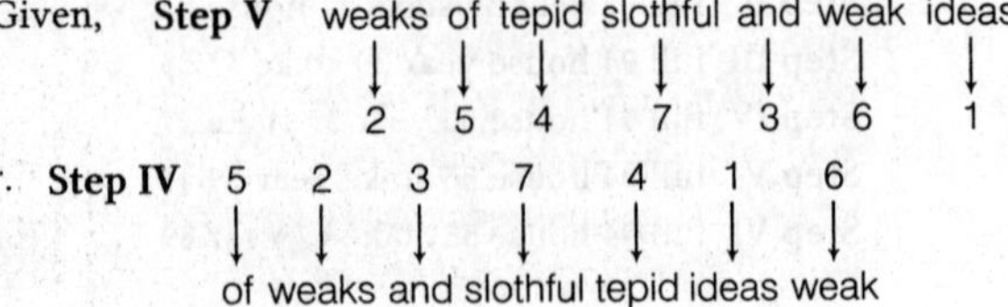

29. (*e*) Given,

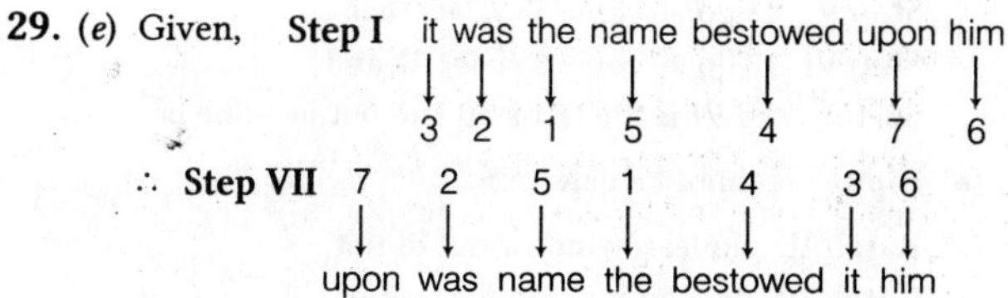

30. (*e*) Given,

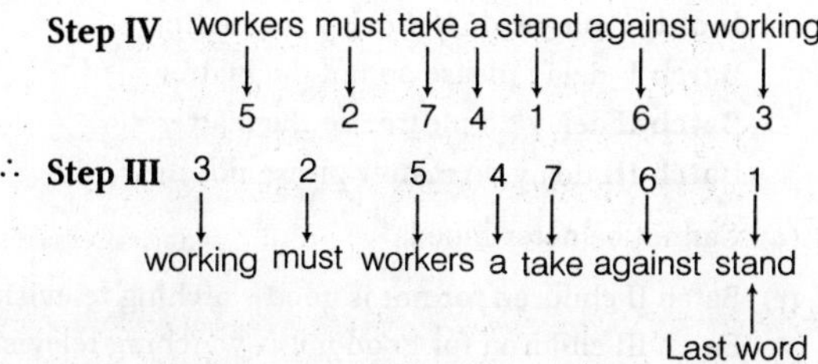

31. (*c*) Given, **Step III**

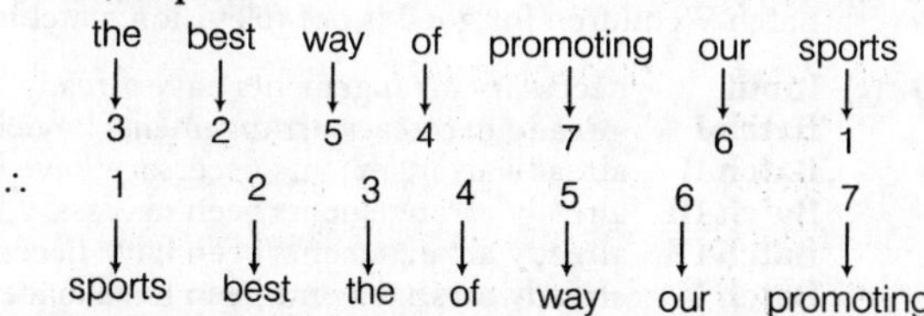

32. (*b*) Given, **Input**

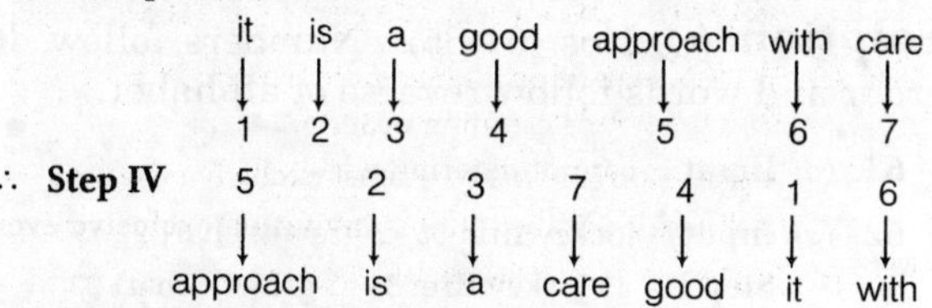

33. (*d*) **Input** how was your stay 56 25 36 64
Step I 64 how was your stay 56 25 36
Step II 64 how 56 was your stay 25 36
Step III 64 how 56 stay was your 25 36
Step IV 64 how 56 stay 36 was your 25
Step V 64 how 56 stay 36 was 25 your
So, sixth step is not possible because fifth step will be last step.

34. (*e*) **Input** power fail now 52 24 75 gate 34
Step I 75 power fail now 52 24 gate 34
Step II 75 fail power now 52 24 gate 34
Step III 75 fail 52 power now 24 gate 34
Step IV 75 fail 52 gate power now 24 34
Step V 75 fail 52 gate 34 power now 24
Step VI 75 fail 52 gate 34 now power 24
Step VII 75 fail 52 gate 34 now 24 power
So, the first step from the last is Step VI

35. (*d*) **Input** cannot be determined.

36. (*a*) **Step II** 75 down 16 24 farm eager 62 sky
Step III 75 down 62 16 24 farm eager sky
Step IV 75 down 62 eager 16 24 farm sky
Step V 75 down 62 eager 24 16 farm sky
Step VI 75 down 62 eager 24 farm 16 sky
Four more steps are required to complete the rearrangement.

37. (*c*) **Input** 14 35 when they came 61 48 home
Step I 61 14 35 when they came 48 home
Step II 61 came 14 35 when they 48 home
Step III 61 came 48 14 35 when they home
Step IV 61 came 48 home 14 35 when they
Step V 61 came 48 home 35 14 when they
Step VI 61 came 48 home 35 they 14 when
To complete the rearrangement 6 steps are required.

38. (*c*) **Step II** 15 yes 62 51 48 talk now gone
Step III 15 yes 48 62 51 talk now gone
Step IV 15 yes 48 talk 62 51 now gone
Step V 15 yes 48 talk 51 62 now gone
Step VI 15 yes 48 talk 51 now 62 gone

39. (*e*) **Step III** 21 victory 30 joint 64 47 all gone
Step IV 21 victory 30 joint 47 64 all gone
Step V 21 victory 30 joint 47 gone 64 all
So, Step V is the last step. Hence, two steps will be required.

40. (*c*) **Input** 89 bind 32 goal house 61 12 joy
Step I 12 89 bind 32 goal house 61 joy
Step II 12 joy 89 bind 32 goal house 61
Step III 12 joy 32 89 bind goal house 61
Step IV 12 joy 32 house 89 bind goal 61
Step V 12 joy 32 house 61 89 bind goal
Step VI 12 joy 32 house 61 goal 89 bind
Step VI is the last step. So, to complete the arrangement, six steps will be required.

41. (*e*) **Input** save 21 43 78 them early 36 for
Step I 21 save 43 78 them early 36 for
Step II 21 them save 43 78 early 36 for
Step III 21 them 36 save 43 78 early for
Step IV 21 them 36 save 43 for 78 early
Step IV is the last step and from last but one step is Step III.

42. (*b*) **Input** desire 59 63 all few 38 46 zone
Step I 38 desire 59 63 all few 46 zone
Step II 38 zone desire 59 63 all few 46
Step III 38 zone 46 desire 59 63 all few
Step IV 38 zone 46 few desire 59 63 all
Step V 38 zone 46 few 59 desire 63 all
So, the last step is Step V.

43. (*e*) **Input** win 92 task 73 59 house range 34
Step I 34 win 92 task 73 59 house range
Step II 34 win 59 92 task 73 house range
Step III 34 win 59 task 92 73 house range
Step IV 34 win 59 task 73 92 house range

44. (*e*) Cannot be determined.

45. (*e*) **Step I** 34 fire dress well 63 43 prime 52
Step II 34 dress fire well 63 43 prime 52
Step III 34 dress 43 fire well 63 prime 52
Step IV 34 dress 43 fire 52 well 63 prime
Step V 34 dress 43 fire 52 prime well 63
Step VI 34 dress 43 fire 52 prime 63 well
So, the last but one is step V.

46. (*a*) **Input** just in time for 36 48 14 59
Step I 14 just in time for 36 48 59
Step II 14 for just in time 36 48 59
Step III 14 for 36 just in time 48 59
Step IV 14 for 36 in just time 48 59

47. (*d*) **Step III** 23 fine 38 49 sixty rely 56 next
Step IV 23 fine 38 next 49 sixty rely 56
Step V 23 fine 38 next 49 rely sixty 56
Step VI 23 fine 38 next 49 rely 56 sixty
So, to complete the arrangement four steps are required.

48. (*c*) **Step III** 17 do 29 foreign 95 74 heights mountain
Step IV 17 do 29 foreign 74 95 heights mountain
Step V 17 do 29 foreign 74 heights 95 mountain

49. (*e*) **Input** yes 21 far 32 17 12 wide goal
Step I 12 yes 21 far 32 17 wide goal
Step II 12 yes 17 21 far 32 wide goal
Step III 12 yes 17 wide 21 far 32 goal
Step IV 12 yes 17 wide 21 goal far 32
Step V 12 yes 17 wide 21 goal 32 far

50. (*d*) **Step IV** 17 hotel 29 father 83 76 door eye
Step V 17 hotel 29 father 76 83 door eye
Step VI 17 hotel 29 father 76 eye 83 door
So, there will no such steps.

51. (*e*) **Step III** 25 win 32 85 73 tax break home
Step IV 25 win 32 tax 85 73 break home
Step V 25 win 32 tax 73 85 break home
Step VI 25 win 32 tax 73 home 85 break
So, three more steps are required to fulfil rearrangement.

52. (*a*) **Step III** 37 yellow 42 61 53 violet green red
Step IV 37 yellow 42 violet 61 53 green red
Step V 37 yellow 42 violet 53 61 green red
Step VI 37 yellow 42 violet 53 red 61 green
So, three more steps are required to complete rearrangement.

53. (*a*) **Input** can you go there 22 36 13 46
Step I 13 can you go there 22 36 46
Step II 13 you can go there 22 36 46
Step III 13 you 22 can go there 36 46
Step IV 13 you 22 there can go 36 46
Step V 13 you 22 there 36 can go 46
Step VI 13 you 22 there 36 go can 46
Step VII 13 you 22 there 36 go 46 can
So, seven steps are required to complete rearrangement.

54. (*b*) **Input** 42 36 go and come back 20 15
Step I 15 42 36 go and come back 20
Step II 15 go 42 36 and come back 20
Step III 15 go 20 42 36 and come back
Step IV 15 go 20 come 42 36 and back
Step V 15 go 20 come 36 42 and back
Step VI 15 go 20 come 36 back 42 and
So, the Step VI is the last step and but last one is step V.

55. (*d*) **Input** cannot be determined.

56. (*d*) **Batch II** do lean window out of not
Batch III do lean not window out of
Batch IV do lean not of window out

57. (*b*) **Input** please do not delay the matter
Batch I delay please do not the matter
Batch II delay do please not the matter
Batch III delay do matter please not the

58. (*d*) Cannot be determined.

59. (*e*) Batch II children for not is good watching television
Batch III children for good not is watching television
Batch IV children for good is not watching television
Batch V children for good is not television watching.

60. (*c*) **Input** necessary arrangements have already been made
Batch I already necessary arrangements have been made
Batch II already arrangements necessary have been made
Batch III already arrangements been necessary have made
Batch IV already arrangements been have necessary made
Batch V already arrangements been have made necessary
So, five steps are required to complete rearrangement.

Solution (Q. Nos. 61-65) Numbers follow decreasing order and words follow reverse of alphabet.

61. (*d*) **Input** cannot determined.

62. (*a*) **Input** jockey firm 36 43 growth chart 22 45
Step I 45 jockey firm 36 43 growth chart 22
Step II 45 jockey 43 firm growth 36 chart 22
Step III 45 Jockey 43 growth firm 36 chart 22

63. (*b*) **Step II** 53 window 42 50 door lock key 36
Step III 53 window 50 42 door lock key 36
Step IV 53 window 50 lock 42 door key 36
Step V 53 window 50 lock 42 key door 36
Step VI 53 window 50 lock 42 key 36 door
So, four more steps are required to complete rearrangement.

64. (*c*) **Step I** 85 journey train 36 54 daily 28 mansion
Step II 85 train journey 36 54 daily 28 mansion
Step III 85 train 54 journey 36 daily 28 mansion
Step IV 85 train 54 mansion journey 36 daily 28
Step V 85 train 54 mansion 36 journey daily 28

65. (*e*) **Step II** 63 sour 18 56 grapes healthy 32 rise
Step III 63 sour 56 18 grapes healthy 32 rise
Step IV 63 sour 56 rise 18 grapes healthy 32
Step V 63 sour 56 rise 32 18 grapes healthy
Step VI 63 sour 56 rise 32 healthy 18 grapes
So, the last step is Step VI.

Advanced Level

Solution (Q. Nos. 1-5) Carefully observing the input and steps, we observe that two words have given arranged in each step.

Starting word from vowel arranged from left to right in reverse alphabetical order and starting word from consonant arranged from right to left in alphabetical order.

Input	gem stat ace cast omit fan rate uncut era input
Step I	uncut gem stat ace omit fan rate era input cast
Step II	uncut omit gem stat ace rate era input fan cast
Step III	uncut omit input stat ace rate era gem fan cast
Step IV	uncut omit input era stat ace rate gem fan cast
Step V	uncut omit input era ace stat rate gem fan cast

1. (*c*) uncut omit input era ace stat rate gem fan cast
2. (*a*) Step III uncut omit input stat ace rate era gem fan cast

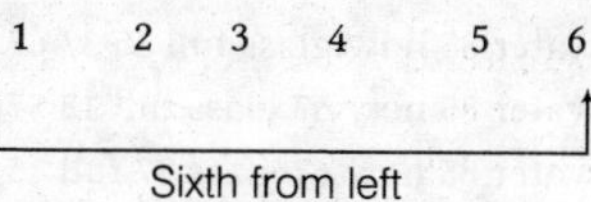

Hence, sixth from the left is 'rate'.

3. (*a*) Step II uncut omit gem stat ace rate era input fan cast
4. (*d*) Step IV one word is between omit and era also one word between rate and fan. Similarly in Step IV, one word is between ace and gem.
5. (*e*) Step V is the last step of the given input. Hence, there will be no such step as the input gets rearranged before step VII.

Solution (Q. Nos. 6-9)

After careful analysis of the given input and various steps of rearrangement, it is evident that in each step one number and one word are rearranged. The lowest number is moved to the left end while the word which will come first in alphabetical order is moved to the right end. In the second step the second lowest number is moved to the left end and the word which will come second in the alphabetical order is moved to the right end. The procedure is continued till all the numbers and words get rearranged accordingly.

Input	84 why sit 14 32 not best ink feet 51 27 vain 68 92
Step I	14 84 why sit 32 not ink feet 51 27 vain 68 92 best
Step II	27 14 84 why sit 32 not ink 51 vain 68 92 best feet
Step III	32 27 14 84 why sit not 51 vain 68 92 best feet ink
Step IV	51 32 27 14 84 why sit vain 68 92 best feet ink not
Step V	68 51 32 27 14 84 why vain 92 best feet ink not sit
Step VI	84 68 51 32 27 14 why 92 best feet ink not sit vain
Step VII	92 84 68 51 32 27 14 best feet ink not sit vain why

6. (*e*) There is no such step.
7. (*d*) The word 'best' is at the fifth position from the right in Step V.
8. (*b*) There are three elements 27, 14 and best – between feet and 32 in the last step of the output.
9. (*c*) The word 'why' is sixth from the left and ninth from the right in the Step IV.

Solution (Q. Nos. 10-14) The arrangement will be as follow

10. (*d*) **Input** ropes 12 33 strong 35 19 in blue ample kite 47 77 57

Step I	ample ropes 33 strong 35 19 in blue kite 47 77 57 12
Step II	ample blue ropes 33 strong 35 in kite 47 77 57 19 12
Step III	ample blue in ropes strong 35 kite 47, 77 57 33 19 12

11. (*b*) **Step IV** ample blue in kite ropes strong 47 77 57 35 33 19 12

Step V ample blue in kite ropes strong 77 57 47 35 33 19 12

12. (*d*) 13. (*e*) 14. (*a*)

Solution (Q. Nos. 15-19)

After careful analysis of the given input and various steps of rearrangement, it is evident that in the first step the highest number is placed at the extreme left position and in the second step, the word which comes first in the alphabetical order is placed at the extreme right position. In the next step the second highest number is placed at the second position from the left. After that step, the word which comes second in the alphabetical order is placed at the extreme right position. These two steps are continued alternately till all the numbers get arranged in the descending order from the left and all the words get arranged in alphabetical order after the numbers.

Input	class 25 war 15 race 73 heap 58 just 88 take 38
Step I	88 class 25 war 15 race 73 heap 58 just take 38
Step II	88 25 war 15 race 73 heap 58 just take 38 class
Step III	88 73 25 war 15 race heap 58 just take 38 class
Step IV	88 73 25 war 15 race 58 just take 38 class heap
Step V	88 73 58 25 war 15 race just take 38 class heap
Step VI	88 73 58 38 25 war 15 race just take class heap
Step VII	88 73 58 38 25 war 15 race take class heap just
Step VIII	88 73 58 38 25 15 war take class heap just race
Step IX	88 73 58 38 25 15 war take class heap just race
Step X	88 73 58 38 25 15 war class heap just race take
Step XI	88 73 58 38 25 15 class heap just race take war

and Step XI is the last step.

15. (*e*) The word war is six th from the left end in step VIII.
16. (*b*) '38' is the ninth from the right in Step VI.
17. (*d*) '15' is seventh from the right end in Step IX.
18. (*a*) Eleven Steps were required to complete the arrangement.
19. (*c*) Option (c) is the Step X.

Solution (Q. Nos. 20-24) After careful study the given input and various steps of rearrangement, we may conclude that the word which comes last in dictionary is placed at the first position from the left and numbers are placed in ascending order from the right.

Input for 52 all 96 25 jam road 15 hut 73 bus stop 38 46
Step I all for 52 25 jam road 15 hut 73 bus stop 38 46 96
Step II bus all for 52 25 jam road 15 hut stop 38 46 96 73
Step III for bus all 25 jam road 15 hut stop 38 46 96 73 52
Step IV hut for bus all 25 jam road 15 stop 38 96 73 52 46
Step V jam hut for bus all 25 road 15 stop 96 73 52 46 38
Step VI road jam hut for bus all 15 stop 96 73 52 46 38 25
Step VII stop road jam hut for bus all 96 73 52 46 38 25 15

20. (*a*) **Step V** jam hut for bus all 25...
1 2 3 4 5 6
... road 15 stop 96 73 52 46 38
Hence, 25 will be 6th position from the left.

21. (*d*) Option (d) would be the III step.

22. (*b*) **Step IV** hut for bus all 25 jam ... road 15 stop 38 96 73 52 46
Hence, road will be at 8th position from the right.

23. (*c*) **Step VII** stop road jam hut for bus all 96 73 52 46 38 25 15

24. (*c*) Step II

Solution (Q. Nos. 28-27)

After careful analysis of the given input and various steps of rearrangement, it is evident that words and numbers rearranged from right to left. In the first step one word is rearranged and in the second step one number is rearranged. The words are rearranged in alphabetical order and the numbers are rearranged in ascending order from right to left.

Input 23 you 13 wake 81 me 43 before 72 go 34 up
Step I 23 you 13 wake 81 me 43 72 go 34 up before
Step II 23 you wake 81 me 43 72 go 34 up 13 before
Step III 23 you wake 81 me 43 72 34 up go 13 before
Step IV you wake 81 me 43 72 34 up 23 go 13 before
Step V you wake 81 43 72 34 up me 23 go 13 before
Step VI you wake 81 43 72 up 34 me 23 go 13 before
Step VII you wake 81 72 43 up 34 me 23 go 13 before
Step VIII you 81 72 wake 43 up 34 me 23 go 13 before
Step IX 81 you 72 wake 43 up 34 me 23 go 13 before

25. (*a*) me

26. (*d*) It is step V.

27. (*d*) Option (d) is step II.

28. (*a*) **Step III** 15 window 29 93 86 sail tower buy
Step IV 15 window 29 tower 93 86 sail buy
Step V 15 window 29 tower 86 93 sail buy
Step VI 15 window 29 tower 86 sail 93 buy

29. (*b*) **Input** station hurry 39 67 all men 86 59
Step I 39 station hurry 67 all men 86 59
Step II 39 station 59 hurry 67 all men 86
Step III 39 station 59 men hurry 67 all 86
Step IV 39 station 59 men 67 hurry all 86
Step V 39 station 59 men 67 hurry 86 all

30. (*d*) **Input** cannot be determined

31. (*b*) **Input** news 79 53 glory for 46 29 task
Step I 29 news 79 53 glory for 46 task
Step II 29 task news 79 53 glory for 46
Step III 29 task 46 news 79 53 glory for
Step IV 29 task 46 news 53 79 glory for

32. (*d*) **Step III** 27 tube 34 gas chamber row 74 53
Step IV 27 tube 34 row gas chamber 74 53
Step V 27 tube 34 row 53 gas chamber 74
Step VI 27 tube 34 row 53 gas 74 chamber
So, last but one Step is V.

33. (*b*) **Step II** 19 year 85 74 near gone 26 store
Step III 19 year 26 85 74 near gone store
Step IV 19 year 26 store 85 74 near gone
Step V 19 year 26 store 74 85 near gone
Step VI 19 year 26 store 74 near 85 gone
So, four more steps are required to complete rearrangement.

34. (*d*) **Input** glass full 15 37 water now 85 67
Step I water glass full 15 37 now 85 67
Step II water 85 glass full 15 37 now 67
Step III water 85 now glass full 15 37 67
Step IV water 85 now 67 glass full 15 37
Step V water 85 now 67 glass 37 full 15
Step V is the last step and Step VI is not possible.

35. (*d*) **Step II** ultra 73 12 16 mail sort 39 kite
Step III ultra 73 sort 12 16 mail 39 kite
Step IV ultra 73 sort 39 12 16 mail kite
Step V ultra 73 sort 39 mail 12 16 kite
Step VI ultra 73 sort 39 mail 16 12 kite
Step VII ultra 73 sort 39 mail 16 kite 12
So, last step is step VII and last but one Step is step VI.

36. (*d*) **Input** cannot determined.

37. (*a*) **Step II** tube 83 49 34 garden flower rat 56
Step III tube 83 rat 49 34 garden flower 56
Step IV tube 83 rat 56 49 34 garden flower
Step V tube 83 rat 56 garden 49 34 flower
Step VI tube 83 rat 56 garden 49 flower 34
Hence, four steps will be required to complete the rearrangement.

38. (*b*) **Input** hunt for 94 37 good 29 48 book
Step I hunt 94 for 37 good 29 48 book
Step II hunt 94 good for 37 29 48 book
Step III hunt 94 good 48 for 37 29 book
Step IV hunt 94 good 48 for 37 29 book
Step V hunt 94 good 48 for 37 book 29
Hence, five steps will be required to complete the arrangement.

39. (*c*) **Input** tobacco chewing is harmful for teeth.
Chewing of tobacco is harmful for teeth.
So, Rule I follows.

40. (*b*) In this due to comes so rule III follows.
Students are benefited *due* to coachings.

41. (*a*) **Rule IV** coaching in any form are beneficial for the students.
Rule I taking of coachings is beneficial to the students.

42. (*d*) **Rule III** will follow rule due to. So, joints are harmed due to excessive weightlifting is the answer